KINN'S

THE
ADMINISTRATIVE

MEDICAL

ASSISTANT

An Applied Learning Approach

EIGHTH·EDITION

8

KINN'S

THE ADMINISTRATIVE MEDICAL ASSISTANT

An Applied Learning Approach

Alexandra Patricia Adams, MA, BA, RMA, CMA (AAMA)
Former Health Information Specialist Program Director
  & Administrative Medical Assisting Instructor
Ultrasound Diagnostic School (now Sanford-Brown College)
Professional Writer
Grand Prairie, Texas

EIGHTH EDITION

8

ELSEVIER

ELSEVIER
SAUNDERS

3251 Riverport Lane
St. Louis, Missouri 63043

Vice President and Publisher: Andrew Allen
Executive Content Strategist: Jennifer Janson
Content Developmental Specialist: Laurie Vordtriede
Publishing Services Manager: Julie Eddy
Senior Project Manager: Richard Barber
Design Direction: Paula Catalano

Printed in Canada

Last digit is the print number: 9 8 7 6 5 4 3 2 1

Working together
to grow libraries in
developing countries

www.elsevier.com • www.bookaid.org

To Susan Cole, Executive Editor, whom we lost far too soon.
Susan was greatly respected by her peers and was a dedicated professional at Elsevier.
We dedicate this edition to her memory.

To the students who will use this textbook as they begin their careers in the
medical profession. It is our hope that they will use this text as a reference manual
during their studies, their externship, and throughout their careers.

To my children, Jimmie, Stacey, Jonathan, and Jessica.
Thank you for your patience as your mom spent hours at the computer
working on "the book."

To my loving husband, Bentley Adams. Your hugs are the best part of my day!
I love you for your support, your guidance, your care, and your patience.
I'm looking forward to our rocking chair days!

Alexandra Patricia Adams, *MA, BBA, RMA, CMA (AAMA)*

PREFACE

Medical assisting as a profession has changed dramatically since *The Office Assistant in Medical and Dental Practice,* by Portia Frederick and Carol Towner, was first published in 1956. Each subsequent edition of this textbook has reflected the age in which it was published. Now, *Kinn's The Medical Assistant: An Applied Learning Approach,* twelfth edition, continues to represent a long-standing commitment to high-quality medical assisting education with its engaging, straightforward writing style and demonstrated positive outcomes. Hundreds of instructors in classrooms across the country have used this text to teach thousands of students over the years. Many of these students have gone on to teach students of their own with this very same trusted resource. To continue the use and growth of this text and its features, the twelfth edition continues to offer the most comprehensive, up-to-date, and innovative approach to teaching this subject today. We appreciate the opportunity to explore the exciting field of medical assisting with you!

▍DISTINCTIVE FEATURES OF OUR APPROACH

This textbook has endured throughout the years because it has been able to keep pace with an ever-changing profession while producing students who are well trained and qualified to enter medical practices across the country. This dependability is the reason the market continues to rely on this text, edition after edition. Underlying this dependability is a foundation of pedagogic features that has stood the test of time and that has been expanded and improved upon yet again in this latest edition. Such features include the following:

- An easy-to-read, highly interactive writing style that engages students through practical applications of medical assistant competencies.
- An emphasis on skill development, with procedural steps outlining each skill, supported by rationales that provide meaning to each step.
- An organizational approach that addresses each body system with its own chapter, with additional chapters dedicated to specialty medical assistant skills.
- Each clinical chapter begins with a review of that system's anatomy and physiology, then moves to the common disorders found in that system, and concludes with patient education and legal and ethical issues.
- A pedagogic framework based on the use of learning objectives, vocabulary terms, and supportive student supplements.
- A package of supportive materials to accommodate a wide variety of student learning types and instructor teaching styles.

▍KEY FEATURES IN THIS EDITION

This edition of *Kinn's The Administrative Medical Assistant* incorporates a unique approach that is reflected in the subtitle: *An Applied Learning Approach.* Learning is believed to take place only when students are engaged, and when the learning requires something from them in response to the information being imparted to them.

This "applied" theme is set upfront in the first chapter, which introduces students to the concepts of critical thinking and the effect of individual learning styles on student success. This, in turn, transitions into time management and problem-solving skills, as well as effective study skills and test-taking strategies. The text develops from there, true to the original Kinn textbook, with its distinctive administrative and clinical sections, and is rounded out by the last chapter, which helps the student focus on preparing for and nurturing a career as a medical assistant.

This pedagogic theme and other new enhancements can be found throughout the book and its supplements in the following new features of the twelfth edition:

- The artwork throughout has been updated and modernized, providing a more attractive textbook for student use. Many new photographs throughout better support the revised content and are more relevant to the actual medical office. Many photographs were replaced with new images that show up-to-date equipment, provide more disease examples, and better illustrate key procedural steps.
- Separate chapters covering paper medical records and electronic medical records teach students about the intricacies of each system.
- Customer service is heavily stressed throughout the chapters. As patients become more involved in their healthcare, medical assistants must realize that the healthcare field is a service industry and that patients should be treated as customers.
- New compliance regulations in medical billing and coding have put a far greater emphasis on reimbursement practices than ever before. The billing and coding unit has been updated to include the basics of diagnostic coding, basics of procedural coding, basics of health insurance, and the health insurance claim form, as well as a brief introduction to ICD-10 coding.
- The sections on emergency preparedness have expanded so that medical assistants will know what to do in emergency situations. This critical information benefits not only the medical assistant but also aids patients, other staff members, and physicians in the medical facility.
- The Connections heading at the end of each chapter integrates text content with the accompanying Evolve Resources website and Student Study Guide.

▍EVOLVE

The Evolve site features a variety of student resources, including Chapter Quizzes and Review Activities, Clinical Skills Videos, Medical Terminology, Audio Glossary, practice CMA and RMA exams, and much more! The instructors' Evolve Resources site consists of TEACH Instructor Resources, including Lesson Plans, PowerPoint Presentations, Answer Keys for Chapter Quizzes and

Review Activities, and an extensive Test Bank with more than 5000 questions.

To access this comprehensive online resource, the student can simply go to the EVOLVE home page at *http://evolve.elsevier.com* and enter the user name and password provided by the instructor. If your instructor has not set up a Course Management System, you can still access all the learning resources available free with this textbook by going to http://evolve.elsevier.com/Kinn/.

STUDY GUIDE AND PROCEDURE CHECKLISTS

The Study Guide provides students with the opportunity to review and build on information they have learned in the text through vocabulary reviews, case studies, workplace applications, and more. The updated Procedure Checklists include CAAHEP and ABHES competencies that can be traced to the online correlation grid, and work products in the study guide ensure that students grasp all the medical assisting competencies.

KINN'S MEDICAL ASSISTING ONLINE

The Medical Assisting Online course closely maps content from the text to CAAHEP and ABHES competencies. Each module is competency focused and outcome oriented, providing the proof and documentation needed to demonstrate the student's knowledge to accrediting organizations.

SPECIAL FEATURES

A Scenario is presented at the beginning of each chapter so that the student can think about a real-world situation when reading the chapter content.

Each chapter contains a Vocabulary with definitions.

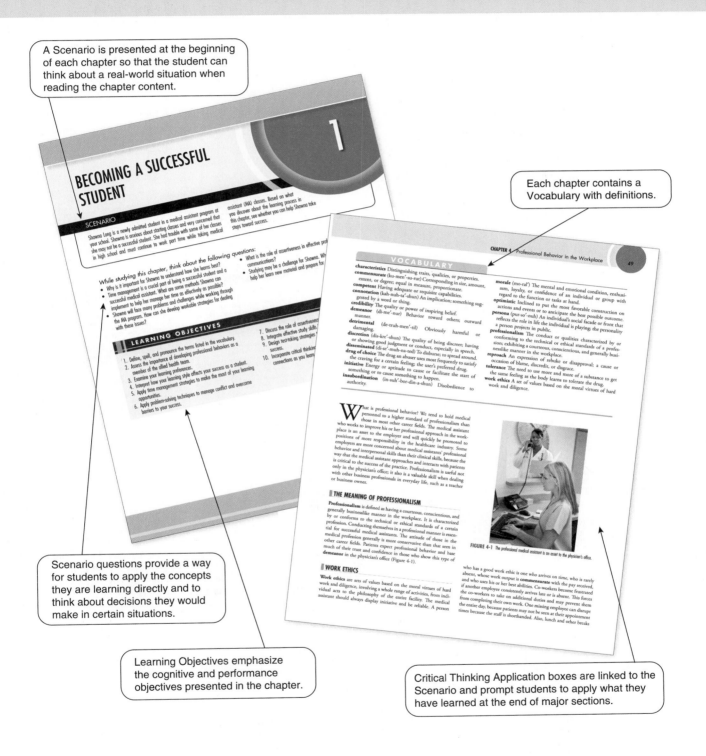

Scenario questions provide a way for students to apply the concepts they are learning directly and to think about decisions they would make in certain situations.

Learning Objectives emphasize the cognitive and performance objectives presented in the chapter.

Critical Thinking Application boxes are linked to the Scenario and prompt students to apply what they have learned at the end of major sections.

Illustrated, step-by-step Procedures show how to perform and document administrative and clinical procedures encountered in the healthcare setting.

At the end of the chapter, the Summary of Scenario provides students with relevant information they may encounter as a professional in the field.

Summary of Learning Objectives reviews important points of the chapter's focus, reinforcing content that students must master.

Connections information at the end of the chapter presents ancillary products and resources available to assist students' comprehension of concepts and to enhance their learning experience.

REVIEWERS

Kathy Cline, RN, ASN MA
Instructor
Blue Cliff College
Alexandria, Louisiana

Nelda Davis, RN, RMA
Program Director, Medical Assisting
Northeast Texas Community College
Mount Pleasant, Texas

Ruth E. Dearborn, CCS, CCS-P
Instructor
University of Alaska Southeast
Sitka, Alaska

Brian Dickens, MBA, RMA, CHI
Regional Program Director, Medical Assisting
Keiser Career College
Greenacres, Florida

Debra Downs, LPN, AAS, RMA (AMT)
Instructor and Program Director, Medical Assisting
Okefenokee Technical College
Waycross, Georgia

Deborah S. Gilbert, RHIA, CMA
Program Director, Medical Assisting
Dalton State College
Dalton, Georgia

Jen Gouge, XRT
Coordinator, Medical Assistant Program
Peninsula College
Port Angeles, Washington

Susanna M. Hancock, AAS-MOM, RMA, CMA, RPT, COLT
Retired Medical Assistant Director and Instructor
American Institute of Health Technology
Boise, Idaho

Carolyn Rowe Helms, BS, RMA
Extern Coordinator/Instructor
Atlanta Technical College
Atlanta, Georgia

Judith Kimelman-Kline, CMA, RMA
Instructor
Miami Lakes Educational Center (MDPS)
Miami Lakes, Florida

Colleen A. Lace, BLS, AA, LPN
Instructor and Allied Health Program Director
Moraine Park Technical College
Fond du Lac, Wisconsin

Loreen W. MacNichol, CMRS, RMC, CCS-P
Faculty, Health Science Department
Kaplan University
Portland, Maine

Laura Melendez, BS, RMA, RT BMO
Instructor
Keiser Career College
Greenacres, Florida

Maureen E. Russell Messier, CMA, RMA, AS, BA
Instructor
Branford Hall Career Institute, a division of Premier Education Group
Southington, Connecticut

Joyce A. Minton, Ed.S, CMA (AAMA), RMA
Director, Medical Assisting Health Sciences
Wilkes Community College
Wilkesboro, North Carolina

Kim Smith Norris, BSM, CPC
Instructor
Everest University
Orange Park, Florida

Julie Pepper, CMA (AAMA), BS
Instructor
Chippewa Valley Technical College
Eau Claire, Wisconsin

Andrea Potteiger, CCS, CCS-P, CPC, CHI, CMAA, CBCS
Lead Healthcare Instructor
New Horizons Harrisburg
Mechanicsburg, Pennsylvania

Macie Rubida, CPC, AA, LPN, BA
Instructor
Kaplan University
Council Bluffs, Iowa

Lynn G. Slack, BS, CMA (AAMA)
Director, Business Programs and Medical Programs
Kaplan Career Institute
Pittsburgh, Pennsylvania

Judith D. Symons, MA, Voc Ed Cert
Medical Assistant
Geisinger Medical Center
Danville, Pennsylvania
Former Instructor
McCann School of Business and Technology
Pottsville, Pennsylvania

Amy D. Tabak, MBA/HR, CPC, CMAA, CBCS
Full-Time Online Instructor
Ultimate Medical Academy Online
Tampa, Florida

Gail Van Grieken, CCMA-C
Teacher, Medical Assistant Program
San Joaquin County Office of Education
Stockton, California

Shannon Ydoyaga, MS, BBA
Associate Dean of Health Professions, School of Mathematics
    Science and Health Professions
Richland College
Dallas, Texas

La Tanya Young, PA-C, MMSc, MPH, CHES
Assistant Professor, College of Professional Studies
Coordinator, Medical Assisting Program
Clayton State University
Morrow, Georgia

ACKNOWLEDGMENTS

Years before I became the author of this book, I used it to teach my own students. All medical assistants owe a great debt to the original author, Mary E. Kinn. Her contributions to this discipline changed the playing field for our medical assisting students, and my gratitude to her is heartfelt and sincere.

I would like to express appreciation to the Elsevier Team, including Susan Cole, Laurie Vordtriede, Richard Barber, all the sales professionals who introduce us to instructors and program managers all over the country, as well as the other employees who worked on the text. We appreciate your insight and assistance as Deb and I do our best to make the Kinn text the finest medical assisting text available.

Deb Proctor has now been my partner for almost 12 years as we revise, rewrite, and rethink the ideas that have made this an outstanding textbook. I appreciate that Deb is so well informed and so willing to share of herself so that medical assisting students gain the knowledge they need to become successful in the medical field. It's been a great 12 years getting to know you and your family and sharing bits and pieces of life with you. I look forward to many more years of working together.

Without our families, writers could not do the work we are called to do. I would like to thank my brothers and sisters, LaNell Crumley, Alisha Crumley, Karry Chapman, Dr. Terry Watson, and Shawn Crumley, and their families for their support. Many thanks to my mom, Patricia Crumley, and my dad, Jim Crumley, for all the things they taught me. Without my mom using flashcards to help me with medical terminology, I might never have become a medical assistant! My dad, who was an attorney and a veteran of the Korean War, instilled a love for law and ethics in me, as well as a strong work ethic. I so appreciate the patience and support that my kids give to me. Jimmie, Stacey, Jonathan, and Jessica consistently stick with me when I have to be at the computer instead of being out and about with them. There are no words to describe my appreciation for my husband, Bentley. You truly take great care of me and are so supportive of my work. Those "rocking chair days" are soon to come! Thank you all for your belief in me and my abilities as a writer. Thank you for making our home a haven where love exists and grows every day.

To all medical assistants using this text: never doubt that you can accomplish your goals. You are the only person who can make a difference in your life, and your life will influence generations to come. Refuse to allow anything to keep you from realizing your dreams. Never stop setting new goals and striving to reach them.

Alexandra Patricia Adams, MA, BBA, RMA, CMA (AAMA)

CONTENTS

PROCEDURES

BECOMING A SUCCESSFUL STUDENT

SCENARIO

Shawna Long is a newly admitted student in a medical assistant program at your school. Shawna is anxious about starting classes and very concerned that she may not be a successful student. She had trouble with some of her classes in high school and must continue to work part time while taking medical assistant (MA) classes. Based on what you discover about the learning process in this chapter, see whether you can help Shawna take steps toward success.

While studying this chapter, think about the following questions:

- Why is it important for Shawna to understand how she learns best?
- Time management is a crucial part of being a successful student and a successful medical assistant. What are some methods Shawna can implement to help her manage her time as effectively as possible?
- Shawna will face many problems and challenges while working through the MA program. How can she develop workable strategies for dealing with these issues?

- What is the role of assertiveness in effective professional communications?
- Studying may be a challenge for Shawna. What skills can she use to help her learn new material and prepare for examinations?

LEARNING OBJECTIVES

1. Define, spell, and pronounce the terms listed in the vocabulary.
2. Assess the importance of developing professional behaviors as a member of the allied health team.
3. Examine your learning preferences.
4. Interpret how your learning style affects your success as a student.
5. Apply time management strategies to make the most of your learning opportunities.
6. Apply problem-solving techniques to manage conflict and overcome barriers to your success.
7. Discuss the role of assertiveness in effective communication.
8. Integrate effective study skills into your daily activities.
9. Design test-taking strategies that help you take charge of your success.
10. Incorporate critical thinking and reflection to help you make mental connections as you learn material.

VOCABULARY

critical thinking The constant practice of considering all aspects of a situation when deciding what to believe or what to do.

empathy (em'-puh-the) Sensitivity to the individual needs and reactions of patients.

learning style The way an individual perceives and processes information to learn new material.

perceiving (pur-sev'-ing) How an individual looks at information and sees it as real.

processing (pro'-ses-ing) How an individual internalizes new information and makes it his or her own.

professional behaviors Actions that identify the medical assistant as a member of a healthcare profession, including being dependable, providing respectful patient care, exercising initiative, demonstrating a positive attitude, and working as an effective team member.

reflection (re-flek'-shun) The process of considering new information and internalizing it to create new ways of examining information.

You have taken the first step toward becoming a successful student by choosing your profession and field of study. The medical assistant profession is both challenging and rewarding. Becoming a medical assistant opens the doors to a wide variety of opportunities in both administrative and clinical practice at ambulatory or institutional healthcare facilities. Medical assistants are important members of the healthcare team, and as a healthcare professional, you will be expected to practice certain **professional behaviors** (Figure 1-1). These professional behaviors include demonstrating dependability, respectful patient care, **empathy,** initiative, a positive attitude, and teamwork. To become a successful medical assistant, you first must become a successful student. This chapter helps you discover the way you learn best and provides multiple strategies to assist you in your journey toward success.

CRITICAL THINKING APPLICATION   1-1

Consider your history as a student. What do you think helped you to succeed? What do you think needs improvement? Create a plan for improvement that includes two or three ways you can become a more successful student. Be prepared to share this plan with your classmates.

WHO YOU ARE AS A LEARNER: HOW DO YOU LEARN BEST?

Think about what you do when you are faced with something new to learn. How do you go about understanding and learning the new material? Over time you have developed a method for **perceiving** and **processing** information. This pattern of behavior is called your **learning style.** Learning styles can be examined in many different ways, but most professionals agree that a student's success depends more on whether the person can "make sense" of the information than on whether the individual is "smart." Determining your individual learning style and understanding how it applies to your ability to learn new material are the first steps toward becoming a successful student (Figure 1-2).

Learning Style Inventory

For you to learn new material, two things must happen. First, you must *perceive* the information. This is the method you have developed over time that helps you examine new information and recognize it as real. Once you have developed a method for learning about the new material, you must *process* the information. Processing the information is how you internalize it and make it your own.

FIGURE 1-1 Professional interaction with patient.

FIGURE 1-2 Student learning.

Researchers believe that each of us has a preferred method for learning new material. By investigating your learning style, you can figure out how to combine different approaches to perceiving and processing information that will lead to greater success as a student.

The first step in learning new material is determining how you perceive the information. When faced with a new learning experience, students decide how they will go about learning the new material; that is, either by watching and observing the new activity or by doing something active to learn about it. Individuals who learn by analysis, observation, and **reflection** are considered *abstract perceivers.* Abstract learners analyze new material as ideas that require thought to process. They study the information and build theories to help them understand it. Abstract perceivers prefer structured learning situations and use a step-by-step approach to problem solving.

Individuals who learn by "doing" are *concrete perceivers,* who learn information through direct experiences of acting, sensing, or feeling the new material. Concrete learners prefer to learn things that have a personal meaning or that they believe are relevant, and they rely on detailed information to learn new material.

The second step in learning new material is information processing, which is the way learners internalize the new information and make it their own. New material can be processed by two methods. *Active processors* prefer to jump in and start doing things immediately. They make sense of the new material by using it immediately. They look for practical ways to apply the new material and typically do not mind taking risks to get the desired results. They learn best with practice and hands-on activities. *Reflective processors* have to think about the information before they can internalize it. They prefer to observe and consider what is going on. The only way they can make sense of new material is to spend time thinking and learning a great deal about it before acting. Complete the activity in the Student Study Guide to help you determine your learning style preference.

CRITICAL THINKING APPLICATION   1-2

- Consider the two ways to perceive new material. Are you a concrete perceiver, who ties the information to a personal experience, or are you an abstract perceiver, who likes to analyze or reflect on the meaning of the material? Choose the type you think most accurately describes your method of investigating new information.
- Now, think about the way you process learning. Are you an active processor, who always looks for the practical applications of what you learn, or are you a reflective processor, who has to think about new material before internalizing it?
- After completing this activity, write down the combination of your perceiving and processing learning styles and share it with your instructor.

Using Your Learning Profile to Be a Successful Student: Where Do I Go from Here?

No one falls completely into one or the other of the categories just discussed. However, by being aware of how we generally prefer first to perceive information and then to process it, we can be more sensitive to our learning style and can approach new learning situations with a plan for learning the material in a way that best suits our learning preferences.

Your preferred perceiving and processing learning profile will fall into one of the following four stages of the Learning Style Inventory, which was created by David Kolb of Case Western Reserve University.

- *Stage 1* learners have a *concrete reflective* style. These students want to know the purpose of the information and have a personal connection to the content. They like to consider a situation from many points of view, observe others, and plan before taking action. They feel most comfortable watching rather than doing, and their strengths include sensitivity toward others, brainstorming, and recognizing and creatively solving problems. If you fall into this stage, you enjoy small-group activities and learn well in study groups.
- *Stage 2* learners have an *abstract reflective* style. These students are eager to learn just for the sheer pleasure of learning, rather than because the material relates to their personal lives. They like to learn lots of facts and arrange new material in a clear, logical manner. Stage 2 learners plan studying and like to create ways of thinking about the material, but they do not always make the connection with its practical application. If you are a stage 2 learner, you prefer organized, logical presentations of material and therefore enjoy lectures and readings and generally dislike group work. You also need time to process and think about new material before applying it.
- *Stage 3* learners have an *abstract active* style. Learners with this combination learning style want to experiment and test the information they are learning. If you are a stage 3 learner, you want to know how techniques or ideas work, and you also want to practice what you are learning. Your strengths are in problem solving and decision making, but you may lack focus and may be hasty in making decisions. You learn best with hands-on practice by doing experiments, projects, and laboratory activities. You enjoy working alone or in small groups (Figure 1-3).
- *Stage 4* learners are *concrete active* learners. These students are concerned about how they can use what they learn to make a difference in their lives. If you fall into this stage, you like to relate new material to other areas of your life. You have leadership capabilities, can create on your feet, and usually are vocal in a group, but you may have difficulty completing your work on time. Stage 4 learners enjoy teaching others and working in groups and learn best when they can apply new information to real-world problems.

To get the most out of knowing your learning profile, you need to apply this knowledge to how you approach learning. Each of the learning stages has pluses and minuses. When faced with a learning situation that does not match your learning preference, see how you can adapt your individual learning profile to make the best of the information. For example, if you are bored by lectures, look for an opportunity to apply the information being presented to a real problem you are facing in the classroom or at home. If you are an abstract perceiver, take time outside of class to think about new information so that you are ready to process it into your learning system. If you benefit from learning in a group, make the effort to organize review sessions and study groups. If you learn best by

FIGURE 1-3 Learning in a small group.

FIGURE 1-4 Time management in a busy medical practice.

teaching others, offer to assist your peers with their learning. By taking the time now to investigate your preferred method of learning, you will perceive and process information more effectively throughout your school career.

CRITICAL THINKING APPLICATION   1-3

Take a few minutes to reflect on a time when you really enjoyed learning about something new. How was the material presented, and what did you do to "make it your own"? What do you need to do to become a more effective learner?

TIME MANAGEMENT: PUTTING TIME ON YOUR SIDE

One of the most complicated tasks for a professional medical assistant is to manage time effectively. No other workplace can compete with the distractions and demands of a busy healthcare practice. Do you think you practice effective time management skills? Do you believe that you are in control of your time, or do you think that other people or situations control it? How frequently do you say that you just do not have enough time to do what you are supposed to do, let alone those things you would like to do? Time management gives you the opportunity to spend time in the way you choose. Effective time management is also crucial to your success as a student and as a future healthcare professional (Figure 1-4).

How to Put Time on Your Side

The following time management skills are designed to help you deal effectively with the demands on your time. Highlight the ones that you think will be most useful in helping you deal with your situation.

1. **Determine your purpose.** What do you want to accomplish this semester, in this course, or in this unit of study? What do you

want to achieve as a student? What is one thing you can do to help achieve your goals?

2. **Identify your main concern.** Besides school, what other demands do you have on your time? Based on the learning goals you have established, what do you need to do to accomplish your goals?
   - *Plan time:* Schedule projects in advance, and make notes to yourself on deadlines.
   - *Use down time:* Take your work with you everywhere you go. Do small bits at every opportunity.
   - *Guard time:* Avoid distractions (e.g., television, music) that interfere with your concentration. Notice how others abuse your time. Learn to say no to outside demands on your time.
   - *Discover time:* Steal time from other activities in your schedule.
   - *Assign time:* Ask for help when you need it from friends and family.

3. **Be organized.** What materials (e.g., books, research, supplies) do you need to have an effective study session? What preparation is needed to make the most of your time?
   - *Record time:* Use a day planner or calendar, either paper or electronic, to note the due dates for assignments and tests. If a paper or project is due on a specific date, put a reminder in your day planner to start the project on a specific date so that you are sure to have it done when it is due.
   - *Optimal time:* Take advantage of the time of day when you study and learn the best. Schedule study time during your peak performance time. If you are an early riser, make time for homework first thing in the day; if you are a night owl, do your homework at night. Plan on dedicating at least some of your optimal time to your school work.

4. **Stop procrastinating.** If you avoid working on your goals, you may not achieve them. Examine the following suggestions as ways to break the procrastination cycle.

- *Make the work meaningful:* What is important about the work you are putting off and what are the benefits of getting it done? Reflect on your long-range goals. Is it important to do a good job on the work so you can earn an acceptable grade, do well in the course, complete the medical assisting program, and ultimately find employment?
- *Plan work deadlines:* Break assignments into achievable sections that can be completed in the time slots available. Schedule those work sections in your day planner so that you do not forget deadlines for assignments.
- *Ask for help:* Let your support system know you have work to get done. Ask them for encouragement to stay on track. If you have school-age children, you can set an excellent example by planning "family" homework sessions. You can get some of your work done while acting as a role model for learning behaviors for your children. Let your partner know when due dates are looming or tests are scheduled. Ask for help in meeting day-to-day demands so that you can study or prepare for school.
- *Prioritize:* If you keep avoiding a certain task, re-evaluate its priority. If it is really worth worrying about, get started now, not later. Don't waste time worrying about how you are going to get things done. Spend that time actually working on the projects that worry you the most.
- *Reward yourself:* Create a reward that is meaningful and something for which you will work. If you want to spend time with your family or friends on the weekend, develop a plan and stick to it so that you can share that special time as a reward.

5. **Remember you.** It is very easy to become overwhelmed with responsibilities both in school and at home. Part of successful time management includes setting aside time to do things you enjoy. You have chosen a profession that can be very demanding. Now is the time to remember that you have to take care of yourself in addition to meeting your professional and personal responsibilities.

CRITICAL THINKING APPLICATION   **1-4**

How do you spend your time? For 3 days this week, write down the amount of time you spend on each activity. How much television do you watch? How much time do you spend talking on the phone? How about driving time, visiting time, work time for family and friends, and so on? At the end of the 3-day period, add up the amount of time you spend on your daily activities. Do you recognize any time you might be wasting? Can you implement any of the suggested time management strategies to make more time available?

▌PROBLEM SOLVING AND CONFLICT MANAGEMENT

As a future member of the healthcare team, you frequently will face problems and conflict. Although we usually look at these situations as negative factors in our lives, problem solving and conflict management actually give us the opportunity to affect a potentially negative situation in a positive way. Learning how to manage problems can be very useful for your practice as a medical assistant, as well as for your success as a student.

The first step in reaching an equitable solution to a problem or conflict is to identify the central issue. How many times have you known that you were upset about something but were not really sure why you felt that way? You cannot solve a problem or resolve a negative situation unless you are sure of what is at the root of your feelings. You need to understand the problem and gather as much information about the situation as possible before you decide to act. One way of doing this is to ask yourself these questions:

- When does the situation occur and under what circumstances?
- How does it make me feel?
- Is someone else involved?
- What interferes with making a decision or resolving the conflict?

Once you understand the situation and how you feel about it, you need to decide whether it is worth the effort to resolve it. Prioritize your involvement. Sometimes situations and problems may arise that you are unable to resolve or that you may decide are not important enough to act on. For example, if one of your co-workers refuses to take out the garbage when it is his or her turn, does that really bother you? If it does, you need to deal with the issue. However, if the individual helps out in other ways, then perhaps the garbage isn't worth the effort to resolve the conflict.

After you have gathered the details about the problem or conflict and you have decided it is important enough to act on, it is time to determine possible solutions. One way to do this is to ask for advice or brainstorm ideas with individuals you respect. Sometimes another person can give you special insight into the problem that you were unable to see on your own. After brainstorming for possible solutions, you should then get feedback regarding the workability of the suggested solutions. An alternative to brainstorming possible solutions to the problem is to list on a piece of paper the pros and cons of possible solutions. Simply looking at a list of the positive and negative aspects of the solution may clarify how you could solve the problem. Before deciding on a particular solution, make sure you critically analyze the consequences of each proposed solution: Which one best meets your needs and has the potential for providing an outcome you can live with?

Finally, you are ready to implement the chosen solution. However, your work is not over yet. You need to evaluate the outcome of your decision and see whether it truly did meet your needs. If not, it may be time to review other possible solutions and try another approach.

Conflict management requires some additional consideration. If you are in conflict with a peer, an instructor, or a co-worker, it is important to follow certain guidelines. You should attempt to solve the conflict in a private place at a prescheduled time. This ensures that the person will meet with you and that neither one has to worry about others overhearing the conversation. At the meeting, clearly state your feelings about the conflict and how you would like it resolved. Then try to come to an agreeable solution. The best way to deal with conflict situations is through open, honest, assertive communication. However, just as with problem solving, it is important to follow up on the decided course of action to see whether it effectively dealt with the source of the conflict (Figure 1-5).

FIGURE 1-5 Dealing with conflict.

CRITICAL THINKING APPLICATION   1-5

Think about a serious problem you are currently facing. Use the brainstorming and/or pros and cons method for creating solutions to the problem. Implement your chosen solution, and follow up on its effectiveness. Did the problem-solving process help you manage the situation more effectively?

Assertive Communication

One of the challenges faced by workers in a healthcare environment is acting assertively when necessary. Assertive communication allows you to express your thoughts and feelings honestly and enables you to stand up for yourself in a reasonable, rational manner without an emotional scene. However, most of us are not born assertive; it is a behavior that must be learned, and many of us must practice it over and over again before it becomes a natural response.

Passive, or nonassertive, individuals often feel hurt when they are taken advantage of or are anxious about dealing with conflict. Just because they comply with what they are told to do or do not argue when they are treated unfairly does not mean that they are not upset about the situation. Often these individuals internalize their hurt and anxiety and eventually have an angry outburst because of built-up stress. Aggressive individuals, on the other hand, take advantage of others, appear self-righteous, and act in a superior way to get what they want. People who act aggressively may humiliate or hurt others to achieve their goals or to have their own needs satisfied.

NONASSERTIVE AND AGGRESSIVE BEHAVIORS AND LANGUAGE

An individual with nonassertive body language displays the following behaviors when attempting to deal with conflict and may use some of the following words:

- Keeps eyes downcast
- Shifts weight when talking
- Has a slumped posture or wrings the hands
- Whines or uses a hesitant tone of voice
- May use the following phrases:
  - "Maybe" or "I guess"
  - "I wonder if you could…"
  - "Would you mind very much if…"
  - "It's not really important."

An aggressive person displays the following behaviors:
- Leans forward and points a finger when talking
- Raises the voice or sounds arrogant
- May use the following phrases:
  - "You'd better…"
  - "If you don't watch out…"
  - "Do it or else!"
  - "You should do it this way!"

Learning how to respond assertively in a potentially challenging situation enables us to be honest and direct with others while at the same time being emotionally honest with ourselves. The goal of assertive behavior is to treat others with respect while acknowledging our own feelings about the problem.

The first step in becoming assertive is to describe the situation and how it makes you feel. Perhaps you have a co-worker who is taking advantage of you; coming to work late, taking long breaks, not answering the phones, and so on. How does that make you feel? Are you angry, hurt, or disappointed? Decide which word best describes your feelings and, using an "I" sentence, clearly state how you feel about the situation. Be specific about the problem. If your statement is too general (e.g., "I am very hurt when you act like that"), the person you are confronting can either misunderstand or ignore you, because the individual does not know specifically what is wrong. A statement such as, "I am very hurt that you take advantage of me by consistently being late for work, taking long breaks, and not helping with answering the phones," makes the problem very clear and how you feel about it.

Acting assertively takes practice, practice, practice. In addition, just because you deliver a clear, concise, assertive message does not mean that the problem will be solved that quickly. Your assertive words must be combined with assertive body language to deliver a clear message about how serious you consider the situation. Remember, 80% to 90% of a message is nonverbal. Therefore, your "I" message must be accompanied by assertive behavior, including establishing eye contact and slightly raising your voice to get the individual's attention. And just because you deliver the perfect message does not mean you will always get what you want. The message may have to be repeated; do you really think someone who is habitually late for work is going to start showing up on time because of one assertive message? However, regardless of the outcome, you will feel better because you have honestly communicated how you feel about the situation, and you are working on a resolution of the problem.

CRITICAL THINKING APPLICATION   1-6

Do you consider yourself passive (nonassertive), assertive, or aggressive? Think about a recent conflict situation. How did you respond? Could assertive behaviors help you solve the problem while making you feel better about yourself?

STUDY SKILLS: TRICKS FOR BECOMING A SUCCESSFUL STUDENT

So far in this chapter, we have looked at the influence of individual learning styles and time management on learning success. Now we will investigate some ideas that are useful for learning new material. These study skills include memory techniques, active learning, brain tricks, reading methods, and note-taking strategies.

Several techniques can help you store and remember information. The first of these involves organizing information into recognizable groups so that the brain can find it easily. You can organize information by getting the big picture first before trying to learn the details. One way to implement this strategy is to skim a reading assignment before actually reading and taking notes on the material, thus getting a general impression of what you need to learn before tackling the details. Depending on your learning style, it may also help to find a way of making the new information meaningful. Think about your educational goals and how the new material will help you achieve those goals. Another way of remembering material is to create an association with something you already know. If new material is grouped with already stored material, the brain remembers it much more easily.

A useful study skill for some learners is to be physically active while learning. Some students learn best if they walk or talk out loud while studying. Besides encouraging learning, moving and talking while studying relieves boredom and keeps you awake. Another way to be actively involved in learning is to use pictures or diagrams to represent the material you are studying. Some people are visual learners, and creating pictures of the material is the easiest method for them to retain the information. Other students find that rewriting notes or making lists of information helps them retain the material. Writing also helps students who need to "do" something to learn.

Studying goes much more smoothly if you work *with* your brain rather than *against* it. If you tend to get anxious and worried while studying, you may be acting as your own worst enemy. One way of dealing with a topic you are anxious about is to overlearn it. If material is overlearned, you are much less likely to experience test anxiety. Another method for remembering material is to review it quickly after class. This minireview helps the new information become part of your long-term memory system. Many students find creating songs, dances, or word associations an effective way to learn and remember new material. Putting details into a familiar song and moving to it can help trick the brain into remembering the information. This is especially helpful when trying to learn anatomy and physiology. Another excellent way of learning information is to actually teach it to someone else. Teaching requires you to have a good understanding of the material and the ability to describe it for others. It can be an effective reinforcement of complicated material.

A great deal of the learning process is expected to take place from assigned readings. You can use several methods to make reading assignments more meaningful. If you find a reading assignment challenging or difficult to understand, the first step is to take the time to read it again. Sometimes the first time through the material is not enough to gain understanding. As you read, highlight important words or thoughts and stop periodically to summarize the material. If you get bored while reading, use your body; walk or talk your way through the assignment. Take the time to look up words

or terms you do not understand or ask your instructor or tutor for help. Outlining the material can help you create a brief overview of what you need to learn. The best way to determine whether you have learned anything from your reading is to try to explain the material to someone else. If you can do that effectively, you know you have acquired the knowledge needed from the reading assignment.

Many students find effective note taking a challenge. The big question is, "How much of what the instructor says do I actually need to write down?" The first step in effective note taking is to come to class prepared. The more familiar you are with the material, the easier it will be to determine the important parts of the instructor's lecture. Pay attention to the instructor and look for clues to what he or she thinks is important. Ask questions about the material if you do not understand it, rather than writing down information that makes no sense to you. Think critically about what you hear before you write it down so you can start to build relationships among the things you want or need to know.

When it comes to actual note taking, some strategies can make the process of recording notes an active learning tool. Organize the information as much as possible while you are writing or typing, either in an outline or a paragraph format. If you take notes directly into a laptop or tablet, make sure your keyboarding skills are good enough for you to keep up with the flow of information and that you review your notes shortly after class to fill in any missing details. If you take notes on paper, use only one side of the page (for easier reading) and leave blank spaces where needed to fill in details later. Use key words to help you remember the material, and create pictures or diagrams to help visualize it. If permitted, use tape recorders when appropriate and make sure you have any handouts or notes that cover material written on the board or provided in a PowerPoint presentation. If your instructor refers the class to a YouTube video, make sure you have transcribed the site address correctly to refer to it at a later time. Another helpful tool is to develop your own system of abbreviations to help simplify the note-taking process.

The most effective way to use your notes is to review them shortly after class. This is the time to add details, clarify information, or make notes about asking the instructor for explanations during the next class. You could even exchange notes with students you trust to compare information (Figure 1-6). Some students find it beneficial to type their notes (if they took them on paper) or to rewrite them. This can give you an opportunity to learn the material as you

FIGURE 1-6 Sharing notes.

transcribe it. As you are reviewing your notes, you also can draw mind maps of the information or diagram outlines to help you better understand and remember the material.

Creating mind maps is a way of representing the main idea of a topic and supporting important details with a figure or picture. Healthcare textbooks present complicated concepts with multiple main ideas, each with its own important details. Mind maps are a way of consolidating complex details and organizing them into a format that is easier to remember. The spider map (Figure 1-7) presents a method for including several main ideas with details in one study guide. The fishbone map (Figure 1-8) can be used to learn complicated causes of disease. The chain-of-events map (Figure 1-9) displays the cause and effect of events, such as infection control or the history of medicine. The cycle map (Figure 1-10) shows the connection between factors, such as in the chain of infection.

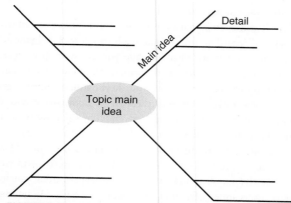

FIGURE 1-7 Spider map showing multiple main ideas with supporting details.

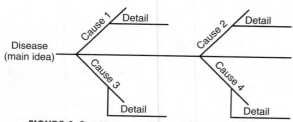

FIGURE 1-8 Fishbone map used to describe causes of disease.

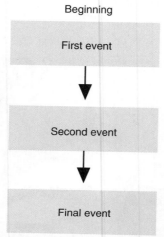

FIGURE 1-9 Chain-of-events map showing the cause and effect of events.

Creating your own mind maps is a way of making the information more meaningful and easier for you to understand.

Although many techniques can help you study, perhaps the most important one is your attitude toward learning. Some students fall into the "I can't possibly learn this material" trap. That type of attitude only leads to self-defeat. The way to overcome barriers is first to recognize that they exist. Once you know your weak spots, use the suggested study skills to improve in those areas. Do not be afraid to ask questions or to ask for help if you do not understand the material. Use as many different strategies as necessary to become a successful student.

CRITICAL THINKING APPLICATION   1-7

Write down at least two barriers to learning that you face. Review the study skills suggestions and choose four to try out. Use them over the next week to help you learn new material. Reflect on whether the chosen study skills helped you learn the material better.

TEST-TAKING STRATEGIES: TAKING CHARGE OF YOUR SUCCESS

What happens when you do not know the answer to the first question on a test? What if you do not know the next one? Are you able to go on without panicking? Many people find taking tests the most challenging part of being a successful student. Multiple approaches are available that you can use to take charge of your success and improve your ability to take tests. These include such strategies as adequate preparation, controlling negative thoughts during test time, and understanding ways to manage various types of questions.

The first step is to go into a test adequately prepared. Use the time management skills already outlined in this chapter to prepare for the big day. Recognize and use your preferred learning style to overlearn the material and increase your confidence. Use memory tools (e.g., flash cards, checklists, and mind maps) to help you visualize the material. Form a study group if you are the type of learner who benefits from studying in groups. Schedule and plan study time, and reward yourself for your hard work. It also is important to go

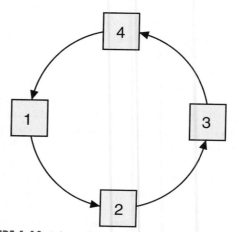

FIGURE 1-10 Cycle map illustrating the way one action leads to another.

into the test rested and relaxed; therefore, you should eat, exercise to relieve stress, and sleep before the test so that you are as alert as possible.

Before you start the test, make sure you read the directions carefully. If possible, begin with the easiest or shortest questions to build your confidence. Be aware of the amount of time allotted for the examination, and pace yourself accordingly. As you go through the test, look for clues to answers in other questions. During test time, remember to use positive self-talk at the first indication of panic. Repeatedly remind yourself that you are well prepared; relax and think about the material before you get worried. You need to stop negative thoughts as soon as they arise and instead visualize yourself being successful. Use slow, deep breathing to relax and, if helpful, close your eyes for a minute and visualize a relaxing place before you go on with the test. You may find it helpful to wear a thick rubber band on your wrist and snap it as soon as you start to think negatively. The sting of the rubber band provides a physical reaction that interferes with the power of your negative thoughts and serves as a reminder to focus on the exam and not on your anxiety.

Certain strategies are useful for answering different types of questions. With multiple choice questions, try to identify key words or clues in each question. Read the question carefully and answer it in your head before you review the provided answers. If you are not absolutely sure of the answer, make an educated guess or follow your instincts in choosing an answer. "True or false" questions give you a 50/50 chance of being correct. Remember that if any part of the question is not true, then the statement is false. Again, check the statements for key words that help indicate the direction of the answer. Look for qualifying terms (e.g., *always, never, sometimes*) that are the key to understanding the meaning of the true or false statement.

CRITICAL THINKING APPLICATION   1-8

Think about a time you experienced test anxiety. Write down the details of the situation and how you felt. Choose four test-taking strategies you think would be beneficial in handling similar situations in the future.

BECOMING A CRITICAL THINKER: MAKING MENTAL CONNECTIONS

The ability to process information and arrive at reasonable conclusions is crucial to all healthcare workers. The process of **critical thinking** involves (1) sorting out conflicting information, (2) weighing your knowledge about that information, (3) ignoring or letting go of personal biases, and (4) deciding on a reasonable belief or action. Critical thinking is actually an active search for the truth.

Critical thinking could be described as thorough thinking, because it requires learners to keep an open mind to all possibilities. Successful students are thorough thinkers, because they must determine the facts about the topic being learned and come to logical conclusions about the material. Critical thinkers also are inquisitive learners, who constantly analyze and sort out conflicting information to reach conclusions.

A crucial step in critical thinking is evaluating the results of your learning. Reflection is the key to critical thinking. "How did I learn what I learned?" and "What does it mean in my life?" are questions that must be asked consistently to continue to learn. Becoming a successful student, and ultimately a successful member of the allied health team, requires critical thinking skills.

SUMMARY OF SCENARIO

One of the things Shawna can do to improve her learning is to determine her individual learning style. By understanding how she typically perceives and processes new information, she can plan the best methods for learning the material. In addition to understanding who she is as a learner, Shawna needs to practice successful time management skills to keep up with school and work responsibilities. Effective problem solving and developing study skills that work for her are also keys to her success as a student.

SUMMARY OF LEARNING OBJECTIVES

1. **Define, spell, and pronounce the terms listed in the vocabulary.**

   Spelling and pronouncing medical terms correctly bolster the medical assistant's credibility. Knowing the definitions of these terms promotes confidence in communication with patients and co-workers.

2. **Assess the importance of developing professional behaviors as a member of the allied health team.**

   Medical assistants play a vital role on the healthcare team and are expected to show such professional behaviors as being dependable, practicing respectful patient care, displaying empathy, showing initiative, demonstrating a positive attitude, and functioning as an effective member of the healthcare team.

3. **Examine your learning preferences.**

   Learning preferences are the ways you like to learn and that have proven successful in the past.

4. **Interpret how your learning style affects your success as a student.**

   Your learning style is determined by your individual method of perceiving or examining new material and the way you process it or make it your own. People are either concrete or abstract perceivers and either active or reflective processors.

5. **Apply time management strategies to make the most of your learning opportunities.**

   Effective time management strategies, such as setting goals, prioritizing, getting organized, and avoiding procrastination, will make you a more successful student and an effective medical assistant.

6. **Apply problem-solving techniques to manage conflict and overcome barriers to your success.**

   Problem-solving and conflict management techniques are crucial to your success. First, identify the central issue and how you feel about it; then, consider possible solutions and their potential results, implement the chosen solution, and analyze the results.

7. **Discuss the role of assertiveness in effective communication.**

   Assertive communication allows you to express your thoughts and feelings honestly and enables you to stand up for yourself in a reasonable, rational manner without an emotional scene. Learning how to respond assertively in a potentially challenging situation enables us to be honest and direct with others while at the same time being emotionally honest with ourselves. The goal of assertive behavior is to treat others with respect while acknowledging our own feelings about the problem.

8. **Integrate effective study skills into your daily activities.**

   Study skills, such as memory techniques, active learning, brain tricks, effective reading methods, note-taking strategies, and mind maps, all help students to be more successful.

9. **Design test-taking strategies that help you take charge of your success.**

   Test-taking strategies include preparing adequately for the examination, controlling negative thoughts during the examination, and understanding how to deal with different types of questions.

10. **Incorporate critical thinking and reflection to make mental connections as you learn material.**

    Critical thinking can be defined as thorough thinking, because it considers all sides of the information without bias. Reflection is the process of thinking about or reviewing information before acting.

CONNECTIONS

Study Guide Connection: Go to the Chapter 1 Study Guide. Read and complete the activities.

Evolve Connection: Go to the Chapter 1 link at *evolve.elsevier.com/kinn* to complete the Chapter Review and Chapter Quiz. Check out the other resources listed for this chapter to make the most of what you have learned from Becoming a Successful Student.

THE HEALTHCARE INDUSTRY

2

SCENARIO

Carlos Santos, CMA, is a medical assisting instructor with 10 years' experience in the clinical area. He worked for a group of family practitioners and for an allergist during his career as a medical assistant before becoming an instructor. Mr. Santos believes that it is very important to give his students an overview of the history of medicine early in their training. He knows that it is exciting to show them the progress of medicine and to introduce students to the pioneers who contributed to the field. This helps the student to understand where he or she fits into the whole picture as a medical assistant. Often Mr. Santos assigns the students a short report on one person who played a role in the progress of medicine. He finds that this is a good way to encourage students to use the Internet and to conduct research right from the start of their training; also, the students get a chance to grow more comfortable speaking in front of a group when they give their reports in class. Mr. Santos knows that his students will develop an appreciation for those who contributed to the medical profession, which will influence their own dedication to both peers and patients.

Mr. Santos knows that his students must recognize the different members of the healthcare team and their responsibilities. Once the students begin their externship or practicum, they will be able to work effectively with each person in the facility and understand each one's role in the treatment of patients. Mr. Santos also introduces them to the current types of facilities available for patient care on both a national and a local level. The knowledge the students gain about the different areas of patient care will be useful once they graduate and begin working in a healthcare facility. All of these skills will make Mr. Santos' students more versatile and valuable to their eventual employers.

While studying this chapter, think about the following questions:

- What recent events could be included as groundbreaking discoveries in medicine?
- Why are continuing medical education and research so important to the healthcare industry and specifically to the medical assistant?
- How can the individual medical assistant contribute to the progress of medicine in today's world?
- What is the value of gaining an overview of the history of medicine as one begins a career in medical assisting?

LEARNING OBJECTIVES

1. Define, spell, and pronounce the terms listed in the vocabulary.
2. Identify the ancient cultures that contributed a major portion of our medical terminology.
3. Distinguish between and describe the staff of Aesculapius and the caduceus.
4. Explain the philosophy behind the phrase "physicians must learn to despise money."
5. Explain why a medical education at Johns Hopkins University School of Medicine was considered superior, even in its early years.
6. List several medical pioneers and discuss the importance of their contributions to the medical profession.
7. Explain the roles of the national health organizations.
8. Identify the role of the Centers for Disease Control and Prevention (CDC) regulations in healthcare settings
9. Discuss the various types of ambulatory care.
10. Name the three main provider portals of entry into the healthcare system and distinguish among the different types of physicians and medical practices.
11. Become familiar with the medical specialties recognized by the American Board of Medical Specialties.
12. Understand both the allied health professions and how they relate to medical assisting.

VOCABULARY

accreditation (u-kre-duh-ta'-shun) The process through which an organization is recognized for adherence to a group of standards that meet or exceed the expectations of the accrediting agency.

advent Coming into being or use.

allopathic (al-o-path'-ik) A term used to contrast homeopathic medicine with mainstream medicine; allopathic medicine is characterized by an effort to counteract the symptoms of a disease by administration of treatments that produce effects opposite to the symptoms.

ambulatory (am'-bu-la-to-re) Able to walk about and not be bedridden.

amenities Things that contribute to comfort, enjoyment, or convenience.

case management The process of assessing and planning patient care, including referral and follow-up, to ensure continuity of care and quality management.

chiropractic (ki'-ruh-prak-tik) A medical discipline that focuses on the nervous system and involves manual adjustment of the vertebral column to affect the nervous system, and thereby treat various disorders, as well as to promote patient wellness.

cited Quoted by way of example, authority, or proof or mentioned formally in commendation or praise.

complementary and alternative medicine (CAM) A group of diverse medical and healthcare systems, practices, and products that are not generally considered part of conventional medicine. Complementary medicine is used in combination with conventional medicine (allopathic or osteopathic); alternative medicine is used instead of conventional medicine.

contamination (kun-ta-mu-na'-shun) The process by which something is made impure, unclean, or unfit for use by the introduction of unwholesome or undesirable elements.

conventional medicine Medicine as practiced by holders of the Doctor of Medicine (MD) and Doctor of Osteopathy (OD) degrees and by their allied health professionals, such as physical therapists, psychologists, and registered nurses.

credentialing (kri-den'-shuh-ling) The process of extending professional or medical privileges to an individual; the process of verifying and evaluating that person's credentials.

dissection (di-sek'-shun) The separation into pieces and exposure of parts for scientific examination.

encounter Any contact between a healthcare provider and a patient that results in treatment or evaluation of the patient's condition; it is not limited to in-person contact.

fermentation (fur-men-ta'-shun) An enzymatically controlled transformation of an organic compound.

holistic (ho-lis'-tik) A health viewpoint that considers all the systems of the body and their interdependence, rather than breaking down the body into discrete parts.

homeopathy (ho-me-uh'-puh-the) A type of alternative medicine that attempts to stimulate the body to recover by itself; a system of therapy based on the concept that disease can be treated with minute doses of drugs thought capable of producing the same symptoms in healthy people as the disease itself.

hospice (hos'-pus) A concept of care that involves health professionals and volunteers who provide medical, psychological, and spiritual support to terminally ill patients and their loved ones.

indicators An important point or group of statistical values that, when evaluated, indicates the quality of care provided in a healthcare facility.

indicted (in-di'-ted) Charged with a crime by the finding of a jury according to due process of law.

indigent (in'-di-junt) A needy or poor person who is unable to provide the basic necessities of life; totally lacking in something of need.

innate Existing in, belonging to, or determined by factors present in an individual since birth.

innocuous (i'-nuh-kyu-wus) Having no effect, adverse or otherwise; harmless.

integrated Formed, coordinated, or blended into a functioning or unified whole; to incorporate into a larger unit.

integrated delivery system (IDS) A network of healthcare providers and organizations that provides or arranges to provide a coordinated continuum of services to a defined population and is willing to be held clinically and fiscally accountable for the clinical outcomes and health status of the population served.

mysticism The experience of seeming to have direct communication with God or ultimate reality.

naturopathy (na-chu-ra'-puh-the) An alternative to conventional medicine in which holistic methods are used, in addition to herbs and natural supplements, with the belief that the body will heal itself. Naturopathic physicians currently can be licensed in 15 states, Puerto Rico, and the Virgin Islands.

osteopathic (us-te-uh-path'-ik) A term describing the type of medicine that is based on the theory that disturbances in the musculoskeletal system affect other bodily parts, causing many disorders that can be corrected by various manipulative techniques in conjunction with conventional medical, surgical, pharmacologic, and other therapeutic procedures.

pandemic (pan-de'-mik) A condition in which most people in a country, a number of countries, or a geographic area are affected.

peer review organizations (PROs) Groups of medical reviewers contracted by the Centers for Medicare and Medicaid Services (CMS) to ensure quality control and the medical necessity of services provided by a facility.

philanthropist (fu-lan'-thruh-pist) An individual who makes an active effort to promote human welfare.

putrefaction (pyu-truh-fak'-shun) Decomposition of animal matter, which results in a foul smell.

robotics Technology dealing with the design, construction, and operation of robots in automation.

staff privileges The permission granted by a facility to a healthcare professional to practice in that facility.

standards Items or indicators used as a measure of quality or compliance with a statutory or accrediting body's policies and regulations.

subluxations (suh-bluk-sa'-shuns) Slight misalignments of the vertebrae or a partial dislocation.

telemedicine The use of telecommunications in the practice of medicine to compensate for the great distances that can separate healthcare professionals, colleagues, patients, and students.

teleradiology The use of telecommunication devices to enhance and improve the results of radiologic procedures.

treatises (tree′-te-ses) Systematic expositions or arguments in writing, including a methodic discussion of the facts and principles involved and the conclusions reached.

triage (tree′-azh) Identification of the severity of patients' conditions and the allocation of treatment according to a system of priorities, which is designed to maximize the number of survivors and provide treatment for the sickest patients first.

The growth of today's healthcare industry seems unstoppable. Thanks to modern technologic advances, medicine speeds forward faster than ever in its quest to improve the health of humankind. Modern advances, such as **telemedicine**, are experiencing significant growth, and the images produced with **teleradiology** have vastly improved in their resolution. **Robotics** is assisting healthcare professionals in surgery and even delivers drugs to hospital floors using laser sensors. Education in medicine has grown exponentially: computers, the Internet, and video have enabled an instructor in New York to communicate with a student in Los Angeles. The key to this technology lies in the development and widespread use of elaborate information systems that have revolutionized the way medicine is practiced today. Technology is advancing at an astounding rate; the healthcare environment of the future is barely imaginable. This chapter looks back at the history of medicine, gazes at its present, and glances toward its future.

THE HISTORY OF MEDICINE

Medical Language and Mythology

Today's medical professional uses words with origins stemming from the romance and fantasy of classical and ancient languages. The study of anatomy reaches back to the dawn of recorded history. Today's modern terms often are similar to their original versions. Some terms are inaccurate when translated literally, because the ancients did not fully understand bodily functions. The word *artery*, for example, which comes from the Greek word *arteria*, literally means "a windpipe." The early Greeks believed that the arteries carried air, not blood. Greek and Roman mythologies have contributed a major portion of our medical terminology, but we have also borrowed liberally from Arabic, Anglo-Saxon, and Germanic sources. Several terms originate from the Bible.

The human head rests on the first cervical vertebra, which is called the *atlas*. Atlas was the famous Greek Titan who was condemned by Zeus to bear the heavens on his shoulders. Achilles' mother held him by the heel as she dipped him into the river Styx so that he would become invulnerable. However, his heel was not immersed, and he later died from a wound in that area. *Achilles heel* is a common expression used today to indicate a point of weakness. Aphrodite, the Greek goddess of love and beauty, is the source of the name for drugs used to enhance sexual arousal, called *aphrodisiacs*. The equivalent Roman goddess of love, Venus, is associated with lustful desires. A portion of the female anatomy, the mons *veneris* (mons pubis), and *venereal* diseases were named after her.

Aesculapius, the son of Apollo, was revered as the god of medicine. The early Greeks worshiped the healing powers of Aesculapius

and built temples in his honor where patients were treated by trained priests. His daughters were Hygeia, goddess of health, and Panacea, goddess of all healing and restorer of health. Our modern word *hygiene* has its origin in Hygeia, and the modern meaning for *panacea* is "a remedy for all ills and difficulties." The staff of Aesculapius is a common medical icon. It depicts a serpent encircling a staff and signifies the art of healing. The staff of Aesculapius has been adopted by the American Medical Association as the symbol of medicine. The mythological staff belonging to Hermes, the messenger of the gods, is the caduceus, which was thought to have magical powers. The caduceus is a winged staff encircled by two serpents. This icon is the medical insignia of the U.S. Army Medical Corps, although it often is misused as a symbol of the medical profession (Figure 2-1).

Medicine in Ancient Times

Although religious and mythological beliefs were the basis for care for the sick in ancient times, evidence suggests that drugs, surgery, and other treatments based on theories about the body were used as early as 5000 BC. In the well-developed societies of the Egyptians, Babylonians, and Assyrians, certain men acted as physicians and used the little knowledge they had to try to treat illness and injury.

Moses presented rules of health to the Hebrews in approximately 1205 BC. He was the first advocate of preventive medicine and is considered the first public health officer. Moses knew that some animal diseases could be passed to humans and that **contamination** existed; therefore a religious law was developed forbidding humans to eat or drink from dirty dishes. The people of that era believed that doing so would defile their bodies and they would lose their souls.

Hippocrates, known as the Father of Medicine, is the most famous of the ancient Greek physicians (Figure 2-2). He was born in 450 BC on the island of Cos in Greece. He is best remembered for the Hippocratic Oath, which has been administered to physicians

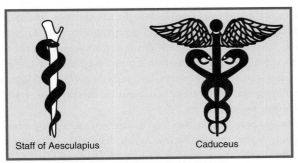

FIGURE 2-1 Staff of Aesculapius and the caduceus.

FIGURE 2-2 Hippocrates is known as the Father of Medicine. (Courtesy National Library of Medicine, Bethesda, Md.)

for more than 2,000 years. Hippocrates is credited with taking **mysticism** out of medicine and giving it a scientific basis. During this period of history, most believed that illness was caused by demonic possession; for the illness to be cured, the demon had to be removed from the body. Hippocrates' clinical descriptions of diseases and his volumes on epidemics, fevers, epilepsy, fractures, and instruments were studied for centuries. He believed that the body had the capacity to heal itself and that the physician's role was to help nature. He described four "humors"—blood, phlegm, yellow bile, and black bile—that he believed must be in balance for the body to maintain a healthy state.

Galen was a Greek physician who migrated to Rome in AD 162 and became known as the Prince of Physicians. He is said to have written more than 500 **treatises** on medicine. He wrote an excellent summary on anatomy as it was known at the time, but his work was faulty and inaccurate, because it was largely based on the **dissection** of apes and swine. He is considered the Father of Experimental Physiology and the first experimental neurologist. He was the first to describe the cranial nerves and the sympathetic nervous system, and he performed the first experimental section of the spinal cord, producing hemiplegia. Galen was a champion of medical ethics; he thought that physicians "must learn to despise money," and that if a physician was interested in profit, he was not serious in his devotion to the art of medicine. Galen's beliefs about monetary profit from medicine parallel the views of many modern healthcare professionals, who understand the nature of the healthcare crisis the world faces today. Although much of what he believed about the body was incorrect, Galen's teachings remained intact until human dissections began and physicians were able to visualize exactly what was inside the human body.

Because both Hippocrates and Galen were highly respected, the authority of their observations went unquestioned. This had a negative effect on the progress of science throughout the Dark Ages and well into the sixteenth century. Their theories and descriptions were

considered immutable principles; therefore, few physicians were innovative and curious enough to challenge them. Those who did experiment in medicine were scorned by their colleagues, and physicians continued to use methods that were at best ineffectual or **innocuous** and at worst harmful to the patient. However, the establishment of universities led to a study of theories of disease rather than observation of the sick.

Early Development of Medical Education

Medical knowledge developed slowly, and distribution of such knowledge was poor. Before the printing press was invented in the middle of the fifteenth century, very little exchange of scientific knowledge and ideas occurred; scientists were not well informed about the investigations of other scientists. The printing press allowed books to be distributed faster and over a widespread area.

In the seventeenth century, European academies or societies were established, consisting of small groups of men who met to discuss subjects of mutual interest. The academies provided freedom of expression that, with the stimulus of exchanging ideas, contributed significantly to the development of scientific thought. One of the earliest of the academies was the Royal Society of London, formed in 1662. The development of communication during this era was important, and these societies contributed to the exchange of information.

In the United States, medical education was greatly influenced by the Johns Hopkins University School of Medicine in Baltimore, Maryland, established in the early 1890s. The school admitted only college graduates with at least one year's training in the natural sciences. The clinical education at Johns Hopkins was superior, because the school partnered with Johns Hopkins Hospital, which had been created expressly for teaching and research by members of the medical faculty.

The earliest medical school **accreditation** resulted from a report published by Abraham Flexner. He received a grant from the Carnegie Foundation Commission to study the quality of medical colleges in the United States and Canada. His report, called the Flexner Report, resulted in the closure of many low-ranking schools and the upgrading of others. These events legitimized medical education and opened new doors for many individuals to the world of medicine.

CRITICAL THINKING APPLICATION   2-1

- Mr. Santos asks his class to identify which of the individuals involved in early medicine have had the greatest impact on modern healthcare. Whom would you choose and why?
- The students point out that early research often was viewed in a negative manner. How does research affect us now, and how is it viewed by the public?

Early Medical Pioneers

Andreas Vesalius (1514-1564) was a Belgian anatomist known as the Father of Modern Anatomy (Figure 2-3). At the age of 29, he published his great *De Corporis Humani Fabrica*, in which he described the structure of the human body. This work marked a turning point by breaking with the traditional belief in Galen's theories. Vesalius introduced many new anatomic terms, but because of his radical

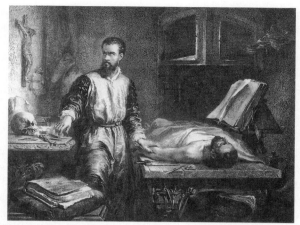

FIGURE 2-3 Andreas Vesalius is known as the Father of Modern Anatomy. (Courtesy National Library of Medicine, Bethesda, Md.)

approach, he was subjected to persecution by his colleagues, teachers, and pupils.

Other important advances and discoveries took place throughout the world. Gabriele Fallopius (1523-1562), an Italian student of Vesalius, also was an accurate dissector. He described and named many parts of the human anatomy. He named the fallopian tubes after himself and also named the vagina and placenta. In 1628 English physician William Harvey (1578-1657) announced his discovery that the heart acts as a muscular pump, forcing and propelling the blood throughout the body. He revealed that the blood's motion is a continuous cycle. He based his conclusion on his experimental vivisection, ligation, and perfusion, as well as brilliant reasoning. Harvey's writings were recognized in Germany before the English permitted their publication at home. Modern England considers Harvey its medical Shakespeare.

The unseen world of microorganisms was first revealed by Anton van Leeuwenhoek (1632-1723), a Dutch linen draper and haberdasher. He ground more than 400 lenses during his lifetime, some of which were no larger than a pinhead. In the grinding process, Leeuwenhoek learned how to use a simple biconvex lens to magnify the minute world of organisms and structures never before seen. Leeuwenhoek was the first ever to observe bacteria and protozoa through a lens, and his accurate interpretations of what he saw led to the sciences of bacteriology and protozoology.

Marcello Malpighi (1628-1694) was born near Bologna, Italy, and attended the University of Bologna, where he earned a doctorate in both medicine and philosophy. He pioneered the use of the microscope in the study of plants and animals. Microscopic anatomy became a prerequisite for advances in physiology, embryology, and practical medicine. In 1661 he described the pulmonary and capillary network connecting the smallest arteries with the smallest veins. This was one of the most important discoveries in the history of science, and it validated Harvey's work. Malpighi is commonly regarded as the first histologist.

Medical Advances in the Eighteenth and Nineteenth Centuries

English scientist John Hunter (1728-1793) is known as the Founder of Scientific Surgery. An army surgeon, he became an expert on gunshot wounds and experimented with tissue transfer. His surgical procedures were soundly based on pathologic evidence. He was the first to classify teeth in a scientific manner, and he introduced artificial feeding by means of a flexible tube passed into the stomach. He provided a classic description of the syphilitic chancre, which sometimes is called a *hunterian chancre*. During his studies of venereal diseases, he inoculated himself with what he thought was gonorrhea, but instead he acquired syphilis. His results in this study actually caused confusion in the medical community, because he mistakenly thought that gonorrhea was a symptom of syphilis. This misconception was not corrected until the beginning of the twentieth century. His collection of anatomic and animal specimens formed the basis for the museum of the Royal College of Surgeons. Hunter is considered the Founder of Scientific Surgery, and today, the John Hunter Hospital in Australia serves more than 600 inpatients and 1,000 outpatients a day.

Edward Jenner (1749-1823) was a student of John Hunter and a country physician from Dorsetshire, England. He is considered one of the immortals of preventive medicine for his development of the smallpox vaccine. While Jenner was serving as an apprentice, he assisted in treating a dairymaid. Smallpox was mentioned, and she commented, "I cannot take that disease, for I have had cowpox." Smallpox at that time was a deadly **pandemic**. Jenner observed that those who had contracted cowpox never contracted smallpox. Later, as a practicing physician, Jenner continued investigating the relationship between cowpox and smallpox almost obsessively, but the medical society members grew bored with his obsession and threatened to expel him from their ranks. On May 14, 1796, Dr. Jenner took purulent matter from a pustule on the hand of Sarah Nelmes, a dairymaid, and inserted it through two small superficial incisions into the arm of James Phipps, a healthy 8-year-old boy. This was the first vaccination. Phipps' vaccination kept him safe from the dreaded disease, and Jenner's method of vaccination spread throughout the world. Today smallpox has been eradicated worldwide as a result of a planned program of global vaccination.

Austrian physician Leopold Auenbrugger (1722-1809) developed the use of percussion in diagnosis. Although scorned and ignored by his contemporaries, his techniques later made him famous and are still used today during physical examinations. René Laënnec (1781-1826) was a French physician who developed the stethoscope in 1819. At first he used only a cylinder of rolled paper in his hands; later he used a wooden device because of its sound-conducting properties. With today's sophisticated stethoscopes, physicians are able to hear sounds in the body, including a fetus inside the mother. Laënnec's book, *Treatise on Mediate Auscultation and Diseases of the Chest,* was readily accepted and translated into many languages. The book is said to be the most important treatise on diseases of the thoracic organs ever written.

Several men of the early 1800s are remembered for their fight against puerperal fever and their concern for women's health. Puerperal fever, an infectious disease that can be contracted during childbirth, was also called *puerperal sepsis* or *childbed fever.* The term *puerperal,* denoting a woman in childbed, originates from the Latin *puer,* "a child," and *pario,* "to bring forth."

The best known of these men was the Hungarian physician Ignaz Philipp Semmelweis (1818-1865); history has called him the Savior of Mothers. His fight against puerperal fever is a sad story

FIGURE 2-4 Louis Pasteur was a brilliant chemist who made numerous contributions to medicine. (Courtesy National Library of Medicine, Bethesda, Md.)

of hardships. His theories were resisted by many professionals, including his instructors. Semmelweis noted that the fever often attacked women who were delivered by medical students coming straight from the autopsy or dissecting rooms. Semmelweis directed that in his wards the students were to wash and disinfect their hands before going to examine the women and deliver the children. As his theories were proved correct, Semmelweis felt an incredible guilt that doctors themselves had caused so many deaths. He died at the age of 47, ironically, from the very disease he had fought. He was infected with puerperal fever from a cut on his finger during an autopsy. His grave had hardly been closed when scientists began to understand the causes of this disease, largely as a result of the investigations of two great scientists, Louis Pasteur and Joseph Lister.

Louis Pasteur (1822-1895) was a Frenchman who did brilliant work as a chemist, but it was his studies in bacteriology that made him one of the most famous men in medical history (Figure 2-4). The title of Father of Bacteriology was bestowed on him, and he also has been honored as the Father of Preventive Medicine. Pasteur's adventures included studying the difficulties involved in the **fermentation** of wine. He averted disaster in France's critical winemaking industry by a process he developed, now called *pasteurization.* This achievement alone would have made him an immortal among the French. Through a process of supplying enough heat to destroy microorganisms, wine was prevented from turning to vinegar. Pasteur's research efforts were impeded when he was stricken with hemiplegia, but after a long, difficult recovery, he was able to continue with a stiff hand and a limp.

Convinced that the infinite world of bacteria held the key to the secrets of contagious diseases, Pasteur left chemistry again to continue studying his theory. Many renowned scientists denied the germ theory of disease and devoted themselves to degrading Pasteur's theories and experiments. In the midst of this controversy, he became involved in the prevention of anthrax, which threatened the health

of cattle and sheep. Pasteur eventually was honored for his work with many other diseases, such as rabies, chicken cholera, and swine erysipelas. He devoted the last 7 years of his life to the Pasteur Institute, which was founded as a clinic for rabies treatment, a research center for infectious disease, and a teaching center. The Pasteur Institute still exists. Pasteur died in 1895, with his family at his bedside. It is said that his last words were, "There is still a great deal to do."

Joseph Lister (1827-1912) revolutionized surgery through the application of Pasteur's discoveries. He understood the similarity between infections in postsurgical wounds and the processes of **putrefaction**. Pasteur proved that these processes were caused by microorganisms. Before this time, surgeons accepted that infections in surgical wounds were inevitable. Lister reasoned that microorganisms must be the cause of infection and should be kept out of wounds. His colleagues were indifferent to his theories, because most believed infections were God-given and natural. Lister disagreed, and he developed antiseptic methods by using carbolic acid for sterilization. By spraying the rooms with a fine mist of the acid, soaking instruments in carbolic solutions, and washing his hands in a similar solution, he was able to prove his theories. He is honored as the Father of Sterile Surgery. Pasteur and Lister met after years of great mutual admiration. The meeting was filled with emotion, and it was written in *Pathfinders in Medicine* that "a new star should have appeared in the heavens to commemorate the event." Medicine truly owes a deep gratitude to these two pioneers for the knowledge they imparted to the art.

Robert Koch (1843-1910) was a German physician, famous for his Koch's Postulates; that is, his theory of rules that must be followed before an organism can be accepted as the causative agent in a given disease. He introduced many of the tools used in the laboratory, such as the culture plate method of isolating bacteria. He discovered the cause of cholera and demonstrated its transmission by food and water. This discovery completely transformed health departments and proved the importance of bacteriology in everyday life. Koch's greatest disappointment was his failure to find a cure for tuberculosis, but in his attempt, he isolated tuberculin, the substance produced by tubercle bacteria. Its use as a diagnostic aid was of immense value to medicine. He became a Nobel Laureate in 1905.

One of Koch's students was a German physician named Paul Ehrlich (1854-1915). He pioneered the fields of bacteriology, immunology, and especially chemotherapy. Ehrlich was only 28 when he wrote his first paper on typhoid, but his greatest gift to humanity was called his "magic bullet," or formula 606, which was designed to fight syphilis. With the organism identified by scientists Bordet and Wasserman, Ehrlich set out to find a chemical that would destroy the organism but not harm the host, specifically, the human body. The six hundred sixth drug Ehrlich tried finally brought about healing. He called it *salvarsan,* because he believed that it offered humankind salvation from the disease. This endeavor also marked the beginning of the practice of injecting chemicals into the body to destroy a specific organism. In 1908 Ehrlich shared the Nobel Prize with Eli Metchnikoff, who is remembered for his theory of phagocytosis and immunology.

Crawford Williamson Long (1815-1878) was the first to use ether as an anesthetic agent. Early in 1842, a group of students would have a social gathering after chemistry lectures and inhale ether, a chemical commonly found in chemistry laboratories, as a form of amusement. Ether, an intoxicant similar to nitrous oxide, functions as a *soporific,* or sleep-inducing agent. However, at one of these "ether frolics," as they were called, Dr. Long also observed that people under the influence of ether did not seem to feel pain. After considerable thought, he decided to use ether for a surgical procedure. In March, 1842, he removed a tumor from the neck of James M. Venable after placing him under the influence of ether. Dr. Horace Wells was a dentist who reported using nitrous oxide as an anesthetic in 1844. Another dentist, Dr. William T. G. Morton, reported using ether in 1846 when he extracted a tooth from a patient, and he also used the gas at Massachusetts General Hospital for a surgical procedure.

Surgeons are grateful to Wilhelm Konrad Roentgen (1845-1923), a professor of physics at the University of Wurzburg, Germany. Roentgen discovered the x-ray in 1895 while experimenting with electrical currents passed through sealed glass tubes. He was awarded the Nobel Prize in Physics in 1901. Although he called it an *x-ray,* history has honored him by calling it the *roentgen ray.* Marie and Pierre Curie discovered radium in 1898, and they were awarded the 1902 Nobel Prize in Physics for their work on radioactivity. Unfortunately, Pierre was killed 3 years later while crossing a street in a rainstorm. Marie was awarded his teaching position at the Sorbonne, a medical university in France; no woman had taught at the school in its 650-year history. In 1911 she was awarded the Nobel Prize for her discoveries of radium and polonium, the first person to receive the award twice. She died in 1934 from pernicious anemia, which was believed to have been caused by her overexposure to radiation and years of overwork.

Nineteenth Century Women in Medicine

Many women made great contributions to medicine in the early nineteenth century, at a time when women were not considered to be as capable as men outside the home environment. Florence Nightingale (1820-1910) is known as the founder of nursing and is fondly called the Lady with the Lamp (Figure 2-5). She was of noble birth, and somewhat late in life she sought nursing training in both England and Europe. By the dawn of the Crimean War in 1854, she had established a fine reputation for her work in hospital organization. She was invited by the British Secretary of War to visit the Crimea to help correct the terrible conditions that existed in caring for the wounded. She created the Women's Nursing Service in Scutari and Balaklava. The physicians treated her and the other 38 nurses poorly until a crisis brought thousands of wounded and sick soldiers to the army hospitals. The bravery and competence of the nurses helped the doctors realize their value to the medical profession. In 1860 she founded the Nightingale School and Home for Nurses in London, which marked the beginning of professional nursing education.

Clara Barton (1821-1912), an American, began her nursing career early in life. When she was 11 years of age, her brother fell from the roof of their barn, and Clara nursed him back to health over a 2-year period. She later was a battlefield nurse and **philanthropist**, whose work during the Civil War led her to recognize that very poor records were kept in Washington to aid in the search for missing men who were wounded or killed in combat. Her efforts to remedy this led to the formation of the Bureau of Records. Her organization and recruitment of supplies for the wounded led to her eventual involvement with the Red Cross in the Franco-Prussian War. In 1881 she organized a Red Cross Committee in Washington, the original formation of the American Red Cross. She served as its first president, from 1881 to 1904. She retired at the age of 82, just after personally leading dangerous expeditions to help victims of fires, hurricanes, and floods. The American Red Cross remains a vital organization to this day.

Elizabeth Blackwell (1821-1910) was the first woman in the United States to receive the Doctor of Medicine degree from a medical school. She began her medical education by reading medical books and later obtained private instruction. Medical schools in New York and Pennsylvania initially refused her applications for formal study, but finally, in 1847, she was accepted at the Geneva Medical College in New York.

Lillian Wald (1867-1940), a social worker and nurse, made great contributions to medical care when she founded the Henry Street Settlement in New York City. Wald operated a visiting nurse service from this establishment. When one of her nurses was assigned to the city's public schools in 1902, the New York City Municipal Board of Health established the world's first public school nursing system.

Margaret Sanger (1883-1966) was born in Corning, New York, and trained as a nurse at the White Plains Hospital. She became the American leader of the birth control movement. While working among the poor in New York City, she came to understand the public's need for information about contraception. In 1873 the federal Comstock Law declared it illegal to import or distribute any device, medicine, or information designed to prevent conception or induce abortion or to mention in print the names of sexually transmitted diseases. Nurses and physicians were legally prohibited from providing this information to their patients. In 1914 Sanger was **indicted** for circulating the magazine *The Woman Rebel,* in which she attacked the legislative restrictions of the Comstock Law. The case was dismissed 2 years later. In the same year, she established the first American birth control clinic; this led to her arrest, conviction, and incarceration in the county jail. She continued her work, and after World War II, she successfully advocated research into hormonal contraception because of the newfound concern about

FIGURE 2-5 Considered the founder of nursing, Florence Nightingale is also known as the Lady with the Lamp. (Courtesy National Library of Medicine, Bethesda, Md.)

population growth. This research ultimately led to development of the birth control pill. When the Planned Parenthood Federation of America was formed in 1941, she was named honorary chairperson.

CRITICAL THINKING APPLICATION   **2-2**

Mr. Santos asks his students to tell him which of these early pioneers they would most like to have worked with. Whom would you choose and why?

- What difficulties would these early medical workers have faced as they explored medicine?
- What difficulties do researchers face today?

MODERN MILESTONES IN MEDICINE

In recognition of the achievements of scientists of the past, Sir Isaac Newton spoke of our innovative ability in the medical field. He humbly said, "If I have seen a little further than others, it is because I have stood on the shoulders of giants." Great strides in medicine occurred in the twentieth century, and technology began to advance rapidly. Medical leaders continued their contributions, and knowledge, treatment, and research grew by leaps and bounds.

Walter Reed, a U.S. Army pathologist and bacteriologist, proved that yellow fever was transmitted by the bite of a mosquito. Individuals with diabetes should be grateful to Sir Frederick Grant Banting, a Canadian physician who isolated insulin for treatment, along with Charles Herbert Best, a Canadian physiologist. In 1928 Sir Alexander Fleming discovered penicillin accidentally while researching influenza and working with staphylococcal bacteria. He found a substance in mold that prevented the growth of bacteria even when the substance was diluted 800 times.

Cardiologist Helen Taussig and surgeon Alfred Blalock explored the health issues of children born with cyanosis resulting from a malformed heart. Dr. Taussig collaborated with Dr. Blalock to develop a lifesaving operation for these children, called "blue babies." History often omits the contributions of Vivien Thomas, an African-American man who was Dr. Blalock's surgical research technician at Johns Hopkins Hospital. Thomas was a former carpenter who constructed several of the medical instruments used in the Blalock-Taussig procedure. Thomas actually created the blue baby condition in dogs, on which he regularly practiced the surgical procedure. When Dr. Blalock and Dr. Taussig performed the first blue baby operation at Johns Hopkins University, Thomas stood over Blalock's shoulder and advised him during the procedure, because Thomas had done the surgery several more times than Blalock. This happened at a time when African-Americans were not allowed on the main floors of the hospital, much less in the surgical suite. This surgery became known as the Blalock-Taussig procedure, and although the first blue baby operation prolonged the patient's life by only 2 months, subsequent operations were successful, and children were able to leave the hospital with the hope of a healthy life.

Jonas Edward Salk and Albert Sabin almost eradicated poliomyelitis, once the killer and crippler of thousands in the United States. Salk's injectable vaccine was developed in 1952, and after wide-scale testing in 1954, it was distributed nationally, greatly reducing the incidence of the disease. Sabin's live-virus vaccine, in a form that could be swallowed, became available less than a decade later.

Werner Forssmann, a German surgeon, originated a cardiac technique called *catheterization* that is used in the diagnosis and treatment of heart disease. Christiaan Barnard, a South African surgeon, performed the first human heart transplantation in 1967. Dr. Elisabeth Kübler-Ross, a Swiss-born psychiatrist who died in 2004, was shocked at the treatment of terminally ill patients at her hospital in New York. She wrote the best-selling book *On Death and Dying,* which helped professionals and laypersons alike understand the stages of grief.

Edwin Carlyle "Carl" Wood is best known for his pioneering work developing and commercializing the technique of in vitro fertilization (IVF). Although some of Dr. Wood's work was controversial, his medical career spanned over 50 years. He wrote 23 books, 59 chapters, and over 400 papers in refereed medical and scientific journals.

Some diseases, conditions, and anatomical structures are named for the person who first discovered them or pioneered the disease. Dr. Virginia Apgar (1909-1974) founded neonatology. She developed the Apgar score, which is a method of assessing the health of newborns at the time of birth. The assessment has greatly reduced infant mortality by quickly determining whether a newborn needs immediate medical treatments. Henry Jay Heimlich, MD, is credited for the Heimlich maneuver, which uses abdominal thrusts to relieve choking. Aloysius Alzheimer (1864-1915) was a German physician who was credited with identifying the first published case of presenile dementia, later known as Alzheimer's disease. Parkinson's disease is named for Dr. James Parkinson, an English surgeon, geologist, and paleontologist. Down's syndrome, which is a chromosomal condition caused by an extra twenty-first chromosome, was first described by British doctor John Langdon Haydon Down. Asperger syndrome was named for Hans Asperger of Austria, who wrote hundreds of publications about autism. Asperger's is characterized by significant difficulties in social interaction along with restricted and repetitive patterns of behavior and interests. Thomas Hodgkin (1798-1866) was considered one of the most prominent pathologists of his time and pioneered preventative medicine. Dr. Hodgkin provided the first description of Hodgkin's disease or Hodgkin's lymphoma, characterized by the orderly spread of disease from one lymph node to another and by the development of systemic symptoms with advanced disease. Those familiar with the common diseases related to human immunodeficiency virus infection (HIV) and acquired immunodeficiency syndrome (AIDS) will recognize Kaposi's sarcoma, a skin tumor discovered by Hungarian physician Moritz Kaposi. In the 1980s, Kaposi's sarcoma, or KS, was determined to be caused by a viral infection and became widely known as one of the AIDS-defining illnesses.

CRITICAL THINKING APPLICATION   **2-3**

- During a class discussion, Mr. Santos points out that the leaders in the healthcare industry had specific goals for their careers and achieved worldwide recognition for their contributions. What individuals have made contributions to medicine in recent years?
- How can the individual medical assistant make a contribution to medicine?

Many modern physicians are making important discoveries in and contributions to the field of medicine. Dr. David Ho is considered by many to be one of the most brilliant minds in medicine today, helping to piece together the puzzle of HIV. A professor at Rockefeller University, Ho is the scientific director and chief executive officer (CEO) of the Aaron Diamond AIDS Research Center in New York City, which is the largest private HIV/AIDS research organization in the world. He was born in Taiwan and his family immigrated to the United States when he was 12 years old. He eventually entered college to study physics—medicine was actually his second choice—but once he discovered molecular biology and the concept of gene splicing, he decided to become a researcher. In 2011, he won the Avant-Garde Award, presented by the National Institute on Drug Abuse, which contributes $500,000 per year for 5-years. The award is given to stimulate high-impact research that may lead to groundbreaking opportunities for the prevention and treatment of HIV/AIDS in drug abusers.

Dr. C. Everett Koop graduated from Cornell University as a medical doctor in 1941 and spent most of his career as a pediatric surgeon. During his terms as the U.S. Surgeon General, he became a proponent of tobacco awareness, insisting that tobacco advertisements must be less attractive to the youth of today. Dr. Koop is a professor at Dartmouth Medical School. He founded the Koop Institute, an organization that has a mission to "promote the health and well-being of all people." Dr. Koop has been honored with many awards, including 41 honorary doctorates.

Dr. Marcia Angell is the former editor in chief of the *New England Journal of Medicine* (NEJM), one of the most prestigious medical publications in the United States. Her career with NEJM began in 1979, and her excellent articles spanned a variety of subjects, from the pharmaceutical companies' profit margins to the effects of socioeconomic status on Americans seeking healthcare services. Dr. Angell was named one of the 25 most influential Americans in 1997 by *Time* magazine. She has written and contributed to several books, including *Science on Trial: The Clash of Medical Evidence and the Law in the Breast Implant Case.* Dr. Angell is a board-certified pathologist and currently serves as senior lecturer in the Department of Global Health and Social Medicine at Harvard Medical School.

As the director of the National Institute of Allergy and Infectious Diseases at the National Institutes of Health (NIH), Dr. Anthony Fauci leads research efforts on immune-mediated disorders. Many of his studies now relate to HIV and the body's response to AIDS, in addition to ways to improve HIV treatment and prevention, including the development of an HIV vaccine. In 2003, an Institute for Scientific Information study indicated that in the 20-year period from 1983 to 2002, Dr. Fauci was the 13th-most-cited scientist among the 2.5 to 3 million authors in all disciplines throughout the world who published articles in scientific journals during that time frame. Dr. Fauci was the world's 10th-most-cited HIV/AIDS researcher in the period between 1996 to 2006. He received his MD degree from Cornell University Medical College, and his career with the NIH has spanned more than 40 years. In 2009, *Forbes* magazine named Dr. Fauci one of the seven most powerful people in medicine.

Vice Admiral Regina M. Benjamin, MD, the current Surgeon General of the United States, took office in 2006 (Figure 2-6). She

FIGURE 2-6 Vice Admiral Regina Benjamin was the first female and first African-American to be elected to the American Medical Association board of directors. Dr. Benjamin is the current Surgeon General of the United States.

earned her bachelor's degree in chemistry at Xavier University in New Orleans, her MD from the University of Alabama at Birmingham, and her MBA from Tulane University in New Orleans; she also holds 18 honorary degrees. In 1995, she was the first female and first African-American woman to be elected to the American Medical Association's board of directors. After establishing a clinic in a small fishing village in Alabama, Dr. Benjamin persevered through Hurricanes Georges and Katrina, in addition to a devastating fire, often contributing her own money to keep the clinic open. She became nationally prominent for her business acumen and her humane approach to preventative medicine.

Armando E. Giuliano, MD, is the executive vice-chair of surgery and surgical oncology at Cedars-Sinai Medical Center in Los Angeles, California. The co-director of the Saul and Joyce Brandman Breast Center, Dr. Giuliano has been honored extensively for his treatment and research on breast cancer. His most recent research on breast cancer was published in the *Journal of the American Medical Association.*

Ching-Hon Pui, MD, is the chair of the Department of Oncology at St. Jude's Children's Research Hospital in Memphis, Tennessee. Dr. Pui received his medical education in Taiwan and uses his experience as a pediatrician, educator, and humanitarian to advance the cure rate and understanding of acute lymphoblastic leukemia in children. Many of his research findings have stimulated changes in clinical practice that are now widely accepted in the global pediatric oncology community. He has authored more than 700 original articles and chapters, edited seven books and monographs, and serves as section editor or editorial board member for several prestigious journals. He is also one of the most highly cited authors in clinical medical research. A series of Dr. Pui's innovative treatment protocols boosted cure rates at St. Jude from about 70% in the early 1980s to an unprecedented 90% in the past decade.

The director of the Center to Advance Palliative Care, a national organization devoted to increasing the number and quality of palliative care programs in the United States, Dr. Diane E. Meier has served as professor of medical ethics at Mount Sinai School of Medicine in New York City, where she has served on the faculty since 1983. Dr. Meier has published extensively in all major peer-reviewed medical journals, including the *New England Journal of Medicine* and the *Journal of the American Medical Association*. She edited the first textbook on geriatric palliative care and four editions of *Geriatric Medicine*. Dr. Meier has appeared on television and in print, including ABC World News Tonight, *The New York Times*, the *Los Angeles Times*, and *Newsweek*.

Keith Black, MD, is the chairman of the Department of Neurosurgery at Cedars-Sinai Medical Center in Los Angeles. Throughout his medical career, Dr. Black has been fascinated with the human brain. He hopes to change cancer treatment by reducing and possibly eliminating the need for chemotherapy, surgery, and radiation treatments, believing that the body's immune system was critical in fighting tumors. His aggressive treatments and leadership have made Cedars-Sinai one of the top neurosurgical centers in the country.

One of the nation's top obstetricians, Dr. Linda Bradley, is considered an innovative leader in the field of obstetrics and gynecology. She has researched hysterectomy alternatives and abnormal uterine bleeding extensively and pioneered the use of hysteroscopy and new procedures such as endometrial ablation and myomectomy. Dr. Bradley is the vice chairman of obstetrics, gynecology, and the Women's Health Institute at the Cleveland Clinic.

THE NATIONAL VIEW OF HEALTHCARE

World Health Organization

The World Health Organization (WHO), founded in 1948, is a specialized agency of the United Nations. The organization promotes cooperation among nations in their efforts to control and eliminate diseases worldwide. The purposes of WHO are:

- To provide worldwide guidance in the field of health
- To set global standards for health
- To cooperate with governments in strengthening national health programs
- To develop and transfer appropriate health technology, information, and standards

One of the greatest accomplishments of this agency was the eradication of smallpox. Other diseases, such as polio and leprosy, are on the verge of eradication. The agency also created and maintains the International Classification of Diseases (ICD) coding system. ICD-9 is used today to identify diseases and conditions with a specific code number (ICD-10 goes into effect in fall 2013). The original purpose of this system was to track worldwide morbidity and mortality statistics. WHO is committed to research and delivery of needed drugs and medical supplies to various areas of the world.

In addition, WHO promotes the sharing of health information, and WHO officials meet with the leaders of the worldwide health industry to discuss various ethical and moral implications that face today's healthcare professionals.

U.S. Department of Health and Human Services

The Department of Health and Human Services (DHHS) is the principal U.S. agency for providing essential human services and protecting the health of all Americans, especially those unable to help themselves. The DHHS is made up of more than 300 programs involved in:

- Medical and social science research
- Immunization services
- Financial assistance for low-income families
- Child support enforcement services
- Improvement of infant and maternal health
- Child and elder abuse prevention services
- Assistance programs for elderly Americans

The DHHS also oversees the Medicare and Medicaid programs. Medicare is the nation's largest health insurer, and the DHHS processes more than 1 billion claims every year.

U.S. Army Medical Research Institute of Infectious Diseases

The primary focus of the U.S. Army Medical Research Institute of Infectious Diseases (USAMRIID) is to protect members of the military, but the institute conducts key research programs in national defense and infectious diseases that benefit everyone (Figure 2-7). USAMRIID, located at Fort Detrick in Maryland, works extensively with the Centers for Disease Control and Prevention (CDC) and WHO. USAMRIID also controls an internationally known reference laboratory with state-of-the-art facilities. This laboratory is instrumental in identifying biologic threats and the diseases those threats produce. USAMRIID is the only laboratory facility operated by the Department of Defense that is equipped to study biosafety level IV viruses and pathogens, the most deadly organisms.

Four biosafety levels are commonly accepted among laboratory professionals. Biosafety level I includes well-known agents that pose a minimal or low biohazard potential to laboratory personnel and

FIGURE 2-7 U.S. Army Medical Research Institute of Infectious Diseases in Fort Detrick, Maryland. (Courtesy USAMRIID, Fort Detrick, Md.)

to the environment as a whole. At this level, the laboratory is not necessarily separated from the regular areas of the facility. Examples of level I pathogens include *Pneumococcus* and *Salmonella* organisms. In the biosafety level II section of the laboratory, substances with a moderate biohazard potential are studied. For biosafety level I and level II areas, laboratory personnel receive specific training in handling pathogens, and specialized equipment is used to prevent splashes and splatters. Pathogens classified as biosafety level II include the hepatitis, Lyme disease, and influenza viruses.

Personnel working in the biosafety level III section receive very specific training in working with the potentially deadly pathogens found at this level. All procedures performed on level III pathogens have a high biohazard risk and are done inside protective safety cabinets. Laboratory personnel are required to wear heavy personal protective equipment. Special regulations concerning exhaust air and ventilation are strictly followed, and access to the laboratory is limited when work is in progress. HIV; *Bacillus anthracis,* which causes anthrax; and *Rickettsia typhi* and *Rickettsia prowazekii,* which cause typhus, are some of the pathogens classified as biosafety level III.

Biosafety level IV includes the most deadly pathogens, which often produce incurable diseases. The biohazard risk of transmission of these agents is extreme and includes the risk of airborne transmission. Laboratory personnel are highly trained in the manipulation and handling of these dangerous pathogens. Laboratory access is strictly controlled in this section. Some of the pathogens studied at biosafety level IV include the Ebola virus, Lassa virus, and hantavirus.

Centers for Disease Control and Prevention

The headquarters of the CDC is in Atlanta, Georgia (Figure 2-8). The CDC is the principal U.S. federal agency concerned with the health and safety of people throughout the world and is part of the DHHS. It is a clearinghouse for information and statistics associated with healthcare. Several divisions in the CDC focus on specific health-related issues, such as the National Center for HIV, STD, and TB Prevention; the Public Health Practice Program Office; the National Center on Birth Defects and Developmental Disabilities; and the National Center for Health Statistics. Branch offices

FIGURE 2-8 Headquarters of the Centers for Disease Control and Prevention (CDC) in Atlanta, Georgia. (Courtesy Centers for Disease Control and Prevention, Atlanta, Ga.)

are located throughout the United States and in several foreign countries. The CDC provides regulations that affect all healthcare facilities. When the virus now known as HIV was discovered, the CDC was one of the first organizations to research and attempt to isolate the virus. When a pandemic begins, the CDC information services offer guidelines that help facilities ensure the health of their employees, patients, and the public at large. The agency also conducts research into the origin and occurrence of diseases and develops methods to control and prevent them. In addition, it develops immunization services and aids in the training of healthcare workers.

National Institutes of Health

The NIH began as a one-room laboratory in the Marine hospital on New York's Staten Island in 1887. Its first major contribution to medicine was the isolation of the bacterium that causes cholera. In 1930 the laboratory became the NIH, an agency of the DHHS. The mission of the NIH is to develop knowledge that will lead to better health for everyone. As a part of the public health service, it seeks to improve the health of the American people, supports and conducts biomedical research into the causes and prevention of diseases, and uses a modern communications system to furnish biomedical information to the healthcare professions.

The NIH moved from Washington, D.C., to Bethesda, Maryland, in 1938 and today occupies more than 60 buildings covering 30 acres. It consists of 27 different institutes and centers, in addition to the National Library of Medicine. Thousands of research projects are underway in NIH laboratories and clinics at any given time. The NIH also provides support to other research projects conducted at universities, medical schools, and hospitals.

TYPES OF HEALTHCARE FACILITIES

Hospitals

Hospitals are classified according to the type of care and services they provide to patients, as well as by the type of ownership. *Acute care* hospitals offer intensive care units and emergency or trauma departments and are equipped to handle the most severely ill or injured patients. *Subacute care* hospitals offer patient care for those who do not require extensive services but still need hospital supervision and treatment. *Specialty* hospitals, such as a psychiatric hospital, offer specific services. *Teaching* hospitals provide a learning environment and often also have research departments. These hospitals usually are affiliated with medical schools, and interns or residents provide care supervised by licensed physician instructors. *Community* hospitals provide care in rural areas or in specific areas within a metropolis. *Regional* hospitals usually are acute care facilities and serve a large area in which intensive care may not be offered in local communities.

Private hospitals are run by a corporation or other organization and usually are designed to produce a profit for the owners or stockholders. *Nonprofit* hospitals exist to serve the community in which they are located and are normally run by a board of directors. The term *nonprofit* sometimes is misleading, because "profit" is different from "making money." A nonprofit hospital or organization may make money in a campaign or fund raiser, but all of the money is returned to the organization. Nonprofit hospitals and organizations must follow strict guidelines in the area of finance and must account to the government for the money brought in and the purposes for which it is used.

A *hospital system* is a group of facilities that are affiliated and work toward a common goal. Hospital systems may include a hospital and a cancer center in a small community or may consist of a group of separate hospitals in a specific geographic region. Many hospital systems are designed as integrated health delivery systems. An integrated delivery system (IDS) is a network of healthcare providers and organizations that provides or arranges to provide a coordinated continuum of services to a defined population and is willing to be held clinically and fiscally accountable for the clinical outcomes and health status of the population served. An IDS may own or could be closely aligned with an insurance product, such as a type of insurance policy. Services provided by an IDS can include a fully equipped community and/or tertiary hospital, home healthcare and hospice services, primary and specialty outpatient care and surgery, social services, rehabilitation, preventive care, health education and financing, usually using a form of managed care. An IDS can also be a training location for health professional students, including physicians, nurses, and allied health professionals.

Sometimes the term *county hospital* is used to designate the hospital to which **indigent** patients are taken. These hospitals provide emergency care to those who cannot pay for medical expenses. Today, however, many people without insurance go to the emergency department (ED or ER) for routine illnesses. This is one reason EDs are busy and full. If patients have no other options, the ED physicians become primary care providers. This is a major cause of the long waiting times in hospital EDs. Managed care has eased this problem somewhat by refusing to cover visits to the ED that are not true emergencies. **Triage**, performed by physicians, nurses, and some other licensed medical professionals, determines which patients have the most severe conditions and should be seen first.

Hospitals have various departments that are organized to provide efficient patient care. The admissions department gathers information and enters it into a computer for use by the rest of the hospital staff. Nursing service supervises all of the nursing care given to the patients and is involved in **case management**. The laboratory provides diagnostic testing on blood, body fluids, and tissues, and the radiology or nuclear medicine department offers diagnostic imaging and radiographic services. The respiratory services department offers a broad spectrum of diagnostic tests and various treatments. Most hospitals also have a physical medicine and rehabilitation department, which offers both physical and occupational therapy. The dietary department employs professionals who carefully plan menus to meet the needs of each patient served. Most modern hospitals have a surgery department, and many offer day surgery services that allow patients to undergo a procedure and return home the same day, if they recover as expected. The medical records department is responsible for the patient records related to every **encounter** that takes place in the facility. Social services works with patients to ensure continuity of care, patient education, and social intervention, all of which assist patients with emotional, economic, and social concerns.

Hospital administrators manage the hospital on a day-to-day basis, and human resource responsibilities usually are a part of the administration department. Almost every hospital has a board of directors to assist the administrators in governing the hospital; in addition, a medical staff committee, led by the hospital's chief of staff, usually assists in the management of the facility and the credentialing process for the physicians who have **staff privileges**. **Credentialing** involves determining whether a practitioner should be allowed to practice medicine in a facility, based on his or her education, license, past performance, and other qualifications.

The National Practitioner Data Bank (NPDB) also gathers information that helps healthcare facilities ensure that physicians who might be brought on staff are competent. The intent of the NPDB is to improve the quality of healthcare by encouraging state licensing boards, hospitals, healthcare entities, and professional societies to identify and discipline those who engage in unprofessional behavior and to restrict the ability of incompetent physicians to move from state to state without disclosure or discovery of previous medical malpractice payment or adverse action history. NPDB provides information about physicians who have had licensure problems, made malpractice settlements, had clinical privileges revoked or restricted, or had action taken against them by a professional society to registered entities, but not to the general public.

Peer review organizations (PROs) are also critical to good healthcare facility management. A medical peer review is defined by the American Medical Association as a process conducted by physicians to ensure that other physicians consistently maintain optimum standards of fitness to practice medicine. Peer review also can be applied to other medical professionals. Credentialing, as mentioned, is the verification process that takes place before assignment or reappointment of staff privileges; peer reviews help ensure that physicians or other medical professionals maintain the high standards necessary to practice medicine in an accurate and effective way.

Accreditation is considered the highest form of recognition for the quality of care a facility or organization provides. Not only does it indicate to the public that the facility is concerned with providing high-quality care, it also provides professional liability insurance benefits and plays a role in regulatory agency relicensure and certification efforts. Hospitals and other healthcare facilities are often accredited by the Joint Commission, an organization concerned with the quality of care in healthcare facilities. **Standards** or **indicators** have been developed that help determine when patients are receiving high-quality care. The term *quality* refers to much more than whether the patient liked the food served or had to wait to have a procedure or test performed. Categories of compliance include:

- Assessment and care of patients
- Use of medication
- Plant, technology, and safety management
- Orientation, education, and training of staff
- Medical staff qualifications
- Patients' rights

Ratings from 1 to 5 are given to the facility on its performance in specific areas. A 1 rating means that the facility is in full compliance with that standard, and the other ratings indicate levels of noncompliance. The DHHS also regulates healthcare facilities, as does the federal Occupational Safety and Health Administration (OSHA), a division of the U.S. Department of Labor that enforces many laws related to workplace safety.

CRITICAL THINKING APPLICATION 2-4

- Mr. Santos has assigned his students to groups and asked them to investigate local hospitals. What types of hospitals are found in your local area, and what services do they provide? How might a hospital board decide what services to offer to the community?

- How might Mr. Santos' students find out whether a physician has staff privileges at a certain hospital?

- What areas or populations are underserved, and why might this be the case?

Ambulatory Care

Many other types of healthcare facilities operate in the industry today. **Ambulatory** care centers include a wide range of facilities that offer healthcare services to patients who are able to walk around (are not bedridden). Physicians' offices, group practices, and multispecialty group practices are common types of ambulatory care facilities. Group practices may involve a single specialty, such as pediatrics, or may be multispecialty. A multispecialty practice might consist of an internal medicine specialist, an oncologist, a family practitioner, and an endocrinologist. Usually the physicians in the practice refer patients to each other when indicated. This is not only more convenient for the patients, but also more profitable for the physicians in the practice. A patient seeing a physician for the first time is considered a *new* patient, whereas a patient who has seen the physician on previous occasions is called an *established* patient. Most physicians charge new patients more than established patients, because the levels of decision making, the extent of the physical examination, and the complexity of the medical history require that more time be directed toward the new patient. This information is critical to the coding process (see Chapters 18 and 19).

Occupational health centers are concerned with helping patients return to work and productive activity. Often, physical therapy is used in conjunction with rehabilitation services that assist the patient in regaining as much of his or her previous level of ability as possible. Also, freestanding rehabilitation centers can assist patients with a wide range of services. Pain management centers help patients deal with discomfort associated with their condition. Sleep centers diagnose and treat people with sleep problems. As is pain, difficulty sleeping is a symptom, and the cause of the disturbance must be found so that proper treatment can be provided. Freestanding urgent or emergency care centers provide patients with an alternative to hospital EDs. They are less expensive, have a shorter waiting time, and are conveniently located in many areas. Most have flexible hours, many are open well into the evening, and walk-in appointments usually are accepted.

Surgery has become more convenient because of the number of ambulatory surgical centers that exist today. Day surgery performed in hospitals continues to provide patients with alternatives to overnight hospital care after surgery. Many insurance companies now prefer day surgery, because it is more cost-effective. Not many years ago, the only alternative to inpatient surgery was the same hospital's day surgery department. Today, more and more freestanding surgical centers are becoming available. Patients can be treated with laser surgery, radial keratotomy, and cataract removal during the day and recover at home the same evening. Plastic surgeons are becoming very innovative in the physical structure of their offices and the types of surgery they offer on an outpatient basis. Many plastic surgeons offer breast augmentation and reduction and even abdominoplasty ("tummy tuck") and liposuction in the office. Not long ago, an abdominoplasty meant staying in the hospital for several days. The new trend is becoming more accepted, partly as a result of the "office-based surgery" accreditation offered by the Ambulatory Care Accreditation Program of The Joint Commission.

A number of rehabilitation services are available to patients, based on their need and the type of illness or injury. Rehabilitation services may be obtained from acute care hospitals, rehabilitation hospitals, or various ambulatory rehabilitation facilities. Patients may use these services for a few weeks after an illness or injury or may continue them for several years. Rehabilitation usually involves several members of the healthcare team working together to ensure that the patient recovers to the greatest extent possible.

Dialysis centers offer services to patients with severe kidney disorders, and many of the larger cities across the country have cancer centers for patients who need treatment by oncologists. Many other types of ambulatory care facilities exist, including centers that provide magnetic resonance imaging (MRI), student health clinics, dental clinics, endoscopy centers, community health centers, mobile health services, podiatric care centers, and women's health centers.

Geriatric and long-term patients have more options today for ambulatory care than ever before. In the past, nursing homes were the only alternative to keeping elderly patients in their own homes. These nursing homes provided care for residents who needed more than just assistance with day-to-day activities. Now, many attractive options to traditional nursing homes or skilled nursing facilities are available. One of the most popular is assisted living. Most assisted-living facilities provide 24-hour supervision of their residents, most meals, and a broad range of services, from the very basic, such as transportation to physician office visits and errand running, to the extravagant, such as shopping trips and daylong outings. Most also provide exercise programs, social services, laundry and linen services, and housekeeping. The cost ranges from approximately $1,000 to $3,000 per month, depending on the location and the **amenities** desired by the resident. Many new assisted-living facilities are designed specifically for patients with Alzheimer's disease or other impaired memory conditions. Independent retirement communities offer residents the opportunity to come and go as they please. Many have a resortlike design, catering to the desire of retirees to enjoy their golden years. Usually the communities consist of apartments or duplex units, and some even offer small cottages.

Other Healthcare Facilities

Several other types of healthcare facilities deserve attention in the broad overview of the healthcare industry. Diagnostic laboratories offer testing services for patients referred by their physicians. Since the enactment of the Clinical Laboratory Improvement Act (CLIA) in 1967 and its amendment i in 1988, many physicians have stopped providing laboratory tests in their offices. These types of laboratories are called *physician office laboratories* (POLs). CLIA was enacted to ensure high-quality laboratory testing. The regulations set forth by both OSHA and CLIA rules often made it more cost-effective to have the patient go to an outside laboratory to have the tests done. The medical assistant should note that, as mentioned previously, OSHA is an organization and division of the U.S. Department of Labor that enforces many laws related to workplace safety. CLIA is a law, not an agency. However, both influence safety and quality testing. (CLIA is discussed in more detail in Chapter 7).

Home health agencies were tremendously successful in the late 1980s to the mid-1990s, but cuts in Medicare funding have caused them to suffer severe losses in recent years. This concept of care is very popular. Unfortunately, the influx of too many home health agencies and the subsequent drop in payments made to them have resulted in fewer home healthcare providers over the past several years. In addition, many hospitals began offering home healthcare, which added to the already heavy competition that smaller firms faced. Home healthcare offers its patients home care, therapy services, administration of and assistance with medications, and other services so that the patient can remain at home yet still obtain the care needed.

Medical suppliers are retail operations that offer all types of medical devices and products. Patients with diabetes can purchase glucose monitoring machines. Special hospital beds can be ordered for those who need them. All types of durable medical equipment (DME), such as bedpans, crutches, bathing assistance devices, wheelchairs, and walkers, are available, often without a physician's prescription. Most medical suppliers serve both the public and the profession.

Hospice centers play an important role in the acceptance of terminal illnesses. These facilities are designed to care for the patient with a terminal disease and provide support to family members. The goal of hospice is to provide peace, comfort, and dignity while controlling pain and promoting the best possible quality of life for the patient. Most patients involved in hospice care have a life expectancy of less than 6 months.

TYPES OF MEDICAL PRACTICE

Medical practices today generally are organized according to one of three types of business structures: the sole proprietorship, the partnership, or the corporation. Sole proprietorships dominated medical practice until the last quarter of the twentieth century. These practices are on the decline as a result of the **advent** of managed care, which favors the multispecialty group practice.

Sole Proprietorship

A sole proprietor is an individual who holds exclusive right and title to all aspects of the medical practice. The sole proprietor may employ other physicians to participate in the practice. The employed physician is entitled to employee benefits; the owner, however, is not considered an employee and is not so entitled. In addition, the owner is potentially liable for all the acts of his or her professional employees and staff members. Although practicing alone has many advantages, including flexibility and independence, it also has significant disadvantages. For example, the owner has total responsibility for covering the practice 24 hours a day, 7 days a week. In an unincorporated solo practice, the business dies when the owner leaves it unless it is sold to someone else. Many modern

physicians do not see sole proprietorship as an avenue for a decent income as a doctor, because managed care companies often offer participation to group practices over the single-practice physician, enabling them to provide more options to the patients. Some doctors organize associate practices. In this case, physicians share office space and often equipment and employees, but they operate their practices as sole proprietorships. Agreements such as these should always be put in writing to prevent misunderstandings and legal problems.

Partnership

When two or more physicians elect to associate in the practice of medicine, they may enter into a partnership agreement. This agreement specifies all the rights, obligations, and responsibilities of each partner. The participants have a greater potential for profit as a partnership than they would in practice as sole proprietors, because various expenses are shared and resources are pooled. Each physician has more freedom, because the doctors rotate an "on call" schedule so that each has some time away from the office and patients. One disadvantage of the partnership is the liability of each for the actions and conduct of all the others. In a partnership arrangement, the partners often pool employees, equipment, insurance, facilities, and even profits, and these resources are divided according to the specifications of the partnership agreement or contract.

A *group practice* is a body of at least three licensed physicians who engage in full-time practice in a formally organized and legally recognized entity. A group practice may take the form of a partnership, or it may be formed as a corporation. The group may share income and expenses, equipment, records, and personnel and may combine patient care and business management. The group practice may be an association of the same specialty or may be a multispecialty organization. Usually a group practice takes the form of a partnership or corporation.

Corporation

A *corporation* may be defined as an artificial entity having a legal and business status that is independent of its shareholders or employees. Corporations are regulated by the statutes of the state in which the incorporation takes place. In most cases the physician shareholders are employees of the corporation. Even a physician in a solo practice can incorporate the practice. All employees of the corporation receive income and tax advantages. Corporations are usually able to offer better benefits packages, which may include pension and profit-sharing plans, medical expense reimbursement, life insurance, disability income insurance, and many other benefits.

HEALTHCARE PROFESSIONALS

Physicians and providers are portals of entry (first contacts) into the healthcare system. Patients who have a medical problem go to a physician or provider to obtain help. Some patients must be referred to a medical specialist for further examinations and treatments. Many insurance policies will not pay for a patient to see a specialist without first consulting with their primary provider. Medical doctors, osteopathic doctors, and chiropractors are three of the portals of entry into the healthcare system.

Title of "Doctor"

Doctors of Medicine

Medical doctors (Doctor of Medicine [MD]) are considered **allopathic** physicians and are the most widely recognized type of physician. They diagnose illness and disease and prescribe treatment for their patients. MDs are allowed to write prescriptions and perform surgery. They offer advice on nutrition and preventive medicine. Becoming an MD usually requires 4 years of undergraduate training (premed) and 4 years of medical school. Some extraordinary students are allowed entry after 3 years of undergraduate studies; however, because competition for entry into medical school is intense, grades and other experience in healthcare are strongly considered. Premed students study biology, physics, organic and inorganic chemistry, mathematics, English, humanities, and social sciences. There are approximately 125 allopathic medical schools in the United States. After medical school, the student faces 3 to 8 years of internship and residency programs. An *intern* is a medical student still in training at medical school who treats patients under the supervision of licensed physicians. A *residency* is a graduate medical education program, often in a specialty, and usually is a paid, on-the-job training hospital position.

Often MDs specialize in a certain field, such as cardiology or pediatrics. These doctors usually invest 3 to 6 years of training in the specialty after medical school and can obtain board certification in one or more of 24 different specialty areas recognized by the American Board of Medical Specialties (ABMS) (Table 2-1). An MD must have a state license to practice, and continuing education is required to maintain the license. Graduates of foreign medical schools usually can obtain a license in the United States after passing an examination and completing a residency program in this country.

Doctors of Osteopathy

Osteopathic physicians (Doctor of Osteopathy [DO]) complete requirements similar to those of MDs to graduate and practice medicine. Osteopaths use medicine and surgery, in addition to osteopathic manipulative therapy (OMT), in treating their patients. Andrew Taylor Still is considered the Father of Osteopathic Medicine, which he began in 1874. He believed in a more **holistic** approach to medicine, and although he was an MD, he founded the American School of Osteopathy in Kirksville, Missouri. The school originally was chartered to offer an MD degree but later focused more on the osteopathic approach. DOs stress preventive medicine and holistic patient care, in addition to a special focus on the musculoskeletal system and OMT. Osteopathic medicine also promotes the **innate** ability of the body to heal itself, and many osteopaths tend to take a more conservative approach to using medications and surgical procedures than allopathic physicians. Many DOs practice **homeopathy**, believing in the body's ability to heal itself. Premed students moving toward osteopathic medicine study biology, physics, organic and inorganic chemistry, mathematics, English, humanities, and social sciences. They also usually complete 4 years of undergraduate studies and then begin 4 years of medical studies at a school for osteopathic medicine. Most DOs participate in a 12-month rotating internship in the various specialty areas before entering a residency program that lasts 2 to 6 years, and they are eligible for board certification through either the American Board of Medical Specialists or the American Osteopathic Association. Approximately one in 20 physicians in the United States is a DO. DOs participate in continuing education programs to renew their licenses annually.

Doctors of Chiropractic

Chiropractors (Doctor of Chiropractic [DC]) typically are thought of as "bone doctors," but they actually focus on the nervous system to help patients live healthier lives. The nervous system is the master system of the body, controlling and coordinating all the other systems. Information from the environment, both internal and external, moves through the spinal cord to get to the brain, and in the same manner, information from the brain moves through the spinal cord to reach the body in a two-way flow of communication. The intention of the **chiropractic** adjustment is to remove any disruptions or distortions of this energy flow that may be caused by slight misalignments, which chiropractors call **subluxations**. Chiropractic colleges require undergraduate studies in biology, organic and inorganic chemistry, physics, English, and the humanities and then 3 to 4 years studying chiropractic. Each state offers licensing. Some chiropractors devote their practices to a specialty, but more often they practice general chiropractic. Continuing education is required for relicensure. Chiropractic is one of the most common fields of **complementary and alternative medicine (CAM)**. Chiropractic can be used along with both allopathic and osteopathic medicine to enhance the results of treatment.

Hospitalists

Hospitalists are physicians whose primary professional focus is the general medical care of hospitalized patients. Most hospitalists are employed by the healthcare facility instead of having individual free-standing offices in which patients are seen and treated. Perhaps the most attractive benefit of becoming a hospitalist is the quality of life for the physician and his or her family. Hospitalists work a specific, set number of hours each week and do not directly experience the economic pressures of managed care, because they usually are placed on a salary. Although the hospitalist is in charge of the patient while the person is in the hospital, if the patient has a primary care provider (PCP), he or she may still visit the patient. Of course, the patient is not required to use the services of a hospitalist and may be cared for by the PCP. However, patients admitted from the emergency department or those in a location away from the PCP may find the hospitalist to be an excellent alternative to their regular physician.

CRITICAL THINKING APPLICATION   2-5

- Mr. Santos challenges his new medical assisting students to interview several types of doctors at some point during their studies. The class discusses the different philosophies of medicine among allopathic, osteopathic, and chiropractic physicians. Discuss with your class the similarities and differences of these three aspects of medicine.

- Most of Mr. Santos' students have visited one or more of these types of doctors. What experiences have you had with medical doctors (MDs), osteopaths (DOs), or chiropractors (DCs)?

TABLE 2-1 Examples of Medical Specialties Recognized by the American Board of Medical Specialties

SPECIALTY	PRACTITIONER'S TITLE	DESCRIPTION
Allergy and Immunology	Allergist/ Immunologist	Allergists/immunologists are trained to evaluate disorders and diseases of the immune system. This includes conditions such as adverse reactions to drugs and food, anaphylaxis, and problems related to autoimmune diseases, asthma, and insect stings.
Anesthesiology	Anesthesiologist	Anesthesiologists provide pain relief and pain management during surgical procedures and also for patients with long-standing conditions accompanied by pain such as cancer patients. Anesthesiologists also provide critical care and resuscitation for patients during cardiac or respiratory emergencies.
Colon and Rectal Surgery	Colon and rectal surgeon	Colorectal surgeons diagnose and treat conditions affecting the intestines, rectum, and anal area, in addition to organs affected by intestinal disease. They often treat cancers that appear in these areas. They also treat disorders such as hemorrhoids and fissures.
Dermatology	Dermatologist	Dermatologists work with adult and pediatric patients in treating disorders and diseases of the skin, hair, nails, and related tissues. Dermatologists are specially trained to manage conditions such as skin cancers, cosmetic disorders of the skin, scars, allergies, and other disorders, both malignant and benign.
Emergency Medicine	Emergency physician	Emergency physicians are experts in triage and treating a patient to prevent the patient's death or serious disability. This physician gives immediate care to stabilize the patient, and then refers to the appropriate professional for further care. These physicians are usually found in hospital emergency rooms or freestanding emergency centers.
Family Medicine	Family practitioner	Family practitioners offer care to the whole family, from newborns to elderly adults. They are familiar with a wide range of disorders and diseases. However, preventive care is their primary concern. This is one of the specialties most often chosen by physicians.
General Surgery	Surgeon	General surgeons correct deformities and defects and treat diseases or injured parts of the body by means of operative treatment. A general surgeon must be familiar with the various specialties to treat patients effectively. General surgery includes all aspects of surgery other than those classified into a subgroup specialty.
Genetics	Medical geneticist	Geneticists are physicians trained to diagnose and treat patients with conditions related to genetically linked diseases. They also may provide genetic counseling when indicated. Often associated with research projects, geneticists may participate in screening programs for defects and abnormalities, sometimes before the birth of an infant.
Internal Medicine	Internist	Internists are concerned with comprehensive care, often diagnosing and treating those with chronic, long-term conditions. They also offer treatment for common illnesses and preventive care. Internists must have a broad understanding of the body and its ailments to be able to diagnose conditions and provide treatment.
Neurological Surgery	Neurosurgeon	Neurosurgeons provide surgical and nonsurgical care for patients with conditions of the central, autonomic, and peripheral nervous systems, including the supporting structures and vascular supplies of related organs.
Neurology/Psychiatry	Neurologist/ psychiatrist	Neurologists diagnose and treat disorders of the brain, spinal cord, and nerves and the blood vessels that support those organs. Generally, neurologists manage infectious, metabolic, degenerative, and systemic involvement of the nervous system. Psychiatrists are physicians who specialize in the diagnosis and treatment of people with mental, emotional, or behavioral disorders. A psychiatrist is qualified to conduct psychotherapy and to prescribe medications when necessary.
Nuclear Medicine	Nuclear medicine specialist	Specialists in nuclear medicine use radioactive substances to diagnose and treat disease. Radiation and imaging instruments are used to detect diseases often before the organ is assessed as abnormal by other methods. Nuclear medicine specialists are aware of the effects of radiation on various structures and are educated in the fundamental principles of radiation and physics.

TABLE 2-1 Examples of Medical Specialties Recognized by the American Board of Medical Specialties—cont'd

SPECIALTY	PRACTITIONER'S TITLE	DESCRIPTION
Obstetrics and Gynecology	Obstetrician/gynecologist	Obstetricians provide care to women of childbearing age and monitor the progress of the developing child. They deliver the baby and care for the mother for approximately 6 weeks after birth. Gynecologists are concerned with the diagnosis and treatment of the female reproductive system.
Ophthalmology	Ophthalmologist	Ophthalmologists diagnose, treat, and provide comprehensive care for the eye and its supporting structures. These physicians also offer vision services, including corrective lenses. Screening tests are promoted as preventive care.
Otolaryngology	Otolaryngologist	Otolaryngologists treat diseases and conditions that affect the ear, nose, and throat and structures related to the head and neck. Problems that affect the voice and hearing are also referred to this specialist.
Pathology	Pathologist	Pathologists study the causes of diseases that affect the body and determine what may have caused a patient's death. These physicians study tissues and cells, body fluids, and the organs themselves to aid in the diagnosis of a patient's ailments. Pathologists often perform autopsies.
Pediatrics	Pediatrician	Pediatricians promote preventive medicine and treat diseases that affect children and adolescents. They monitor the child's growth and development and provide a wide range of health services to keep their patients healthy.
Physical Medicine and Rehabilitation	Physiatrist	Physiatrists assist patients who have physical disabilities, which may include rehabilitation; patients with musculoskeletal disorders; and patients suffering from pain as a result of injury or trauma. Their primary goal is to restore the patient to the state of health he or she had before the injury or trauma, as nearly as possible, through rehabilitation.
Plastic Surgery	Plastic surgeon	Plastic surgeons work with patients who have a physical defect as a result of some type of injury or condition. These surgeons perform reconstructive procedures using grafts, flaps, and tissue transfer and replanting. They also provide cosmetic enhancements and elective procedures.
Preventive Medicine	Preventive medicine specialist	Preventive medicine specialists are concerned with preventing mental and physical illness and disability. They also analyze current health services and plan for future medical needs. Preventive medicine consists of several components, including biostatistics, environmental studies, occupational studies, and clinical preventive medicine activities.
Radiology	Radiologist	Radiology is a specialty in which x-rays are used to diagnose and treat disease. A diagnostic radiologist specializes in using x-rays, ultrasound, nuclear medicine, computed tomography, and magnetic resonance imaging to detect abnormalities throughout the body.
Thoracic Surgery	Thoracic surgeon	Thoracic surgeons are concerned with the operative treatment of the chest and chest wall, lungs, and respiratory passages. They also are involved with heart surgery, including both valvular and coronary heart surgery.
Urology	Urologist	Urologists are concerned with the treatment of diseases and disorders of the urinary tract. They diagnose and manage problems with the genitourinary system and practice endoscopic and percutaneous procedures related to these structures.

Data from http://www.abms.org/who_we_help/physicians/specialties.aspx.

Dentists

The two basic types of dentists in the United States are Doctors of Dental Medicine (DMDs) and Doctors of Dental Surgery (DDSs). Dentists treat and prevent problems of the teeth and gums and the tissue surrounding them. They can perform oral surgery and write prescriptions for antibiotics and analgesics. Some specialist dentists perform straightening, called *orthodontics,* and some perform root canal therapy, called *endodontics.* Dental school usually lasts 4 years after completion of undergraduate studies, and state licensing is required.

Optometrists

The optometrist (OD) is trained and licensed to examine the eyes to test visual acuity and to treat vision defects by prescribing correctional lenses and other optical aids. A program of exercise may be planned for the patient's eyes. Optometrists study at accredited schools of optometry for 4 years after completing undergraduate studies in the sciences, mathematics, and English. They must be licensed in the state in which they practice. Optometrists should not be confused with ophthalmologists, who are licensed MDs.

Podiatrists

Podiatrists (Doctors of Podiatric Medicine [DPMs]) are educated in the care of the feet, including surgical treatment. Most people spend an extraordinary amount of time on their feet, resulting in wear and tear and chronic pain. Podiatrists are trained to find pressure points and weight-distribution problems. These doctors train for 4 years at accredited colleges after undergraduate studies in the sciences.

Other Doctorates

Other individuals may be called "doctor" based on the degree they have earned in their field. For instance, a person with a PhD has a doctor of philosophy degree in his or her field of expertise and may be addressed as "doctor." This individual might work as a professor at a university or in a field related to his or her discipline. An individual with a PsyD degree is a doctor of psychology, and someone with an EdD degree is a doctor of educational psychology. Doctors who practice **naturopathy**, called *naturopathic physicians,* use only natural means to help the body to heal. These medical professionals are licensed in 15 states.

Nurses

Registered Nurses

The RN has many career options. Many nurses work in an administrative capacity as managers in hospitals or other types of healthcare facilities. They also provide direct patient care, a role in which they are vital for assessing the patient and providing a care plan. Nurses usually find a specialty area that they enjoy and practice within that area, although they may also "float" to different departments in the hospital. Some function as home health nurses, visiting patients and providing home care. Others work in nursing homes, in public health, or in physicians' offices.

Licensed Practical and Vocational Nurses

Licensed practical nurses (LPNs) and licensed vocational nurses (LVNs) offer bedside care, assisting with the day-to-day personal care required by inpatients. They assess patients, chart their progress, and administer medications and intravenous fluids where allowed by law. They often work in hospitals or skilled nursing facilities and also are found in physicians' offices. They sometimes supervise nursing assistants and may also provide patient education services.

Nurse Practitioners

Nurse practitioners (NPs) provide basic patient care services, including diagnosing and prescribing medications for common illnesses. These professionals must have advanced academic training beyond the registered nurse (RN) degree and also have vast clinical experience. Nurse practitioners usually focus on preventive care and disease prevention. An NP is allowed to practice independently or as a part of a team of healthcare professionals.

Nurse Anesthetists

Nurse anesthetists are registered nurses (RNs) who administer anesthetics to patients during care by surgeons, physicians, dentists, or other qualified health professionals. They practice in many different settings, including offices, traditional hospitals, labor and delivery units, ophthalmology offices, plastic surgery offices, and many others. This practice is quite advanced, and they are compensated well for their skills. Nurse anesthetists can be found in both metropolitan and rural communities.

Other Healthcare Professionals

Many different healthcare professionals contribute to the patient's care and recovery. Some work in a hospital setting, and others perform their duties in other types of medical facilities or in the patient's home. The *Healthcare Careers Directory,* published by the American Medical Association, lists many of the various allied healthcare professionals who provide care to patients (Table 2-2). Additionally, more information about licensed healthcare professionals is available in Table 2-3.

▌CLOSING COMMENTS

The healthcare industry is certainly one of the most exciting career fields in today's world. The constant change in and development of new technology and theories make medicine an attractive option for career choices. The needs of medicine extend far beyond the boundaries of the United States, and collaborative efforts among countries promote a faster move forward, with new discoveries and hope for those affected by disease. Headlines daily grace newspapers and computer screens, detailing stories of human cloning, "designer" babies, genetic discoveries, and computer capabilities that amaze us all. Medications are being developed that will bring us to the brink of eliminating certain diseases. The mapping of the human genome may lead to incredible breakthroughs in the study of colon, breast, and ovarian cancers, cystic fibrosis, neurologic degeneration, sickle cell anemia, and countless other conditions. There has never been a more thrilling time to become part of the world of medicine and to make a contribution as a healthcare professional.

▌Patient Education

Some patients have very little knowledge about the healthcare industry and may need instruction and explanations about details important to their healthcare. For instance, many patients do not understand that they may receive several bills after a hospital stay. They often call the physician's office with questions; therefore medical assistants must understand hospital systems to be able to help the patients. Become familiar with community resources to make referrals for patients that need help from various sources. If a patient seems to have a need, speak with him or her privately and determine whether any agency or organization could help with the issues at hand. Patients will appreciate the medical assistant's willingness to look for ways to help when confronted with problems. Always have an attitude of enthusiasm at every opportunity to assist a patient.

▌Legal and Ethical Issues

The medical assistant should have a good understanding of the history of medicine and develop an appreciation of those who paved the way to the achievement of today's level of medical technology. These pioneers of medicine should be respected for their efforts to expand and improve healthcare, because many of them sacrificed their reputations and even their lives to prove their theories. Often,

TABLE 2-2 Allied Health Occupations Recognized by the American Medical Association

TITLE	CREDENTIAL	JOB DESCRIPTION
Anesthesiologist Assistant	AA	Functions as a specialty physician assistant under the direction of a licensed and qualified anesthesiologist; assists in developing and implementing the anesthesia care plan.
Art Therapist	ATR	Uses drawings and other art and media forms to assess, treat, and rehabilitate patients with mental, emotional, physical, and/or developmental disorders.
Athletic Trainer	ATC	Provides a variety of services, including injury prevention, assessment, immediate care, treatment, and rehabilitation after physical injury or trauma.
Audiologist	CCC-A	Identifies individuals with symptoms of hearing loss and other auditory, balance, and related neural problems; assesses the nature of those problems and helps individuals manage them.
Blindness and Visual Impairment professionals	LVT, O&M, VRT	Help people learn to use their vision more efficiently, both with and without optical devices; provide training and offer recommendations to help patients function more successfully in their environments.
Blood Bank Technology Specialist	SBB	Performs routine and specialized tests in blood center and transfusion services, using methods that conform to the accepted standards in the blood bank industry.
Diagnostic Cardiovascular Sonographer/Technologist	RDCS, RVT	Using invasive or noninvasive techniques (or both), performs diagnostic examinations and therapeutic interventions for the heart and blood vessels at the request of a physician.
Clinical Laboratory Science/ Medical Technologist	MT, MLT	In conjunction with pathologists, performs tests to diagnose the causes and nature of disease; also develops data on blood, tissues, and fluids of the human body using a variety of methodologies.
Counseling-related professional	LPC, LMHC	Deals with human development through support, therapeutic approaches, consultation, evaluation, teaching, and research; practices the art of helping people to grow.
Cytotechnologist	CT	Works with pathologists to evaluate cellular material from all body sites, primarily through use of the microscope; examines specimens for normal and abnormal cytologic changes, including malignancies.
Dance Therapist	DTR, ADTR	Uses the psychotherapeutic properties of movement as a process that furthers the emotional, cognitive, social, and physical integration of the patient as a tool for healing.
Dental Assistant, Dental Hygienist, Dental Laboratory Technician	CDA, RDH, CDT	Performs a wide range of tasks, from assisting the dentist to teaching patients how to prevent oral disease and maintain oral health.
Diagnostic Medical Sonographer	RDMS	Uses medical ultrasound to gather sonographic data, which can aid the diagnosis of a variety of conditions and diseases; also monitors fetal development.
Dietician, Dietetic Technician	DTR	Integrates and applies the principles of food science, nutrition, biochemistry, physiology, food management, and behavior to achieve and maintain health status.
Electroneurodiagnostic Technologist	REEG-T	Records and studies the electrical activity of the brain and nervous system; obtains interpretable recordings of patients' nervous system function.
Emergency Medical Technician, Paramedic	EMT, Paramedic	Provides medical care to people who have suffered an injury or illness outside the hospital setting, most often in an emergency; provides basic or advanced life support (or both).
Genetics Counselor	IGC	Provides genetic services to individuals and families seeking information about the occurrence or risk of a genetic condition or birth defect.
Health Information Management professional	RHIA, RHIT	Provides expert assistance in the systems and processes for health information management, including planning, engineering, administration, application, and policy making.
Kinesiotherapist	RKT	Provides rehabilitation exercise and education designed to reverse or minimize debilitation and enhance the functional capacity of medically stable patients.

Continued

TABLE 2-2 Allied Health Occupations Recognized by the American Medical Association—cont'd

TITLE	CREDENTIAL	JOB DESCRIPTION
Massage Therapist	MT	Applies manual techniques, and may apply adjunctive techniques, with the intention of positively affecting the health and well-being of a patient or client.
Medical Assistant	CMA, RMA	Functions as a member of the healthcare delivery team and performs both administrative and clinical procedures and duties; a multiskilled health professional.
Medical Illustrator	MI	Specializes in the visual display and communication of scientific information; creates visuals and designs communication tools for teaching both medical professionals and the public.
Music Therapist	MT-BC	Uses music in a therapeutic relationship to address the physical, emotional, cognitive, and social needs of individuals of all ages; assesses the strengths and needs of clients and patients.
Nuclear Medicine Technologist	RT	Uses the nuclear properties of radioactive and stable nuclides to make diagnostic evaluations of anatomic or physiologic conditions of the body; also provides therapy with unsealed radioactive sources.
Occupational Therapist	OTR	Uses purposeful activity and interventions to achieve functional outcomes, thereby maximizing the independence and maintaining the health of those limited by physical injury or illness.
Ophthalmic Laboratory Technician, Medical Technician/Technologist	COT, COMT	Collects data and performs clinical evaluations; performs tests and protocols required by ophthalmologists; assists in the treatment of patients.
Orthoptist	CO	Performs a series of diagnostic tests and measurements on patients with visual disorders; helps design a treatment plan to correct disorders of vision, eye movements, and alignment.
Orthotist/Prosthetist	RTO, RTP, RTPO	Designs and fits devices (orthoses) to patients who have disabling conditions of the limbs and spine and/or partial or total absence of a limb.
Perfusionist	CCP	Operates extracorporeal circulation and autotransfusion equipment during any medical situation where the patient's respiratory or circulatory function must be supported or temporarily replaced.
Pharmacy Technician	CPhT	Assists pharmacists with duties that do not require the expertise or judgment of a licensed pharmacist.
Physical Therapist	PT	Helps to improve a patient's strength and mobility, relieve pain, and prevent or limit permanent physical disabilities; takes a personal, direct approach to meeting individual health goals.
Physician Assistant	PA	Practices medicine under the direction and supervision of a licensed doctor of medicine or osteopathy; makes clinical decisions and provides a range of services.
Radiation Therapist, Radiographer	RRTD	Delivers prescribed dosages of radiation to patients for therapeutic purposes; provides appropriate patient care and maintains accurate records of the treatment provided.
Rehabilitation Counselor	CRC	Determines and coordinates services to assist people with disabilities in moving from psychological and economic dependence to independence.
Respiratory Therapist, Respiratory Therapy Technician	RRT, CRT, RPFT, CPFT	Evaluates, treats, and manages patients of all ages with respiratory illnesses and other cardiopulmonary disorders; advanced respiratory therapists exercise considerable independent judgment.
Surgical Assistant	CSA	Assists in exposure, hemostasis, closure, and other intraoperative technical functions that help the surgeon carry out a safe operation with optimal results for the patient.
Surgical Technologist	ST, CST	Helps prepare patients for surgery and maintains the sterile field in the surgical suite, making sure all members of the surgical team follow sterile technique.
Therapeutic Recreation Specialist	CTRS	Uses treatment, education, and recreation services to help people with illnesses, disabilities, and other conditions develop and use their leisure in ways that enhance their health.

TABLE 2-3 Licensed Healthcare Professions

TITLE	CREDENTIAL	JOB DESCRIPTION
Physician Assistant	PA	Physician assistants provide direct patient care services under the supervision of licensed physicians. They are trained to diagnose and treat patients as directed by the physician, and in 46 states and the District of Columbia, they are allowed to write prescriptions. These professionals take patient histories, order and interpret tests, perform physical examinations, and even make diagnostic decisions. They work in physicians' offices and hospitals, on military bases, and in other healthcare facilities.
Nurse Practitioner	NP	Nurse practitioners provide basic patient care services, including diagnosing and prescribing medications for common illnesses. These professionals must have advanced academic training, beyond the registered nurse (RN) degree, and also must have extensive clinical experience. Nurse practitioners usually focus on preventive care. A nurse practitioner is allowed to practice independently as part of a team of healthcare professionals.
Nurse Anesthetist	NA	Nurse anesthetists are registered nurses who administer anesthetics to patients during care provided by surgeons, physicians, dentists, or other qualified health professionals. They practice in many different settings, including offices, traditional hospitals, labor and deliver units, ophthalmology offices, and plastic surgery offices. This practice is quite advanced, and nurse anesthetists are compensated well for their skills. They can be found in both metropolitan and rural communities.
Registered Nurse	RN	A registered nurse has many career options. Many nurses work in administration as managers in hospitals or other types of healthcare facilities. They also provide direct patient care, a role in which they are vital for assessing the patient and providing a care plan. Nurses usually find a specialty area that they enjoy and practice in that area, although they may also "float" to different departments in the hospital. Some function as home health nurses, visiting patients at home and providing home care. Others work in nursing homes, in public health, or in physicians' offices.
Licensed Practical or Vocational Nurse	LPN or LVN	Licensed practical nurses (LPNs) and licensed vocational nurses (LVNs) offer bedside care, assisting with the day-to-day personal care required by inpatients. They assess patients, chart their progress, and administer medications and intravenous fluids where allowed by law. They often work in hospitals or skilled nursing facilities and also are found in physicians' offices. They sometimes supervise nursing assistants and may also provide patient education services.
Medical Technologist	MT	Medical technologists perform diagnostic testing on blood, body fluids, and other types of specimens to assist the physician in arriving at a diagnosis. These professionals work with bacteria and viruses and use their technical skills, combined with their knowledge of disease, to perform their duties. They can make quality control decisions and can act independently in their profession. Hospitals, teaching universities, research organizations, and laboratories employ most of the medical technologists. These professionals usually have a Bachelor of Science (BS) degree in addition to certification or licensure.
Medical Laboratory Technician	MLT	Medical laboratory technicians perform most of the same test procedures that the medical technologist performs; the difference between the two is that the MLT does not work independently. MLTs usually are supervised by an MT and have at least an associate's degree and certification or a licensure. MLTs work in the same types of facilities as MTs.
Physical Therapist	PT	Physical therapists assist patients in regaining their mobility and improving their strength and range of motion, which may have been impaired by an accident or injury or as a result of disease. After assessing the patient, the physical therapist devises a treatment plan in conjunction with the patient's physician. The goal of the physical therapist is to improve how the patient functions at work and at home.
Respiratory Therapist	RT	Most respiratory therapists work in hospitals. All types of patients receive respiratory care, including newborns and geriatric patients. Respiratory therapists commonly use oxygen therapy to assist with breathing, and they also perform diagnostic tests that measure lung capacity.
Occupational Therapist	OT	Occupational therapists work with patients who have developed conditions that disable them developmentally, emotionally, mentally, or physically. Occupational therapists assist in helping the individual to compensate for loss of function; their goal is to bring patients to a functional level where they can live healthy, productive lives.

Continued

TABLE 2-3 Licensed Healthcare Professions—cont'd

TITLE	CREDENTIAL	JOB DESCRIPTION
Diagnostic Cardiac Sonographer or Vascular Technologist	DCS or DVT	Diagnostic cardiac sonographers (DCSs) or vascular technologists (DVTs) assist in the diagnosis and treatment of cardiac and vascular diseases and disorders. They perform noninvasive tests, including echocardiographs and electrocardiographs. Often the cardiovascular technician uses ultrasonography to assist the physician in identifying malfunctions of the heart and its structures.
Radiology Technician	RT	Radiology technicians use various machines to help the physician diagnose and treat certain diseases. These machines may include x-ray equipment, ultrasonographic machines, and magnetic resonance imaging (MRI) scanners. Radiology technicians explain procedures to patients. They also are knowledgeable about the correct positioning techniques used for each examination; these techniques ensure that the images recorded are accurate and helpful for the diagnosing physician.
Paramedic	Paramedic	Paramedics are specially trained to provide emergency care to patients in life-threatening situations. Paramedics are highly efficient and well versed in the functions of the body. They perform advanced skills and, with more experience, are able to supervise or direct the operations of an emergency care ambulance facility.
Emergency Medical Technician	EMT	Emergency medical technicians progress through several levels of training, each providing more advanced skills. Their medical education encompasses managing respiratory, cardiac, and trauma cases and often emergency childbirth. Some states also recognize specialties in the EMT field, such as EMT-Cardiac, which includes training in cardiac arrhythmias, and EMT—Shock Trauma, which includes starting intravenous fluids and administering specific medications.
Registered Dietician	RD	Registered dieticians are thoroughly trained in nutrition and the different types of diets patients require to improve or maintain their condition. They use the advice of the physician and information about the patient to design healthy diets during hospital stays and even help plan menus for home use. In addition, they teach patients about their recommended diet and also about alternatives that can help the patient choose attractive foods.

Modified from the American Medical Association: *Healthcare careers directory (2012-2013)*. Accessed [02-19-2013] at http://www.ama-assn.org/ama/pub/education-careers/careers-health-care/directory.page

they broke the laws of the time to advance medical science. Their historical legacy represents enormous endeavors by these discoverers of new principles, theories, treatments, and cures.

Ethical medical assistants must always strive to serve the patient above the call of duty and continuously work within their scope of practice. Patients expect everyone in the medical field to have ethics above reproach; remember that all actions are under an ethical microscope and must be professional, accurate, and performed in a competent manner. Put the patient first every day at work and always treat the individual with respect and compassion.

SUMMARY OF SCENARIO

Mr. Santos is an effective instructor, and one who is concerned about providing interesting material for his students. He wishes to instill a strong respect in the students for the people who played a role in early medical advances. His classroom discussions will help the students to think about what it was like to present new ideas to the public and often be ridiculed.

In addition to teaching his students about the history of medicine and the state of healthcare today, he provides opportunities for the students to work together in discussion groups and present information to the class. He encourages Internet research, a valuable skill that will help the medical assisting student in many areas of training. By allowing the students to speak in front of the class to give reports on the medical pioneers, Mr. Santos teaches them to be more at ease when speaking in public and when articulating instructions and details to patients and co-workers. All of these skills make a well-rounded medical assistant who will become a great asset to the facility in which he or she is employed.

Mr. Santos explains that continuing medical research is critical to the healthcare industry, because new and more effective drugs and treatments are necessary, and because many diseases and conditions do not as yet have a cure. Medical research constantly looks for better ways to make patients well and continually strives to find cures for diseases that medicine has not yet conquered. Medical assistants may work for physicians who are involved in research projects, and this may afford them the opportunity to contribute to medical research.

By providing his students with an overview of the healthcare industry, Mr. Santos helps them to become more familiar with the professionals whom they will encounter in various medical facilities and to have a better awareness of their duties and responsibilities.

SUMMARY OF LEARNING OBJECTIVES

1. **Define, spell, and pronounce the terms listed in the vocabulary.**
   Spelling and pronouncing medical terms correctly bolster the medical assistant's credibility. Knowing the definition of these terms promotes confidence in communication with patients and co-workers.

2. **Identify the ancient cultures that contributed a major portion of our medical terminology.**
   Greek and Roman mythology contributed the major portion of the medical terms we use today. Terms have also been borrowed from Anglo-Saxon, German, Arabic, and other sources, including the Bible.

3. **Distinguish between and describe the staff of Aesculapius and the caduceus.**
   The American Medical Association adopted the staff of Aesculapius as the symbol of medicine. The symbol is a staff encircled by a serpent. The caduceus often is mistakenly used to represent medicine but is actually the medical insignia of the U.S. Army Medical Corps. This icon is a winged staff encircled by two serpents.

4. **Explain the philosophy behind the phrase "physicians must learn to despise money."**
   Galen was a champion of medical ethics and believed that physicians could not truly be devoted to the practice of medicine if they were concerned about profit. Many modern medical professionals agree with Galen's theory and argue that physicians must base their decisions on what is best for the patient as opposed to focusing on monetary profit.

5. **Explain why a medical education at Johns Hopkins University School of Medicine was considered superior, even in its early years.**
   Johns Hopkins University School of Medicine has been recognized as a leader in healthcare education for more than a century. The university was one of the first institutions to partner with a hospital for training purposes, resulting in its superior medical education. The School of Medicine also had a research department, where faculty members investigated new methods and treatments for patients. The combination of a medical education with readily available patients brought the discovery of illness and disease into a new light for those early medical students. Today, the Johns Hopkins medical system is a multibillion-dollar organization, incorporating three acute care hospitals and other facilities into an integrated healthcare system.

6. **List several medical pioneers and discuss the importance of their contributions to the medical profession.**
   Numerous early pioneers made tremendous contributions to the medical field. Constant growth and research have pressed the medical profession forward, and with the assistance of technology, the growth speeds along today faster than ever.

7. **Explain the roles of the national healthcare organizations.**
   National healthcare organizations provide information, medication, and personnel to attempt to eradicate diseases and treat the diseases for which no cure exists. Many of these organizations operate with restricted funding and rely often on donations and volunteer workers to operate. These agencies often work together in an effort to solve problems of epidemics effectively and learn more about diseases. All of the national healthcare organizations are a vital part of the medical industry today.

8. **Identify the role of the Centers for Disease Control and Prevention (CDC) regulations in healthcare settings.**
   The CDC is a clearinghouse for information and statistics associated with healthcare. Several divisions within the CDC focus on specific health-related issues, such as the National Center for HIV, STD, and TB Prevention; the Public Health Practice Program Office; the National Center on Birth Defects and Developmental Disabilities; and the National Center for Health Statistics. Branch offices are located throughout the United States and in several foreign countries. The CDC provides regulations that affect all healthcare facilities. When the virus now known as HIV was discovered, the CDC was one of the first organizations to research and attempt to isolate the virus. When a pandemic begins, the CDC information services offer guidelines that help facilities ensure the health of their employees, patients, and the public at large.

9. **Discuss the various types of ambulatory care.**
   Physicians' offices, group practices, and multispecialty group practices are a few types of ambulatory care. This division of medicine also includes occupational health centers, dialysis centers, rehabilitation clinics, and sleep centers. Patients who are ambulatory are able to move from place to place, usually on their own or with the assistance of a wheelchair or walker.

10. **Name the three main provider portals of entry into the healthcare system and distinguish among the different types of physicians and medical practices.**
    The three main provider portals of entry into the healthcare system are medical doctors, osteopathic physicians, and chiropractic physicians. These different disciplines have some similar training, but osteopathic physicians usually use a holistic approach, and chiropractors concentrate many of their efforts on the alignment of the spine in an effort to promote healing of the body. Most physicians work in a sole proprietorship, a group practice, or a healthcare corporation.

11. **Become familiar with the medical specialties recognized by the American Board of Medical Specialties.**
    Numerous specialties focus on particular areas of the practice of medicine. The American Board of Medical Specialties recognizes 24 specialty groups, which support various organizations designed to promote that particular branch of medicine. Although other specialties and subspecialties of medicine exist, the most common and most generally recognized are those associated with the American Board of Medical Specialties.

12. **Understand both the allied health professions and how they relate to medical assisting.**
    The American Medical Association recognizes more than 60 allied health-care occupations. These allied health professionals contribute to the field of medicine, each playing a specific role in the healthcare industry. The medical assistant works as a part of the healthcare team with all of these professionals.

CONNECTIONS

📖 **Study Guide Connection:** Go to the Chapter 2 Study Guide. Read and complete the activities.

ⓔ **Evolve Connection:** Go to the Chapter 2 link at evolve.elsevier.com/kinn to complete the Chapter Review and Chapter Quiz. Check out the other resources listed for this chapter to make the most of what you have learned from The Healthcare Industry.

THE MEDICAL ASSISTING PROFESSION

3

SCENARIO

Sandra Ramirez is a single mother who has decided on medical assisting as a career. She has always been interested in the medical field and wants a job that will allow her to spend evenings and weekends with her 3-year-old son, Roberto. The idea of working in a physician's office appeals to her, and she has applied to a school that is close to her apartment and day care provider. She plans to attend day classes and work part-time after school until it is time to pick up her son.

Sandra is very excited about her new career and has set several goals for her training. First, she hopes to attain perfect attendance, and second, she would like to graduate with honors. She has budgeted her study time and plans to ask her instructors during the first 2 weeks of school for suggestions on how she can better prepare for classes and examinations. Sandra will find medical assisting to be a rewarding career and respected profession.

While studying this chapter, think about the following questions:

- What obstacles might prevent Sandra from attending all her classes, and how can she prepare in advance to overcome them?
- How can Sandra begin to explore the type of physician's office in which she would enjoy being employed after graduation?
- What goals might Sandra have at the commencement of her training? At the end of training?
- How can Sandra make the most of her time attending school to become a medical assistant?

LEARNING OBJECTIVES

1. Define, spell, and pronounce the terms listed in the vocabulary.
2. Briefly discuss the history of medical assisting as a profession.
3. Discuss the versatility of a career in medical assisting.
4. Differentiate between administrative and clinical medical assisting duties and recognize the importance of becoming knowledgeable about the general responsibilities of the medical assistant.
5. Comprehend the current employment outlook for the medical assistant.
6. Give the reasons that hiring an individual with no formal training often is more expensive than hiring a professional medical assistant.
7. Identify several considerations to keep in mind, other than financial compensation, when choosing a position as a medical assistant.
8. Discuss the aspects of the medical assistant's performance on a successful externship.
9. List three unacceptable behaviors on the externship site.
10. Explain why continuing education is so important to the medical assistant.
11. Understand medical assistant credentialing requirements, the importance of credentialing, and the process of obtaining credentials.
12. Discuss the difference between a CMA and a RMA.

VOCABULARY

allied health fields Occupational disciplines in which professionals involved with the delivery of healthcare or related services assist physicians with the diagnosis, treatment, and care of patients in many different specialty areas.

benefits Services or payments provided under a health plan, employee plan, or some other agreement, including programs such as health insurance, pensions, retirement planning, and many other options that may be offered to employees of a company or organization.

certification (ser-tuh-fuh-ka'-shun) The attesting of something as being true as represented or as meeting a standard; the result of having been tested, usually by a third party, and awarded a certificate based on proven knowledge.

continuing education units (CEUs) Credits for courses, classes, or seminars related to an individual's profession that are designed to promote education and to keep the professional up to date on current procedures and trends in the field; CEUs often are required for licensing.

cross-training Training in more than one area so that a multitude of duties may be performed by one person or so that substitutions of personnel may be made in an emergency or at other necessary times.

externship (or **internship**) A training program that is part of the medical assisting course of study in an educational institution. This part of training is taken in the actual business setting of that field of study; the terms are interchanged in some areas of the country.

intangibles (in-tan'-juh-buls) Qualities that cannot be perceived, especially by touch, or cannot be precisely identified or realized by the mind.

invasive Involving entry into the living body, as by incision or insertion of an instrument.

perks Extra advantages or benefits of working in a specific job that may or may not be commonplace in that particular profession; a shortened form of perquisites.

phlebotomy (fli-bah'-tuh-me) An invasive procedure used to obtain a blood specimen for testing, experimentation, or diagnosis of disease.

practicum Another word for the externship; a training program that is a part of the medical assisting course of study in the actual business setting of a medical office or facility. (This term is used by the Commission on Accreditation of Allied Health Education Programs [CAAHEP] to designate the externship.)

profit sharing Offer of a part of a company's profits to employees or other designated individuals or groups.

stock options Offers of stocks for purchase to a certain group of individuals or certain groups, such as employees of a for-profit hospital.

versatile (vur'-suh-til) Embracing a variety of subjects, fields, or skills; having a wide range of abilities.

According to the U.S. Department of Labor's *Occupational Outlook Handbook,* medical assisting employment will grow 31% in the decade between 2010 and 2020, making this career field one of the fastest growing occupations in the United States. Much of this growth will be the result of an increase in the number of group practices, clinics, and other facilities that need a high number of support personnel. This makes the medical assistant who can handle both clinical and administrative duties particularly valuable to the physician.

A career as a medical assistant is challenging and offers job satisfaction, opportunities for service, financial reward, and possibilities for advancement. Men and women can be equally successful as medical assistants. Individuals considering the medical assisting discipline must be dedicated and committed and must have a strong desire to become caregivers. Caregivers are people who have the ability to put the needs of the patient first, and they have a sincere concern for those who are not at their best. A caregiver must feel an obligation to assist the patient in whatever way possible and must have patience with those who, at times, are more difficult. This strong inner desire is one of the most important qualities of the successful professional medical assistant. Through the development of this "care giving" mentality, many personal rewards will follow, as will a long and beneficial career.

THE HISTORY OF MEDICAL ASSISTING

The first medical assistant was probably a neighbor of a physician who was called on to help when an extra pair of hands was needed. As time passed and the practice of medicine became more organized and more complicated, some physicians hired nurses to help in their office practices. Gradually, record keeping, data reporting, and an increasing number of business details became important to physicians, and they realized a need for an assistant with both administrative and clinical training. Nurses were likely to have training only in clinical skills; therefore, many physicians began training them or other individuals to assist with all of the office duties. Community and junior colleges began offering training programs that focused on both administrative and clinical skills in the late 1940s. Medical assistant organizations at the local and state levels began developing around 1950, and soon after, certifying examinations became available. Today medical assisting is one of the most respected **allied health fields** in the industry, and training is readily available through community colleges, junior colleges, and private educational institutions throughout the United States.

The American Association of Medical Assistants (AAMA) was co-founded by Mary E. Kinn, who served as the organization's president in 1958. She helped to establish a certifying program for members of the AAMA and chaired the certifying branch in 1959. Kinn authored this textbook from 1967 through 1999 and then retired. She is greatly respected for her contributions to the field of medical assisting.

THE SCOPE OF PRACTICE OF A MEDICAL ASSISTANT

Today's medical assistant is a **versatile** professional. The duties that medical assistants perform vary not only from office to office, but even within the same office. Medical assistants perform routine duties within the offices of many types of health professionals, including physicians, chiropractors, podiatrists, and others. According to the *Occupational Outlook Handbook,* more than half of the total number of medical assistants work in a physician's office. Individuals with medical assisting training can accomplish various jobs in the hospital environment, and some are employed by freestanding emergency centers or surgery centers. Opportunities for medical assistants are growing because of the constant change within the medical profession and the surge of **cross-training**, which means that one individual is trained to do a variety of duties. Medical assistants work under the direct supervision of a physician in the office and perform tasks delegated by the doctor or supervisor.

The AAMA once defined the scope of practice as the "performance of delegated clinical and administrative duties within the supervising physician's scope of practice consistent with the medical assistant's education, training, and experience." This definition remains accurate today. The duties performed by the medical assistant do not constitute the practice of medicine. Students should review the definition and requirements of the scope of practice for medical assistants in their individual states.

The two major categories of duties that medical assistants perform are administrative tasks and clinical tasks (Figure 3-1). On the administrative end of the spectrum, medical assistants greet patients who arrive in the office or clinic and obtain basic registration information. They may enter information into a computer and assemble the patient's paper or electronic medical record. They are trained to do office bookkeeping, which may be done electronically or manually. The medical assistant is trained in filing procedures and in proper techniques for adding information to the medical record. A

basic knowledge of procedure and diagnosis coding is important today, and some medical assistants concentrate strictly on the billing and coding career option. They are able to complete insurance claim forms and determine insurance coverage and limitations for the patient. Medical assistants answer telephones, schedule appointments, update medical records, and handle all types of correspondence. Often the medical assistant schedules outpatient procedures and hospital admissions and may coordinate consultations with physicians. Those who enjoy the administrative side of the profession often enter office management positions.

The clinical duties that medical assistants perform are just as broad as the administrative duties. These professionals prepare patients and the equipment needed before examinations and assist the physician during patients' office visits. They assist with or perform basic testing procedures and are usually proficient in **phlebotomy**. Medical assistants are trained in first aid skills and cardiopulmonary resuscitation. They collect and prepare laboratory specimens, and they know how to follow the regulations established by the U.S. Occupational Safety and Health Administration (OSHA) and the Clinical Laboratory Improvement Amendments (CLIA). Often medical assistants working in the clinical area are responsible for inventorying and ordering supplies. When directed by a physician and allowed by the state, they may administer various types of medications and perform x-ray examinations, if trained to do so. Medical assistants also perform electrocardiograms and prepare patients for x-ray evaluations. They assist in minor surgical procedures, prepare sterile trays, and perform autoclave sterilization procedures for instruments. Other clinical duties involve taking medical histories from patients, patient teaching, and obtaining and recording vital signs. Medical assistants who enjoy the clinical side of the profession may become office managers or may supervise other medical assistants.

Duties and restrictions related to medical assisting vary from state to state, but in most of the United States, the medical assistant performs as an agent of the physician and is under the physician's supervision. This means that the medical assistant performs actions that he or she is told to perform by the physician and that the physician is responsible for those actions. The command may be relayed to the medical assistant from the physician verbally, through a

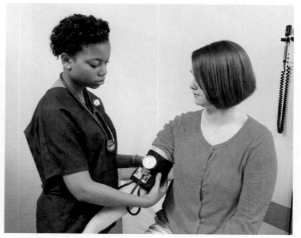

FIGURE 3-1 The responsibilities of a medical assistant include both administrative and clinical duties.

supervisor, or by way of the office policy and procedure manual. *Respondeat superior* is a Latin term meaning "let the master answer." Physicians are responsible not only for their own actions, but for the actions of employees performing within the scope of their employment.

CRITICAL THINKING APPLICATION   3-1

- Sandra is not sure whether she would enjoy administrative or clinical assisting more. How can she begin to explore both avenues during her classroom training? During her externship or practicum?
- How could Sandra explore the medical specialties and determine what areas might be of interest to her as a career?

A CAREER IN MEDICAL ASSISTING

Trained medical assistants are equipped with a flexible, adaptable career in which they experience the rewards of helping other people (Figure 3-2). The skills acquired by the medical assistant are valuable, and employment is readily available anywhere in the world where medicine is practiced. Many medical assistants pursue their careers far beyond the usual retirement age, because physicians realize the value of the experienced, mature employee. This career attracts the nontraditional student who may be older than the average postsecondary student by a decade or more. Although many older students feel intimidated by the classroom, they often have excellent experiences in school and reach the top of the class. Medical assisting is more than suitable for the student just exiting high school. Many individuals plan to work as medical assistants to earn a viable income while pursuing further academic studies.

The practice of medicine has changed dramatically in the past several decades. Increasing costs have created a trend away from hospital-based treatment and toward the delivery of care in physicians' offices and in outpatient ambulatory clinics. Although physicians have employed medical assistants in their practices for many years, computerization and technologic advances have created more opportunities for formally trained medical assistants, and their responsibilities have similarly increased. Clearly defined educational requirements have been established, and this has resulted in improvement of the quality and accessibility of medical assistant training. These requirements have also helped create a healthy respect for medical assistants, who are considered an integral part of today's allied health field.

Employment for medical assistants is abundant. As mentioned previously, the Labor Department projects that the medical assisting field will grow much faster than the average for all occupations; a growth of 31% is expected in the medical assisting field between 2010 and 2020. In 2010, medical assistants held approximately 527,600 jobs in the United States, and about one half of those were in physicians' offices. The projected employment for 2020 is 690,400 medical assistants. According to the Department of Labor, job growth will be so great because of the increasing number of group practices, clinics, and other healthcare facilities that need a high proportion of support personnel, particularly medical assistants who can handle both administrative and clinical duties. Additionally, the movement toward electronic medical records has resulted in a strong demand for medical assistants who can manage health information. Jobs may also be available with federal agencies, such as the Department of Veterans Affairs, the Public Health Service, and armed forces clinics or hospitals.

Most medical assistants derive a high degree of satisfaction from their work. Job turnover among medical assistants is surprisingly low; some begin working with a physician when the practice is opened and stay until the physician's retirement. In the past, physicians often would hire any individual to perform office and clinical duties, but these people frequently were untrained and unprofessional; they therefore could be paid a minimum amount for their work. Most physicians have learned that hiring an untrained person to work in the medical office usually is more expensive in the long run. Untrained assistants often make errors that are costly to the practice, and these assistants require much more supervision; this means that the supervisor's time is not used for the duties that he or she would normally perform because the medical assistant is not completely able to work alone. Formal training and **certification** are valuable not only to the medical assistant, but also to the physician-employer.

Medical assistants are compensated in various ways, some by hourly wages and some by salary. The earnings vary from place to place. Overall, medical assistants can expect a healthy return on their investment in training, experience, and skills. Most physicians realize that a good medical assistant is worth a higher than average wage, and a medical assistant with formal training is almost always compensated on a higher scale than one with no training. The *Occupational Outlook Handbook* reports statistics on the average salaries for many different career fields, including medical assisting. (This information can be accessed at www.bls.gov/oco. Annual salary updates are also available on the Web site.) More information on salaries may be obtained by monitoring the local classified advertisements and by checking online job information on sites such as Yahoo! Careers. Medical assistants must determine a realistic entry-level salary for their geographic area. Often graduates expect to make a much higher salary than is reasonable right after graduation with little or no experience.

FIGURE 3-2 Medical assisting is a career with many benefits and perks, not to mention the innate rewards of assisting patients in need.

The medical field offers great **benefits** to employees. Usually, the larger the organization, the better the benefits and **perks**. Most employers offer a health insurance plan or managed care plan to their employees. Often a life insurance program is included, and dental insurance is always a valuable benefit. Some companies have **profit-sharing** plans and **stock options**, as well as a retirement plan. Some organizations give their employees access to credit unions, and many have discount options at local businesses, such as uniform shops. Other benefits may include uniform stipends or reimbursement, tuition reimbursement, and continuing education allowances.

Remember that you should consider benefits and perks when contemplating a job opportunity. Many medical assistants may choose to work for less money if the benefits and the opportunities for advancement are good. Consider driving time, holidays, paid parking, sick days, vacation days, and facilities when choosing a job. Do the co-workers seem to enjoy one another's company and get along? Is the physician friendly or more aloof? All of these should be weighed carefully before the final decision is made as to which position to accept. Some facilities pay more and offer fewer benefits, whereas others pay less and offer more benefits. It is a truism that "money is a byproduct of services rendered." Nowhere is this more accurate than in the medical field. When the patients are served well, the medical assistant becomes more and more valuable to the employer and is compensated accordingly.

CRITICAL THINKING APPLICATION   3-2

- Sandra knows that she needs certain benefits as a single mother. What might she need to look for in a job after she graduates?
- What are some ways Sandra can compare positions and opportunities?
- What types of Web sites might help Sandra learn about opportunities in her geographic location?

▌PROFESSIONAL APPEARANCE

A well-groomed medical assistant in appropriate attire has a positive psychological effect on patients. The essentials of a professional appearance are good health, good grooming, and suitable dress.

Good health requires adequate sleep, balanced meals, and enough exercise to keep fit. Medical assistants can set a good example by living a sensible, healthy lifestyle that includes regular checkups for their own physical condition, both medical and dental. A radiantly healthy office staff presents the best possible public relations image for the physician.

Good grooming is little more than attention to the details of personal appearance. Personal cleanliness, which includes taking a daily bath or shower, using deodorant, and practicing good oral hygiene, is vital. Perfume and aftershave cologne should not be used or should be applied lightly, because patients and co-workers may be allergic to some scents. Makeup should be conservative and applied moderately. Heavy or exaggerated makeup is out of place in the professional office; subtle eye and lip makeup is best. Clear or muted shades of nail polish are best, and long nails are not only inappropriate but can be dangerous to the patient and the medical assistant. Nails must be kept clean and at a very conservative length.

The medical assistant's hair should be shiny, clean, neatly styled, and off the collar.

Medical assistants usually wear a uniform or laboratory coat; this not only presents a professional appearance, but also identifies the assistant as a member of the healthcare team (Figure 3-3). Medical professionals rarely wear traditional white in today's medical facilities, although it is appropriate if allowed in the office policy manual. Fashionable styling makes it possible for the medical assistant's uniform to be both practical and attractive. Women may choose to wear pantsuits, which are available in white or a variety of colors; a two-piece dress uniform in white or a color; an attractively styled traditional white uniform; or a scrub set. Scrubs have become increasingly popular and much more attractive over the past decade. They now are often made of pretty fabrics in rich colors and patterns and are much better suited for the professional office than the old green or blue scrubs worn in the surgical suites of hospitals.

Men may also wear the newer scrubs or may choose white slacks with a white or colored shirt, jacket, or pullover top. If it is acceptable in the facility, a lab coat may be worn over street clothes, but it is important that the lab coat be buttoned when **invasive** procedures are performed. Uniforms should be laundered daily and neatly pressed, because medical assistants are exposed to ill patients throughout the workday. Shoes should be appropriate for a uniform, spotless, and comfortable. Many attractive styles that resemble running or tennis shoes are available at uniform shops, specially conditioned for the medical professional who is on his or her feet most of the day. White shoes must be kept white by daily cleaning and touchups. Remember that if laced shoes are worn, the laces also need cleaning.

In some facilities, the physician prefers that the staff not wear uniforms. Some psychiatrists and some pediatricians, for example, believe that the clinical appearance of a uniform may affect patients adversely. However, today's uniforms reflect so many styles and patterns that the right one for the particular office should be readily available. Some of the fabrics depict cartoon characters or drawings that will appeal to children yet still function as a durable uniform. A medical assistant who does not wear a uniform should follow the dictates of good taste and should be conservative in choosing a

FIGURE 3-3 Medical assistants must have a professional appearance and demeanor in the medical office.

professional wardrobe. Jeans are rarely acceptable in the medical facility, unless the office is extremely casual or it is a special day.

The garments worn while on duty must be comfortable, allow for easy movement, and still look fresh at the end of a busy day. Whatever uniform style the assistant chooses, it should be personally becoming and worn over appropriate undergarments. The lines, colors, and ornamentation of the undergarments should not be seen through the uniform; therefore, it is best to wear undergarments that have a neutral color and not a pattern. Thongs and high-cut underwear should be avoided. When a uniform is worn, jewelry should be limited to an engagement ring, wedding band, and professional pin. No more than two earrings per ear lobe should be worn, and the clothing or hairstyle should always cover tattoos.

Facial and tongue piercings are unacceptable in the medical setting and must be removed during working hours. A name badge will help patients identify each staff person by name.

Make sure the dress code required in the office setting is clearly understood. Adherence to that code is a demonstration of responsibility and willingness to cooperate with office rules. Compliance with office regulations is a factor in decisions on office promotions.

EDUCATION AND TRAINING

Ideally, a medical assistant should have both administrative and clinical skills, although he or she may have a personal preference for one over the other. The physician's staff must be able to handle all responsibilities of the office except those requiring the services of the physician or another licensed professional. In an office with several assistants, each should be able and willing to substitute in an emergency for any of the others, and all should be cross-trained to perform each others' duties. Teamwork is a very important part of any occupation and even more so in the medical environment.

Certain knowledge and skills are expected of a trained medical assistant. The skills mentioned in this chapter are not all-inclusive; rather, they suggest what may be expected on entry into employment as a professional medical assistant.

Classroom Training

Formal training is essential for today's medical assistant. Many community colleges, junior colleges, and private career institutions offer courses in medical assisting. After satisfactory completion of the program, the student usually receives a certificate or diploma. Private career institutions offer training that usually takes 7 to 10 months to complete, and they offer enrollment as often as monthly. Students who attend community colleges, junior colleges, and some private career institutions to study medical assisting may complete the educational requirements to obtain an associate's degree in medical assisting. Courses at the community college level usually take 1 to 2 years to complete and offer enrollment from every few weeks to two or three times a year.

Currently the trend is toward offering the medical assisting program in modules, so that the student receives some clinical training, some administrative training, and some theory in each module. Some classes are taught in traditional classrooms, and the clinical aspect usually is taught in a laboratory at the school. Much of the equipment the medical assistant will use in practice is found in the laboratory, such as an autoclave, medical instruments and trays, and specimen collection equipment. Medical assistant training usually involves the study of medical terminology, anatomy and physiology, aseptic technique, clinical procedures, medical law and ethics, principles of pharmacology, insurance billing and coding, receptionist and telephone technique, patient communication, human relations, management duties, and receptionist duties, among other subjects.

Instructors are important allies of medical assisting students, and the relationship between instructor and student should be one of mutual respect. Students must realize that instructors have a strong desire to share their knowledge and that they want each student to succeed. Individual schools have certain rules and regulations that must be enforced, many of them a result of state or federal regulation or legislation. The guidelines that students must follow are not designed to hinder their education, but rather to ensure that graduates are competent medical assistants. Students should complete assignments accurately, turn them in on time, and take pride in all the work they do for class. They should never miss school days unless absolutely necessary, and they should develop good habits in school so that they become valuable assets to future employers.

CRITICAL THINKING APPLICATION 3-3

- How can Sandra develop a positive, nurturing relationship with her instructors?
- What should she do if she has difficulty in the classroom or if her grades begin to fall?
- How can Sandra study effectively and prepare for examinations?

Externship (Practicum)

Medical assistant training programs require an **externship** or a **practicum** before the student graduates. Some schools call this the **internship**. This on-the-job training allows students to put the skills they have learned in the classroom to use with real patients and staff members. In most cases, externships are unpaid positions that are part of the medical assistant training program, not a separate entity. Most accreditation organizations do not allow student externs to be paid.

The physician, probably more than any other employer, expects employees to carry out their duties independently, with little or no direct supervision. Someone at the externship site is designated as the student's supervisor. Medical assisting students should consult frequently with their externship supervisors to determine what is expected of them and the progress they are making (Figure 3-4).

The student must be open to constructive criticism and must be a willing learner. Techniques may be learned on the externship that were not included in the classroom training, or optional methods may be taught for various procedures. The medical assisting student should never argue with the staff at the clinical site that a method taught by the school is the only correct way. Often several methods can be used to obtain the same result. The medical assisting student should treat the externship experience as if it were a probationary period on an actual job. Remember, the externship often is the first medical reference the student will be able to list on the resume.

FIGURE 3-4 The externship or internship provides practical experience in the skills learned in the classroom. It is usually listed first on the medical assistant graduate's resumé; therefore, it is vital to perform well and make a good impression.

Several general rules must be remembered on the externship site. First, the medical assisting student must gain the trust of the employees there. The student should perform the assigned duties eagerly, in a timely manner, and to the best of his or her ability. If questions arise at any time, the student should ask the externship supervisor for clarification instead of assuming or performing the duties incorrectly.

It often is helpful to read the job description of the medical assistant in the facility so that the student will understand what is expected. The student medical assistant must show responsibility and dependability. The student must remain busy while at the externship site. If all assigned duties have been completed, the extern should offer to assist others in their duties or ask for additional responsibilities. Counters always need cleaning, and filing always needs to be done. The student who performs these duties without being told shows initiative and a strong work ethic. In addition, all the rules for professional appearance apply to the site and should be followed meticulously, because the student medical assistant will be working with actual patients.

The medical assistant may find it necessary to educate the patient about what a medical assistant is and does. Patients often assume that those assisting in the office are nurses, but medical assistants should never represent themselves as such. When making introductions or assisting with patients, the student medical assistant should state, "I am Sandra Ramirez, Dr. Patrick's medical assistant extern," or "I am Sandra, a medical assistant intern here in Dr. Patrick's office." These words accurately portray the duties performed and let patients know who is caring for them in the physician's office.

Externs need to know a few other rules. A medical assisting student must never attempt to form a romantic relationship with patients or co-workers on the externship site. Patient confidentiality must be respected at all times; therefore, anything the student discovers about a patient must not be revealed or discussed under any circumstances. The student can never use any of the drug samples at the office unless specifically given permission by the physician. The student should not go to the drug storage area alone without permission or unless directed to do so by the supervisor or physician. Externs should be extremely careful if asked to handle petty cash in the office. No student wants to be accused of any impropriety while performing externship duties. Students must never ask the physician to treat them or any members of their family or friends. If the physician offers this as a benefit, it is acceptable, but it must not be assumed that the physician is available for and willing to give free treatment. An extern must not ask the physician to provide prescriptions; for liability reasons, most physicians will not prescribe medications for people who are not their patients.

The extern should bring to the physician's office **intangibles** that are not found in any job description. Courtesy toward others, a capacity for teamwork, a positive attitude, enthusiasm, initiative, and dedication are important personal attributes for the professional medical assistant. After becoming comfortable with the expectations of the externship, the student should concentrate on developing his or her skills and learning as much as possible during this short period. An extern becomes a valuable team player by assisting others and by being reliable. By performing at peak level, the student gains the respect and trust of those on the externship site, and these people can serve as excellent references when the search begins for that first paid position. Remember, the professional services of a medical assistant are extremely personal. Therefore, the manner in which these services are performed can affect the health and welfare of a patient in either a positive or a negative way. When medical assisting students do their best to make sure all contact with patients is positive, they win the praise of patients, supervisors, and co-workers alike.

BENEFITS OF AN EXTERNSHIP

- The school has a line of communication to the community and is better able to assess the needs and expectations of the public for which it is training prospective employees.
- The externship agency benefits from the new ideas and methods that the trainee may introduce. If the facility is looking for additional help, this is an ideal way to evaluate the performance of a trainee without involvement in the hiring process.
- The trainee benefits most of all by exposure to practical experience in a variety of settings. This experience in the real world removes a great deal of the anxiety that might otherwise be present in a first employment situation.

CRITICAL THINKING APPLICATION   3-4

- If Sandra has any difficulty on her externship, whom should she contact?
- What should Sandra do when she has completed her normal duties for the day at the externship site but it is not yet time to leave the clinic?
- How can Sandra gain more knowledge from her co-workers during her externship?

Continuing Education

Education does not end with the completion of formal training. The amount of medical knowledge gained in a given year is astounding. The practicing medical assistant must keep current with the rapid changes in the profession. Most physicians appreciate medical assistants who ask questions about unfamiliar conditions and procedures, and they are willing to teach students about the functioning of the body and treatments that benefit the patient. Much can be learned by reading or reviewing the medical literature that arrives in the daily mail or articles that appear in newspapers, magazines, and medically related newsletters.

Continuing education classes are available to enhance the knowledge of the professional medical assistant. **Continuing education units (CEUs)** may be required to maintain the medical assistant's certification. These credits can be obtained through many sources, including the AAMA, the American Medical Technologists (AMT), and various other agencies and educational institutions. Professional seminars and workshops often offer CEUs. Notices of continuing education classes are sent in bulk to medical facilities and physicians' offices, and staff members should watch for courses that pertain to their particular job duties and take advantage of them.

PROFESSIONAL ORGANIZATIONS

By joining a professional organization and taking part in the activities it offers, a medical assistant can grow personally and professionally, keeping abreast of current trends. Participation in a recognized professional organization shows that the employee takes his or her career seriously and wants to be an asset to the employer. Often, a medical assistant is qualified to sit for more than one type of exam; for instance, a medical assistant with 1,020 hours of clinical experience, including venipuncture, skin puncture, and specimen processing, may be able to take the phlebotomy exam. A medical assistant with 2 years' experience working as an administrative medical assistant may be eligible to take the Certified Medical Administrative Specialist (CMAS) exam. Several billing and coding certifications are available (these are discussed in more detail in Chapter 16). National organizations, state chapters of these organizations, and local groups meet to promote the profession of medical assisting. The organizations offer many benefits to members. Some offer health, disability, and malpractice insurance programs. Some offer credit card options and discount programs that are exclusive to their membership. All extend an opportunity for continuing education and learning beyond the classroom. Some schools that offer medical assistant training form local or school-based chapters of professional organizations. Both the AAMA and AMT offer discounted student memberships.

> ### CRITICAL THINKING APPLICATION   3-5
> - When should Sandra get involved with professional organizations for medical assistants?
> - How can she contribute to professional organizations in her area once she has graduated and secured a position as a medical assistant?
> - Why is it important that Sandra participate in volunteer organizations?

American Association of Medical Assistants and Certified Medical Assistants

The AAMA was organized formally in 1955 as a federation of several state associations that had been functioning independently. Today, the AAMA has 45 state societies and 250 local chapters. The

organization, which has its national headquarters in Chicago, was the driving force behind the establishment of a national certification program for medical assistants. The AAMA also has been instrumental in the accreditation of medical assistant training programs in community colleges and private career institutes and in setting the minimum standards for entry-level medical assistants. At meetings held on national, state, and local levels, medical assistants can participate in workshops, learn about all types of advancement in the field, listen to prominent speakers, and network with other medical assistants from other parts of the country. The AAMA publishes a bimonthly journal, *CMA Today*, which includes articles with tests that may be submitted for CEU credit.

Since 1963, the AAMA has administered the Certified Medical Assistant (AAMA) examination. Those who pass the examination are awarded the CMA (AAMA) credential (Figure 3-5). Examinations are computerized and are offered continuously, year-round, at Prometric Testing and Assessment Centers throughout the United States. Certification is available to graduates of medical assisting programs accredited by the Commission on Accreditation of Allied Health Education Programs (CAAHEP) or by the Accrediting Bureau of Health Education Schools (ABHES). Recertification is required every 5 years and can be accomplished through CEUs or re-examination. Exam applications and additional information are available on the AAMA's Web site at www.aama-ntl.org.

American Medical Technologists and Registered Medical Assistants

In the early 1970s, the AMT, a national certifying body for laboratory professionals, began offering a certifying examination for medical assistants. This led to the formation of the Registered Medical Assistant (RMA) program within the AMT in 1976. The AMT offers this credential to medical assistants who meet established standards and pass the certifying examination (Figure 3-6).

Several other certification examinations are offered by the AMT that may be of interest to medical assistants. The Certified Office Laboratory Technician (COLT) examination is available to those who have completed certain educational and work experience requirements. Most medical assistants who work in the clinical area and have at least 6 months of experience are qualified to take the examination. Medical assistants also may qualify to take the examination for certification as a Registered Phlebotomy Technician (RPT), which is offered by the AMT, after meeting

FIGURE 3-5 This pin is worn by the Certified Medical Assistant (AAMA). (Courtesy American Association of Medical Assistants, Chicago, Ill.)

FIGURE 3-6 This pin is worn by the Registered Medical Assistant. (Courtesy RMA/American Medical Technologists, Park Ridge, Ill.)

specific work-related requirements. The examination for Certified Medical Administrative Specialist (CMAS) is offered to those who have graduated from an accredited administrative program or who have 5 years of experience in the field. RMAs with 2 years of administrative experience may also take the examination. All of these exams are computerized and can be taken at Pearson VUE centers throughout the United States. More information about the RMA examination is available on the American Medical Technologists' Web site at www.americanmedtech.org.

The AMT provides societal benefits, including publications such as *AMT Events,* a quarterly magazine with useful information and articles relating to the professions served by the organization. The AMT also offers national, state, and local meetings to enhance the knowledge and networking opportunities of its members. CEU credits are available to help increase a medical assistant's level of competence and are a requirement for those who first became certified (or will recertify) after January 1, 2006. (For more information on the AMT, visit the Evolve Web site at *evolve.elsevier.com/kinn*).

National Healthcareer Association

Some schools also offer certification through the National Healthcareer Association (NHA). Examinations and credentials available from the NHA include those for Certified Medical Administrative Assistant (CMAA), Certified Clinical Medical Assistant (CCMA), Certified Billing and Coding Specialist (CBCS), and Certified Medical Transcriptionist (CMT). The cost for these certification examinations ranges from about $100 to $150. More information is available on the NHA Web site at www.nhanow.com.

American Registry of Medical Assisting

The purpose of the American Registry of Medical Assistants (ARMA) is to certify and advance the position of the qualified medical assistant, to provide updated medical and social information of interest to the medical assistant through publications, and to be of service to its members. This registry is accomplished through a recommendation system, and medical assistants are not required to test to receive the registration designation; however, the organization does require CEUs. More information can be obtained on the ARMA Web site at www.arma-cert.org.

National Center for Competency Testing

The National Center for Competency Testing (NCCT) is an independent certification agency that has tested more than 240,000 individuals since 1989. The organization offers certification as a medical assistant, billing and coding specialist, medical office assistant, phlebotomy technician, patient care technician, and electrocardiography (ECG) technician. To earn an NCCT credential, candidates must meet all eligibility requirements and pass an examination based on the knowledge, skills, and abilities required at job entry. The NCCT's Web site is www.ncctinc.com.

Taking Certification Examinations

Both the CMA and RMA certifications are national credentials. As mentioned, the CMA credential is offered by the AAMA, and the RMA credential is offered by the AMT. Because medical assistants are not required to be licensed, both of these examinations are voluntary. A medical assistant may practice in the United States without either certification, but most employers today require at least one certification. Both organizations have committees that develop their certifying examinations, which are based on the roles that medical assistants fulfill in the workplace.

Students should take the examination soon after graduation; the intricate knowledge gained in school is easier to recall the sooner the exam is taken. In addition, the fee for the CMA examination goes up 1 year after the graduation date. Although the graduate is not guaranteed higher wages with certification or registration, most employers are willing to pay more for a graduate who has been through formal training and the certification or registration procedure. By registering for certification examinations soon after beginning the medical assistant training, the student can prepare throughout the classroom experience.

The CMA examination covers three general categories, including administrative, clinical, and transdisciplinary competencies. The examination is scored by tallying correct responses; therefore, making a guess does not count against the student. The minimum score to obtain the CMA credential currently is 425, and students are allowed 3 hours to complete the examination. Once the student has been approved to take the exam, the AAMA sends a testing center scheduling permit to the candidate, who then schedules the exam. The test can be scheduled at the candidate's convenience within a 90-day assigned period of the student's choice. The AAMA offers two practice tests on its Web site; these tests cover anatomy and physiology and include a medical terminology review. The AAMA requires either continuing education credits or re-examination to maintain the CMA credential.

The RMA examination can be scheduled nearly every day of the year other than Sundays and holidays at more than 200 testing centers throughout the United States, its territories, and Canada. Applicants for the RMA examination must be graduates of a medical assisting course accredited by ABHES or CAAHEP, or they must meet requirements related to their experience. The RMA examination covers administrative skills, clinical skills, and general skills and comprises more than 200 questions. Examinees are allowed 3 hours to take the test. Scoring is based on a scale, and the minimum passing score is 70. Practice examinations are available on the AMT Web site.

The AMT recently mandated a point system to prove compliance with continuing education requirements. RMAs, CMASs, and COLTs are required to earn 30 points, and RPTs are required to earn 20 points. Points can be earned through continuing education, employer evaluations, professional and formal education, and various other methods.

THE MEDICAL ASSISTANT CREED

I believe in the principles and purposes of the profession of medical assisting.

I endeavor to be more effective.

I aspire to render greater service.

I protect the confidence entrusted to me.

I am dedicated to the care and well-being of all patients.

I am loyal to my physician-employer.

I am true to the ethics of my profession.

I am strengthened by compassion, courage, and faith.

The Difference Between CMAs and RMAs

The two major differences between the CMA and RMA credentials are the examination consultant organizations and the cost. The current CMA examination fee is $125 for recent CAAHEP or ABHES graduates. The fee is $250 for nonrecent graduates and individuals who are not members of the AAMA, which administers this exam. The annual membership fees for the AAMA vary from state to state and are substantially lower if a person joins while still a student. The cost of student membership ranges from $20 to approximately $35, but the student must apply for membership before graduating. Annual dues thereafter are $67 to $107, depending on the state association. The RMA examination fee is $95, which includes the first year's dues. Annual dues thereafter currently are $50. Table 3-1 presents a detailed comparison of the CMA and RMA.

CRITICAL THINKING APPLICATION   3-6

- Why is it important for Sandra to obtain one of the medical assisting certifications after graduation?
- How important are continuing education units to the new graduate?
- How might certification help her career as a medical assistant?
- When and where can the tests be taken in your area?

CLOSING COMMENTS

This chapter has presented the advantages of becoming a trained medical assistant and some of the many career opportunities available. The skills that must be developed and the general knowledge that must be acquired to perform the duties of a medical assistant effectively have been presented. However, skills and knowledge alone do not ensure success. Personality traits and professional appearance are also critical. Professional societies and continuing education are vital to the medical assistant's career. The individual who chooses this career must be willing to accept the responsibilities inherent in its standards. The importance of obtaining national certification cannot be stressed enough.

Patient Education

Medical assistants may find it necessary to educate the patient about their scope of practice. Patients often assume that those assisting in the office are nurses, but medical assistants should never present themselves in this manner. When making introductions, the medical assistant should state, "I am Sandra Ramirez, Dr. Patrick's medical assistant." These words accurately portray the medical assistant's role and help the patient identify who is who in the physician's office.

Medical assisting has grown into one of the most respected professions in the allied health field. When asked, medical assistants should share information about their roles in the office and the training that has prepared them for their duties. Some of those who ask may be interested in a career change or have the desire to enter the medical field. Medical assistants should always be good ambassadors for their profession.

Legal and Ethical Issues

In the course of medical assistants' daily work, they must deal with a vast amount of personal and intimate information about the patients who have entrusted their care to the physician and those employed by the practice. Such information must be held in strict confidence and must never be discussed with or relayed to others, including professional associates, unless the lack of knowledge would hinder the patient's care.

On an externship or practicum, a medical assisting student should expect to observe all the office protocols of regular attendance, punctuality, and dress code. The extern should hold the rules and regulations of the office in high regard and not expect special treatment. Never expect or ask for payment for serving as an extern, because this is a part of the school curriculum.

During the externship, medical assisting students should restrict their practice to areas in which they have been trained. Know the boundaries within which medical assistants are expected to perform and do not exceed them. Some medical assistants carry their own malpractice or medical liability insurance policies; externs may be covered by a blanket policy held by their school. Remember, if ever in doubt about what is acceptable during the externship, or even in actual practice as a medical assistant, ask the physician or supervisor.

TABLE 3-1 Differences Between the Certified Medical Assistant and the Registered Medical Assistant

	CERTIFIED MEDICAL ASSISTANT (CMA)	REGISTERED MEDICAL ASSISTANT (RMA)
Credentialing organization	American Association of Medical Assistants (AAMA)	American Medical Technologists (AMT)
Address of certification or registration organization	American Association of Medical Assistants 20 N. Wacker Drive, Suite 1575 Chicago, IL 60606-2903 Telephone: 800-228-2262 or 1-312-899-1500	American Medical Technologists 10700 W. Higgins Road, Suite 150 Rosemont, IL 60018 800-275-1268 1-847-823-5169
Organization Web site	www.aama-ntl.org	www.americanmedtech.org
Mailing address for certification applications	AAMA Certification 7999 Eagle Way Chicago, IL 60678-1079	RMA Certification/AMT 10700 W. Higgins Road, Suite 150 Rosemont, IL 60018
Requirement for certification or registration	Federal licensing is not required; certification or registration is optional in most states.	Federal licensing is not required; certification or registration is optional in most states.

Qualifications for taking the examination	Applicants must fall into one of three categories to qualify to take the CMA examination:
	• Category one: Graduating student or recent graduate of a medical assisting program accredited by the Commission on Accreditation of Allied Health Education Programs (CAAHEP) or the Accrediting Bureau of Health Education Schools (ABHES)
	• Category two: Non-recent graduate of a medical assisting program accredited by CAAHEP or ABHES
	• Category three: Recertificant
		• Good moral character and at least 18 years old
		• High school graduate or acceptable equivalent
		• Graduate of or scheduled to graduate from one of the following:
		Must meet one of five eligibility routes, including:
		  ○ Route 1 — Education: a recent graduate of, or scheduled to graduate from, an accredited medical assistant program;
		  ○ Route 2 — Military: a recent graduate of, or scheduled to graduate from, a formal medical services training program of the United States Armed Forces;
		  ○ Route 3 — Work Experience: employed as a medical assistant for five of the last seven years, no more than two years as a medical assisting instructor;
		  ○ Route 4 — Instructor: must be currently instructing and must have completed a course of instruction in a healthcare discipline related to medical assisting;
		  ○ Route 5 — Passed another certifying organization's certification exam approved by the AMT Board of Directors
		• Must have 5 years of work experience unless graduated from the medical assisting program within the last 3 years

Examination approval organization	National Board of Medical Examiners (NBME) www.nbme.org	National Commission for Certifying Agencies (NCCA) www.noca.org/ncca/ncca.htm
Cost of examination	AAMA members and recent graduates: $125 Non-recent graduates and nonmembers: $250	$95 (membership in the AMT is not required)
Duration of examination	3 hours	3 hours
Content of examination	200 computerized questions covering general or transdisciplinary skills, clinical skills, and administrative skills	More than 200 computerized questions covering general subject areas, clinical areas, and administrative areas
Testing sites	More than 200 centers throughout the United States; applicants are assigned to a center after they have been approved to take the examination. A list of testing sites is available at www.prometric.com.	More than 200 centers throughout the United States A list of testing sites is available at www.pearsonvue.com/amt.
Web sites for obtaining a practice test	www.aama-ntl.org/becomeCMA/exam_outline.aspx	AMT Web site: www.amt1.com
Testing dates	Apply for a 90-day window, then schedule the exam within that window at a convenient date and time. Testing dates are ongoing and are arranged at Prometric Testing and Assessment Centers throughout the United States.	Testing dates are ongoing and are arranged at Pearson VUE Centers throughout the United States.

SUMMARY OF SCENARIO

Sandra has chosen to embark on an exciting career and will find her work rewarding. She knows that she will be proud of her efforts and looks forward to becoming a respected member of the healthcare team in a physician's office. She has set goals for her class work and attendance and is determined to meet them. Obstacles usually arise whenever a person embarks on a new project, and Sandra must plan for the days that she or her child may be ill or her transportation fails. She should have a backup plan in place to help her overcome minor setbacks.

Many opportunities exist for the medical assistant in both administrative and clinical positions, and as Sandra progresses through her training, she will find areas that appeal to her more than others. However, all her courses will be vital to her development as a versatile medical assistant, able to perform front-office and back-office duties. She will be exposed to various duties during her externship, and these experiences will help her determine where she might enjoy working once she graduates. It is important that Sandra gain as much experience and knowledge as possible while in school, so that she will have more options after her training.

Sandra should develop a good relationship with her instructors and go to them when she has questions or concerns. These professionals are anxious to share their knowledge and experience with students to best prepare them for the work environment. If Sandra's grades ever drop or if she is struggling, she should seek the advice of the instructor to determine how to improve her performance. The externship also is crucial, because it usually is the first medical reference a new graduate will have. Sandra should bring any difficulties at the externship site to the attention of the externship supervisor or an instructor at her school. Learning to set goals will help her achieve more throughout her education, and this is a habit she should carry into her career.

With so many benefits available at different facilities in the medical field, Sandra must carefully weigh what she needs for herself and her son before taking any position. Many physicians' offices now offer evening and weekend hours; Sandra may have to adjust her schedule to fit those working hours, or she may stick to her original desire to find a job without evening or weekend shifts. She should look at all of her options and choose the best one after careful evaluation.

For now, Sandra should spend her time in school getting to know her instructors and understanding their expectations. In addition, she should study hard, learn to budget time and money, and discover as much as possible about the field of medical assisting. These efforts will pay off in satisfaction with her chosen career and in the job she ultimately accepts.

SUMMARY OF LEARNING OBJECTIVES

1. **Define, spell, and pronounce the terms listed in the vocabulary.**
   Spelling and pronouncing medical terms correctly bolster the medical assistant's credibility. Knowing the definition of these terms promotes confidence in communication with patients and co-workers.

2. **Briefly discuss the history of medical assisting as a profession.**
   The first medical assistants probably were neighbors and friends of the physician. The field has grown into one of the most respected and versatile professions in allied health.

3. **Discuss the versatility of a career in medical assisting.**
   Medical assistants are versatile enough to work in many different settings. Most are employed in physicians' offices, but they also work in hospitals, insurance companies, clinics, laboratories, and many other facilities. The combination of administrative and clinical training makes the medical assistant quite valuable to the employer.

4. **Differentiate between administrative and clinical medical assisting duties and recognize the importance of becoming knowledgeable about the general responsibilities of the medical assistant.**
   Administrative duties involve running the office, such as scheduling appointments and filing insurance claims. Administrative medical assistants usually spend most of the day in the front office of the facility. Clinical duties include more patient contact and assisting the physician in the back office. New graduates often move toward one or the other division, but they should always be ready and willing to adapt to new duties or to substitute in other areas when necessary.

5. **Comprehend the current employment outlook for the medical assistant.**
   According to the Department of Labor, the medical assisting field is projected to grow much faster than the average for all occupations, with a 35% expected growth from 2006 to 2016. The projected employment for 2016 is 565,000 medical assistants.

6. **Give the reasons that hiring an individual with no formal training often is more expensive than hiring a professional medical assistant.**
   Untrained assistants often make errors that are costly to the practice, and these assistants require much more supervision; this means that the supervisor's time is not used for the duties that he or she would normally perform, because the medical assistant is not completely able to work alone. Formal training and certification are valuable not only to the medical assistant, but also to the physician-employer.

7. **Identify several considerations to keep in mind, other than financial compensation, when choosing a position as a medical assistant.**
   The medical assistant should consider many factors other than the salary when choosing a position. Location, perks, benefits, and the atmosphere of the office all are important. Many assistants are interested in growth within the organization and welcome those opportunities. Working for a friendly, caring physician and/or supervisor is invaluable. Sometimes, taking a lesser position in a well-known and reputable facility is

temporarily worth a lower wage because of future opportunities. Consider all aspects of a position before accepting a job offer.

8. **Discuss the aspects of the medical assistant's performance on a successful externship.**

The medical assisting externship offers the student an opportunity to put the skills learned in the classroom to good use. If completed successfully, the externship is an excellent reference for the resumé. Students should perform at the optimal level and never hesitate to complete duties assigned. Offer to go above and beyond to secure the support of the externship site as the job search begins.

9. **List three unacceptable behaviors on the externship site.**

A student medical assistant extern should never attempt to form relationships with patients outside the office or read patients' charts for personal information. Do not ask the physician to treat family members, and do not take medications without explicit permission from the physician or supervisor. Be very careful when handling cash and drugs in the office. The student should make every effort never to be late to the externship site unless a true emergency occurs.

10. **Explain why continuing education is so important to the medical assistant.**

Continuing education is important to medical assistants because it enables them to learn the latest trends and information and understand how to use them. Take advantage of local seminars and continuing education classes. Often the employer will agree to pay for classes or seminars that the medical assistant takes if they relate to his or her employment at the facility. Some employers will provide tuition reimbursement for college expenses, often even if the college courses are not related to the position the employee holds at the facility.

11. **Understand the medical assistant credentialing requirements, the importance of credentialing, and the process of obtaining credentials.**

Most physicians prefer a credentialed medical assistant when making hiring decisions. Information about the credentialing process is available from the AAMA and AMT Web sites and from other certifying organizations.

12. **Discuss the difference between a CMA and a RMA.**

The main difference between the CMA and RMA credentials is the agency that provides the certification. The CMA credential is awarded by the AAMA, and the RMA credential is awarded by the AMT. Both are nationally recognized certifications.

CONNECTIONS

Study Guide Connection: Go to the Chapter 3 Study Guide. Read and complete the activities.

Evolve Connection: Go to the Chapter 3 link at *evolve.elsevier.com/kinn* to complete the Chapter Review and Chapter Quiz. Check out the other resources listed for this chapter to make the most of what you have learned from The Medical Assisting Profession.

4

PROFESSIONAL BEHAVIOR IN THE WORKPLACE

Karen Yon has wanted to work in the medical field for most of her adult life. She studied very hard in high school and graduated with honors. She volunteered in a local hospital and then, after working as a server in restaurants for 3 years, she enrolled in medical assisting classes. After her externship, she was asked to continue as a regular employee at a family practice in her area.

Karen strives to perform all her duties professionally and compassionately. She maintains a professional image for patients and co-workers. She had found it difficult to learn to be professional at all times and show compassion to patients through just the classroom experience. However, she knew that these were important aspects of her job, and she was able to gain valuable experience in these areas during her externship. Because this is her first job in the medical field, she wants to make a good impression on her employer and to be a team player.

Throughout most of Karen's training as a medical assistant, her grandmother was confined to a rehabilitation center after a stroke. Although she has progressed well with treatment, Karen is the only relative who lives close to the rehabilitation center, and her family depends on her to check on her grandmother from time to time. Karen enjoys spending time at the center reading to her grandmother, because they are close. Still, Karen realizes that the stroke has caused permanent damage, and her grandmother's health seems to be declining.

While studying this chapter, think about the following questions:

- How do professional medical assistants put aside personal issues and devote themselves to the patients in the office?
- How can Karen meet her family and work obligations equally well?
- What steps should Karen take to ensure that both her family and her supervisors understand her obligations to the other?
- How can Karen exhibit professional behavior and compassion for patients on a daily basis at the physician's office?

LEARNING OBJECTIVES

1. Define, spell, and pronounce the terms listed in the vocabulary.
2. Explain the reasons professionalism is important in the medical field.
3. Discuss several of the characteristics of professionalism.
4. Explain why confidentiality is so important in the medical profession.
5. Discuss the importance of the medical assistant's attitude in caring for patients.
6. List some examples of office politics.
7. Identify specific ways teamwork can be promoted in the physician's office.
8. Discuss the meaning of *insubordination* and why it is grounds for dismissal.
9. Identify and implement time management principles to maintain efficient office function.
10. Talk about goal setting and how it helps a person achieve career success.
11. Discuss how substance abuse can impact the medical assistant's employment.

VOCABULARY

characteristics Distinguishing traits, qualities, or properties.

commensurate (ku-men'-su-rut) Corresponding in size, amount, extent, or degree; equal in measure, proportionate.

competent Having adequate or requisite capabilities.

connotation (kah-nuh-ta'-shun) An implication; something suggested by a word or thing.

credibility The quality or power of inspiring belief.

demeanor (di-me'-nur) Behavior toward others; outward manner.

detrimental (de-truh-men'-til) Obviously harmful or damaging.

discretion (dis-kre'-shun) The quality of being discreet; having or showing good judgment or conduct, especially in speech.

disseminated (di-se'-muh-na-ted) To disburse; to spread around.

drug of choice The drug an abuser uses most frequently to satisfy the craving for a certain feeling; the user's preferred drug.

initiative Energy or aptitude to cause or facilitate the start of something or to cause something to happen.

insubordination (in-suh'-bor-din-a-shun) Disobedience to authority.

morale (mo-ral') The mental and emotional condition, enthusiasm, loyalty, or confidence of an individual or group with regard to the function or tasks at hand.

optimistic Inclined to put the most favorable construction on actions and events or to anticipate the best possible outcome.

persona (pur-so'-nuh) An individual's social facade or front that reflects the role in life the individual is playing; the personality a person projects in public.

professionalism The conduct or qualities characterized by or conforming to the technical or ethical standards of a profession; exhibiting a courteous, conscientious, and generally businesslike manner in the workplace.

reproach An expression of rebuke or disapproval; a cause or occasion of blame, discredit, or disgrace.

tolerance The need to use more and more of a substance to get the same feeling as the body learns to tolerate the drug.

work ethics A set of values based on the moral virtues of hard work and diligence.

What is professional behavior? We tend to hold medical personnel to a higher standard of professionalism than those in most other career fields. The medical assistant who works to improve his or her professional approach in the workplace is an asset to the employer and will quickly be promoted to positions of more responsibility in the healthcare industry. Some employers are more concerned about medical assistants' professional behavior and interpersonal skills than their clinical skills, because the way that the medical assistant approaches and interacts with patients is critical to the success of the practice. Professionalism is useful not only in the physician's office; it also is a valuable skill when dealing with other business professionals in everyday life, such as a teacher or business owner.

THE MEANING OF PROFESSIONALISM

Professionalism is defined as having a courteous, conscientious, and generally businesslike manner in the workplace. It is characterized by or conforms to the technical or ethical standards of a certain profession. Conducting themselves in a professional manner is essential for successful medical assistants. The attitude of those in the medical profession generally is more conservative than that seen in other career fields. Patients expect professional behavior and base much of their trust and confidence in those who show this type of **demeanor** in the physician's office (Figure 4-1).

WORK ETHICS

Work ethics are sets of values based on the moral virtues of hard work and diligence, involving a whole range of activities, from individual acts to the philosophy of the entire facility. The medical assistant should always display initiative and be reliable. A person

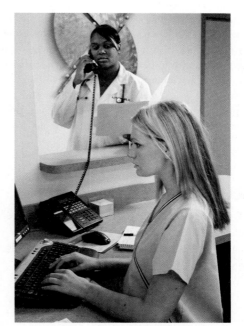

FIGURE 4-1 The professional medical assistant is an asset to the physician's office.

who has a good work ethic is one who arrives on time, who is rarely absent, whose work output is **commensurate** with the pay received, and who uses his or her best abilities. Co-workers become frustrated if another employee consistently arrives late or is absent. This forces the co-workers to take on additional duties and may prevent them from completing their own work. One missing employee can disrupt the entire day, because patients may not be seen at their appointment times because the staff is shorthanded. Also, lunch and other breaks may be shortened because the staff cannot process cases as quickly when an employee does not show up. All employees should know the attendance policies in their facility as outlined in the policy and procedure manual.

Most new hires have a probationary period that may last 30 to 90 days. Any absences or tardiness during the probationary period can be grounds to terminate the employee once the probationary period is up or even before that if multiple attendance issues arise. If the medical assistant has an emergency and must be absent or tardy, he or she should make sure to notify the supervisor according to office policy. All employees must be on time and in attendance every day in the medical office. Physicians and patients alike expect this reliability.

Work ethics also apply to other situations. If another employee is seen taking drugs from the supply cabinet or money from the cash box, the act should certainly be reported. However, if the guilty employee is also a close friend of the person who witnesses the act, an ethical dilemma arises. A medical assistant must always act in such a way that his or her actions are above **reproach**.

CHARACTERISTICS OF PROFESSIONALISM

Many **characteristics** make up the professionalism required of medical assistants. Student medical assistants should begin developing these characteristics while in school; these qualities do not appear magically when the student begins working with actual patients. Although we might think that we would always behave appropriately during an externship or in a job setting, the habits developed in school will carry over into these experiences. If the behavior is unacceptable, it will be **detrimental** to the medical assistant's professional career. If the medical assistant wishes to advance and receive wage increases, promotions, and the trust of the employer, the characteristics discussed in the following sections must be a part of his or her **persona**.

> ### CRITICAL THINKING APPLICATION 4-1
> - How can students practice professional behavior while still in the classroom situation?
> - When students are practicing clinical skills, how can they demonstrate proficiency in professional behavior?

Loyalty

Loyalty is faithfulness or allegiance to a cause, ideal, custom, institution, or product. Loyalty to an employer means that the employee is appreciative of the opportunity provided by the job and supports the company by giving the best effort possible. Many individuals today are interested only in what the employer can provide for them. However, this is an immature approach to take toward a job. When a person is employed by a company, use of skills is exchanged for different types of compensation. Each benefits the other. Often we forget that experience alone is a great benefit from working. Loyalty to the employer is important, and in return the employee should feel a sense of loyalty from the company.

> ### CRITICAL THINKING APPLICATION 4-2
> - How can Karen demonstrate loyalty to her employer?
> - What are some ways her employer can reciprocate Karen's loyalty?

Dependability

One of the most valuable traits of a successful medical assistant is dependability. The physician and supervisors must know that they can depend on the medical assistant to perform all of the assigned duties each day. A medical assistant must follow through when the physician or supervisor gives an order. Be responsible enough to know the job description and what is expected on a daily, weekly, and monthly basis. Supervisors should be confident that once given a task to do, the medical assistant will carry it out accurately and in a timely manner.

Courtesy

Show courtesy to the patients and your co-workers in the physician's office. Kind words and compassion go far in building trust between the medical assistant and patients (Figure 4-2). All visitors and staff members in the office should be shown kindness and consideration. The fact that a medical assistant is having a bad day is no excuse for inflicting anger or irritation onto patients. Always demonstrate a good attitude and offer patients and visitors a sincere smile.

Initiative

Lack of **initiative** is one of the more common complaints from supervisors about employees. Taking initiative means that the medical assistant looks for opportunities to be of help, assisting others as the workload demands. Instead of waiting to be told to perform a task, the **competent** medical assistant looks for jobs that need to be completed. Never remain idle. Employees can always find tasks to complete in the medical office. For example, filing is a continual need. Supplies can be inventoried, ordered, or restocked when extra time is available. Cleaning countertops and straightening areas as work is done helps keep the facility tidy. The medical assistant should also keep an eye on the reception area, which may need attention several times during the day.

FIGURE 4-2 Taking a few moments to explain forms and bills to a patient is a courteous way to prevent misunderstandings and to promote goodwill.

CRITICAL THINKING APPLICATION   4-3
- How can Karen show her initiative on the job?
- What types of duties can she perform if she has finished her work for the day and some time is left before she is scheduled to leave?

Flexibility

A medical assistant must be able to adapt to a wide variety of situations. An emergency could occur in the office, and the staff must be flexible enough to adjust the schedule and care for all patients. Being flexible also means that staff members are willing to assist one another in the performance of their duties. No one in the physician's office should ever say, "That's not my job." The patients must come first, and every staff member must be willing to lend a hand where needed. Some medical assistants trade or rotate their duties. If one assistant does not particularly enjoy doing a certain task, perhaps another assistant would be willing to trade tasks. This way, both are more satisfied with their jobs. If the medical assistant is able to adapt to various situations quickly and cheerfully, he or she becomes a valuable asset to the office.

Credibility

Credibility is the perceived competence or character of a person, leading to the belief that the individual can be trusted. Because trust is a vital component of the physician-patient relationship, the credibility of the physician and those who assist in the office should be strong. The information provided to patients must be accurate. Patients expect that the physician and medical assistant instruct them in a manner that enhances their health and provides positive results. A medical assistant must take care in giving any advice to patients, because they view the medical assistant as an agent of the physician. Patients may not distinguish between the medical assistant's comments and the physician's orders. Remember that giving anything that could be construed as medical advice is outside the scope of the duties of the medical assistant. To avoid facing charges of practicing medicine without a license, a medical assistant must be sure to suggest only what the physician has authorized.

Confidentiality

The importance of confidentiality in the medical environment cannot be stressed enough. Patients are entitled to privacy where their health is concerned, and they should be confident that medical professionals use information only to care for them. Never reveal any information about any patient to anyone without specific permission to do so. Always verify that the person seeking information has the right to see it and that the patient has signed a consent form allowing a third party to view the record. Casual conversations in hallways, elevators, and break rooms between staff members can be overheard by a family member or friend of the patient. Confidentiality is often breached in these areas of the medical office.

The rules regarding confidentiality extend beyond the medical office. At home, medical assistants should not discuss details about patients with their families and friends. Those outside the medical profession do not understand how vital it is to keep information confidential and may pass along private or damaging facts to others. Medical assistants must make it a rule never to discuss a patient with

FIGURE 4-3 A good attitude goes a long way in supporting good patient and staff relationships.

anyone unless information must be shared for the patient's care and treatment. The Health Insurance Portability and Accountability Act (HIPAA) was passed in part to ensure patient confidentiality. (HIPAA is discussed in more detail in later chapters.)

Attitude

Possibly the most important asset a medical assistant brings to the office is a good attitude. A good attitude is characterized by courtesy and kindness to others, refraining from jumping to conclusions, giving the other person the benefit of the doubt, and being **optimistic**. This trait alone can influence promotions, terminations, and the entire atmosphere of the office (Figure 4-3). Individuals are able to control their attitudes with practice. It takes skill to react calmly to people who are very upset rather than to respond in kind, especially if you are being harassed or accused. Speaking in an even tone and perhaps a little softer than normal forces the listener to lower his or her voice to hear. Offer to help resolve the problem and attempt to move to a private room to talk, out of the hearing of other patients. Always have a good attitude with co-workers and be willing to assist them with their duties, especially on hectic days.

OBSTRUCTIONS TO PROFESSIONALISM

At times it is not easy to be a professional. Sometimes patients, co-workers, and supervisors try our patience, and it can be difficult to maintain a professional attitude in these cases. Some of the obstructions to professional behavior are discussed in this section.

Personal Problems and "Baggage"

Everyone has a life outside the workplace, and sometimes we face challenges and difficult times that are hard to put aside. During working hours, our thoughts should be on the job at hand, especially when we are dealing with patients. However, some situations in our lives may be so critical or distracting that we find ourselves thinking of them constantly. This personal baggage can interfere with our ability to perform job duties properly.

When a situation intrudes on our thoughts at work, it often is best to take the time to talk with a supervisor. It is not always necessary to share the intimate details, but a quick explanation that some difficulties are occurring outside of work helps the supervisor to understand any changes in habit or attitude. Some supervisors are uncaring and are concerned only with satisfactory job performance. The medical assistant must use some **discretion** in discussing private affairs with the supervisor.

The professional medical assistant never transfers personal problems or baggage to anyone at the medical facility, especially patients. The workday should be centered around patient care; therefore, do not allow personal business to impinge on time that should be spent assisting patients and the physician. The patient must be the prime concern of all the employees in a medical facility.

CRITICAL THINKING APPLICATION   4-4
It often is difficult to keep from thinking about a problem while you are working. How can Karen do this if she is concerned about a grandmother who is critically ill?

Rumors and the "Grapevine"

A rumor is talk or widely **disseminated** opinion with no discernible source, or a statement that is not known to be true. The definition alone suggests that spreading rumors should be avoided. Most people enjoy working in an environment in which employees cooperate and get along with each other, but rumors can cause problems with employee **morale** and often are great exaggerations or manipulations of the truth. By promoting the grapevine, rumors are passed along and become more and more outrageous with each retelling. A medical assistant should refuse to participate in the office rumor mill and should attempt to be cordial and friendly to everyone at work (Figure 4-4). Supervisors regard those who spread or discuss rumors as unprofessional and untrustworthy. Avoid passing along work-related rumors to patients, family, and friends.

Personal Phone Calls and Business

The medical assistant should not take unnecessary phone calls from friends and family at the office. The office phone is a business line and must be used as such, except in emergencies. Using personal cell phones during working hours is not acceptable. Use breaks and lunch hours to take care of business on the phone. Never take a personal call or respond to text messages on a cell phone while working with a patient. If a phone must be carried, place it on the vibrate setting and always step into a hall or break area if a call absolutely must be taken. This should happen only in rare cases. Visitors should not frequent the office, especially the area where the medical assistant is working. If someone must come to the office, always offer the reception area as a waiting room. Visitors should never be allowed to enter patient areas.

Checking personal e-mail also should be avoided in the workplace. Any type of personal business, such as studying, looking up information on the Internet for personal use, Internet shopping,

FIGURE 4-4 Gossip and rumors have no place in the medical profession. Avoid employees who participate in this type of activity.

or balancing a personal checkbook should be done at home and not in the office. All of these actions distract the medical assistant from the job at hand; the focus should be on serving the patients in the office at all times. Many employees are fired each year for surfing or shopping on the Internet for personal reasons or for checking personal e-mail. Make sure all personal business is handled outside of business hours.

CRITICAL THINKING APPLICATION   4-5
- Karen has a friend who works in a video store a few doors down from her office. Her friend has started stopping in daily on her lunch hour to chat with Karen. How can Karen politely discourage this?
- Karen feels the need to check on her grandmother's condition as often as possible during the days she is ill. How might she accomplish this in a professional way?

Office Politics

Most people associate office politics with some underhanded scheme or plans to move upward in the company in whatever way possible, whether the methods used are ethical or not. The tendency is to give the word *politics* a negative **connotation**, and that is usually correct. Politics can be defined as the art or science of influencing and guiding government or some other organization. The same can be applied to medical office politics. When an individual wishes to move upward in an organization, he or she may use a positive or negative strategy. Many people develop a specific plan regarding how they will advance and in what time period they will accomplish their goals. Medical assistants who want to advance should be productive workers, accept responsibility, be dependable, and always conduct themselves in a professional manner. Using underhanded techniques and instigating trouble is not an effective method of career advancement. Those who use negative office politics often find that their methods turn into disasters and they lose the support of co-workers

FIGURE 4-5 Teamwork is a vital part of the medical profession. All staff members must work together to care for the patient and perform required duties in the physician's office.

and supervisors, making the work environment tense and anxious. Often, they seek other employment, but if they continue negative office politics in their new office, they will likely face the same results and find themselves without a job.

PROFESSIONAL ATTRIBUTES

Teamwork

If managers were asked to name the most important attributes for medical professionals, teamwork would be high on the list (Figure 4-5). Staff members must work together for the good of the patients. They must be willing to perform duties outside the formal job description if they are needed in other areas of the office. Many supervisors frown on employees who state, "That's not in my job description." Any order that is given by a supervisor becomes mandatory, and an individual who refuses to perform an assigned task can have his or her employment terminated for **insubordination**. A medical assistant should perform the duty and later discuss with the supervisor any valid reasons that the task should have been assigned to someone else. However, if the task is illegal, unethical, or places the patient or anyone else in danger, it should not be done. Discuss the situation with the supervisor above the one who ordered the task; in many cases, this would be the physician.

Although we all would enjoy working in an office where everyone gets along and likes every other employee, this does not always happen. Personal feelings must be set aside at work, and all employees must cooperate with others to get the job done efficiently. If a medical assistant has an issue with another employee, the first move would be to discuss it privately with the other person. If the situation does not improve, perhaps a supervisor should be involved for further discussions.

Time Management

We have often heard the expression "work smart." This means that we are to use our time efficiently and concentrate on the most important duties first. To do this, we must first prioritize our duties and arrange our schedules to ensure that these duties can be performed. The first way to improve time management is to plan the tasks that need to be done that day. Taking 10 minutes to write down the tasks for the day helps ensure that they are done. Then, stay on

schedule throughout the day, unless you are interrupted by emergencies. Even then, when office days are well planned, allowances can be made for emergencies and most tasks can still be completed. The key to managing time is prioritizing.

Prioritizing

Prioritizing is simply deciding which tasks are most important. Many people make a "to do" list for the day's activities, but the secret to success is prioritizing those activities into categories that give order to the tasks.

Most tasks can be prioritized into three general categories: those that *must* be done that day, those that *should* be done that day, and those that *could* be done if time permits. Once a general list of tasks has been established, review the list and further prioritize it, using a code such as *M* for must, *S* for should, and *C* for could (or this might be further simplified by using the letters *A, B,* and *C*). Once the tasks have been divided into these categories, they can be further classified in each section. For instance, if category *A* (must be done that day) has six tasks, they can be numbered in the order they should be performed. The same process is completed with the tasks in categories *B* and *C*. As the tasks are completed, they are checked off for that day. Other categories can be added to customize the list. For example, an *H* category can be used for duties to perform at home, *P* could represent phone calls that need to be made, *E* could represent errands to run, and *EM* might represent e-mails to be sent. Customizing the categories makes the list more user-friendly and helps the user to meet his or her individual needs.

Setting Goals

Individuals who succeed in life are planners and goal setters. The first step in becoming a proficient goal setter is to take the time to really think about what is to be accomplished throughout one's lifetime. These goals must be written down and reviewed often. Goals should be set for all areas in a person's life, including personal growth, career, home life, family, spiritual needs, and any others that apply to the individual. The goals should not be unreasonable. They should be measurable and specific, with written steps detailing how they will be reached. Determination and persistence in reaching the goals helps make them happen, along with hard work. The goals should be reviewed often and progress evaluated. Reset goals whenever necessary and celebrate accomplishments.

> **CRITICAL THINKING** APPLICATION   4-6
> - What are some goals Karen might set regarding her behavior on the job?
> - List several goals for the new medical assistant to work toward during his or her first year on the job.

KNOWING THE FACILITY AND ITS EMPLOYEES

A much-circulated story tells of a college professor who used to end a critical test with the question, "What is the name of the woman who cleans our wing of the building?" This would perplex most students, but the question makes a good point. A professional medical assistant should attempt to get to know the people who work in the facility and should have a good idea of

FIGURE 4-6 Knowing which employee to call when help is needed promotes goodwill among employees and often gets a task done more efficiently.

who handles which duties (Figure 4-6). When patients have specific problems with which they need help, they can be referred to the person who knows the most about that particular issue. It is wise to express appreciation to others whenever possible. Say "thank you" or "I appreciate your help" often when working with others. This makes co-workers more likely to assist at other times when their help is needed.

DOCUMENTATION

From the standpoint of professional behavior, documentation skills are vital to medical assistants. Charting accurately with legible, neat handwriting can make a difference in the perception of professionalism in the medical office. Complete, accurate EMR entries are critical as well, and a thorough knowledge of the computer program used in the office will enhance the providers' ability to provide competent patient care. Be complete in any narrative regarding patients. Be sure to state facts, not opinions, and never use sarcastic remarks when charting. Phone messages must be documented carefully as well and handled in a professional manner. Never use sarcasm when reporting messages to the physician or anyone else in the office. Use conservative speech, proper wording, and good grammar in all situations in the medical facility.

Note Taking

Whenever office meetings or seminars are held, be prepared by having a pad and pencil ready for note taking. A medical assistant should never be without paper and pen so that accurate information from the meeting can be jotted down for future reference. It is wise to keep a notebook or file on office meetings for reference in case clarification of an order or a point is needed. Keep a small spiral notebook in a pocket with a pen so that if an order is given in passing by the physician, you have a place to jot it down until you have access to the patient's chart. This can help you avoid administering incorrect dosages of medication or forgetting to order a laboratory

test, in addition to many other errors that could be made by relying on memory. If notebook, pad, or personal desk assistants (PDAs) are used, notes can be easily uploaded and organized in whatever manner the medical assistant finds helpful. However, do not hold up meetings or disrupt them as information is typed into the machines (long nails are especially disruptive and should be kept trimmed and neat).

INTERPERSONAL SKILLS

Interpersonal skills are paramount in working with patients and other health professionals. A medical assistant should work to perfect his or her communication techniques. Often the success of a business is directly related to the ability of its employees to communicate effectively.

When speaking to patients and providing them with information, remember that most do not have any medical background and do not understand many of the phrases used by the medical community. A medical assistant must be patient and explain in a courteous manner any aspect of the instructions or details that the patient does not understand. When educating the patient, the medical assistant should have a professional attitude of concern and helpfulness. Assure the patient that medical assistants and the rest of the staff in the facility are bound by rules of patient confidentiality if the patient seems concerned about revealing information.

SUBSTANCE ABUSE

All employees of medical facilities must avoid drug and alcohol abuse (also called *substance abuse*), which is defined as the repeated and excessive use of a substance, despite its destructive effects, to produce pleasure and escape reality. Substance abuse includes the use of illegal and legal drugs. Many facilities require screening before employment, and some perform screenings randomly during employment. Because drugs and alcohol remain in the body for various lengths of time, an individual who uses on a Sunday afternoon may still have residual effects on Monday. This can prevent a medical assistant from performing at maximum capacity and can cause mistakes that may even be life-threatening to the patient. Also, the drive to and from work can result in an accident. Fatal or not, anytime substance abuse results in harm to another person, the user is at risk of lawsuits and legal problems. By abusing drugs even once, the medical assistant can damage his or her career irreparably.

A person is considered to have a substance abuse problem if at least one of the following four criteria is met:
- Continued use despite social or interpersonal problems
- Repeated use that results in failure to fulfill obligations at work, school, and/or home
- Repeated use that results in physically hazardous situations
- Use that results in legal problems

Before a person is labeled an abuser, however, the medical assistant should understand the differences between use, dependence, abuse, and addiction. Most people use some type of drug or supplement, many on a daily basis. If a patient takes a blood pressure medication, he or she uses that drug for a specific purpose that provides a health benefit. Physical dependence is not always part of the definition of addiction. Some drugs cause a physical dependence but not an addiction, such as a medication for diabetes. The patient depends on the drug to relieve the symptoms of the disease, but the drug usually is not abused or used in a way that would be considered an addiction. *Abuse* is the use of illegal drugs or the misuse of prescription and over-the-counter drugs.

Anyone who experiences at least three of the following seven criteria in the same 12-month period could be considered an abuser and should seek drug and alcohol counseling:

- Tolerance for the drug
- Withdrawal symptoms
- Difficulty controlling drug use
- Negative consequences from drug use
- Significant time or emotional energy spent seeking drugs
- Neglect of regular activities
- A desire to cut down on the use of a certain drug

Addiction is the compulsive use of a substance despite its negative and sometimes dangerous effects. The abuse of prescription drugs is a growing concern in the United States. Many of these drugs alter brain activity and are highly addictive, and as a result, the user's behavior changes. Opioids, central nervous system depressants, anti-anxiety drugs, and stimulants are the most common categories of prescription drug abuse. Once users are addicted, their ability to make voluntary decisions changes and a craving leads to a state of constantly seeking the **drug of choice**. Most physicians are opposed to hiring a person with a history of or convictions for substance abuse. Often, personal relationships and careers are destroyed, and this can lead to theft to buy drugs or alcohol. (For more information on the most commonly abused drugs and symptoms of substance abuse, visit the Evolve site at *evolve.elsevier.com/kinn.*)

According to the National Institute on Alcohol Abuse and Alcoholism (NIAAA), alcohol abuse is a disease that has the following four symptoms:

- *Craving*—a strong urge or need to drink
- *Loss of control*—the inability to stop drinking once it has begun
- *Physical dependence*—the occurrence of withdrawal symptoms after drinking (e.g., shakiness, nausea, sweating, and anxiety)
- **Tolerance**—the need to increase the amount of alcohol taken in to get the same effect

The potential to abuse alcohol is partly inherited, and the individual lifestyle may also influence whether a person becomes an alcoholic. This does not mean that a person who is a child of an alcoholic will definitely become an alcoholic, but the risk is greater when alcoholism is prevalent in the family. Treatment for alcoholism works for many people. Some never drink again, but others may go for months or years without drinking and still suffer a relapse; still others are simply unable to stop drinking for any length of time.

In the physician's office, one question opens the door to talk about alcoholism and helps to diagnose patients, including employees, with alcohol problems. That question is, "On any single occasion in the past 3 months, have you had more than five drinks containing alcohol?" A positive answer should lead to more questions about the individual's drinking habits. Detecting abuse issues early leads to the initiation of treatment, and this can help a person avoid becoming an alcoholic. The earlier in life abuse issues are identified, the more likely it is that treatment will be effective and further abuse will be prevented.

Substance abuse has the potential to end a medical assistant's career and can lead to incarceration. A medical assistant who is under the influence of controlled substances or alcohol can easily make medication errors and fail to document correctly and, in addition, cannot care for the patient to his or her optimal ability. Almost all physicians report missing medications to the police, and in subsequent investigations, the medical assistant may be arrested and jailed. Convictions for substance abuse can make finding a job in a healthcare facility almost impossible. Many facilities conduct pre-employment and random drug testing, and the chances of not being caught are extremely slim, especially if a substance is still in the system several days after use. Avoid any behavior that can threaten loss of a career in the medical field and legal action.

CLOSING COMMENTS

Patients expect and deserve professional behavior from those who work in medical facilities. Always show compassion, caring, and consideration for a person who comes to the office, whether a patient, visitor, or co-worker. By displaying these traits, the medical assistant earns the respect of co-workers and becomes indispensable to the physician-employer. Behaving in a professional manner in the medical office helps gain the patient's trust. Trust is one of the most important factors in preventing cases of medical professional liability. The medical assistant must never be judgmental when dealing with patients who have substance abuse problems; these patients have a disease just as difficult as cancer or any chronic illness. They deserve empathy and concern. Treating patients with care and not subjecting them to poor attitudes keeps the patient-physician relationship strong and conducive to the health and recovery of the patient.

Patient Education

Remember that most patients do not have any medical background and do not understand many of the phrases used by the medical community. Always be patient and courteously explain any aspect of the instructions or details the patient does not understand. Project a professional attitude of concern and helpfulness. If the patient seems concerned about revealing pertinent information, assure the person that medical assistants and the rest of the staff in the facility are bound by rules of patient confidentiality. Before the patient leaves the exam room, make sure to ask, "Do you have any questions?" This gives patients the opportunity to get all their questions answered before they leave the office.

A professional medical assistant does not share personal information with anyone at the medical facility. Refrain from passing along rumors of any type to patients or their families.

Legal and Ethical Issues

Confidentiality is perhaps the most important aspect of professionalism. Release of any information about patients without their permission is not only unethical, it is against the law. The American Medical Association (AMA) suggests that the purpose of a physician's ethical duty to maintain patient confidentiality is to allow the patient to feel free to make a full and frank disclosure of information to the physician, knowing that the physician will protect the confidential nature of the information. Patients must feel that their confidences will be protected by each member of the physician's staff, including the medical assistant. The workday should be centered around patient care, so never allow personal business to intrude on time that should be spent assisting patients and the physician. Otherwise, the patient may be left with the impression that the medical assistant, or the entire staff, is unprofessional and this often leads to trust issues between physician and patient.

SUMMARY OF SCENARIO

Karen is happy to be employed in a family practice in which providing quality patient care is paramount. She is learning to be careful of what she says and to remain focused on the patient instead of any difficulties she may be having. Karen knows it is her responsibility to be a team player and to assist the other staff members as much as possible. She maintains a good attitude, even when personal issues could distract her from her duties. Karen gets a strong sense of pride from being a member of the medical profession. She is meticulous about presenting a neat appearance and arrives on time for each workday. She always asks others whether they need help when she has any extra time throughout the day. Karen looks forward to a long relationship with her employer. The rewards she feels as a member of the health team are second to none.

Although Karen is concerned about her grandmother's health, those concerns must be minimally intrusive on her work duties and her attitude toward her patients and co-workers. By taking time to speak with her supervisor and explaining the situation with her grandmother, Karen takes a proactive role in ensuring that the supervisor understands the pressures Karen is facing. Most supervisors are sympathetic and understanding when issues outside the practice affect employees; however, this should not happen on a regular basis. By encouraging Karen to call and check on her grandmother periodically, the supervisor helps Karen to feel more confident and less distracted during the day. Because she has found her supervisor to be a supportive ally, Karen can relax and carry out her duties professionally and competently throughout the workday. Karen puts the patients first, and this is a fine example of both professionalism and patient compassion.

SUMMARY OF LEARNING OBJECTIVES

1. **Define, spell, and pronounce the terms listed in the vocabulary.**
   Spelling and pronouncing medical terms correctly bolster the medical assistant's credibility. Knowing the definition of these terms promotes confidence in communication with patients and co-workers.

2. **Explain the reasons that professionalism is important in the medical field.**
   Professionalism is the characteristic of conforming to the technical or ethical standards of a profession. It involves showing courtesy, being conscientious, and conducting oneself in a businesslike manner at the workplace. Professionalism is vital in the medical profession, because patients expect and deserve to be treated in a professional way. When the medical assistant acts in a professional way, he or she creates trust with the patient. Patients notice professional behavior, even when it is not directed at them specifically. They notice how others are treated in the reception room and in other areas of the office. Always act in a professional manner while at work.

3. **Discuss several of the characteristics of professionalism.**
   Some of the characteristics of professionalism are loyalty, dependability, courtesy, initiative, flexibility, credibility, confidentiality, and a good attitude.

4. **Explain why confidentiality is so important in the medical profession.**
   Confidentiality is crucial in the medical profession, because patients depend on medical personnel to keep their health information private. Breach of patient confidentiality is one reason an employee could be terminated immediately and can result in litigation between the patient and the physician-employer.

5. **Discuss the importance of the medical assistant's attitude in caring for patients.**
   Because most patients are not at their best when visiting the physician's office, the attitude of the staff plays an important role in patients' attitudes while in the office. Medical assistants need patience when working with those who are ill. A smile or a reassuring pat on the back goes a long way and can be encouraging.

6. **List some examples of office politics.**
   Office politics can be negative or positive. A person who uses others to gain promotion in the company or who takes credit for a team effort may be using office politics in a negative way; a person who strategically plans advancement through outstanding performance, dependability, and teamwork uses office politics in a positive manner. Knowing when to speak and when to listen helps the medical assistant play the game of politics well in the medical facility.

7. **Identify specific ways teamwork can be promoted in the physician's office.**
   Teamwork makes any job easier to complete. By helping those who may be overwhelmed with duties, the medical assistant may find willing co-workers who will help when the situation is reversed in the future. If two assistants both have duties they dislike, they might trade the duties, to the satisfaction of both. All must work together for the good of the facility and the patients it serves.

8. **Discuss the meaning of insubordination and why it is grounds for dismissal.**

   Insubordination is disobedience to any type of authority figure, usually the supervisor, and it can be grounds for immediate dismissal. When given a task to complete, the medical assistant should carry out the order unless it is unlawful or unethical. If the medical assistant does not carry out an order, the patient's life may be at risk. If the medical assistant feels that the duty should be performed by someone else or should not be performed for some reason, he or she should consult the supervisor. Discuss the issue and attempt to reach an agreement about the appropriateness of performing the task in the future.

9. **Identify and implement time management principles to maintain efficient office function.**

   Prioritizing tasks can help the medical assistant accomplish more tasks. Prioritizing can be used for work, home, and extracurricular activities. Tasks can be identified as those that must, should, or could be done that day. Then, within each of these categories, the tasks can be numbered in the order in which they should be completed. Prioritizing tasks is the most important time management principle.

10. **Talk about goal setting and how it helps a person achieve career success.**

    Goals should be written down and reviewed often to check progress. Taking small steps toward goals helps ensure that they eventually are reached. Individuals should set goals in each area of their lives, breaking the tasks down into manageable parts. Goals should not be unreasonable or unattainable, but rather should provide the opportunity for small successes along the way to reaching the ultimate goal.

11. **Discuss how substance abuse can impact the medical assistant's employment.**

    Substance abuse can lead to arrest and conviction. The medical assistant may face legal action if he or she is abusing drugs or alcohol. This can lead to the end of a career in the healthcare industry. Additionally, the medical assistant could injure a patient by giving incorrect doses of medication or failing to document information properly in the medical record. In extreme cases, patients could die from the medical assistant's actions while under the influence of controlled substances. Any medical assistant struggling with a substance abuse problem should seek professional help immediately.

CONNECTIONS

Study Guide Connection: Go to the Chapter 4 Study Guide. Read and complete the activities.

Evolve Connection: Go to the Chapter 4 link at *evolve.elsevier.com/kinn* to complete the Chapter Review and Chapter Quiz. Check out the other resources listed for this chapter to make the most of what you have learned from Professional Behavior in the Workplace.

5

INTERPERSONAL SKILLS AND HUMAN BEHAVIOR

Many types of patients seek medical attention and care in the physician's office. Each has different needs and different concerns, even if the diagnoses are similar. Communication and interpersonal skills are vital in meeting these needs and providing optimum care to the patient. However, the patient is not the only individual to consider. Family members often are crucial to the health and well-being of the patient.

Lucille Cloyd is an 83-year-old patient who has been diagnosed with pancreatic cancer and is seeing Dr. Neill for treatment. Her daughter, Sarah Smithson, helps to care for her; she is close to her mother emotionally. Sarah also is Dr. Neill's patient. Although Sarah does not want to see her mother in pain,

she suffers with the knowledge that life will be very different without her. Mrs. Cloyd is widowed and visits the physician once a month in addition to receiving hospice services. She is a good-humored woman who feels that she has led a fruitful life, yet she has moments of depression. She has been living with Sarah and her family for 2 months and enjoys interacting with her two grandchildren and the family's pets.

The medical assistant must consider not only Mrs. Cloyd, but also her extended family. Compassion and sensitivity are necessary to care for this patient, in addition to excellent listening skills. A good knowledge of human relations helps the medical assistant make Mrs. Cloyd's medical care as pleasant as possible under the circumstances.

While studying this chapter, think about the following questions:

- How can the medical assistant treat patients as individuals during a busy workday?
- How does the medical assistant effectively communicate with a patient's family members?
- How will developing good listening skills make the medical assistant more effective?
- How do friends and family members play a role in the health of the patient?

LEARNING OBJECTIVES

1. Define, spell, and pronounce the terms listed in the vocabulary.
2. Explain why first impressions are crucial.
3. Differentiate between verbal and nonverbal communication.
4. Identify styles and types of verbal communication.
5. Explain the different levels of spatial separation.
6. Analyze the effect of hereditary, cultural, and environmental influences on communication.
7. Discuss the value of touch in the communication process.
8. Recognize the elements of oral communication using a sender-receiver process.
9. Explain the value of active listening.
10. Define and understand abnormal behavior patterns.
11. Recognize commonly used defense mechanisms.
12. Discuss the role of assertiveness in effective professional communication.

13. Identify the roles of self-boundaries in the healthcare environment.
14. List several ways to deal with conflict.
15. Recognize communication barriers.
16. Identify techniques for overcoming communication barriers.
17. Differentiate between adaptive and nonadaptive coping mechanisms.
18. Identify common stages that terminally ill patients go through and discuss the support that can assist them and their families during their struggle.
19. Discuss using empathy when treating terminally ill patients.
20. Identify resources and adaptations that are required based on individual needs.
21. List and explain the levels of Maslow's hierarchy of needs.
22. Discuss why physical and emotional needs affect our daily performance at work.

VOCABULARY

adage (a´-dij) A saying, often in metaphoric form, that embodies a common observation.

aggressive Forceful or intended to dominate; hostile, injurious, or destructive, especially when referring to a behavior caused by frustration.

ambiguous (am-bi´-gu-wus) Capable of being understood in two or more possible senses or ways; unclear.

animate To fill with life; to give spirit and support to expressions.

battery An offensive touching or use of force on a person without his or her consent.

caustic (kos´-tik) Marked by sarcasm.

channels Means of communication or expression; courses or directions of thought.

comfort zone A place in the mind where an individual feels safe and confident.

congruent (kun-gru´-unt) Being in agreement, harmony, or correspondence; conforming to the circumstances or requirements of a situation.

decodes Converts, as in a message, into intelligible form; recognizes and interprets.

defense mechanisms Psychological methods of dealing with stressful situations that are encountered in day-to-day living.

encodes Converts from one system of communication to another; converts a message into code.

encroachments Actions that advance beyond the usual or proper limits.

enunciate (e-nun´-se-at) To utter articulate sounds; the act of being very distinct in speech.

external noise Sounds or factors outside the brain that interfere with the communication process.

externalization The attribution of an event or occurrence to causes outside the self.

feedback The transmission of evaluative or corrective information to the original or controlling source about an action, event, or process.

grief Reaction to an unfortunate outcome; a deep distress caused by bereavement, a loss, or a perceived loss.

internal noise Factors inside the brain that interfere with the communication process.

language barrier Any type of interference that inhibits the communication process and is related to languages spoken by the people attempting to communicate.

litigious (luh-ti´-jus) Prone to engage in lawsuits.

malediction (ma-luh-dik´-shun) Speaking evil or the calling of a curse.

media A term applied to agencies of mass communication, such as newspapers, magazines, and telecommunications.

paraphrasing To express an idea in different wording in an effort to enhance communication and clarify meaning.

perception Capacity for comprehension; an awareness of the elements of the environment.

physiologic noise Internal interferences comprised of biological factors within a speaker or listener that hinder effective and accurate communication.

pitch Highness or lowness of a sound; the relative level, intensity, or extent of some quality or state.

proxemics (prok-se´-miks) The study of the nature, degree, and effect of the spatial separation individuals naturally maintain.

sarcasm A sharp and often satirical response or ironic utterance designed to cut or inflict pain.

stereotype Something conforming to a fixed or general pattern; a standardized mental picture that is held in common by many and represents an oversimplified opinion, prejudiced attitude, or uncritical judgment.

stressors Stimuli that cause stress.

subtle Difficult to understand or perceive; having or marked by keen insight and ability to penetrate deeply and thoroughly.

thanatology (tha-nuh-tah´-luh-je) The study of the phenomena of death and of psychological methods of coping with death.

vehemently (ve´-uh-ment-le) In a manner marked by forceful energy; intensely, emotionally.

volatile (vah´-luh-til) Easily aroused; tending to erupt in violence.

The interpersonal skills developed by the medical assistant help to set the tone of a medical office. Interpersonal skills include the communications process and how we relate to one another during that process. Human relations can be defined as the study of the problems that arise from organizational and interpersonal contact. The two entities intersect, and the successful medical assistant continually works to enhance these attributes. Patients who visit the healthcare facility may not be at their best, and the way in which the medical assistant reacts to and interacts with them can make an incredible difference in their **perception** of the office, the physician, and the medical staff. These interactions may also affect the patient's treatment and recovery.

FIRST IMPRESSIONS

Our elders have stressed all our lives that first impressions are lasting ones, and this old **adage** is still true! The opinions formed in the early moments of meeting someone remain in our thoughts long after the first words have been spoken. The first impression involves much more than just physical appearance or dress; it includes attitude and compassion, and the all-important smile (Figure 5-1).

One of the primary objectives of the professional medical assistant is to care for and about the people being served. Patients are the reason the facility exists, and they should be offered the best customer service possible. They must be welcomed warmly, and it is

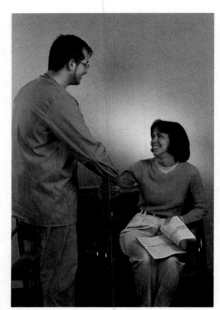

FIGURE 5-1 First impressions are critical in gaining the patient's trust.

important to call patients by their names. People enjoy hearing their names, and it gives a patient confidence that the medical staff members know for whom they are caring.

Think for a moment about how it feels to be a new patient entering the unknown territory of the physician's office. Staff members of the facility are in familiar surroundings and already have some information about the new patient. However, the patient knows nothing about the staff members. One way to break that barrier is to have all staff members wear name badges, with letters large enough to be read at a distance of 3 feet. Include the staff position if several divisions of responsibility exist (e.g., "medical assistant," "insurance biller," and "office manager"). When the patient approaches, if you are wearing a name badge, make introductions and smile. Smiles should show in the voice and the eyes. Genuinely welcome the patient to the office. This small effort helps put the patient at ease in the office environment.

Some physicians make brief notes in the medical record about the personal life of the patient. When the patient arrives for an appointment, the physician can ask about a recent trip abroad or a new grandchild. This tells the patient that the doctor and the office staff see him or her as more than just an illness or a medical record number. It gives the impression that they truly care, and that impression should be an accurate one. Once an impression is formed in the patient's mind, it is very difficult to change; therefore, make the first impressions of your office positive ones. The events in a patient's life can drastically influence the person's health, and any information that would be beneficial to the physician in treating the patient belongs in the medical record.

PATIENT-CENTERED CARE

Healthcare professionals have embraced patient-centered care, an innovative approach to plan, deliver, and evaluate healthcare that is grounded in mutually beneficial partnerships among healthcare providers, patients, and families. Patient- and family-centered care applies to patients of all ages and may be practiced in any healthcare

setting. Each patient that seeks care from the physician has a unique set of needs, including clinical symptoms that require medical attention and issues specific to the individual that can affect his or her care. As patients navigate the healthcare delivery system, physicians and their employees must be prepared to identify and address not just the clinical aspects of care, but also the spectrum of each patient's demographic and personal characteristics. Good communication skills are vital to meeting the needs of the patient and his or her support system.

COMMUNICATION PATHS

Verbal Communication

Peter Urs Bender suggests several types of verbal communication in his book "Guide to Strengths and Weaknesses of Personality Types," including:

1. Expressive – talkative, excited, enthusiastic.
2. Decisive – domineering, controlling, authoritarian.
3. Amiable – nurturing, positive, helpful.
4. Analytical – supportive, questioning, perfectionist.

The medical assistant can develop enough perception to determine the type of verbal communication that a patient uses most often. Then, by studying these four types, it will be easier to communicate verbally with each of the personality types. Think about family members and close friends – what personality type might they be?

The **pitch** of the voice is a part of verbal communication. The voice lifts at the end of a question. It drops at the end of a statement. Usually when a speaker intends to continue a statement, the voice holds the same pitch, the head remains straight, and the eyes and hands are unchanged. This is not an appropriate time to interrupt. If the message is interrupted, the train of thought may not be completed. The tone of voice and choice of words also affect messages.

The medical assistant should speak clearly and **enunciate** words properly. Speak loudly enough that the patients are able to hear clearly, and pay particular attention to those who wear some type of hearing assistance device. It is wise to note this information on the patient's medical record to jog the memory when a patient with a hearing problem visits the office. Never assume that just because a patient is elderly, he or she has a hearing problem. When talking with patients, be sure to use the volume of speech to an advantage. Always speak at a clearly audible level, but at times it will be necessary to increase or decrease the volume of speech. When a patient is upset, for instance, it often helps to lower the volume of speech, because the patient tends to get quieter to hear the person speaking.

Eye contact is critical, especially in the age of electronic medical records. Look at the person to whom you are speaking and do not forget a genuine smile. Look at the person more than at the computer. Many people feel that a person who speaks and cannot look another in the eyes is being deceptive. It also can mean that the speaker is very shy and has little self-confidence. Use gestures where appropriate to liven speech and **animate** the conversation.

Medical assistants must become aware of how they express themselves and how they affect the feelings of others. The tone of voice is vital. **Sarcasm** and **caustic** remarks have no place in the medical office. For example, telling a patient, "I hope you can manage to be on time for your next appointment" is needless and rude. The

PROCEDURE 5-1

Recognize and Respond to Verbal Communications

GOAL: *To be able to recognize verbal communication and respond to it in a professional manner.*

EQUIPMENT and SUPPLIES

- Cards with various patient scenarios (available on Evolve)

PROCEDURAL STEPS

1. Select a classmate as a partner who will play the role of a patient for this procedure. Use patients of varying cultural backgrounds and ability to communicate in English while practicing the procedure. Make sure your partner understands the patient's role on the card.
   <u>PURPOSE:</u> To practice communication with a patient whose responses will not be predictable.

2. Taking turns, draw a card and role-play the scenario described on it.

3. State the message to your patient. Demonstrate sensitivity appropriate to the message being delivered.
   <u>PURPOSE:</u> To send a clearly communicated message.

4. Demonstrate empathy and be impartial when communicating with patients, family, and staff.
   <u>PURPOSE:</u> To treat each person fairly and with professionalism.

5. Demonstrate awareness of the territorial boundaries of the person with whom you are communicating.
   <u>PURPOSE:</u> To recognize and protect personal boundaries in communicating with others.

6. Allow your patient to respond to the sent message. Apply active listening skills.

   <u>PURPOSE:</u> To make sure your patient understood your message and to allow him or her to communicate a response.

7. Restate your patient's response.
   <u>PURPOSE:</u> To make sure you understand the patient's message.

8. Clarify any issues that are unclear.
   <u>PURPOSE:</u> To make sure the meaning of each message sent is understood.

9. Demonstrate awareness of diversity in providing patient care.
   <u>PURPOSE:</u> To respect the diversity of the patient population.

10. Refrain from using slang or other unprofessional terms.
    <u>PURPOSE:</u> To maintain professional communication.

11. Demonstrate recognition of the patient's level of understanding in communications.
    <u>PURPOSE:</u> To ensure that the message sent is worded or expressed in a way the patient can understand and to communicate on the recipient's level of comprehension.

12. Continue to communicate back and forth, making sure that your message to each patient is understood correctly.

13. Analyze communications in providing appropriate responses and feedback.
    <u>PURPOSE:</u> To continually improve the communications process between healthcare professionals, other staff members, and patients.

---

medical assistant must be conservative when speaking and must not be too familiar. The patient expects professionalism and has the right to demand this in the healthcare setting. Never make an inappropriate remark and follow with "I was just kidding." This is never used in a medical facility or in any type of interpersonal communication. Take special care not to hurt anyone's feelings with words and phrases. Be very careful about what is said, especially to patients (Procedure 5-1).

Remember that patients are in the facility to be treated by the physician and staff. They usually are concerned about their illness and may have great apprehension and fear about the future. It is completely out of place for the medical assistant to talk about his or her personal life and challenges with the patients. Allow the patient to speak, and listen instead of offering personal information. Often patients casually mention details to the medical assistant that might influence their care. The saying that we are given "one mouth and two ears" stresses which should get more use!

Nonverbal Communication

Both verbal and nonverbal communications are important in the art of expression, and both are needed to succeed in the communication exchange. Nonverbal communication involves messages conveyed without the use of words. They are transmitted by body language, gestures, and mannerisms that may or may not be in agreement with the words the person speaks. Body language is partly instinctive, partly taught, and partly imitative. It involves eye contact, facial expression, hand gestures, grooming, dress, space, tone of voice, posture, touch, and much more. We are often unaware of our own nonverbal signals and consciously recognize only a small number of the signals sent by others. Our ability to help others increases as we hone our own skills in interpreting nonverbal communication; it is almost always more accurate than verbal communication and tends to convey our true feelings and beliefs (Procedure 5-2).

Appearance is an integral part of nonverbal communication. Our appearance influences the way others view us and can present a conflicting message, or even a totally incorrect message. When we see someone who dresses or grooms in a way that is very different from our own style, we tend to assume that the personalities are also very different. This is not always true. Although we should not judge people by the way they dress, it is difficult not to form opinions based on what we see. Visible piercings and tattoos often are regarded unfavorably in the medical profession, as are long, brightly painted nails. Although these do not signify that the wearer is not professional, many patients, especially older patients, are uncomfortable with these trends. For this reason alone, the medical assistant who is less conservative may diminish his or her chances for certain jobs and advancements. Expressing oneself is healthy, yet in the medical profession, a conservative appearance is mandatory so as not to raise obstacles to communication.

PROCEDURE 5-2

Recognize and Respond to Nonverbal Communications

GOAL: *To be able to recognize nonverbal communication and respond to it in a professional way.*

EQUIPMENT and SUPPLIES

- Cards with various statements that can be communicated in a nonverbal way (available on Evolve)

PROCEDURAL STEPS

1. Select a classmate as a partner who will play the role of a patient for this procedure. Use patients of varying cultural backgrounds and ability to communicate in English while practicing the procedure.
   PURPOSE: To practice nonverbal communications with a patient whose responses will not be predictable.
2. Taking turns, draw a card and communicate the thought on the card to your patient.
3. Use appropriate body language and other nonverbal skills in communicating with patients, family, and staff.
   PURPOSE: To make certain that the nonverbal communication sends the same message as the verbal communication.

4. Demonstrate respect for individual diversity, incorporating awareness of one's own biases in areas including gender, race, religion, age, and economic status. Refrain from influencing the patient toward personal ethics and beliefs.
   PURPOSE: To demonstrate awareness of diversity when providing patient care and to avoid offending patients of any culture.
5. Determine whether the receiver understood the message correctly.
   PURPOSE: To send a nonverbal message that is understood by the receiver.
6. Continue to communicate back and forth, making sure each message sent is conveyed to the receiver accurately. Remain impartial and show empathy when dealing with patients.
7. Analyze communications in providing appropriate responses and feedback.
   PURPOSE: To continually improve the communications process between healthcare professionals, other staff members, and patients.

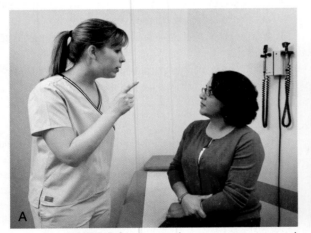

FIGURE 5-2 A, Pointing often is an accusatory gesture and causes discomfort. **B,** A bright smile helps to put the patient at ease and to relax.

The successful medical assistant expresses self-esteem and confidence by stance, vocabulary, facial expression, and a caring attitude. The experience of speaking to someone who does not make eye contact helps one realize the importance of greeting the patient with the eyes as well as the voice and body language. Facial expressions often convey our true feelings and are not masked by the words we use. Our eyes often tell the truth when our words are misleading or false. Use an open body stance when dealing with patients. Crossed arms and legs hint that you are "closed" to the person to whom you are speaking, and this may be construed as disinterest or disbelief. Nonverbal and verbal communication are interdependent (Figure 5-2); they must be in harmony to convey an accurate message that the receiver can easily interpret. If the two are not **congruent**, the nonverbal presentation usually is dominant and expresses the true message.

The need for boundaries, or personal space, is demonstrated by how patients in the reception area choose a seat. **Proxemics** is the study of the nature, degree, and effect of the spatial separation individuals naturally maintain and how this separation relates to heredity, cultural, and environmental factors. Seldom does a person sit in a space next to a stranger if another option is available. Although the need for space varies with the individual culture, some might even remain standing to satisfy the need for personal space. Public space usually is accepted as a distance of 12 to 25 feet, and social space usually is considered to be 4 to 12 feet. Personal space ranges from 1½ to 4 feet, and intimate contact includes physical touching to approximately 1½ feet. The medical assistant often can tell when he or she has invaded someone's personal space, because the person tends to back up a step or two. If this happens, take a small step back and respect the boundaries being set. The more familiar and

FIGURE 5-3 Touching the patient communicates care and compassion. Careful listening and asking questions helps the patient express thoughts and feelings.

CRITICAL THINKING APPLICATION   5-1
- How might touch be an important communication tool with Mrs. Cloyd?
- How can using touch affect Sarah?
- Could laughter affect either of these women as they deal with death?

THE PROCESS OF COMMUNICATION

Anyone who works in the realm of public service should develop good communication skills. It is important to be able to interact with others and to put them at ease so that their comfort level increases and they develop trust. To communicate well, we first must have a general understanding of the process of communication. Once a message has been sent, it cannot be retrieved and restated or expressed in a different way. Especially in the medical profession, communication must be clear and concise, and the message we intend to send must match what the receiver understands.

Although many different scientific models of communication exist, the one that best fits most types of communication is the transactional communication model. Before students can understand how this model works, they must understand the elements we use to communicate.

When two people interact, both people usually act as senders and as receivers (or communicators). The sender is the person who sends a message through a variety of different channels. **Channels** can be spoken words, written messages, and body language. The sender **encodes** the message, which simply means that he or she chooses a specific means of expression using words and other channels. The receiver **decodes** the message according to his or her understanding of what is being communicated. However, sometimes the receiver misunderstands the message. This often is a result of *noise,* which is anything that interferes with the message being sent. It can be literal noise, such as a radio or a jackhammer on the street outside; this is called **external noise**. Or it can be **internal noise**, which includes the receiver's own thoughts or prejudices and opinions. **Physiologic noise** also interferes with communication. This includes any biologic factor that would prevent the communicator from sending or receiving accurate messages, such as not feeling well or being overly tired. **Feedback** can be given through verbal expressions or body language, such as a simple nod of understanding. The perception of the receiver is very important and is discussed later in this chapter.

The transactional communication model (Figure 5-4) depicts "communicators" instead of one sender and one receiver. If two people are communicating, both are sending and receiving messages and both are encoding and decoding messages. Even when two people are speaking one at a time, messages are continually sent with words, body language, facial expressions, and gestures. Various channels of communication are used, and both communicators offer feedback, including subconscious feedback. Noise may or may not be present, but even the best communicators experience some type of noise, even if that is only thinking of what to say next.

comfortable patients are with the medical assistant, the closer the space they allow. Other types of boundaries are discussed later in the chapter.

Touch is a powerful communicator. The soft acceptance of shaking someone's hand, to the good-natured pat on the back, to the harsh slap on the face all relay different messages that need no words to express accurately. In the medical profession, as in any business, touch can be comforting or can lead to a sexual harassment suit. Individuals who have experienced sexual abuse or other traumatic experiences may not want to be touched at all. Unfortunately, one must be extremely careful when using this effective communication tool. In today's **litigious** society, any nonconsensual touching may be considered **battery**, and touch should be used with great discretion and caution.

The medical assistant should not be afraid to touch patients appropriately, such as giving a pat on the back or a squeeze of the hand (Figure 5-3). Some patients are receptive to a brief sideways hug, whereas others would take this as an intrusion into their personal space. Certainly patients with serious illnesses appreciate touch as an expression of empathy. Never be afraid to touch sick patients, especially those with diseases such as acquired immunodeficiency syndrome (AIDS), as long as proper precautions are followed where indicated. If unsure, ask a patient whether he or she minds being hugged. These patients need to feel acceptance, and the attitude of the medical staff members they encounter directly influences their adherence to keeping their appointments with the physician. If they do not feel accepted and cared for, they will not return to the physician's office. A gentle touch and a smile do wonders for showing care and concern.

Posture can signal depression, excitement, anger, or even an appeal for help. When the physician sits at the front of the chair and leans forward, he or she is sending a message of care and interest. Positioning also is important. Sitting behind a desk promotes an air of authority. Standing or sitting across a room may convey a negative message of denying involvement or reluctance to talk. Sitting side by side with a patient helps initiate trust and promote open conversation. The medical assistant should practice good postural techniques as a part of projecting a positive image and for personal health reasons.

Listening

Listening is just as important to good communication as the spoken word. *Hearing* is the process, function, or power of perceiving sound,

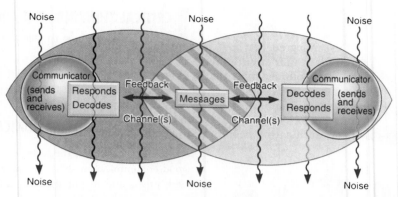

FIGURE 5-4 The transactional communication model. (From Adler RB, Towne N: *Looking out, looking in: interpersonal communication,* San Antonio, 1996, Harcourt Brace.)

whereas *listening* is defined as paying attention to sound or hearing something with thoughtful attention. Patients need to know that the medical assistant is listening. This is actually true in all interpersonal relationships, including husband-wife, parent-child, supervisor-employee, and doctor-patient interactions. When listening to someone who is attempting to communicate, the first rule is to look at the speaker and pay attention. Sometimes it is important not to respond immediately but to remain silent and offer an understanding and reassuring nod.

Sometimes it is hard to listen. We may not be able to listen effectively, because we are distracted by our own thoughts. Perhaps the situations occurring in our own lives make the conversation we are hearing seem meaningless and unimportant. Or so many messages may be attacking at once that we are unable to focus on any specific one to listen to what is being communicated. At other times, such as in anger, we are so rapidly preparing our response that we cannot listen to what is being said. We may simply be too tired to listen, or we may have prejudged the speaker and decided that we do not need to listen. However, while working with patients, the medical assistant must be diligent not only in *hearing* the words being spoken, but also in *listening* to them and to what the patient is attempting to communicate.

Active listening is a skill that enables a person to paraphrase and clarify what the speaker has said. **Paraphrasing** is listening to what the sender is communicating, analyzing the words, and restating them to confirm that the receiver has understood the message as the sender intended. This process clarifies the speaker's thoughts and helps indicate that a common understanding of the message exists between the speaker and the receiver. When communicating in this way, the receiver should reword what the sender has said and then ask a clarifying question. Consider the following example:

| Patient: | *"I haven't been feeling well lately."* |
| Medical assistant: | *"You say you have not been feeling well. What exactly is the trouble?"* |

This type of communication may seem awkward at first, because most of us believe that listening involves lack of speech. *Active listening* means that the speaker's words are heard, and a restatement is used to verify that the message was understood correctly. This statement gives the speaker the opportunity to correct any misconceptions or misunderstandings. Consider the following example:

Patient:	*"My back hurts."*
Medical assistant:	*"Where does it hurt?"*
Patient:	*"In the middle."*
Medical assistant:	*"Can you point to exactly where it hurts?"*
Patient:	*"Yes, right here (points)."*
Medical assistant:	*"Is it a sharp or dull pain?"*
Patient:	*"Very sharp."*
Medical assistant:	*"How often does it occur?"*
Patient:	*"Several times a day."*
Medical assistant:	*"Can you tell me on an average day how many times it bothers you?"*
Patient:	*"About six times."*
Medical assistant:	*"How long does it last?"*
Patient:	*"About 10 or 15 minutes."*
Medical assistant:	*"How long have you felt this pain?"*
Patient:	*"For about 2 weeks."*
Medical assistant:	*"So you have had a sharp pain in this part of your back about six times a day lasting for up to 15 minutes for 2 weeks? Is that correct?"*
Patient:	*"Yes."*

It would have been easier if the patient had said, "I have had a sharp pain in my back that lasts up to 15 minutes, and it happens about six times a day." This example shows how the medical assistant can continue clarifying until the answer is specific enough, which is critical when obtaining information from the patient.

It also is best to ask "open" rather than "closed" questions. An open question requires more than a "yes" or "no" answer. It forces the patient to provide more detail and expand on his or her thoughts. A closed question can be answered with "yes" or "no" and compels the medical assistant to spend more time obtaining the answers needed to document the patient's needs thoroughly.

CRITICAL THINKING APPLICATION   5-2

- How can the medical assistant be sure that Mrs. Cloyd understands how she is to take her medication?
- Often older patients do not appreciate instructions being given to their caregiver instead of directly to them. How can the medical assistant place the primary focus on communicating with Mrs. Cloyd, yet at the same time make sure Sarah understands the instructions and care?

Often when a person or patient is talking with the medical assistant, the person is looking for a specific type of response. Some patients want advice, some want sympathy, and others are looking for reassurance. Many patients open up more quickly and more completely to the medical assistant than to the physician. This can be a very positive aspect of the relationship the medical assistant has with patients, because it is important to build good rapport with them. However, the medical assistant should never agree to withhold information from the physician under any circumstances. If the patient asks that the assistant not reveal something to the physician, the medical assistant should politely explain that he or she has an ethical obligation to report any and all pertinent information to the physician, especially if it affects medical care. For example, if the patient asks the medical assistant not to tell the physician that the patient has been smoking against medical advice, the assistant could be jeopardizing the patient's care if the information is not reported.

This does not mean that specific details must always be aired. If the patient reveals that her stress levels have been high because she has filed a sexual harassment suit against her boss, but she does not want to share each detail with the physician, the medical assistant could report to the physician that the patient is having some legal problems that have resulted in additional stress at work. The physician will understand that the patient's stress level is elevated and can effectively treat the patient without knowing the specific, intimate details of the acts between the patient and her employer. However, the medical assistant must *never* agree to lie to the physician. The patient must understand that if the physician questions any information given by the patient, it must be revealed so that the physician is assured that the care provided is appropriate. Remember that the physician may have worked with the patient for a long time and has a better understanding of the patient's needs than the medical assistant. One patient may be able to handle a high stress level, and another may crumble at the first sign of stress. Good physicians know their patients and keep accurate, complete records that aid decision making in these situations.

If the medical assistant is ever in doubt about telling the physician something a patient has said, the best solution is to tell. Medical professionals are legally bound to confidentiality, and the patient may need to be reminded of this. Encourage the patient to talk to the physician and communicate all concerns, no matter how insignificant they may seem. Never display a judgmental attitude or express negativity about the patient's activities, thoughts, or behavior. Offer to be with the patient, if he or she desires, during difficult discussions with the physician or to make arrangements for a special counseling session with the physician if this is indicated. Some patients are hesitant to initiate a conversation with the physician because they feel they are taking too much time. The medical assistant can help ensure that critical issues receive the doctor's attention.

WARNINGS AGAINST ADVISING A PATIENT

The medical assistant must be extremely careful when making suggestions or comments to a patient to prevent legal accusations of practicing medicine without a license. Often a patient asks for an opinion as to which course of action to take. Medical assistants are not qualified to give any type of advice to a patient. Strict laws in most states prohibit anyone other than a licensed physician from offering medical advice. Even if the patient asks what the medical assistant would do if presented with the same options, the assistant cannot encourage the patient to choose one option over another. The assistant can offer a listening ear, though, and help the patient process his or her own thoughts. This can be done in much the same way as using active listening techniques. When a patient expresses a concern, the medical assistant should restate the concern and then ask a clarifying question. For example:

Patient:	*"I don't know whether I should take the chemotherapy treatments the doctor wants me to have."*
Medical assistant:	*"You seem worried about the treatments. What are you concerned about specifically?"*

Patients must make their own decisions about treatment options when faced with a medical decision. The medical assistant often is looked upon not only as an authority figure, but also as an extension of the physician. Patients may mistakenly think that the medical assistant has the same opinion as the physician. All communication with the patient must be professional and accurate. Always attempt to get the patient to discuss all concerns and fears openly with the physician.

The medical assistant should never agree to withhold any information from the physician, because even a small detail could completely change the plan of treatment. When giving instructions to patients, offer them in writing and keep a copy for the patient's medical record so that a written record of what was communicated to the patient is available. Use excellent documentation technique when adding information to the patient's medical record. Remember that all the patients in the facility deserve to be treated with respect and compassion. Help the physician establish trust with the patient. An open, trusting relationship helps to prevent legal issues in the future.

CRITICAL THINKING APPLICATION   5-3
- How should the medical assistant handle Sarah's questions about the various aspects of her mother's treatments?
- How does her mother's decision not to have chemotherapy affect Sarah? What barriers to communication might exist between them?

OBSERVING CAREFULLY

In the fast-paced world of medicine, medical professionals sometimes miss the nonverbal signals sent by patients; however, these signals play a critical role in patients' care. If the patient hesitates when speaking, it may be an indication that he or she has more to say. As mentioned previously, the inability to look a person directly in the eyes sometimes, but not always, indicates deception. The medical assistant must pay close attention both to what is seen and what is heard when communicating with the patient. Look into the patient's eyes and watch intently for signs of trouble.

When a patient cries, the medical assistant should always question what is causing the tears. Some patients may refuse to discuss the issue or insist that nothing is wrong, but tears are always a sign of some emotion, whether anger, frustration, fear, pain, or some other concern. Do not allow patients who are obviously emotionally upset to leave the office without reasonable assurance that they are going to be safe. The medical assistant might wish to suggest that a friend come to the office and escort the patient home. On rare occasions, it is better to be firm with the patient and insist on help getting home if the person is in a **volatile** state. This action may save patients from hurting themselves or someone else. Careful observation of the patient as a whole is worth the time investment and may even save the patient's life. By using observational skills, the medical assistant can begin to identify abnormal behaviors and use these observations to provide better patient-centered care. Remember that any observations that the medical assistant makes and documents in the medical record cannot be misconstrued as diagnoses. Communicate with the physician if there is any question or concern about proper documentation methods.

PSYCHOLOGICAL DISORDERS

A *psychological disorder* is defined as a psychological or behavior pattern that occurs in an individual and is thought to cause distress or disability that is not expected as a part of normal development and culture. The roots of psychology extend to beliefs in witchcraft and demon possession, but today, the science of psychology is a vast field involving the study of the brain and how it works.

Numerous abnormal behavior patterns affect humans. Some are better understood than others, and many can be controlled with medications. In his introductory psychology textbook, Rod Plotnik argues that treating abnormal behavior is accomplished by using one or more of three basic methods: the psychoanalytic, the cognitive-behavioral, and the medical-model approaches. When using a psychoanalytic approach, a psychiatrist or psychologist engages in therapy with the patient, usually face-to-face. The patient identifies and discusses the issues or conflicts that cause his or her abnormal behavior in an effort to understand it; then the psychiatrist or psychologist and the patient explore alternative actions that may allow the patient to live normally with the abnormal behavior or to eliminate it completely. The cognitive-behavioral approach is based upon the belief that mental disorders result from a deficit in a thought process and that the patient suffers from maladaptive thinking processes, so treatment focuses on changing the patient's maladaptive thoughts and behaviors. The medical-model approach involves using psychoactive drugs to treat mental disorders.

The *Diagnostic and Statistical Manual of Mental Disorders* contains standard classifications of mental disorders as used by mental health professionals in the United States. Some of the abnormal behaviors include:

- *Phobia:* An exaggerated, usually inexplicable and illogical fear of a particular object or situation
- *Obsessive-compulsive disorder:* An anxiety disorder characterized by recurrent, unwanted thoughts and/or repetitive behaviors
- *Antisocial behavior:* An inability to distinguish right from wrong or to feel remorse, characterized by dysfunctional thinking and perception of situations
- *Panic disorder:* Sudden, sometimes chronic, episodes of intense fear that develops for no apparent reason

- *General anxiety disorder:* An ongoing anxiety that interferes with day-to-day activities and relationships
- *Major depressive disorder:* A condition affecting both mind and body that can cause a variety of emotional and physical problems

DEFENSE MECHANISMS

Anxiety or stress causes the human body to react in many different ways. Some people handle **stressors** more easily than others. Most people use **defense mechanisms** when they feel pressured or attacked in some way. These often are subconscious reactions designed for emotional protection; they help us deal with whatever difficult event has triggered such a response. Often people may not even realize that they are using these mechanisms and may **vehemently** deny that they are doing so. Many types of defense mechanisms exist; the medical assistant should be familiar with them to better communicate with patients and others with whom they come in contact in the course of their duties.

Verbal Aggression

When a person verbally attacks another without addressing the original complaint, or disregards it, he or she is being verbally **aggressive** (Figure 5-5). Such people may attack, or they may change the subject. Some individuals get very angry at any suggestion of wrongdoing. They lash out, usually quite loudly, and attack quickly in hopes of diminishing their role in any wrongdoing. For example:

"When are you going to clean the drug sample closet?"

"Who are you to ask me that? You haven't finished your duties today, either!"

Handling Verbal Aggression

When a person is verbally aggressive, diffuse the situation by using communication techniques. Some people wildly exaggerate with accusations such as, "You always act that way…" You can partially agree by responding with, "I sometimes say things like that, but…" Giving the aggressor an unsatisfying agreement, such as, "You may be right" or "You have a point," will not add to the argument but will not indicate agreement, either.

FIGURE 5-5 Remain calm even if a patient becomes verbally aggressive. Attempt to calm the person by listening and expressing empathy whenever possible.

Sarcasm

The word *sarcasm* comes from the Greek word *sarkasmos,* which means "to tear flesh" or "to bite the lips in rage." This is quite an accurate definition of the nature of sarcasm. It is a biting edge added to words that a person states with the intent to cause pain or anger. Sarcasm is hostile and cruel in most cases, and some individuals use it constantly, thinking it is quite witty. On the contrary, it often makes bitter enemies of its victims. For example, "Of course it's a nice dress, if you like tents."

Handling Sarcasm

Although ignoring the sarcasm is often suggested, it is not always effective. Sarcasm is a type of bullying, and the best way to deal with any kind of bullying is to stand up to it. For instance, if a co-worker makes a sarcastic remark, even if it is done in front of others, the medical assistant might say, "That was an awfully sarcastic remark…" Just the open confrontation itself may cause the person to rethink making such statements in public.

Rationalization

Rationalizing is attributing actions to rational and credible motives without analyzing underlying methods. When people rationalize their behavior, they are offering excuses for what has been done or said and trying to convince others that the behavior was completely justified. For example, "He only hits me because he is stressed at work."

Handling Rationalization

Often, when a person is rationalizing, the medical assistant can simply ask a more probing question, such as, "Now, is that the real reason that you were late for work, or did you wake up late?" Often the person will immediately admit the real reason for his or her actions.

Compensation

A person who compensates makes up for one behavior by stressing another. Compensation is a psychological mechanism through which feelings of inferiority, frustration, or failure in one area are counterbalanced by achievement in another. Compensation is not always a negative response, but it often is used as an excuse for not accomplishing what should be accomplished. For example, "I know I gained 5 pounds, Dr. George, but I exercised three times last week."

Handling Compensation

Using the method of further questioning, described previously, also is effective in dealing with a person who is compensating for his or her behavior. Say, "How long did you exercise?" or "What was your diet like last week?" Often, by asking questions and not making judgmental statements, the person will realize that he or she was compensating and will eventually admit inappropriate behavior.

Regression

Regression is the reversion to an earlier mental or behavioral level. Some people regress to a childlike state or period or exhibit qualities inherent to an earlier time in life. This can include making excuses for not doing a certain thing, saying that it cannot be done, instead of telling the truth, which is that the person does not want to do it. Replacing the word "can't" with "won't" is a good gauge of the use of regression. For example, "I'd like to get better grades, but I can't find time to study."

Handling Regression

Preceding your response with a positive statement may make the person exhibiting regression feel more comfortable admitting inappropriate behavior. For instance, reply to the statement about grades, in the preceding section, by saying, "I know you are really smart, and I'll bet you can make more time to study if you look for opportunities to do your reading and other work."

Repression

The process whereby unwanted desires or impulses are excluded from the consciousness and left to operate in the unconscious is called *repression.* Blocking a problem from the mind and changing the subject when it is mentioned are both types of repression. The repressed urges or desires may seethe beneath the surface, absorbing energy, and force continual repression of the desires, which takes more and more concentration to do successfully. For example, "I had a fight with my brother and I should phone him, but I just can't deal with that now."

Handling Repression

A person who is repressing his or her feelings may truly be unable to handle stressful situations temporarily. The best approach may be to simply be supportive and lend an ear if the person is willing to talk. Say, "I understand that you're in a difficult situation. If you want to talk about it, I will be there to listen." Severe cases may prompt a referral to a professional counselor.

Apathy

Apathy is a lack of feeling, emotion, interest, or concern. It is an indifference to what is happening or a pretense of not caring about a situation. Usually, apathy is not a true reflection of the inner feeling. It is a defense mechanism similar to repression but with a more flippant attitude. For example, "I don't care what grade I got on the test, because I am not going to pass the class anyway."

Handling Apathy

Attempt to get past the pretense that the person is expressing by saying, "Now, I know you really do care about your grades and of course you can pass the class. How can I help you study and prepare?" When you express confidence, the person may open up about the true concerns or may eventually develop more confidence in his or her abilities.

Displacement

Displacement is the redirection of an emotion or impulse from its original object, such as an idea or person, to another object. When challenged or attacked by one person or event, the person uses displacement to channel negative feelings to some other area, which gives a false sense of control over issues that may not be controllable. The venting of hostile feelings is directed somewhere other than where it should be directed; however, this usually is a result of a lack of confidence in addressing the true issues at hand. For example, "I have enough problems at work; I don't need to come home to a nagging wife!"

Handling Displacement

Sometimes, simply stating, "Are you really mad at me or are you upset about issues at work?" will diffuse a person using displacement. However, if displacement is used often, professional counseling may be indicated.

Denial

Denial is a psychological defense mechanism in which a person avoids confronting a personal problem or reality by denying the existence of the problem or reality. The common expression, "He's in denial," originates from this situation. For whatever reason, the person is unable to cope with the stress of a situation and completely pushes it away, and any person or thing representing it. For example, "I can't possibly have cancer; I just had a checkup, and I'm completely healthy."

Handling Denial

Listening is an important technique to use when a person is in denial. Express empathy, using phrases such as, "I know it is devastating to receive a cancer diagnosis, especially in an otherwise healthy patient. What concerns do you have about the diagnosis and what lies ahead for you?" This technique gently brings the person back to dealing with the situation and moving his or her thought process forward to deal with the issues at hand. Avoid suggesting that you "know how he feels," because no patient wants to hear about another person's problems or experiences when trying to deal with a major life event.

Physical Avoidance

Some events are so painful that a person may completely avoid any representation of the event. This could be a person, a place, an object, or just about anything that serves as a reminder of the event that induces the negative feelings. If the problem is a person, that person may be avoided forever. If it is a place, such as a home that a couple lived in before one of them died, the other person may move. In some cases, such as physical abuse, the avoidance may be necessary, but it also can be quite unhealthy and may need to be explored further through therapy. For example, "I will never go to that restaurant again, because that's where my ex-husband told me he wanted a divorce."

Handling Physical Avoidance

Being unwilling to revisit painful experiences is not always unhealthy. A person who doesn't want to be in a physical place that brings painful memories really should not have to confront those feelings unless physical avoidance becomes a pattern of behavior. Say, "Let's go to that new Mexican restaurant and just start new memories." This may be a more positive move forward than insisting on confronting old hurt.

Projection

Projection, as a defense mechanism, is the attribution of one's own ideas, feelings, or attitudes to other people or to objects. This especially includes the **externalization** of blame, guilt, or responsibility

as a defense against anxiety. Some people project their feelings about a certain issue onto others, who may not be affected by the negative connotations the first person feels. Projection is a way to avoid dealing with the root issues of a problem. For example, "Everyone else is always late, so why am I getting reprimanded for it?"

Handling Projection

Bring the person back to dealing with his or her behavior. Say, "We are dealing with your behavior right now. I realize that situations will make us late periodically, but this has become a pattern that we need to deal with." Insist that the conversation remain about only this person's behavior.

CONFLICT

Conflict is defined as the struggle resulting from incompatible or opposing needs, drives, or wishes or external or internal demands. We deal with conflict in our lives in some capacity almost daily. Knowing how to recognize the signs of conflict and the patterns people use to deal with conflict can be of great benefit to the medical assistant. This enables the professional to be understanding and empathetic to patients, co-workers, supervisors, and others in the day-to-day work environment.

Conflict is not always negative; sometimes it is beneficial to relationships. It can be constructive and allow people to learn more about each other. This may promote a stronger understanding and deeper levels of intimacy. Unless both parties are aware that a problem exists between them, no conflict exists. The conflict begins when both realize that a problem needs to be resolved. People handle conflict in different ways. Some avoid it at all costs; on the other end of the spectrum, some seem to thrive on conflict.

The knowledge of some of the many types of conflict can help the medical assistant understand the thought processes of others and how best to respond to them and also to discern how others respond. Of itself, assertion is not conflict; assertion is stating or declaring positively. Often being forcefully assertive or aggressive can be very productive. Assertive people often receive job promotions and reach the goals they set for their lives. However, too much aggression can make a person seem pushy; therefore, it should be controlled and used at the appropriate times. Remember, there is a difference between assertion and aggression, which are discussed in the following paragraphs.

Nonassertion is the inability to express needs and thoughts or the refusal to express them. Some avoid conflict and some accommodate by putting others' desires before their own. Sometimes nonassertion is justifiable. Anyone who has been involved in a long-term relationship realizes that sometimes the other person's needs must come first. Many have learned the truth of the old saying, "Choose your battles wisely."

CRITICAL THINKING APPLICATION   5-4

- Why might Mrs. Cloyd and Sarah experience conflict at this stage in their lives?
- How might each deal better with disagreements, especially regarding Mrs. Cloyd's decisions about her medical care?

Aggression is defined in several ways. It can be a hostile, injurious, or destructive behavior or outlook, especially when caused by frustration. It is also the practice of making attacks or **encroachments**, especially if the acts are unprovoked. In the realm of psychological studies, there are different types of aggression. Direct aggression occurs when a person directly attacks another, whether by criticism, **malediction**, ridiculing, or other methods. This behavior causes the victim to feel embarrassment, shame, anger, or a range of other emotions. *Passive aggression* is a familiar term, but many may not know its definition. A passive-aggressive person expresses himself or herself in an obscure, **ambiguous** way. People who experience passive aggression may have feelings of rage, inadequacy, or resentment that they cannot articulate in a direct manner. Unfortunately, this behavior does not usually provide the results needed or expected.

Resolving Conflict

Conflict exists in all relationships, whether they are at work, home, or in social situations. In most cases, the person or persons involved in conflict do not intend to cause problems, and the conflict should not be considered personal. The first impulse in response to conflict is often the fight-or-flight response, either to attack or retreat. Professionalism dictates that the first response be put aside so that the medical assistant can apply logical thought to the situation. Personal beliefs are developed based on each individual's unique experiences and perspectives.

Resolving conflict can range from being simple to excruciatingly difficult. Also, the medical assistant must remember that conflict presents an opportunity for growth and increased maturity at the workplace. The following tips can help resolve conflicts.

- Expect conflict, because people do not agree on every viewpoint or situation all the time. Do not dread or fear conflict.
- Realize that conflict can be a healthy process that allows input from various points of view. That input can lead to better decisions.
- Accept that others have legitimate, viable opinions that they should be allowed to express.
- Listen to other opinions and then consider them in an honest, fair manner. People are rarely wrong 100% of the time.
- Never attack a person with a different opinion. Instead, keep the focus on the situation at hand and how it can be resolved.
- Do not insist on being right all the time. Welcome input from those with alternative, original ideas.
- Avoid judgment or assigning blame; do not immediately assume that the other person is wrong.
- Deal with conflict as it happens. Never let several situations build up to an explosion. Do not say that nothing is wrong when hurt feelings are quietly accumulating.

BOUNDARIES

Remember that a patient has physical boundaries or personal space, as discussed earlier in this chapter. The patient's personal space ranges from 1½ to 4 feet, so be aware of any nonverbal communication from the patient that you may be infringing on his or her space.

Keep in mind, too, that spacial boundaries are not the only ones that affect patients.

Boundaries indicate a limit or fixed extent. Setting boundaries at work helps prevent awkward situations and misunderstandings. The first step in setting boundaries is to perform a self-inventory. Determine what is important in the work environment and the type of environment most conducive to strong performance on the job.

Life Coach David B. Bohl suggests five steps in setting self-boundaries at work:

1. Know how you expect to be treated and be clear about it with others. If you prefer to be called "Ms. Roberts" instead of "Linda," correct anyone who uses your first name directly and politely.
2. Do not feel that you have to offer explanations for your boundaries. Adults should respect the preferences of other adults in the workplace. Do not feel that you have to explain boundary choices.
3. Be respectful, thoughtful, and responsible when setting boundaries. Do not make unreasonable demands, and consider your motives in each situation. For instance, do not insist that the staff call you by your last name simply to remind them that you are the boss, but do use last names when promoting a more professional environment for workers and patients alike.
4. Respect other people's boundaries if you want yours to be respected, even if you do not agree with their boundaries. If boundaries are incompatible, work toward an acceptable, fair compromise. If the person with whom you share office space enjoys listening to country music during the day and you prefer classical music, compromise by listening to country in the morning and classical in the afternoon or determine another fair arrangement. Or, both could agree to wear earphones if that is allowed in the office policies manual.
5. Be proactive when dealing with other people's boundaries. If unsure, ask. Do not make assumptions when unsure. Ask co-workers questions, such as how they prefer to receive communications and how they prefer to be addressed.

Self-Boundaries

Individuals also may want to set self-boundaries in the workplace, forming a sort of "rule book" for personal actions when on the job or standards of behavior that the individual will or will not accept. For instance, a medical assistant may decide to pair up with another employee whenever each one takes a medication from the supply closet or takes money from the petty cash drawer, serving as each other's witness. This may take some cooperation and time management skills, but it makes each accountable to the other and provides a witness in case of some impropriety in those areas. Of course, always team with a co-worker who has a track record of being trustworthy. A medical assistant may decide to avoid checking personal e-mail at work or to refrain from Internet use unless completing a job duty. Additionally, some medical assistants may prefer to be addressed by just their first name, whereas others prefer their last name. Self-boundaries allow medical assistants to keep their focus on work duties and concentrate on performing at an optimum level every day.

The Crazy-Makers: Passive-Aggressive Communication

In their book, *Looking Out, Looking In: Interpersonal Communication*, Ronald B. Adler and Neil Towne discuss the concept of "crazy-makers," which is credited to psychologist George Bach. Bach developed the theory of creative aggression; he nicknamed this passive-aggressive behavior "crazy-making." According to Bach, two types of aggression exist: clean fighting and dirty fighting. Crazy-making was his name for dirty fighting, which is a detrimental behavior for all involved. The term *partner* is used loosely to indicate the opposite side or victim of the crazy-maker. Bach described the characteristic types of passive-aggressive individuals:

The Avoider

Avoiders refuse to fight. When a conflict arises, they leave, fall asleep, pretend to be busy at work, or keep from facing the problem in some other way. This behavior makes it difficult for the partner to express feelings of anger and hurt, because avoiders will not fight back.

The Pseudoaccommodator

Pseudoaccommodators refuse to face up to a conflict either by giving in or by pretending nothing is wrong. This drives the partner crazy, because the partner definitely feels a problem exists; the partner also feels guilty and resentful toward the pesudoaccommodator for having brought up the situation for discussion in the first place.

The Guilt-Maker

Instead of saying straight out that they do not want or do not approve of something, guilt-makers try to make their partners feel responsible for causing pain. A guilt-maker's favorite line is, "It's okay, don't worry about me…," followed by a long sigh.

The Subject Changer

The subject changer is an avoider who escapes facing up to aggression by shifting the conversation whenever it approaches an area of conflict. Because of their tactics, subject changers and their partners never have the chance to explore their problems and do something about them.

The Distracter

Rather than come out and express their feelings about an object of dissatisfaction, distracters attack other parts of their partners' lives. Thus they never have to share what is really on their minds and can avoid dealing with painful parts of their relationships.

The Mind Reader

Instead of allowing their partners to express feelings honestly, mind readers go into character analysis, explaining what the other person really means or what is wrong with the other person. By behaving this way, mind readers refuse to handle their own feelings and leave no room for their partners to express themselves.

The Trapper

Trappers play an especially dirty trick by setting up a desired behavior for their partners; then, when the behavior is manifested, they attack the very thing they requested. For example, the trapper may say, "Let's be totally honest with each other," then attack the partner's words of honesty.

The Crisis Tickler

Crisis ticklers bring what is bothering them almost to the surface but never quite express their true feelings. For instance, instead of admitting concern about the finances, they innocently ask, "Gee, how much did that cost?" dropping a rather obvious hint but never really dealing with the crisis.

The Gunnysacker

Gunnysackers do not respond immediately when angry. Instead, they put their resentment into a gunnysack, which after a while begins to bulge with both large and small gripes. Then, when the sack is about to burst, the gunnysacker pours out all the pent-up aggression on the overwhelmed and unsuspecting partner.

The Trivial Tyrannizer

Instead of honestly sharing their resentments, trivial tyrannizers do things they know will bother their partners, such as leaving dirty dishes in the sink, clipping fingernails in bed, belching out loud, turning up the television too loud, and so on.

The Beltliner

Everyone has a psychological "beltline," and below it are subjects too sensitive to be approached without damaging the relationship. Belt-lines may have to do with physical characteristics, intelligence, past behavior, or deeply ingrained personality traits a person is trying to overcome. In an attempt to "get even" or hurt their partners, beltliners use intimate knowledge to hit below the belt, where they know it will hurt.

The Joker

Because they are afraid to face conflicts squarely, jokers kid around when their partners want to be serious, thus blocking the expression of important feelings.

The Blamer

Blamers are more interested in finding fault than in resolving a conflict. Needless to say, they usually do not blame themselves. Blaming behavior almost never resolves a conflict and is an almost surefire way to make partners defensive.

The Contract Tyrannizer

Contract tyrannizers do not allow their relationships to change from the way they once were. Whatever the agreements the partners had for roles and responsibilities at one time, they will remain unchanged.

The Kitchen Sink Fighter

Kitchen sink fighters are so named because in an argument, they bring up things that are totally off the subject, as in everything, including the kitchen sink. Perhaps it is the way the other person behaved last New Year's Eve, or bad breath, or the unbalanced checkbook; any past imperfection is fair game for picking a fight.

The Withholder

Instead of expressing their anger honestly and directly, withholders punish their partners by holding something back, such as courtesy, affection, good cooking, humor, or sex. Such withholding is likely to build up even greater resentments in the relationship.

The Benedict Arnold

Benedict Arnolds get back at their partners by sabotage, by failing to defend them from attackers, and even by encouraging ridicule or disregard from outside the relationship.

BARRIERS TO COMMUNICATION

Physical Impairment

Patients may have physical conditions that impair their ability to communicate effectively. This could be a vision or hearing problem or one of many other conditions that make communicating a bit more difficult than usual. The medical assistant should use more descriptive language when speaking with the patient who has a visual disturbance. This helps the patient "see" what is being discussed. The person with diminished hearing may be very sensitive and in denial of the condition. Make sure you have his or her attention and that you are face-to-face with the person while speaking. People who are hearing impaired often are very dependent on lip reading for comprehension.

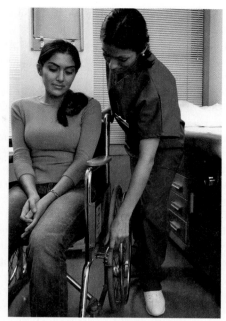

FIGURE 5-6 Bilingual staff members are valuable in ensuring accurate communication with patients who speak a different language.

> ## CRITICAL THINKING APPLICATION   5-5
> - What must be considered when communicating verbally with Mrs. Cloyd? With Sarah?
> - How can the medical assistant show compassion to a terminally ill patient during her appointment when the office is extremely busy?

Language

With non-English-speaking patients, the medical assistant may need to use gestures and more body language to convey messages. In such cases, be alert to the possibility of misunderstanding. Confirm that the message sent is the message the listener received by asking for feedback. Ask the listener to repeat the message, and if family members are present, make sure they, also, have a good understanding of what was communicated.

The clinic may employ a bilingual staff member to reduce the chance of miscommunication with those who speak a different language (Figure 5-6).

Prejudice

Personal and social bias, or prejudice, brings about discrimination. Discrimination is unfair treatment of a person because of race, gender, religious affiliation, or handicap or for any other reason. Discrimination is unethical, morally and socially wrong, and in many situations illegal; it also prevents us from communicating effectively.

Some discrimination is very **subtle** and is not expressed openly or in a blatant manner. Subtle discrimination is based on a person's appearance, values, lifestyle, or some other personal factor. Examples include discrimination against those who are obese, divorced individuals, homosexuals, welfare recipients, or those with sexually transmitted diseases. Sometimes we are not aware that our words or actions reflect subtle discrimination against others.

Personal prejudices must be recognized before one can change them. Medical professionals are exposed to a wide variety of people who need excellent medical care. The professional cannot allow personal prejudice to affect the care of any individual. Everyone has the right to be honored as a human being and treated respectfully. This enforces the Golden Rule: treat others as you would wish to be treated. Realize the worth of each individual and allow that attitude to be reflected in all actions taken with a patient.

Stereotyping

Stereotyping is defined as the application of a standardized mental picture that is held in common by members of a group; it represents an oversimplified opinion, prejudiced attitude, or uncritical judgment. It is unfair to **stereotype** anyone or categorize the person based on preconceived and often incorrect assumptions. Although sometimes an assumption based on stereotypic categories may have a degree of truth, people should not be judged before you have gotten to know them as individuals. The medical assistant should push preconceived notions aside and look at the individual when forming and building a relationship. In the medical profession, stereotypic categories should not be considered when caring for patients and developing good rapport with them.

Perception

Perhaps one of the most important issues to consider when discussing barriers to communication is the concept of perception. Perception is the capacity for comprehension or the discernment of what is being communicated according to the message receiver's point of reference. When we discussed the transactional communication model earlier in the chapter, it was obvious that because of different types of noise and channels, the message sent sometimes would be distorted; the receiver would not always get the message the sender meant to send. The receiver's perceptions could completely alter the message, no matter how clearly it was sent. If the receiver believes that all attorneys are corrupt, he or she will probably be unable to get past this perception when speaking with one and therefore may not be able to trust any attorney.

Often our perceptions stem from some experience that happened in the past with a certain group of people. This perception goes unresolved or has affected us so strongly that we group all people from that walk of life into a negative category. This is an unfair way to deal with people; everyone should be viewed as an individual, not as a part of a stereotypic group. Remember, perception is an individual's point of view, right or wrong. The issue of interpretation also plays a role: the determination of what is meant by a certain message. An attempt must be made to understand both points of view, and the participants must be willing to discuss them calmly, even when discussing subjects that evoke anger. Most people do not truly enjoy conflict. Have a healthy respect for others' opinions. The differences among individuals are part of what makes each of us unique.

OVERCOMING BARRIERS TO COMMUNICATION

We know that communication barriers exist – but how do we overcome them? Most people who enter the medical field have a natural sense of caring and empathy, but the medical assistant can nurture their skills in using patience, perception, and listening skills. If a patient has a physical impairment, being observant will help with communication issues. Often, these patients want to be self-sufficient, so they may not appreciate help with simple tasks while at the physician's office. Be patient with them, as well as those who have a language barrier. Encourage these patients to bring an interpreter so that accurate, quality information can be placed into the medical records. Prejudice can be overcome with facts about the source of the social bias, and the same is true for stereotyping and perception issues. Even highly abrasive patients can be tolerated when the medical assistant wants to be an effective communicator with all patients. If nothing seems to work, talk to the office manager or physician. In severe cases, the physician may have to speak to the patient, or even suggest that he or she seek a different provider.

COMMUNICATION DURING DIFFICULT TIMES

Communication is not an art that comes easily to everyone. It often is difficult to express feelings in an honest, open way. When a crisis occurs, it is much harder to communicate effectively, and we sometimes say things we do not mean. Medical assistants must develop communication skills that can be used in times of trouble. They must be able to understand the reason or reasons a patient or co-worker is unable to communicate.

Patience is important, too, because people are not always at their best when they are concerned about their condition or that of a loved one. Always remain calm when dealing with a person who is experiencing a traumatic event or has any depressive condition. Remember that he or she may be reacting to many emotions, such as fear, anger, doubt, inadequacy, or many others. The key is to listen, to determine the best way to help the patient out of any

immediate danger and to help him or her establish some type of support system.

Anger

One of the most difficult times to communicate is when we are angry. Anger is a normal emotion that all of us feel at one time or another. Usually the expression of anger is a healthy thing. Some people bottle up their emotions and do not express what they truly feel inside. If this is done repeatedly, at some point the anger erupts, possibly over a tiny event or at an inappropriate time. Others explode over every little situation; people who do this need anger management skills and training.

Anger, like most emotions, can cause physiologic changes. When a person feels anger, the blood pressure rises and the heart rate increases. Many things can trigger anger, from a simple traffic backup to a real or perceived betrayal, the diagnosis of a disease, or the death of a close relative. "Road rage" is one example of anger out of control and is a serious problem on our public highways today. Unexpressed anger can cause or contribute to all types of health problems, including depression and hypertension.

The medical assistant can help pacify an angry patient by speaking calmly and refusing to return the emotion. If the volume is gradually lowered with every sentence spoken, the angry person also must lower the volume to hear what the assistant is saying. Suggest that the person breathe deeply and stop talking for a few minutes. Remember that the anger being expressed usually is not directed intentionally at the medical assistant. Be a good listener and allow the person to speak, as long as it is not abusive speech. Using logic with the angry individual may also help. Some use words such as *never* and *always;* for example, "My wife never balances the checkbook!" or "You always make me wait for my appointment!" These statements are broad generalizations and usually untrue. Using a logical approach and maintaining a calm attitude help the angry individual.

Address the root of the problem and be willing to admit it if the physician's office has made a mistake or contributed to a problem. Do not be afraid to say, "I'm sorry, I/we made an error." If you made the mistake, own it and apologize. Arguing never resolves the situation and only increases the intensity of the patient's feelings. Four words that often can disarm an angry person are, "Let me help you." Sometimes in a medical professional's career, a patient, a co-worker, or even the physician will lash out, even though the medical assistant is not the cause of the anger. Realize that this is a part of being human, and be as caring and kind as possible. If the anger becomes abusive, either refer the situation to a supervisor or, if that is not possible, tell the patient that you can no longer discuss the situation and offer to schedule an appointment so that the matter can be discussed at a later time. By then, the patient probably will have calmed down and will be able to discuss the situation rationally.

Shock

When an event or a circumstance arises that is especially painful, an individual may experience emotional shock. This may happen when a person has just been told that a family member has been killed in an automobile accident or some other catastrophe has taken place. Many different types of shock occur, but in this chapter, the emotional aspect is discussed. Often the person cannot think or move, and other coping reactions may take place. One person may scream in agony, whereas another may sit down and begin to talk about a completely unrelated subject. The person who appears calm is probably more at risk, because in addition to shock, he or she may be experiencing denial. We never really know in advance how we will react to events that are traumatic. Also, our reactions may differ from time to time. A person is able to cope with a traumatic event based on the other stressors in his or her life at the time.

David Straker, in his book, *Changing Minds*, describes adaptive and nonadaptive coping mechanisms. An adaptive coping mechanism is one that offers some type of positive help. Logically, a nonadaptive coping mechanism would be negative in nature. Consider the sleep requirement. A person who is in some type of shock may have some insomnia and needs to sleep. Getting several nights of recuperative sleep is an adaptive coping mechanism. If, however, he or she begins to sleep consistently during the day and at night, sleep may be considered a nonadaptive coping mechanism, because the individual is using sleep to avoid stressful issues.

Never leave a person in emotional shock alone. If the healthcare professional cannot stay close by, arrangements should be made for someone to stay near, especially during the early stages, if at all possible. Because the thought processes the person is experiencing may not be under control, he or she could be a danger to himself or herself or others.

The medical assistant should watch for several signs of emotional shock, including hyperactivity, disruptions in breathing patterns, blank staring, sudden hysterics, and shaking. Humans have an innate sense of threat or danger, and this sense may initiate the fight-or-flight syndrome. When a person feels a threat of some kind, the hormone adrenaline is released in the body quickly, producing an increased heart rate and blood pressure. The oxygen level in the body increases, which prepares the muscles to help the body flee. Awareness is increased, as are energy and performance. The individual either runs, avoiding the danger, which is the "flight" aspect, or stays to "fight," facing the stressors or threat. With either choice, the body must have this increased energy level and awareness to deal with the situation. When the immediate period of shock abates, the individual may feel a debilitating, drained sensation as the hormonal levels return to normal.

CRITICAL THINKING APPLICATION 5-6

- Is it possible that Sarah might experience shock months after her mother's death?
- How can the medical assistant help Sarah deal with these emotions?

Death and Dying

Years ago patients who were considered terminally ill were placed in hospital wards and left to their demise. The medical community did not focus on understanding the fears and concerns of the dying, and very few measures were offered to them that preserved their dignity. However, in 1969, Dr. Elisabeth Kübler-Ross, a Swiss psychiatrist, wrote a ground-breaking book, *On Death and Dying*. Kübler-Ross, who studied **thanatology**, realized that terminally ill patients were somewhat ignored, even by medical professionals, and she spent many hours interviewing these patients and discovering their fears and concerns. Kübler-Ross listened to them and realized that patients passed through certain stages as they dealt with their

impending death. She held seminars, during which she interviewed dying patients as medical students listened. When the book was published, she was recognized internationally as an authority on the subject of death. She wrote more than 20 books about the process of dying. In *Life Lessons,* she shares many of the truths she had learned from the dying to encourage us to live. Kübler-Ross died in August, 2004.

Kübler-Ross believed that the process of dealing with death or loss has five specific stages: denial, bargaining, anger, depression, and acceptance. She believed that all people go through each stage in the grieving process, but they may not go through the stages in the same order. A stage could take days to work through or several months. Although she related these stages to dying patients, they are not exclusively limited to those who are dying. Anyone experiencing **grief** may progress through these five stages, and having a good understanding of them can help the medical assistant to better care for the patient.

On Death and Dying identifies denial as the first stage, during which the patient or grieving person denies the issue that is causing the grief and thinks, "No, not me." The person is shocked and rejects the facts. The denial is a defense mechanism that helps the individual deal with the news. The second stage is anger, when the dying patient begins to ask, "Why me?" The anger often is directed at others, who may include the people in the family taking care of the patient or healthcare workers who cannot produce a cure. In the third stage, the patient begins to bargain in an attempt to postpone death or eliminate it altogether. This bargaining usually is with God, and the patient may pray to see a child marry or to witness some other upcoming event. The event is not the true hope of the patient, but life itself is. These patients say, "Yes, me, but…" in the attempt to postpone death. The fourth stage is depression. During this stage, patients realize that they are going to die and may feel regret for the goals they did not accomplish or for not taking better care of themselves. These patients say, "Yes, it's me…" and they must be allowed this period of grieving. However, family and friends should watch the patient carefully for signs of deep depression. The final stage of grief is acceptance, during which the patient is able to say, "Yes, me, and I'm ready." The reality of the impending death or distressing situation is accepted, and although the patient may continue to experience some depression, he or she is better equipped to deal with the arrangements that have to be made and may even demonstrate good humor during this time.

Patients who are dying must be treated with empathy, dignity, and respect. This does not mean that they are unable to laugh and enjoy the life they are still living. Gentle touch and kind words reassure patients that the medical assistant cares for them. It is important to be careful with words and phrases around dying patients, but be natural in your conversations with them and do not be afraid to laugh. Never suggest to such patients that you "know how they feel." This phrase belittles their situation, and we never truly know how another person feels. Asking questions is a good method of communication when you are unsure about what to say. Use questions such as, "How do you feel about that?" or "What does your family think about your plans to discontinue treatment?" Then listen to the patient and make eye contact with him or her as you listen. You may also ask, "How can I help you?" as opposed to "Is there anything I can do?" There will be a natural tendency for the patient to say "No" to the second question. However, if you ask specifically how to help, they may open up and allow you or the office staff to be of help. They may simply need suggestions about who could cut their grass or how to contact Meals on Wheels. Hospice services provide terminally ill patients and their families with care and support, often from the point of diagnosis to bereavement. Many have found hospice services invaluable in the process of coping with a loved one close to death. The medical office should have listings of community resources to assist in these types of situations. Always use empathy when talking with the patient by being aware of, and sensitive to, the feelings that the patient may be experiencing.

CRITICAL THINKING APPLICATION   5-7
- People often put off writing a will. Could this be procrastination or a fear of death?
- When is it important to have a will?
- How can the medical assistant help Sarah to deal with her mother's impending death?
- What stage of grief might Mrs. Cloyd currently be experiencing? What stage might Sarah be experiencing?

MULTICULTURAL ISSUES

Cultural differences influence the way we deal with people from various parts of the world. We often become isolated in our thinking and incorrectly assume that people all over the world think and do things the same way we do. However, vast differences in cultures exist from country to country, and even in areas within the same country.

We sometimes stereotype people of other cultures and think we understand what they are like and how they live. Often, the **media** have influenced our thinking. Much can be learned from other cultures, and sharing is a way to gain an understanding of experiences in other places.

EXAMPLES OF CULTURAL TRADITIONS
- A husband speaks for his wife. The wife does not speak to the physician.
- The palm of the hand, facing down, is used to beckon someone. The hand motion signaling one to come or follow, performed with the back of the hand toward the patient, is used only when calling an animal. An open hand is used to point, rather than one finger.
- A female's clothing is not removed without the presence of another female family member.
- Emotional crying and sobbing denote femininity.
- Going to the doctor is a sign of weakness.
- The female medical assistant never touches the male patient.
- Acquaintances are not permitted to stand within 3 feet of the patient; only immediate family members are permitted to stand within this space.
- The Chinese do not like to be touched by people they do not know.
- The Laotian's "yes" response may not mean "yes," because it is considered rude to say "no" to others or to cause conflict.

- A native of Cambodia, as well as a Laotian, will not look into the eyes of the person being addressed because long eye contact means disrespect and is impolite.
- Cambodians do not like to have their blood drawn, because they believe it will weaken them.
- Afghans and Mexicans have a concept of time that is less precise than in the United States.
- Vietnamese consider the head to be a sacred part of the body and are offended by being touched on the head or shoulders. Only the elderly may touch the head of a child without giving offense.

Communicating with People of Other Cultures

People from other cultures want to be treated just as you would like to be treated if you were visiting another country; they want to be respected and treated fairly. Much can be learned about the background of others, and much can be shared about the culture we know, too. Cultural differences are responsible for many misunderstandings. We must make an attempt to understand people from other walks of life.

When we speak with those from a foreign country, a **language barrier** may exist. Even if the person knows some English, some words and phrases may not make sense in the way we use them in the United States.

It is important to be sensitive to and aware of the beliefs of the many cultures represented in the patient population. If you work in a practice that predominantly serves a distinct ethnic group, discuss possible cultural differences with the physician and with influential people in the cultural group. Learning to understand cultural differences helps you gain the confidence and respect of patients. Always use language and verbal skills that enable patients to understand the details of their medical care. Even if the traditions and cultures are vastly different and difficult to understand, the medical assistant must demonstrate respect for diversity in approaching patients and their families.

Communicating with patients who speak another language is difficult without an interpreter. If the physician serves a large population of non-English speakers, he or she should make certain that at least one staff member is bilingual and available to assist with interpreting when necessary. If none of the employees are bilingual, the appointment scheduler should tell patients to bring a friend or relative to their office visits to assist with paperwork and interpreting. The office policy should state that an interpreter must be present for the physician to treat the patient, so that the entire staff is able to communicate properly with the patient. Appropriate communication is vital to ensure that the patient understands the physician and the instructions to be followed, especially medication dosages.

COMMUNICATING DURING THE PATIENT ENCOUNTER

Remember that patients often are apprehensive during their appointments with the physician. Some questions can elicit information the patient has not voiced aloud. Many hospitals have added the phrase "Are you safe at home?" to their basic intake to ensure that the patient is not being abused or is the victim of violence. Even the simplest tasks, such as collecting a urine specimen, can cause nervousness and

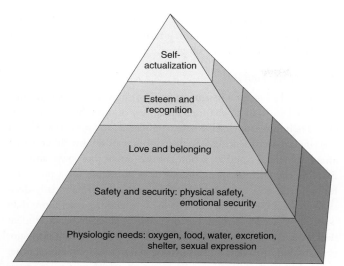

FIGURE 5-7 Maslow's hierarchy of needs. (From Adler RB, Towne N: *Looking out, looking in: interpersonal communication,* San Antonio, 1996, Harcourt Brace.)

anxiety. Always explain the purpose of tests the physician orders, and when performing treatments, explain each step to put the patient more at ease. Patients may not understand that a "blood glucose" simply means a blood sugar test in lay terms. Be sensitive to the patient rights and feelings when collecting specimens.

Maslow's Hierarchy of Needs

Psychologist Abraham Maslow created what he called the "hierarchy of needs" (Figure 5-7). A *hierarchy* is defined as things arranged in order, rank, or a graded series. Maslow believed that our human needs can be categorized into five levels and that the needs on each level must be satisfied before we can move to the next level. These levels often are depicted as a triangle, with the most basic needs at the bottom and the highest potential for growth as a human being at the top.

The needs we have as humans, at the most basic level, are those that involve our physical well-being: food, rest, sleep, water, air, and sex. The second level includes issues related to our safety. We need to feel safe and secure in our homes and our environments, as well as the places where we work. The third level involves our social needs for love, a sense of belonging, and interaction with others. The fourth level relates to our self-esteem. We have an inner need to feel good about ourselves and to know that others view us in a positive manner. The last level is the self-actualization stage, in which we maximize our potential. In this level, we attempt to be at our best and to live our lives to the fullest extent possible.

People adapt to life based on their individual needs, and many entities influence that adaptation, such as cultural and other elements of the environment, language abilities, and even physical threats, such as situations in which a woman refuses to leave her abusive husband for fear of harm. The medical assistant should actively investigate the resources that will allow patients to adapt to situations that affect their health status, and almost any life event can influence the patient's well-being.

Approval, Acceptance, and Achievement

Three specific needs that we have, apart from Maslow's hierarchy of needs, are critical to our happiness. These three are approval,

acceptance, and achievement. Although most would agree that we do not need everyone's approval at all times, we do seek the approval of specific people. Children usually want to please their parents, even when the child is an adult. We seek to please our supervisors, and even our own children. However, the need to please can be taken too far. Various books address personalities called *pleasers,* who often place their own needs second to the needs of those they feel they must please to feel of worth.

We have a healthier self-esteem if we feel accepted by others. This resembles the sense of belonging discussed earlier but is a bit more extensive. A feeling of acceptance includes the belief that our actions, words, dress, mannerisms, and other personality traits are acceptable to others we wish to impress.

Last, we have an inner need for achievement. Most humans want to do something great and contribute to their world in some way. A great thing to one person may be winning an Olympic race, but to another it may be reading to an elderly grandmother at a nursing home. We all enjoy praise for a job well done, or for losing weight, or for passing a difficult examination. Everyone benefits when legitimate praise is shared freely and appreciated. This is especially true in our close relationships but is just as important in the workplace. It is much easier to work for a supervisor who praises for work well done than for one who never offers a pat on the back.

A Good Night's Sleep

Many of us do not realize the value of our sleep time. Sleep is one of the most important physical needs we have, and it is the one most often sacrificed during busy, stressful periods. This is called *sleep deprivation.* Human beings need approximately 8 hours of sleep each night, although many can function for a period of time with less sleep. Eventually this lack of sleep takes a physical and emotional toll on the body.

Healthy Nutrition

We have been taught since we were children that good nutrition is vital to a healthy body. Our bodies are machines, and their performance depends on good health. We care for the body with a balance of good nutrition, activity, and healthcare. A balanced diet is essential to ensure that the organs and systems within us function at optimal levels. When the body is not receiving the nutrients and vitamins it needs, various parts may malfunction, and this can lead to conditions or diseases or to worsening of problems already present.

CRITICAL THINKING APPLICATION   5-8
- Could Sarah's sleep and nutrition habits affect her ability to care for her mother?
- How might these affect Sarah's personal stress levels, and how can she ensure that she is caring for herself, when her thoughts are primarily on her mother?

Positive Relationships

As mentioned earlier in this chapter, all of us need to feel approval, acceptance, and achievement. These also are vital components of our relationships. When we are involved in a relationship that is not going well, it naturally is reflected in our attitude, our opinions, and our sense of self-esteem. This can greatly influence our performance at work. Often, because of infatuation, we find ourselves in a situation that might not be a positive one. Once the relationship is in progress, it sometimes is difficult to end it and find a connection with a supportive, caring individual.

Many individuals really have not determined what they need from a relationship. It is helpful to make a list of what you are looking for in a partner and to commit to refusing to compromise on the critical points. The sparks and fireworks that appear in the beginning of a relationship may lose their intensity as time goes on, and a firm foundation must be present after the newness wears off. Choose carefully and wisely, and the chances of becoming involved in healthy relationships greatly increase. In addition, more and more individuals are choosing to remain single and are enjoying life to the fullest. Certainly this choice is better than being a part of a destructive partnership.

Harmful relationships are not always just between partners. Often we experience stress and strain with relatives, friends, and co-workers. Sometimes contact with the person causing the discontent cannot be avoided, at least for a period of time. In these cases, we must learn coping techniques for dealing with the difficult relationship. Open, honest communication is paramount. By making wise relationship choices, medical assistants may prevent additional stress and worry during working hours, which can help keep their focus on the patients and duties to be performed and not on stressful situations outside of work.

CRITICAL THINKING APPLICATION   5-9

- Often survivors feel a sense of "unfinished business" with a person who has died, and they have a more difficult time bringing closure to the relationship. How might Sarah spend high-quality time with her mother and come to terms with her death in a positive way?
- Is there anything that should not be discussed with a terminally ill patient?

Healthy Self-Esteem

Self-esteem is confidence and satisfaction in oneself. To have high self-esteem, an individual must also be self-aware, and that takes some honesty. It means taking a look at your strengths and your weaknesses and knowing what you have to offer as a person. To feel well and accomplish goals in life, you must develop positive attitudes and positive responses to the pressures in life. It sometimes can be difficult to keep a positive attitude when others are being negative. Some people believe that if they inflict their bad feelings on others, they will feel better about themselves. It is important to remember, though, that no one can make you feel a certain way; it is a choice you make. Blaming others for one's situation in life or negative emotions is self-defeating.

We are able to control two things in life: our attitude and our actions. Even when faced with a potentially volatile situation, our attitude and reactions are decisions we make. These decisions should be made with careful thought, even if the reaction must be a swift one. Think before speaking. Pause a moment, if needed, before reacting. Take a timeout. Choose your battles wisely. All of these suggestions can help you react in a more positive, constructive way when faced with a difficult situation.

Improving Yourself

No matter how great a person's training or how many opportunities are placed in front of the individual, fear and doubt can sabotage efforts to improve one's self-image, confidence, and potential. Almost every failure or mistake can be traced to fear or doubt; either we are afraid to take a specific action, or we doubt our own abilities. Blaming the circumstances around us is no excuse for a poor performance. It also is important to remember that small, daily decisions make a huge impact on our lives, sometimes even more than what we consider critical life decisions. For example, a student decides not to study for 30 minutes daily for an upcoming major examination, then fails it. This small decision to do something other than study results in failing an examination, which may force course repetition and delay the graduation date.

Self-esteem improves if a person is able to adapt to situations well. To be human is to be a changing, growing, imperfect but amazing living creation. Adapting means being flexible and open to the actions of others. Although we should have empathy for others, we cannot allow others to ruin our day or lower our confidence level. Inventor-philanthropist Charles Kettering once said, "The only time you can't afford to fail is the last time you try." Our failures often teach us much more than our successes. The important thing is to get up, evaluate why the failure occurred, then move forward armed with the new knowledge gained from mistakes.

Procrastination is often a symptom of the fear of failure and the fear of success. Many people procrastinate because they feel it gives them an excuse for their failure. They say, "There is no way I could pass that test; I only had 2 days to study!" Others are perfectionists and put off doing a job or delegating because they feel no one can do it as well as they can. The best way to stop procrastinating is to do something! Divide projects into small steps and complete one at a time. This makes tasks much less overwhelming.

Comfort Zones

We all have comfort zones. When faced with new ideas or changes, many of us tend to be a bit unsure of ourselves. Think back to the first day of school, the first day on a new job, the first time at a fancy restaurant, a first date; these events often made us feel a bit uncomfortable. New experiences may be outside our comfort zone. Psychologists often speak about a **comfort zone**, which is a place in the mind where we feel safe and comfortable, where we can perform comfortably and confidently. For most goals, however, we have to move outside our comfort zone to reach them.

CLOSING COMMENTS

Interpersonal skills are critical to success as a medical assistant. Communication is a part of all interactions throughout the day, and the better developed these skills are, the better the medical assistant can serve the patients in the facility. Every attempt should be made to enhance the interpersonal and human relations skills the medical assistant currently has and to strive continually to better these skills. This ensures that effective communication is part of the relationship with patients and with others with whom the medical assistant interacts.

Patient Education

The medical assistant has the opportunity to provide an educational service to every patient who enters the healthcare facility. Patients often have questions about their care or treatment, and the medical assistant with good communication skills can assist the patient in understanding.

Patients must have a clear knowledge of the role they play in their own care. The medical assistant can communicate information to the patient in many ways other than verbally. Leaflets and brochures can help patients understand their illness better and can educate them, but the medical assistant should always explain each piece of literature given to a patient. Never just hand out printed information and expect it to be read. Have the patient repeat instructions to clarify them if a question exists as to whether the patient understands.

Remember that physical care is not the only aspect of patient care; patients also have emotional needs. Often the very things we take for granted, such as food and shelter, are a struggle for some patients. The resulting stress can worsen their physical condition. Ask questions to remain aware of what the patient is communicating to the staff and what is not being said. This helps the medical assistant to best serve the patient.

Legal and Ethical Issues

Patients see the medical assistant as an extension of the physician; therefore, it is important that all communication with the patient be professional and accurate. Never give a patient advice that is not approved by the physician, to prevent accusations of practicing medicine without a license. Always discuss with the physician any issues that might affect the patient's care. Never agree to withhold any information from the physician, because even a small piece of information could completely change the plan of treatment. When giving instructions to patients, it is always best to have them in writing and to keep a copy for the patient's medical record so that a record exists of what was communicated to the patient. Use excellent documentation technique when adding information to the patient's chart. Remember that all the patients in the facility deserve to be treated with respect and compassion. Help the physician establish trust with the patient. An open, trusting relationship with the patient helps to prevent legal issues in the future.

SUMMARY OF SCENARIO

Mrs. Cloyd and her daughter are facing a difficult time. Death is inevitable for everyone, but when a loved one is diagnosed with a terminal illness, it is particularly distressing. Both of these women need compassion and caring from the medical team. They need to feel as if they are being heard and that their opinions are important. Some of their needs are similar, but they also have differing needs. A gentle touch and laughter can brighten their day, and these expressions are critical to a person experiencing the stress of a devastating illness.

The medical assistant must ensure that Mrs. Cloyd understands her medications and treatments. The office should assist her and her daughter in finding community resources for which she might be eligible. Be sure to instruct Mrs. Cloyd primarily, and make certain that Sarah also understands any directions her mother should follow. Sarah needs compassion as she deals with her mother's illness and impending death. Because she likewise is a patient of the clinic, she should be given care and attention and may have emotional needs or periods of great stress also. Even on the busiest of days, these two women deserve warmth from the staff and should be made as comfortable as possible as they seek medical care.

Although the medical office is always a busy place, medical assistants can take a moment to individualize the care that they provide to patients. Looking into the patients' eyes and genuinely asking how they have been getting along demonstrates interest in them. Call patients by their name and ask about their families. These techniques allow the medical assistant to develop rapport, which results in a more pleasant office visit for the patient.

Often, the patient is accompanied by a relative or friend, and the medical assistant may find it necessary to interact with these individuals. Remember that all information about the patient must be kept in strict confidence. Friends and family play a role in the overall health of the patient. When relations are strained, patients may feel depressed and stressed. This can affect their health in a negative way. The patient with strong family support often heals faster and has a better outlook on health issues.

Listening is a skill that must be practiced and refined. Patients need to know that the medical assistant is focusing attention on them, listening to their concerns, and paraphrasing to make sure the patient is understood correctly. Listening is one of the most important skills the medical assistant can develop.

SUMMARY OF LEARNING OBJECTIVES

1. **Define, spell, and pronounce the terms listed in the vocabulary.**

   Spelling and pronouncing medical terms correctly bolster the medical assistant's credibility. Knowing the definition of these terms promotes confidence in communication with patients and co-workers.

2. **Explain why first impressions are crucial.**

   First impressions are crucial in the medical profession because dress, attitude, and appearance all influence the credibility of the medical assistant. The medical assistant should always treat patients and visitors to the office as individuals who deserve the best in customer service.

3. **Differentiate between verbal and nonverbal communication.**

   Verbal communication depends on words and sound, whereas nonverbal communication consists of messages conveyed to another without the use of words. Body language, eye contact, facial expressions, and hand gestures are some of the many ways we use body language. Sometimes our body language conflicts with verbal communication, and a mixed signal is sent to the receiver. Often we are unaware of nonverbal signals and notice only a small number of the signals that other people send.

4. **Identify styles and types of verbal communication.**

   Medical assistants communicate casually in day-to-day life but use a professional style when communicating in the medical facility. Tone and diction are important. All information must be clear and accurate when communicating with patients. Although a personal or casual type of verbal communication is used in normal discussion, professional verbiage and attitude are required in medical facilities.

5. **Explain the different levels of spatial separation.**

   Spatial separation can be defined as the space of comfort between individuals. Public space usually is considered to be 12 to 25 feet, whereas social space is approximately 4 to 12 feet. Personal space is a range of 1½ to 4 feet, and intimate space includes touching up to approximately 1½ feet.

6. **Analyze the effect of hereditary, cultural, and environmental influences on communications.**

   Communication is affected by heredity when an individual inherits a gene that plays a part in the communication process; for example, a person with delayed speech and language skills may find it more difficult to communicate with others. Many conditions, such as autism, affect communication and social interaction. A patient's cultural heritage may prevent or hinder communication, depending on the beliefs related to culture that are held by the patient. Additionally, our environment may hinder communication. A person who is physically or emotionally abused may refuse to share information about the abuser.

7. **Discuss the value of touch in the communication process.**

   Touch is important in the process of communication because it projects an air of care and compassion to the receiver. The medical assistant should never be afraid to touch patients, as long as precautions are taken with those who are contagious. Touching the patient shows empathy and often can be more eloquent than the spoken word.

8. **Recognize the elements of oral communication using a sender-receiver process.**

   The transactional communication model includes a sender and a receiver, who offer messages to each other using various channels. The sender encodes a message, then the receiver decodes it to the best of his or her ability. Often some type of noise interferes, such as internal, external, and physiologic noise. Perception is important when communicating, because messages sometimes can be easily misinterpreted.

9. **Explain the value of active listening.**

   Listening is one of the most important skills the medical assistant can develop. Listening involves not only silence, but also active feedback. Open-ended questions help the medical assistant restate what the patient is saying to make sure the patient is understood clearly.

10. **Define and understand abnormal behavior patterns.**

    Patients may exhibit various abnormal behavior patterns that affect their physical and emotional health, such as phobias, obsessive-compulsive disorder, antisocial behavior, panic disorder, general anxiety disorder, and major depressive disorder. Some degree of knowledge about each of these disorders can help the medical assistant understand individual patients and allows the medical assistant to approach patients with empathy and professionalism.

11. **Recognize commonly used defense mechanisms.**

    Defense mechanisms are psychological methods of dealing with stressful situations. They include sarcasm, denial, repression, compensation, and several others. Often these mechanisms are our only way of dealing with circumstances with which it is difficult to cope.

12. **Discuss the role of assertiveness in effective professional communication.**

    There is a difference between assertion and aggression. Being assertive can mean that a person is forcefully stating his or her beliefs or point of view, often with no support or attempt at proof. An aggressive individual is acting in a forceful, dominant, hostile, injurious, or destructive manner. However, being either assertive or aggressive can be positive and productive. Assertive people often receive job promotions and reach the goals they set for their lives. However, too much aggression can make a person seem pushy; therefore, it should be controlled and used at the appropriate times.

13. **Identify the roles of self-boundaries in the healthcare environment.**

    Self-boundaries can include the physical space between people, but they also can apply to communications in a way that affects interaction with others. Each medical assistant must determine the workplace boundaries that are personally important to him or her; such as the use of first or last names, off-the-clock interactions with co-workers and supervisors, and e-mail forwarding of inappropriate materials.

14. **List several ways to deal with conflict.**

    Everyone experiences conflict in daily living; therefore, it is necessary to develop skills in dealing with conflict in as positive a way as possible. Conflict is not always negative and can be quite beneficial to relationships. Knowing the different types of conflict and the ways people attempt to process conflict help the medical assistant to recognize patterns and respond appropriately. Some individuals deal with conflict by being aggressive, assertive, or nonassertive. In addition, many passive-aggressive methods of dealing with conflict can be used, such as avoidance, changing the subject, distraction, blaming, and several others.

15. **Recognize communication barriers.**

Some of the barriers to communication include physical impairment, language differences, prejudice, stereotyping, and perception. Barriers may also be present during difficult times, such as when a crisis occurs, when a person is angry or in shock, or when a patient or family member is experiencing an impending death or illness or has experienced a serious accident.

16. **Identify techniques for overcoming communication barriers.**

The medical assistant who approaches the patient with understanding and respect often wins the trust of the patient, who in turn will offer the information needed to help the person. Sincerity, empathy, and kindness make a difference, and a caring attitude also helps to overcome communication barriers.

17. **Differentiate between adaptive and nonadaptive coping mechanisms.**

An adaptive coping mechanism is one that offers some type of positive help. Logically, a nonadaptive coping mechanism would be negative in nature. Consider the sleep requirement. A person who is in some type of shock may have some insomnia and needs to sleep. Getting several nights of recuperative sleep is an adaptive coping mechanism. If, however, he or she begins to sleep consistently during the day and at night, sleep may be considered a nonadaptive coping mechanism, because the individual is using sleep to avoid stressful issues.

18. **Identify common stages that terminally ill patients pass through and discuss the support that can assist them and their families during their struggle.**

Dr. Elisabeth Kübler-Ross suggested that the process of grief has five stages: denial, bargaining, anger, depression, and acceptance. She believed that all stages are experienced while grieving, but not necessarily in the same order. A medical assistant with a good understanding of the grieving process can better care for the patient and the patient's loved ones.

19. **Discuss the use of empathy when treating terminally ill patients.**

Empathy is the ability to understand another person's feelings, situation, or motives. The medical assistant should look at situations from the patient's point of view and be considerate of his or her wishes at all times, even if the patient's needs and desires differ from the medical assistant's opinions. Terminally ill patients should never be pushed toward unwanted treatments or procedures by the healthcare professional.

20. **Identify resources and adaptations that are required based on individual needs.**

Each medical office should keep accurate, up-to-date information about available resources on hand so that it can be accessed quickly when needed. Be sure to check the physician's notes to determine whether he or she made a referral for a patient, and follow up to make sure the patient sought assistance from the person or organization named in the referral.

21. **List and explain the levels of Maslow's hierarchy of needs.**

Maslow's hierarchy of needs includes five levels, beginning with our most basic needs, such as food, rest, sleep, water, and anything that involves our physical well-being. The second level is related to safety issues; and the third, to our social needs, such as love and interaction with others. The fourth level deals with our self-esteem, and the fifth is self-actualization, where our potential is maximized.

22. **Discuss why physical and emotional needs affect our daily performance at work.**

Everyone needs physical and emotional rest to function throughout the day. A good night's sleep, consisting of at least 8 hours; regular exercise; and healthy nutrition help keep the medical assistant fit for duty. When these needs are not met, work performance may suffer, and the medical assistant may not be able to give proper attention and care to patients. Exhaustion affects the ability to perform, as do pressing concerns that linger in the mind. Make every effort to clear all negative thoughts and completely focus on the patients.

CONNECTIONS

📖 **Study Guide Connection:** Go to the Chapter 5 Study Guide. Read and complete the activities.

℮ **Evolve Connection:** Go to the Chapter 5 link at *evolve.elsevier.com/kinn* to complete the Chapter Review and Chapter Quiz. Check out the other resources listed for this chapter to make the most of what you have learned from Interpersonal Skills and Human Behavior.

6

MEDICINE AND ETHICS

SCENARIO

Monica Johnson has been employed for 6 months as a medical assistant in a family practice. She works as the clinical medical assistant for Dr. Richard Wray. One of Dr. Wray's patients, Anna Walsh, recently adopted a baby after 8 years of trying to conceive a child. The baby, Delaney Gracelia, was born to a single mother, Susan, who participated in an open adoption in which she and the Walshes met and got to know each other during her pregnancy. Susan dated the baby's father for about 6 months before discovering that she was pregnant, and they are no longer dating. Susan wanted to make a good decision for the baby and decided to place her for adoption. Dr. Wray performed some genetic testing on Delaney, and the adoptive parents were involved throughout the pregnancy, even meeting Delaney's birth mother for physician appointments from time to time. Monica observed both Susan and the Walshes and saw many benefits from the arrangement, noticing that everyone was primarily concerned with Delaney and her happiness and well-being. However, some periods were difficult for both sides. This prompted Monica to give some thought to her own feelings and ideas about many different ethical situations and issues and how she would react in the face of having to make ethical decisions.

While studying this chapter, think about the following questions:

- What difficulties do patients placing their babies for adoption face?
- What difficulties do adoptive parents face when participating in an open adoption?
- How can the medical assistant be supportive of both the adoptive parents and the birth mother?
- Should the medical assistant discuss personal beliefs about ethical situations with patients?

LEARNING OBJECTIVES

1. Define, spell, and pronounce the terms listed in the vocabulary.
2. Differentiate between legal, ethical, and moral issues affecting healthcare.
3. Compare personal, professional, and organizational ethics.
4. Identify the effect personal ethics may have on professional performance.
5. Recognize the role of patient advocacy in the practice of medical assisting.
6. Explain rights and duties as related to ethics.
7. List and define the four types of ethical problems.
8. Discuss the process used to make an ethical decision.
9. Detail the impact of the American Medical Association's Council on Ethical and Judicial Affairs (CEJA) on the ethical decisions made by healthcare professionals.
10. Discuss several of the CEJA's opinions and how they might differ from the views of the class as a whole.
11. Explore the role of confidentiality as it applies to the medical assistant.
12. Discuss the role of cultural, social, and ethnic diversity in ethical performance of medical assisting practice.
13. Describe the way unique identifiers can help patients infected with the human immunodeficiency virus (HIV) avoid discrimination.
14. Note some of the concerns about ethics that apply to genetic information.

VOCABULARY

advocate (ad'-vuh-kat) One who pleads the cause of another; one who defends or maintains a cause or proposal.

allocating (a'-luh-ka-ting) Apportioning for a specific purpose or to particular persons or things.

annotations (a-nuh-ta'-shuns) Notes added by way of comment or explanation.

beneficence (buh-ne'-fuh-sens) The act of doing or producing good, especially performing acts of charity or kindness.

clinical trials Research studies that test how well new medical treatments or other interventions work in the subjects, usually human beings.

disparities (di-spar'-uh-tes) Marked differences or distinctions.

disposition (dis-puh-zi'-shun) The tendency of something or someone to act in a certain manner under given circumstances.

duty Obligatory tasks, conduct, service, or functions that arise from one's position, as in life or in a group.

euthanasia (yu-thuh-na'-zhe-uh) The act or practice of killing or permitting the death of hopelessly sick or injured individuals in a relatively painless way for reasons of mercy.

fidelity (fuh-de'-luh-te) Faithfulness to something to which one is bound by pledge or duty.

gametes (ga'-mets) Mature male or female germ cells, usually possessing a haploid chromosome set and capable of initiating formation of a new diploid individual; a sex cell, whether sperm or ovum.

genome (jeh'-nom) The genetic material of an organism.

idealism The practice of forming ideas or living under the influence of ideas.

impaired Being in a less than perfect or less than whole condition; it includes having handicaps or functional defects and being under the influence of drugs, alcohol, and/or controlled substances.

infertile Not fertile or productive; not capable of reproducing.

introspection (in-truh-spek'-shun) An inward, reflective examination of one's own thoughts and feelings.

justice With regard to medical ethics, the fair distribution of benefits and burdens among individuals or groups in society with legitimate claims on those benefits.

nonmaleficence (non-mal-fe'-zens) Refraining from the act of harming or committing evil.

opinions Formal expressions of judgment or advice by an expert; formal expressions of the legal reasons and principles on which a legal decision is based.

philosopher A person who seeks wisdom or enlightenment; an expounder of a theory in a certain area of experience.

postmortem Done, collected, or occurring after death.

procurement (pro-kuhr'-ment) To get possession of, to obtain by particular care and effort.

public domain The realm embracing property rights that belong to the community at large, are unprotected by copyright or patent, and are subject to use or appropriation by anyone.

ramifications (ra-muh-fuh-ka'-shuns) Consequences produced by a cause or following from a set of conditions.

reparations (re-puh-ra'-shuns) Amends, acts of atonement, or satisfaction given as a result of a wrong or injury.

sociologic Oriented or directed toward social needs and problems.

surrogate (suhr'-uh-gat) A substitute; to put in place of another.

unique identifiers Codes used instead of names to protect the confidentiality of the patient in a method of anonymous HIV testing.

veracity (vuh-ra'-suh-te) A devotion to or conformity with the truth.

*E*thics can be defined as the thoughts, judgments, and actions on issues that have implications of moral right and wrong. Various beliefs exist about what is and is not ethical in everyday life and in the medical profession. The decisions that people make based on ethical beliefs can quite possibly alter the course of human existence. Ethics are different from legal issues mainly because something that is legal is not necessarily ethical. Ethics is considered a higher authority than legality. The American Medical Association's Council on Ethical and Judicial Affairs (CEJA) clarifies the relationship between law and ethics as follows: Ethical values and legal principles are usually closely related, but ethical obligations typically exceed legal duties. In some cases, the law mandates unethical conduct. In general, when physicians believe a law is unjust, they should work to change the law. In exceptional circumstances of unjust laws, ethical responsibilities should supersede legal obligations. Ethics and morals are more closely related, although ethics often are attributed to professional interactions, whereas morals are usually personal in nature. Medical assistants not only must have a strong knowledge base about ethical issues they might face throughout their careers, they also must come to terms with some of the deeply rooted value systems that have been a part of their lives since youth. The trials and tribulations we have experienced, as well as the joys, all influence our thought patterns when we are faced with an opportunity to make a good ethical decision.

Personal, professional, and organizational ethics all contribute to the way the medical assistant approaches the patient. For instance, if a medical assistant personally believes that a patient should be taken off life support when there are no signs of brain activity, he or she must understand that professionally, this decision must be left to the patient's family members. The medical assistant must not force his or her personal ethical beliefs on the patient or family members. Organizations will offer ethical guidelines as well in the form of policies and procedures; for example, each medical assistant is required to maintain patient confidentiality. This practice reflects the organizational ethic that all patients have the right to confidentiality of their information and records (Procedure 6-1). Personal and professional ethics must be kept separate so that patients can make their own decisions regarding their healthcare (Procedure 6-2).

PROCEDURE 6-1

Respond to Issues of Confidentiality

GOAL: *To ensure that medical assistants treat all information regarding patient care as completely confidential.*

Unless otherwise noted, all equipment and supplies are to be provided by the instructor.

EQUIPMENT and SUPPLIES

- Copy of the Code of Ethics of the American Association of Medical Assistants (AAMA)
- Copy of the Medical Assistant Creed
- Copy of the Oath of Hippocrates
- Copy of the guidelines from the Health Insurance Portability and Accountability Act (HIPAA)
- Notepad and pen
- Patient medical record
- Patient role-play cards (provided by instructor)

PROCEDURAL STEPS

1. Read through each document, paying particular attention to the references to confidentiality.
   PURPOSE: To gain insight into documents that stress confidentiality as a critical aspect of the healthcare process, to reinforce the importance of patient confidentiality, and to understand the roots of ethical behavior.
2. Select a student with whom to role-play as a patient. The patient should present with a situation or an illness that he or she wants to keep confidential.
   PURPOSE: Apply ethical behaviors, including honesty and integrity, in performance of medical assisting practice.
3. Greet each patient by name.
4. Take the patient to a private exam room or other area suitable for a private conversation and attend to his or her needs and questions.
   PURPOSE: To restrict the conversation to medical personnel and the patient.

5. Listen carefully to what the patient says, taking notes if necessary, asking clarifying questions, and using restatement to clear up any misunderstandings.
   PURPOSE: To demonstrate to patients an interest in what they say and to make sure all their concerns are addressed and answered.
6. Assure the patient that his or her concerns and health issues are confidential.
   PURPOSE: To put the patient at ease, so that he or she feels comfortable in sharing each detail of the condition or of the concerns that need to be discussed.
7. Explain to the patient that information cannot be kept from the physician.
   PURPOSE: To make sure the medical assistant will not be asked to withhold information from the physician.
8. Discuss the information with the physician or ask the physician to speak personally with the patient, depending on which is appropriate to the circumstances.
   PURPOSE: To act only with authorization from the physician.
9. Instruct the patient according to the physician's orders, if necessary.
10. Document the patient's concerns, information given by the patient, and the physician's orders in the medical record.
    PURPOSE: To provide a record of the conversation and the circumstances of the patient's concerns and the physician's plan for resolution.
11. Do not share information about the patient with anyone not directly related to the patient's care.
    PURPOSE: To ensure complete patient confidentiality.

PROCEDURE 6-2

Develop a Plan for Separating Personal and Professional Ethics

GOAL: *To determine one's ethical views before having to confront an ethical decision.*

Unless otherwise noted, all equipment and supplies are to be provided by the instructor.

EQUIPMENT and SUPPLIES

- Pen and paper
- Copy of the Council on Ethical and Judicial Affairs Opinions
- Patient Role-Play Cards (provided by instructor)

PROCEDURAL STEPS

1. Set aside time to study and consider the ethical issues outlined in this chapter (e.g., abuse, abortion, organ donation, stem cell research, and so on).

   PURPOSE: To make any ethical decision, research the subject and give thought to each issue so that the decision is credible.
2. For each issue, make notes regarding personal thoughts, paying particular attention to whether you agree with the current opinion of the Council on Ethical and Judicial Affairs.
   PURPOSE: To examine the impact that personal ethics and morals may have on the medical assistant's practice.

3. Look at each issue as a separate ethical problem and apply the ethical decision-making process to each.
   PURPOSE: To consider each issue in an organized way.
4. Gather relevant information by researching each problem.
   PURPOSE: To make certain that all facts are considered when determining personal views about each issue.
5. Identify the type of ethical problem that each issue represents.
   PURPOSE: By accumulating information about the issue and matching it with an ethical problem, the medical assistant will be able to apply knowledge and determine personal views more easily.
6. Determine the ethical approach to use.
   PURPOSE: Knowing the type of problem that each ethical issue represents helps the medical assistant to determine the best approach to each decision.
7. Explore practical alternatives.
   PURPOSE: Considering all practical alternatives helps the medical assistant make the best ethical decisions.
8. Decide your personal stand on each issue.
   PURPOSE: By gathering information, identifying the problem and the best ethical approach to use, then considering all practical alternatives, the medical assistant can arrive at a sound ethical decision about his or her personal stand on each issue.
9. Determine the Council on Ethical and Judicial Affairs stance on each issue.

PURPOSE: By determining the personal stance and knowing the professional stance for each ethical issue, the medical assistant will not be faced with having to make a decision on the spot.
10. Continue the process until each ethical issue has been addressed.
11. Conduct further research about other ethical issues using the American Medical Association Web site.
    PURPOSE: To discover additional ethical issues that medical assistants may face throughout their career.
12. Refrain from inflicting personal ethical views on any patient.
    PURPOSE: To ensure that patients determine their own ethical views and make medical decisions based on their own views as opposed to those of the medical staff.
13. Interact with patients in a professional way, regardless of their or your own ethical views.
    PURPOSE: All patients must be treated in a professional way, regardless of their ethical views or healthcare choices.
14. Re-evaluate personal ethical views periodically and apply new knowledge and experience to determine whether ethical views have changed.
    PURPOSE: To be open to change based on experience in the medical field and new discoveries or technology. Healthcare is an ever-changing profession; therefore a medical assistant must develop an attitude of being a lifelong learner. New trends may change the medical assistant's position on ethical issues.

HISTORY OF ETHICS IN MEDICINE

From earliest recorded history, humans have pondered ethics, or the judgment of right and wrong. Ethics should not be confused with etiquette. *Etiquette* refers to courtesy, customs, and manners, whereas *ethics* explores the moral right or wrong of an issue. It is not surprising that for centuries, the field of medicine has set for itself a rigid standard of ethical conduct toward patients and professional colleagues.

The earliest written code of ethical conduct for medical practice was conceived in approximately 2250 BC by the Babylonians. It was called the Code of Hammurabi. It elaborated on the conduct expected of a physician and even set the fees a physician could charge. The code was quite lengthy and detailed, which is probably the reason it did not survive the ages. In approximately 400 BC Hippocrates developed a brief statement of principles that remains an inspiration to the physicians of today. The Oath of Hippocrates has been administered to many medical graduates. The most significant contribution to medical ethics after Hippocrates was made by Thomas Percival, an English physician, **philosopher**, and writer. In 1803 he published his Code of Medical Ethics. Percival was very concerned about **sociologic** matters and took great interest in the study of ethical concepts as they related to the medical profession.

In 1846, as the American Medical Association (AMA) was being organized in New York City, medical education and medical ethics already were considered important aspects of the profession. At the first annual AMA meeting in 1847, a Code of Ethics was formulated and adopted. It specifically acknowledged Percival's code as its foundation, and this document became a part of the fundamental standards of the AMA and its components. Even today, sections of the AMA Code of Ethics stem from Percival's writings.

WHO DECIDES WHAT IS ETHICAL?

When we weigh the question of who decides what is ethical, the answer is evident: you do. Every day medical professionals face the task of making ethical decisions. As with any important choice, the short- and long-term effects and consequences must be considered. Although depending on groups and committees to guide ethical decisions is a completely acceptable practice, the responsibility for making these decisions ultimately rests with the individual (Figure 6-1).

Organizations that study ethical dilemmas may decide that a concept such as abortion is an ethical medical practice. But if an individual does not find abortion to be an acceptable practice for religious or other reasons, abortion is not ethical for that individual. A great freedom that Americans often take for granted is that we can exercise free will in decisions related to individual conscience in this country and that we can choose from a variety of options; however, we must exercise this responsibility carefully.

FIGURE 6-1 Medical assistants may find themselves making ethical decisions on a daily basis.

CRITICAL THINKING APPLICATION   6-1

- Monica knows that she has deep-rooted thoughts and ideas about many ethical matters. However, she has never really thought about where she formed her ideas. Where do we get most of our opinions on ethical or moral issues?

- What is the difference between an opinion's being personal and its being someone else's?

THE ROLE OF THE AMERICAN MEDICAL ASSOCIATION AND ITS COUNCIL ON ETHICAL AND JUDICIAL AFFAIRS IN ISSUES OF ETHICS

The AMA serves physicians as a national organization that provides various types of information and support. One of the most important facets of the AMA is its Council on Ethical and Judicial Affairs. The CEJA consists of nine active members of the AMA, including one resident physician member and one medical student member. It is responsible for interpreting the *AMA Principles of Medical Ethics* as adopted by the House of Delegates of the AMA. The AMA's Code of Ethics has four components:

- Principles of medical ethics
- The fundamental elements of the patient-physician relationship
- Current opinions of the CEJA with **annotations**
- Reports of the CEJA

The *Code of Medical Ethics: Current Opinions with Annotations* contains the first three components, with discussion of more than 135 ethical issues encountered in medicine. A separate publication, *Reports of the Council on Ethical and Judicial Affairs,* discusses the rationale of the council's **opinions**. The *AMA Principles of Medical Ethics* has been revised several times to take into account

developments in medicine, but the moral intent and overall **idealism** of these principles have not changed.

■ MAKING ETHICAL DECISIONS

An understanding of a few of the elements of ethics, the different types of ethical problems, and how a good ethical decision is made is important before we discuss the opinions of the CEJA. Then, as some of the opinions are presented in this text, students can begin to evaluate their own positions on each issue. This section enables the medical assistant to recognize the types of ethical problems that might arise in the physician's office and provides a pattern to follow in making an ethical decision.

■ Elements of Ethics

Dr. Ruth Purtilo, an authority on ethics in medicine, has written a book on the subject, *Ethical Dimensions in the Health Professions.* She presents three general elements of ethics: duties, rights, and character traits. A **duty** is an obligation a person has or perceives himself or herself to have. A daughter may feel the obligation to care for her elderly parents, or a husband who has hurt his spouse may feel an obligation to somehow make up for his act.

Purtilo mentions several types of duties related to the medical profession. **Nonmaleficence** means refraining from harming oneself or another person. **Beneficence** means bringing about good. **Fidelity** is the concept of keeping promises, and **veracity** is the duty of telling the truth. **Justice**, in relation to medical ethics, deals with the fair distribution of benefits and burdens among individuals or groups in society having legitimate claims on those benefits. When a person has wronged another, he or she has a duty to make **reparations**, or right the wrong. Last, a person should feel grateful if he or she is a beneficiary of someone else's goodness. This also is a type of duty.

Rights are defined as claims a person or group makes on society, a group, or an individual. The Bill of Rights appended to the U.S. Constitution guarantees certain liberties that we enjoy as American citizens. However, some individuals think that they have rights, but those rights are actually privileges. For instance, Americans do not have the "right" to healthcare services. Individuals may expect to be cared for when sick, but this is not a right guaranteed to anyone in America. Some countries provide medical care to all their citizens, but the United States is not one of those countries. A right applies to all people within a group, without prejudice.

Purtilo defines *character traits* as a **disposition** to act a certain way. A person who believes that honesty is an important character trait usually can be trusted to speak the truth. One who feels comfortable with taking small items from work for use at home may not be able to resist an opportunity to take something more valuable. Character traits certainly do not always indicate how a person will react in all situations. No human being is perfect, and we sometimes are unpredictable. Stress also can interfere with our normal reactions, and other factors, such as depression or anger, influence how we act. The phrase that someone is acting "out of character" usually means that the person is deviating from his or her normal behavior patterns.

With an understanding of these basic elements of ethics, we have a good foundation to help us look more objectively at ethical problems and solve them to the best of our ability.

Types of Ethical Problems

Purtilo presents four basic types of ethical problems (Figure 6-2):
- Ethical distress
- Ethical dilemmas
- Dilemma of justice
- Locus of authority issues

Ethical distress is a problem in which a certain course of action is indicated, but some type of hindrance or barrier prevents that action. A professional knows the right thing to do but for some reason cannot do it.

WHAT SHOULD BE DONE?

1. **Ethical Distress**
   I know which course of action I (the "agent") should take for the patient's benefit, but there is a structural barrier to my being able to do it.

   A = Agent
   C = Course of Action
   O = Outcome

2. **Ethical Dilemma**
   There are two (or more) courses of action, each of which is right (or wrong). No matter which one I (the "agent") choose, something of value will be compromised.

   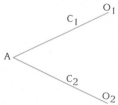

3. **Distributive Justice**
   There are benefits to be distributed among several potential beneficiaries. Not everyone can receive a full measure of the benefit. On what basis should the distribution be made?

   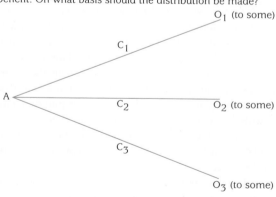

WHO SHOULD DO IT?

4. **Locus of Authority**
   There are 2 (or more) agents or "authorities" in this situation. Each believes he or she knows what outcome will benefit the patient the most, but only one authority will prevail.

   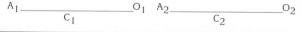

FIGURE 6-2 Summary of the types of ethical problems. (From Purtilo R: *Ethical dimensions in the health professions,* ed 4, Philadelphia, 2005, WB Saunders.)

An *ethical dilemma* is a situation in which an individual is faced with two or more acceptable or correct choices, but doing one precludes another. A choice must be made, and something of value may be lost if a second choice is eliminated. This could be viewed as the proverbial "being caught between a rock and a hard place," when the effect of a choice made may be greater than is immediately obvious.

The third type of ethical problem is the *dilemma of justice.* This problem focuses on the fair distribution of benefits to those who are entitled to them. Choices must be made regarding who receives these benefits and in what proportion. Examples include organ donation and distribution of scarce or costly medications.

In *locus of authority issues,* two or more authority figures have their own ideas about how a situation should be handled, but only one of those authorities can prevail. If one physician feels that a patient should have surgery and another does not, how does the patient decide?

Recognizing the type of ethical problem is not always easy. Sometimes an issue is a mixture of one or more types of ethical problems. When possible, it is wise to take time to weigh the courses of action before making an important decision. Unfortunately, with the fast pace of the medical profession, this is not always possible. Some decisions must be made in a split second; therefore, having a thorough grasp of ethical decision making before the need arises is important.

The Ethical Decision-Making Process

Purtilo proposes a five-step process for ethical decision making:
1. Gathering relevant information
2. Identifying the type of ethical problem
3. Determining the ethical approach to use
4. Exploring the practical alternatives
5. Completing the action

To gather information, a medical professional should ask questions, review charts, talk to the patient and other professionals, and search for other data so that the entire situation is available for scrutiny. Once the information has been gathered, the medical professional must decide which ethical problem or problems are presented. In determining the ethical approach to use, we must consider the duties, rights, and character traits of all the individuals involved, paying close attention to the **ramifications** of all possible decisions. All of the alternatives must be considered and evaluated, after which an action should be taken.

Although taking time to give these areas some thought is best, it may not be possible. Therefore, those entering the medical profession should take stock of their core beliefs. Scan the newspapers and search professional journals for ethical situations, think about the facts, then decide how you would react to each one. This is excellent preparation for the day you are faced with making a quick ethical decision.

CRITICAL THINKING APPLICATION   6-2
- What are the ramifications of an open adoption such as Delaney's? What problems might occur during the first year of her life?
- How might these problems be prevented?
- What are the positive aspects of the adoption?

CURRENT OPINIONS OF THE COUNCIL ON ETHICAL AND JUDICIAL AFFAIRS AND MEDICINE'S ETHICAL ISSUES

Now, armed with a basic knowledge of the types of ethical problems and the process for solving them, we take a look at some of the CEJA's opinions. Remember, physicians and other medical professionals are not bound to abide by these opinions. They are free to make their own decisions, but many of the medical professionals in our country tend to agree with the decisions made by the council. In the study guide, students will find cases to discuss relating to many of these ethical situations.

Abortion

In 1973 the U.S. Supreme Court heard the case of *Roe v. Wade*. Norma McCorvey (using the name Jane Roe) petitioned the court for permission to have an elective abortion when, at age 21, she found herself pregnant with her third child. The class action suit she filed against Henry Wade, then the district attorney in Dallas, Texas, eventually was appealed to the Supreme Court. Although she won her case, it was too late for her to have an abortion, and her child was born and placed for adoption. McCorvey went public with her true identity in the early 1980s and later became a staunch opponent of abortion and has spent many years promoting the overturn of *Roe v. Wade*.

Since the ruling was handed down in 1973, abortion has been one of the most volatile issues in medical ethics. According to the *AMA Principles of Medical Ethics,* the AMA does not prohibit a physician from performing an abortion in accordance with good medical practice and under circumstances that do not violate the law. In recent years laws have been passed in some states requiring mandatory parental notification of a minor's intent to have an abortion. In some cases this means that the minor must have parental consent, and in others, parents only must be notified of their daughter's intent to have an abortion. Some states also require a 24-hour or longer waiting period after the notification. However, the CEJA states that the patient, even if an adolescent, should ultimately be in control of the decision on whether parents should be involved in the abortion decision.

The AMA strongly encourages physicians to attempt to persuade the minor to seek counseling from someone she trusts, such as a school counselor, teacher, or relative, if the minor's parent will not be involved in the abortion decision. However, the AMA agrees that the physician should not feel compelled to require minors to involve the parent in the decision. Medical professionals must be aware of the laws in their respective states that deal with the mandatory notification requirements and should contact the medical societies in their region to determine what constitutes proper notification.

Abuse

The AMA requires that a physician be familiar with the signs of physical, psychological, and sexual abuse of spouses, children, mentally incompetent persons, and the elderly. Discovery of abuse creates a difficult situation for a medical professional. The patient may be the object of abuse but may deny its existence because of fear of further attacks. The law requires that abuse be reported, and if the physician does not report abuse, ethical standards have been breached. In addition, the abuse may continue. Any medical assistant who suspects abuse must report this information to the physician immediately. Then, the physician must determine whether the incident is reportable by law and take action. If the physician does not take action, but the medical assistant is confident that abuse has happened, he or she is responsible for making a report to the proper authority in the city or state.

Allocation of Health Resources

Sometimes society must decide who receives care when serving all who need care is not possible. Decisions must be made fairly and should be weighed carefully. The criteria to consider when **allocating** health resources include urgency of need, likelihood of benefit, duration of benefit, amount of resources required for successful treatment, and potential for change in the quality of life. Nonmedical criteria should not be considered; these include ability to pay, the social worth of the individual, age, obstacles to treatment, and the patient's contribution to the illness. The physician must remain the patient's **advocate** and should not be involved in making allocation decisions for that patient. Procedures for such allocations are determined in an objective manner by the institutions involved in the patient's care.

Artificial Insemination/In Vitro Fertilization

Any individual or couple considering artificial insemination or in vitro fertilization must be thoroughly counseled and must endure lengthy screening procedures for communicable and genetic diseases that the donor and/or recipient may have. Artificial insemination is performed when donated sperm is used to impregnate a woman. Egg cells are fertilized outside the womb and then, if fertilization takes place, the embryo is placed inside the woman's uterus. Before in vitro fertilization can happen, the physician must determine the woman's most fertile time in the month and harvest the eggs at that time. The technique of in vitro fertilization and embryo transplantation enables certain couples previously incapable of conception to bear a child. The CEJA holds that because of serious ethical and moral concerns, any fertilized egg that has the potential for human life and that will be implanted in the uterus of a woman should not be subjected to laboratory research. All fertilized ova not used for implantation that are maintained for research purposes must be handled with the strictest adherence to the *AMA Principles of Medical Ethics,* to the guidelines for research and medical practice expressed in the CEJA's opinion on fetal research, and to the highest standards of medical practice.

Informed consent must be provided, and further regulations are based on the marital status of the people involved. If the recipient is married to the donor, the resultant child has all the rights of a child naturally conceived. If the donor is anonymous, the husband must sign a consent if he is to become the legal father of the resultant child. If the donor and recipient are not married, the recipient is considered the sole parent, unless both parties agree to recognize a right to paternity. Providing artificial insemination or in vitro fertilization to a single woman or a woman who is part of a homosexual couple is not considered unethical. It usually is considered unethical to offer compensation to donors other than reimbursement of actual expenses and/or compensation for the donor's time.

Much discussion is ongoing about the use of extra embryos harvested for reproductive purposes. The control and use of these **gametes** logically should be left to the man and woman who produced them, but the AMA agrees that both must give their consent to how they are used. Artificial insemination/in vitro fertilization is considered an ethical procedure.

Stem Cell Research

Many organizations believe that using human embryos for stem cell research destroys the most vulnerable of beings, and laws have been passed to protect these embryos. Others want to explore the possibility of developing cures from this research for conditions such as Alzheimer's disease, diabetes, Parkinson's disease, and heart disease. Stem cell research continues to be an area of disagreement because of the controversy regarding the point at which life begins. Those who believe that life begins at conception usually oppose stem cell research, because it involves experimentation and testing on a "viable human being." Many physicians believe that their commitment is first to "living persons," as opposed to embryos, and therefore support stem cell research.

Surrogate Motherhood

Surrogate motherhood introduces many different ethical, legal, and social problems for the individuals involved. However, it may be the only opportunity for an **infertile** couple to have a child. The benefits of surrogacy must be heavily weighed against the possible risks and psychological problems that might arise. The AMA believes that the birth mother must be given a period during which she can reverse her decision to give up the child she has delivered and void the contract. However, in cases of gestational surrogacy, the legality and ethical implications are more complicated. In gestational surrogacy, the child is not genetically linked to the birth mother. Usually the couple engaging the surrogate mother are the genetic parents of the resultant child. One must also consider what will happen if the child is born with a deformity or handicap. This is a contract that should never be enacted without strong forethought and counseling.

Genetic Counseling

Genetic counseling is another area in which the AMA recommends caution. Through genetic counseling, parents of tomorrow may be able to choose eye color, talents, and intellect levels for their children. Human beings already have been conceived as "designer babies." In 1980 the Repository for Germinal Choice (more commonly known as the "Genius Sperm Bank") was founded. Although it was not established to create a perfect "master race," it did attempt to produce leaders and creators. As with cloning, the AMA recommends that much more research be done before genetic counseling is instituted on a global scale.

CRITICAL THINKING APPLICATION 6-3
- How might the genetic testing done in Delaney's case have caused an ethical dilemma?
- Discuss whether genetic testing can be counted on to predict disease.
- How many in your class would have genetic testing done on their own child before birth?

Family and Intimate Partner Violence

The CEJA believes that all forms of family and intimate partner violence are major public health issues and urges the profession, both individually and collectively, to work with other interested parties to prevent such violence and to address the needs of victims. Physicians have a major role in lessening the prevalence, scope, and severity of child maltreatment, intimate partner violence, and elder abuse, all of which fall under the rubric of family violence. To support physicians in practice, the AMA will continue to campaign against family violence and remains open to working with all interested parties to address violence in American society. The AMA's efforts are guided, in part, by its Advisory Council on Family Violence.

Ethical Responsibility to Study and Prevent Error and Harm

In the context of healthcare, an error is an unintended act or omission or a flawed system or plan that harms or has the potential to harm a patient. Patient safety can be enhanced by studying the circumstances surrounding healthcare errors. According to the CEJA, physicians should participate in the development of reporting mechanisms that emphasize education and systems change, providing a substantive opportunity for all members of the healthcare team to learn. Physicians also must show professional and compassionate concern for patients who have been harmed, regardless of whether the harm was caused by a healthcare error.

Physician-Assisted Suicide

The AMA believes that physician-assisted suicide interferes with the fundamental purpose of being a physician—to be a healer. The CEJA advocates that physicians aggressively provide care and treatment alternatives for those near the end of life but that they avoid promoting or providing the means by which patients could end their own lives. Such means include not only assisting the patient to inject chemicals that induce death, but also prescribing drugs and providing information about lethal doses or administering a lethal dose of a drug to a patient to promote death. This is sometimes called **euthanasia**, or mercy killing.

Surrogate Decision Making

According to the CEJA, physicians should encourage patients to document their preferences about advance directives through a living will or durable power of attorney. However, many patients do not have any type of documentation of their wishes available when tragedy strikes. In these cases, a surrogate may be asked to make decisions for the patient about medical treatment. Even when such provisions have been made, the documents sometimes are unavailable in an emergency; therefore, patients should discuss treatment options in advance with those who may be called on to act as a surrogate decision maker. If patients cannot make medical decisions for themselves and documented advance directives are unavailable or nonexistent, absent any state regulation to the contrary, the physician should approach the patient's family, domestic partner, or a close friend to act as the surrogate decision maker. In some cases family members may disagree about decisions necessary for the patient's health and well-being. In these instances the physician should work to resolve the conflict through mediation or should consult the facility's ethics committee. The physician's ultimate goal is to act in the best interests of the patient, and in the absence of any other basis for interpreting how a patient would wish to proceed with treatment, the physician should make the decision that, in the physician's professional opinion, would most benefit the patient.

Withholding or Withdrawing Life-Prolonging Treatment

A physician is committed to saving life and relieving suffering. Sometimes these two goals are incompatible, and a choice between them must be made. If possible, the patient should decide what treatment is given. Often the patient makes his or her wishes known to a responsible relative or other representative in case the patient becomes incapacitated. Some patients want a "do not resuscitate" (DNR) or "no code" order added to their charts. Usually such an order is established so that no heroic measures are taken in a situation in which a patient would be unable or incompetent to make a decision. In any case, the decision to withdraw life support should be made before any mention of organ donation is made by the medical professionals tending the patient. In the best situation, the patient has formally completed advance directives. Two types of advance directives usually are used in the United States: a living will and a durable power of attorney. These documents are written instructions for healthcare and are strongly recommended by the AMA.

A durable power of attorney is a legal document that allows the patient to appoint someone who is trusted to make medical decisions for the patient in the event the patient cannot. This person is sometimes called a *patient advocate* or *healthcare proxy*. Federal law requires that patients be given information about advance directives by all facilities that participate in the Medicare and Medicaid programs.

Quality of Life

Physicians sometimes must participate in or advise others on decisions affecting the fate of a person whose prognosis is poor, such as a deformed newborn or a person of advanced age with many physical problems. The first thought may be the burden that the patient's care places on the family or society. However, the AMA insists that the physician's primary consideration must be what is best for the patient.

Fees for Medical Services

Concern for the quality of patient care should be the physician's first consideration. However, the physician should be conscious of costs and should not provide or prescribe unnecessary services. Access to an adequate level of healthcare for all members of our society is now a moral expectation but certainly not a right. Cost must be considered when these services are provided, in addition to the degree of benefit to the patient, the duration of the benefit, and the number of people who will benefit.

Organ Donation

Organ donation is not only considered ethical by the AMA, it is encouraged. However, it is considered unethical to participate in proceedings in which the donor receives payment, except reimbursement of expenses directly incurred in the removal of the donated organ. The rights of the patient and the donor must be protected equally. If the donor is deceased, the death must be certified by a physician other than the recipient's physician.

Because the need for donated organs is so extreme, protocols have been established by healthcare facilities to determine when it is proper to harvest organs. Organ **procurement** may be performed immediately after a person has died, or it may be done after a patient has been kept alive artificially for a time. Hospitals also have specific guidelines for the donation of organs from living donors, such as a kidney donation. When donations are made from one living person to another, both patients must have an advocate team that includes a physician, so that the interests and well-being of each patient are addressed. Payment to a living donor other than legitimate expenses incurred in connection with removal of the organ is considered unethical. Blood donations probably are the most common form of organ donation.

The CEJA has recommended consideration of two proposals with regard to organ donation: the mandated choice model and the presumed consent model. These proposals are aimed at increasing organ donations and would change the approach to consent for deceased donations. The mandated choice model would require individuals to express their preferences about organ donation when they perform some state-regulated task, such as renewing a driver's license. This method would be ethically appropriate only if the individual's choice was made in accordance with the principles of informed consent. Under the presumed consent model, deceased individuals would be presumed to be organ donors unless they had indicated a refusal to donate.

CRITICAL THINKING APPLICATION   6-4

- Monica has often thought about being an organ donor. She is very much in favor of organ donation because of her interest in the medical field. Her parents are very opposed to this because of their religious beliefs. How can Monica deal with this conflict within her family?
- If Monica dies before her parents do, how can she ensure that her wishes are carried out?

Capital Punishment

The CEJA does not consider participation by a physician in the act of capital punishment to be ethical. The physician may certify the person's death but should not administer a lethal injection or induce death in any way. This will conflict with the physician's role as a healer, much in the same manner as does physician-assisted suicide.

Potential Patients

According to the CEJA, physicians must keep their professional obligations to provide care to patients in accord with their prerogative to choose whether to enter into a patient-physician relationship and must respond to the best of their ability in cases of medical emergency. The Emergency Medical Treatment and Active Labor Act (EMTALA) is a statute that ensures public access to emergency services regardless of ability to pay. Physicians also cannot refuse to care for patients based on race, gender, sexual orientation, gender identity, presence of infectious diseases, or any other criteria that would constitute discrimination. However, if a physician does not feel he or she is qualified to treat a certain condition or disease, the patient can ethically be referred to a more qualified physician.

Withholding Information from Patients

The practice of withholding pertinent medical information from patients in the belief that disclosure is medically contraindicated is known as "therapeutic privilege." It creates a conflict between the physician's obligations to promote patients' welfare and respect for their autonomy by communicating truthfully. Withholding medical information from patients without their knowledge or consent is ethically unacceptable. Physicians should encourage patients to specify their preferences regarding communication of their medical information, preferably before the information becomes available. Moreover, physicians should honor patients' requests not to be informed of certain medical information or to convey the information to a designated proxy, provided these requests appear to genuinely represent the patient's own wishes.

Healthcare Fraud and Abuse

The following guidelines encourage physicians to play a key role in identifying and preventing fraud: (1) Physicians must renew their commitment to the Principles of Medical Ethics, which state that "a physician shall deal honestly with patients and colleagues, and strive to expose those physicians deficient in character, competence, or who engage in fraud or deception"; and (2) physicians should make no intentional misrepresentations to increase the amount of payment they receive or to secure noncovered health benefits for their patients.

National Health Information Technology

The AMA supports the development, adoption, and implementation of national health information technology standards through collaboration with public and private interests and consistent with current efforts to establish health information technology standards for use by the federal government.

Genetic Information and the Criminal Justice System

The release of genetic information from a physician's records without the consent of the patient constitutes a breach of confidentiality. However, according to the CEJA, the confidentiality laws acknowledge that law and overriding social considerations may permit physicians to disclose confidential information in limited circumstances. Physicians should follow the AMA's guidelines when releasing information to criminal justice authorities.

Gifts to Physicians from Industry

Many gifts given to physicians by companies in the pharmaceutical, device, and medical equipment industries serve an important and socially beneficial function. However, there is a growing concern about certain gifts from industry to physicians. To avoid the acceptance of inappropriate gifts, physicians should observe the following guidelines: (1) Any gifts accepted by the physicians individually should primarily be of benefit to patients and not be of substantial value; (2) individual gifts of minimal value are permissible as long as the gifts are related to the physician's work (e.g., pens and notepads); (3) gifts for conferences or meetings must meet the CEJA's definitions; and (4) subsidies from industry must contribute to patient care. If a question ever arises as to the ethics regarding acceptance of any gift from industry, the physician or office manager should consult the AMA.

FIGURE 6-3 One of the duties of a medical assistant is to ensure that the patient understands the instructions given. Only when the patient fully understands the choices available can he or she make sound decisions.

Informed Consent

The patient's right of self-decision can be effectively exercised only if the patient possesses enough information to enable an informed choice (Figure 6-3). The CEJA holds that the patient should make his or her own determination about treatment. The physician's obligation is to present the medical facts accurately to the patient or to the individual responsible for the patient's care and to make recommendations for management in accordance with good medical practice. The physician has an ethical obligation to help the patient make choices from among the therapeutic alternatives consistent with good medical practice. Physicians should also sensitively and respectfully disclose all relevant information to patients.

Interprofessional Relationships

If a medical assistant recognizes or suspects an error in a physician's orders, he or she has an ethical obligation to report this to the physician. A possible error must be questioned, even if it means risking the physician's or supervisor's displeasure. This could save a life or prevent a lawsuit.

Physicians often refer a patient to another physician for diagnosis and treatment. Physicians should make these referrals only when they are confident that the patient will receive competent treatment. Offering a financial incentive or other valuable consideration to patients in exchange for recruitment of other patients is unethical.

Unless the state imposes legal restrictions, a physician in private practice is free to choose whom he or she will treat. Although private practitioners may refuse certain patients, they must treat those who have already been accepted in the practice or face possible charges of neglect. This does not include referring a patient to another physician for a condition that is not within the scope of practice of the original physician.

A sports medicine physician must keep in mind that the professional responsibility at a sporting event is to protect the health and

FIGURE 6-4 Confidentiality applies to all information about the patient, including what is charted and what is said between the patient and the medical assistant.

safety of the participants, and personal judgments are governed only by medical considerations. Players should not be allowed to play and risk injury to ensure that a game is won.

In years past, it was considered unethical for a physician to have any type of romantic relationship with nurses or assistants in the office or hospital. Although this is not as stringent a rule today, fraternizing with co-workers, especially subordinates, is unwise.

Confidentiality and Patient Privacy

Confidentiality is one of the cardinal rules of the medical profession. It is completely unethical and unacceptable to divulge any information about a patient to any other person not directly related to the patient's care. The places where confidentiality often is breached are elevators, hallways, waiting or reception areas, break rooms, and lunch rooms. A relative may be standing behind the medical assistant, listening to conversations that are inappropriate for those not personally involved in the patient's care to hear. Breach of patient confidentiality is grounds for immediate termination from a healthcare facility or physician's office.

Confidentiality restrictions apply to information in a patient's records and charts and also to what the medical assistant is told by the patient or the patient's family (Figure 6-4). Never investigate a patient's record strictly for curiosity. All information in the record must be kept in confidence. If records are computer based, accessing records of patients who do not fall directly under the medical assistant's realm of duty also is considered unethical. Never share information about patients with anyone outside the medical facility or office, including your own immediate family.

The prime objective of the medical profession is to render service to humanity, and this also must be a medical assistant's first concern. The importance of respecting the confidentiality of information learned from or about patients in the course of employment cannot be overemphasized. It is unethical to reveal patient confidences to anyone, including family members, a spouse, best friends, and other medical assistants. A medical assistant must never mention the names of patients outside the place of employment, because sometimes the doctor's specialty reveals the patient's reason for consultation. Confidential papers, case histories, and even the appointment book should be kept out of sight of curious eyes.

Outside observers should be present during the patient's encounters with the physician only with the patient's explicit permission.

Outside observers may include a friend who drove the patient to the physician's office or a medical student or intern observing in the clinic. This permission should be documented in the patient's chart.

Never discuss one patient's case with another patient. If curious patients ask questions about others, simply explain that medical assistants are obligated to keep all patient information confidential. This can be done in a tactful, kind manner. Patients who ask questions of a medical nature about their own case should be referred to the physician for information and instructions unless the physician has authorized the medical assistant to provide this information. When minors request confidential services, physicians should encourage them to include their parents. However, if the minor does not want to involve them and the law does not require otherwise, physicians should allow competent minors to consent to medical care and should not notify the parents without the minor's consent.

Remember that the Health Insurance Portability and Accountability Act (HIPAA) has established strict regulations for patient confidentiality and disclosure of private health information. Make sure the physician's office is abiding by its own privacy policy and that all patients have been given a chance to review that policy. A document stating that the patient has read and understands the privacy policy or that he or she has refused to sign should be part of the patient's medical record.

Patients may not always understand the ethical standards to which physicians and medical assistants adhere. They may ask questions about their own health or the health of a fellow patient. Medical assistants must educate patients about the issues of confidentiality in such a way that patients are not offended; they should explain that all patients deserve to have their medical and personal information kept private. Now more than ever, the medical assistant's obligation to keep information private is not only an ethical but also a legal responsibility. All patients should understand that they are entitled to confidential treatment of their records and that the facility is dedicated to that principle.

CRITICAL THINKING APPLICATION   6-5

- Susan, Delaney's birth mother, comes to the office for a checkup 6 weeks after the baby was born. She looks a little sad, and when Monica questions her, she asks how Delaney is doing. What should Monica tell her?
- How can the office protect itself from issues involving confidentiality in this unusual adoption scenario?

Advertising

The only restrictions on advertising by physicians are those that specifically protect the public from deceptive practices. Standards on advertising and publicity have been liberalized over the years, but any advertisement or publicity must be true and not misleading. Testimonials of patients, for instance, should not be used in advertising, because they are difficult to verify or measure by objective standards. Statements regarding the quality of media services are highly subjective and difficult to verify.

Communication with the Media

Although information about some patients, such as celebrities and politicians, may be considered news, the physician cannot discuss any patient's condition with the press without authorization from the patient or the patient's legal representative. The physician may release only authorized information or that which is public knowledge. Certain kinds of news are part of public records; such news in the **public domain** includes births, deaths, accident reports, and police cases.

A medical assistant must be aware that only the physician is authorized to release information, and under no circumstances should the medical assistant violate the confidential nature of the physician-patient relationship. It is unethical even to certify or verify that a patient is under the physician's care without the patient's permission. A policy must be in place for every medical office regarding how media inquiries should be handled and to whom they should be referred. Never voluntarily speak to the press without authorization from the physician. Communication with the media falls under the HIPAA guidelines. Do not release a patient's health information without written permission.

Physician Obligations in Emergency Preparedness and Response

Physicians are ethically obligated to provide urgent medical care during disasters. Because extensive physician involvement is required during national, state, regional, and local disasters, physicians are expected to contribute both their time and their skills in such emergencies. Examples of instances when physicians would be obligated to act include natural disasters, epidemics, terrorist attacks, and emergencies on a local and national scale.

Malevolent Use of Biomedical Research

Because biomedical research may produce information that has potential for both harmful and beneficial applications, the physician must assess the possible ramifications of participation in such research before engaging in projects. One of the most harmful uses of biomedical research involves biologic weapons. Physicians are expected to hold public trust as sacred and consider the welfare of society as a whole, in addition to the welfare of individual patients.

Racial and Ethnic Healthcare Disparities

No **disparities** in medical care based on race or ethnic background are acceptable. Patients are entitled to the same quality of care regardless of their race or ethnic background. The CEJA demands that physicians strive to eliminate biased behavior toward patients. Discrimination toward any patient or patient group cannot be tolerated. In addition, physicians must take into account any language barriers that might hinder effective treatment of the patient. Every effort must be made to ensure that the patient understands the physician and vice versa. The medical assistant must recognize that patients will have cultural, social, and ethnic diversities and that these diversities should be respected.

Diagnostic Imaging on Request

Patients may request diagnostic imaging services for reasons such as determination of a baby's gender. Physicians should perform diagnostic imaging only when they believe the benefits of the imaging service outweigh the risks involved.

FIGURE 6-5 With the advent of advanced computer technology, a medical assistant must be particularly careful about using information about patients on the computer.

Computers

The expanding uses of computer technology permit the accumulation of an unlimited amount of medical information. With the use of computers in the physician's office and the employment of computer service organizations, confidentiality becomes even more difficult to maintain. In general, all information must be entered and accessed only by authorized personnel, and a tracking system should be used to identify which employees access information. Breaches in computer policies should be considered a breach of patient confidentiality, and the consequences should be stringent enough to deter employees from accessing information to which they are not entitled (Figure 6-5). Computerized information should be disseminated only to those with a legitimate need for it.

Fees and Charges

Charging or collecting an illegal or excessive fee is unethical. The medical assistant is responsible for keeping informed about current billing regulations and to see that they are followed conscientiously.

Requesting that payment be made at the time of treatment is entirely appropriate and very common in today's medical offices. Often, managed care patients are asked to remit their co-payment before seeing the physician on the day of the visit. If the patient is notified in advance, adding interest or other reasonable charges to delinquent accounts also is considered ethical. Most offices use a patient information booklet, which provides a written reference for all policies, that is given to new patients on the first visit. A reasonable fee may be charged for duplicating patients' records.

Physicians should never base their decision whether to order a diagnostic test on the patient's insurance coverage. If an expensive diagnostic test is needed, such as a magnetic resonance imaging (MRI) scan, the physician should order it instead of withholding the order for financial reasons. However, if the physician is aware of a way that the patient could get financial assistance with the test, he or she should relay that information to the patient.

Fee Splitting and Contingent Fees

If a physician accepts payment from another physician solely for referral of a patient, both are guilty of an unethical practice called *fee splitting.* This practice is unethical whether it involves another physician, a clinic, a laboratory, or a drug company.

Although attorneys often accept a case on a contingency fee basis, it is unethical for a physician to engage in this practice. The fee in this case is contingent on a successful outcome, but a physician should never set his or her fee on the successful outcome of medical treatment. A physician's fee must always be based on the value of service provided to the patient.

Insurance Forms

Although in times past physicians' offices willingly filed insurance claims for their patients, some have changed to a payment up front system and give patients the information needed to file the claim themselves. Many offices still file at least one insurance claim for established patients, but they may charge for multiple or complex insurance filing. This practice is entirely ethical if it conforms to local custom.

Waiver of Insurance Co-Payments

Physicians may opt to write off or waive co-payments to facilitate a patient's access to medical care. If access to care is directly threatened because the patient cannot make the co-payment, the physician may forgive the payment. However, routine waiver of co-payments may violate the policies of some insurers, both public and private. Physicians should ensure that their policies on co-payments are consistent with applicable law and within the legal boundaries of their contracts with insurers.

Professional Courtesy

Professional courtesy is defined as the provision of medical care to physician colleagues or their families and staff free of charge or at a reduced fee. This is a long-standing tradition but certainly not an ethical requirement. Physicians make the decision as to who receives professional courtesy in their offices, and this should be written into the office policy manual. In some cases, extending professional courtesy is contrary to insurance and/or managed care contracts. In addition, some physicians have stopped offering professional courtesy because of the rising costs of healthcare and shrinking reimbursements.

Appointment Charges

It is ethical for a physician to charge for a missed appointment or one that was not cancelled within a stated time if the patient was fully advised in advance that such a charge may be made. Discretion should be used in applying such charges, however, because the patient may have encountered an emergency. Often, adding a missed appointment charge to the bill of a patient who never cancels in advance prompts a call in the future when the appointment cannot be kept.

Prescribing Drugs and Devices

The physician should not be influenced in the prescription of drugs, devices, or appliances by a direct or indirect financial interest in the supplier. A physician may own or operate a pharmacy but generally may not ethically refer his or her patients to that pharmacy. Patients should enjoy the same freedom of choice in deciding who fills their prescriptions as they do in choosing a physician.

Professional and Contractual Relationships

Physicians often enter into contractual relationships, which may be as simple as monthly pest control services for the office. However, contracts can be quite complicated and contain numerous provisions, requiring an attorney's assistance. Physicians should negotiate the wording of contracts so that no question exists of financial incentives for the physician that would in any way compromise professional judgment or integrity.

Physician Ownership of a Health Facility

A physician ethically may own or have a financial interest in a for-profit or other healthcare facility, such as a freestanding clinic or health club. However, before admitting or referring a patient to that facility, the physician has an ethical obligation to reveal such ownership to the patient. In general, physicians should not refer patients to a health facility outside their office practice and at which they do not directly provide care or services.

Ghost Surgery

Substitution of another surgeon without the patient's consent is called *ghost surgery.* Patients have the right to choose their own physician or surgeon. Ghost surgery may happen when the patient has already received anesthesia and has no idea that a substitution has been made. To make a substitution without consulting the patient is deceitful and unethical.

Discipline Within Medicine

A physician should expose incompetent, corrupt, dishonest, or unethical conduct on the part of members of the profession without fear of loss of favor. A physician may be subject to civil or criminal liability, including loss of license to practice medicine, for violating government laws. Expulsion from membership is the maximum penalty that may be imposed by a medical society for violation of ethical standards.

Physician Health and Wellness

Physicians are responsible for maintaining their own good health and for being well enough to treat their patients. When physicians are not well, both physically and mentally, their health can interfere with the ability to provide good care to patients and engage in the safe execution of professional medical activities and decision making. Physicians not in such good health are said to be **impaired**.

The CEJA recommends that all physicians have their own personal doctor, who will use uncompromised objectivity in caring for the physician's health. Healthcare providers are expected to intervene promptly when the health or wellness of a colleague appears to have become compromised. The CEJA suggests types of intervention, such as offers of encouragement and referrals to physician health programs or other programs that restore and maintain the physician's health and wellness.

Substance Abuse

It is unethical for a physician to practice medicine while under the influence of a controlled substance, alcohol, or other chemical agents that could impair the ability to care for the patient properly or perform procedures. The physician's staff also must avoid all types of substance abuse. Healthcare providers who are aware of other providers or staff members with substance abuse problems must take action to ensure patients' safety, which may include reporting the user to the appropriate authority in the city or state in which the person practices medicine or works in the medical industry.

Unethical Conduct by Members of the Health Professions

In rare instances, a medical assistant is faced with a situation in which the physician-employer's conduct appears to violate established ethical standards Before making any judgments, the medical assistant must be absolutely sure of all the information and circumstances. If unethical conduct occurs, the medical assistant must then make his or her own decision about continued employment in the facility and whether the unethical behavior should be reported to a law enforcement agency, the local medical society, or the hospital where the physician has been granted privileges. Would it be wise to remain in the office under the circumstances? Would it be better to seek other employment? Would remaining adversely affect future opportunities for employment with another physician?

These decisions are difficult, especially if the relationship and employment conditions have been favorable and congenial. An ethical medical assistant does not want to participate in known substandard or unlawful practices, especially those that might be harmful to patients. In addition, the medical assistant must never make inaccurate reports regarding unethical behavior and should realize that some states can prosecute individuals who file a false report. Be absolutely certain of the facts before making such accusations against any health professional. When the physician's ethical standards conflict with those of the medical assistant, the medical assistant must decide whether staying with the physician is the best option. That decision may require a degree of soul searching and perhaps listing the pros and cons of each decision. Never compromise ethical standards for monetary gain. Remember that we must live with the decisions we make today, tomorrow.

ETHICAL ISSUES REGARDING HIV

Infection with the human immunodeficiency virus (HIV) creates a whole new world of ethical concerns for patients and those who support and care for them. When the HIV crisis first came to public attention, much about the virus was unknown, and a wealth of misinformation resulted. Those infected with the virus often were forced to leave their homes and lost their jobs; they were shunned by society, and they faced rejection seemingly everywhere they turned, all because of fear of the illness.

Clinical trials currently are underway for vaccinations against HIV, but clinical trials need volunteers for testing. Because vaccinations often are made of an *attenuated,* or weakened, strain of a virus, serious concerns exist about who receives the vaccination. Researchers have considered testing the vaccines in several Third World countries with a high number of prostitutes and a thriving sex industry. These people, who have no intention of changing their lifestyle regardless of the risks, may see vaccination trials as a chance to avoid contracting HIV. However, this raises the ethical question of whether testing should be done on people from disadvantaged countries rather than our own citizens.

Even today, people infected with HIV face discrimination. Consequently, problems arise with testing in some states in which the names of patients who test positive for HIV are reported to various health departments and agencies. Although the stated intention is to ensure that these patients receive care, the accompanying effect is the risk of discriminatory practices. Some states use code systems, called **unique identifiers**, to help maintain the confidentiality of those tested. However, other states insist by statute that the names be reported. Some states require mandatory HIV testing for prisoners and those who have committed sex crimes. Insurance is a difficult issue when a person is infected with HIV, and some policies can be cancelled if HIV infection is discovered. This may prompt providers who want to treat patients infected with HIV to delay reporting the infection as long as possible, using other diagnoses regarding symptoms as opposed to the underlying cause of the patient's problems. Many details are involved when HIV is a factor, even the reporting of HIV-positive status on the **postmortem** report. All of these ethical issues are difficult to resolve, and great care must be taken in making decisions that affect a patient who tests positive for HIV.

ETHICS AND THE HUMAN GENOME

The mapping of the human **genome** has been in the news for several years. The genome project formally began in 1990 with the goals of identifying all 20,000 to 25,000 genes present in the human body; determining the sequences of the 3 billion chemical base pairs that make up human deoxyribonucleic acid (DNA); and finding ways to catalog this information in databases to make it readily available to those who need it. The project was completed in 2003, but the data discovered during the 13 years of the project will be studied for years.

The mapping of the human genome and the information provided have raised concerns about privacy and confidentiality issues. Who actually owns genetic information, and who will be allowed to control it? Logically, the patient would seem to own his or her own genetic information; however, if that is so, the patient should be able to control access to it. Also, decisions must be made regarding fair use of genetic information. Employers, schools, courts, insurance companies, adoption agencies, and the military are just a few examples of organizations that might misuse genetic information and discriminate against those whom they may wish to target for inclusion or exclusion. Reproductive issues also arise, along with questions about the reliability of genetic testing.

CLOSING COMMENTS

Medical assistants have an ethical obligation to keep abreast of current developments that affect the practice of medicine and the care of patients. Membership in a professional organization provides access to continuing education for maintaining knowledge and skills pertaining to the performance of medical assisting.

The study of ethics requires much thought and honest appraisal of what the medical assistant believes. Sometimes **introspection** of this type is difficult. Often our beliefs are a result of our environment, upbringing, and other factors that have influenced our thinking and actions from the time we were small children to our current age. It is important that our belief system be one that we have created personally, not just a set of beliefs accepted from another source.

Medical assistants should take a serious look at the thoughts and concepts that make up their own concepts of ethics. It is important to approach ethical decisions calmly, logically, and without haste.

Patient Education

Patients may not always understand the ethical standards to which physicians and medical assistants adhere. They may ask medical assistants questions about their own health or the health of a fellow patient. Medical assistants must educate patients about confidentiality in such a way that the patient does not take offense, explaining that all patients deserve to have their medical and personal information kept private. Now more than ever, ethical obligations for privacy, in addition to legal ones, are imperative. A medical assistant must be certain that all patients understand that they are entitled to confidential treatment of their records and that the facility is dedicated to that principle.

Legal and Ethical Issues

The prime objective of the medical profession is to render service to humanity, and this also must be a medical assistant's first concern.

The importance of respecting the confidentiality of information learned from or about patients in the course of employment cannot be overemphasized. It is unethical to reveal patient confidences to anyone, including family members, a spouse, best friends, and other medical assistants. Never mention patient names outside the place of employment; sometimes, the physician's specialty reveals the patient's reason for consultation.

Do not discuss one patient's case with another patient. If curious patients ask questions about others, simply explain that the staff is obligated to keep all patient information confidential. This can be done in a tactful and kind manner. Patients who ask questions of a medical nature about their case should be referred to the physician for information and instructions unless the physician has authorized the medical assistant to provide such information. A medical assistant should never give advice of a personal or professional nature to the patient, because patients tend to identify remarks made by any of the assistants as reflecting the advice of the physician. By avoiding these situations, medical assistants protect themselves, the physician, and the patient. Confidential papers, case histories, and even the appointment book should be kept out of sight from curious eyes.

SUMMARY OF SCENARIO

Pregnancy usually is a joyous time, but Monica has learned that even such an anticipated event can bring ethical issues to light. She has realized that every situation has two or more sides and that she must be open and willing to look at all sides when making an ethical decision.

Medical assisting is a rewarding career, but sometimes the decisions medical professionals face are quite difficult. Monica must learn to be nonjudgmental and not to inflict her opinions on her patients. They must make their own decisions about their health and emotional well-being, and the medical assistant should not influence their thinking unfairly.

Monica must continue to evaluate her own ideas and beliefs throughout her career as a medical assistant. Periodic self-evaluation is good for everyone, and she will grow emotionally from the experiences that patients bring about where ethical issues are concerned.

Patients who place their babies for adoption often feel the same type of grief experienced on the death of a loved one. Sometimes this loss does not register with the patient for many years after the event. Adoptive parents also face many fears, such as the concern that the adoptive mother will change her mind about the proceedings and want the child back. Some families find the adjustment to having an adopted child in the family a difficult one. Siblings may be less than accepting of the new child, and later in life other children may tease the adopted child. However, adoption is most often a positive event in the life of a family.

The medical assistant should be supportive of both the adoptive parents and the birth mother. Personal beliefs should be set aside, so that the patient and others involved are able to make the best decisions they can for their own lives.

SUMMARY OF LEARNING OBJECTIVES

1. **Define, spell, and pronounce the terms listed in the vocabulary.**
Spelling and pronouncing medical terms correctly bolster the medical assistant's credibility. Knowing the definition of these terms promotes confidence in communication with patients and co-workers.
2. **Differentiate between legal, ethical, and moral issues affecting healthcare.**
Legal issues are related to an actual law or a regulation that affects medical practice. Ethical issues are not as strict as laws and vary from person to person, but most physicians follow the ethical guidelines set forth by the AMA. Moral issues are related to a person's concept of right and wrong.

3. **Compare personal, professional, and organizational ethics.**
Personal ethics are those beliefs held by an individual. Professional ethics are those generally held by most people in a profession. Organizational ethics are closely related to professional ethics and are outlined by organizations as policy.
4. **Identify the effect personal ethics may have on professional performance.**
The medical assistant may hold personal ethical beliefs that contradict professional ethics. However, the medical assistant must agree to the ethical policies and procedures set forth by the employer and follow them in every situation. If the ethical policies and procedures differ greatly

from personal ethical beliefs, the medical assistant should look for employment opportunities that are more in line with those personal beliefs.

5. **Recognize the role of patient advocacy in the practice of medical assisting.**

   All medical professionals should be patient advocates, providing support as the patient makes decisions related to his or her health. Personal ethical opinions and beliefs cannot be forced upon patients or used to coerce the patient's decisions.

6. **Explain rights and duties as related to ethics.**

   Ethics are judgments of right and wrong or actions on issues that have implications of a moral right and wrong. *Etiquette* deals with courtesy, customs, and manners. A *duty* is an obligation that a person has or perceives himself or herself to have. *Rights* are claims made by a person or a group on society, a group, or an individual. Although these terms have different definitions, the concepts are interrelated, and often all are involved in ethical questions.

7. **List and define the four types of ethical problems.**

   Ethical distress is caused when a problem has an obvious solution but some type of barrier hinders the action that needs to be taken. An *ethical dilemma* is a situation that has two or more solutions, but if one is chosen, something of value is lost in not choosing the other. A *dilemma of justice* involves allocation of benefits and how they are to be distributed fairly. Two or more authority figures, each with his or her idea of how to handle a certain situation, are the center of the *locus of authority* ethical problem. Only one of the authority figures can prevail. Often an ethical problem has several aspects, and more than one type of problem is presented.

8. **Discuss the process used to make an ethical decision.**

   Making an ethical decision is easier when the situation is approached logically and considered using a five-step process. First, relevant information is gathered; then the type of problem is identified. After the ethical approach to use has been determined, alternatives are explored. Finally, all that is left is to complete the action and make the decision.

9. **Detail the impact of the American Medical Association's Council on Ethical and Judicial Affairs on the ethical decisions made by healthcare professionals.**

   Although healthcare professionals do not have to abide by the opinions of the CEJA, the council's opinions are highly regarded, and many professionals practice in accordance with these opinions. Often providers abide by the opinions to prevent controversy, but many still openly oppose the decisions of the CEJA.

10. **Discuss several of the CEJA's opinions and how they might differ from the views of the class as a whole.**

    The opinions put forth by the CEJA are just one group of opinions. Class members may share very differing views based on culture, experience, or serious consideration of the issues. Each individual is entitled to an opinion, and these opinions should be discussed and shared calmly and respectfully.

11. **Explore the role of confidentiality as it applies to the medical assistant.**

    Confidentiality is of major importance in the medical profession. The patient's privacy should be a prime concern of the medical assistant. It is a serious enough issue that a breach of patient confidentiality is sufficient reason for immediate termination of an employee. Because confidentiality is such a critical aspect of patient care, it is considered highly unethical to reveal any information about a patient to anyone else. All medical assistants are required and expected to uphold the confidentiality of the information with which they come in contact.

12. **Discuss the role of cultural, social, and ethnic diversity in ethical performance of medical assisting practice.**

    Our cultural, social, and ethical beliefs are all related to our personal views. When practicing their profession, medical assistants must set aside personal beliefs if they conflict with the patient's care, and the patient's cultural, social, and ethical beliefs must be honored.

13. **Describe the way unique identifiers can help patients infected with HIV avoid discrimination.**

    Unique identifiers maintain the confidentiality of patients who are tested for HIV. Some individuals might hesitate to be tested if they are concerned that their names would be reported to various agencies. If unique identifiers are used, patients may have much more confidence that the chances of discrimination because of HIV status are reduced.

14. **Note some of the concerns about ethics that apply to genetic information.**

    Many ethical concerns apply to genetic testing. Many patients are concerned about how the information gained will be used and who will have access to it. Questions arise about the ownership of the information. When negative information is found, other ethical problems arise that must be addressed. Knowledge of a person's genetic blueprint could lead to discrimination. Countless issues must be examined before the use of genetic information becomes widespread.

CONNECTIONS

Study Guide Connection: Go to the Chapter 6 Study Guide. Read and complete the activities.

Evolve Connection: Go to the Chapter 6 link at *evolve.elsevier.com/ kinn* to complete the Chapter Review and Chapter Quiz. Check out the other resources listed for this chapter to make the most of what you have learned from Medicine and Ethics.

Barbara Johnson is the new office manager for two neurologists in an urban area. Recently she was subpoenaed to appear in court with medical records to testify about a patient. This particular patient was referred to one of the physicians in the clinic, Dr. Rebecca Patrick. Dr. Patrick saw the patient several years ago, and the patient has brought a medical professional liability case against a surgeon in another city. Barbara is considered the custodian of medical records and will take them to court and answer questions about the information in them.

One of Barbara's first priorities at her new job is to make sure the office is operating in compliance with the legal regulations that affect the facility. She is knowledgeable about the requirements of the Occupational Safety and Health Administration (OSHA), as well as other legal issues. She is familiar with legal issues and has testified as a custodian of records several times during her tenure as an office manager.

Two of the employees Barbara supervises, Samantha and Lynda, are newly graduated from medical assisting school and are anxious to learn more about the statutes and laws that affect the physicians' office. Barbara is more than happy to share what she has learned with them. She is excited about her new job and eager to be a great success.

While studying this chapter, think about the following questions:

- How can the medical assistant help the staff comply with legal regulations in the medical office?
- How can new graduates learn about the laws that affect them in their state?
- What are some ways medical professional liability suits can be prevented?
- What should the medical assistant do if the employer is not in compliance with legal regulations?

LEARNING OBJECTIVES

1. Define, spell, and pronounce the terms listed in the vocabulary.
2. Discuss all levels of government legislation and regulation as they apply to medical assisting practice, including regulations established by the U.S. Food and Drug Administration (FDA) and the federal Drug Enforcement Administration (DEA).
3. Discuss the legal scope of practice for medical assistants.
4. Distinguish among an act, a statute, and an ordinance.
5. Compare criminal and civil law as they apply to the practicing medical assistant.
6. Explain the three basic categories of criminal law.
7. Distinguish which type of civil law deals with medical professional liability.
8. Provide an example of tort law as it would apply to a medical assistant.
9. Describe liability, professional and personal injury, and third-party insurance.
10. Explain the four essential elements of a valid contract.
11. Distinguish between interrogatories and depositions.
12. List three things to remember when testifying in court.
13. Discuss the advantages of arbitration.
14. Differentiate among malfeasance, misfeasance, and nonfeasance.
15. Explain the "four Ds" of negligence.
16. Define the types of damages.
17. Compare and contrast physician and medical assistant roles in terms of standard of care.
18. Explain the importance of informed consent.
19. List several legal disclosures the physician must make.
20. Identify where to report illegal and/or unsafe activities and behaviors that affect the health, safety, and welfare of others.
21. Explain how the medical assistant's practice is affected by negligence, malpractice, statutes of limitation, Good Samaritan laws, the Uniform Anatomical Gift Act, Living Wills/Advanced Directives, and the Medical Durable Power of Attorney.
22. Summarize the Patient's Bill of Rights.
23. Describe the implications of the Health Insurance Portability and Accountability Act (HIPAA) for the medical assistant in various medical settings.
24. Describe personal protective equipment.
25. Discuss requirements for responding to hazardous materials disposal.
26. Describe the importance of Material Safety Data Sheets (MSDS) in a healthcare setting.
27. Distinguish between the OSHA and CLIA; indicate which one is an actual agency.
28. Identify how the Americans with Disabilities Act (ADA) applies to the medical assisting profession.

VOCABULARY

abandonment To withdraw protection or support; in medicine, to discontinue medical care without proper notice after accepting a patient.

act The formal action of a legislative body; a decision or determination of a sovereign state, a legislative council, or a court of justice.

allegation (a-li-ga′-shun) A statement by a party to a legal action of what the party undertakes to prove; an assertion made without proof.

appeal A legal proceeding by which a case is brought before a higher court for review of the decision of a lower court.

appellate (uh-pe′-lut) Having the power to review the judgment of another tribunal or body of jurisdiction, such as an appellate court.

arbitration (ar-buh-tra′-shun) The hearing and determination of a cause in controversy by a person or persons either chosen by the parties involved or appointed under statutory authority.

arbitrator (ar-buh-tra′-ter) A neutral person chosen to settle differences between two parties in a controversy.

assault An intentional, unlawful attempt of bodily injury to another by force.

assent To agree to something, especially after thoughtful consideration.

bailiff An officer of some U.S. courts who usually serves as a messenger or usher and who keeps order at the request of the judge.

battery A willful and unlawful use of force or violence on the person of another.

Code of Federal Regulations (CFR) A coded delineation of the rules and regulations published in the Federal Register by the various departments and agencies of the federal government. The CFR is divided into 50 titles that represent broad subject areas and chapters that provide specific detail.

concurrently Occurring at the same time.

contributory negligence Statutes in some states that may prevent a party from recovering some damages if he or she contributed in any way to the injury or condition.

damages Loss or harm resulting from injury to person, property, or reputation; compensation in money imposed by law for losses or injuries.

decedent (di-se′-dent) A legal term for a deceased person.

defendant A person required to answer in a legal action or suit; in criminal cases, the person accused of a crime.

docket A formal record of judicial proceedings; a list of legal cases to be tried.

due process A fundamental constitutional guarantee that all legal proceedings will be fair; that one will be given notice of the proceedings and an opportunity to be heard before the government acts to take away life, liberty, or property; a constitutional guarantee that a law will not be unreasonable or arbitrary.

emancipated minor A person under legal age who is self-supporting and living apart from parents or a guardian; a mature minor considered by the courts to possess a sufficient understanding of self-care and responsibility.

expert witnesses People who provide testimony to a court as experts in certain fields or subjects to verify facts presented by one or both sides in a lawsuit, often compensated and used to refute or disprove the claims of one party.

felony A major crime, such as murder, rape, or burglary; punishable by a more stringent sentence than that given for a misdemeanor.

fine A sum imposed as punishment for an offense; a forfeiture or penalty paid to an injured party or the government in a civil or criminal action.

guardian ad litem Legal representative for a minor.

implied consent Presumed consent, such as when a patient offers an arm for a phlebotomy procedure.

implied contract A legally enforceable agreement that arises from conduct, from assumed intentions, from some relationship among the immediate parties, or from the application of the legal principle of equity.

informed consent A consent, usually written, which states understanding of what treatment is to be undertaken and of the risks involved, why it should be done, and alternative methods of treatment available (including no treatment) and their attendant risks.

infractions (in-frak′-shuns) Breaking the law; minor offenses against the rules, usually punishable by fines.

judicial (ju-di′-shuhl) Of or relating to a judgment, the function of judging, the administration of justice, or the judiciary.

jurisdiction (jur-uhs-dik′-shun) A power constitutionally conferred on a judge or magistrate to decide cases according to law and to carry sentence into execution; jurisdiction is original when it is conferred on the court in the first instance, called original jurisdiction; or it is appellate when an appeal is given from the judgment of another court.

jurisprudence (jur-uhs-proo′-dens) The science or philosophy of law; a system or body of law or the course of court decisions.

law A binding custom or practice of a community; a rule of conduct or action prescribed or formally recognized as binding or enforceable by a controlling authority.

liable (li′-uh-buhl) Obligated according to law or equity; responsible for an act or circumstance.

libel A written defamatory statement or representation that conveys an unjustly unfavorable impression.

litigious (luh-ti′-juhs) Prone to engage in lawsuits.

manifestation (ma-nuh-fuh-sta′-shun) Something that is easily understood or recognized by the mind.

misdemeanor (mis-duh-me′-nuhr) A minor crime, as opposed to a felony, punishable by fine or imprisonment in a city or county jail rather than in a penitentiary.

municipal (myu-ni′-suh-puhl) **courts** Courts that sit in some cities and larger towns and that usually have civil and criminal jurisdiction over cases arising within the municipality.

negligence (ne′-gli-jents) Failure to exercise the care a prudent person usually exercises; implies inattention to one's duty or business; implies want of due or necessary diligence or care.

ordinance (or'-di-nens) Authoritative decree or direction; law set forth by a governmental authority, specifically, municipal regulation.

other potentially infectious materials (OPIM) Substances or materials other than blood that have the potential to carry infectious pathogens, such as body fluid, urine, semen, and others.

perjured testimony The voluntary violation of an oath or vow either by swearing to what is untrue or by omission to do what has been promised under oath; false testimony.

physician office laboratories (POLs) Laboratories owned by a private physician or corporation, such as the laboratory inside a physician's office or a freestanding laboratory.

plaintiff The person or group bringing a case or legal action to court.

precedence (pre-sed'-ens) To surpass in rank, dignity, or importance; to be, go, or come ahead or in front of.

precedents (pre'-suh-dens) A person or thing that serves as a model; something done or said that may serve as an example or rule to authorize or justify a subsequent act of the same kind.

preponderance of the evidence Evidence of greater weight or more convincing than the evidence offered in opposition to it; evidence that as a whole shows that the fact sought to be proven is more probable than not.

prudent Marked by wisdom or judiciousness; shrewd in the management of practical affairs.

reasonable doubt Doubt based on reason and arising from evidence or lack of evidence; it is not doubt that is imagined or conjured up, but doubt that would cause reasonable persons to hesitate before acting.

reciprocity The mutual exchange of privileges; a recognition of one state or institution of the licenses or privileges granted by the other.

recourse A turning to something or someone for help or protection.

relevant Having significant and demonstrable bearing on the matter at hand.

respondent (ri-spahn'-dunt) The person required to make answer in a civil legal action or suit; similar to a defendant in a criminal trial.

slander Oral defamation; a harmful, false statement made about another person.

statutes (sta-choots) Laws enacted by the legislative branch of a government.

stipulate To specify as a condition or requirement of an agreement or offer; to make an agreement or covenant to do or forbear from doing something.

subpoena (suh-pe'-nuh) A writ or document commanding a person to appear in court under a penalty for failure to appear.

subpoena duces tecum A legally binding request to appear in court and provide records or documents that pertain to a particular case.

testimony A solemn declaration usually made orally by a witness under oath in response to interrogation by a lawyer or authorized public official.

Uniform Commercial Code (UCC) A unified set of rules covering many business transactions; it has been adopted in all 50 states, the District of Columbia, and most U.S. territories. It regulates the fields of sales of goods; commercial paper, such as checks; secured transactions in personal property; and particular aspects of banking, letters of credit, warehouse receipts, bills of lading, and investment securities.

verdict The finding or decision of a jury on a matter submitted to it in trial.

The **law** is a fascinating subject. When law is applied to medicine, it can provoke interesting case studies and complex decisions. In today's **litigious** society, medical assistants, in addition to physicians and other staff members, must take steps to protect themselves from lawsuits. Legal issues underlie many aspects of the provision of healthcare in a physician's office. Although the wording of **statutes** and regulations often is long and complicated, medical assistants must stay abreast of the rules governing medical facilities and do everything possible to remain in compliance with the standards and regulations for all organizations that oversee the medical industry.

Generally, the law holds that every person is **liable** for the consequences of his or her own **negligence** when another person is injured as a result. In some situations, this liability also extends to the employer. Physicians may be held responsible for the mistakes of those who work in their healthcare facility, and sometimes they must pay **damages** for the negligent acts of their employees.

Under the doctrine of *respondeat superior,* physicians are legally responsible for the acts of their employees when the employees are acting within the scope of their duties or employment. Physicians are also responsible for the acts of assistants who are not their own employees if the assistant commits acts of negligence in the presence of the physician while under the physician's immediate supervision. *Respondeat superior* is a Latin term meaning "let the master answer." When physicians practice as partners, they are liable not only for their own acts and those of their partners, but also for the negligent acts of any agent or employee of the partnership. A medical assistant acting within the scope of the employment contract is considered an agent of the employer.

Medical assistants guilty of negligence are liable for their own actions, but the injured party generally sues the physician, because the chance of collecting damages is greater. However, even an assistant who has no money can be liable for any negligent action. This fact illustrates the continuing importance of exercising extreme care in performing all duties in the professional office and maintaining liability coverage once employed in the healthcare industry.

JURISPRUDENCE AND THE CLASSIFICATIONS OF LAW

Jurisprudence, the science and philosophy of law, comes from the Latin words *juris,* which means "law, right, equity, or justice," and *prudentia,* which means "skill or good judgment."

Law is a custom or practice of a community. It is a rule of conduct or action prescribed or formally recognized as binding or enforceable by a controlling authority. Law is the system by which society gives order to our lives. The U.S. Constitution is the supreme law of the United States; it takes **precedence** over federal statutes, court opinions, and state constitutions. The state constitution is the supreme law within the boundaries of each state unless it conflicts with the U.S. Constitution. States cannot pass laws that conflict with the U.S. Constitution, nor can local governments pass laws that conflict with the state constitution.

A law enacted at the federal level, which must be passed by Congress, is called an **act**. *Statutes* are laws that have been enacted by state legislatures. Local governments create and enact **ordinances**. Much of our law is based on previous **judicial** and jury decisions, which are called **precedents**. Often judges and juries follow precedents when making a decision on a case. The two basic categories of jurisprudence are criminal law and civil law.

Criminal Law

Criminal law governs violations of the law punishable as offenses against the state or the federal government. Such offenses involve the welfare and safety of the public as a whole rather than of one individual. Criminal offenses are classified into three basic categories: misdemeanors, felonies, and treason. To ensure fair treatment under the law, all physicians are entitled to **due process**, which guarantees that the accused will have an opportunity to defend himself or herself against any charges brought in opposition. Several crimes can be committed **concurrently**, such as a criminal who robs and assaults a convenience store clerk or a man who commits rape and murder.

Misdemeanors

A minor crime is called a **misdemeanor**. Such a crime is punishable by **fine** or imprisonment in a city or county jail rather than in a penitentiary. Misdemeanors vary from state to state and often are divided into subgroups or classes, such as class A, class B, or class C misdemeanors. In most states the subgroups are divided from most serious offenses to lesser offenses. Some states have created a subcategory of misdemeanors for **infractions**, which often are called *violations*. Infractions are minor offenses, such as traffic tickets, which are punishable only by a fine.

Felonies

A **felony** is a major crime, such as murder, rape, or burglary. It is punishable by a more stringent sentence than for misdemeanors. Federal law and most state statutes classify felonies as crimes punishable by imprisonment for more than 1 year, whereas misdemeanors are punishable by imprisonment for 1 year or less. Usually a convicted felon cannot vote, hold public office, or own a firearm. Felonies often are divided into subgroups or degrees, such as first degree, second degree, and third degree. A first-degree offense is normally the most serious.

Treason

Treason, the most serious crime, is the offense of attempting to overthrow the government. High treason constitutes a serious threat to the stability or continuity of the government, such as an attempt to kill the president. The president of the United States has the right to declare an action against the United States an act of war rather than an act of treason, which is considered a crime. For instance, although the terrorist attacks of September 11, 2001, were certainly a threat against the United States, they were declared acts of war.

Civil Law

Civil law is concerned with acts that are not criminal in nature but involve relationships of individuals with other individuals, organizations, or government agencies. Many types of civil law address numerous issues. The three that most directly affect the medical profession include tort law, contract law, and administrative law.

Tort Law

Tort law provides a remedy for a person or group that has been harmed by the wrongful acts of others. Four elements must be established in every tort action: (1) the **plaintiff** must establish that the **respondent** or **defendant** was under a legal duty to act in a particular fashion; (2) the plaintiff must demonstrate that the defendant breached this duty by failing to conform his or her behavior accordingly; (3) the plaintiff must prove that the breach of the legal duty proximately caused some injury or damage; and (4) the plaintiff must prove *damages*, the injury or loss suffered. Medical professional liability, or medical malpractice, falls into the category of tort law. **Libel** and **slander** are common complaints that fall into the category of tort law. When a person is liable for an act, he or she is obligated or responsible according to the law. Professional and personal injuries are types of torts, meaning that a person or group has injured someone or something else. Physicians carry professional liability insurance, a type of third-party insurance, to help guard them from liability costs. Medical assistants can also invest in liability insurance. Remember, "libel" and "liable" are defined differently although they sound the same. Refer to the vocabulary list for clarification.

Contract Law

A contract is an agreement that creates an obligation. Contract law touches our lives in many ways practically every day, but we usually do not give much thought to its influences. If a person parks a car in a parking garage for a monthly fee and signs a contract for a year, then begins parking elsewhere and refuses to pay the fee, the person may be liable for the fees for the duration of the entire contract. If the person's vehicle is damaged while parked in the garage, the garage may be responsible for reimbursement, if the contract does not **stipulate** otherwise. A contract does not have to be formalized in writing to be binding on the parties involved. Oral contracts also are valid in many states in most situations. The **Uniform Commercial Code (UCC)** is a long, elaborate act that attempts to harmonize the law of sales and other commercial transactions in all 50 states. This code directly affects contract law.

Administrative Law

Administrative law involves regulations set forth by governmental agencies. For example, the Internal Revenue Service (IRS) has thousands of regulations and codes, and the typical American does not understand all of them, which may result in errors when filing taxes. The laws that allow the IRS to collect taxes and pursue restitution are administrative laws. Other agencies that are involved with administrative law are the Social Security Administration (SSA),

Citizenship and Immigration Services (USCIS), and the Centers for Medicare and Medicaid Services (CMS).

ANATOMY OF A MEDICAL PROFESSIONAL LIABILITY LAWSUIT

A medical liability case often stems from a breach of trust or miscommunication between the physician and the patient. These cases fall into the category of tort law. Even when the physician has made an error, often the level of trust between the physician and patient determines whether a lawsuit is pursued. First, the physician-patient relationship must be formed. Before this relationship can be discussed, the requirements for a valid, enforceable contract must be understood.

What Constitutes a Valid Contract?

A valid legal contract has four essential elements. First, a **manifestation** of **assent** or "meeting of the minds" must exist. This element is proven by an "offer" and the "acceptance" of that offer. The parties to the contract must understand and agree on the intent of the contract. Second, the contract must involve legal subject matter. An obligation that requires an illegal action, such as a gambling contract, is not an enforceable contract. Third, both parties must have the legal capacity to enter into a contract. This means that each party must be an adult of sound mind or an emancipated minor. Fourth, some type of consideration must be involved. Consideration is an exchange of something of value (e.g., money) for the physician's time.

> ### CRITICAL THINKING APPLICATION   7-1
> Barbara works for Dr. Rebecca Patrick, who saw the patient bringing the lawsuit against the surgeon as a referral patient. Does Dr. Patrick have a contract with the patient, based on a physician-patient relationship? Why or why not?

The physician-patient relationship is generally held by courts to be a contractual relationship that is the result of three steps:
- The physician invites an offer by establishing his availability (e.g., posting office hours or making himself available during office hours).
- The patient accepts the appointment and makes an offer by arriving for or requesting treatment.
- The physician accepts the patient's offer by examining the patient and beginning treatment. Physicians also accept the offer by exercising independent medical judgment on behalf of the patient.

Before accepting a patient, the physician is under no obligation, and no contract exists. However, once the physician has accepted the patient, an **implied contract** exists (Figure 7-1). An implied contract in this case assumes that the physician will treat the patient using reasonable care and that the physician has a degree of knowledge, skill, and judgment that might be expected of any other physician in the same locality and under similar circumstances. It is extremely important that no express promise of a cure be made by anyone in the office, including the physician, because this would become a part of the contract.

FIGURE 7-1 The physician-patient relationship is built on a strong foundation of trust, but it also is a contractual relationship.

The patient's responsibility in this agreement includes the liability of payment for services and a willingness to follow the advice of the physician. Most physician-patient contracts are implied contracts. Although many forms may be completed by the patient before he or she is accepted by the physician, they do not in most cases constitute a formal contract for each specific visit to the physician.

> ### CRITICAL THINKING APPLICATION   7-2
> - If the patient does not pay for the services rendered by the physician, does this negate the physician-patient contract?
> - How might Barbara, Samantha, and Lynda ensure that patients understand that they are expected to follow the advice of the physician?

After the physician-patient relationship has been established, the physician is obligated to attend the patient as long as attention is required, unless the physician or patient terminates the contract. When a physician terminates the contract, the patient must be given notice of the physician's intentions so that the patient has sufficient time to secure another physician. The physician may write a letter of withdrawal from medical care of the patient, and it should be delivered by certified mail, return receipt requested. A copy of the letter and the return receipt should be attached to the patient's chart and permanently retained. Reasonable time should be allowed for the patient to secure other medical care.

To protect the physician against a lawsuit for **abandonment**, the details of the circumstances under which the physician is withdrawing from the case should be included in the patient's medical chart. The letter of withdrawal does not have to specify a reason for withdrawal unless the physician so chooses. However, some physicians include a brief reason in the letter, such as missing appointments or failing to comply with treatment orders. In either case, the letter should state the following:
- That professional care is being discontinued
- That the physician will provide copies of the patient's records to another physician on request
- That the patient should seek the attention of another physician as soon as possible

A patient who wants to terminate the physician-patient relationship simply no longer seeks the physician for treatment. The patient does not have to inform the office; however, if this is done, the office manager or physician should follow up with a confirmation letter, stating that the patient has ended the relationship.

Breach of Contract

An unjustifiable failure to perform all or some part of a contractual duty is a breach of contract. For example, if a surgeon prepares a surgery estimate and says that the fee will be no more than $6,500, but then charges the patient $7,200, a breach of contract exists. Although most physicians state that the document is just an estimate, this particular physician stated a clear amount that the surgery costs would not exceed.

The Statute of Frauds

In 1677 a statute was adopted in England to reduce the occurrence of **perjured testimony**. It provided that certain contracts could not be enforced if they depended on the **testimony** of witnesses alone and were not evidenced in writing. The provisions of this English statute have been closely followed by statutes adopted in all 50 states in the United States.

A promise to pay the debts of another person is an example of a contract that usually must be made in writing. If a third party who is not otherwise legally responsible for a patient's medical bills agrees to pay them, the agreement cannot be enforced unless it is in writing. If a physician were to enter into an agreement to perform a series of treatments for a given sum and this series covered a time span of more than 1 year, the contract would have to be in writing to be enforceable.

> ### CRITICAL THINKING APPLICATION 7-3
> - For what reasons might a physician not want to accept a patient?
> - Must the physician treat every patient who attempts to make an appointment?
> - How might Barbara tactfully explain that the physician will not accept the patient into treatment?

Preliminaries of Litigation

Lawsuits are filed in a variety of different courts, and different states have different types of courts at various levels. The state judiciary has several branches. At the local level are usually **municipal courts**. These are courts in a city or town that usually deal with ordinance violations. Municipal judges may issue search and arrest warrants. Some states also have justice of the peace courts, which have **jurisdiction** over many misdemeanors and some civil matters, in addition to concurrent jurisdiction over some matters along with the municipal courts. The judges that preside over justice of the peace courts may also issue search and arrest warrants. They often function as small claims courts, with which the medical assistant may have contact in cases of patients who do not pay their bills. Both municipal and justice of the peace courts are local trial courts with limited jurisdiction.

County courts are higher than municipal and justice of the peace courts. These courts handle misdemeanors and civil matters up to a certain monetary limit. District courts have unlimited jurisdiction in criminal and civil matters. They are the highest state courts, other than **appellate** courts. If one party to a lawsuit is dissatisfied with a lower court's decision, it has the right to **appeal** to a higher court

for review and possible reversal of the decision. Most states have an appellate court for both criminal and civil matters. The U.S. District Court handles federal matters of a criminal or a civil nature. States also have Supreme Courts that handle a limited number of appellate cases.

Under Article III, Section One of the U.S. Constitution, the U.S. Supreme Court has the authority to ensure equal justice under the law (Figure 7-2). The Supreme Court interprets and guards the Constitution. The court's one chief justice and eight associate justices are appointed by the president and confirmed by Congress. Approximately 8,000 cases are on the **docket** per term, which runs from the first Monday in October to the first Monday in October of the next year. Only 80 to 90 cases are chosen each year for full oral argument in front of the justices.

> ### CRITICAL THINKING APPLICATION 7-4
> Samantha and Lynda are curious as to how Supreme Court's decisions affect the individual physician's office. What Supreme Court decisions have affected the medical profession?

Preparing for Court

Medical professional liability suits are far from rare, and every physician faces the probability of being sued at least once during his or her career. When a suit is filed, preparation for court should start expeditiously. A medical assistant may be involved in preparing materials for court and scheduling or participating in depositions. The best advice for a medical assistant in this position is to remember to tell the truth. Attorneys help prepare the defense of the physician and the staff, but everyone should be truthful in answering in court to prevent the loss of his or her credibility in the trial and charges of perjury. Be especially careful to present a true, complete statement to the representing attorney. Unless he or she knows the whole truth, an appropriate defense cannot be prepared.

Interrogatories

Before the trial, the physician may be asked to complete an interrogatory, which is a list of questions from each party to the other in the lawsuit. Answers to the interrogatory must be provided within

FIGURE 7-2 The U.S. Supreme Court. The Supreme Court decides cases that involve interpretation of the Constitution of the United States.

a specified time, and the answers are considered to be given under oath. Only the parties named in the lawsuit may be questioned through interrogatories.

Depositions

A deposition is testimony taken from a party or witness to the litigation and is not limited to the parties named in the lawsuit. A witness who is not a party to the lawsuit may be summoned by **subpoena** for the deposition. The deposition usually is taken in an attorney's office in the presence of a court reporter and is taken under oath. The person giving the deposition is called the *deponent*. The transcribed deposition, once finished, is sent to the deponent for review, and the deponent is at liberty to request any necessary changes or corrections in the document.

CRITICAL THINKING APPLICATION   **7-5**

■ Samantha and Lynda are anxious to hear about Barbara's previous experiences in testifying in court. She mentions that attorneys often advise witnesses to "answer the question, then be quiet." What might be meant by this advice?

■ Discuss the phrase, "the truth, the whole truth, and nothing but the truth."

Subpoenas

A subpoena is a document issued by a court that requires a person to be in court at a specific time and place to testify as a witness in a lawsuit, either in a court proceeding or in a deposition. A **subpoena duces tecum** is a legally binding request to provide records or documents to appear in court and usually is issued to the person considered the custodian of the records. This may be the medical assistant or office manager. A fee may be demanded for the time spent in compiling the records and for photocopying charges, but this fee must be requested at the time the subpoena duces tecum is served, or it is considered to be waived. Physician approval must be obtained to release or to copy any patient records. Original records should never be released under any circumstances. If an original record is demanded in the subpoena, it usually is taken to court or to mediation by the physician or an employee of the physician's office. Copies can be released in advance of the court date. Release only the information requested in the subpoena and provide only information that originated in the physician's office. Do not provide records sent from previous or consulting physicians. Those records must be subpoenaed separately from the originating office.

Before responding to a subpoena, make sure it is valid. Although variances may occur from state to state, some general rules can be used to judge the validity of a subpoena:

- A subpoena issued in one state court generally is not valid in another state. Always verify the state in which the subpoena was issued.
- A subpoena issued by a federal court in one state generally is not valid in another state unless a federal statute authorizes nationwide service of process.
- Any duly authorized law officer may execute a valid subpoena anywhere in the same state. The officer notifies the issuing court once the subpoena has been served.

- Generally, the person or entity subpoenaed has 21 days to respond, but this period can differ from place to place.
- A subpoena duces tecum should be filed no less than 15 days before a trial. One served less than 15 days before a trial should not be honored.

Read the subpoena carefully to determine exactly what records are requested. The physician should always be notified of subpoenas served to the medical facility. Never copy records required in a subpoena without bringing the matter to the attention of the physician or office manager, or both. It also is advisable to keep a log of subpoenas served to the office, what records were involved, and the disposition of the request, including when the records were presented to the court. Always inform the physician about the subpoena, because he or she may want to present the document to an attorney for review before any information is released.

Discovery

Discovery is the pretrial disclosure of pertinent facts or documents by one or both parties to a legal action or proceeding. Many states have extensive discovery statutes that require each side to reveal to the other the facts that they "discover" while investigating the case. Discovery is also considered the process of uncovering facts in a lawsuit before the court proceedings.

Presentation of evidence may be done by testimony. A witness is called who has some information about an aspect of the case and is asked questions by one or both attorneys. The witness does not know about every part of the case, but something the person knows is **relevant**.

Another type of evidence may be documentary evidence. This is any type of evidence brought before the court by document or display. It could be a patient's chart, a letter, a laboratory result, or a photograph. All of these are usually entered into evidence and numbered for easy reference.

CRITICAL THINKING APPLICATION   **7-6**

Samantha wonders what she should do if she ever finds information during a medical professional malpractice case that might harm her employer's defense. What advice would you offer? Would it be considered an obligation or a choice to report the employer for wrongdoing?

Preparing Witnesses and Testifying

Attorneys prepare witnesses who may be called to testify during the court proceedings. They review the questions that will be asked and potential questions the opposite side may present. The attorney helps the witness to clarify the answers he or she gives so that they are sharp and succinct. One of the first rules law students learn is never to ask a question to which they do not already know the answer.

Witnesses should always be on time for a court appearance, because the judge and jury may frown on those who appear late; and that frown may include a fine or confinement in jail for contempt of court! It is critical that witnesses dress conservatively and in a manner that shows respect for the court. If any documents are to be referenced while testifying, the witness should review the documents before the court appearance if possible, so that the needed information is easy to locate and discuss. The witness should speak clearly and at a volume audible to the attorneys and parties to the suit, the judge, the jury, and the court reporter. The witness should always answer each question aloud, because the court reporter must record those answers and cannot specify that the witness "nodded yes" as a response to a question.

If a question is confusing, the witness should ask the attorney to restate or repeat it. If the witness does not know the answer to a question or does not recall, that should be stated clearly and confidently. Above all, the parties involved are expected to tell the truth and must be seen as credible witnesses (Figure 7-3). Lying under oath constitutes perjury, which carries stiff penalties. Listening is as important as speaking; therefore the witness should be sure to listen to the question and answer it, elaborating only if the attorney asks for more details.

If an attorney lodges an objection to a question, the witness should be silent until the judge rules on the objection. The objection may be sustained or overruled. Sustaining the objection means that the judge agrees with the objection and will not allow the question stated in that manner. If the judge allows the question, he or she will overrule the objection. Then the witness will be allowed to answer. The witness should never display a combative or hostile attitude and should not make sarcastic remarks while testifying in court. The witness should be professional at all times and restrain inappropriate comments and belligerent behavior. Using "yes, sir" and "no, ma'am" is appropriate in the courtroom. Always address the judge as "Your Honor."

Inside the Courtroom

Today's courtrooms are a far cry from the ones depicted on television shows representing the Old West. Modern courtrooms are equipped with computer and video equipment, and elaborate security systems often monitor those entering the building. The advent of truTV has changed the way Americans see the justice system. By simply turning on our televisions, we can watch justice at work.

Knowing the role of each person in a court of law can be helpful. The person or body bringing the lawsuit to court is referred to by different terms, depending on the type of case. In a criminal court, the government brings the case and is represented by a prosecutor. For example, in criminal cases, legal documents read, *The State of Texas v. Robert Smith*. In this case, the fictitious Robert Smith is the defendant. In civil court, the person or group bringing the case to court is called the *plaintiff* (or *complainant* in some court systems), and the opposite party is called the *defendant* or *respondent*. A judge presides over the case, giving instructions concerning the law to the jury, if a jury is present. If no jury is present, the judge decides the case; this is called a *bench trial*. A witness is a person who knows some pertinent information about the case and gives testimony. Often a court reporter takes notes of the proceedings, and a **bailiff** may be present, who assists in keeping order. All of these individuals should be treated with respect and courtesy.

Burden of Proof

In a criminal case the burden of proof is on the prosecution, which must prove guilt beyond any **reasonable doubt**. Reasonable doubt is defined as the level of certainty a juror must have to find a defendant guilty of a crime. It is real doubt, based on reason and common sense after careful and impartial consideration of all the evidence, or lack of evidence, in a case.

Civil cases must be proven by a **preponderance of the evidence**. This means that the greater weight of evidence must point to the defendant or respondent as being responsible for the act involved in the case.

To understand the difference between reasonable doubt and preponderance of the evidence, think of the scales of justice (Figure 7-4). For a case to be proven beyond a reasonable doubt, the scales should tip heavily toward either guilt or innocence. However, for a case to be proven by preponderance of the evidence, the scales need tip only slightly one way or the other.

FIGURE 7-3 Witnesses must be credible and must tell the truth on the stand in court to avoid charges of perjury.

FIGURE 7-4 Lady Justice. Justitia was the Roman goddess of justice and is the figure depicted in statues across the world, often holding both scales and a sword. Her scales imply the weighing of justice, and the blindfold represents the impartiality of justice.

To illustrate the difference in the burden of proof in criminal and civil cases, consider *The People of the State of California v. Orenthal James Simpson*. In O.J. Simpson's criminal trial, much circumstantial evidence was presented; however, enough doubt also existed that the scales could not tip heavily toward a **verdict** of guilty, and Mr. Simpson was acquitted. In the civil trial brought by family members of Nicole Brown Simpson and Ron Goldman after the criminal trial had ended, just enough evidence existed to tip the scales in favor of the families' claim that Mr. Simpson was somehow responsible for the deaths of the two victims. This is the equivalent of a preponderance of the evidence.

CRITICAL THINKING APPLICATION   7-7

A discussion of the burden of proof prompts Barbara, Samantha, and Lynda to discuss the case of O.J. Simpson. Discuss whether reasonable doubt existed in his criminal trial.

Outcome of the Case

Once both sides have presented their case to the judge or jury, they usually are given the opportunity to present a final summation of their case. The jury then retires to consider the verdict. This can take minutes, hours, days, or weeks. After the jury reaches a decision, the judge may enter it as a final verdict or may disregard it if the evidence does not support the jury's decision. The judge may also revise the verdict to comply with statutes, such as statutory limits on the amount of punitive damages. The final decision of the trial court is reflected in the judgment, signed by the judge.

Either side normally has the right to appeal the decision to a higher court. However, not all appellate courts are required to hear all cases. For instance, the U.S. Supreme Court chooses the cases it hears each year, and it is restricted to cases that involve interpretation of the Constitution and how that interpretation affects the people it governs.

In criminal cases, if the defendant is found guilty of the crime, a sentencing date is set, usually a few weeks to a few months after the verdict is announced. At this time the punishment is announced.

ARBITRATION

Arbitration is an alternative to trial in which a third party is chosen to hear evidence and make a decision because of the individual's familiarity with or knowledge of the law or the issues involved. Arbitration is common in modern business life. It is recognized by statute in most states and usually is available to the medical profession, offering an alternative for resolving legal disputes between physician and patient. Many physicians and attorneys see arbitration as one way to solve the crisis of litigation in this country. Court battles can take years and can be extremely expensive, and much of the money reverts to the attorneys rather than the victors in the lawsuit.

In arbitration, the patient and the physician agree to submit the dispute to an **arbitrator** in an informal hearing. The arbitrator renders a legally binding decision based on very specific rules of arbitration. Arbitration applies essentially the same rights and the same measure of damages as a court. It is fair, less expensive, faster, and more confidential than court litigation.

The staff of each medical office should know whether arbitration statutes exist in the state where the office conducts business. The state medical board or local medical society should be able to provide this information. An arbitration agreement is a contract and is subject to the judgment of the courts only as to the fairness of the agreement. The agreement is precisely worded by an attorney and should not be paraphrased when explained to a patient. Signing the agreement is a voluntary act by the patient, who has a grace period in which to revoke the agreement if he or she later decides against it. Likewise, a physician always has the option to decide not to care for a patient but must formally notify a patient if the decision is made to no longer render care.

If a physician elects to implement an arbitration agreement procedure with patients, every member of the physician's staff should know the details of the agreement, how and when the patient should sign up, and how to answer the patient's questions. The way the program is presented to the patient and the office staff's willingness to answer the patient's questions play a large part in whether courts uphold the arbitration agreement as fair and legal.

The patient and the physician both have the opportunity to agree on who will arbitrate the case, so that one side is not favored over the other. By prior agreement, the arbitrator (or arbitrators) may be appointed by or from the American Arbitration Association, which is a neutral, private, nonprofit association dedicated to the advancement of out of court remedies. Its panels of arbitrators are made up of people from business, the professions, and public interest groups.

MEDICAL PROFESSIONAL LIABILITY AND NEGLIGENCE

When a patient is injured as a result of a physician's negligence, the patient may initiate a malpractice lawsuit to recover financial damages. However, experience has shown that the incidence of malpractice claims is directly related to the personal relationship and trust that exist between the physician and the patient. Deterioration of the physician-patient relationship is a common reason patients sue physicians for malpractice, even when the patient has sustained no real injury.

Medical professional liability, commonly called *medical malpractice,* is governed by the law of torts. The term *medical professional liability* encompasses all possible civil liability that can be incurred during the delivery of medical care. Medical professional liability is much more easily prevented than defended.

To understand medical malpractice, the term *negligence* first must be understood. Negligence, in general, implies inattention to one's duty or business, or the implication of a lack of necessary diligence or care. In medicine, negligence is defined as the performance of an act that a reasonable and **prudent** physician would not do or the failure to do an act that a reasonable and prudent physician would do. This, of course, also applies to any other healthcare professional. The standard of prudent care and conduct is not defined by law but is left to the determination of a judge or jury, usually with the help of **expert witnesses**. Expert witnesses are members of the profession involved—in this case, medicine. To be considered an expert witness, a person usually belongs to a certifying or qualifying organization, against which the defendant's qualities may be compared.

Professional negligence in medicine falls into one of three general classifications:

- *Malfeasance,* or performance of an act that is wholly wrongful and unlawful
- *Misfeasance,* or improper performance of a lawful act
- *Nonfeasance,* or failure to perform an act that should have been performed

A physician who performs an operation carelessly or fails to render care that should have been given may be found to have been negligent. Although a medical assistant acts as an agent of the physician in carrying out most of his or her duties, the medical assistant may perform an act that can result in litigation. For instance, if the medical assistant gives a patient the wrong medication or the wrong dose of medication, both the physician and the medical assistant can be held liable for the error. Some states limit the scope of practice of medical assistants where medications are involved; however, if medical assistants are performing within the realm of duties for which they have received training and the physician is accepting responsibility for the actions of those in the medical office, they usually are allowed to dispense and administer medications unless prohibited by state law. The medical assistant should always practice within the legal boundaries of the state (Procedure 7-1).

> **CRITICAL THINKING** APPLICATION   **7-8**
>
> Lynda is curious as to whether a physician is guilty of medical professional liability if he or she makes a mistake in diagnosing a patient. When might this be considered malpractice and when might it not be considered malpractice?

What if the patient makes his or her condition worse? Is the physician then fully responsible? **Contributory negligence** exists when the patient contributes to his or her own condition, and it can lessen the damages that can be collected or even prevent them from being collected altogether.

The Four Ds of Negligence

Negligence is not presumed; it must be proven. The Committee on Medicolegal Problems of the American Medical Association (AMA) has determined that patients must present evidence of four elements before negligence has been proven. These elements have become known as the four Ds of negligence:

1. *Duty:* Duty exists when the physician-patient relationship has been established. The patient has sought the assistance of the

---

PROCEDURE 7-1

Perform Within the Scope of Practice

GOAL: To perform duties within legal boundaries and within the scope of practice in the state where employed as a medical assistant.

EQUIPMENT and SUPPLIES

- Computer with Internet access
- Access to text of laws and regulations affecting the practice and scope of practice for medical assistants

PROCEDURAL STEPS

1. Read the laws and regulations that apply to medical practices thoroughly.
   PURPOSE: To understand the content and intent of the laws and regulations.
2. Become familiar with the laws that affect medical practices in your state.
   PURPOSE: To understand which laws apply to the employer's facility.
3. Obtain additional training on compliance with the laws and regulations, if necessary.
   PURPOSE: To make sure all actions and procedures in the office are in compliance with the current applicable laws.
4. Read journals and other information, either in print or on the Internet, about the laws and regulations.
   PURPOSE: To remain current in compliance activities.
5. Stay aware of licensure issues that affect the physician, including:
   - Licensure
   - Registration
   - Certification
   - Suspension
   - Revocation
   PURPOSE: To ensure that the physician is practicing medicine legally according to all laws and regulations.
6. Know the scope of practice for a medical assistant.
   PURPOSE: To ensure that the medical assistant is practicing legally according to the scope of practice.
7. Make certain information is available on current laws and regulations at all times.
8. Perform all activities in accordance with applicable laws and regulations.
   PURPOSE: To ensure compliance with applicable laws and regulations.
9. Demonstrate an awareness of the consequences of not working within the legal scope of practice.
   PURPOSE: Follow the laws and regulations to ensure compliance in the medical facility.
10. Prepare a brief report for your instructor summarizing the laws in your state that apply to medical offices or choose one specific law to summarize. Turn in the report to your instructor.

physician, and the physician has knowingly undertaken to provide the needed medical service.

2. *Dereliction:* Dereliction is failure to perform a duty. Proof must exist that the physician somehow neglected the duty to the patient.

3. *Direct cause:* Proof must exist that the patient was harmed directly because of the physician's actions or failure to act and that the harm would not otherwise have occurred.

4. *Damages:* The patient must prove that a loss or harm has resulted from the physician's actions.

If all four of these elements exist, the patient may obtain a judgment against the physician in a medical professional liability case.

Types of Damages

Five types of damages are common in tort cases: nominal, punitive, compensatory, general, and special damages.

Nominal damages are small awards that are token compensations for the invasion of a legal right in which no actual injury was suffered. For instance, if an unauthorized medical facility employee accesses a patient's medical record and is discovered but has not revealed any of the information in the record, the patient has not actually been harmed but may be awarded nominal damages in a lawsuit for the invasion of the patient's privacy.

Punitive damages are designed to punish the party who committed the wrong in such a way so as to deter repetition of the act; these are sometimes called *exemplary damages.* These damages were historically set so that the amounts would discourage intentional wrongdoing, misconduct, and outrageous behavior. The amount of damages awarded coincides in some percentage with the wealth of the defendant. Tort reform, currently a much-discussed subject, would cap the amount of money that could be collected during personal injury litigation, including medical malpractice cases. A specific monetary figure (e.g., $500,000) has been suggested as a limit on punitive damages; some believe that plaintiffs should be allowed to collect only up to three times the amount of compensatory damages. Some states have passed legislation that caps one or more of the categories of damages.

CRITICAL THINKING APPLICATION   7-9

Samantha and Lynda disagree as to whether punitive damages should be awarded in medical professional liability cases. Samantha believes that nothing compensates for certain losses, but Lynda believes that monetary compensation is reasonable when a loss has been suffered. Discuss both sides of the issue, and whether providers should be punished AND compensated if the liability proves to be true.

Compensatory damages are designed to compensate for any actual damages caused by the negligent person. They are intended to make the injured person "whole." Of course, nothing can substitute for the loss of an arm or a leg, for example, but compensatory damages help the patient or the family recover from the loss.

General damages include compensation for pain and suffering, for loss of a bodily member or faculty, for disfigurement, or for other similar direct losses or injuries. The fact of the losses has to be proven, but the monetary value does not.

Special damages are awarded for injuries or losses that are not a necessary consequence of the physician's negligent act or omission. These may include the loss of earnings or costs of travel. Both the fact of these losses and the monetary value must be proven.

Standard of Care

The standard of care as it pertains to a medical assistant must be distinguished from the medical assistant's scope of practice. From a legal perspective, each medical assistant is required to perform all duties in a manner that meets or exceeds that of a reasonably competent and knowledgeable medical assistant. Also, medical assistants cannot perform any duties for which they have not been trained. A medical assistant should treat every chart touched as if it will end up in a court of law. Remember, if it is not in the chart, there is no way to prove an event happened. The courts hold that a physician must do the following:

- Use reasonable care, attention, and diligence in the performance of professional services
- Follow his or her best judgment in treating patients
- Have and exercise reasonable skill and care that are commonly had and exercised by other reputable physicians in the same type of practice in the same or a similar locality

In the worst case, a physician or medical facility may be faced with wrongful death litigation. A wrongful death **allegation** is one in which the physician or medical facility is blamed for the death of a patient because of error or inappropriate treatment. A wrongful death suit usually is brought by the family of the **decedent** against the physician or others involved with the patient.

Consent

A physician must have consent to treat a patient, even though this consent usually is implied by the patient's appearance at the office for treatment. This **implied consent** is sufficient for common or simple procedures generally understood to involve little risk, such as phlebotomy and taking vital signs. When more complex procedures are anticipated, the physician must obtain the patient's **informed consent.** A physician who fails to secure some formal expression of consent could be charged with the crime of **battery.** Make sure the patient's identity has been verified before asking him or her to sign the consent form.

Informed consent involves a deeper understanding of the patient's condition and a full explanation of the plan for treatment. Informed consent is not satisfied merely by having the patient sign a form. A discussion must occur during which the physician provides the patient or the patient's legal representative with enough information to decide whether the patient will undergo the treatment or seek an alternative. The medical assistant cannot hold this conversation about consent with the patient; the discussion must be initiated by the physician. However, the medical assistant can witness the document and ask the patient to sign the consent form. After such discussion, the patient either consents to the proposed therapy and signs a consent form or refuses to consent. According to the AMA's standards for informed consent, the discussion should include at least the following elements:

- Patient's diagnosis, if known
- Nature and purpose of the proposed treatment or procedure
- Risks and benefits of the proposed treatment or procedure

- Alternative treatments or procedures, regardless of the cost or the extent to which the treatment options are covered by health insurance
- Risks and benefits of the alternative treatment(s) or procedure(s)
- Risks and benefits of not receiving or undergoing a treatment or procedure

The discussion should be fully documented in the patient's medical record, and a copy of the signed form should be placed in the record. Treatment may not exceed the scope of the consent that the patient has given. Often the consent forms are lengthy and mention excessive possibilities and complications. Some language may attempt to be all inclusive (e.g., "included, but not limited to") when risks are listed. It is wise to have an attorney review the forms used for informed consent, because those that are too broad or too specific can be detrimental to the physician in a medical professional liability case.

Patients cannot be forced to undergo any type of medical treatment or care. The ultimate decision about care must be left to the patient, and although medical professionals should disclose information to help the patient make a good, informed decision, the patient should never be persuaded to act in any manner or accept any treatment with which he or she does not agree. Should the patient decide not to undergo treatment the physician feels is necessary, an informed refusal of treatment or care should be signed. This should be a statement similar to the informed consent, but it indicates that the patient has elected not to undergo treatment. Some physicians discontinue all treatment if a patient does not participate in the care the physician recommends. This document, once signed, should be added to the patient's medical record.

Each state has its own consent laws. Some states and insurance programs require a certain period to pass between the signing of the consent and the actual medical procedure; for instance, Medicaid sometimes requires a 30-day waiting period between the signing of a consent for a tubal ligation and performance of the procedure. Medical assistants should be familiar with the laws in their own state that apply to their particular facility. Most of the laws can be found easily by searching on the Internet. More information about consent can be found in Chapter 17, along with a sample consent form.

CRITICAL THINKING APPLICATION   7-10

Barbara stresses to Samantha and Lynda that at some time in their professional career, a patient will ask for their advice regarding whether the patient should undergo a certain procedure or treatment. Barbara explains that patients often consider advice from the medical assistants in the office to be an extension of the physician's opinions. How might they handle such questions from patients? Should a medical assistant offer any type of advice?

Giving Consent to Medical Procedures

Mentally competent adults certainly are able to consent to medical procedures. However, if an act is unlawful, the consent is invalid.

For instance, if an abortion is performed in a state where abortion is illegal, the consent to that procedure is null. Consent is also invalid if it is given by a person who is unauthorized to do so or if it is obtained by misrepresentation or fraud.

In an emergency, one may render aid or care to prevent loss of life or serious illness or injury. However, implied consent in this circumstance lasts only as long as the emergency exists, and formal consent must be obtained for further treatment as soon as the emergency has passed.

Physicians sometimes are reluctant to render aid in an emergency to someone who is not their patient for fear they will later be charged with negligence or abandonment. In 1959 California passed the first Good Samaritan law. Under this law, volunteers at the scene of an accident are given immunity to liability for any civil damages resulting from the rendering of emergency care. Most states now have either Good Samaritan or Volunteer Protection statutes. As long as the emergency care is given in good faith and without gross negligence, and the healthcare worker provides only emergency care that he or she has been trained to provide, the likelihood of a successful lawsuit against that individual is very slim.

Adults who have been found by a court to be insane or incompetent usually cannot consent to medical treatment. Consent must be obtained from the guardian, except in emergency situations.

Generally, when the patient is a minor, consent for surgery or treatment must be obtained from a parent, guardian, or **guardian ad litem**, except in an emergency requiring immediate treatment. If the parents are legally divorced or separated, consent should be obtained from the custodial parent, but if the child is visiting the second parent, consent may be obtained from that parent, because in such a situation that parent has temporary custody.

Consent is not required for minors in the following circumstances:

- When consent may be assumed, such as in a life-threatening situation
- When a certain treatment is required by law, such as a vaccination or x-ray evaluation for school entry or safety
- When a court order has been issued, as in a situation in which parents withhold consent for a necessary treatment because of religious reasons

In many states, treatment of sexually transmitted diseases, drug abuse, alcohol dependency, pregnancy, or providing birth control measures does not require parental consent. Even if there are age of consent laws, physicians can still treat minors with these issues; the fact that the patient disregarded age statutes does not mean that he or she cannot receive medical treatment.

Emancipation is defined by statute and varies from state to state. An **emancipated minor** is a person younger than the age of majority (usually 18 to 21 years) who meets one or more of the following conditions:

- Married
- In the armed forces
- Living separately and apart from parents or a legal guardian
- Self-supporting

Some states include a minimum age for emancipation. Unless a statute declares otherwise, a minor who has the right to consent to treatment is entitled to the protection of his or her confidences, even from parents.

Statute of Limitations

A statute of limitations is a period after which a lawsuit cannot be filed. The statute of limitations varies from state to state and differs for various types of litigation. Many states have a 2-year statute of limitations for medical malpractice issues. However, in some instances, the statute of limitations may be extended because of a delay in the discovery of an injury. For example, a patient has surgery to replace a valve in the heart, and the surgery seems successful. Two years later, the patient undergoes a routine echocardiogram and the physician discovers that the surgeon mistakenly replaced the aortic valve when the surgery was intended for the pulmonary valve. Although 2 years have already passed, the statute of limitations begins at the point of discovery of the injury; therefore the patient could now bring suit against the surgeon for the error.

Confidentiality

Confidentiality is one of the most sacred trusts the patient places in the hands of the physician and staff (Figure 7-5). Breach of patient confidentiality is grounds for immediate dismissal of a healthcare professional. The strictest care must be taken when handling patient records and discussing information about patients.

In many special cases, patient confidentiality plays a vital role. A patient who tests positive for the human immunodeficiency virus (HIV) may face discrimination if the information surfaces. Physicians who treat such patients may want to take extra care when leaving phone messages or sending mail. Instead of leaving a message for a patient from "Dr. Watson's office," the medical assistant could say that the message is from "Terry Watson's office." This could indicate an attorney, accountant, or real estate broker. Curious co-workers or relatives may not grow as suspicious as they might if they were to encounter a message from a physician's office.

Patients receiving treatment for substance abuse are protected by federal statutes. Confidentiality also is of utmost importance to patients receiving treatment for mental health issues, sexually transmitted diseases, sexual **assault**, and any type of abuse.

LAW AND MEDICAL PRACTICE

Law affects the physician's day-to-day practice. Some of the ways the medical assistant encounters legal issues in the physician's office are discussed in this section. Medical assistants must comply with both state and federal laws and regulations while performing the duties associated with their job (Procedure 7-2).

FIGURE 7-5 Patient confidentiality is the most important trust that exists between the physician and the patient.

PROCEDURE 7-2

Practice Within the Standard of Care for a Medical Assistant

GOAL: To perform duties within the standard of care in the state where employed as a medical assistant.

EQUIPMENT and SUPPLIES

- Computer with Internet access
- Access to text of laws and regulations affecting the standard of care for medical assistants

PROCEDURAL STEPS

1. Become familiar with the standard of care expected of a medical assistant in your state.
   PURPOSE: To make certain that the laws and regulations that apply to the specific practice are applied with each patient.
2. Approach every patient, every day, in a professional manner.
3. During your introduction, identify yourself as a medical assistant.
   PURPOSE: To ensure that the patient understands the medical assistant's position.
4. Use reasonable care, attention, and diligence during each encounter with patients.
   PURPOSE: To make certain that each patient is treated carefully and with the utmost professionalism during each encounter.

5. Follow your best judgment while working with each patient.
   PURPOSE: To ensure that patients are given optimum care.
6. Exercise reasonable skill and care, as would be expected from other area physicians' medical assistants in the same practice area.
   PURPOSE: Each patient must be treated with equal quality care.
7. Stay abreast of medical developments and techniques.
   PURPOSE: To consistently provide patients with the best care available.
8. Refrain from performing a procedure or treatment if it is beyond the scope of technical skill and/or training.
   PURPOSE: To ensure that the patient's care is provided by those who are confident and competent in their work.
9. Document treatments and care as required in the patient's medical record.
   PURPOSE: To provide a legal, permanent record of the patient's care.
10. Follow this standard of care while performing the remainder of the procedures in this chapter.

Legal Disclosure

The physician is charged with safeguarding patient confidences within the constraints of the law, but according to state laws, which vary somewhat across the nation, certain disclosures must be made. Frequently the medical assistant is involved with the responsibility for reporting these events.

Births and deaths must be reported. In some states, detailed information about stillbirths is required. Physicians also must report cases that may have been a result of violence, such as gunshot wounds, knife injuries, or poisonings. Any death from accidental, suspicious, or unexplained causes must also be reported. In some states, occupational diseases and injuries must be reported within specific time limits.

Sexually transmitted diseases are reportable in every state. All 50 states require that patients with confirmed cases of acquired immunodeficiency syndrome (AIDS) be reported by name to the local health department. Furthermore, more than half of the 50 states require that patients who test positive for HIV be reported. Individuals are reported either by name or by unique identifiers. A continuing controversy exists as to whether the reporting prompts patients to receive care or deters individuals in high-risk groups from seeking care.

Child abuse is a leading cause of death among children younger than 5 years of age, and healthcare professionals are required by law to report any suspected cases of child abuse. The report should be made as soon as evidence is discovered that gives the physician "cause to believe" that abuse or neglect has occurred. Even if the evidence is uncertain, the physician should report it and allow the government to investigate and determine what action to take to protect the child. However, it is essential to make every attempt to ensure that the report is legitimate, because it could lead to the child's being removed from the home and placed in foster care. Cases of spousal and elder abuse are difficult, because the person being abused often is reluctant to report the situation for fear of further mistreatment. The law requires that suspected cases of abuse of children, the elderly, or any others at risk be reported to the authorities.

Local health departments publish lists of reportable diseases and the method to use in reporting them. Often this can be done by telephone or mail. Appropriate forms must be used for mail reporting and are supplied by the health departments or available on their Web sites. County and state health departments periodically issue bulletins that are sent to healthcare providers with information about disease outbreaks and various statistics. Local health departments should be consulted for specific procedures and reporting protocols.

Patient Self-Determination Act

The Patient Self-Determination Act of 1990 brought the term *advance directives* to the forefront of medical care. This act requires healthcare facilities to develop and maintain written procedures that ensure that all adult patients receive information about living wills, durable powers of attorney for healthcare, and advance directives. These documents place the decision-making power in the hands of the patient and the family, providing them with written notification of their right to consent to or refuse medical treatment.

Patient's Bill of Rights

In March of 1998, President Bill Clinton received the final report from the President's Advisory Commission on Consumer Protection and Quality in the Healthcare Industry. The commission was created to advise the president on current issues in the healthcare industry and to make recommendations to ensure that patients would receive high-quality healthcare services. The report, "Quality First: Better Healthcare for All Americans," led to the development of a Consumer Bill of Rights and Responsibilities for the healthcare industry. This usually is called the Patient's Bill of Rights. The document, which has eight sections, lists three specific goals:

1. To strengthen consumer confidence by ensuring that the healthcare system is fair and responsive to consumers' needs, provides consumers with credible and effective mechanisms to address their concerns, and encourages consumers to take an active role in improving and ensuring their health
2. To reaffirm the importance of a strong relationship between patients and their healthcare professionals
3. To reaffirm the critical role consumers play in safeguarding their health by establishing rights and responsibilities for all participants in improving their health

Most healthcare facilities have adopted a Patient's Bill of Rights that provides a condensed version of the entire report. Often this information is presented to patients when they are admitted to healthcare facilities, or it may be posted in a prominent place in the facility. The medical assistant must consider the rights of the patient in each encounter. Explain procedures to patients and make sure they consent to treatment. The Patient's Bill of Rights is honored when written consent is obtained from patients, but the medical staff must always consider the patient and his or her individual desires and preferences in all phases of medical treatment. Office information booklets or bulletin board postings often contain information on where a patient may make a complaint about the care received at a facility. Policies and procedures should honor the provisions of the Patient's Bill of Rights that apply in that particular medical facility (Procedure 7-3).

PATIENT'S BILL OF RIGHTS

I. Information Disclosure
You have a right to receive accurate and easily understood information about your health plan, healthcare professionals, and healthcare facilities. If you speak another language, have a physical or mental disability, or just don't understand something, assistance will be provided so you can make informed healthcare decisions.

II. Choice of Providers and Plans
You have the right to a choice of healthcare providers that is sufficient to provide you with access to appropriate high-quality healthcare.

III. Access to Emergency Services
If you have severe pain, an injury, or a sudden illness that convinces you your health is in serious jeopardy, you have the right to receive screening and stabilization emergency services whenever and wherever needed, without prior authorization or financial penalty.

IV. Participation in Treatment Decisions

You have the right to know all your treatment options and to participate in decisions about your care. Parents, guardians, family members, or other individuals whom you designate can represent you if you cannot make your own decisions.

V. Respect and Nondiscrimination

You have a right to considerate, respectful, and nondiscriminatory care from your doctors, health plan representatives, and other healthcare providers.

VI. Confidentiality of Health Information

You have the right to talk in confidence with healthcare providers and to have your healthcare information protected. You also have the right to review and copy your own medical record and request that your physician amend your record if it is not accurate, relevant, or complete.

VII. Complaints and Appeals

You have the right to a fair, fast, and objective review of any complaint you have against your health plan, doctors, hospitals, or other healthcare personnel. This includes complaints about waiting times, operating hours, the conduct of healthcare personnel, and the adequacy of healthcare facilities.

VIII. Consumer Responsibilities

In a healthcare system that protects consumer rights, it is reasonable to expect and encourage consumers to assume reasonable responsibilities. Greater individual involvement by consumers in their care increases the likelihood of achieving the best outcomes and helps support a quality-improvement, cost-conscious environment.

AFFORDABLE CARE ACT OF 2010

The Affordable Care Act, signed into law in March of 2010, was designed to provide better health security by enacting comprehensive health insurance reforms that hold insurance companies accountable, lower healthcare costs, guarantee more choice, and enhance the quality of care for all Americans. The law restricts the use of annual limits and bans lifetime limits on healthcare benefits; for example, if a patient has cancer, the insurance company cannot put a limit on the amount of coverage provided to that patient, even if it is a catastrophic amount. Additionally, the act prohibits discrimination against children with pre-existing conditions.

Additional benefits went into effect on September 23, 2011, including:

- Preventive services, such as mammograms, colonoscopies, immunizations, prenatal and new baby care, will be covered and insurance companies will be prohibited from charging co-payments or co-insurance for these services.
- Patients will have the right to appeal coverage decisions to a third party.
- Patients are guaranteed their choice of primary care physicians and do not have to get a referral for an obstetrician/gynecologist or pediatrician.

Health insurers and employers are also now required to provide clear and consistent information about health plans, including an easy-to-understand Summary of Benefits and Coverage and a uniform Glossary of terms commonly used in health insurance coverage. More benefits will take effect through 2014.

Controlled Substances Act

On May 1, 1971, the Controlled Substances Act of 1970 became effective. In October, 1973, the Drug Enforcement Administration became a part of the U.S. Department of Justice. The DEA works with local, state, federal, and international agencies and organizations to address and regulate the serious issues of drug use and abuse in the United States.

Before administering, prescribing, or dispensing any drugs, a physician is required to register with the regional office of the DEA. This registration is renewable every 3 years. If a physician works from more than one office, he or she must register each individual office. Regulations on the writing, telephoning, and refilling of prescriptions vary, depending on which drug schedule is involved.

Under the Controlled Substances Act, drugs are categorized into schedules I to V. Drugs in schedule I have the highest potential for abuse and addiction, and those in schedule V have the lowest abuse potential.

Schedule I substances have no accepted medical use in the United States (e.g., heroin and lysergic acid diethylamide [LSD]). Only a physician involved in research with such drugs is concerned with schedule I substances.

Schedule II drugs have a high abuse potential, with severe risk of mental and physical dependence. These include certain narcotic, stimulant, and depressant drugs (e.g., opium, morphine, codeine, and methylphenidate [Ritalin]). Controlled substances in schedule II can be obtained only with a federal triplicate order form obtained from the DEA. A special inventory must be maintained on controlled substances and retained for 2 to 3 years, depending on state requirements. When a controlled substance is removed from inventory, it must be recorded. The record must show the date, the name of the drug, the dosage, and the name of the patient, physician, and employee involved. Substances in schedules III, IV, and V do not require triplicate forms.

Schedule III substances have an abuse potential that is lower than that of drugs in the first two schedules. They include compounds that have limited amounts of certain narcotic drugs combined with nonnarcotic substances (e.g., acetaminophen [Tylenol] with codeine, hydrocodone (Lortab, Norco, Vicodin), butalbital with aspirin and caffeine (Fiorinal) and several steroids.

Schedule IV substances have still lower potential for abuse; for example, phenobarbital, diazepam (Valium), propoxyphene (Darvon and Darvocet), alprazolam (Xanax), chlordiazepoxide (Librium), and pentazocine lactate (Talwin).

Schedule V substances have lower abuse potential than those in schedule IV but still warrant control. They include preparations that contain moderate amounts of certain narcotics, as may be found in cough medicines and antidiarrheal products.

The physician may call in a prescription to the pharmacist, but the pharmacist must transcribe it in writing before filling it. With permission from the physician, the medical assistant may orally transmit a prescription for controlled substances only in schedules

Incorporate the Patients' Bill of Rights into Personal Practice and Medical Office Policies

GOAL: *To ensure that the patient's rights are honored in the daily procedures performed and policies enacted in the physician's office.*

Unless otherwise noted, all equipment and supplies are to be provided by the instructor.

EQUIPMENT and SUPPLIES

- Copy of the Patient's Bill of Rights
- Office policy and procedure manuals
- Patient Role-Play Cards (provided by instructor)

PROCEDURAL STEPS

1. Review the eight points in the Patient's Bill of Rights.
   PURPOSE: To become familiar with the points and content of the document.
2. Review the office policy regarding information disclosure to make sure patients have the right to receive information about their health plan, professionals, facilities, and personal care.
   PURPOSE: To comply with the first article in the Patient's Bill of Rights.
3. Review the office policy regarding choice of providers, realizing that some patients may have restrictions on those choices according to their insurance plan.
   PURPOSE: To comply with the second article in the Patient's Bill of Rights.
4. Review the office policy regarding emergency treatment, paying close attention to the procedures for referral to emergency facilities and for emergency treatment in the office.
   PURPOSE: To comply with the third article in the Patient's Bill of Rights.
5. Review the office policy regarding consent for treatment and discussion of healthcare options to ensure that patients are given the ultimate choice in making decisions about their medical care.
   PURPOSE: To comply with the fourth article in the Patient's Bill of Rights.

6. Review the office policy regarding discrimination to make sure the policy is nondiscriminatory and that all employees are expected to be courteous and considerate to every patient and visitor to the office.
   PURPOSE: To comply with the fifth article in the Patient's Bill of Rights.
7. Review the office policy's sections on confidentiality to make certain that they comply with the patients' right to see their records and to expect confidential treatment of their healthcare information.
   PURPOSE: To comply with the sixth article in the Patient's Bill of Rights.
8. Review the office policy regarding patients' complaints and appeals (if applicable) to ascertain whether patients are given information about filing such grievances.
   PURPOSE: To comply with the seventh article in the Patient's Bill of Rights.
9. Review the office policy regarding quality improvement and cost-consciousness to make certain the office maintains the utmost level of quality while remaining cost-conscious.
   PURPOSE: To comply with the eighth article in the Patient's Bill of Rights.
10. Consider each of the eight articles while completing daily duties and performing patient care and treatment in the medical facility.
    PURPOSE: To incorporate the Patient's Bill of Rights into everyday practice.
11. Demonstrate sensitivity to patients' rights.
    PURPOSE: To reassure patients so that they know healthcare professionals are sensitive to their needs and desires.
12. Explain the Patient's Bill of Rights while role-playing with another student.

III, IV, or V, and the dispensing pharmacist must put the prescription into writing before filling it. The medical assistant cannot under any circumstances orally transmit a prescription for a schedule II drug. These prescriptions must be presented in writing to the pharmacist on the appropriate form.

Stored controlled substances must be kept in a locked cabinet or safe. Any loss of controlled drugs by theft must be reported to the regional office of the DEA when the theft is discovered. If a physician discovers that his or her DEA number is being used in the unauthorized prescription of controlled substances, he or she should report the incident to the DEA, to the state regulatory agency, and to the local police. This is especially important in the case of employees whose employment has been terminated and who are suspected of drug theft in the office. In numerous cases fired employees have

retaliated by reporting to the DEA exactly what they themselves took, but they accuse the physician or other staff members of taking the controlled substances. This results in messy investigations and months of follow-up; therefore any suspected employee drug use or abuse should be documented and reported to the local authorities. Periodic drug testing of employees is one way to help prevent office drug abuse. Many states now have laws to prevent the filing of false reports; therefore, if the physician is wrongly accused by a disgruntled employee, the physician often has some **recourse**.

A physician who discontinues medical practice must return the registration certificate and any unused order forms and triplicate prescription pads to the nearest office of the DEA. The regional DEA office advises the physician on the disposition of any controlled drugs still on hand.

CRITICAL THINKING APPLICATION   **7-11**

Barbara explains the importance of reporting any employee who is suspected of using drugs or taking drugs from the office. This may be difficult, because co-workers often are friendly with one another and may hesitate to report such acts. Discuss ways to handle this situation.

The Uniform Anatomical Gift Act

The Uniform Anatomical Gift Act was approved by the National Conference of Commissioners on Uniform State Laws in 1968. Although many states already had passed laws that permitted living persons to make a gift of their body or portions of it after death, the laws were so different from state to state that arrangements for a donation in one state might not be recognized in another. All states have adopted the Uniform Anatomical Gift Act or similar legislation.

Essentially, the model law for donation states the following:

- Any person of sound mind and 18 years of age or older may give all or any part of his or her body after death for research, transplantation, or placement in a tissue bank.
- A donor's valid statement of gift is paramount to the rights of others except when a state autopsy law may prevail.
- If a donor has not indicated an intent to donate during his or her lifetime, his or her survivors, in a specified order of priority, may do so.
- Physicians who accept organs or tissues, relying in good faith on the documents, are protected from lawsuits. The physician attending at the time of death, if acquainted with the donor's wishes, may dispose of the body under the Uniform Anatomical Gift Act.
- The time of death must be determined by a physician who is not involved in the transplantation, and the attending physician cannot be a member of the transplant team.
- The donor may revoke the gift, or the gift may be rejected by the proposed recipient.

The most important clause of the act permits the donation to be made by a will (without waiting for probate) or by other written or witnessed documents, such as a card designed to be carried by the person or a Uniform Donor Card (Figure 7-6). The Uniform Donor Card is considered a legal document in all 50 states. Many states now list donor preference on the driver's license as well.

The provisions of the Uniform Anatomical Gift Act are so designed that the offer is exercised only after death. Therefore,

donors should reveal their intentions to as many of their relatives and friends as possible and to their physician. Because the human body and its parts are not commodities in commerce, no money can be exchanged in making an anatomic donation itself. Fees are charged for performing the transplant and various procedures, but organs cannot be bought and sold. It also is important to note that family members should be prepared to receive the body of the person who has donated his or her entire body to research once the research facility has completed its study. This can often be a traumatic experience that rekindles the grief process, so the procedures and final disposition of the body should be decided at the time of the donation to avoid this difficult situation.

The Health Insurance Portability and Accountability Act

HIPAA was signed into law on August 21, 1996, and all healthcare providers were required to comply with HIPAA's privacy standards by April 2003. Its history began in the Clinton healthcare reform proposals. HIPAA was designed for several purposes, with many goals in mind. Limiting the administrative costs of healthcare and privacy issues and preventing fraud and abuse are of primary importance in the HIPAA regulations. The law has two provisions: Title I (Insurance Reform) and Title II (Administration Simplification). The use of electronic transmissions ideally lowers the administrative costs of providing healthcare, but it has led to problems with privacy regarding health information. The law also had to provide security and confidentiality guarantees for the individual patient. Extensive privacy rules, including the use of unique identifiers, have shaped the law.

The final regulations regarding the privacy legislation sections of HIPAA were published in December, 2000, after the Centers for Medicare and Medicaid Services (CMS) reviewed more than 50,000 comments on and concerns about this important subject. All healthcare organizations that transmit any health information electronically must comply with HIPAA; fines as well as prison terms can be imposed on those who do not comply with the regulations.

HIPAA has had a tremendous effect on the healthcare industry. All healthcare providers, clearinghouses, and health plans that use electronic information must comply with HIPAA regulations. The benefits of HIPAA compliance include:

- Lower administrative costs
- Increased accuracy of data
- Increased patient and consumer satisfaction
- Reduced revenue cycle time
- Improved financial management

Title I, which deals with insurance reform, includes several provisions that protect individuals and their insured dependents if they change jobs or lose a job.

Title II details the process of administrative simplification. Standardization of the exchange of healthcare data is one way HIPAA promotes computer-to-computer transactions. This standardization process helps reduce the number of forms and methods used in the claims processing cycle, including electronic transactions and standard code sets (e.g., diagnosis, procedure, and supply codes). It also provides for unique identifiers for providers, employers, health plans, and patients. Medical professionals who access medical information must use log-in and password systems that prevent unauthorized individuals from accessing protected health information.

DONOR

DONOR CARD

I _____, have spoken to my family about organ and tissue donation. I wish to donate:
__ any needed organs and tissue
__ only the following organs and tissue: _____
The following people have witnessed my commitment to be a donor.
donor signature _____ date _____
witness_____
witness_____
next of kin _____ ph _____

FIGURE 7-6 Organ donation card.

The Occupational Safety and Health Act and the Bloodborne Pathogens Standard

In 1970 President Richard Nixon signed the Occupational Safety and Health Act, which created what has become the Occupational Safety and Health Administration. OSHA is a division of the U.S. Department of Labor, and since its creation, workplace injuries, illnesses, and fatalities have been reduced significantly. OSHA's mission is to ensure workplace safety and a healthy environment in the workplace.

OSHA commonly is considered the regulatory agency that requires steel-toe boots and hard hats; however, the medical industry moved into the OSHA spotlight in the late 1980s, when the threat of HIV infection extended to healthcare workers. Hepatitis and other pathogens already were a concern for healthcare workers, but when HIV, the virus that causes AIDS, was identified, action was needed to better protect the individuals who cared for patients with these infectious diseases. OSHA's Final Ruling on Bloodborne Pathogens became fully effective in July, 1992, and since then various additions have been made to update the regulations in light of new information about blood-borne pathogens.

The law requires medical facilities to comply with the Bloodborne Pathogens standard and to be able to prove their compliance to OSHA inspectors if necessary. The actual standard can be found in 29 **Code of Federal Regulations (CFR)** 1910.1030. The following information details the legal requirements of the OSHA standard as it pertains to the physician's office.

General Duty Clause

No law can cover every single situation that may arise in the course of daily living. Because of this, OSHA's general duty clause is a catchall regulation that fits almost any situation not specified in any other section of the law. The general duty clause simply states that a workplace must be free of any hazard that might cause serious harm or death. For example, one breach of the general duty clause is failure of a facility to provide reasonable security procedures at a retail store. Although not a specific breach of any regulation, this fits nicely into the general duty clause.

Emergency Preparedness

OSHA requires that all facilities with more than 10 employees have a written emergency action plan in place. The plan must include procedures that cover:

- Reporting a fire or other emergency
- Performing an emergency evacuation, including the type of evacuation and exit route assignments
- Establishing rules for employees who remain to run critical equipment before they evacuate
- Accounting for all employees after evacuation
- Establishing procedures to be followed by employees performing rescue or medical duties
- Providing the name or title of the person (or persons) to be contacted for information about the plan or an explanation of the individual's duties under the plan
- A list of the Personal Protective Equipment (PPE) to be used by each employee who will be exposed to bloodborne pathogens, such as lab coats, protective glasses, or gloves, as well as an indication of which tasks require what PPE

The plan also must have an alarm system to notify employees in case of an emergency, and the system must use a separate, distinct signal for each type of emergency. The employees must be trained in safe evacuation procedures. Also, the employer must review the plan with each employee at four specific times: (1) when the plan is developed, (2) when the employee is initially assigned to a job, (3) when the employee's responsibilities change, and (4) and when the plan is changed.

Facilities with more than 10 employees also must have a written fire prevention plan. The fire prevention plan must include:

- A list of all major fire hazards and the proper handling and storage of each
- The type of fire prevention equipment necessary to control each major hazard
- Procedures to control accumulations of flammable and combustible waste materials
- Procedures for regular maintenance of safeguards installed on heat-producing equipment to prevent the accidental ignition of combustible materials
- The name or job title of the person responsible for maintaining equipment, preventing or controlling sources of ignition or fires, and controlling fuel source hazards.

Employers must tell employees about the fire hazards associated with their job, in addition to ways the employee can protect himself or herself. The office policy manual should include information about procedures to follow during natural disasters, such as hurricanes, tornadoes, and other weather-related events, and during crime incidents at the facility (e.g., robbery and vandalism). Large-scale events, such as terrorist attacks or bioterrorism, also should be addressed, because medical professionals will be called upon to help in these situations. Obtain a copy of the local hospital's emergency preparedness plan and use it as a guideline if the office needs a written plan. (More information about emergency preparedness can be found in Chapters 27 and 58.)

OSHA inspectors can recommend fines when a facility is found to be out of compliance with an OSHA standard. One of the most common infractions involves a facility that has an Exposure Control Plan but is not using it or following its procedures and policies. This could cause an inspector to declare the facility willfully negligent. Willful negligence exists when "an employer representative was aware of the requirements of the [OSHA] Act, or the existence of an applicable standard or regulation, and was also aware that the condition or practice was in violation of those requirements, and did not abate the hazard." Fines for noncompliance can quadruple for willful negligence.

COMMON OSHA VIOLATIONS

- No eyewash facilities available
- No labeling or improper labeling of hazardous chemicals
- No MSDS for each hazardous chemical
- Storage of contaminated laboratory coats with clean ones
- Not communicating hazards to employees
- No documentation of initial employee training
- No documentation of annual employee training

- No annual hazard assessment
- Having an Exposure Control Plan but not following it
- No proof of destruction of hazardous waste
- No Emergency Action Plan in the facility
- No written Exposure Control Plan
- OSHA Form 300 not posted during required period
- No records of hepatitis B vaccinations or declination forms

MSDS, Material Safety Data Sheet; *OSHA*, Occupational Safety and Health Administration.

Exposure Control Plan

The Exposure Control Plan can be a part of the regular safety plan written for the medical facility or a stand-alone document, but it must cover all the elements required by OSHA. The plan must be put in writing, must be reviewed annually, and written documentation must exist that the plan was reviewed and updated or revised, if needed. A hard copy must be provided to employees on their request within 15 working days, and the plan must be available at all times in the workplace.

The plan must delineate the tasks employees perform in which the risk of blood exposure is present. It also must classify jobs in the facility according to the likelihood of exposure. For instance, some job duties always expose the employee to blood or **other potentially infectious materials (OPIM)**, often on a daily basis. Some duties only occasionally expose the employee, and other duties never expose the employee to blood or OPIM. Employees must be told to which category they belong and what duties they will perform that could lead to exposure. In addition, a clear follow-up procedure must be in place that details how the medical facility will track employee exposures. The employee cannot be abandoned after an exposure incident. Periodic counseling must take place in which the facility determines and documents the progress of the employee who has had an exposure, including laboratory tests and medical treatment received.

The Exposure Control Plan must contain a Waste Management section that details how waste is removed from the facility and destroyed. Most medical offices contract with companies that specialize in removing and destroying hazardous medical waste. The office must keep the receipts given by the company that prove that the waste was taken away from the facility and then incinerated or otherwise destroyed.

The plan must also contain a section on Hazardous Materials Communication, which explains what substances in the facility are hazardous and how to handle a spill or exposure to those products. Only the manufacturer of a chemical can determine whether it is hazardous, and Material Safety Data Sheets must be kept on almost all chemicals and reagents in the facility. Recent rulings have exempted some chemicals, but without the MSDS information, a medical assistant could not determine what type of health, reactivity, flammability, or other risks the chemical could have.

If the facility has equipment for x-ray studies, a Radiation Safety Plan must also be written and followed. All facilities should have an Emergency Action Plan in place, which provides procedures in case of tornadoes, fires, floods, or any other type of emergency that might occur in the office. This plan should contain floor plans of the facility, diagrams depicting the most efficient exits from the building, and the chain of command in an emergency. Diagrams with exit routes should be posted in every room of the medical office. At least annually, a hazard assessment must be performed on the entire facility. The hazard assessment is an inspection for problem areas in which the facility might be out of compliance. The facility must have documentation that the hazard assessment was done.

OSHA Record-Keeping Regulations

An injury or illness is considered to be work related when an event or exposure in the work environment contributed to or caused the condition or significantly aggravated a pre-existing condition. OSHA made several changes in the regulations covering record keeping on work-related injury to simplify forms, protect employee privacy, encourage employee involvement, and enable computer use for meeting OSHA requirements. The revised rules took effect January 1, 2002. Three basic forms now are used to keep records on injuries, accidents, and illnesses related to the workplace.

- OSHA Form 300—Log of Work-Related Injuries and Illnesses: Information is posted on form 300 regarding work-related deaths and every work-related injury or illness that involves loss of consciousness, restricted work activity or job transfer, days away from work, or medical treatment beyond first aid. An OSHA Form 301 (Injury and Illness Incident Report) should be completed for each entry on the log.
- OSHA Form 300A—Summary of Work-Related Injuries and Illnesses: Form 300A must be completed even if no injuries or illnesses that were work related occurred during the year. It must be posted in a common area for viewing by all employees, and provides the total number of accidents, illnesses, and injuries in the facility for the previous year. The length of time that this information must be posted has increased from 1 month to 3 months, specifically from February 1 to April 30 each year. An additional change is the certification of the form. A company executive must examine the document and certify that it is accurate.
- OSHA Form 301—Injury and Illness Incident Report: Form 301 is used to report what actually happened when an employee suffers a work-related injury or illness. This form, or an acceptable substitute, such as a state worker's compensation form, must be completed within 7 calendar days after notification of the illness or injury. The form should be completed as quickly as possible so that an exact recollection of events can be documented (Procedure 7-4). Now that the new record-keeping regulations have become effective, employees are guaranteed access to their OSHA 301 forms for the first time.

The log and summary forms must be kept on file for a minimum of 5 years. Only the Summary should be posted during the specified period from February 1 to April 30 each year, reflecting information from the previous calendar year. The forms are not sent to OSHA unless specifically requested. (To view these forms, visit the Evolve site at *evolve.elsevier.com/kinn*)

CRITICAL THINKING APPLICATION   7-12
Barbara quickly realizes that the office is using older versions of OSHA forms 300 and 301. Where might she look for or go to find updated information and forms?

PROCEDURE 7-4

Complete an Incident Report

GOAL: *To fill out an accurate, complete incident report that provides all legally required information.*

Unless otherwise noted, all equipment and supplies are to be provided by the instructor.

EQUIPMENT and SUPPLIES

- OSHA Form 301 (or other incident report form)
- Pen
- Notes taken regarding incident (Patient Role-Play Cards on Evolve)

PROCEDURAL STEPS

1. Interview the employee(s) involved in the incident using Patient Role-Play cards (choose cards that detail an employee or patient incident).
2. Review the notes taken by those who witnessed the incident.
   PURPOSE: To gain an understanding of what happened during the incident.
3. Interview those who may have additional information or those who provided the original notes, if clarification on the issues is needed.
   PURPOSE: To be clear about the exact sequence of events during the incident.
4. Read through OSHA Form 301 before filling out any sections.
   PURPOSE: To avoid making mistakes while putting the information in the spaces on the form.

5. Complete information about the employee(s) and the healthcare professional who treated the employee(s).
   PURPOSE: To document the incident and the principles involved.
6. Detail the information requested about the incident, including the actual injury or illness, a narrative of what happened, and what object(s) was involved in the injury.
   PURPOSE: To document the incident and the sequence of events.
7. Sign the report and, if possible, review it with the employee(s).
   PURPOSE: To prove that the report was submitted and reviewed by a supervisor.
8. If the injured employee(s) completes the incident report, make sure it is reviewed and signed by a supervisor.
   PURPOSE: Some facilities have incident reports the employee completes that detail the events surrounding the incident. These must be reviewed by a supervisor.
9. Make sure the incident was reported in a timely manner and within any state regulatory times.
10. Refer the employee(s) to the proper persons for medical care.
    PURPOSE: To make sure the employee(s) obtains timely and proper medical care.
11. Submit the completed report to your instructor.

It is wise to keep a communication log of calls to OSHA in which questions were asked or information verified. Note the day and time called, the first and last name of the person spoken to, the person's title, and the question asked and response given. Take detailed notes while discussing the issue on the phone. This log could be invaluable if a question ever arises about a subject discussed with a local OSHA official. It may make the difference when an OSHA inspector suggests a hefty fine. If the medical facility can show documentation that a certain procedure was discussed with an OSHA official and decisions were made based on that discussion, the facility may have sufficient evidence that the law was considered and the facility did its best to comply.

Needlestick Safety and Prevention Act

An estimated 600,000 to 800,000 injuries occur annually among healthcare workers. One third of these injuries happen during the disposal process. In an effort to reduce these injuries, which can lead to exposure to HIV, hepatitis B virus (HBV), or other blood-borne pathogens, OSHA revised its Bloodborne Pathogens standard to comply with the Needlestick Safety and Prevention Act, which became law on November 6, 2000. The regulations became effective on April 18, 2001.

Employers are now required to involve employees in the selection of needle safety devices. The facility must be able to prove that consideration was given to various types of devices that promote needle safety, what led to the decision to choose the device currently in use, and which employees were involved in these decisions. A list should be kept of which employees contributed to the selection decisions. Minutes from meetings, copies of employee response forms, and the forms used to solicit input are good methods of proving that employees were involved in the selection process.

CRITICAL THINKING APPLICATION   7-13

Barbara needs input about the needle safety devices used in the facility. Should she call a meeting of the entire office or should just specific employees present? If so, discuss who should have input in these decisions.

A needlestick and sharps injury log must also be kept in the medical facility. At a minimum, the log must include the following information:

- Description of the incident
- Type and brand of device used when the incident took place
- Location of the incident

The regulations that took effect in 2001 require all needlestick and sharps injuries to be reported and documented, not just the ones that result in injury or illness.

OSHA Training Requirements

All employees, including full-time, part-time, and temporary employees with a risk of occupational exposure, must receive training in the facility in which they are employed at two very specific times. Initial training must be conducted before a new employee starts any work-related duties. In addition, training must be conducted annually to update and inform employees about new regulations and procedures related to OSHA compliance. The initial training requirement is one of the most frequently breached regulations, yet it is critical to the employee's safety. Training must include the following:

- Making accessible a copy of the regulatory text of the OSHA standard and an explanation of its content.
- General discussion of blood-borne diseases and their transmission
- Universal precautions and body substance isolation
- The Exposure Control Plan
- Engineering and work practice controls, including handling of needles and sharps
- Personal protective equipment
- Hepatitis B vaccine
- Response to emergencies involving blood
- Potential sources of infection and tasks that might pre-empt exposure
- Written schedules for cleaning
- Handling of contaminated laundry
- Handling of exposure incidents and spills
- Post-exposure evaluation and follow-up program
- Reading of MSDS, signs, labels, and color coding (Figure 7-7) and the locations of these items

The employee must be given an opportunity to ask questions and receive answers, and the trainer must be knowledgeable about the subject matter. Documentation of the training sessions should be kept in each employee's personnel file or a special file for OSHA-related information.

CRITICAL THINKING APPLICATION   7-14

Barbara reviews the employee files and finds that neither Samantha nor Lynda received OSHA training when they were initially hired. How might Barbara rectify this, and what documentation would be helpful?

Hepatitis B Vaccination

The hepatitis B vaccination series must be offered to employees at risk of occupational exposure at no cost to the employee. The employee cannot be asked to pay in advance for the vaccination and be reimbursed, nor can the employee be asked to put the vaccination series on his or her personal health insurance policy. It must be made available to the employee within 10 working days of initial hire or assignment. The vaccination series can be declined by the employee, who must sign a declination form. If at any time the employee decides to receive the vaccination series, this must still be offered at no cost. The employee does not have to offer a reason for the declination. Prescreening and postvaccination serologic tests cannot be required.

The vaccination series is completed within a 6-month period. The second vaccination is given 1 month after the first, and the third 5 months after the second. Documentation should be provided to the employee for each vaccination received. Currently a booster dose of the hepatitis B vaccine is not required. However, if a routine booster is recommended by the U.S. Public Health Service in the future, it must be made available at no cost to employees.

CRITICAL THINKING APPLICATION   7-15

Lynda has not disclosed to anyone at the facility that she has had a case of hepatitis. Should she discuss this matter with Barbara? Is Lynda required to discuss this matter with Barbara? Is Lynda placing her patients at risk? If Lynda declines the hepatitis vaccination, must she explain why on the declination form?

Clinical Laboratory Improvement Amendments

The Clinical Laboratory Improvement Amendments (CLIA) were the result of a congressional investigation of **physician office laboratories (POLs)** and the deficiencies in the quality of the services and results provided by these laboratories. A set of minimum standards for laboratories was established, which improved the quality of test procedures. Quality control and assurance, as well as personnel and proficiency testing, are of utmost importance to the facility complying with CLIA.

CLIA regulations set the minimum standard for laboratory practice and quality. Remember that CLIA is not a governmental agency, but a law. CLIA is enforced by the Department of Health and Human Services (DHHS). OSHA is both a law (Occupational Safety and Health Act) and an agency (Occupational Safety and Health Administration). This is an important difference between CLIA and OSHA.

Some tests conducted in the laboratory are exempt from CLIA standards:

- Nonautomated dipstick or tablet urinalysis
- Fecal occult blood
- Ovulation using visual color comparison
- Urine pregnancy using visual color comparison
- Erythrocyte sedimentation rate
- Hemoglobin by copper sulfate method
- Spun microhematocrit
- Blood glucose testing using certain devices cleared by the U.S. Food and Drug Administration (FDA) for home use
- Specialized self-contained hemoglobin tests

Offices that perform only these tests may obtain a certificate of waiver and are not routinely inspected for CLIA compliance. Tests of moderate or high complexity must be performed by trained personnel with education and experience in the test areas in which they are working. A list of the moderate- and high-complexity procedures can be found in the July 26, 1993, issue of the *Federal Register*, and updates are published periodically that detail any changes in the list or regulations for testing procedures. Laboratories apply for a CLIA certificate through their local health departments and are periodically inspected for compliance.

Material Safety Data Sheets communicate hazards to employees about the products and chemicals used in the medical office. They also inform the employee as to what to do in case of an exposure. OSHA requires that MSDS are kept on all hazardous chemicals, unless exempted. Only the manufacturer can determine if a product is hazardous. MSDS can be obtained from either the manufacturer or the medical supply company from which the product was ordered. They must be provided after requested from the manufacturer within 30 days. Keep copies of requests to prove that an attempt has been made to obtain the MSDS information.

Typical label for a hazardous chemical

The appropriate number should be placed inside each box that applies in the figure above. Most offices use the National Fire Protection Association Rating System. Many MSDS provide the labeling information on the sheet. Others must be read thoroughly to determine how the labels should be completed. If the MSDS says that a chemical has a "moderate to high" hazard, label it high. If it says "low to moderate," label it moderate. Never guess at the numbers used for the label—always consult the MSDS. If individual containers are labeled, the facility is said to always be out of compliance, because it is easy to miss a container that may have just arrived in a shipment. Many medical facilities place labels on a permanent fixture next to where the product is stored, but it must be permanently stored in that area.

Simple Rating Guide
0—no hazard
1—slight hazard
2—moderate hazard
3—high hazard
4—extreme hazard

NFPA Rating Summary

Health (Blue)			Reactivity (Yellow)		
4	Danger	May be fatal on short exposure. Specialized protective equipment required.	4	Danger	Explosive material at room temperature.
3	Warning	Corrosive or toxic. Avoid skin contact or inhalation.	3	Danger	May be explosive if shocked, heated under confinement, or mixed with water.
2	Warning	May be harmful if inhaled or absorbed.	2	Warning	Unstable or may react violently if mixed with water.
1	Caution	May be irritating.	1	Caution	May react if heated or mixed with water but not violently.
0		No unusual hazard.	0	Stable	Not reactive when mixed with water.
Flammability (Red)			**Special Notice Key (White)**		
4	Danger	Flammable gas or extremely flammable liquid.	W		Water reactive.
3	Warning	Flammable liquid flash point below 100° F.	Oxy		Oxidizing agent.
2	Caution	Combustible liquid flash point of 100° to 200° F.			
1		Combustible if heated.			
0		Not combustible.			

FIGURE 7-7 Labeling and the National Fire Protection Association (NFPA) Rating System. (Courtesy National Fire Protection Association, Quincy, Mass.)

Americans with Disabilities Act

In 1990 the Americans with Disabilities Act (ADA) was signed into law with the intent of eliminating discrimination against individuals with disabilities. The act is comprehensive legislation that addresses many areas in which a person might experience discrimination, including telecommunications, housing, public transportation, air carrier access, voting accessibility, education, and rehabilitation. The physician's office falls in the category of public accommodations, which are defined as private entities that own, lease, lease to, or operate public facilities.

Public accommodations must comply with basic nondiscrimination requirements that prohibit exclusion, segregation, and unequal treatment. They also must comply with specific requirements related to architectural standards for new and altered buildings; reasonable modifications to policies, practices, and procedures; effective communication with people with hearing, vision, or speech disabilities;

and other access requirements. Public accommodations also must remove barriers in existing buildings, where it can be done without much difficulty or expense given the public accommodation's resources.

These regulations affect the physician's office because individuals with disabilities must be able to enter and exit the facility without difficulty. This means that individuals in wheelchairs need a ramp to enter and exit the building. They also must be able to navigate throughout the office without major barriers. Any facility with 15 or more employees must comply with the ADA. To be protected by the act, a person must have a disability or a relationship or association with an individual with a disability. An individual with a disability is defined by the ADA as a person who has a physical or mental impairment that substantially limits one or more major life activities; a person who has a history or record of an impairment; or a person who is perceived by others as having an impairment. The ADA does not specifically name all the impairments covered. Every medical facility must comply with the ADA. The law requires that public medical facilities must allow persons with disabilities to easily and safely:

- Reach door handles for opening and closing
- Enter and exit buildings
- Move through doors and hallways
- Use drinking fountains, phones, and restrooms
- Move from floor to floor (elevators are required for multilevel buildings)
- Do everything the general public can do in a public place

HITECH Act of 2009

The Health Information Technology for Economic and Clinical Health was signed into law in February, 2009, to promote the adoption and meaningful use of health information technology. The law encourages physicians and healthcare entities to comply with HIPAA regulations by enacting stiff penalties for noncompliance. Physicians who do not adopt electronic medical records will eventually be penalized in Medicare payments. The HITECH Act also imposes data breach notification requirements for unauthorized uses and disclosures of "unsecured PHI"; in other words, patients must be notified if there is a breach that exposes the patient's protected health information (PHI) (Procedures 7-5, 7-6).

PROCEDURE 7-5

Apply Local, State, and Federal Healthcare Laws and Regulations for Medical Assisting

GOAL: To be aware of local, state, and federal, laws and regulations that apply to the employer's facility and recognize the importance of compliance with such laws and regulations.

EQUIPMENT and SUPPLIES

- Computer
- Access to organizational Web sites that have established legislation and regulations that pertain to medical facilities
- Information about changes to and new federal and state legislation and regulations

PROCEDURAL STEPS

1. Consistently review applicable legislation and regulations that apply to the facility.
   PURPOSE: To ensure compliance with the law.
2. Discover the federal and state ramifications of issues related to healthcare workers, such as:
   - Regulatory bodies
   - Education and credentials
   - Scope of practice
   - Job qualifications
   - Continuing education unit (CEU) requirements
   - Loss of credentials
   PURPOSE: To ensure full compliance in the medical facility.
3. Review and understand federal and state legislation and regulations related to:
   - Americans with Disabilities Act
   - Controlled substance schedules
   - Occupational Safety and Health Administration (OSHA)
   - Centers for Disease Control and Prevention (CDC)

- Local Public Health Departments
- Material Safety Data Sheets (MSDS)
  PURPOSE: To ensure full compliance in the medical facility.
4. Review and understand accrediting agency requirements that affect the facility.
   PURPOSE: To recognize the importance of local, state, and federal legislation and regulations in the practice setting.
5. Stay aware of new state and federal legislation and regulations and the consequences of noncompliance.
6. Always follow office policy when performing any action at the facility.
   PURPOSE: To ensure full compliance in the medical facility.
7. Apply all local, state, and federal regulations to the daily duties of the medical facility.
   PURPOSE: To ensure full compliance with laws and regulations that affect the medical facility.
8. Report new or changed regulations to the appropriate supervisor in the medical facility.
   PURPOSE: To incorporate new regulations or changes into the office policy manual.
9. Facilitate or attend training sessions that explain new or changed regulations.
   PURPOSE: To ensure full compliance with laws and regulations that affect the medical facility.
10. Research one federal or state law that has recently been updated or changed. Prepare a report summarizing the change and submit it to your instructor.

PROCEDURE 7-6

Report Illegal and/or Unsafe Behaviors That Affect Health, Safety, and Welfare of Others to Proper Authorities

GOAL: To provide a proper procedure for the medical assistant to follow when legal or ethical regulations have been breached.

EQUIPMENT and SUPPLIES

- Contact information for regulatory and law enforcement agencies.
- Written reports or documentation of breaches of regulations, if available.

PROCEDURAL STEPS

1. Compile a list of all regulatory and law enforcement agencies that have jurisdiction over the medical facility.
2. Construct an office directory of contact information for each agency.
   <u>PURPOSE:</u> To have contact information close at hand when needed.
3. Document any illegal and/or unsafe act that occurs in the medical office.
   <u>PURPOSE:</u> To have a record of questionable incidents so that the medical assistant will not have to rely on memory.
4. Consider each aspect of the incident and make sure that it was truly a breach of law or ethics before acting. If unsure, discuss the situation with a trusted peer.
   <u>PURPOSE:</u> To prevent false accusations and the filing of a false report.

5. Report the incident to the direct supervisor and give him or her an opportunity to act.
   <u>PURPOSE:</u> To follow the chain of command.
6. If the situation is not resolved, report the incident to the next person in the chain of command unless the situation is critical and could cause harm to the patient.
   <u>PURPOSE:</u> To follow the chain of command.
7. If the situation still is not resolved, report the incident to the proper authorities, depending on the nature of the incident.
   <u>PURPOSE:</u> To comply with the law and ethical standards for medical practice.
8. Turn in your directory to your instructor.

CLOSING COMMENTS

Most patients never entertain the thought of taking legal action against their physicians, and a medical assistant should not develop an attitude of skepticism. However, a medical assistant can play an important role in preventing medical claims.

- Give scrupulous attention to the needs of each patient and do not leave patients alone for long periods. This especially applies to young children and elderly patients. Do not criticize other physicians or healthcare facilities. Never give out any information about the patient without written consent, and verify the identity of anyone asking for information about a patient.
- Use discretion in phone and office conversations. One never knows who may be standing nearby. Be aware of tone of voice and attitude during spoken conversations. Communicate office policies and procedures to patients clearly before treatment whenever possible.
- Keep accurate records that show exactly what was done to the patient and when it was done. The medical assistant must never make any promises as to the outcome of treatment. Record cancelled and no-show appointments and record the facts if a patient discontinues treatment.
- Check office equipment often to ensure that it is working properly. Keep drug samples and prescription pads out of sight. Never diagnose, prescribe, or offer a prognosis. Perform only the tasks for which you are trained and keep abreast of new findings and procedures in healthcare. Correctly follow all federal and state regulations.

- Play a positive part in the prevention of medical liability claims. Take care of the patient in a compassionate and competent way, and malpractice will not be a frequent issue in the medical facility.

Patient Education

Perhaps the most important detail to remember with regard to patient education and law is patience. Many medical forms are complicated, and regulations change often. Patients usually are not as well educated as the medical assistant on matters concerning legal policies and procedures. Often patients become frustrated with the number of changes with which they are expected to contend, and they unintentionally may project this frustration onto the medical assistant. Remain calm and answer questions, offering as much assistance to the patient as possible.

Legal and Ethical Issues

Generally, the law holds that every person is liable for the consequences of his or her own negligence when another person is injured as a result. In some situations, this liability extends to the employer. Physicians may be held responsible for the mistakes of those who work in their healthcare facility, and sometimes they must pay damages for the negligent acts of their employees.

Under the doctrine of *respondeat superior*, physicians are legally responsible for the acts of their employees when they are acting within the scope of their duties or employment. Physicians also are responsible for the acts of assistants who are not their own employees if they commit acts of negligence in the presence of the physician while under the physician's immediate supervision. When physicians practice as partners, they are liable not only for their own acts and those of their partners, but also for the negligent acts of any agent or employee of the partnership.

Medical assistants guilty of negligence are liable for their own actions, but the injured party generally sues the physician, because the chances of collecting damages are better. However, even assistants with no money can be held liable for any negligent action, and liens can be placed on their property in anticipation of its sale and potential profit. This fact illustrates the continuing importance of exercising extreme care in performing all duties accurately and professionally in the healthcare facility.

SUMMARY OF SCENARIO

Barbara is enthusiastic about her new job and duties. She is confident about appearing in court to represent Dr. Patrick and discuss the contents of the medical record of the patient suing his surgeon. Dr. Patrick is not a party to the lawsuit but has a physician-patient relationship with the patient just the same. An offer existed, as did the acceptance of that offer. The relationship was based on legal subject matter, and the physician and the patient had the legal capacity to enter into a contract. Consideration also existed, because the patient paid for services and the physician treated the patient. Both received something of value. Samantha and Lynda would like to accompany Barbara to the court proceedings to watch and learn.

Even if a patient does not pay for treatment, a contract still exists. The physician may elect to terminate the physician-patient relationship if the patient does not pay, but the trust that the patient places in the physician can be considered a thing of value.

Patients should understand their role in their treatment and their responsibilities to the physician. Often this information is communicated in the patient policy brochure, or it may be discussed orally with the patient. Physicians are not required to accept all patients; for instance, not all physicians deliver babies. Some physicians do not treat patients with workers' compensation claims. Physicians do have the right to see the types of patients they want to and are competent to treat, but they should never discriminate on the basis of race, gender, or any other protected status.

A physician may not always be correct in his or her diagnoses, but this does not mean that the physician has committed malpractice. However, if expert witnesses feel that the physician should have made a different diagnosis based on the case, then the physician might be held liable for negligence. If an employee has information about a case that is damaging to the physician, he or she is ethically obligated to report the information, but rarely legally liable to speak up unless a law has been broken.

Samantha and Lynda have learned many new concepts about law from Barbara and are anxious to follow the court proceedings. They will learn more by watching the actual process of law at work. Barbara looks forward to sharing more knowledge with the employees as they continue to work together.

Medical assistants can help the physician comply with legal regulations in the office by making sure that they understand the policies and procedures required by the facility. Rules are made to ensure compliance so that both patients and employees are kept safe and risks in the office are kept to a minimum. Patient confidentiality is one of the most important rules to remember. New graduates can learn about the laws that affect medical facilities in their area by discussing them with their supervisors and by attending seminars and training. Much information is available on the Internet regarding legal issues.

Trust is a critical factor in avoiding medical professional liability lawsuits. When the patient trusts the physician, he or she is much more likely to work through issues that otherwise might lead to legal action against the physician. Keeping accurate patient records and documenting all information required in the patient chart helps prove that the physician adequately cared for the patient. Clearly, legible handwriting is vital in this process.

The medical assistant may find that the physician is not in compliance with certain rules and regulations. Never jump to conclusions and assume that the physician has no intention of complying. There are various reasons for noncompliance, and any issues should be brought to the attention of the office manager or the physician for clarification. It is the medical assistant's responsibility to question noncompliance and make every effort to bring the facility into compliance with the cooperation of supervisors, co-workers, and the physician. As a team, medical professionals can remain in compliance and deliver excellent care to all patients.

SUMMARY OF LEARNING OBJECTIVES

1. **Define, spell, and pronounce the terms listed in the vocabulary.**
   Spelling and pronouncing medical terms correctly bolster the medical assistant's credibility. Knowing the definition of these terms promotes confidence in communication with patients and co-workers.

2. **Discuss all levels of government legislation and regulation as they apply to medical assisting practice, including regulations established by the FDA and the DEA.**
   An exhaustive listing of government legislation and regulation is available to the medical assistant through Internet research, useful for those situations when asked to keep the facility in compliance with the law. The person charged with this duty must be able to interpret lengthy legalese and determine the exact tasks and precautions required of the facility. Some offices form a compliance committee to help ensure that all pertinent laws that govern the medical practice are followed meticulously.

3. **Discuss the legal scope of practice for medical assistants.**
   From a legal perspective, each medical assistant is required to perform all duties in a manner that meets or exceeds that of a reasonably competent and knowledgeable medical assistant. Also, medical assistants cannot perform any duties for which they have not been trained.

4. **Distinguish among an act, a statute, and an ordinance.**
   Different types of laws and regulations affect us, depending on the origination of the law. *Acts* are introduced at the federal level and must be passed by Congress. State legislative bodies develop *statutes,* and local governments create *ordinances.*

5. **Compare criminal and civil law as they apply to the practicing medical assistant.**
   Criminal law governs violations punishable as offenses against the state or government. *Civil law* is concerned with acts that are not criminal but involve relationships between individuals and other individuals, groups, or government agencies. The medical assistant needs to understand the differences between the types of law and how they affect the physician's medical practice. Medical assistants must personally review those laws that influence medical assistant practice and make sure that they are followed on a constant basis, with documentation to prove so if necessary in a courtroom.

6. **Explain the three basic categories of criminal law.**
   Infractions are the lowest on the criminal law scale, usually resulting in a fine. *Misdemeanors* are minor crimes punishable by a fine or imprisonment in a city or county jail. *Felonies* are major crimes, such as rape, murder, or burglary. Most felonies carry punishment of imprisonment for at least 1 year, and they are divided into subgroups, usually first-, second-, and third-degree felonies. *Treason* is a higher crime, usually an attempt to overthrow the government. High treason constitutes a serious threat to the stability of the government, such as an attempt on the life of the president.

7. **Distinguish which type of civil law deals with medical professional liability.**
   Tort law is the division of civil law that deals with medical professional liability. Tort law provides relief for those who have suffered harm from the actions of others. The plaintiff must establish duty, breach of duty, and damages as a result of the breach of duty, and the extent of the damages suffered.

8. **Provide an example of tort law as it would apply to a medical assistant.**
   If a medical assistant committed a breach of patient confidentiality, his or her error would fall under the category of tort law, and the medical assistant could be held liable for the error, resulting in damages being paid to the patient by the physician and/or his liability insurer.

9. **Describe liability, professional and personal injury, and third-party insurance.**
   When a person is liable for an act, he or she is obligated or responsible according to the law. Professional and personal injuries are types of torts, meaning that a person or group has injured someone or something else. Physicians carry professional liability insurance, a type of third-party insurance, to help guard them from liability costs. Medical assistants can also invest in liability insurance.

10. **Explain the four essential elements of a valid contract.**
    Four elements are essential to a valid legal contract: (1) there must be a "meeting of the minds," or manifestation of assent; (2) the contract must involve legal subject matter; (3) the parties to the contract must have the legal capacity to enter into a contract; and (4) some type of consideration must be offered.

11. **Distinguish between interrogatories and depositions.**
    Interrogatories are lists of questions directed from each party of a lawsuit to the other. Interrogatories are answered under oath and directed only to the parties actually named in the lawsuit. *Depositions* can be taken from any witness or party to the lawsuit. They also are taken under oath, and often witnesses are subpoenaed to offer a deposition.

12. **List three things to remember when testifying in court.**
    Testifying in court can be an intimidating experience, but good preparation can alleviate many anxieties. Discussing potential questions with the attorney helps prepare the witness for giving testimony. Always tell the truth to prevent charges of perjury. Speak clearly and distinctly, and do not hesitate to ask the attorney to repeat a question. A brief pause to think about an answer causes no harm. Dress conservatively, know the location and room of the court in advance, and always arrive on time. Credibility is critical in a medical professional liability trial.

13. **Discuss the advantages of arbitration.**
    Arbitration is a popular alternative to court trials. It involves the use of a third party familiar with law or the issues at hand. It is recognized by statute in most states and provides a faster, confidential, fair, and less expensive resolution to a dispute.

14. **Differentiate among malfeasance, misfeasance, and nonfeasance.**
    Malfeasance, misfeasance, and nonfeasance are types of negligence often involved in medical professional liability cases. *Malfeasance* is performing an act that is completely wrong or unlawful. *Misfeasance,* comparable to a mistake, is the improper performance of a lawful act. *Nonfeasance* is the failure to perform some act that should have been performed.

15. **Explain the "four Ds" of negligence.**

The four Ds of negligence are (1) the *duty* to care for the patient; (2) *dereliction,* or failure to perform that duty; (3) proof that this failure was the *direct* cause of a patient's injury; and (4) proof that the patient suffered *damages* from the injury.

16. **Define the types of damages.**

Nominal damages are token compensations for invasion of a legal right. *Punitive damages* are designed to punish an offender and discourage repetition of an act. *Compensatory damages* are designed to compensate for the actual damages suffered, whereas *general damages* include compensation for pain and suffering, loss of a body member, disfigurement, and other similar losses. *Special damages* can include such losses as earnings or travel costs.

17. **Compare and contrast physician and medical assistant roles in terms of standard of care.**

Physicians are highly trained and skilled professionals who are licensed to diagnose and treat patients. Medical assistants cannot diagnose, treat, or advise patients toward any course of action and must be careful to remain within the medical assistant scope of practice when carrying out their duties at work.

18. **Explain the importance of informed consent.**

Informed consent gives the patient a full understanding of the condition that has been diagnosed, including what could happen if the patient undergoes treatment, refuses treatment, or delays treatment. It provides the patient with information on the advantages and risks of a medical procedure and alternative treatments the patient may want to consider. Informed consent places control in the hands of the patient, who is given the opportunity to make the decisions about his or her healthcare. Patients can never be forced to undergo any type of procedure or treatment.

19. **List several legal disclosures the physician must make.**

The physician must make several types of legal disclosures with regard to a patient's health that do not require the patient's consent. Information about births and deaths, injuries or illnesses as a result of violence, accidental or suspicious deaths, sexually transmitted diseases, and any type of abuse are examples of legal disclosures that must be made by healthcare professionals.

20. **Identify where to report illegal and/or unsafe activities and behaviors that affect the health, safety, and welfare of others.**

In any emergency situation, the medical assistant should call 911. Keep a list of contact information for agencies that provide community assistance. Hospitals often keep an exhaustive list of agencies that can help patients receive various types of assistance. Government agencies are usually listed in the blue pages of a telephone directory and can be easily found using Internet search engines.

21. **Explain how the medical assistant's practice is affected by negligence, malpractice, statutes of limitations, Good Samaritan acts, the Uniform Anatomical Gift Act, Living Wills/Advanced Directives, and the Medical Durable Power of Attorney.**

Because medical assistants are required to perform all duties in a manner that meets or exceeds that of a reasonably competent and knowledgeable medical assistant, they must be aware of state and federal laws and regulations that affect their practice. Many physicians keep copies of the laws that affect the practice in the policy and procedure manual. All employees are responsible for knowing the law and following procedures that are outlined in the policy manual.

22. **Summarize the Patient's Bill of Rights.**

The Patient's Bill of Rights was designed to (1) strengthen consumer confidence by ensuring that the healthcare system is fair and responsive to consumers' needs; (2) provide consumers with credible and effective mechanisms to address their concerns; (3) encourage consumers to take an active role in improving and ensuring their health; (4) affirm the importance of a strong relationship between patients and their healthcare professionals; and (5) affirm the critical role consumers play in safeguarding their health by establishing rights and responsibilities for all participants in improving patients' health.

23. **Describe the implications of the Health Insurance Portability and Accountability Act (HIPAA) for the medical assistant in various medical settings.**

Passage of the Health Insurance Portability and Accountability Act (HIPAA) in 1996 established extensive privacy rules and regulations for the healthcare profession concerning the electronic transfer of information. The act also limited administrative costs by supporting the use of electronic transfer of information and presented guidelines for preventing fraud and abuse. However, the privacy issues raised by HIPAA have been the most discussed and debated topics related to this law.

24. **Describe personal protective equipment.**

Personal protective equipment is designed to protect the wearer from blood-borne pathogens and/or other potentially infectious materials. OSHA requires that employers provide personal protective equipment (PPE) if the employee is at risk of exposure to blood-borne pathogens.

25. **Discuss requirements for responding to hazardous materials disposal.**

Hazardous materials must be disposed of according to the information provided on the MSDS. Spill kits, used to dispose of waste safely, are required in medical facilities. Most biologically hazardous waste is disposed of by waste removal companies and is usually incinerated. The medical facility is provided with receipts both when the waste is picked up and when it is finally incinerated. OSHA requires that these receipts be kept for a specific time.

26. **Describe the importance of the Material Safety Data Sheet (MSDS) in a healthcare setting.**

The Material Safety Data Sheet (MSDS) provides vital information about a product or chemical used in the medical facility. The MSDS explains the proper use of the product and the appropriate action when a spill occurs.

27. **Distinguish between OSHA and CLIA; indicate which one is an actual agency.**

The Occupational Safety and Health Administration (OSHA) is an agency, a division of the U.S. Department of Labor. More than 2,300 employees work for OSHA, and the agency runs on an annual budget of approximately $443 million as of 2002. Twenty-six states have their own OSHA programs, which adds 3,100 employees. The Occupational Safety and

Health Act of 1970 created this agency to ensure safety in the work-place. The Clinical Laboratory Improvement Amendments (CLIA) is a law that regulates the quality of services provided by laboratories. CLIA is enforced by the Department of Health and Human Services.

28. **Identify how the Americans with Disabilities Act (ADA) applies to the medical assisting profession.**

Medical assistants must comply with the ADA as it applies to the medical facility employer. Know the provisions of the act and assist in making certain that the facility is in full compliance. Assist patients with disabilities as they make their way into, through, and out of the facility. Offer to help with disrobing and dressing before assuming that the patient needs assistance.

CONNECTIONS

📖 **Study Guide Connection:** Go to the Chapter 7 Study Guide. Read and complete the activities.

🅔 **Evolve Connection:** Go to the Chapter 7 link at *evolve.elsevier.com/kinn* to complete the Chapter Review and Chapter Quiz. Check out the other resources listed for this chapter to make the most of what you have learned from Medicine and Law.

8

COMPUTER CONCEPTS

Dr. Michael Bouchard is aware of the advantages of networking his office computers and having Internet access to meet the needs of his facility. Every day he and his staff send and receive many important e-mail messages to and from patients and other individuals. His staff members use the computer for communications and to access sources of online information. Patient tracking, accounting functions, and health information retrieval are immensely faster on a computer than with a paper-based system. The scheduling features of the software are a distinct advantage, because the schedule is shared; everyone in the office knows the doctor's schedule, which prevents double-booking and miscommunication. Dr. Bouchard sends his staff members for regular computer training so that all of them can use the computers in the most efficient ways.

The requirements of the Health Information Portability and Accessibility Act (HIPAA) have altered the methods by which information may be used in medical facilities. No employee is allowed to access information in the clinic that is not necessary for that employee to provide patient care and assistance. Dr. Bouchard takes the HIPAA guidelines seriously and makes sure that his entire staff understands the importance of keeping health information secure.

While studying this chapter, think about the following questions:

- How do computers help the physician's office to run more efficiently?
- Can an employee in the physician's office invade a patient's right to privacy by accessing medical records?
- How can information on the computer be kept secure from curious employees who do not need to access the information for the purpose of patient care?
- How does logging in and logging out of the office network help ensure proper access to medical records?
- How could the computer be considered a co-worker in the medical office?

LEARNING OBJECTIVES

1. Define, spell, and pronounce the terms listed in the vocabulary.
2. List several ways the computer can be effective in a medical office.
3. Explain the basic functions a computer performs.
4. Explain the basic parts of a computer.
5. List the three elements that differentiate microprocessors.
6. Discuss the differences among various types of printers.
7. Explain the importance of a motherboard.
8. Explain and give examples of peripheral devices.
9. List and discuss several types of file formats.
10. Explain the concept of computer networking.
11. Define the function of browsers.
12. Discuss the importance of computer security.
13. Locate the keys on a keyboard.

VOCABULARY

application software Computer programs designed to perform specific tasks.

artificial intelligence The aspect of computer science that deals with computers taking on the attributes of humans, such as mimicking human thought. For example, expert systems can make decisions, such as software designed to help a physician diagnose a patient, given a set of symptoms.

backup Any type of storage that prevents the loss of files with hard disk failure.

bits The smallest units of information inside the computer, each represented either by the digit "0" or "1"; 8 bits equal 1 byte.

bookmark A command in a browser that marks the Internet protocol (IP) address of a Web site so that it can be saved and recalled quickly without typing the entire Web address.

browsers Software programs that allow users to view Web pages on the Internet (e.g., Internet Explorer, Firefox).

byte A unit of data that contains 8 binary digits, or bits.

cache (kash) Special, high-speed storage that either can be part of the computer's main memory or a separate storage device. One function of a cache is to store Web sites visited in the computer memory for faster recall the next time the Web site is requested.

CD burner A device that can "write" data on a blank compact disk (CD) or copy data from one CD to a blank CD.

cookies Messages sent to a Web browser from a Web server that identify users and can prepare custom Web pages for them, possibly displaying their name on return to the site.

cursor A symbol on the monitor screen that shows the location of the next character to be typed.

cyberspace The nonphysical space of the online world of computer networks in which communication takes place.

database A collection of related files that serves as a foundation for retrieving information.

device driver The program or commands given to a device connected to a computer that enable the device to function. For instance, a printer may come equipped with software that must be loaded onto the computer first so that the printer will work.

digital subscriber line (DSL) A high-speed, sophisticated modulation scheme that operates over existing copper telephone wiring systems; often referred to as "last-mile technologies," because DSL is used for connections from a telephone switching station to a home or office and not between switching stations.

digital video disk (DVD) An optical disk that holds approximately 28 times more information than a CD; a DVD is most commonly used to hold full-length movies. Compared with a CD, which holds approximately 600 megabytes, a DVD can hold approximately 4.7 gigabytes. Also called a *digital versatile disk.*

disk drives Devices that load a program or data stored on a disk into the computer.

domain name The initial part of a URL listing; the domain and name of the host or server, indicating the publisher of a Web page or site.

e-commerce Short for *electronic commerce;* used to describe the sale and purchase of goods and services over the Internet; doing business over the Internet.

e-mail Short for *electronic mail;* communications transmitted via computer or computer network.

environment The state of a computer, usually determined by the programs running and hardware and software characteristics.

flash drive A small, portable device that can carry 2 to 8 gigabytes or more of information and that plugs into a USB port; also called a *thumb drive, jump drive,* or *portable drive.*

gigabyte (GB) Approximately 1 billion bytes.

hard copy The readable paper copy or printout of information.

hardware The physical components of the computer system, such as the central processing unit (CPU), monitor, and printer.

HTML The acronym for *hypertext markup language,* the language used to create documents for the Internet.

HTTP The acronym for *hypertext transfer protocol,* which defines how messages are formatted and transmitted over the Internet. When a URL is entered into the computer, an HTTP command tells the Web server to retrieve the requested Web page.

hub A common connection point for devices in a network with multiple ports, often used to connect segments of a local area network (LAN).

icons Pictures, often on the monitor screen "desktop," that represent programs or objects. Clicking on an icon directs the user to the program.

input Information entered into and used by the computer.

kilobyte (KB) Approximately 1,024 bytes.

megabyte (MB) Approximately 1 million bytes.

megahertz (MHz) The measuring device for microprocessors. A megahertz is 1 million cycles of electromagnetic currency alternation per second and is used as a unit of measure for the clock speed of computer microprocessors.

modem Short for *modulator-demodulator;* a device that allows information to be transmitted over telephone lines at speeds measured in bits per second (bps). The modem speed generally is listed somewhere on the unit.

multimedia The presentation of graphics, animation, video, sound, and text on a computer in an integrated way or all at once. CD-ROMs are efficient multimedia devices.

notebook Although often used interchangeably with "laptop," this term was created to identify a smaller, thinner, and lighter device, partially designed to fit on tray tables on airplanes.

output Information processed by the computer and transmitted to a monitor, printer, or other device.

personal digital assistant (PDA) A handheld computer capable of functions such as mobile telephony, Web browsing, and media playing. PDAs typically include an appointment calendar, to-do list, address book, note programs, and e-mail and/or Web capabilities.

queries Requests for information from a database.

router (rau´-ter) A device used to connect any number of LANs, which communicate with other routers and determine the best route between any two hosts.

scanner A device that reads text or illustrations on a printed page and can translate the information on that page into a form the computer can understand.

search engines Programs that search documents for keywords and return a list of documents containing those words.

server A computer or device on a network that manages shared network resources.

switch In networks, a device that filters information between LAN segments and reduces overall network traffic and increases speed and bandwidth use efficiency.

system software The operating system and all utility programs that allow the computer to function and perform operations.

tablet A wireless, portable personal computer with a touch screen interface, usually smaller than a notebook but larger than a smart phone (e.g., Apple iPad, Samsung Galaxy, Dell Streak).

TCP/IP The acronym for *transmission control protocol/Internet protocol;* a suite of communications protocols used to connect users or hosts to the Internet.

telecommunications The science and technology of communication by transmission of information from one location to another via telephone, television, telegraph, or satellite.

terabyte (TB) Approximately 1 trillion bytes.

URL The acronym for *uniform resource locator;* specifies the global address of documents or information on the Internet. The URL provides the IP address and the domain name for the Web page, such as microsoft.com.

virtual reality An artificial environment presented to a computer user that feels as if it were a real environment, often involving use of special gloves, earphones, and goggles to enhance the experience.

Today's business world is almost unimaginable without computers, although the computer industry is less than a century old. Within this short time, a computer upsurge has taken place, and today our lives are affected by computers daily. Personal computers (PCs), laptops or notebook computers, and cell phones that send and receive **e-mail** are commonplace. Our world is now one of enhanced **telecommunications**, where faster processing of information is both needed and expected. Advances in technology happen daily; as soon as one "new and improved" device is on the market, its "better and faster" competitor is released. Most people venture into **cyberspace** on a daily basis, where a world of information is waiting with the simple click of a mouse!

Computers are critical in the physician's office and in other types of healthcare facilities. The development of medically specific software, the decrease in the cost of computer **hardware**, and the time savings the computer brings to the office make it well worth the investment. A medical assistant must have more than computer literacy; a good understanding of the way computers work and their capabilities is essential in a medical office.

Since the emergence of the electronic medical record (EMR), patients are likely to see physicians using laptops, tablets, smart phones, and/or personal digital assistants (PDAs) in the exam room, an indication that the entire medical industry is steadily moving toward a paperless environment. The EMR makes the physician's office more efficient and patient information more accessible. The EMR is covered extensively in Chapter 15; before the medical assistant can grasp the concepts of the EMR, he or she needs a strong foundation in basic computer operation. In the current economy, many displaced workers who have found themselves without employment have had to improve their computer skills to be marketable. Some have worked in fields that required little or no computer use, and certainly in any medical facility, computer skills will be mandatory.

COMPUTER BASICS

Getting Started

Even with a basic knowledge of a computer's components and capabilities, without hands-on knowledge the beginner may have some

initial fear of the unknown. The most basic setup of a computer system includes a microprocessor, monitor, keyboard, and mouse (Figure 8-1). The computer is only a machine that takes direction from the operator, performing the tasks it is told to do. A computer can simulate the thought process and make decisions, but most computers found in medical facilities wait for commands that prompt it to act. Dialog boxes appear that ask for **input** from the user; this is how the computer communicates with the user. Computers assist workers in medical offices in several ways, such as:

- Performing repetitive tasks
- Reducing errors
- Speeding up production
- Recalling information on command
- Saving time
- Reducing paperwork and storage space
- Allowing for more creative and productive use of workers' time

The more familiar medical assistants become with the computer, the better skilled they become in its use. Occasionally errors are made, and the computer may respond with an error message. However, the monitor's screen normally indicates what to do next.

FIGURE 8-1 Computers are an invaluable tool for today's medical office. This photograph shows *(left to right)* a CPU, monitor, keyboard, and mouse. The keyboard and mouse are types of input devices that allow data to be entered into the computer, where they are processed. (Courtesy Dell Corp., Round Rock, Texas.)

The computer usually allows the operator the opportunity to figure out the correct information and input it. A help menu can always be accessed, or the instruction manual can be consulted; help lines and technical support also are available when problems occur. The problem may be with the software or with the computer itself. Usually, determining which has caused the problem is fairly easy.

Rarely does a computer "break," although this is a common fear among new users. Records are unlikely to be destroyed by accident; usually, very specific commands are needed to delete stored information. However, a medical assistant must take care not to shut off the computer without saving the information that has been entered. By using a computer in the classroom and practicing at home or at a library, if possible, the medical assistant can become familiar with computer operation and gain confidence that it can be mastered. However, mastery is accomplished only through practice.

With a knowledge of computer terms, the ability to follow step-by-step instructions, and reasonable expertise with a keyboard, a medical assistant can rapidly learn and use almost any computer system. Although computers and software may vary from facility to facility, basic computer operation is similar, and if the instructions given by the computer are carried out, the user should be successful in the tasks attempted.

Although it seems elementary, the first step in computer use is to turn on the system. If nothing happens when the power button is pressed, the primary troubleshooting protocol is to make sure the system is plugged into the power outlet. If a surge protector or an uninterruptible power supply (UPS) is used, be sure this device has power. Then, check all the cords that attach the hardware to determine whether they are fastened securely. Once the power is on, the computer goes through a process called *booting*. The boot sequence is a set of operations the computer performs to load the operating system and prepare it for use.

Once the computer is on, the desktop appears, along with several **icons**. To open a certain program, double-click on its icon. Once a program has been opened, many functions can be performed, such as creating a document, a spreadsheet, or a presentation or maintaining a **database**. Some basic computer functions include:

- *Opening a document.* A document stored on the computer can be opened by clicking on its icon, if the icon appears on the desktop. If the document is stored in a folder, open the folder and click on the document icon.
- *Saving a document.* Most toolbars have a button that allows a document to be saved to a folder or to the desktop. Click the button, then name the file so that it can be easily found when it is needed. Word processing programs also usually have a "Save As" option so that a document can be saved and edited without changing the original file. Be sure to check the compatibility of the versions of the software being used. Most programs are backward compatible; for instance, MS Office 2010 can open MS Office 2007, but older software versions cannot open newer versions.
- *Creating a folder.* Folders in which documents can be stored are easily created. For instance, in a Windows **environment**, a folder can be created on the desktop. To do this, right-click on the desktop away from other files, folders, and icons, then select the command "New." When the second dialog box appears, select "Folder." Click "Folder" and a folder titled "New Folder" will appear on the desktop. To rename it, click twice on the words "New Folder" and type in the words "Study Guides" or whatever title is to be used. The folder is ready for use. To move documents into the folder, click on the document icon and hold the left mouse button down while dragging the document on top of the folder. This is called "drag and drop" or sometimes "click and drag." To place documents not on the desktop in the folder, use the "Save As" feature and save the document to the desired folder. Or the document can be saved to the desktop, after which the "drag-and-drop" feature can be used to place it in the desired folder.
- *Copying, moving, deleting, and renaming files.* Most word processing programs allow the user to copy, move, delete, and rename files. In Windows, a file may be copied easily by right-clicking on the document icon and then clicking "Copy." Then, open the folder to which the file is to be copied, right-click inside the folder, and click "Paste." A copy of the file will appear in the folder. Files can be moved from one place to another by using the drag-and-drop method. To delete a file, right-click on the document icon and click "Delete." A dialog box will open that confirms the user's choice to delete the file. The file remains in the Recycle bin on the desktop for a brief period once deleted; therefore, if a mistake was made and the file is needed, the user should look to see whether it is still available. Renaming files is as simple as clicking twice on the file name and typing in the new one. The user also can right-click on the document icon and select "Rename," which will allow the user to change the name of the document.
- *Cutting, copying, and pasting text.* Text can be moved from one place to another by cutting and pasting. First, highlight the text to be moved, then press the "Cut" button. This function can also be accomplished by right-clicking the mouse and selecting "Cut." Next, place the **cursor** at the point where the text should be inserted, then click the "Paste" or right-click the mouse and select "Paste." Text is copied in the same manner. Instead of clicking the "Cut" button, press the "Copy" button. These functions allow the user to be more efficient when creating documents.
- *Finding files.* Computers have a search mechanism that allows the user to search for a file with certain keywords or extensions. In the Windows environment, click the "Start" button, then click on "Search." The dialog box that appears asks the user for what to search (e.g., picture, audio file, document, or other file type). An option to search all files and folders also is available. Enter keywords that pertain to the desired file, and click "Search."
- *Copying an entire disk.* An entire diskette or compact disk (CD) can be copied. First, click on "Start" and then click on "My Computer." Find the drive that has the diskette or CD and right-click on that icon. Then, click on "Copy." Open the folder to which the contents should be copied, and click "Paste." The actual diskette or CD could also be opened, then under the "Edit" drop-down menu, the user can choose "Select All." This allows all the files on the diskette or CD to be copied or permanently moved to another location.
- *Exiting a program.* Click on the "X" button in the upper right corner of the document to exit a program. If the work has not

yet been saved, the user is prompted either to save the document or cancel the action. The user also can exit the program by clicking on "File" then "Close."

When the user has finished with the computer for the day, it always should be shut down properly. To do this, click the "Start" icon, then click "Shut down Computer." The dialog box that appears allows the user to turn off the computer, restart it, stand by, or cancel the action. The restart function is helpful when the computer "freezes" or fails to function as it should. This takes the computer back through the booting sequence and often corrects problems and allows the user to continue working. Never attempt to fix problems on the computer that are beyond the medical assistant's scope of knowledge. Often a technical assistance desk can guide the user through various steps to correct basic issues. Always report computer malfunctions to the proper person or department.

Computer systems have user manuals which can usually be easily accessed and referenced online, and can usually be saved to the local computer system or the computer desktop. These manuals can be consulted when functions do not perform as they should or when a user is working with an unfamiliar system. Tutorials may be available to help the new user learn the system or to refresh the skills of the experienced user. Software programs have a *help* function, usually accessed on the tool bar. The help function allows the user to type in keywords to search for instructions on using certain features or to reference an index of help topics. The help function is written into the program, and users do not pay a fee for its use. However, most of the major software programs, such as Microsoft Office and Adobe Creative Suite, have entire books devoted to details about the use and capabilities of the software, and classes often are available.

PROCESSING INFORMATION

A computer is a machine designed to accept, store, process, and provide information (Figure 8-2). Computers serve the following basic functions:

- *Input:* Input includes any information that enters the computer. It can take a variety of forms, from commands entered from the keyboard to data from another computer or device, such as a **scanner**. The device that feeds data into a computer, such as a mouse, scanner, keyboard, or voice recognition system, is called an *input device.*
- *Processing:* Processing is the act of manipulating the data that are currently inside the computer to carry out a certain task.
- *Output:* **Output** is anything that exits the computer. Output can appear in many forms, such as binary numbers, characters, pictures, printed pages, or a simple image on the computer screen. Output devices include monitors, speakers, printers, scanners, and modems.
- *Storage:* The act of retaining data or applications is called *storage.* Data can be stored on the hard drive, on CDs, or on separate drives, such as an external hard drive or a **flash drive** (two different types of storage devices). The type of storage device used depends on the amount of information that needs to be saved and where it needs to be used. CDs and flash drives are common portable storage devices used in the business world.

CRITICAL THINKING APPLICATION   **8-1**

- Dr. Bouchard plans to send two of his employees to a training class on using a new software program designed to perform all computer functions needed for his practice. Although he can send only two employees, how can the others learn the system?
- Would it be beneficial or detrimental to close the office for a day to educate the other employees about the system? What should the physician consider before losing a day of patient visits?

TYPES OF COMPUTERS

Various types of computers meet the needs of staff in today's medical office. The most common type is the desktop computer, which usually consists of a central processing unit (CPU), monitor, mouse, and keyboard. The laptop, **notebook**, **tablet**, and **personal digital assistant (PDA)** have grown in popularity because they are compact and portable (Figures 8-3 and 8-4). Some physicians and office employees carry the computer from room to room while treating patients. Information can be entered directly into the computer, which saves time and is much more efficient than handwritten or transcribed notes. The PDA and some tablets are small enough to carry in a pocket or purse. Physicians may use this device when treating patients or making hospital rounds, because it is lighter and even more convenient than a laptop. The PDA also organizes personal information, such as addresses and phone numbers, and most models allow the user to access the Internet and read e-mail. The PDA also can be used as a day planner to keep track of appointments, meetings, and other important events.

Embedded computers are computers inside another device, such as an ultrasound unit or electrocardiograph (ECG). These computers allow data input and output and usually analyze information.

FIGURE 8-2 The keyboard and mouse are types of input devices that allow data to be entered into the computer, where they are processed. These are the main two types of input devices used with computer systems, although the evolution of technology continually provides faster, easier methods of getting data from outside the computer system to its internal processing system. (Courtesy Dell Corp., Round Rock, Texas.)

FIGURE 8-3 Laptop computers vary in size and weight and are easily portable. (Courtesy Dell Corp., Round Rock, Texas.)

FIGURE 8-4 The personal digital assistant (PDA) is a handheld device that usually contains an address, a phone book, and a personal organizer and allows the user to access the Internet. (Courtesy Dell Corp., Round Rock, Texas.)

PARTS OF THE COMPUTER

A medical assistant must understand the function of the different parts of a computer. The physical pieces that can be touched and seen are called *hardware.* Computers using Windows software have an option in the control panel for adding hardware. This shortcut makes adding new equipment easy and provides instruction all along the way. Many types of software have an automatic setup that allows for installation and an uninstall feature; for example, Microsoft also has installation Wizard to assist in installation of programs. Hardware provides the medium on which software can be used. Most PCs have a microprocessor, monitor, keyboard, and mouse, and many are connected to a printer.

Microprocessor

The microprocessor is housed inside the casing of the main computer hardware. The microprocessor is the central unit of the computer; it contains the logic circuitry, which carries out the instructions of a

computer's programs. It is considered the most important piece of hardware in a computer system. Microprocessors act as the brain of the computer and interpret instructions from a program. Microprocessors, sometimes called *CPUs,* are differentiated by three basic elements:

- *Bandwidth:* Bandwidth is the amount of information that can be sent over a connection at one time or how many **bits** can be processed in a single instruction. *Bits* (short for binary digits) are the smallest pieces of information on the computer. Eight bits make up 1 **byte**. A **kilobyte (KB)** is approximately 1,024 bytes, and a **megabyte (MB)** is approximately 1 million bytes. A **gigabyte (GB)** consists of approximately 1 billion bytes. A **terabyte (TB)** provides a huge amount of storage, consisting of approximately 1 trillion bytes.
- *Clock speed:* Clock speed determines how many instructions per second the processor can handle. Clock speed is measured in **megahertz (MHz)**. One megahertz equals 1 million cycles per second; therefore, a processor that operates at 300 MHz executes 300 million cycles per second.
- *Instruction set:* The instruction set is the set of instructions the microprocessor can execute.

The higher the bandwidth and clock speed, the faster and more powerful the microprocessor. For instance, a 32-bit microprocessor that runs at 50 MHz is more powerful than a 16-bit microprocessor that runs at 25 MHz.

A microprocessor contains memory consisting of electronic and magnetic cells, each of which contains information. The two kinds of memory are read-only memory (ROM) and random-access memory (RAM). ROM is internal memory, which contains a portion of the operating system and computer language; this is sometimes known as *main memory.* Data that have been "burned" onto a ROM chip cannot be removed and can only be read, similar to a CD-ROM, unless the CD is a "rewriteable" type. With this permanent memory, much less information has to be transferred from a disk to start the computing process. ROM cannot be overwritten and is not erased when the power is shut off. RAM can be thought of as an internal scratch pad for the computer. It contains the program instructions and the data currently processing. RAM normally is erased when the power is shut off.

> **CRITICAL THINKING APPLICATION   8-2**
>
> A colleague of Dr. Bouchard has mentioned that he knows of a Web site with several computer programs that can be downloaded for free. Dr. Bouchard investigates the site and realizes that the software has been pirated. What concerns could this cause if he uses the software in his office? What would happen if any of this software were to malfunction?

Monitor

A monitor, which looks very much like a television screen, is a device used to display computer-generated information. Monitors can be adjusted for brightness, sharpness, and other settings of the user's choice. Many are high-definition monitors that rival the best plasma TV screens. Color monitors allow for a high-quality display, and the more advanced models have resolutions capable of reproducing high-quality pictures good enough for viewing a **digital video disk (DVD)**. The monitor provides the user with instant feedback on entries into the computer. Monitors sometimes are referred to as *displays*.

Keyboard

For most computers, the keyboard is the primary text input device. Keyboards have special function keys, such as the escape key, tab key, cursor movement keys, numeric keys, shift keys, and control keys. Additional function keys, numbered F1 to F12, are used to perform specific word processing or other computer-related operations. Used alone, a function key may create bold print, underline, indent, or call up a help screen. Used in conjunction with the Ctrl, Alt, or Shift key, the function keys can produce other effects, such as activating the printer, inserting the current date into a document, retrieving a file, or moving a designated block of text. Wireless keyboards are a popular alternative that allow the user to move around more freely while operating the computer. Wave keyboards, and others designed with ergonomics in mind, also are popular.

Mouse

A wireless mouse allows the user to manipulate the cursor without a cord attached. The mouse is a pointing device with a ball on the bottom that is moved by rolling it on a flat tabletop or mouse pad. An optical mouse has a photosensor instead of the rolling ball device. Some computers, especially laptops, have a built-in device, called a *trackball,* that is moved with the finger or thumb and serves the same function as a mouse. Other computers have a touchpad or trackpoint that is manipulated to control the cursor. The cursor is a pointer or flat bar that appears on the monitor to show where the next character will appear (i.e., the insertion point). The mouse allows the user to navigate around the screen quickly and to click on links to access Web sites.

Printer

Printers are output devices. Documents on the monitor may be directed to a printer to produce a printout, or **hard copy**, of a document. Many printers are bidirectional, which means they print from both left to right and right to left. The type of printer used should depend on the job being performed.

Impact printers are inexpensive and produce a fair to moderate quality hard copy. They form letters or shapes that they are directed to print by arranging patterns of dots on the paper. They often operate faster than letter-quality or color machines, but the print lacks the clarity generally desired for a truly professional look. These printers are often used in laboratories and larger departments in healthcare facilities that run lengthy reports or produce output that does not need a pristine appearance.

Inkjet printers use an ink cartridge that feeds an array of nearly microscopic tubes, each of which has a heating element that is energized during the printing process. The ink cartridge may be black or color. Inkjet printers cost less than laser printers, but the ink cartridges they use are fairly expensive and increase the operating cost.

Laser printers use xerographic technology similar to that in photocopiers; therefore, a laser printer can produce an almost limitless variety of forms and sizes as well as complex graphics. One disadvantage of inkjet and laser printers is that they cannot produce multiple copies with carbon sets or multicopy forms, which often are used by insurance companies for their filing forms.

Some printers today are multifunctional, serving as printers, fax machines, scanners, and copiers. Although these are excellent for home offices, they may not be the best investment for offices that use these machines often during the day. Many larger offices have networked printers that allow users to send jobs to a specific printer from any point within the network.

CRITICAL THINKING APPLICATION   8-3

Dr. Bouchard has asked his office manager to perform a cost comparison on printers for three of the office computers. He prefers that they have scanning and fax capability. What are some features the office manager will be interested in knowing about on these machines?

INSIDE THE COMPUTER

A basic knowledge of the parts of a computer and their function can help a medical assistant deal with minor technical issues and more easily communicate with technical support personnel.

Motherboard

A motherboard is the main circuit board for the computer, to which other devices can be attached. Usually it contains the processor, the memory, and other controllers and devices that allow the system to operate and function.

Disk Drives

Today's computers have various **disk drives** on which information can be stored or accessed. The hard disk or hard drive is a magnetic disk inside the computer that holds approximately 10 MB to 400 to 500 GB of information (Figure 8-5). Application software normally is saved to the hard disk and stored there on the computer for use when needed. This is commonly called the *C drive.*

CDs normally are used in the computer's A drive, although the drives can have different names or labels, depending on the brand of computer. Flash drives make transporting information from one computer to another quick and easy.

FIGURE 8-5 Hard drives store data and applications for fast, effective access and retrieval. Although a program installed on a hard drive can be removed, most are intended for permanent use, such as Microsoft Office or Peachtree Accounting.

Dr. Bouchard mentions that he noticed CD-R disks on sale over the weekend. The price was $30 for 100 CD-Rs. One of the medical assistants noticed a 30-pack of CD-Rs for $7.99. Which is the better buy?

CD-ROM

Most of today's PCs are equipped with CD-ROM drives, which allow the storage of data on a CD. CDs hold much more information than their predecessors, floppy disks. A single CD can store the equivalent of about 300,000 text pages. A CD-RW is one on which data can be written, erased, and rewritten. Computers with a **CD burner**, or CD-R drive, can take information from one CD or another source and write it to a second CD. The computer must also have software that enables the burner to work. Software installed on a computer to allow a hardware device to function is called a **device driver**. Unlike most other storage media, CDs can easily be mailed in a flat envelope.

Software

Software comprises the programs and utilities loaded onto or inside a computer that carry out the work performed by the machine. The two types of software are system software and application software.

System software serves as the operating system of the computer and allows it to run and carry out the functions the computer performs. For instance, Windows XP is a type of operating system software. **Application software** refers to the programs loaded onto the computer that carry out the work for the actual users of the computer. Examples of application software are Microsoft Office, MediSoft, and Medical Manager. Applications (programs) are designed to perform specific tasks, such as word processing, billing, accounting, appointment setting, insurance form preparation, payroll, and database management. Many software applications are available for complete medical practice management (Procedure 8-1).

Modems

A **modem**, short for *modulator-demodulator,* is a device over which data can be transmitted via telephone lines and other media, such as a coaxial cable. Modems can be internal or external. An internal modem is built into or added to the inside of the computer casing. A cable modem operates over cable TV lines and uses the coaxial cable to provide faster Internet access. **Digital subscriber line (DSL)** modems operate over phone lines, as do normal modems, but they use a different frequency; as a result, the telephone can be used while the computer is accessing the Internet. Often a filter is attached to the phone that removes other frequencies in which the DSL is working; this prevents interference with the telephone line operation.

PROCEDURE 8-1

Use Office Hardware and Software to Maintain Office Systems

GOAL: To use the office computer system to maintain the hardware and software systems used in the physician's office.

EQUIPMENT and SUPPLIES

- Computer system
- Computer software applications
- Software manuals
- Description of office systems
- Hardware user manuals
- Patient data
- Business data

PROCEDURAL STEPS

1. Determine the types of data the physician's office needs to computerize.
   PURPOSE: To effectively plan the needs of the physician's office.
2. List these data in a Word document.
3. Research each type of data and determine how often it should be backed up to maintain accuracy and follow regulations.
   PURPOSE: To make certain that the office is in compliance with all rules and regulations regarding the data produced in the medical office.
4. Research computer systems and software that can handle the tasks that need to be completed daily in the physician's office.

5. Determine a schedule for maintaining the hardware of the computer system.
   PURPOSE: To comply with manufacturers' recommendations for hardware maintenance.
6. Determine a reasonable backup schedule for the data contained on the office computer system.
   PURPOSE: To plan a workable time period in which data should be backed up.
7. Develop a spreadsheet that includes a timeline for hardware and software maintenance in the physician's office.
8. Discuss the spreadsheet and the choices with the instructor, including any changes that might be indicated.
   PURPOSE: To receive input on the spreadsheet and suggestions for changes, if indicated.
9. Revise the spreadsheet if necessary.
10. Submit the spreadsheet to the instructor.

Speakers and Microphones

Some computers have external speakers to provide a higher quality sound from the computer. Many computers also have built-in speakers that provide a fair quality of sound. Microphones can be built in or attached so that the user can speak directly into the computer, even to someone on the other side of the world!

PERIPHERAL DEVICES

Peripheral devices are those that are not essential to the operation of the computer. For instance, the computer can operate without a modem, although a modem is necessary to access the Internet. Even a mouse is considered a peripheral device, because everything the mouse can access also can be reached by pressing certain buttons on the keyboard, although often multiple keys must be pressed at once. This section discusses some of the peripheral devices in use today.

Scanners

Scanners read text, illustrations, or photographs printed on paper and put them into a format the computer can understand. Photographs can be placed in the scanner, saved on the computer, and then used in a document. Some advanced scanners are used like highlighters and can collect notes from printed text.

Digital Cameras

Many digital cameras can be attached directly to a computer or printer, and photographs can be downloaded directly from the camera. Other cameras use a disk to load the pictures onto the computer.

> **CRITICAL THINKING** APPLICATION   8-5
>
> How might a digital camera be of use to a physician in the medical practice? What care should be taken when the camera is used with a patient?

Flash Drives

Individuals who use numerous computers in different places find the flash drive to be a convenient way to transfer files. The flash drive (also known as a *thumb drive* or *jump drive*) allows the user to save files from the originating computer to the drive so that only the drive is transported to the second computer (Figure 8-6). To use the device, after a document is completed, use the "Save As" function and find the flash drive in the "My Computer" location. After the file has been saved to the flash drive, it can be removed from the computer. Flash drives can be carried in a pocket or purse and have a cap that should be left on to protect the USB mechanism. Flash drives commonly have a storage capacity of 2 to 4 GB and can be purchased with a capacity of 64 GB or more.

External Hard Drives

An external hard drive is a disk drive with a very high storage capacity that is attached externally to a computer. These drives are used as a **backup** device for important data. The first external hard drives

FIGURE 8-6 A flash drive (also called a *thumb* or *jump drive*) allows the user to store documents for use on a different computer.

were called Zip drives, which held 100 to 250 MB of data. Today's internal hard drives can hold 400 to 500 GB, whereas high-end external hard drives commonly hold 500 GB. Some are sold with two drives in one unit, which have a capacity of a terabyte or more. These drives can even be stored somewhere other than the facility so that they are safe in case of fire or some other destructive event. Some external hard drives can be set up to back up the main hard drives at a specific date and time.

ADDING A PROGRAM TO A COMPUTER

Adding or loading a program onto a computer is relatively easy. Most programs today come on a CD-ROM. The program usually includes instructions for loading it onto the computer. Watch the monitor for steps to complete and information about the user's preferences, then follow all the directions.

In a Windows environment, the Control Panel provides an option to "Add/Remove Programs." Once clicked, this allows the program in the CD disk drive to be loaded onto the computer. At several points the computer may ask the user questions about his or her preferences for the program. Often the computer needs to be restarted after installation.

To remove a program from the computer, access the "Add/Remove Programs" icon and follow the directions for removing the program. This may be the only way to remove the program completely from the computer system.

FILE FORMATS

A file is a collection of data. Computers use many types of files. A text file, for example, contains some type of text, which is the main body of printed words or written matter on a page. Often an extension is used at the end of the filename to designate the type of file. A few of the common file extensions include the following:

- *jpg:* JPG (or JPEG) stands for "joint photographic experts group"; this format often is used for photographs.
- *gif:* GIF stands for "graphics interchange format," which supports color and often is used for scanned images and illustrations rather than photographs.
- *doc:* The extension .doc usually indicates a file created by a word processor or word processing software; *doc* stands for document.
- *txt:* A text file usually has the extension .txt.
- *rtf:* RTF stands for "rich text format."

- *bmp:* Bit-mapped graphics are indicated by the extension .bmp. These are compiled by a graphics image set in rows or columns of dots.

A medical assistant familiar with these types of files can save and open them correctly and use the computer to the fullest advantage in the medical office.

COMPUTER NETWORKING

A network is a group of two or more computer systems that are linked together. Several types of networks exist:

- *LAN:* A *local area network,* or a computer network spanning a relatively small area. Most LANs are contained in a single building or group of buildings and are connected by a **router**, but LANs can be connected to other LANs even at a distance. A **hub** is a device that connects several computers or networks, and a **switch** is designed to help the LAN run more efficiently by controlling local network traffic.
- *MAN:* A *metropolitan area network.* A MAN spans an area that does not exceed a metropolitan area or city and connects several LANs.
- *WAN:* A *wide area network,* which spans a relatively large geographic area. Typically, a WAN consists of two or more LANs or MANs. These networks can be connected through public networks, such as a telephone system, or through leased lines or satellites. The largest WAN is the Internet.
- *HAN:* A *home area network,* which connects computers inside a user's home.
- *CAN:* A *campus area network,* often used on college campuses and sometimes on military bases.

A computer network enables resource and information sharing. A group of computers may be liked to one printer, and print jobs are completed as they are requested by users, one at a time. Computers may also be linked by a network to an insurance company database, so that insurance claims can be transmitted electronically. A group of businesses operating in different locations may also share a network. All networks are designed to make computer systems more efficient.

SERVERS

A **server** is important to the network, because it is the computer that manages the shared network resources. Several types of servers exist. When many computers are connected to one printer, often a print server manages these printers. File servers are used for file storage, and database servers are used to process database **queries**.

THE INTERNET

The Internet is a global network that connects millions of computers. This fascinating structure has made the world a smaller place. Through chat programs one can talk with individuals literally on the other side of the world and be introduced to cultures that 20 years ago would never have been understood. Through Web pages, we can visit different parts of the world and learn and see many things that previously were impossible for the average person to experience. **E-commerce** allows us to shop on the Internet, from the most exclusive stores in Beverly Hills to the corner grocer. The Internet has changed the way we learn, do business, communicate, and entertain ourselves.

Each computer connected to the Internet is called a *host* and is independent of all the others. The users of each computer determine which services to make available to other users on the Internet. Often a company or organization also has an Intranet, which is a local network that uses Internet technology within a company or single location but does not have access to the Internet directly.

Internet service providers (ISPs) are companies that provide access to the Internet (e.g., AT&T, America Online, Verizon, Earthlink, Yahoo, and scores of others). ISPs issue each user an IP address, which is a unique identifier for that user's particular computer on a transmission control protocol/Internet protocol (**TCP/IP**) network. An IP address is a 32-bit number written as four numbers separated by a period. Each number can be zero to 255; therefore a valid IP address could be 10.145.32.254. Messages are defined and transmitted over the Internet when a uniform resource locator (**URL**) is entered into the browser and a hypertext transfer protocol (**HTTP**) command tells the Web server to retrieve the requested Web page (Box 8-1).

A **domain name** identifies an IP address, such as microsoft.com or ama-assn.org. A limited number of top-level domains are available

---

BOX 8-1 READING A WEB SITE URL ADDRESS

URL is an acronym for *uniform resource locator.* A URL specifies the global address of documents or information on the Internet. An example of a URL is: http://www.hhs.gov/policies/index.html

Using this example, the information in the Web site address can be broken down as follows:

http://www.hhs.gov/

http:

Hypertext Transfer Protocol: This allows the user to access a server that stores Web pages.

ftp:

File Transfer Protocol: This allows the user to access a section of a Web site onto which files and documents can be uploaded.

mailto:

Mailto: This initiates an outgoing message to the e-mail address that follows

http://www.hhs.gov/policies/index.html

This section of the URL defines the Web address and is the part that is usually typed into the address bar to reach the Web site.

http://www.hhs.gov/**policies/**index.html

This section of the URL is the pathname, containing directory/subdirectory names, indicating where information can be found on a server's hard drive.

http://www.hhs.gov/policies/**index.html**

This section represents the filename (index) and the format, or extension (.html); it indicates what the Web browser is to do with the downloaded file. Other examples of filename extensions include .htm, .exe, .jpg, and .gif.

to which a domain name can be attached. Some of these top-level domains are *.com* (familiarly called *dot-com)* for commercial businesses; *.org* for organizations, usually nonprofit; *.edu* for educational institutions; *.gov* for government agencies; and *.net* for network organizations. Others include *.biz, .info, .tv, .name,* and *.pro.* The IP address can also be used to locate information on a computer; for instance, if the IP address reads as follows: *www.smithclinic.com/documents/mailings/patient_address_list/* then the list used for sending mailings to patients can be found in the Documents section in a file named Mailings, and the document is named patient_address_list.

Most Internet sites use a language called *hypertext markup language* **(HTML),** which was one of the first and is still one of the most popular languages used to create Web pages.

Hotspots are locations that offer an access point, providing public wireless broadband network services. They are found in places such as airports, libraries, convention centers, and hotels. Users may be able to connect to the network for no charge or may be required to place a credit card number on file or make a deposit. This service is convenient for the medical professional who is traveling or attending events away from the office.

Many physicians and health organizations offer a Web site with information about their services. In today's data-driven society, this is an excellent way to educate the public about the services the organization offers and to provide all types of information to the audience the organization wants to reach. To obtain a domain name, the desired name must be available, and one must pay a small fee to have the name registered and added to a central database. Companies such as register.com or verisign.com offer domain name registration services.

A word of caution: Because most medical offices have some type of connection to the Internet, the medical assistant may be tempted to check personal e-mail, "surf" the Web, or participate in instant messaging during working hours. Remember, personal business should not be conducted while at work. Supervisors appreciate the medical assistant who is honest with his or her time and spends it in productive, work-related activities.

BROWSERS

Web **browsers** are software applications that allow the user to locate and display Web pages. Two commonly used browsers are Microsoft Internet Explorer and Mozilla Firefox. These browsers can display graphics and text and can also present **multimedia** information, the quality of which depends on the computer system in use and the Internet connection speed. Browsers also have a **bookmark** capability that allows the user to mark a certain Web page and then easily return to it by clicking on its link in a drop-down box in the browser's menu. The **cache** allows quick retrieval of previously viewed sites, because the computer remembers and saves the information on the hard drive. **Cookies** are stored information about individual users, such as screen names and passwords.

Browsers and other Web sites also have **search engines**. These are programs in which a topic, word, or group of words can be entered, and the program searches the Internet for matches. A listing of those matches appears, and the user can click on each match to reference information and perform research. Information on just about any subject can be found by using search engines.

USING A PHONE TO PERFORM COMPUTER FUNCTIONS

Most of today's cell phones have Web browsing capabilities. The costs depend on what services are ordered. Smart phones offer advanced capabilities, often with PC-like functionality. Some mobile phones and most smart phones allow the user to read and edit business documents in a variety of formats, such as .doc and .pdf. PDAs are handheld computers and can have the same capabilities as a mobile phone or smart phone. Even the telephony industry has difficulty defining the differences among these three items, but in general, they differ in how they are built and what they can do. A physician can see magnetic resonance imaging (MRI) reports on some devices, which eliminates the need to sit at a computer to make medical decisions, allowing the physician more mobility. The medical assistant can expect to see these devices become almost standard in the future.

THE COMPUTER AS A CO-WORKER

The computer is a valuable tool in the medical office. It can assist in filing insurance claims by sending information from the computer in the office to the computers at the insurance company via a modem. Electronic processing of insurance claims not only saves time but also provides immediate information as to whether a claim will be accepted. Errors in coding or procedure are immediately evident, and many rejections can be avoided even before the claim is transmitted. Most insurance companies require that providers file claims electronically.

A patient's demographics can appear on computerized patient ledgers, listing the name, address, telephone number, and insurance information. As services are rendered, charges are entered into the computer, and payments also are displayed. This helps the medical facility maintain an accurate balance of all patient accounts.

At the appropriate time each month, the computer can print a patient's billing statement, which shows a detail of charges, payments, adjustments, and the current balance. In addition, the computer can be programmed to age the accounts according to any criteria selected and to include this information on the billing statement. A series of collection letters can be developed and personalized for individual patients as they are needed.

Database software makes it possible to organize a large volume of information, which can be used in a number of ways. One of the most practical uses is the organization of identifying information on each patient. The computer also can store clinical information about patients using much less space and with greater security than papers in a patient's chart. Access to records can be limited with passwords.

The computer has virtually replaced the appointment book in many medical offices today. Software for setting appointments ranges from relatively simple programs to very sophisticated systems. An advantage of computer scheduling is that more than one person can access the system at one time, and the same information is available to all users.

Computers are even being used as marketing tools and virtual secretaries in some modern medical offices (Figure 8-7). Computers can be used for functions such as automatic routing to call all patients with appointments for the next day and remind them to visit the doctor, or perhaps to call all patients due for a 6-month eye or dental examination. The program often gives the patient the opportunity to cancel and reschedule before the 24-hour cutoff time. As a marketing tool, computers can be programmed to call all phone numbers in a certain area code with a prerecorded message about a new procedure available at the office or a new physician in the area. Although many individuals are annoyed by the telemarketing concept and being called by a computer, the success rate is good. Computers can call thousands upon thousands of phone numbers, relay a message, and track replies within a matter of hours. Even if only a handful of new patients are obtained, over the life of the patients, the doctor may see a strong profit. Remember, the physician's office is a business, and businesses need to make a profit to survive. This number of calls could never be accomplished in the same time period by humans. These methods of using the computer open all kinds of doors for the medical practice of the future.

The medical office should routinely perform a file backup to make sure valuable data can be retrieved in the event of a system failure. Many medical office computer programs have an automatic backup function, but some must be backed up manually. It is wise to keep backup copies of the database and other critical documents off the premises in case of fire or other tragedy.

COMPUTER SECURITY

Patients are entitled to the utmost confidentiality with respect to their medical records and the release of any information of a personal nature. Computer technology allows the accumulation and storage of a vast amount of data that may be accessible to a variety of individuals, making it imperative that guidelines be set up for the protection of such data.

Encryption is the translation of data into a code that is not readily understood by most users. It is one effective way to achieve data security. To access or read an encrypted file, the user must have a password that enables the code to be decrypted. Once the code has been decrypted, the file can be used by the application. Encrypted data are called *cipher text.*

Some individuals attempt to access information in a computer without the owner's consent. These people may intend to use the information just for fun or may have a malicious intent, such as to steal or corrupt the data. Although these people are commonly called *hackers,* computer enthusiasts insist that the correct term for individuals who break into computers with dishonorable intent is *crackers.* The term *hacker* originally simply described a person who enjoyed learning about using computers and becoming proficient in their use.

Various methods may be used to protect networks, computers, and data from unauthorized access. Firewalls are systems designed for just such a purpose and can be integrated into both the hardware and the software of the computer. Firewalls often are used to prevent individuals from accessing private networks. Each message sent and received is examined, and the firewall blocks those that do not meet specific security criteria. Passwords, frequent password changes, and user logs also help protect data and the integrity of the database.

Viruses are programs or pieces of code that are loaded onto a computer, usually without the owner's knowledge, and can act like a physical virus in that they can make the computer "sick." Viruses can replicate themselves, copying themselves over and over again, and can be passed to other computers through e-mails, usually without the sender's knowing that a virus was passed along. Even simple viruses can quickly use all available memory and bring the system to a standstill; some can completely corrupt the computer's hard drive. More dangerous types of viruses can transmit over networks, bypassing security systems and destroying valuable data. This is why antivirus software is an important part of any computer system. Check for updates to the antivirus program at least weekly.

HIPAA REGULATIONS AND COMPUTERS

The Health Insurance Portability and Accountability Act (HIPAA) was passed in part to ensure that patient health information would be kept private and confidential. The wide use of computers in healthcare facilities sometimes makes this a difficult goal. The law limits who can look at and/or receive a patient's health information. Health information may be used and shared as follows:

FIGURE 8-7 Inside a computer. Today's microprocessors are designed so that memory, additional drives, and other hardware can easily be added to the system. (Courtesy Dell Corp., Round Rock, Texas.)

- For patient care and treatment coordination
- To pay physicians and facilities for healthcare
- With family, friends, and relatives whom the patient has identified as being involved in the patient's healthcare
- To make sure good care is provided in clean facilities
- To protect public health
- To make required reports to law enforcement officials

Health information cannot be shared or used without the patient's permission in most cases. Specifically, the provider cannot:

- Give health information to a patient's employer
- Use or share health information for marketing purposes
- Share mental health information obtained in counseling sessions

The healthcare facility must train those who use computer systems in what information can and cannot be shared. Individual computer users should have their own log-in names and passwords that are not provided to anyone else. All users should be required to use the log-in name and password every time they use the computer system. Patient information must not be accessed unless the user needs to know the contents of the patient's file to provide care. Be careful when releasing any type of medical information to anyone. Questions should be directed to the office manager or physician. Additional information about HIPAA can be found in Chapter 17.

ELECTRONIC SIGNATURES

Electronic signature programs are offered both as stand-alone products and as part of computerized medical record systems. After a report has been reviewed for accuracy, a physician can use a password and personal identification number (PIN) to electronically "sign" the document by clicking on an icon. Once the document has been signed, it cannot be altered; only additions are allowed.

COMPUTERS AND ERGONOMICS

The increased use of computers in the workplace has underscored the need to choose comfortable, safe furniture and equipment. Repetitive strain injury (RSI) accounts for most work-related injury claims. This includes a number of conditions caused by repeatedly straining certain nerves, muscles, or tendons. Carpal tunnel syndrome is an example of an RSI.

To prevent such injuries, office staff should use posture chairs that support the lumbar section of the back, with a correct angle of the knee and the feet resting on the floor. Of the many designs for keyboards available, one should be chosen that allows the correct angle at the elbow and the wrist to be held in a neutral position. Learn where all of the keys are located, because the last computer in use may have had a different key placement. Practicing keyboard skills and typing speed are the best way to learn key location. If work stations are shared, know how to adjust the components so that they are in the best position each day.

Eyestrain is another danger arising from continuous use of a computer. The monitor should be just below eye level and an arm's length away. At least once an hour, the user should take a break from looking at the monitor. (Ergonomics is discussed in more detail in Chapter 12 and on the Evolve Web site.)

CLOSING COMMENTS

Computers should be considered additional workers in the office. A medical assistant who learns how best to use the computer and discovers as many of its capabilities as possible is a valuable employee.

Read the manuals that accompany equipment and programs and try new applications for old procedures. Computers are designed to save time, so look for ways to make the day's workload lighter by taking full advantage of the computer.

The future promises more rapid technologic advances; computer equipment can become archaic in as short a time as 6 months after purchase. **Artificial intelligence**, voice recognition, **virtual reality**, and retinal scanning, seen mostly in the movies, will become commonplace in our homes and businesses. These tools will make the work environment even faster and more efficient as the world becomes a smaller place.

The evolution of computers will continue to bring about changes in medical facilities of the future. Medical staffs will find themselves educating their patients about computer use, because numerous programs in development will allow patients to "check in" once they arrive at the office and verify their identity. A medical assistant will need patience to teach these procedures and assure the patients that these new methods will increase their security and the protection of their medical records.

Patient Education

Patients commonly enter the physician's office having researched their symptoms and illnesses on the Internet. This practice is an indication that the patient is interested in health matters and in being part of the process of maintaining their health. No patient should substitute their regular physician for information obtained on the Internet. The medical assistant can encourage patients who are interested in learning about their condition but should remind them to discuss any concerns and questions with the physician.

With the growing number of medical databases online, physicians now can use information on the Internet to help educate their patients about the illnesses they face right from the exam room. While consulting with the patient, with a few clicks of the mouse the physician can print excellent information, which often can assist the patient with referrals to help agencies and suggestions for better healthcare.

Legal and Ethical Issues

The medical assistant should use the computer at work for business purposes only. Never allow it to become a distraction from doing the job at hand. Many medical assistants and other office personnel have been terminated for using the office computer for personal reasons. Always follow office policy on computer use and make sure patients are the priority during office hours.

SUMMARY OF SCENARIO

Dr. Bouchard is a progressive physician who believes that the use of technology will assist him in the care of his patients and help his office run more efficiently. The computer helps the staff complete tasks in a timely manner and provides records of business transactions. Staff members are able to function much faster than when records were kept by hand. Dr. Bouchard understands the need to train his staff and to keep them up-to-date on the latest versions of their computer software. His willingness to close his office for staff-wide training demonstrates his commitment. He is cost conscious and looks for the best available equipment for the investment he is willing to make.

Dr. Bouchard often uses digital camera equipment to take "before" and "after" pictures of his patients, but only with their special written consent. He also uses the computer to send his patients a monthly e-mail newsletter with health information and special news about the practice.

He monitors his staff's Internet use but is reasonable about allowing them a small degree of personal access on breaks and at lunch. The doctor cautions his staff about accessing medical records that they are not actively involved

with in patient care to avoid invading the patient's privacy. The computer system prints a daily log of all employees and what information they accessed throughout the day, and he stresses the importance of logging on and off the computer using their individual passwords and log-on IDs. Dr. Bouchard's employees realize the importance of keeping medical information private. Unless a staff member needs to know the information in the chart to care for the patient, he or she may be accused of invading the patient's privacy when accessing medical information.

Dr. Bouchard is very interested in new developments for healthcare facilities, such as those that will allow his patients to check themselves in and gain access to limited information about their own medical record. He has a vision that one day his patients will be able to download their statements or perhaps their child's immunization records from their home computers, reducing the staff's workload and providing instant access to some information for his patients. Insightful physicians such as Dr. Bouchard see the computer as a co-worker in the medical facility.

SUMMARY OF LEARNING OBJECTIVES

1. **Define, spell, and pronounce the terms listed in the vocabulary.**
   Spelling and pronouncing medical terms correctly bolster the medical assistant's credibility. Knowing the definition of these terms promotes confidence in communication with patients and co-workers.

2. **List several ways the computer can be effective in a medical office.**
   The computer performs repetitive tasks, reduces errors, speeds up production, recalls information on command, saves time, reduces paperwork, and allows for more creative and productive use of staff members' time.

3. **Explain the basic functions a computer performs.**
   The computer performs four basic functions: input, processing, output, and storage. *Input* includes information that is put into the computer, and *output* is information that comes out of the computer. *Processing* is the manipulation of data that occurs between input and output. *Storage* is the retention of data in the computer or on storage media.

4. **Explain the basic parts of a computer.**
   The *microprocessor* is the brains of the system that interprets the instructions given to it by an application program. The *monitor* allows the user to see immediate output on a screen, and *printers* allow the output to be produced as a hard copy. The *keyboard* and *mouse* are input devices.

5. **List the three elements that differentiate microprocessors.**
   (1) The *bandwidth* describes the amount of information that can be sent over a connection at one time; (2) the *clock speed* determines the number of instructions per second the processor can handle; (3) the *instruction set* is the instructions the microprocessor can execute.

6. **Discuss the differences among various types of printers.**
   Three main types of printers are used in medical offices. *Impact* printers produce output of moderate quality and are inexpensive. *Inkjet* printers use a cartridge and a heating element to produce an image on a page. *Laser* printers use technology similar to a photocopier.

7. **Explain the importance of a motherboard.**
   The motherboard is the main board to which all other devices are connected inside the computer. It holds all the essential wiring and expansion devices needed to operate the computer and the battery that keeps the clock and calendar running when the computer is turned off.

8. **Explain and give examples of peripheral devices.**
   Peripheral devices (e.g., scanners, Zip drives) perform special functions but are not necessary to the computer's functioning.

9. **List and discuss several types of file formats.**
   The *file format* is the extension just after the file name that describes the method used to save the file. It also helps identify the type of file. For example, a *.jpeg* file often is used for photographs, a *.gif* file is used for scanned illustrations or images, and a *.txt* file is usually specifically for text for a printed page.

10. **Explain the concept of computer networking.**
    Computer networks are groups of two or more computers linked together. These networks can be local or can cover a city or wide geographic area. Some are limited to a few buildings. Networks often share resources, such as printers.

11. **Define the function of browsers.**

Browsers are software applications that allow a user to find information on the Internet. They can show graphics and often multimedia (e.g., videos). Internet Explorer and Netscape Navigator are commonly used browsers.

12. **Discuss the importance of computer security.**

Computer security is critical, especially because confidential patient information is stored on computers in medical facilities. Several methods may be used to enhance computer security, such as firewalls and antivirus programs. Restrictions on who may log in and the use of passwords also help the facility ensure that only authorized individuals have access to confidential information.

13. **Locate the keys on a keyboard.**

Examine the keyboard used in the educational or medical facility and determine the location of the keys. The medical assistant may need to adjust to different keyboard types at various work stations.

CONNECTIONS

Study Guide Connection: Go to the Chapter 8 Study Guide. Read and complete the activities.

Evolve Connection: Go to the Chapter 8 link at *evolve.elsevier.com/ kinn* to complete the Chapter Review and Chapter Quiz. Check out the other resources listed for this chapter to make the most of what you have learned from Computer Concepts.

TELEPHONE TECHNIQUES

9

SCENARIO

Ashlynn McDowell, a recent graduate of a medical assisting program, has begun her first position as a receptionist in an obstetrician's office. Ashlynn's lifelong goal has been to work in obstetrics, and she is determined to perform to the best of her abilities. However, she has never held a job in a professional office. She knows that she needs to practice all the skills she learned in school to be an effective receptionist.

Ashlynn works for Dr. Stella Frank, who is customer-service oriented and wants her patients to feel cared for and special. She insists that all their concerns be taken seriously. Ashlynn is anxious to build trust with the patients and offer them help with the problems they encounter that fall into her realm of responsibility.

Dr. Frank recently purchased computer software that allows Ashlynn to record phone messages on the computer, and these messages are automatically routed both to an inbox for the physician and as an entry in the patient's medical record.

Although the system is new to everyone in the office, Ashlynn is determined to become proficient at its use as quickly as possible.

She knows that she must speak clearly and distinctly and must be adept at follow-up skills. She plans to dress professionally each day so that she projects the right image to the patients with whom she comes in contact. Ashlynn will strive to be the type of employee who has a willingness to learn, an ability to adapt, and a heart full of compassion for the patient. She is a team player who sincerely wants to cooperate with other staff members who might need her help.

Dr. Frank is pleased that she has found such an eager person to add to her staff and will assist and guide Ashlynn as she learns how to make the patients feel like a part of the clinic family. Ashlynn's self-esteem has increased because she feels she is making a great contribution to healthcare.

While studying this chapter, think about the following questions:

- How can Ashlynn's telephone demeanor convince patients she wants to help them?
- Why does the tone of voice play an important role in patient perception?
- How does the medical assistant speaking to patients on the telephone strike a balance between too much and too little time?
- How can the medical assistant reduce patients' frustration with telephone issues?

LEARNING OBJECTIVES

1. Define, spell, and pronounce the terms listed in the vocabulary.
2. Determine and discuss the source of incoming and outgoing calls to a physician's office.
3. Describe how to develop a pleasing telephone voice.
4. Demonstrate the correct way to hold a telephone handset.
5. Explain why courtesy is so important when speaking on the telephone.
6. Demonstrate the correct way to answer the telephone in the office.
7. Discuss different ways to handle callers who want to speak to the physician.
8. List the seven elements of a correctly handled telephone message.
9. Demonstrate the correct way to record a message accurately and take a request for action.
10. Demonstrate the most efficient way to call in a prescription or a prescription refill to a pharmacy.
11. Discuss how the medical assistant should handle callers who have a complaint.
12. Explain how angry callers might be handled.
13. List several questions to ask when handling an emergency call.
14. Discuss several useful sections of the introductory pages of the phone directory.

VOCABULARY

clarity The quality or state of being clear.

competent Having adequate abilities or qualities; having the capacity to function or perform in a certain way.

cultivate To foster the growth of; to improve by labor, care, or study.

diction The choice of words, especially with regard to clearness, correctness, or effectiveness.

enunciation (e-nun-se-a′-shun) The utterance of articulate, clear sounds.

inflection (in-flek′-shun) A change in the pitch or loudness of the voice.

invariably (in-var′-e-uh-buh-le) Consistently; not changing or capable of change.

jargon The technical terminology or characteristic idiom of a particular group or special activity, as opposed to lay terms.

monotone A succession of syllables, words, or sentences in an unvaried key or pitch.

multitasking Performing multiple tasks at the same time.

pitch The property of a sound, especially a musical tone, that is determined by the frequency of the waves producing it; the highness or lowness of sound.

provider An individual or company that provides medical care and services to a patient or the public.

salutation (sal-yu-ta′-shun) An expression of greeting, goodwill, or courtesy by words or gestures.

screen Something that shields, protects, or hides; to select or eliminate through a screening process.

STAT Medical abbreviation for immediately; at this moment.

tactful Having a keen sense of what to do or say to maintain good relations with others or to prevent offense.

tedious (te′-de-yus) Tiresome because of length or dullness.

The telephone is the lifeline of a medical practice and a powerful public relations tool. Most patients seen in a medical facility make the initial appointment by telephone. When used appropriately, the telephone can help build a medical practice from its beginning and throughout its life (Figure 9-1). If used inappropriately, it can destroy a flourishing practice. Always remember that the voice on the other end of the line is that of the patient, and telephone calls can never be considered an interruption of the workday. The patients are the reason the practice exists.

Most incoming calls are from the following sources:

- Established patients calling for appointments or to ask questions
- New patients making a first contact with the physician's office
- Patients and medical workers reporting treatment results or emergencies
- Other physicians making referrals or discussing a patient
- Laboratories reporting vital patient information
- Pharmacies and patients calling in to refill prescriptions

EFFECTIVE USE OF THE TELEPHONE

Active Listening

Although great emphasis is placed on rules for speaking, the importance of active listening often is overlooked. The same attention should be given to a telephone conversation that would be given to a face-to-face conversation (Box 9-1). Concentration is not always easy for a medical assistant who is juggling several duties at once in the medical office; therefore, he or she must practice focusing on the call at hand. Effective active listening also provides vital information about the nature of the call—whether the caller is distressed, agitated, or has a concern that must be addressed immediately. Review listening skills in Chapter 5.

FIGURE 9-1 The telephone plays a vital role in the success of a medical practice.

Developing a Pleasing Telephone Voice

Individuals who call a physician's office should be greeted by a pleasant, friendly voice. A common sales technique is to make sure the caller "hears a smile." Customer service is critical in today's medical offices, and this technique is quite useful for medical assistants, because they are likely to be the caller's first point of contact with the practice. Be sure to enunciate clearly, pronouncing each word separately and distinctly. **Diction**, **pitch**, and **clarity** also are important. Avoid speaking in a **monotone**; instead, use **inflection**, or a change in the pitch and loudness of the voice. This helps the speaker emphasize certain points during the conversation.

When a telephone call is received from a stranger, one usually tries to visualize that person's appearance and perhaps forms an opinion of the individual's personality. The caller may sound mature, somewhat

BOX 9-1   HOW TO LISTEN

- Quiet the mind to absorb what the speaker is saying.
- Focus on the conversation.
- Look at the speaker's eyes.
- Don't interrupt.
- Allow the speaker to express the complete thought.
- Repeat your interpretation of what has been said, using the speaker's words when possible.
- Ask whether the interpretation is correct.
- Respond to the speaker.
- Don't look at a watch or clock or answer a cell phone when listening.
- Remain on the speaker's subject.
- Respect differing opinions.
- Be empathetic.

FIGURE 9-2 The handset should be held in the center, with the mouthpiece approximately 1 inch in front of the lips.

worried, well educated, or frantic. Because communication is a two-way street, the caller also forms an impression of the person answering the phone. Sometimes these impressions are incorrect, but much can be inferred from what is heard on the telephone.

The tone of voice used by the medical assistant and other medical staff members plays a role in the patient's attitude. A study by Harvard University claims that the tone of voice used by surgeons is directly linked to medical professional liability claims. How something is said to a patient is just as important as what is said. Always use a friendly, warm tone of voice and project confidence when speaking with patients. Be courteous and **tactful** and choose your words carefully. Every caller should be made to feel that the medical assistant has time to attend to his or her needs. If the medical assistant is rushed to pick up the telephone, he or she should wait a few seconds until able to answer graciously without seeming breathless or impatient.

Be alert and interested in the person calling. Always give your full attention to the caller, and do not allow distractions to interfere with the conversation. Build a pleasant, friendly image for the office. Talk naturally and avoid repetition of mechanical words or phrases, such as "uh-huh" and "you know." Do not use professional **jargon**, such as referring to *otalgia* when the patient reports an earache. Using correct grammar adds to a favorable impression. Speak distinctly; clear pronunciation and **enunciation** are vital. Move the lips, tongue, and jaw freely. Talk directly into the mouthpiece. Never answer the telephone while eating, drinking, or chewing gum. A well-modulated voice carries best. Use a normal tone of voice, neither too loud nor too soft. Talk at a moderate rate, neither too quickly nor too slowly. Be expressive, and vary the tone of voice.

CRITICAL THINKING APPLICATION   9-1

Ashlynn has a tendency to speak a little fast in her normal conversations. How will she need to adjust as she is answering phones in the medical office? She also is a friendly person and enjoys talking on the phone. What precautions should she take so that this does not become an issue on the job?

This brings out the meaning of sentences and adds color and vitality to what is said.

Holding the Telephone Handset Correctly

A medical assistant must develop professional telephone habits and correct the more casual ones that are used at home. The handset should be placed so that the medical assistant's voice is relayed distinctly and accurately. Practice holding the handset around the middle, with the mouthpiece approximately 1 inch from the lips and directly in front of the teeth (Figure 9-2). Never hold it under the chin. Check the proper distance by taking the first two fingers and passing them sideways through the space between the lips and the mouthpiece. If the fingers just squeeze through, the lips are the correct distance from the telephone and the voice will go over the line in as close to its natural tone as possible. When using a headset, speak directly into its mouthpiece, positioning it the same distance from the mouth as a telephone handset.

Speak directly into the telephone immediately after removing it from its cradle. When turning to face another part of the room, make sure the handset moves, too; otherwise, the voice will be lost. A medical assistant who speaks too quickly, enunciates poorly, or fails to speak directly into the transmitter may not be easily understood by the person on the other end of the line.

Maintaining Confidentiality

Keep in mind that all communications in a healthcare facility are confidential. If others are nearby, use discretion when mentioning the name of the caller. Be careful about being overheard when repeating any symptoms or other information received by telephone. Never use a speaker phone to listen to voice mail or hold a phone conversation within the hearing range of others. Do not place patients on speaker phone at any time. Another individual may hear private medical information, which is a violation of regulations established by the Health Insurance Portability and Accountability Act (HIPAA).

CRITICAL THINKING APPLICATION   9-2

Ashlynn hears an employee speaking on the intercom to a patient. How should she handle this situation? To whom, if anyone, should Ashlynn report this activity and why? What problems might be caused if this type of conversation is overheard?

Each employee must be courteous on the phone since it is the lifeline of the office. The medical assistant's phone manner sets the tone for the caller's perception of the entire practice. Patients expect good customer service, and because they can decide who their providers are, courtesy must be a part of every patient encounter. Additionally, if patients are happy with the experience they had, they may refer others to the physician's office.

Thinking Ahead

Always think ahead when an important call must be made. Have the patient's chart or the bill in question at hand before dialing the phone and a pen and pad nearby ready to take notes. Write down a list of questions to ask or goals for the conversation. Keep the call short and simple, then free the line for other calls.

Most offices keep a list of frequently called phone numbers both for staff use and to offer to patients. A list of local pharmacies, hospitals, and their departments is helpful. All of these are time-savers that help the medical assistant better serve patients.

MANAGING TELEPHONE CALLS

A medical office receives many calls during the course of a single day. Each deserves the medical assistant's complete and **competent** attention, no matter how busy the office. The following section can assist the medical assistant with managing and following up on common incoming calls.

Answering Promptly

Whenever possible, answer the telephone on the first ring and always by the third ring. If the facility has several incoming lines or more than one telephone, a conversation sometimes must be interrupted to answer another call. It is courteous to say, "Excuse me just a moment; the other line is ringing." Answer the second call and determine who is calling. If it is not an emergency, ask that person to hold while the first call is completed. If possible, get the phone number of the second caller, but do not allow that request to turn into a lengthy conversation. Do not make the mistake of continuing with the second call while the first caller waits. Return to the first call as soon as possible and apologize briefly for the interruption. Think of what would happen during a face-to-face conversation. A second person who approaches people involved in a conversation should not expect to interrupt and be heard at length. However, if the second call is an emergency, take a moment to return to the first line and alert the caller that he or she will have to be kept waiting or be called back.

Never answer a call by saying, "Please hold" without first finding out who is calling. The call could be an emergency, and this type of greeting is extremely discourteous. It takes only a moment to be polite. If the call is an emergency, prompt attention to it could save

a life. The medical assistant must know how to activate emergency medical services (EMS) in his or her area. Usually this is as easy as calling 911; however, each medical assistant should be able to communicate quickly and efficiently with the EMS staff.

Keep the focus on the call. Do not attempt to multitask while answering the telephone, because this practice takes attention away from the patient. Callers can hear keyboard strokes and other office activity; a caller therefore might assume that the medical assistant is not giving full attention to the person on the phone. Treat the phone call just as if the patient were standing in the office (Procedure 9-1).

Identifying the Facility

The medical assistant should identify the facility first, then state his or her name. Numerous telephone greetings can be used. Discuss which are best with the physician or office manager. Some physicians prefer a very formal statement when answering the phone, whereas others allow a more casual script. Always follow the procedure outlined in the policy manual. Examples of telephone greetings include:

"This is Dr. Frank's office, Miss McDowell speaking. How may I help you?"

"Frank Maternal Health Clinic, this is Ashlynn McDowell. How may I help you?"

"Stella Frank's office, this is Miss McDowell. How may I help you?"

"Dr. Frank's office, this is Ashlynn. How may I help you?"

Some physicians avoid using the title "Doctor" to protect their patient's confidentiality. For instance, if a physician needs to call a work number and leave a message for a patient, curious co-workers might attempt to investigate what type of physician is being seen. Dropping the "Doctor" when leaving messages and when answering the telephone can be an effective means of protecting a patient's privacy. However, merely saying "Hello" is unsatisfactory; the name of the facility should always be mentioned to callers. Otherwise, the caller **invariably** asks if he or she has reached the physician's office, which wastes time, and the opportunity to create a favorable impression of the facility has been lost.

The use of a **salutation** in telephone identification is optional. Sometimes adding "Good morning" or "Good afternoon" to the identification is awkward. A rising inflection or a questioning tone of voice indicates interest and a willingness to assist and eliminates the need for an additional greeting. When the type of greeting has been chosen, practice until it can be said easily and smoothly. Never rush, so that all callers can clearly understand exactly what is said.

CRITICAL THINKING APPLICATION   9-3

Most offices dictate how the phone is to be answered. What should Ashlynn do if she is very uncomfortable with the way she is asked to answer the phone? Who ultimately should decide how the phone is answered?

Identifying the Caller

If the caller does not identify himself or herself, ask who is calling. Write the name down immediately on a pad of paper or phone message form. Repeat the caller's name by using it in the

PROCEDURE 9-1

Demonstrate Telephone Techniques

GOAL: *To answer the telephone in a physician's office in a professional manner and respond to a request for action.*

EQUIPMENT and SUPPLIES

- Telephone
- Message pad
- Pen or pencil
- Appointment book
- Computer
- Notepad

PROCEDURAL STEPS

1. Demonstrate telephone techniques by answering the telephone by the third ring, speaking directly into the mouthpiece, which should be positioned 1 inch from the mouth.
   <u>PURPOSE:</u> To convey interest in the caller by answering promptly. Proper positioning of the handset allows for an audible tone and carries the voice well.

2. Speak distinctly with a pleasant tone and expression, at a moderate rate, and with sufficient volume for the person to understand every word.

3. Identify the office and/or physician and yourself.
   <u>PURPOSE:</u> To assure the caller that the correct number has been reached and to identify the staff member.

4. Verify the identity of the caller, and if using a computerized messaging system, bring the patient's medical record to the active screen of the computer.
   <u>PURPOSE:</u> To confirm the origin of the call.

5. Screen the call if necessary.
   <u>PURPOSE:</u> To determine whether the caller has an emergency and needs immediate attention or referral to a hospital emergency department.

6. Apply active listening skills to assess whether the caller is distressed or agitated and to determine the concern to be addressed.
   <u>PURPOSE:</u> To make sure the medical assistant hears and understands the message being sent by the patient and to show that the patient has the medical assistant's full attention.

7. Determine the needs of the caller and provide the requested information or service if possible. Provide the caller with excellent customer service. Be as helpful as possible.
   <u>PURPOSE:</u> To allow the medical assistant to handle many calls and conserve the physician's and staff members' time and energy.

8. If unable to assist the caller, transfer the call to the appropriate person. However, first provide the person to whom the call is being transferred with as much information as possible about the caller and his or her needs.
   <u>PURPOSE:</u> To provide good customer service and be as helpful to the caller as possible.

9. Take a proper message for further action, if required, and suggest a time the patient will likely get an answer from the physician's office.
   <u>PURPOSE:</u> Not all calls can be resolved immediately.

10. Terminate the call in a pleasant manner and replace the receiver gently. Always allow the caller to hang up first.
    <u>PURPOSE:</u> To promote good public relations, provide excellent customer service, and ensure that the caller has no further questions.

---

conversation as soon as possible. Individuals like to hear their own names, and name repetition assures the patient that he or she has been identified correctly. Try to use the person's name at least three times during the call, and remember other courteous expressions, such as "thank you," "please," and "you're welcome," as often as possible. However, if other patients are within the range of your voice, remember that the caller's privacy must be respected.

Occasionally a caller refuses to identify himself or herself to the medical assistant and may be quite insistent on speaking with the physician. The individual could be a patient; therefore, every attempt to identify the patient and assist him or her should be made. Such callers may also be salespersons who are fully aware that if their identity is revealed, they will never get the opportunity to speak to the physician. These people may be firmly told, "Dr. Frank is busy with a patient and has asked that we take messages for her. If you

will not leave a message, you may wish to write a letter to her and mark it 'personal.'" This phrase usually prompts the caller to provide his or her name, and the call then can be handled according to office policy. Rarely does the caller choose to write a letter to the physician and deal with the wait time that course of action requires. If the patient agrees, the situation may be best handled with a regular appointment, during which the patient can speak privately with the physician.

Screening Incoming Calls

Most physicians expect the medical assistant to **screen** all telephone calls. The physician and office manager provide guidance on the type of calls to be routed to the physician and those that he or she will return at a later time. The medical assistant should become familiar with their preferences and also use good judgment, much of which comes with experience, in deciding whether to put through a call to the physician.

If it is office policy, put calls from other physicians through at once. If the physician is busy and cannot possibly come to the telephone, explain this briefly and politely, then say that the physician will return the call as soon as possible.

Many callers ask, "Is the doctor in?" or "May I speak to the doctor?" Avoid answering with a simple "Yes" or "No" or by responding with the question, "Who is calling, please?" If the physician is not in, say so before asking the identity of the caller. Otherwise, the impression may be created that the physician is just not willing to talk with this person.

If the physician is away from the office, the rule of offering assistance still holds. The medical assistant may say, "No, I am sorry, Dr. Frank is not in. May I take a message?" or "No, I am sorry, but Dr. Frank will be at the hospital most of the morning. May I ask her to return your call after 1 o'clock?"

If the physician is in and is available for telephone calls, a typical response would be, "Yes, Dr. Frank is in; may I say who is calling, please?"

When physicians prefer to keep telephone calls to a minimum, say, "Yes, Dr. Frank is in the office, but she is not free to come to the phone. May I take a message, please?" By responding in this way, the physician is not committed to taking the call.

During the time a physician is examining a patient, he or she will not wish to be interrupted with a routine call. In such cases you might say, "Yes, Dr. Frank is in, but she is with a patient right now. May I help you?" or "Yes, Dr. Frank is in, but she is with a patient right now. Is there anything you would like me to ask her?"

Try to guard against being overprotective. A patient should be able to talk with the physician when absolutely necessary, but unless it is an emergency, the patient probably is willing to do so at the physician's convenience. The medical assistant who answers the telephone acts as a screen, not a roadblock.

Although no one wants to sit next to a telephone waiting on a physician to call, this is the reality in most cases. In fact, physicians almost always rely on their staff to give them messages from patients and then follow up on the instructions the physician gives for each patient. Staff members should provide an approximate time frame within which the patient's call will be returned, but they must always stress that the time is an estimate. Emergencies cannot be predicted, and it may be impossible to abide by that time frame. Always ask for the patient's cell phone number, if available, then ask him or her to keep the phone handy for the rest of the day. Make every effort to return calls by noon for morning messages and by the time the office closes for afternoon messages. By cross-training all employees to take accurate messages and document calls, any employee can return calls, even if he or she did not take the original message.

Find out exactly how calls are to be handled when the physician is out of the office and under what circumstances he or she can be interrupted when on the premises. **Cultivate** a reputation for being helpful and reliable. A medical assistant can save the physician many interruptions if patients develop confidence in the medical assistant's ability to help them and have faith in his or her promises to take messages and deliver them properly. (For more tips on handling telephone calls, visit the Evolve site at *evolve.elsevier.com/kinn*.)

CRITICAL THINKING APPLICATION   9-4

Ashlynn answers the phone; the caller is a male pharmaceutical representative who has been visiting the clinic for several months. She cheerfully greets him and asks if he is calling to make an appointment. He states that he wants to make an appointment with Ashlynn—for a date. How should she handle this call? What problems could arise if this were a patient and Ashlynn were to accept the date?

Minimizing Wait Time

When a call cannot be put through immediately, ask, "Would you prefer to wait, or should I call you back when Dr. Frank is free?" If the caller elects to wait, remember that waiting with a silent telephone can be irritating and **tedious**. The waiting time always seems long, no matter how brief it really is. Many of today's phones are equipped with timers that tell the caller exactly how long they have been waiting on hold. The longer they wait, the more irritated they may become. Let no more than 1 minute pass without breaking in with some reassuring comment. For instance: "I'm sorry, Dr. Frank is still busy. Would you like to continue to hold?" or "I'm sorry to keep you waiting so long, Ms. Hughes. Would you prefer to have me return your call when Dr. Frank is free?" If the wait is longer than expected, the caller may wish to reconsider and call back at another time or have the call returned. By going back on the line at frequent intervals, the medical assistant allows the caller an opportunity to express such concerns. In any event, be considerate and remember that irritation can be lessened each time the medical assistant returns to the call by saying, "Thank you for waiting, Ms. Hughes."

When it is necessary to leave the telephone and obtain information, ask the caller, "Will you please wait while I get the information?" Listen for a reply. If getting the information will take longer than a few seconds, give some estimate of the time required and offer to call back. When returning to the telephone, always thank the caller for waiting. Requests that might require pulling the patient's chart from the files are best handled with a call back to the patient.

Remember that leaving a person on hold ties up one of the physician's telephone lines, and an emergency call could be coming through or new patients might be attempting to call. Most phone calls to a physician's office during the day are important, therefore the lines should be kept clear as much as possible.

Transferring a Call

Always ask the patient's permission to place him or her on hold and to transfer the call. Identify the person on the phone when a call is transferred to the physician or another person in the facility. Transferring the call to a co-worker's voice mail without warning the caller that the person is not available is considered poor customer service. Any person who refuses to give a name should not be put through unless the medical assistant has been specifically instructed to do so. If the person is not immediately available, ask the caller whether he or she would prefer to be put through to voice mail. Some callers simply believe their call will receive more attention if a human takes the message. If the caller insists, take a written message and deliver it to the proper person as soon as possible.

All medical assistants should learn "who does what" in the medical facility. Knowing about the functions of the office and which person is responsible for which areas makes a significant difference in the customer service provided to the patient. For example, suppose that the medical office employs one insurance receptionist, named Sarah, and three insurance billers. Opel handles names that begin with A through G, David handles names that begin with H through P, and Andrea handles names that begin with Q through Z. If a call comes to the office and the patient has an insurance question, the medical assistant could put the call through to Sarah. However, better customer service dictates that the medical assistant ask the name of the patient and put the call through to the person who handles that patient's particular claims. If the patient's name is Rebecca Whitehead, the medical assistant should call Andrea and ask if she may transfer Ms. Whitehead's call to her. The fewer times the caller is transferred, the happier the caller.

When the caller is a patient, the physician or clinical medical assistant probably will need his or her medical record at hand during the conversation. Remember, protecting the patient's right to privacy is vital. If others are in hearing range, take the chart to the person responsible for the call and say, "This patient is waiting on the telephone." Because the physician's office often is a hectic place, most require that a message be taken so that the medical record can be reviewed, the patient's request considered, and the patient called back with questions or instructions from the doctor.

Taking a Telephone Message

If the office uses a manual message-taking system, always have a pen or pencil in hand and a message pad nearby when answering the telephone. Several calls may be answered before an opportunity arises to relay a message or carry out a promise of action. The telephone message, whether taken through a computer system or by hand, is a vital part of competent patient care (Procedure 9-2).

Many types of message pads are available today (Figure 9-3). Ordinary spiral-bound notebooks are inexpensive, sturdy, and well proportioned. These usually lie flat on a desk and can be filed for future reference. Never use small scraps of paper for messages; they are too easily lost. Message books should be kept indefinitely in the medical office, because they could be used as evidence in a court of law. Once the caller's request has been acted upon, a copy of a phone message could be added to the patient's chart, or at a minimum the information could be noted in the chart if it concerns the patient's medical care.

A minimum of seven items are needed to take a telephone message correctly:

1. Name of the person to whom the call is directed
2. Name of the person calling

PROCEDURE 9-2

Take a Telephone Message

GOAL: *To take an accurate telephone message and follow up on the requests made by the caller.*

EQUIPMENT and SUPPLIES

- Telephone
- Computer
- Message pad
- Pen or pencil
- Notepad

PROCEDURAL STEPS

1. Demonstrate telephone techniques by answering the telephone using the guidelines in Procedure 9-1.
   <u>PURPOSE:</u> To answer promptly and courteously, which conveys interest in the caller and promotes good customer service.
2. Using a message pad or the computer, take the phone message (either on paper or by data entry into the computer) and obtain the following information:
   - Name of the person to whom the call is directed
   - Name of the person calling
   - Caller's telephone number
   - Reason for the call
   - Action to be taken
   - Date and time of the call
   - Initials of the person taking the call
   <u>PURPOSE:</u> To have accurate information, which allows the staff member to address the caller's issues quickly and efficiently.

3. Apply active listening skills and repeat the information back to the caller after recording the message.
   <u>PURPOSE:</u> To verify that all the information was recorded accurately.
4. Provide the caller with an approximate date and time the call will be returned, if possible.
   <u>PURPOSE:</u> To show consideration for the patient's time and to prevent the person from sitting by the phone, awaiting a call.
5. End the call and wait for the caller to hang up first.
6. Deliver the phone message to the appropriate person. Separate trays or slots for each staff member are helpful.
7. Follow up on important messages.
   <u>PURPOSE:</u> To make sure important issues are addressed in a timely manner.
8. Keep old message books for future reference. Carbonless copies allow the facility to keep a permanent record of phone messages.
   <u>PURPOSE:</u> To have a permanent source of messages in case a number is needed after the paper message has been discarded.
9. File pertinent phone messages in the patient's medical record. Make sure the computer record is closed after the documentation has been done.
   <u>PURPOSE:</u> To keep a permanent record of important information in the patient's chart.

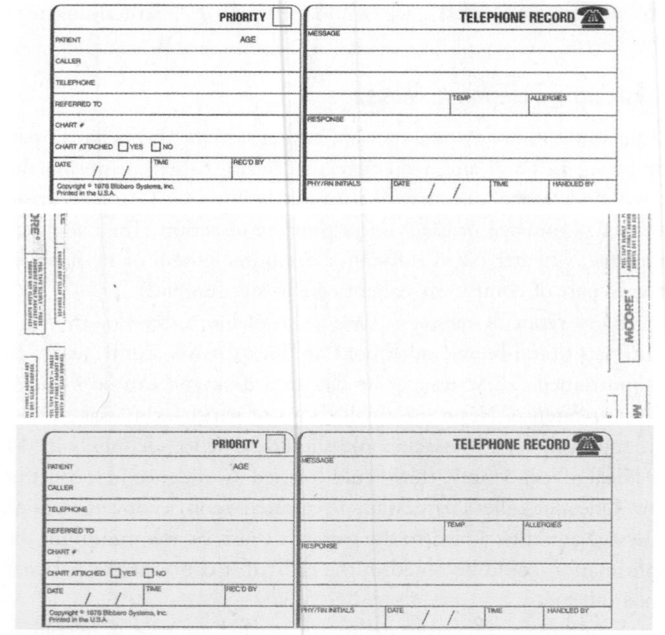
PRIORITY
PATIENT AGE
CALLER
TELEPHONE
REFERRED TO
CHART #
CHART ATTACHED YES NO
DATE / / TIME REC'D BY
Copyright © 1978 Bibbero Systems, Inc. Printed in the U.S.A.
TELEPHONE RECORD
MESSAGE
TEMP ALLERGIES
RESPONSE
PHY/RN INITIALS DATE / / TIME HANDLED BY

FIGURE 9-3 Phone message forms with self-adhesive backing make charting calls easier and more time efficient. (Courtesy Bibbero Systems, Petaluma, Calif.)

3. Caller's daytime, evening, and/or cell phone number
4. Reason for the call
5. Action to be taken
6. Date and time of the call
7. Initials of the person taking the call

Impression-sensitive message pads, which provide a copy of each page, ensure that no message is forgotten and are the best way to keep track of handwritten messages. These pads also provide a copy of the message in case one is lost, and they help ensure that all messages are delivered and receive follow-up action. Make certain that the handwriting on all phone messages is legible.

Electronic software systems usually populate the name, address, phone number, date, and time of a message; therefore, the medical assistant needs only to type in the reason for the call and what the patient would like the physician to do. The software may also offer ways to flag the messages for various actions once it has been taken, such as a flag for a call back or for a prescription refill. Electronic flags also can indicate the message's level of urgency.

The nature of the message determines whether it should be reported immediately. The person who completes the call must sign and date the message. If the call is from a patient and relates in any way to the medical history or if any instructions were given or queries answered, this information must be placed in the patient's medical record. Message forms are available that have a self-adhesive backing and can be placed permanently in the patient's case history.

Taking Action on Telephone Messages

The message procedure is not complete until the necessary action has been taken. Place notations on the memo pad or in the computerized day planner to carry over to the following day if they have not been completed, but this should be a rare occurrence. Do not trust to memory messages that were not attended to from previous days; always carry them forward either electronically or in writing.

Make brief notations of patients' attitudes while talking to them on the telephone, if they are significant. The physician does not require a character study, but it is helpful to know when a patient appears fearful, apprehensive, or nervous. If a patient shows such symptoms, it may be wise to consult with or transfer the call to the physician or clinical medical assistant.

Ending a Call

When a caller's requests have been satisfied, do not encourage inappropriate chatting or permit the call to monopolize your time unnecessarily. The telephone lines should be cleared for other calls. Thank the person for calling, close the conversation with some form of "good-bye," and replace the telephone on its cradle gently. Allow the caller to hang up first.

Retaining Records of Telephone Messages

Each office must develop a policy on the retention of telephone message records. Electronic medical record systems will likely be capable of sending message information directly to the computerized medical record. Many offices elect to keep handwritten message pads for the same period that the statute of limitations runs for medical professional liability cases. Remember that phone records include telephone bills, especially those that detail long-distance charges. Keeping message records can be of assistance in proving any number of claims, including the number of times patients called the office and the fact that calls to the patient were attempted or returned. Make sure accurate telephone records are kept to ensure good patient care and customer service.

TYPICAL INCOMING CALLS

Medical assistants answer incoming calls to spare the physician unnecessary interruptions during visits with patients. Outgoing calls may be made to follow up with patients or to conduct the general business of the office, such as ordering supplies and obtaining laboratory results. Many calls relate to the administrative aspects of the office and actually can be better handled by the medical assistant. The policy on handling calls should be clearly set forth in the office procedures manual.

New Patients and Return Appointments

Procedures for handling appointments for new patients and scheduling return appointments are discussed in Chapter 10. Always provide excellent customer service to the caller. Remember that the routine questions that may be asked should be answered in a polite, cheerful manner. Health matters are important to the individual patients whom the practice serves. Follow the designated office procedure as to what information should be gathered and recorded when appointments are made.

Directions

Each office should have a clear set of directions written out that can be read to the caller who requests directions. Prepare them from various points in the area; for instance, one set would guide a patient who is coming from the north, and another set would be for a patient coming from the south. Place these directions close to the telephone so that all employees can access them easily. Not all employees live close to the clinic or are familiar with the area; therefore, the written set of directions will be helpful to all staff members and those who call the facility. Place a map on the office Web site and direct patients there for printable instructions. Never simply suggest that the caller refer to an Internet map when he or she asks for directions.

Inquiries about Bills

A patient may ask to speak with the physician about a recent bill. Ask the caller to hold for a moment while the ledger is obtained from the computer or files. If nothing irregular is found on the ledger, return to the telephone and say, "I have your account in front of me now. Perhaps I can answer your question." Most likely the caller will have some simple inquiry, such as whether the insurance has paid, or he or she may want to delay making a payment until the next month. Not all patients realize that the medical assistant usually makes such decisions and is the best person with whom to discuss these matters. When necessary, create a note in the electronic medical record (EMR) or the physical ledger card about the patient's call, such as a promise to pay on a certain date.

A patient may have a question about a statement that came in the mail. If billing matters are handled by another employee, tell the patient that the call will be transferred to the billing office. If you are responsible for billing, politely ask the patient to hold the line while you obtain the patient ledger. On returning to the line, thank the patient for waiting and explain the charges carefully. If an error has occurred, apologize and say that a corrected statement will be sent out at once. Always remember to thank the patient for calling. If patients are properly advised about charges at the time services are rendered, the number of these calls can be reduced considerably.

Inquiries about Fees

Fees vary widely in each medical office, and quoting an exact fee before the physician sees the patient is difficult. However, a good estimate should be given to the patient as to what they should expect to pay, especially on the first visit. Asking a patient to just appear at the office without having any idea of the cost is unreasonable. Discuss with the physician or office manager what range should be quoted to the patient, then follow your quotes with the statement that the fees vary, depending on the patient's condition and tests the physician orders. If fees are regularly discussed on the telephone, write a suggested script in the policy manual. Do not be evasive. Have a schedule of fees available.

Participating Provider

Patients may call the office to inquire whether the physician is a participating **provider** with their particular insurance plan or managed care organization. The physician should keep a carefully updated list of which plans are valid. This is important, because insurance benefits vary for participating and nonparticipating providers, and a claim will be denied or reimbursement lessened if the physician is not a provider for the patient's insurance company.

Requests for Assistance with Insurance

In today's environment of managed care, co-pays, Medicaid, and Medicare, insurance claims will more than likely be completed and filed by the healthcare facility. Nevertheless, patients may call to inquire about their coverage or ask whether any response to claims has been made. A medical assistant or member of the staff responsible for insurance filing must have the knowledge to answer these inquiries. Be patient with these inquiries; insurance is a difficult subject to understand, even for trained individuals familiar with the various forms and procedures. Some patients, especially elderly ones, can become quite confused when dealing with insurance companies. Help them as much as possible so that they can collect the benefits to which they are entitled.

Radiology and Laboratory Reports

When results are urgently needed, laboratory and radiologic findings may be telephoned, faxed, or e-mailed to the physician's office on the day the procedures are performed. The medical assistant should take these reports and relay them to the physician. If the test has been marked **STAT**, which means that the physician wants the results immediately, reports may be faxed to the physician's office. Original reports usually are delivered by mail for the medical record. Some facilities are equipped to receive laboratory results directly from the laboratory by computer.

Satisfactory Progress Reports from Patients

Physicians sometimes ask patients to phone the office to report on their condition a few days after the office visit. The medical assistant can take such calls and relay the information to the physician if the report is satisfactory. Assure the patient that you will inform the physician about the call. The physician should always be immediately informed about unsatisfactory progress reports. The doctor should provide instructions for the patient to follow in such situations.

Routine Reports from Hospitals and Other Sources

Routine calls may be received from hospitals and other sources reporting a patient's progress. Take the message carefully and make sure that the physician sees it. The message should then be placed in the patient's medical record.

Office Administration Matters

Not all calls concern patients. Calls may come from the accountant or the auditor or about banking procedures, office supplies, or office maintenance, most of which the medical assistant can handle or refer to the appropriate person. For some of these calls, the medical assistant may need to gather additional information and return the call.

Requests for Referrals

Physicians who are liked and respected by their patients frequently are called for referrals to other specialists. If the physician has furnished the medical assistant with a list of practitioners for this purpose, these inquiries may be handled without consulting the physician, unless the patient's insurance plan requires a written referral. However, the physician should always be informed of such requests. Document referrals in the patient's medical record.

Some managed care organizations require a physician referral before a patient may see a specialist. This referral should come from the physician, unless he or she has authorized automatic referrals. Most physicians require the patient to come in for an office visit to discuss the referral. Afterward, a staff member calls the referral physician and notifies the office staff of the referral. Handle these calls as

PROCEDURE 9-3

Call the Pharmacy with New or Refill Prescriptions

GOAL: To call in an accurate prescription to the pharmacy in the most efficient manner.

EQUIPMENT and SUPPLIES

- Prescription information
- Notepad
- Patient medical record
- Telephone
- Computer and/or fax machine

PROCEDURAL STEPS

1. Receive the call from the patient or a fax from a pharmacy requesting a prescription; use appropriate telephone technique.
   <u>PURPOSE:</u> To provide consistently good customer service when speaking with callers.

2. Obtain the following information from the patient:
   - Patient's name
   - Telephone number where he or she can be reached
   - Patient's symptoms and current condition
   - History of this condition
   - Treatments the patient has tried
   - Pharmacy name, telephone number, and/or fax number
   <u>PURPOSE:</u> To have the information the physician will need to determine whether a prescription will be called in for the patient or whether the person needs to come to the office to be seen by the doctor.

3. Write in the patient's chart the prescription the physician wants the patient to have. Be very careful to transcribe the information correctly. Analyze communications in providing appropriate responses and feedback by reading it back to the physician.
   <u>PURPOSE:</u> To have a permanent record of the prescription in the chart and to make sure the prescription is exactly what the physician wants the patient to take, eliminating errors in medication name and dosage.

4. If the prescription is a refill, give the physician the patient's chart with the message requesting a refill attached, along with the information in step 2.

<u>PURPOSE:</u> To have the patient's chart as a reference and to provide the physician with the information needed to determine whether the medication requested should be refilled.

5. Note the comments the physician writes in the chart. If the prescription is written or a refill is approved, call the patient's pharmacy and ask to speak to a member of the pharmacy staff. (If the prescription was requested by fax, complete the requested information and send the fax back to the pharmacy.)

6. Ask the pharmacy staff member to repeat the prescription back to you.
   <u>PURPOSE:</u> To verify that the pharmacy staff member took down the prescription accurately.

7. Note in the chart the date and time the prescription was called to the pharmacy.
   <u>PURPOSE:</u> To create a permanent record of the medication being called to the pharmacy, along with the correct dose and frequency of doses.

8. Call the patient to notify him or her that the prescription has been called in. Provide any information about the prescription doses, frequency, and so on requested by the physician. Tell the patient when to return to the office, if necessary. Ask the patient to write this information down.
   <u>PURPOSE:</u> To inform the patient of the dosage and frequency, so that if an error is made by the pharmacy, the patient will note the discrepancy and the error can be corrected before the patient takes any of the medication.
   <u>NOTE:</u> Many physicians use an electronic medical record system that allows them to use e-prescribing functions. E-prescribing works in a similar way to electronic faxing. The physician usually enters the desired prescription information into the patient's electronic record while in the exam room. The patient's pharmacy is listed in the record, so once the prescription is completed, the physician clicks "send" and it is on its way to the pharmacy. This method is becoming more common and helps to eliminate prescribing errors and forged prescriptions.

quickly as possible so that the patient may make an appointment to see the referral physician.

Prescription Refills

Pharmacies periodically call the physician's office to obtain approval for a patient to refill a prescription. Prescriptions have a specific notation as to the number of times the prescription can be refilled. However, the physician may have noted in the chart that a certain medication is to be taken for 6 months, but the prescription was written only for 1 to 2 months. Any prescription refills should be authorized only with the physician's approval. Tell the pharmacist that you will have to check with the physician and call back. Many pharmacies today handle prescription refills by fax so that they

have a written record that the refill was authorized. Make sure state regulations and procedures are followed any time you deal with prescription refills or calls (Procedure 9-3). Some medications require a written prescription.

SPECIAL INCOMING CALLS

Patients Refusing to Discuss Symptoms

Occasionally patients call and want to talk with the physician about symptoms they are reluctant to discuss with a medical assistant. Patients have a right to privacy, but the physician cannot be expected to take numerous calls from patients who do not want to speak to the medical assistant. If the patient refuses to discuss any symptoms, suggest that he or she make an appointment with the physician to discuss the problem in person.

Unsatisfactory Progress Reports

If a patient under treatment reports that he or she is still not feeling well or that the prescription the doctor provided is not helping, do not practice medicine illegally by giving the patient medical advice. Make detailed notes about the patient's comments, then present them to the physician. He or she may make a medication change or may decide that the patient should return to the office. Follow up with the patient and convey the physician's instructions.

Requests for Test Results

When the physician orders special tests for the patient, the patient may be told to call the office in a couple of days for the results. It is ultimately the responsibility of the physician to notify the patient of test results, especially if they are abnormal. Make sure the physician has seen the results and has given permission before sharing the results with the patient. If specified in the office policy, the medical assistant can give test results to the patient. Patients do not always understand that the medical assistant does not have the privilege of giving out information without the permission of the physician. If the result is unfavorable, the physician should be the one to inform the patient and give further instructions. This call must be handled tactfully; otherwise, the patient may feel as if the staff is concealing information.

Most physicians prefer that medical assistants provide only normal test results to the patients. However, the medical assistant may provide abnormal test results if authorized by the physician. For example, when a patient has a questionable Pap smear, the medical assistant usually is the person who calls the patient with the results and further instructions from the physician. If the patient then has any questions about the test results, he or she must be referred to the physician. The medical assistant needs good communication skills to relay information such as this without crossing the line of practicing medicine without a license.

The best policy for dealing with more serious abnormal test results is to schedule an appointment for the patient to see the physician. These results are best related in person instead of on the telephone. Human immunodeficiency virus (HIV) test results should never be given on the telephone; the physician should always insist that the patient return to the office to obtain these results.

Patients who call the office for test results must be appropriately identified before the results are given. Some offices use a special code that is written in the chart, and knowledge of this code or password gives the person access to the information. Make sure the right individual is on the line before offering test results. Especially be careful in situations in which the family includes a "Senior" and "Junior." If the medical assistant calls and asks for Robert Smith, the elder Mr. Smith may answer, whereas the younger Mr. Smith is the one who came to the office for tests. Staff members may breach HIPAA regulations if they do not identify the patient accurately.

Requests for Information from Third Parties

The patient must give written permission before any member of the physician's staff can give information to third-party callers. This includes insurance companies, attorneys, relatives, neighbors, employers, and any other third party.

Complaints about Care or Fees

A medical assistant may be able to offer a satisfactory explanation to a patient who complains about the care he or she received or the fee charged. Often, the patient simply does not understand a charge, and the medical assistant can provide assistance by reviewing the bill. If a patient seems angry, offer to pull the chart, research the problem, and if needed, discuss it with the physician. Four magic words often calm the angry patient: "Let me help you." This reassures the patient that someone is willing to talk about the problem. However, if you are unable to appease the patient easily, the physician or office manager may prefer to talk directly to the patient.

Calls from the Physician's Family and Friends

Personal calls to the physician from family members or friends are handled in accordance with instructions from the physician. If the physician does not want to take the calls, the medical assistant must tactfully tell the caller that the physician cannot be disturbed at that time.

Calls from Staff Members' Family and Friends

The telephone lines should never be burdened with an excess of personal calls to the staff. A call is necessary in emergencies, but staff members should never monopolize the telephone for personal business and conversations. Emergency calls could be coming through, and the lines must be clear. Keep personal calls to an absolute minimum.

HANDLING DIFFICULT CALLS

Angry Callers

No matter how efficient the medical assistant is on the telephone or how well liked the employer may be, sooner or later an angry caller will be on the line. The anger may have a legitimate cause, or the caller's irritation may have resulted from a misunderstanding. Handling such calls is a real challenge. First, take the required action, even if it is to say that the matter will be discussed with the physician as soon as possible and the patient will be called back later. If answers are not readily available, a friendly assurance that the situation is important and that every attempt will be made to find the answer quickly usually calms the angry feelings.

The medical assistant may find that lowering the tone of voice and volume of speech may force the angry caller to do the same to hear. This method does not always work, but it usually is true that when dealing with an angry person, calm promotes calm. Some patients may misread this method and become even angrier, thinking that their complaint is not being taken seriously. Interpersonal skills are critical when dealing with other individuals, because the more skilled the medical assistant becomes, the better able he or she is to deal with multiple types of personalities.

Always avoid getting angry in response and try to get to the root of the real problem. Express interest and understanding, take careful notes, and follow through with the problem to the most appropriate resolution. Never "pass the buck" by saying, "That isn't my job," or "I am not the person who filed that insurance claim." No matter whose fault the problem is, it is best to deal with it and find a solution instead of placing blame.

CRITICAL THINKING APPLICATION   9-5

An angry caller raises his voice at Ashlynn over an issue that happened before she began to work at the facility. She suggests that he speak with the office manager, but he refuses and continues to berate Ashlynn.
- What choices does Ashlynn have in this situation?
- Should she simply hang up on the patient?
- How can the call be handled diplomatically?

Aggressive Callers

Aggressive callers insist that they receive whatever action they feel is necessary, and they usually insist on action immediately. Treat these callers with a calm, poised attitude, but do not allow the caller's aggression to initiate inappropriate action. Reassure the caller that the concern being shared is valid and will receive the full attention of the right person. Explain when the caller can expect a response from the office, and be sure to follow up that the appropriate action was taken.

Unauthorized Inquiry Calls

Some individuals call the physician's office requesting information to which they are not entitled. These callers must be told politely but firmly that such information cannot be provided to them because of privacy laws. Insistent callers should be referred to the office manager or physician.

Sales Calls

Sales calls often are thought of as an interruption to the physician's busy day, but some salespersons may have important information on products, equipment, or services the office uses regularly. Do not completely disregard salespersons, but do not allow them to monopolize time or telephone lines, either. Keep these calls quick and to the point. Most professional salespersons realize that the physician's and staff's time is extremely valuable and respect this. Developing a good rapport with representatives ("reps") from the companies whose products are frequently used in the practice may result in discounted prices and first news of sales and promotions. In turn, these people rarely waste the time of office personnel.

Physician Shopping

Some calls are from prospective patients seeking information about the office and the types of illnesses or conditions the physician treats. Because managed care plans require the patient to choose a primary care provider, patients may call to obtain an idea of the physician's background before selecting him or her to be their physician. Often patients must choose from a list of physicians they do not know. Consider these callers future patients or as people who may refer patients to the office. Always be polite and answer questions respectfully. Remember, even if the caller does not become a patient, he or she may share his or her impressions of the practice with another prospective patient.

Not to be confused with physician shopping, "doctor shopping" has become a serious issue in the medical community. Patients who see multiple physicians requesting prescriptions for narcotics without the provider's knowledge of the other prescriptions, are said to be doctor shopping, which is now illegal in many states. The Center for Disease Control defines this act as obtaining drugs through fraud, deceit, misrepresentation, or concealment. Over a period of time, the medical assistant who answers the phone will learn to spot many drug seekers when they call for an initial appointment. Always share any concerns or suspicious activity with the physician or the office manager.

If reference needed for above information: http://www.cdc.gov/homeandrecreationalsafety/Poisoning/laws/dr_shopping.html Accessed on 5-15-2013

Complaints

When callers complain, use an approach similar to the one used with angry callers. Do not attempt to blame someone else and never argue with the patient. Find the source of the problem, then present the options to the caller as to how the situation can be resolved. Remember to treat callers in the same manner that you would wish to be treated. A complaint may seem small and insignificant to the office staff, but to the patient it could be paramount. Provide good customer service to patients, and complaints will be few and far between.

Callers with Difficulty Communicating

Occasionally, calls will come to the office from patients or family members who have difficulty with the English language. In some cases, English is not the caller's primary language, so the medical assistant must use listening skills to ensure understanding. If a certain language is predominant in the area, the physician should consider hiring a medical assistant who is bilingual. Some patients speak English, but have a heavy accent, so listen carefully and ask questions to be sure that he or she is properly understood. Some physicians may have a population of deaf patients and will need to either employ an individual who uses sign language or have access to some other type of device designed to communicate with the hearing impaired.

EMERGENCY CALLS

Many emergency calls require judgment on the part of the person answering the phone in the medical practice. Good judgment comes from experience and proper training by the physician with regard to what constitutes a real emergency in each type of practice and how such calls should be handled. The person answering the telephone first should determine whether the call is truly urgent. If so, never hang up the phone until an ambulance reaches the patient or other help arrives. When necessary, ask another staff member to call 911 while remaining on the line with the patient. Emergency calls could include such conditions and/or symptoms as chest pain, profuse bleeding, severe allergic reactions, cessation of breathing, injuries resulting in loss of consciousness, and broken bones. An urgent call could be an adult patient with a fever over 102° F, an animal bite, or an increasingly painful ear infection. Emergency calls are life-threatening, whereas an urgent call requires prompt attention but is not life-threatening. Often the physician instructs the patient to go straight to the closest hospital emergency department instead of the office. Policy and procedure manuals should dictate the action to take in emergency situations.

If the physician is in, the call may need to be transferred to him or her immediately. All offices should have a written plan of action for the times the physician is not physically present in the office to handle the call. The physician and medical assistant may also jointly develop typical questions to ask the caller to determine the validity and disposition of an emergency. Some examples of questions to ask include:

- At what telephone number can you be reached?
- Where are you located?
- What are the chief symptoms?
- When did they start?
- Has this happened before?
- Are you alone?
- Do you have transportation?

Screening Guidelines

In a facility with multiple employees, the physician may designate one individual as the screening nurse or assistant. In the managed care environment, every physician would be wise to have a written telephone protocol for handling urgent situations and emergencies. The protocol should state that the employees are bound by the written guidelines and that any giving of advice by unauthorized personnel may be grounds for dismissal.

A special sheet of instructions listing specific medical emergencies, such as chest pain, heavy bleeding, fainting, seizure, and poisoning, should be posted by each telephone. The phone numbers for the nearest poison control center, hospital, and ambulance should be listed. Such calls should be routed to a physician immediately. Additional instructions should include what action to take if no physician is available, such as sending the patient to an emergency department or calling an ambulance. Most offices have some means of constant contact with the physician, whether by pager, cell phone, or another method.

Getting the Information the Physician Needs

As the medical assistant gains experience and knows the physician better, he or she begins to have a sense of the questions the physician will have for patients who call the facility. For instance, the physician is interested in how long the patient has had symptoms, what makes the symptoms better or worse, what remedies have been tried, what has worked and not worked, and other specifics about the condition. If the patient complains of painful urination, the medical assistant learns to ask about pain in the back, blood in the urine and/or stool, and cramping. One way to learn about questions to ask is to listen to the physician carefully as he or she questions patients about their symptoms. This can help the medical assistant learn more about signs and symptoms and enable him or her to be a better assistant to the physician.

Remember to always be "patient with your patients." Those who call the medical office for help are almost never at their best. When feeling ill, people often are short-tempered and even display poor manners. Some can be verbally abusive. Care for patients as if they were family members, and they will feel care and compassion in the medical facility.

TYPICAL OUTGOING CALLS

Most outgoing calls in a physician's office are responses to the incoming calls. The same rules for courtesy and diction apply to calls made from the office to patients, other individuals, and businesses.

It is helpful to plan outgoing calls in advance. For instance, if the medical assistant is placing an order for office supplies, a list should be made that includes the product, the price, the quantity needed, and a catalog page number, if applicable. Questions about the various products ordered should be noted so that they can be asked while the sales representative is on the phone.

Some medical assistants find it helpful to make all outgoing calls at once, when possible. This way the calls can be made one after another, and if a call back is necessary, the medical assistant is likely to still be by the phone. Organizing calls helps increase office efficiency.

Never be rude to an individual on the phone. Remember to treat those on the other end of the phone as you would wish to be treated. Do not forget that the medical assistant is a representative of the physician and should behave in a professional manner at all times.

TELEPHONE SERVICES

Voice Mail

Voice mail is widely used in today's business offices because it affords an around-the-clock method for receiving patient messages. Unfortunately, it can prove frustrating to those who find themselves speaking to an electronic device more often than a human being. Voice mail allows the caller to hear a recorded message that may also provide information about what to do in case of an emergency. Similar to an answering machine, voice mail records a caller's message, which can later be retrieved, and allows special temporary greetings when the user is away from the office. Keep patients happy by answering voice mail messages promptly.

Answering Services

Because a physician's telephone is an all-important tool of the practice, someone must be able to answer it at all times, day and night, weekends and holidays. This presents no problem during weekdays, but nights and weekends require special attention. Most physicians subscribe to telephone answering services that provide round-the-clock coverage. Answering services normally provide an operator (rather than a recording device) to answer the phones, which often is preferred over standard voice mail. Two types of operator-answered services are available. With the first type, physician-subscribers leave messages with or obtain patients' messages from a service for which a number appears in the local telephone directory after the physician's number, with a notation to call the second number after hours. This form of service is somewhat inconvenient for the patient but is far better than no coverage at all. With the second type, the answering service has a direct connection with the office telephone. When the telephone rings in the physician's office or at home, it also signals on the switchboard of the answering service. As long as the telephone rings, it continues to signal at the answering service. If no one answers within a certain agreed-on number of rings (or immediately in some cases), the answering service operator takes the call. This method provides continuous live telephone coverage.

Even during the day, such an answering service can function effectively. Sometimes the staff members may be assisting the physician and unable to answer the telephone. Not answering the telephone is extremely poor policy; therefore, if the office has an agreement with the answering service, its operators accept calls in such situations. With this direct-wire answering method, the operator answers the telephone in the same manner as the regular staff.

The answering service greatly appreciates receiving a call every day from a member of the physician's staff before leaving the office with information on where the physician will be during the evening or other special messages. The next morning, a staff member should call the service and ask for any messages that may have been taken or collect the messages through e-mail. Usually there will be messages from patients who called after office hours but whose calls were not urgent enough to merit an emergency call to the physician. An answering service can act as a buffer for the physician and help eliminate too frequent, unnecessary calls during the late evening or night hours. Some physicians in smaller practices or in rural areas have a recorded message that plays after hours. The message directs patients with an emergency either to go to the nearest emergency department or to call a secondary number to reach the physician on call. In rare cases, a physician's message simply states to call back during regular office hours.

Automatic Call Routing

In automatic call routing, a call is answered by an automated operator's message that presents a list of options, such as "If you are calling about your account, press 1; to make an appointment, press 2 …" and so forth. The impersonal nature of automation does not lend itself well to answering the telephone in a small to medium-sized physician's office, but the medical assistant encounters it frequently when placing outgoing calls. Some larger clinics and hospitals may use automatic call routing on a daily basis.

CRITICAL THINKING APPLICATION　　9-6

Ashlynn has had many complaints from patients about the new call routing system, because it takes so long to "get to a human being." How can she get her patients to be more accepting of modern call routing systems? What methods might help elderly patients to deal with automated call routing more easily?

Call Forwarding

Call forwarding allows the user to forward calls to another designated number, such as a cell phone. Usually a code is entered, then the phone number to which the calls should be forwarded. This prevents the user from missing important calls when away from the main telephone.

Caller ID

Caller ID allows the user to see who is calling before picking up the handset to answer the phone. The caller's phone number and name appear on a screen, and the user can decide whether to take the call.

If the user subscribes to call-waiting services, another benefit called call-waiting caller ID is often available. Call-waiting caller ID allows the user to see who is calling even when the user is already on the phone.

Caller ID Blocking

Patients may have a feature on their phones that prevents anonymous or private calls from connecting and ringing. The feature, which works with caller ID, shows the words "anonymous," "private," "out of area," or "unavailable." The user has several options when using this feature. He or she can accept the call, reject the call, or send it directly to voice mail. Some physicians often use a blocker (e.g., *67) before calling patients, so that the patient will not have access to the physician's personal phone numbers. The caller hears a message stating that the person being called does not accept unidentified calls and then must choose from several menu options. This system is most commonly used when a patient calls a physician after hours and the physician subsequently returns the patient's call. Patients may need to be educated about this procedure so that the physician can reach them easily when calling after established office hours.

Cellular Phones

Considered a luxury item only 10 years ago, cellular (or cell) phones have become commonplace. Many people no longer have a home phone because of the expense of having two phones, and the cell phone usually is the better buy for the money. Several of the more popular cell phone companies offer free long distance calls in the United States and may provide users free night and weekend minutes as a bonus. Most of today's advanced cell phones even allow the user to access the Internet and check e-mail through the telephone. Cell phone companies usually offer a text messaging service, which allows the user to type a message with the cell phone keys, which then is sent directly to a cell phone number. Encourage staff members who use mobile telephones to take advantage of Bluetooth technology for hands-free talking.

Fax Machines

A fax machine can be a great time and labor saver in conveying patient information from physician to physician or from physician to hospital. It allows its user to send and receive copies of printed documents over telephone lines to other facilities that have fax machines (Figure 9-4). Most offices find this machine indispensable. Unless precautions are taken to ensure the security of information arriving by fax, the danger of loss of confidentiality is present. When sensitive material is sent, it is wise to telephone ahead to alert the receiver that this information will be arriving so that the appropriate person is on hand to receive it. A fax cover sheet should be used that instructs individuals who receive faxes in error to destroy them and states that the information contained in the fax is strictly confidential. Many offices use a printer that also functions as a fax, scanner, and copier. Fax services are also available online, such as Ring Central, through which documents are uploaded from the computer but sent to a fax machine. These services also usually offer a fax number, so that a fax sent from a machine to that fax number will be received in the e-mail inbox. The cost of these services varies and is usually quite affordable; however, the user must still have access

FIGURE 9-4 Fax machines allow written data to be transferred from one place to another simply by dialing a telephone. (Courtesy Dell Corp., Round Rock, Texas.)

FIGURE 9-5 Using a headset helps the medical assistant keep the hands free while using the telephone and is better ergonomically.

to a scanner to fax documents that are not loaded onto the computer, such as a request for records that the patient has signed.

Headsets

In today's world of **multitasking**, the headset helps a medical assistant keep hands free while speaking on the phone. A popular headset is a very lightweight plastic earphone and microphone combination that allows the wearer to move about the room with the hands free (Figure 9-5). Some units weigh less than 1 ounce and are worn behind the ear or clipped to the wearer's glasses. Some headsets can be equipped with a cord that allows for easy mobility. Some also have a quick-disconnect feature that allows the user to separate the headset even during a call without breaking the connection.

USING LONG DISTANCE AND SPECIAL SERVICES

Long distance calls are simple to place, usually inexpensive, and efficient. When information is needed in a hurry, telephoning is much more expedient. Before placing a long distance call, have the correct number ready. If you do not have the number, you may obtain directory assistance by dialing 1, then the area code of the party you are calling, followed by 555-1212. In some areas, numbers are available by calling 1-411. Directory assistance is now an automated service in many regions, and you will be asked for the name of the city and the person you are calling. Often a fee is charged for using directory assistance, so look for the phone number using free sources whenever possible.

The Internet makes searching for phone numbers much easier. Try to find phone numbers through the Internet (try *www.yellowpages.com* or *www.whitepages.com*) or use a printed phone book to avoid directory assistance charges on the monthly phone bill. A search for the business or physician needed may yield the information. If the company has a Web site, there is usually a "Contact Us" page that directs the user to the individual departments and even personnel who can assist in finding the correct phone numbers. Some Internet services allow the user to call long distance, and sometimes even internationally, through the computer with no long distance charges.

Time Zones

The continental United States is divided into four standard time zones: Pacific, Mountain, Central, and Eastern (Figure 9-6). When it is noon Pacific time, it is 3 PM Eastern time. When calling from San Francisco to New York, plan to make the call no later than 2 PM if the call is to a business or professional office. When it is 2 PM on the West Coast, it is 5 PM on the East Coast.

International Service

International Direct Distance Dialing (IDDD) is available in many areas. International dialing codes are the same for all companies offering IDDD. Depending on the long distance company, additional numbers or codes may preface the international access, country, and city codes. IDDD is still not available in all areas. If it is available, you may place international station-to-station calls by dialing the following in sequence:

1. International code 011
2. Country code
3. City code
4. Local telephone number
5. The pound sign (#) button if the telephone is touchtone

After dialing any international code, allow at least 45 seconds for the ringing to start. Consult the Internet for updates on international calling procedures and country or city codes.

Wrong Numbers

One slip in direct distance dialing can mean a call to Los Angeles or New York instead of Dallas. If you reach a wrong long distance number, be sure to obtain the name of the city and state that was called. Report this information promptly to the local operator so that the facility will not be charged for the call. If you are cut off before terminating a call, also report this. The operator will either reconnect the call or adjust the charge.

Conference Calls

Conference telephone service is of great value to the medical profession in notifying and explaining to a family how a patient is

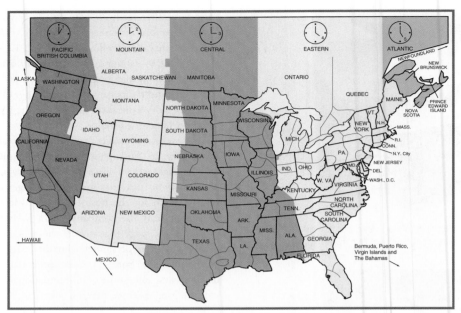

FIGURE 9-6 Time zones across the United States.

progressing. It has exceptional value in family conferences, at which a quick decision by the entire family regarding a patient's condition is required.

This service can connect numerous points for a conference in which each person can hear or talk to all others participating. Conference calls may be local or long distance. Charges are added for the number of places connected, the distance between parties, and the length of the conversation.

Conference calls can be set up by a normal long distance operator or through conference call services, many of which can be found online. To schedule a call, contact either an operator or the calling service and relay the pertinent information about time, date, and the individuals who are to be included in the call. Many businesses have conference call capabilities on their phone or computer systems. Notify everyone participating in the call of the time, date, number to call, and subjects to discuss. If prior arrangements are made with all parties, there is a better chance of reaching everyone and having a successful conference.

Operator-Assisted Calls and Services

Operator-assisted calls include the following:

- Person to person
- Billing to a third party
- Collect calls
- Requests for time and charges
- Certain calls placed from hotels
- Credit for wrong numbers
- Conference calls
- Some international calls

Operator-assisted calls through most phone service providers have an initial charge and a service charge. Fewer and fewer calls are operator assisted in today's business world, because the cost for these calls often is high. Try other alternatives before making an operator-assisted call.

FIGURE 9-7 Multiline telephones allow numerous calls to come into the office at once. Each call deserves the same kind of attention and care from the medical assistant.

OFFICE TELEPHONE EQUIPMENT NEEDS

Number and Placement of Telephones

Familiarity with a multiple-line telephone system is a must for medical assistants. Few healthcare facilities can get along with just one telephone line. Two incoming lines, along with a private outgoing line with a separate number for the physician's exclusive use, is the minimum recommended number of lines.

One medical assistant can handle no more than two incoming lines; therefore, the addition of more lines may involve additional staffing (Figure 9-7). If a staff member is assigned solely to dealing with insurance and billing, a separate line and listing in the telephone directory for this service may considerably lessen the load on the main incoming lines.

Telephones should be placed where they are accessible but private. Some facilities also place a telephone in the reception room for the convenience of patients and to prevent their asking to use the facility's phones. However, recent trends suggest that a separate telephone line with a limited calling area for the convenience of patients who need to call out may be preferable. This telephone should not be in the reception room but in an area available to patients on request. It should be placed low enough for use by patients in wheelchairs. Wherever possible, other telephones should be placed on the wall to conserve desk space.

USING A TELEPHONE DIRECTORY

As previously mentioned, online telephone directories are convenient and provide the user with a fast response after a query. Some television programming systems provide service right on the television screen, which is helpful to patients. To use the television-based service, the remote control guides the user to the correct channel, and then the name of an individual or business is entered with the remote control.

The primary purpose of the telephone directory is to provide lists of those who have telephones, their telephone numbers, and in most cases their addresses. In addition, the directory is an aid in checking the spelling of names and in locating certain types of businesses through the yellow pages. Some directories are color coded, with residence listings on white pages, business numbers on pink pages, and business by categories and advertisements on yellow pages. Often, federal, state, county, and city government listings are included as blue pages. Directories usually are organized into three sections:

- Introductory pages
- Alphabetic pages (white pages)
- Yellow pages

The introductory pages sometimes are entirely overlooked by subscribers. This section precedes the white alphabetic pages and provides basic information concerning the telephone services in the area.

Some directories include ZIP code maps for the local area. Take a few moments to become familiar with the local directory, then use it frequently for getting information fast.

The white pages are an alphabetic listing of telephone subscribers with their telephone numbers and often their addresses.

The yellow pages directory, sometimes published separately, contains listings for businesses arranged by the product or services they sell. Physicians are listed alphabetically, usually under the heading Physicians and Surgeons, and have the option of another listing by type of practice.

In some metropolitan areas, a street address and telephone directory is published that is arranged by street address, followed by the name and telephone number of the person or business at that address.

Organizing a Personal Phone Directory

Organize telephone numbers in a tabbed 3 × 5-inch desktop file or a rotary file. Binders with clear sheet protectors also work well as personal phone directories. Emergency numbers might be typed on a colored card or flagged with a colored tab. A personal directory of telephone numbers should include all the numbers frequently called.

Identifying Community Resources

Patients often call the physician's office looking for information on various community resources. Those who are fighting cancer may be interested in programs offered by the American Red Cross. Those who are diabetic may wish to know the options for ordering blood glucose testing supplies through online services. Some patients may benefit from Meals on Wheels. The medical assistant should be concerned with providing good customer service to patients and visitors with whom they come in contact. Therefore, it is helpful to keep a list of the community resources that might be of assistance to patients. Often information can be found in the first few sections of the telephone book. The physician may want to keep a list of services most often used by the clinic's patients. Patients appreciate staff members who try to offer assistance and resources outside the physician's office.

CLOSING COMMENTS

A telephone is a tool; it can be used to build a physician's practice or to destroy it. Medical assistants must become proficient in good telephone technique and must make sure callers hear compassion and patience in their voices, even over the phone. A medical assistant must convey a genuine sense of caring for the patients who call the facility, just as if they were standing in the office. By keeping this in mind, the medical assistant plays a major role in patient satisfaction, and patients will find their medical care a pleasant process.

Patient Education

Today's telephone systems allow physicians to educate patients while they are on hold; recordings may be played that offer health information on subjects from A to Z. These messages can be professionally recorded and/or custom designed by the physician and staff. Special events may be announced, with the option to press a certain number for more information about the event.

Some phone directories offer listings of health information in the introductory pages. A patient may call a main number, then press a second number to reach the desired subject. Such features help address the needs of today's more information-oriented healthcare consumers, who are interested in healthy lifestyles and in gaining useful information immediately. Always be willing to teach and assist patients who must deal with these informational resources.

Legal and Ethical Issues

The guidelines for medical confidentiality apply equally to telephone conversations; therefore, take care that no one overhears sensitive information. Use discretion when mentioning the name of a caller or patient.

Do not place or receive personal phone calls during work hours. Time limitations for personal phone use should be described in the office policy manual. The telephone is a business line and should be reserved for patients and others conducting business with the office. The medical assistant should encourage friends and family to call at home so that all patient calls get through to the office.

Telephone and message records may be brought into court as evidence; make sure all messages are complete and legible. Most offices should keep these records for at least the same period as the statute of limitations in that state.

SUMMARY OF SCENARIO

Ashlynn is quickly becoming a part of the team at Dr. Frank's office and is developing into a well-liked asset to the staff. She has learned to slow down when speaking on the phone and to adjust her volume and pitch, depending on the patient with whom she is speaking. Although she tends to be quite talkative, she is balancing just the right amount of friendly chat with the business at hand. She does this by offering a friendly greeting to callers, getting to the business at hand, then being affable before ending the call. By expressing her concern and asking how she can be of help to the patients, Ashlynn shows them that she sincerely cares about their problems. She is careful about her tone of voice, realizing that patients may take her comments the wrong way if she does not treat them in a cordial manner. Dr. Frank is very pleased with her performance.

Ashlynn takes care when she speaks to patients and others on the phone so that she does not breach confidentiality in any way. She has become comfortable with the way she is to answer the telephone. The pace of her speech and the wording are now a habit. Ashlynn is determined to maintain a professional relationship with all the people related to her work environment. She is adept now at handling calls from angry patients and can maintain control with even the most aggressive callers. She leaves callers on hold for a minimum amount of time and reassures them frequently that she is attending to their situation. By treating callers as she would want to be treated, Ashlynn reduces frustration, and she feels that the office is more efficient at handling the large volume of calls that come in each day. She shows much promise for a long and rewarding career in the medical field and is satisfied with the current track of her career. As she continues to settle into her position, she looks forward to learning more about efficiency and time management. Her good attitude and desire to learn will only enhance her performance at work, making her a valuable employee and one worth promoting.

SUMMARY OF LEARNING OBJECTIVES

1. **Define, spell, and pronounce the terms listed in the vocabulary.**
   Spelling and pronouncing medical terms correctly bolster the medical assistant's credibility. Knowing the definition of these terms promotes confidence in communication with patients and co-workers.

2. **Determine and discuss the source of incoming and outgoing calls to a physician's office.**
   Incoming calls to a physician's office come from a wide variety of sources. Established or new patients may be calling to set appointments. Insurance companies may be seeking information about a claim. Hospitals, nursing facilities, or other healthcare units may need to report the progress of a patient. Laboratory results may be coming in for a patient who is very ill. Routine sales calls and telemarketing calls also come to the office, in addition to personal calls to the physician and staff members.

3. **Describe how to develop a pleasing telephone voice.**
   A pleasing telephone voice is one that is friendly and conveys a favorable impression of the physician's practice. Enunciate words and pronounce them clearly and distinctly. Vary the pitch of your voice, avoiding a monotonous or droning manner. Always be courteous and use tact. Both incoming and outgoing calls should be businesslike and handled in a professional manner.

4. **Demonstrate the correct way to hold a telephone handset.**
   The telephone handset should be held around the middle of the shaft, with the mouthpiece approximately 1 inch from the lips, in front of the teeth. Talk directly into the handset so that the caller can clearly hear what is said. Do not hold the mouthpiece beneath the chin, because the voice may not be heard clearly. To prevent sore muscles and neck problems, do not lean the head downward to hold the phone between the ear and the shoulder.

5. **Explain why courtesy is so important when speaking on the telephone.**
   Courtesy to patients and other callers is vital. First impressions are important, and a medical assistant's phone manner sets the tone for the caller's perception of the physician's practice. Customer service is important to today's physician, because many patients have choices among their healthcare providers, and the attitude of staff members may play a large part in such a decision. Patients who receive good customer care not only will continue to see the provider, they also will refer other patients to the physician. This is one of the best ways to help a practice grow.

6. **Demonstrate the correct way to answer the telephone in the office.**
   Medical assistants should answer the telephone promptly and professionally. The physician's image is affected by the way telephone calls are handled. Be courteous and polite to all callers.

7. **Discuss different ways to handle callers who want to speak to the physician.**
   The physician's time is valuable, but it also is centered on the patients. It is physically impossible for the physician to take all the calls each day. The medical assistant therefore must screen the calls and decide which ones should be put through to the physician. The medical assistant should offer to take a message and attempt to find out exactly what the caller's needs are and how they can be resolved. The patient should not feel that the physician is totally inaccessible but must also understand that patients in the office must have the physician's full attention.

8. **List the seven elements of a correctly handled telephone message.**
   The seven elements of a correctly handled phone message are (1) the name of the person to whom the call should be directed; (2) the name of the person calling; (3) the caller's telephone number; (4) the reason for the call; (5) the medical assistant's description of the action to be taken; (6) the date and time of the call; and (7) the initials of the

person taking the call, so that if any question arises, that person can be consulted.

9. **Demonstrate the correct way to record a message accurately and take a request for action.**

When taking a telephone message, strive for accuracy. Be sure to get all the information that the physician will need to act. Repeat any words or numbers that are not heard clearly.

10. **Demonstrate the most efficient way to call in a prescription or a prescription refill to a pharmacy.**

The medical assistant should follow the office policy and procedure manual when calling in new prescriptions or refills to a pharmacy. If a question ever arises as to what the physician meant, ask — do not guess. Mistakes with medications can cost the patient's life.

11. **Discuss how the medical assistant should handle callers who have a complaint.**

Callers who have a complaint should be handled in a manner similar to that for angry callers. Remain calm and offer to help. Take a serious interest in what the caller has to say. Let the caller know that his or her concerns are important to the staff and the physician. Find the source of the problem and determine exactly what the caller wants or expects as a resolution. Always follow up on complaints and make sure they were resolved as much to the caller's satisfaction as possible.

12. **Explain how angry callers might be handled.**

Never return anger when a caller is angry. Remain calm and speak in tones that are perhaps slightly quieter than those of the caller. This often prompts the caller to lower his or her tone of voice. Offer to help the angry person and ask questions to gain control of the conversation, moving it toward resolution. Do not argue with angry callers.

13. **List several questions to ask when handling an emergency call.**

First, ask for a phone number where the caller can be reached in case of a sudden disconnection. Ask about the chief symptoms and when they started. Find out whether the patient has had similar symptoms in the past and what happened in that situation. Determine whether the patient is alone, has transportation, or needs an ambulance. In severe cases, do not hang up the phone until the ambulance or police arrive.

14. **Discuss several useful sections of the introductory pages of the phone directory.**

Useful sections of the introductory pages include area codes, emergency service information, long distance calling information, time zones, government listings, and community service numbers. It may be helpful to tear these pages out, place them in clear sheet protectors, and add them to a binder for easy reference.

CONNECTIONS

Study Guide Connection: Go to the Chapter 9 Study Guide. Read and complete the activities.

Evolve Connection: Go to the Chapter 9 link at *evolve.elsevier.com/ kinn* to complete the Chapter Review and Chapter Quiz. Check out the other resources listed for this chapter to make the most of what you have learned from Telephone Techniques.

10

SCHEDULING APPOINTMENTS

SCENARIO

Ramona West is the medical assistant in charge of scheduling appointments for Dr. Charlotte Brown. Ramona is an extremely organized person who thinks quickly and creatively. One of her professional goals is to ensure that the office remains on schedule throughout the day and that patient's waiting time is kept to an absolute minimum. She is fortunate that Dr. Brown is cooperative and time oriented, and they work well together to reach this common goal.

Ramona usually arrives at work at least 15 minutes early to begin her preparations for the day. She reviews the electronic medical record for each patient to make sure test results from previous visits are available to the physician and that the medical record is complete. She pays special attention to the patients who arrive in the office as she completes her daily tasks, remembering the importance of providing patients with good customer service. Ramona greets each patient by name and carries on a brief but cordial conversation. Patients appreciate that she goes the extra mile to remember something about them, and this promotes excellent patient relations.

Ramona leaves a little time in the morning and afternoon for emergency appointments. The office uses an automatic call routing system to contact patients and confirm appointments in advance, which increases her show rate. Her friendly, caring attitude makes her a favorite among the patients, and Dr. Brown is pleased with the relationship-building skills Ramona has developed.

While studying this chapter, think about the following questions:

- How can the medical assistant contribute to an efficient daily routine?
- How does the medical assistant contribute to keeping the daily schedule on track?
- How can the schedule be put back on track when emergencies disrupt the day?
- How does the flexibility of the medical assistant contribute to office efficiency?

LEARNING OBJECTIVES

1. Define, spell, and pronounce the terms listed in the vocabulary.
2. Describe scheduling guidelines.
3. Discuss the advantages of computerized appointment scheduling.
4. Explain the features that should be considered when choosing an appointment book.
5. Explain how self-scheduling can reduce the number of calls to the medical office.
6. Discuss pros and cons of various types of appointment management systems.
7. Explain the importance of legible writing in the appointment book.
8. Explain the basic procedure to follow when the office is behind schedule.
9. Discuss the benefits of offering choices to patients when scheduling appointments.
10. Identify critical information required for scheduling patient admissions and/or procedures.
11. Discuss several methods of dealing with patients who consistently arrive late.
12. Name several reasons for failed appointments.
13. Recognize office policies and protocols for handling appointments.

VOCABULARY

automatic call routing A software system that answers phones automatically and routes calls to staff after the caller responds to prompts; also used to call a large number of patients to remind them of appointments or make announcements.

disruption An unexpected event that throws a plan into disorder; an interruption that prevents a system or process from continuing as usual or as expected.

established patients Patients who are returning to the office who have previously been seen by the physician.

expediency (ik-spe'-de-un-se) A means of achieving a particular end, as in a situation requiring haste or caution.

integral (in'-ti-grul) Essential; being an indispensable part of a whole.

interaction A two-way communication; mutual or reciprocal action or influence.

intermittent Coming and going at intervals; not continuous.

interval Space of time between events.

matrix Something in which a thing originates, develops, takes shape, or is contained; a base on which to build.

no-show A person who fails to keep an appointment without giving advance notice.

preauthorization A process required by some insurance carriers in which the provider obtains permission to perform certain procedures or services or refers a patient to a specialist.

precertification A process required by some insurance carriers in which the provider must prove medical necessity before performing a procedure.

prerequisite (pre-re'-kwe-zut) Something that is necessary to an end or to carry out a function.

proficiency (pruh-fi'-shun-se) Competency as a result of training or practice.

reimbursement Payment of benefits to the physician for services rendered according to the guidelines of the third-party payer.

screening A system for examining and separating into different groups; in the medical office, determining the severity of illness that patients experience and prioritizing appointments based on that severity.

socioeconomic Relating to a combination of social and economic factors.

template A predeveloped page layout used to make new pages with a similar design, pattern, or style; a standardized file type used in computer software as a preformatted example on which to base other files.

The physician's time is the most valuable asset of a medical practice. The person responsible for scheduling this time must understand the practice, be familiar with the working habits and preferences of the physician (or physicians), and have clear guidelines for time management in the practice.

Appointment scheduling is the process that determines which patients the physician sees, the dates and times of appointments, and how much time is allotted to each patient based on the complaint and the physician's availability. Time management involves the realization that unforeseen interruptions and delays always occur. Most medical care providers find that efficient appointment scheduling is one of the most important factors in the success of the practice. Scheduling can be done in a number of ways, and each facility must find the way that suits it best.

USING ESTABLISHED PRIORITIES FOR APPOINTMENT SCHEDULING

Patients often complain that the amount of money they pay to see the physician does not correspond with the amount of time the physician spends with the patient. A patient may say, "I only saw the doctor for 5 minutes and could not even remember all the questions I wanted to ask!" The patient must feel confident that the physician will take enough time to understand his or her concerns. Well-planned scheduling and adherence to that schedule allow the physician to do more than run in and out of examination rooms with little time for the patient to talk with the physician.

The person scheduling appointments must learn the physician's habits and desires. If the physician suggests scheduling patients every 15 minutes but always spends 20 to 25 minutes with a patient, the schedule must be adjusted. Talk with the physician and/or office manager and compromise so that the schedule is workable. Some physicians need prompting to end the patient visit and move to the next patient. The medical assistant assisting in the examination room can help the physician remain on schedule, because he or she teams with the scheduler and they work together for an efficient flow of patients through the office.

The scheduling system must be individualized to the specific practice. The following general guidelines can be applied to any practice, whether computer or paper based. Four factors must be considered in scheduling: the patient's needs, the physician's preferences and habits, the facilities available, and the duration of office visits.

Patient Needs

Consider the **socioeconomic** status of the area being served when determining office hours and appointment times. The office staff should answer the following questions:

- Is the office in a busy metropolitan area or a rural agricultural community?
- Are the patients young, middle aged, or retirement age?
- Is the area more industrial or residential?
- What type of patients are seen? Are they of a specific age or gender? Do they have common diagnoses? Is the physician a general practitioner?

- Are evening and weekend appointments essential for most of the patients served?

After these elements have been considered, the scheduler must allot time based on the patient's needs for each individual office visit. These needs can be assessed by determining the following:

- What is the purpose of this visit?
- What is the patient's age?
- Will the patient require the physician's time for the entire visit or will another staff member perform all or part of the service?
- Is the patient a parent who prefers to schedule appointments while the children are at school?
- Does the patient object to traveling after dark?
- Is the patient a day worker who cannot take time off from a job?
- Is the patient a child whose parents both work during the day?

The office should make every attempt to meet the patient's needs while balancing the physician's preferences and the available facilities.

Physician Preferences and Habits

Consider the preferences and habits of the physicians in the practice before establishing and implementing a scheduling plan. Ask the following questions:

- Does the physician become restless if the reception room is not packed with waiting patients?
- Does the physician worry if even one patient is kept waiting?
- Is the physician methodic and careful about being in the facility when patient appointments are scheduled to begin?
- Is the physician habitually late?
- Does the physician move easily from one patient to another?
- Does the physician require a "break time" after a few patients?
- Would the physician rather see fewer patients and spend more time with each one or schedule more patients each day?

All of these preferences and habits become an **integral** part of the scheduling process (Figure 10-1). Keep in mind that the physician cannot spend every moment of the day with patients. The physician also has telephone calls to make and receive, reports to examine and dictate, meetings to attend, mail to answer, and many other business responsibilities. An experienced staff can handle many but not all of these tasks.

> ### CRITICAL THINKING APPLICATION   10-1
> - Ramona has noticed that Dr. Brown is taking a little longer with patients than normal and that she is running consistently behind schedule by approximately 5 to 15 minutes. How can Ramona help rectify this situation?
> - Discuss ways of approaching the physician when he or she is the cause of the delays in the schedule. What opening remarks can the medical assistant use to start the discussion in a positive way?

Available Facilities

Getting a patient into the office at a time when no facilities are available for the services needed is pointless. For example, suppose that an office with two physicians has only one room that can be used for minor surgery. Do not schedule two patients requiring

FIGURE 10-1 The habits and preferences of the physician must be considered when appointments are scheduled for patients.

minor surgery for the same time block, even if both doctors could be available. If the office has only one electrocardiograph, do not book two electrocardiographic procedures at the same time. As the medical assistant gains **proficiency** in scheduling, it becomes easier to pair patient needs with the available facilities according to the physician's preference. Major equipment frequently used or a certain room with such equipment may need its own scheduling column in the appointment book or software system.

Duration of Office Visits

The medical assistant who performs scheduling duties must know the amount of time required for various office visits and procedures. The office policy and procedure manual should have a list of the procedures performed in the physician's office with a notation of the time required for the procedure using established priorities. The time blocks are important, because the physician's **reimbursement** from insurance companies is based partly on the time requirements of the procedure or office visit. When scheduling, make sure to allow enough time to complete a procedure; for example, never schedule a Pap smear or minor surgery in a 10- or 15-minute time slot.

METHODS OF SCHEDULING APPOINTMENTS

The two most common methods of appointment scheduling are computerized scheduling and appointment book scheduling. Each has advantages and disadvantages, and the physician's office should weigh the benefits and choose the method that best suits the physician and the staff.

Computer Scheduling

The computer has replaced the appointment book in many practices. Software for appointment scheduling ranges from relatively simple programs that merely display available and scheduled times to more sophisticated systems that perform several other functions. Many programs can display such information as the length and type of appointment required and day or time preferences. The computer then can select the best appointment time based on the information entered into the computer.

The computer also can be used to keep track of future appointments. For example, when a patient calls and inquires about an appointment, the system can search by his or her name to find the time and date. Printouts also can be run to show the physician's daily schedule, including the patients' names and telephone numbers and the reason for the visit. Multiple copies of these schedules can be made, according to the needs of the practice.

Computer scheduling allows more than one person to access the system at once, and the information is available to all operators. The medical assistant can generate a hard copy of the next day's appointments before leaving each evening. In some facilities, employees keep an appointment book as a backup to computer scheduling.

Appointment Book Scheduling

Office suppliers carry a variety of appointment book styles. Some appointment books show an entire week at a glance, and many are color coded, with a special color used for each day of the week (Figure 10-2). This is very helpful when the physician asks the patient to return, for instance, in 2 weeks. If Wednesdays are colored yellow, the medical assistant can flip quickly to the correct day 2 weeks later and schedule the appointment. Multiple columns may be available to correspond with the number of doctors in a group practice, and the time can be divided according to their preferences.

Self-Scheduling

The future of appointment scheduling includes self-scheduling, which is a method by which a patient can log on to the Internet and

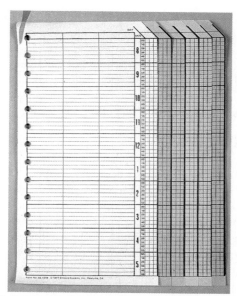

FIGURE 10-2 Color-coded appointment book pages help the medical assistant flip to the right day of the right week quickly. Appointments for multiple physicians can be color-coded in the book.

view a facility's schedule, then select his or her own appointment time and make the appointment right then. The system should allow for patient confidentiality by showing only available times. Other patients' names should never be visible on an online system.

Software is available that allows the patient to self-schedule through secure links to the physician's appointment book. The software or Internet site for the physician's office should give the patient guidelines as to the amount of time needed for certain appointments or should allow only a certain length of time to be self-scheduled, such as 15 minutes. These systems will reduce the number of calls to the office and are available to the patient 24 hours a day. Some of these systems also send an automatic e-mail reminder to the patient the day before the appointment, requesting a reply to confirm. These systems are less frustrating to patients, who do not have to wait on hold to speak to the person who does scheduling for the office. Lengthy or complicated appointments should be scheduled through the office staff.

Although this type of system for making appointments appeals to most technologically savvy people, some patients stringently reject online scheduling because it requires at least minimal computer skills, which the patient may not have or be comfortable performing. If this method is used, some allowance must be made for patients who do not have computers. Other patients may object to online scheduling because they do not want their name anywhere on the Internet. This is a valid issue, and the office should allow these patients to schedule over the phone.

CRITICAL THINKING APPLICATION   10-2

The software used in Dr. Brown's office can allow patients to self-schedule. Ramona has heard about patient self-scheduling and would like to try this method in her office, but Dr. Brown is concerned that her patients enjoy personal contact and is not sold on the idea.

- What can Ramona say to convince Dr. Brown to try this new, time-saving method of scheduling?
- What challenges might the use of this system bring?

ADVANCE PREPARATION

After an appropriate method of setting appointments has been chosen, some advance preparation should be done. This is sometimes called establishing the **matrix** (Procedure 10-1). Block out time slots when the physician routinely is not available to see patients, such as days off, holidays, lunch or dinner breaks, time for hospital rounds, and meetings. In the space where a patient's name normally would appear, note the reason the time is blocked off. Most electronic scheduling software allows the user to create a **template** that can be used repeatedly when new appointment pages are needed. The template can be set to block time slots unavailable for appointments automatically, such as lunch hours and regular meeting times. Always try to account for every time period in each day.

Legality of the Appointment Book

Because the appointment book can be used as a legal record, it must be accurate and maintained so that it provides correct information about the patients at the office. Patients are expected to follow the physician's orders; this includes keeping appointments. If a patient

PROCEDURE 10-1

Manage Appointment Scheduling Using Established Procedures

GOAL: *To establish the matrix of the appointment page and enter information according to office policy.*

EQUIPMENT and SUPPLIES

- Appointment book or computer
- Office procedure manual
- Information about physician's office hours and availability
- Clerical supplies
- Calendar

PROCEDURAL STEPS

1. Determine the proper methods for scheduling an appointment by consulting the office procedure manual; make sure to follow established priorities when managing appointments.
   PURPOSE: To follow prescribed office policy and established priorities for appointment scheduling.
2. Become familiar with any software used for scheduling appointments.
   PURPOSE: To become proficient with the scheduling software used in the office.
3. Determine the hours the physician (or physicians) will not be available.
   PURPOSE: To make sure patients are not scheduled when the physician is unavailable and to prevent rescheduling issues.
4. Make a column in the appointment book or program for each provider.
   PURPOSE: Some medical facilities have multiple providers who maintain a schedule of patients. For example, many physicians employ physician assistants or nurse practitioners who also see patients.

5. Establish the matrix of the appointment book by blocking out the times the physician is unavailable or the office is closed.
   PURPOSE: To leave available only time slots that can be used for patient appointments.
6. Allow buffer time in the morning and afternoon.
   PURPOSE: To allow for emergencies and short rest or catch-up times for the staff and providers.
7. Determine the number of rooms available for patient examinations, treatments, and procedures.
   PURPOSE: The number of available rooms affects the number of patients that can be seen during a day.
8. Establish a list of procedures that details the amount of time needed for an appointment; use established priorities according to the office policy.
   PURPOSE: To better gauge how much time the physician will spend with patients, according to established priorities.
9. Put the appointment book in a convenient place for all employees who schedule appointments.
   PURPOSE: To make sure the appointment book is always readily available.

---

does not show up for an appointment or cancels it and does not reschedule, a notation of this fact should be placed in the patient's medical record. If a patient reschedules an appointment and subsequently keeps it, there is no need to document that it was rescheduled.

Pencil is used in the appointment book so that making changes is easier. The information in the book includes the patient's name and a phone number where the patient can be reached. Some offices list the reason for the appointment, but most note only the name and phone number. The reason for the visit is not necessary if the medical assistant references the time needed for the appointment and blocks off that amount of time. Although the appointment book can be used as a legal record, actual medical records are more likely to be used in matters of litigation. Because progress notes are dated, a copy of the medical record shows all pertinent information about the patient's adherence to the physician's orders, including the appointments with the physician. Pens are permanent, but the book can become illegible if a number of patients change or cancel their appointments. Because the appointment book could be produced in litigation as a legal record, it should be kept for the number of years that constitute the statute of limitations in that individual state. If the appointment book is discarded, its contents should be shredded to protect patient privacy.

TYPES OF APPOINTMENT SCHEDULING

Different types of appointment scheduling are used to meet the various needs of the medical facility, the providers, and the patients. Some offices use a combination of methods to create the right mix of activity during the day and to ensure that the day runs smoothly and efficiently. The medical assistant should become proficient at managing appointments (Procedure 10-2). The following section presents several methods of appointment scheduling.

Open Office Hours

With the open office hours method, the facility is open at given hours of the day or evening, and the patients are "scheduled" by the physician, who mentions to the patient that he or she should return "in a couple of weeks" for follow-up. The patients come in at **intermittent** times, knowing they will be seen in the order of their arrival. Physicians who use this method say that it eliminates the annoyance of broken appointments and an office running behind schedule. The open office hours method also has been called *tidal wave scheduling*. Some of these facilities allow online or telephone check-in, and patients are notified when it is close to their turn with the provider.

Few healthcare facilities in metropolitan areas have open office hours with no scheduled appointments, but this system still is found

PROCEDURE 10-2

Schedule and Monitor Appointments

GOAL: *To manage appointments as they are cancelled, not kept, or rescheduled throughout the business day.*

EQUIPMENT and SUPPLIES

- Appointment book or computer
- Office procedure manual
- Appointment cards
- Clerical supplies
- Telephone

PROCEDURAL STEPS

1. Determine the names of patients who have appointments either the day before or the morning of the appointment.
   <u>PURPOSE:</u> To prepare the medical records for the patients who have appointments.
2. Confirm the appointments if required.
   <u>PURPOSE:</u> To make sure the patient plans to keep the appointment and to provide an opportunity to reschedule or to call in a patient on the waiting list.
3. Make note of any patient arriving late in the appointment book. If this behavior has become a pattern, also note it in the medical record.
   <u>PURPOSE:</u> Repeated behavior that disrupts the clinic schedule should be documented.
4. Document failure to arrive for an appointment in the appointment book or scheduling program and in the patient's medical record.

5. Call the patient to attempt to reschedule the appointment and obtain a reason for the no-show.
   <u>PURPOSE:</u> To document failure to comply with physician's recommendation to return.
6. Reschedule missed appointments, if possible, after talking with the patient.
   <u>PURPOSE:</u> To keep the patient on schedule for medical care.
7. Write the new appointment time, date, and day on an appointment card or give the information to the patient over the telephone.
   <u>PURPOSE:</u> To ensure that the patient is aware of the new appointment time.
8. If the physician is running more than 15 minutes late, inform patients of the delay.
   <u>PURPOSE:</u> To offer the patients the opportunity to reschedule if necessary.
9. As patients arrive, place a check next to the name in the appointment book.
10. Offer the sign-in sheet to the patient for his or her signature.
    <u>PURPOSE:</u> To verify that the patient arrived in the clinic.

---

in some rural areas, where the way of life is governed not so much by the clock as by the needs of the people in the area. Open office hours scheduling is most commonly used at laboratories, imaging facilities, urgent care clinics, and emergency departments. Many emergency departments are open 24 hours a day. Although called *emergency departments,* many of these facilities deal with general practice cases.

The open office hours system can have many disadvantages. The office may already be crowded when the physician arrives, resulting in an extremely long wait for some patients. Patients may arrive in waves throughout the day, which causes parts of the day to be very busy and parts to be slow. This makes getting other office duties accomplished difficult. Without planning, the facilities and staff can be overburdened.

Scheduled Appointments

Studies have shown that practitioners can see more patients with less pressure when their appointments are scheduled. Unfortunately, the skill required for scheduling appointments often is not fully appreciated by the practitioner or office manager, and the responsibility is delegated to the least-qualified medical assistant. An efficient, bright individual proficient at multitasking should be assigned to the scheduling of duties. Although the skill and attitude of the assistant who manages the appointment schedule are very important, the ultimate success of the system lies in the cooperation of the physicians.

Different procedures require different amounts of time; the scheduler must understand how long it takes to draw blood, fill out new patient paperwork, and weigh and check the patient in; all procedures, even the simplest, must have an associated amount of time needed to complete the task. If the patient needs an average of 15 minutes to do new patient paperwork, this time must be included in the schedule. (This is why many offices ask new patients to arrive 15 minutes early for their appointment.) If an allergy shot takes only 20 minutes from check-in to checkout and does not require the patient to see the physician, the scheduler knows that other patients can see the physician while the medical assistant gives the allergy shot. The scheduler cannot efficiently set appointments without developing the skill of accurately assessing how long an office procedure takes.

Flexible Office Hours

Most scheduling practices are carryovers from the days when expectant mothers of families with young children relied on one wage earner. Today families commonly have two working parents. As a result, many healthcare providers are turning to extended day and flexible office hours. Staff hours are affected by these schedules, but this flexibility works to the advantage of the patient and the staff at the physician's office. Patients appreciate flexible office hours, because they can schedule an appointment after work or after children's school hours. Evening and weekend hours may increase the size of the practice because of the convenience offered to patients.

Wave Scheduling

Wave scheduling is an attempt to create short-term flexibility within each hour. Wave scheduling assumes that the actual time needed for all the patients seen will average out over the course of the day. Instead of scheduling patients at each 20-minute **interval**, wave scheduling places three patients in the office at the same time, and they are seen in the order of their arrival. This way, one person's late arrival does not disrupt the entire schedule.

Modified Wave Scheduling

The wave schedule can be modified in several ways. For example, one method is to have two patients scheduled to come in at 10 AM and a third at 10:30 AM. This hourly cycle is repeated throughout the day. In another version, patients are scheduled to arrive at given intervals during the first half of the hour, and none are scheduled to arrive during the second half of the hour.

Double-Booking

Booking two patients to come in at the same time, both of whom are to be seen by the physician, is poor practice. Of course, if each appointment is expected to take only 5 minutes, no harm is done by telling both to come at the same time and reserving a 15-minute period for the two. This is simply one method of wave scheduling. However, if each patient requires 15 minutes, two require 30 minutes. This must be reflected in the scheduling. It is not considered double-booking if a patient comes to the office to receive a treatment by someone other than the physician, such as a patient receiving physical therapy or an antiallergy injection.

Grouping Procedures

Grouping or categorizing of procedures is another method of scheduling that appeals to many practitioners. For instance, an internist might reserve all morning appointments for complete physical examinations, or a pediatrician might keep that time for well-baby visits. A surgeon might devote one day each week to seeing only referral patients. Obstetricians often schedule pregnant patients on different days from gynecology patients. The physician and staff can experiment with different groupings until the plan that works best for the practice eventually becomes evident. In applying a grouping system of appointments, the medical assistant may find it helpful to color-code the sections of the appointment book reserved for designated procedures.

Advance Booking

Often appointments are made months in advance. When any appointment is made, an appointment card should be completed and given to the patient. All appointment cards should mention that patients must give 24 hours' notice if they are unable to keep the time reserved for them. Most offices have some type of confirmation procedure by which patients are called the day before to verify that they intend to keep the appointment.

TIME PATTERNS

When booking appointments, a medical assistant should make it a policy to leave some open time during each day's schedule so that if a patient calls with a special problem that is not an immediate emergency, time will be available to book the patient for at least a brief visit. Mondays and Fridays generally are the most hectic days of the week. Keeping one time slot available in the morning and the afternoon specifically for emergencies also is a wise practice. A busy physician always fills these open slots, and having them in the schedule causes the least **disruption** during the day. If possible, set aside time in the morning and afternoon for a break. Even 15 minutes can give the physician time to return calls from patients, verify prescription calls, or answer questions.

PATIENT WAIT TIME

Be aware of the amount of time the patient sits in the reception area. Ideally, the patient's name is called to go to the examination room precisely at the scheduled appointment time (Figure 10-3). However, the scheduling process has failed if the patient then waits in the back office for 30 minutes to see the physician. Make it clear to the patient whether he or she is free to leave the office after the physician has finished the examination. Some patients mistakenly wait in the examination room until told they are free to leave. Always make sure the patient knows when to go where.

If a patient has waited longer than 15 minutes in the reception area, the medical assistant should briefly explain the delay and offer to reschedule the appointment. The longer patients sit and wait, the more anxious and frustrated they become. Remember, some patients are there to see the physician for test results or may be expecting a negative diagnosis. Do not make their visit more stressful by forcing them to wait for a long time. Briefly explain the situation and allow the patient to decide whether to wait or reschedule. If a delay is forthcoming, attempt to call patients who may be en route to the

FIGURE 10-3 One of the most common patient complaints is the time spent in the reception area.

office and inform them that there will be a delay. Always ask for the patient's cell phone number for just such events.

TELEPHONE SCHEDULING

A pleasant manner and expressing a willingness to help are just as important on the telephone as when meeting patients face to face. This is especially true when making appointments, because the telephone contact may be the patient's first impression of the facility. Often the manner in which the booking is made makes more of an impact than the convenience of the appointment time.

Be especially considerate if the time requested for an appointment must be refused. Briefly explain why the time is not available and offer a substitute date and time. Comply with the patient's desires as much as possible, and do not show annoyance if the patient does not understand the scheduling process. Most people, however, understand the need for a well-managed office and are willing to cooperate.

Many offices offer the patient a choice when scheduling the appointment and let the patient decide which option is best for him or her. For example, the following dialog might take place during the scheduling call:

Medical assistant: *"Mrs. Thomas, Dr. Stern is available to see you in the office next Tuesday or Wednesday, January 6 or 7. Which day is better for you?"*

Patient: *"I will be working on Wednesday, so I would like to come in on Tuesday."*

Medical assistant: *"Do you prefer a morning or afternoon appointment?"*

Patient: *"The afternoon is best for me."*

Medical assistant: *"Great. Would 1:30 or 3:30 be a better time?"*

Patient: *"I can be there at 1:30."*

Medical assistant: *"Then Dr. Stern will see you at 1:30 next Tuesday, January 6. Thank you for calling, Mrs. Thomas. We'll see you then!"*

These small courtesies give patients the feeling they control their time. Always repeat the time to reinforce the appointment and do not hesitate to ask the patient if he or she has a pen with which to jot down the time and date. While repeating the information to the patient, check the appointment book or computer screen to ensure that it was posted correctly.

Write legibly when using an appointment book. These records could be called into court, and the medical assistant must be able to read his or her own writing if asked to testify. Form the habit of entering the patient's daytime telephone number after every entry. The appointment may need to be canceled or the schedule rearranged in a hurry, and many precious minutes can be saved if

the telephone number is handy. Cell phone numbers also are quite useful for tracking down a patient quickly.

SCHEDULING APPOINTMENTS FOR NEW PATIENTS

Arranging the first appointment for a new patient requires time and attention to detail (Procedure 10-3). This first encounter provides the first impression of the office and may set the tone for all subsequent visits. Tact, courtesy, and professionalism are extremely important. During the conversation with the new patient, request preliminary information to help determine how much time to allot for the visit on the appointment schedule. The physician may also expect the medical assistant to give general instructions to patients seeking care for specific complaints. For example, the patient may be required to bring a urine specimen or to make sure laboratory tests are completed before the appointment. Some offices obtain enough information to build a patient medical record before the office visit; others wait until the patient actually arrives to construct the medical record.

After the necessary information has been recorded, offer the patient the first available appointment. Whenever possible, offer a choice between two dates and times. Ask the patient whether he or she knows the directions to the office or offer the physical address for those who want to obtain exact directions from one of the many Internet directions sites, such as MapQuest. Tell the patient whether any special parking conveniences are available and whether the office provides a token or parking validation. The patient's options for the first payment should also be discussed. If payment is expected immediately, inform the patient. The office staff should expect patient concerns about the amount of the first bill and should address this issue before the appointment so that there are no surprises or misunderstandings. Before ending the conversation, repeat the appointment date and time and then thank the patient for calling.

Some medical offices mail an information packet about their facility to new patients, especially if the appointment is several days away. With today's technology and the patient's e-mail address, such information can also be sent via the Internet. This information should inform the patient about the nature of the practice, introduce the medical staff, and explain appointment policies and financial arrangements.

If another physician has referred the patient, the medical assistant may need to call the referring physician's office to obtain additional information before the patient's appointment. This information should be printed out and given to the attending physician before the patient arrives. Remember to send a thank you note to anyone who refers a patient to the facility.

Many offices call each patient the day before the appointment as a reminder and a courtesy. This can be a time-consuming procedure, but most patients appreciate this service, and it may open appointments for others if the original patient cannot keep the scheduled time slot. E-mail and automatic dialers also can be programmed to call or send electronic reminders to patients about their appointments. This procedure can run automatically if the office has access to the proper equipment, which takes no time away from the medical assistant's other duties. Often, the medical assistant will need to conduct **preauthorization** or **precertification** to determine whether a patient is eligible for treatment or for certain procedures. The office

PROCEDURE 10-3

Schedule Appointments for New Patients

GOAL: *To schedule a new patient for a first office visit.*

EQUIPMENT and SUPPLIES

- Appointment book or computer
- Scheduling guidelines
- Appointment card
- Telephone

PROCEDURAL STEPS

1. Obtain the patient's full name, birth date, address, and telephone number.
   NOTE: Verify the spelling of the name.
2. Determine whether the patient was referred by another physician.
   PURPOSE: You may need to request additional information from the referring physician, and your physician will want to send a consultation report.
3. Determine the patient's chief complaint and when the first symptoms occurred.
   PURPOSE: To help gauge the time needed for the appointment and the degree of urgency.
4. Search the appointment book for the first suitable appointment time and an alternate time.

5. Offer the patient a choice of these dates and times to demonstrate sensitivity appropriate to the message being delivered.
   PURPOSE: Patients are better satisfied if they are given a choice.
6. Enter the mutually agreeable time in the appointment book, followed by the patient's telephone number.
   NOTE: Indicate that the patient is new by adding the letters NP.
7. If new patients are expected to pay at the time of the visit, explain this financial arrangement when the appointment is made.
   PURPOSE: The payment policy is explained to the patient, who can come prepared to pay.
8. Offer travel directions for reaching the office as well as parking instructions. E-mail or mail new patient paperwork.
   PURPOSE: To relieve any anxiety about being able to find the medical facility.
9. Analyze communications in providing appropriate responses and feedback by repeating the day, date, and time of the appointment before saying goodbye to the patient.
   PURPOSE: To verify that the patient understands the date and time of the appointment.

---

manager must make certain that these procedures are being done and assign these duties to a specific person(s). More about preauthorization and precertification is included in Chapter 20.

SCHEDULING APPOINTMENTS FOR ESTABLISHED PATIENTS

In Person

Most return appointments for **established patients** are arranged when the patient is leaving the office. A good policy is to have all patients stop by the front desk before leaving in case any information is needed from the patient or any outside scheduling must be done. The patient's medical record can be reviewed to see whether the physician ordered any laboratory tests or procedures, and these can be scheduled and discussed with the patient. When making a return appointment, follow the same procedures as for scheduling any appointment by phone, offering the patient choices in the day and time slots (Procedure 10-4). If a certain time the patient specifically requests is not available, offer two alternatives. Always give the patient an appointment card and any necessary instructions at this time, along with a bright smile (Procedure 10-5). Never forget to provide excellent customer service.

By Telephone

Usually the medical assistant needs only to determine when the patient must return and to find a suitable time in the schedule.

Established patients do not usually need directions and parking information unless the office has recently moved. If some time has passed since the patient's last visit, recheck certain information and enter any changes on the patient's medical record. Be sure to ask whether insurance companies or benefits have changed; also, verifying the patient's address and phone numbers is always a good idea. If an e-mail address is not on file, obtain one so as to have a quick, easy way to notify the patient of appointments and other events.

SCHEDULING OTHER TYPES OF APPOINTMENTS

The medical assistant also will make other types of appointments, and these will appear on the appointment schedule. They include surgeries the physician will perform at a hospital or other facility, hospital rounds and consultations, outside appointments and meetings, and even house calls if the physician makes them. The physician also must have time to get from one location to another, so driving time must be considered when arranging all appointments.

Some critical information is required when scheduling admission or treatments in other facilities. Always provide the scheduler with the patient's name, address, phone numbers (both home and cell), Social Security number, and insurance information and relay the procedures that are to be performed. Patient allergies should be mentioned if the patient is being admitted. Additionally, the facility may have forms that the patient needs to complete, so an e-mail address is helpful in such cases. Always send the admitting diagnosis and orders to the healthcare facility prior to admission time or with

PROCEDURE 10-4

Schedule Appointments for Established Patients or Visitors

GOAL: *To schedule a general appointment either by telephone or in person.*

EQUIPMENT and SUPPLIES

- Appointment book or computer
- Office procedure manual
- Clerical supplies
- Appointment cards
- Telephone

PROCEDURAL STEPS

1. Learn the proper methods for scheduling an appointment by consulting the office procedure manual.
   <u>PURPOSE:</u> To follow prescribed office policy for appointment scheduling.
2. Ask the name of the person wanting to make the appointment and obtain his or her phone number.
   <u>PURPOSE:</u> To be able to speak professionally with the individual and to identify the person in the patient database, if applicable. Ask for the phone number in case the line is disconnected or the appointment needs to be changed.
   <u>SAY:</u> *"To whom am I speaking, please?"*
3. Ask the reason for making the appointment.
   <u>PURPOSE:</u> To determine the time needed for the appointment.
   <u>SAY:</u> *"What is the reason for making this appointment?"*
4. Determine for whom the appointment is being made, if necessary.
   <u>PURPOSE:</u> To schedule the individual with the right provider or person.
   <u>SAY:</u> *"Mr. Adams, would you like to see Dr. Blake, or would you like to see our nurse practitioner, Mrs. Jackson?"*
5. Analyze communications in providing appropriate responses and feedback by giving the person a choice between 2 days of the week.
   <u>PURPOSE:</u> To allow the individual to choose a convenient time; this reduces the number of missed appointments. If the suggested days are not satisfactory, allow the person to suggest an alternate day.
   <u>SAY:</u> *"Would you prefer to come on Monday or Tuesday, Mr. Adams?"*
6. Give the person a choice between a morning or an afternoon appointment.
   <u>PURPOSE:</u> To allow the individual to choose a convenient time of day.
   <u>SAY:</u> *"Would morning or afternoon be better for you?"*
7. Give the person a choice between two specific times.
   <u>PURPOSE:</u> To allow the individual to choose the best time for his or her needs.
   <u>SAY:</u> *"Mr. Adams, would you prefer 9 AM or 11 AM?"*
8. Write the person's name and the phone number on the appropriate line of the appointment book or enter this information into the scheduling system.
   <u>PURPOSE:</u> To document the appointment and ensure that the time is reserved.
9. Analyze communications in providing appropriate responses and feedback by repeating the appointment day, date, and time back to the person.
   <u>PURPOSE:</u> Repeating the appointment time reduces errors and misunderstandings.
   <u>SAY:</u> *"I have you scheduled for 9 AM on Tuesday, March 14, Mr. Adams. If you are not able to keep your appointment, please let us know."*
10. If the person scheduling the appointment is in the office instead of on the phone, give the individual an appointment card.
    <u>PURPOSE:</u> Providing appointment cards reduces the number of missed appointments.

---

the patient. Some facilities require a history form prior to admission. The patient will be required to bring a form of picture identification, such as a state driver's license, and his or her insurance card.

Inpatient Surgeries

When scheduling a surgery, call the facility where the procedure will be performed as soon as the operation is planned. Most surgical departments and centers have a surgical secretary who makes these arrangements. Provide all necessary information and state any special requests the physician may have, such as the amount of blood to have available for the patient. The secretary may want all the patient's insurance information and certainly will want a phone number so that the patient can be contacted before the surgery if necessary. Make sure all this information is handy before placing the call.

Outpatient and Inpatient Procedure Appointments

A medical assistant often is asked to arrange laboratory or radiography appointments for patients. Before calling the facility to schedule the appointment, be sure all necessary information is handy. When the patient is informed of the time and place of the appointment, relay any special instructions, then note these arrangements in the patient's medical record. Some offices make a reminder call to the patient or send a reminder e-mail message.

Outpatient testing is common, because most physicians do not have extensive x-ray or laboratory equipment in their offices. Magnetic resonance imaging (MRI), computed tomography (CT) scans, numerous x-ray evaluations, ultrasonography, and simple blood tests all may need to be scheduled (Procedure 10-6). Provide the patient

PROCEDURE 10-5

Document Appropriately and Accurately

GOAL: To document appropriately and accurately on all patient medical records and other office paperwork that concerns the patient.

EQUIPMENT and SUPPLIES

- Any medical document
- Clerical supplies
- Computer or word processor
- Office policy and procedure manual

PROCEDURAL STEPS

1. Determine the information that needs to be added to the patient's medical record, appointment book, telephone message, or other office paperwork that concerns the patient.
   PURPOSE: To place pertinent, accurate information into the document.
2. Make sure the information is factual, timely, and accurate.
   PURPOSE: To ensure that the information is usable.
3. Document accurately in the medical record by writing or typing the information into the document.
4. Reread the information to make sure it is legible.
   PURPOSE: To be sure the information can be read even after several years by anyone who needs to access the information.
5. Date and sign the entry if necessary.
   PURPOSE: To authenticate the entry.

6. Make sure the entry meets any local, state, or federal guidelines that may apply to the information contained in the document.
   PURPOSE: To remain in compliance with local, state, and federal rules and regulations.
7. Make sure the entry is written in compliance with office policies and procedures.
   PURPOSE: To comply with office policy.
8. If the entry needs to be corrected, draw one line through it and make the new entry below or in the required place in the document.
   PURPOSE: To correct the document according to office policy and procedure guidelines.
9. Make sure the correction has not obliterated any part of the medical record or documentation that affects the patient.
   PURPOSE: No obliteration is acceptable in any part of the medical record.
10. Place the date and initial the corrected entry.
    PURPOSE: To authenticate the correction.

PROCEDURE 10-6

Schedule Outpatient Admissions and Procedures

GOAL: To schedule a patient for outpatient admission or procedure within the time frame needed by the physician, confirm with the patient, and issue all required instructions.

EQUIPMENT and SUPPLIES

- Diagnostic test order from physician
- Name, address, and telephone number of diagnostic facility
- Patient's demographic information
- Patient's medical record
- Test preparation instructions
- Telephone
- Consent form

PROCEDURAL STEPS

1. Obtain an oral or written order from the physician for the exact procedure to be performed.
   PURPOSE: To have a documented order for the procedure to be performed
2. Precertify the procedure with the patient's insurance company if necessary.
   PURPOSE: To make sure expected insurance benefits are valid and the procedure will be covered by the patient's insurance policy.

3. Determine the physician's and patient's availability.
   PURPOSE: To make sure the patient will be able to comply with the arrangements for the test and that the physician is available, if he or she must be present for the procedure. The urgency of the needed test results affects the time and date of the appointment needed.
4. Telephone the diagnostic facility and schedule the patient's procedure or test.
   - Order the specific test.
   - Provide the patient's diagnosis and orders.
   - Establish the date and time for the procedure.
   - Give the patient's name, age, address, and telephone number.
   - Provide the patient's demographic information, including identification and insurance policy numbers and addresses for filing claims.
   - Determine any special instructions for the patient or special anesthesia requirements.
   - Notify the facility of any urgency for test results.

PROCEDURE 10-6—cont'd

<u>PURPOSE:</u> To schedule the procedure or admission and provide needed information.

5. Notify the patient of the arrangements:
   - Give the name, address, and telephone number of the diagnostic facility.
   - Specify the date and time to report for the test.
   - Give instructions on preparation for the test (e.g., eating restrictions, fluids, medications, enemas).
   - Explain any preadmission testing.
   - Remind the patient to take a form of picture identification and the insurance card.
   - Explain whether the patient needs to pick up orders or whether they will be forwarded to the facility in advance.
   - Ask the patient to repeat the instructions.

<u>PURPOSE:</u> To make sure the patient understands the necessary preparations and the importance of keeping the appointment. If time permits, provide written instructions to the patient.

6. Have the physician review the consent form with the patient. The patient should sign the consent form, and a copy should be placed in the medical record. Note the arrangements on the patient's medical record.

<u>PURPOSE:</u> To make sure the patient understands the risks, benefits, and alternatives to the procedure. To ensure follow-up on the diagnosis and/or treatment.

7. Implement time management principles to maintain effective office function by placing a reminder on the physician's tickler or desk calendar. Make sure the information is listed on the office schedule. Check the patient's postsurgical status. Follow up if results are not received in a timely manner.

<u>PURPOSE:</u> To check whether the appointment was kept and a report was received from the testing facility.

---

with the name, address, and phone number of the facility where the tests will be done.

Some patients may require a series of appointments (e.g., at weekly intervals). Try to set up these appointments on the same day each week at the same time of day. This considerably reduces the risk of the patient forgetting an appointment.

In some cases the medical assistant may be responsible for scheduling inpatient admissions or inpatient surgical procedures (Procedures 10-7 and 10-8). This is similar to scheduling outpatient testing, but the medical assistant coordinates with a hospital rather than an outside facility.

Outside Visits

If the physician regularly makes house calls or visits patients in skilled nursing facilities, a special block of time must be reserved in the appointment schedule. The physician needs demographic information, such as addresses, room numbers, and the best route to each home or facility. Remember to allow for travel time. Most physicians do not make house calls, because seeing patients in the office is easier; however, such visits may be necessary in certain situations. The physician's medical bag should always be prepared and well stocked before he or she has to make any outside visits.

SPECIAL CIRCUMSTANCES

Late Patients

Probably every medical practice has a few patients who are habitually late for appointments. This seems to be a problem for which no cure has been found. Emergencies and small delays can happen to anyone, but a patient who constantly arrives late can put a strain on the practice. Such patients can be booked as the last appointment of the day. Then, if closing time arrives before the patient does, the staff

has no obligation to wait. Some medical assistants tell the patient to come in 30 minutes before the appointment time actually scheduled. Make an attempt to work with patients who have occasional difficulties arriving on time, but do not allow the schedule to be constantly disrupted by late patients.

CRITICAL THINKING APPLICATION   10-5
Seth Jones is always late for his appointments. How might Ramona approach him about this? What can Ramona do to assist Mr. Jones in arriving for appointments on time?

Rescheduling Canceled Appointments

Changes sometimes must be made in the appointment schedule. Unexpected conflicts might arise that force a patient to change the appointment time. When rescheduling an appointment, make sure the first appointment day and time is removed from the appointment book or database, then set the new appointment. Otherwise, the patient will be expected in the office on 2 days, and time will be wasted with calls and follow-up, only to discover that the appointment was rescheduled.

Emergency Calls

Periodically, emergency or urgent calls come into the office, and an appointment needs to be scheduled. To some extent, all calls that come in go through a **screening** process, and emergencies are prioritized to evaluate the urgency of the need to see the physician. Screening is an extremely important function that requires experience, a knowledge of signs and symptoms, and tact.

Emergencies may involve emotional crises in addition to the more obvious physical problems. Patients with emergencies and those who are acutely ill should be seen the same day. The urgency

PROCEDURE 10-7

Schedule Inpatient Admissions

GOAL: *To schedule a patient for inpatient admission within the time frame needed by the physician, confirm with the patient, and issue all required instructions.*

EQUIPMENT and SUPPLIES

- Admission orders from physician
- Name, address, and telephone number of inpatient facility
- Patient's demographic information
- Patient's medical record
- Any preparation instructions for the patient
- Telephone
- Admission packet

PROCEDURAL STEPS

1. Obtain an oral or written order from the physician for the admission.
   PURPOSE: To have a documented order for the admission.
2. Precertify the admission with the patient's insurance company if necessary.
   PURPOSE: To make sure expected insurance benefits are valid and the admission will be covered by the patient's insurance policy.
3. Determine the physician's and patient's availability if the admission is not an emergency.
   PURPOSE: To make sure the patient will be able to comply with the arrangements for the admission and that the physician is available to care for the patient during the admission. The urgency of the admission affects the time and date of the appointment needed.
4. Telephone the diagnostic facility and schedule the patient's admission.
   - Order any specific tests needed.
   - Provide the patient's admitting diagnosis.
   - Establish the date and time.
   - State the patient's room preferences.
   - Give the patient's name, age, address, and telephone number.

- Provide the patient's demographic information, including identification and insurance policy numbers and addresses for filing claims.
- Determine any special instructions for the patient.
- Notify the facility of any urgency for test results.
PURPOSE: To schedule the admission and provide needed information.
5. Notify the patient of the arrangements:
   - Give the facility's name, address, and telephone number.
   - Specify the date and time to report for admission.
   - Provide any necessary instructions on preparation for the procedure (e.g., eating restrictions, fluids, medications, enemas).
   - Outline any preadmission testing.
   - Ask the patient to repeat the instructions.
   PURPOSE: To make sure the patient understands the preparation necessary and the importance of admittance. If it is the office policy, give the patient an admission packet that contains the orders and basic instructions for the admission.
6. Note the arrangements and the admission on the patient's medical record.
   PURPOSE: To ensure follow-up on the diagnosis and/or treatment.
7. Implement time management principles to maintain effective office function by placing a reminder on the physician's tickler or desk calendar. Make sure the information is listed on the office schedule. If the physician keeps a list of all inpatients, add the patient's name to that list.
   PURPOSE: To keep a record of the number of days the patient was seen in the hospital by the physician during rounds for insurance billing purposes.

PROCEDURE 10-8

Schedule Inpatient Procedures

GOAL: *To schedule a patient for inpatient surgery within the time frame needed by the physician, confirm with the patient, and issue all required instructions.*

EQUIPMENT and SUPPLIES

- Orders from the physician
- Inpatient facility's name, address, and telephone number
- Patient's demographic information
- Patient's medical record
- Any preparation instructions for the patient
- Telephone
- Consent form

PROCEDURAL STEPS

1. Obtain an oral or written order from the physician for the admission.
   PURPOSE: To have a documented order for the admission.
2. Precertify the admission with the patient's insurance company if necessary.
   PURPOSE: To make sure expected insurance benefits are valid and the admission will be covered by the patient's insurance policy.

PROCEDURE 10-8—cont'd

3. Determine the physician's availability if the surgery is not an emergency. Another physician may be the surgeon. If so, the surgery also must be coordinated with that office.
   PURPOSE: To make sure the physician is available to care for the patient during the admission and the surgery. The urgency of the surgery affects the time and date of the appointment needed.
4. Telephone the hospital surgical department and schedule the patient's procedure.
   - Order any specific tests needed.
   - Provide the patient's admitting diagnosis.
   - Establish the date and time.
   - Give the patient's name, age, address, and telephone number.
   - Provide the patient's demographic information, including identification and insurance policy numbers and addresses for filing claims.
   - Determine any special instructions for the patient.
   - Notify the facility of any urgency for the surgery.
   PURPOSE: To schedule the surgery and provide the facility with the needed information.
5. If the patient has not already been admitted to the hospital, notify him or her of the arrangements:
   - Give the facility's name, address, and telephone number.
   - Specify the date and time to report for admission.
   - Provide any necessary instructions on preparation for the procedure (e.g., eating restrictions, fluids, medications, enemas).

- Explain any preadmission testing.
- Ask the patient to repeat the instructions.
   PURPOSE: To make sure the patient understands the preparation necessary and the importance of surgery. If it is the office policy, give the patient an admission packet that contains the orders and basic instructions for the surgery.
6. The physician should review the consent form with the patient. Have the patient sign a consent for the surgical procedure. Keep the original consent in the patient's medical record and give the patient a copy.
   PURPOSE: To ensure that the patient understands the risks, benefits, and alternatives to the surgical procedure.
7. Note the arrangements on the patient's medical record.
   PURPOSE: To ensure follow-up on the diagnosis and/or treatment.
8. Implement time management principles to maintain effective office function by placing a reminder on the physician's tickler or desk calendar. Be sure the information is listed on the office schedule. If the physician keeps a list of all inpatients, add the patient's name to that list. After the procedure, follow up with the hospital on the patient's condition as required by the physician.
   PURPOSE: To check on the patient's status and keep a record of the number of days the patient was seen in the hospital by the physician during rounds for insurance billing purposes.

---

of the call initially can be determined by having a list of questions prepared for reference. The physician should help with this list; he or she should determine what is considered an emergency (life-threatening) or urgent (serious but not life-threatening). The patient may need to be referred directly to a hospital emergency department, or the physician may want to see the patient that day in the office. Remember to keep the patient on the phone until emergency medical technicians (EMTs) or other help arrives at the patient's location. Never place an emergency call on hold. Always obtain the name, phone number, and location at the start of the call so that the patient can be found if he or she loses consciousness or is disconnected.

Physician Referrals

If another physician telephones and requests that a patient be seen today, most offices honor that request if at all possible. It is important to keep a schedule that is not intolerant of this type of request.

Patients Without Appointments

The physician must agree to a policy for patients without appointments, and the medical assistants must carry it out. A patient who requires immediate attention most likely will be accommodated in the schedule somehow. If the patient does not need immediate care, a brief visit with the physician and a scheduled appointment at a later time may be the answer. Also, the medical assistant may simply have to turn down the request. Follow established office policy.

FAILED APPOINTMENTS

Why do patients fail to keep appointments? Some are simply forgetful. Once this tendency is detected in a patient, form the habit of telephoning or e-mailing a reminder the day before the appointment. **Automated call routing** offers the patient the option of canceling an appointment and can be programmed to keep calling until the patient responds and confirms or cancels the appointment.

A patient who has been pressed for payment may stay away because of an inability to pay for medical services. Do not make the mistake of classifying all such patients as "deadbeats." Many have every desire to pay, but they cannot afford to and feel embarrassed about their situation, so they avoid their appointments.

Patients also may fail to keep appointments because they are in a state of denial about their condition. For instance, if a patient recently tested positive for the human immunodeficiency virus (HIV), he or she may avoid appointments because going to see the physician forces the patient to face the reality of the disease. Take special care with such patients, and if denial is suspected, discuss this with the physician, who may want to refer the patient for counseling.

It is important to determine the reason for failed appointments and to do whatever is possible to remedy the situation. Telephone the patient to make sure no misunderstanding has occurred. If the patient's health is such that medical care must continue, write a letter and explain this to the patient. Send the letter by certified mail with return receipt requested. Keep the letter in the patient's medical record for legal protection.

NO-SHOW POLICY

Some patients may not realize the importance of keeping their appointments. The patient who does not arrive for a scheduled appointment or reschedule it is called a **no-show**. A busy practice must have a very specific policy on appointment no-shows and must enforce it effectively. The first time a patient fails to show, note the fact on the medical record and/or ledger card. The second time, warn the patient, and if a third no-show occurs, consider dropping the patient by using the customary methods that provide legal protection for the physician.

The physician may wish to charge patients for not showing up or for rescheduling the appointment. Be understanding whenever possible, but do not let a patient take advantage of the physician's time. The office policy manual must state that patients may be charged for missed appointments, especially if the time slot could not be filled with another patient. Because the time slot was scheduled and the physician was ready and available to treat the patient, it is ethical to charge the patient for missing an appointment, especially if he or she did not call to cancel or reschedule. Many physicians do not press this issue, but it is an available tool if needed.

Recording the Failed Appointment

When a patient fails to keep an appointment, a notation should be made in the patient's medical record and in the appointment book or database. If the patient is seriously ill, the physician should also be told about the failure to show.

INCREASING APPOINTMENT SHOW RATES

Everyone benefits from a full schedule of kept appointments. Appointment show rates can be increased in several ways.

Automated Call Routing

As mentioned earlier, automated call reminders can contact patients scheduled for appointments. The patient is asked to press a certain key on the phone to confirm the appointment and a different key to cancel the appointment. This same tool can be used to send messages to patients (e.g., a reminder that it is the time of year to get a flu vaccination), to introduce a new physician at the office, or announce the availability of a new procedure. The call can even be recorded by the physician so that it sounds more personal.

Appointment Cards

Most healthcare facilities use appointment cards to remind patients of scheduled appointments and to eliminate misunderstandings about dates and times (Figure 10-4). Make a habit of reaching for an appointment card while writing an entry in the appointment book. After the date and time have been written on the card, double-check with the book to make sure the entries agree.

Confirmation Calls

Patients who have made appointments in advance may appreciate a confirmation call to remind them they have a time set aside to see the physician. Always note the phone number the patient prefers the office to use for such calls. Many individuals now have home phone, cell phone, and work phone numbers; however, they may want calls from the physician to go only to their home phone. The preferred phone number can be highlighted in the medical record or on the computer. The office must use caution in making calls to patients because of the significance of privacy guidelines and standards. Some offices may want to prepare a release form in which the patient grants the office staff permission to contact the patient. Many physicians insist that messages left on voice mail not mention the term "doctor" or "doctor's office" for confidentiality reasons. The medical assistant might say, "This is Pam at Robert Welch's office confirming your appointment tomorrow at 2 PM. Please call us if you cannot make the appointment. Our number is 555-212-0909. Thank you!"

If the patient has signed the privacy policy and the policy states that messages from the physician's office may be left at certain numbers, the office certainly can leave messages at that number and mention that the call is from the physician's office. Still, it is a good idea to have an established policy on leaving messages that does not breach any patient's confidentiality.

E-Mail Reminders

Many computer scheduling programs can send an e-mail to patients the day before an appointment to remind them of it. This is a great timesaver for the office staff, because no time is taken to perform this duty other than the original scheduling of the appointment.

Mailed Reminders

The office staff may mail reminder cards to patients. This method is a bit time-consuming but worth the effort if the patients show up for their appointments.

A patient who is due for an appointment but has not yet arranged a date and time may be sent a reminder. A simple way of handling this is to have a supply of postcards on hand, and while patients are still in the office, have them write their name and address on the postcard. Then place the card in a tickler file under the date it is to be mailed.

HANDLING CANCELLATIONS AND DELAYS

When the Patient Cancels

Inevitably, cancellations occur. If a list is kept of patients with advance appointments who would like to come in sooner, the medical assistant can begin calling to try to get one of them in to fill the available opening. By keeping a list of patients willing to take the first cancelled appointment, the medical assistant can readily identify which patients to call to fill the vacancy. Each cancellation should be noted in the medical record, along with a reason for the cancellation if that information is available. If the patient simply reschedules an appointment, a notation need not be made in the medical record unless a pattern develops that might be significant to the patient's medical treatment.

When the Physician is Delayed

Some days the physician will be delayed in reaching the office. If advance notice of the delay is received, start calling patients with

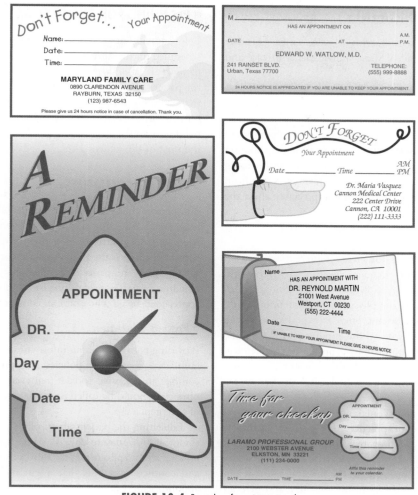

FIGURE 10-4 Examples of appointment cards.

early appointments and suggest that they come later. If some patients arrive before the office learns of the delay, explain that an emergency has detained the physician.

Show concern for the patient, but do not be overly apologetic, which might imply some degree of guilt. Most patients realize that a physician has certain priorities. The patient in the office may be inconvenienced, but it is not a "life or death" matter. If this kind of situation occurs frequently, however, consider devising a different scheduling system.

When the Physician Is Called to an Emergency

Physicians are conscious of their responsibilities for responding to medical emergencies, and most patients are understanding if the medical assistant takes time to explain what has happened. The medical assistant may say, "Dr. Wright has been called away to answer an emergency. She asked me to tell you she is very sorry to keep you waiting. There will be at least a 1-hour delay." The medical assistant should then ask the patient, "Do you want to wait? If that is inconvenient, I'll be glad to give you the first available appointment on another day. Or perhaps you'd like to have some coffee or do some shopping and return in an hour."

As quickly as possible, call the patients scheduled for a later hour. In many offices, especially those of obstetricians, surgeons, and general practitioners, a whole day's appointments sometimes must be cancelled. For this reason, it is particularly important to have the daytime telephone number of each patient available so that the appointment can be rescheduled. If at all possible, cancel appointments before the patient arrives in the office to find that the physician is not available. The **expediency** of the office staff in contacting patients who will be affected by an emergency is most appreciated.

When the Physician Is Ill or Out of Town

Physicians get ill, too, and patients scheduled to be seen during the course of the physician's recovery must be informed of this. They need not be told the nature of the illness.

When the physician is called out of town for personal or professional reasons, appointments must be canceled or rescheduled. Customarily, the patient is given the name of another physician, or possibly a choice of several, who will provide care during such absences. For security reasons, merely state that the doctor is unavailable. Stating over the telephone that the physician is out of town could lead to attempted burglary or other unauthorized intrusion on the premises.

OTHER TYPES OF APPOINTMENTS

The physician will need to meet with a wide range of other unscheduled callers. Handle all of these individuals with care and courtesy.

Physicians

Another physician dropping into the facility should be ushered in to see the physician as soon as possible, regardless of the appointment schedule. If the physician is seeing a patient, explain the situation and, if possible, take the visiting physician into a private room to wait. Then notify the physician as soon as possible. Visits from other physicians are usually brief and do not appreciably affect the schedule.

Pharmaceutical Representatives

Also known as *detail persons* or *reps,* representatives from pharmaceutical companies are frequent visitors to physicians' offices and generally are welcomed when the schedule permits. They are well trained and bring the physician valuable information on new drugs. The medical assistant often is expected to screen such visitors and turn away those whose products would not be used in that practice. If the representative or the pharmaceutical company is unknown to the office, ask for a business card and then check with the physician, who will decide whether to see the caller.

Specialists usually limit their conferences with pharmaceutical representatives to their line of practice. The medical assistant, together with the physician, can prepare a list of the representatives with whom the physician is willing to spend time; the list is the determining factor in future conferences. The medical assistant can say whether the physician will be available that day and give an estimate of the waiting time or suggest a later time at which the caller may return. The caller then can decide whether to wait or return later. The pharmaceutical representative usually is quite understanding and cooperative and willing to wait patiently a long while for just a brief visit with the physician. In turn, the medical assistant should treat the representative with courtesy, showing as much cooperation as possible.

Salespeople

Salespeople from medical, surgical, and office supply houses call regularly at physicians' offices. Sometimes they want to see the physician, but the office manager or the medical assistant in charge of ordering supplies usually can handle these calls.

Unsolicited salespeople sometimes can present a problem in the professional office. If the physician does not want to see such callers, the medical assistant must firmly but tactfully send them away. Suggest that they leave their literature and cards for the physician to study and say that the physician will contact them if further information is desired.

PLANNING FOR THE NEXT DAY

Before leaving at the end of the day, look over the appointments scheduled for the next day. Review the medical records for scheduled patients. If laboratory tests or other procedures were scheduled on the patient's last visit, determine whether the reports are available in the medical record. If the patient is scheduled for specific procedures on this visit, make sure everything needed for the procedure is on hand and available. Planning can save many precious moments at the time of the patient visit.

CLOSING COMMENTS

The person charged with the responsibility of scheduling appointments has a huge impact on the efficiency of the medical office. A friendly, helpful attitude is a **prerequisite** for cordial **interaction** with patients, as is the ability to make compromises that benefit both the physician and patient. An office that runs smoothly and stays on schedule indicates professionalism and competence and is greatly appreciated by all who come in contact with it.

Patient Education

Providing patients with an information booklet about the office can familiarize them with policies and procedures. Many physicians compile an extensive booklet that even provides tips as to when the physician should be called immediately, listing symptoms and signs of emergencies.

Educating the patient about office policies helps the facility run smoothly from day to day. All patients should be familiar with the policies about appointments. This leads to fewer misunderstandings and conflicts over bills that might include a charge for a missed appointment.

If the facility offers Internet-based appointment scheduling, patients must be taught how to use the system. A printed pamphlet or information sheet is helpful for providing instructions to the patient. A wise option is to have a special phone number patients can call if they have problems with the scheduling system. For best results, choose a program that is simple to use, easy to understand, and does not breach patient confidentiality.

Legal and Ethical Issues

The appointment schedule may be used as a legal record and could be brought by subpoena into a court of law. Make sure all handwriting in the book is completely legible and that information is routinely collected in a consistent manner for each entry. Do not fail to note a no-show both in the patient's medical record and the appointment schedule. This often is helpful when a physician must prove that the patient did not follow medical advice or that the patient contributed to his or her poor condition by missing appointments. Old appointment schedules should be kept for a time equal to that of the statute of limitations in the state where the practice is located.

SUMMARY OF SCENARIO

Ramona is an asset to the medical office, because her dedication and customer service skills help her interact with patients in a positive way. She genuinely cares about the patients and makes every effort to meet their needs while following Dr. Brown's preferences. She has found that her bright smile is a valuable aid when patients have been waiting and are growing restless.

Ramona cooperates with other staff members to get the patients seen as quickly as possible and to minimize wait time. She is flexible and can change the order of the patients seen, if needed, to maximize the use of time and facilities in the office. Because she is so cheerful and friendly, patients do not seem to mind when she asks for their cooperation. She keeps current phone numbers and cell phone information so that she can notify a patient quickly if Dr. Brown is running behind schedule. Ramona's proficiency on the computer also is an asset, and she makes frequent use of e-mail to take care of patient problems or rescheduling requests.

Because of the cooperation she receives from staff and patients alike, Ramona successfully runs an efficient office. She contributes to that efficiency by constantly refining her knowledge about her job. She pays attention to the times during the day that do not run as smoothly as others, evaluates the problems at those times, and then corrects them. Ramona also keeps the schedule moving by communicating with the clinical medical assistants, keeping them informed about arriving patients and those who have come early or are running late. She can quickly adjust and substitute a patient who already has arrived. Ramona has learned how to manipulate the schedule to accommodate an emergency. She knows that by making minor adjustments and keeping the waiting patients informed, the staff can handle any emergency.

All medical assistants need to develop skills in flexibility. Establishing a system that works, and using it correctly, makes patients and staff members more content with their experience in the physician's office.

SUMMARY OF LEARNING OBJECTIVES

1. **Define, spell, and pronounce the terms listed in the vocabulary.**
   Spelling and pronouncing medical terms correctly bolster the medical assistant's credibility. Knowing the definition of these terms promotes confidence in communication with patients and co-workers.

2. **Describe scheduling guidelines.**
   When appointments are scheduled, a medical assistant must consider (1) the patients' needs, (2) the physician's preferences, and (3) the available facilities. Make every attempt to schedule a patient at his or her most convenient time; this helps prevent no-shows. The physician will outline his or her preferences, which should be a high priority to the medical assistant. However, most physicians are flexible and make adjustments according to the needs of the office. The availability of facilities in the office is perhaps the most inflexible factor. If a certain room or piece of equipment is being used for one patient, it usually cannot be used for another.

3. **Discuss the advantages of computerized appointment scheduling.**
   Computerized scheduling programs are in demand, because they are easy to operate and simplify both the scheduling and changing of appointments. The computer can find the first available time much faster than a person scanning an appointment book. Most programs can prepare reports and even notify patients of the impending appointment automatically by e-mail. Web-based self-scheduling programs are becoming popular; these allow a patient to see the physician's available appointments and book his or her own date and time.

4. **Explain the features that should be considered when choosing an appointment book.**
   When an appointment book is chosen, all the needs of the office should be considered. If the practice has multiple physicians, the book should be arranged so that each physician is readily identified. Books that open flat on the desk surface are much easier to handle, but another style

might be better if not enough space is available to open the book completely. The book also should provide enough space to write all the patient information needed in the various time slots, such as the name, phone number, and reason for the visit.

5. **Explain how self-scheduling can reduce the number of calls to the medical office.**
   Self-scheduling can vastly reduce the number of calls to the office, because a high number of everyday calls are requests to schedule appointments. Patients can even make an appointment at midnight if they desire.

6. **Discuss pros and cons of various types of appointment management systems.**
   Open office hours allow patients to come to the physician's office when it is convenient and wait their turn to see the physician. Scheduling of specific appointments is the most popular method of seeing patients. Flexible office hours allow patients to see the physician during the evening and often on weekends. Many of today's medical offices have some flexible scheduling, because most families now consist of two working parents. Wave scheduling brings two or three patients to the office at the same time, and they are seen in the order of their arrival. This type of scheduling can be modified in many ways to suit the needs of the facility. Other scheduling methods include double-booking and grouping of like procedures.

7. **Explain the importance of legible writing in the appointment book.**
   Because the appointment schedule might be called into a court of law, completely legible handwriting in the book is vital. Even if the book is 5 years old, the person charged with testifying in court should be able to read all entries clearly. Scribbled, messy handwriting implies incompetence and reflects on the practice.

8. **Explain the basic procedure to follow when the office is behind schedule.**

   When the office is running more than 15 minutes behind schedule, the medical assistant should briefly explain the delay to the waiting patients and then offer to reschedule their appointments. The patients should be kept informed of wait times until the schedule resumes.

9. **Discuss the benefits of offering choices to patients when scheduling appointments.**

   Giving a patient a choice in appointment times to better meet his or her needs is good customer service. Offering the patient a choice of 2 days, morning or afternoon, and two times helps ensure that the patient will keep the appointment.

10. **Identify critical information required for scheduling patient admissions and/or procedures.**

    Always provide the scheduler with the patient's name, address, phone numbers (both home and cell), Social Security number, insurance information, and relay the procedures that are to be performed. Patient allergies should be mentioned if the patient is being admitted. Additionally, the facility may have forms that the patient needs to complete, so an e-mail address is helpful in such cases. Always send admitting diagnosis and orders to the healthcare facility prior to admission time or with the patient. Some facilities require a history form prior to admission. The patient will be required to bring a form of picture identification, such as a state driver's license, and his or her insurance card.

11. **Discuss several methods of dealing with patients who consistently arrive late.**

    Patients who are habitually late for appointments might be told to arrive 15 minutes before the time written in the book. Some offices book these patients as the last appointment of the day, so that if they do not arrive promptly, they do not see the physician. Usually talking with the patient and gaining an understanding of why the patient arrives late improves the situation. The office can work with the patient to choose the best times that will result in a kept appointment.

12. **Name several reasons for failed appointments.**

    Some patients forget the appointment with the physician, and some are habitually careless about remembering their scheduled time. Small emergencies often come up, and in today's busy business world, some patients just cannot get away from their own offices or other obligations to visit the physician. In some cases patients do not keep appointments because they do not want to deal with a health issue confronting them.

13. **Recognize office policies and protocols for handling appointments.**

    Always follow written office policies and procedures when handling appointment setting. Each patient should be treated cordially, respectfully, and in the same manner as other patients. Follow these guidelines, but be flexible when a patient has a special problem or situation in scheduling. Whenever a question arises, discuss an action plan with a supervisor.

CONNECTIONS

Study Guide Connection: Go to the Chapter 10 Study Guide. Read and complete the activities.

Evolve Connection: Go to the Chapter 10 link at *evolve.elsevier.com/kinn* to complete the Chapter Review and Chapter Quiz. Check out the other resources listed for this chapter to make the most of what you have learned from Scheduling Appointments.

PATIENT RECEPTION AND PROCESSING

SCENARIO

Most people enter the healthcare field for very specific reasons. Georgina Robertson recalls being in a serious car accident when she was 6 years old. As a result, her vision was temporarily impaired. She remembers seeing a woman in a white uniform who offered words of comfort. The woman seemed to have a haze around her; combined with the hospital lights, it made her look as if she had wings. That vision of an "angel" never left Georgina, and it led to her decision to enter the medical field.

Today, Georgina works for Dr. Stuart Wade, a cardiologist in a large metropolitan area. Georgina is an experienced medical assistant, and she enjoys getting to know her patients. She makes notes on the medical record that remind her of special events in the lives of the patients who visit Dr. Wade's office. The patients feel that she truly cares about them, aside from her duties at the clinic. Although she is efficient and time conscious, she always has a moment to share a warm smile or hear about a new grandchild. Georgina is a valued member of the medical team in her office. She currently is attending a state college in the evening hours, gaining credits toward her bachelor's degree. She plans to continue her education and apply to medical school in the future.

While studying this chapter, think about the following questions:

- What are some ways to develop good rapport with patients?
- Why is the sign-in register a potential breach of patient confidentiality?
- What is the value of knowing some information about patients' personal lives?

LEARNING OBJECTIVES

1. Define, spell, and pronounce the terms listed in the vocabulary.
2. Explain the purpose of the office mission statement.
3. List several patient amenities and why these are important additions to the medical office.
4. Describe how to prepare for patient arrivals.
5. Explain why using the patient's name as often as possible is important.
6. Discuss how the medical assistant can help the patient prepare for an examination.
7. Discuss ways to make the patient feel at ease and comfortable in the medical office.
8. Explain how to place the medical record to prevent breach of confidentiality.
9. Discuss how the medical assistant might deal with talkative patients.

VOCABULARY

amenity (uh-me´-nuh-te) Something conducive to comfort, convenience, or enjoyment.

demographic (de-muh-gra´-fik) The statistical characteristics of human populations (as in age or income) used especially to identify markets.

fervent Exhibiting or marked by great intensity of feeling.

harmonious Marked by accord in sentiment or action; having the parts agreeably related.

incidental disclosure A secondary use or disclosure that cannot reasonably be prevented, is limited in nature, and occurs as a result of another use or disclosure that is permitted.

intercom A two-way communication system with a microphone and loudspeaker at each station for localized use.

perception A quick, acute, and intuitive cognition; a capacity for comprehension.

phonetic (fuh-ne´-tik) Constituting an alteration of ordinary spelling that better represents the spoken language, that uses only characters of the regular alphabet, and that is used in a context of conventional spelling.

progress notes Notes used in the medical record to track the patient's progress and condition.

sequentially (si-kwen´-shuh-le) Of, relating to, or arranged in a sequence.

The patient reception area should be an inviting place where patients feel comfortable. Visits to the physician can be times of great stress, and the office staff must do everything possible to make the experience pleasant for patients. A patient usually has a choice of healthcare providers and should be given excellent customer service. Good patient relations result in referrals to the physician, and this helps the practice grow. When patients have a good experience with a physician, they are likely to tell others. When the office staff is committed to making the patient feel welcome and the focus is on care of the patient, success of the practice is inevitable.

THE OFFICE MISSION STATEMENT

Healthcare providers often have a **fervent** reason for entering the medical field. For example, a physician remembers the heritage of her immigrant grandfather. She has fond memories of her grandfather's pride and is thankful for the opportunities he found in America after coming to the United States with nothing but the clothes on his back. The grandfather's dream was to see his granddaughter become a physician. On the most trying days, she can step into her office and look at a picture of her grandfather. Her memories help her find the strength and determination to care for her patients. This is the source of that physician's mission statement.

A mission statement defines the predominant goals of the organization in a succinct declaration consisting of a few sentences. The statement reflects the reasons that the practice exists. The physician develops the mission statement alone or may consult the office staff for input. Many offices display the mission statement prominently in the reception area and on printed material, such as patient information booklets. Whatever the contents, each employee of the facility should be familiar with the statement and have a personal commitment to promoting the physician's philosophy in everyday practice.

THE RECEPTION AREA

A first impression is lasting. Nowhere is this more important than in the healthcare facility, where the environment must appear orderly and faultlessly clean. The facility may be a physician's office, a hospital, a health maintenance organization, an insurance company, or one of the many other healthcare establishments. No matter the type of facility, the appearance of the reception room and the front desk, as well as a cordial greeting from the medical assistant, influence patients' **perception** of the entire facility and of the care they will receive.

The reception room is just that—a place to receive patients and visitors. The area should be planned for patients' comfort; it should be as attractive and cheerful as possible and kept clean and uncluttered. Some medical assistants have the opportunity to assist in the design and decoration of this very important area. Consider the traffic flow (the movement of patients from place to place in the reception room) and the flow of traffic through the rest of the office, so that it is unhindered and logical (Figure 11-1).

CRITICAL THINKING APPLICATION   11-1

Georgina believes that her patients enjoy a homey atmosphere, which is less intimidating than the sterile, clinical feel of some medical offices. How might she give her office this type of ambiance?

Fresh, **harmonious** colors and cleanliness are the foundation of an attractive room (Figure 11-2). Select comfortable furniture that can accommodate the peak load of patients seen each day and arrange it in conversational groups. Individual seating usually is the best choice for the physician's office. Provide good lighting, ventilation, and a regulated temperature. Reduce room clutter by providing a place to hang coats, rainwear, and umbrellas.

Most physicians' offices are well supplied with recent magazines, and some have various books. Publications with short items of popular interest are favorites, such as *Reader's Digest*. Any reading material placed in the reception room should be of interest to the general public; *Good Housekeeping*, *U.S. News and World Report*, *Real Simple*, *Oprah*, and *People* are examples of interesting magazines that most people enjoy reading. Some patients may donate magazines to the office; if there is a name in the subscription area, be sure to mark through it so that the patient's name cannot be read. The reception

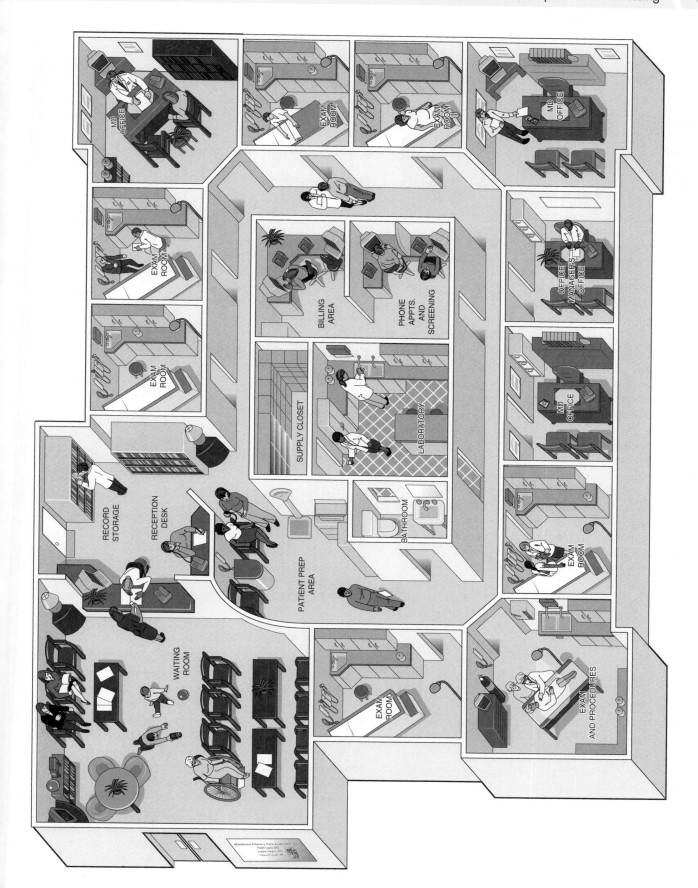

FIGURE 11-1 The medical office should be arranged so that the flow of traffic is conducive to the movement of patients throughout the office.

FIGURE 11-2 Patients appreciate cleanliness, restful colors, good ventilation, and light to read by when waiting in the reception area.

room, incidentally, is not the place for the physician's professional journals.

A writing desk with writing paper in the reception area for the convenience of patients is a nice touch, as is restful music from a concealed speaker. A lighted aquarium or an educational display of some sort enhances the attractiveness and individuality of the reception area in the professional practice. Patients often are interested in health-related brochures. The physician also may have a DVD or healthcare book library that allows patients to check out items of interest to them. A telephone in the reception area is an asset and can be programmed by the phone company not to allow long distance calls. A television or DVD player can help the time pass much faster, especially in pediatric offices. Children enjoy Disney movies and cartoon programs, and these hold their interest until it is time to see the physician. A children's corner equipped with small-scale furniture and some playthings works well. Youngsters who might otherwise get into mischief are kept pleasantly occupied. Toys should be easily cleanable; plastic washable items are especially good. Take extra care to ensure that no toy has sharp corners that could cause injury or small parts that could be swallowed. When selecting toys, make sure they will not stimulate the child toward noisy activity. Never place any type of ball in the reception area, because small children tend to throw them, and the balls can injure a patient or visitor.

CRITICAL THINKING APPLICATION   11-2

Georgina has a few patients who bring young children to their appointments. Sometimes the children are a bit disruptive and make other patients feel uncomfortable. How might Georgina handle this problem in the medical office? Some children misbehave in public, and the parents do not respond or correct them. How might Georgina deal with this situation if it arises?

Many modern offices offer a computer for patients to use while waiting to see the physician. This is a great **amenity**, because patients can make good use of their time in the reception area. Some patients may bring their personal laptop computers and use their wait time to complete projects. Providing Internet access for patients also is helpful; an amazing amount of work can be done just by checking

office e-mail. If patients are allowed to connect to the office network, the wise course is to provide one specific log-on name and password just for them so as to maintain control over access to private health information.

Periodically, take an objective look around the reception room. Could it use a little brightening or freshening up? Try to look at the room as if seeing it for the first time. The medical assistant is responsible for the appearance of the area by making sure the room remains neat and orderly throughout the day. Check the temperature and lighting for comfort. Scan the room at intervals during the day to ensure that it is in good order.

If the medical assistant's desk is in the reception area or in open view of patients, it should be free of clutter. In particular, patients' medical and financial records should not be in sight. Keep computer monitors out of view to protect patient confidentiality. Some offices use privacy screens that allow only the user to see the monitor, or they use a screen saver that activates after being idle for a few minutes. Medical assistants should not keep personal items on their desks.

PREPARING FOR PATIENT ARRIVAL

Advance preparation helps make the day go smoothly and contributes to a more relaxed atmosphere for all. Some offices prepare for the next day on the evening before, whereas others prepare each morning. The office should be consistent, and the same routine should always be performed so that important preparations are not left undone.

CRITICAL THINKING APPLICATION   11-3

Housekeeping chores will always be associated with preparing for each day in the physician's office. What are some ways Georgina can divide these tasks fairly among the staff members? How should Georgina handle the employee who feels that general housekeeping duties are not a part of the job description?

Preparing Medical Records

Review a list of patients who will visit the physician during the next appointment period. If an electronic medical record system is used, this task could be as simple as pulling up and printing a report. If a paper-based system is used, pull the medical records for the day (or the next day if this is done in the evenings) and check off the patient's name on a copy of the appointment schedule; this helps ensure that all the records have been located and are ready (Figure 11-3). Occasionally two or more patients may have the same or a similar name. Check the patient's Social Security number, date of birth, or other pertinent information to make sure the right medical record has been pulled. Review each record to verify that any recently received information (e.g., laboratory reports, radiograph readings) has been entered correctly and permanently attached to the record (Procedure 11-1); if a document is missing, attempt to obtain it prior to the patient's arrival using a fax or other electronic means. Arrange the medical records **sequentially** in the order in which the patients are scheduled to be seen. The medical assistant may be expected to place

PROCEDURE 11-1

Organize a Patient's Medical Record: Preparing the Medical Record for Use During Office Visits

GOAL: *To prepare patients' medical records for the daily appointment schedule and have them ready for the physician during the patient's office visit.*

EQUIPMENT and SUPPLIES

- Appointment schedule for current date
- Patient medical records
- Clerical supplies (e.g., pen, tape, stapler)

PROCEDURAL STEPS

1. Review the appointment schedule.
2. Identify the full name of each scheduled patient.
3. Pull the patients' medical records, checking each patient's name on your list as the record is pulled.
   PURPOSE: To determine that the correct medical records have been pulled and that no medical records have been omitted.
4. Review each medical record.
   PURPOSE: To reaffirm that:
   - The correct patient medical record has been pulled.
   - Any previously ordered tests have been performed.

- The results of the tests have been posted or entered in the medical record.
- Forms have been replenished inside the medical record (e.g., progress notes and others).

5. Annotate the appointment list with any special concerns.
   PURPOSE: To alert the physician about matters that should be checked or discussed with the patient.
6. Arrange the medical records sequentially according to each patient's appointment.
7. Place the medical records in the appropriate examination room or other specified location.

FIGURE 11-3 More physicians and their staff members are using electronic medical records to reduce paperwork and provide better, more efficient patient care. (From Bonewit-West K: *Today's medical assistant*, ed 2, St Louis, 2013, Saunders.)

FIGURE 11-4 Greet all patients with a warm smile and assist them with forms they need to complete for the medical record.

the records of all the patients to be seen that day on the physician's desk, but the physician is more likely to prefer reviewing each record just before entering the examination room. Make sure enough space is available on the **progress notes** for the physician to write in the record. If not, place additional progress notes pages in the record.

GREETING THE PATIENT

Every patient has the right to expect courteous treatment in a physician's office. Regardless of the patient's economic or social status, each person who enters the reception room should receive a cordial, friendly greeting (Figure 11-4). A personal touch, such as greeting the patient by name, is an easy way to develop patient rapport. Use

the patient's last name and title unless the patient insists on the use of his or her first name or prefers a nickname. For example, the medical assistant may say:

"How are you today, Mr. Roberts?"

"Ms. Nelson, the doctor will be in to see you shortly."

If the office has a policy of obtaining a copy of all patients' photo identification cards, such as the driver's license, these can be used to identify patients and greet them by name, even if they do not visit the office often. This practice also ensures that the person receiving benefits is actually the person covered by the insurance policy.

Patient Check-In

The reception desk should be in clear view of all visitors who come into the office. If only one medical assistant is present, welcoming each new visitor personally sometimes is impossible. Develop an announcement system that alerts the staff when people enter the office. Patients who enter an empty reception room do not know whether to sit down, knock on the glass partition, or try to announce themselves in some other way. Glass partitions are used to maintain some privacy; however, some physicians have eliminated them because they are so impersonal and they send the signal that the physician and staff are off limits to patients. If the partition is used, the office policy and procedure manual should dictate when the glass should remain open and when it should be closed.

A sign placed in the reception room that reads, "Please sign in and sit comfortably. We will be with you shortly," assures patients that their presence will be acknowledged. However, the best solution is to keep a staff member at the front desk at all times to greet patients and answer questions. Make sure no patient medical records are lying on the reception desk in view of patients signing in or approaching the desk when they arrive at the office. This prevents violation of the regulations established by the Health Insurance Portability and Accountability Act (HIPAA).

The medical assistant should check the reception room each time he or she has been away from the desk to see whether more patients have arrived. Greet these patients by name; if you do not know the person who has entered the reception area, ask the individual's name. Use a sign-in register that promotes patients' privacy. Although patients can read the names of others who are in the office to visit the physician, this is not considered a violation of HIPAA policy as long as the information disclosed is appropriately limited. This is one type of **incidental disclosure**, as described in Chapter 17. The sign-in sheet should have only the information needed to sign in, such as the patient's name, the provider's name, the arrival and appointment times, and a place to note that patients are new to the practice or that their address, insurance coverage, or other demographic information has changed (Figure 11-5). The best registers allow the staff to remove the patient's name and information after the person signs the document. Pressure-sensitive labels printed with lines for the patient's name, the appointment time, and a "yes" or "no" question about changes in insurance coverage are a practical, inexpensive solution for confidential patient registers. The signed label then can be placed in a separate log book or even inside the patient's medical record. The office can order custom registers that work like a pegboard, making the identifying information invisible to subsequent patients. Patients should not be expected to provide details of the reason for their visit in a public area.

Patient Sign-In Date: ______

Please sign in and notify us if:
you are a new patient, your insurance, telephone number or address have changed.

NO.	Please Print Name Sign-In on next available line	Arrival Time	Appt. Time	Appointment with	New Patient (✓)	Any change in address/phone/ insurance since last visit?
1	1					
2	2					
3	3					
4	4					
5	5					
6	6					
7	7					
8	8					
9	9					
10	10					
11	11					
12	12					
13	13					
14	14					
15	15					
16	16					
17	17					
18	18					
19	19					
20	20					
21	21					
22	22					
23	23					

14037

FIGURE 11-5 Sign-in sheets contain very basic information about the patient and provide information for the medical assistant about changes that need editing on the patient's demographic information.

Patient Interaction

Although the medical office can make patients feel jittery, the medical assistant should try to make everyone feel at ease and comfortable. Cultivate the habit of greeting each patient immediately in a friendly, self-assured manner. Establish eye contact and smile while introducing yourself to the patient. For example, "Good morning, I'm Elizabeth, Dr. Wade's medical assistant." Remember to ask about the patient before asking about insurance coverage; no patient wants to feel that the physician's main interest is the collection of an insurance check.

Patients like to be acknowledged when they arrive. All staff members should review the day's schedule in the morning to be prepared to greet patients by name and to know whether the patient is new or established. Learn how to pronounce each patient's name correctly; incorrect pronunciations may offend or irritate some people. If the name is unusual, write the **phonetic** spelling on the record for reference. Note if the patient prefers a nickname. Make notes on the medical record that help staff members remember names when talking to patients on the phone or in person. By using the patient's name often, the medical assistant also ensures that the correct patient is being treated.

Physicians and staff members sometimes make brief notes in the medical record about the current events in the patient's life. With this information, the medical assistant and the physician can read

CRITICAL THINKING APPLICATION 11-4

A patient passes Georgina in the hallway as she is leaving for lunch and stops to greet her. The patient's face is familiar, but Georgina cannot recall the patient's name. Occasionally, Georgina sees a patient outside of the office, such as in a grocery store, the library, and other places around town. Everyone forgets someone's name on occasion.

- How might Georgina and her staff members remember names?
- What special tips or techniques can help you remember names?
- What can Georgina do the next time she sees a patient and does not remember the person's name?

those notes before entering the examination room and share a short dialog with patients at the beginning of their visits. For example:

Medical assistant:	*"Hello, Mrs. Williams, how are you today?"*
Mrs. Williams:	*"I am doing very well, Georgina, how are you?"*
Medical assistant:	*"I'm fine. How was the cruise you took with your husband last month?"*
Mrs. Williams:	*"It was wonderful! The water was the bluest I have seen!"*
Medical assistant:	*"You went to Cozumel, didn't you?"*
Mrs. Williams:	*"Yes, we did! I'm surprised you remember, as many patients as you see each day!"*

This brief chat confirms that the staff members care about the individual patient, because they take an interest in their personal lives (Figure 11-6). Because the patient does not see the medical assistant or physician look at the notes before entering the patient room, the patient assumes that the information is recalled from memory. This is an impressive customer service technique. Most patients appreciate the physician's and staff's interest in their families, hobbies, and work. Computer-based medical records systems usually have a notes option where such information can be recorded.

Patients may feel somewhat anxious when visiting the physician's office, especially if they know they may be receiving bad news; perhaps a tumor has been discovered to be cancerous, or a family member may have been diagnosed with Alzheimer's disease. Watch the patient's body language. If a patient does not maintain good eye contact or seems otherwise uneasy, a gentle touch or a reassuring smile may be helpful as the office visit progresses. Remember to keep the patient's safety in mind and make certain that he or she has some type of support that will assure a safe arrival back home or at a family or friend's home after the office visit.

Some state regulations prohibit the placement of information other than health details in the medical record; however, most health professionals agree that a patient's mental and emotional health are connected to the person's physical health. Details about what is happening in patients' lives provide clues to their physical problems. As a simple example, a patient going through a divorce may experience depression that needs to be treated with medication. Without knowledge of the divorce, the physician does not have all the information needed to make a sound medical decision. Physicians can treat patients more effectively when such information is available in the medical record.

REGISTRATION PROCEDURES

On a patient's first visit to the physician's office, the staff performs certain registration procedures (Procedure 11-2). Most physicians use a patient information or registration form to gather **demographic** information about the patient. The form may be attached to a clipboard and handed to the patient with instructions to complete sections. The medical assistant must be ready and willing to answer any questions (Figure 11-7). The patient's name should appear prominently at the top of the form, followed by other pertinent facts in logical order. Most information sheets contain the following:

- Patient's full name and date of birth
- Responsible person's name and relationship to the patient
- Address and telephone number
- Name, address, and telephone number of spouse
- Occupation
- Place of employment
- Social Security number
- Driver's license number
- Nearest relative not living with the patient and his or her relationship
- Source of referral, if any

When the completed form is returned, check carefully to verify that all the necessary information has been provided.

Some practices place their registration paperwork on their Web site, and the patient can download, complete, and print the paperwork prior to their first office visit. If a good length of time will pass between making the appointment and arriving for the office visit,

FIGURE 11-6 Patients appreciate being called by name and remembered from visit to visit. The medical assistant should develop a good relationship with the patient and be a caring advocate.

FIGURE 11-7 The medical assistant should take time to explain forms the patient does not understand and should always be willing to answer questions.

PROCEDURE 11-2

Register a New Patient

GOAL: *To complete a registration form for a new patient with information for credit and insurance claims and to inform and orient the patient to the facility.*

EQUIPMENT and SUPPLIES

- Registration form
- Clerical supplies (pen, clipboard)
- Private conference area

PROCEDURAL STEPS

1. Determine whether the patient is new to the practice.
2. Obtain and record the necessary information:
   - Patient's full name, birth date, and name of spouse (if married)
   - Home address, telephone number (include ZIP and area codes)
   - Occupation, name of employer, business address, telephone number
   - Social Security number and driver's license number, if any
   - Name of referring physician, if any
   - Name and address of person responsible for payment
   - Method of payment
   - Health insurance information (photocopy both sides of the insurance ID card)

- Name of primary carrier
- Type of coverage
- Group policy number
- Subscriber number
- Assignment of benefits, if required

   <u>PURPOSE:</u> This information is necessary for credit and insurance claims.
3. Review the entire form and confirm the patient's eligibility for insurance coverage.
   <u>PURPOSE:</u> To verify that the given information is complete and legible.
4. Determine that required referrals have been received, if applicable.
   <u>PURPOSE:</u> Insurance coverage may not be valid without a referral.
5. Explain medical and financial procedures to patients.
   <u>PURPOSE:</u> To help the patient develop a comfort level and know what to expect.
6. Collect co-payments or balance payment charges.
   <u>PURPOSE:</u> To keep accounts current and prevent the need to mail statements.

---

the paperwork can be mailed to the patient, with instructions to bring the completed documents to the office visit. More information about patient forms used in the medical practice is found in Chapter 14; examples of many different forms are available on the Evolve Web site.

> **CRITICAL THINKING** APPLICATION   **11-5**
> Often some time is needed to complete forms when a new patient arrives in the office. How might Georgina keep the office on schedule when new patients arrive, requiring medical record construction and form completion? What are some ways to trim time from these activities?

Obtaining a Patient's History

The patient's personal history, medical history, and family history may be obtained by asking him or her to complete a questionnaire; the physician can augment this information during the patient interview. Some experienced medical assistants conduct the interview to obtain the patient's personal and medical history, family history, and chief complaint. This is a specialized procedure, and the medical assistant should be specifically trained to perform it for the individual practice.

When taking a patient history, talk with the patient in a private area or in the exam room. Follow the questionnaire and discuss the issues the patient relates as a past illness or injury, in addition to current health problems. Watch the patient's body language while listening. Use reflection, restatement, and clarification (see

Chapter 5) when obtaining patient information. Discuss the patient's history thoroughly and make accurate notations in the medical record. Describe the current chief complaint, using the patient's own words whenever possible in documenting the problem. Remember that the medical assistant can never offer the patient any type of medical advice.

SHOWING CONSIDERATION FOR PATIENTS' TIME

The patient expects to see the physician or practitioner at the appointed time. The medical assistant should bring the patient to the examination room for treatment or consultation as close to the appointment time as possible or explain delays. All patients want to be kept informed about how long they should expect to wait to see the physician. Any delay longer than 10 to 15 minutes should be explained. A crowded reception room is not always an indication of a physician's popularity. It may simply mean that the physician or assistant is inefficient at scheduling patients. Always consider the patient's time and make every effort to streamline the office visit.

A solo or small practice should seldom have more than three to five patients in the reception room. Patients complain that the wait time in medical facilities is one of the most frustrating aspects of the medical profession. The patient who complains about medical fees or the care received may first have become agitated during a long wait to see the physician. Many patients are fearful and tense; long wait times intensify these feelings. The medical assistant can often put patients in a better frame of mind with just a friendly smile and a show of concern.

Patients with Special Needs

Some patients are physically challenged, some are very ill, and some are severely uncomfortable. Language or cultural barriers may exist. Observe the patient's appearance and behavior. Is the patient pale? Do the eyes or voice reflect pain or discomfort? Find out how the patient is feeling before suggesting that he or she be seated to wait for the physician. The patient may need to lie down in a cool room or perhaps be seen as an emergency case. Patients with disabilities, such as those who use a wheelchair, cane, walker, or crutches, may need extra attention. Some patients may need help disrobing even if a disability is not obvious. Ask if the patient needs assistance.

ESCORTING AND INSTRUCTING THE PATIENT

While in the physician's office, most patients prefer to be escorted rather than simply told where to go. This usually is the clinical medical assistant's responsibility, but the task may be assigned to an administrative medical assistant. Pronounce the patient's name correctly when calling the person to the clinical area (Figure 11-8). If unsure of the pronunciation, ask the patient. Write the name phonetically on the medical record for quick retrieval at the next appointment.

Some patients bring a family member or friend with them to their appointment. On occasion, several people want to accompany the patient when the person sees the physician. The office policy and procedure manual should address the maximum number of patients allowed in. If the patient insists on more visitors, explain that the exam rooms are small and have only one chair; suggest that the additional people may be uncomfortable standing in such a small room. If the patient still insists, make every attempt to satisfy the patient's needs.

Remember that to an employee of the practice, the office surroundings may become as familiar as home. A stranger to the practice's environment may be confused or disoriented by all the hallways, doors, and rooms. Uncertainty creates anxiety. Take the time to escort the patient personally to the appropriate examination or treatment room; do not point to the room and expect the patient to find the way. If a urine specimen is needed, direct the patient to the restroom and always explain what to do with the specimen.

FIGURE 11-8 Pronounce the patient's name correctly and use it often. This promotes good customer service and pleases the patient. Announcing the patient's name does not violate HIPAA regulations.

On arrival in the examination room, tell the patient whether he or she needs to disrobe. Explain what garments, if any, can be left on, whether shoes are to be removed, whether jewelry needs to be removed, and any other necessary instructions. If a gown is to be worn, specify whether the opening should be in the front or back and tell the patient where he or she can hang up clothes if this is not obvious. An examination table should never be placed in such a position that the patient is exposed to passersby in the hallway if the door is opened. Imagine a patient ready for a Pap smear facing the door as the physician enters! Allow patients a sense of modesty at all times, and make all instructions completely clear. Be equally clear when the examination has been completed. Do not assume that patients know what is expected of them. Tell patients whether they should go to the physician's office for consultation or return to the reception area to wait, or whether they are free to check out with the front office and leave.

The medical assistant helps keep the schedule operating smoothly by immediately tidying each examination room and escorting the next patient in so that the physician has no idle moments waiting for a patient to be prepared. Try not to place a patient in an examination room just to clear out the reception area. Keeping the patient waiting after being gowned, draped, and positioned on the examining table is especially inconsiderate. Medical offices often are chilly or even cold, which makes a draped patient quite uncomfortable. A magazine rack on the wall of the treatment room is a welcome addition in some practices.

Remember that in today's litigious society, physicians prefer a second person in the room during examinations to avoid claims of sexual assault or harassment. The office may be equipped with a buzzer that alerts the medical assistant to enter the examination room after the physician has initially consulted with the patient. Be prompt in answering the buzzer and provide assistance during the examination. Patients may be uncomfortable and uneasy; offer words of encouragement, a smile, and a pat on the shoulder.

MEDICAL RECORD PLACEMENT

Medical records should never be left in the examination room to be picked up and read by a patient. This can cause misunderstandings, because patients rarely know medical terms and abbreviations. A number of methods are used to signal that a patient is ready to be seen. Often file holders are located on the doors of the examination rooms, and the medical record can be placed in the holder horizontally when the patient is ready to be seen. The physician can signal the medical assistant that he or she is finished examining the patient by placing the medical record in an upright position on leaving the exam room. Place the medical record so that the patient's name cannot be seen by other patients in the hallway. HIPAA considers names on medical records to be incidental disclosures; however, protecting patient privacy by simply turning the chart so that the name cannot be read is a good habit to cultivate.

Some offices have light call systems, by which a physician can press a button to call the medical assistant for help with the examination. Others have a visual item outside the door that signals what that particular patient needs next. Other offices place patients in examination rooms in a certain order, and the physician knows, for instance, that when he or she has finished with the patient in room

1, the next patient will be waiting in room 2. The office should develop a method that allows the most efficient use of time while providing high-quality care, and at the same time, protects patient confidentiality.

CHALLENGING SITUATIONS

Talkative Patients

Any professional office has problem patients. Talkative patients, for example, take up far more of the physician's time than is justified. An alert medical assistant usually can spot this tendency during the initial interview. The patient's history can be flagged with a symbol to alert the physician. The medical assistant can buzz the physician's **intercom** and remind him that the next patient is ready. Once the medical assistant has learned which patients take extra time, they can be booked for the end of the day, or more time can be allowed for them.

CRITICAL THINKING APPLICATION   11-6
Georgina has one patient who insists on sitting close to her desk and attempting to chat the entire time she is waiting to see the physician. Even worse, she comes to her appointments at least an hour early. How might Georgina subtly deal with this patient?

Children

Children frequently present special management challenges, whether they are patients or they accompany a patient. Usually, the parent or guardian accompanies the child into the exam room, but some exceptions exist, such as a case of suspected child abuse. Older children certainly can see the doctor without a parent, especially for routine visits, such as a school sports physical. However, minors still need a parent to consent to treatment in most cases. The physician cannot force the parent to leave the examination room by any means. Although this practice of separating children from their parents to treat their needs is not always feasible, it sometimes can be applied with great success.

Parents are responsible for their children's behavior while at the physician's office. If children are doing something that could harm themselves or other patients, quietly speak to the parents and allow them to handle the situation. When children behave badly, the medical assistant can go to the child, kneel down to his or her level, and offer a book or toy, leading the child away from any objects that could be broken or from other patients. The medical assistant can say, "Let's come over here and play next to your mom!" If the child continues to behave badly, call the parent to the exam room early, so that others in the reception area can relax and enjoy a pleasant office visit. The medical assistant should not discipline the child. Some patients may be anxious about receiving test results or have other issues, and an unruly child can make the situation even worse.

Angry Patients in the Reception Area

Every medical assistant eventually is confronted with an angry patient. The anger may simply reflect the patient's pain or fear of what the physician may discover during the examination. If possible, invite the patient into a room out of the reception area. Usually the best course is to let the patient talk out the anger. Pacify the patient using a calm attitude and speak in a low tone of voice. Under no circumstances should the medical assistant return the anger or become argumentative. Medical assistants must use good listening skills with angry people and must be empathetic.

Patient's Relatives and Friends

Patients sometimes are accompanied by a relative or well-meaning friend who may become restless waiting for the patient and attempt to discuss the patient's illness. The medical assistant should sidestep any discussion of a patient's medical care, except by direction of the physician. Avoid a too casual attitude, such as, "I'm sure there's nothing to worry about." A show of moderate concern and reassurance that "the patient is in good hands" usually takes care of the situation. Remember that health information cannot be released to anyone, including concerned friends and relatives, without the patient's consent.

THE FRIENDLY FAREWELL

As soon as the visit with the physician has been completed, the medical assistant should be ready to help the patient dress, if necessary, and make sure any questions the patient may have are answered. Answer questions if they can be addressed ethically and legally; otherwise, direct the patient to the physician. Some questions can be answered only by the physician; in such cases, the assistant can offer to get answers for the patient or bring the physician back to the examination room to answer the questions. Remember, patients view the medical assistant as an extension of the physician, and the medical assistant must be very careful to prevent accusations of practicing medicine without a license.

The medical assistant can help convey a sense of caring by terminating the visit cordially. If the patient will return for another visit, the assistant can say something like, "We'll see you next week." If this is the patient's last visit, a pleasant "I hope you'll be feeling better soon" is appropriate. Whatever words of goodbye are chosen, all patients should leave the facility feeling that they have received top-quality care and were treated with friendliness, respect, and courtesy.

PATIENT CHECKOUT

When the patient returns to the front office for checkout, greet him or her with a friendly smile and call the individual by name. Form the habit of asking patients whether they have any questions. Check the medical record to determine when the physician wants the patient to return. Most physicians note this information on the encounter form. Make the return appointment, remembering the technique of giving the patient choices for which day to come, morning or afternoon, and specific times. Then ask the patient for payment, using phrases such as, "Your co-pay today is $15, Mrs. Williams. Will you be writing a check or would you like to charge this visit to your Visa?"

Some offices insist that co-pays be collected before the office visit; this matter is handled according to the physician's discretion. Some

FIGURE 11-9 Always thank the patient for coming and wish him or her well.

patients do not believe they should have to pay before seeing the physician; they simply are not used to paying at the start of the visit. The medical assistant can say, "Mr. Thomas, would you like to go ahead and pay your co-pay now?" By giving the patient the option, it seems as if the medical assistant is helping the patient save time instead of insisting on collecting before seeing the physician. Follow the procedures outlined in the office policy and procedure manual for patient checkout.

Be sure to thank the patient for coming and wish the person well as he or she leaves the office (Figure 11-9).

CLOSING COMMENTS

A personal touch is vital to projecting a sense of care to the patients seen in the physician's office. Many medical offices are not concerned enough about the customer service aspect of the business. Patients talk about their experiences with their friends and relatives and may be an excellent source of referrals if they are treated with dignity and courtesy. If they have a good experience, they tell several people. If they have a poor experience, they tend to tell everyone they know. Make sure to play a part in having each patient feel a sense of satisfaction as he or she leaves the office. All patients should feel that their time and money have been well spent.

Patient Education

Offering a patient education center in the reception area is an effective way to provide patients with up-to-date information about healthcare issues. Brochures and information sheets can be displayed, and DVD programs that deal with health topics can be available for viewing while the patient is waiting to see the physician.

Both the physician and the medical assistants caring for patients should ask whether the patient has any questions during the office visit. Patients often complain that they did not get to speak to the physician long enough to get their questions answered completely.

Legal and Ethical Issues

A medical assistant must never offer medical advice to a patient unless specifically instructed to do so by the physician. The patient sees the medical assistant as an extension of the physician and tends to weigh advice and comments by the medical assistant with the same validity as if they came from the physician. Provide only information the physician has approved or that is included in the office policy and procedure manual.

When a patient complains, listen carefully and try to resolve the problem or assure the patient that the issue will be discussed with the appropriate staff member to find a solution. If someone other than the patient asks for information about the patient, refrain from discussion unless the patient or physician has authorized the release of information.

SUMMARY OF SCENARIO

Georgina is a person who truly makes a difference in the healthcare profession. She takes her role as a patient advocate seriously and strives to make her patients feel comfortable in Dr. Wade's office. She keeps the mission statement posted close to her desk and rereads it often to keep her focus clear. She shares the vision with the other staff members, who are supportive and in agreement with the purpose for which the office exists.

Dr. Wade promotes continuing medical education and encourages his staff members to participate in courses and seminars that will help them be more effective patient advocates. The office sends birthday and Christmas cards to the patients in the database, and at the annual holiday party, the staff hand-signs each Christmas card. Georgina sends a monthly newsletter to patients, some by mail and some by e-mail, to keep them up-to-date on office policies and interesting health information. All of these activities indicate a strong, caring attitude toward the patients. Georgina considers each one a customer of the clinic, and she is determined that they all receive excellent customer service.

Wait times are at a minimum in Dr. Wade's office. Cell phone numbers and e-mail addresses are gathered at registration and updated frequently so that the staff can quickly contact patients. Georgina offers new patients a form for evaluation of the office so that they can provide input about their experience as a new patient. All these efforts promote a trusting, caring relationship among physician, staff, and patients.

Medical assistants can develop a strong rapport with patients by treating them as they themselves would want to be treated. Patients enjoy hearing their own names and being recognized by staff members. Georgina remembers to greet each patient on his or her arrival at the clinic and always asks the names of patients she does not know. She knows that having a bit of personal knowledge about the patients will be of benefit to Dr. Wade, and the entire staff is cordial and friendly to all patients.

Georgina knows that she must keep the sign-in register confidential and uses a form that complies with HIPAA regulations. This prevents patients from obtaining private health information during check-in procedures. By protecting patient confidentiality, the office not only remains in compliance with federal regulations, but also puts the patients' interests first, ensuring that they can enter the office with confidence and trust.

SUMMARY OF LEARNING OBJECTIVES

1. **Define, spell, and pronounce the terms listed in the vocabulary.**
   Spelling and pronouncing medical terms correctly bolster the medical assistant's credibility. Knowing the definition of these terms promotes confidence in communication with patients and co-workers.

2. **Explain the purpose of the office mission statement.**
   The office mission statement is the philosophy of why the office exists. Often physicians themselves develop the mission statement, which outlines their vision and reasons for entering medical practice. Some physicians allow the office staff to assist in its development. All employees should become familiar with the mission statement and promote its ideas to all patients and visitors.

3. **List several patient amenities and why these are important additions to the medical office.**
   Patient amenities include such things as a VCR, television, computer, telephone, and a desk where patients can sit and balance a checkbook or review work while away from the office. These features turn the time spent in the physician's office into productive minutes instead of wasteful ones.

4. **Describe how to prepare for patient arrivals.**
   Some offices prepare for patient arrivals the evening before and some in the morning. Patients' medical records must be pulled; they should be checked for completed laboratory tests and posted results and to ensure that the progress notes for this visit are ample. Rooms should be checked and inventoried to make sure they are neat and clean and that sufficient supplies are on hand.

5. **Explain why using the patient's name as often as possible is important.**
   People like hearing their own names; a better relationship is built between the staff and patients when the names are used often. Patients feel that the office staff cares enough about them to acknowledge them, and this custom adds a personal touch.

6. **Discuss how the medical assistant can help the patient prepare for an examination.**
   The medical assistant should escort the patient to the examination rooms and other areas of the office. Always tell the patient when to disrobe and exactly what should be removed. Offer to assist with disrobing if the patient needs extra help. Take care that the patient's purse or wallet is in a secure place. Make sure doors do not open and expose the disrobed patient. Instruct the patient whether he or she may leave or should wait after seeing the physician. Ask whether the patient has any questions.

7. **Discuss ways to make the patient feel at ease and comfortable in the medical office.**
   The personal touch helps the patient feel at home and comfortable in the office. An attractive reception area with various patient amenities provides a warm atmosphere. Using the patient's name often and a gentle touch impart a sense of caring. Watch body language for clues and offer a reassuring smile when appropriate.

8. **Explain how to place the medical record to prevent breach of confidentiality.**

Some medical offices place patient medical records in a door file, which alerts the physician that the patient is ready to be seen. Other offices place the medical records in door files in a certain order. For example, if examination rooms 1, 2, and 3 are available, patients are seen in that order by the physician. Make every effort to place the medical record so that the patient's name is not visible to anyone passing by in the hallway.

9. **Discuss how the medical assistant might deal with talkative patients.**
Talkative patients may be lonely and may enjoy the social interaction of their visits to the physician's office. Be as courteous as possible with talkative patients, letting them know when necessary that another patient is waiting or that the physician needs assistance. When this is said with a smile, most patients understand.

CONNECTIONS

📖 **Study Guide Connection:** Go to the Chapter 11 Study Guide. Read and complete the activities.

⊖ **Evolve Connection:** Go to the Chapter 11 link at *evolve.elsevier.com/ kinn* to complete the Chapter Review and Chapter Quiz. Check out the other resources listed for this chapter to make the most of what you have learned from Patient Reception and Processing.

12

OFFICE ENVIRONMENT AND DAILY OPERATIONS

SCENARIO

Kayla Kemper performed her externship at Dr. Richard Tarago's office, a general practice clinic downtown that serves lower income patients, most of whom do not have medical insurance. Some patients have a co-payment of $5 to $25; others have no co-payment, depending on their income level. Kayla's family is quite wealthy, and working with patients whose lifestyle is very different from hers has been an eye-opening experience. On many days she wanted to leave the clinic, because she realized that a large number of patients were unable to seek medical care at the start of an illness, and when they finally came to the clinic, they were in worse condition.

Kayla is a caring person, and she saw the suffering many patients experienced daily. She found it tough to see people who had difficulty obtaining health care, yet she realized that a large number of Americans have no insurance coverage at all. Kayla discussed her feelings with the clinic manager, Elaine Mays, and expressed her concern for the patients in the clinic. Elaine asked whether Kayla would like to continue working with the patients, and Kayla admitted that she would, although it was not easy for her. Elaine then suggested that because Kayla's background is so different from the patients, she might want to stay at the clinic as a volunteer for a few months to add to her learning experience. She accepted the offer, and after 3 months as a volunteer, Elaine hired Kayla to work in the clinical area full time. The patients consistently commented on how compassionately and considerately Kayla treated them. Kayla truly learned the meaning of giving as it relates to the medical profession. Her externship was the start of her full-time career.

While studying this chapter, think about the following questions:

- What are some issues that might prevent a medical assistant from showing compassion to all patients? How can these issues be resolved?
- Why is it a good practice to allow the person who uses a certain supply to order it?
- Why might outsourcing be less expensive than doing testing or procedures in the office?
- How might an extensive list of community resources be helpful to patients?

LEARNING OBJECTIVES

1. Define, spell, and pronounce the terms listed in the vocabulary.
2. List five specific actions that must be taken to prepare for patients before the office opens in the morning.
3. Explain why patient traffic flow is an important consideration in the office design.
4. List some of the expenses involved in the operation of a medical practice.
5. Describe how prices can be compared for medical office supplies.
6. Discuss the importance of routine maintenance of office equipment.
7. List several ways to save money and prevent waste in the medical office.
8. Discuss fire safety issues in a healthcare environment.
9. Discuss critical elements of an emergency plan for response to a natural disaster or other emergency.
10. Identify emergency preparedness plans in the community.
11. Discuss potential roles of the medical assistant in emergency preparedness.
12. Describe the fundamental principles for evacuation of a healthcare setting.
13. Explain the difference between medical waste and regular waste.
14. Identify principles of body mechanics and ergonomics.

VOCABULARY

advance An amount of money or credit furnished in anticipation of repayment.

backorder An ordered item that is not delivered when promised or demanded but will be filled at a later date.

budget A plan for the coordination of resources and expenditures; the amount of money available or required for a particular purpose.

depleted Lessened markedly in quantity, content, power, or value.

discrepancies Differences between conflicting facts, claims, or opinions.

fiscal year An accounting period of 12 months during which a company determines earnings and profit; the fiscal year does not necessarily begin in January; the business determines the beginning of its fiscal year.

honorarium A payment in recognition of acts or professional services, usually on a special occasion.

incurred To become liable or subject to; to bring down upon oneself.

mitigating To cause to become less harsh or hostile; to make less severe or painful.

outsourcing The practice of subcontracting work to an outside company.

overhead The ongoing administrative expenses of a business that cannot be attributed to any specific business activity but are still necessary for the business to function (e.g., rent, utilities, insurance).

packing slip A list of items included in a shipment.

per diem By the day; per day. An allowance for daily expenses.

proactive Acting in anticipation of future problems, needs, or changes.

New medical assistants may have difficulty putting all their skills together and using them at the same time throughout the course of a day. Medical assistants must be multitaskers and must develop a good memory. They also must be efficient workers. While in school, medical assisting students spend several days learning a specific skill, such as phlebotomy. However, during the externship and on the job, the medical assistant may need to perform a phlebotomy, chart a procedure, and check out a patient, all within a matter of minutes.

Most of the general tasks in the physician's office are done daily, weekly, or monthly. Such tasks include preparing for the day, using the office policy manual, ordering and receiving supplies, cleaning, office budgeting, lunches and breaks, office security, travel arrangements, and ergonomics. The physician's office is a busy environment where the medical assistant encounters new challenges each day. This chapter details the general office environment and the daily operations that the medical assistant may perform in the physician's office. Multitasking is a critical skill that all medical assistants should strive toward; during a typical day, many duties will be carried out at one time and the medical assistant must keep track of the progress of each responsibility.

The more flexible the medical assistant, the more valuable he or she is to the physician. By learning and refining adaptation skills, medical assistants increase office efficiency, allowing the schedule to handle interruptions and emergencies. Remember that the patient is the reason the office exists and is of primary importance to the office staff. However, various tasks demand attention in the daily operation of the medical office.

THE OFFICE POLICY AND PROCEDURES MANUAL

Virtually all businesses have some type of policy and/or procedures manual, but it is especially important in the physician's office and other medical facilities. The manual should be easy to read, detailed, and logically organized. Besides providing administrative information, the manual also should provide procedural sheets that outline the steps of each procedure performed in the office. The manual should be a "living" document, constantly updated as technology advances and changed whenever regulations change. The manual must be reviewed annually for corrections and additions; this review must be documented as a step in the compliance with regulations established by the Occupational Safety and Health Administration (OSHA). Documentation can be a statement verifying that the manual has been reviewed; this statement should be dated and signed by the office manager or physician. One of OSHA's most common citations for noncompliance is having a policy manual but not following the stated policy in various areas. The medical assistant must form the habit of going to the office policy manual whenever in doubt about any procedure.

Using the Office Policy Manual

All employees should read the office policy manual when they begin working in the physician's office. Manuals and other office policy documents may be posted on the physician's Web site, often in the sections pertaining to employees. Some physicians make these and other employee-related documents available in pdf format. Reading the manual helps the medical assistant become informed about the expectations of supervisors. However, the office policy manual is not only used for new employees (Procedures 12-1 and 12-2). The manual should be a reference that all employees use whenever necessary. OSHA requires that the policy manual be reviewed at least annually to make sure all the information is accurate and up-to-date. Whenever revisions are made, insert a page in the manual giving the date the revisions become effective.

After the revised manual has been reviewed and accepted, a memo can be distributed detailing the changes made and where to look for them.

PROCEDURE 12-1

Explain General Office Policies

GOAL: *To communicate office policies and procedures effectively to employees, patients, and visitors in the office.*

EQUIPMENT and SUPPLIES

- Office policy manual
- Office procedure manual (if not included in policy manual)
- Patient information sheets (if needed)
- Patient information brochure (if needed)

PROCEDURAL STEPS

1. Design an office policy manual and a patient information brochure that provide general information for employees and patients. At a minimum, the information should include:
   - Philosophy statement
   - Goals
   - Description of the medical practice
   - Location and/or map
   - Phone numbers
   - Pager numbers
   - E-mail and Web site addresses
   - Staff names and credentials
   - Services offered
   - Hours of operation
   - Appointment system
   For employees:
   - Vacation, sick leave
   - Confidentiality
   - Grievances
   - Benefits
   - Payroll information
   - Other employee information

   <u>PURPOSE:</u> To give employees and patients a written document that details general information that can be used as a reference when needed.
2. Offer the brochure to new employees and patients or to any other employees and patients who do not have a current brochure.
3. Briefly discuss each section of the brochure with new employees and patients.
   <u>PURPOSE:</u> To acquaint employees and patients with the contents of the policy manual and answer questions that might arise about each section.
4. Watch for verification of understanding from the employee or patient, both verbally and nonverbally. Apply active listening skills.
   <u>PURPOSE:</u> By watching a patient's body language and listening to his or her questions, the medical assistant can determine whether the patient truly understands the information presented.
5. Demonstrate empathy in communicating with patients, family, and staff.
6. Ask the employee or patient if he or she has any questions.
   <u>PURPOSE:</u> To ensure understanding of the information presented.
7. If required, document in the medical record that the employee or patient received the information.
   <u>PURPOSE:</u> To help prove an employee or patient was given certain information about policies and procedures.

PROCEDURE 12-2

Explain the Physician's Instructions to Patients, Staff Members, and Visitors

GOAL: *To communicate office policies and procedures effectively to employees, patients, and visitors in the office so that they understand instructions from the physician.*

EQUIPMENT and SUPPLIES

- Office policy manual
- Office procedure manual (if not included in policy manual)
- Patient information sheets (if needed)
- Physician's orders, if applicable
- Patient information brochure

PROCEDURAL STEPS

1. Determine the communication needs of the employee, patient, or visitor.
   <u>PURPOSE:</u> To discover the best way to communicate information to a person who may have special needs.
2. Arrange for an interpreter, if needed, or involve a family member to assist the patient with the treatment procedures.
   <u>PURPOSE:</u> To make sure information is communicated and received accurately.
3. Provide instructions to the employee, patient, or visitor.
4. Watch for verification of understanding from the individual, both verbally and nonverbally. Apply active listening skills.
   <u>PURPOSE:</u> By watching body language and listening to questions, the medical assistant can determine whether the person truly understands the information presented.
5. Ask whether the person has any questions.
   <u>PURPOSE:</u> To ensure understanding of the information presented.
6. If required, document in the medical record that the employee, patient, or visitor (if necessary) received the instructions.
   <u>PURPOSE:</u> To help prove an employee or patient was given certain instructions about policies, procedures, and expectations or directions about treatment.

The office policy manual should include sections that deal with several topics, such as:

- Expected employee performance
- Tardy and absentee policy
- Sexual harassment
- Confidentiality
- Vacations, sick time, and paid time off
- Employee evaluation
- Continuing education
- Chain of command
- How to deal with certain patients and visitors

Some offices require employees to sign a document stating that they have read and understand the entire policy. The manual should be written clearly and concisely in language that is easily understood. It should be used if a question arises about policy matters and also when an employee is unsure of the reason for or way to proceed with a task. A procedures manual often is combined with the policy manual. Regardless of the setup, every office task should be detailed in one of the two documents.

FIGURE 12-1 The telephone is the lifeline of a medical practice. The medical assistant will take several phone messages throughout the course of the day and must see that all of them are given proper attention and follow-up.

OPENING THE OFFICE

Employees arrive earlier than patients so that the office can be prepared for the day. Some office policies dictate that the office be readied for the next day the evening before, but for the purposes of this chapter, assume that the policy requires preparation in the morning.

Although the physician may trust the employees, office policy should demand that supervisors be **proactive** in preventing theft. Depending on the size of the clinic, a certain number of employees will have keys and will know the alarm codes for the facility. The best policy is to monitor this access and information strictly. When numerous keys are distributed, more employees have after-hours access to the office. By limiting this access, the physician may prevent some losses to theft. Two things in particular make the physician's office a target: money and drugs. Usually, only a limited amount of cash is kept in the office. However, most offices keep some medications, often narcotics, which can be addictive or sold for a profit on the street. If such items are used, they must be protected, not only for safety but also to remain in compliance with the law. Even during regular office hours, the staff should practice careful methods, such as keeping back doors locked securely, so that only those authorized are able to enter the building.

PREPARING FOR THE DAY AHEAD

Once the employees have arrived for work, all of them should begin preparing for patients and visitors. Each employee is responsible for his or her own work space, and the staff may work as a team to prepare common areas of the office, such as the reception area. When each person understands the duties required and when they are divided up among the staff, work can be completed quickly and efficiently.

Several duties are completed before the patients arrive. The voice mail or answering service should be checked to collect any messages left since the last time the staff was in the office (Figure 12-1). Some answering services send calls by e-mail or fax. Make sure a phone

message book is handy when retrieving messages; write each one into the message book and include all information needed to respond to the message properly. This ensures that copies of the messages are available if one happens to get lost. Patients' records may need to be pulled so that the medical assistant can take action and follow up on the messages.

Print two copies of the day's appointments and place one copy on the physician's desk unless he or she chooses to view the appointments on a computer system. Use the other copy to pull medical records for the patients who will visit the office during the day if paper records are kept. If the office does not use electronic health records, keep the paper medical records in a convenient, central area so that staff members can find them easily once the patients begin to arrive. Make sure the physician has enough room in the progress notes section of the medical record to write the details of the office visit. If needed, add a new sheet of progress notes. Glance over the notes from the last visit to determine whether laboratory work or treatments were ordered and find out whether the results are available.

Patient exam rooms should be restocked with all the regular supplies used in the individual rooms. Items such as cotton balls, bandages, gauze pads, patient gowns, and drapes need to be replenished daily. The physician and patient should never be forced to wait in the examination room while the medical assistant searches for supplies. Check the restrooms to make sure adequate toilet paper, soap, and hand towels are available. If urine specimen cups and towelettes are kept in patient restrooms, make sure enough are available to last throughout the day.

Be sure prescription pads are available for the physician, although they should not be left in open areas or on counters in exam rooms (Figure 12-2). Many physicians keep one pad in their pocket and the extras stored in a locked cabinet. Physicians using electronic health records can print prescriptions directly from their computer system or have them sent to the pharmacy electronically. Patients should never have access to prescription pads, because they might try to forge a prescription; this is a breach of federal or state law

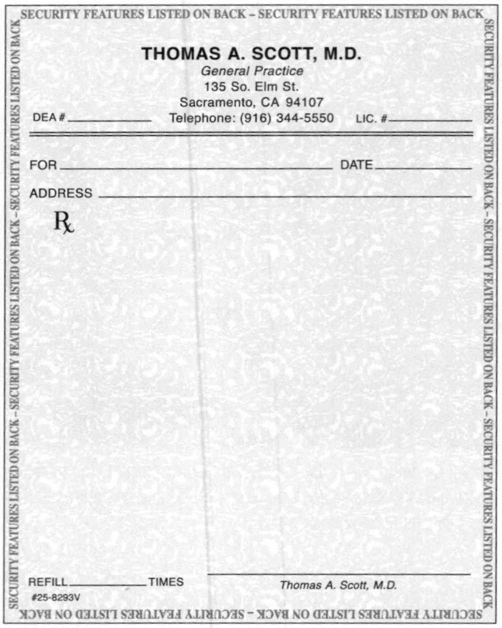
SECURITY FEATURES LISTED ON BACK - SECURITY FEATURES LISTED ON BACK

THOMAS A. SCOTT, M.D.
General Practice
135 So. Elm St.
Sacramento, CA 94107
DEA #_______ Telephone: (916) 344-5550 LIC. #_______

FOR_______ DATE_______
ADDRESS_______
℞

REFILL_______TIMES Thomas A. Scott, M.D.
#25-8293V

FIGURE 12-2 Keep a close watch on prescription pads, so that patients do not have access to them. Many electronic medical records (EMR) systems allow the physician to write prescriptions directly from the computer.

or both. Take extra care to keep prescription pads out of patients' sight.

Certain equipment may need to be turned on, such as computers, laboratory equipment, and copy machines. Lights should be turned on in all the examination rooms. If quality assurance tests need to be performed on any of the laboratory machines, run the tests and record the results.

Some specimens from previous days may need to be checked for results or additional testing, although many physicians today use outside laboratories. Always record test results in the patient's medical record. The medical assistant cannot decide whether a test result is abnormal; however, if that information is clearly indicated on the lab's report form, then act according to office policy. Some physicians only want to see the test results if they fall outside normal ranges. Most laboratories print test results so that abnormal results are emphasized; they may be printed in a different color ink or in a separate column labeled "Abnormal." If results are abnormal, the physician may need to do follow-up work or see the patient again. As mentioned, the medical assistant cannot judge whether a test result is abnormal, but if that information is clearly indicated, the medical assistant can file the document according to office policy.

CRITICAL THINKING APPLICATION 12-1

Kayla realizes that the office does not have a set method for letting the medical assistants know that laboratory results are ready to be filed. How might she handle this and what suggestions can Kayla make to Elaine?

The patient accounting system should be prepared for the day. Secure enough encounter forms for each patient in the appointment book. Stock the patient checkout area with plenty of appointment cards. If the office gives small gifts to patients, such as refrigerator magnets or coffee mugs, make sure they are available for use. Many offices place the physician's business card just outside the receptionist's window or in the patient reception area. Because patients often take one of the cards, this supply should also be checked.

Various specialty offices may need to prepare additional equipment; therefore, make sure everything necessary is available for the physician and staff members. The day runs smoother when the office is completely prepared for the patients. When all of these duties have been completed, the last task is to unlock the front door and begin welcoming patients to the practice.

PATIENT TRAFFIC FLOW

Ideally, the physician's office is located in an area of town that is easy to find, has ample parking, and does not force the patient to do any excess walking, especially upstairs. The medical assistant is usually not involved with designing the interior of the office; however, the placement of all furniture and equipment is an important factor in the efficient flow of traffic. Patients should be able to quickly determine the location of the patient waiting room. It is helpful if one room is designated as a "sick room" so that well patients will not be stricken with an illness just from visiting the office (when space is short, a face mask may be issued to patients with symptoms of communicable disease). Good traffic flow is important so that the patients and employees can maneuver through the office easily and avoid retracing their steps. Additionally, patients should be able to locate separate parts of the office, such as the lab or check-out areas. Neither patients nor employees should be subjected to dodging furniture or tripping over equipment cords. When moving through the hallways, guide the patient along the right side and leave the left for those traveling in the opposite direction.

CRITICAL THINKING APPLICATION 12-2

One of the older patients seems concerned that an ill child is coughing excessively in the waiting area. How can Kayla help alleviate the patient's concern? What can Kayla do to resolve the issue?

VISITORS TO THE OFFICE

Many people besides patients visit the physician's office. Some of these individuals have appointments; others stop by at random. The office policy manual should detail the procedure to follow in dealing with such individuals. Most physicians prefer to set aside a specific time for pharmaceutical representatives (also called *detail persons* or *drug reps*). These professionals usually are quite competent and knowledgeable about various drugs, and they should be treated with respect by all members of the office staff. In the past, pharmaceutical representatives were allowed to leave memo pads, pens, and other gift items for the physicians and staff that advertised a certain drug or treatment. Many states have laws that prevent pharmaceutical companies from providing these perks. However, some states may not have passed such laws, and physicians still can receive these items. Lawmakers are more concerned about perks such as an **honorarium** for serving as a guest speaker than about pens and notepads. However, many lawmakers believe that physicians' prescribing habits are directly related to pharmaceutical company perks. The company's goal is to educate the physician about their products so that the physician can better care for patients. Some states are developing laws that require reporting of any gifts of more than $25; in most states, this does not include the free samples of the actual drugs. In general, most physicians have decided not to accept these gifts so that no question arises of any breach of ethical conduct.

Pharmaceutical representatives are not the only salespersons who may visit the physician's office. Salespeople from office supply stores, medical equipment sellers, and others may stop by to make appointments or take orders for various items. The office manager usually can address the needs of salespeople and normally is authorized to place orders.

CRITICAL THINKING APPLICATION   12-3

One of the pharmaceutical representatives is extremely pushy. How can Kayla express that the physician cannot meet with the rep? What can Kayla do if the rep continues to be insistent about seeing the physician?

At times, other physicians stop by the office to see the doctor. They may not have an appointment, but the physician should be notified at once when another doctor is waiting in the reception area. If office policy allows, take the visiting physician to the doctor's office instead of forcing him or her to wait in the patient reception area. Because doctors understand busy schedules, most do not stop by another doctor's office without an important reason.

The physician's family members or friends may visit the medical office. Never send family members or friends away without notifying the physician of their presence and asking whether he or she has time to speak to them.

DAILY, WEEKLY, AND MONTHLY DUTIES

Develop a list of duties that are performed daily, weekly, and monthly. Checklists are helpful when staff members want to make sure all duties are completed. The lists help the supervisors divide work evenly among staff members. Be specific on the checklist and include every task that needs to be done, even the most insignificant ones. If a staff member is struggling to finish her daily duties, other staff members should assist so that all required jobs are completed for the day. Take the initiative and work as a team; the effort may be important when supervisors choose employees to promote or terminate.

Constant Cleaning

Patients expect the physician's office to be immaculate. Nothing should be or appear dirty in any part of the facility. Keeping the office truly clean helps curb the spread of germs and communicable diseases. Effective cleaning products should be used daily, especially

in high traffic areas. Countertops, sinks, door handles, and restrooms should be checked frequently and cleaned whenever necessary. When and if slow periods occur between patients or during lengthy office visits, take a cloth and use a disinfectant on nearby counters or around door handles. Look for things to clean in the office. By being conscientious about these things, the medical assistant becomes more valuable to the physician. Supervisors and physicians notice this productivity; good cleaning habits reflect positively on the medical assistant and are important factors in employee evaluations.

Cleaning Services

Many offices employ a cleaning service that performs more intensive chores. These professionals usually come to the facility during the evening, when patients and staff are gone. They clean and disinfect the bathrooms, vacuum, dust, and empty trash. They also may perform other specific tasks as required by the office staff. The office manager should establish some means of communicating with the head of the cleaning team. Many offices leave a notebook for the cleaning crew that details specific cleaning tasks to be performed in addition to regular cleaning tasks. The office manager should delegate a staff member to be the contact person for the service. If any task is not completed in a satisfactory manner, immediately contact the cleaning supervisor and resolve the problem. Make sure a log is kept so that tasks are listed and note whether they were completed or the reason they were not completed. Always inspect what is expected; the cleaning service must perform the jobs it is being paid to do. Do not allow situations to go unresolved. Be open and frank with services that do not meet expectations.

CRITICAL THINKING APPLICATION   12-4

Kayla has noticed that on the days after the cleaning crew has come, sodas, plastic ware, and other small items seem to be missing from the kitchen area. Today, she notices that an entire box of paper towels is gone from the office. Kayla knows the box was there the day before, because she personally checked in the shipment. How can Kayla handle this situation? How is the situation complicated if one of the people who cleans the office at night is a co-worker's sister?

Filing

The medical assistant rarely has a shortage of documents ready to be filed. Although this task sometimes is monotonous, filing is a critical job that must be completed accurately and in a timely manner (Figure 12-3). If a laboratory result is not placed in the right medical record, important information that may affect the patient's health could be lost.

SUPPLIES AND EQUIPMENT IN THE PHYSICIAN'S OFFICE

The medical assistant is responsible for stocking exam rooms and making sure all supplies and equipment are available and in good working order. The following sections describe the process of ordering and receiving medical supplies and equipment.

FIGURE 12-3 Filing is a critical job that must be done daily. Filing often is necessary even when an EMR system is used. Office administration files usually are kept in a manual system.

Identifying the Need for Specific Supplies

The medical assistant orders supplies periodically to ensure that the physician has everything needed to treat patients. The office policy and procedures manual details how employees should identify the need for certain supplies, order them, check them in, and place them in the office inventory for use. Nothing is more frustrating to the physician than reaching for an item during a procedure, only to find it is unavailable. Communication is the key to keeping supplies in stock.

Budgeting

Most offices use an annual **budget** to determine the amount of money to be spent on various categories of expenses (Figure 12-4). Some expenses involved in the operation of a medical practice include:

- Salaries
- Medical supplies
- Business equipment
- Medical equipment
- Utilities
- Rent or mortgage
- Insurance
- Maintenance
- Taxes
- Laboratory fees
- Office supplies

Expense categories are important, because most business expenses can be deducted on tax returns, and staff salaries are directly related to the physician's **overhead** costs. Always keep receipts for items to be used in the medical office and submit them in a timely manner to the office manager or other designated individual.

CRITICAL THINKING APPLICATION   **12-5**

Elaine has asked Kayla to prepare a budget for next year for her department. Kayla has never done this before. How can she prepare for this challenging task? What references can she use to develop an accurate budget for the coming year?

Businesses usually plan expenses for the year in advance, allocating expected income into various categories of expenses. Then, at least monthly, expenses are logged into a ledger or spreadsheet and separated into specific categories. This allows tracking of expenses to ensure that a category is not over budget. If a specific category of expenses is over budget, adjustments may need to be logged in, either to allot more funds to that category or to stop spending in that category until the next year. Exceeding the allowed amount in a budget is not necessarily uncommon; however, good business practice dictates that budgets come in very close to the estimations made at the beginning of the budget year. When a category goes over budget, money often must be taken from another budget category to cover the amount. This reduces the money available in the second category. Employees should not be allowed to spend money needlessly or wastefully. The physician should designate a minimum number of people to make purchases on behalf of the facility.

Comparing Prices

A good shopper is an asset to the physician's office. Compare prices when shopping for supplies and equipment. Tell salespeople that comparisons will be conducted and that price will be a strong consideration when the time comes to make a purchase. However, price should not be the only consideration. Warranties, bulk purchase opportunities, maintenance agreements, and other factors may influence the best deal available on a certain item. Quality is another important factor; the physician may be willing to pay more for an item based on its quality and durability. Personal preference also influences purchasing decisions. The clinical medical assistant may prefer one brand of needles over another, even though they are the same price. In most circumstances, those who regularly use a certain item should be allowed to decide the brand, model, or other specifics before the item is purchased.

Most companies produce a catalog, whether online or printed. When a need has been identified, compare the prices from at least three sources before placing an order. For instance, if 70% isopropyl alcohol is needed, and the stock must last 6 months, first determine how much is needed. Suppose that approximately one 16-ounce bottle is used per month in each of five treatment rooms. Further suppose that the following prices are listed:

Smith's Medical Supply	1 dozen bottles	$10.53
Argosy Medical and Dental Supply	2 dozen bottles	$17.44
Walgreens	1 bottle	$.53
CVS Pharmacy	1 gallon	$6.12

If these prices are compared, and assuming all other aspects of the products are equal, buying bottles of alcohol at Walgreens clearly is a better deal than buying one or two dozen at either Smith's Medical Supply or Argosy Medical and Dental Supply. The alcohol at Smith's costs approximately 87¢ per bottle; at Argosy, the cost is approximately 72¢ per bottle. Is the gallon a better buy? Let's work it out. The alcohol can always be poured into containers from the gallon bottle. A gallon has 128 ounces; it therefore can provide only 8 16-ounce bottles; the cost per bottle is approximately 76¢. Walgreens, at 53¢ per bottle, has the lowest price. Still, if Walgreens is 15 miles away, the gas used to get the alcohol may push the total

Chart of Accounts - Variance Analysis Template

	Budget	This month	Last month	This month last year	This year to date	Last year to date
ALL EXPENSES	100%					
Capital (IRS section 179) purchases						
Donations and contributions						
Dues						
Fees: Lab						
Fees: Retirement plan						
Insurance: Business						
Insurance: Malpractice						
Janitorial/maintenance						
Journals						
Lease payments: Equipment						
Legal, accounting and consultants						
Loan payments: Principal						
Loan payments: Interest						
Marketing: Ads, promotion and yellow pages						
Marketing: Meals and entertainment						
Meals: Business/staff meetings						
Miscellaneous						
Outside services						
Postage						
Rent and utilities						
Repairs and maintenance: Building						
Repairs and maintenance: Contracts						
Repairs and maintenance: Equipment						
Staff wages						
Staff benefits						
Staff retirement plan						
Staff continuing education						
Supplies: Clinical						
Supplies: Office						
Taxes and licenses						
Telephone/answering service/pager						
Travel and professional meetings						
Uniforms and laundry						
Doctor associate wages						
Doctor associate benefits						
Doctor associate retirement plan						
Doctor associate continuing education						
Ancillary provider wages						
Ancillary provider benefits						
Ancillary provider retirement plan						
Ancillary provider continuing education						
Owner's wages/draws						
Owner's benefits						
Owner's retirement plan						
Owner's auto						
Owner's dues						
Owner's individual and student loans						
Owner's insurances						
Owner's journals						
Owner's marketing: Meals and entertainment						
Owner's other						
Doctor-owner net income (practice profit)						

Adapted with permission from *Medical Practice Forms: Every Form You Need to Succeed.* Copyright © 2004 PMIC. Physicians may adapt for use in their own practices; all other rights reserved. "Three Steps to an Effective Practice Budget." Borglum K. *Family Practice Management.* January 2004:46-50, http://www.aafp.org/fpm/20040100/46thre.html.

FIGURE 12-4 Chart of accounts. Most physicians' offices operate on an annual budget to control expenditures and to make sure supplies and equipment are readily available.

cost higher than the total cost of driving 2 miles to Argosy to buy the product. Also consider delivery and shipping and handling charges, in addition to sales taxes, that might be added to the cost of the order. Some suppliers may cut the cost on certain items to get the order, either meeting or beating the deal offered by another supplier. Examine all costs before placing the order with a supplier.

Ordering Supplies

Responsibility for ordering supplies in the medical office should be assigned to one person. The medical assistant who assumes this task can use various methods to track the needed supplies and then place orders to replenish them. One simple method is to develop a spreadsheet that lists all the products and supplies that need to be ordered periodically (Procedure 12-3). Post the sheets in areas where supplies are stored. When staff members take supplies from storage, they should make a note on the spreadsheet. When it is time to place an order, the sheets are gathered and used to determine which supplies need to be replenished. Some offices use software programs to prepare orders, and others use a computer system to enter products taken from the supply area. Still others may use a sticker system, in which a coded sticker is removed when a product is used and placed on a card or form; that amount then is charged to the patient. Others use a note card system, in which a note card is prepared for each supply item, and after the inventory has been performed; orders are completed based on the needs reflected by the note cards. After determining the items that need to be ordered, browse medical or office supply catalogs to shop for the best prices (Procedure 12-4). The order may need to be divided and offered to two different suppliers if certain items can be obtained at a better rate.

The Internet is a valuable tool for shopping for supplies. Businesses often can find excellent prices and great discounts by ordering online (Figure 12-5). Some physicians and office managers may be hesitant to use credit card accounts online; however, if an account is established with an online supply company, they will hold payment information or perhaps extend credit, and the company credit card need not be used. Most physicians establish accounts with suppliers and pay the accounts monthly. Because credit card purchases involve fees and interest payments, the balance should be paid off monthly to prevent additional charges. These charges increase each month a balance is carried on the account, which makes the actual cost higher than just paying cash for the order.

FIGURE 12-5 Competitive prices can be found using Internet research. Purchasing through the Internet is easy, safe, and convenient.

PROCEDURE 12-3

Inventory Office Supplies and Equipment

GOAL: *To establish an inventory of all expendable supplies in the physician's office and follow an efficient plan or order control.*

EQUIPMENT and SUPPLIES

- Computer
- Inventory and order control cards or stickers
- Computer spreadsheet or list of supplies on hand
- Pen or pencil

PROCEDURAL STEPS

1. Inventory all supplies on hand and enter this information into a computer spreadsheet.
   <u>PURPOSE:</u> To establish a record of all items in the current inventory.
2. Enter into the spreadsheet the name of the item, the number of items currently in stock, the usual price per item, and any bulk discounts.
   <u>PURPOSE:</u> To establish a beginning inventory.
3. Determine the point where the supply should be replenished and highlight or otherwise tag those items.
   <u>PURPOSE:</u> The notation or tag serves as an alert that supply is low.

4. Review the spreadsheet to determine which items are ready to be reordered.
5. When the order has been placed, note the date and quantity ordered on the spreadsheet.
6. When the order is received, note the date and quantity in the appropriate column, and add the new inventory to the spreadsheet.
   <u>NOTE:</u> If the order is only partially filled, make note of items that are backordered and monitor until the order is complete.
7. Repeat the inventory and ordering process each month.
   <u>PURPOSE:</u> To ensure that all supplies are available in the facility when needed.
8. Periodically ask for input from staff members about specific supplies purchased for use in the facility.
   <u>PURPOSE:</u> To provide the people who use the individual supply items an opportunity to suggest products they prefer and that are easy to use, reliable, and efficient.

PROCEDURE 12-4

Prepare a Purchase Order

GOAL: *To prepare an accurate purchase order for supplies or equipment.*

EQUIPMENT and SUPPLIES

- List of current inventory
- Phone
- Purchase order
- Fax machine
- Pen

PROCEDURAL STEPS

1. Review the current inventory and determine what items need to be ordered.
   <u>PURPOSE:</u> To determine what is needed so that the office will not be overstocked or understocked.
2. Complete the purchase order accurately, filling in all applicable spaces and blanks with the information requested.
   <u>PURPOSE:</u> To create an accurately completed purchase order, which helps eliminate mistakes in the order and in shipments.
3. List the items to be ordered, including quantity, item numbers, size, color, price, and extended price. Be sure all applicable information is included.
   <u>PURPOSE:</u> To help ensure accurate orders.

4. Provide the physician's signature, Drug Enforcement Administration (DEA) certificate, and medical license when needed.
   <u>PURPOSE:</u> Some items require these documents to verify that the physician is eligible to order them.
5. Call in, fax, mail, or electronically submit the order to the vendor. Keep a copy for your records. Keep any verification provided that the order was received, such as a fax receipt.
   <u>PURPOSE:</u> To document exactly what was ordered on what date and provide proof that the order was received.
6. Note on the inventory which items are on order.
   <u>PURPOSE:</u> To keep other staff members from preparing duplicate orders.
7. Keep a copy of the order in the appropriate place in the office filing system.
   <u>PURPOSE:</u> To reference the order if needed and have a copy of the items ordered to compare with the packing list once the items arrive at the office.

Replenishing Supplies

Replenish supplies at the reception desk regularly. Stationery, appointment cards, charge slips, sharpened pencils, pens, telephone message pads, and any items likely to be needed should be on hand when the day begins. Discovering that supplies are **depleted** during a busy day can seriously interrupt the flow of patient care. One person should be in charge of checking the inventory of supplies regularly and ordering as necessary. In a practice with several employees, a clinical assistant usually is responsible for checking clinical supplies and preparing the patient rooms; however, in a small practice, only one assistant may be available for all duties. Everything should be ready for the day before patients begin to arrive, so that the physician and medical assistant can give their undivided attention to the patients' needs.

Ordering Equipment

Ordering equipment is more involved than ordering simple supplies. Much of the equipment acquired for the physician's office is considered a capital purchase. Before purchasing this type of equipment, compare price, features, and benefits. The physician or office manager almost always is involved in the purchase of capital equipment. Different businesses use different monetary amounts to classify capital purchases; some use $1,000, whereas others may consider a capital purchase as one that exceeds $5,000. Physicians consult with accountants to determine the limits on capital purchase amounts. At least three estimates should be obtained before making a major equipment purchase.

The physician and staff members who will use the equipment will have questions about the features and benefits, in addition to the cost to purchase and the cost to use in the facility. Sometimes the cost of using certain equipment may exceed the cost of **outsourcing**. For instance, performing a complete blood count (CBC) in the office may cost $10. If the test can be outsourced by sending it to an outpatient laboratory and the resulting cost is $8, the physician could avoid equipment and maintenance costs. Also, if the physician continues to charge $10 for a CBC, he or she will make a profit of $2 on every test. Physicians should not order unnecessary tests; however, making a profit on procedures and treatments performed is certainly ethical. Remember, the physician's office is a business, and there is nothing unethical about making a profit.

CRITICAL THINKING APPLICATION   12-6

Kayla is talking with a patient who tells her husband that she doesn't know how they will afford lab tests. When Kayla walks by them, they stop talking. How can Kayla help the patient in this situation? Should Kayla mention to the patient that she overheard her concerns?

The medical assistant has numerous options when looking for equipment to purchase. Start the search on the Internet to get an idea of the price range of the equipment, both new and used. Local suppliers offer catalogs detailing the products and equipment available, and the suppliers' sales representatives can answer questions. Investigate whether used equipment might be for sale from the supplier. Physicians selling their practice or retiring might have equipment for sale. Obviously, some items should be purchased only from a medical supplier, but many great deals are available from various sources.

Receiving an Order

When an order arrives from a supplier, notify the person in charge of inventory. Boxes should be opened only if enough time is available to check them in properly. Carefully open the package and look for the **packing slip**, which is a list of items ordered and the items shipped. Occasionally an ordered item will not be included in the package because it has been placed on **backorder**. The item may be out of stock but will be sent to the physician as soon as it becomes available. Compare the items listed on the packing slip to the items found inside the box. If any **discrepancies** are found, bring them to the attention of the supplier immediately. Employees should never take items from the package before they have been checked against the packing slip. Once the order has been checked in, make a note on the packing slip that the package was received as expected and then place new stock in the proper place. Make sure stock is rotated, with the new items placed at the back and older items or those with earlier expiration dates placed at the front so that they are used first.

Warranty Information

Many purchased items include a warranty. Always mail warranty information to the manufacturer. Warranty cards usually resemble a postcard and have several questions about the purchaser. If the warranty card is completed and returned, the manufacturer can contact those who have purchased a certain product if defects are discovered or recalls are necessary. The warranty period begins on the date of purchase and usually lasts 1 year, but it can be longer, depending on the item purchased. Keep a copy of the completed warranty in a file with other information on the specific product or piece of equipment, such as the receipt for the purchase, expense records, owner's manuals, and maintenance records.

Invoices and Statements

An invoice is an itemized list of goods shipped that specifies the price and the terms of a sale. A statement is a summary of a financial account that shows the balance due and transactions that affect the account. Invoices precede statements. A medical supplier may send an invoice when a sale has been completed, and statements are mailed whenever an account has a balance. Some invoices request payment upon receipt, whereas others allow a certain period to make a payment (Figure 12-6). Read invoices and statements carefully and make sure they are free of errors before making a payment.

Troubleshooting Equipment Failure

When equipment fails to function properly, consult the owner's manual to determine the steps for troubleshooting. The owner's manual includes contact information so that the purchaser can reach the manufacturer if necessary. Today, purchasers have additional contact options, such as e-mail and live chat via the Internet; both offer fast access for problems that need to be solved quickly.

Equipment Maintenance

Medical office equipment must be maintained regularly, especially machines that perform testing procedures. The Clinical Laboratory

FIGURE 12-6 Invoices and statements must be compared carefully to orders actually received at the physician's office.

Improvement Amendments (CLIA) require that controls and calibrations be performed. All these requirements are designed to ensure that patient testing is accurate and that those results are reliable. Remember that the maintenance must be performed by an authorized user of the equipment; in general, if an employee is authorized to use the equipment, he or she also can take care of maintenance issues.

The maintenance process is similar to maintaining a car in good working condition. Periodically, the oil, filters, and tires must be changed, brake pads must be removed and replaced, and the engine must be kept clean. Similarly, medical office machines must be kept in good repair and working condition (Procedure 12-5).

Maintenance guidelines are included in the owner's manual, and they should be the basis of any maintenance plan. The medical assistant can develop a maintenance schedule to ensure that all office equipment receives proper, timely attention. Keep all information about each equipment item in a separate file and add maintenance records as they are produced. Routine maintenance is important for keeping equipment in top working order, so that patient care is not affected by the availability of equipment. Some machines may require proof of maintenance records to honor warranties. Some physicians prefer to lease equipment, such as copiers, that have a maintenance plan included in the monthly rate. This often proves to be more economical than purchasing expensive machines; the maintenance plan is usually in effect the entire time the equipment is leased, and better warranties are often attached to leased equipment. The medical assistant may be asked to perform comparative pricing on such items and help determine the most efficient direction the office should take with regard to leasing or making a purchase.

PREVENTING WASTE

Waste prevention reduces the production of waste or eliminates it entirely. Companies can reduce the cost of waste management, reduce long-term liability for the disposal of hazardous waste, and become more efficient to enhance profit margins. The key to successful waste management is the cooperation of employees; unless they are willing to participate in waste management efforts, most

Perform and Document Routine Maintenance of Office Equipment

GOAL: *To ensure that all office equipment is in good working order at all times.*

EQUIPMENT and SUPPLIES

- Spreadsheet with information on each piece of office equipment, including serial number and servicing schedule
- Pen or pencil
- Computer
- Access to all office equipment

PROCEDURAL STEPS

1. Gather information about each piece of equipment, including at least:
   - Name of equipment
   - Type of equipment
   - Manufacturer's or maker's name
   - Manufacturer's address
   - Contact phone numbers for technical support
   - Contact phone numbers for main office
   - Date purchased
   - Cost of product
   - Original receipt showing where the item was purchased
   - Date warranty begins and ends
   - Addresses to which equipment should be sent if under warranty
   - Number of times the equipment needs service in a year
   - Last date of service
   - Explanation of what was done during last servicing
   - Number assigned by the office manager to identify the equipment

   <u>PURPOSE:</u> To give the medical assistant all the information needed for maintenance and servicing of the equipment.

2. Place all the information about each piece of equipment into a spreadsheet.
   <u>PURPOSE:</u> To create a written record and documentation of all information about each piece of equipment.

3. Make a list of the months of the year. Note which equipment needs servicing in which months.
   <u>PURPOSE:</u> To create a calendar for equipment servicing.

4. Check the spreadsheet monthly to determine which equipment needs servicing that month.

5. Schedule equipment servicing and maintenance during the current month.
   <u>PURPOSE:</u> To establish a specific time the equipment will be available for servicing.

6. Check with co-workers to make sure servicing dates work with all schedules, especially if a piece of equipment will be out of service for any length of time.
   <u>PURPOSE:</u> To prevent scheduling conflicts during times the staff needs the equipment.

7. Schedule servicing appointments.

8. Oversee appointment scheduling to make sure the appointments are kept.

9. Record new information on the document or spreadsheet to reflect new times for servicing and any additional information.
   <u>PURPOSE:</u> To ensure that the most accurate information is on file about every piece of equipment in the office and that all maintenance records are documented.

---

efforts will be unsuccessful. Employees in a physician's office can reduce waste while saving money in the following ways:

- Use solar-powered calculators and battery rechargers
- Use refillable pens, pencils, and tape dispensers
- Use refillable calendars
- Use two-way billing envelopes
- Reuse file folders and binders
- Refurbish office equipment
- Use bulletin boards
- Reuse printer toner and ribbon cartridges
- Retrofit exit sign bulbs
- Convert to high-efficiency fluorescent lighting
- Reuse dishware
- Use reusable forced air filters
- Reuse single-sided paper

Avoiding waste and being conservative with products at the office save money and may result in an increase in employee wages and benefits. Always participate in efforts to preserve products and be open to trying new conservation methods.

LUNCH AND BREAK TIMES

Even though the physician's office is a busy place and often hectic, all staff members should take a morning and afternoon break and a lunch period. Many offices close between noon and 2 PM so that the staff can have lunch and use the time to rest and refocus (Figure 12-7). Often, office managers rotate lunches so that there is always someone at the front desk; some assistants go to lunch during the first hour and some during the second hour. Although many people run errands and try to complete personal tasks during lunch, health-care workers should make every effort actually to use breaks for their intended purpose so that they can serve patients to the best of their ability.

Be respectful of lunch hours and break times by leaving and returning at the appropriate time. Remember to clean any dishes used and put them away and to return food to the refrigerator that belongs there. If food produces a strong odor, close the lunchroom door and use ventilation if it is available in the room. Patients expect a clean, fresh smell in the office, Medical supplies that need to be refrigerated cannot be stored with food. Leftovers should be removed at least once a week. All employees should keep the lunch or break area clean. Always wash your hands or use hand sanitizer after lunch and all breaks and between patients.

SENDING AND RECEIVING E-MAIL

Electronic communications are sent and received frequently throughout the business day. E-mail used in the professional office should have a professional tone, good grammar, and accurate spelling. Never use Internet slang or abbreviations in any professional message. Treat e-mail information as confidential if it relates to a patient. Use the office e-mail system for work-related messages only. Use a separate, personal e-mail address for information that is not business related. The information on the company computer belongs to the company;

FIGURE 12-7 Use lunch periods and breaks to relax. Don't skip lunch or breaks, because this practice can lead to burnout.

it does not belong to the user. If family and friends send jokes or off-color comics, the user can be held responsible for them and ultimately terminated for their content. Refrain from sending and receiving such messages on business computers. A good general rule to follow is to refrain from sending any e-mail at the workplace that supervisors should not read. Remember that the information services staff often can find e-mails and other improper files on computers, even if they have been deleted. Also, some computer systems can be monitored in real time, with every keystroke recorded and every Web site visited logged. Many businesses require employees to sign a statement that explains acceptable use of the Internet, e-mail, and computer systems policies. Employees may be terminated for noncompliance with these policies or improper use of the computer system.

INTERNET RESEARCH

The medical assistant may be asked to research various types of information using the Internet (Procedure 12-6). If a word or phrase is entered into a search engine, various Web sites containing the word or phrase appear on the results screen. Not all articles found on the Internet are reliable; some are completely false, and others are simply one person's or group's opinion. Look for information from sites that can be trusted, such as the American Heart Association or the American Medical Association. Once a good, informative site has been found, read through it carefully, because it may lead to more sites that provide additional information.

TRAVELING FOR BUSINESS PURPOSES

Throughout the course of a **fiscal year**, employees may attend seminars or workshops to gain additional information, learn new techniques or procedures, and obtain continuing education units (CEUs), which may be needed to maintain certification.

PROCEDURE 12-6

Use the Internet to Access Information Related to the Medical Office

GOAL: To use the Internet to research any topic related to the medical office.

EQUIPMENT and SUPPLIES

- Computer
- Topic for research
- Printer

PROCEDURAL STEPS

1. Start the computer, if necessary.
2. Open a Web browser (e.g., Internet Explorer or Firefox).
   <u>PURPOSE:</u> The Web browser allows the user to access a home page, from where a search engine can be activated.
3. Open a search engine (e.g., Yahoo, Google, Dogpile, Alta Vista, WebCrawler).
4. Type the subject of the research in the Search box.

5. Review the results.
   <u>PURPOSE:</u> To make sure the search results contain valuable information on the subject.
6. Determine whether the search results are from a reliable source.
   <u>PURPOSE:</u> To obtain quality, accurate information from a source that can be trusted.
7. Decide what information is pertinent to the research project.
8. Print the information, if desired.
   <u>PURPOSE:</u> To make a hard copy of the information for later reference.
9. Create a file on the computer to store information about the research subject.
   <u>PURPOSE:</u> To allow referencing of the research information without repeating the search.

Seminars and Workshops

Both physicians and office staff members periodically attend seminars or workshops to participate in continuing education events or to learn new skills. Physicians are required to accumulate a certain number of continuing education credits each year, and a medical assistant also may need continuing education credits, depending on his or her type of certification. When planning to attend a seminar, consider not only the cost of the sessions, but also the cost of travel to and from the seminar and of lodgings, gas, and food. Invitations to attend seminars often arrive in the mail, although some arrive by e-mail. Watch for enrollment deadlines and make sure registration is done before the deadline date. Some seminars offer great discounts if registration is completed early.

Scheduling Travel, Hotel Rooms, and Car Rentals

The location of the event often dictates the type of travel arrangements that should be made (Procedure 12-7). Distant locations usually require an airline flight. A travel agent sometimes is used to book flights and hotel rooms, but more and more, companies are booking their own flights using the Internet. Other trips involve car travel. Staff members who travel by car are entitled to reimbursement for mileage expenses; in fact, the company should reimburse any reasonable business expense **incurred**.

Many organizations suggest hotels on the brochures for events. If the physician prefers a certain hotel, reservations should be made at that location if possible. However, do not hesitate to suggest a different hotel if one is closer to the event or offers a better price for the same amenities.

Renting a car may be necessary so that staff members can travel from place to place while attending the seminar. Take care when using a debit card to pay for rentals or deposits. Many establishments place a hold on the estimated total balance due, even if the balance may be paid in cash. This process could place a hold on available funds until the payment actually clears.

Travel Receipts

Travelers should keep all receipts obtained during the trip and turn them in to the office manager. Most business trip expenses are tax deductible. After the traveler returns to the office, a travel expense

---

PROCEDURE 12-7

Make Travel Arrangements

GOAL: *To make travel arrangements for the physician or another staff member.*

EQUIPMENT and SUPPLIES

- Travel plan
- Telephone
- Telephone directory
- Computer

PROCEDURAL STEPS

1. Verify the dates of the planned trip; consider:
   - Desired date and time of departure
   - Desired date and time of return
   - Preferred mode of transportation
   - Number in party
   - Preferred lodging and price range
   - Ticketing method
2. Telephone a trusted travel agency to arrange for transportation and lodging reservations or book the trip using Internet resources.
   PURPOSE: A travel agent might be better suited to answer questions about regulations for international travel. The Internet is an easy way to book trips and compare costs.
3. Arrange for traveler's checks, if desired.
   PURPOSE: Using traveler's checks is better than carrying large amounts of cash; they can be easily replaced if lost or stolen.
4. Print tickets or e-receipts from the computer.
5. Using the travel plan, check the tickets for errors.
   PURPOSE: To prevent errors resulting from misunderstanding and to verify compliance with travel requests.

6. Check to see that hotel and airline reservations have been confirmed and note the confirmation numbers.
7. Prepare an itinerary:
   - Date and time of departure
   - Flight numbers or identifying information for other modes of travel
   - Mode of transportation to hotel (or hotels)
   - Name, address, and telephone number of hotel and confirmation numbers if available
   - Name, address, and telephone number of travel agency
   - Date and time of return
   PURPOSE: The itinerary provides the details of the entire trip at a glance and is a more organized way to keep up with times, dates, confirmation numbers, and other details all in one document.
8. Keep one copy of the itinerary in the office files and e-mail or give one to the office manager and/or physician.
   PURPOSE: To help locate the traveler, if necessary, at every point of the trip.
9. E-mail or give several copies of the itinerary to the traveler.
   PURPOSE: To provide the traveler with extra copies for family or friends.
10. Collect all travel receipts when the traveler returns.
    PURPOSE: To prove all expenses during business travel, for tax purposes.

report should be completed, which details the expenses incurred and any repayment due the employee. Some businesses provide the traveler with **advance** money, which must be reconciled once all receipts have been collected. Remember that some businesses allow a set dollar amount for meals, such as $10 for breakfast, $20 for lunch, and $35 for dinner. This is called a **per diem**, which is an allowance for daily expenses. Account for each expense on the report and attach the receipts, then turn the report in to the designated person. Make a copy for personal records. Taxes should not be taken out of business expense reimbursements.

BASIC SAFETY AND SECURITY IN THE MEDICAL OFFICE

No one knows when the safety and the security individuals enjoy will be jeopardized. The saying "better safe than sorry" has never been truer than today. Never assume that any place of business is immune to crime.

Suspicious Persons

If a suspicious person enters the office, make every effort to keep a distance. Staff members should stay behind the counter or desk so that the person cannot grab or gain control of one of the employees. If you feel a serious concern about a suspicious individual, try to notify another employee early in the conversation. Pick up the telephone and dial the office manager's extension. Plan a code in advance for different emergency situations. For instance, use the phrase, "Norman is here to see you," which relates to Norman Bates of the movie *Psycho*, a frightening character. This alerts the office manager that a potential problem has arisen at the front desk and the police should be called. Even if the situation isn't life-threatening, the police would rather respond to a false alarm than arrive to find a crisis.

Robbery

Although physicians' offices rarely have an excess of cash on hand, thieves may assume that there is money to steal or, more likely, narcotics. Do not argue or fight with such people. Give them what they want; the object is to get them out of the office as quickly as possible. Once they are out, lock the doors and call the police. Do not touch any items the robber touched so that the crime scene is preserved. When such a situation occurs, employees clearly will be under duress; however, they should make every effort to remember basic identifying markers:

- Height
- Weight
- Hair color and length
- Clothing, especially the color
- Race
- Distinctive marks (e.g., scars, tattoos)

Make the observations as subtly as possible; criminals rarely react well to being sized up for later identification. If the criminal refuses to leave the office and the situation escalates, make every effort to find out what the person wants that will prompt him or her to leave. Remain as calm as possible throughout the ordeal. For more safety tips for employees, visit the Evolve site at *evolve.elsevier.com/kinn*.

Office Security

Various valuable items can be found in the medical office. Narcotics are stored in a locked cabinet, and cash and checks are kept in the office. Prescription pads, cash, and checks must be locked up securely and kept out of sight. For these reasons, the office must always be secure. A thief does not know whether the office has narcotics or cash but will assume that they are available. Even if the office has neither, the staff must be prepared for office crime and be proactive in preventing such situations.

Alarm systems often are used to protect the medical office. Either the office is monitored, or an alarm sounds when tripped. Monitored alarms go off when a door or window is opened and the security code is not entered into the unit. When the alarm is tripped, an employee of the alarm company attempts to call the office to determine whether a true emergency exists. If no one answers, the alarm company sends the police to the facility. Occasionally a false alarm sounds, prompting the police to investigate. Many alarm companies charge the business a fee when the alarm is not a valid emergency.

Only a few staff members need to know the alarm code. The office manager and those who open and close the facility need to know the code, as does the physician. The fewer people who know the code, the better. A combination of letters and numbers is best for alarms, rather than a strictly numeric or alphabetic code.

The office manager should make daily bank deposits, putting all the cash and check payments from patients into the physician's checking account. The only cash that should remain in the office is a minimum amount of petty cash. Remember, a person who decides to rob the facility may assume that the physician has an abundance of cash on hand. Unless daily deposits are made, that assumption may be true. Never keep deposits in a purse or car, or put off going to the bank until the next day, or keep deposits at home overnight. Once the medical assistant takes the deposit out of the office to any location other than the bank, he or she is responsible for those funds.

Smoke Alarms and Fire Extinguishers

Smoke alarms should be installed in every physician's office. The two basic types of smoke alarms are photoelectric alarms and ionization alarms. If nuisance alarms continually sound (e.g., from making popcorn in the lounge area), changing the type of alarm may solve the problem. Smoke alarm batteries must be changed twice a year; the best time to do this is when daylight savings time occurs. Although the old batteries may not be dead, new ones will be fresh and certainly will last 6 months.

Fire extinguishers must be readily available and prominently mounted in a visible, convenient place. The extinguishers must be serviced annually by a fire professional certified to perform inspections. Also, staff members should be trained in the use of fire extinguishers; most fire departments offer this training for free or at a nominal charge. A multipurpose ABC fire extinguisher is appropriate for a small business. Staff members can remember the basic use of the fire extinguisher by memorizing the mnemonic device PASS:

P—Pull the pin
A—Aim the hose
S—Squeeze the handle
S—Sweep the nozzle

In addition, remember to "RACE":

R—Rescue
A—Alarm
C—Confine
E—Extinguish

To determine whether a physician's office is safe, answer the following questions:

- Are all exits accessible and unobstructed?
- Are all fire extinguishers operable and properly located?
- Are all emergency lighting units and exit signs operable?
- Are any extension cords or multiplug adaptors in use?
- Does an escape plan exist with two ways out and do employees know how to use it?
- Are fire alarms and the sprinkler system functioning correctly and easily accessible?
- Are all materials stored neatly and orderly without obstructing the sprinkler heads?
- Are all flammable liquids and materials stored away from heat sources?
- Are all plumbing, mechanical, and electrical systems functioning properly?

Fire Exits and Exit Routes

At least two exits in the medical facility must be designated fire exits. These exits must be clearly marked and easily accessible. The exit doors must remain unlocked during business hours so that people can get out in case of a fire or other emergency. For security reasons doors can be locked on the outside, but they must have an exit bar on the inside that allows people to leave by pushing on the exit bar. In case of a fire during office hours, remember to assist patients and visitors to exit the facility.

Employees should have regular drills that allow them to practice evacuating the building. An escape plan must be posted in every room of the facility showing the exit routes from that particular room. Two escape routes from each room should be posted, a primary route and a secondary route. Before leaving through a door, feel it; if it feels warm, exit by another route. If the facility is two stories tall, have ladders ready that attach to a window and unfold to allow escape. Buildings with two or more stories also should have stairwells that can be used in case of fire.

EMERGENCY PREPAREDNESS

According to the Federal Emergency Management Agency (FEMA), an emergency is any unplanned event that can cause death or significant injury to employees, patients, or the public. Emergencies can immediately shut down a business, disrupt operations, cause physical or environmental damage, or threaten a facility's financial standing or public image. All the following events are considered emergencies:

- Fire
- Hazardous materials spill
- Flood
- Hurricane
- Tornado
- Winter storm
- Earthquake
- Communications failure
- Terrorist act or attack
- Bioterrorism
- Civil disturbance
- Explosion

The event does not have to be a large-scale disaster to affect the medical community adversely.

Emergency management is the process of preparing for, **mitigating**, responding to, and recovering from an emergency (Procedure 12-8). Every medical office needs an emergency operations plan (EOP). The objectives of the plan should include:

1. Protecting the safety of patients, visitors, and staff
2. Providing prompt, efficient medical care
3. Establishing a clear chain of command
4. Maintaining and restoring essential services as quickly as possible
5. Protecting clinic property, facilities, and equipment

The first critical step in emergency preparedness planning is to determine what emergencies or disasters might happen in a single medical facility or in a general area. Kaiser Permanente has created a Hazard Vulnerability Assessment (HVA), which can be used by any medical facility to identify the hazards in a particular geographic area (Figure 12-8). After considering all the information gained by reviewing the HVA, outline an EOP that addresses each of the hazards that might affect the physician's office. Once those hazards have been identified, determine the steps that must be taken to enable the facility to respond properly to each hazard. Consider whether additional equipment and supplies must be purchased or whether the office list of community resources is up-to-date and can handle several referrals at once (Procedure 12-9). How would the office staff handle a mass influx of emergency patients, if need be, while still treating the patients scheduled on a particular day? What type of documentation would be necessary when caring for mass emergency patients? What medications are necessary to treat patients in an emergency? The HVA can help the physician and staff answer these and other questions, which will prepare them for many different types of emergencies.

The physician and staff should be ready to offer their services if disaster strikes, especially during a natural disaster such as a hurricane, flood, fire, or other emergency situation. Remember, the medical assistant can only perform duties for which he or she has been trained but can certainly assist a physician and take his or her direction as emergency care is given to a patient.

After the EOP has been written and reviewed, every employee on staff must be trained in how the plan should be followed. Written copies must be easily accessible. Employees should hold emergency drills once a quarter to practice their response. Without practice, the EOP will not work as smoothly as when employees know their roles and responsibilities during emergencies. One person should be designated the facility's safety officer. Make sure the chain of command is clear and all employees know to whom they should report for assignments during activation of the EOP. When additions are made to the EOP, make certain that they are dated so that users will know when the change became effective.

The medical assistant plays an important role in an emergency. All medical assistants must have current training in cardiopulmonary resuscitation (CPR) and first aid, and they must be able to

PROCEDURE 12-8

Develop a Personal (Patient and Employee) Safety Plan

GOAL: *To ensure patient and employee safety during any hazard or emergency situation.*

EQUIPMENT and SUPPLIES

- Hazard assessment for facility
- Office policy manual
- Community resource information
- List of contact information for all employees
- Clerical supplies for emergency action plan

PROCEDURAL STEPS

1. Complete a hazard vulnerability assessment for the facility.
   <u>PURPOSE:</u> To determine any potential hazards that could affect the facility and its patients and employees.

2. Consult the other health facilities in the area, in addition to emergency providers and law enforcement, to determine their roles in hazardous or emergency situations.
   <u>PURPOSE:</u> To determine the facility's role in a city or area-wide emergency and to gain an understanding of the services likely to be available or unavailable.

3. Review the hazard vulnerability assessment with the physician, supervisors, and employees.
   <u>PURPOSE:</u> To discuss the findings from the assessment and determine where action should be taken to plan for various potential safety issues.

4. Determine the method personnel will use to report their readiness for duty during any hazardous or emergency situation.
   <u>PURPOSE:</u> To account for each employee and evaluate additional personnel needs.

5. Develop an emergency operations plan (EOP) for each type of hazard that exists for the facility, based on its location, common weather issues, and disasters that might occur.
   <u>PURPOSE:</u> To be able to act quickly and efficiently if a hazard or disaster occurs.

6. Discuss and determine what hazards might exist both for patients and for employees and then make provisions for patient and employee safety and evacuation.
   <u>PURPOSE:</u> To protect patients and employees as a primary concern and to determine how best to care for both in a hazardous or emergency situation.

7. Determine what, if any, medical care can be given in the various hazards or emergencies that might affect the facility.
   <u>PURPOSE:</u> To be able to access and begin medical care quickly where needed during a hazardous situation or emergency.

8. Establish a clear chain of command for any hazard or emergency situation.
   <u>PURPOSE:</u> To make sure all employees know the chain of command so that the safety plan can be executed quickly and efficiently.

9. Make sure all employees remain within their scope of practice while carrying out the steps in the emergency action plan.
   <u>PURPOSE:</u> To continue to respect the scope of practice during emergency situations.

10. Act as a team and assist other workers as tasks are completed during the emergency. Relieve workers and allow for breaks and rest periods when necessary. Be compassionate toward all patients.
    <u>PURPOSE:</u> To recognize the effects of stress on all persons involved in emergency situations.

11. Continually evaluate personal stress and the need for breaks and rest during emergency situations.
    <u>PURPOSE:</u> To demonstrate self-awareness in responding to emergency situations.

12. Determine how resources will be restored for essential services and develop a list of contacts for every utility and service that affects the facility.
    <u>PURPOSE:</u> To maintain information to help the facility restore essential services (e.g., electricity) as quickly as possible.

13. Determine what areas of the facility might be vulnerable during an emergency and determine how those areas will be protected.
    <u>PURPOSE:</u> To protect vulnerable property and equipment against loss.

14. Conduct quarterly drills to practice initiating the emergency plan.
    <u>PURPOSE:</u> To be ready for hazardous situations and emergencies before the actual event and to make sure that each employee understands his or her role during an emergency.

---

perform the procedures for which they were trained in both capacities. Be willing to help wherever help is needed. Realize that stress compounds medical emergencies and can complicate other medical problems. Be aware of the personal need to step away for a few moments and collect your thoughts or to just take a few moments to breathe in and out slowly. Often only a few minutes away from the situation provides a new surge of energy to take back to the job at hand. The smallest acts are vital in an emergency; even the simple task of taking down names and injuries helps emergency workers process patients faster and get them the care they need. Make it a habit to be a volunteer and put to use the valuable medical skills you have learned in class, during the externship, and on the job.

Before an emergency arises, the office must make contingency plans for information. All healthcare facilities need backup plans for the following:

- Communications
- Emergency power

Medical Center Hazard and Vulnerability Analysis

This document is a sample Hazard Vulnerability Analysis tool. It is not a substitute for a comprehensive emergency preparedness program. Individuals or organizations using this tool are solely responsible for any hazard assessment and compliance with applicable laws and regulations.

INSTRUCTIONS:

Evaluate potential for event and response among the following categories using the hazard specific scale. Assume each event incident occurs at the worst possible time (e.g., during peak patient loads).

Issues to consider for **probability** include, but are not limited to:
1 Known risk
2 Historical data
3 Manufacturer/vendor statistics

Issues to consider for **response** include, but are not limited to:
1 Time to marshal an on-scene response
2 Scope of response capability
3 Historical evaluation of response success

Issues to consider for **human impact** include, but are not limited to:
1 Potential for staff death or injury
2 Potential for patient death or injury

Issues to consider for **property impact** include, but are not limited to:
1 Cost to replace
2 Cost to set up temporary replacement
3 Cost to repair
4 Time to recover

Issues to consider for **business impact** include, but are not limited to:
1 Business interruption
2 Employees unable to report to work
3 Customers unable to reach facility
4 Company in violation of contractual agreements
5 Imposition of fines and penalties or legal costs
6 Interruption of critical supplies
7 Interruption of product distribution
8 Reputation and public image
9 Financial impact/burden

Issues to consider for **preparedness** include, but are not limited to:
1 Status of current plans
2 Frequency of drills
3 Training status
4 Insurance
5 Availability of alternate sources for critical supplies/services

Issues to consider for **internal resources** include, but are not limited to:
1 Types of supplies on hand/will they meet need?
2 Volume of supplies on hand/will they meet need?
3 Staff availability
4 Coordination with MOB's
5 Availability of back-up systems
6 Internal resources ability to withstand disasters/survivability

Issues to consider for **external resources** include, but are not limited to:
1 Types of agreements with community agencies/drills?
2 Coordination with local and state agencies
3 Coordination with proximal health care facilities
4 Coordination with treatment specific facilities
5 Community resources

FIGURE 12-8 Hazard and vulnerability analysis as an emergency preparedness tool for physicians' offices. (Modified from Kaiser Foundation Health Plan, Oakland, Calif.)

- Information systems support
- Electronic medical records
- Human resource information

Also, identify employees with special skills that might be useful in an emergency. For example, those who speak another language could help with patients of other cultures. All personnel at the medical facility need to know their role and where they should report in emergencies. By being prepared in advance, the physician's office team can execute its EOP efficiently and in a timely manner. Identify and learn as much as possible about the EOPs of other local and regional medical facilities and determine how the physician's office can assist if a larger scale emergency occurs. Remember that in a serious regional emergency, community emergency workers such as fire, police, and paramedic personnel focus their efforts where the need is greatest. Be prepared to support their efforts and to contribute to the emergency response.

Evacuating the Health Facility

An evacuation cannot commence until an order has been given by the safety officer. All lights should be on, and the exits must be clear, allowing for the unhindered evacuation of both patients and employees. Attempt the first exit route; if it is impassable, use the second exit route. Evacuate the people nearest the danger first, and then systematically evacuate all other persons, closing doors as they are passed. If traveling through smoke, keep low; do not allow anyone to run in smoke-filled areas. Do not enter doors that feel warm or those that emit smoke when opened slightly. Take everyone to the designated assembly area, leaving one staff member there to ensure that no one returns to the facility for any reason. Keep a count on all persons and notify the safety officer if someone is missing.

A fire in a medical facility can be devastating, not only because of the financial loss, but also because of the chemicals inside, which can make it much more intense. MSDS sheets are critical to the practice, since information about the flammability of each chemical is given. Additionally, the MSDS sheet provides information about other chemicals that can react with each other. Employees should immediately put the evacuation plan into action and get all patients out of the facility. Take first aid supplies only if an emergency kit has been assembled previously and can be reached safely. The patient sign-in sheet and an employee list will help to account for everyone who might have been in the office prior to evacuation. Make certain that each employee knows his or her duties during a fire, or in any emergency, in advance.

WASTE STORAGE AND DESTRUCTION

Two basic types of waste are found in physicians' offices: medical waste and regular waste. Medical waste includes anything that once was part of the human body. Not everything that originates in the human body is considered medical waste; the place where it is encountered makes the distinction. A used Kleenex in the trashcan in the reception area restroom is considered regular waste; however, that same tissue left in an exam room is considered medical waste. Most offices use a trash service to remove regular waste. Removing medical waste is slightly more complicated (Figure 12-9). OSHA requires records to prove that (1) medical waste was collected by the removal waste service, and (2) that the same waste was destroyed by the waste

PROCEDURE 12-9

Maintain a Current List of Community Resources for Emergency Preparedness

GOAL: To help patients find organizations that can assist with their needs during an emergency and to establish a list of community resources that can be used for referral purposes during any type of emergency or for everyday use.

EQUIPMENT and SUPPLIES

- Phone book
- Internet access
- Library access
- Newspapers
- Local volunteer guides
- Computer
- Pen or pencil
- Notepad

PROCEDURAL STEPS

1. Research the emergency resources available locally, regionally, and state-wide using the Internet, phone book, newspapers, and other guides.
   PURPOSE: To become familiar with various agencies that provide services in the local area.
2. Open a document on the computer in either a word processing program or a spreadsheet. Create a list of the resources in the document. Include the following information:
   - Name of agency
   - Purpose or mission of agency
   - Physical address
   - Mailing address, if different
   - Phone numbers
   - Web site address
   - Contact name and e-mail information
   - Hours of operation
   - Services offered or performed
   PURPOSE: To make information readily available before an emergency occurs.
3. Update the information whenever a change is needed.
   PURPOSE: To provide the most accurate information possible and shorten response time during an emergency.
4. Provide referrals to agencies when patients and their friends or families ask for it or when the physician recommends referral.
   PURPOSE: To get patients the help they need.
5. Ask patients for feedback, if possible, after they have used the agency's services.
   PURPOSE: To make sure the agencies are hospitable and provide the expected services.
6. Make note of those referred to the agencies and their experience, if applicable.
   PURPOSE: To provide a record of the referral.
7. When faced with an emergency, remain as calm as possible and keep the focus on the needs of the individuals who require assistance.
   PURPOSE: Emergencies can be extremely stressful for medical personnel, just as they are for patients. To be helpful, the medical assistant must remain calm and stay focused on the task at hand.
8. Step away from emergencies for brief breaks whenever possible.
   PURPOSE: To reduce stress and allow the medical assistant to regain a sharp focus on the tasks at hand.

FIGURE 12-9 OSHA requires proper disposition of medical waste. The office must keep records of waste removal and incineration.

service. The medical waste service usually comes every few days, and the waste is picked up and then destroyed by incineration.

ERGONOMICS

Ergonomics is the applied science concerned with designing and arranging items so that they interact efficiently and safely. Most office injuries are caused by falls, repetitive movements, awkward postures, reaching, bending over, lifting heavy objects, or applying pressure or force (Figure 12-10). Most workplace injuries can be prevented by using proper body mechanics (Procedure 12-10). OSHA developed a four-pronged approach to addressing musculoskeletal disorders in the workplace. The approach includes a combination of industry-specific and task-specific guidelines, outreach, enforcement, and research. Since the implementation of these measures, OSHA has seen significant improvement in these problems. Plenty of information on ergonomics is available online, both through a general search and on the OSHA Web site. Most employers include information about ergonomics in the employee orientation and training and in handbooks.

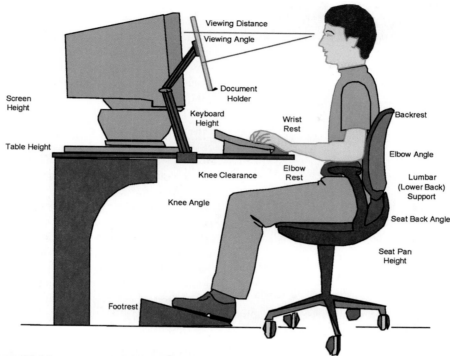

Figure 12-10 Medical assistants should use good body mechanics to prevent repetitive motion injuries. (Modified from Oregon Occupational Safety & Health Division [OR-OSHA]. Available at *www.orosha.org*).

PROCEDURE 12-10

Use Proper Body Mechanics

GOAL: *To prevent workplace injuries through the use of proper body mechanics.*

PROCEDURAL STEPS: LIFTING

1. Take a moment to evaluate the job and determine the best approach to the task.
   <u>PURPOSE:</u> To think before acting, so that proper body mechanics can be used to prevent injuries.
2. Test the weight of the load to lift and determine whether help is needed to move it safely.
   <u>PURPOSE:</u> To avoid lifting weight that is too heavy for one person.
3. Bow forward, then squat at the knees in front of the object.
   <u>PURPOSE:</u> To steady the body and prepare for the lift.
4. Lift the object, moving straight up, and steady the body before beginning to walk.
5. When placing the object, squat down and bend at the knees.
   <u>PURPOSE:</u> To avoid injury during the lifting and placing process.
6. Stand carefully, placing equal weight on both feet.

PROCEDURAL STEPS: COMPUTER USE

1. Sit directly in front of the computer monitor, avoiding a left or right placement, and use scroll bars on the screen to keep the working text in a comfortable position.
   <u>PURPOSE:</u> To eliminate neck twisting.

2. Adjust the monitor to a comfortable height, so that the user's eyes line up 2 to 3 inches below the top of the monitor casing.
   <u>PURPOSE:</u> To avoid neck and shoulder pain.
3. Adjust the viewing distance to approximately an arm's length.
   <u>PURPOSE:</u> At this distance, the user should be able to see the monitor clearly without making any bodily movements.
   <u>NOTE:</u> Remember that the text size can be adjusted in most software programs, which makes it easier to read and edit.
4. Keep the wrists straight and flat as they are placed on the keyboard.
   <u>PURPOSE:</u> To avoid repetitive motion injuries.
5. Keep the upper arms and elbows close to the body while typing and using a mouse.
6. Sit all the way to the back of the chair instead of leaving space between the chair and the body.
   <u>PURPOSE:</u> To prevent back and shoulder strain.
7. Keep the head and neck as straight as possible while working at the computer.
8. Place the feet flat on the floor or on a footrest.
9. Take a short break to stretch after 1 hour of steady work.
   <u>PURPOSE:</u> To allow the body to move and rest.

ERGONOMICS AND PREVENTING WORKPLACE INJURIES

Eye Strain

- Make sure the lighting is as even as possible in the office; check for glaring or flickering lights.
- Place the computer monitor at a comfortable horizontal distance for viewing.
- Reduce glare by using an antiglare filter or a liquid crystal display (LCD) display.
- Use a high-quality computer monitor; text characters should look sharp and clear.
- Set up the monitor to reduce eye strain; the monitor should be placed directly in front of the user, just below the straight ahead gaze.
- Take an eye break every 15 minutes or so to give the eyes a chance to relax and reduce strain.

Back, Neck, and Shoulder Pain and Injuries

- Take frequent breaks and change positions every 20 to 30 minutes.
- Warm up or stretch before starting activities that include repetitive movements or prolonged positions.
- Avoid twisting or bending movements.
- Position equipment directly in front of the user.
- Place the back and shoulders against the backrest of the chair.
- Avoid overstretching or overreaching; keep feet flat on the floor.
- Avoid bending the neck forward for prolonged periods.
- When lifting heavy objects, bend from the hips and not the waist.

Back Pain

- Refrain from twisting when lifting.
- Get close to the object.
- Bend the knees and grasp the object firmly.
- Lift straight up in one fluid movement.
- Hold the object close to the body.
- Move close to where the object is to be placed.
- Bend the knees when lowering the object.
- Avoid bad posture.
- Keep the feet slightly apart.
- Knees should be straight.
- Tuck the chin in slightly.
- Keep the shoulders back.
- Exercise and avoid a sedentary lifestyle.
- Never ignore pain.
- Stop smoking. Nicotine blocks the transport of oxygen and important nutrients to the spine's disks, and the lack of oxygen can impair the disks' ability to repair themselves. If the disks cannot repair themselves, the spine may suffer from degenerative disk disease.

Modified from articles on www.spineuniverse.com.

Guidelines are designed to educate individual workers about the ways ergonomics can affect them and how they can be injured in performing their everyday work duties. OSHA enforces ergonomic standards to ensure that employers take the necessary precautions to prevent ergonomic injuries and protect their employees. Ergonomic injuries must be reported annually on the appropriate OSHA forms.

IDENTIFYING AND SHARING COMMUNITY RESOURCES

Medical assistants must be able to identify community resources so that they can assist patients with needs that are not office-related and possibly not medical. At various times, patients need help with meals, rehabilitation, Medicare issues, exercise groups, and other services. Grocery stores that deliver are a great convenience for older patients. Get to know the people in the community, trade information, and refer patients when they need help with a particular issue. (See the following box, Community Resources, which lists organizations and services in which patients commonly are interested.) A phone directory can be created for a local community resource list (Procedure 12-11).

COMMUNITY RESOURCES

Check with these organizations for services available in the local area:
- Alcoholics Anonymous
- Alzheimer support organizations
- American Cancer Society
- American Heart Association
- American Red Cross
- Child Protective Services
- Civic organizations
- Council on Aging
- Family services
- Homeless organizations
- Hospice services
- Legal Aid societies
- Mental health and mental retardation services
- Public Health Department
- United Way

To expand the knowledge base regarding resources available in the community, get involved in various organizations, especially health industry councils and organizations for medical assistants or other office staff members. Make introductions and be prepared to talk about the services the clinic offers. Ask questions about other facilities. Exchange business cards, if they are available; if so, send a thank you note to the contact and periodically get in touch. Patients appreciate that the office staff can refer them to local resources and help them gather information.

Emergency Phone Numbers

Every medical facility should keep a list of emergency and frequently called numbers close to each telephone in the office. The list

PROCEDURE 12-11

Develop and Maintain a Current List of Community Resources Related to Patients' Healthcare Needs

GOAL: To help patients find organizations that can assist with their needs beyond the physician's office and to establish a list of community resources that can be used for referral purposes.

EQUIPMENT and SUPPLIES

- Phone book
- Internet access
- Library access
- Newspapers
- Local volunteer guides
- Computer
- Pen or pencil
- Notepad

PROCEDURAL STEPS

1. Research the resources available in the local community using the Internet, phone book, newspapers, and other guides.
   PURPOSE: To become familiar with various agencies that provide services in the local area.

2. Open a document on the computer in either a word processing program or a spreadsheet. Create a list of the resources in the document. Include the following information:
   - Name of agency
   - Purpose or mission of agency
   - Physical address
   - Mailing address, if different
   - Phone numbers
   - Web site address
   - Contact name and e-mail information
   - Hours of operation
   - Services offered or performed

   PURPOSE: To make information readily available.

3. Update the information whenever a change is needed.
   UNDERLINE_PURPOSE: To provide the most accurate information possible.

4. Provide referrals to agencies when patients and their friends or families request it or when the physician recommends referral.
   PURPOSE: To get patients the help they need.

5. Ask patients for feedback, if possible, after they have used the agency's services.
   PURPOSE: To make sure the agencies are hospitable and provide the expected services.

6. Make note of those referred to the agencies and their experience, if applicable.
   UNDERLINE_PURPOSE: To provide a record of the referral.

---

should include 911, which summons police and fire departments in most areas of the country. Other numbers on the list might include:

- Local hospitals, including extensions that connect to the emergency department
- Local pharmacies
- Numbers of all physicians associated with the practice
- All employees' phone numbers
- Nonemergency police number
- Numbers of physicians periodically on call

Each office will have different numbers on the emergency phone list. The physician and office manager often provide input about the numbers included. The numbers must be updated periodically. If the list is kept on a computer, a new one can be printed out and distributed each time a phone number changes. Because the list is used in emergencies, it must always be current and accurate.

▌CLOSING THE OFFICE

When the day comes to an end, several duties must be performed before locking the doors and closing the office. First, check to see that all patients have left the facility. Walk through all exam rooms and treatment areas to make sure they are empty. At the same time, straighten the exam rooms so that they are ready for tomorrow's patients.

Other duties include locking file cabinets that contain patients' records, placing laboratory specimens in the outside lockbox for pick up, performing general housekeeping duties, running accounting reports, balancing the day sheet, and preparing the bank deposit. The phones must be turned over to the answering service or to voice mail.

▌CLOSING COMMENTS

Although the tasks discussed in this chapter include duties performed daily, the medical assistant should not be lazy about doing them. When the physician sees that the medical assistant is competent in completing small duties, he or she will consider the person competent at completing more difficult tasks. By consistently proving to be a skilled, dependable worker, the medical assistant will be promoted to higher levels of responsibility.

Always keep in mind that the patient is the primary concern in the physician's office. The medical assistant's efforts should be directed at making patients feel more at ease and encouraging them to follow the treatment plan devised by the physician. In this way, even the most unimportant office duties play a part in the patients' health and well-being.

▌Patient Education

Medical offices often use brochures and printed material to educate their patients. These materials must look professional and reflect a positive image of the physician and the facility. Make sure copied material is clean, without streaks, and attractively presented. If the information is written by an office staff member, make sure correct grammar is used and that several office members proofread the work for errors and proper use of the English language. Good first impressions are important, but every impression in the medical office molds public opinion about professionalism and competence.

Legal and Ethical Issues

Keep copies of all communications leaving the office that relate to patient care. If any information is handwritten, it must be completely legible to the patient. Because the appointment book and telephone messages also are considered a form of written communication, they must be clear and easy to read. Take enough time to write legibly so that no confusion arises if the document is referenced at a later date.

SUMMARY OF SCENARIO

Kayla learned much more during her externship than she had ever thought she would. She saw patients who had few belongings and no health insurance. Her experience helped her realize just how difficult obtaining medical care is without insurance. Kayla is happy that her clinic sees these patients and allows them to pay what they can to obtain medical care. She feels slightly guilty that she has had such an easy life as she listens to her patients' stories and their problems.

Kayla has developed a sense of caring for the people she helps in the clinic. She does not treat the patients disrespectfully; on the contrary, she treats them as individuals who are entitled to dignity. She understands that although she might not connect with all the patients, she can make a difference to the ones who enter the clinic by expressing an emotion she truly feels—compassion.

Elaine allowed Kayla to order many of the supplies she needs, because Kayla is the primary user of those items. This allows Kayla to use the items she has found perform best and with which she is most comfortable. Kayla suggested that the clinic outsource some of their laboratory tests because of the expense of buying the supplies to run the tests. This has allowed the clinic to keep prices lower, a great help to the patients.

Kayla found that most of the patients who come to the clinic need referrals, whether for food, clothing, other medical services, child care, or other needs. She designed a lengthy list of community resources, and she can tell patients where to go to receive help with various problems. The patients appreciate Kayla's willingness to help them. Even though Kayla comes from a completely different background, the patients have accepted her as a medical assistant who truly cares.

SUMMARY OF LEARNING OBJECTIVES

1. **Define, spell, and pronounce the terms listed in the vocabulary.**
   Spelling and pronouncing medical terms correctly bolster the medical assistant's credibility. Knowing the definition of these terms promotes confidence in communication with patients and co-workers.

2. **List five specific actions that must be taken to prepare for patients before the office opens in the morning.**
   The office should be cleaned, whether it is done the evening before or as one of the morning duties. Exam rooms should be checked for supplies and replenished, if necessary. The phone should be taken off of voice mail or the answering service should be called to inform them that the office staff has arrived for the day. Computers should be booted up and medical equipment turned on. Patients' records should be pulled for the patients who have appointments. Two copies of the appointment book should be made; one is placed on the physician's desk, and the other is used to pull the medical records. Individual offices may assign additional duties to the medical assistants who work in the office.

3. **Explain why patient traffic flow is an important consideration in the office design.**
   Patient traffic flow is important, because patients should not have to retrace their steps repeatedly as they move through the clinic. Furniture should be arranged so that getting from one place to another is easy and does not require dodging furniture and décor.

4. **List some of the expenses involved in the operation of a medical practice.**
   Operation of a physician's office involves many types of expenses. Lease or mortgage payments are among the largest expenses. Utilities, payroll, equipment and supplies, professional organization dues, insurance, maintenance, and taxes are examples of expenses that must be worked into the annual budget.

5. **Describe how prices can be compared for medical office supplies.**
   Compare unit prices by determining the cost of each individual item. If a bulk of 8 containers of White Out costs $9. 99, then each individual bottle costs $1. 25. If another company offers the same product at 10 for $12, then the individual cost is $1. 20, which is the better buy of the two. However, the cost to buy the product, meaning the gas to get to the store or the shipping and handling costs, if any, may increase the price. Be aware of these factors and figure all possible costs before placing an order.

6. **Discuss the importance of routine maintenance of office equipment.**
   Office equipment must be periodically and regularly maintained to ensure proper working order and accurate testing results. The failure to perform regular maintenance may not only result in malfunction when the equipment is needed, but may also void warranties.

7. **List several ways to save money and prevent waste in the medical office.**

Make sure trash bags are completely full before taking out the trash. Use refillable print cartridges and solar-powered calculators and adding machines. Print on both sides of the paper when possible. Monitor ordering to determine where budget cuts could be made. Watch carefully for areas where money could be saved or items could be bought in bulk.

8. **Discuss fire safety issues in a healthcare environment.**

Fire prevention is critical in a healthcare facility, because fire and smoke are so dangerous. All healthcare facilities must have a fire safety plan in place, and both a primary and a secondary exit route must be posted in each room in case of fire or other emergency.

9. **Discuss critical elements of an emergency plan for response to a natural disaster or other emergency.**

Emergency management is the process of preparing for, mitigating, responding to, and recovering from an emergency. Every medical office needs an emergency operations plan (EOP). The objectives of the plan should include protection of patients, visitors, and staff; provisions for prompt, efficient medical care; establishment of a clear chain of command; rapid maintenance and restoration of essential services; and protection of clinic property, facilities, and equipment.

10. **Identify emergency preparedness plans in the community.**

Determine the emergency plans that exist in the local community by contacting large health facilities, regional hospitals, and fire/police stations. When establishing the physician's office emergency plan, consider these other facilities and agencies, incorporating them into the physician's plan where applicable.

11. **Discuss potential roles of the medical assistant in emergency preparedness.**

The medical assistant must follow established office policies and procedures during any emergency. All employees should document that they have read the EOP, and this document should be displayed prominently and easily accessed.

12. **Describe the fundamental principles for evacuation of a healthcare setting.**

An evacuation cannot commence until an order has been given by the safety officer. All lights should be on and the exits must be clear, allowing for the unhindered evacuation of both patients and employees. Attempt the first exit route, then use the second if the first route is impassable. Evacuate the people nearest the danger first, and then systematically evacuate all other persons, closing doors as they are passed. If traveling through smoke, keep low; do not allow anyone to run in smoke-filled areas. Do not enter doors that feel warm or those that emit smoke when opened slightly. Take everyone to the designated assembly area, leaving one staff member there to ensure that no one returns to the facility for any reason. Keep a count on all persons and notify the safety officer if someone is missing.

13. **Explain the difference between medical waste and regular waste.**

Medical waste includes any disposed item that was once a part of the human body or used to clean up blood or body fluids. Regular waste is any other trash that does not have to go into a biohazard waste container.

14. **Identify principles of body mechanics and ergonomics.**

OSHA developed a four-pronged approach to addressing musculoskeletal disorders in the workplace. The approach includes a combination of industry-specific and task-specific guidelines, outreach, enforcement, and research. Since the implementation of these measures, OSHA has seen significant improvement in these problems. Plenty of information on ergonomics is available online, and most employers include information about ergonomics in the employee orientation and training and in handbooks.

15. **Explain why keys and alarm codes should be shared with only a few people.**

It is easier to keep track of alarm codes and keys if they are entrusted to only a few people. Also, if fewer people have the codes and keys, there is less chance someone will be able to use them to enter the office and steal equipment and supplies.

CONNECTIONS

Study Guide Connection: Go to the Chapter 12 Study Guide. Read and complete the activities.

Evolve Connection: Go to the Chapter 12 link at *evolve.elsevier.com/kinn* to complete the Chapter Review and Chapter Quiz. Check out the other resources listed for this chapter to make the most of what you have learned from Office Environment and Daily Operations.

13

WRITTEN COMMUNICATIONS AND MAIL PROCESSING

SCENARIO

Brandon Tipps is a medical assistant who works with his father, Dr. Rick Tipps. Brandon has considered continuing his education to become a doctor, but he is not sure whether he would like to be a medical doctor, an osteopathic physician, or a chiropractor. He decided to spend his summer off from college working in his father's family practice so that he can get a closer look at the inner workings of a physician's office.

Brandon has assisted with every procedure in the clinic, including the administrative skills required in the front office. The staff has been impressed with Brandon's ability to do any task, no matter how small, as if it were the most important task in the office. He continuously moves from employee to employee to ask what he can do to help. When the administrative medical assistant working in the front office, Darla Grover, was injured in a car accident and had to be off work for a while, Brandon stepped right in to do her job and quickly learned her duties. His help enabled the office to continue to run smoothly even with one employee absent for several weeks.

Brandon has an excellent command of the English language and types about 60 words per minute. Because he is organized and efficient, he can handle the enormous amount of incoming and outgoing mail with very little assistance from the office manager. He also is able to answer phones and schedule appointments. He speaks clearly and is an expert in customer service. Many of Dr. Tipps' patients have known Brandon since he was a small child, and they enjoy seeing him helping in his father's office. The patients and staff alike will certainly miss him once he returns to college.

While studying this chapter, think about the following questions:

- What types of difficulties can arise when a physician's family member works at the office?
- How do proofreader's marks help the medical assistant save time?
- What types of impressions could be formed by people who receive mail from a physician's office?
- Explain why any written communication discussed in this chapter should be worded in a professional manner.

LEARNING OBJECTIVES

1. Define, spell, and pronounce the terms listed in the vocabulary.
2. Recognize the elements of fundamental writing skills.
3. Explain the various parts of speech.
4. Name some essential references for the medical assistant's library.
5. Discuss applications of electronic technology in effective communication.
6. List the four common sizes of letterhead stationery.
7. Discuss the differences in the four letter styles.
8. Explain the four standard parts of a business letter.
9. Discuss the process of developing and the value of keeping a communications portfolio.
10. Discuss how to open, sort, and annotate incoming mail.
11. Explain how to save money when mailing.
12. Describe how to compose, proofread, and mail a business letter.
13. Organize technical information and summaries.
14. Describe the proper way to send a fax.
15. Explain how to process incoming mail.
16. Explain how to address an envelope according to the U.S. Postal Service's optical character reader guidelines.

VOCABULARY

academic degree A title conferred by a college, university, or professional school upon completion of a program of study.

amiable (a'-me-uh-buhl) Having qualities that make one liked and easy to deal with.

annotating Furnishing with notes that are usually critical or explanatory.

archived To have filed or collected records or documents.

bond A durable, formal paper used for documents.

categorically Placed in a specific division of a system of classification.

clauses Groups of words containing a subject and predicate and functioning as a member of a complex or compound sentence.

collect on delivery (COD) A method of payment used when an article or item is delivered and payment is expected before it is released.

concise (kun-sis') Expressing much in brief form.

condescending Assuming an air of superiority.

continuation pages The second and following pages of a letter.

courier A messenger, especially one on official or diplomatic business; a service that provides delivery and transportation services for documents and/or packages.

curt Marked by rude or peremptory shortness.

disseminate (di-se'-muh-nat) To disperse throughout.

domestic mail Mail sent within the boundaries of the United States and its territories.

editing To prepare for publication or public presentation; to alter, adapt, or refine, especially to bring about conformity to a standard or to suit a particular purpose.

flush Directly abutting or immediately adjacent, as set even with an edge of a type page or column; having no indention.

girth A measure around a body or an item.

grammar The study of the classes of words, their inflections, and their functions and relations in the sentence; a study of what is preferred and what should be avoided in inflection and syntax.

international mail Mail that is sent outside the boundaries of the United States and its territories.

intrinsic (in-trin'-zik) Belonging to the essential nature or constitution of a thing; indwelling, inward.

phrases Groups of words with a specific grammatical function, such as a noun phrase or an adjective phrase.

portfolio A set of pictures, drawings, documents, or photographs either bound in book form or loose in a folder.

ream A quantity of paper weighing 20 lb or consisting of, variously, 480, 500, or 516 sheets.

recipient The receiver of some thing or item.

stationers (sta'-shuh-nerz) Sellers of stationery.

substance number A number based on the weight of a ream of paper containing 500 sheets.

superfluous (suh-puhr'-flu-uhs) Exceeding what is sufficient or necessary.

template Something that establishes or serves as a pattern.

watermark A marking in paper resulting from differences in thickness usually produced by the pressure of a projecting design in the mold or on a processing roll; it is visible when the paper is held up to the light.

Written correspondence and mail processing consume a large part of the day of the administrative medical assistant. When asked what skills they most want in an administrative assistant, many physicians specify the ability to spell accurately and to write a good letter. When a physician delegates the responsibility for composing letters or reports with the potential to reflect positively or negatively on the practice, he or she is expressing confidence in the medical assistant's abilities.

IMPORTANCE OF WRITTEN COMMUNICATIONS

Written communications offer the perfect opportunity for making a good impression on others. However, communications that make such an impression do not just happen; they require thought, preparation, skill, and a positive attitude. Written communications include original letters, memorandums, replies to inquiries, responses to requests for information, telephone messages, e-mail, transcriptions, orders for supplies, instructions for patients, and a variety of other forms. Communications that are courteous to the reader, correct in content, and **concise** without being **curt** are most appreciated. Remember that people may misjudge the "tone" of an e-mail and determine that the sender was rude or hateful, when the sender may have just been very direct and pointed. Communication truly is both

an art and a skill. The ability to communicate effectively is extremely important to the administrative medical assistant who wants to succeed and advance his or her career.

CRITICAL THINKING APPLICATION 13-1

Brandon has just found a small backlog of correspondence that accumulated during the first 3 days Darla was out of the office. A large amount of mail comes to the office each day. How can Brandon manage the daily mail and clear the pile of communications that accumulated over those 3 days?

Reflection on the Physician

Each member of the staff must be conscientious about the documents and materials in the office and those that leave it. An envelope addressed carelessly or a patient information sheet that has been photocopied over and over implies that the office staff is not concerned about the appearance of documents that leave the office. If the staff is careless in this respect, many patients assume the staff is careless with everything, including patient care.

Everything that happens in the medical office reflects on the physician or physicians who practice there. Letters with misspelled

TABLE 13-1 150 Frequently Misspelled or Misused English Words

absence	corroborate	inimitable	persistent	ridiculous
accede	definitely	inoculate	personal	sacrilegious
accessible	description	insistent	personnel	seize
accommodate	desirable	irrelevant	possession	separate
achieve	despair	irresistible	precede	siege
affect	development	irritable	precedent	similar
agglutinate	dilemma	judgment	predictable	sizable
all right	disappear	labeled	predominant	stationary
altogether	disappoint	led	predominate	stationery
analyses (pl.)	disastrous	leisure	prerogative	subpoena
analysis (s.)	discreet	license	prevalent	succeed
analyze	discrete	liquefy	principal	suddenness
anoint	discriminate	maintenance	principle	superintendent
argument	dissatisfaction	maneuver	privilege	supersede
assistant	dissipate	miscellaneous	procedure	surprise
auxiliary	drunkenness	mischievous	proceed	tariff
balloon	ecstasy	misspell	professor	technique
believe	effect	necessary	pronunciation	thorough
benefited	eligible	newsstand	psychiatry	tranquility
brochure	embarrass	noticeable	psychology	transferred
bulletin	exceed	occasion	pursue	truly
category	exhilaration	occurrence	questionnaire	tyrannize
changeable	existence	oscillate	rearrange	unnecessary
clientele	February	paid	recede	until
committee	forty	pamphlet	receive	vacillate
comparative	grammar	panicky	recommend	vacuum
concede	grievous	parallel	referring	vicious
conscientious	height	paralyze	repetition	warrant
conscious	incidentally	pastime	rheumatism	Wednesday
coolly	indispensable	perseverance	rhythmical	weird

words or errors give the reader a negative impression of the physician and the practice itself. Great care must be taken to ensure that each document in the office and sent from the office is well written and grammatically correct. Table 13-1 lists some frequently misspelled and misused words. For a list of more misspelled medical words, visit the Evolve site at *evolve.elsevier.com/kinn*.

WRITING SKILLS AND COMPOSING TIPS

All medical assistants must know the fundamental skills of proper business writing. Most business letters should be less than one page long and carefully organized (Procedure 13-1). This takes practice and preparation. Everyone who writes letters develops a personal style.

The medical assistant should carefully read the letter to be answered. Make note of or underline any questions asked or materials requested. Decide on the answers to the questions and verify the information; this is called **annotating**. Draft a reply, proofread it, and then rewrite for clarity (Procedure 13-2). Keep most sentences short. Put only one idea in each sentence and eliminate **superfluous** words. Be careful about using medical terms in correspondence with patients. Instead, use language the reader can easily understand.

PROCEDURE 13-1

Compose Professional Business Letters

GOAL: *To compose a professional business letter that conveys accurate, helpful information that is easily understood, clearly written, and free of both spelling and grammatical errors.*

EQUIPMENT and SUPPLIES

- Computer
- Word processing software
- Draft paper
- Letterhead
- Printer
- Pen or pencil
- Highlighter
- Envelope
- Correspondence to be answered
- Other pertinent information needed to compose a letter
- Electronic or paper dictionary and thesaurus
- Writer's handbook
- Portfolio and/or templates

PROCEDURAL STEPS

1. Determine the reason for initiating a letter or other type of communication.
   UPURPOSE: To ensure that the goals of the correspondence are fulfilled and that relevant information has been identified and included.
2. Make any necessary notes on the letter or a copy of the letter. A scrap sheet of paper may be used.

3. Prepare a draft of the letter, using good grammar, and save it in the computer.
   UPURPOSE: To put the thoughts on paper for later revision and to make the letter easy to understand.
4. Proofread a printed copy of the letter, using proofreader's marks to make corrections.
   UPURPOSE: To see the document as it will look once printed and to speed the process by using proofreader's marks.
5. Make any necessary corrections.
6. Allow the physician or other interested parties to proofread the letter, if the medical assistant is not the person whose signature will appear at the bottom.
   UPURPOSE: To give the physician an opportunity to correct the letter and add thoughts, if desired.
7. Make any final changes, then print the letter on stationery. Allow the person whose name appears at the bottom to sign the letter.
8. Address the envelope using optical character reader (OCR) guidelines and place the letter and any supporting documents inside (see Procedure 13-5 for OCR guidelines).
9. Mail the letter using the correct postage.
   UPURPOSE: Using incorrect postage or guessing can delay delivery of the document.

PROCEDURE 13-2

Organize Technical Information and Summaries

GOAL: *To compose information accurately and in an organized manner, using strong spelling and grammatical skills, so that it meets the goals of the writer and is usable by the receiver.*

EQUIPMENT and SUPPLIES

- Stationery
- Computer or typewriter
- Correspondence to be answered or notes
- Guide for proofreader's marks

PROCEDURAL STEPS

1. Scan the letter or memo to be answered or the notes about the correspondence to be written and highlight any questions that should be answered or points to be made.
   UPURPOSE: To ensure that the goals of the correspondence are fulfilled and that relevant information has been identified and included.
2. Write the letter or memo using good grammar.
3. Print a draft copy of the letter or memo. Read it carefully and highlight changes to be made or note any additions to be made. Use proofreader's marks.

UPURPOSE: Reading a hard copy of a letter or memo is more conducive to finding errors and grammatical mistakes.
4. Revise the letter or memo using the notes and proofreader's marks.
5. Read the letter or memo once again on the screen. Perform spelling and grammar checks if those tools are available on the computer.
   UPURPOSE: To locate any missed errors or misspelled words.
6. Print a final draft. Read the letter word for word and check once again for errors.
7. Have another person proofread correspondence that is especially important.
   UPURPOSE: Often another person can find missed errors quickly.
8. Complete the final preparations for mailing the letter or distributing the memo. Address the letter using guidelines for optical character reader (OCR) and fast processing at the post office.

Most physicians use a highly professional and formal style in their dictation. The medical assistant responsible for composing correspondence for the office should strive for the same degree of formality the physician uses. It would be inappropriate for the assistant to write in a breezy, informal style when acting as the representative of an employer with a more formal approach. The principal point to remember is that every letter produced in your office should project the image of the physician, regardless of who composes or signs the letter.

Grammar Review

Good **grammar** is essential to the writing of effective, professional business letters. Medical assistants must understand the elements of acceptable grammar and writing skills.

Parts of Speech

Nouns. A noun is a person, place, or thing. Nouns can also be thoughts, ideas, or concepts, such as *freedom* or *courage*. Common nouns name general persons, places, or things (e.g., *teacher* and *city*). Proper nouns are specific (e.g., *Mrs. Adams* and *New York City*).

Pronouns. Pronouns replace nouns and provide the writer with shortcuts so that proper nouns do not have to be repeated constantly. Pronouns include words such as *it, you, he, she, her, his, them, mine, you, yours, its, ours,* and *theirs.*

Verbs. Action verbs are words that express movement, such as *run, drive,* or *type.* Linking verbs express a condition or state of being; they include *is, am, are, was, be,* and *been.* Linking verbs also express the senses, as in *smell, hear, taste, touch, feel,* and *look.*

Adjectives. Adjectives can describe nouns and pronouns, or they may show which one, how many, and what kind of. *A, an,* and *the* are special types of adjectives called *articles.* Examples of adjectives include a *golden* sunset, a *playful* dog, and a *crooked* nose.

Adverbs. Just as adjectives describe nouns, adverbs describe verbs, adjectives, or other adverbs. Adverbs specify when, where, to what extent, or how. Examples include *unusually* warm, *never* won, and *quite* cold.

Prepositions. Connecting words that show a relationship between nouns, pronouns, or other words in a sentence are called *prepositions.* Examples of prepositions include *by, from, of, to, in, at, with, into,* and *on.*

Conjunctions. Conjunctions join words or **phrases**. These helpful words include *and, or, nor,* and *but.*

Interjections. Interjections show strong feeling. They often are followed by an exclamation point and sometimes by a comma. *"Ouch! That really hurt!"* is a sentence that uses an interjection.

Making Sense of Sentences

Sentence structure is important when writing a professional letter or document. Medical assistants should know the basics of good sentence structure so that written documents make sense and represent the medical facility and staff in a positive way.

Types of Sentences. The four basic types of sentences are declarative, interrogatory, imperative, and exclamatory. Declarative sentences make a statement, whereas interrogatory sentences ask a question. Imperative sentences state a command or request. Exclamatory sentences express strong feeling.

Declarative:	*She was the last person here.*
Interrogatory:	*Are we going to the fair today?*
Imperative:	*Clean your room before dinner.*
Exclamatory:	*I am so excited for you!*

Sentence Structure. When written correctly, sentences follow certain patterns. Three very basic patterns are used to construct sentences:

- Subject—predicate
- Subject—object
- Subject—complement

The *subject* of a sentence usually is a noun; it is the word or group of words that acts, or that is acted on or described by the verb. The *predicate* is the part of the sentence that contains the verb; it tells what the subject is doing or experiencing, or what is being done to the subject. The *object* is a noun, pronoun, or group of words functioning as a noun or pronoun that receives the action of the verb. The complement is a word or group of words in the predicate that renames or describes a subject or object in the sentence.

Sentence Errors. Three main sentence errors plague most writers: the sentence fragment, the run-on sentence, and the comma splice.

A sentence fragment is an incomplete thought or a part of a sentence that is punctuated as though it were a complete sentence: *Although the doctor had seen the patient.*

A run-on sentence contains independent **clauses** that do not have a semicolon, a comma, or a conjunction between them. These are also called *run-together* or *fused* sentences: *The office was clean when the staff left on Friday the doors were locked.*

A comma splice is a sentence in which a comma alone joins independent clauses: *The storm grew worse, it began to snow.*

Personal Tools

Competent handling of written communications requires a basic knowledge of composition. A personal reference library that includes an up-to-date standard dictionary, a medical dictionary, a composition handbook, an English language reference manual, and a thesaurus is a tremendous help.

Those who have difficulty with spelling should keep a small, loose-leaf, indexed notebook or card index of troublesome words. If you need to look up the spelling of a word in the dictionary, record the word in the notebook or card index for quick reference. The physician or a medical assistant familiar with the practice might compile a basic list of frequently used medical terms and abbreviations as a reference.

EQUIPMENT AND SUPPLIES

To create a favorable impression with letters, the medical assistant must use good equipment and high-quality supplies. Regardless of the kind of equipment available, the medical assistant is responsible for knowing how to use it to the best advantage and how to keep it in good working condition. If the equipment manual is available, study it and keep it handy for reference when problems occur. Know how to maintain equipment so that the effort invested in composing correspondence has a high-quality appearance.

Equipment

Computers

Computer applications and electronic technology have made all types of communication easy, efficient, and effective. Various letters and documents can be saved and reused time after time by changing the name and the basic information in the text. Computers can add graphics to text, compute figures, and use multimedia in communications, all of which enhance the document's appearance and effectiveness.

Copiers

Maintain the copier so that copies are crisp and clear. The toner cartridge must be replaced or refilled when necessary, and this can be expensive. Multiple copies of documents usually are made on a copier rather than printed from the computer.

Scanners

Occasionally documents are scanned and sent by e-mail. Scanners provide high resolution and can produce images of written text and photos. Scanners often are used to create images so that older documents can be stored.

Printers

Machines that function only as printers are available and quite inexpensive; however, most medical offices can benefit from an all-in-one printer. These machines print, fax, copy, and scan laser-quality documents. Many all-in-one printers available today have advanced features, such as lab-quality photo printing, printing on both sides of the paper, and wireless connectivity.

Supplies

Stationery

Paper quality unquestionably affects the reader's overall impression of the communication. **Stationers** or printing companies are qualified to advise on the selection of paper, which can range from all sulfite (wood pulp) to all cotton fiber (sometimes called *rag*). Letterhead paper usually is **bond** paper that has a cotton fiber content of 25% or higher.

The weight of a type of paper is described by the **substance number**. This number is based on the weight of a **ream** that consists of 500 sheets of 17- × 22-inch paper. The higher the substance number, the heavier the paper. If the ream weighs 24 pounds (lb), the paper is referred to as *Sub 24* or *24-lb weight*. Letterhead stationery and matching envelopes are usually 16-, 20-, or 24-lb weight. This often is abbreviated as 16#, 20#, or 24#.

Sizes and Types of Letterhead Paper. Letterhead paper is available in four basic sizes:

Standard or letter	8½ × 11 inches
Monarch or executive	8½ × 10½ inches
Baronial	5½ × 8½ inches
Legal	8½ × 14 inches

Standard letterhead is used for general business and professional correspondence. Letterhead should be well designed and of a high-quality paper. The letter represents the sender and can help the receiver form an impression of the professionalism of the business.

Bond paper has a felt side and a wire side. When a sheet of letterhead is picked up and held to the light, a design or letters can be read from the printed side. This design, called a **watermark**, is an indication of quality. The side from which the watermark can be read is the felt side of the paper and the side on which printing or typing should be done. The watermark should always read across the page in the same direction as the typing.

CRITICAL THINKING APPLICATION   13-2

Brandon realizes that his father's office does not have a method of logging letters sent by certified mail. This forces the receptionist to dig through a patient's file to determine whether certified mail was actually sent and the notice of delivery received. How can this issue be resolved?

Continuation Pages. The second and continuing pages of a letter are placed on plain bond that matches the letterhead in weight and fiber content; these are called **continuation pages**. The stationery used for continuation pages should exactly match the letterhead but should not have the letterhead printing. Using different paper for the continuation pages is considered unprofessional.

Envelopes. Just as the continuation pages should be the same type of paper as the letterhead stationery, so should the envelopes. Envelopes are available in three basic sizes or types:

- No. 10
- No. 6¾
- Window

No. 10 envelopes are the general business size used for letter and legal stationery. No. 6¾ envelopes and window envelopes often are used for statements.

LETTER STYLES

A business letter usually is arranged in one of three styles: block, modified block or standard, or modified block indented. A fourth style, *simplified*, occasionally is used. The block and modified block styles are most commonly used in the physician's office.

Block Letter Style

When the block letter style is used, all lines start **flush** with the left margin (Figure 13-1). This style is considered the most efficient but is less attractive on the page.

Modified Block Letter Style

In the modified block style, the dateline, complimentary closing, and typed signature all begin at the center. All other lines begin at the left margin (Figure 13-2).

Modified Block Letter Style with Indented Paragraphs

The modified block letter style with indented paragraphs is identical to the block style except that the first line of each paragraph is indented five spaces (Figure 13-3).

Simplified Letter Style

In the simplified letter style, all lines begin flush with the left margin (Figure 13-4). The salutation is replaced with an all-capital subject

Elizabeth Blackwell, M.D.
223 Orange Avenue, N.W.
Cottonwood, UT 84121

January 26, 20—

Mr. Richard Fluege
3678 North Willow Avenue
Palm Beach, FL 33480

Dear Mr. Fluege:

Please send me full particulars on the professional suites you expect to offer for sale or rent in the Medical Arts Professional Annex.

In about six months, I will be ready to open my practice, and I am interested in locating in Florida. My preference is a street-level suite of approximately 2,000 square feet.

After I have had an opportunity to study the information you send me, I will write or telephone you if I have further questions.

Very truly yours,

Elizabeth Blackwell, M.D.

EB:mek

FIGURE 13-1 Block letter style.

MEDICAL ARTS PROFESSIONAL ANNEX
3678 North Willow Avenue
Palm Beach FL 33480

January 29, 20—

Elizabeth Blackwell, M.D.
223 Orange Avenue, N.W.
Cottonwood, UT 84121

Dear Doctor Blackwell:

We have two remaining street-level suites available for occupancy about July 1. These are marked on pages 3 and 4 of the enclosed descriptive brochure. If one of these suites appeals to you, we will be pleased to customize it for your practice.

Please feel free to call me collect at the number on the brochure for further discussion of your needs.

Sincerely yours,

Richard Fluege
Business Manager

RF:ab
Enclosure

FIGURE 13-2 Modified block letter style.

line on the third line below the inside address. The body of the letter begins on the third line below the subject line. The complimentary closing is omitted. An all-capital typed signature is entered on the fifth line below the body of the letter.

Types of Punctuation for Letter Styles

Traditionally the punctuation pattern used is based on the letter style. Normal punctuation is always used in the body of a business letter. In the other parts, either standard or open punctuation is used.

When standard punctuation is used, a colon is placed after the salutation, and a comma is placed after the complimentary closing. This is the punctuation pattern most often used, and it is appropriate with the block or modified block letter styles. When open punctuation is used, no punctuation is used at the end of any line outside the body of the letter unless that line ends with

WILLIAM OSLER, M.D.
1000 South West Street
Park Ridge, NJ 07656

January 26, 20—

Robert Koch, M.D.
398 Main Street
Park Ridge, NJ 07656

Dear Doctor Koch:

Mrs. Elaine Norris

Thank you for referring your patient, Mrs. Elaine Norris, for consultation and care. She was examined in my office today.

FINDINGS: The patient complained of pain in the left lower quadrant and some abdominal tenderness. She had a temperature of 100.2 degrees.

RECOMMENDATIONS: The patient was placed on a soft, low-residue, bland diet, antibiotics, and bed rest for a few days. Upper and lower gastrointestinal x-rays will be performed next week.

TENTATIVE DIAGNOSIS: Diverticulitis of large bowel.

Mrs. Norris has been asked to return here for reevaluation in about ten days.

Sincerely yours,

William Osler, M.D.

WO:gm

FIGURE 13-3 Modified block letter style with indented paragraphs.

ROBERT KOCH, M.D.
398 Main Street
Park Ridge, NJ 07656

January 30, 20—

William Osler, M.D.
1000 South West Street
Park Ridge, NJ 07656

ANNABELLE ANDERSON

You will be pleased to know, Bill, that Mrs. Anderson is progressing nicely. Her wound is healing. Her temperature has returned to normal, and she is beginning to resume her usual activities.

Mrs. Anderson has an appointment to return here for one more visit next week. At that time, I will ask her to return to you for any further care.

ROBERT KOCH, M.D.

RK:hb

FIGURE 13-4 Simplified letter style.

an abbreviation. This pattern is always used with the simplified letter style.

SPACING AND MARGINS

Generally, centering a letter on the page is the most attractive presentation. This is easily done with computer programs, such as Microsoft Word or WordPerfect. Business letters almost always are single spaced. If a letter consists of only a few lines, double-space both the inside address and the message and indent the first line of each paragraph five spaces.

The first typed entry, which is the date on the first page of the letter, usually is placed on the third line below the letterhead or on line 13 if the paper has no letterhead. The typing on continuation pages begins 1 inch from the top.

On standard letterhead, the side margins are usually 1 to 1½ inches on each side. If a letter is very short, making the margins wider creates a better appearance.

A 1-inch margin is the minimum at the bottom of the page. This can be increased if the letter will be carried over to a second page. Never use a second page to type only the complimentary closing and signature. Carry over a minimum of two lines of the body of the letter onto a continuation page. The heading of continuation pages is single spaced.

THE PARTS OF A LETTER

The structure of a letter and its placement on the page have been fairly well standardized into four main parts:
- Heading
- Opening
- Body
- Closing

Heading

The heading includes the letterhead and the dateline. The printed letterhead usually is centered at the top of the page and includes the name of the physician or group and the address. It may include the telephone number and the medical specialty or specialties. In a group or corporate practice, the names of the physicians may also be listed. Occasionally, the heading also includes the name of an office manager.

The dateline consists of the name of the month written in full, followed by the day and year. The date should not be abbreviated, nor should ordinal numbers (e.g., 1st, 2nd, 3rd) be used after the name of the month.

Opening

The opening consists of the inside address, the salutation, and the attention line, if one is used. The inside address has two or more lines, starts flush with the left margin, and contains at least the name of the individual or firm to whom the letter is addressed and the mailing address. When the letter is addressed to an individual, the name is preceded by a courtesy title, such as Dr., Mr., Mrs., Miss, or Ms. When addressing a letter to a physician, omit the courtesy title and type the physician's name, followed by his or her **academic degree**, such as *Rick P. Tipps, MD.* The name also could be written as *Dr. Rick P. Tipps.* However, do not use both a courtesy title and a degree that means the same thing, as in *Dr. Rick P. Tipps, MD.* Although this construction is often seen, even on the sign in front of physicians' offices, writing a doctor's name in this way is incorrect.

CRITICAL THINKING APPLICATION 13-3

Brandon has noticed that some of the correspondence leaving the office is signed incorrectly, with "Dr. Rick P. Tipps, MD" in the typed signature line. This is an uncomfortable situation, because Brandon realizes that the person who is typing the signature this way is the office manager.
- How might he approach her so that the mistake can be corrected?
- Is it wise to approach the office manager, or should Brandon go to his father? Why or why not?

The salutation is the letter writer's introductory greeting to the person being addressed; it is typed flush with the left margin on the second line below the last line of the address and is followed by a colon unless open punctuation is used. The words in the salutation vary, depending on the letter's degree of formality.

The attention line, if used, is placed on the second line below the inside address. If the medical assistant knows the name of the person for whom the letter is intended, that person's name is used in the inside address, and he or she is addressed personally. If the letter is addressed to a company or organization and directed to a division or department, the division or department name is placed on the attention line.

Body

The body of a letter includes the subject line, if one is used, and the message. In medical office correspondence, the subject of a letter frequently is a patient; in that case, the patient's name is used as the subject line or may be noted with the abbreviation "Re:". Because the subject line is considered part of the body of the letter, it is placed on the second line below the salutation. It may start flush with the left margin or at the point of indentation of indented paragraphs, or it may be centered. The word "Subject," followed by a colon, may be used or omitted entirely.

Begin typing the message on the second line below the subject line or on the second line below the salutation if no subject line is used. The first line of each paragraph may be indented five spaces, or it may start flush with the left margin, depending on the letter style chosen.

Closing

The closing includes the complimentary closing, the typed signature, the reference initials, and any special notations.

The complimentary closing is the writer's way of saying good-bye. This closing is placed on the second line below the last line of the body of the letter and is followed by a comma unless open punctuation is used. Only the first word is capitalized. The words used are determined by the degree of formality in the salutation. For example, if the salutation is *Dear Herb,* the closing might be *Cordially, Very truly yours,* or *Sincerely yours,* with consistent punctuation. If the letter is addressed to a business, the complimentary closing most often used is *Sincerely.*

A typed signature is a courtesy to the reader, especially if the name does not appear on the printed letterhead or if the personal signature is difficult or impossible to decipher. The typed signature is placed on the fourth line directly below the complimentary closing.

Reference initials that identify the writer and typist are placed flush with the left margin on the second line below the typed signature. If the writer's name is included on the signature line, the writer's initials need not be included in the reference block unless desired. The writer's initials, if used, should precede the typist's initials and are separated by a colon or diagonal line: GB:mek *(writer:typist)* and GB/mek *(writer/typist).*

Special notations sometimes are needed to indicate that enclosures are included with the letter or that copies of the letter are being distributed to others. If the letter has an enclosure, type the word *Enclosure* or *Enc.* on the first line below the reference initials. If more than one enclosure is involved, specify the number (e.g., *Enclosures 3*) or the name of the actual enclosure (e.g., *map* or *brochure*). If copies are to be sent to others, type this notation in the same manner as the enclosure notation or after it if both notations are needed. The copy notation usually is written as *c:* or *copy to:* followed by the name or names of those to whom a copy will be sent. If the person to whom the letter is addressed is not to know that copies are being distributed to others, use the notation *bc:* for "blind copy" on all copies except the original. Place this notation either in the upper left of the letter at the margin or below the last notation at the lower left margin.

Postscripts

Although a postscript sometimes may be used to express an afterthought, it often is used to emphasize an idea or statement. Begin the postscript on the second line below the last special notation. Follow the style of the letter, indenting the first line if paragraphs were indented in the body of the letter or starting at the margin if indentation was not used in the letter.

Continuation Pages

If the letter requires one or more continuation pages, the heading of the second and subsequent pages must have three items:
- Name of the addressee
- Page number
- Date

The heading should begin on the seventh line from the top of the page. Continuation of the body of the letter begins on the tenth line or the third line below the heading. The three accepted forms for the continuation page heading are:

RICK P. TIPPS, M.D.	Rick P. Tipps, M.D.	Rick P. Tipps, M.D.
Page 2	Page 2	-2-
July 5, 2010	July 5, 2010	July 5, 2010
	Subject: Susan Clemmons	

Signing the Letter

Some physicians prefer to compose and sign all letters that leave their offices. However, most are more than pleased to delegate the responsibility of composing and signing business letters to a competent assistant. Although not all authorities agree on the form to be followed, most recommend that a woman's typed signature include a courtesy title (Miss, Mrs., or Ms.) and that the title not be enclosed in parentheses. The courtesy title need not be included in the handwritten signature.

In general, the physician signs all of the following:
- Letters dealing with medical advice to patients
- Letters to officers or committees of the medical society
- Referral and consultation reports to colleagues
- Medical reports to insurance companies
- Personal letters

The medical assistant usually composes and signs letters concerning the following:
- Routine matters (e.g., arranging or rescheduling appointments)
- Orders for office supplies
- Notification to patients about surgery or hospital arrangements
- Collection of delinquent accounts
- Letters of solicitation

OTHER TYPES OF WRITTEN COMMUNICATION

The physician's office must deal with many types of written communications other than business letters. Remember, every piece of written communication that leaves the office reflects on the office. Make sure to follow the rules of grammar even when sending a simple business e-mail.

Telephone Messages

One of the most common types of written communication in the medical office is the telephone message. Seven items must be recorded when a phone message is taken:
- Name of the person to whom the call is directed
- Name of the person calling
- Caller's daytime or cell phone number (or both)
- Reason for the call
- Action to be taken
- Date and time of the call
- Initials of the person taking the call

E-Mail and Text Messages

E-mail and texting are popular ways to send written communications in today's computer-literate society. E-mail messages can be saved, printed for the patient's chart, and **archived** for storage. E-mails pertinent to the patient's care or a conflict situation should be printed, and a copy should be placed in the patient's medical record. E-mails that show a pattern of cancelled appointments should also be added to the patient's medical record. Any e-mail sent in a professional capacity from the physician's office or by a physician's representative should adhere to proper rules of grammar and should have accurate spelling. People tend to classify e-mail as casual communication, but because it is so frequently used in business, it should be written in the same professional manner as a mailed letter. Use of the proper letter format, including the inside addresses and date, is not necessary. However, the rest of the e-mail should read similarly to a letter. Never send e-mails or texts from the medical office that use abbreviations such as "r" for "are," or "u" for "you." Internet abbreviations of any kind are not acceptable in business communications. Use single spacing and do not use terms or sentences in all-capital letters (e.g., ARE THE TEST RESULTS AVAILABLE?); this implies shouting in e-language.

The medical assistant also should not immediately answer an e-mail that is derogatory, accusatory, or negative in some other way. Print the e-mail and go through it calmly, marking what needs to be addressed. Because attitude often is easily detectable in an e-mail, make sure the response has no hint of negativity. Once a professional response has been crafted, type and send it. In this situation, the best course often is to send a copy to the office manager, either openly or blindly, depending on the situation. This way, the medical assistant includes the supervisor in the conflict and keeps that individual aware of the brewing situation. The office manager can get involved if necessary or just monitor the situation and how the medical assistant handles it.

Realize that e-mails are not guaranteed to be a secure form of communication. Consider the alternatives before sending an e-mail containing privileged or confidential information. Many offices use a disclaimer with their e-mails, such as:

> This e-mail, including attachments, contains information that may be confidential, protected by attorney/client privilege, or exempt from disclosure under applicable law. This e-mail, including attachments, constitutes nonpublic information intended to be conveyed only to the designated recipient(s). If you are not an intended recipient of this communication, please be advised that any disclosure, dissemination, distribution, copying, or other use of this communication is strictly prohibited. If you have received this communication in error, please notify the sender immediately by reply e-mail and destroy all electronic and printed copies of the communication and any attached documents.

Text messages of a personal nature should not be sent during office hours. If the phone belongs to the office, it should never be used for personal texting. The office policy manual should address e-mailing and texting, and those policies should be strictly followed when communicating in this manner with patients or other business entities. Critical or confidential information may be e-mailed according to office policy but should never be sent via text or as an attachment to a text.

Patients must indicate their agreement to receive e-mail and text messages as outlined on the office privacy practices forms, which are usually given to the patients upon their first visit to the office. Some offices send appointment reminders through e-mail or texts, in addition to other types of information. The indications that the patient lists on the privacy practices forms can be changed whenever the patient wishes; if the patient wants to make a change, a new form must be signed. This document will contain information on sending e-mails and texts, so if a patient is willing to receive information from the physician's office via e-mail and text, he or she will indicate that on the privacy practices form. Texts may also be used throughout the business day from employee to employee, but patients should never be given the physician or other employees' cell phone numbers for texting purposes.

Faxed Messages

All faxes should have a cover sheet that states that the information in the fax is confidential and intended only for the person to whom the fax was sent (Procedure 13-3). Use correct grammar in all faxed messages. Use a fax only when absolutely necessary or when the information sent will not breach patient confidentiality. This helps prevent other individuals on the receiving end from reading faxed information. Most businesses use a disclosure statement similar to the example shown for e-mails on all faxed transmissions. Call ahead when faxing information to alert the person who is to receive the fax. This practice helps ensure that the fax goes to the right person, which promotes confidentiality.

Memorandums

Most offices **disseminate** various memorandums throughout the business week (Figure 13-5). These written documents also must be clear, concise, and grammatically correct. Remember that people reading memos, e-mails, faxes, and letters often can detect attitudes in written communications; therefore, make the document sound professional, even if the subject matter is frustrating or difficult.

When sending information to employees, make sure the important points are all included and presented in a way that does not sound **condescending**. Sometimes, it is wise to include a supervisor's initials on memos that might not receive a positive response so that employees realize the writer's supervisor is aware of and supports the information in the memo. Although e-mail is used on a daily basis in the medical office, memos are often necessary to denote policy changes and are often printed and added to the office policy manual. Some physicians and office managers require that employees initial memos to verify that they were read prior to filing them or adding them to policy manuals.

CRITICAL THINKING APPLICATION 13-5

- E-mail is used more and more often to communicate with employees. Brandon has noticed that very few printed memos circulate throughout the office. What are the advantages and disadvantages of communicating through e-mail with employees?
- The office manager has given Brandon information to disseminate to all the employees of the clinic. She did not specify whether to give out the memo by hand or by e-mail, but she did state that the information was very important. Which would be the best method?

EDITING

All documents should go through an **editing** process before mailing or delivery. First proofread the document and then review it for accuracy in grammar and spelling. Table 13-2 shows proofreader's marks. Although these marks usually are used in copyediting, medical assistants who take the time to learn them will be able to process documents that need revision or need an answer twice as fast as those who make lengthy notes. Most software programs have spelling and grammar checks, as well as a dictionary and thesaurus. The programs also have a *Find* feature that allows the user to move through the document quickly and locate certain words or phrases that need to be changed. For instance, if a document uses the phrase "paper-based medical record," using the *Find* feature, each place that the word "paper" occurs can be edited to say "electronic." Editing also allows the user to track changes in a document and to compare the current version to a previous one.

Users can learn advanced features of the software program used in the medical office by taking courses online or at local community colleges. This extra effort can make editing documents go much faster. The more users know about the program, the more efficient they become in its use. Some programs offer free tutorials on their Web site. Also, textbooks available at local libraries or bookstores often include a tutorial CD that corresponds to lessons in the text.

PROCEDURE 13-3

Prepare a Fax for Transmission

GOAL: *To compose and transmit a clearly written, grammatically correct fax that is easily understood, free of spelling and grammatical errors, and sent in a manner that provides for patient confidentiality.*

EQUIPMENT and SUPPLIES

- Stationery
- Computer or typewriter
- Correspondence to be answered or notes
- Guide for proofreader's marks
- Fax machine or all-in-one device

PROCEDURAL STEPS

1. Determine the information and/or documents that need to be included in the fax transmission.
   <u>PURPOSE:</u> To ensure that the goals of the correspondence are fulfilled and that relevant information has been identified and included.

2. Complete a fax cover sheet to include as the first document to be faxed, using acceptable business grammar. Make certain that the fax cover sheet contains a disclosure statement.

3. Print a draft copy of the letter or memo. Read it carefully and highlight changes to be made or note any additions to be made. Use proofreader's marks.
   <u>PURPOSE:</u> Reading a hard copy of a fax is more conducive to finding errors and grammatical mistakes.

4. Revise the fax using the notes and proofreader's marks.

5. Read the fax once again on the screen. Perform spelling and grammar checks if those tools are available on the computer.
   <u>PURPOSE:</u> To locate any missed errors or misspelled words.

6. Prepare a final draft. Read the fax word for word and check once again for errors.

7. Have another person proofread a fax that is especially important.
   <u>PURPOSE:</u> Often another person can find missed errors quickly.

8. Scan any attachments that might need to be sent with the fax into the computer.

9. Make certain that the medical facility confidentiality statement is included on the bottom of the fax cover sheet.
   <u>PURPOSE:</u> To promote patient confidentiality once the fax arrives at its destination.

10. Send the fax.

11. Document that the fax was sent and received if required by office policy.
    <u>PURPOSE:</u> To have proof that the information was sent via fax and proof that the fax was received at its destination, if the fax machine has this capability.

12. When sending critical information via fax, call the receiving office to make certain that the fax was received. Document the person's name who verified that the fax and all attachments were received.
    <u>PURPOSE:</u> To provide documentation that information was sent and received.

13. If a fax is received in error, contact the sender immediately and inform him or her of the mistake. Do not read the fax any further than necessary to determine that it was sent in error.

Take advantage of these learning opportunities and show initiative and a willingness to learn.

DEVELOPING A PORTFOLIO

Letter composition can be made faster and easier by developing a **portfolio** of sample letters to suit the various situations that frequently arise. As the physician approves letters, add them to the office portfolio. For instance, suppose a letter is needed for a patient who wants to change an appointment. Compose a letter that is clear, concise, and courteous and make an extra copy to put in the portfolio. Alternatively, if a computer is used, store the letter on a disk or on the computer's hard drive. Do this each time a new kind of letter is written. Soon you will be able to select a letter from the portfolio and change it slightly to suit the current situation.

Templates also can help the medical assistant build a portfolio. A **template** is a guide or pattern that can be followed to create a new document. Microsoft keeps a wide array of templates on its Web site that can be downloaded to the user's computer and adapted for individual use. New templates are added to the Web site often, and most are available at no cost to the user.

U.S. POSTAL SERVICE

The U.S. Postal Service (USPS) is an independent establishment of the executive branch of the U.S. government. The Postal Service has been transformed from messages sent to neighbors in colonial times to an agency dedicated to providing mail service to every single home and business in the United States. Today, many operations can be done online at *www.usps.com.*

MAIL PROCESSING

Incoming Mail

Each day a great variety of mail comes into the professional office and must be processed (Procedure 13-4). Common items in the daily mail include:

INTEROFFICE MEMORANDUM

TO	All Staff
FROM	Office Manager
DATE	December 1
SUBJECT	Holiday Schedule

Our entire facility will be closed on December 24, December 25, December 31, and January 1. The office will be on reduced staff during the days of December 26, 27, 28, 29, and 30. Assignments will be based on seniority of staff members. Please submit your preferences as soon as possible.

A

MEMO TO:	George Walker
FROM:	Stanley Barr
DATE:	February 8
SUBJECT:	Office rental

We are experiencing unexpectedly rapid growth in our business office and will soon need additional space for our increased number of employees. Do you have a larger facility available in this building? If so, I would like to hear from you regarding the location, square footage, and anticipated rental costs.

B

FIGURE 13-5 Examples of memorandums. Memos are intended to be short, specific, and to the point; memos can be delivered via e-mail if allowed by the office procedure manual.

TABLE 13-2 Proofreader's Marks

Symbol or Margin Notation	Meaning	Example
ℛ or ᖷ or ᕫ	Delete	take it out
⌒	Close up	print as o ne word
ℨ	Delete and close up	cloße up
∧ or ⟩ or ⋏	Insert	insert here (something
#	Insert a space	put onehere
ℯ#	Space evenly	space evenly ∧ where indicated
stet	Let stand	let marked text stand as set
tr	Transpose	change order the
[	Set farther to left	⌞ too far to the right
]	Set farther to right	tool far to the left
¶	Begin a new paragraph	the same is true. ¶In conclusion
ⓢⓟ	Spell out	set ⑤ lbs as five pounds
cap	Set in CAPITALS	set nato as NATO
lc	Set in lowercase	set South as south
ital	Set in *italic*	set oeuvre as *oeuvre*
bf	Set in **boldface**	set important as **important**
⋁	Superscript or superior	ᒾ as in πr²
⋀	Subscript or inferior	₂ as in H₂O
⋏	Comma	red blue, and yellow
⋎	Apostrophe	Calvin's lizard was green.
⊙	Period	The end is near ⊙
; or j/	Semicolon	1, this 2, that
: or ⊙	Colon	is the following :
⌄⌄ or ⌣⌣	Quotation marks	He said, I did it.
( )	Parentheses	Run fast now.

- General correspondence
- Payments for service
- Bills for office purchases
- Insurance claim forms to be completed
- Laboratory reports
- Hospital reports
- Medical society mailings
- Professional journals
- Promotional literature and samples from pharmaceutical houses
- Advertisements
- Interoffice envelopes

In large clinics and medical centers, the mail is opened by specially designated people in a central department to speed up this daily task. In the average medical office, however, a medical assistant, often the receptionist, opens the mail using the ordinary letter-opening method.

Opening the Mail

Before any mail is opened, the physician and medical assistant should establish the procedure to follow for incoming mail; that is, what letters should be opened and what pieces, if any, the physician prefers to open personally. For example, the physician may prefer to open any communications from an attorney or accountant, even if they are not marked *Personal*. If you have any doubt about whether you should open an envelope, do not open the item; forward it to the person to whom it is addressed. Even a simple procedure such as opening the daily mail can be done more efficiently if a good system is followed.

Annotating

Annotating the mail is an additional service the medical assistant can perform. Read through each letter, underline the significant words

---

PROCEDURE 13-4

Receive, Organize, Prioritize, and Transmit Information Expediently

GOAL: To efficiently sort through the mail that arrives daily in the medical office.

EQUIPMENT and SUPPLIES

- Computer
- Draft paper
- Letterhead stationery
- Pen or pencil
- Highlighter
- Staple remover
- Paper clips
- Letter opener
- Stapler
- Transparent tape
- Date stamp

PROCEDURAL STEPS

1. Clear a working space on the desk or countertop.
2. Sort the mail according to importance and urgency:
   - Physician's personal mail
   - Ordinary first-class mail
   - Checks from insurance companies and patients
   - Periodicals and newspapers
   - All other pieces, including drug samples

   PURPOSE: To prioritize the mail for the physician so that the most important issues can be dealt with first.

3. Open the mail neatly and in an organized manner.
4. Stack the envelopes so that they all face in the same direction.
5. Pick up the top one and tap the envelope so that when you open it you will not cut the contents.

   PURPOSE: To avoid damaging the envelope's contents.
6. Open all envelopes along the top edge for easiest removal of contents.
7. Remove the contents of each envelope and hold the envelope to the light to make sure nothing remains inside.
8. Make a note of the postmark when this is important.
9. Discard the envelope after you have checked to see that the message inside has a return address. Some offices make it a policy to attach the envelope to each piece of correspondence until it has received attention.
10. Date-stamp the letter and attach any enclosures.

    PURPOSE: The date stamp identifies when the envelope and its contents were received at the office.
11. If an enclosure notation is present at the bottom of the letter, make sure the enclosure was included. If it is missing, indicate this on the notation by writing the word "No" and circling it.

    PURPOSE: To document that the enclosure or enclosures mentioned in the letter were not found inside the envelope.
12. Organize the mail for transmission to each person, and at the appropriate time, distribute it to the proper individuals.

---

and phrases, and note in the margin any action required; this makes taking action on the mail much easier. If the letter needs no reply, code it for filing at this time. A highlighter that does not photocopy may be used for annotating. When mail refers to previous correspondence, obtain this from the file and attach it or a copy. If the patient's chart is needed when replying to an inquiry, pull the chart and place it with the letter.

The medical office should have a specific place for the opened, annotated mail. After sorting, opening, and annotating the mail, place the items the physician will want to see in the established place, with the most important mail on top. Personal mail, of course, remains unopened. If a piece of personal mail addressed to the employer is opened by mistake, fold and replace it inside the envelope and write *Opened in error* across the outside, followed by the initials of the person who opened it. Use the same procedure with a piece of mail addressed to another office that may have been opened in error. In such cases, reseal the envelope with transparent tape and hand it to the mail carrier.

Responding to the Mail

In some offices the physician and medical assistant go over the mail together. Once the medical assistant has gained confidence, drafting a reply to most inquiries will be easy. Usually, the physician is very pleased to delegate this responsibility, especially for matters that do not relate to patient care.

Letters of referral from other physicians should be noted carefully so that an answer can be sent after the patient has been seen and the physician can give a report. If considerable time may pass before such information can be sent, a courteous gesture is to write a letter to the referring physician advising that a detailed report will follow. Some physicians send printed cards expressing thanks for referrals; others prefer to write thank you letters to professional colleagues.

Mail Requiring Special Handling

Payment Receipts

Payments from patients and insurance companies arrive at the office daily. All payments should be separated and recorded immediately in the day's receipts. A payment received on Monday should be recorded on Monday. Most patients consider their cancelled check a receipt; if the patient requests a receipt, one should be mailed. Otherwise, the receipt may be placed in the patient's chart for delivery on a future office visit.

CRITICAL THINKING APPLICATION   13-6

Brandon notices that Mrs. Attaway, a widow and long-time patient of his father, sent in a check for $125 for a bill. However, her insurance company had already paid $112 toward the bill. Brandon knows that Mrs. Attaway must be very careful with her money and has always paid her bills quickly. The policy of the office is to route the overpayment through the system, but refund checks are cut only once per month. What should Brandon do in this situation?

Insurance Information

Insurance information should be put in a predetermined place for handling by the billers. Documents relating to insurance should be passed to the appropriate person immediately to prevent delays and to comply with time limits that might result in the claim going unpaid.

Drug Samples

Sample drugs and related literature usually are delivered by pharmaceutical representatives, but they occasionally may arrive by mail. Determine from the physician what types of literature and samples should be saved. Most physicians keep pertinent new samples in a locked sample storage area, along with the accompanying literature for immediate reference. Other drug samples are **categorically** stored. Drugs should never be tossed into the trash.

Vacation Mail

When the physician is away from the office, a medical assistant generally is responsible for handling all mail. In this circumstance, all pieces should be examined carefully. The medical assistant then can decide how to handle each piece by asking the following questions:

- Is it important enough to warrant phoning or faxing the physician?
- Should it be forwarded for immediate attention?
- Should I answer it myself or send a brief note to the correspondent, explaining that the physician is out of the office and the reply will be delayed a bit?
- Can this wait for attention until the physician returns or would that give the appearance of negligence?

If the medical assistant is unable to contact the physician or forward important mail, he or she should always answer the sender immediately, explaining the delay and requesting cooperation. Instead of forwarding an original piece of mail and risking possible loss, make a copy for forwarding. Then, if the physician wants the letter answered, notations can be made on the copy and the copy can be returned to the office staff for answering, without defacement of the original letter.

When the physician is traveling from place to place, the envelopes for all communications sent to him or her should be numbered consecutively. This helps the physician to determine easily whether any mail has been lost or delayed. If a record is kept of each piece of mail sent out and its corresponding number, anything that might be lost can be identified and remailed if necessary.

Correspondence that does not require immediate action and that the medical assistant cannot answer until the physician returns should be placed in a special folder marked *Requires Attention;* this folder is placed on top of other accumulated mail. Mail the medical assistant can compose but that requires the physician's approval before mailing should be put into another special folder marked *For Approval.* When the physician returns, these letters can be rapidly checked and signed.

Any letters marked *Personal* may be acknowledged to the return address on the envelope. The brief acknowledgment should state that the physician is out of town for a certain length of time and will attend to the letter immediately on returning. This acknowledgment also should offer help in any way possible in the meantime.

Discard any mail that ordinarily would not be brought to the physician's attention. Some promotional literature falls into this category. Make sure mailings from professional organizations are saved.

In rare cases, the entire facility may be closed for a time. In such cases the post office can be contacted to hold mail until the facility reopens. The postal carrier cannot accept an oral request; a formal written request must be made. Never leave mail unattended to gather outside a mailbox or clutter up a doorway in a hall. Far too much money and mail of a confidential nature are sent to physicians' offices to run the risk of mail theft or destruction.

Outgoing Mail

Preparing outgoing mail is a daily duty and the medical assistant must stay on top of the mail so that it does not become outdated. Three basic envelopes are used for outgoing mail in the physician's office, including the No. 10, No. 6¾, and window envelopes.

Addressing the Envelope

Delivery Addresses. The USPS attempts to have all mail in standard-sized envelopes read, coded, sorted, and canceled automatically at regional sorting stations where mail can be processed at a rate of more than 30,000 letters per hour. The success of automatic sorting depends on the cooperation of mailers in preparing envelopes in a format that can be read by automatic equipment (Procedure 13-5).

The Postal Service provides three special sets of abbreviations: (1) state names; (2) long names of cities, towns, and places; and (3) names of streets and roads and general terms, such as *University* or *Institute.* The information can be obtained from the Postal Service, or a program can be purchased for the computer. When these abbreviations are used, it is possible to limit the last line of any **domestic mail** address to 27 strokes. The next-to-last line in the address block should have a street address or post office box number.

The address block should start no higher than 2¾ inches from the bottom. Leave a bottom margin of at least ⅜ inch and left and right margins of at least 1 inch. Nothing should be written or printed below the address block or to the right of it.

The regulations for addressing envelopes were developed mainly for volume mailers with computerized mailing lists (Figure 13-6). Some exceptions are acceptable to the Postal Service and its scanning equipment. For example, the traditional style of typing an address in lower case with initial capital letters can be read by the optical scanners. Also, if the ZIP code cannot fit on the line with the city and state, it can be placed on the line immediately below. When a suite number is used, most people place it after the delivery address,

PROCEDURE 13-5

Address an Envelope According to Postal Service Optical Character Reader Guidelines

GOAL: *To correctly address business correspondence so that the mail arrives at the post office and is processed by the U.S. Postal Service as efficiently as possible.*

EQUIPMENT and SUPPLIES

- Envelopes
- Computer or typewriter
- Correspondence

PROCEDURAL STEPS

1. Place the envelope in the printer.
2. Enter the word processing program, such as Microsoft Word, and check the *Tools* section for envelopes. The address block should start no higher than 2¾ inches from the bottom. Leave a bottom margin of at least ⅝ inch and left and right margins of at least 1 inch. Nothing should be written or printed below the address block or to the right of it.
   PURPOSE: To ensure correct placement of the address for accurate reading by the optical character reader (OCR).
3. Use dark type on a light background, no script or italics, and capitalize everything in the address.
   PURPOSE: To ensure that the OCR can read the address.
4. Type the address in block format using only approved abbreviations and eliminating all punctuation. If a suite number is to be included, type it above the delivery address on a separate line.
5. Type the city, state, and ZIP code on the last line of the address.
6. No line should have more than 27 total characters, including spaces.
7. Leave a ⅝- × 4¾-inch space blank in the bottom right corner of the envelope.
   PURPOSE: To allow for bar code scanning (BCS).
8. Mail addressed to other countries includes the city and postal code on the third line and the name of the country on a fourth line.

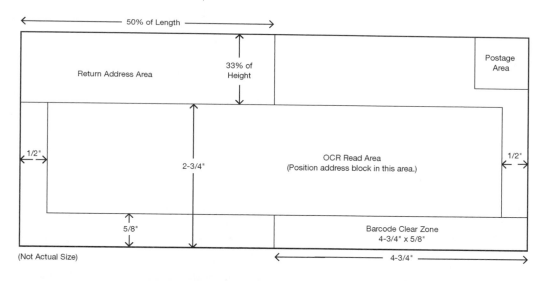

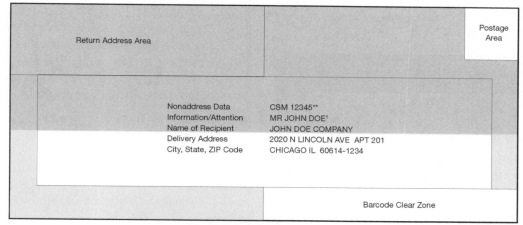

FIGURE 13-6 Addressing envelopes.

which is fine. However, if it does not fit in that space, it should be placed *above* the delivery address, not below it.

Return Addresses. Always place a complete return address on the envelope. If the envelope is mailed without a stamp or if the stamp falls off and the envelope has no return address, it will go to the dead letter office. There, postal employees open the mail to try to identify the sender, but huge delays may make the mail useless on delivery. If an address is found for the sender, the mail is returned in an official envelope with a notice of postage due. If an address is not found for the sender, the mail is destroyed.

Notations. Any notations on the envelope directed to the addressee (e.g., *Personal* or *Confidential*) should be typed and underlined on line 9 or on the third line below the return address, whichever is lower. Align it with the return address on the left edge of the envelope.

Any notations directed to the Postal Service (e.g., special delivery or certified mail), should be typed in all capital letters on the upper right side of the envelope immediately below the stamp area. If an address has an attention line, it should be typed above the organization line or on the line immediately above the street address or post office box number.

Sealing and Stamping Hints

When many envelopes need to go into the mail at one time (e.g., at statement time), the process can be speeded up by sealing several at a time:

- Fan out unsealed envelopes, address side down, in groups of six to 10.
- Draw a damp sponge over the flaps, and starting with the lower piece, turn down the flaps and seal each one.

Do not use too much moisture, because this may cause the glue to spread and several envelopes to stick together. A similar process simplifies stamping several letters at one time if a postage meter is not used. If possible, purchase stamps by the roll. Tear off about ten stamps from the roll. Fanfold the stamps on the perforations so that they separate easily. Fan the envelopes address side up. Starting at one end of the fanned envelopes, attach the stamp at the end of the strip, tear it off, and proceed to the next envelope. Automated sealers and stampers are also available to make this procedure easier and more efficient. Alternative stamping options are available on the Internet. Stamps can be purchased online and printed on the office printer. Personalized stamps are also available that allow the user to upload a photo or drawing to a stamp template and then print the stamps for use on office mail.

BASIC U.S. POSTAL SERVICE DELIVERY ADDRESS GUIDELINES

- Always put the address and the postage on the same side of the mail piece.
- On a letter, the address should be parallel to the longest side.
- Use the following:
  - All capital letters
  - No punctuation
  - At least 10-point type
  - One space between city and state

- Two spaces between state and ZIP code
- Simple type fonts
- Left-justified format
- Black ink on white or light paper
- No reverse type (white printing on a black background)
- If the address appears inside a window, make sure at least ⅛-inch clearance is present around the address. Sometimes parts of the address slip out of view behind the window, and the mail processing machines cannot read the address.
- If address labels are used, make sure no important information is cut off. Also make sure the labels are on straight. Mail processing machines have trouble reading crooked or slanted information.

More Tips

- Always put the attention line on top; never below the city and state or in the bottom corner of your mail piece.
- If the suite or apartment number cannot fit on the same line as the delivery address, put it on the line above the delivery address, not on the line below.
- Words such as "east" and "west" are called directionals, and they are very important. A missing or bad directional can prevent the mail from being delivered correctly.
- Use the free ZIP code lookup and the ZIP+4 code lookup on the Postal Service Web site to find the correct ZIP codes and ZIP+4 codes for the addresses.
- Almost 25% of all mail pieces have something wrong with the address, such as a missing apartment number or a wrong ZIP code. Some of those mail pieces may be delivered despite the incorrect address, but it costs the Postal Service time and money.
- If a first-class mail letter weighs 1 ounce or less and the address is parallel to the shortest side, the piece may be nonmailable or will be charged the nonmachineable surcharge.
- Sometimes it is not important that the mail piece reach a specific customer, just that it reach an address. One way to do this is to use a generic title such as "Postal Customer" or "Occupant" or "Resident," rather than a name, plus the complete address.
- Fancy fonts, such as those used on wedding invitations, do not read well on mail processing equipment. Fancy fonts look great on the envelopes, but they may slow down the mail.
- Use common sense. If you cannot read the address, the automated mail processing equipment cannot read the address, either.
- Some types of paper interfere with the machines that read addresses. The paper on the address side should be white or light in color. No patterns or prominent flecks, please! Also, the envelope shouldn't be too glossy; avoid shiny, coated paper stock.

Modified from the U.S. Postal Service Web site: www.usps.com. Accessed 9/25/12.

Cost-Saving Mailing Procedures

Using ZIP Codes. The ZIP code is a very important part of an address, just as the area code is a very important part of a telephone number. ZIP codes start with the number 0 on the East Coast and gradually become higher, up to number 9, on the West Coast and in Hawaii.

The five-digit ZIP code was introduced in 1961. The first three digits identify a major city or distribution point, and all five digits identify an individual post office, zone of a city, or other delivery unit. The Postal Service later developed the nine-digit ZIP code, consisting of the original five digits followed by a hyphen and four additional digits that further identify the addressee's street location. The ZIP code is transformed electronically into a bar code. The office computer may have this capability. The Postal Code claims that the ZIP+4 code, when used with the automated letter-sorting machinery, can eliminate 20 mail-handling steps and result in considerable savings. These savings are passed on to bulk mailers on mailings of 250 or more pieces that have typed addresses in machine-readable format along with the nine-digit ZIP+4 code.

Presorting. Bulk mailers can get a discount on postage for presorting their mail. A discounted presort rate is charged on each piece that is part of a group of 10 or more pieces sorted to the same five-digit code or a group of 50 or more pieces sorted to ZIP codes with the same first three digits. The USPS uses the words "presorting" and "bulk" interchangeably.

Using Correct Postage. Although mailing fees are still one of our better bargains, the mailing costs for even a small office are a sizable item in the annual budget, and carelessness can cause them to soar. If the facility does not have a postage meter that dispenses postage exactly, make sure you are not putting too many stamps on your outgoing mail. Use an accurate postage scale and remember that only the first ounce requires the base rate; additional ounces are charged at a lower rate. Also remember, the USPS does not deliver mail without postage.

Getting Faster Mail Service

Postage Meters. A postage meter is the most efficient way of stamping the mail in a large business office. It can print postage onto adhesive strips, which are placed on envelopes or packages, or it can print the postage directly onto an envelope. Metered mail does not have to be canceled or postmarked when it reaches the post office. This means that it can move on to its destination more quickly.

CRITICAL THINKING APPLICATION   13-7

- Brandon knows the mail processing would go much faster if the office invested in a postage meter. The office manager states that she has mentioned this to Brandon's father several times, but he did not purchase a meter. How might Brandon approach his father about this issue?
- What should Brandon do before discussing the postage meter with his father?

Mailing Practices. For large mailings, local letters should be separated from out-of-town letters. Letters or packages that need to be rushed should be taken directly to the post office for mailing. Others can be placed in street boxes or the building's mail chute for pickup. Packages should always be taken to a post office and weighed for proper postage. Place a letter tray on the desk or in some other convenient place so that all outgoing mail is kept together until it is ready to leave the office.

Classifications of Mail

Mail is classified according to type, weight, and destination. The ounce (oz) and the pound (lb) are the units of measurement. Domestic mail is sent to a destination within the United States and its territories; **international mail** is sent to a destination outside the United States. Letters to distant points of the globe are in almost all cases sent by air and can be expected to reach their destination within a few days. The rates for international mail are based on increments of ½ to 1 ounce. A table of mailing rates and current postage can be obtained from the post office or found online at *www.usps.com*.

Express Mail. Express mail is available 7 days a week, 365 days a year for items weighing up to 70 lb and measuring 108 inches in combined length and **girth**. This includes delivery on Sundays and holidays to most locations. It is the fastest mail service offered by the USPS. Service features include:

- Noon delivery between major business markets
- Merchandise and document reconstruction insurance
- Express mail shipping containers
- Shipment receipt
- Optional return receipt service
- Optional **collect on delivery (COD)** service
- Waiver of signature option
- Collection boxes
- Optional pickup service
- Automatic insurance up to $100 free of charge

First-Class Mail. First-class mail comprises sealed or unsealed handwritten or typed material, such as letters, postal cards, postcards, and business reply mail. Postage for letters weighing 13 oz or less is based on weight, in 1-oz increments. Envelopes larger than the standard No. 10 business envelope should have the green diamond border to expedite first-class delivery. The minimum quantity to mail at discount prices is 500 mail pieces. First-class mail over 13 oz automatically becomes Priority Mail. At the time of this publishing, first-class stamps cost 46¢. Postage rates usually are adjusted each May, although rates do not necessarily increase for all services annually.

The forever stamp, first issued by the USPS in 2007, is used as first-class postage on envelopes weighing 1 oz or less. Regardless of postal rate increases, and no matter the original purchase price, the forever stamp will always be valid for first-class mail.

Priority Mail. First-class mail weighing more than 13 oz is classified as priority mail, and the postage is calculated on the basis of destination and weight (maximum of 70 lb). Remember these tips about priority mail:

- If using an envelope or box not purchased from the USPS, make sure to mark it *Priority Mail*.
- Priority mail drop shipment is a special way to get mail delivered sooner. Sacks or trays of standard mail are sent to the post office nearest the zip code for delivery and then sent by standard mail.
- Priority mail parcels weighing more than 15 lb and larger than 84 inches in combined length and girth are charged a balloon rate.

Standard Mail. Standard mail consists of advertising, promotional, directory, or editorial material (or any combination of such material). It must be securely bound by permanent fastenings such as staples, spiral binding, glue, or stitching and cannot have the nature of personal correspondence. Loose-leaf binders and similar fastenings are not considered permanent. Mail in this class cannot weigh more than 15 lb.

Media Mail. Media mail is used for books, film, manuscripts, printed music, printed test materials, sound recordings, play scripts, printed educational charts, loose-leaf pages and binders consisting of medical information, videotapes, and computer-recorded media such as CD-ROMs and flash drives. Media mail cannot contain advertising or weigh more than 70 lb.

Business Mail. Businesses may want to consider the benefits of using business mail to acquire new customers and retain current customers and to develop new services for them, in addition to filling orders and completing transactions. Research business mail options on the USPS Web site.

Nonprofit Mail. Nonprofit organizations are eligible for additional mail discounts. Look for more information on the USPS Web site.

Special Services

Insured Mail. Insurance coverage against loss or damage is available for priority mail, first-class mail, and parcel post.

Registered Mail. Mail of all classes, particularly that of unusually high value, can be additionally protected by registering it. The sender may request evidence of its delivery. Registering a piece of mail also helps to trace delivery if necessary.

A registered letter is sent by going to the post office and completing the required forms. All articles to be registered must be thoroughly sealed with USPS tape; cellophane tape is not permitted. On receiving the item, the **recipient** must sign a form acknowledging delivery. A registered letter may be released to the person to whom it is addressed or to his or her agent. For an additional fee, a personal receipt may be requested (Figure 13-7, *A*). This ensures that the letter is released only to the individual to whom it is addressed. Such pieces bear the label *To Addressee Only.* Registered mail can be insured for up to $25,000.

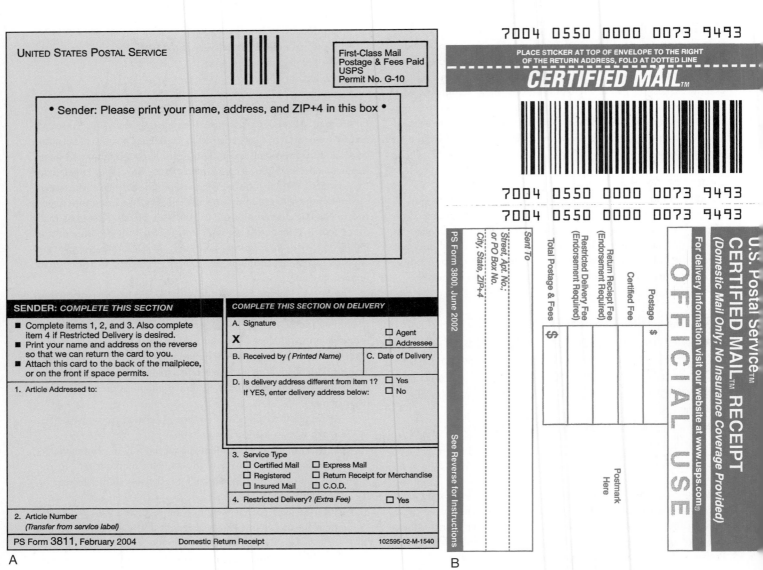

FIGURE 13-7 A, Delivery receipts for certified mail, registered mail, and insured mail. Attach to the back of the article and endorse the front with the phrase *Return Receipt Requested* adjacent to the article number. **B,** Receipt for certified mail. Attach the bottom portion of the receipt to the top of the envelope, just to the right of the return address.

Registered mail is tracked by number from the time of mailing until the time of delivery and is transported separately from other mail under a special lock. In case of loss or damage, the customer may be reimbursed up to certain limits, provided the value of the registered article was declared at the time of mailing and the appropriate fee was paid.

Postal Money Orders. Postal money orders are a convenient way to mail money, especially for a person who does not have a personal checking account. Domestic money orders may be purchased in amounts as high as $1,000.

Special Delivery. Mail of any class that has been marked *Special Delivery* is charged at the special delivery rate. Such pieces may be regular first- or second-class, registered, insured, or COD pieces. The *Special Delivery* designation generally does not speed up the normal travel time between two cities but does ensure immediate delivery of the item when it arrives at the designated post office.

Special Handling. Third- and fourth-class mail sent by special handling receives the fastest service and ground transportation practicable; about the same as for first-class mail. A special handling fee is charged in addition to the required postage and is determined by weight. This fee does not include insurance or special delivery at the destination; special delivery, if desired, is available at an added cost. If a parcel is sent by priority mail, special handling offers no additional advantage, because the mail already is traveling as quickly as possible.

Certified Mail. Any piece of mail without **intrinsic** value and on which postage is paid at the first-class rate will be accepted as certified mail. Items that should be certified include contracts, deeds, mortgages, bank books, checks, passports, insurance policies, money orders, and birth certificates; these are not themselves valuable but would be difficult to duplicate if lost. Certified mail often is used to aid debt collection.

Regular postage in addition to a certified mail fee must be affixed. For an additional fee, a receipt verifying delivery can be requested (see Figure 13-7, *B*). Certified mail can be sent special delivery if the prescribed fees are paid. A record of delivery of certified mail is kept for 2 years at the post office of delivery; however, no record is kept at the post office of origin. Furthermore, this type of mail does not provide insurance coverage unless it is purchased separately. In most offices, the office manager handles any mail that requires a signature for delivery. The liability for delivered items rests with supervisors or is designated by the office policy manual. The medical assistant should keep a supply of certified mail forms and return receipts on hand. These may be obtained at any post office. Full instructions are included on the forms. Fees and postage may be paid using ordinary postage stamps, meter stamps, or permit imprints. Certified mail can be mailed at any post office, station, or branch or can be deposited in mail drops or in street letter boxes if specific instructions are followed.

Certificate of Mailing. If a sender needs proof of mailing but is not especially concerned with proof of receipt of an item, the most economic method is to obtain a certificate of mailing. Obtain this form at the post office and fill in the required information. Attach a stamp for the current fee and hand the form to the postal clerk along with the piece of mail. The clerk will postmark the receipt, initial it, and hand it back as acknowledgment of having received the piece of mail at the post office. This is sometimes used when mailing tax reports or other items that must be postmarked by a certain date.

Private Delivery Services

Not all mail is delivered by the USPS. Actually, the USPS delivers only about 44% of the mail in the United States. Many private services pick up and deliver mail overnight. Among these are FedEx, United Parcel Service, Emery, Airborne Express, and DHL. These services are highly advertised and competitive. All large cities and many smaller communities have centralized points where packages can be dropped off for the service of the sender's choice. Pickup service also is available in many communities. Most moderately large cities have privately owned **courier** services that transfer mail and packages from place to place; the fees for courier services vary widely and often depend on the delivery times and distances that the items must travel.

> ## CRITICAL THINKING APPLICATION 13-8
> The office has always used FedEx for sending packages. However, Brandon wonders whether FedEx offers the best rates. How might he gather this information?
> ■ What should be considered in the choice of a private delivery service?

Handling Special Situations

Forwarding and Obtaining a Changed Address. If a piece of mail is marked *Forwarding Service Requested,* the post office will forward mail to the new address if it is sent within 12 months of the change or if the receiver has left a forwarding order with the post office. At that time, the forwarding order expires unless the receiver requests that it be continued. Between 12 and 18 months, the piece is returned to the sender with the new address noted. After 18 months, mail usually is returned with the reason for nondelivery noted. Forwarding is free when priority or first-class mail is used.

If the mailer wants to know an addressee's new address, this service can be obtained from the post office by placing the words *Address Correction Requested* beneath the return address on the envelope. This can be handwritten, stamped, typed, or printed. The new address is noted on a sticker and returned to the sender; this service has no charge if the item is sent priority or first-class mail. The post office charges a weighted fee for this service for standard mail and packages. If the envelope is marked *Change Service Requested,* the post office disposes of the piece of mail and returns a card to the sender showing the forwarding address of the addressee. If the piece was sent priority or first class, no charge is incurred for the service unless the notification is sent electronically, which involves a small charge.

Recalling Mail. If a letter has been dropped in the mailbox by mistake, do not ask the mail collector to give it to you; he or she is not permitted to do so. However, mail can be recalled by making written application at the post office, together with an envelope addressed identically to the one being recalled. If the letter has already left the local post office, the postmaster, at the sender's expense, can notify the postmaster at the destination post office to return the letter. However, there is no guarantee that the letter will be retrieved.

Returned Mail. If a letter is returned to the sender after an attempt has been made to deliver it, it cannot be mailed again without new postage. It is best simply to prepare a new envelope with the correct address, affix the proper postage, and place it in the mail.

When mail is returned to the medical office, be sure to correct the database, indicating that mail to a certain patient has been returned, so that postage is not wasted sending mail to that address again.

Tracing Lost Mail. Receipts issued by the post office, whether for money orders, registered mail, certified mail, or insured mail, should be retained until receipt of the item has been acknowledged. If no acknowledgment of receipt for such mailing arrives after an adequate interval, notify the post office to trace the letter or package. Regular first-class mail is not easily traced, but the post office makes every attempt to find it. In tracing a lost letter or package, the post office requires that a special form be filled out; information from any original receipt should be written on this form, along with any other identifying information.

USING MAIL MERGE

The *Mail Merge* feature in Microsoft Word is a useful way to create a group of documents that are similar in text but have unique identifying features. For instance, the physician wants to send a letter to all the patients informing them that the office is moving to a new address. However, the physician wants to personalize the letters rather than sending the same one with the greeting, "Dear Patients." *Mail Merge* can help the user create a set of letters, e-mails, and faxes; a set of labels and envelopes; or numbered items, such as tickets or coupons. Many assume that *Mail Merge* is very complicated, but easy-to-follow instructions can be found on the Internet at *www.microsoft.com.*

Closing Comments

Remember that every document sent from the medical office should project a professional image. Use neat handwriting when correspondence is not computer generated. All the office staff must be able to read items written years ago. It is worth the time and effort to brush up on English skills so that writing documents becomes as comfortable as setting an appointment or assisting in a procedure.

Patient Education

Medical offices often use brochures and printed material to educate their patients. It is critical that these materials look professional and reflect a positive image of the physician and the facility. Make sure copied material is clean, has no streaks, and is attractively presented. If the information was written by an office staff member, make sure correct grammar has been used and that several office members proofread the work for errors and proper use of the English language.

Legal and Ethical Issues

Keep copies of all communications leaving the office that relate to patient care. If any information is handwritten, it must be completely legible to the patient. As always, every document containing patient information must be treated as strictly confidential.

SUMMARY OF SCENARIO

Brandon has been a tremendous help to the office staff over the summer months. He has learned about every area of the medical clinic and has mastered several of the office procedures, both clinical and administrative. He has a greater understanding now of the business aspect of the medical office.

His duties as a temporary administrative medical assistant have opened his eyes to the value and importance of administrative personnel. He can easily see that everyone, from the receptionist to the scheduler to the insurance billers, plays a vital role in the smooth operation of the facility.

Toward the end of the summer, the office staff honors Brandon with a going-away party. He announces with a smile that he has decided he wants to become a pediatrician, based on his experience in his father's family practice. He tells the staff he plans to hire them all away from his father! Then, on a serious note, he thanks all the employees for their patience and for their willingness to let him learn from them. Everyone expects Brandon to be a complete success.

Sometimes, working with a member of the physician's family is difficult. Employees should understand that family members often have as much at stake in the success of the practice as the employee. Make every attempt to get along with family members, even if they are less than **amiable**.

Learning proofreader's marks helps the medical assistant work through a document needing revision or simple grammatical corrections much easier and faster. Once learned, the marks are simple to use, and they will be helpful throughout the medical assistant's career.

Every document makes an impression, and that impression can be positive or negative. Each document generated by the medical assistant needs to make a positive impression. Proofread everything, including e-mails and memos, and look for ways the wording can be made more accurate or more fitting to communicate the message. All documents must be professional—each one, each day, every single time—because they reflect on the physician and the medical office.

SUMMARY OF LEARNING OBJECTIVES

1. **Define, spell, and pronounce the terms listed in the vocabulary.**

   Spelling and pronouncing medical terms correctly bolster the medical assistant's credibility. Knowing the definition of these terms promotes confidence in communication with patients and co-workers.

2. **Recognize the elements of fundamental writing skills.**

   The medical assistant must be able to write general business letters, memos, meeting minutes, and various other documents necessary in the physician's office. The needed skills include spelling, grammar, basic sentence structure, and the parts of speech that make up a complete sentence. These fundamental writing skills apply not only to letters, but also to e-mails, reports, and all other documents.

3. **Explain the various parts of speech.**

   The medical assistant should be familiar with the various parts of speech and the way to use them correctly in a sentence. *Nouns* name something, such as a person, place, or thing; *pronouns* are substitutes for nouns. Action *verbs* are words that express movement; linking verbs express a condition, a state of being, or the senses. *Adjectives* usually describe nouns, whereas *adverbs* usually describe verbs. *Prepositions* are connecting words, as are *conjunctions*. *Interjections* show strong feelings and are often followed by an exclamation point.

4. **Name some essential references for the medical assistant's library.**

   Developing a personal tool collection that can assist the medical assistant with written communications in the medical office is very helpful. An up-to-date dictionary, a medical dictionary, a composition handbook, an English language reference manual, and a thesaurus are valuable additions to the references library.

5. **Discuss applications of electronic technology in effective communication**

   Using electronic technology to communicate allows the medical assistant to complete tasks faster and more efficiently. Letters can be saved and used again by simply changing names and pertinent data. A portfolio of commonly used forms and letters can be stored electronically and used when needed.

6. **List the four common sizes of letterhead stationery.**

   Standard (or letter) stationery, which is most commonly used for business purposes, is 8½ × 11 inches. Monarch (or executive) stationery is 8¼ × 10½ inches and is used for informal business correspondence. Baronial stationery is 5½ × 8½ inches, and legal stationery is 8½ × 14 inches.

7. **Discuss the differences in the four letter styles.**

   Block is an efficient but less attractive letter style in which all lines begin flush with the left margin of the paper. Modified block is similar, but some lines begin at the center of the page instead of the left margin. Modified block with indented paragraphs is identical to block style, except for the indention of the paragraphs. Simplified letter style has lines that begin flush at the left margin, but other items, such as the salutation and complimentary closing, are omitted.

8. **Explain the four standard parts of a business letter.**

   The four standard parts of a business letter are (1) the heading, (2) the opening, (3) the body, and (4) the closing. The heading includes the letterhead and dateline, and the opening includes the inside address and any attention or salutation line. The body is the message of the document, and the closing includes the signature, complimentary closing, reference initials, and special notations.

9. **Discuss the process of developing and the value of keeping a communications portfolio.**

   Subsequent letters are much easier to draft if the medical assistant develops a portfolio that contains sample letters and other types of communications. Once a letter has been written, it can be saved on the computer hard drive, a CD, or a flash drive, or it can be printed and placed in a binder for easy viewing. If the letter is kept in a binder, the file name under which it is saved on the computer should be noted on each example so that the document can be easily found again. This is an excellent way to save time in the busy medical office.

10. **Discuss how to open, sort, and annotate incoming mail.**

    Mail is one of the most common types of communication used in the physician's office and is handled according to the preferences of the physician, office manager, or office policy manual specifications The process for responding to and initiating written correspondence is outlined in Procedure 13-4.

11. **Explain how to save money when mailing.**

    The medical assistant should consult the post office when mailing, checking for better rates, and using ZIP codes.

12. **Describe how to compose, proofread, and mail a business letter.**

    Business letters must look professional and have sentences that are grammatically correct. The process for proofreading a business letter or publication for accuracy is outlined in Procedure 13-1.

13. **Organize technical information and summaries.**

    Most written documents include the four standard parts of a basic business letter or memo—the heading, opening, body, and closing. If a list of questions is to be answered, address them in the same order as presented. When responding to any review of information, present it in the order that it was given. Follow office policies and procedures when organizing technical information and/or summaries.

14. **Describe the proper way to send a fax.**

    Transmissions sent by fax must arrive at their destination in a confidential manner. The process for preparing a fax for transmission should be outlined in every office policy and procedure manual. Simply enter the phone number into the machine and place the document in the letter tray. If faxing from the computer, click on the fax icon and enter the number, then designate the document to send. Most fax machines provide a sender's receipt once the document has reached its destination.

15. **Explain how to process incoming mail.**
Most physicians' offices have a process for dealing with mail and other types of information that arrives at the facility. Fax transmissions are covered in Procedure 13-3, while the method for receiving, organizing, prioritizing, and transmitting information, including mail, is outlined in Procedure 13-4.

16. **Explain how to address an envelope according to the U.S. Postal Service's optical character reader guidelines.**
Addresses should be written in such a way that they are quickly and efficiently read by postal service machines. The process for addressing an envelope according to the Postal Service's optical character reader guidelines is outlined in Procedure 13-5.

CONNECTIONS

Study Guide Connection: Go to the Chapter 13 Study Guide. Read and complete the activities.

Evolve Connection: Go to the Chapter 13 link at *evolve.elsevier.com/kinn* to complete the Chapter Review and Chapter Quiz. Check out the other resources listed for this chapter to make the most of what you have learned from Written Communications and Mail Processing.

THE PAPER MEDICAL RECORD

14

SCENARIO

Susan Beezler has just begun her career in the medical assisting profession. She is attending medical assisting school in the morning and works part-time for a family practitioner in the afternoons as a clerical record assistant. Susan is eager to learn about medicine and looks forward to taking on more responsibility at the office.

The practice is growing swiftly and recently added a new physician, Dr. Alex Thomas. Dr. Thomas has enjoyed working with Susan and feels that her energy will be just what his patients need. He has taken a professional interest in Susan and often lets her assist him with patients when her other duties allow.

Susan knows that although she is a beginner in the office, she will gain trust from her supervisors and patients as long as she projects a teachable attitude. The office has not yet converted to an electronic records system, so

Susan uses the information she learned in school about paper medical records. She cheerfully performs filing and even does some transcription for Dr. Thomas. The other staff members are pleased with her willingness to perform the most mundane tasks.

Susan enjoys sharing her experiences with her classmates. She is the only one currently working in the medical field, and the other students ask her lots of questions about the "real world" of medicine. She is very careful not to breach patient confidentiality; she discusses situations only in general, never mentioning any patients' names.

Susan feels a great sense of pride that she is already a member of the healthcare team and able to contribute to the lives of her patients.

While studying this chapter, think about the following questions:

- How can the medical assistant earn the patient's trust so that the person is comfortable revealing the very private information required by a health history?
- Why is the simple task of filing such a critical duty in the physician's office?

- How can filing, often considered boring, be made more enjoyable?
- Why is it important that the medical record be legible?

LEARNING OBJECTIVES

1. Define, spell, and pronounce the terms listed in the vocabulary.
2. State several reasons accurate medical records are important.
3. Explain who owns the medical record.
4. Explain how to document appropriately and accurately.
5. Explain the difference between a traditional medical record and a problem-oriented medical record.
6. Explain how to establish and organize a patient's medical record.
7. Identify systems for organizing medical records.

8. Differentiate between subjective and objective information.
9. Describe various types of information kept in the medical record.
10. Explain how to make additions to a medical record.
11. Discuss correction of an entry in the patient's record.
12. Identify both equipment and supplies needed to file medical records.
13. Discuss filing procedures.
14. Describe indexing rules.
15. Discuss the pros and cons of various filing methods.
16. Identify types of records common to the healthcare setting.

VOCABULARY

alphabetic filing Any system that arranges names or topics according to the sequence of the letters in the alphabet.

alphanumeric Of or relating to systems made up of combinations of letters and numbers.

audit A formal examination of an organization's or individual's accounts or financial situation; a methodic examination and review.

augment To make greater, more numerous, larger, or more intense.

caption A heading, title, or subtitle under which records are filed.

chronologic order Of, relating to, or arranged in or according to the order of time.

continuity of care Continuation of care smoothly from one provider to another, so that the patient receives the most benefit and no interruption in care.

dictation (dik-tay'-shun) The act or manner of uttering words to be transcribed.

direct filing system A filing system in which materials can be located without consulting an intermediary source of reference.

gleaned Gathered bit by bit (e.g., information or material); picked over in search of relevant material.

indirect filing system A filing system in which an intermediary source of reference (e.g., a card file) must be consulted to locate specific files.

microfilm A film with a photographic record of printed or other graphic matter on a reduced scale.

numeric filing The filing of records, correspondence, or cards by number.

objective information Information gathered by watching or observing a patient.

obliteration (uh-bli-tuh-ra'-shun) The act of making undecipherable or imperceptible by obscuring or wearing away.

OUTfolder A folder used to provide space for the temporary filing of materials.

OUTguide A heavy guide used to replace a folder temporarily removed from the filing space.

power of attorney A legal instrument authorizing a person to act as the attorney or agent of the grantor.

pressboard A strong, highly glazed composition board resembling vulcanized fiber; heavy card stock.

procrastination (pruh-kras-tuh-na'-shun) Intentional postponement of doing something that should be done.

provisional diagnosis A temporary diagnosis made before all test results have been received.

purging The process of moving active files to inactive status.

quality control An aggregate of activities designed to ensure adequate quality, especially in manufactured products or in the service industries.

requisites (re'-kwuh-zuhts) Entities considered essential or necessary.

retention schedule A method or plan for retaining or keeping medical records and for their movement from active, to inactive, to closed filing.

reverse chronologic order Arranged in order so that the most recent item is on top and older items are filed further back.

shingling A method of filing in which a report is laid on top of the older report, resembling the shingles of a roof.

subjective information Information gained by questioning the patient or taking it from a form.

tickler file A chronologic file used as a reminder that something must be dealt with on a certain date.

transcription A written copy of something made either in longhand or by machine.

vested Granted or endowed with a particular authority, right, or property; to have a special interest in.

A medical records management system is only as good as the ease of retrieval of the data in the files. A fast pace is the norm in the medical office; therefore, staff members must be able to find patients' medical records quickly, and the records must be functional so that the needed information can be obtained easily.

Few things are more frustrating to the patient than being told, "We cannot locate your records." Patients have every right to question the competence of the medical care they are receiving if the office has problems simply finding a chart. Organization and adherence to set routines help ensure that medical records are accessible when needed.

In today's medical facilities, records are either paper based or computer based. The versatile medical assistant is knowledgeable about both systems and able to perform well with either.

THE IMPORTANCE OF ACCURATE MEDICAL RECORDS

Medical records are kept for four basic reasons. First, the medical record helps the physician provide the best possible medical care for the patient. The physician examines the patient and enters the findings in the patient's medical record. These findings are clues to the diagnosis. The physician may order many types of tests to confirm or **augment** the clinical findings. As the reports of these tests come in, the findings fall into place, much like the pieces of a jigsaw puzzle. Then, with the confirmation data to support the diagnosis, the physician can prescribe treatment and form an opinion about the patient's chances of recovery, assured that every resource has been used to arrive at a correct judgment. The medical record provides a complete history of all the care given to the patient.

The medical record also provides critical information for others. By reading through the record and discovering the methods used to treat the patient, healthcare professionals can provide **continuity of care**. Each person knows what the patient has experienced and can provide continuous care, even from one facility to another. For example, when a patient is transferred from a hospital to a skilled nursing facility, the information from the patient's hospital record helps the nursing facility staff to better care for the patient. When patients move from place to place or caregivers change, copies of the pertinent information should move with the patient to provide this continuity of care.

Second, medical records are kept as legal protection for those who provided care to the patient. A documented medical record is excellent proof that certain procedures were performed or that medical advice was given. An accurate record is the foundation for a legal defense in cases of medical professional liability. This is one reason writing legibly in the record and documenting exactly what happened to the patient, in addition to the provider's response, are critical. Remember: If it isn't charted, it didn't happen (Procedure 14-1).

Third, medical records provide statistical information that is helpful to researchers. The patient's record provides information about medications taken and the reactions to them. Medical records may be used to evaluate the effectiveness of certain kinds of treatment or to determine the incidence of a given disease. Physicians often take part in drug studies that track adverse reactions and side effects. The effects of various treatments and procedures also can be tracked and statistics **gleaned** from the information gathered from patients' records. Correlation of such statistical information may result in a new outlook on some phases of medicine and can lead to revised techniques and treatments. The statistical data from medical records also are valuable in the preparation of scientific papers, books, and lectures.

Fourth, medical records are vital for financial reimbursement. The information in the medical record supports claims for reimbursement and is required by most third-party payers.

OWNERSHIP OF THE MEDICAL RECORD

Who owns the medical record? Patients often assume that because the information in the medical record is about them, ownership of the record rightfully is theirs. However, the owner of the physical medical record is the physician or medical facility, often called the "maker," that initiated and developed the record. The patient has the right of access to the information within the record but does not own the physical chart or other documents pertaining to the record. The patient has a **vested** interest and therefore has the right to demand confidentiality of all information placed in the chart.

The actual medical record should never leave the medical facility where it originated. Even the physician should refrain from taking the record from the office to the hospital or nursing facility. If information from the record is needed, copies can be placed in a file, and progress notes can be written on site and inserted into the original record later. Patients' records should be kept in a locked room or locked filing cabinets when the office is closed.

Written medical records must be legible. Each record should be written as if the physician and staff expect it to eventually be involved in a lawsuit; therefore, every word must be legible to an average reader years after written. The record can help the physician prove that he or she treated a patient in a competent manner, or it can prove that the patient was not given competent care. Every person

---

PROCEDURE 14-1

Document Patient Care Accurately

GOAL: *To document appropriately and accurately on all medical records and other office paperwork that concerns the patient.*

EQUIPMENT and SUPPLIES

- Any medical document
- Clerical supplies
- Computer
- Office policy and procedures manual
- Progress notes

PROCEDURAL STEPS

1. Determine the information that needs to be added to the patient's medical record, appointment book, telephone message, or other office paperwork that concerns the patient.
   <u>PURPOSE:</u> To place pertinent, accurate information into the document or medical record.

2. Make sure the information is factual, timely, and accurate.
   <u>PURPOSE:</u> To ensure that the information is usable.

3. Write or type the information into the document.

4. Reread the information to make sure it is legible and makes grammatical sense.
   <u>PURPOSE:</u> To make certain that anyone who needs to access the information will be able to read it, even after several years.

5. Date and sign the entry, if necessary.
   <u>PURPOSE:</u> To authenticate the entry.

6. Make sure the entry meets any local, state, or federal guidelines that may apply to the information in the document.
   <u>PURPOSE:</u> To comply with local, state, and federal rules and regulations.

7. Make sure the entry is written so as to comply with office policies and procedures.
   <u>PURPOSE:</u> To meet the requirements of the facility's own office policy and procedures manual.

8. If the entry needs to be corrected, draw one line through it and make the new entry above it or directly after the information that needs to be corrected.
   <u>PURPOSE:</u> To correct the document according to the office policy and procedures guidelines.

9. Date and initial the corrected entry.
   <u>PURPOSE:</u> To authenticate the correction.

10. Make sure the correction has not obliterated any part of the medical record or documentation that affects the patient.
    <u>PURPOSE:</u> To comply with the rule that no obliteration is acceptable in any part of the medical record.

11. File the medical record in its proper place according to the facility's filing system.
    <u>PURPOSE:</u> To ensure that the medical record can be easily retrieved.

on staff at the physician's office is responsible for writing legibly in every medical record.

CREATING AN EFFICIENT MEDICAL RECORDS MANAGEMENT SYSTEM

The medical records management system should provide an easy method of retrieving information. The files should be organized in an orderly fashion The information also must be accurate, and corrections should be made and documented properly. The wording in the record should be easily understood and grammatically correct. An efficient method of adding documents to the chart must be established so that the physician or other provider always has the most up-to-date information.

Above all, the medical records management system must work for the individual facility.

Types of Records

The two major types of patient records are the paper medical record and the electronic medical record. As computer technology advances, the paper medical record seems more and more inefficient. It is difficult to use a paper-based record for multiple purposes. In most cases, only one person at a time can use the paper record. Misfiled information is common, and the entire record also can be misfiled. Data cannot be accessed easily for research and **quality control**, and in facilities with multiple departments, the information is difficult to share. The paper-based record is good evidence of patient care, but it is not nearly as useful in other capacities.

The electronic medical record (also called the *electronic health record*) is much more efficient than the paper record. Chapter 15 covers the electronic medical record in more detail.

ORGANIZATION OF THE MEDICAL RECORD

Source-Oriented Records

The traditional patient record is source oriented; that is, observations and data are cataloged according to their source—physician, laboratory, radiology department, nurse, technician—with no recording of a logical relationship among them. Forms and progress notes are filed in **reverse chronologic order** (most recent on top) and in separate sections of the record according to the type of form or service rendered (e.g., all laboratory reports together, all x-ray reports together, and so on). Some files are placed in **chronologic order**; that is, the items inside are filed according to the order of time. However, most patient files are in reverse chronologic order so that the physician and staff members do not have to search to the bottom of the chart to find a recent lab report on a test.

Problem-Oriented Medical Records

The problem-oriented medical record (POMR) is a departure from the traditional system of keeping patient records. It sometimes is referred to as the Weed system, because it was originated by Dr. Lawrence L. Weed, a professor of medicine at the University of Vermont College of Medicine.

The POMR is a record of clinical practice that divides medical action into four bases:

- The *database,* which includes the chief complaint, present illness, patient profile, review of systems, physical examination, and laboratory reports.
- The *problem list,* a numbered, titled list of every problem the patient has that requires management or workup. This may include social and demographic troubles in addition to strictly medical or surgical ones.
- The *treatment plan* includes management, additional workups needed, and therapy. Each plan is titled and numbered with respect to the problem.
- The *progress notes* include structured notes that are numbered to correspond with each problem number.

Several companies have developed file folders for organizing patient data according to the POMR (Figure 14-1). The problem list is entered on the divider cover for laboratory reports. Special sections are provided for current major and chronic problems and for inactive major or chronic problems. The divider cover for progress notes is a chart for listing medications and other therapeutic modalities. Progress notes follow the SOAP approach. SOAP is an acronym for the following:

- *S*ubjective impressions
- *O*bjective clinical evidence
- *A*ssessment or diagnosis
- *P*lans for further studies, treatment, or management

Some medical offices also use an *E* in the record to represent evaluation; others include *E* for education and *R* for response. The education notation documents that the patient was educated about his or her condition or given a patient information sheet. The response section is used to record an assessment of the patient's understanding of and possible compliance with the treatment plan.

The POMR has the advantage of imposing order and organization on the information added to a patient's medical record. The records are more easily reviewed, and the likelihood of overlooking a problem is greatly reduced. The SOAP method forces a rational approach to the patient's problems and assists the formulation of a logical, orderly plan of patient care (Figure 14-2). The POMR has continued to grow in popularity since its introduction in the 1970s. It is especially advantageous in clinics, group practices, and hospitals,

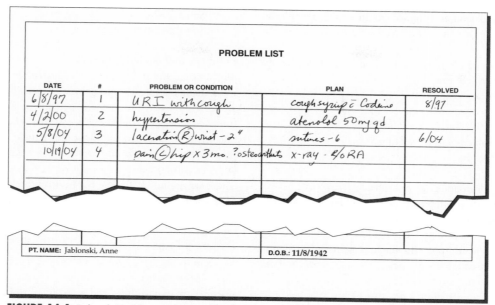

PROBLEM LIST

DATE	#	PROBLEM OR CONDITION	PLAN	RESOLVED
6/8/97	1	URI with cough	cough syrup c̄ Codeine	8/97
4/2/00	2	hypertension	atenolol 50mg qd	
5/8/04	3	laceration ®️ wrist - 2"	sutures - 6	6/04
10/19/04	4	pain Ⓛ hip X 3 mo. ?osteoarthritis	x-ray - r/o RA	

PT. NAME: Jablonski, Anne   D.O.B.: 11/8/1942

FIGURE 14-1 A chart designed for a problem-oriented medical record (POMR). Some charts are specifically adapted to the POMR. (Courtesy Bibbero Systems, Petaluma, Calif.)

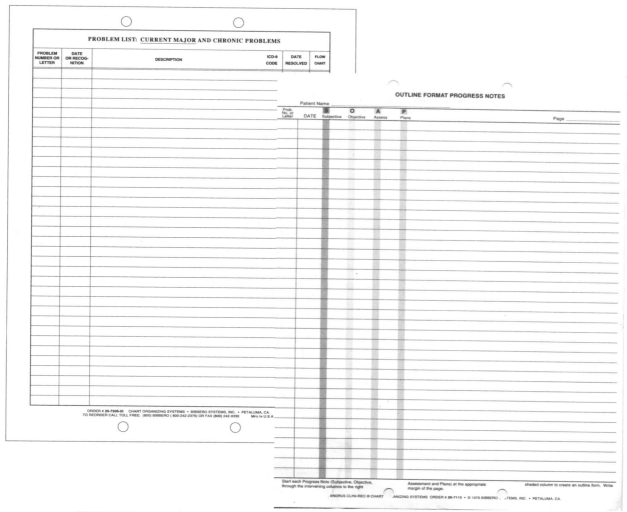

FIGURE 14-2 SOAP progress notes. The SOAP method keeps information organized and in a logical sequence. An actual progress note would include the physician's signature or initials after this entry. (Courtesy Bibbero Systems, Petaluma, Calif.)

where more than one person must be able to find essential information in the chart. Note that the SOAP method often is used in the POMR.

Some facilities use the CHEDDAR method in medical records. CHEDDAR signifies the following:

C—Chief complaint

H—History

E—Examination

D—Details (of problem and complaints)

D—Drugs and dosages

A—Assessment

R—Return visit information, if applicable

The physician decides which recording method he or she prefers, and the medical assistant must conform to that standard. The office policy and procedures manual provides specific instruction, if the standard used is different from one the medical assistant has used in the past. Never hesitate to ask the physician if you are unclear about any part of the documentation standard.

CRITICAL THINKING APPLICATION   14-3

Dr. Thomas wants Susan to thoroughly understand the SOAP method of charting, but she is more comfortable with the CHEDDAR method.

■ How does the SOAP method differ from the CHEDDAR method?

■ What are the pros and cons of each method?

■ How can Susan adjust quickly to the new standard?

CONTENTS OF THE COMPLETE CASE HISTORY

The medical case history is the most important record in a physician's practice. For completeness, each patient's record should contain **subjective information** provided by the patient and **objective information** provided by the physician. If all entries are completed, the case history will stand the test of time. No branch of medicine is exempt from the need to keep patient history records.

Subjective Information

Personal Demographics

The patient's case history begins with routine personal data, which the patient usually supplies on the first visit when the medical record is established (Procedure 14-2). Most patients are required to complete a patient information form (Figure 14-3). The basic facts needed are:

- Patient's full name, spelled correctly
- Names of parents if the patient is a child
- Patient's gender
- Date of birth
- Marital status
- Name of spouse if married
- Number of children if any
- Home address, telephone number, and e-mail address
- Occupation
- Name of employer
- Business address and telephone number
- Employment information for spouse
- Healthcare insurance information

- Source of referral
- Social Security number

Personal and Medical History

The personal and medical history, which often is obtained by having the patient complete a questionnaire, provides information about any past illnesses or surgery the patient has had and about injuries or physical defects, whether congenital or acquired (Figure 14-4). It also includes information about the patient's daily health habits. Stickers can be used on the front of the medical record to indicate allergies, advance directives, and other information (Figure 14-5). These are useful for helping the health professional keep important facts about the patient in the forefront of the mind while treating the individual.

Patient's Family History

The family history comprises the physical condition of the various members of the patient's family, any illnesses or diseases individual members may have had, and a record of the causes of death. This information is important, because certain diseases may have a hereditary pattern. Most physicians are interested in the immediate family: children, parents, grandparents, and siblings.

Patient's Social History

The social history includes information about the patient's lifestyle. If the patient drinks, how many drinks per day or per week are consumed? If the patient smokes cigarettes, how many packs a day are smoked? Drug use and even marital information can be considered part of the social history.

CRITICAL THINKING APPLICATION   14-4

While taking a patient's medical history, Susan asks about his social history. She asks whether he drinks alcohol. The patient immediately becomes defensive and accuses Susan of getting too personal about his affairs.

■ How might Susan explain her reasons for asking these questions? What options are available if the patient refuses to discuss his social history with Susan?

■ Could this opposition to questions about the social history raise suspicion in Susan's mind? What might she suspect?

Patient's Chief Complaint

The patient's chief complaint is a concise account of the patient's symptoms, explained in the patient's own words. It should include the following:

- The nature and duration of pain, if any
- When the patient first noticed the symptoms
- The patient's opinion about the possible causes of the problem
- Remedies the patient may have applied before seeing the physician
- Whether the patient has had the same or a similar condition in the past
- Other medical treatment received for the same condition in the past

PROCEDURE 14-2

Organize a New Patient's Medical Record

GOAL: *To create a medical file for a new patient that will contain all the personal data necessary for a complete record and any other information required by the facility.*

EQUIPMENT and SUPPLIES

- Computer
- Clerical supplies (pen, clipboard)
- Registration form
- File folder
- Color-coded labels for folder
- Index label for folder tab
- Identification (ID) card (if using numeric system)
- Cross-reference card, if needed
- Financial ledger, if needed
- Routing slip
- Private conference area

PROCEDURAL STEPS

1. Determine that the patient is new to the office.
2. Obtain and record the required personal data.
   <u>PURPOSE:</u> To gather complete information for credit and insurance claim processing.
3. Write the information on the patient history form.
4. Review the entire form.
   <u>PURPOSE:</u> To make sure the information is complete and correct.
5. Select a label and folder for the record.
   <u>PURPOSE:</u> To choose the appropriate color for the patient's name if color coding is used.
6. Type the caption on the label and apply it to the folder.
   <u>PURPOSE:</u> To use the patient's name for alphabetic filing or an appropriate number for numeric filing.
7. For a numeric filing system, prepare a cross-reference card and a patient ID number.
   <u>PURPOSE:</u> To use numeric filing correctly. It is an indirect system that requires a cross-reference to a patient's name for locating the chart. The patient uses the number on the ID card when arranging appointments or making inquiries.
8. Prepare the financial card or put the patient's name in the computerized ledger.
9. Put the patient history form and all other forms required by the agency into the prepared folder as specified in the office policy and procedures manual.
10. Make a copy of the patient's health insurance identification card and driver's license.
    <u>PURPOSE:</u> To make a record of health insurance coverage and to keep the phone number and claims address on hand. The driver's license identifies the patient and ensures that the right person is receiving healthcare benefits.
11. Clip an encounter form on the outside of the patient's folder.

Most medical facilities use a pain scale to determine the severity of the patient's discomfort. The medical assistant might ask, "How bad is your pain on a scale of 1 to 10, with 1 being almost no pain, and 10 being the worst pain you've ever experienced?" The pain scale or wording used in individual facilities should be documented in the office policy and procedures manual and followed by the medical assistant.

Objective Information

Objective findings, sometimes referred to as *signs,* become evident from the physician's examination of the patient. These findings can be observed and measured.

Physical Examination Findings and Laboratory and Radiology Reports

After the physician has examined the patient, the physical findings are recorded in the history. The results of other tests or requests for these tests are then recorded or, if they appear on separate sheets, are attached to the history.

Diagnosis

Based on all the evidence provided in the patient's past history, the physician's examination, and any supplementary tests, the physician notes his or her diagnosis of the patient's condition in the medical record. If some doubt remains, this may be labeled a **provisional diagnosis**. A *differential diagnosis* is the process of weighing the probability of one disease causing the patient's illness against the probability that other diseases are causative. For example, the differential diagnosis of rhinitis, or a runny nose, could indicate allergic rhinitis (hay fever), the common cold, or even abuse of drugs or nasal decongestants.

Treatment Prescribed and Progress Notes

The physician's suggested treatment is listed after the diagnosis. Generally, instructions to the patient to return for follow-up treatment within a specific period also are noted here. If surgery or other treatment is needed, the patient must sign a consent form (Procedure 14-3).

Thank you for selecting our health care team!
To help us meet all your health care needs, please
fill out this form completely in ink. If you have any questions
or need assistance, please ask us - we will be happy to help.

Welcome

Patient #_____

Soc. Sec. #_____

Date_____

Patient Information (CONFIDENTIAL)

Name_____ Birth date _____ Home phone_____

Address_____ City _____ State____ Zip____

Check appropriate box: ☐ Minor ☐ Single ☐ Married ☐ Divorced ☐ Widowed ☐ Separated

If student, name of school/college _____ City_____ State__ ☐ Full time ☐ Part time

Patient's or parent's employer_____ Work phone _____

Business address_____ City_____ State____ Zip____

Spouse or parent's name_____ Employer_____ Work phone _____

Whom may we thank for referring you?_____

Person to contact in case of emergency_____ Phone _____

Responsible Party

Name of person responsible for this account _____ Relationship to patient _____

Address_____ Home phone _____

Driver's license #_____ Birth date _____ Financial institution_____

Employer_____ Work phone _____ SSN#_____

Is this person currently a patient in our office? ☐ Yes ☐ No

Insurance Information

Name of insured _____ Relationship to patient _____

Birth date _____ Social Security #_____ Date employed_____

Name of employer_____ Union or local #_____ Work phone _____

Address of employer_____ City _____ State____ Zip____

Insurance company_____ Group #_____ Policy/ID #_____

Ins. co. address_____ City _____ State____ Zip____

How much is your deductible? _____ How much have you used?_____ Max. annual benefit _____

DO YOU HAVE ANY ADDITIONAL INSURANCE? ☐ Yes ☐ No   IF YES, COMPLETE THE FOLLOWING:

Name of insured _____ Relationship to patient _____

Birth date _____ Social Security #_____ Date employed_____

Name of employer_____ Union or local #_____ Work phone _____

Address of employer_____ City _____ State____ Zip____

Insurance company_____ Group #_____ Policy/ID #_____

Ins. co. address_____ City _____ State____ Zip____

How much is your deductible? _____ How much have you used?_____ Max. annual benefit _____

I authorize release of any information concerning my (or my child's) health care, advice and treatment provided for the purpose of evaluating and administering claims for insurance benefits. I also hereby authorize payment of insurance benefits otherwise payable to me directly to the doctor.

X _____

Signature of patient or parent if minor   Date

FIGURE 14-3 The patient information form provides all the information the medical assistant needs to construct the patient's chart.

On each subsequent visit, the date must be entered on the chart, and information about the patient's condition and the results of treatment, based on the physician's observations, must be added to the history. Notations of all medications prescribed or instructions given, and the patient's own progress report, should be placed in the record. Any home visits are noted. If the patient is hospitalized, the name of the hospital, the reason for admission, and the dates of admission and discharge are recorded. Much of this information can be obtained from the hospital discharge summary.

Condition at the Time of Termination of Treatment

When the treatment is terminated, the physician records that information. For example: *August 18, 2013. Wound completely healed. Patient discharged.*

Obtaining the History

The medical assistant usually collects the routine personal data. The personal and medical history and the patient's family history may be obtained by asking the patient to complete a questionnaire, with the physician augmenting the information provided during the patient interview.

The Medical Assistant's Role

When the medical assistant is responsible for recording the patient's history, care must be taken to ensure that the patient's answers are not heard by others in the reception room. If privacy is not possible, the patient should be given a form to fill out, and the information should be transferred to the permanent record later. When privacy is available, the medical assistant may ask the patient questions and

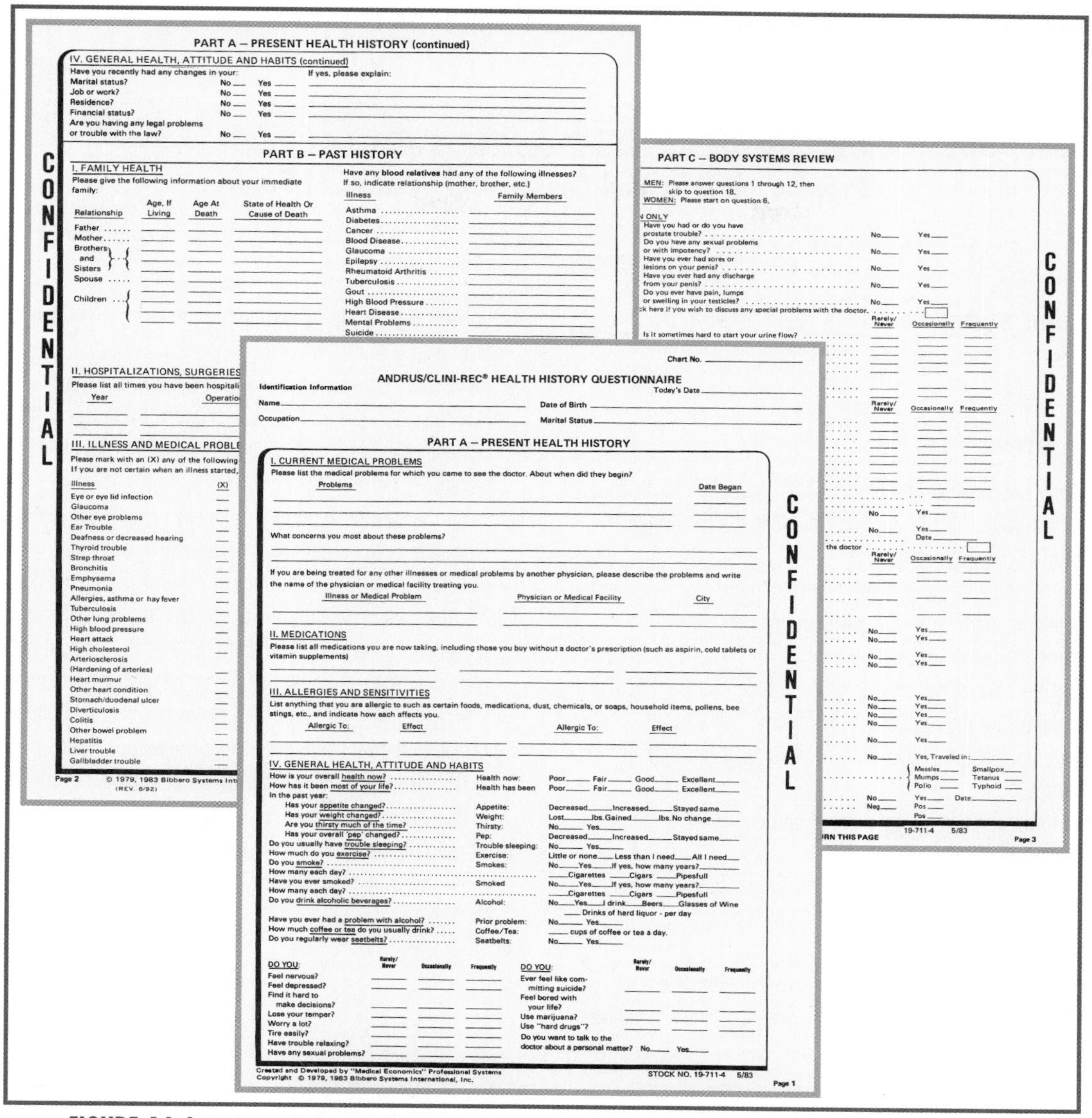

FIGURE 14-4 Database self-administered general health history questionnaire. Lengthy questionnaires should be completed by the patient before the individual is seen by the physician. Either mail the information to the patient in advance or ask the patient to come in early to complete the paperwork. (Courtesy Bibbero Systems, Petaluma, Calif.)

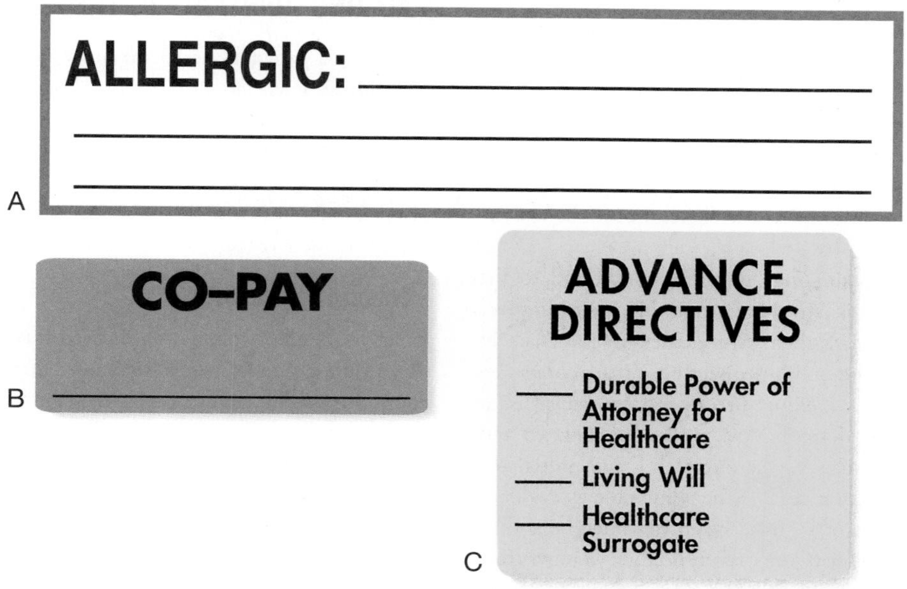

FIGURE 14-5 Chart stickers. Information on stickers on the outside of the chart allows the physician and medical staff to see important information about the patient quickly. (Courtesy Bibbero Systems, Petaluma, Calif.)

PROCEDURE 14-3

Prepare an Informed Consent for Treatment Form

GOAL: To inform the patient adequately and completely about the treatment or procedure he or she is to receive and to provide legal protection for the facility and the provider.

EQUIPMENT and SUPPLIES

- Pen
- Consent form

PROCEDURAL STEPS

1. After the physician has provided the details of the procedure to be done, prepare the consent form. Be sure the form includes the following:
   - Nature of the procedure or treatment
   - Risks and/or benefits of the procedure or treatment
   - Any reasonable alternatives to the procedure or treatment
   - Risks and/or benefits of each alternative
   - Risks and/or benefits of not receiving the procedure or treatment
   PURPOSE: To make sure the patient is fully informed about the procedure or treatment and the risks and/or benefits of having and not having it performed.
2. Personalize the form with the patient's name and any other demographic information the form lists.
   PURPOSE: To correctly identify the patient and the procedure.
3. Deliver the form to the physician for use as the patient is counseled about the procedure.
   PURPOSE: To prevent charges of practicing medicine without a license. The physician should explain procedures, risks, benefits, and alternatives and answer all the patient's questions.
4. Witness the patient's signature on the form, if necessary. The physician also usually signs the form.
5. Provide the patient with a copy of the consent form.
   PURPOSE: To ensure that the patient is fully informed about the procedure and has a copy of the information for his or her personal records.
6. Place the consent form in the patient's chart. The facility where the procedure is to be performed may require a copy.
   PURPOSE: To keep a permanent copy of the signed consent form.
7. Ask the patient whether he or she has any questions about the procedure. Refer questions that you cannot or should not answer to the physician. Make sure all the patient's questions are answered.
   PURPOSE: To make sure the patient has been fully informed by the physician before undergoing the procedure.
   NOTE: The medical assistant does not explain the consent form to the patient; this is the physician's responsibility.
8. Provide the patient with the date and time of the procedure and any other instructions required.

---

write or type the answers directly into the record. This method offers an opportunity to become better acquainted with the patient while completing the necessary records. If new patients must complete a lengthy questionnaire, the questionnaire may be mailed to the patient with a request that it be completed and returned to the physician before the appointment. If the record is to be computerized, requesting the information ahead of time gives the office staff the opportunity to transfer information to the computer before the new patient's visit.

The patient's chief complaint may have been indicated to the medical assistant, but the physician will question the patient in more detail. Many practitioners write their own entries on the chart in longhand. Some may type the findings directly into the computer. Others may dictate the material, either directly to the medical assistant or by using a recording device. If the material is dictated and typed, the physician should check each entry and then initial the entry to verify its accuracy. For a chart to be admissible as evidence in court, the person dictating or writing the entries must be able to attest that they were true and correct at the time they were written. The best indication of this is the physician's signature or initials on the typed entry.

MAKING ADDITIONS TO THE PATIENT'S RECORD

As long as a patient is under the physician's care, the medical history is building. Each laboratory report, radiology report, and progress note is added to the record, with the latest information always on top (Procedure 14-4). Although each item is important, the most recent usually is most significant to the patient's care. Again, the physician should read and initial each of these reports before it is placed in the record.

Laboratory Reports

Paper of different colors often is used for reporting different procedures. For example, urinalysis report forms may be yellow, blood count forms pink, and so on. When laboratory slips are smaller than the history form, they should be placed on a standard 8½- × 11-inch sheet of colored paper. Type or print the patient's name in the upper right corner, and then, with transparent tape, fasten the first report even with the bottom of the page. The second laboratory report is taped or glued in place on top of and approximately ½ inch above the first slip, allowing the date to show on the first report. With this method, called **shingling**, the latest report always appears on top

PROCEDURE 14-4

Add Supplementary Items to Patients' Records

GOAL: *To add supplementary documents and progress notes to patients' histories, observing standard steps in filing while creating an orderly file that facilitates ready reference to any item of information.*

EQUIPMENT and SUPPLIES

- Assorted correspondence, diagnostic reports, and progress notes
- Patients' files
- Computer
- Mending tape
- FILE stamp or pen
- Sorter
- Stapler

PROCEDURAL STEPS

1. Group all papers according to patients' names.
   <u>PURPOSE:</u> To expedite the filing process.
2. Remove any staples or paper clips.
   <u>PURPOSE:</u> Staples in the file folders are hazardous; paper clips are bulky and inadvertently may become attached to other materials.
3. Mend any damaged or torn records.
4. Attach any small items to standard-size paper.
   <u>PURPOSE:</u> Small items are easily lost or misplaced in files.
5. Group any related papers together.
6. Place your initials or stamp FILE in the upper left corner.
   <u>PURPOSE:</u> To indicate that the document has been released for filing.
7. Code the document by underlining or writing the patient's name in the upper right corner.
   <u>PURPOSE:</u> To indicate where the document is to be filed.
8. Continue steps 2 through 7 until all documents have been conditioned, released, indexed, and coded.
9. Place all documents in the sorter in filing sequence.
   <u>PURPOSE:</u> To allow the sorter to be taken to the file cabinet or shelf for insertion of documents into patients' folders.

(Figure 14-6). When checking previous reports, it is necessary only to run a finger down the slips until the desired date is found and then flip up the slips above.

Radiology Reports

Radiology reports usually are typed on standard letter-size stationery from the facility where the imaging was done. They are placed in the patient's history folder, with the most recent report on top. All radiology reports may be stapled together or kept behind a special divider in the chart.

Progress Notes

Reports on the patient's progress are continually added to the medical record. Each of the patient's visits should be entered into the chart, with the date preceding any notations about the visit. The medical assistant can type or stamp the date on the chart when readying the charts for the patient's visit. Every instruction, prescription, or telephone call for advice should be entered with the correct date. A wise course is to initial each entry, especially when several people are handling and making entries in a patient's record. This helps trace entries if some question arises.

MAKING CORRECTIONS AND ALTERATIONS TO MEDICAL RECORDS

Corrections sometimes must be made to medical records. The first step is to verify the proper procedure for making corrections in the facility's policy and procedures manual. Some physicians prefer a specific method for correcting errors in the medical record. Erasing, using correction fluid, or any other type of **obliteration** is never acceptable. To correct a handwritten entry:

1. Draw a line through the error.
2. Insert the correction above or immediately after the error, in a spot where it can be read clearly.
3. If indicated by the policy and procedures manual, write "Correction" or "Corr." in the margin.
4. The person making the correction should write his or her initials or signature below the correction and the date. Follow the format indicated in the policy and procedures manual (Figure 14-7).

Errors made while using the computer are corrected in the usual way. However, an error discovered in an entry at a later date is corrected in the same manner as for a handwritten entry. This is sometimes called an *addendum.* Never attempt to alter medical records without using this specific correction procedure, because this alteration of records may indicate a fraudulent attempt to cover up a mistake made by a staff member or the physician. Do not hide errors. If the error could in any way affect the patient's health and well-being, it must be brought to the physician's attention immediately.

CRITICAL THINKING APPLICATION 14-5

Susan has been using an incorrect abbreviation for several weeks and is having a difficult time remembering the right abbreviation. After taking a call from Mrs. Johnston, she remembers that she used the incorrect abbreviation in her chart last week. When Susan pulls the chart, she notices that entries have been made after the ones that Susan made on Mrs. Johnston's last visit. How does Susan correct her error?

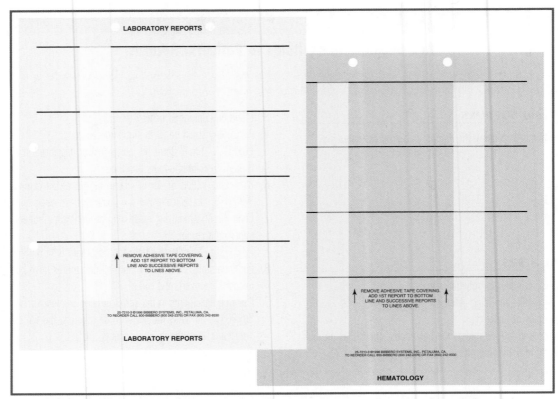

FIGURE 14-6 Shingled laboratory report forms. These forms make filing laboratory reports easy and provide a good adhesive so that the reports do not fall out of the chart if they are not standard size. (Courtesy Bibbero Systems, Petaluma, Calif.)

	error 10/15/XX ——— D. Bennett, CMA (AAMA)	
10/15/XX	9:30 a.m. Tubersol Mantoux test: 9mm induration. ———————	
	12 ——— D. Bennett, CMA (AAMA)	

FIGURE 14-7 Corrections to medical records must be done in a legible manner and must be clearly understood. Always initial and date corrections to medical records. (From Bonewit-West K: *Today's medical assistant,* ed 2, St Louis, 2013, WB Saunders.)

KEEPING RECORDS CURRENT

One of the greatest dangers to good record keeping is **procrastination**. The record must be methodically kept current. The medical assistant is responsible for seeing that this is done.

Case histories and reports may accumulate on the physician's or the medical assistant's desk during the day. After the last patient has gone, check each history to make sure all necessary information has been recorded and that each entry is sufficiently clear for future understanding. Give the physician all abnormal reports to read and initial so that action can be taken and they can be filed in the patient's case history folder. Some physicians want to see every laboratory report, whether normal or abnormal; others prefer the abnormal results be circled or highlighted. Always adhere to written policy when reporting abnormal results and filing documents. If the medical assistant decides what the physician does and doesn't need to see, the assistant is practicing medicine without a license. Follow the requirements as set forth in the office policy and procedures manual.

While the physician is reviewing these reports, pull the histories of any patients seen outside the office that day and those of patients given special instructions by telephone or for whom prescriptions were ordered. These entries are made in the same manner as for an office visit, but the type of call is explained in parentheses after the date.

A prescription pad, printed on no-smear, carbonless paper, is available for a timesaving, write-it-once system. By placing the prescription blank over the patient's record, the prescription is automatically copied on the record as it is written. Prescription carriers with adhesive strips are also available for the physician who uses duplicate prescription blanks. Be very careful that prescription pads are not stolen by patients in an effort to obtain drugs illegally.

The patient's record should not leave the office. A physician's pocket call record can be used for outside calls, and the information can be transferred to the chart in the office. Notations should be made of any missed appointments or of refusals to cooperate with instructions as they occur.

After all records have been reviewed for the day, and if time is too short to file them, they should be placed in a file tray and locked away for the night. Do not leave histories out in view at night, especially if the facility has a cleaning service. On arrival the next morning, the medical assistant can index the histories for filing. Attach extra reports and information sheets. Always attach material to the chart permanently; do not simply drop forms into the folders. When this has been done, the records are ready for filing.

The physician may prefer to dictate progress notes rather than write them in longhand. Patient histories, physical examination findings, medications prescribed, follow-up findings, and summaries of telephone conversations all can be dictated. At the end of the day, the recorded information is either given to the medical assistant for transcribing into the records or prepared for an outside transcriber.

A great deal of time may be saved in transcribing these notes by using a continuous roll or pages of self-adhesive strips. After the **transcription** is complete, the physician may want to check the notes, underline important points, and initial each entry to verify that each is correct, in the event of an **audit** or litigation. The notes then are returned to the medical assistant for insertion into the charts. The use of self-adhesive strips saves the time and effort involved in removing the sheet from a chart that may be bound with metal fasteners, inserting the sheet into the typewriter, and putting the sheet back into the folder. It also simplifies the physician's part in checking and initialing the notes, because only the transcribed material is handled, rather than the bulky chart. These forms also are useful for shingling telephone message records kept in the patient's record (Figure 14-8).

TRANSFER, DESTRUCTION, AND RETENTION OF MEDICAL RECORDS

Regular Transfer of Files

In most medical offices, records are filed according to three classifications:

- *Active files,* which are the files of patients currently receiving treatment.
- *Inactive files,* which generally are the files of patients whom the doctor has not seen for 6 months or longer. When these individuals return for care, their folders are replaced among the active files.
- *Closed files,* which are the records of patients who have died, moved away, or otherwise terminated their relationship with the physician.

Some system must be established for regular transfer of files from active to inactive status or possibly destruction. The expansion of charts and the file space available can influence the transfer period. Charts for patients currently hospitalized may be kept in a special section for quick reference and then placed in the regular active file when the patient is discharged from the hospital. In a surgical practice, the chart frequently includes the specific date on which the patient is discharged from the physician's care, and the notation is made on the chart, "Return prn" (from the Latin *pro re nata,* "as the occasion arises" or "when needed"). This record may safely be placed in the inactive file. The process of moving a file from active to inactive status is called **purging**. In a general practice office, the outside

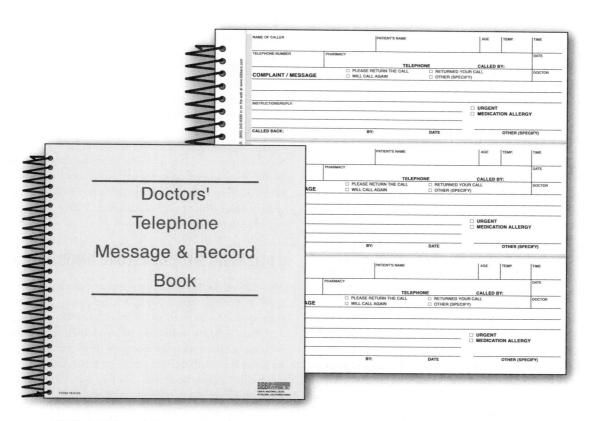

FIGURE 14-8 Shingled telephone message forms. These self-adhesive forms allow several telephone messages to be filed chronologically. (Courtesy Bibbero Systems, Petaluma, Calif.)

of the folder may be stamped with the date of the visit each time the patient is seen. It then is a simple matter to determine when the chart should be transferred to the inactive status; this is called the *perpetual transfer method.*

Most medical facilities use a year sticker on the file folder that indicates the last year the patient visited the clinic. If the file has a sticker showing that the patient's last visit was in 2011, and he or she presents to the clinic on January 5, 2013, a *2013* sticker should be placed over the one that indicates *2011.* These stickers often are included with color-coded filing systems. The medical assistant can easily look at a group of files and see which ones need to be changed to inactive or closed status.

Retention and Destruction

Physicians have an obligation to retain patient records that may reasonably be of value to a patient, according to the American Medical Association (AMA) Council on Ethical and Judicial Affairs. Currently, no standard, nationwide rule exists for establishing a records **retention schedule**.

Medical considerations are the primary basis for deciding how long to retain medical records. For example, operative notes and chemotherapy records should always be part of the patient's chart. The laws regarding the retention of medical records vary from state to state, and many governmental programs have their own guidelines for specific records retention. When no rules specify the retention of medical records, the best course is to keep the records for 10 years. However, for minors, the facility should keep the records until the minor reaches the age of majority plus 3 years.

If a particular record no longer needs to be kept for medical reasons, the physician should check the state law for any requirement that records be kept for a minimum time (most states do not have such a provision). The time is measured from the last professional contact with the patient. In all cases, medical records should be kept for at least the period of the statute of limitations for medical malpractice claims, which may be 3 years or longer, depending on state law. In the case of a minor, the statute of limitations may not apply until the patient reaches the age of majority. In summary, know the state requirements related to medical records retention and follow those guidelines; the office policy manual should address records retention pertaining to the state where the practice exists.

The records of any patient covered by Medicare or Medicaid must be kept at least 10 years. The Health Insurance Portability and Accountability Act (HIPAA) privacy rule does not include requirements for the retention of medical records. However, the privacy rule does require that appropriate administrative, technical, and physical safeguards be applied so that the privacy of medical records is maintained (Chapter 17 presents more detailed information about HIPAA).

Some physicians refuse to destroy or discard old records. The records should be stored somewhere other than the medical facility unless an abundance of storage space is available. The records should be kept in a facility where the temperature is controlled and the unit is locked. Always refer to state laws when discarding medical records, because state law varies with regard to medical record retention. For instance, some states require that pediatric records be kept 7 years after the patient turns 18; others require a 7-year retention period, to begin when the patient reaches his or her twenty-first birthday.

Before old records are discarded, patients should be given an opportunity to claim a copy of the records or have them sent to another physician. To preserve confidentiality when discarding old records, destroy the documents by shredding or through a professional document destruction service. HIPAA does not require any particular disposal method, but facilities must review their own circumstances to determine what steps are reasonable to safeguard patient information. The medical facility should keep a master list of all records that have been destroyed.

Protection of Records

Do not release original case histories to anyone outside the healthcare facility. Instead, prepare a summary or photocopy the materials needed for reference and retain the original in the physician's office. Because the facsimile machine is standard equipment in business offices, the transfer of information is simplified and the records remain in safekeeping. Often only certain aspects of the record are requested, and these can easily be supplied by faxing the required pages, observing precautions for confidentiality. Send only the information requested and make sure a release has been signed to provide the information. If possible, call before faxing confidential patient information and ask the person who is to receive it to retrieve it from the fax.

Occasions may arise when records are temporarily out of the office, although this should be an extremely rare occurrence. Some physicians release case histories to their colleagues, or an original record may be subpoenaed by a court. In such instances, a colored **OUTfolder** should be inserted into the file in place of the regular folder and a notation made of the name, date, and to whom the record was released. Interim papers may be placed in the OUTfolder until the original is returned.

Long-Term Storage

Large healthcare facilities may find it advisable to convert their records to **microfilm** for storage if the facility has not yet begun to scan documents into an electronic medical record system. If documents are stored electronically, they must be regularly backed up for storage. Another option is the transfer of paper records onto optical disks. Microfilm and optical disk technology are both expensive and probably are not practical for any but a very large group practice or health maintenance organization, so the facility should be moving toward some form of electronic storage. Using that method, medical records can be kept indefinitely.

RELEASING MEDICAL RECORD INFORMATION

The medical facility must be extremely careful when releasing any type of medical information. The patient must sign a release for information to be given to any third party (Procedure 14-5).

Often a family member calls to inquire about a patient, but without the patient's specific request or release, no information may be given. Some offices have a code system, whereby the patient gives the facility a code word that a family member must use to receive medical information about the patient.

Requests for medical information should be made in writing (Figure 14-9). Accepting a faxed request for medical information or a faxed release of information from a patient is unwise. Even requests

PROCEDURE 14-5

Prepare a Record Release Form

GOAL: *To provide a legal document indicating the patient's consent to the release of his or her medical records to another provider or healthcare facility.*

EQUIPMENT and SUPPLIES

- Medical record release form
- Pen
- Envelope

PROCEDURAL STEPS

1. Explain to the patient that a medical record release form is required to obtain records from another provider. If the patient is having records sent to another provider, a release also is required for that purpose.
   <u>PURPOSE:</u> To make sure the patient understands the record release procedure and purposes.

2. Review the record release form with the patient and ask whether the person understands the form or has any questions about it.
   <u>PURPOSE:</u> To provide the opportunity for questions and to make sure the patient understands the form.

3. Have the patient sign the form in the space indicated. If other demographic information is required (e.g., Social Security number or other names used), complete that information as well.

<u>PURPOSE:</u> The patient must sign the form for records to be released by any medical facility.

4. Make a copy of the form for the file, then mail it to the appropriate facility. Note the date the form was sent. Give the patient a copy if it is requested.
   <u>PURPOSE:</u> To have a record that the information or documents were actually requested on a certain date.

5. Check that the requested records arrived.
   <u>PURPOSE:</u> To make sure the records the physician needs to treat the patient accurately and competently are available in a timely manner.

6. Check the patient's medical record to determine whether a signed, current privacy policy document is on file. If not, have the patient sign one and place it in the record.
   <u>PURPOSE:</u> To ensure that all patients are notified of the office privacy policy.

RECORDS RELEASE AUTHORIZATION

TO _____
                        Doctor or Hospital

_____
                            Address

I HEREBY AUTHORIZE AND REQUEST YOU TO RELEASE TO:

ALL RECORDS IN YOUR POSSESION CONCERNING _____

_____ILLNESS AND/OR

TREATMENT DURING THE PERIOD FROM _____TO _____.

NAME _____TEL. _____

ADDRESS_____

SIGNATURE _____DATE_____
                    (If relative, state relationship)
WITNESS_____DATE_____

25-8104 © 1973 BIBBERO SYSTEMS, INC., PETALUMA,, CA.

FIGURE 14-9 Authorization to release medical records. All requests for medical records should be made in writing, and the request should be kept in the patient's chart. (Courtesy Bibbero Systems, Petaluma, Calif.)

from the patient's attorney or third-party payers must be cleared by the patient for them to obtain information. Some attorneys may present a legal document called a **power of attorney** or a subpoena, which authorizes them to see the records. A durable power of attorney is used often in the medical field; it allows another person (usually an attorney) to make transactions during the time that the patient is suffering from an incapacitating medical condition. It may allow the attorney to pay a utility bill for a hospitalized patient, make bank transactions, cash a Social Security check, and perform other types of transactions that the patient is too ill to perform.

As both parties to a lawsuit begin to prepare their cases, they enter the discovery process. Each side must disclose the pertinent facts of the case that may influence the final outcome of that case. On each occasion that information is needed from the provider, a separate request must be sent. Because this request form is signed by the patient, it serves as a release.

Most offices charge a fee to copy medical records, whether it is a per-page charge or a per-chart fee. Before releasing medical records, make sure you have a written, up-to-date release that has been signed by the patient. Follow the steps in the policy and procedures manual. Some physicians designate the office manager to handle requests for records releases.

Pay particular attention to records release requests involving a minor. In most cases, the parent or legal guardian is entitled to read through the patient's medical records; however, according to the Department of Health and Human Services, there are three situations in which the parent may not be legally entitled to review the records of his or her minor child, including:

- When the minor is the one who consents to care and the parent is not required to also consent to care under state law
- When the minor obtains medical care at the direction of a court or a person authorized by the court
- When the minor, parent, and physician all agree that the doctor and minor patient can have a private, confidential relationship

If the physician believes that the minor might be in an abuse situation or that the parent or legal guardian may be harming the patient, the physician is required to act, both legally and ethically.

Remember that the patient ultimately decides whether a record can be released. If any question arises about what is to be released, consult the office manager or the physician.

CRITICAL THINKING APPLICATION 14-6

Susan has never seen a power of attorney and is curious about this type of document. How might she investigate and learn more about it? Whom should Susan approach first for this information? The physician has an attorney whom Susan has met once. Should she call her and ask about the document without notifying the physician? Why or why not?

The time may come when a patient decides that he or she no longer agrees to the release of medical information. In this case, the patient should sign a revocation form, and it must become part of the medical record (Figure 14-10).

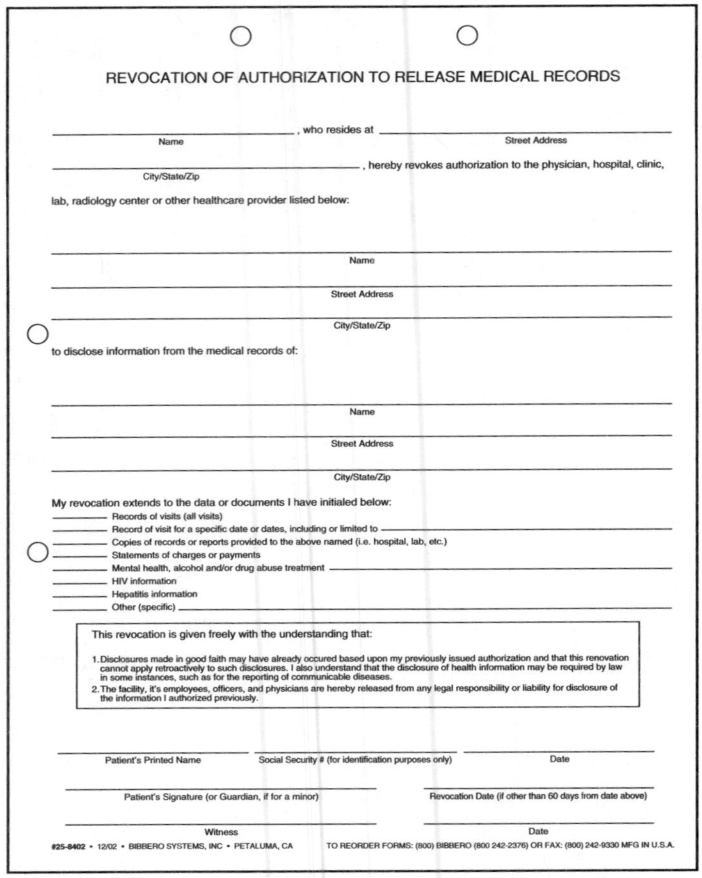
REVOCATION OF AUTHORIZATION TO RELEASE MEDICAL RECORDS

____________, who resides at ____________
Name / Street Address

____________, hereby revokes authorization to the physician, hospital, clinic,
City/State/Zip

lab, radiology center or other healthcare provider listed below:

____________ Name

____________ Street Address

____________ City/State/Zip

to disclose information from the medical records of:

____________ Name

____________ Street Address

____________ City/State/Zip

My revocation extends to the data or documents I have initialed below:

- ______ Records of visits (all visits)
- ______ Record of visit for a specific date or dates, including or limited to ______
- ______ Copies of records or reports provided to the above named (i.e. hospital, lab, etc.)
- ______ Statements of charges or payments
- ______ Mental health, alcohol and/or drug abuse treatment ______
- ______ HIV information
- ______ Hepatitis information
- ______ Other (specific) ______

This revocation is given freely with the understanding that:

1. Disclosures made in good faith may have already occured based upon my previously issued authorization and that this renovation cannot apply retroactively to such disclosures. I also understand that the disclosure of health information may be required by law in some instances, such as for the reporting of communicable diseases.
2. The facility, it's employees, officers, and physicians are hereby released from any legal responsibility or liability for disclosure of the information I authorized previously.

Patient's Printed Name ____ Social Security # (for identification purposes only) ____ Date ____

Patient's Signature (or Guardian, if for a minor) ____ Revocation Date (if other than 60 days from date above) ____

Witness ____ Date ____

#25-8402 • 12/02 • BIBBERO SYSTEMS, INC • PETALUMA, CA TO REORDER FORMS: (800) BIBBERO (800 242-2376) OR FAX: (800) 242-9330 MFG IN U.S.A.

FIGURE 14-10 Revocation of release of medical records. (Courtesy Bibbero Systems, Petaluma, Calif.)

Sometimes patients want to look at their own records. They certainly have a right to see this information, but some patients may not understand the terminology used in the record. A staff member should always remain with a patient who is looking at his or her medical record. Remember, the original medical record should never leave the medical facility. The physician can ethically charge for any copies of the medical record, both in full or in part. Always follow office policy when releasing medical records.

When a release is presented to the office, copy only the records requested in the release. Do not provide additional information that is not requested. The person requesting the information can be charged reasonable copying fees.

DICTATION AND TRANSCRIPTION

Administrative medical assistants may find that transcribing **dictation** is a job they perform periodically. Transcription can be done from handwritten notes, such as those in shorthand, or from machine dictation. Smooth operation of the facility may depend on the timely, accurate performance of assigned responsibilities, such as record documentation and preparation of special reports. Accuracy and speed are primary **requisites**, as is a strong grasp of medical principles, especially anatomy and physiology.

Dictation may be done using a machine transcription unit or a portable transcription unit. Many healthcare facilities now use a system that is accessed by telephone; the physician calls the system using passwords or access codes and records the information for the medical record while speaking into the telephone. Later, employees transcribe the information into the medical record.

Voice Recognition Software

Some healthcare facilities use voice recognition software for transcription. These software systems are loaded onto an office computer and work through a USB port or the line-in jack of a telephone. When first installed, the software requires the user to say several sentences into the unit so that it "learns" to recognize the user's voice. The system can be used to dictate progress notes, letters, e-mails, and virtually any document in the medical office that needs to be created. Some systems have an authentication component that allows a type of electronic signature, such as those needed for hospital record dictation.

FILING EQUIPMENT

The vertical, four-drawer steel filing cabinet, used with manila folders with the patient's name on the tab, was the traditional system of choice for years. The most popular system today is color-coding on open shelves. Rotary, lateral, compactable, and automated files also are available. Some records are kept in card or tray files. Regardless of the type or style of equipment, the best quality is always an economy. Some factors that should be considered when selecting filing equipment are:

- Office space availability
- Structural considerations
- Cost of space and equipment
- Size, type, and volume of records
- Confidentiality requirements
- Retrieval speed
- Fire protection

Drawer Files

Drawer files should be full suspension; they should roll easily, close securely, and be equipped with a locking device. The best cabinets have a center trough at the bottom of each drawer with a rod for holding divider guides. A drawback of the vertical four-drawer files is that only one person can use a file cabinet at a time. Filing also is slower, because the drawer must be opened and closed each time a file is pulled or filed.

File cabinets are heavy and can tip over, causing serious damage or injury unless reasonable care is taken. Open only one file drawer at a time, and close it when the filing has been completed. A drawer left even slightly open can injure a passerby.

Shelf Files

Shelf files should have doors to protect the contents. A popular type of shelf file has doors that slide back into the cabinet; the door from a lower shelf may be pulled out and used for work space. Open shelf units hold files sideways and can go higher on the wall because no drawers need to be pulled out (Figure 14-11). File retrieval is faster, because several individuals can work simultaneously. Open shelf units without doors are the most economical, but they offer little protection or confidentiality for the records. They are susceptible to water and fire damage.

FIGURE 14-11 Open shelf filing is an efficient method, especially for color-coded filing systems. The shelf doors often can be used as workspace.

Rotary Circular Files

Rotary circular files can hold a large volume of records. They save space and clerical motion. The files revolve easily; some have push-button controls. Several people can work at one rotary file and use records at the same time. One disadvantage is that they afford less privacy and protection than files that can be closed and locked.

Lateral Files

Lateral files are good for personal files and are especially attractive for the physician's private office. They use more wall space than the vertical file but do not extend so far out into the room. The folders are filed sideways in the lateral file, left to right, instead of front to back as in a vertical file.

Compactable Files

An office with little space and a great volume of records might use compactable files, which are a variation of open shelf files. The files are mounted on tracks in the floor, and the units slide along the tracks so that access is gained to the needed records. One drawback is that not all records are available at the same time.

Automated Files

Automated files are very expensive initially and require more maintenance than other types of filing equipment. They are likely to be found only in very large facilities, such as clinics or hospitals. These files bring the record to the operator instead of the operator going to the record. When the operator presses a button indicating the appropriate shelf, the shelf automatically moves into position in front of the operator for record retrieval. The automated or power file is fast and can store large numbers of records in a small amount of space. However, only one person can use the unit at one time.

Card Files

Almost every office has some occasion to use a card file. This may be for patient ledgers, a patient index, a library index, an index of surgical tray setups, telephone numbers, or numerous other records. A good-quality steel box or tray is a sound investment.

Special Items

Metal framework is available that can convert a regular drawer file into suspension-folder equipment. The assistant with a great deal of filing may want to purchase a portable filing shelf that fits on the side of an opened drawer and can be moved from place to place as needed. Another special filing item is a sorting file, which can be a great time-saver. A portable file cart for temporary filing of unbilled insurance claims may be quite useful. It also may be used for preliminary sorting of charts to be refiled; this is sometimes called a *suspense file*.

FILING SUPPLIES

Divider Guides

Each file drawer or shelf should be equipped with plenty of dividers or guides. Some authorities recommend one guide for approximately each 1½ inches of material, or every eight to 10 folders. Guides should be of good-quality **pressboard** or strong plastic. Less well constructed guides soon become bent and frayed and have to be replaced. Divider guides have a protruding tab, which may be an integral part of the card or may be made of metal or plastic. The guides reduce the area of search and serve as supports for the folders. They are available in single, third, or fifth cut (one, three, or five different positions).

OUTguides

OUTguides are heavy guides used to replace a folder that has been removed temporarily (Figure 14-12). They should be of a distinctive color for quick detection. This makes refiling simpler and alerts the file clerk that a file is missing. Several colors may be used, each color designating the temporary location of the file. The OUTguide may have lines for recording information, or it may have a plastic pocket for inserting an information card.

File Folders

Most records to be filed are placed in covers or tabbed folders. The most commonly used is a general purpose, third-cut manila folder that may be expanded to ¾ inch. These are available with a double-thickness, reinforced tab, which greatly extends the life of the folder. Folders kept in drawers have tabs at the top; those kept on shelves have tabs at the side. Many folder styles are available for special purposes.

The vertical pocket, which is of heavier weight than the general purpose folder, has a front that folds down for easy access to contents and is available with up to a 3½-inch expansion. These are used for bulky histories or correspondence.

Hanging, or suspension, folders are made of heavy stock and hang on metal rods from side to side in a drawer. They can be used only with files equipped with suspension equipment.

Binder folders have fasteners that are used to bind papers in the folder. These offer some security for the papers, but filing the materials is time-consuming.

The number of papers that will fit in one folder depends on the thickness of the papers and the capacity of the folder. Near the bottom edge of most folders are one or more score marks, which should be used as the contents of the folders expand. Papers should never protrude from the folder edges, and they should always be inserted with their tops to the left. When papers start to ride up in any folder, the folder is overloaded.

FIGURE 14-12 OUTguides allow tracking of a file not in its proper location by providing information on the location of the file. (Courtesy Bibbero Systems, Petaluma, Calif.)

Labels

The label is a necessary filing and finding device. Use labels to identify each shelf, drawer, divider guide, and folder. A label on the drawer or shelf identifies the nature of its contents. It should also indicate the range (alphabetic, numeric, or chronologic) of the material filed in that space.

The label on the divider guide identifies the range of folder headings following that divider guide up to the next divider (e.g., BaBo). The label on the folder identifies the contents of that folder only. This may be the name of the patient, subject matter of correspondence, a business topic, or anything at all that needs to be filed. Label a folder when a new patient is seen, existing folders are full, or materials need to be transferred within the filing system.

Labels are available in almost any size, shape, or color to meet the individual needs of any facility. Visit an office supply store and review the catalogs to find the best product to meet the needs of the facility.

A narrow label applied to the front of the folder tab is the easiest to use and satisfactory for folders kept in a drawer file. Labels for shelf filing should be identifiable from both front and back. Always type the label before separating it from the roll or protective sheet. Type the **caption** on the label in indexing order.

FILING PROCEDURES

Filing of all materials involves five basic steps: conditioning, releasing, indexing and coding, sorting, and storing and filing.

Conditioning

Conditioning of papers involves removing all pins, brads, and paper clips; stapling related papers together; attaching clippings or items smaller than page size to a regular sheet of paper with rubber cement or tape; and mending damaged records.

Releasing

The term *releasing* simply means that some mark is placed on the paper indicating that it is now ready for filing. This usually is either the medical assistant's initials or a FILE stamp placed in the upper left corner.

Indexing and Coding

Indexing means deciding where to file the letter or paper, and coding means placing some indication of this decision on the paper (Table 14-1). This may be done by underlining the name or subject, if it appears on the paper, or writing the indexing subject or name in some conspicuous place. If the paper logically could be filed in more

TABLE 14-1 Applying Indexing Rules

INDEXING RULE	NAME	UNIT 1	UNIT 2	UNIT 3
1	Robert F. Grinch	Grinch	Robert	F.
	R. Frank Grumman	Grumman	R.	Frank
2	J. Orville Smith	Smith	J.	Orville
	Jason O. Smith	Smith	Jason	O.
3	M. L. Saint-Vickery	Saint-Vickery	M.	L.
	Marie-Louise Taylor	Taylor	Marielouise	
4	Charles S. Anderson	Anderson	Charles	S.
	Anderson's Surgical Supply	Andersons	Surgical	Supply
5	Ah Hop Akee	Akee	Ah	Hop
6	Alice Delaney	Delaney	Alice	K.
	Chester K. DeLong	Delong	Chester	
7	Michael St. John	Stjohn	Michael	
8	Helen M. Maag	Maag	Helen	M.
	Frederick Mabry James	Mabry	Frederick	
	E. MacDonald	Macdonald	James	E.
9	Mrs. John L. Doe (Mary Jones)	Doe	Mary	Jones (Mrs. John L.)
10	Prof. John J. Breck	Breck	John	J. (Prof.)
	Madame Sylvia	Madame	Sylvia	
	Sister Mary Catherine	Sister	Mary	Catherine
	Theodore Wilson, M.D.	Wilson	Theodore (M. D.)	
11	Lawrence W. Sloan, Jr.	Sloan	Lawrence	W. (Jr.)
	Lawrence W. Sloan, Sr.	Sloan	Lawrence	W. (Sr.)
12	The Moore Clinic	Moore	Clinic (The)	

than one place, the original is coded for the main location and a cross-reference sheet is prepared, indicating this location, and coded for the second location. Every paper placed in a patient's chart should have the date and the patient's name on it, usually in the upper right corner. Include the chart number if a numeric system is used.

Sorting

Sorting is arranging the papers in filing sequence. Sort papers before going to the file cabinet or shelf. Do any necessary stapling of papers at the desk or filing table. Invest in a desktop sorter with a series of dividers, between which papers are placed in filing sequence. In the preliminary sorting, place the papers in the appropriate division in the sorter. It then is comparatively simple to arrange these groups into the proper sequence for filing.

Storing and Filing

When storing or filing papers in the folder, place items face up, top edge to the left, with the most recent date at the front of the folder. Lift the folder 1 or 2 inches out of the drawer before inserting new material, so that the sheets can drop down completely into the folder. However, the best course is to attach items to the file folder permanently so that they cannot fall out accidentally. When filing completed folders, arrange them in indexing order before going to the file cabinets.

Locating Misplaced Files

Unless files are promptly replaced after use, they may become lost. Papers may be misfiled, requiring a thorough search to find them, which wastes valuable time. After a methodic and complete search through the proper folder, check several places for the misplaced paper: (1) in the folder in front of and the one behind the correct folder; (2) between the folders; (3) at the bottom of the file under all the folders; (4) in a folder of a patient with a similar name; and (5) in the sorter.

INDEXING RULES

Indexing rules are fairly well standardized and based on current business practices. The Association of Records Managers and Administrators takes an active part in updating these rules. Some establishments adopt variations of these basic rules to accommodate their needs. In any case, the practices need to be consistent within the system.

1. Last names are considered first in filing; then the given name (first name), second; and the middle name or initial, third. Compare the names beginning with the first letter of the name. When a letter is different in the two names, that letter determines the order of filing.

> abe
> abi
> abm
> abx
> acl
> acm
> ada
> ade
> adi

2. Initials precede a name beginning with the same letter. This illustrates the librarian's rule, "Nothing comes before something."

> Smith, J.
> Smith, Jason

3. With hyphenated personal names, the hyphenated elements, whether first name, middle name, or surname, are considered to be one unit.

> Carlotta Freeman-Duque is filed as Freemanduque, Carlotta
> Cindy-Jean Green is filed as Green, Cindyjean

4. The apostrophe is disregarded in filing.

> Andersons' Surgical Supply
> Andersons Surgical Supply

5. When indexing a foreign name in which you cannot distinguish between the first and last names, index each part of the name in the order in which it is written.

> Cau Liu
> Talluri Devi

If you can make the distinction, use the last name as the first indexing unit.

> Liu, Jason

6. Names with prefixes are filed in the usual alphabetic order, with the prefix considered part of the name.

> von Schmidt is filed as Vonschmidt
> DeLong is filed as Delong
> LaFrance is filed as Lafrance

7. Abbreviated parts of a name are indexed as written if that form generally is used by that person.

> Ste. Marie is filed as Stemarie
> St. John is filed as Stjohn
> Wm. is filed as Wm
> Edw. is filed as Edw
> Jas. is filed as Jas

8. Mac and Mc are filed in their regular place in the alphabet.

> Maag
> Mabry
> MacDonald
> Machado
> MacHale
> Maville
> McAulay
> McWilliams
> Meacham

If the files have a great many names beginning with Mac or Mc, some offices file them as a separate letter of the alphabet for convenience.

9. The name of a married woman is indexed by her legal name (her husband's surname, her given name, and her middle name or maiden surname).

> Doe, Mary Jones (Mrs. John L.)
> not Doe, Mrs. John L. (unless first name is unknown)

10. When followed by a complete name, titles may be used as the last filing unit if needed to distinguish the name from another, identical name.

> Mr. James D. Conley
> Conley James D Mr.
> Dr. James D. Conley
> Conley James D Dr.

Titles without complete names are considered the first indexing unit.

> Madame Sylvia
> Sister Theresa

11. Terms of seniority or professional or academic degrees are used only to distinguish the name from an identical name.

> Theodore Wilson, PhD
> Theodore Wilson, Sr.
> Theodore Wilson, Jr.
> Theodore Wilson, MD
> These examples would be filed in the following order:
> Theodore Wilson, Jr.
> Theodore Wilson, MD
> Theodore Wilson, PhD
> Theodore Wilson, Sr.

12. Articles (e.g., the, a) are disregarded in indexing.

> Moore Clinic (The)

FILING METHODS

The three basic filing methods used in healthcare facilities are:
- Alphabetic by name
- Numeric
- Subject

Patients' charts are filed either alphabetically by name or by one of several numeric methods. Subject filing is used for business records, correspondence, and topical materials.

Alphabetic Filing

Alphabetic filing by name is the oldest, simplest, and most commonly used system. It is the system of choice for filing patients' records in most physicians' offices.

The alphabetic system of filing is traditional and simple to set up, requiring only a file cabinet or shelf, folders, and some divider guides (Procedure 14-6). It is a **direct filing system** in that the person filing needs to know only the name to find the desired file. Alphabetic filing does have some drawbacks:
- The correct spelling of the name must be known.
- As the number of files increases, more space is needed for each section of the alphabet. This results in periodic shifting of folders to allow for expansion.
- As the files expand, more time is required for filing or retrieving each folder because of the greater number of folders involved in the search. The time can be greatly reduced by color-coding.

Numeric Filing

Some form of **numeric filing** combined with color and shelf filing is used by practically every large clinic or hospital. Management consultants differ in their recommendations; some recommend numeric filing only if more than 5,000 to 10,000 charts are involved. Others recommend nothing but numeric filing. Numeric filing is an **indirect filing system**, or one that requires use of an alphabetic cross-reference to find a given file. Some object to this added step and overlook the advantages of numeric filing, which are:
- It allows unlimited expansion without periodic shifting of folders, and shelves usually are filled evenly.
- It provides additional confidentiality to the chart.
- It saves time in retrieving and filing records quickly. One knows immediately that the number 978 falls between 977 and 979. By contrast, an alphabetic system, even with color-coding, requires a longer search for the exact spot.

Several types of numeric filing systems can be used. In the straight, or consecutive, numeric system, patients are given consecutive numbers as they visit the practice. This is the simplest numeric system and works well for files of up to 10,000 records. It is time-consuming, and the chance for error is greater, when documents with five or more digits are filed. Filing activity is greatest at the end of the numeric series.

In the terminal digit system, patients also are assigned consecutive numbers, but the digits in the number usually are separated into groups of twos or threes and are read in groups from right to left instead of from left to right. The records are filed backward in groups. For example, all files ending in 00 are grouped together first, then those ending in 01, and so on. Next the files are grouped by their middle digits so that the 00 22s come before the 01 22s. Finally, the files are arranged by their first digits, so that 01 00 22 precedes 02 00 22.

Middle-digit filing begins with the middle digits, followed by the first digit and finally by the terminal digits.

Some practices use the last four digits of each patient's Social Security number to file patient records. However, no law requires every U.S. resident to have a Social Security number; if a patient does not, a "pseudo number" would have to be issued.

Numeric filing requires more training, but once the system has been mastered, fewer errors occur than with alphabetic filing (Procedure 14-7).

PROCEDURE 14-6

File Medical Records Using an Alphabetic System

GOAL: *To file records efficiently using an alphabetic system and to ensure quick, easy retrieval of the records.*

EQUIPMENT and SUPPLIES

- Medical records
- Physical filing equipment
- Cart to carry records, if needed
- Alphabetic file guide
- Staple remover
- Stapler

PROCEDURAL STEPS

1. Using alphabetic guidelines, place the records to be filed in alphabetic order. If a stack of documents is to be filed, place them in alphabetic order inside an alphabetic file guide or sorter. Use rules for filing documents alphabetically.
   PURPOSE: To organize the filing process and file the record or document quickly without retracing steps and skipping from letter to letter.

2. Go to the filing storage equipment (shelves, cabinets, or drawers) and locate the correct spot in the alphabet for the first file.
3. Place the file in the cabinet or drawer in correct alphabetic order.
4. If adding a document to a file, place it on top so that the most recent information is seen first. This puts the information in the file in reverse chronologic order.
   PURPOSE: To provide access to the most pertinent and recent information.
5. Securely fasten documents to the chart. Do not just drop the documents inside the chart.
   PURPOSE: To keep vital information from falling out of the chart and being lost.
6. Refile the chart in its proper place.

PROCEDURE 14-7

File Medical Records Using a Numeric System

GOAL: *To file records efficiently using a numeric system and to ensure quick, easy retrieval of the records.*

EQUIPMENT and SUPPLIES

- Medical records
- Physical filing equipment
- Cart to carry records, if needed
- Numeric file guide
- Staple remover
- Stapler
- Paper clips

PROCEDURAL STEPS

1. Using numeric guidelines, place the records to be filed in numeric order. If a stack of documents is to be filed, write the chart number on the document. Use rules for filing documents numerically.
   PURPOSE: To organize the filing process and file the records or documents quickly without retracing steps and skipping from letter to letter.

2. Go to the filing storage equipment (shelves, cabinets, or drawers) and locate the numeric spot for the first file.
3. Place the file in the cabinet or drawer in correct numeric order.
4. If adding a document to a file, place it on top so that the most recent information is seen first. This puts the information in the file in reverse chronologic order.
   PURPOSE: To provide access to the most pertinent and recent information.
5. Securely fasten documents to the chart. Do not just drop the documents inside the chart.
   PURPOSE: To keep vital information from falling out of the chart and being lost.
6. Refile the chart in its proper place.

Susan is unsure whether alphabetic or numeric filing is best in the medical office. What are some advantages and disadvantages of each method?

Subject Filing

Subject filing can be either alphabetic or **alphanumeric** (A 1-3, B 1-1, B 1-2, and so on) and is used for general correspondence. The main difficulty with subject filing is indexing, or classifying; that is, deciding where to file a document. Many papers require cross-referencing. All correspondence dealing with a particular subject is filed together. The papers in the folders are filed chronologically, the most recent on top. The subject headings are placed on the tabs of the folders and filed alphabetically.

Color-Coding

When a color-coding system is used, both filing and finding files is easier, and misfiling of folders is kept to a minimum. The use of color visually restricts the area of search for a specific record. A misfiled chart is easily spotted even from a distance of several feet. In color-coding, a specific color is selected to identify each letter of the alphabet. Any selection of colors may be used, and the division of the alphabet is determined by one's own needs. However, studies have shown that the frequency with which different letters occur varies widely.

Alphabetic Color-Coding

Files can be color-coded in several ways. One alphabetic system uses five different colored folders, with each color representing a segment of the alphabet. The second letter of the patient's last name determines the color.

As medicine continues to consolidate into larger facilities with more patients under one management, the filing of patients' charts becomes more complicated, and color-coding becomes more useful. Several color-coding systems use two sets of 13 colors: one set for letters A to M, and a second set of the same colors on a different background for letters N to Z.

Many ready-made systems are available for use. Self-adhesive, colored letter blocks with either two or three letters in the specific colors are supplied in rolls. The color blocks with the appropriate letter are placed on the index tab of the folder, along with the patient's full name. The letters are in pairs so that they can be seen from either side of the chart. Strong, easily differentiated colors are used, creating a band of color in the files that makes spotting out-of-place folders easy (Figure 14-13).

Numeric Color-Coding

Color-coding is also used in numeric filing. Numbers 0 through 9 are each assigned a different color. In a terminal digit filing system, the colors for the last two numbers are affixed to the tab. If the number 1 is red and 5 is yellow, all files with numbers ending in 15 form a red and yellow band. Usually a predetermined section of the number is color-coded.

Other Color-Coding Applications

Color can work in many other ways for the efficient medical office. Small tabs in a variety of colors can be used to identify certain types

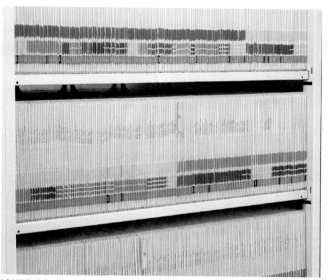

FIGURE 14-13 With color-coding of patients' charts, a misplaced file is easily spotted. (Courtesy Bibbero Systems, Petaluma, Calif.)

of insured patients and other specific information. For example, a red tab over the edge of the folder may identify a patient on Medicaid; a blue tab may identify a Medicaid patient; a green tab may identify a workers' compensation patient; matching tabs may be attached to the insured's ledger card; research cases may be identified by a special color tab; and brightly colored labels on the outside of a patient's chart can indicate certain health conditions, such as drug allergies. In a partnership practice, a different color folder or label may identify each physician's patients. Color also can be used to differentiate dates; one color for each month or year.

The use of color in filing is limited only by the imagination. One word of caution: Every person in the facility who uses the files must know the key to the coding, and the key should also be written in the facility's policy and procedures manual.

ORGANIZATION OF FILES

Physicians find studying a disorganized history very difficult. Some systematic method must be followed in placing items in the patient folder. From the filing standpoint, it should be emphasized that when a patient record is not in actual use, it should be in only one place—the filing cabinet or on the shelf. Many precious hours can be lost searching for misplaced or lost records carelessly left unfiled (Procedure 14-8).

The patient's full name, in indexing order, should be typed on a label and the label attached to the folder tab. A strip of transparent tape can be placed on the label to prevent smudging. The patient's full name should also be typed on each sheet in the folder. Some of the types of records common to the healthcare setting, other than patient records, include health-related correspondence, general correspondence, practice management files, miscellaneous files, and tickler or follow-up files.

Health-Related Correspondence

Correspondence pertaining to patients' medical records should be filed with the case history. Other medical correspondence should be filed in a subject file.

Maintain Organization by Filing

GOAL: *To make sure various office filing systems are maintained and usable by all parties at the medical facility.*

EQUIPMENT and SUPPLIES

- Documents to be filed
- Various file folders
- Office filing systems (e.g., equipment maintenance, general office, and so on, if the facility's files are not kept in one general grouping)
- Clerical supplies

PROCEDURAL STEPS

1. Identify the correct filing system for the document. For example, equipment maintenance information may be placed in its own separate grouping of files, or it may be put in a general office filing system.
   <u>PURPOSE:</u> To determine the best place to put the document so that it can be easily retrieved.

2. Inspect the document to be added.
   <u>PURPOSE:</u> To condition, release, index, code, and/or sort the document if needed.

3. Add the document to the proper file in the correct filing system.
   <u>PURPOSE:</u> To make sure the forms the physician needs are available at all times.

4. Attach the document to the file permanently or according to office policy.
   <u>PURPOSE:</u> To keep information from falling out of the file and getting lost or misplaced.

5. Attach documents in the file with the most recent on top. Then place the record in the designated place in the filing system.
   <u>PURPOSE:</u> To allow easy access to the most recent data.

6. Continue the process until all documents have been filed in the filing system.

7. Consider staff needs and limitations when establishing a filing system.

General Correspondence

The physician's office operates as both a business and a professional service. Correspondence of a general nature pertaining to the operation of the office is part of the business side of the practice. Usually, a special drawer or shelf is set aside for the general correspondence. The correspondence is indexed according to subject matter or the names of the correspondents. The guides in a subject file may appear in one, two, or three positions, depending on the number of headings, subheadings, and subdivisions.

Practice Management Files

Of course, the most active financial record is the patient ledger. In facilities that still use a manual system, this is a card or vertical tray file, and the accounts are arranged alphabetically by name. At least two divisions are used: active accounts and paid accounts.

Miscellaneous Files

Papers that do not warrant an individual folder are placed in a miscellaneous folder. In that folder, all papers relating to one subject or with one correspondent are kept together in chronologic order, with the most recent on top, and then filed alphabetically with other miscellaneous material. Related materials may be stapled together. Never use paper clips for this purpose. When as many as five papers accumulate with one correspondent or subject, a separate folder should be prepared. Other business files include records of income and expenses, financial statements, income and payroll tax records, canceled checks, and insurance policies. These papers may be filed chronologically.

Tickler or Follow-Up Files

The most frequently used follow-up method is a **tickler file**, so called because it tickles the memory that something needs to be done or followed up on a particular date. The tickler file is always a chronologic arrangement. In its simplest form, it consists of notations on the daily calendar. If information, such as an x-ray report or laboratory report, is expected about a patient with an appointment to come in, the medical assistant might make a note on the calendar or tickler file a day ahead to check on whether the report has arrived.

The tickler file can be a part of a computerized medical record system or could be as simple as an e-mail sent to oneself. Many people put reminders on their cell phones using an application (app) specially designed for memos and reminders. The tickler file could also be a card file; 12 guides, one for each month, are placed at the front of the cabinet, container, or other object used to hold the folders. Notations of actions to be taken are placed behind the guides for specific days of the current month. Notations for future months are placed behind the guide for that month. To be effective, the tickler file must be checked the first thing each day.

CRITICAL THINKING APPLICATION   14-8
Susan is responsible for checking the tickler file daily. What types of documents and duties might she find inside these files?

The tickler file can be used in many ways. It is a useful reminder of recurring events, such as payments, meetings, and so forth. On the last day of each month, all the notations from behind the next month's guide are distributed among the daily numbered guides, and the guide for the month just completed is placed at the back of the file.

Transitory or Temporary File

Many papers are kept longer than necessary because no provision is made for segregating those with a limited usefulness. This situation can be prevented by having a transitory or temporary file. For example, if a medical assistant writes a letter requesting a reprint, the file copy is placed in the transitory folder. When the reprint is received, the file copy is destroyed. The transitory file is used for materials with no permanent value. The paper may be marked with a T and destroyed when the action is completed.

Temporary files also are useful when the physician sees patients who are physically transitory. For example, consider the patient who becomes ill while on vacation in New York City. She sees a physician there. However, the patient lives in Dallas and therefore is not likely to return to the physician in New York. Nevertheless, some documentation must exist that details the patient's treatment. A temporary file can be created and shredded after the state statute of limitations has expired. Some medical facilities keep all temporary or transient patient files in one expanded folder. Refer to the office policy and procedures manual to find the procedure for handling these patients' files.

CLOSING COMMENTS

Just as in every aspect of the medical profession, advances in medical records management are occurring rapidly, allowing physicians and other caregivers to perform their duties more efficiently and accurately. A medical assistant must constantly be willing to learn and to adapt to changes arising from legislation and technologic advances. Because many patients are computer literate, computers have become generally accepted as a means of recording medical information. This is a positive change, because many patients and providers were not in favor of computer-based medical records when the concept was first presented to the general public.

Patient Education

The medical assistant should always explain to the patient any paperwork the person may be required to complete or sign. Patients do not like simply to be told, "Sign here." Take the time to explain any form that needs completion or a signature so that the patient understands the reason for collecting the information and the medical staff's need to have it available.

Many forms are similar, and patients may complain about answering the same questions on multiple forms. Review and revise the forms used in the office often so that they are user friendly and nonrepetitive for the office staff and patient alike.

Patients may need reassurance that each staff member is committed to complete patient confidentiality. Always be open to answering questions about a patient's medical record.

Legal and Ethical Issues

The authority to release information from the medical record lies solely with the patient unless such a release is required by law through a subpoena. Ownership of the record often is a subject of controversy. The record belongs to the physician; the information belongs to the patient.

When a medical record is used as evidence in a court case, the person who entered information must be able to read it, no matter how long ago the entry was created.

Be sure to understand the laws governing records retention. Records should be kept through the period of the statute of limitations and possibly longer in certain situations. Take care with the medical chart, because it is the lifeline of patient care in the medical facility. When a chart is corrected, the proper method must be followed, and the record should never be obliterated (see steps 8 through 10 in Procedure 14-1).

SUMMARY OF SCENARIO

Susan looks forward to attending her medical assisting classes each day and works diligently to perform to the best of her ability in the classroom. She strives to do well on each procedure check-off and each examination she completes. Her instructors provide excellent feedback and appreciate her contributions to the class.

Susan has the attitude that everything she is allowed to do in the medical office is a learning tool. She regularly asks for additional responsibilities and is always ready to assist a co-worker. Dr. Thomas has recognized that she has the desire to learn, and he gives her many opportunities to glean more knowledge through the everyday activities in the office.

Although she is new to the medical profession, Susan learns quickly and thinks logically. She knows the rules and regulations on patient confidentiality and is always careful about the information she provides to those who request it. She is never hesitant about asking her office manager for guidance if she is unsure about any aspect of her duties. Susan is understanding and respectful when patients are concerned about their privacy. Her confidence and warm personality play a role in the trust she earns from the patients at the clinic.

Susan is willing to admit when she has made an error and has sought advice from Dr. Thomas and her office manager when an error needed correction.

Although filing is not one of her favorite duties, she can be counted on to do her best while completing this important task. She realizes that filing is critical, because the documents in the patient's medical record direct the care provided to the patient. An abnormal laboratory report that is missing can make a crucial difference in the patient's care. She takes pride in her work and is efficient and accurate where medical records are concerned. When she is faced with a task new to her, she considers it a learning experience and asks for help if she is not completely sure about the way to handle a situation.

Susan's co-workers are supportive and always willing to assist her as she learns to be the best medical assistant she can be. Her future as a professional medical assistant certainly holds opportunity and chances for advancement. Just as important, patients trust her. She has alleviated patients' concerns about electronic medical records by taking the time to explain privacy policies and exactly what information will be accessible to third parties. This trust also gives patients the confidence to reveal personal information and to know that it will be held in the strictest confidence, not just by Susan, but by each employee in the physician's office.

SUMMARY OF LEARNING OBJECTIVES

1. **Define, spell, and pronounce the terms listed in the vocabulary.**
   Spelling and pronouncing medical terms correctly bolster the medical assistant's credibility. Knowing the definition of these terms promotes confidence in communication with patients and co-workers.

2. **State several reasons accurate medical records are important.**
   Medical records must be accurate primarily so that the correct care can be given to the patient. The record also helps ensure continuity of care between providers so that no lapse in treatment occurs. The record serves as indication and proof in court that certain treatments and procedures were performed on the patient; therefore, it can be excellent legal support if it is well maintained and accurate. Medical records also aid researchers with statistical information.

3. **Explain who owns the medical record.**
   The physician owns the physical medical record, but the patient owns the information contained in it.

4. **Explain how to document appropriately and accurately.**
   All medical documentation must be correct, complete, and timely. Entries should be written in compliance with office policy and local, state, and federal law. Never obliterate any portion of the record. Re-read all entries to make certain that they are legible and that the entry makes grammatical sense (see Procedure 14-8).

5. **Explain the difference between a traditional medical record and a problem-oriented medical record.**
   The POMR categorizes each of the patient's problems and elaborates on the findings and treatment plan for all concerns. Detailed progress notes are kept for each individual problem. This method addresses each of the patient's concerns separately, whereas a traditional record may address all problems and concerns at one time, usually covering one to three patient concerns per office visit. The POMR helps ensure that individual problems are all addressed.

6. **Explain how to establish and organize a patient's medical record.**
   The patient's chart must be established and organized so that the components are easy to find (see Procedure 14-2). Use the data on the patient information forms to build the patient's medical record and to create a financial record. Follow office policy when creating new patient records.

7. **Identify systems for organizing medical records.**
   Alphabetic filing is a simple, traditional filing system in which documents are filed in alphabetic order. Numeric filing systems use a number code to give order to the files. An alphanumeric system is a combination of the two.

8. **Differentiate between subjective and objective information.**
   Very simply, subjective information is provided by the patient, whereas objective information is provided by the physician or provider. Examples of subjective information include the patient's address, Social Security number, insurance information, and description of what he or she is experiencing. Objective information is obtained through the physician's questions and observations made during the examination.

9. **Describe various types of information kept in the medical record.**
   Both subjective and objective information are kept in the progress notes. Demographic information about the patient can be found, in addition to many types of reports, including consultations, lab reports, radiology and other imaging reports, and various types of correspondence.

10. **Explain how to make additions to a medical record.**
    Items periodically must be added to patients' records, such as when test results arrive or new information becomes available. Determine where the document should be placed in the record, then condition, index, and code the documents, making sure that they have been released for filing. Sort them for easier filing, then place them in the correct medical record. (see Procedure 14-4).

11. **Discuss correction of an entry in the patient's record.**
    The appropriate procedures must be followed to make corrections in a patient's chart. A single line should be drawn through the incorrect information and then initialed and dated. Some offices also require a notation of "Corr." or "Correction" on the chart. A medical assistant should never try to alter the medical record or cover up an error in charting.

12. **Identify both equipment and supplies needed to file medical records.**
    Several types of equipment and supplies are needed to manage patients' records. A variety of shelving units and filing containers must be available. Open shelving allows maximum use of color-coded charts, which makes finding misfiles quick and easy. Many file folder styles are available, and several types of forms can be used in patients' charts. The preference of the physician and staff members who use these tools is important, as are concerns such as cost and availability. A medical assistant should be conservative when ordering supplies and purchasing equipment, ordering only the number needed to save on office supply costs.

13. **Discuss filing procedures.**
    Some offices use an alphabetic filing system (see Procedure 14-6). Some offices use a numeric filing system (see Procedure 14-7). Review office policy to determine which system to use and the correct procedures to follow when filing documents.

14. **Describe indexing rules.**
    Five basic steps are involved in document filing. (1) The papers are conditioned, which is the preparatory stage for filing. (2) The documents are released, which means they are ready to be filed because they have been reviewed or read and some type of mark has been placed on the document to indicate this. (3) The documents are indexed, which involves deciding where each document should be filed and coding it with some type of mark on the paper indicating that decision. (4) Sorting involves placing the files in filing sequence. (5) The actual filing and storing of the documents is the last step.

15. **Discuss the pros and cons of various filing methods.**
    Both the alphabetic and numeric filing systems have advantages and disadvantages. Perhaps most important is the staff's preference. Some

find it easier to retrieve files that are in standard alphabetic order, whereas others prefer a numeric system. The numeric system is more confidential than an alphabetic system. Some staff members prefer a combination of the two, the alphanumeric system. Both effectively keep medical records in good order and allow the medical assistant to spot a misfiled record quickly.

16. **Identify types of records common to the healthcare setting.**
Medical offices keep numerous files on hand for the administration and business aspects. For example, maintenance and supply records, personnel and human resources records, and budget and bill-paying records all are examples of files that help the staff conduct the facility's business. Some offices keep several different filing systems according to subject, whereas others keep one comprehensive system. The facility should use whatever system most benefits the employees and allows the fastest retrieval of files.

CONNECTIONS

Study Guide Connection: Go to the Chapter 14 Study Guide. Read and complete the activities.

Evolve Connection: Go to the Chapter 14 link at *evolve.elsevier.com/ kinn* to complete the Chapter Review and Chapter Quiz. Check out the other resources listed for this chapter to make the most of what you have learned from The Paper Medical Record.

15

THE ELECTRONIC MEDICAL RECORD

Sloan Swarten was hired as a medical assistant at the Southwest Family Medical Clinic in Tempe, Arizona, in October. Dr. Adkins and Dr. Brooks opened the practice 2 years ago. The clinic is fully electronic; no paper records are used at all. Sloan is more interested in the clinical aspect of medical assisting, but because she waited 6 months after finishing school to start looking for work, she had a difficult time finding a job. She accepted the position in medical records at Southwest, known to be a sizeable, busy practice, in the hope that she could soon transfer to the clinical side. Her supervisor, Jennifer Sanchez, stressed that the only available position was in the medical records department, but she also said she would consider moving Sloan to the clinical side after a few months if she performed well and if it proved to be a beneficial move for the clinic.

Sloan does not particularly like the medical records department, and she spends her breaks and lunch periods with the clinical medical assistants. She often remarks that she really would like to work on the clinical side. Sloan is computer literate, but she did not take the administrative classes at school very seriously, because she planned to do clinical work. Her probation period is 6 weeks, and she has decided to make the best of the medical records job until she is transferred. Sloan works with Alex, who supervises the electronic medical records aspect of the clinic. Since most of her previous experience was working with paper records, Alex had to learn the entire program when Southwest opened, and she has enjoyed becoming an expert, or **superuser**, on the system. Alex likes to learn new things and is able to find solutions to records issues quickly and efficiently. Sloan and Alex get along well, although Alex is concerned that Sloan doesn't really want to learn the electronic systems.

While studying this chapter, think about the following questions:

- Do you believe Sloan will make it to the clinical side of the office?
- Why is the medical records department one of the most important areas of the physician's office?
- From the information given in this scenario, what mistakes has Sloan already made, if any?
- Why is it important to know both administrative and clinical skills in the physician's office?

LEARNING OBJECTIVES

1. Define, spell, and pronounce the terms listed in the vocabulary.
2. Discuss the presidential Executive Order that led to the implementation of electronic medical record systems across the nation.
3. Discuss the principles of using the electronic medical record (EMR).
4. Distinguish between an electronic health record (EHR) and an electronic medical record (EMR).
5. Explain how the American Recovery and Reinvestment Act applies to the healthcare industry.
6. Define meaningful use.
7. List the three main components of meaningful use legislation.
8. Discuss the advantages and disadvantages of an electronic medical record system.
9. Explore the capabilities of an electronic medical record system.
10. Give several reasons patients are hesitant in accepting electronic health records.
11. Discuss the importance of nonverbal communication with patients when an EMR system is used.
12. Summarize the goals of the Nationwide Health Information Network (NHIN).
13. List the core capabilities of the NHIN.
14. Summarize the role of the medical assistant with regard to the changing technology in healthcare facilities and organizations.

VOCABULARY

alleviate To partly remove or correct; to relieve or lessen.

computerized physician/provider order entry (CPOE) A process of electronic data entry of medical practitioner or provider instructions for the treatment of patients.

culpability Meriting condemnation, responsibility, or blame, especially as wrong or harmful.

e-prescribing The use of electronic devices to communicate with pharmacies and send prescribing information, taking the place of writing a prescription by hand and physically giving it to a patient; new or refill prescriptions can be submitted electronically, cutting down on fraud and errors.

electronic health record (EHR) An electronic record of health-related information about a patient that conforms to nationally recognized interoperability standards and that can be created, managed, and consulted by authorized clinicians and staff from *more than one healthcare organization.*

electronic medical record (EMR) An electronic record of health-related information about an individual that can be created, gathered, managed, and consulted by authorized clinicians and staff *within a single healthcare organization.*

interoperable The capability of a system to work with or use the parts or equipment of another system.

parameters Any set of physical properties, the values of which determine characteristics or behavior.

personal health record (PHR) An electronic record of health-related information about an individual that conforms to nationally recognized interoperability standards and that *can be drawn from multiple sources but that is managed, shared, and controlled by the individual.*

prevalent Generally or widely accepted, favored, or practiced.

reasonable cause Circumstances that would make it unreasonable for the covered entity, despite the exercise of ordinary business care and prudence, to comply with the administrative simplification provision that was violated.

reasonable diligence The business care and prudence expected from a person seeking to satisfy a legal requirement under similar circumstances.

superuser A special account on a computer system that is used for system administration; also, a person in a facility who is able to make system-wide changes to a computer system.

willful neglect Conscious, intentional failure or reckless indifference to the obligation to comply with the administrative simplification provision violated.

With technology advancing at such a rapid pace, it is no surprise that the number of offices using an electronic medical record (EMR) system is growing steadily. Some physicians may not budge and will never change to electronic health records. However, because more and more hospitals are using electronic records, physicians, medical assistants, and other healthcare professionals must learn to communicate electronically about patients and to originate information by electronic means. For those who have worked in the healthcare industry for some time, this may present a challenge; however, today's medical students are being trained in the use of the EMR as a standard practice. In the not too distant future, the EMR will be the standard, and paper medical records will be much less common.

EXECUTIVE ORDER TO PROMOTE INTEROPERABILITY OF EMR SYSTEMS

On August 22, 2006, President George W. Bush issued an Executive Order designed to promote the interoperability of health records and the overall quality and efficiency of healthcare. He set a goal of establishing electronic health records for most Americans by 2014. The order took effect on January 1, 2007. It listed five requirements:

1. The agencies involved will implement **interoperable** systems as their current systems are upgraded (e.g., Centers for Medicare and Medicaid Services [CMS]).

2. Providers (e.g., a regional Veterans Affairs Hospital) and payers with whom the agencies do business also will implement interoperable systems as their current systems are upgraded. In other words, a hospital that receives federal funding, such as Medicare, must adopt electronic health record systems.

3. The prices paid by health insurance issuers will be available both to beneficiaries and enrollees in the health plan.

4. The agencies and providers will participate in the development of information about the overall cost of healthcare services and treatments.

5. The agencies and providers will develop and identify, for beneficiaries, enrollees, and providers, approaches that encourage the provision and receipt of high-quality, efficient healthcare.

An interoperable system sounds complicated; however, it simply is a system that is able to work with another system. For example, a physician could use his office EMR system to access the EMR system of a hospital to check the hospital's records on his patients. Although the language of the presidential order is complex and the technologic features such systems require are overwhelming to most medical assistants, keep the end goal in mind—providing high-quality, efficient care to patients.

The EMR is becoming the healthcare facility's most important business and legal record. The legal requirements are more intricate than those for a paper medical record. Just as a paper medical record is considered a legal record in court, so is the EMR.

TECHNOLOGIC TERMS IN HEALTH INFORMATION

Some confusion has arisen regarding the acronyms *EMR* and *EHR.* The National Alliance for Health Information Technology (NAHIT) identified 18 to 63 definitions for the five main terms that relate to the electronic medical record. To **alleviate** the confusion, NAHIT has established definitions for EMR and EHR that are easy to understand. The **electronic health record (EHR)** is an electronic record of health-related information about a patient that conforms to nationally recognized interoperability standards and that can be created, managed, and consulted by authorized clinicians and staff from *more than one healthcare organization.* The **electronic medical record (EMR)** is an electronic record of health-related information about an individual that can be created, gathered, managed, and consulted by authorized clinicians and staff *within a single healthcare organization.*

A **personal health record (PHR)** is defined by the NAHIT as an electronic record of health-related information about an individual that conforms to nationally recognized interoperability standards and that can be drawn from multiple sources but that is managed, shared, and controlled by the individual. Few PHRs currently exist, and most Americans do not know what a PHR is or how it can be of value to them.

The Health Insurance Portability and Accountability Act (HIPAA) uses the term *protected health information* (PHI), which is any information about health status, the provision of healthcare, or payment for healthcare that can be linked to an individual patient.

For the purposes of this chapter, *EMR* refers to the electronic system the physician uses in the ambulatory setting, because it is used within a single healthcare organization. To help yourself understand the difference between the EMR and the EHR, consider this scenario: If the Southwest Family Medical Clinic uses an EMR, their records are in electronic form, but the records are available electronically only inside the office or to staff members who log on to the system remotely. If the clinic were using an EHR, the physicians and staff would be able to see not only records generated in their clinic, but also records on their patients created at multiple other healthcare facilities, such as the local hospital, a regional imaging facility, or a freestanding laboratory. The clinic would have an interoperable access to the records created at other facilities. Healthcare professionals envision that the EHR eventually will provide a patient's medical records from birth to death.

In "Defining Key Health Information Technology Terms," a report published in 2008, NAHIT acknowledged the need to define three additional vital terms: health information exchange, health information organization, and regional health information organization. *Health information exchange* is the electronic movement of health-related information among organizations according to nationally recognized standards. *Health information organization* is an organization that oversees and governs the exchange of health-related information among organizations according to nationally recognized standards. A *regional health information organization* is a health organization that brings together healthcare stakeholders in a defined geographic area and governs health information exchange among them for the purpose of improving health and care in that community. The report stated that as multiple groups grappled with how to achieve the president's vision, these terms emerged to characterize some of the key building blocks of the envisioned health technologic infrastructure: electronic medical records and/or electronic health records for healthcare professionals; personal health records for individuals and healthcare consumers, and electronic health information exchange to enable efficient communication among these various records.

AMERICAN RECOVERY AND REINVESTMENT ACT (ARRA)

The American Recovery and Reinvestment Act of 2009 (ARRA), commonly known as the Economic Stimulus Package, was passed to promote economic recovery. This legislation was signed into law by President Barack Obama on February 17, 2009. The health information technology aspects of the bill provide slightly more than $31 billion for healthcare infrastructure and EHR investment. The sections of the ARRA that pertain to healthcare are collectively known as the Health Information Technology for Economic and Clinical Health Act, or HITECH Act.

HITECH ACT AND MEANINGFUL USE

The HITECH Act provides financial incentives for the meaningful use of certified EHR technology to achieve health and efficiency goals. It was incorporated into the ARRA to promote the adoption and meaningful use of health information technology. Remember, HIPAA was created in large part to simplify administrative processes using electronic devices. *Meaningful use,* defined simply, means that providers must show that they are using EHR technology in ways that can be measured significantly in quality and quantity. If providers meet the meaningful use requirements, they will qualify for incentive payments. Three main components of meaningful use can be identified, including:

- Use of certified EHR in a meaningful manner, such as **e-prescribing**
- Use of certified EHR technology for electronic exchange of health information to improve the quality of health care
- Use of certified EHR technology to submit clinical quality reports, procedure and diagnosis codes, surveys, and other measures

Criteria for meaningful use will be implemented in three stages:

- Stage 1 (2011 and 2012): Sets the baseline for electronic data capture and information sharing
- Stage 2 (expected to be implemented in 2013): Continues to expand on the baseline
- Stage 3 (expected to be implemented in 2015): Continues to expand on the baseline and will be further developed through future rule making

In Subtitle D of the HITECH Act, privacy and security concerns related to the electronic submission of health information are addressed. Several provisions strengthen the civil and criminal penalties of the HIPAA rules, most of which became effective in February, 2009. More of the provisions will become effective over the next few years, subject to future lawmaking.

Included in the February, 2009, modifications of HIPAA were:

- Establishment of categories of violations that reflect increasing levels of **culpability**
- Requirements that penalties be determined based on the nature and extent of the violation and the nature and extent of the harm resulting from the violation
- Establishment of tiers of increasing penalty amounts that determine the range of and authority to impose civil monetary penalties (Table 15-1)

TABLE 15-1   Categories of HIPAA Violations and Associated Penalties

CATEGORY: SECTION 1176(A)(1)	EACH VIOLATION	ALL SUCH VIOLATIONS OF AN IDENTICAL PROVISION IN A CALENDAR YEAR
(A) Did not know	$100 to $50,000	$1.5 million
(B) Reasonable cause	$1,000 to $50,000	$1.5 million
(C) (i) Willful neglect— corrected	$10,000 to $50,000	$1.5 million
(C) (ii) Willful neglect—not corrected	$50,000	$1.5 million

As indicated in Table 15-1, minimum and maximum penalty amounts are established and can be assessed by the Department of Health and Human Services (DHHS), depending on the nature of the violation. The DHHS determines the penalties on a case-by-case basis and may provide or continue to provide a waiver for violations that arise from a **reasonable cause** and are not **willful neglect** incidents that are not corrected in a timely manner. The DHHS will also consider whether the covered entity has provided **reasonable diligence** in its attempts to bring the facility into compliance with the law. Physicians can expect reductions in the amounts they are paid from Medicare and Medicaid if they are not in compliance by 2015. Remember, the computer system in the medical office must be more than a tool for data recall to be considered an EMR system; the physician must use the system for tasks, at a minimum, such as e-prescribing and **computerized physician/provider order entry (CPOE)**.

ADVANTAGES AND DISADVANTAGES OF THE EMR

According to a 2010 mail survey of 10,301 physicians done by the Centers for Disease Control and Prevention (CDC), 50.7% of physicians in office-based practices use full or partial EMR systems. The use of EMR systems in physicians' offices increased steadily from 2001 through 2010. The primary reason physicians have not yet adopted an EMR system is the expense. Other reasons include:

- Inability to find an EMR system that meets the practice's needs
- Uncertainty about a return on investment
- Physician resistance
- Loss of productivity or down time for installation and learning curve

The EMR has several advantages over a paper medical record. Most experts agree that the EMR can reduce medical errors by keeping prescriptions, allergies, and other information organized; it also can reduce costs by preventing duplicate tests. Staffing needs also may be reduced, because fewer personnel are needed to manage an EMR system. Because a computer keyboard is used to enter information into the record, the record is not nearly as likely to be illegible. Typed copy certainly is easier to read than handwriting, even if the record is several years old. EMR systems require individual user names and passwords, which secure the system from unauthorized users.

Compared to walls and file cabinets full of paper medical records, the EMR requires less storage space. One or two external hard drives with a terabyte of disk space each conceivably could hold all the medical records of all patients throughout the life of a physician's practice. This would eliminate the need to purge inactive files, and the resulting space requirement for the external hard drive may be no bigger than a large shoebox. The files may be duplicated regularly and placed off site as a backup.

Information can be accessed in a variety of locations, and more than one person can see the record at any given time. The patient database usually allows various types of statistical information to be recalled, which is a valuable tool. Patient information is available quickly in an emergency, even when the patient is not in his or her hometown. The physician and medical assistants can access progress notes, test results, and any other information about the patient, including patient education and appointment no-shows. The physician and medical assistants can access patient information using a smart phone or personal digital assistant (PDA).

Once the physician and staff become familiar with the system, they may find that they are able to see more patients in the course of a day than when paper records were used. All these advantages lead to cost savings and more efficient patient care.

However, the EMR system is not without disadvantages. Studies show that lack of capital is the most significant obstacle to adoption of the system; another stumbling block is the reluctance of employees in physicians' offices to make such substantial changes and to learn a new computer system. Employees may not be the only individuals resistant to a changeover to electronic records; patients often are fearful that their private health information will be available to unauthorized individuals, and they often assume that their records will be posted on the Internet. The startup costs of conversion to an EMR system usually are quite high, although most physicians realize that the system eventually will be worth the cost. "The Financial and Nonfinancial Costs of Implementing Electronic Health Records in Primary Care Practices," an article in the online journal *Health Affairs,* suggests that the startup cost for a five-physician practice is approximately $162,000, with $85,500 going toward maintenance costs during the first year (Fleming et al., 2011). The study also suggested that the implementation team would need an average of 611 hours to prepare for the implementation, and end-users, such as the physicians, medical assistants, and other staff members, would need about 134 hours of training to use the system. Both the physician and staff require extensive training in the EMR system and must be receptive to even more training to use the system to its full capacity. Training is time-consuming and takes the physician and staff away from treating patients for certain periods. Because not all computer systems are user friendly, care must be taken to choose a system that has technologic support, both live and online, that is available during the hours the healthcare facility is operating. Space for the equipment can be an issue, although usually less space is required than for a paper record system. Because healthcare facilities use different sets of abbreviations and terms, issues can arise with interaction of the office system with other systems. Finally, security and confidentiality are major concerns of both the healthcare professionals and the patients.

SUCCESSFUL CONVERSION TO AN EMR SYSTEM

- Get the entire facility "on board" with the change.
- Provide leadership to the staff.
- Encourage and praise the staff's hard work in making the conversion successful.
- As a medical assistant, be loyal and promote loyalty to the facility during the change.
- Use good people management skills, especially with those who are against the conversion. Many people who were initially averse to conversions later say they do not know how they ever worked without the EMR.
- Always give patients, visitors, and co-workers excellent customer service.
- Work as a team with other staff members.
- Use every employee's strong qualities where they are needed.
- Be willing to venture into a new system and keep a positive attitude.
- Remember that if medicine is anything, it is constant change.

CRITICAL THINKING APPLICATION   15-1

Some of the patients who visit Dr. Adkins and Dr. Brooks have expressed concern that electronic medical records may not be private enough and that their health information will be "floating around on the Internet." They are worried that unauthorized individuals could somehow access their information on the computer and do them harm.

- How might Sloan alleviate the patients' fears about their records being available on the Internet to so many people?
- What disadvantages with regard to confidentiality are associated with the EMR?
- Should a patient be allowed to decide whether his or her records will be kept on computer or on paper?

INCENTIVES FOR IMPLEMENTING EMR SYSTEMS

As mentioned earlier, the CMS has established an incentive program for health facilities that is based upon three specific stages and a set of objectives the facility must meet to receive the incentive payment. The incentive program includes stages and objectives with associated measures for determining whether the facility has met the objective. Stage 1 began in 2011, and Stages 2 and 3 will take effect in 2013 and 2015, respectively. To meet the requirements of Stage 1, Meaningful Use, eligible professionals must complete 15 core objectives, 5 of 10 objectives from the menu set, and 6 total clinical quality measures.

CAPABILITIES OF EMR SYSTEMS

The EMR system (also sometimes called a *practice management system*) can perform a multitude of tasks, saving time and money in the physician's office (Figure 15-1). As these systems become more

prevalent and technology advances, these capabilities will multiply. The following are some of the features of a typical EMR system.

- **Specialty software.** Patient data are captured and processed into a system that is specialty-specific, so that the terminology and patient care treatments are compatible with the physician's specialty. However, additional features can allow the physician to include terminology from other specialties.
- **Appointment scheduler.** The appointment scheduler allows the staff to track and schedule appointments, matrix the schedule, and account for recurring time blocks (Figure 15-2). The appointments can be merged into specific types with default times so that lengthy procedures are not scheduled in short appointment blocks. The scheduler features also allow various search **parameters**; if a patient calls because he or she cannot remember the appointment time, a search can be initiated using the date, physician's name, patient's name, or other search keywords.
- **Appointment reminder and confirmation.** The system can be programmed to initiate automatic reminder or confirmation calls to patients. The staff can record the reminders, and patients are prompted to choose options, such as "Press one," to confirm or reschedule appointments.
- **Prescription writer.** The EMR system can produce electronic prescriptions, which can be printed and given to patients or automatically submitted to a pharmacy. Lists can be created with the physician's most common drug choices and dosages. A patient allergies function can block the prescription of drugs the patient cannot take, and the system can generate a patient information sheet on new prescriptions.
- **Medical billing system.** The EMR billing system can manage all of the practice's billing and accounting systems. The system also can interface with clearinghouses for electronic claims submission and tracking. Reports can be generated that provide accurate details of the financial state of the practice at certain intervals or whenever requested.
- **Charge capture.** The charge capture functions can store lists of billing codes (e.g., International Classification of Diseases [ICD] and Current Procedural Terminology [CPT]) in addition to charges associated with procedures, supplies, and laboratory tests. Evaluation and Management (E/M) codes are used during office visits to obtain the highest possible reimbursement; these help the physician maximize profits while remaining in compliance with the law. Alerts can let the user know when a certain charge does not match a diagnosis code; for instance, a male patient would not undergo a gynecologic exam. In such cases, the software alerts the user and helps prevent errors that can lead to denial of insurance claims.
- **Eligibility verification.** EMR billing systems can perform online verification of insurance eligibility and can capture demographic data.
- **Referral management.** Current and referring physicians can be coordinated and automated, allowing the physician to share patient information with another physician. This reduces the patient's physical effort of transporting copies of records back and forth to referring physicians, eliminates the costs of such copies, and is faster and more efficient than copying and mailing patient records.

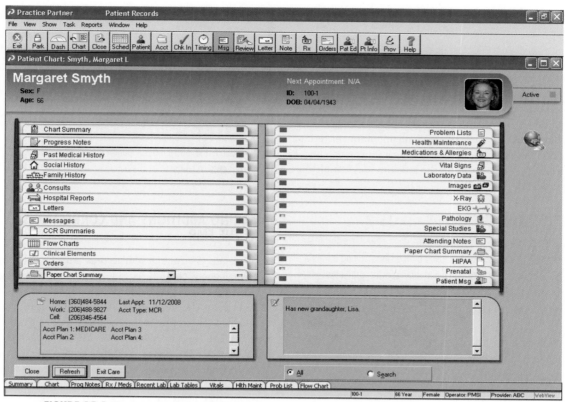

FIGURE 15-1 The electronic medical record (EMR) can perform numerous tasks in addition to displaying personal information about the patient. This allows the physician and medical assistants to interact with patients and provide better service. (Courtesy McKessan Corp., Alpharetta, Ga.)

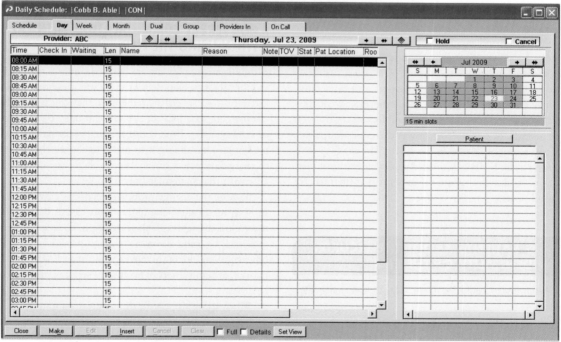

FIGURE 15-2 The EMR usually has a scheduling system that can be changed to manage the needs of the physician and office staff. (Courtesy McKessan Corp., Alpharetta, Ga.)

- **Laboratory order integration.** The laboratory order integration feature allows the user to interact with outside laboratories and to receive and post laboratory results to patients' records. Tests can be ordered from the physician's laptop, PDA, or smart phone. Results can be transmitted by fax, scan, or e-mail and uploaded directly into the patient's record.
- **Patient portal.** User-friendly patient portals can be added to the system that allow the patient to access medical records and perform other functions, such as setting an appointment, printing a child's immunization record, reviewing a statement, checking whether insurance has paid on the account, and completing new patient records online.

CRITICAL THINKING APPLICATION   15-2

Jennifer, the office manager, has noticed that Sloan seems frustrated in the training classes for the EMR system used by the clinic. During a break, Jennifer asks Sloan whether she is having any specific problems with the training classes. She also asks for Sloan's input on the system. Sloan says that she just prefers clinical work and that her typing skills are a little "rusty."

- How might Jennifer respond to Sloan's comments?
- Why might this be a warning sign that Sloan will not be a good match for the clinical side of the practice?

PATIENTS' CONCERNS ABOUT THE EMR

Patients worry about the security of their information, particularly about who can access it. Lawsuits often are filed when patients discover that an unauthorized person has accessed their protected health information. The medical assistant should listen to a patient's concerns and explain the safety procedures that apply to the EMR in language the patient can understand. Some facilities prepare a brochure to explain the conversion process to the patient and the advantages of the EMR system.

The medical assistant should expect hesitation and even reluctance from patients who are concerned about the privacy of their health information. Patients are concerned about lack of control over who views their records. Be prepared to answer their questions about the safety of their records as related to the EMR. The medical assistant must know how the EMR is protected and what security measures are in place to be able to reassure the patients that their records are protected at all times.

REASSURING PATIENTS ABOUT THE SECURITY AND CONFIDENTIALITY OF THE EMR

- Explain the conversion before the office changes and during the conversion.
- Never display a negative attitude about the change to an electronic medical record system; patients tend to reflect the attitude you show them.
- Prepare a pamphlet explaining the processes that will change in your particular office with use of the EMR.

- Take a moment to show the patient a little about the software once it has been implemented (using only their record). Most patients are interested in and perhaps even amazed by what the EMR can accomplish. Show the individual the log-in process (without revealing passwords) to reassure him or her that access to records is private and secure.
- Explain the records backup process to help alleviate patients' fears that their health information may be lost.
- Explain the office access policy regarding who can access and view patients' records.

MAKING ADDITIONS AND CORRECTIONS TO THE EMR

Additions to electronic health records must be made by making an additional entry. Never delete a previous entry or change it unless it is in the process of being entered. A good rule of thumb is to avoid changing any electronic entry after the initials of the maker have been added. This, of course, should take place immediately after the note is placed in the record. Once this has happened, a new entry must be made to correct information in a previous entry. Some EMR programs do not allow any changes to the record; in this case, the user must create a new entry to make corrections or add notes. Virtually all EMR systems place a date and time stamp on entries and log which employee has entered the record. This method also prevents another user from changing a record previously entered. Never share passwords to the EMR system with other employees; in some facilities, password infractions are grounds for immediate termination of employment.

NONVERBAL COMMUNICATION WITH THE PATIENT WHEN USING THE EMR

Although many patients are covered under a type of insurance that requires them to choose a primary care provider (PCP) and to have a referral to a specialist, remember that the patient has the option of changing that PCP or specialist, usually by making a phone call or sending a fax. Even if the change process takes a little longer, the patient still has the right to make a change. The patient may decide to change providers simply because he or she does not feel comfortable with that particular provider.

Because the change process is relatively easy, the physician wants to keep his or her patients (in most cases), because losing patients means loss of income. If the care begins to seem impersonal, patients may feel a strong desire to change providers, even though most offices and providers are moving toward an EMR system. Remember, patients are consumers of healthcare services, and they expect quality healthcare.

When using the EMR, the medical assistant must make sure his or her nonverbal communication sends the right message to the patient. Eye contact is absolutely essential (Figure 15-3). If the medical assistant constantly looks at the computer screen, the patient feels quite alienated from the information exchange process. Do not insinuate by physical action that the EMR is a "hidden entity"; for example, do not necessarily shield the computer screen from the patient's view when entering information. Although patients may not understand anything they see on the screen, they will feel more at ease if their information is not hidden from them. Also, modify your stance so that the patient feels like a part of the information process. Just as sitting in a chair across from a supervisor's desk can be intimidating, the patient may feel the same emotions sitting across from a medical assistant entering information into the EMR.

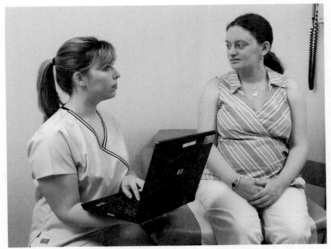

FIGURE 15-3 The medical assistant must make eye contact with the patient when using an EMR.

Take an open stance; sit next to or at an angle to the patient to support the impression that those in the healthcare facility and the patient are partners in the healthcare plan.

Remember that patients deserve to choose in most aspects of their healthcare plans; therefore, offer choices wherever possible. Never expect patients to make quick decisions about their care. They may want to consult family members or give some thought to important medical decisions. The medical assistant needs to promote time to think unless the patient is faced with a critical, time-sensitive decision. Physicians often assume that patients will automatically follow their instructions or orders; however, some patients prefer some time to think. Always follow up and make note of any wait time the patient requests, notify the physician, and enter that information into the EMR (Procedure 15-1). Make sure timely communication is kept with the patient and that any additional orders that need to be put in place are completed. The many features of the EMR allow the medical assistant to be efficient and highly competent if he or she is willing to make an extra effort to master the EMR system.

Also make sure patients understand all instructions given to them regarding test procedures or preparation for procedures. Most EMRs can print an instruction sheet, which the medical assistant can review with the patient. The customer service aspect of patient care is even more important when the facility uses an EMR system. Chapter 26 presents more customer service tips for the medical office.

PROCEDURE 15-1

Execute Data Management Using Electronic Healthcare Records such as the EMR

GOAL: *To obtain and enter patient data using the electronic health record (EHR) and/or electronic medical record (EMR).*

EQUIPMENT and SUPPLIES

- Patient's medical records
- Data to be included in medical records
- Computer

PROCEDURAL STEPS

1. Take a laptop computer or handheld device into the treatment room with the patient.
2. Welcome the patient warmly, maintaining eye contact.
   PURPOSE: To interact with the patient before opening the computer; the computer cannot become a barrier that blocks interpersonal interaction between the medical assistant and the patient.
3. Place the laptop on a secure, flat surface and open the patient's record. Do not place the device on a flimsy stand or try to operate it while holding the unit.
   PURPOSE: To avoid dropping and damaging the computer.
4. Stand so that the computer is more to the side rather than placed between you and the patient.
   PURPOSE: To keep the computer from becoming a barrier between patient and medical assistant.
5. Verify the patient's basic demographics (e.g., mailing address and phone number).

   PURPOSE: To make sure the computer has the most recent data needed to contact the patient.
6. Discuss the reason for the patient's visit to the office.
   PURPOSE: To record the chief complaint.
7. Enter data offered by the patient into the EMR. Follow office policy guidelines and enter the data as directed by the EMR instructional materials.
   PURPOSE: To comply with office policy and to enter data in the correct format.
8. Continue to maintain eye contact with the patient; do not constantly look down at the keyboard while entering data.
   PURPOSE: To maintain the human connection with the patient, so that the computer does not become a deterrent to interaction with the patient.
9. Use the proper technique for entering patient data (e.g. SOAP, CHEDDAR).
   PURPOSE: To follow the method of charting used in the facility.
10. After entering pertinent data, ask the patient whether he or she has any additional information or questions for the physician.
    PURPOSE: To make sure the data are complete and to document questions for the physician's attention.

11. Briefly read back to the patient the data about the chief complaint and symptoms.
    PURPOSE: To make sure all pertinent data have been entered and that the patient's explanations of symptoms and other issues were understood.
12. If data such as paper reports need to be entered, scan them into the computer and save them in the patient's EMR.
13. Electronically sign all entries.
    PURPOSE: To document who entered data into the record.

14. Save the data as indicated by the office policies and procedures manual and the EMR user manual.
    PURPOSE: To ensure that the data entered are retained in the EMR.
15. Follow the process specified in the EMR user manual for closing the EMR program and shutting off the computer.
    PURPOSE: To comply with instructions and to guard against loss of patient data.

CRITICAL THINKING APPLICATION   15-3

Jennifer walks behind Sloan's desk and notices that she is looking at the progress notes on a patient who was recently arrested and indicted for child abuse. The case has been in the newspaper and on television consistently for several weeks. Jennifer asks Sloan why she has accessed that record. Sloan hesitates and then says she must have entered the wrong patient ID number.

- Does Sloan's explanation sound convincing?
- Why is Jennifer concerned about Sloan looking at the patient's record?
- Just because the individual is a patient at the clinic, does that mean any employee has the right to look at the patient's EMR?

THE NATIONWIDE HEALTH INFORMATION NETWORK

The Nationwide Health Information Network (NHIN) was developed to provide a secure, national, interoperable health information infrastructure that will connect providers, consumers, and others involved in supporting healthcare. The organization is a critical part of the national information technology agenda. It will enable health information to follow the consumer, making it available for clinical decision making, and support appropriate use of healthcare information beyond direct patient care, so as to improve health. The goals of the organization are to:

- Develop capabilities for standards-based, secure data exchange nationwide
- Improve the coordination of care information among hospitals, laboratories, physicians' offices, pharmacies, and other providers
- Ensure that appropriate information is available at the time and place of care
- Ensure that consumers' health information is secure and confidential
- Give consumers new capabilities for managing and controlling their personal health records and provide access to their health information from electronic health records and other sources
- Reduce risks from medical errors and support the delivery of appropriate, evidence-based medical care
- Lower healthcare costs resulting from inefficiencies, medical errors, and incomplete patient information

NHIN has several core capabilities, including:

- Finding and retrieving healthcare information within and between health information exchanges and other organizations
- Delivering a summarized patient record to support patient care and the patient's health
- Supporting consumers' preferences regarding the exchange of their information, including the ability to choose not to participate in the NHIN
- Supporting secure information exchange
- Supporting a common trust agreement that establishes the obligations and assurances to which all NHIN participants agree; also, providing the ability to match patients to their data without a national patient identifier
- Supporting harmonized standards developed by voluntary consensus standards bodies for the exchange of health information among all such entities and networks

BACKUP SYSTEMS FOR THE EMR

Even the best or most expensive EMR system cannot function without power. If a natural disaster occurs and the physician's office is without electricity for several days or weeks, the physician must have a backup system for the EMR so that the office can function. HIPAA requires that the facility adopt a backup and recovery plan that includes daily off-site software backup for the EMR system. Several alternatives can be used for data preservation and backup.

- *External hard drive.* An external hard drive connects to the main computer and with fairly simple programming can copy the information in the EMR daily. Seven folders, one for each day of the week, can hold the information from the previous day; these folders are replaced with new, updated information at designated periods. CDs and DVDs can hold daily data, and some thumb drives have enough capacity to perform this task. Once a habit of a daily backup to the external hard drive has been established, the method is relatively simple and reliable.
- *Full server backup.* The physician may want to back up the EMR system on a dedicated server, which is a large-capacity computer set aside specifically for the EMR system. With these servers, a full backup should be performed monthly. Many large medical facilities and hospitals have one or more dedicated servers for the EMR system.

- *Online backup systems.* An online backup system can be used, usually for a subscription fee. Although the cost may be higher than for some other methods, online systems are easy to use, because there is no external drive to carry and no CD or thumb drive to put through the process of downloading data. However, a time investment is involved, because the process of contacting the company that offers the service and then downloading all the data takes several hours. Also, the initial download can take quite a while. Even so, an online system is very stable and reliable.

All these backup methods require an alternative power source in case of a disaster that interrupts electricity. Remember that backup systems are not effective if the data are stored at the medical facility, and the disaster happens at or affects that physical address. Information technology professionals usually recommend using two of these three methods for the best protection. The system must be protected from theft and unauthorized use, just as is the on-site system.

Medical assistants should keep their paper medical records skills sharp in case the EMR system is down for an extended period. Always have supplies available for alternative use in such instances.

THE MEDICAL ASSISTANT AND THE EMR

Once the medical assistant has trained on the EMR system and has had the opportunity to use it for a time, daily use should become second nature. In fact, it may be difficult to imagine a workday without the system! By being open to change and willing to learn, the medical assistant can set a good example for all employees and will be more receptive to the process of change. Be encouraging to other staff members while training on the system, and if technology comes easily to you, share your knowledge with others and assist wherever possible. Do not expect to master the system in a week; instead, realize that a new system has a learning curve and be patient with and receptive to the educational process. Keep technical support phone numbers handy and feel free to use them whenever a new or complicated issue arises. Work as a team, and if possible, help others who might find learning the system more of a struggle. Above all, while getting used to the new technology, make sure your attitude is one of enthusiasm, interest, and curiosity.

CLOSING COMMENTS

A primary goal of all healthcare facilities is to provide efficient, high-quality patient care. The EMR system can help the staff reach that goal. In the future, every physician's office, hospital, pharmacy, and other healthcare facilities may be able to access information in minutes, which will improve patient care and save lives. Stay abreast of news and articles related to EMR systems. Remember, the healthcare industry is one of constant growth and learning, and today's information technology provides the medical assistant with endless opportunities to make that growth personal and rewarding.

Patient Education

When educating patients about the EMR system, allow them to watch as their information is entered into the computer. Showing patients just a few of the system's capabilities may reassure them of its efficiency and possibilities. Always maintain eye contact with patients whose information is being entered into the computer. Physicians and medical assistants alike may have to relearn how to interact with patients in a natural way while using the laptop or PDA in the examination rooms. Realize that during the implementation period, processing and serving patients may take longer, because the staff is using new technology. Most patients are understanding about this if the medical assistant explains that a new system is in place and asks for patience. Because patients are not always technologically savvy, most will be supportive and interested in the EMR system.

Legal and Ethical Issues

Remember that the EMR system contains information that is confidential at all times. The patient must authorize the release of health information in electronic form, just as if it were a piece of paper. Electronic medical records systems must:

- Maintain the security and confidentiality of data
- Be easily retrievable
- Have safeguards against the loss of information
- Protect patients' rights to confidentiality and privacy
- Require identification and authentication for access

By supporting these requirements, the medical facility remains in compliance with applicable laws and gains the trust of patients, who are reassured that their health information is secure and safe.

SUMMARY OF SCENARIO

Jennifer has decided that Sloan is just not a good match for the practice. One week before Sloan's probationary period is up, Jennifer brings her into the office to talk. She reminds Sloan that she originally was hired to work in the administrative part of the office. She explains that, although Sloan's desire and enthusiasm for the clinical side were evident, Jennifer did not feel that Sloan was addressing her duties in a responsible way and that her work ethic needed improvement. Jennifer reminded Sloan of the patient's record she had accessed and explained that this was a breach of patient confidentiality and medical ethics.

Sloan was clearly affected by Jennifer's evaluation of her work. She opened up to Jennifer and expressed her remorse that she had waited so long after graduation to look for employment. She also said that she was beginning to feel desperate for a job and felt that she needed to take the administrative job in hopes of later getting the position she wanted. Sloan apologized for accessing the patient's record and said she understood that this breach alone was grounds for immediate termination.

Jennifer was impressed that Sloan was able to admit her mistakes and feel remorse for them. She agreed to allow Sloan to volunteer at the clinic in the back office two afternoons a week until she found permanent employment. Sloan was thankful that Jennifer was willing to help her reach her career goals. She said she would take the knowledge of her mistakes to heart and work very hard for Jennifer as a volunteer. Jennifer reiterated to Sloan that her breach of confidentiality would be a difficult issue to overcome in future employment.

SUMMARY OF LEARNING OBJECTIVES

1. **Define, spell, and pronounce the terms listed in the vocabulary.**
   Spelling and pronouncing medical terms correctly bolster the medical assistant's credibility. Knowing the definition of these terms promotes confidence in communication with co-workers and patients.

2. **Discuss the presidential Executive Order that led to the implementation of electronic medical record systems across the nation.**
   President George W. Bush issued an Executive Order in August, 2006, that presented the goal of having electronic health records for most Americans by the year 2014. The order included five requirements that outlined the relationship between the agencies involved in the initial implementation process and the beneficiaries they serve. In general, when computer upgrades were initiated, these agencies and beneficiaries agreed to implement interoperable systems that would lead to nationwide electronic medical record systems in the near future.

3. **Discuss the principles of using the electronic medical record (EMR).**
   Electronic medical records systems allow record sharing among various healthcare entities in a geographic area. This leads to better patient care, because healthcare professionals can put together a more detailed picture of the patient's health. Using the EMR or EHR, a physician can access hospital records on his or her patients, even if he or she was not the attending physician. Also, laboratory reports can be viewed on smart phones and PDAs without having to be mailed or faxed to the office. Having the whole picture about a patient's health enables the physician to make better treatment choices and provide the best care.

4. **Distinguish between an electronic health record (EHR) and an electronic medical record (EMR).**
   The electronic health record (EHR) is an electronic record of health-related information about an individual that conforms to nationally recognized interoperability standards and that can be created, managed, and consulted by authorized clinicians and staff from more than one healthcare organization The electronic medical record (EMR) is an electronic record of health-related information about an individual that can be created, gathered, managed, and consulted by authorized clinicians and staff within one healthcare organization.

5. **Explain how the American Recovery and Reinvestment Act applies to the healthcare industry.**
   The American Recovery and Reinvestment Act (ARRA) of 2009, commonly known as the Economic Stimulus Package, was meant to promote economic recovery. The health information technology aspects of the bill provide slightly more than $31 billion for healthcare infrastructure and EHR investment. The sections of the ARRA that pertain to healthcare are collectively known as the Health Information Technology for Economic and Clinical Health (HITECH) Act.

6. **Define meaningful use.**
   Meaningful use, defined simply, means that providers must show that they are using EHR technology in ways that can be measured significantly in quality and quantity. If providers meet the meaningful use requirements, they will qualify for incentive payments.

7. **List the three main components of meaningful use legislation.**
   The three main components of meaningful use are (1) use of certified EHR in a meaningful manner, such as e-prescribing; (2) use of certified EHR technology for electronic exchange of health information to improve quality of health care; and (3) use of certified EHR technology to submit clinical quality reports, procedure and diagnosis codes, surveys, and other measures.

8. **Discuss the advantages and disadvantages of an electronic medical record system.**
   Advantages of an EMR system include savings in time and money, reduced staffing needs, fewer medical errors, faster retrieval of information, and enormous technologic capabilities. Disadvantages include patient concerns about confidentiality, staff training, staff acceptance, and space and storage issues.

9. **Explore the capabilities of an electronic medical record system.**
   Some capabilities of an EMR system include specialty practice components, appointment scheduling features, prescription writers, medical billing systems, charge capture, eligibility verification, referral management, laboratory order integration, patient portals, and many other features that vary from system to system.

10. **Give several reasons patients are hesitant in accepting electronic health records.**
    The medical assistant should expect hesitation and even reluctance from patients with regard to the EMR system, because they are concerned about the privacy of their health information. Patients worry about lack of control over who views their records. Be prepared to answer their questions about the safety of their records as related to the EMR. Medical assistants must know how the EMR is protected and what security measures are in place so that they can reassure patients that their records are protected at all times.

11. **Discuss the importance of nonverbal communication with patients when an EMR system is used.**
    Eye contact is critical when an EMR system is used with patients. Body language must indicate that the medical assistant is open to and listening to the patient's concerns, not just concentrating on data entry. Physicians and medical assistants alike may have to relearn how to interact with patients in a natural way while using the laptop or PDA in the examination room. Realize that during the implementation period, processing and serving patients may take longer, because the staff is using new technology. Most patients are understanding about this if the medical assistant explains that a new system is in place and asks for patience. Because patients are not always technologically savvy, most will be supportive and interested in the EMR system.

12. **Summarize the goals of the Nationwide Health Information Network (NHIN).**
    The goals of the NHIN include developing capabilities for standards-based, secure data exchange nationwide; improving the coordination of care information among hospitals, laboratories, physicians' offices, pharmacies, and other providers; ensuring that appropriate information is available at the time and place of care; ensuring that consumers' health

information is secure and confidential; giving consumers new capabilities for managing and controlling their personal health records and providing access to their health information from electronic health records and other sources; reducing risks from medical errors and supporting the delivery of appropriate, evidence-based medical care; and lowering healthcare costs resulting from inefficiencies, medical errors, and incomplete patient information.

13. **List the core capabilities of the NHIN.**

The core capabilities of the NHIN are to find and retrieve healthcare information within and between health information exchanges and other organizations; to deliver a summarized patient record to support patient care and to support the patient's health; to support consumers' preferences regarding the exchange of their information, including the right to choose not to participate in the NHIN; to support secure information exchange; to support a common trust agreement that establishes the obligations and assurances to which all NHIN participants agree; to match patients to their data without a national patient identifier; and

to support harmonized standards developed by voluntary consensus standards bodies for the exchange of health information among all such entities and networks.

14. **Summarize the role of the medical assistant with regard to the changing technology in healthcare facilities and organizations.**

By being open to change and willing to learn, the medical assistant sets a good example for all employees and is more receptive to the process of change. Be encouraging to other staff members while training on the system, and if technology comes easily to you, share your knowledge with others and assist wherever possible. Do not expect to master the system in a week; realize that new systems have a learning curve and be patient with and receptive to the educational process. Keep technical support phone numbers handy and feel free to use them whenever a new or complicated issue arises. Work with others as a team, and if possible, offer to help those who might find learning the system more of a struggle. Above all, while getting used to the new technology, make sure your attitude is one of enthusiasm, interest, and curiosity.

CONNECTIONS

📖 **Study Guide Connection:** Go to the Chapter 15 Study Guide. Read and complete the activities.

ⓔ **Evolve Connection:** Go to the Chapter 15 link at *evolve.elsevier.com/ kinn* to complete the Chapter Review and Chapter Quiz. Check out the other resources listed for this chapter to make the most of what you have learned from The Electronic Medical Record.

Reference

Fleming NS, Culler SD, McCorkle R, et al: The financial and nonfinancial costs of implementing electronic health records in primary care practices. *Health Affairs* Mar 1;30(3):481-489, 2011. Available at http://content.healthaffairs.org/content/30/3/481.abstract. Accessed November 12, 2011.

16

HEALTH INFORMATION MANAGEMENT

Laura Kelly graduated from her medical assistant training 1 year ago and is now employed at a freestanding urgent care center. She works with the quality assurance staff and also performs front office duties. She enjoys working with statistics, is very detail oriented, has excellent computer and coding skills, and is able to comprehend lengthy regulatory text, such as that used in the rules and guidelines established by the Health Insurance Portability and Accountability Act (HIPAA). She has proven to be a valuable employee, and her efforts help the center comply with privacy laws.

Laura thought that quality assurance involved only patient satisfaction when she began working for the center. She has learned that this is just a small part of the total quality picture of the facility. The center has developed a patient questionnaire to solicit input from patients, and she enjoys talking with them about their experiences. Laura rarely encounters complaints, and she is proud to work for a medical facility that employs individuals who are concerned about giving exceptional care to patients. She understands that providing quality in a healthcare facility has many aspects.

Laura also realizes that health information encompasses much more than the patient's medical record. She knows that health statistics are vital to research and that physicians rely on statistical information when prescribing drugs, giving treatments, planning for future growth, deciding on which services to offer, and performing other services. Providers frequently contact Laura to determine how many procedures of a certain type were done at the center during a given period. The facility's database is very sophisticated and allows her to access many types of statistics quickly. Her office also monitors people who enter the database and what information is accessed. Monitoring access is one method of ensuring that privacy is maintained.

Laura has attended continuing education workshops, which provided up-to-date information and enabled her to help the staff stay in compliance with the numerous regulations that govern the facility. She is eager to learn and assist her employers in keeping the center safe for all patients and visitors.

While studying this chapter, think about the following questions:

- How is health information used in today's medical facilities?
- What can the individual medical assistant do to improve the quality of care given in his or her employer's facility?
- Why is quality management an important aspect of today's healthcare industry?
- How do statistics affect healthcare?

LEARNING OBJECTIVES

1. Define, spell, and pronounce the terms listed in the vocabulary.
2. Describe several ways health information is used.
3. Explain the nine characteristics of quality health data.
4. Explain the four concerns of quality assurance.
5. Explain the functions of the National Center for Health Statistics (NCHS).
6. Give some types of statistics kept by the NCHS.
7. Define total quality management.
8. Explain the function of The Joint Commission (formerly the Joint Commission on Accreditation of Healthcare Organizations [JCAHO]).
9. Discuss the importance of healthcare standards in medical facilities.

VOCABULARY

adverse event An injury caused by medical management rather than the underlying condition of the patient.

authenticated Proved; with regard to medical records, it applies to a signature, initials, or computer keystroke by the maker of the record to verify that the record is correct.

benchmarks Items or factors that serve as standards against which other items or factors can be measured or judged.

circumvent (suhr-kuhm-vent′) To manage to get around, especially by ingenuity or strategy.

contraindications (kahn-truh-in-duh-ka′-shuns) Factors, such as symptoms or conditions, that make a particular treatment or procedure inadvisable.

disparities (di-spar′-uh-tez) Fundamentally different and often incongruous elements; elements that are markedly distinct in quality or character.

encrypted (in-kript′-ed) Encoded; converted from one system of communication to another.

erroneous (eh-ro′-ne-uhs) Containing or characterized by error or assumption.

gradients A change in parameters or the value of a quantity, such as temperature or pressure; a change in response with distance from the stimulus; a graded difference in physiological activity along an axis, as of the body or embryonic fluid.

near miss A situation in which an error is caught or corrected before it affects the patient.

nosocomial (no-suh-ko′-me-uhl) Originating or taking place in a hospital.

potentially compensable event (PCE) An adverse occurrence, usually involving a patient, that could result in a financial obligation for a business or organization.

quality assurance (QA) Activities designed to increase the quality of a product or service through process or system changes that increase efficiency or effectiveness.

sentinel events Unexpected occurrences involving death or serious physical or psychological injury, or the risk thereof.

standards Models or examples established by authority, custom, or general consent; something set up and established by authority as a rule for the measure of quantity, weight, extent, value, or quality.

transposed Altered in sequence; interchanged.

Before the 1990s, practitioners in the healthcare field were barely familiar with the term "health information management." Today, this well-respected profession employs thousands of individuals across the United States. As more medical facilities move toward computer-based medical records, more trained health information management professionals are needed. The medical assistant may want to pursue employment in this growing field.

The health information management profession is supported by a national organization, the American Health Information Management Association (AHIMA). In 1994 the association's House of Delegates developed the following statement:

Health information management is the profession that focuses on healthcare data and the management of healthcare information resources. The profession addresses the nature, structure, and translation of data into usable forms of information for the advancement of health and healthcare of individuals and populations. Health information professionals collect, integrate, and analyze primary and secondary healthcare data; disseminate information; and manage information resources related to research, planning, provision, and evaluation of healthcare services.

EVOLUTION OF THE PROFESSION

In 1928 the American College of Surgeons realized that accurate medical records promoted good medical care. This desire for quality led to the establishment of the Association of Record Librarians of North America. In 1970 the organization changed its name to the American Medical Record Association. Medical records professionals found employment in hospitals, health clinics, insurance companies, and other organizations that used medical records. In 1991 the organization became known as the American Health Information Management Association. Advances in technology have brought the health information management profession from a paper-based environment into a highly sophisticated computer age, where physicians can access patient and statistical data in seconds.

HEALTH INFORMATION CERTIFICATIONS

AHIMA offers certifications in health information management, coding, and healthcare privacy and security. Because healthcare facilities are now provided financial incentives for converting to electronic medical records, the need for individuals in health information careers grows each year. Medical facilities need employees who can manipulate data and, at the same time, can keep patient records accurate and confidential. Health Information Technology certifications include:

- Registered Health Information Administrator (RHIA)
- Registered Health Information Technician (RHIT)
- Certified Coding Associate (CCA)
- Certified Coding Specialist (CCS)
- Certified Coding Specialist—Physician-based (CCS-P)
- Certified Health Data Analyst (CHDA)
- Certified in Healthcare Privacy & Security (CHPS)
- Certified Documentation Improvement Practitioner (CDIP)

Additional information about each certification and the eligibility requirements can be found in Table 16-1 and on the Evolve site at *evolve.elsevier.com/kinn*.

TABLE 16-1 Certifications in Healthcare Technology

CERTIFICATION INITIALS	CERTIFICATION NAME	OVERVIEW	ELIGIBILITY REQUIREMENTS
RHIA	Registered Health Information Administrator	Works as a manager in multiple healthcare settings as a critical link between providers, patients, providers, co-workers, and office visitors.	Complete the requirements of a baccalaureate program in Health Information Management accredited by the Commission on Accreditation for Health Informatics and Information Management Education (CAHIIME) or a comparable foreign program
RHIT	Registered Health Information Technologist	Works in multiple healthcare settings with solid potential for advancement into management, especially with a baccalaureate degree	Complete the requirements of an associate program in Health Information Management accredited by CAHIIME or a comparable foreign program
CCA	Certified Coding Associate	Exhibits a professional capability and competency in medical coding	U.S. high school diploma or equivalent; strongly recommended that candidate have 6 months of experience or have completed a program recommended by the American Health Information Management Association (AHIMA) or another formal coding training program
CCS	Certified Coding Specialist	Classifies medical data from patients' records into accurate diagnosis and procedure codes	U.S. high school diploma or equivalent; strongly recommended that candidate have at least 3 years of on-the-job experience in a hospital and have an academic background in anatomy and physiology, pathophysiology, and pharmacology
CCS-P	Certified Coding Specialist—Physician-based	Specializes in a physician-based setting	U.S. high school diploma or equivalent; strongly recommended that candidate have at least 4 years of on-the-job experience in multiple specialties for physician services and have an academic background in anatomy and physiology, pathophysiology, and pharmacology
CHDA	Certified Health Data Analyst	Develops an expertise in health data analysis and transforms data into accurate, consistent, and timely information	Associate's degree and 5 years of health data experience; RHIT credential or bachelor's degree and 3 years of experience; RHIA credential or master's degree and 1 year of experience
CHPS	Certified in Healthcare Privacy & Security	Develops competency in designing and implementing privacy and security systems in all types of healthcare organizations	Bachelor's degree and 4 years of experience in healthcare management; master's degree or higher, or RHIA or RHIT credential, with 2 years of experience
CDIP	Certified Documentation Improvement Practitioner	Captures and analyzes health information and can fluently translate the technoclinical language of the electronic medical record	RHIA, RHIT, CCS, CCS-P, registered nurse (RN), doctor of medicine (MD), or doctor of osteopathy (DO) credential and 2 years of experience in clinical documentation improvement; associate's degree or higher and 3 years of experience in clinical documentation improvement; must also have completed coursework in medical terminology and in anatomy and physiology

USES OF HEALTHCARE DATA

Healthcare data are used primarily to plan patient care, to plan for the future growth and development of the facility, and to ensure that patients receive continuity of care from one healthcare provider to another. However, the information provided by healthcare records can be useful in other ways.

Primary data are the information in the actual medical record; *secondary data* are generated from the information in the medical record. For example, when a drug is evaluated, statistics must be kept to help the manufacturers determine its effectiveness. Information on side effects and other **contraindications** is reviewed and used to make the drug safer and more marketable.

Healthcare organizations gather information on the number of patients who enter the facility with the same diagnosis. This and other information helps them plan the types of equipment required to meet the needs of this patient group. For instance, if the facility is located in a geographic area with a large number of patients with cardiac disease, the hospital may need to add a cardiac intensive care unit. Healthcare data and statistics guide planning for the needs of next week and the next decade.

The *Federal Register* (FR), which is published by the Office of the Federal Register, National Archives and Records Administration (NARA), provides daily access to rules, proposed rules, and notices of federal agencies and organizations, including those dealing with healthcare. Today's technology allows NARA to e-mail the FR's table of contents each day (Monday through Friday). Also, healthcare information can be accessed on the agency's Web site, which offers updated information about rules and regulations currently in effect, changes, new proposals, and final rulings. The FR is an excellent source of health data, and every medical facility should receive at least the daily table of contents e-mail, which can help the medical facility stay up-to-date on new regulations and changes in current ones.

CRITICAL THINKING APPLICATION 16-1

- Laura has noticed that the center keeps extensive records on the admitting diagnosis and the final diagnosis. Why is this information important to the center?
- If a certain physician is admitting numerous patients with the same diagnosis or for a certain procedure, what concerns might this raise for the facility? For what logical reason might this happen?

Third-party payers use healthcare information to determine whether claims should be paid. The data provide proof that a certain procedure or treatment was medically necessary and therefore its cost should be reimbursed. Government and regulatory agencies use data to ensure that healthcare facilities are in compliance with the various statutes and **standards** that govern them. Facilities use data to help determine whether they are providing high-quality healthcare to their patients.

WHAT ARE HIGH-QUALITY DATA?

The information in a database is only as reliable as the person who enters it into the computer. Nine characteristics of quality healthcare data have been identified: validity, reliability, completeness, recognizability, timeliness, relevance, accessibility, security, and legality.

- **Validity.** The validity of healthcare data is synonymous with accuracy. Accuracy is a primary characteristic of data, whether in paper-based or computer-based records. Great care must be taken that letters and numbers are not **transposed** when characters are typed on the keyboard.
- **Reliability.** The healthcare professional must be able to rely on the data. If a patient's medical chart indicates that he or she has no allergies, the medical assistant must be able to trust that information and give an injection, confident that the patient is not allergic to the medication. Reliability also pertains to the degree to which the information in the database can be trusted.
- **Completeness.** The information must be not only accurate, but complete. If the medical assistant gives an injection but fails to document it in the patient's chart, the record is incomplete. A court probably would rule that the injection could not be considered to have been given, because it was not documented in the patient's record. If a computer system is designed to upload new information into the database every night and the system malfunctions, the strong possibility exists that the records in the system are incomplete, possibly lacking vital information needed for the patient's care.
- **Recognizability.** All users of health information must be able to interpret the data in the health record. The facility should insist on consistent use of abbreviations to prevent misunderstandings when a patient's chart is reviewed. Some systems display charts to show an increase or a decline in basic vital signs (e.g., blood pressure, weight, and temperature). Such a system allows the physician to track symptoms over time without having to search through a paper record (Figure 16-1).
- **Timeliness.** Health information must be entered into the chart or database as soon as it is available. The medical assistant should never commit information to memory with the intention of entering it later. Reports from laboratories or medical testing centers also should be placed in the chart as soon as the physician has reviewed them so that patient care decisions are supported by the latest information. Whether paper or electronic, the medical record must be accurate, timely, complete, and accessible so that the patient receives optimum care from all providers.
- **Relevance.** The information in the database must be relevant to be useful. Needless and meaningless statistics about patient treatments or drug interactions do not benefit providers or users of health information.
- **Accessibility.** An advantage of a computer-based patient record is its accessibility; it can be viewed by more than one user at a time. The facility must take care to provide access only to individuals authorized to view the records. The computer system should have a log-in process that prompts for a password, and it should keep records of who accesses information by time and date. Paper-based patient records must be returned to their proper place when not in use so that they are accessible to all staff members.
- **Security.** Only certain employees should be allowed to access health information, and precautions must be taken to prevent access by intruders. Firewalls, which are similar to filters, allow

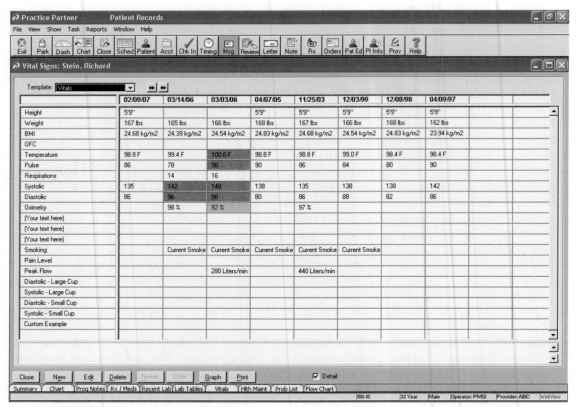

FIGURE 16-1 Electronic medical records allow the physician to determine whether changes in basic vital signs over time are significant. This type of data can help physicians determine the number of patients who have hypertension, and the information can then be used to contact patients with that diagnosis when a new hypertensive drug is available. (Courtesy McKessan Corp., Alpharetta, Ga.)

only certain types of data to enter or exit. Information can be **encrypted**, which means that it is changed into a code that can be read only after it has been unencrypted. These precautions are necessary because of the sensitivity of patient information. Also, care must be taken to ensure that no one can change the information already in the record.

- **Legality.** Medical records are regulated by many statutes. The laws on retention of records vary from state to state. Medical records cannot be altered, and they should be corrected according to accepted guidelines. The record must be completely legible and must be **authenticated** properly (Figure 16-2).

CRITICAL THINKING APPLICATION   16-2

- One of Laura's duties is to make sure medical records have been authenticated. Why is authentication of records important?
- One physician, Dr. Anthony, is consistently careless about record authentication. How can the center encourage him to complete this critical duty?

▌ CHALLENGES OF QUALITY ASSURANCE PROBLEMS

Many larger medical facilities today have entire departments devoted to quality assurance. **Quality assurance (QA)** comprises activities designed to improve the quality of a product or service through process or system changes that increase efficiency or effectiveness. Although many people assume that quality is determined solely by

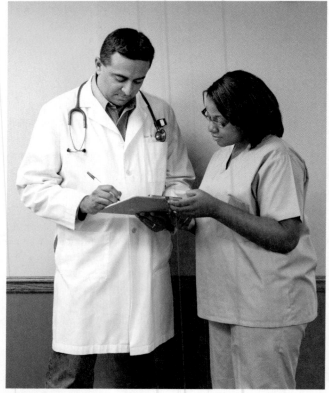

FIGURE 16-2 Physicians must authenticate medical records by initialing or signing their entries. Some computer systems automatically authenticate records.

the patient, much more is involved in quality assurance than just the patient's satisfaction with services rendered. The four concerns of quality assurance are overuse, underuse, misuse, and variations in the use of healthcare services. No medical assistant should attempt to **circumvent** any co-worker's attempts, especially in an attempts to make the co-worker look less competent. Instead, all of the staff members must work together toward the common goals set by the physician and office manager.

Costs rise when providers order excessive, unnecessary healthcare services. Overused treatments and services include hysterectomies, tympanostomy tubes, and antibiotics. Antibiotics are prescribed widely for common colds and acute bronchitis, but the drugs do not benefit patients with these illnesses.

Underuse of services and treatments can be equally costly. Mammograms and cervical cancer screening tests can detect medical problems early, yet many at-risk patients do not take advantage of these services (Figure 16-3). Beta blockers have been proved to reduce mortality in patients who have had heart attacks by as much as 43%, but they often are not prescribed for these patients. Patients with diabetes should have their eyes checked regularly, but many do not. All these are examples of underuse of services that can affect the quality of healthcare.

CRITICAL THINKING APPLICATION 16-3

- How might a medical assistant encourage patients to have screening tests done, such as mammograms and tests for cervical cancer?
- What marketing strategies could Laura help develop that would prompt more patients to take advantage of health screening opportunities?
- How do these services benefit the health facility?

Some healthcare services are misused. These errors can cause death, delay of correct diagnosis, unnecessary injuries, and increased healthcare costs. Laboratory tests that provide **erroneous** results are an example of misuse. Medication errors can be fatal to patients or can cause complications in a current illness. Hospital injuries and **nosocomial** infections promote further complications.

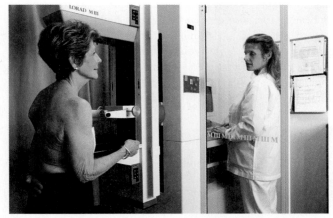

FIGURE 16-3 Healthcare professionals must encourage at-risk patients to have screening tests, such as those for breast and cervical cancer.

Services vary widely across the country. Live discharge rates (i.e., the number of patients who leave the hospital without expiring) are higher in some areas of the United States than in others. Individuals who seek medical care are more conscientious and are likely to seek health services in a different geographic area if they believe they will receive better care. All these issues contribute to the concept of high-quality healthcare.

CRITICAL THINKING APPLICATION 16-4

- Laura is concerned about the number of employees in her facility who are allowed to access patient information. For instance, all employees have access to all health information on all patients. Is this a good policy? Why or why not?
- Should all physicians have access to all patient records? Why or why not?

NATIONAL CENTER FOR HEALTH STATISTICS

The National Center for Health Statistics (NCHS), a division of the Centers for Disease Control and Prevention (CDC), is the primary provider of the health information statistics used to guide actions and policies affecting the health of the American public. The functions of the NCHS include:

- Documenting the health status of the U.S. population and important subgroups
- Identifying **disparities** in health status and the use of healthcare by race, ethnicity, socioeconomic status (SES), region, and other population **gradients** or **parameters**.
- Describing experiences with the healthcare system
- Monitoring trends in health status and healthcare delivery
- Identifying health problems
- Supporting biomedical and health services research
- Providing information to effect changes in public policies and programs
- Evaluating the impact of health policies and programs

Statistics are vital to many entities interested in the healthcare industry. Some statistics available through the NCHS are related to the following:

- Teenage pregnancy
- Incidence of infection with the human immunodeficiency virus (HIV)
- Alcohol and drug use
- Births
- Deaths
- Communicable diseases
- Infant health and mortality
- Leading causes of death
- Life expectancy
- Sexually transmitted diseases
- Suicide

TOTAL QUALITY MANAGEMENT

Total quality management is defined as management or control activities based on the leadership of top-level management and supported by the involvement of all employees and departments, from planning and development to sales and service. These management and control activities focus on quality assurance. Ideally, qualities that satisfy the customer are built into products and services as they are received from providers.

For total quality management practices to be effective, all employees must commit to providing patients with the best care possible. This includes both top-level management and the staff members who work directly with patients.

> ### CRITICAL THINKING APPLICATION   16-5
>
> - Laura has noticed that many employees are frustrated when confronted with quality assurance regulations. Often employees complain that the policies are a waste of time. How can Laura convince these employees that the regulations are important, and how can she gain cooperation from these people?
> - Should adherence to quality assurance policies be a mandatory part of the employee's job description?

The Concept of Total Quality Management

Much of the thrust of today's interest in total quality management originated from the teachings of W. Edwards Deming, who earned a doctorate in mathematical physics from Yale University in 1928. Deming is perhaps best known for the work he did on quality management with Japanese managers and engineers. He developed 14 points for managers to institute that emphasize quality rather than quantity. By following these guidelines, medical assistants can help prevent medical liability claims.

1. Create constancy of purpose in improving the product or service, with the aims of becoming competitive, staying in business, and providing jobs.
2. Adopt a new philosophy. Western management must awaken to the challenge, learn their responsibilities, and take on leadership for change.
3. Stop depending on inspection to achieve quality. Eliminate the need for inspection on a mass basis by building quality into the product or service in the first place.
4. End the practice of awarding business on the basis of the price tag. Instead, minimize total cost. Move toward a single supplier for any one item, based on a long-term relationship of loyalty and trust.
5. Continually improve the system of production and service so as to improve quality and productivity and thus constantly reduce costs.
6. Institute training on the job.
7. Institute leadership. The aim of supervision should be to help people, machines, and gadgets to do a better job. Supervision of management is in need of overhaul, in addition to supervision of production workers.
8. Drive out fear so that everyone can work effectively for the company.
9. Break down barriers between departments. People must work as a team to foresee problems in production and in use that may be encountered.
10. Eliminate slogans, exhortations, and targets for the work force that ask for zero defects and new levels of productivity; these only create adversarial relationships. Eliminate quotas and substitute leadership. Eliminate management by objective. Eliminate management by numbers and numeric goals. Substitute leadership.
11. Remove barriers that rob hourly workers of their right to pride in their workmanship. The responsibility of supervisors must be changed from sheer numbers to quality.
12. Remove barriers that rob people in management and engineering of their right to pride in their workmanship. This means abolishing the annual merit rating and management by objective.
13. Institute a vigorous program of education and self-improvement.
14. Put everybody in the company to work to accomplish the transformation. The transformation is everybody's job.

Deming believed that these points could help managers and employees achieve quality in their facility or business. They are widely used in countless business and service organizations today.

The Joint Commission

The Joint Commission is a nonprofit organization that provides accreditation services for healthcare facilities. Earning accreditation is a voluntary process, but more than 17,000 healthcare facilities in the United States are accredited by and comply with the standards of The Joint Commission. The organization sees its mission as one of continuously improving the safety and quality of care provided to the public by providing healthcare accreditation and related services, which help healthcare organizations improve their performance. Many think The Joint Commission deals only with hospitals; however, the organization has vastly expanded its services over the years to include ambulatory care, assisted living, behavioral healthcare, critical access hospitals, home care, laboratory services, long-term care, and office-based surgical centers. Administrative or clinical medical assistants may be employed in all of these; therefore, they should have some knowledge of The Joint Commission, its purpose, its regulations, and the types of facilities it serves.

Ambulatory care and office-based surgery centers, in addition to many other facilities, have found that competitive pressures in the healthcare market, combined with the rapidly changing healthcare field, have prompted them to seek accreditation. Providing high-quality patient care and continually striving for improved performance, both of which are proven by meeting accreditation standards, are **benchmarks** of success. For many years, healthcare facilities were interested in meeting the minimum standards that would reflect quality healthcare. Partly because of the fierce competition in the medical market, the goal recently has shifted from simply meeting minimum standards to exceeding standards and providing optimum healthcare (Figure 16-4).

RISK MANAGEMENT

A risk is any occurrence that could result in patient injury or any type of financial loss to the healthcare facility. Risk management is a program designed to identify, contain, reduce, or eliminate the potential for harm and financial loss to a facility if a compensable event occurs. In a healthcare facility, it usually involves the delivery system and actual workplace.

FIGURE 16-4 Accreditation of a healthcare facility takes teamwork and a commitment to quality assurance.

A facility's policies and procedures are designed to manage risk and prevent situations that could result in harm to people or property for which the healthcare facility could be held liable. Both the Occupational Safety and Health Administration (OSHA) and Clinical Laboratory Improvement Amendments (CLIA) have established regulations that promote risk management.

Effective risk management benefits the physician's office by cutting financial losses and improving the quality of healthcare provided by the staff. Risk management programs stress the prevention of financial loss and reduce the possibility of negative publicity resulting from **sentinel events**. The Joint Commission defines a sentinel event as an unexpected occurrence that involves death or serious physical or psychological injury or the risk of either. Sentinel events must be reported immediately and investigated thoroughly, and their contributing factors must be rectified to prevent recurrence of the problem. Records are kept of the sentinel events that happen in a facility, especially those involving a patient injury or death.

The Joint Commission defines sentinel events and monitors and investigates them in the facilities it accredits. A physician's office may have similar incidents, such as:

- Medication errors
- Delayed treatment
- Medical equipment failure
- Patient falls
- Fire
- Wrong-site surgery
- Unintended retention of foreign objects

Traditionally, hospitals are the facilities that have formed QA departments. However, numerous physicians' offices are appointing QA committees to help reduce risk and liability. Some physicians designate the office manager or another staff member as the site safety officer.

Risk and liability are synonymous with financial loss in the healthcare facility. For this reason, policies and procedures must be followed as specified in the office policy and procedures manuals. Attorneys are quite shrewd about using office policy and procedures manuals against the medical facility during a lawsuit. If the manual states that quality control procedures are to be performed daily, but no logs exist to prove they were, the attorney can surmise that the office does not follow its own policy; if this can be proved once, the

attorney will look for every other breach in office policy and will emphasize this during the court proceedings. If the office cannot follow its own policies, it likely will be judged as incompetent. This could result in a **potentially compensable event (PCE)**, creating a financial obligation for the healthcare facility. For the physician, a court award to a patient can mean that the physician will have to pay higher liability insurance premiums, which affects the overhead costs of running the facility and keeping it open. A higher overhead also may mean that the salaries of medical assistants and other employees must be frozen for a specified period or indefinitely.

All employees of healthcare facilities can help avoid liability by strictly following the office policy and procedures manual and by paying close attention to situations that might lead to office liability.

RISK MANAGEMENT: HELPING YOUR PHYSICIAN TO AVOID BEING SUED

1. Communication is the first step to preventing claims. Keep an open dialog with the patient and be sure to ask repeatedly whether the patient has any questions and whether he or she understands the physician's instructions.
2. Show that you care about patients. Form a professional but genuine relationship with them. Sincerely chat with them and express your hope that they will feel better soon. Never guarantee a cure or say that the doctor will "take care of everything." Patients who have a good relationship with the physician are much less likely to bring a medical liability claim to court.
3. Consider patients as active participants in their own healthcare. Explain their responsibility to follow instructions, take their medicine, and discuss questions with the physician whenever they arise. Without patients' cooperation, the physician cannot effectively help them overcome or deal with their illnesses.
4. Encourage patients to do research about their condition on reputable Web sites. Patients need to have a basic knowledge of their disease or condition. The more they know, the better they will be able to recognize serious symptoms or problems.
5. Suggest that patients write down questions and bring them to the office. Encourage them to take notes or provide them with information sheets on their disease or what to expect during a procedure.
6. Remember that if an event is not charted in the medical record, it didn't happen. Make sure comprehensive information about the patient, including attitude and compliance with orders, is included in the medical record.

ACKNOWLEDGING AND DISCLOSING MEDICAL ERRORS

One of a medical professional's most difficult tasks is dealing with a mistake that involves a patient. Most medical professionals do not intentionally make errors in any aspect of patient care, but unfortunately, mistakes happen from time to time in any business. Mistakes in the medical industry can cost patients their lives. Most errors are minor and easily rectified, but some lead to medical professional liability cases. All medical facilities need a plan for addressing errors when they occur, and they should use errors as an opportunity to learn. This allows supervisors to change procedures that led to the mishap and to train employees in ways to prevent mistakes.

The Institute of Medicine defines an error as "failure of a planned action or the use of a wrong plan" and an **adverse event** as "an injury caused by medical management rather than the underlying condition of the patient" (Table 16-2). However, patients often define errors much differently. A patient may consider rude attitudes or poor customer service as medical errors, although most physicians would not define these as errors. Earlier in this chapter, the term *sentinel event* was introduced, which is defined as an unexpected occurrence involving the death of or serious physical or psychological injury to a patient. Both an adverse event and a sentinel event can be considered errors; however, an adverse event is not necessarily a sentinel event. The least destructive type of medical error is a **near miss**, in which an error is caught or corrected before it affects the patient.

COMMON MEDICAL ERRORS

- Medication errors
- Documentation and follow-up on adverse drug reactions
- Lack of follow-up on abnormal test results
- Lack of follow-up on consultations
- Failure to educate the patient
- Lack of follow-up on no-show appointments

An intensive study by physicians Kathleen Mazor, Steven Simon, and Jerry Gurwitz reviewed information on the ways physicians deal with medical errors and how they inform patients and their families of those mistakes. The authors found that communication is the key to handling medical errors, and they concluded that physicians are ethically obligated to disclose such errors to the patient (Mazor et al., 2004). Likewise, medical assistants are ethically obligated to report every error they make directly to the physician responsible for the patient's care.

The most significant obstacle to disclosure usually is the fear of litigation. Some individuals will sue a physician for even the most insignificant mistakes. In Chapter 7, four elements were presented that must be offered as evidence to prove negligence: the physician must have the *duty* to care for the patient; proof of *dereliction of duty* must exist, meaning that the physician somehow failed to perform his or her duty as the patient's caregiver; the physician's action or lack of action must be the *direct cause* of the patient's condition; and the patient must prove that he or she suffered *damages* as a result of the physician's action or lack of action.

Medical assistants have important responsibilities when a medical error is made in the physician's office. They should never hide the error, especially when documenting the medical record. The error should be reported not only to the supervisor or office manager, but also to the physician, who can adjust the patient's course of care if necessary. The medical assistant also should allow the physician to be the person who talks with the patient about the error, because a medical assistant cannot answer the patient's questions about how the mistake will affect the person. Although many believe that an

TABLE 16-2 Preventable Adverse Events and Errors Identified by Family Physicians During Patient Visits

CLASSIFICATION	EXAMPLES	PATIENT VISITS WITH ERRORS (NUMBER/ PERCENT)
Office administration errors		57/16.5
Charting	Any part of record is not present, is in the wrong place, entire record is missing	37/10.5
General office administration	Staffing problems, missing or incorrect forms or paperwork, laboratory, x-ray, or imaging processing errors	21/6
Physician-related errors	Skill problems, time management problems (feeling rushed, interrupted)	28/8
Patient communication errors	Problems communicating with patient by physician, staff, or other physicians; appointment and screening errors	16/4.5
Preventable adverse events	Missed diagnosis, misdiagnosis, delayed treatment, incorrect treatment	15/4.3

From Elder NC, Vonder Meulen M, Cassedy A: The identification of medical errors by family physicians during outpatient visits, *Ann Fam Med* [online] 2(2):125-129, 2004. Accessed 9-21-2012.

apology is an admission of guilt, a sincere apology, when indicated, goes a long way in mending the relationship between the patient and physician or staff member and may even enhance the relationship, strengthening it and resulting in greater trust.

ACKNOWLEDGING AND REPORTING MEDICAL ERRORS MADE BY THE MEDICAL ASSISTANT

1. IMMEDIATELY inform the physician and supervisor when an error is discovered, no matter how insignificant the error.
2. Document the error in the medical record. Do not obliterate or change any part of the medical record as it stands; add an addendum or begin a new entry in the patient's progress notes.
3. Complete an incident report if indicated by the office policy and procedures manual.
4. Call the patient and ask him or her to come to the office. Use a phrase such as, "We'd like you to come into the office to discuss some things that have happened with your care. When would you like to come in?"

5. Do not disclose information prematurely. Allow the physician to make all the decisions about talking with the patient and make sure all the facts are available before the discussion with the patient.

6. Meet with the patient with the physician when the patient is told an error has been made. Conduct the meeting in a private area free of interruptions, preferably one that does not have a desk. The patient will be less intimidated if the physician sits next to him or her rather than behind a desk. Never relay information about a medical error via telephone or e-mail.

7. Use layman's terms when talking with the patient.

8. Offer a sincere apology for the error if appropriate.

9. A gentle touch on the patient's hand shows compassion and sincere sympathy.

10. Allow the patient to ask questions, both immediately and after the meeting has ended. The physician might say, "I know this is unexpected and upsetting news. If you think of other questions, I'd be happy to meet with you again or talk with you on the telephone. Here's the number where you can reach me."

11. Never make excuses for the mistake. The patient will receive the news much better if the blame is not placed on another person or facility.

12. Explain to the patient how the people involved will learn from the mistake. Explain any policy changes that the error may have prompted to assure the patient that supervisors or the physician have corrected the processes that led to the mishap.

13. Assure the patient that the staff and physician care about him or her and want the best for those who receive medical care at the facility. Patients need to feel that the physician and staff are sympathetic to their concerns.

14. Document all communication with the patient regarding the medical error.

Common sense must prevail in dealing with a medical error. To encourage admissions of error, some states now prevent the use of apologies as evidence of guilt in court in medical professional liability cases. Although many believe that apologies should be avoided so that there is no admission of guilt or liability, the medical assistant must cope with the feelings that he or she has after making a mistake. The apology may help reconcile those feelings and help the medical assistant move past the adverse event. Remember to discuss any patient contact after an error with the supervisor and the physician and to document such encounters in the patient's medical record when indicated.

CLOSING COMMENTS

Health information management is a critical aspect of today's healthcare facility. Although the regulations may seem stringent, the value of protecting the patient's privacy is immeasurable. Patients have the right to be cared for in a professional manner and to expect their health information to be kept confidential. The medical assistant should focus on following office policies and procedures and privacy guidelines. Take care when working with medical records and information.

Patient Education

Patients today are more health conscious than ever before, largely because of the abundance of medical information available on the Internet. Most large healthcare facilities employ patient advocates, who work with other professionals (e.g., insurance companies, case managers, and lawyers) to ensure that the patient receives quality medical care. The patient advocate helps resolve various issues regarding the patient's medical condition.

In general, an **advocate** is a person who supports or promotes the interests of another person. Medical assistants can serve as patient advocates in the physician's office. The National Patient Safety

BREAKDOWN OF OUTPATIENT ERRORS

Where do community-based physicians make errors? The California Academy of Family Physicians analyzed errors made over the course of a year by a group of 50 family physicians. The following chart shows a breakdown of the outpatient errors.

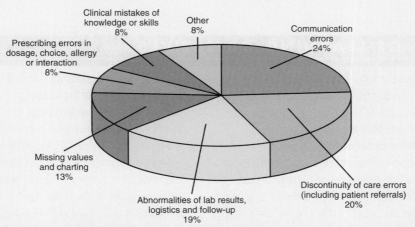

- Clinical mistakes of knowledge or skills 8%
- Other 8%
- Communication errors 24%
- Prescribing errors in dosage, choice, allergy or interaction 8%
- Missing values and charting 13%
- Abnormalities of lab results, logistics and follow-up 19%
- Discontinuity of care errors (including patient referrals) 20%

From Daftary AV: Diagnosing and treating medical errors in family practice, California Academy of Family Physicians, Monograph, March/April 2004.

Foundation (NPSF) encourages medical professionals to partner with patients and help them learn about the steps they can take to become more involved in their own healthcare.

The patient's good health is a team effort. Numerous professionals perform their duties to the best of their abilities toward a common goal—quality care. Communicating with the patient and working together build trust, reduce risk, and lessen liability in the medical facility. Each medical assistant must do his or her part to provide the patient with exceptional, first-rate care.

Legal and Ethical Issues

The medical assistant must be familiar with the laws affecting medical issues and must be able to guide patients as concerns arise. Be prepared to answer questions or direct such patients to the right source for information. Seminars that target compliance issues affecting the physician's office often are available to the medical assistant. Most employers are willing to pay for such seminars so that the office can remain in strict compliance with the law and regulations. Just as individuals practice defensive driving to keep a ticket off their driving record, physicians must practice some defensive medicine to prevent liability suits. Remember that the medical profession is one of constant change. The medical assistant must have a positive attitude about the learning process, especially when new rules and regulations take effect. When a problem arises, patients want their concerns to be acknowledged. They expect the medical professional to be truthful and empathetic and to apologize if necessary.

SUMMARY OF SCENARIO

Laura is learning more about health information management each day. She has earned the respect of her supervisors, who often give her lengthy, complicated documents on regulations and ask her to read and summarize them for the staff. She has a knack for picking out the actual requirements amid the excess of legalese.

Laura has developed good relationships with many of the staff physicians at the hospital. She has approached several of them about record authentication, and her bright personality helps foster a sense of cooperation between the medical staff and the center's staff. She has even received approval to give coupons good for one lunch at a popular nearby restaurant when physicians form the habit of authenticating their records in a timely manner. The physicians appreciate the recognition for completing their duties on schedule and definitely enjoy the lunch!

Laura has given thought to continuing her education in the health management field and possibly gaining certification in this area. She knows that this will lend credibility to the knowledge she has gained on the job. Her supervisors are pleased with her performance and know they can count on Laura to complete any task she is assigned on time and with accurate results. Laura looks forward to a long career at the center, serving both the patients and staff in the years to come.

Health information is used daily in medical facilities. The medical record probably is the most common source of health information that healthcare professionals use, but they also access databases that provide statistical and other information that affects patient care. Laura knows that she can contribute to quality healthcare by making sure records are accurate, complete, and reliable for the medical professionals who use them. Providing quality healthcare is mandatory in today's society, because physicians are susceptible to lawsuits and complaints when patients believe that they did not receive optimum care. Also, patients have the right to choose their healthcare providers, and they deserve and insist upon quality healthcare.

Laura has noticed that today's patients are more sophisticated and knowledgeable about health-related issues, primarily because of the ease of looking up their health issues on the Internet. Patients often tell the doctor what they think their diagnosis is, based on their own Internet research. This is proof that even patients are using healthcare information. Statistical information helps Laura's employers determine the diseases and disorders most likely to affect patients in their urgent care center. Computers are an invaluable tool that allows healthcare providers and facilities to share information so that they can better provide quality patient care.

SUMMARY OF LEARNING OBJECTIVES

1. **Define, spell, and pronounce the terms listed in the vocabulary.**
   Spelling and pronouncing medical terms correctly bolster the medical assistant's credibility. Knowing the definition of these terms promotes confidence in communication with patients and co-workers.

2. **Describe several ways health information is used.**
   Health information helps ensure continuity of care from provider to provider. It assists manufacturers in determining side effects of drugs. It provides statistical information about primary and secondary diagnoses. Health information also helps the medical facility plan for future needs and capital equipment.

3. **Explain the nine characteristics of quality health data.**
   (1) *Validity* means that the information is accurate; (2) *reliability* means that the information can be counted on to be accurate and that medical decisions can be based on it; (3) *completeness* means that the information is available in its entirety; (4) *recognizability* means that the data can be understood by users; (5) *timeliness* means that the information is the latest available to the provider about a patient or treatment; (6) *relevance* is the usefulness of the health data; (7) *accessibility* means that the information is easily available to the provider; (8) *security* involves efforts to keep unauthorized people from accessing the data; and (9) *legality*

refers to the correctness of the information and its authentication by the healthcare provider.

4. Describe the four concerns of quality assurance.

The four concerns of quality assurance are overuse, underuse, misuse, and variations in the use of healthcare services. Overuse (excessive use) of services raises costs (e.g., using the emergency department for nonemergencies). In underuse, patients do not take advantage of many services they should be using, especially if they are at-risk patients. Misuse of services often reflects errors, such as laboratory errors or misdiagnoses. Variations in services simply means that in different parts of the country, individuals use services in different ways, which can influence the quality of care overall in the United States.

5. Explain the functions of the National Center for Health Statistics (NCHS).

The NCHS, a division of the CDC, is the primary provider of health information statistics. Health statistics are important, because they enable providers to better treat their patients. For instance, if a certain area has a high number of outbreaks of a particular disease, physicians armed with this knowledge and with up-to-date information on the disease's treatment may be able to treat affected patients more quickly, promoting a full recovery. The NCHS also helps compile information such as the number of HIV infections, the number of teen pregnancies, and other vital health data useful to medical professionals.

6. Give some types of statistics kept by the NCHS.

The NCHS compiles statistics on alcohol and drug use, births, deaths, communicable diseases, infant health and mortality, and life expectancy.

7. Define total quality management.

Total quality management comprises management and control activities based on the leadership of top-level management and supported by the involvement of all employees and departments in an effort to provide quality assurance.

8. Explain the function of The Joint Commission (formerly the Joint Commission on Accreditation of Healthcare Organizations [JCAHO]).

The Joint Commission, a nonprofit organization, offers accreditation to facilities that want to excel in healthcare services. Accreditation is voluntary, but more than 17,000 healthcare facilities in the United States are accredited by the agency, including many that employ medical assistants and coders.

9. Discuss the importance of healthcare standards in medical facilities.

Without strong healthcare standards, quality cannot exist. The focus of quality assurance has shifted in recent years from just meeting the minimum standards to providing optimum quality. People expect high-quality healthcare. Organizations that seek accreditation or that focus their efforts on quality will exceed standards, not just meet them.

CONNECTIONS

Study Guide Connection: Go to the Chapter 16 Study Guide. Read and complete the activities.

Evolve Connection: Go to the Chapter 16 link at *evolve.elsevier.com/kinn* to complete the Chapter Review and Chapter Quiz. Check out the other resources listed for this chapter to make the most of what you have learned from Health Information Management.

Reference

Mazor KM, Simon SR, Gurwitz JH: Communicating with patients about medical errors: a review of the literature, *Arch Intern Med* 164:1690-1697, 2004.

Bibliography

Abdelhak M, Grostick S, Hanken MA, et al: *Health information: management of a strategic resource,* ed 3, St Louis, 2007, Mosby/Elsevier.

Institute of Medicine, Committee on Quality of Healthcare in America: *Crossing the quality chasm: a new health system for the 21st century,* Washington, DC, 2001, National Academy Press. Available at: www.nap.edu/catalog/10027.html

Maguire P: Strategies to tackle outpatient errors, *ACP-ASIM Observer* June 2002. Available at: www.acpinternist.org/archives/2002/06/errors.htm

Malaty W, Crane S: How might acknowledging a medical error promote patient safety? *J Fam Pract* 55:775-780, 2006.

Weiss GG: Medical errors: should you apologize? *Med Econ* 83:50-54, 2006.

Sabrina Ragland, a medical assistant with 12 years of experience, works for a gastroenterologist, Dr. Tim Taylor. Her mother-in-law, Elsa Ragland, has been a registered nurse (RN) for 40 years. For more than half of her career, Elsa has worked for a local internist, Dr. Royce Berry. A casual comment at a Ragland family picnic resulted in a medical professional liability lawsuit based on violation of patient privacy. Sabrina's and Elsa's careers were jeopardized by a simple exchange of what seemed to be innocent information.

Vivian Adams, a 42-year-old hospital insurance biller, saw Dr. Berry in his office for pain in the lower left quadrant. Ms. Adams was not a new patient, but she had not visited the office in approximately 2 years.

When she arrived for her appointment, she was presented with the office privacy policy and was asked to sign the document. Vivian glanced through it, signed it, and saw the doctor. He performed an examination and found that Vivian likely was suffering from irritable bowel syndrome (IBS); he then prescribed medication. Ms. Adams called the physician 1 week later, complaining that she was no better. Dr. Berry changed her medication without seeing her and did not hear from her again, other than her requests for refills of the IBS medication.

After 6 months with no improvement, Ms. Adams went to Dr. Taylor; he performed several diagnostic tests and told Ms. Adams that she had colon cancer. She was given a **bleak** prognosis. She told Dr. Taylor that she blamed Dr. Berry for not being more thorough in his testing. Sabrina was in the room and heard the comment.

That weekend at the picnic, Sabrina mentioned Ms. Adams to her mother-in-law and stated that the patient might sue Dr. Berry, although the patient never said those words. Elsa defended Dr. Berry and proclaimed that he was a good doctor, then expressed her hope that Ms. Adams would not sue her employer. One week later, Elsa was in a grocery store and saw Ms. Adams. Elsa immediately expressed her sympathy about the diagnosis and then asked whether there was anything she could do. Her intent was to be kind and to try to **avert** litigation against Dr. Berry. Her gesture might have been well received had Ms. Adams' daughter, Terri, not been with her. Terri was not yet aware that her mother had been diagnosed with cancer. Ms. Adams had told no one about her illness at that point. After the incident at the grocery store, the first person Ms. Adams called was her attorney.

While studying this chapter, think about the following questions:

- When can the medical assistant discuss a patient, with whom, and under what circumstances?
- What has the Health Insurance Portability and Accountability Act (HIPAA) done for the medical industry and the patients it serves?

- When new policies and procedures are implemented, how can the staff embrace the changes and ease the transition?
- What happens if the patient refuses to sign the privacy policy?

LEARNING OBJECTIVES

1. Define, spell, and pronounce the terms listed in the vocabulary.
2. Explain how the HIPAA Privacy Rule benefits the healthcare industry and patients.
3. Explain the difference between Title I and Title II of the Privacy Rule.
4. List the rights of patients under the Privacy Rule.
5. List the elements that must be included in a Notice of Privacy Practices.
6. Briefly explain what is expected of healthcare providers under the Privacy Rule.
7. Describe an incidental disclosure.
8. List the three instances when a parent is not considered the child's representative.
9. Explain the circumstances under which a provider may discuss protected health information with a patient's friends and family.
10. Discuss the role of the Notice of Privacy Practices in emergencies.

VOCABULARY

avert To see coming and ward off or avoid.

bleak Not hopeful or encouraging.

business associates Individuals or organizations that perform or assist a covered entity in the performance of a function or activity involving the use or disclosure of individually identifiable health information.

complainant (kuhm-pla′-nuhnt) The person making a complaint against another person and/or organization.

covered entities As defined by HIPAA, organizations that transmit information in an electronic form during a transaction.

divulge (duh-vuhlj′) To make known, as a confidence or secret.

due diligence The effort made by an ordinarily prudent or reasonable party to prevent harm to another party or oneself; doing everything possible to prevent something negative from happening; also called *due care*.

electronic fund transfer (EFT) The movement of funds between different accounts in the same or different banks using wire transfer, automated teller machines (ATMs), or computers, without the use of paper documents.

electronic media The means of electronic transmission, including the Internet, private networks, dial-up phone lines, and fax modems; includes information moved from one place to another while stored on an electronic device.

electronic remittance advice (ERA) An explanation that accompanies checks and relays details of the payment sent to the provider from the insurance company or other third-party provider.

healthcare providers Providers of medical or health services, individually or as organizations, that furnish, bill for, or are paid for services or products.

incidental disclosure A secondary use of health information that cannot reasonably be prevented, is limited in nature, and occurs as a result of another use or disclosure that is permitted.

individually identifiable health information Any part of a patient's health record that is created or received by a covered entity.

inferred Derived as a conclusion from facts and premises.

Office for Civil Rights (OCR) The division of the federal government that enforces privacy standards.

Office of the Inspector General (OIG) An office of the U.S. Department of Health and Human Services that conducts audits, investigations, and inspections involving laws pertaining to health and human services.

personal health information (PHI) The patient's own information that pertains to his or her health.

preclude To rule out in advance.

prevalent Generally or widely accepted, practiced, or favored.

privacy officer A person designated to ensure compliance with privacy standards for a covered entity.

protected health information (PHI) Any individually identifiable health information that may be transmitted and/or maintained in electronic form.

transactions As defined by HIPAA, transmissions of information between two parties to carry out financial or administrative activities related to healthcare.

verbiage A manner of expressing oneself in words.

The creation of privacy and security laws was a huge step toward more efficient healthcare and faster reimbursements. However, technology often forces organizations to move forward somewhat quickly. Healthcare facilities with already strapped budgets sometimes view such innovations as a hindrance. Compliance officers at larger facilities may wonder whether additional federal regulations are necessary.

Many healthcare workers believe that they can say nothing to anyone, about any patient, at any time. When employees of the physician's office gain an understanding of the compliance HIPAA requires, they can feel secure in their dealings with patients and other individuals.

HEALTH INSURANCE PORTABILITY AND ACCOUNTABILITY ACT

The Health Insurance Portability and Accountability Act, or HIPAA, was enacted in 1996. The act is a group of laws that affect employees of healthcare facilities, insurance companies, or other **covered entities** and the patients they serve. The federal government required all covered entities to be in compliance with HIPAA by April 14, 2003 (small healthcare plans received an extra year to comply). As technology advances and health records become computerized, legislation

dealing with privacy is imperative. HIPAA was developed partly to help ensure the confidentiality of medical records. The statute applies to records created or maintained by healthcare providers, health plans, and health clearinghouses that engage in certain electronic transactions. The Office for Civil Rights, a division of the Department of Health and Human Services (DHHS), oversees the administration of HIPAA.

HIPAA's Privacy Rule includes the following requirements.

- Patients must give specific authorization before entities covered by the regulation can use or disclose protected information in most nonroutine circumstances, such as releasing information to an employer or for use in marketing activities. Doctors, health plans, and other covered entities must follow the rule's standards for the use and disclosure of personal health information.

- Covered entities generally must provide patients with written notice of their privacy practices and patients' privacy rights. The notice must include information that might be useful for patients choosing a health plan, physician, or other provider. Patients generally are asked to sign or otherwise acknowledge receipt of the privacy notice from direct treatment providers.

- Pharmacies, health plans, and other covered entities must obtain an individual's specific authorization before sending marketing materials. Pharmacies and other covered entities are explicitly forbidden to sell personal medical information to a business that would market its products or services under a business associate agreement. Physicians and other covered entities are allowed to communicate freely with patients about treatment options and other health-related information, including disease management programs.

- Ultimately, patients generally will be able to access their personal medical records and request changes to correct any errors. In addition, patients generally could request an accounting of non-routine uses and disclosures of their health information. Remind patients that they may be charged for copies of their medical record; this is an ethical practice for the physician's office.

Many healthcare organizations are concerned about the cost of implementing and maintaining measures for complying with the privacy regulations. However, the benefits of the Privacy Rule far outweigh the inconveniences of compliance.

Effect of the HIPAA Privacy Rule

The HIPAA Privacy Rule created national standards to protect individuals' medical records and other **personal health information (PHI)**. This group of laws was the first enacted to protect patients' privacy. The Privacy Rule benefits both patients and **healthcare providers**:

- Patients have more control over their medical records.
- Patients are able to make informed choices about the use of their PHI.
- Boundaries are set on the use and release of health records.
- Safeguards are established that healthcare providers must ensure to protect the privacy of health information.
- Violators are held accountable and face both civil and criminal penalties if patients' privacy rights are compromised.
- Public health is protected by the balance struck between public responsibility and disclosure of PHI.

Under the few laws that existed before the HIPAA Privacy Rule, personal health information could be distributed to others without notifying the patient or obtaining his or her authorization, even if the information exchange had nothing to do with the patient's medical treatment or healthcare reimbursement. A health plan could pass patient information to a financial lender, who might then deny the patient a home mortgage or credit card based on the health history. Employers could obtain health information and use it in personnel decisions. Because computers make information exchange so much easier, laws had to be enacted to protect patients' privacy.

Note that the abbreviation PHI has more than one meaning in medical terminology. PHI stands for both *personal* health information, which relates to the patient, and *protected* health information, which relates to information transmitted electronically. Always consider the context in which these abbreviations are used when interpreting information related to the electronic medical record.

Title I and Title II Provisions

HIPAA has two provisions, Title I and Title II. Title I covers insurance reform, and Title II deals with administrative simplification. Title I limits the use of pre-existing health conditions, which in the past prevented an employee from obtaining health insurance coverage or limited that coverage. If an individual left a job with insurance coverage and attempted to secure new coverage, a pre-existing health condition often would **preclude** that person from obtaining coverage for that illness. Many individuals were refused any coverage at all, especially if the condition was a serious one, such as a heart condition or high blood pressure. Today, because of HIPAA laws, discrimination against individuals in poor health now or in the past is prohibited. The regulations limit the use of pre-existing condition exclusions and guarantee that certain individuals can purchase healthcare insurance after leaving or losing a job.

The Consolidated Omnibus Budget Reconciliation Act (COBRA) was passed by Congress in 1986. COBRA provides certain former employees, retirees, spouses, former spouses, and dependent children with group health coverage. The premium usually is higher than that paid during employment but still usually lower than for individual health coverage. Most people who lose their job for any reason have difficulty paying for COBRA coverage.

Certain criteria must be met to qualify for COBRA coverage. The company must have at least 50 employees to be required to offer COBRA to its employees. The employees need not all be full-time workers; certain calculations allow part-time workers to be counted to reach the 50-employee benchmark. Also, the employee must be a "qualified beneficiary" to receive COBRA benefits. A *qualified beneficiary* is an individual who was covered under the healthcare plan the day before a qualifying event. A *qualifying event* is an incident that would cause an employee to lose healthcare coverage.

The goal of Title II is to reduce administrative costs in the healthcare industry. Often goals sound simple, but many steps must be taken to reach a goal. Many different objectives must be met to simplify the administrative costs involved in patient care. Several agencies must work together and agree on various regulations. They must share information and resources. Agencies must compromise and "give and take" when forming policies or working toward administrative goals.

CRITICAL THINKING APPLICATION   17-1
- How does information sharing help to cut patient healthcare costs?
- What other reasons might exist for sharing patient information?

Provisions of Administrative Simplification

Electronic media are used daily in modern physicians' offices and healthcare facilities. Because computer use has become **prevalent**, patients have begun to express concern about who sees **protected health information (PHI)** and what is done with that information.

Title II of HIPAA has two parts:
- Development and implementation of standardized electronic **transactions** using standard code sets
- Implementation of privacy and security procedures to prevent the misuse of health information by ensuring confidentiality

The second part of the administrative simplification provision deals with the privacy, confidentiality, and security of PHI and is the focus of this chapter.

Patients' Rights

Separate from the Patient's Bill of Rights, HIPAA provides for several patients' rights:

- The right to notice of a facility's privacy practices
- The right to have access to, view, and obtain a copy of their PHI
- The right to restrict certain parts or uses of their PHI
- The right to request that communications from the facility be kept confidential
- The right to request that the facility amend the PHI
- The right to receive notice of all disclosures of their PHI

These rights are the heart of the HIPAA Privacy Rule. They must be protected by all involved in the healthcare profession.

Right to Notice of Privacy Practices

Patients have the right to a copy of the Notice of Privacy Practices used in the physician's office (Figure 17-1). A copy of this document also must be prominently displayed in the office. These privacy practices are developed by the individual facility and must be written in language that patients will understand. Patients should be given a copy of the Notice of Privacy Practices and should sign an acknowledgment that they received it. If a patient refuses to sign the acknowledgment, the medical assistant can note that the document was offered to the patient and the person refused to sign. This proves **due diligence** on the part of the office and that a good faith effort was made to provide the patient with privacy information. Most patients sign the document. Be prepared to explain the Notice of Privacy Practices to patients. It must include:

- How PHI is used and disclosed by the facility
- The duties of the provider in protecting health information
- The patient's rights regarding PHI
- How complaints can be filed if patients believe their privacy has been violated
- Whom to contact at the facility for more information
- The effective date of the Notice of Privacy Practices

WALNUT HILL FAMILY AND PREVENTIVE MEDICINE CLINIC, PA
1701 W. Walnut Hill Lane, Suite 200
Dallas, Texas 75229
214-549-1111 214-549-1222 (FAX)
info@walnuthillclinic.com

NOTICE OF PRIVACY PRACTICES

THIS NOTICE DESCRIBES HOW MEDICAL INFORMATION ABOUT YOU MAY BE USED AND DISCLOSED AND HOW YOU CAN GET ACCESS TO THIS INFORMATION.
PLEASE REVIEW IT CAREFULLY.

YOUR MEDICAL RECORD (CHART) contains your symptoms, examination, and test results, diagnoses, treatment, and plan for follow-up. This is protected health information (PHI), and is used for many reasons. Your medical record serves as a:

- basis for planning your care and treatment (this includes scheduling and appointment reminders)
- means of communication among the many health professionals who contribute to your care
- legal document describing the care you received
- means by which you or a third-party payer can verify services billed
- tool in educating health professionals
- source of data for quality control programs and medical research
- source of information for public health officials (by law, certain illnesses must be reported)

YOUR HEALTH INFORMATION RIGHTS
Although your medical record (chart) is the physical property of the clinic, the information contained within the record belongs to you. You have the right to:

- request a restriction on certain uses and disclosures of your information
- obtain a paper copy of this notice
- inspect and obtain a copy of your medical record as provided in our office policy manual
- amend your health record (requests must be made in writing)
- request communications of your health information by alternative means or at alternative locations
- revoke your authorization to use or disclose health information except to the extent that action has already been taken
- obtain an accounting of any non-routine disclosures of your health information

OUR RESPONSIBILITIES
The Walnut Hill Family and Preventive Medicine Clinic is required to:

- maintain the privacy of your medical record (chart)
- abide by the terms of this notice
- notify you if we are unable to agree to a requested restriction
- accommodate reasonable requests you may have to communicate health information by alternative means or at alternative locations or phone numbers

We reserve the right to change our practices and to make new provisions effective for all protected health information we maintain. We will post a copy of our current notice in a visible location at all times. We will not use or disclose your protected health information without your authorization, except as described in this notice.

FOR MORE INFORMATION OR TO REPORT A PROBLEM
Please contact Sue Singer or Ron Rachels during regular office hours at 214-549-1111 or you can email or mail questions or complaints to Dr. Robbie Speasak at the above address. If you believe that your privacy rights have been violated, you can file a complaint with the Secretary of the Department of Health and Human Services. You will not be penalized in any way for filing a complaint.

FIGURE 17-1 HIPAA Notice of Privacy Practices.

Right to Access Protected Health Information

Patients must be allowed access to their personal health information (Procedure 17-1). The maker, not the patient, owns the record; however, the HIPAA Privacy Rule grants patients the right to access, inspect, and obtain a copy of their health information. Most physicians' offices require patients to request access in writing and to act on that request within 30 days (Figure 17-2). HIPAA restricts access to psychotherapy notes, information compiled for use in legal proceedings, and information exempted from disclosure by the Clinical Laboratory Improvement Amendments (CLIA).

CRITICAL THINKING APPLICATION   17-2
- Why is patients' access to protected health information important?
- When might the patient need access to his or her health records?

Right to Request Restrictions on Certain Uses and Disclosures of Protected Health Information

Patients can request restrictions on the use of their PHI. For instance, if a patient had an abortion many years ago and does not want that information released, she has the right to ask a provider not to **divulge** that information. The provider does not have to agree to the request but must review it and give a good reason for the restriction not to be honored. An appeal process should be in place for cases in which the provider does not agree with the restriction.

Right to Request Confidential Communications

Patients have the right to determine where they want to receive communications from the provider. The patient may prefer to be contacted on a cell phone instead of a home phone, or through e-mail. Providers must accommodate reasonable requests. Suppose a married female patient comes to the clinic for a pregnancy test. Further suppose that her husband has had a vasectomy. Clearly, a call to her home phone number with test results could initiate personal and private difficulties for the patient. Document the preferred method of communication in the patient's medical record and make certain that method is used for each contact until the patient dictates otherwise.

Right to Request Amendment of Protected Health Information

If patients inspect their medical record and find an error, they can request that changes be made to the record. This request should be made in writing. Providers must review the request and act on it in a timely manner, generally within 60 days. The request may be denied if the provider was not the creator of the record, as in the case of records provided by a consulting physician. Or, the provider may believe that the information is correct and complete. A review process must be in place by which such requests can be considered.

Right to Receive an Accounting of Disclosures of Protected Health Information

Patients may request that the physician provide an accounting of all disclosures of the patient's PHI that are nonroutine (as defined in the facility's Notice of Privacy Practices). Patients are entitled to receive this accounting annually without charge, but the provider can charge patients for additional accountings.

PROCEDURE 17-1

Apply HIPAA Rules in Regard to Privacy/Release of Information

GOAL: To follow HIPAA guidelines so that the patient's confidentiality is kept and the patient's health information is protected.

EQUIPMENT and SUPPLIES

- Copy of the HIPAA guidelines
- Office policy and procedures manual
- Release of information forms
- Notice of privacy policy

PROCEDURAL STEPS

1. Review the HIPAA law, office policy and procedures manual, and the facility's notice of privacy practices.
   PURPOSE: To make certain that all applicable laws and policies are followed when releasing medical information.
2. Examine the document requesting release of patient information.
   PURPOSE: To determine whether the document is valid and the information can be released to the requesting party. Most medical facilities require that all information requests be addressed in writing, and some require a specific time period for response, such as 1 week.
3. Compare the request to the facility's own information release form. Send the requestor a facility form, if necessary, by mail or fax.

PURPOSE: To obtain all of the information that the facility requires in releasing information. Some requests are not complete when received, and the medical assistant must make certain that all of the required information is provided before the release of a patient's information.

4. Determine what information is being requested.
   PURPOSE: The medical facility should not release any information other than what is specifically requested.
5. Make copies of the information for the requestor.
6. Mail or fax the information, depending upon the requested method of delivery. Make certain that fax submissions contain a confidentiality statement.
   PURPOSE: To ensure the patient's confidentiality.
7. Document the release of information in the patient's medical record, if required by office policy.
   PURPOSE: To provide a reference point for when the request was completed and mailed.

REQUEST TO ACCESS MEDICAL RECORD

Patients have the right to access their personal health information. We will be happy to accommodate any patient who wishes to exercise this access to inspect or obtain a copy of the record. Please provide the information requested on this form. This request will be acted upon within thirty (30) days. Standard copy charges will apply.

Patient Name _____

Date of Birth _____ Phone _____

Address _____

City _____ State _____ ZIP _____

Email Address _____

Date of Last Office Visit _____

Please note below what information should be copied or provided:

_____
_____

Please note below the following change(s) that need to be addressed:

_____
_____

I wish to receive a regular accounting of non-routine disclosures of my protected health information.

❐ Yes   ❐ No

_____   _____
Patient Signature   Date

FOR OFFICE USE ONLY

Date Copied _____ Date Mailed _____

Certified Mail # _____

FIGURE 17-2 Request to access a medical record.

SEVEN COMPONENTS OF A HIPAA COMPLIANCE PROGRAM

The Office of the Inspector General (OIG) of the Department of Health and Human Services has developed seven components of an effective HIPAA compliance program:
1. Conducting internal monitoring and auditing
2. Implementing compliance and practice standards
3. Designating a compliance officer or contact
4. Conducting appropriate training and education
5. Responding appropriately to detected offenses and developing corrective action
6. Developing open lines of communication
7. Enforcing disciplinary standards through well-publicized guidelines

Responsibilities of Providers or Health Plans

The responsibilities placed on providers and health plans seems extensive when one reads the actual **verbiage** of the law. Do not be intimidated when reading a publication written by the federal government. These documents are rarely written for ease of understanding and may need to be reread several times before the reader grasps the meaning of a regulation.

In general, the HIPAA Privacy Rule requires that providers perform activities such as the following.
- Notifying patients of their privacy rights
- Explaining how their health information might be used
- Developing privacy procedures in the facility
- Implementing those privacy procedures
- Training employees so that they understand the procedures
- Designating an individual to be responsible for implementation
- Securing medical records so that they are not available to those who do not need them

HIPAA AND ELECTRONIC FUND TRANSFERS

As discussed earlier in this chapter, one of the main goals of HIPAA legislation is administrative simplification. After HIPAA was enacted, an amendment was added to place the **electronic fund transfer (EFT)** on the list of electronic health care transactions that are addressed in HIPAA.

Not only do EFTs cut costs, they help the provider to maintain patients' privacy, because checks and other written documents might be seen by other patients. By computerizing all of these transactions, privacy is maximized for the patient. The new legislation addresses both the EFT and **electronic remittance advice (ERA)**, the document that explains the payment being sent to the provider.

Because EFTs eliminate the need for paper, printing, and postage costs, using EFTs is more economical. Also, the facility saves staff time and expenses, because staff members are not required to manually process and deposit checks, According to the Centers for Medicare and Medicaid Services (CMS), the benefits of changing to an electronic system are obvious; however, many providers and health facilities have still not converted to electronic processing. This forces the physicians and employees to do paperwork instead of using that time to deliver health care to patients. Although all covered entities are required to comply with the adopted standards of HIPAA transactions, the health care EFT standards are expected to have the most substantial cost and benefit impacts on physician practices, hospitals, and commercial and government health plans. The CMS estimates that these entities will save $3 billion to $4.5 billion over the next 10 years. The EFT regulation became effective in January, 2012, and HIPAA-covered entities must be in compliance by January 1, 2014.

PERMISSION TO DISCLOSE PROTECTED HEALTH INFORMATION

Once the patient has signed the Notice of Privacy Practices, the physician may disclose PHI in the manner that is described in the policy. Virtually all the daily operations that involve PHI are covered under the privacy practices document.

Some offices ask patients to sign a receipt of the Notice of Privacy Practices annually. Others simply post the current policy prominently in the office and state where it can be found on the original notice that the patient signs. With either method, every current medical record should contain a signed Notice of Privacy Practices, an acknowledgement that the patient received the Notice of Privacy Practices, or a statement that the patient refused to sign it. Physicians also use separate release of information forms that detail exactly where to call a patient, whether the patient prefers e-mail communications, and/or specific releases for information related to human immunodeficiency virus (HIV) infection or psychotherapy (Figures 17-3 and 17-4).

At times, conflicting permissions may be an issue in the disclosure of PHI. Suppose a patient requests that a copy of his or her medical record be sent to a third party, such as an attorney. The patient signs the release at an office visit. Before the medical record is copied and sent, the attorney forwards a signed release for just the progress notes. Call the patient first and attempt to verify what he or she wants sent. Another option is to adhere to the most restrictive request; in this case, send only the progress notes. Always document any form of communication about the patient's preference in writing. The medical assistant may find it necessary to ask the patient to sign a new permission form. Do not hesitate to contact the patient if any question arises about what the person wants released.

New HIPAA legislation has been enacted that will require physicians to track any disclosure of a patient's medical information. Additionally, HIPAA will now affect the physician's **business associates**, such as clearinghouses, attorneys, accountants, and others who have access to protected health information. This is the first time the federal government has regulated the business associates of providers, and it means that business associates will have more culpability with

regard to privacy violations. When a breach of privacy happens, the provider or business associate must provide notification to the patient in writing. Providers have until January 1, 2014, to comply with these regulations; however, patients will be able to request an accounting of disclosures back to 2011.

Identifying the Patient

Providers see numerous patients each day, and the medical assistant may not know each one by sight. Always insist on identification when releasing any type of health information to anyone. A state-issued driver's license or identification card is the best means of identification, but alternates may be necessary for those who do not have that particular document. The office policy and procedures manual should list acceptable forms of identification. When making any type of disclosure, make sure to note the reason the person has the authority to request and receive the PHI.

Patients' Names and Sign-In Sheets

A staff member in a physician's office may call out a patient's name when it is time to see the physician. Sign-in sheets that list patients' names may also be used. Covered entities are permitted to make such incidental disclosures if they comply with the minimum necessary requirements of HIPAA (Figure 17-5). An **incidental disclosure** is a secondary use that cannot reasonably be prevented, is limited in nature, and occurs as a result of another use or disclosure that is permitted.

The Privacy Rule is not intended to impede customary and necessary healthcare communications or practices or to require that all risk of incidental use or disclosure be eliminated to satisfy the rule's standards. Disclosures that could occur as a byproduct of engaging in healthcare communications or practices may be considered acceptable under the Privacy Rule. Incidental disclosures might include:

- Confidential conversations between providers or with patients, if a possibility exists that they may be overheard (e.g., by hearing the patient and physician talking through the wall when in an adjacent examination room)
- Seeing other patients' names when signing in
- A person not authorized to see PHI walks by medical equipment and sees material containing **individually identifiable health information** (e.g., sees a patient's name on an ultrasound screen)
- Physicians speaking with patients in semiprivate hospital rooms
- Healthcare staff orally coordinating patient care services at a nurses' station or central location in an office
- A pharmacist discussing a patient with a physician on the phone when another person is standing nearby

Most physicians' offices have implemented sign-in sheets that ideally allow only one patient to sign in at a time and that prevent the person from seeing other patients' names. Sign-in sheets that use pressure-sensitive stickers are a good example. The patient signs in on the form, then the sticker is removed and placed either in the patient's medical record or on a log sheet. Some offices are more technologically advanced and have a computer sign-in system. The patient arrives and goes to the computer screen, sees his or her name, and then presses "enter" to signify that he or she has arrived for the

**Patient Consent to the Use and Disclosure of Health Information
for Treatment, Payment, or Health Care Operations**

I understand that as part of my health care, the practice originates and maintains paper and/or electronic records describing my health history, symptoms, examination and test results, diagnoses, treatment, and any plans for future care or treatment. I understand that this information serves as:

- A basis for planning my care and treatment,
- A means of communication among professionals who contribute to my care,
- A source of information for applying my diagnosis and treatment information to my bill,
- A means by which a third-party payer can verify that services billed were actually provided,
- A tool for routine health care operations, such as assessing quality and reviewing the competence of staff.

I have been provided the opportunity to review the *"Notice of Patient Privacy Information Practices"* **that provides a more complete description of information uses and disclosures. I understand that I have the following rights:**

- The right to review the *"Notice"* prior to acknowledging this consent,
- The right to restrict or revoke the use or disclosure of my health information for other uses or purposes, and
- The right to request restrictions as to how my health information may be used or disclosed to carry out treatment, payment, or health care operations.

Restrictions:

I request the following restrictions to the use or disclosure of my health information:

_____

_____

May discuss treatment, payment, or health care operation with the following persons:

(Please check all that apply) Spouse [　] **Your Children** [　] Relatives [　] Others [　] **Parents** [　]

Please list the names and relationship, if you checked "Relatives" or "Others" above

_____

_____

Messages or Appointment Reminders: (Please check all that apply)

May we leave a message on your answering machine at home [　] or at work [　]? **Do not leave a message** [　]
May we leave a message with someone at your **home** using the doctor's name or the practice name? Yes [　] No [　]
May we leave a message with someone at your **work** using the doctor's name or the practice name? Yes [　] No [　]
Messages will be of a nonsensitive nature, such as appointment reminders.

I understand that as part of treatment, payment, or health care operations, it may become necessary to disclose health information to another entity, i.e., referrals to other health care providers, labs, and/or other individuals or agencies as permitted or required by state or federal law.

I fully understand and accept the information provided by this consent.

_____   _____   _____
Signature   Print name of person signing   Date

*If other than patient is signing, are you the parent, legal guardian, custodian, or have Power of Attorney for this patient for treatment, payment, or health care operations? Yes [　] No [　]

FOR OFFICE USE ONLY
[　] Patient refused to sign the consent form.
[　] Restrictions were added by the patient (see restrictions listed above)
[　] "Consent form" received and reviewed by _____ on (date) _____
[　] "Consent form" placed in the patient's medical record on (date) _____

FIGURE 17-3 Example of a HIPAA-compliant patient disclosure form. (From Klieger DM: *Saunders essentials of medical assisting,* ed 2, St Louis, 2010, WB Saunders.)

appointment. The patient's name appears only for 15 minutes or so before the appointment and for 15 minutes after. If the name is not on the screen, the patient is directed to see the office staff. This subtly teaches the patient to be on time for appointments. These devices save time, although the patient must receive brief training in how to use the system. The short time the patient's name is on the screen is an incidental exposure, but it is acceptable according to HIPAA guidelines, as explained previously.

Placement of Patient Medical Records

Many physicians' offices place medical records inside a wall folder just outside the examination room. By turning the record so that the name cannot be seen by someone passing in the hallway, the facility meets the minimum necessary requirement to protect patient privacy. The hallway area should be supervised, and nonemployees should be escorted when in the clinical area of the office.

CRITICAL THINKING APPLICATION 17-3

- Why is it important to safeguard the names of patients in hallways?
- How might Patient A be affected if Patient B sees Patient A's name on a chart in the medical facility?

GENERAL MEDICAL HEALTH CARE

AUTHORIZATION FOR RELEASE OF MEDICAL INFORMATION

I, _____ ____/____/____ _____ hereby authorize
　　　　Print Patient's Name　　　　　Date of Birth　　Social Security Number

General Medical Health Care 1234 Riverview Road, Anytown, FL 33333

to release medical, including HIV Antibody Testing, Psychiatric/Psychological, Alcohol and/or Drug Abuse, information records to:

To: _____

Address _____
　　　　　(Street)　　　　　　　　　(City)　　　　　　(State)　　　　(ZIP)

For the purpose of:　1. Drs. appointment on: _____

　　　　　　　　　　2. Other: _____

　　　　　　　　_____
　　　　　　　　　　Please Specify Reason for Disclosure

I understand that if I consent to the release of any of my medical records, the results of any HIV Antibody Testing, Psychiatric/Psychological, Alcohol and/or Drug Abuse information will be released.

I understand this consent may be cancelled upon written notice to the hospital, except that action by the hospital has been taken in reliance on this authorization, and that this authorization shall remain in force for a 90-day period in order to effect the purpose for which it is given. Alcohol and drug abuse information, if present, has been disclosed from records whose confidentiality is protected by Federal Law. FEDERAL REGULATIONS (42CFR, part II) prohibit making any further disclosure of records without the specific written authorization of the undersigned, or as otherwise permitted by such regulations. The confidentiality of HIV antibody test results is protected by Florida Law [Fla. Stat.ANN. 381.609 (2) (F)], which prohibits any further disclosure by a person to whom this information has been disclosed, without specific written consent of the undersigned or as otherwise permitted by state law.

_____ From: _____ To: _____
　　(Date of Authorization)　　　(Dates to be Released)

_____
　　　Patient's Signature

_____
Parent, Legal Guardian, or Authorized
　Representative Signature

_____
　Relationship to Patient

_____
　　　　Witness

FIGURE 17-4 Example of a HIPAA-compliant patient disclosure form that includes permission for release of human immunodeficiency virus (HIV) and psychological information. (From Klieger DM: *Saunders essentials of medical assisting*, ed 2, St Louis, 2010, WB Saunders.)

Children's Health Records

The Privacy Rule does allow parents to see the medical records of their children as long as this is not inconsistent with state law. In most cases the parent is the child's personal representative under the Privacy Rule (Figure 17-6). However, under some circumstances, the parent is not considered the child's personal representative, such as:

- When the minor is the one who consents to care and the parent's consent is not required under state or other applicable law (e.g., an emancipated minor)
- When the minor obtains care at the direction of a court or a person appointed by the court
- When the parent agrees that the minor and healthcare provider may have a confidential relationship

A minor may need treatment for a sexually transmitted disease, pregnancy, or other issue that may best be treated with discretion, without involving the parent. The office manager may wish to identify such patients or individual office visits in a manner different from their normal record to ensure their privacy. Always be certain

HIPAA MINIMUM NECESSARY STANDARD
[45 CFR 164.502(b), 164.514(d)]

Background

The minimum necessary standard, a key protection of the HIPAA Privacy Rule, is derived from confidentiality codes and practices in common use today. It is based on sound current practice that protected health information should not be used or disclosed when it is not necessary to satisfy a particular purpose or carry out a function. The minimum necessary standard requires covered entities to evaluate their practices and enhance safeguards as needed to limit unnecessary or inappropriate access to and disclosure of protected health information. The Privacy Rule's requirements for minimum necessary standards are designed to be sufficiently flexible to accommodate the various circumstances of any covered entity.

How the Rule Works

The Privacy Rule generally requires covered entities to take reasonable steps to limit the use or disclosure of, and requests for, protected health information to the minimum necessary to accomplish the intended purpose. The minimum necessary standard does not apply to the following:

- Disclosures to or requests by a health care provider for treatment purposes.
- Disclosures to the individual who is the subject of the information.
- Uses or disclosures made pursuant to an individual's authorization.
- Uses or disclosures required for compliance with the Health Insurance Portability and Accountability Act (HIPAA) Administrative Simplification Rules.
- Disclosures to the Department of Health and Human Services (HHS) when disclosure of information is required under the Privacy Rule for enforcement purposes.
- Uses or disclosures that are required by other law.

The implementation specifications for this provision require a covered entity to develop and implement policies and procedures appropriate for its own organization, reflecting the entity's business practices and workforce. While guidance cannot anticipate every question or factual application of the minimum necessary standard to each specific industry context, where it would be generally helpful we will seek to provide additional clarification on this issue in the future. In addition, the Department will continue to monitor the workability of the minimum necessary standard and consider proposing revisions, where appropriate, to ensure that the Rule does not hinder timely access to quality health care.

http://www.hhs.gov/ocr/hipaa/

FIGURE 17-5 Overview for HIPAA's minimum necessary standard.

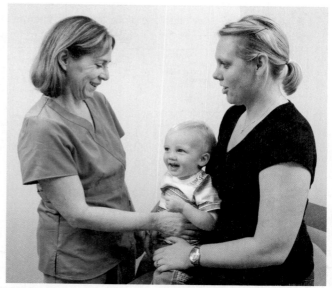

FIGURE 17-6 In most cases the parent is considered the child's representative and is allowed to see the child's medical records.

members, friends, or other individuals identified by the patient. The covered entity also may share relevant information with the family and these other people if it can reasonably be **inferred**, based on professional judgment, that the patient does not object or that the action is in the patient's best interest. Remember that if the patient has requested that such information not be shared with others, the provider must honor that request unless it is deemed unreasonable.

Both covered entities and business associates can discuss a patient's bill with a person other than the patient to obtain reimbursement. No limit is placed on those to whom such a disclosure may be made. However, the Privacy Rule does require a covered entity or business associate to reasonably limit the amount of information disclosed for such purposes to the minimum necessary and to abide by any reasonable requests by the patient for confidential communications and restrictions.

Telephone Messages and Faxes

Medical assistants must communicate with patients, and that communication often is initiated with a telephone call. At times the patient is not at home or available, and the medical assistant must use professional judgment about leaving a message and how much information to disclose to the person who answers the telephone. Even leaving a message on an answering machine can be questionable, because no one is sure who will hear a message containing PHI.

If the patient has requested that the provider or provider's employees communicate only in a confidential manner, such as by alternative means or at an alternative location, the provider must honor that request if it is reasonable. For instance, requests to receive calls at work instead of at home are reasonable requests, unless there are extenuating circumstances.

A fax can be sent containing PHI to another healthcare provider for treatment purposes or to another individual as requested by the patient. Use reasonable care in sending a fax, such as verifying the correct numbers, directing the fax to a certain person, and using

that state and national laws are not being broken when dealing with patients who are minors.

Discussing Information with Family and Friends

The Privacy Rule specifically permits covered entities to share information directly relevant to the patient's care with a spouse, family

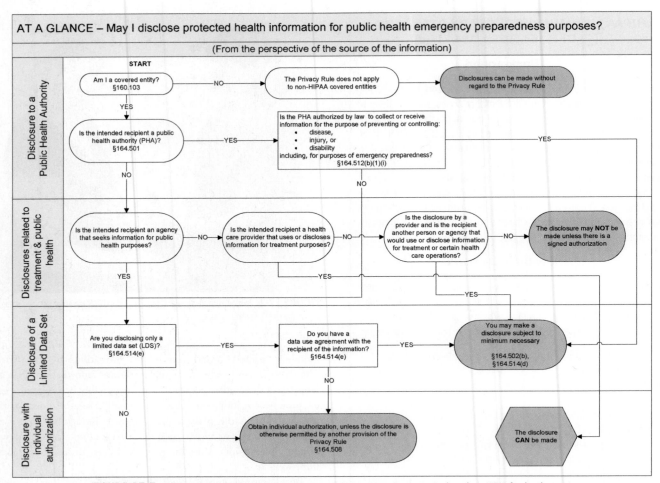

FIGURE 17-7 Guidelines for compliance with HIPAA's privacy regulations. (From Burton B: *Quick guide to HIPAA for the physician's office,* St Louis, 2003, WB Saunders.)

cover sheets that stress confidentiality. All fax machines should be located in secure areas to prevent unauthorized access to PHI. Information used for treatment purposes can be shared by fax, e-mail, or telephone with other healthcare providers.

Emergencies

Healthcare providers and facilities, such as hospitals, with a direct treatment relationship with individuals are not required to provide their Notice of Privacy Practices to patients at the time they are providing emergency treatment (Figure 17-7). In such situations, the HIPAA Privacy Rule requires only that providers give patients a notice when it is practical to do so after the emergency situation has resolved. In addition, the Privacy Rule does not require that providers make a good faith effort to obtain the patient's written acknowledgment of receipt of the notice.

Complaints About Privacy Violations

When a patient has a complaint about a violation of the privacy of his or her information, the first person he or she should talk to is the **privacy officer** at the facility where the incident occurred. If the complaint is not resolved, the patient should be directed to the office manager or physician. In the event the patient's issue has still not been resolved, he or she may file a written complaint, either on paper or electronically, with the **Office for Civil Rights (OCR)**. The

complaint must be filed within 180 days of when the **complainant** knew or should have known that the act had occurred. The OCR may waive the 180-day time limit if good cause is shown. Complaints must meet the following criteria:

- They must be filed in writing, either on paper or electronically.
- They must name the entity that is the subject of the complaint.
- They must describe the acts or omissions believed to be in violation of the Privacy Rule.
- They must be filed within 180 days of the incident.
- They must apply to an incident that occurred after April 14, 2003 (2004 for small health plans).

The OCR has 10 regional offices, each covering certain states. Complaints must be filed with the regional office that has jurisdiction over the state in which the incident occurred. A complaint form is available on the OCR Web site. The **Office of the Inspector General (OIG)** conducts investigations and audits when a question arises regarding privacy laws.

HIPAA AND EMERGENCY PREPAREDNESS

During major catastrophes and evacuations, healthcare providers face significant challenges in keeping their patients and staff members

PROCEDURE 17-2

Perform Risk Management Procedures

GOAL: *To prevent risk and liability in the physician's office.*

EQUIPMENT and SUPPLIES

- Copy of laws affecting the physician's practice
- Computer with Internet access
- Office policy and procedure manual

PROCEDURAL STEPS

1. Research laws that affect the medical office on the Internet. Make certain that the sites used for research are reliable.
   <u>PURPOSE:</u> To determine the laws that will influence the operations of a medical office and how they affect the role of the medical assistant.
2. Research your individual state on the Internet and look for patient confidentiality and disclosure laws.
3. Become familiar with office policies and procedures.
   <u>PURPOSE:</u> To make certain that policies and procedures are followed when carrying out daily operations at the medical facility.

4. Determine common risks that occur in the medical facility.
   <u>PURPOSE:</u> To learn what issues or situations might result in losses at a medical facility and determine ways to avoid such risks.
5. Perform a risk assessment at the medical facility.
   <u>PURPOSE:</u> To determine specific risks that are present at a medical facility.
6. Discuss the risks with office management or in a staff meeting.
7. Determine ways to eliminate the risks found during the assessment.
   <u>PURPOSE:</u> To work as a team to eliminate possible risks.
8. Devise a plan to eliminate or reduce risk in the medical office based upon the risk assessment.
   <u>PURPOSE:</u> To take specific steps toward the reduction of risk in the facility.
9. Document all risk assessments and management efforts.
   <u>PURPOSE:</u> To provide proof that risks were addressed and managed as required by regulatory and/or compliance agencies.

---

safe while providing continuity of their healthcare plans. Also, individuals with disabilities make the process more difficult; sometimes the healthcare provider and the patient are the only two resources available to find a safe place for themselves.

Medical offices must have a safety evacuation plan that covers major disasters and allows healthcare professionals to be available in case they are needed at a disaster site. The best plans are developed by the actual site that will use them, so that they are customized for that particular facility, area, and its resources. For instance, if the medical office is next door to the hospital where the physician has staff privileges, transporting patients would be easier than if the hospital were several blocks away. For this reason, the office staff should discuss the problems they would face in an emergency and plan for the individual needs of both the staff members and the patients. The patients' privacy is a primary factor during any emergency, so the plan must include contingencies for maintaining that privacy. By pre-planning, the medical facility performs one type of risk management; planning efforts and the subsequent use of the plan helps the physician and employees to avoid new or additional injuries and/or illnesses (Procedure 17-2).

The office staff must be aware of the acceptable times to communicate with others about patient care, especially in emergency situations. Just because an emergency exists does not mean that the medical assistant is automatically free to release health information about the facility's patients.

CLOSING COMMENTS

Every employee of the physician's office must read the policy and procedures manual to make sure he or she clearly understands the

CIRCUMSTANCES IN WHICH HEALTHCARE PROVIDERS MAY COMMUNICATE WITH FAMILY, FRIENDS, OR OTHERS INVOLVED IN A PATIENT'S CARE

- If the patient does not object and office policy is followed, healthcare providers can communicate with family, friends, and others involved in the patient's care. This should be indicated on the appropriate form and placed into the patient's medical record.
- If the patient is unconscious, healthcare providers may communicate with others if they believe it is in the patient's best interests; however, they may not share with any person information about a past condition unrelated to the current incident.
- The provider should obtain written permission from the patient to share information; however, this is not always mandatory and not always practical, especially during emergencies.
- Healthcare providers must set their own rules for verifying requests for information (e.g., a driver's license must be shown before copies of a patient's records are discussed or provided) and for determining whether the individual is entitled to the information.
- Other people designated by the patient can pick up medical supplies, x-ray films, or prescriptions. Most facilities and offices insist on some type of identification in these instances.
- Healthcare providers can discuss information with an interpreter, who then communicates with family and friends about the patient's healthcare.
- Through the healthcare facility's privacy policy, patients should designate in advance the individuals who can access and discuss their health information.

Guidelines for HIPAA Privacy Compliance

1. Consider that conversations occurring throughout the office could be overheard. The reception area and waiting room are often linked, and it is easy to hear the scheduling of appointments and exchange of confidential information. It is necessary to observe areas and maximize efforts to avoid unauthorized disclosures. Simple and affordable precautions include using privacy glass at the front desk and having conversations away from settings where other patients or visitors are present. Health care providers can move their dictation stations away from patient areas or wait until no patients are present before dictating. Phone conversations by providers in front of patients, even in emergency situations, should be avoided. Providers and staff must use their best professional judgment.

2. Be sure to check in the patient medical record and in the computer system to see if there are any special instructions for contacting the patient regarding scheduling or reporting test results. Follow these requests as agreed by the office.

3. Patient sign-in sheets are permissible, but limit the information requested when a patient signs in, and change it periodically during the day. A sign-in sheet must not contain information such as reason for visit because some providers specialize in treating patients with sensitive issues. Showing that a particular individual has an appointment with the physician may pose a breach of confidentiality.

4. Make sure patients sign a form acknowledging receipt of the NPP. The NPP allows the physician to release the patient's confidential information for billing and other purposes. If the practice has other confidentiality statements and policies besides HIPAA mandates, these must be reviewed to ensure they meet HIPAA requirements.

5. Format policies for transferring and accepting outside PHI must address how the office keeps this information confidential. When using courier services, billing services, transcription services, or email, ensure that transferring PHI is done in a secure and compliant manner.

6. Computers are used for a variety of administrative functions, including scheduling, billing, and managing medical records. Computers typically are present at the reception area. Keep the computer screen turned so that viewing is restricted to authorized staff. Screensavers should be used to prevent unauthorized viewing or access. The computer should automatically log off the user after a period of being idle, requiring the staff member to reenter their password.

7. Keep usernames and passwords confidential, and change them often. Do not share this information. An authorized staff member such as the PO will have administrative access to reset passwords if they are lost or if someone discovers the password. Also, practice management software can track users and follow their activity. Do not ever give out a password. Safeguards include password protection for electronic data and storing paper records securely.

8. Safeguard the work area; do not place notes with confidential information in areas that are easy to view by nonstaff. Cleaning services will access the building, usually after business hours; ensure that PHI is protected.

9. Place medical record charts face down at reception areas so the patient's name is not exposed to other patients or visitors to the office. Also, when placing medical records on the door of an examination room, turn the chart so that the identifying information faces the door. If medical record are kept on countertops or in receptacles, ensure that non-staff persons will not access the records. Handling and storing medical records will certainly change because of HIPAA guidelines.

10. Do not post the health care provider's schedule in areas viewable by non-staff individuals. The schedules are often posted for professional staff convenience, but this may be a breach in patient confidentiality.

11. Fax machines should not be placed in patient examination rooms or in any reception area where non-staff persons may view incoming or sent documents. Only staff members should have access to the faxes.

12. Direct mail and phone calls only to the appropriate staff members.

13. Recognize, learn, and use HIPAA TCS if involved in coding and billing.

14. Send all privacy-related questions or concerns to the appropriate staff member.

15. Immediately report any suspected or known improper behavior to supervisors or the PO so that the issue may be documented and investigated.

16. Direct all questions to the supervisors or PO.

FIGURE 17-8 Guidelines for HIPAA Privacy Rule compliance.

HIPAA Privacy Rule and how it relates to the individual office. Medical assistants are responsible for learning and following the guidelines set forth by HIPAA (Figure 17-8). If they are uncertain about any situation, they should contact the office's privacy officer for direction, or they should research the question on the HIPAA Web site. Never assume that a patient will not mind if certain information is disclosed. Always check the medical record to determine the patient's preferences. Keep current on changes in HIPAA regulations. Embrace changes designed to improve patient care and treatment.

Patient Education

HIPAA regulations can be confusing to even seasoned medical professionals, so imagine the confusion patients might feel in attempting to understand privacy regulations. Be patient when explaining the uses of health information in the medical facility. Take the time to review the information with the patient and to use terms the person understands. The medical assistant should stress that the privacy regulations put the patient more in control of his or her health information. Remember to tell patients that they can change expressed preferences, if necessary, by completing a new privacy notification.

Legal and Ethical Issues

Any government regulation takes several readings to understand. One of the facility's primary goals must be to remain in strict compliance, not only with HIPAA, but also with all laws and regulations that affect the medical office. The medical assistant may have to devote some study time to federal regulations to understand them adequately and to be able to act on the provisions.

Patient confidentiality is one of the most important facets of medical practice, but some medical professionals believe that the information about the patient belongs only to the physician or the facility. The information about the patient belongs to the patient and must be disclosed, according to office policies, when the patient requests it. Never release medical information without a written release signed by the patient.

SUMMARY OF SCENARIO

Sabrina and Elsa will experience many challenges as a result of the information exchange they shared at the family picnic. Their conversation probably began like any other, but once Sabrina told Elsa the details of Ms. Adams' visit, they violated patient privacy laws. Their future in the medical field is now uncertain.

Ms. Adams suffered emotionally after the breach of privacy. Her daughter, Terri, does not understand why her mother did not tell her about the illness. The relationship between the mother and daughter is now stressful, an interference with their normal bond during this critical time. The family questions whether to pursue the matter legally or spend the time they have left together in more productive ways. They have many decisions to make.

Dr. Taylor placed Sabrina on probation for 3 months. Before this incident, she had never received any type of disciplinary action. Elsa was not formally disciplined, largely because of her long-standing relationship with Dr. Berry. Still, there is sharp tension between them in the office now, as he faces a possible medical professional liability lawsuit and complaints about the privacy of Ms. Adams' PHI. Neither Sabrina nor Elsa will look at her job the same as before the incident; everything is different. They both feel that they have disappointed their employers, their patients, and themselves.

The medical assistant must remember that patients should be discussed only with others who are directly involved in the patient's medical care. The HIPAA Privacy Rule has made great strides in protecting patient privacy and in simplifying administrative processes. However, the rule is effective only if office policies are established and practiced. New policies may be difficult to implement, but gaining an understanding of the reason for the policy and its major goals can help the medical assistant embrace changes more readily.

SUMMARY OF LEARNING OBJECTIVES

1. **Define, spell, and pronounce the terms listed in the vocabulary.**

   Spelling and pronouncing medical terms correctly bolster the medical assistant's credibility. Knowing the definition of these terms promotes confidence in communication with patients and co-workers.

2. **Explain how the HIPAA Privacy Rule benefits the healthcare industry and patients.**

   HIPAA's Privacy Rule gave patients more control over their medical records. They are able to make informed choices on how their personal health information is used, and boundaries are set on the use and release of health records. Safeguards are established that healthcare providers must ensure to protect the privacy of health information. Violators are held accountable and face both civil and criminal penalties if a patient's privacy rights are compromised. The Privacy Rule also protects public health by striking a balance when public responsibility supports disclosure of personal health information.

3. **Explain the difference between Title I and Title II of the Privacy Rule.**

   Title I of the Privacy Rule covers the insurance industry. It limits the use of pre-existing health conditions that in the past would have either prevented an employee from obtaining health insurance coverage or limited the coverage. Title II deals with administrative simplification. This section is the source of the privacy and security laws that affect the patient. The goal of Title II is to reduce administrative costs in the healthcare industry.

4. **List the rights of patients under the Privacy Rule.**

   Patients have several rights under the Privacy Rule, including the right to notice of a facility's privacy practices; the right to have access to, view, and obtain a copy of their personal health information; the right to restrict certain parts or uses of their PHI; the right to request that communications from the facility be kept confidential; the right to ask the facility to amend the PHI; and the right to receive notice of all disclosures of their PHI.

5. **List the elements that must be included in a Notice of Privacy Practices.**

   A Notice of Privacy Practices must include details on how PHI is used and disclosed by the facility; the duties of the provider to protect health information; the patient's rights regarding PHI; how complaints can be filed if patients believe their privacy has been violated; whom to contact at the facility for more information; and the effective date of the Notice of Privacy Practices.

6. **Briefly explain what is expected of healthcare providers under the Privacy Rule.**

   Healthcare providers are expected to notify patients of their privacy rights; explain how their health information might be used; develop privacy procedures in the facility; implement those privacy procedures; train employees so that they understand the procedures in place; designate an individual to be responsible for implementation; and secure medical records so that they are not available to those who do not need them.

7. **Describe an incidental disclosure.**

   An incidental disclosure is a secondary use or disclosure that cannot reasonably be prevented, is limited in nature, and occurs as a result of another use or disclosure that is permitted.

8. **List the three instances when a parent is not considered the child's representative.**

   A parent is not considered the child's representative if (1) the minor consents to care and the parent's consent is not required under state or other applicable law (e.g., in the case of an emancipated minor); (2) the minor obtains care at the direction of a court or a person appointed by the court; or (3) the parent agrees to confidentiality between the minor and healthcare provider.

9. **Explain the circumstances under which a provider may discuss protected health information with a patient's friends and family.**

   A provider may discuss PHI with a patient's family or friends unless the patient has limited disclosure and has requested that he or she receive only confidential communication with the provider. Unless the patient makes this request, which should be in writing, the provider may discuss the patient with others as long as good judgment is used and the communication is related to the patient's treatment.

10. **Discuss the role of the Notice of Privacy Practices in emergencies.**

    Healthcare providers and facilities (e.g., hospitals) with a direct treatment relationship with individuals are not required to provide their notices of privacy practices to patients at the time they provide emergency treatment. The HIPAA Privacy Rule requires only that providers give patients a privacy notice when it is practical to do so after the emergency situation has resolved.

CONNECTIONS

Study Guide Connection: Go to the Chapter 17 Study Guide. Read and complete the activities.

Evolve Connection: Go to the Chapter 17 link at *evolve.elsevier.com/ kinn* to complete the Chapter Review and Chapter Quiz. Check out the other resources listed for this chapter to make the most of what you have learned from Privacy in the Physician's Office.

BASICS OF DIAGNOSTIC CODING

Sharon Oliver

18

SCENARIO

Mike Simeone has been employed by Dr. Buckner and Dr. Walker in their gastroenterology practice for the past 2 years. He works as an administrative assistant in medical records and simultaneously has been enrolled in the medical assisting program at his local college. As he has become more knowledgeable, Mike has been given more responsibility in tasks related to diagnostic coding, such as abstracting a diagnostic statement and selecting the most accurate diagnostic code for billing and reimbursement. To perform diagnostic coding, Mike uses a manual called the *International Classification of Diseases, Ninth Revision, Clinical Modification,* or ICD-9-CM.

Mike's experience working in medical records gives him an understanding of the importance of correct, thorough documentation. His strong skills in reading and understanding physicians' orders, treatment plans, chart notes, diagnostic statements, and other medical records will prove invaluable as Mike learns more about diagnostic coding and refines his coding skills.

Mike is aware of the legalities and importance of proper billing as it affects reimbursement. He knows that the practice is committed to compliance with all the regulations affecting the operation of the facility, and he knows the patients' charts are well documented, which makes his new tasks easier to accomplish. Mike is a conscientious worker and looks forward to using his experience to advance his position in the practice and in the medical assisting profession.

While studying this chapter, think about the following questions:

- How do the format, layout, and conventions of the ICD-9-CM manual help the medical assistant search for the most accurate and specific diagnostic code?
- Why is medical record documentation critical with regard to diagnostic coding?
- Why does the medical assistant need to know the steps for performing diagnostic coding?
- What are the benefits of using the diagnostic codes found in the ICD-9-CM?

LEARNING OBJECTIVES

1. Define, spell, and pronounce the terms listed in the vocabulary.
2. Identify three purposes of the most current diagnostic coding system.
3. Describe how to use the most current diagnostic coding system.
4. Explain and apply the basic coding rules in the use of the ICD-9-CM.
5. Explain where diagnostic information can be found and demonstrate how to abstract the diagnostic statement from the medical record.
6. Demonstrate the use of the Alphabetic Index in the selection of main and modifying terms and the appropriate code (or codes) or code ranges.
7. Explain the importance of the Tabular Index.
8. Correctly use instructional terms and symbols as defined in the ICD-9-CM.
9. Explain the use of V and E codes.
10. Perform diagnostic coding.

VOCABULARY

abstract An outline or summary of the diagnostic statement and/or procedures and services performed. In procedural coding, the outline or summary helps ensure that all procedures and services are included in an insurance claim submission and that nothing is omitted from or added to the encounter form or charge ticket; as a verb form, *abstract* means to compile this outline or summary for use in procedural coding.

Alphabetic Index Volume 2 of the ICD-9-CM coding manual; it lists conditions, injuries, illnesses, and diseases in alphabetical order by main terms, modifying terms, and subterms. It also contains the Classification of Factors Influencing Health Status and Contact with Health Service (V Codes) and the index for Supplemental Classification of External Causes of Injury and Poisoning (E Codes).

ancillary diagnostic services Services that support patient diagnoses (e.g., laboratory or radiologic services).

and In the context of the ICD-9-CM, *and* should be interpreted as *and/or.*

assessment The physician's determination of what is or may be wrong with the patient based on the findings from the history and physical examination (H&P). The assessment includes a preliminary, interim, or final diagnosis.

chief complaint (CC) The reason the patient has sought medical care, usually taken down in the patient's own words. It is recorded in the history documentation in the medical record, preceded by the abbreviation CC.

code first When more than one code is necessary to identify a given condition, *code first* or *use additional code* is used. A *code first* note is found at a manifestation code. A *use additional code* note is found at the etiology code when the underlying condition is sequenced first followed by the manifestation.

coding Converting verbal or written descriptions into numeric and alphanumeric designations.

conventions Abbreviations, punctuation, symbols, instructional notations, and related entities that help guide the medical assistant or coder in the selection of an accurate, specific code.

diagnosis The concise, technical description of the cause, nature, or manifestations of a condition or problem. *Initial diagnosis:* The physician's temporary impression, sometimes called a *working diagnosis. Differentiated diagnosis:* A comparison of two or more diseases with similar signs and symptoms. *Clinical diagnosis:* The conclusion the physician reaches after evaluating all findings, including laboratory and other test results.

diagnostic statement Information about a patient's diagnosis or diagnoses that has been extracted from the medical documentation.

etiology The science and study of the causes of disease. The cause of a disorder; a claim may be classified according to the etiology.

excludes Exclusion terms are always written in italics, and the word *excludes* often is enclosed in a box to draw particular attention to these instructions. Exclusion terms may apply to a chapter, a section, a category, or a subcategory. The applicable code number usually follows the exclusion term. An *excludes* note under a code indicates that the terms excluded from the code are to be coded elsewhere. The term *Excludes* means "DO NOT CODE HERE."

history and physical examination (H&P, HPE) At the patient's first visit with a new physician or an established provider or upon admission to a hospital, the history and physical examination (H&P) are documented. The H&P normally includes the chief complaint, a review of systems (ROS), the patient's personal and family medical history, a physical examination, an assessment of the findings from the history and physical exam, and a treatment plan for the patient, also referred to as Medical Decision Making (MDM).

includes When this term appears under a subdivision, such as a category (three-digit code) or two-digit procedure code title, it indicates that the code and title include these terms. Other terms also classified to that particular code and title are listed in the Alphabetic Index.

***International Classification of Diseases, Ninth Revision, Clinical Modification* (ICD-9-CM)** The manual that establishes the system for classifying disease to facilitate collection of uniform and comparable health information for statistical purposes, for indexing medical records for data storage and retrieval, and to facilitate payment.

***International Statistical Classifications of Diseases and Related Health Problems, Tenth Revision, Clinical Modification* (ICD-10-CM)** The current ICM rules manual, which contains the greatest number of changes in the ICD-CM system in ICD history. To allow more specific reporting of diseases and newly recognized conditions, the ICD-10-CM contains approximately 55,000 more codes than the ICD-9-CM.

manifestation An indication of the existence, reality, or presence of something, especially an illness.

notations Found in both the Alphabetic Index and the Tabular Index, notations are instructions or guides in classification assignments, defining category content or the use of subdivision codes; also called *instructional notations.*

notes Used to define codes and give coding instructions; often they are used to list the fifth-digit subclassification (or subclassifications) for certain categories.

principal diagnosis The initial identification of the condition or complaint the patient expresses in the outpatient medical setting based on the physician's assessment as documented in the medical record.

see A direction to the coder to look in another place; this instruction must always be followed. It is found in the Alphabetic Index, volumes 2 and 3.

see also A direction to the coder to look elsewhere if the main term or subterm (or subterms) for that entry are not sufficient for coding the information. If a code number follows, *see also* is enclosed in parentheses. If there is no code number, *see also* is preceded by a dash.

see category A direction to the coder to see a specific category (three-digit code); this instruction must always be followed.

SOAP notes A system of charting comprising the *s*ubjective findings, *o*bjective findings, *a*ssessment, and *p*lan for treatment.

Tabular Index Volume 1 of the ICD-9-CM coding manual; it contains all the diagnostic codes in numeric order, which are grouped into 17 chapters of diseases and injuries.

use additional code A *use additional code* note is found at the etiology code when the underlying condition is sequenced first, followed by the manifestation. A term that appears only in the Tabular Index (Volume 1) in subdivisions in which the user should add further information, by means of an additional code, to give a more complete picture of the diagnosis. In some cases, *if desired* follows the term. For the purpose of coding, the *if desired* phrase will not be used. When the term *use additional code if desired* appears, disregard "if desired" and assign the appropriate additional code.

with In the context of the ICD-9-CM, the terms *with, with mention of,* and *associated with* in a title dictate that both parts of the title must be present in the diagnostic statement to allow assignment of the particular code.

Accurate medical record keeping and efficient claims processing are possible only if *each and every* procedure and service provided during an office visit or encounter is identified. An encounter is any contact between a patient and a provider of service. The term *encounter* is used for all settings, including hospital admissions.

The physician or provider also must provide diagnostic information that demonstrates the need for the procedures and services. A **diagnosis** is the determination of the nature of a condition, illness, disease, injury, or congenital defect. In medical **coding**, the terms **assessment** and **diagnostic statement** are synonymous with diagnosis.

Both components (i.e., the diagnostic findings and the procedures and services) are used to determine the charges for an encounter and to generate an insurance claim. This chapter focuses on teaching the medical assistant how to gather diagnostic information and translate it into a diagnostic code. The *International Classification of Diseases, Ninth Revision, Clinical Modification* (**ICD-9-CM**) coding manual is used for this purpose. Two main parts of the ICD-9-CM are the Tabular Index (Volume 1) and the Alphabetic Index (Volume 2). The **Tabular Index** describes conditions, illnesses, diseases, and injuries; it also includes the sections Classification of Factors Influencing Health Status and Contact with Health Service (V Codes), and an index for Supplemental Classification of External Causes of Injury and Poisoning (E Codes). The **Alphabetic Index** is used to locate the codes in the Tabular Index based on the diagnosis provided in the medical record.

The ICD-9-CM manual is used to assign a standardized numeric or alphanumeric code to the diagnostic statement written by the provider. Diagnostic statements are found in operative reports, discharge summaries, history and physical (H&P) reports, and reports on ancillary diagnostic services that support the patient's diagnosis or diagnoses. **Ancillary diagnostic services** include radiology, pathology, and laboratory service reports. These reports are used by healthcare providers to code and report clinical information, as required for participation in Medicare and Medicaid insurance programs, and by most third-party payers and insurance carriers. The ICD-9-CM also is used to track healthcare statistics. Practice management software, clearinghouses, and third-party payers recognize these codes, which simplify the reimbursement process and speed payment to healthcare providers.

GETTING TO KNOW THE ICD-9-CM

What Is Diagnostic Coding?

Diagnostic coding is the translation or transformation of written descriptions of diseases, illnesses, or injuries into numeric or alphanumeric codes. Use of the ICD-9-CM facilitates accurate medical record keeping and efficient claims processing. The manual identifies the disease or injury for which a patient was treated as a three-, four-, or five-digit code. ICD-9-CM codes are used in the claims submission process to request reimbursement from payers, to track the diagnoses treated by the physician to provide statistical data for research, and for other purposes.

The CMS publication *"Avoiding Medicare Fraud and Abuse: A Roadmap for Physicians"* maintains that the five most important federal fraud and abuse laws that apply to physicians include the:

- False Claims Act (FCA)
- Anti-Kickback statute
- Physician Self-Referral Law (Stark Law)
- Social Security Act
- United States

Violations of these laws may result in non-payment of claims, Civil Monetary Penalties (CMPs), exclusion from the payor program, criminal and civil liability, and in extreme cases, jail time. These laws may be changed or updated, so the person who is responsible for coding must pay close attention to detail and act as a sort of "medical detective" to build a case against a physician or clinic. Both the ICD-9-CM and the CPT coding manuals are updated annually. The Federal Register announces most changes and new coding manuals often have a few pages dedicated to the updates for that particular year. Accurate use of the ICD-9-CM manual is essential for correct translation of the diagnostic statements in the medical record into numeric or alphanumeric codes.

Why Use ICD-9-CM Codes?

The ICD-9-CM codes are important for several reasons. They are used to:

- Standardize a system of diagnostic coding accepted and understood by all parties in the reimbursement cycle
- Create a more convenient method of data storage and retrieval

- Help maximize reimbursement to the provider
- Shortening the claims processing time
- Facilitate and assess regulatory compliance through the use of guidelines and other instructions
- Help evaluate the appropriateness and timeliness of medical care

Evolution of ICD Coding

Classification systems are used by healthcare organizations to organize healthcare data and make retrieval meaningful. The early Greeks were the first to group data by disease processes. Captain John Graunt of London was the first to publish mortality and morbidity statistics, in the London Bills of Mortality (1662), which was the first real attempt to study disease processes from a statistical viewpoint. Later, in the 1830s, William Farr introduced uniformity in the use of statistics. His work helped classify diseases by anatomic site. He published the International List of Causes of Death and provided the foundation for current vital statistics.

In 1893 Dr. Jacques Bertillon developed the Bertillon Classification of Causes of Death. The American Public Health Association (APHA) recommended adoption of this classification system for Canada, Mexico, and the United States and further recommended that the system be revised every 10 years. Subsequent revisions were called the International Classification System of Causes of Death. Revisions were completed in 1900, 1910, 1920, 1929, and 1938.

In the 1950s the U.S. Public Health Service published the International Classification of Diseases, which was adapted for indexing hospital records by diseases and operations. This became the International Classification of Diseases, Adapted (ICDA). Subsequent modifications in 1962 provided greater detail and introduced a classification for surgical procedures. In 1968, because of the need for even greater detail and specificity, the eighth revision of the ICDA was adapted for use in the United States (ICDA-8). ICDA-8 provided the basis for coding morbidity and mortality statistics in the United States and served as a method of indexing all diagnoses and operative procedures in hospital records.

In 1975 the ICDA was renamed the *International Classification of Diseases, Ninth Revision* (ICD-9). In 1979 the National Center for Health Statistics (NCHS) developed a modification of the ICD-9 for use in the United States. That modification, the ICD-9-CM, has been used in the United States ever since.

Legislation has been passed to formally adopt the tenth revision, or modification, of the diagnostic and procedural coding manuals (ICD-10) for use in the United States. ICD-10 is a significant upgrade and improvement to the coding manual currently in use. (See Appendix B for more information about the ***International Statistical Classifications of Diseases, Tenth Revision, Clinical Modification*** (**ICD-10-CM**) and the Procedural Coding System (ICD-10-PCS.) The effective date for these publications is October 1, 2014.

ICD-9-CM Codes

ICD-9-CM codes are listed in the Tabular Index (Volume 1) of the ICD-9-CM coding manual. The coding system consists of a three-digit category code that represents a specific disease, illness, condition, or injury within a general disease category. For example, 250 is the disease classification, or category, for diabetes mellitus. Up to two digits can be added for further definition and specificity. The two additional digits are the fourth digit, or subcategory, and the fifth digit, or subclassification.

Consider the example of diabetes category code 250 (Figure 18-1). Using this code and the conventions and guidelines (discussed later) in the ICD-9-CM manual, it can be determined that a fourth digit must be added that describes whether any disease manifestation is present that was caused by the diabetes, such as kidney disease or diabetic retinopathy. A fifth digit must also be added that describes the type of diabetes (e.g., type 1 controlled or type 2 uncontrolled).

The ICD-9-CM conventions, notes, and guidelines, combined with the diagnostic statement or statements from the medical record, provide the details needed to select the most accurate three-digit category code and, if applicable, a fourth digit (subcategory) and fifth digit (subclassification) code.

STRUCTURE OF THE ICD-9-CM

The ICD-9-CM is published in various media, including book, CD, and downloadable file. Every year the ICD-9-CM manual is reviewed for changes. Additions, revisions, and deletions are made to many of the diagnostic codes, code descriptions, and guidelines. The medical assistant must always use the current year's coding manual to ensure correct coding and billing and to comply with regulatory guidelines.

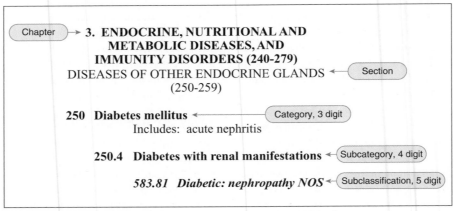

FIGURE 18-1 Example of category, subcategory, and subclassification.

Depending on the publisher, the layout, symbols, color coding, and some other features vary somewhat; however, the format, conventions, tables, appendixes, content, and basic structure are the same. The basic ICD-9-CM manual is made up of three volumes.

- Volumes 1 and 2, mentioned earlier, are used for diagnostic coding by hospitals, physicians, and all other providers of service. Volume 1, the Tabular Index, contains all the diagnostic codes, which are grouped into 17 *chapters* of disease and injury. Chapters are broad sections of the ICD-9-CM coding manual grouped by disease or illness (e.g., Chapter 10 contains diagnostic codes for diseases of the genitourinary system).
- Volume 2, the Alphabetic Index, is used the same way as an alphabetic index in any textbook, except that it refers the user back to the category codes in the Tabular Index rather than to page numbers.
- Volume 3 is used by hospitals to code inpatient procedures and services performed in the hospital environment. Most physician providers do not use Volume 3.

Most coding manuals, depending on the publisher, have an Introduction that provides the historical background. The ICD-9-CM coding manual also contains other useful information. In the ICD-9-CM, the coder will find the format and conventions of the coding manual; anatomic illustrations; special coding instructions for many conditions, illnesses, and injuries; and the current year's ICD-9-CM Official Coding Guidelines for using ICD-9-CM codes. The Centers for Medicare and Medicaid Services (CMS) prepares the guidelines for using the ICD-9-CM codes and instructions on how to report them on claim forms. The guidelines are a set of rules that have been developed to accompany and complement the official conventions and instructions provided in the ICD-9-CM manual.

Annual modifications are made to the ICD-9-CM through the ICD-9-CM Coordination and Maintenance Committee. The committee holds meetings twice a year, at which time modification proposals are submitted to the committee. Modification proposals that are approved are incorporated into the official government version of the ICD-9-CM and become effective for use October 1 of the year after their presentation.

Tabular Index (Volume 1)

The Tabular Index is a numeric listing of diagnosis codes and detailed descriptions. As mentioned earlier, a diagnosis is the determination of the nature of a disease, injury, condition, or congenital defect. The Tabular Index consists of the following:

- Seventeen chapters that classify diseases and injuries
- Two sections containing supplementary classification codes (V and E codes)
- Four appendixes (Appendix B, Glossary of Mental Disorders, was deleted October 1, 2004)

A chapter is a group of three-digit code numbers that describes a general category. For example, the code range 240-279 comprises Chapter 3: Endocrine, Nutritional and Metabolic Diseases, and Immunity Disorders.

Each of the 17 chapters is subdivided into four levels (see Figure 18-1):

- *Section*: A group of three-digit categories that represent a group of conditions or related conditions.

- *Category*: A three-digit code that represents a specific disease, illness, condition, or injury within a chapter (e.g., in Figure 18-1, Category 250 represents diabetes mellitus). A three-digit code is used only if it is not further subdivided.
- *Subcategory:* A fourth digit that adds information or description to the category code. For example, in Figure 18-1, under Category 250, a fourth digit is used to describe whether any disease process or manifestation exists that was caused by the diabetes mellitus. Category 250 has 10 fourth-digit subcategory codes. Fourth digits sometimes describe the location of the illness (e.g., code 410.2 indicates *of inferolateral wall*).
- *Subclassification:* A fifth digit which, when used appropriately, adds the highest level of detail to the illness or injury. In Figure 18-1, under Category 250, fifth digits are used to describe the type of diabetes mellitus (e.g., type 1 controlled or type 2 uncontrolled). Fifth digits sometimes describe the episode of care (e.g., code 410.21 indicates *MI* [myocardial infarction] *of inferolateral wall, initial*).

Supplemental Classifications

The two supplementary chapters in the Tabular Index contain V codes, which describe factors that influence health status and contact with health services that cannot be classified elsewhere, and E codes, which describe external causes of injury or poisoning.

V Codes. V codes are used either when the patient is not currently ill or to explain problems that influence a patient's current illness, condition, or injury. The Supplementary Classification of Factors Influencing Health Status and Contact with Health Service (V01-V89) is used in cases such as preventive vaccination or when a patient encounter is only for administration of a treatment, such as dialysis, chemotherapy, or screening.

E Codes. The E code chapter, the Supplemental Classification of External Causes of Injuries and Poisoning (E800-E999), classifies environmental or external causes of injury, poisoning, or other adverse effects on the body. For example, an E code would be used to describe the details of an automobile accident to explain how a patient's injuries occurred. E codes also identify the place of occurrence (i.e., where the event happened) and not the patient's activity at the time of the event.

Appendixes

The Tabular Index currently has the following four appendixes (as mentioned, Appendix B, Glossary of Mental Disorders, was deleted October 1, 2004).

- *Appendix A: Morphology of Neoplasms.* The term *morphology* means the form or structure, and *neoplasms* means new growth. Morphology code numbers consist of the letter M followed by five digits. The first four digits identify the histologic (tissue) type of the neoplasm, and the fifth digit indicates the neoplasm's behavior. M codes are used for statistical data only and are not used in physician billing. This appendix is used primarily by inpatient coders and morbidity and morphology statisticians.
- *Appendix C: Classification of Drugs.* The adverse effects of drugs are coded according to the American Hospital Formulary Service (AHFS) list. This section is used almost exclusively by pharmacies.

Example

NEC

Diagnosis:	Pneumonia due to gram-negative bacteria
Index:	Pneumonia gram-negative bacteria NEC 482.83
Tabular:	482.8 Pneumonia due to other specified bacteria 482.83 Other gram-negative bacteria
Code:	482.83 Pneumonia due to gram-negative bacteria

Code 482.83 identifies gram-negative bacterial pneumonia that cannot be classified more specifically. The other subclassifications within 482.8 are for anaerobes (482.81), Escherichia coli [E. coli] (482.82), other than gram-negative bacteria (482.83), Legionnaire's disease (482.84), and other specified bacteria (482.89). None of these other subclassifications can be assigned to the diagnostic statement; therefore, 482.83 is the most appropriate code assignment.

NOS

Diagnosis:	Bronchitis
Index:	**Bronchitis** 490
Tabular:	**490 Bronchitis, not specified as acute or chronic** Bronchitis NOS
Assign:	490 Bronchitis

The diagnosis was not specified by the physician as acute or chronic; therefore, the "not otherwise specified" code 490 must be assigned. In this situation, it would be appropriate for the coder to query the physician for more specific information.

FIGURE 18-2 Example of NEC and NOS abbreviations. (Modified from Buck CJ: *Step-by-step medical coding: 2012 edition,* St Louis, 2012, WB Saunders.)

- *Appendix D: Classification of Industrial Accidents.* This appendix concerns the Statistics of Employment Injuries categorized by the type of industry in which the accident occurred. This section usually is used by government organizations, such as the Occupational Safety and Health Administration (OSHA). It is seldom used by physician providers.
- *Appendix E: List of Three-Digit Categories.* All the three-digit category codes from the Tabular Index are listed in order, by chapter.

Conventions Used in the Tabular Index

Conventions are abbreviations, punctuation, symbols, instructional notations, and related entities that help the medical assistant or coder select an accurate, specific code. Conventions are found in the Tabular Index. Understanding their meaning and using them as guides are crucial to accurate coding. Each publisher offers its version of the ICD-9-CM, and some differences may be seen in the symbols, notations, colors, or other reference marks used. The most common conventions are described here.

Abbreviations. Two primary abbreviations are used in the Tabular Index: NOS and NEC (Figure 18-2).

- *NOS (not otherwise specified).* This abbreviation is the equivalent of "unspecified" and means that the diagnostic statement does not provide more specificity or definition. An NOS code typically is used when an illness has not been fully diagnosed (e.g., the physician documents a diagnosis as flu, with no other documentation). Because no additional documentation is available, the medical assistant can use a code with a description of "flu, NOS."

[ ]	Brackets enclose synonyms, alternative wording, or explanatory phrases.
( )	Parentheses are used to enclose supplementary words, which may be present or absent in the statement of a disease or procedure. These supplementary words do not usually affect the code number selected, but instead provide further definition or specificity to the code description.
:	Colons are used in the Tabular Index after an incomplete term that needs one or more of the modifiers or adjectives that follow to make it assignable to a given category.
{ }	Braces enclose a series of terms, each of which is modified by the statement appearing to the right of the brace.

FIGURE 18-3 Example of punctuation usage in the ICD-9-CM.

- *NEC (not elsewhere classifiable).* The category number for the term including NEC is used only when the coder lacks the information necessary to code the term to a more specific category. NEC means that the diagnostic statement contains specific wording but no specific classification exists to match the wording.

Punctuation. Four basic forms of punctuation are used in the Tabular Index: brackets, parentheses, colon, and braces (Figure 18-3). Each form serves a different purpose for reading and understanding the code descriptions.

Symbols. Symbols are used to designate the requirement of a fourth or fifth digit (or both), new entries, and revised text or codes. Other symbols may be included, depending on the publisher. Regardless of publisher, all symbols or other changes are described completely in the Introduction to the ICD-9-CM,. The most commonly used symbols are shown in Figure 18-4.

Other Conventions. Two other conventions used in both the Alphabetic Index and the Tabular Index are bold and italic fonts.

- **See category:** an instruction to the coder to see a specific category (three-digit code), and this instruction must always be used when it is present.
- **Bold:** Bold type is used for all codes and titles in the Tabular Index.
- *Italics:* Italic type is used for exclusion notes and to identify any diagnosis that should not be used as the **principal diagnosis**.

Instructional Notations. Instructional **notations** are critical to correct coding practices. The instructional notations appear in red type in the Tabular Index (Figure 18-5). The instructional notations include the following:

- **Includes:** A notation indicating that under a chapter, subchapter, category, subcategory or subclassification, separate terms can be found that further define, give examples of, or provide modifying adjectives, in addition to sites or conditions.
- **Excludes:** Exclusion terms are enclosed within a box and are printed in italics. The terms after the word *Excludes* are not

classified to the chapter, subchapter, category, subcategory, or specific subclassification code under which they are found.

- **Notes:** Notes are used to define terms and give coding instructions. They often are used to list the fifth-digit subclassification (or subclassifications) for certain categories.
- **See:** The *See* instruction follows a main term and indicates that another term should be referenced. It is necessary to go to the main term referenced with the *See* note to locate the correct code.
- **See also:** The *See also* instruction is found after a main term in the Alphabetic Index. *See also* indicates that another main term may be referenced that may provide additional useful index entries. It is not necessary to follow the *See also* note when the original main term provides the necessary code.
- **See category:** This notation directs the coder to see a specific category (three-digit code). This instruction must always be followed.
- **Code first:** *Code first* notes are found under certain codes that are not specifically manifestation codes but that may indicate an underlying cause to the patient's problem. When a *Code first* note is present, and the patient has an underlying condition, the underlying condition should be sequenced first.
- **Use additional code:** According to an ICD-9-CM coding convention, an underlying condition must be sequenced first, followed by the manifestation. Wherever such a combination exists, a *Use additional code* note is found with the etiology code, and a *Code first* note is found with the manifestation code.

Related Terms

- **And:** In the context of the ICD-9-CM, *and* should be interpreted as *and/or*.
- **With:** The word *with* should be interpreted to mean *associated with* or *due to* when it appears in a code title, the Alphabetic Index, or an instructional note in the Tabular Index. The word *with* in the Alphabetic Index is sequenced immediately after the main term, not in alphabetical order.

Alphabetic Index (Volume 2)

The Alphabetic Index consists of an alphabetic list of diagnostic terms and related codes; three supplementary sections (the Hypertension Table, Neoplasm Table, and Table of Drugs and Chemicals), and a separate Alphabetic Index for E Codes (Index to External Causes). In most published versions of volumes 1 and 2, a Summary

☐ or ◯	The lozenge or circle symbol is found to the left of a disease code. The symbol will contain the number 4 or 5 and indicates that use of a fourth or fifth digit is required.
§	The section mark symbol is only used in the Tabular Index of Diseases and precedes a code denoting a footnote on the page.
•	The bullet symbol indicates a new entry.
△	The triangle symbol indicates a revision in the Tabular Index and a code change in the Alphabetic Index.

FIGURE 18-4 Symbols in the ICD-9-CM.

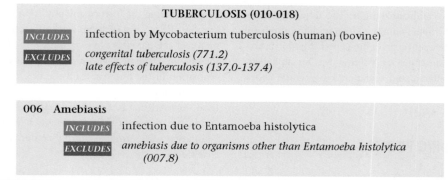

FIGURE 18-5 Example of instructional notations. (Modified from Buck CJ: *Step-by-step medical coding: 2012 edition,* St Louis, 2012, WB Saunders.)

of the Additions, Deletions, and Revisions to the Tabular Index for the current year is included and typically is found at the end of the main Alphabetic Index (Volume 2).

The Alphabetic Index includes main terms, nonessential modifiers, modifying terms, and subterms.

- *Main terms:* These terms appear in bold type.
- *Nonessential modifiers:* These terms are enclosed in parentheses and appear after the main term. They are supplementary words or explanatory information; they do not affect the code assignment.
- *Modifying terms:* These terms are indented two spaces to the right under the main term. They are called *essential modifiers,* because they change the description of the diagnosis in bold type.
- *Subterms:* These terms are indented two spaces under the level of the preceding line. These diagnoses are used when all conditions exist.

A diagnostic statement from the physician may contain many medical terms, but typically only one main term describes the patient's illness or injury.

Supplementary Sections of the Alphabetic Index

The Alphabetic Index includes three tables and one supplementary index (these are discussed in detail later in the chapter):

- *Hypertension Table:* Lists the types of hypertension and the manifestations and causes of hypertension.
- *Neoplasm Table:* Lists neoplasms by anatomic location. Neoplasms are further classified into four categories: malignant, benign, in-situ, and uncertain histologic behavior.
- *Table of Drugs and Chemicals:* Presents a classification of drugs and other chemical substances to identify poisonings and external causes of adverse effects.
- *Index to External Causes of Injuries and Poisoning (E Codes):* A supplementary index that lists E codes, which classify environmental events, circumstances, and other conditions as the cause of injury; the place of occurrence; and other adverse effects.

▌ Procedures (Volume 3)

Volume 3 of the ICD-9-CM contains a Tabular Index and an Alphabetic Index of procedures. Unlike volumes 1 and 2, it is not used by physicians or providers. It is used primarily in hospitals and other facilities to code the inpatient procedures performed in those settings. The procedure codes consist of two digits followed by a decimal and then one or two additional digits. The Tabular Index of Volume 3 has 17 chapters, which contain codes and descriptions for surgical, diagnostic, and therapeutic procedures performed in a hospital setting. The Alphabetic Index of Volume 3 is an alphabetic listing of the surgical, diagnostic, and therapeutic procedure codes; it is used as a guide to find a specific code or codes in the Tabular Index of Volume 3.

▌ BEGINNING THE CODING PROCESS

▌ Medical Documentation

The steps for using the ICD-9-CM manual actually begin with interpreting and abstracting the medical documentation.

Information pertinent to code selection is culled from a variety of medical documents. Sources of diagnostic statements include the encounter form; treatment notes; discharge summary; operative report; and radiology, pathology, and laboratory reports.

Encounter Form

The encounter form is also known as a *superbill, fee slip,* or *charge ticket* (see Chapter 22).

In the physician's practice, the encounter form generally is a preprinted form. It also is the form the medical assistant uses most often to obtain the charges and diagnosis when performing charge and payment data entry and insurance billing. Although it is a convenience for the physician and medical staff, the encounter form can also be a source of errors that can reduce or delay reimbursement. It is vital that the preprinted form be reviewed annually to ensure that any diagnosis or procedure codes used on it have been updated, revised, or deleted according to the latest information from the *Current Procedural Terminology* (CPT) and ICD-9-CM coding manuals. If the preprinted encounter form is not updated annually, a code that has been revised or even deleted may be used for a diagnosis or procedure in data entry or insurance billing, and this will cause problems with reimbursement.

▌ Treatment or Progress Notes

Treatment notes are the second most common medical document from which diagnostic information can be obtained. Chapter 14 discussed treatment notes and finding the assessment (or diagnosis) using SOAP notes. **SOAP notes** are a system of charting in which information is divided into the *s*ubjective findings, *o*bjective findings, *a*ssessment, and *p*lan for treatment.

History and Physical Exam

The **history and physical examination (H&P, HPE)** are the starting point of the patient's "story" regarding the reason the person sought or is receiving medical attention. The H&P begins with a statement in the patient's own words that describes the reason for seeking medical attention. This statement is called the **chief complaint (CC)** and is often abbreviated CC in the history documentation in the medical record. After the chief complaint, the physician documents any other pertinent history about medical, behavioral, and social factors, such as smoking, drinking, drug use, family history, previous surgeries, and hospitalizations. (To see an example of an H&P report, visit the Evolve site at *evolve.elsevier.com/ kinn.*)

After taking the history, the physician performs a physical examination (PE). This includes both objective and subjective assessments of the patient's physical status. The final sections of an H&P include an assessment and a plan. The assessment is the physician's evaluation of the findings from the H&P, and it includes a preliminary, interim, or final diagnosis. The plan is the plan for treatment (also referred to as *Medical Decision Making* [MDM]) for the conditions noted in the assessment; it may include x-ray studies, laboratory tests, surgery, administration of medications, or other treatments.

Discharge Summary

The discharge summary is used primarily for extracting procedure and diagnostic information for patients who were hospitalized rather than seen in the physician's office. The main elements of a discharge summary are the patient's demographic information, admission date, date of discharge, H&P findings, clinical course, condition on discharge, discharge diagnosis, and aftercare plan. Diagnostic statements are obtained from the discharge diagnosis section. (To see an example of a discharge summary, visit the Evolve site at *evolve.elsevier.com/kinn*.)

Operative Report

For patients who underwent surgery as an outpatient or inpatient, the operative report also is used to extract procedure and diagnostic information. An operative report includes the preliminary diagnosis and procedure, the final diagnosis and procedure, and a detailed description of the operative procedure from start to finish. The medical assistant uses the final diagnosis when searching for and selecting a diagnosis code. (To see an example of an operative report, visit the Evolve site at *evolve.elsevier.com/kinn*.)

Radiology, Laboratory, or Pathology Report

Radiology, laboratory, and pathology reports are used to support and/or establish the diagnostic statement or statements. Any findings from these reports must be documented in the treatment notes in the medical record to be used for diagnostic coding, charge entry, or insurance billing purposes.

Extracting Diagnostic Statements

The basic steps in diagnostic coding are to analyze and abstract the diagnosis or assessment documented in the medical record. Then, in the ICD-9-CM manual, the medical assistant uses the Alphabetic Index, the Tabular Index, and the conventions and guidelines to select the most accurate and applicable diagnostic code. As a verb form, **abstract** means to create an outline or summary of information from a text or record. In diagnostic coding, an abstract is created to find all the diagnostic statements recorded during a patient encounter. The abstracted diagnostic statements then are broken down into the main term (or terms) and any modifying terms or subterms.

Main and Modifying Terms

The Alphabetic Index is organized by main terms, modifying terms (nonessential and essential), and subterms. Main terms indicate the condition, disease, illness, or injury. Modifying terms, as described earlier, modify (i.e., act as adjectives for) main terms. Modifying terms are indented two spaces below the main term. Subterms are indented two spaces below the modifying term and add more detail or information to the modifying term. Modifying terms and subterms further describe or add information or definition needed to narrow the search for an appropriate diagnostic code. Modifying terms and subterms affect the selection of appropriate codes; therefore, when selecting a code or code range, it is important to review the Alphabetic Index carefully, not only for main terms, but also for modifying terms and subterms.

As mentioned, a main term typically is the primary condition, disease, or injury. Modifying terms provide further specificity, or detail, such as the anatomic site or additional manifestations of the condition. For example, in the diagnostic statement "atherosclerotic heart disease," the condition (and thus the main term) is *disease*. The modifying term *heart* adds the anatomic location, and the subterm *atherosclerotic* adds the type of heart disease.

Main terms also can be found by eponym, synonym, or acronym. An *eponym* describes a disease, condition, or injury named after a person (e.g., Hodgkin's disease). *Acronyms* are abbreviations of words that create a new word; for example, the acronym for gastroesophageal reflux disease is GERD. GERD and gastroesophageal reflux disease both are medical terms. *Abbreviations* are slightly different; they are "shorthand" for common medical terms. For example, the abbreviation for upper respiratory infection is URI. *Synonyms* are words that are similar in meaning and can be used interchangeably. It is important that medical coders keep reference books on hand, including a medical dictionary that lists abbreviations, so that they can clearly understand the diagnostic statement.

Figure 18-6 shows diagnostic statements taken from various documents, including encounter forms, treatment notes, discharge

Diagnostic Statement	Main Terms	Modifying or Sub-Terms
Methicillin-resistant *Staphylococcus aureus* (MRSA)	*Staphylococcus*	*Aureus*
	Staphylococcus aureus	Methicillin-resistant Resistant Medication resistant
	MRSA	
Cerebrovascular accident (CVA)	accident	Cerebrovascular
	CVA	
Arteriosclerotic heart disease (ASHD)	Disease	Heart Arteriosclerotic
	Heart	Arteriosclerotic
	ASHD	
Varicosities, left leg	Varicose, Varicosity	Leg, veins
GERD	GERD	
Gastroesophageal reflux	Reflux	Gastroesophageal
URI	Infection	Respiratory, upper
	Respiratory	Infection, upper
Upper riratory infection	Infection	Respiratory, upper
	Respiratory	Infection, upper

FIGURE 18-6 Extracting main and modifying terms from a diagnostic statement.

summaries, and operative reports. The first column contains the diagnostic statement, including any related acronym or abbreviation. The second column lists the main term (or terms) which can be extracted from the diagnostic statement. The last column lists modifying and subterms that further define the main term.

In addition to using the conventions, notes, punctuation, and guidelines when choosing the diagnotic code or codes from the ICD-9-CM, the medical assistant must keep in mind two important considerations:

1. Nothing can be omitted from or added to the diagnostic statement that is not documented in the patient's medical record.
2. When the diagnostic statements are compared with any code description, the description of that code must match, in accordance with the conventions and guidelines, with no essential element of the statement added or missing.

CRITICAL THINKING APPLICATION   18-1

Mike sometimes is confused as to which term is the main term and which are modifying terms. What documents or references can help him determine the main term? Whom can he consult in the practice to make sure he understands the main term? What can happen if he selects a modifying or subterm instead of a main term?

STEPS IN ICD-9-CM CODING

Ten basic steps are required for accurate ICD-9-CM coding. The first step involves abstracting the diagnostic statement from the medical record and determining the main and modifying terms. The next four steps are performed using the Alphabetic Index to search for the code, codes, or code ranges that best fit the diagnostic statement. The remaining five steps are performed using the Tabular Index to verify and confirm that the code (or codes) located in the Alphabetic Index fully matches the diagnostic statement and is the most specific and accurate diagnostic code. Procedure 18-1 describes the basic coding steps and explains the purpose of each step.

Using the Alphabetic Index (Volume 2)

Once the medical assistant has abstracted the diagnostic statement from the medical record and identified the main terms, he or she begins searching for the best code in the Alphabetic Index. As mentioned previously, the Alphabetic Index is a comprehensive, alphabetic listing of all diagnoses, conditions, illnesses, diseases, and injuries in the ICD-9-CM manual. The most important thing to remember about the Alphabetic Index is that it should be used only as an aid to locating possible code matches. The Tabular Index, with its conventions, punctuation, notes, and guidelines, must always be used to confirm that the code (or codes) selected is accurate and specific and that no contraindications exist to use of the code found in the Alphabetic Index.

Never code directly from the Alphabetic Index. Even if only one code is found in the Alphabetic Index, it may be used only if a thorough review of the conventions and instructional notations in the Tabular Index does not contraindicate it. The Alphabetic Index does not tell you whether there are instructional notes for any possible additional coding rules.

Figure 18-7 presents an excerpt from the Alphabetic Index that includes cysts. Note first the nonessential modifiers in parentheses beside the bolded main term **cyst**. Nonessential modifiers add detail, but they do not have to be present in the diagnostic statement for the code to be acceptable for use. The nonessential modifiers are *mucus, retention, serous,* and *simple.* Directly below the main term **cyst** is a notation that provides guidance on the proper selection of codes in this category. The first modifying term indented under the main term **cyst** is *accessory, fallopian tube.* Directly under this modifying term, not indented, is another modifying term, *adenoid (infected),* for the main term **cyst**. Because there is additional indention, these are two separate modifying terms for the main term **cyst**. The third description indented under cyst is *adrenal gland.* Note that directly below *adrenal gland* is a second indention. This is a subterm that directly modifies *adrenal gland,* not the main term **cyst**.

Using the Tabular Index (Volume 1)

Figure 18-8 presents an excerpt from the Tabular Index that uses the category code for **cyst** (see Figure 18-7). Note that category code 364 refers to disorders of the iris and ciliary body. Indented below category code 364 are the subcategories 364.0 through 364.9. The code selected for the diagnosis of exudative cyst of the anterior chamber of the eye was 364.62. Look at 364.6. The description of subcategory 364.6 is *cyst of the iris, ciliary body, and anterior chamber.* Remember, *and* can mean either *and* or *or.* To the left of code 364.6 is a convention indicating that a fifth digit must be used. At this point, most but not all of the diagnostic statement has been included in the description of code 364.6; all except for the term *exudative.*

Knowing that the convention requires a fifth digit and that an essential word is missing from the diagnostic statement, the medical

Cyst *(Continued)*
   breast (benign) (blue dome)
      (pedunculated) (solitary)
      (traumatic) 610.0
     involution 610.4
     sebaceous 610.8
   broad ligament (benign) 620.8
     embryonic 752.11
   bronchogenic (mediastinal)
     (sequestration) 518.89
     congenital 748.4
   buccal 528.4
   bulbourethral gland (Cowper's) 599.89
   bursa, bursal 727.49
     pharyngeal 478.26
   calcifying odontogenic (M9301/0) 213.1
     upper jaw (bone) 213.0
   canal of Nuck (acquired) (serous) 629.1
     congenital 752.41
   canthus 372.75
   carcinomatous (M8010/3) - *see*
     Neoplasm, by site, malignant
   cartilage (joint) - *see* Derangement, joint
   cauda equina 336.8
   cavum septi pellucidi NEC 348.0
   celomic (pericardium) 746.89
   cerebellopontine (angle) - *see* Cyst,
     brain
   cerebellum - *see* Cyst, brain
   cerebral - *see* Cyst, brain
   cervical lateral 744.42

FIGURE 18-7 Excerpt from the Alphabetic Index illustrating main and modifying terms for a cyst.

PROCEDURE 18-1

Performing ICD-9-CM Coding

GOAL: *To perform accurate diagnosis coding using the ICD-9-CM manual.*

EQUIPMENT and SUPPLIES

- ICD-9-CM manual (volumes 1 and 2, current year)
- Encounter form or charge ticket
- Medical record
- Paper
- Pen or pencil

PROCEDURAL STEPS

Preparation

1. Abstract the diagnostic statement or statements from the encounter form and/or the patient's medical record.
   a. Determine the main terms in the diagnostic statement that describe the patient's condition.
   b. Determine what modifying words describe the main term in the diagnostic statement.
   PURPOSE: To extract all diagnoses or diagnostic statements from the medical record and to ensure that all parts of the diagnostic statement are included in the encounter form or medical record, with nothing missing or added. To identify the main, modifying, and subterms to be used to search the Alphabetic Index.

Alphabetic Index (Volume 2)

1. Locate the main terms taken from the diagnostic statement in the Alphabetic Index (Volume 2) of the ICD-9-CM manual.
   PURPOSE: To provide a starting point for searching the Alphabetic Index.
2. Locate the modifying words listed under the main term in the Alphabetic Index.
   PURPOSE: To ensure further specificity of the codes found in the Alphabetic Index.
3. Review the conventions, punctuation, and notes in the Alphabetic Index.
   PURPOSE: To ensure that no additional searches, exclusions, or similar terms are needed to complete the search in the Alphabetic Index
4. Choose a tentative code, codes, or code range from the Alphabetic Index that matches the diagnostic statement as closely as possible.
   PURPOSE: To prevent backtracking and repeated searches in the Alphabetic Index.

Tabular Index (Volume 1)

1. Look up the codes chosen from the Alphabetic Index in the Tabular Index (Volume 1).
   PURPOSE: To begin the process of determining whether the codes selected from the Alphabetic Index are appropriate and accurate.
2. Review notes, conventions, and the ICD-9-CM Official Coding Guidelines associated with the code and code description in the Tabular Index.
   a. Review conventions and punctuation.
   b. Review instructional notations:
      - Includes or excludes statements
      - Code first, code also, and code additional statements
      - and, or, and/or with statements
   PURPOSE: To ensure that the code or codes selected are appropriate for use and to determine whether they require additional codes, further specificity, or are excluded from use.
3. Verify the accuracy of the tentative code in the Tabular Index.
   a. Make sure all elements of the diagnostic statement are included in the codes selected.
   b. Make sure the code description does not include anything not documented in the diagnostic statement.
   PURPOSE: To ensure that the most accurate and specific code is selected and that no contraindication exists to use of the code or codes selected.
4. Carry the codes to their highest level of specificity (fourth and fifth digits if they are available).
   PURPOSE: To ensure further specificity of the codes found in the Alphabetic Index.
5. Assign the code (or codes) selected from the Tabular Index as the appropriate code for the patient's condition by documenting it in the patient's medical record.
   PURPOSE: To ensure that the medical record or encounter form contains documentation of the code or codes selected.

assistant must next review possible fifth digits available for code 364.6. The fifth-digit codes in Figure 18-8 range from 364.60 to 364.64. The code description for 364.62 contains the missing essential word: *exudative*. A review of the punctuation, instructional notes, *excludes* comments, and conventions does not contraindicate the use of code 364.62; therefore, it can be selected as the most specific and accurate code. *Note:* Beneath the codes requiring a fifth digit, brackets show which fifth digit is appropriate to use with the respective code.

CRITICAL THINKING APPLICATION   18-2

Mike found a tentative code in the Alphabetic Index for a diagnostic statement for one of his patients. When he turned to the Tabular Index, he found an instruction in the code description that stated that the diagnostic statement was excluded from use of the code he had selected. What steps might Mike have taken when searching in the Alphabetic Index that led him to the wrong code in the Tabular Index? What steps can he take to restart his search and find the appropriate code?

ICD-9-CM

● **364 Disorders of iris and ciliary body**
 ● **364.0 Acute and subacute iridocyclitis**
   Anterior uveitis, acute, subacute
   Cyclitis, acute, subacute
   Iridocyclitis, acute, subacute
   Iritis, acute, subacute
   Excludes *gonococcal (098.41)*
   herpes simplex (054.44)
   herpes zoster (053.22)
  ■ **364.00 Acute and subacute iridocyclitis,
   unspecified**
   364.01 Primary iridocyclitis
   364.02 Recurrent iridocyclitis
   364.03 Secondary iridocyclitis, infectious
   364.04 Secondary iridocyclitis, noninfectious
   Aqueous:
    cells
    fibrin
    flare
   364.05 Hypopyon
 ● **364.1 Chronic iridocyclitis**
   Excludes *posterior cyclitis (363.21)*
  ■ **364.10 Chronic iridocyclitis, unspecified**
  ● **364.11 Chronic iridocyclitis in diseases classified
   elsewhere**
    Code first underlying disease, as:
    sarcoidosis (135)
    tuberculosis (017.3)
    Excludes *syphilitic iridocyclitis (091.52)*
 ● **364.2 Certain types of iridocyclitis**
   Excludes *posterior cyclitis (363.21)*
   sympathetic uveitis (360.11)
   364.21 Fuchs' heterochromic cyclitis
   364.22 Glaucomatocyclitic crises
   364.23 Lens-induced iridocyclitis
   364.24 Vogt-Koyanagi syndrome
 ■ **364.3 Unspecified iridocyclitis**
   Uveitis NOS

 ● **364.4 Vascular disorders of iris and ciliary body**
   364.41 Hyphema
    Hemorrhage of iris or ciliary body
   364.42 Rubeosis iridis
    Neovascularization of iris or ciliary body
 ● **364.5 Degenerations of iris and ciliary body**
   364.51 Essential or progressive iris atrophy
   364.52 Iridoschisis
   364.53 Pigmentary iris degeneration
    Acquired heterochromia of iris
    Pigment dispersion syndrome of iris
    Translucency of iris
   364.54 Degeneration of pupillary margin
    Atrophy of sphincter of iris
    Ectropion of pigment epithelium of iris
   364.55 Miotic cysts of pupillary margin
   364.56 Degenerative changes of chamber angle
   364.57 Degenerative changes of ciliary body
  ■ **364.59 Other iris atrophy**
    Iris atrophy (generalized) (sector shaped)
 ● **364.6 Cysts of iris, ciliary body, and anterior chamber**
   Excludes *miotic pupillary cyst (364.55)*
   parasitic cyst (360.13)
   364.60 Idiopathic cysts
   364.61 Implantation cysts
    Epithelial down-growth, anterior chamber
    Implantation cysts (surgical) (traumatic)
   364.62 Exudative cysts of iris or anterior chamber
   364.63 Primary cyst of pars plana
   364.64 Exudative cyst of pars plana

◄ New   ◄▥ Revised   ~~deleted~~ Deleted   ● Use Additional Digit(s)   ■ Nonspecific Code
● Not first-listed DX   OGCR Official Guidelines   Coding Clinic   Excludes   Includes   Use additional   Code first   Omit code

FIGURE 18-8 Excerpt from the Tabular Index illustrating codes 364 through 364.64.

▌ Diagnostic Coding Decision Tree

A series of questions, called a *decision tree*, can help the medical assistant navigate the Alphabetic Index and Tabular Index in performing the steps for diagnostic coding. The decision tree for the main text is designed to guide the selection of the appropriate ICD-9-CM diagnostic code (Figure 18-9). (To see an example of the use of a diagnostic coding decision tree, visit the Evolve site at *evolve.elsevier.com/kinn*.)

EXAMPLES OF STEPS IN DIAGNOSTIC CODING

1. The diagnostic statement is *cholecystitis*. There is only one main term: *Cholecystitis*. In the Alphabetic Index, the main term, **Cholecystitis**, has a single code, 575.10. Turning to the Tabular Index, 575.10 states, *Cholecystitis, unspecified*. The surrounding codes all add information that is not contained in the diagnostic statement; for example, 575.1 states, *Cholecystitis,* but a symbol convention to the left of

the code contains the number 5, which means a fifth digit must be used for this diagnosis. Code 575.0 states, *Acute cholecystitis.* The diagnostic statement does not specify acute; therefore, 575.0 adds inaccurate information. In the same way, codes 575.11, 575.12, and 575.2 add information that is not contained in the diagnostic statement. Therefore, the final and most accurate code for the diagnostic statement, *Cholecystitis,* is 575.10.

2. Changing the diagnostic statement, *cholecystitis,* only slightly by adding *with calculus (cholelithiasis)* changes the Alphabetic Index search and also the code. The main term remains **Cholecystitis,** although **Cholelithiasis** also could be used as the main term. The choice of either as a main term guides the coder to the same place in the Tabular Index. Using **Cholecystitis** again as a main term guides the coder to 575.10; however, indented below the main term is the subterm *with calculus,* followed by *See Cholelithiasis.* The code for cholelithiasis is 574.2, but again, indented below *cholelithiasis* is the

subterm *with cholecystitis* and the code 574.1. In the Tabular Index, code 574.2 refers only to the cholelithiasis, code 574.1; however, it is a combination code that includes cholelithiasis with cholecystitis. There is one more step, according to the symbol convention to the left of the code, which indicates that a fifth digit must be added. At the beginning of the subcategory for cholelithiasis (574), an instructional note provides the fifth digit definitions: 0 means *without mention of obstruction* and 1 means *with obstruction.* Because the diagnostic statement did not mention an obstruction, the most specific and accurate code to choose from the Tabular Index is 574.10.

CRITICAL THINKING APPLICATION 18-3

Mike is working with a medical record that has the terms "cholelithiasis" and "acute cholecystitis with calculus." How will the coding steps and decision tree questions affect or change the selection of a diagnosis code?

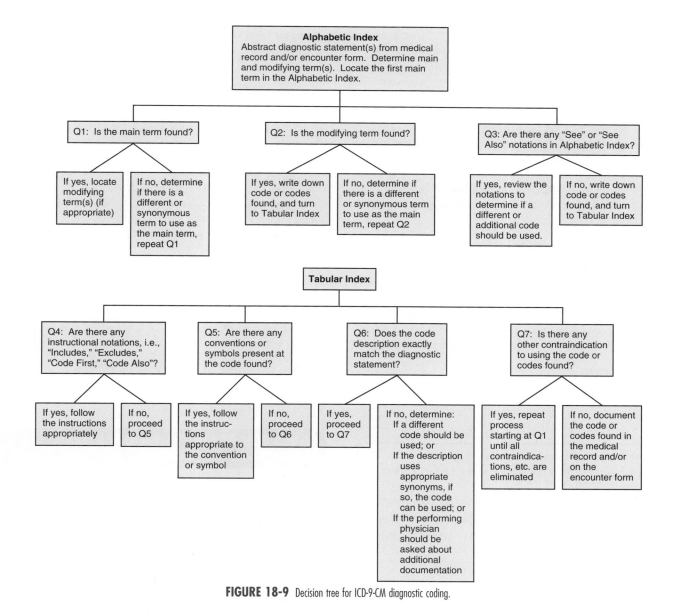

FIGURE 18-9 Decision tree for ICD-9-CM diagnostic coding.

SPECIAL CODING INSTRUCTIONS

Remember that all ICD-9-CM coding manuals, regardless of the publisher, have comprehensive instructional notes and conventions to help the coder select the most accurate diagnostic code or codes. When any discrepancy occurs between reference sources, including this text, the current year's ICD-9-CM coding manual is the final authority. This fact cannot be overemphasized. The medical assistant must always thoroughly review and refer to the conventions, instructional notations, code definitions, and other guidelines in the Alphabetic Index and Tabular Index when coding.

The following instructions are designed to provide some additional guidance in selecting diagnostic codes from various chapters in the ICD-9-CM; however, they are not to be considered a replacement for the ICD-9-CM manual, nor do they provide all the coding information, definitions, or explanations found in the manual. The steps for diagnosis coding in Procedure 18-1 are the same for all chapters of the ICD-9-CM, but special rules and considerations apply to some chapters that affect the code selection process.

Coding of Signs and Symptoms

Signs and symptoms are coded only if the physician has not yet reached a determination of the final diagnosis. If the physician's notes contain terminology such as "rule out" or "suspected," for example, the medical coder should use the patient's documented signs and symptoms, including subjective and objective findings. Subjective findings include the patient's chief complaint (CC) or statements regarding why the patient is seeing the physician. Objective findings are any measurable indicators found during the physical examination. Ill-defined conditions, signs, and symptoms are found in Chapter 16 of the Tabular Index (Volume 1). Figure 18-10 presents an illustration of the Signs and Symptoms section in Chapter 16.

Coding Suspected Conditions

When a diagnosis is stated as "questionable," "probable," "likely," or "rule out," code the patient's documented symptoms, signs, or CC. For outpatients, do not code the suspected condition if no final assessment or diagnosis has been made. If a patient is asymptomatic or has a family or personal history of a condition, a screening code from the Supplementary Classification of V Codes should be used.

Multiple Coding

Some conditions require the use of more than one code. In the Tabular Index, the instructional notation *Use additional code* means to use another code in conjunction with the one selected; *Code first* means that if more than one code is used, the code with the notation *Code first* should be the first or primary diagnosis. Multiple codes may be needed for late effects, complication codes, and obstetric codes to describe a condition more fully. Always review the ICD-9-CM manual guidelines, instructional notes, and conventions to determine when the use of multiple codes is appropriate. A patient diagnosed with diabetic retinopathy with type 1 diabetes requires multiple codes. The first code, 250.51, represents diabetes with ophthalmic manifestations; code 362.01 represents the diabetic retinopathy. The subclassification 1 designates type 1 diabetes. Figure 18-11 shows an example of multiple coding. Manifestation codes are ALWAYS a secondary code.

Using Combination Codes

A combination code is used to identify two diagnoses or a diagnosis with a secondary process (manifestation) or complication. A combination code contains descriptions of both conditions in the code definition in the Tabular Index. Combination codes are identified by referring to the subterms in the Alphabetic Index or by looking for *inclusion* and *exclusion* terms in the Tabular Index. An example of a combination code from the ICD-9-CM is shown in Figure 18-12.

Coding Late Effects and the Past Medical History

A *late effect* is a problem that remains after the acute phase of an illness or injury has ended. There is no time limit on when a late effect code can be used. Coding of late effects generally requires two codes: the condition or nature of the late effect is coded first (e.g., hemiplegia); then, the condition or nature of the effect is coded as a late effect. A late effect sometimes is described in the medical documentation as "old" or "residual" or as a "sequela," or some other phrase is used that indicates the passage of time since the onset of the original condition. A personal history of a condition more often is described as "history of …".

Be sure to distinguish between a late effect and a historical statement in a diagnosis. Whenever the diagnosis includes the term "effects of old …", "sequela of …", or "residuals of …", "due to …," the condition should be coded as a late effect. If the diagnosis is expressed in terms of "history of …", a V code is used to indicate a personal history of the condition.

Coding Impending or Threatened Conditions

Code any condition described at the time of discharge as "impending" or "threatened" as shown in the box.

- Use only if there is no final or determining diagnosis
- Use if "rule out" or "suspected" are included in the assessment or diagnostic statement.
- Signs and symptoms can be subjective and/or objective findings
  - Subjective: Chief complaint (CC) or patient's verbal statements
  - Objective: Any measurable indicators found during the physical examination
- Signs and Symptoms are found in Chapter 16, Ill-Defined Conditions, Signs and Symptoms, Volume 1 of the ICD-9-CM.

FIGURE 18-10 Rules for coding signs and symptoms.

RULES FOR CODING IMPENDING OR THREATENED CONDITIONS

1. If it did occur, code as a confirmed diagnosis.
2. If it did not occur, reference the Alphabetic Index to determine whether the condition has a subentry term for *impending* or *threatened;* also reference main term entries for *Impending* and *Threatened.*
3. If the subterms are listed, assign the given code.
4. If the subterms are not found, code the existing underlying condition or conditions, signs, or symptoms and not the condition described as "threatened" or "impending."

MULTIPLE CODING (ALSO KNOWN AS DUAL CODING)

Diagnosis: Diabetic retinopathy with type I diabetes

(Note: Retinopathy is the manifestation and diabetes is the etiology (cause) of the retinopathy or retinal hemorrhage.)

Diagnosis: Index: **Retinopathy**, diabetic 250.5 *[362.01]*
                          diabetic 250.5 *[362.01]*

The Index subterm "diabetic" located under "Retinopathy" identifies the code for the etiology as 250.5 and directs you to the code for the manifestation of *[362.01]* retinopathy. The italicized code is never sequenced first as the first-listed diagnosis but is assigned to identify a manifestation.

Tabular: **250 Diabetes mellitus**

              250.5 Diabetes with ophthalmic manifestations
                  Use additional code to identify manifestation
              250.51 Type I, not stated as uncontrolled

Note that the diagnosis of diabetes mellitus will always be reported with a five-digit code because the fifth digit indicates the type of diabetes. See the fifth-digit codes listed after code 250 in the Tabular of your ICD-9-CM.

  Code 250.51 is the correct code to describe the diabetes (etiology). The statement "Use additional code to identify manifestation..." in the Tabular at 250.5 directs you to assign a code that identifies the manifestation (retinopathy).

Tabular: **362 Other retinal disorders**

              362.0 Diabetic retinopathy
                  Code first diabetes (250.5)
              362.01 Background diabetic retinopathy

Note that the "*Code first diabetes 250.5*" directs you to the etiology code (diabetes).

Codes: 250.51, 362.01 Diabetic retinopathy with type I diabetes

The multiple codes fully describe the diagnostic statement. The Guideline directs you to place the etiology code first, followed by the manifestation code.

FIGURE 18-11 Example of multiple coding. (Modified from Buck CJ: *Step-by-step medical coding: 2012 edition,* St Louis, 2012, WB Saunders.)

COMBINATION CODES

Diagnosis: Acute cholecystitis with cholelithiasis

Index: **Cholecystitis** with calculus (stones in the gallbladder) directs you to
                  See Cholelithiasis

Index: **Cholelithiasis** with, cholecystitis, acute 574.0

Tabular: **574 Cholelithiasis**

              574.0 Calculus of gallbladder with acute cholecystitis

A fifth-digit subclassification is indicated as 0 for a case without mention of obstruction and as 1 when there is obstruction. There was no mention of obstruction in this case, so assign the fifth digit 0.

Code: 574.00 Acute cholecystitis with cholelithiasis

The single code 574.00 fully describes the diagnosis of acute cholecystitis with cholelithiasis.

FIGURE 18-12 Example of combination codes. (Modified from Buck CJ: *Step-by-step medical coding: 2012 edition,* St Louis, 2012, WB Saunders.)

Coding Infectious and Parasitic Diseases

Most often, multiple codes are needed to code infectious or parasitic diseases. The first code identifies the disease or condition (e.g., bacterial infection), and the second code identifies the organism causing the disease (e.g., streptococcal bacteria). The basic coding principles for the use of either combination or multiple codes apply throughout this section of the ICD-9-CM.

Coding Organism-Caused Diseases

Two categories for identifying the organism that causes a disease are found in other sections or categories. These codes, 041 and 079, may be used either as additional codes or as solo codes, depending on the diagnostic statement. For example, for a urinary tract infection (UTI) caused by *Escherichia coli*, the UTI is coded first (599.0) and the *E. coli* is coded second (041.4X).

Human Immunodeficiency Virus (HIV) Infection and Acquired Immunodeficiency Syndrome (AIDS)

For coding of HIV infection and AIDS, it is essential first to understand the descriptions of the codes available. The key is whether the patient has symptoms.

- Human immunodeficiency virus (HIV): This indicates only that the virus is present.
- Acquired immunodeficiency syndrome (AIDS): AIDS is a syndrome; a *syndrome* is defined as a "group of symptoms occurring together." AIDS is the manifestation (or manifestations) of and/or symptoms that can occur as a result of HIV infection.

Never code a patient as having HIV unless it is clearly documented as confirmed. Probable and suspected cases are never coded; instead, the signs and symptoms present should be coded. The code for a confirmed diagnosis of HIV infection is 042. The codes for illnesses and symptoms associated with AIDS are found primarily in Chapter 3 of the ICD-9-CM manual. Remember that stringent restrictions are placed on the disclosure of medical information regarding patients with HIV infection and/or AIDS. Make sure the patient has signed the appropriate release of medical information form before any disclosures are made to third parties.

Coding Complications of Care

A complication of medical or surgical care generally results in additional procedures or services for a patient, but often the complication is not mentioned as part of the diagnostic statement, which results in reduced reimbursement. It is important to review the medical documentation to determine whether a complication exists and to code the complication in addition to the diagnostic statement.

- Postoperative complications that affect a specific anatomic site or body system are classified according to the appropriate chapter (1 through 16) of the Tabular Index.
- Postoperative complications that affect more than one anatomic site or body system are classified according to Chapter 17 (Injury and Poisoning) of the Tabular Index.
- If the Alphabetic Index does not provide a specific main term and/or subterm to identify a postoperative complication, classify the complication to categories 996 through 999, Complications of Surgical and Medical Care, Not Elsewhere Classified.

Coding the Etiology and Manifestation

Etiology refers to the underlying cause or origin of a disease. **Manifestation** describes the signs and symptoms of the disease. In the Alphabetic Index, the etiology and manifestation codes are listed together. The etiology code is listed first, with the manifestation listed beside it in italicized brackets. These italicized codes are always listed secondary to the etiology code.

Coding Neoplasms

A neoplasm, or new growth, is coded by the site or location of the neoplasm and its behavior. The Neoplasm Table (Figure 18-13) is located in the Alphabetic Index under the main term **Neoplasms**. This table gives the code numbers for neoplasms by anatomic site in alphabetic order. Six possible code numbers exist for each anatomic site, depending on whether the neoplasm is malignant or benign, exhibits uncertain behavior, or is of an unspecified nature. Malignant

	Malignant					
	Primary	Secondary	Ca in situ	Benign	Uncertain Behavior	Unspecified
Neoplasm *(continued)*						
bone (periosteum)	170.9	198.5	—	213.9	238.0	239.2
Note—Carcinomas and adenocarcinomas, of any type other than intraosseous or odontogenic, of the sites listed under "Neoplasm, bone," should be considered as constituting metastatic spread from an unspecified primary site and coded to 198.5 for morbidity coding and to 199.1 for underlying cause of death coding.						
acetabulum	170.6	198.5	—	213.6	238.0	239.2
acromion (process)	170.4	198.5	—	213.4	238.0	239.2
ankle	170.8	198.5	—	213.8	238.0	239.2
arm NEC	170.4	198.5	—	213.4	238.0	239.2
astragalus	170.8	198.5	—	213.8	238.0	239.2
atlas	170.2	198.5	—	213.2	238.0	239.2
axis	170.2	198.5	—	213.2	238.0	239.2
back NEC	170.2	198.5	—	213.2	238.0	239.2
calcaneus	170.8	198.5	—	213.8	238.0	239.2

FIGURE 18-13 Neoplasm Table from the ICD-9-CM manual. (Modified from Diamond MS: *Mastering medical coding,* St Louis, 2006, WB Saunders.)

neoplasms are categorized into three separate subclassifications: primary, secondary, and in situ.

Terms Defining Malignant Neoplasm Sites

- *Primary:* Identifies the originating anatomic site of the neoplasm. A primary malignancy is defined as the original site or sites of the cancer.
- *Secondary:* Identifies sites to which the primary neoplasm has metastasized (spread). A secondary malignancy is defined as a second location to which the cancer has spread from the primary location.
- *In situ:* Carcinoma in situ is defined as the absence of invasion of surrounding tissues. Tumor cells are undergoing malignant changes but are still confined to the point of origin, without invasion of surrounding normal tissue. The In Situ column is used only if the physician uses that precise terminology.

Definitions of Benign, Uncertain Behavior, and Unspecified Nature Neoplasms

- *Benign:* The growth is noncancerous, nonmalignant, and has not invaded adjacent structures or spread to distant sites.
- *Uncertain behavior:* The pathologist is unable to determine whether the neoplasm is benign or malignant.
- *Unspecified nature:* Neither the behavior nor the histologic type of neoplasm is specified in the diagnostic statement.

The ICD-9-CM instructional notes state that the behavior of the neoplasm should be determined first when coding.

- Most coding decisions for malignant neoplasms are between primary and secondary.
- *In situ* is used only when the diagnostic statement contains that exact phrase.
- *Unspecified* is used only when no pathology study has been done and the neoplasm is still described with a term such as "tumor" or "growth."
- *Uncertain* is used only when the neoplasm's behavior is not malignant, the tumor is not in situ, or the behavior is unpredictable.

Note that there is also a code beginning with M that is called the *morphology code.* The morphology code is not typically used by physicians or providers when coding diagnoses.

Five Steps for Coding Neoplasms

The following steps can help the medical assistant determine the most specific and accurate diagnostic code for a neoplasm. These steps should be considered in addition to the basic diagnostic steps.

1. Using the Neoplasm Table in the Alphabetic Index, determine the site (anatomic location) of the neoplasm and select the row in the Neoplasm Table in which it appears.
2. Determine the neoplasm behavior and select the Neoplasm Table column that best defines the behavior: *Malignant, Benign, In-situ, Uncertain Behavior,* or *Unspecified Nature.*
3. If the neoplasm is malignant, determine whether the malignancy is primary, secondary, or in situ.
4. Link the appropriate Neoplasm Table column to the appropriate row.
5. Check the code in the Tabular Index to make sure the code complies with the guidelines, conventions, and instructional notations in the Tabular Index.

The ICD-9-CM manual also always provides additional information, definitions, and guidelines for coding neoplasms, just as it does for all other diseases, illnesses, and injuries.

Coding for the Circulatory System

Physicians use a wide variety of terms and phrases to identify components of the circulatory system. To code disorders of the circulatory system accurately, the coder must carefully review all inclusions, exclusions, conventions, guidelines, and instructional notations associated with each potential code selected.

Myocardial Infarction

A myocardial infarction (MI) is coded as follows:

- As *acute* if it is documented as such in the diagnostic statement or has a stated duration of 8 weeks or less.
- As *chronic* if it is so stated in the diagnostic statement or if symptoms persist after 8 weeks.

Other MI coding considerations include the following:

- If an MI is specified as "old" or "healed" without any current or presenting symptoms, it should be coded using category 412.
- A history of an MI uses code 412, which describes an *Old myocardial infarct.* This code is used only if the patient has no symptoms and only if the old MI was diagnosed by means of an electrocardiogram.
- If the patient is symptomatic, code the underlying condition or symptoms only if the underlying condition is not known.

Arteriosclerotic Cardiovascular Disease

Arteriosclerotic cardiovascular disease (ASCVD) is classified to subcategory 429.2, with an additional code used to identify whether arteriosclerosis is present. For example, the diagnostic statement "generalized arteriosclerotic cardiovascular disease" should be coded using 429.2 followed by 440.9, *generalized and unspecified atherosclerosis.*

Hypertensive Disease

A distinction is made in the ICD-9-CM between "elevated" and "high" blood pressure. High blood pressure is defined as hypertension. If a diagnostic statement does not contain the word *hypertension* or the phrase *high blood pressure,* the condition is coded as elevated blood pressure, not hypertension.

The Alphabetic Index contains a Hypertension Table (Figure 18-14) under the main term **Hypertension.** The table contains subterms that identify different types of hypertension and any complications caused by the hypertension. Hypertension is classified three ways: malignant, benign, and unspecified.

- *Malignant* hypertension usually is considered acute and life-threatening.
- *Benign* hypertension, although considered dangerous, is not considered acute or life-threatening.
- Unless the diagnostic statement specifically states "malignant" or "benign" hypertension, hypertension should be classified as *unspecified.*

Hypertension frequently is the cause of various forms of heart and vascular disease; however, the mention of hypertension in the diagnostic statement does not mean that a combination code for

	Malignant	Benign	Unspecified
Hypertension, hypertensive (arterial) (arteriolar) (disease) (essential) (fluctuating) (idiopathic) (intermittent) (labile) (low rennin) (orthostatic) (paroxysmal) (primary) (systemic) (uncontrolled) (vascular)	401.0	401.1	401.9
with			
heart involvement (conditions classifiable to 428, 429.0-429.3, 429.8, 429.9 due to hypertension) (*see also* Hypertension, heart)	402.00	402.10	401.90
with kidney involvement – *see* Hypertension, cardiorenal			
renal involvement (only conditions classifiable to 585, 586, 587) (excludes conditions classifiable as 584) (*see also* Hypertension, kidney)	403.00	403.10	403.90
with heart involvement – *see* Hypertension, cardiorenal			
failure (and sclerosis) (*see also* Hypertension, kidney)	403.01	403.11	403.91
sclerosis without failure (*see also* Hypertension, kidney)	403.00	403.10	403.90
accelerated (*see also* Hypertension, by type, malignant)	401.0	—	—
antepartum – *see* Hypertension, complicating pregnancy, childbirth, or the puerperium			

FIGURE 18-14 Hypertension Table from the ICD-9-CM manual. (Modified from Diamond MS: *Mastering medical coding,* St Louis, 2006, WB Saunders.)

hypertensive heart disease should be used. If a cause-and-effect relationship exists between the hypertension and the heart disease, it should be clearly documented in the clinical record or diagnostic statement.

Coding for Complications of Pregnancy, Childbirth, and the Puerperium

Coding for the obstetric patient is like using a specialty codebook within the main codebook. This is challenging for those who do not code obstetrics often. Some important terms regarding pregnancy are:

- *Antepartum*—meaning pregnancy (applies as soon as a pregnancy test result is positive)
- *Childbirth*—meaning delivery
- *Peripartum*—the period from the last month of pregnancy to 5 months' postpartum
- *Postpartum*—the puerperium (6 weeks after delivery)

Obstetric Coding Guidelines

To begin searching for obstetric codes, start at either of the main terms **Pregnancy** or **Delivery**. Look for a subterm regarding the condition, or start at the main term for the condition and look for a subterm that states *affecting pregnancy* or *during pregnancy.*

- Normal, uncomplicated prenatal and postpartum care for the mother and routine visits for the baby are coded with V codes as long as no current problem exists.
- Some mothers have conditions that put them at high risk; these situations are also coded with V codes unless a problem manifests itself during the pregnancy.
- Normal, uncomplicated delivery for the mother is coded using category 650, and a V code is used to describe the outcome of the delivery.

USE OF CATEGORY 650 AND V CODES IN PREGNANCY CODING

- In the ICD-9-CM manual, use codes from the Tabular Index (Volume 1), Chapter 11, in the 630-677 range. If the pregnancy is documented as a normal pregnancy or is unrelated to the reason for the physician encounter, use a V code (V22.2) in place of any Chapter 11 code.
- Chapter 11 codes are used only on the maternal record, not on the newborn record.
- Categories 640-648 and 651-676 require a fifth digit. The fifth digit indicates whether the encounter is antepartum or postpartum or whether the delivery occurred.

A normal, uncomplicated delivery is described as one in which no problem or complication occurred during the entire encounter and no procedures were performed other than those deemed normal. The available V codes used to describe the outcome of delivery are V27.0-V27.9. If the mother delivered a single baby, born live, without complication, the code would be V27.0.

In obstetric care, fifth digits are used only for obstetric patients with complications. In Figure 18-15, note that the fifth digits divide the pregnancy into three different "time zones," which are described in the ICD-9-CM as episodes of care:

- Before delivery (antepartum)
- Delivery (the episode of care when the delivery occurs)
- After delivery (postpartum)

The fifth-digit codes for the episode of care are:

0—Unspecified as to episode of care or not applicable
1—Delivered, with or without mention of antepartum condition
2—Delivered, with mention of postpartum complication
3—Antepartum condition or complication
4—Postpartum condition or complication

● **637 Unspecified abortion**
    Requires following fifth digit to identify stage:
    Coding Clinic: 1994, Q2, P14

> ■ 0 unspecified
>   1 incomplete
>   2 complete

    Includes   abortion NOS
            retained products of conception following
            abortion, not classifiable elsewhere

● ■ **637.0 Complicated by genital tract and pelvic**
    [0-2] **infection** ♀   M

● ■ **637.1 Complicated by delayed or excessive hemorrhage** ♀ M
    [0-2]

● ■ **637.2 Complicated by damage to pelvic organs or**
    [0-2] **tissues** ♀   M

● ■ **637.3 Complicated by renal failure** ♀   M
    [0-2]

● ■ **637.4 Complicated by metabolic disorder** ♀   M
    [0-2]

● ■ **637.5 Complicated by shock** ♀   M
    [0-2]

● ■ **637.6 Complicated by embolism** ♀   M
    [0-2]

● ■ **637.7 With other specified complications** ♀ M
    [0-2]

● ■ **637.8 With unspecified complication** ♀   M
    [0-2]

● ■ **637.9 Without mention of complication** ♀   M
    [0-2]

FIGURE 18-15 Excerpt from ICD-9-CM: pregnancy codes and use of fourth and fifth digits.

If the baby has a problem while the mother is still pregnant, code it only if it affects the mother's condition or management. Code the baby's problem on the mother's chart only if it creates a medical concern or a medical need for the mother to undergo testing or treatment. When it is appropriate to code a fetal condition that affects the mother's management, use codes for pregnant patients, not codes for babies.

Cesarean Delivery

Cesarean codes only define the reasons a cesarean delivery was performed; they do not describe cesarean deliveries as separate from vaginal births. A cesarean delivery is considered the treatment for a problem or condition that exists at the time of delivery.

Outcome of Delivery and Liveborn Infant Codes

- Outcome of Delivery codes (V27) are reported on the mother's health record after the delivery.
- A Liveborn Infant code or codes (V30-V39) describe the condition of the baby at delivery (e.g., liveborn or stillborn) and are reported on the newborn's record.

Newborn Coding

Babies are considered newborn or perinatal for the first 28 days. The code range used for these patients, 760-779, is found in Chapter 15 of the Tabular Index. After the twenty-eighth day of life, do not use codes specific to perinatal patients. Newborn codes should never be used on the maternal record. If a newborn is healthy, a code from the V code category 30 should be used in addition to any other Chapter 15 code.

Liveborn Infant Category

A fifth digit from the Liveborn Infant category is used only when a fourth digit of 0 is assigned. A fourth digit of 0 means that the baby was born in the hospital; the fifth digit then specifies whether the birth was cesarean. The other fourth digits (i.e., 1 and 2) represent births that occurred other than in the hospital. Cesarean deliveries are presumed to occur only in the hospital; therefore, no fifth digit is provided.

Coding Injuries

Injuries constitute a major section of the ICD-9-CM. They are classified first according to the type of injury and then by anatomic site.

- When coding injuries, separate codes should be assigned for each individual injury unless a combination code is provided.
- If a patient has multiple injuries, the most severe injury should be coded first.
- Superficial injuries, such as abrasions or contusions, are not coded when associated with more severe injuries at the same site.
- If an injury results in minor or major damage to peripheral nerves or blood vessels, the injury is coded first, with additional codes from categories 950-957, Injury to Nerves and Spinal Cord, and/or 900-904, Injury to Blood Vessels.

Coding Fractures

Fractures are coded first by anatomic site and then by type of fracture. The category code range for fractures, 800-829, is found in Chapter 17 (Injury and Poisoning) in the Tabular Index. Fractures can be classified as open or closed. A fracture is said to be *open* if the skin has been broken and the bone protrudes through the skin surface, or when a wound, such as a puncture, allows the bone to be seen. In a *closed* fracture, the bone is not exposed to the outside of the body. If no indication is given whether the fracture was open or closed, it should be coded as if it were closed.

Burns

The same principles for combination and multiple coding apply to burns. Code each burn separately unless specific combination codes are given in the Tabular Index. There are many combination codes. Because burns are coded by site and degree and by the extent of body surface involvement, all burn cases should have at least two codes, and a third if the wound is infected. Other types of wounds, lacerations, punctures, and so on use a different fifth digit to show that they are infected and therefore complicated. Because burn codes use the fifth digit for other information, an additional code is necessary to indicate infection.

Table 18-1 presents the Lund-Browder Chart for Determining Burn Percentages in Children. First, determine the child's age and then the body part or parts burned. Next, add the percentage listed in the Age column for each body area burned. The sum represents the percentage of the body burned. For example, if the entire left leg of a 10-year-old child were burned, the burn percentage would be calculated as follows:

$$\tfrac{1}{2} \text{ of thigh: } (4.25\%) \times 2 = 8.5\%$$

$$\tfrac{1}{2} \text{ of lower leg: } (3\%) \times 2 = 6\%$$

$$8.5\% + 6\% = 14.5\% \text{ of the body burned}$$

TABLE 18-1 Lund-Browder Chart for Determining Burn Percentages in Children

	UP TO 1 YEAR	1 YEAR	5 YEARS	10 YEARS	15 YEARS
½ of head	9.5%	8.5%	6.5%	5.5%	4.5%
½ of 1 thigh	2.75%	3.25%	4%	4.25%	4.25%
½ of lower leg	2.5%	2.5%	2.75%	3%	3.25%

http://medical-dictionary.thefreedictionary.com/rule+of+nines

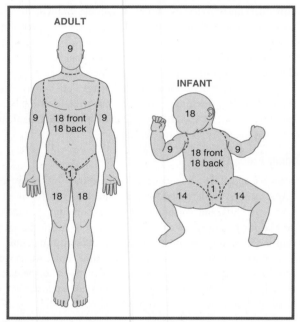

FIGURE 18-16 Rule of Nines for determining burn percentages in adults and infants.

Figure 18-16 presents the Rule of Nines, which is used to determine burn percentages in adults. Using the Rule of Nines, add the percentage listed for each body area burned. The sum is the percentage of the body burned. For example, the burn percentage for burns on the entire head and front and back torso in an adult would be calculated as follows:

$$\text{Front and back of head: } 4.5\% \times 2 = 9\%$$

$$\text{Front and back of torso: } 9\% \times 2 = 18\%$$

$$9\% + 18\% = 27\% \text{ of the body burned}$$

When evaluating burns on growing children, providers may find it necessary to change the percentage assignments to accommodate proportionally larger heads than adults. The percentages may also be changed if a patient has large buttocks, thighs, or a large abdomen that is involved in the burn.

Steps for Coding Burns

1. Code the burn to the site by degree. Under the main term **Burn**, find the subterm for the site and then the subterm for the degree. If the burn is stated to be at the same site but of a different degree,

code to the highest degree. Omit the code for the lower level burn at the same site.

2. Determine the percentage of the body burned using category 948 (Chapter 17 in the Tabular Index). The fourth digit describes the total burned surface; the fifth digit describes the percentage of only third-degree burns; for example, 50% of total body surface burned with 15% third-degree burns.

3. If the burn is said to be infected, use code 958.3 as a third code to identify the infection.

Using E Codes

The ICD-9-CM uses E codes to describe the circumstances of an accident or injury. E codes are listed in a separate Tabular Index and Alphabetic Index (Figure 18-17). E codes describe the following:

- Nature of an event (e.g., fire, fall, collision, abuse)
- Place of occurrence
- Late effect of an injury
- Intent (e.g., self-inflicted, assault, accident)
- Drugs and chemicals that caused the injury or disease

E codes are never principal codes or listed first, because they are only supplementary information. They most often are used with injury codes, but they may be used with any condition that is the result of an external cause, such as a respiratory problem caused by smoke inhalation. The E code describing the initial incident is used only once, the first time the patient is treated for the condition. Some major categories of E codes include the following:

- Transport accidents
- Poisoning and adverse effects of drugs, medicinal substances, and biologics
- Accidents and falls
- Accidents caused by fire and flames
- Accidents caused by natural and environmental factors
- Late effects of accidents, assaults, or self-injury
- Assaults or purposely inflicted injury
- Suicide or self-inflicted injury

It is correct to use as many E codes as necessary to describe all the information provided by the record. It is acceptable to use non-physician documentation to support these codes if it does not conflict with the physician's documentation. This is the only exception to the rule that diagnoses and diagnostic statements must be documented in the medical record by physicians if the information is to be used for code selection or billing purposes.

Table of Drugs and Chemicals

The ICD-9-CM's Table of Drugs and Chemicals contains a classification of drugs and other chemicals. It is used to identify poisoning states and external causes of adverse effects. Each of the substances is assigned a code, which is used based on the type of poisoning (e.g., overdose, wrong substance given or taken, or a prescription drug taken with alcohol). The table also contains a list of external causes of adverse effects caused by the ingestion or exposure to a drug or chemical.

The poisoning codes in the first column of the Table of Drugs and Chemicals should be determined and listed first, followed by the external cause (E code). The Table of Drugs and Chemicals has five E code headings: *Accidental Poisoning, Therapeutic Use, Suicide Attempt, Assault,* and *Undetermined Cause.*

E CODE INDEX

Railway Accidents	E800-E807
Motor Vehicle Traffic Accidents	E810-E819
Motor Vehicle Nontraffic Accidents	E820-E825
Other Road Vehicle Accidents	E826-E829
Water Transport Accidents	E830-E838
Air and Space Accidents	E840-E845
Vehicle Accidents Not Classified Elsewhere	E846-E848
Place of Occurrence	E849
Accidental Poisoning by Drugs, Medicinal Substances, Biologicals	E850-E858
Accidental Poisoning by Other Solid and Liquid Substances, Gases, Vapors	E860-E869
Misadventure to Patients During Surgical/ Medical Care	E870-E876
Surgical/Medical Procedures Cause of Abnormal Reaction of Patient or Later Complication, Without Mention of Misadventure at Time of Procedure	E878-E879
Accidental Falls	E880-E888
Accidents by Fire and Flames	E890-E898
Accidents Due to Natural/Environmental Factors	E900-E909
Accidents Caused by Submersion, Suffocation and Foreign Bodies	E910-E915
Other Accidents	E916-E928
Late Effects of Accidental Injury	E929
Drugs, Medicinal and Biological Substances Causing Adverse Effects in Therapeutic Use	E930-E949
Suicide and Self-Inflicted Injury	E950-E959
Homicide and Injury Purposely Inflicted by Other Persons	E960-E969
Legal Intervention	E970-E978
Injury Undetermined Whether Accidentally or Purposely Inflicted	E980-E989
Injury Resulting from Operations of War	E990-E999

FIGURE 18-17 Example of E codes. (Modified from Diamond MS: *Mastering medical coding,* St Louis, 2006, WB Saunders.)

EXTERNAL CAUSE CODES (E CODES) USED WITH THE TABLE OF DRUGS AND CHEMICALS

- *Accidental poisoning (E850-E869):* Accidental overdose of a drug; wrong substance given or taken, taken inadvertently; accidents in the use of drugs in medical and surgical procedures; and to show external causes of poisonings coded with the Tabular Index (Volume 1), Chapter 19, Injury and Poisoning, category codes 980-989.
- *Therapeutic use (E930-E949):* An adverse effect caused by proper administration of the correct substance in the proper dosage.
- *Suicide attempt (E962):* Self-inflicted injury or poisoning. Never code Suicide Attempt without documentation from the physician.
- *Assault (E961-E962):* Injury or poisoning inflicted by another person with the intent to injure or kill.
- *Undetermined (E980-E982):* Used only when neither accidental nor intentional circumstances can be determined.

E Codes Used with the Table of Drugs and Chemicals

An E code to identify a drug or chemical may be added to clarify the patient's circumstance whenever a drug or chemical is identified in the medical record as a causative substance. In addition to the E codes that identify the causative substances, the Table of Drugs and Chemicals includes a column for poisoning associated with each substance. These codes can be used with an E code from the other columns with one exception: a Poisoning code cannot be used with a Therapeutic Use code. Problems caused by correct substances properly used are considered adverse effects, not poisoning.

V Codes: Classification of Factors Influencing Health Status and Contact with Health Service

V codes are used to describe circumstances or encounters with a physician or healthcare provider when no current illness or injury exists. V codes may stand alone or may be principal or secondary. Some codes have a notation that they cannot be principal or stand-alone.

V Code Index for History Codes

In the Alphabetic Index, under the main term **History**, is the subterm *personal.* This means that the subterms are considered the patient's personal history. The subterm *family* indented two spaces under **History** describes the family history rather than personal history. Watch the subterm indentations closely to ensure that the code selected is the proper history code.

Diabetes Mellitus

Diabetes mellitus codes always require a fourth and fifth digit. The fourth digit describes any manifestations of the diabetes that may be present; the fifth digit describes the type of diabetes. The fourth-digit subcategories for category 250, diabetes mellitus, are divided by the presence or absence of complications and the nature of the complication. Figure 18-18 presents the fourth-digit subcategories 250.0-50.9.

The fifth digit is required to code the type of diabetes mellitus (DM). Determining the type of diabetes is critical to proper code assignment. The two types of DM are type 1, which includes both juvenile-onset DM and insulin-dependent diabetes mellitus (IDDM), and type 2, which sometimes is called adult-onset DM. Type 2 DM is not always treated with insulin and therefore is also called *non-insulin-dependent DM.*

Four fifth digits are used to specify the type of diabetes and whether it is under control:

0—Type II or unspecified type, not stated as uncontrolled. This fifth digit is used for patients with type 2 DM even if the patient requires insulin.

1—Type I (juvenile type), not stated as uncontrolled.

2—Type II or unspecified type, uncontrolled. This fifth digit is used for patients with type 2 DM even if the patient requires insulin.

3—Type I (juvenile type), uncontrolled.

MAXIMIZING THIRD-PARTY REIMBURSEMENT

The most important thing to remember in using the ICD-9-CM is to code the diagnosis to the highest level of specificity, linking the

Fourth Digit Subcategories for Diabetes Mellitus

- 250.0 Diabetes mellitus without mention of complication

- 250.1 Diabetes mellitus with ketoacidosis (defined as a life-threatening condition in which ketones, which result from the breakdown of fat for energy, accumulate in the bloodstream and the pH of the blood decreases)

- 250.2 Diabetes with hyperosmolarity (defined as a concentration of the body fluids that is abnormally increased)

- 250.3 Diabetes with other coma

- 250.4 Diabetes with renal manifestations

- 250.5 Diabetes with ophthalmic manifestations

- 250.6 Diabetes with neurological manifestations.

- 250.7 Diabetes with peripheral circulatory disorders

- 250.8 Diabetes with other specified manifestations

- 250.9 Diabetes with unspecified complication

FIGURE 18-18 Excerpt from ICD-9-CM: fourth-digit subcategories 250.0 through 250.9.

ICD-9-CM code to the *Current Procedural Terminology*, fourth edition (CPT-4) code. Obtaining the correct reimbursement is important to the practice's cash flow and depends on proper coding and billing techniques. Some other crucial points to remember when submitting diagnostic codes for claims include:

- Use the current year ICD-9-CM manual and stay informed of all changes, revisions, and additions published for that year to both the codes and the official coding guidelines.
- Code accurately from documented information, making sure the appropriate code or codes are assigned for all parts of the diagnostic statement, with no additions or omissions.
- Be sure the diagnosis corresponds to the symptoms and treatment. Many codes are specific to age and gender.
- Review data entry to make sure no digits have been transposed.
- Know the insurance carrier's rules and requirements for completion and submission of claims.
- Incomplete or inaccurate codes may result in delay or denial of reimbursement. An inaccurate diagnosis may have a lifelong negative effect on the patient.

CLOSING COMMENTS

Medical assistants have the trust of the physician and practice that employ them. Therefore, a medical assistant must be responsible and knowledgeable to ensure that no fraud takes place in the coding and claims submission process. Medical assistants are expected to adhere to ethical standards, assigning and reporting only codes clearly supported by concise documentation in the patient's chart. When in doubt, a medical assistant should consult the attending healthcare provider for clarification. Maintaining and continually enhancing coding skills and keeping informed of changes in codes, guidelines, and regulations are necessary responsibilities for a coding professional.

Patient Education

Since most patients are uneducated about medical billing and coding, they may not understand how the codes on their encounter forms relate to their diagnosis. If the patient approaches with questions, explain that the codes represent his or her diagnosis to the most specific and accurate level. The system of diagnostic coding standardized the way medical billing is handled by all parties in the reimbursement cycle. Since the coding system is much like a foreign language, be patient when explaining this process and answering questions; otherwise, those who are unfamiliar with its dialogue will have difficulty understanding the billing process.

Legal and Ethical Issues

By using the billing and coding system, providers are able to express the simplicity or complexity of a medical treatment or procedure. This specificity leads to the maximum reimbursement to the provider. The medical assistant must perform coding procedures accurately so that they reflect exactly what happened during the treatment. Codes must not be exaggerated to increase the reimbursement to the provider.

In the next chapter, procedure codes will be introduced; the procedure codes must "match" the diagnosis code – meaning that the procedure code must be a logical treatment for the diagnosis (more than one diagnosis may be listed on the claim form). For example, patients who are diabetic may be checked for a blood glucose level at each visit. Medical assistants should become familiar with the laws and regulations within their state regarding the billing and coding process. Medical assistants who are eager to learn will become successful and valuable employees.

SUMMARY OF SCENARIO

Mike is enthusiastic about his position and enjoys learning more about the coding process. He knows that as he gains experience and earns his certificate, he will be even more valuable as an employee. As Mike progresses with diagnostic coding, he also will be able to help the physicians and nursing staff be attentive to details when documenting a patient's chart.

Although using the superbill to enter the codes for billing is an easy tool, Mike has learned that knowing how to use the ICD-9-CM volumes is a necessary asset to ensure accurate coding. He also knows it is important when coding a diagnosis to make sure the medical documentation matches the encounter form and that all elements of the diagnostic statement must be included.

Furthermore, he must ensure that the diagnosis listed on the encounter form is fully documented in the patient's medical record. In addition, Mike has learned that the layout and structure of volumes 1 and 2 of the ICD-9-CM manual are designed to aid the selection of the most specific and accurate diagnosis code. Every feature of the manual provides guidance in choosing and confirming a diagnostic code that matches the diagnostic statement on the encounter form and in the medical record. The steps and decision tree for diagnostic coding ensure that Mike will be coding to the highest level of specificity and accuracy.

SUMMARY OF LEARNING OBJECTIVES

1. **Define, spell, and pronounce the terms listed in the vocabulary.**
   Spelling and pronouncing medical terms correctly bolster the credibility of the medical assistant. Knowing the definition of these terms promotes confidence in communication with patients and co-workers. Also, understanding the medical terms found in the diagnostic statement is essential for identifying and selecting the most accurate and appropriate diagnostic code or codes.

2. **Identify three purposes of the most current diagnostic coding system.**
   The ICD-9-CM is used to track healthcare statistics and to facilitate accurate medical record keeping and ease in processing claims. Use of the ICD-9-CM is mandatory for participation in many federal, state, and private insurance programs.

3. **Describe how to use the most current diagnostic coding system.**
   Each of the volumes of the ICD-9-CM has a specific use. The Alphabetic Index (Volume 2) is used to look for the disease or diseases documented in the clinical record. The coder then proceeds to the Tabular Index (Volume 1) to find and assign a code. The coder must follow guidelines provided in the specific manual used for coding in the medical facility.

4. **Explain and apply the basic coding rules in using the ICD-9-CM.**
   Several basic rules can assist the medical assistant in coding: (1) Make sure to use the most recent ICD-9-CM manual; (2) keep a medical dictionary handy; (3) proofread the claim and make sure it makes good sense; (4) do not use nonspecific codes; and (5) take care in coding pre-existing conditions.

5. **Explain where diagnostic information can be found and demonstrate how to abstract the diagnostic statement from the medical record.**
   Diagnostic information is found in the medical record and typically also on the encounter form or charge ticket. It can be located in the history and physical examination (H&P), treatment notes and discharge summary and also in various reports from the radiology and pathology departments and the laboratory. Information about the patient's

   diagnosis is extracted from the medical record; this information becomes the diagnostic statement.

6. **Demonstrate the use of the Alphabetic Index in selection of main and modifying terms, and appropriate code (or codes) or code ranges.**
   Main terms are selected from the diagnostic statement to begin the search for the best code or code ranges. A main term typically is the primary condition, disease, or injury. Modifying terms provide further specificity, or detail, such as the anatomic site or additional manifestations of the condition.

7. **Explain the importance of the Tabular Index.**
   Never code directly from the Alphabetic Index. The Tabular Index contains the most specific information. Check and recheck the codes to make sure the documentation supports the codes used on the claim.

8. **Correctly use instructional terms and symbols as defined in the ICD-9-CM.**
   The medical assistant should become familiar with all the symbols used in the ICD-9-CM. Instructional notations should be read thoroughly and all directions followed when coding a claim.

9. **Explain the use of V and E codes.**
   V or E codes may help clarify or further explain a code. V codes are used when the patient is not currently ill but is being seen by health service professionals. E codes are used to explain that some external cause contributed to an adverse effect in the body.

10. **Perform diagnostic coding.**
    The medical assistant's knowledge of accurate diagnostic coding contributes to the legal and financial health of the practice. In most cases ICD-9-CM codes are found on the provider's encounter form (or superbill) and/or in the practice management software. However, with literally thousands of current diagnostic codes, it may be necessary to code from the ICD-9-CM manual. Because these codes are updated yearly, they are an asset in coding compliance. The process for diagnosis coding is outlined in Procedure 18-1.

CONNECTIONS

Study Guide Connection: Go to the Chapter 18 Study Guide. Read and complete the activities.

Evolve Connection: Go to the Chapter 18 link at *evolve.elsevier.com/kinn* to complete the Chapter Review and Chapter Quiz. Check out the other resources listed for this chapter to make the most of what you have learned from Basics of Diagnostic Coding.

19

BASICS OF PROCEDURAL CODING

Carline A. Dalgleish, Sharon Oliver, and Alexandra Patricia Adams

SCENARIO

Sherald Vogt excelled on her diagnostic coding examinations, and she now looks forward to learning procedural coding. The process for coding procedures and services will prove to be similar to that of ICD-9-CM and diagnostic coding, except she will use a different coding manual, the *Current Procedural Terminology* (CPT), for most procedural and services rendered coding. She will also use the *Healthcare Common Procedural Coding System*, or HCPCS (pronounced "hic-pix") manual. As with the ICD-9-CM, accurate coding begins with the proper analysis of clinical information to abstract the correct data and accurately assign a procedure or service code. In the ICD-9-CM, she learned about coding conventions and guidelines. The CPT also has conventions, symbols, guidelines, and formal steps specific to procedural coding that Sherald will use to correctly assign procedure codes. Sherald is beginning to fully understand the impact diagnostic and procedural coding has on reimbursement, and her responsibility to uphold ethical standards when coding to keep her employers, Dr. Shuman, Dr. Taylor, and Dr. Caddell, in compliance with federal and state guidelines. She is excited to begin this new phase of her education and to have the opportunity to learn more skills, which will help her reach her goal of becoming an even more valuable asset to the practice.

While studying this chapter, think about the following questions:

- What will Sherald find similar to what she learned with the ICD-9-CM as she performs procedural coding?
- What will help Sherald in selecting the most specific and accurate CPT code?
- What are the differences between coding for the CPT and coding for HCPCS?
- What will Sherald learn about the legal and compliance implications of improper coding?

LEARNING OBJECTIVES

1. Define, spell, and pronounce the terms listed in the vocabulary.
2. Describe the steps for abstracting procedural data from clinical documentation.
3. Identify four purposes of the CPT.
4. List the six main sections of the CPT and describe their content.
5. Describe the coding conventions, guidelines, and layout of the CPT manual and their importance.
6. Describe the process and steps for selecting the most accurate code based on clinical documentation.
7. Explain the importance of correctly assigning Evaluation and Management (E/M) codes.
8. Discuss the importance of modifiers.
9. Define upcoding and explain why it must be avoided.
10. Explain the process for selecting the correct procedure codes.
11. Explain the process for selecting main and modifying terms.
12. Explain how to find codes in the Alphabetic Index of the CPT manual.
13. Explain how to analyze and select codes using the CPT Main Text.

VOCABULARY

abstract An outline or summary of the diagnostic statement and/or procedures and services performed. In procedural coding, the outline or summary assists in ensuring that all procedures and services are included in an insurance claim submission and that nothing is omitted or added to the encounter form or charge ticket; as a verb form, *abstract* also means to compile this outline or summary for use in procedural coding.

acronyms Abbreviations, such as ECG for electrocardiography.

add-on codes Codes that indicate additional or supplemental procedures carried out along with the primary procedure.

Alphabetic Index The reference section of the CPT manual; it is used to help find a code or code range.

bundled codes CPT codes designating procedures or services that are grouped together and paid for as one procedure or service, according to the National Correct Coding Initiative (NCCI) edits, established by the Centers for Medicare and Medicaid Services (CMS).

category In the CPT manual, the element indented one level below a subsection; it usually refers to a specific anatomic site or to procedures and/or services.

Category I codes Five-digit primary procedure or service codes, found in the Tabular Index, that are selected when performing insurance billing or statistical research.

Category II codes Special codes that can help providers track revenue and reimbursement; these codes are alphanumeric and end in the letter F.

Category III codes Codes for a new or experimental procedure or service, otherwise referred to as "Emerging Technology"; these codes are alphanumeric and end in the letter T.

crosswalked With regard to the coding process, a crosswalk is the reference from a deleted or changed code to its new code location in the manual.

downcoding A change in a code or codes for entries submitted for reimbursement. This change usually is made by the insurance company, generally because the code submitted in some way does not match the company's specifications.

eponym A name or term for something that is based on the name of a person (or occasionally a place or thing). Traditionally in medicine, discoveries often are named after the person or people who made the discovery.

established patient (EP) A patient who has received professional services (face to face) from the physician, or from another physician of the *exact* same specialty *and subspecialty* who belongs to the same group practice, within the past 3 years.

guidelines Found at the beginning of each section of the coding manual, guidelines are the specific definitions of items that must be read to appropriately interpret and report the procedures and services contained in that section.

HCPCS *Health Care Common Procedural Coding System;* also called *Level II codes,* HCPCS codes were created by the CMS to report supplies, materials, injections, and certain procedures and services not defined in the CPT manual.

main term The primary or key word or words abstracted from a medical record that are used to begin the code search in the Alphabetic Index. A main term can identify a procedure or service performed; an organ or anatomic site; a condition, illness, or injury; or an eponym, abbreviation, or acronym.

Main Text See Tabular Index.

modifiers Terms that serve as the means to report or indicate that a service or procedure performed has been altered by some specific circumstance but not changed in its definition or code.

modifying terms Key words selected after the main term has been chosen to help further define or describe the procedure or service performed.

new patient (NP) A patient who has *not* received any professional services (face to face) from the physician or another physician of the *exact* same specialty *and subspecialty* who belongs to the same group practice, within the past 3 years.

patient status (PS) The state of a patient as either new or established; appears in the Evaluation and Management section of the CPT.

physical status The physical condition of the patient.

place of service (POS) codes Codes used on professional claims to specify the facility or location where the service or services were rendered.

providers Individuals qualified by education, training, licensure or regulation, and facility privileging who perform a professional service within their scope of practice and independently report that professional service.

section One of the six primary divisions of the main body of the CPT.

subcategory In the CPT manual, the element indented one level below a category, usually a procedure or service unique to a specific category.

subsection In the CPT manual, the element indented one level below a section; it usually describes an anatomic site or organ system (e.g., Integumentary, Cardiology).

Tabular Index The Main Text of the CPT manual; it contains the alphanumeric listing of all Category I procedure and service codes and their respective descriptions.

unbundled codes Codes in which the components of a major procedure are separated and reported separately.

upcoding A deliberate increase in a CPT code, despite the lack of documentation, to the next highest reimbursable code so as to obtain higher reimbursements.

Procedural coding is defined as the transformation of verbal descriptions of medical services and procedures into numeric or alphanumeric designations. As with diagnostic coding and use of the ICD-9-CM manual, the medical assistant must develop meticulous accuracy when using the *Current Procedural Terminology* (CPT) manual, developed by the American Medical Association (AMA), and the *Healthcare Common Procedural Coding System* (HCPCS), developed by the Centers for Medicare and Medicaid Services (CMS). The medical assistant facilitates accurate medical recordkeeping and efficient processing of insurance claims by using the CPT and HCPCS, which identify appropriate procedures and services common to the physician's office. CPT and HCPCS (discussed later in the chapter) are used in the claims submission process to obtain reimbursement from payers, to track physicians' productivity, and to provide statistical data for research and other purposes.

GETTING TO KNOW THE CPT

The Evolution of CPT Coding

The CPT manual is a list of descriptive terms and identifying codes for reporting medical services and procedures performed by physicians. The CPT provides a uniform, or standard, language that accurately describes medical, surgical, and diagnostic services and enhances reliable communication among physicians, patients, and third parties. The manual was developed after the AMA recognized a need for a standardized description of services that would be universally understood by physicians, hospitals, insurance companies, and all involved in the reimbursement or statistical data collection process.

The second edition of the CPT, published in 1970, presented an expanded system of terms and codes to designate diagnostic and therapeutic procedures in surgery, medicine, radiology, laboratory, pathology, and medical specialties. At that time, the four-digit classification was replaced with the current five-digit coding system. The fourth edition was published in 1977 and included significant updates in medical technology. At the same time, a system of periodic annual updating was introduced to keep pace with the rapidly changing environment. The fourth edition is still in use today; however, at this writing, the AMA is in the process of developing the fifth edition of the CPT, the first major revision since 1977.

Purpose of CPT Procedural Coding

The CPT uses a five-digit classification system that is designed to do the following:

- Encourage the use of standard terms and descriptors to document procedures in the medical record
- Help communicate accurate information on procedures and services to agencies concerned with insurance claims
- Provide the basis for a computer-oriented system to evaluate operative procedures
- Contribute basic information for actuarial and statistical purposes

Before continuing, consider this important fact: there are roughly 150,000 procedure and service codes in the CPT manual and thousands more in the HCPCS manual. Memorizing the codes for each specific procedure and service would be impractical, if not impossible. Instead, the key to success is learning how to use the coding manuals to find the most specific and accurate code based on interpretation of the medical record. This requires a solid understanding of medical terminology, anatomy, and physiology and a knowledge of how to use the CPT manual and its symbols, conventions, guidelines, and notes. The goal of this chapter is to teach the skills, processes, and decisions required to use the CPT and HCPCS manuals. Remember, the CPT and HCPCS manuals for the current year are always the final authority. The symbols, guidelines, conventions, and other instructions found in the CPT manual contain all the information needed to select the correct code for the procedure or service documented in the medical record.

THE CPT CODE

Category I Codes

The CPT code is a five-digit code also known as a **Category I code**. Category I codes are located in the Tabular Index (also called the *Main Text*) of the CPT manual and arranged by sections. For example, codes beginning with 7 (e.g., 70100—a radiologic examination of the mandible, partial, with less than four views) are located in the Radiology section of the manual. Each code has a description of the service or procedure performed. Some CPT codes (e.g., Category II and Category III codes, discussed later) are alphanumeric.

Product Pending U.S. Food and Drug Administration Approval

Occasionally, a new vaccine is assigned a Category I code before the Food and Drug Administration (FDA) has approved the vaccine for use. These vaccines are listed in Appendix K and are identified in the Tabular Index of the CPT in various ways by different publishers. Some publishers use the letter P (approval pending); others use a lightning bolt symbol (⚡) in various colors to designate the pending FDA approval. These codes are tracked by the AMA to monitor FDA approval status. When the FDA status changes to approval, the lightning bolt symbol (⚡) or other "pending" identifier is removed.

Bundled Codes

Bundled codes indicate procedures or services that are grouped together and paid for as one procedure or service, as designated by the NCCI edits. If bundled codes are separated and used individually, a special report should be used to describe the circumstances that made the unbundling necessary.

Unbundled Codes

Unbundled codes are used when the components of a major procedure are separated and reported separately.

Category II

Category II codes are a set of supplemental tracking codes that can be used for performance measurement. Category II codes are optional; they cannot be used as a substitute for Category I codes, and they are not reported as part of the billing process. **Providers** can use Category II codes to help measure performance and outcomes. These codes describe clinical components that may be typically included in Evaluation and Management services or clinical services. No relative value is associated with them. In a Category II code, the fifth digit is the letter F.

Category II codes are described and listed in Appendix H of the CPT manual. They are listed in alphabetic order by condition instead of numerically. Category II codes are reviewed by the Performance Measures Advisory Group, which is composed of members from various medical organizations and government agencies. In some publisher's editions of the CPT manual, Category II codes are also listed in their own section immediately after the Medicine section and before the appendixes.

Category III

Category III codes are temporary codes assigned for emerging and new technology, services, and procedures that have not been officially added to the Main Text of the CPT manual. In a Category III code, the fifth digit is the letter T. Category III codes may be used in billing and reporting if no code in the Main Text accurately describes the technology, service, or procedure performed, and no Category I code matches the medical documentation. Category III codes have no reimbursement value. In most publisher's editions of the CPT manual, Category III codes are also listed in their own section immediately after the Medicine section and before the appendixes.

Modifiers

Modifiers (Table 19-1) give providers a means of indicating that a service or procedure performed was altered by some specific circumstance but was not changed in its definition. Two- or five-digit alphanumeric modifiers, included with the five-digit CPT code, can be used to supply additional information or to describe extenuating circumstances that affect the rendered procedure or service. For instance, modifier -50 adds the detail that a procedure was performed bilaterally, or on both sides of the body. For example, the code 99050 is used to describe care provided after normal business hours. To describe a situation in which an assistant surgeon is needed for a surgical procedure, modifier -80 can be used to allow the assistant surgeon to submit charges for his or her time and services (code 99080 describes a special report).

The modifiers for HCPCS are codes composed of two alphanumeric characters. Like the modifiers for CPT Category I codes, the HCPCS modifiers do not change the description of the code, but rather provide additional information or describe extenuating circumstances.

FORMAT OF THE CPT CODING MANUAL

In the CPT manual, each procedure or service is represented by a five-digit numeric code (Figure 19-1), a type of medical shorthand that saves enormous amounts of time and effort and helps to ensure accuracy of information. Just imagine, for example, if a billing department had to describe, in writing, every single one of the medical procedures and services represented by the codes in the CPT manual. Preparing one bill for one patient could take an hour or longer, and problems with reimbursement still would arise if the health insurance or third-party payer had additional questions or, worse, reduced or even denied payment based on its interpretation of the written narrative. In most instances, using the five-digit CPT codes eliminates the need for written descriptions, thus assuring clear communication, and the standardization of codes ensures that everyone in the reimbursement cycle understands exactly what procedure or service was provided to the patient. In addition, these codes enable automated computer processing of claims, which also saves time and effort.

CPT CONTENT

The CPT manual generally includes the following content, depending on the publisher:
- Comprehensive instructions for use of the manual, including steps for coding
- A complete Alphabetic Index

MODIFIER	DESCRIPTION
-50	Bilateral procedure. If procedure was performed on both sides of the body (e.g., both knees, both eyes) and code description does not indicate that the procedure or service was performed bilaterally, modifier -50 is used.
-62	Two surgeons. When two surgeons work together as primary surgeons performing distinct parts of a procedure, each surgeon should report the procedure he or she performed to the insurance carrier and use modifier -62. (This prevents the insurance carrier from possibly rejecting a surgical charge as a duplicate.)

TABLE 19-1 Commonly Used CPT Code Modifiers

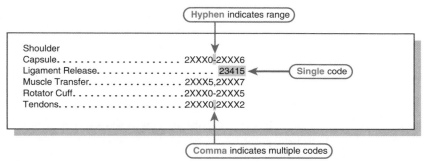

FIGURE 19-1 CPT code example. (From Buck CJ: *Step-by-step medical coding, 2012 edition*, St Louis, 2012, WB Saunders.)

- The Main Text (Tabular Index), composed of:
  - Six sections
  - Guidelines and notes
  - Conventions
  - Fourteen appendixes

The Indexes

The CPT has two primary divisions, the Alphabetic Index and the Main Text (Tabular Index). The **Alphabetic Index** is like any other index in a textbook; it is simply a guide to finding data in the body of the textbook. However, instead of providing the page numbers where the information is located, as a typical index does, the CPT's Alphabetic Index lists the code or code ranges, which are arranged in numeric order in each section of the Main Text.

Main Text

The **Tabular Index (Main Text)** is divided into six broad categories, or **sections,** with codes listed in numeric order in each section. Like the ICD-9-CM, the codes in the Tabular Index include definitions, guidelines and notes, which enable the coder to select the most specific code or codes based on the procedures and services descriptions documented in the medical record. The six sections of the Tabular Index include:

- Evaluation and Management
- Anesthesia
- Surgery (all body systems)
- Radiology
- Pathology and Laboratory
- Medicine

Each of the six sections reflect the general type of service. Sections are subdivided into subsections; subsections are further divided into categories; and categories can be subdivided into subcategories. Each level of a section provides more specificity regarding the procedure or service performed and the anatomic site or organ system involved (Table 19-2). In most instances, all four levels are found, although this is not a hard and fast rule.

In the CPT manual, the **subsection** is listed below the section and indented two spaces. The subsection usually describes an anatomic site or an organ system, as in the following examples:

- Anatomic site: heart, femur, or skull
- Organ system: digestive, integumentary, or cardiology

A **category** is listed below the subsection and indented two spaces. It generally refers to a specific procedure or service, but it can also indicate a more specific anatomic site:

- Procedures: esophagoscopy, incision and drainage, or cardiac catheterization
- Specific anatomic site: mitral valve, distal femur, or occipital bone

Subcategory is the lowest level of code description. The subcategory is listed below the category and indented two spaces. It provides even more specificity about an anatomic site or the procedure or service performed.

Evaluation and Management Section

The Evaluation and Management (E/M) section contains codes for the different types of encounters or visits patients have with providers; these encounters may include office, hospital, and emergency

TABLE 19-2 Section, Subsection, Category, and Subcategory Examples

SECTION	SUBSECTION	CATEGORY	SUBCATEGORY
Surgery	Musculoskeletal System	Application of Casts and Strapping	Body and Upper Extremity
Surgery	Cardiovascular System	Arteries and Veins	Embolectomy/ Thrombectomy
Medicine	Physical Medicine and Rehabilitation	Modalities	
Medicine	Neurology and Neuromuscular Procedures	Sleep Testing	
Radiology	Diagnostic Radiology	Head and Neck	
Radiology	Vascular Procedures	Aorta and Arteries	

department visits; consultations; and physician contact with patients in intensive care units, skilled nursing facilities, nursing homes, and other facilities. The code range in the E/M section is 99201 to 99499. The E/M section is further divided into subsections that include different types of services (e.g., office visits, hospital visits, consultations, skilled nursing facility, or nursing home visits). The subcategories of E/M services are further classified into levels of E/M services that are identified by specific codes. This classification is important, because the nature of a physician's work varies by type of service, place of service, and the patient status. The subsections, categories, and subcategories are written to further modify or describe the service or procedure performed.

Anesthesia Section

The Anesthesia section includes codes for anesthesia services rendered by anesthesiologists and anesthetists before, during, and after surgery. The code ranges in the Anesthesia section are 00100 to 01999 and 99100 to 99140. Codes are included for the types of anesthesia administered (e.g., general, local, and sedation anesthesia); other support services, including the anesthesiologist's preoperative and postoperative encounters with the patient, evaluation of the patient's physical status, and the administration of anesthesia, fluids, and/or blood; and monitoring services, such as blood pressure, temperature, and electrocardiography (ECG). Unusual forms of monitoring (e.g., intra-arterial, central venous, and Swan-Ganz) are not included and can be billed separately.

Surgery Section

The Surgery section, the largest section of the CPT, includes standardized codes for all invasive surgical procedures performed by physicians. An invasive procedure is defined as any medical procedure in which a bodily orifice or the skin must be penetrated by cutting, puncture, or other method. This section is divided into subsections typically identifying specific body systems, beginning with the integumentary (skin) system and ending with the ophthalmologic (eye) and otologic (ear) systems. In most instances, each subsection is further divided into categories and subcategories, which describe procedures and services unique to that anatomic subsection.

Radiology Section

The Radiology section includes codes for diagnostic imaging, including x-ray studies and scans, and for therapy used in the treatment of cancer. The code range in the Radiology section is 70000 to 79999.

Pathology and Laboratory Section

Codes are included for all diagnostic tests performed on bodily fluids and tissue, including urine, blood, sputum, and feces, as well as excised or biopsied cells, tissue, or body organs; and for evaluation of those fluids and tissues to identify any pathology or disease present. The code ranges for the Pathology and Laboratory section are 80047 to 80076 for Organ or Disease–Oriented Panels and 80100 to 89999 for all other tests.

Medicine Section

The codes for the Medicine section range from 90281 to 99199 and 99500 to 99607 (excluding the anesthesia code ranges described in the Anesthesia section). The Medicine section includes many and varied subsections, categories, and subcategories. This section can be considered a catchall section in that it includes codes for services and procedures that do not fit into any of the other sections of the CPT

manual. Medical specialties, such as ophthalmology, otolaryngology, and allergy, which involve procedures and services that vary greatly from the traditional office encounter, are grouped in the Medicine section rather than the E/M section. Noninvasive diagnostic tests are included in the Medicine section rather than in the Surgery section, which typically includes only invasive procedures.

Conventions of the CPT Main Text

Conventions (Figure19-2) are special symbols used to provide additional information about certain codes. Examples of conventions include triangular and round symbols, which indicate that a code or description was revised, removed, or added. A plus sign (+) indicates an **add-on code**. Codes with a plus sign are additional codes that must be used with certain Category I codes. For example, one of the codes in the Surgery section, Integumentary subsection, is +15401. Code 15401 describes "each additional 100 sq. cm...." Just above code 15401 is code 15400, which describes a "xenograft of the skin... the first 100 sq. cm. or less..." If the medical documentation states that a "200 sq. cm. xenograft of the skin" was performed, the medical assistant would code the first 100 sq. cm. using code 15400, and the second 100 sq. cm. by using add-on code 15401 (+15401).

Another example of a symbol convention is a circle with a small round dot in the center. This symbol indicates that conscious sedation, rather than a general anesthetic, was used during a surgical procedure.

In most CPT manuals, the legend explaining the meanings of the convention symbols is found at the bottom of each page of the Tabular Index.

⃠	**Modifier -51 exempt.** This symbol is used to specify when a code is exempt from use of the modifier -51. Modifier -51 allows coders to specify that one procedure was performed multiple times. Normally, in the instance when the same procedure has been performed more than once, reporting of modifier -51 would be required to indicate that the same procedure (with the same definition and code) was performed two or more times; however, when this symbol appears in front of the code, the code description already indicates the procedure was performed more than once, and therefore modifier -51 is not required.
+	**Add-on code.** An add-on code is used when more than one code must be used to completely describe a specific procedure or service. Some medical procedures are commonly carried out at the same time a primary procedure is being performed and are described as procedures performed by the same physician to include an additional treatment or procedure done at the same time or in conjunction with the main procedure being performed. Add-on codes can be readily identified by specific words used in the code description, such as additional digit(s), lesions(s), neurorrhaphy, etc. Add-on codes are always used in addition to the primary service or procedure and must never be reported as a stand-alone code.
•	**New code.** In healthcare, scientific research results in new emerging technology procedures and services. Once a new procedure or service is approved for use or judged to be effective, a temporary **Category III** code is assigned. If the procedure or service is then adopted, and statistics bear out the integration of the new procedure with the more mainstream or traditional codes, then a permanent CPT-4 code is assigned, and the code is added to the main text of the CPT-4 manual.
▲	**Revised code.** In addition to the new codes added to the CPT-4 each year, many code descriptions are revised as well. The change may be only to clarify or improve the wording of the description, or, as is the case in most instances, it may be revised to add or remove terminology or information.
►◄	**New or revised text.** Text within the guidelines is often revised to add or remove information, correct grammar, or further clarify the content.
⊙	**Conscious sedation.** This is a new convention, added in 2005, to describe CPT-4 codes that include conscious sedation use. Codes with this convention do not require the use of separate Conscious Sedation codes from the Medicine Section of the CPT-4.
⁄	**FDA approval pending.** A symbol indicating that a CPT-4 category I code has been assigned to a vaccine product in anticipation of approval for use from the Food and Drug Administration (FDA).

FIGURE 19-2 CPT Main Text conventions.

Guidelines

Guidelines, which are found at the beginning of each section and some subsections of the CPT manual, add definitions and descriptions necessary to appropriately interpret and report the procedures and services in that section or subsection. For example, in the Medicine section, specific instructions are provided for handling unlisted services or procedures, special reports, and supplies and materials provided to the insurance company or the patient (Figure 19-3). Guidelines are written to assist in understanding when and under what circumstances codes may be used. It is important to thoroughly read and understand the guidelines provided throughout the Main Text. This is especially important when first learning to code, or working in a section of the CPT that is rarely used. It is also important to reread the guidelines after the CPT annual revisions, additions, and deletions, are effective January of each year. Selecting a code without reading the guidelines will usually lead to selection of the wrong code. Not only will this result in the potential for delayed or denied reimbursement, but continued inappropriate code selection can be considered fraud or abuse and can result in serious civil or criminal penalties.

Notes

Notes are typically found only in the category, subcategory, or code description area of the CPT. They apply only to the designated group of codes following the note and (unlike guidelines) not to the whole

section. As do guidelines, notes provide additional information to assist in the selection of specific codes.

Unlisted Procedure or Service Code

Occasionally, even with the best documentation and the coder's best efforts, an accurate, specific code to match the procedure or service performed cannot be found in the CPT manual. In each section (and sometimes in subsections, categories, and/or subcategories), nonspecific codes have been provided. These codes are called Unlisted Procedures and Services. For example, code 29999 is found in the Surgery section, Musculoskeletal subsection. It describes an "unlisted procedure, arthroscopy." Unlisted codes can be used only when no Category I or Category III code provides an exact match to the medical documentation. When an unlisted code is used, a Special Report must be sent with the insurance claim that describes the procedure or service thoroughly.

Special Reports

When bills are submitted for services rendered or procedures performed, most insurance carriers or third-party payers require no additional information on the insurance claim form other than the procedure or service CPT code. When a bill is submitted for a service that is unlisted, unusual, or newly adopted, the third-party carrier requires a special report so that the company can determine whether provision of that service or procedure was medically appropriate.

Appendixes

The following appendixes are found in the CPT manual.

- Appendix A: *Modifiers:* Lists all the two-digit numeric or alphanumeric codes used to increase specificity and provide additional information about certain procedures and services.
- Appendix B: *Summary of Additions, Deletions, and Revisions:* For easy reference, at each annual update of the CPT, this appendix lists all changes made from the previous year.
- Appendix C: *Clinical Examples:* Provides helpful narrative examples that aid selection of the correct and most specific level of E/M codes.
- Appendix D: *Summary of CPT Add-on Codes:* Lists codes needed when more than one code is required to fully describe the service or procedure rendered or to identify a procedure performed concurrently with another procedure.
- Appendix E: *Summary of CPT Codes Exempt from Modifier -51:* Lists all procedures and services exempt from the use of modifier -51. Modifier -51 (99051) is the multiple procedures modifier. When multiple procedures are performed at the same session by the same provider, the primary procedure is reported, and the additional procedure or service is identified by appending modifier -51 to the procedure or service code. This is done only when the primary procedure code does not include the additional procedure in its description.
- Appendix F: *Summary of CPT Codes Exempt from Modifier -63:* Lists all procedures exempt from the use of modifier -63. Modifier -63 is used to report procedures performed on infants weighing less than 4 kg to identify the increased complexity common with these patients. Category I codes that state specifically "Exempt from modifier -63" do not require use of this modifier.

99000—99116 Medicine

Miscellaneous Services

99000	Handling and/or conveyance of specimen for transfer from the physician's office to a laboratory
99001	Handling and/or conveyance of specimen for transfer from the patient in other than a physician's office to a laboratory (distance may be indicated)
99002	Handling, conveyance, and/or any other service in connection with the implementation of an order involving devices (e.g., designing, fitting, packaging, handling, delivery or mailing) when devices such as orthotics, protectives, prosthetics are fabricated by an outside laboratory or shop but which items have been designed, and are to be fitted and adjusted by the attending physician
	(For routine collection of venous blood, use 36415)
99024	Postoperative follow-up visit, normally included in the surgical package, to indicate that an evaluation and management service was performed during a postoperative period for a reason(s) related to the original procedure
	(As a component of a surgical "package," see **Surgery Guidelines**)
	(99025 has been deleted)

FIGURE 19-3 Example of Miscellaneous Services in the Medicine section.

- Appendix G: *Summary of CPT Codes that Include Moderate (Conscious) Sedation:* Lists all procedure codes that include conscious sedation as part of the code description; this eliminates the need to code the sedation separately.
- Appendix H: *Alphabetic Index of Performance Measures by Clinical Condition or Topic:* Lists Category II codes used by providers tracking and measuring performance and outcomes.
- Appendix I: *Genetic Testing Code Modifiers:* Lists all modifiers, and their descriptions, unique to genetic testing.
- Appendix J: *Electrodiagnostic Medicine Listing of Sensory, Motor, and Mixed Nerves:* Lists each sensory, motor, and mixed nerve conduction study code. This appendix aids the accurate use of codes 95900, 95903, and 95904.
- Appendix K: *Product Pending FDA Approval:* Lists vaccine products for which FDA approval is pending and those that have been assigned Category I codes before approval.
- Appendix L: *Vascular Families:* Lists the elements of the vascular system, grouped by families, beginning at the aorta and ending at the termination point of each vessel. This appendix is designed to assist coding for the Cardiology subsection of the Surgery and Medicine sections.
- Appendix M: *Deleted CPT Codes:* Provides a summary of **cross-walked**, deleted and renumbered codes and descriptors.
- Appendix N: *Summary of Resequenced CPT Codes:* Provides a summary of CPT codes that do not appear in numeric sequence in the listing of CPT codes. Resequencing allows existing codes to be relocated to an appropriate location for the code concept, regardless of the numeric sequence.

BEGINNING THE CODING PROCESS

Medical Documentation

The steps for using the CPT manual actually begin not in the CPT coding manual but in the medical documentation. Information pertinent to code selection is taken from a variety of medical documents. Sources of information include the following:

- Encounter form (also called a *superbill, fee slip,* or *charge ticket*)
- History and physical report (H&P)
- Discharge summary
- Operative report
- Pathology report
- Radiology report

These documents were discussed in earlier chapters, and examples were given. Although these same forms are used for CPT coding, the information abstracted is different (as shown later in the chapter). As in ICD-9-CM coding, when the medical documentation is compared against any code description, all the elements of that code must substantially match, with nothing added or missing.

Many providers have CPT and ICD-9-CM codes preprinted on their encounter forms or charge tickets. However, it is important also to review the medical record carefully and compile an abstract of all the procedures and services rendered during an encounter. For example, on the encounter form, a provider checks off the procedure for a esophagogastroduodenoscopy (EGD); however, when the medical assistant reviews the medical record, he discovers that the operative report states that an EGD with biopsy was performed.

If the medical assistant had not reviewed the medical record, a code with a lower reimbursement amount for the procedure would have been submitted to the insurance carrier, and the provider would have lost revenue. Update encounter forms annually to ensure that code additions, changes, and revisions appear on the preprinted forms.

The coding steps and process outlined in this chapter, including use of the Alphabetic Index and the Main Text of the CPT, apply to all sections of the CPT manual. Some special considerations and differences apply to the E/M and Anesthesia sections.

The basic steps in medical coding are to (1) read, analyze, and abstract the procedure or service documented in the medical record and (2) compare it with the encounter form, operative report, or other documentation to ensure that all services and procedures have been recorded. The term **abstract**, used as a verb in this context, means to create an outline or summary of information from a text or record.

In procedural coding, an abstract is created to find all the procedures and services performed during a patient encounter and also to ensure that nothing has been omitted from or added to the encounter form or charge ticket that is not documented in the medical record. The abstracted data are then broken down into main terms and modifying terms. A **main term** is usually the primary procedure or service performed, and a **modifying term** further defines or adds information to the main term. Next, the main and modifying terms are used to find the code or code ranges in the Alphabetic Index. Last, the code selected is confirmed by reviewing the guidelines, notes, and conventions in the Main Text to verify that the most accurate code has been chosen.

USING THE ALPHABETIC INDEX

The Alphabetic Index is a comprehensive, alphabetic listing of all procedures and services in the CPT manual. Medical assistants must keep in mind the most important fact about the Alphabetic Index: it should be used only as an aid to finding the area in the Main Text to evaluate for selecting the proper code. The Alphabetic Index is not a substitute for the Main Text. Even if only one code is assigned, the Main Text must be used to ensure that the code selection is accurate.

The Alphabetic Index is used as a guide to search for one or more codes or code ranges. The index is similar to that found in any textbook; it is an alphabetic list of main and modifying terms found in the Main Text of the coding manual. In a typical index, the term or concept listed in the index is followed by a reference page or pages, where detailed information is presented in the body of the book. The Alphabetic Index in the CPT is used in the same way, except that it references codes or code ranges rather than pages. As discussed earlier, the Main Text is divided into sections, and the procedures and services are listed in numeric order by the Category I code.

The Alphabetic Index is organized by main terms that can stand alone. The CPT code set has been developed as stand-alone descriptions of medical procedures. Some of the procedures in the CPT are not printed in their entirety but refer back to a common portion of the procedure listed in a preceding entry. This is evident when an entry is followed by one or more indentations. This is the part before the semicolon (;) in the description. Do not confuse the two-digit modifiers discussed earlier in the chapter with modifying terms. *Modifiers* are numeric supplements to a Category I code, whereas *modifying terms* are words that add to or modify the meaning of the main term.

Modifying terms are indented two spaces below the main term. They further describe or add information or a definition needed to narrow the search for an appropriate procedure or service code. A main term might be a procedure, such as an excision, and each modifying term could provide further information about the anatomic location or the organ excised, the type of instrument used, or a special technique, or whether other procedures were performed at the same time as the excision, such as obtaining biopsy tissue for examination. Modifying terms affect the selection of appropriate codes; therefore, it is important to review the list of modifying terms when selecting a code or code range.

Consider the examples presented in Table 19-3. If the medical documentation contains the narrative description of a procedure as a "diagnostic cystoscopy," the main term is *Cystoscopy*; the modifying term is *diagnostic,* because it describes the type of cystoscopy performed. Another example is "esophagogastroscopy with biopsy and fulguration of lesions." In this example, the main term is *Gastroscopy* (the procedure performed), and the modifying terms are *esophago-* (which adds another anatomic site scoped at the same time as the gastroscopy); *with biopsy* and *fulguration* (two additional procedures performed during the gastroscopy); and *lesions* (describes the object of the biopsy and fulguration).

Two rules should be followed when coding any procedure or service:

- Be as specific as possible in code selection and use all pertinent words in the description given in your documentation.

- Never add any words, modifying terms, or descriptors to the procedure or service code description that change the definition of the procedure or service or that are not documented.

Once the medical documentation has been abstracted to determine the procedures and services performed and the main and modifying term or terms have been identified, the next step is to look for the terms in the Alphabetic Index. Use the Alphabetic Index to search for one or more codes or a code range that best describes the procedure or service documented in the medical record. Using the code or codes found in the Alphabetic Index search, locate each in the appropriate section, subsection, category, or subcategory of the Main Text and select the most specific code that best matches the medical record documentation.

▌Searching the Alphabetic Index

Begin the search by using one or all of the four primary classifications (or types) of main and modifying term entries:

- Procedure or service (e.g., examination, excision, scope, revision, repair, drainage)
- Organ or anatomic site (e.g., clavicle, mandible, humerus, liver, colon, uterus)
- Condition, illness, or injury (e.g., cholelithiasis, ulcer, fracture, pregnancy, fever)
- Eponym, synonym, abbreviation, or **acronym** (e.g., MRI [magnetic resonance imaging], Naffziger operation, Mosenthal test, GERD [gastroesophageal reflux disease])

As described previously, the CPT manual is divided into six sections (i.e., E/M, Anesthesia, Surgery, Radiology, Pathology and Laboratory, and Medicine). The sections may first list the procedure (e.g., excision, incision, repair), the organ or anatomic site (e.g., clavicle, liver), or a condition (e.g., a fracture or laceration).

TABLE 19-3 Identification of Main and Modifying Terms in the Alphabetic Index

| CODE | MAIN TERM(S) | MODIFYING TERMS | | | |
		FIRST	SECOND	THIRD	FOURTH
	Cystoscopy	Diagnostic			
	Gastroscopy	Esophago-	With biopsy	With fulguration	Of lesions
492000	**Cyst**	Abdomen			
		Ankle			
		Bartholin's gland			
		Bile duct			
21030	**Excision**	Cheekbone			
23140		**Clavicle**			
23146				**With allograft**	
23147				With autograft	
27355-27758			Femur		
Cyst excision: 49200					
Cyst excision of clavicle: 23140					
Cyst excision of clavicle with allograft: 23146					

TABLE 19-4 Comparing Codes in the Range 52234 to 52250

CODE	MAIN TERM(S)	FIRST	SECOND	THIRD	FOURTH
				MODIFYING TERM	
52234	Cystourethroscopy	Treatment or fulgurations	Of a lesion or lesions	Using either cryosurgery or laser surgery	With or without a biopsy
52235/52240	Same	Same	Same except for size of lesions	Same	Same
52204	Cystourethroscopy	with biopsy			
52214	Cystourethroscopy	with fulguration	Of bladder, urethra or glands		
52224	Cystourethroscopy	with fulguration	No mention of specific urinary system structure or organ		

Use the name of the performed procedure or service (anastomosis, splint, repair, stress test, therapy, vaccination); the organ or other anatomic site of the procedure (tibia, colon, salivary gland, aorta); the condition, illness, or injury (abscess, fracture, cholelithiasis, strabismus); or, if applicable, synonyms, **eponyms**, or abbreviations (ECG [electrocardiography], Stookey-Scarff procedure, Mohs' micrographic surgery).

Using *See* and *See Also* in the Alphabetic Index

The *see* statement in the Alphabetic Index points to another location in the Alphabetic Index to find the code or code range. The *see also* statement points to additional codes or code ranges in the Alphabetic Index that may be useful to the code found in the original search.

Use of the Semicolon

A semicolon at the end of a main description indicates that modifying terms and descriptions follow. Every indented description below a stand-alone code is related to that stand-alone code. If a main term has no additional modifying terms, the next entry is a stand-alone description of a different procedure, which is positioned flush left, without indentation.

Stand-Alone Codes and Code Ranges

In the Alphabetic Index, a procedure or service may list a single code, called a *stand-alone code,* or a range of possible codes that may match the medical documentation. Remember that the Alphabetic Index is an index; it is designed as a guide to the most suitable codes that match the documentation. It does not provide specificity; that is the purpose of the Main Text. At this point, the search is only for the closest match or matches to the medical documentation.

Because some medical procedures and diagnostic tests can be quite complex, there may be a single (stand-alone) code or a code range that may include one main term but several variations (or modifying terms) of the main procedure or service. For example, the code for *Craterization, phalanges, toe* is 28124, a stand-alone code. However, using the same main term, *Craterization,* but adding *any of the phalanges* (toes or fingers) yields a range of codes: 26235-29236. The code range is shown with a hyphen to indicate that all codes within that range could be appropriate.

In some cases a stand-alone code and a range of codes are listed for the same service or procedure. For example, *Craterization, femur,* lists both the stand-alone code 27360 and the code range 27070-27071. Once a stand-alone code or code range has been found in the Alphabetic Index, the next step is to look up each of those in the Main Text and select the code or codes that most closely match the medical documentation (Table 19-4).

Steps for Using the Alphabetic Index

1. Abstract the procedures and/or services performed from the medical documentation.
2. Determine the main and modifying terms from the abstracted information.
3. Select the most appropriate main term to begin searching in the Alphabetic Index.
4. Once the main term has been located, select one or more modifying terms, if needed, to narrow the search.
5. If no main or modifying term produces an appropriate code or code range, repeat steps 2, 3, and 4 using a different main term.
6. Find the code or code ranges that include all or most of the description of the procedure or service found in the medical record.
7. Disregard any code or code range containing additional descriptions or modifying terms that are not found in the abstracted information or the medical documentation.
8. Write down the code or code ranges that best match the medical documentation.

CRITICAL THINKING APPLICATION 19-1

Sherald is having trouble finding a procedure in the Alphabetic Index. What are some options and alternative ways she can perform an Alphabetic Index search?

USING THE TABULAR INDEX (MAIN TEXT)

Once the code or codes have been selected from the Alphabetic Index, the next stop is the Tabular Index (Main Text), where the final decision is made regarding the choice of code. In the Main Text, the conventions, symbols, guidelines, notes, and even the punctuation all play a part in choosing the most accurate code possible.

In the Main Text, look up each code or code range found in the Alphabetic Index. Read the description of the code thoroughly to ensure that the main elements abstracted from the medical documentation are all included in the code description, with nothing substantial omitted or added. Read the section guidelines and notes to determine whether additional codes should be used, add-on codes or modifiers are required, or use of the code is contraindicated.

Steps for Using the Main Text (Tabular Index)

Except for the special considerations required for coding from the Evaluation and Management (E/M) and Anesthesia sections, the following steps apply to all sections of the CPT manual (Procedure 19-1). The numbering of these steps is continuous with the numbering of the steps for the Alphabetic Index search.

9. Turn to the Main Text and find the first code or code range noted from the Alphabetic Index search.

10. Compare the description of the code with the medical documentation. Verify that all or most of the medical record documentation matches the code description and that there is no additional element or information in the code description that is not found in the documentation.

11. Read the guidelines and notes for the section, subsection, and code to ensure that there are no contraindications to the use of the code.

12. Evaluate the conventions, especially add-on codes (+) and exemption from modifier -51.

13. Determine whether any special circumstances require the use of a modifier.

14. Determine whether a Special Report is required.

15. Record the CPT code selected in the medical record documentation next to the procedure or service performed and in the appropriate block of the insurance claim form.

Coding Decision Tree

A series of questions, sometimes called a *decision tree,* can assist the medical assistant in navigating the Alphabetic Index and Main Text of the CPT. The decision tree for the Main Text is designed to guide the selection of the appropriate CPT Category I code or code range (Figure 19-4). (Visit the Evolve site at *evolve.elsevier.com/kinn* for an example of how to use the decision tree.)

Abstracting the procedure and service information from the patient's medical record or the encounter form is only the first step in the coding decision process. Procedure 19-1 illustrates the steps for using the Alphabetic Index and Main Text to guide the medical

---

PROCEDURE 19-1

Perform Procedural Coding: CPT Coding

CAAHEP COMPETENCIES: IV.C.IV.6., IV.P.IV.3., V.P.V.6., VII.P.VII.1., IX.A.IX.2.

ABHES COMPETENCIES: 3.v

GOAL: *Use the steps for procedure and service coding to find the most accurate and specific CPT Category I code.*

EQUIPMENT and SUPPLIES

- CPT coding manual (current year)
- Encounter form (charge ticket)
- Medical record
- Paper
- Pen or pencil
- Medical dictionary or medical terminology reference book

PROCEDURAL STEPS

1. Abstract the procedures and/or services performed from the medical documentation.
   PURPOSE: To ensure that all procedures and/or services are listed on the encounter form; that all procedures and services on the encounter form match the medical record; and that nothing documented in the medical record is missing from the encounter form.

2. Select the most appropriate main term to begin the search in the Alphabetic Index.
   PURPOSE: To have a starting point for the Alphabetic Index search.

3. Determine the main and modifying terms from the abstracted information.
   PURPOSE: To identify the term or terms to begin the search in the Alphabetic Index.

4. Once the main term has been located, select modifying term or terms if needed.
   PURPOSE: To provide additional specificity and help narrow the search for the code or code range in the Alphabetic Index.

5. If no modifying term produces an appropriate code or code range, repeat steps 2 and 3 using a different main term classification.
   PURPOSE: To aid in finding the most appropriate code or code range by using alternative methods of searching the Alphabetic Index.

6. Find code or code ranges that include all or most of the medical record procedure or service description.
   PURPOSE: To assist in directing the medical assistant to the proper section, subsection, category or subcategory of the Main Text of the CPT.

7. Disregard any code or code range containing additional descriptions or modifying terms not found in the medical record.
   PURPOSE: To prevent upcoding or downcoding errors and other compliance issues.

8. Write down the code or code ranges that best match medical documentation.
   PURPOSE: To prevent repeated reference to the Alphabetic Index by recording all possible matches to the code or code range being sought. This saves time and prevents redundant effort.

9. Turn to the Main Text and find the first code or code range found while searching the Alphabetic Index.
   PURPOSE: To begin the process of finding the most specific and accurate code.

10. Compare the description of the code with the medical documentation. Verify that all or most of the medical record documentation matches the code description and that there is no additional element or information in the code description that is not found in the documentation.
    PURPOSE: To avoid upcoding and downcoding errors and to ensure there are no contraindications to use of the code selected.

11. Read the guidelines and notes for the section, subsection, and code to ensure that there are no contraindications to the use of the code.
    PURPOSE: To ensure there are no instructions that would prevent the use of the code selected.

12. Evaluate the conventions, especially add-on codes (+) and exemption from modifier -51.

PURPOSE: To ensure there are no instructions that would prevent the use of the code selected.

13. Determine whether special circumstances require the use of a modifier.
    PURPOSE: To select, if appropriate, modifiers that provide additional information for the chosen code to explain certain circumstances or provide additional detail.

14. Determine whether a Special Report is required
    PURPOSE: To clarify and add additional detail when an unusual or extenuating circumstance exists or if a Category III or unlisted procedure Category I code is used.

15. Record the CPT code selected in the medical record documentation next to the procedure or service performed and in the appropriate block of the insurance claim form.
    PURPOSE: To complete the documentation and recording requirements.

assistant to the selection of the most specific and accurate procedure or service code from the CPT coding manual.

> **CRITICAL THINKING** APPLICATION   **19-2**
> If a patient were referred for epigastric pain and Dr. Shuman performed an ultrasound examination of the gallbladder, what would Sherald need to consider to properly code this encounter for the ultrasound examination?

SURGERY CODING

The steps for performing Surgery coding were outlined earlier in this chapter and are detailed in Procedure 19-1. Some guidelines and notes related to surgery coding must be considered when researching and selecting a procedure or service code. Always review the current year's guidelines for the Surgery section for the most up-to-date information. The following sections discuss a few of the more common guidelines. When coding procedures and services, be sure to read the guidelines and notes thoroughly; they always provide all the answers needed when determining the most accurate code.

General

Surgical Package Definition

The CPT code descriptions of surgical procedures typically include the following services:
- Local infiltration, digital block, and/or topical anesthesia
- Subsequent to the decision for surgery, one related E/M encounter on the day of, or the day before, the date of the procedure
- Immediate postoperative care, including documentation in the patient's medical record and talking with family and/or other physicians
- Writing orders for postsurgical care

- Evaluating the patient in the postanesthesia recovery area
- Typical postoperative follow-up care (see the list below for follow-up care)
- Typical postoperative follow-up care (includes care for approximately 6-8 weeks after surgery and usually done at the physician's office)

Integumentary System

Excision of Lesions—Benign or Malignant

Excision of benign lesions includes a simple closure and anesthesia. If an incision, excision, or trauma requires intermediate or complex closure, the repair by intermediate or complex closure is coded and reported separately.

Repair (Closure)
- *Simple repair:* Performed when the wound is superficial (epidermis, dermis, or subcutaneous) without significant involvement of deeper structures. This includes local anesthesia and chemical or electrocauterization of wounds not closed.
- *Intermediate repair:* Includes simple repair with a need for a layered closure of one or more of the deeper layers of subcutaneous tissue and superficial fascia in addition to the skin closure. Single-layer closure of heavily contaminated wounds that required extensive cleaning or removal of particulate matter also constitutes intermediate repair.
- *Complex repair:* Includes wounds that require more than layered closure (e.g., scar revision, extensive undermining, or stents or retention sutures). Necessary preparation includes creation of a limited defect for repairs or debridement of complicated lacerations or avulsions. Complex repair does not include excision of benign or malignant lesions, excisional preparation of a wound bed, or debridement of an open fracture or open dislocation.

Instructions for Listing Services for Wound Repair
- The repaired wound or wounds should be measured and recorded in centimeters whether curved, angular, or stellate.

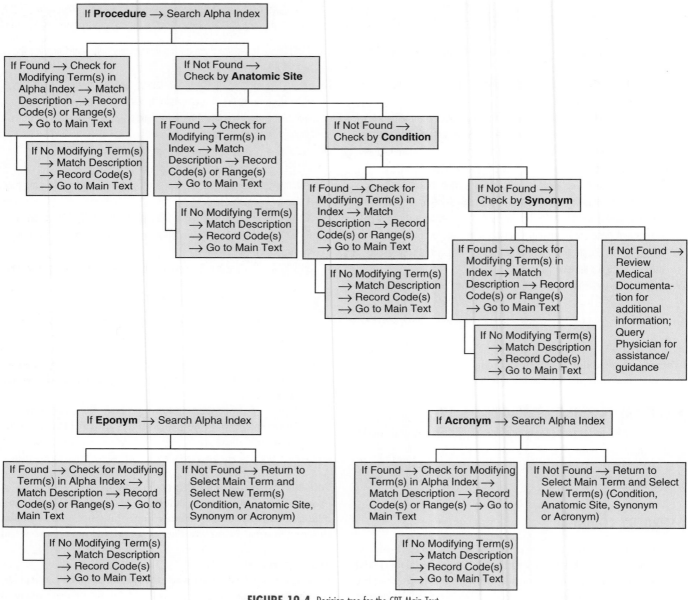

FIGURE 19-4 Decision tree for the CPT Main Text.

- When multiple wounds are repaired, add together the lengths of those in the same classification (simple, intermediate, or complex) and from all anatomic sites that are grouped together into the same code descriptor. Do not add lengths of repairs from different groupings of anatomic sites (e.g., face and extremities, or of different classifications (intermediate and complex).

- When wounds of more than one classification are repaired, list the more complicated repair as the primary procedure and the less complicated repair as the secondary procedure, using modifier -59.

- Debridement is considered a separate procedure only when gross contamination requires prolonged cleansing, when large amounts of dead or contaminated tissue must be removed, or when debridement is carried out separately without immediate primary closure.

- Wound repair that involves nerves, blood vessels, and/or tendons should be reported under the appropriate system for repair of those structures. The repair of these associated wounds is included in the primary procedure unless it qualifies as a complex repair, in which case modifier -59 applies.

Musculoskeletal System

Fractures

- *Closed fracture:* The fractured bone does not protrude through the dermis or epidermis.
- *Open fracture:* The fractured bone cuts through the skin layers and can be directly visualized.
- *Closed treatment:* The fracture site is not surgically opened (exposed to the external environment and directly visualized). The three methods of closed treatment of fractures are (1) without

manipulation, (2) with manipulation, and (3) with or without traction.

- *Manipulation:* Attempted reduction or restoration of a fracture or dislocated joint into its normal anatomic alignment by manually applied forces.
- *Open treatment:* Used when (1) the fractured bone is surgically opened or (2) an opening is made remote from the fracture site to insert an intramedullary nail across the fracture site.
- *Percutaneous skeletal fixation:* Fracture treatment that is neither open nor closed. The fracture fragments are not visualized, but a fixation device (e.g., pins) is placed across the fracture site, usually under x-ray imaging.

Cardiovascular System

Grafting for Coronary Bypass

Venous Grafts

- Venous grafting codes cannot be used as stand-alone codes if arterial grafts are also used during the performance of a bypass graft.
- Procurement of the saphenous vein graft is included in most venous grafting codes and should not be reported as a separate service.
- Procurement of upper extremity or femoropopliteal veins uses the harvesting code, which should be reported in addition to the bypass procedure.

Arterial Grafts

- To report combined arterial-venous grafts, two codes must be used: the arterial graft code and the appropriate combined arterial-venous graft code.
- Procurement of the artery for grafting is included in most venous grafting codes and should not be reported as a separate service, with the following exception: an additional code should be reported for an upper extremity artery or vein or a femoropopliteal vein.

Maternity Care and Delivery

The services normally provided in uncomplicated maternity cases include antepartum care, delivery, and postpartum care.

- *Antepartum care* includes the initial and subsequent history; physical examinations; recording of weight, blood pressure, and fetal heart tones; routine chemical urinalysis; monthly visits up to 28 weeks' gestation; biweekly visits to 36 weeks' gestation; and weekly visits until delivery. Any other visits or services provided within this period should be coded separately.
- *Delivery* includes admission to the hospital, the admission history and physical examination, management of uncomplicated labor, vaginal delivery (with or without forceps or episiotomy), or cesarean delivery. Medical problems complicating labor and delivery should be identified by using the codes in the Medicine and E/M sections in addition to codes for maternity care.
- *Postpartum care* includes hospital and office visits after vaginal or cesarean section delivery.

UNDERSTANDING EVALUATION AND MANAGEMENT

To properly code E/M services, the medical assistant must understand important differences, or variations, from the basic steps outlined earlier. The steps for finding a Category I code for E/M services are quite different from those discussed earlier in this chapter (Procedure 19-2). The instructions include identifying the section, subsection, category, and subcategory of the procedure or service; reviewing the reporting instructions and guidelines for the code chosen; reviewing the level of E/M service; determining the extent of history obtained and examination performed; and determining the complexity of medical decision making.

The E/M section is divided into broad subsections (Figure 19-5), such as *office visit, emergency room visit, hospital visit,* and *consultation.* These subsections are further divided into subcategories, which include the place where the services were rendered (e.g., the provider's office, a hospital emergency department, a skilled nursing facility, or the patient's home) and the **patient status (PS)** (i.e., whether the patient is new or established).

The first two steps in choosing an E/M code are:
1. Identify the place of service (POS)
2. Identify the patient status

Identifying the Place of Service

The "place of service" is the facility where the encounter between the patient and the provider occurred. The two most common places of service are "office" and "hospital." Refer to the Evolve site at *evolve.elsevier.com/kinn* for a complete list of POS locations and their two-digit identifying numbers, or **place of service (POS) codes**.

Identifying the Patient Status

The patient status choices are *new* or *established* patient. A **new patient (NP)** is one who has not received any professional services (face to face) from the physician or another physician of the exact same specialty and subspecialty, who belongs to the same group practice, within the past 3 years. An **established patient (EP)** is one who has received professional services from the physician or another physician of the exact same specialty and subspecialty, who belongs to the same group practice, within the past 3 years.

Once the POS and patient status have been established, the next step in selection of an E/M code is to determine the level of service provided.

Determining the Level of Service Provided

Key Components and Contributing Factors

The three key components for determining the level of service for E/M coding are: history, examination, and medical decision making. The four contributing factors are: counseling, nature of presenting problem, coordination of care, and time. The history, examination, and medical decision making components are considered primary key; that is, they are typically the three most important components for deciding the level of service. Counseling, nature of presenting problem, coordination of care, and time are secondary considerations.

History. To understand the levels of the history, it is important to know the definition and components of the patient history. The history relates to the patient's clinical picture and depends on the patient for answers to specific questions. The patient history is discussed in greater detail in Chapter 14 and later in Chapter 28.

Perform Procedural Coding: Evaluation and Management Coding

CAAHEP COMPETENCIES: IV.C.IV.6., IV.P.IV.3., V.P.V.6., VII.P.VII.1., IX.A.IX.2.

ABHES COMPETENCIES: 3.v

GOAL: *Use the steps for Evaluation and Management coding to find the most accurate and specific CPT Category I E/M section code.*

EQUIPMENT and SUPPLIES

- CPT coding manual (current year)
- Encounter form (charge ticket)
- Medical record
- Paper
- Pen or pencil
- Medical dictionary or medical terminology reference book

PROCEDURAL STEPS

1. Determine the place of service.
   <u>PURPOSE:</u> To determine where the procedure or service was performed.
2. Determine the patient status.
   <u>PURPOSE:</u> To determine whether the patient is a new or an established patient.
3. Review the guidelines and notes for the selected subsection, category, or subcategory.
   <u>PURPOSE:</u> To determine whether there are any contraindications for use of the code selected.
4. Identify the subsection, category, or subcategory of service in the E/M section.

<u>PURPOSE:</u> To ensure that the correct place of service and patient status are used and the appropriate level of service is selected.

5. Review the level of E/M service descriptions for each code in the subsection, category, or subcategory chosen.
   <u>PURPOSE:</u> To assist in the selection of the appropriate level of service.
6. Determine the level of service
   a. Determine the extent of the history obtained.
   b. Determine the extent of the examination performed.
   c. Determine the complexity of medical decision making.
   <u>PURPOSE:</u> To ensure that the correct level is chosen for the history, examination, and medical decision making.
7. If necessary, compare the medical documentation against examples in Appendix C, Clinical Examples, of the CPT manual.
   <u>PURPOSE:</u> To compare the medical documentation to the examples in Appendix C for assistance in selection of the appropriate level of service.
8. Select the appropriate level of E/M service code, and document it on the medical record or encounter form.
   <u>PURPOSE:</u> To complete the documentation and reporting requirements.

Levels of History

- *Problem-focused history:* A problem-focused history concentrates on the chief complaint; it looks at the symptoms, severity, and duration of the problem. It usually does not include a review of systems (ROS) or the family and social histories.
- *Expanded problem-focused history:* The physician proceeds as in the problem-focused history but includes a review of the systems that relate to the chief complaint. Usually past, family, and social histories are not included.
- *Detailed history:* The detailed history consists of the chief complaint; extended history of present illness; problem-pertinent system review extended to include a review of a limited number of additional systems; and the pertinent past, family, and/or social histories directly related to the patient's problems.
- *Comprehensive history:* A comprehensive history includes the chief complaint; extended history of present illness; review of systems that is directly related to the problem or problems identified in the history of the present illness plus a review of all additional body systems; and complete past, family, and social histories.

Examination. The examination is the objective part of the patient's visit. The physician examines the patient, obtains measurable findings, and makes notes referring to body areas and/or organ systems, as follows:

- Body areas: Head, including face and neck; chest, including breasts and axillae; abdomen; genitalia, groin, and buttocks; and back, including spine and extremities
- Organs and organ systems: Constitutional (e.g., vital signs, general appearance); eyes; ears, nose, throat, and mouth; cardiovascular; respiratory; gastrointestinal (GI); genitourinary; musculoskeletal; skin; neurologic; psychiatric; and hematologic, lymphatic, and immunologic

Levels of Examination. The examination is divided into the following levels:

- *Problem-focused examination:* The examination is limited to the single body area or single system mentioned in the chief complaint.
- *Expanded problem-focused examination:* In addition to the limited body area or system, related body areas or organ systems are examined.
- *Detailed examination:* An extended examination is performed on the related body areas or organ systems.
- *Comprehensive examination:* A complete multisystem examination is performed or a complete examination of a single organ system.

Medical Decision Making. When a physician makes medical decisions, the decisions are based on many years of education and

▸Initial Nursing Facility Care◂

New or Established Patient

When the patient is admitted to the nursing facility in the course of an encounter in another site of service (e.g., hospital emergency department, physician's office), all evaluation and management services provided by that physician in conjunction with that admission are considered part of the initial nursing facility care when performed on the same date as the admission or readmission. The nursing facility care level of service reported by the admitting physician should include the services related to the admission he/she provided in the other sites of service as well as in the nursing facility setting.

Hospital discharge or observation discharge services performed on the same date of nursing facility admission or readmission may be reported separately. For a patient discharged from inpatient status on the same date of nursing facility admission or readmission, the hospital discharge services should be reported with codes 99238, 99239 as appropriate. For a patient discharged from observation status on the same date of nursing facility admission or readmission, the observation care discharge services should be reported with code 99217. For a patient admitted and discharged from observation or inpatient status on the same date, see codes 99234-99236.

(For nursing facility care discharge, see 99315, 99316)

▸Typical unit times have not been established for 99304-99306.◂

  ▸(99301-99303 have been deleted)◂

● **99304** Initial nursing facility care, per day, for the evaluation and management of a patient which requires these three key components:

 ■ **a detailed or comprehensive history;**

 ■ **a detailed or comprehensive examination; and**

 ■ **medical decision making that is straightforward or of low complexity.**

Counseling and/or coordination of care with other providers or agencies are provided consistent with the nature of the problem(s) and the patient's and/or family's needs.

Usually, the problem(s) requiring admission are of low severity.

Subsequent Nursing Facility Care

▸All levels of subsequent nursing facility care include reviewing the medical record and reviewing the results of diagnostic studies and changes in the patient's status (i.e., changes in history, physical condition, and response to management) since the last assessment by the physician.◂

● **99307** Subsequent nursing facility care, per day, for the evaluation and management of a patient, which requires at least two of these three key components:

 ■ **a problem-focused interval history;**

 ■ **a problem-focused examination;**

 ■ **straightforward medical decision making.**

Counseling and/or coordination of care with other providers or agencies are provided consistent with the nature of the problem(s) and the patient's and/or family's needs.

Usually, the patient is stable, recovering, or improving.

● **99308** Subsequent nursing facility care, per day, for the evaluation and management of a patient, which requires at least two of these three key components:

 ■ **an expanded problem-focused interval history;**

 ■ **an expanded problem-focused examination;**

 ■ **medical decision making of low complexity.**

Counseling and/or coordination of care with other providers or agencies are provided consistent with the nature of the problem(s) and the patient's and/or family's needs.

Usually, the patient is responding inadequately to therapy or has developed a minor complication.

● **99309** Subsequent nursing facility care, per day, for the evaluation and management of a patient, which requires at least two of these three key components:

 ■ **a detailed interval history;**

 ■ **a detailed examination;**

 ■ **medical decision making of moderate complexity.**

Counseling and/or coordination of care with other providers or agencies are provided consistent with the nature of the problem(s) and the patient's and/or family's needs.

Usually, the patient has developed a significant complication or a significant new problem.

FIGURE 19-5 Example of Evaluation and Management (E/M) coding: new or established patient and place of service.

experience. Three elements comprise the medical decision making process:

1. The number of diagnoses and/or management options
2. The amount and/or complexity of data obtained, reviewed, and analyzed
3. The risk of significant complications and/or morbidity and/or mortality

Number of Diagnoses and Management Options. The physician's notes during the history and examination should help identify whether the patient's problem is minor, acute, stable, or worsening. The medical documentation should also identify whether a new problem exists or whether the physician plans to order any diagnostic tests to further investigate the patient's illness or injury.

Amount and Complexity of Data Reviewed. The medical documentation should also identify what laboratory tests, x-ray diagnostic procedures, and other tests have been ordered or reviewed.

Risk of Complications and Morbidity or Mortality. Risk is often involved in medical care, either from the treatment given to the patient or from the lack of treatment and professional care. *Morbidity,* the relative incidence of disease, and *mortality,* which relates to the number of deaths from a given disease, is an integral part of the assessment of risks made by the physician.

Medical Decision Making Complexity Levels. The four levels of complexity in medical decision making are: straightforward, low complexity, moderate complexity, and high complexity (Table 19-5).

Contributing Factors

Counseling. Counseling is a discussion with a patient and/or family regarding diagnostic results, impressions, recommended diagnostic studies, prognosis, risks and benefits of management or treatment options, and instructions for management, treatment, and/or follow-up. Almost all E/M services contain a degree of counseling with the patient and/or the family. This is factored into the E/M code, and as long as this factor does not exceed 50% of the time spent with the patient, it is included in the E/M code. It can be considered a contributing factor when the counseling exceeds 50% of the encounter.

Nature of Presenting Problem. The presenting problem is usually explained in the chief complaint. It can range from something as simple as a cold in an otherwise healthy patient to a life-threatening problem. Unless dealing with the nature of the presenting problem exceeds half of the patient encounter, it is included in the E/M code description and is not a factor in selecting the level of service.

Coordination of Care. Some patients need assistance in arranging for care beyond the visit or hospitalization. Some will need care in a skilled nursing facility or home health care. Others will need hospice care. The primary physician usually coordinates this care. Coordination of care is also factored into the E/M code and is a consideration for determining the level of service only when it exceeds 50% of the patient encounter.

Time. Time is included in the E/M code descriptions only to assist physicians in selecting the most appropriate level of E/M service. The times expressed in the code descriptions are averages, and time is not a determining factor in code selection unless counseling exceeds more than 50% of the encounter. Only then can time be used as a determining component to code level selection.

At first, E/M coding is difficult to understand and put into practice. The steps for E/M coding provided here can serve as a guide to medical assistants in determining the place of service, patient status, and level of care provided, so that they can select the most accurate E/M code. Using the clinical examples in Appendix C of the CPT manual and comparing them to the medical documentation also can help medical assistants acquire a better understanding of E/M coding.

CRITICAL THINKING APPLICATION   19-3

Dr. Caddell performed a colonoscopy at the hospital on Cecil Matthews, who has been Dr. Caddell's patient for several years. Mr. Matthews came to the office with left lower quadrant pain and a history of colon cancer. What other factors or information would Sherald need to know to properly code Mr. Matthews' office visit (encounter)? What other factors or information would Sherald need to know to properly code Mr. Matthews' colonoscopy?

ANESTHESIA CODING

The codes for anesthesia are listed primarily in the Anesthesia section of the CPT manual, although codes for conscious sedation are found in the Medicine section. The codes selected are based typically on the anatomic location of the surgery performed; for example, code 00402 is used for anesthesia during a reconstructive procedure on the breast in the integumentary system.

Anesthesia coding differs from any other form of coding in the way anesthesia services are billed (Procedure 19-3). A standard formula has been established for payment of anesthesia services: Basic unit values + Time units + Modifying units (B + T + M). This formula is affected by two factors: the patient's **physical status** (PS) and any qualifying circumstances.

TABLE 19-5 Complexity of Medical Decision Making

NUMBER OF DIAGNOSES OR MANAGEMENT OPTIONS	AMOUNT AND/OR COMPLEXITY OF DATA TO BE REVIEWED	RISK OF COMPLICATIONS AND/OR MORBIDITY OR MORTALITY	TYPE OF MEDICAL DECISION MAKING
Minimal	Minimal or none	Minimal	Straightforward
Limited	Limited	Low	Low complexity
Multiple	Moderate	Moderate	Moderate complexity
Extensive	Extensive	High	High complexity

PROCEDURE 19-3

Perform Procedural Coding: Anesthesia Coding

CAAHEP COMPETENCIES: IV.C.IV.6., IV.P.IV.3., V.P.V.6., VII.P.VII.1., IX.A.IX.2.

ABHES COMPETENCIES: 3.v

GOAL: *Use the steps for anesthesia coding to select the most accurate and specific anesthesia code and to perform the anesthesia formula calculation to determine the charge for the service.*

EQUIPMENT and SUPPLIES

- CPT coding manual (current year)
- Encounter form (charge ticket)
- Medical record
- Conversion factor list (issued by an insurance carrier: for the purposes of this exercise, use the example in Figure 19-5)
- Paper
- Pen or pencil
- Calculator

PROCEDURAL STEPS

1. Read the medical documentation to determine what procedure or service was provided.
   <u>PURPOSE:</u> To ensure all procedures and/or services are listed on the encounter form; that all procedures and services on the encounter form are documented in the medical record; and that nothing documented in the medical record was omitted from the charge ticket.

2. Determine the anatomic site or organ system involved.
   <u>PURPOSE:</u> Anesthesia service codes use the anatomic site and organ system as a category.

3. In the Alphabetic Index, go to the heading Anesthesia and find the code or code range that includes all or most of the medical record procedure or service.
   <u>PURPOSE:</u> To avoid selecting a surgery or other type of procedure or service code other than anesthesia-related codes.

4. Write down the code or code range found in the Alphabetic Index, under the Anesthesia heading, that best matches the medical documentation.
   <u>PURPOSE:</u> To prevent repeated references to the Alphabetic Index by recording all possible matches to the code or code range being sought. This saves time and prevents redundant effort.

5. Turn to the Main Text, Anesthesia section, and find the code or code range found while searching the Alphabetic Index.
   <u>PURPOSE:</u> To verify and select the most specific anesthesia code.

6. Read the guidelines and notes for the section, subsection, category, or subcategory.

   <u>PURPOSE:</u> To ensure the correct code is chosen and no instructions prevent the use of the code selected.

7. Evaluate the conventions, especially add-on codes (+) and exemptions from modifier -51.
   <u>PURPOSE:</u> To ensure the correct code is chosen and there are no contraindications to use of the code.

8. Document the code selected.
   <u>PURPOSE:</u> To determine the basic unit value and perform the anesthesia calculation to determine the charge.

9. Determine the basic unit value from the Relative Value Guide.
   <u>PURPOSE:</u> To perform the anesthesia calculation to determine the charge for the anesthesia service.

10. Determine the patient's physical status and document the appropriate modifier.
    <u>PURPOSE:</u> To perform the anesthesia calculation to determine the charge for the anesthesia service.

11. Determine whether any qualifying circumstance modifier should be used. If yes, document the modifier.
    <u>PURPOSE:</u> To perform the anesthesia calculation to determine the charge for the anesthesia service.

12. Determine the total anesthesia time, divide by 15 (minutes), and document the time.
    <u>PURPOSE:</u> To perform the anesthesia calculation to determine the charge for the anesthesia service.

13. Select the appropriate geographic conversion factor.
    <u>PURPOSE:</u> To perform the anesthesia calculation to determine the charge for the anesthesia service.

14. Calculate the charge for the anesthesia service using the anesthesia formula.
    <u>PURPOSE:</u> To determine the charge for the anesthesia service or procedure.

15. Document the anesthesia charge and the code in the medical record and on the encounter form or charge ticket.
    <u>PURPOSE:</u> To complete the documentation and recording requirements.

Anesthesia Formula

Basic Unit Value (B)

The Anesthesia Society of America (ASA) publishes a Relative Value Guide (RVG), which lists the codes for anesthesia services. The RVG compares anesthesia services and assigns a numeric value to each service based on the level of complexity; this numeric value is called the *basic unit value.*

Time Unit (T)

Anesthesia services are provided based on the time during which the anesthesia was administered, in hours and minutes. Typically 15 minutes equals 1 time unit, although this can vary because insurance carriers make that determination independently. The time starts when the anesthesiologist begins preparing the patient to receive anesthesia, continues through the procedure, and ends when the patient is no longer under the personal care of the anesthesiologist. The hours and minutes during which anesthesia was administered are recorded in the patient's record.

Modifying Unit (M)

Modifying units reflect circumstances or conditions that change or modify the environment in which the anesthesia service is provided. The two modifying characteristics for anesthesia services are qualifying circumstances and physical status modifiers. Table 19-6 presents a list of these modifiers and their descriptions; a list also can be found in the Anesthesia section of the CPT manual.

Qualifying Circumstances (QC). Sometimes anesthesia is provided in situations that make administration more difficult. These types of cases include provision of anesthesia in emergency situations, to patients of extreme age, during the use of controlled hypotension, and with hypothermia. There are four qualifying circumstances (QC) codes. Each of the five-digit codes is preceded by a plus sign symbol (+), indicating that it is an add-on code; these codes are used in addition to the Category I anesthesia code.

Physical Status Modifiers. The second type of modifying unit used in anesthesia coding is the physical status modifier. These modifiers are used to indicate the patient's physical condition at the time anesthesia was provided. There are five physical status modifiers, each composed of two characters: first the letter P, followed by a ranking of 1 to 6 (e.g., P1, P2, P3, and so on). P1 represents a normal healthy patient, and P6 represents a brain-dead patient whose organs are being harvested.

Conversion Factors

A conversion factor is the dollar value of each basic unit value. Each third-party payer issues a list of conversion factors. The conversion factor for any given geographic location (Figure 19-6) is multiplied by the number of basic unit values assigned to each procedure.

▌Calculating Anesthesia Services

Using the basic unit value (B), modifying unit (M), time unit (T), and conversion factor, the fee for anesthesia services is calculated according to the anesthesia billing formula (Figure 19-7):

$$(B + M + T) \times \text{Conversion factor}$$

▌RADIOLOGY CODING

The Radiology section (Figure 19-8) contains all diagnostic imaging codes, including not just x-ray studies, but also ultrasound, magnetic resonance imaging (MRI), and nuclear medicine procedures, in addition to radiation oncology and several other types of diagnostic imaging procedures, services, and therapies. The Radiology section is further subdivided into subsections, such as head and neck, then chest, spine, and pelvis, upper and lower extremities, abdomen, gastrointestinal and urinary tracts, gynecologic, obstetric, heart, and vascular procedures. The next subdivision, categories, defines the types or function of various procedures (e.g., diagnostic ultrasound, radiation oncology, hyperthermia, and so on) that are unique to the

TABLE 19-6	Anesthesia Physical Status and Qualifying Circumstances Modifiers
MODIFIER	**DESCRIPTION**
Physical Status Modifiers*	
P1	A normal healthy patient
P2	A patient with mild systemic disease
P3	A patient with severe systemic disease
P4	A person with severe systemic disease that is a constant threat to life
P5	A moribund patient who is not expected to survive without the procedure
P6	A declared brain-dead patient whose organs are being removed for donor purposes
Qualifying Circumstances Modifiers†	
99100	Anesthesia for patient of extreme age, under 1 year or over 70
99116	Anesthesia complicated by utilization of total body hypothermia
99135	Anesthesia complicated by utilization of controlled hypothermia

*A physical status modifier is required for use in performing anesthesia calculations.
†Use a qualifying circumstances modifier code, if appropriate, in addition to the primary CPT Category I Anesthesia code.

Locality Name	Anesthesia Conversion Factor
Manhattan, NY	22.65
NYC suburbs/Long I., NY	22.74
Queens, NY	22.28
Rest of New York	19.91
North Carolina	20.23
North Dakota	19.70

FIGURE 19-6 Anesthesia conversion factors. (From Buck CJ: *Step-by-step medical coding, 2012 edition,* St Louis, 2012, WB Saunders.)

Medical Narrative

A 25-year-old female patient in good physical condition has anesthesia services while undergoing laparoscopy (CPT-4 Code 00840). The time for the anesthesia administration was 2 hours. For the purposes of this example the RBV basic unit value will be 4.

Basic Unit Value	=	4
+ Modifying Units: PS	=	0
+ QC	=	0
+ Time Units	=	8
= 12 Total Units		

The total units value of 12 is then multiplied by the conversion factor for the geographic location of the anesthesiologist's office. For the purposes of this exercise, the conversion factor for Manhattan, NY, will be $20.48, and for North Carolina, $15.77. For the office located in Manhattan, NY, multiply $20.48 by 12. The fee for the anesthesia services would be $245.76. For the office located in North Carolina, multiply 12 times $15.77, for a fee of $189.24.

FIGURE 19-7 Anesthesia formula and calculation example.

Radiology

Diagnostic Radiology (Diagnostic Imaging)

Head and Neck

70010	Myelography, posterior fossa, radiological supervision and interpretation
70015	Cisternography, positive contrast, radiological supervision and interpretation
70030	Radiologic examination, eye, for detection of foreign body
70100	Radiologic examination, mandible; partial, less than four views
70110	complete, minimum of four views
70120	Radiologic examination, mastoids; less than three views per side
70130	complete, minimum of three views per side
70134	Radiologic examination, internal auditory meati, complete
70140	Radiologic examination, facial bones; less than three views

FIGURE 19-8 Radiology section of CPT.

anatomic site subsection. In addition to the radiology procedure codes, codes are included for physician supervision and interpretation of diagnostic imaging data and for clinical and radiation treatment planning and administration of contrast materials during radiologic procedures.

The coding steps for radiologic procedures are the same as for other Category I codes. When searching by main term in the Alphabetic Index, using *Radiology* as the main term; a *See* note directs the coder to the more specific subcategories of nuclear medicine, ultrasound, radiation therapy, and x-ray studies. As always, a thorough review of the conventions, guidelines, and notes in the Main Text is essential to accurate coding.

PATHOLOGY AND LABORATORY SECTION

The subcategories for the Pathology and Laboratory section include organ panels (Figure 19-9) and disease panels, drug testing, therapeutic drug assays, evocative or suppression testing, consultations, urinalysis, chemistry, molecular diagnostics, infectious agents, microbiology, anatomic pathology, cytopathology, cytogenetic studies, and surgical pathology.

Organ or disease panels are groupings of numerous tests performed to diagnose the health or disease status of specific organ systems. To use a panel code, all the tests listed under the code selected must have been performed. Otherwise, the individual tests should be billed using a separate code for each. The codes for drug testing are *qualitative;* that is, they are based on the type of drug found. *Quantitative* assays, on the other hand, are performed to determine the amount of drug present.

CODING FOR THE MEDICINE SECTION

Immune Globulins

When coding administration of immune globulins, identify the immune globulin product administered and the method of administration using the codes in the *hydration, therapeutic, prophylactic, and diagnostic injections and infusions* subsection (Figure 19-10).

Immunization Administration for Vaccines or Toxoids

These codes are for the administration of vaccines and toxoids only and should be reported in conjunction with the appropriate codes in the *immunization administration for vaccine/toxoids* subsection (Figure 19-11).

Vaccines/Toxoids

These codes identify the vaccine product only. Codes in the *immunization administration for vaccines/toxoids* subsection must be used in addition to the vaccine or toxoid product codes. To meet the reporting requirements of immunization registries, vaccine distribution programs, and reporting systems, the exact vaccine product administered must be reported on the insurance claim.

Hydration, Therapeutic, Prophylactic, and Diagnostic Injections and Infusion

Hydration codes are intended to report a hydration intravenous (IV) infusion consisting of prepackaged fluid and electrolytes; they are

Pathology and Laboratory

Organ or Disease Oriented Panels

These panels were developed for coding purposes only and should not be interpreted as clinical parameters. The tests listed with each panel identify the defined components of that panel.

These panel components are not intended to limit the performance of other tests. If one performs tests in addition to those specifically indicated for a particular panel, those tests should be reported separately in addition to the panel code.

80048 Basic metabolic panel

This panel must include the following:

Calcium (82310)

Carbon dioxide (82374)

Chloride (82435)

Creatinine (82565)

Glucose (82947)

Potassium (84132)

Sodium (84295)

Urea nitrogen (BUN) (84520)

(Do not use 80048 in addition to 80053)

80050 General health panel

This panel must include the following:

Comprehensive metabolic panel (80053)

Blood count, complete (CBC), automated and automated differential WBC count (85025 or 85027 and 85004)

FIGURE 19-9 Pathology and Laboratory section of CPT.

Medicine

Immune Globulins

►Codes 90281-90399 identify the immune globulin product only and must be reported in addition to the administration codes 90765-90768, 90772, 90774, 90775 as appropriate. Immune globulin products listed here include broad-spectrum and anti-infective immune globulins, antitoxins, and various isoantibodies.◄

- ⊘ **90281** Immune globulin (Ig), human, for intramuscular use
- ⊘ **90283** Immune globulin (IgIV), human, for intravenous use
- ⊘ **90287** Botulinum antitoxin, equine, any route
- ⊘ **90288** Botulism immune globulin, human, for intravenous use
- ⊘ **90291** Cytomegalovirus immune globulin (CMV-IgIV), human, for intravenous use
- ⊘ **90296** Diphtheria antitoxin, equine, any route
- ⊘ **90371** Hepatitis B immune globulin (HBIg), human, for intramuscular use
- ⊘ **90375** Rabies immune globulin (RIg), human, for intramuscular and/or subcutaneous use
- ⊘ **90376** Rabies immune globulin, heat-treated (RIg-HT), human, for intramuscular and/or subcutaneous use

FIGURE 19-10 Relationship of immune globulins and infusions in CPT.

(Figure 19-12). HCPCS codes, like CPT codes, are updated annually. They are designed to promote standardized reporting and collection of statistical data on medical supplies, products, services, and procedures.

CODING LEVELS: CPT AND HCPCS

Currently, two levels of procedure and services codes are used:
- Level I codes: These are the CPT codes, developed by the AMA and published in the current CPT manual.
- Level II: These are the HCPCS codes, developed by the CMS to describe medical services and supplies not covered in the CPT manual.

HCPCS Codes

The HCPCS (Level II) codes have five alphanumeric digits, beginning with one letter followed by four numerals. HCPCS also uses two alphabetic or alphanumeric character modifiers to add information or to supplement the Level II codes. HCPCS uses five conventions (Figure 19-13).

HCPCS Manual

Like the CPT manual, the HCPCS manual is divided into two parts: the Alphabetic Index and the Tabular Index. As with the CPT, procedures and services can be looked up in the Alphabetic Index and then confirmed as the most accurate and appropriate code by using the Tabular Index. The HCPCS manual has no subsections, categories, or subcategories; it has only sections, as outlined earlier.

not used to report the infusion of drugs or other substances. When multiple drugs are administered, report the service or services and the specific materials or drugs for each.

Home Health Procedures and Services

These codes are used by nonphysician health care professionals only. They are used to report services provided in a patient's residence (including assisted-living apartments, group homes, nontraditional private homes, custodial care facilities, and schools).

HEALTHCARE COMMON PROCEDURE CODING SYSTEM (HCPCS)

As mentioned previously, **HCPCS** is a collection of codes and descriptions that represent procedures, supplies, products, and services not covered by or included in the CPT coding system

An appendix contains all the HCPCS modifiers and their descriptions.

The coding steps for HCPCS are almost identical to those for CPT Category I codes (Procedure 19-4). A main term is determined and used to help find the procedure or service in the Alphabetic Index. The Alphabetic Index lists a code, codes, or code range. These codes or code ranges are then reviewed in the Tabular Index for specificity and accuracy. As with the CPT codes, the clinical documentation is the starting point, and the final code selected should add nothing to or omit anything from the description in the medical documentation. The final step is determining whether the code selected can stand alone or requires a modifier to further define or add needed information.

Coding using the HCPCS manual is essentially the same as coding for a CPT procedure or service. The conventions, layout, and format of the HCPCS manual are different, and the manual has only sections and subsections. The HCPCS codes can be used when a specific procedure or service is not found in the CPT coding manual.

CLOSING COMMENTS

Remember that new coding manuals are published each year and should be ordered in the early fall so that they arrive in a timely manner, allowing the medical assistant to review them. Always use the current years' manual so that the codes used are accurate and specific. The front of new manuals usually contains an introductory section that highlights changes and/or new regulations. If the office uses coding software, the publisher should offer annual updates that can be loaded to the computer. This helps to insure that all codes used are up-to-date for the current year.

Although the billing and coding process can be intimidating and overwhelming, approach it with a good attitude. No provider will

---

Immunization Administration for Vaccines/Toxoids

Codes 90465-90474 must be reported in addition to the vaccine and toxoid code(s) 90476-90749.

Report codes 90465-90468 only when the physician provides face-to-face counseling of the patient and family during the administration of a vaccine. For immunization administration of any vaccine that is not accompanied by face-to-face physician counseling to the patient/family, report codes 90471-90474.

If a significant separately identifiable Evaluation and Management service (e.g., office or other outpatient services, preventive medicine services) is performed, the appropriate E/M service code should be reported in addition to the vaccine and toxoid administration codes.

  (For allergy testing, see 95004 et seq)

  (For skin testing of bacterial, viral, fungal extracts, see 86485-86586)

  ▶(For therapeutic or diagnostic injections, see 90772-90779)◀

90465 Immunization administration under 8 years of age (includes percutaneous, intradermal, subcutaneous, or intramuscular injections) when the physician counsels the patient/family; first injection (single or combination vaccine/toxoid), per day

  (Do not report 90465 in conjunction with 90467)

+ 90466 each additional injection (single or combination vaccine/toxoid), per day (List separately in addition to code for primary procedure)

  (Use 90466 in conjunction with 90465 or 90467)

FIGURE 19-11 Relationship of immune vaccines/toxoids and administration codes in CPT.

☼ **Special coverage instructions.**
Indicates that there are instructions provided regarding circumstances in which the code might be included for reimbursement.

◆ **Not covered by or valid for Medicare.**
These codes might result in reimbursement by private health insurance payors but not by Medicare. Their value may be only for statistical data collection but not for reimbursement.

✳ **Carrier discretion.** These codes may or may not be paid by health insurance carrier including Medicare.

▶ **New.**

➠ **Revised.** The revised symbol is placed in front of codes with any data, payment, or miscellaneous change from the prior year.

FIGURE 19-13 HCPCS conventions.

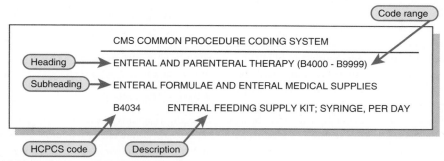

FIGURE 19-12 *Healthcare Common Procedure Coding System* (HCPCS) national codes, established by the Centers for Medicare and Medicaid Services. (Courtesy U.S. Department of Health and Human Services, Centers for Medicare and Medicaid Services, Atlanta, Ga.)

PROCEDURE 19-4

Perform Procedural Coding: HCPCS Coding

CAAHEP COMPETENCIES: IV.C.IV.6., IV.P.IV.3., V.P.V.6., VII.P.VII.1., IX.A.IX.2.

ABHES COMPETENCIES: 3.v

GOAL: *Use the steps for procedure and service coding to find the most accurate and specific HCPCS code.*

EQUIPMENT and SUPPLIES

- HCPCS coding manual (current year)
- Medical record
- Encounter form (charge ticket)
- Paper
- Pen or pencil

PROCEDURAL STEPS

1. Read the medical documentation to determine what procedures or services were provided.
   PURPOSE: To ensure that all procedures and/or services are listed on the encounter form; that all procedures and services on the encounter form match the medical record; and that nothing documented in the medical record is missing from the encounter form.
2. Determine the main and modifying terms from the abstracted information.
   PURPOSE: To identify the term or terms to begin the search in the Alphabetic Index.
3. After the main term has been located, select modifying term or terms if needed.
   PURPOSE: To provide additional specificity and help narrow the search for the code or code range in the Alphabetic Index.
4. Select the most appropriate main term to begin a search in the Alphabetic Index.
   PURPOSE: To start the search for the best code or codes in the Alphabetic Index
5. If no modifying term produces an appropriate code or code range, repeat steps 2 and 3 using a different main term classification.
   PURPOSE: To aid in finding the most appropriate code or code range by using alternative methods of searching the Alphabetic Index.
6. Find the code or code ranges that include all or most of the medical record procedure or service description.
   PURPOSE: To assist in directing the medical assistant to the proper section, subsection, category, or subcategory of the Main Text of the HCPCS manual.

7. Disregard any code or code range containing additional descriptions or modifying terms not found in the medical record.
   PURPOSE: To prevent upcoding or downcoding errors and other compliance issues.
8. Write down the code or code ranges that best match the medical documentation.
   PURPOSE: To prevent repeated references to the Alphabetic Index by recording all possible matches to the code or code range being sought. This saves time and prevents redundant effort.
9. Turn to the Main Text, and find the first code or code range found while searching the Alphabetic Index.
   PURPOSE: To begin the process of finding the most specific and accurate code.
10. Compare the description of the code with the medical documentation. Verify that all or most of the medical record documentation matches the code description and that there is no additional element or information in the code description that is not found in the documentation.
    PURPOSE: To avoid upcoding and downcoding errors and to ensure there are no contraindications to use of the code selected.
11. Read the guidelines for the section and subsection and code to ensure there are no contraindications to the use of the code.
    PURPOSE: To ensure there are no instructions that would prevent use of the code selected.
12. Evaluate the HCPCS manual conventions.
    PURPOSE: To ensure there are no instructions that would prevent use of the code selected.
13. Determine whether any special circumstances require the use of a modifier.
    PURPOSE: To select, if appropriate, modifiers that provide additional information for the code selected to explain certain circumstances or provide additional detail.
14. Record the HCPCS code selected in the medical record documentation next to the procedure or service performed and in the appropriate block of the insurance claim form.
    PURPOSE: To complete the documentation and reporting requirements.

---

have confidence in the medical assistant who complains about the changing nature of the work he or she is assigned to complete. Look for opportunities to learn more about the process; many of the larger hospitals periodically offer free workshops about specific sections of coding manuals. Publishers of coding manuals will often bring authors to a hospital or clinic to conduct a seminar. Additionally, there are numerous online seminars or workshops that can be completed and physicians will often cover the costs of such programs if they are not free. A medical assistant who is eager to learn and takes advantages of such opportunities will be much more valuable to his or her employer.

Patient Education

Like the diagnosis codes, procedure codes must be specific and accurate to ensure the maximum reimbursement for the provider. When patients have questions about items on their bills related to procedure codes, answer them or refer them to the person designated as the biller/coder in the provider's office. Patients who have surgery or other complicated procedures may receive bills from more than one provider. Even if they are confused and frustrated, take the time to educate them as to why they may have received separate bills from, for instance, a radiologist who completed x-ray reports or a pathologist who inspected specimens from surgical procedures. Patient questions are never insignificant and deserve courteous attention from the medical assistant.

Legal and Ethical Issues

Medical assistants must be responsible and remain knowledgeable about CPT to ensure that no fraud takes place in the coding and claims submission process. Medical assistants should also ensure that proper precautions are taken to avoid incorrect coding, data entry errors, and false claims submissions.

Codes or narratives in patient chart documentation should not be altered to increase insurance reimbursement or to accommodate policy coverage requirements. Deliberate misrepresentation, such as **downcoding** or **upcoding**, may carry criminal and/or civil penalties.

Downcoding, in which lower level codes are used even when the diagnostic statement indicates a higher level procedure or service, usually affects reimbursement only by lowering the amount received. However, it may have civil and criminal penalty implications if it is done to skirt insurance policy restrictions or pre-existing condition clauses. It is also common for insurance claims examiners to change the procedure code on a health insurance claim form to a procedure code with a lesser value. This happens most often when there is a mismatch of the official CPT description and the description written on the insurance claim form. It is important to review the explanation sent from the insurance carrier when payment is received to determine whether downcoding occurred and to refile or challenge the lowered code by providing additional information that will result in approval of the higher code used, if appropriate.

Upcoding, in which a higher level procedure or service code is used than is supported by the medical documentation, can result in civil and criminal penalties, including fines, loss of privileges as a participating provider, and even prison time. Stay familiar with laws that affect billing and coding procedures so that the provider receives the highest legal and accurate reimbursement possible for the procedures and treatments performed.

SUMMARY OF SCENARIO

Sherald has learned that procedural coding using the CPT is similar in many ways to ICD-9-CM diagnostic coding. The two coding manuals have unique but similar steps, conventions, and guidelines. She has also learned that proper abstracting of procedural data from the medical record is equally important in the ICD-9-CM and the CPT. In addition, Sherald discovered that HCPCS codes describe procedures and services not found in the CPT, such as medicines, ambulance services, and durable medical equipment. Sherald now knows the legal implications of coding compliance errors, such as upcoding and downcoding.

Sherald enjoys working toward becoming a medical assistant. As she progresses with learning procedural coding, she envisions herself as becoming more well rounded in her knowledge of the practice's administrative operations. The encounter form is a common document used to enter the procedure when a patient checks out, but knowing how to use the CPT manual is essential when notes must be coded from procedures or services performed by Dr. Shuman or Dr. Taylor. As with diagnostic coding, Sherald can pull the patient's chart for research and documentation if any questions arise about a claim. Sherald knows that coding to the highest level of specificity helps ensure accuracy and aids the practice in obtaining maximum reimbursement. Sherald continues to use the Internet to network and research. She stays informed of the changes in procedural coding by ordering the updated CPT manual each year.

SUMMARY OF LEARNING OBJECTIVES

1. **Define, spell, and pronounce the terms listed in the vocabulary.**
   Spelling and pronouncing medical terms correctly bolster the medical assistant's credibility. Knowing the definition of these terms promotes confidence in communication with patients and co-workers.

2. **Describe the steps for abstracting procedural data from clinical documentation.**
   The medical assistant must thoroughly read clinical documentation and look for all of the procedures that were performed and should be charged to the patient. Most physician offices use the encounter form to document procedures and services, but there are instances when the medical assistant will need to read through the medical record to determine what was done to the patient and what charges should be made.

3. **Identify four purposes of the CPT.**
   The CPT is designed to encourage the use of standard terms and descriptors to document procedures in the medical record; to communicate accurate information on procedures and services to agencies concerned with insurance claims; to provide the basis for a computer-oriented system to evaluate operative procedures, and to contribute basic information for statistical purposes.

4. **List the six main sections of the CPT and describe their content.**
   The Main Text has six sections: Evaluation and Management (E/M), Anesthesia, Surgery, Radiology, Pathology and Laboratory, and Medicine. Each section contains subsections, categories, and subcategories that further define, modify, and describe the procedure or service codes.

5. **Describe the coding conventions, guidelines, and layout of the CPT manual and their importance.**

The CPT guidelines, symbols, conventions, notes, and steps are designed to guide a medical coder through the process of analyzing and translating clinical documentation and selecting the most accurate code for the procedure performed or the services rendered. The CPT contains a comprehensive Alphabetic Index, a Main Text listing of the CPT Category I codes, and several appendixes and addenda. The Alphabetic Index is composed of main and modifying terms that help provide specificity in selecting code or code ranges to evaluate in the Main Text. The Main Text numerically lists all the CPT procedure and service codes and provides guidelines and conventions in selecting the most specific and most accurate code for insurance billing, reimbursement, and statistical data collection. The appendixes and addenda provide lists of deletions, additions, and changes to the previous year's CPT, modifiers, Category II and III codes, clinical examples for use of the E/M codes, add-on codes, exempt codes, codes that include conscious sedation, and drugs awaiting U.S. Food and Drug Administration (FDA) approval.

6. **Describe the process and steps for selecting the most accurate code based on clinical documentation.**

To use the CPT properly, the coder begins by reading and abstracting the medical documentation, then follows several specific steps using the CPT Alphabetic Index to find a numeric, Category I, CPT procedure or service code, codes, or range of codes. The steps for using the Alphabetic Index are (1) read the medical documentation; (2) select the main term classification to begin the search; (3) after locating the main term, select the modifying term or terms; (4) if no modifying term produces an appropriate code or code range, repeat steps 2 and 3 using a different main term classification; (5) find the code or code ranges that include all or most of the medical record procedure or service description; (6) disregard any code or code range containing additional descriptions or modifying terms not found in the medical record; (7) write down the code or code ranges that best match the medical documentation. Once the coder has found the code, codes, or code range in the Alphabetic Index, he or she moves to the CPT Main Text to refine the search and find the appropriate code.

7. **Explain the importance of correctly assigning evaluation and management (E/M) codes.**

The physician can only bill for services that are actually rendered to patients and must use the E/M guidelines to determine the correct codes for each patient. The amount of time spent with the patient and the level of medical decision making, in addition to the length and complexity of the history and examination process, all affect the code choice that applies to a particular patient encounter.

8. **Discuss the importance of modifiers.**

Modifiers enable the physician to indicate that a service or procedure was altered in some way but not changed in definition. Modifiers also allow the physician to provide additional information or to describe extenuating circumstances that affect the rendered procedure or service.

9. **Define upcoding and explain why it must be avoided.**

If a code is selected that not only matches the procedure or service performed but also adds modifying information that is not in the medical documentation, the information is considered "upcoded." Consistent upcoding can result in legal charges of fraud or abuse.

10. **Explain the process for selecting the correct procedure codes.**

The medical assistant must understand the process for selecting the correct procedure codes used for billing purposes. The selection directly influences the physician's total reimbursements. The process for code selection is outlined in Procedure 19-1.

11. **Explain the process for selecting main and modifying terms.**

The Alphabetic Index is organized by main terms that can stand alone or can be further detailed by using modifying terms that are indented under the main terms. The medical assistant should be as specific as possible in code selections, using all pertinent words in the description as found in the medical documentation.

12. **Explain how to find codes in the Alphabetic Index of the CPT manual.**

First, analyze the medical documentation to determine what services or procedures were performed. Select the main term from the documentation and search for it in the Alphabetic Index. Modifying terms help the coder find the appropriate code, which should then be located in the Main Text. Determine which code is the most accurate description for the procedure or service provided.

13. **Explain how to analyze and select codes using the CPT Main Text.**

After searching the Alphabetic Index, turn to the appropriate codes in the Main Text to perform the final coding steps. Read the section thoroughly to determine the most accurate code to assign to the procedure or service rendered to the patient. Code the procedure or service. The process for using the Alphabetic Index and Main Texts of the CPT manual are detailed in Procedures 19-2 to 19-4.

CONNECTIONS

Study Guide Connection: Go to Chapter 19 Study Guide. Read the Case Study and Workplace Applications and complete the assignments. Do online research for answers to the questions in the Internet Activities associated with basics of procedural coding.

Evolve Connection: For more information related to basics of procedural coding, go to *evolve.elsevier.com/kinn* and visit related Web links for Chapter 19. Click on the Medical Assisting Exam Review and answer the practice questions to sharpen your test-taking skills.

20

BASICS OF HEALTH INSURANCE

Carline A. Dalgleish, Sharon Oliver, and Alexandra Patricia Adams

SCENARIO

The instructor in Ann Snyder's administrative medical assistant class, Grant Wilson, knows that working with medical insurance can be quite rewarding, and experienced billers also find the field financially rewarding. Mr. Wilson works with Ann and her classmates, answering their questions and helping them to see that medical insurance is not as complicated as it seems.

The medical assistant who is able to pay attention to detail and likes paperwork will usually enjoy billing and coding activities. The person who performs these duties in the physician's office is a critical staff member, because the tasks that are done related to billing influence the physician's income. That income is used to pay clinic expenses and payroll, so all of the employees of the facility indirectly count on accurate and timely billing. The individual who contributes billing and coding skills, in addition to an understanding of health insurance and reimbursement guidelines, will be an asset to the practice and can look forward to a long and rewarding career.

Ann will learn that when insurance billing is broken down into manageable segments of information and applied to real-life situations, it becomes an interesting task. She will learn about the importance of verifying insurance eligibility and the steps for obtaining authorization for referrals and procedures; she also will learn that those benefits differ among insurance carriers, whether private, commercial, federal, or state insurance payers.

While studying this chapter, think about the following questions:

- How will Ann be able to remember all the benefits, exclusions, authorizations, and other required information for the multiple insurance carriers and third-party administrators?
- Why is it important to verify insurance eligibility and benefits before the patient is seen in a provider's office?

- Why is it important to understand the procedures for obtaining referrals and authorizations?
- What will Ann need to know to perform insurance deductible and co-insurance calculations?

LEARNING OBJECTIVES

1. Define, spell, and pronounce the terms listed in the vocabulary.
2. Discuss the purpose of health insurance.
3. Differentiate among the various types of insurance policies.
4. Explain the numerous classifications of insurance benefits available.
5. Explain how insurance benefits are determined.
6. Differentiate among the different types of managed care options.
7. List and discuss other major third-party payers.
8. Explain the procedure for verifying insurance benefits.
9. Discuss the different types of fee schedules.
10. Explain how to make managed care referrals and obtain precertifications.
11. Perform eligibility and verification of benefits procedures.
12. Perform a preauthorization procedure.
13. Demonstrate how insurance benefits are determined by calculating deductible and co-insurance payments.

VOCABULARY

allowed charge (allowable amount) The maximum amount of money that many third-party payers allow for a specific procedure or service.

authorization An alphanumeric/number given by the insurance company authorizing approval of a procedure or service. This does not guarantee payment.

beneficiary The individual entitled to receive benefits from an insurance policy or program or a governmental entitlement program offering healthcare benefits. Also called a *participant, subscriber, dependent, enrollee,* or *member.*

benefits The amount payable by an insurance company for a monetary loss to an individual insured by that company, under each coverage.

birthday rule An insurance rule that applies as follows: when an individual is covered under two insurance policies, the insurance plan of the policyholder whose birthday comes first in the calendar year (month and day, not year) becomes the primary insurance.

capitation A payment method used by many managed care organizations in which a fixed amount of money is reimbursed to the provider for patients enrolled during a specific period of time, no matter what services were received or how many visits were made.

carriers In insurance terms, companies that assume the risk of an insurance policy.

Civilian Health and Medical Program of the Uniformed Services (CHAMPUS) See TRICARE.

Civilian Health and Medical Program of the Department of Veterans Affairs (CHAMPVA) A comprehensive health care program in which the VA pays the cost of covered health care services and supplies for eligible beneficiaries; to be eligible, the individual cannot be eligible for TRICARE, but can be the spouse or child of a disabled veteran, as well as the surviving spouse or child of a veteran who died from a service-connected disability; a veteran who died while suffering a service disability; or a military member who died in the line of duty.

co-insurance A policy provision frequently found in medical insurance whereby the policyholder and the insurance company share the cost of covered losses in a specified ratio (e.g., 80/20 means that 80% is covered by the insurer and 20% by the insured).

commercial insurance plans Plans that reimburse the insured for expenses resulting from illness or injury according to a specific fee schedule as outlined in the insurance policy and on a fee-for-service basis. Sometimes called *private insurance.*

co-payment A sum of money that is paid at the time of medical service; a form of co-insurance.

deductibles Specific amounts of money a patient must pay out of pocket before the insurance carrier begins paying. Usually this amount ranges from $100 to $500. This deductible amount is met on a yearly or per-incident basis.

dependents The spouse, children, and sometimes domestic partner or other individuals designated by the insured who are covered under a healthcare plan.

disability income insurance Insurance that provides periodic payments to replace income when an insured person is unable to work as a result of illness, injury, or disease.

effective date The date on which an insurance policy or plan takes effect so that benefits are payable.

eligibility A term that describes whether a patient's insurance coverage is in effect and eligible for payment of insurance benefits.

exclusions Limitations on an insurance contract for which benefits are not payable.

explanation of benefits (EOB) A letter or statement from the insurance carrier describing what was paid, denied, or reduced in payment. It also contains information about amounts applied to the deductible, the patient's co-insurance, and the allowed amounts.

explanation of Medicare benefits (EOMB) An explanation of benefits from Medicare (see *explanation of benefits* [EOB]).

fee for service An established schedule of fees set for services performed by providers and paid by the patient.

fiscal intermediary An organization that contracts with the government to handle and mediate insurance claims from medical facilities, home health agencies, or providers of medical services or supplies.

government plans Entitlement programs or healthcare plans that are sponsored and/or subsidized by the state or federal government, such as Medicaid and Medicare.

grandfathered A legislative provision that allows the exception based on a preexisting condition.

group policy Insurance written under a policy that covers a number of people under a single master contract issued to their employer or to an association with which they are affiliated.

guarantor The person responsible for paying a medical bill.

health insurance Insurance protection, provided in return for periodic premium payments, that provides reimbursement of expenses resulting from illness or injury. It includes accident, disability income, medical expense, and accidental death and dismemberment insurance. Also known as *accident and health insurance* or *disability income insurance.*

Health Insurance Portability and Accountability Act (HIPAA) A law enacted in 1996 to improve the portability and continuity of health insurance coverage; to combat waste, fraud, and abuse in health insurance and healthcare delivery; to promote the use of medical savings accounts; to improve access to long-term care services and coverage; to simplify the administration of health insurance; and to serve other purposes. As a result, standards have been created for electronic health information transactions and for the privacy of health information. Also known as the Kassebaum-Kennedy Act.

health maintenance organization (HMO) An organization that provides a wide range of comprehensive healthcare services for a specified group at a fixed periodic payment. HMOs can be sponsored by the government, medical schools, hospitals, employers, labor unions, consumer groups, insurance companies, and hospital-medical plans.

indemnity plans Traditional health insurance plans that pay for all or a share of the cost of covered services, regardless of which physician, hospital, or other licensed healthcare provider is used. Policyholders of indemnity plans and their dependents choose when and where to get healthcare services.

individual policy An insurance policy designed specifically for the use of one person and his or her dependents. An individual policy generally does not offer some of the amenities of a group policy (e.g., lower premiums). Often called *personal insurance.*

insured An individual or organization covered by an insurance policy according to the policy terms; usually, the individual or group that pays the premiums. Blue Cross/Blue Shield refers to this person or group as the *subscriber.*

managed care plans An umbrella term for all healthcare plans that provide healthcare in return for preset monthly payments and coordinated care through a defined network of primary care physicians and hospitals.

medical savings accounts (MSAs) Tax-deferred bank or savings accounts that are combined with a low-premium, high-deductible insurance policy; they are designed for individuals or families who choose to fund their own healthcare expenses and medical insurance.

Medicaid A federal- and state-sponsored health insurance program for the medically indigent.

Medicare A federally sponsored health insurance program for those over age 65 and for individuals under age 65 who are disabled.

Medigap A term sometimes applied to private insurance products that supplement Medicare insurance benefits.

participating provider (PAR) A physician or other healthcare provider who enters into a contract with a specific insurance company or program and by doing so agrees to abide by certain rules and regulations set forth by that particular third-party payer.

policyholder A person who pays a premium to an insurance company and in whose name the policy is written in exchange for the insurance protection provided by a policy of insurance.

preauthorization A process required by some insurance carriers in which the provider obtains permission to perform certain procedures or services or refer a patient to a specialist.

premium The periodic (monthly, quarterly, or annual) payment of a specific sum of money to an insurance company, for which the insurer in return agrees to provide certain benefits.

primary care provider (PCP) A general practice or nonspecialist provider or physician responsible for the care of a patient

for some health maintenance organizations. Also called a *gatekeeper.*

referral An insurance term used when a primary care provider wants to send a patient to a specialist. Typically, the provider must obtain authorization from the insurance carrier in advance to refer a patient.

remittance advice (RA) An explanation of benefits from Medicaid (see *explanation of benefits* [EOB]).

resource-based relative value scale (RBRVS) A fee schedule designed to provide national uniform payment of Medicare benefits after adjustment to reflect the differences in practice costs across geographic areas.

rider A special provision or group of provisions that may be added to a policy to expand or limit the benefits otherwise payable. It may increase or decrease benefits, waive a condition or coverage, or in any other way amend the original contract.

self-insured (or self-funded) plan An insurance plan funded by an organization having a large enough employee base that it can afford to fund its own insurance program.

self-referral Occurs when a patient or an insured individual refers himself or herself to a specialist without requesting the referral from the primary provider (e.g., a woman seeking an annual gynecologic examination). Managed care guidelines may require the patient to report the self-referral.

service benefit plans Plans that provide benefits in the form of certain surgical and medical services rendered rather than cash. A service benefit plan is not restricted to a fee schedule.

third-party administrator (TPA) An organization that processes claims and performs other business-related functions for a health plan.

third-party payers Entities that make payment on an obligation or debt but are not parties to the contract that created the debt.

TRICARE A government-sponsored program under which authorized dependents of military personnel receive medical care. Originally called *CHAMPUS.*

utilization review A review of individual cases by a committee to make sure that services are medically necessary and to study how providers use medical care resources.

workers' compensation A system of laws that protects employees against the loss of wages and the cost of medical care resulting from an occupational accident, disease, or death, unless the employee is proven negligent.

THE PURPOSE OF HEALTH INSURANCE

The purpose of health insurance is to help individuals and families offset the costs of medical care. **Health insurance** is defined as a contract for protection against financial losses resulting from illness or injury. This protection provides payment of monetary **benefits** for covered sickness or injury, depending on the insurance policy purchased. There are various types of health insurance, such as accident insurance, disability income insurance, hospitalization, medical expense insurance, and accidental death and dismemberment insurance.

Health insurance typically covers services and procedures considered medically necessary. Most insurance policies do not cover

"elective" procedures, such as certain cosmetic surgeries that are not considered medically necessary. More and more of today's health insurance policies cover "preventive" care, which includes services provided to help prevent certain illnesses or that lead to an early diagnosis.

IMPACT OF INSURANCE BILLING ON THE MEDICAL OFFICE

Nearly all of the physician's income is derived from the insurance payments received for services rendered. Regular expenses, such as rent, salaries, medical and office supplies, equipment, and so on, depend on the practice's cash flow, which arises from proper and timely filing of insurance claims to meet the financial needs of the medical office. This is the most important job function of the coder/biller.

CYCLE OF HEALTH INSURANCE

The information that follows describes common types of insurance coverage and insurance carriers, the steps for obtaining insurance coverage information, and some of the terminology associated with obtaining insurance coverage and insurance billing. The **insured** or **policyholder**, defined as an individual, group, or employer, pays a set amount called a premium. A **premium** is the periodic (monthly, quarterly, or annual) payment of a specific sum of money to an insurance company for which the insurer agrees to provide certain benefits. This premium, in return, pays for an insurance policy that covers the insured for a specific type (or types) of coverage, such as basic and major medical coverage, accidental death or disability, and so on. When an insured or a covered beneficiary or dependent of the insurance policy becomes ill or suffers an injury, treatment is provided by a physician or other provider of service in a doctor's office, emergency department, or hospital, and the fee is paid by the insurance company when medical necessity and covered benefits are met.

Tasks Related to the Cycle of Health Insurance

The medical assistant's tasks are initiated when the patient encounters the provider, either by appointment, as a walk-in, or in the emergency department or hospital. Insurance billing and coding tasks typically completed by the medical assistant include:

- Obtaining information from the patient and the insured, including demographic, employment, and insurance data.
- Verifying the patient's **eligibility** for insurance payment by the insurance carrier or carriers, in addition to the benefits available and exclusions, and determining whether special authorizations are needed to refer the patient to specialists or for the performance of certain services or procedures (e.g., surgery or diagnostic tests).
- Performing diagnostic and procedural coding and reviewing the encounter form or charge ticket for completeness once the patient has been seen by the provider.
- Calculating insurance deductibles and co-insurance amounts and providing the patient with a statement showing the out-of-pocket amount he or she owes.
- Obtaining preauthorization for referral of the patient to a specialist or for special services or procedures that require advance permission.
- Completing an insurance claim form and submitting it to the insurance company for reimbursement for services and procedures performed.
- Posting payments and adjustments on the patient ledger or account and examining the **explanation of benefits (EOB)**, **explanation of Medicare benefits (EOMB)**, or **remittance advice (RA)** from the insurance company to identify what was paid, reduced, or denied and also the deductible, co-insurance, and allowed charges (also called *allowable amounts*).

- Adjusting the account to reflect an allowable amount, which is either written off (adjusted) or passed on to the patient for payment, and also any courtesy, professional, or other type of adjustment.
- Billing the patient for any outstanding balance or, if the patient has a secondary insurance, completing the secondary insurance claim form and submitting it to the insurance company with a copy of the EOB showing payment from the primary insurance carrier.
- Following up on any rejected or unpaid claims, making sure that any requests from the insurance carrier for more information about specific claims are answered as soon as possible.
- Meeting the timely filing requirements of each of the medical office's participating insurance carriers. Failure to do this results in zero payment from the insurance company and inability to bill the patient for the nonpayable amount.

Determining Primary and Secondary Coverage

When the patient is the insured, the patient becomes the guarantor, and the patient's insurance is primary. If the patient also is covered by another policy, that policy becomes the secondary insurance.

The only exception to this convention arises when the patient is not the insurance policy holder, such as when a child is insured by each parent. In such cases, the **birthday rule** applies; that is, under law, the insurance plan of the policyholder whose birthday comes first in the calendar year (month and day, not year) becomes the primary insurance.

Cost of Coverage

In this age of rising healthcare costs, most insurance carriers do not reimburse the full amount for services and procedures rendered. A **carrier** is an insurance company or third party that pays for medical care. The insured, or **beneficiary**, in most instances is required to pay certain out-of-pocket expenses, such as deductibles, co-payment or co-insurance charges, and costs for noncovered services.

A **deductible** is an amount a policyholder agrees to pay per claim or per accident toward the total amount of an insured loss before the insurance company begins payment of benefits. A deductible amount is stated in the insurance contract and normally ranges from $100 to $500. Under most circumstances the deductible must be paid only one time per calendar year; however, some policies have a deductible per occurrence.

The medical assistant should always verify the **effective date**, or date the insurance coverage began, on the patient's insurance card. An excellent policy for any provider's office is to call the insurance company to verify insurance eligibility, benefits, and **exclusions** before the patient's appointment or encounter with the provider. This verification is done by phone or fax and ensures that the insurance is in effect and the patient is eligible for benefits. Most major insurance carriers have a Web site dedicated to verifying eligibility and claims payments. (Verification of benefits is discussed in more detail later in the chapter.)

Co-insurance is a policy provision frequently found in medical insurance. Under this provision, the policyholder and the insurance company share the cost of covered losses in a specified ratio, such as 80/20 (i.e., 80% of services are paid by the insurance carrier and 20% by the insured).

Many plans now require a **co-payment**, which is a type of co-insurance that is collected at the time of service. Co-payments usually range from $10 to $25 for office visits but can vary according to the services rendered. Most managed care plans require a co-payment. In addition, any services or procedures that are not covered under the terms of an insurance policy are the responsibility of the policyholder or insured.

TYPES OF HEALTH INSURANCE

Health insurance is available to most people in this country through group or individual plans. In addition, many people are covered by government plans or entitlement programs. However, although health insurance might be available, it is not always affordable. A recent survey revealed that more than 40 million Americans have no regular source for obtaining medical care, and lack of health insurance was a major obstacle.

The types of health insurance available include group insurance, individual insurance, government-sponsored insurance, self-insured plans, and medical savings accounts. Government plans can be federal and/or state sponsored; they include Medicare, Medicaid, TRICARE, the **Civilian Health and Medical Program of the Department of Veterans Affairs (CHAMPVA)**, and workers' compensation.

Group Policies

Insurance written under a **group policy** covers a number of people under a single master contract (subsidized by employers) that is issued to their employer or to an association with which they are affiliated. Group coverage usually provides greater benefits at lower premiums because of the large pool of people from whom premiums are collected. Physical examinations are normally not required, and pre-existing conditions are often waived. Often the employee shares the cost of coverage through payroll deductions.

Individual Policies

Individuals who do not qualify for inclusion in a group or government-sponsored plan may apply to companies that offer **individual policies**, often called *personal insurance*. The applicant is normally required to fill out an extended health questionnaire and undergo a physical examination before acceptance. Unlike with group policies, with personal insurance there is a risk that coverage may be denied, or the individual may have to accept a **rider**, or limitation, on benefits the policy will cover. Premiums are almost always higher with individual policies, and often the benefits are less.

Government Plans

Many large groups of people are covered by **government plans** or entitlement programs. A patient who is age 65 or older is covered by Part A and Part B of Medicare. A medically indigent patient may be eligible for Medicaid, with or without Medicare. **Dependents** of military personnel are covered by TRICARE (formerly the **Civilian Health and Medical Program of the Uniformed Services [CHAMPUS]**); surviving spouses and dependent children of veterans who died as a result of service-related disabilities are covered by CHAMPVA.

Some wage earners are protected against the loss of wages and the cost of medical care resulting from an occupational accident, disease, or disability through workers' compensation insurance. An individual may collect benefits for health expenses from an automobile policy if the injury is related to a car accident or other such loss.

TRICARE

The federal government first became responsible for insuring a large group of people in 1956 with passage of Public Law 569. This law authorized dependents of military personnel to receive treatment from civilian physicians at the expense of the government. The program administering these benefits became CHAMPUS, which today is known as **TRICARE** (discussed in detail later in this chapter).

Medicaid

In 1965 the federal government provided for the medically indigent through a program known as **Medicaid**. Title XIX of Public Law 89-97, under the Social Security Amendments of 1965, provided for agreements involving cost sharing between federal and state governments to provide medical care for people meeting specific eligibility criteria.

Medicare

Established in 1965, **Medicare** is a federal health insurance program that provides healthcare coverage for individuals age 65 and older. The program also covers certain individuals under age 65 who have disabilities or end-stage renal disease (ESRD). The Medicare program was developed by the Healthcare Financing Administration (HCFA) as part of Title XVIII of the Social Security Act. The HCFA now is known as the *Centers for Medicare and Medicaid Services* (CMS).

Workers' Compensation

All state legislatures have passed workers' compensation laws to protect wage earners against the loss of wages and the cost of medical care resulting from occupational accident or disease, as long as the employee was not proven negligent. State laws differ as to the classes of employees included and the benefits provided by **workers' compensation** insurance.

Self-Insured Plans

Many large companies or organizations have a big enough employee base that they choose to fund their own insurance program. This is called a **self-insured** (or **self-funded**) **plan**. Technically, a self-funded plan is not insurance by true definition. The employer pays employee healthcare costs from the firm's own funds. Usually the costs of benefits and premiums for self-insured plans are similar to those for group plans. Self-funded plans tend to work best for companies that are large enough to offer good coverage and reasonable premium rates and are able to pay large claims for expensive medical services. Often a **third-party administrator (TPA)** or **fiscal intermediary** handles paperwork and claim payments for a self-insured group.

Self-funded healthcare or self-insurance is an arrangement in which an employer provides health or disability benefits to employees with its own funds or employees for health coverage with their personal funds. This is different from fully insured plans, in which the employer contracts an insurance company to cover the employees and dependents. In self-funded healthcare, the employer assumes the direct risk for payment of the claims for benefits. The terms of eligibility and coverage are set forth in a plan document, which includes provisions similar to those found in a typical group health insurance policy. Unless exempted, such plans create rights and obligations under the Employee Retirement Income Security Act of 1974 (ERISA).

Medical Savings Account

In 1996 Congress made tax-free **medical savings accounts (MSAs)** available to 750,000 American workers and their families. This is a type of self-insurance. Under a provision of the Kassebaum-Kennedy health insurance reform bill, small companies (50 or fewer employees), self-employed individuals, and the uninsured can purchase health insurance policies and make tax-free deposits to an MSA. They can use their MSA money to pay small and routine healthcare expenses, reserving a high-deductible medical insurance policy to pay large, catastrophic expenses. Money that remains in the account at year's end earns tax-free interest. People can also elect to use MSA money to pay their health insurance premiums during a job change, which should reduce *job lock,* a situation in which people do not change jobs for fear of losing their health insurance.

In an MSA program, generally associated with self-employed individuals, tax-deferred deposits can be made for medical expenses. Withdrawals from the MSA are tax free if used to pay for qualified medical expenses. The MSA must be coupled with a high-deductible health plan (HDHP). Withdrawals from MSA go toward paying the deductible expenses in a given year. MSA funds can cover expenses related to most forms of healthcare, disability, dental care, vision care, and long-term care, whether the expenses are billed through the qualifying insurance or otherwise.

Once the plan deductible has been met in a given year, the HDHP pays any remaining covered medical expenses in that year. If there are funds remaining in the MSA at the end of the year, the funds can either roll over for the following year or can be withdrawn as taxable income.

MSAs have been superseded by health savings accounts (HSAs), which were established as part of the Medicare Prescription Drug, Improvement, and Modernization Act of 2003. Existing MSAs were **grandfathered**.

CRITICAL THINKING APPLICATION   20-1

Ann understands how medical assistants can easily become intimidated by all the regulations that affect insurance coverage. Discuss differences and similarities between the different types of insurance companies and insurance coverage. How can the medical assistant effectively keep up with all of the rules pertaining to policies that are frequently presented in the office?

TYPES OF INSURANCE BENEFITS

An insurance package is tailored to the needs of each individual or group policy, and the combinations of benefits are limitless. This is also called "cafeteria style," in which employers can choose the benefits they want for their employees. A policy may contain one or any combination of the benefits described in the following sections (Table 20-1).

Hospitalization

Hospital coverage pays the cost of all or part of the insured person's hospital room and board and specific hospital services, such as the costs involved in having surgery in a hospital. Hospital insurance policies frequently set a maximum amount payable per day and a maximum number of days of hospital care, per the diagnosis-related group (DRG). Some insurance companies require that the hospital be accredited or licensed.

Surgical

Surgical coverage pays all or part of a surgeon's fee; some plans also pay for an assistant surgeon. Surgery includes any incision or excision, removal of foreign bodies, aspiration, suturing, and reduction of fractures. Surgery may be performed in a hospital, physician's office, or elsewhere. The insurer frequently provides the subscriber with a surgical fee schedule that establishes the amount the insurer will pay for commonly performed procedures.

Basic Medical

Basic medical coverage pays all or part of a physician's fee for nonsurgical services, including hospital, home, and office visits. Usually there is a deductible that the patient pays, in addition to a co-payment or co-insurance payment each time service is received. The insurance plan may include a provision for diagnostic laboratory, radiology, and pathology fees. Some medical plans do not cover routine physical examinations or preventive health checkups, such as mammograms or prostate examinations, if the patient does not have a specific complaint or illness.

The Affordable Care Act brings major changes to the healthcare industry, and several of its provisions have already taken effect. Beginning on January 1, 2014, all Americans will have access to affordable health insurance options, according to the HHS website. Some of the key provisions include:

- Prohibiting discrimination due to preexisting conditions based on gender or sex
- Eliminating annual limits on insurance coverage
- Ensuring coverage for individuals who are participating in clinical trials
- Making care more affordable through tax credits that will become available to people with income levels between 100% and 400% of the poverty line who are not eligible for other affordable coverage
- Increasing access to Medicaid, making the federal funding to states payable at 100% for the first 3 years, and 90% thereafter
- Promoting individual responsibility by making coverage mandatory or by charging a fee to those who do not have coverage, both of which will help to offset the costs of coverage

The four core categories of the Act include benefits for hospitalization and ER services, physician and midlevel practitioners care, pharmacy benefits, and laboratory and imaging services. In 2015 and beyond, additional provisions will go into effect, such as paying physicians based upon value and not volume.

TABLE 20-1 Types of Health Insurance and Plan Benefits

BENEFIT	COVERED	PAYS
Hospitalization	Cost of all or part of the hospital room and board; and specific hospital services (i.e., costs involved in having surgery in a hospital)	Maximum amount per day and maximum number of days
Surgical	Any surgical procedure, including but not limited to incision or excision; removal of foreign bodies; aspiration; suturing; reduction of fractures	Surgeon's fee Assistant surgeon's fee
Basic medical	Outpatient and/or physician office procedures and services	Physician's fees diagnostic, radiologic, laboratory, and pathology fees
Major medical	Catastrophic or prolonged illness or injury	Takes over when basic medical, hospitalization, and surgical benefits end
Disability	Accident or illness resulting in an inability for patient to work; can be paid whether work-related or not work related.	Cash benefits paid in lieu of salary while patient is unable to earn an income
Dental care	Preventive care and/or treatment and repair of teeth and gums	Typically pays 100% for preventive care, 50% for repair and treatment
Vision care	Eye exam and glasses	Set benefit amount, depending on vision care policy for examination and/or glasses
Medicare supplement	Deductible and co-insurance amounts unpaid by Medicare	Deductible and co-insurance amounts unpaid by Medicare
Special risk	Certain specific illnesses (cancer, heart failure) or accidents (automobile, airplane)	Typically pays a maximum benefit
Life insurance	Loss of life	Usually a lump sum payment of the life insurance benefit
Long-term care	Long-term skilled nursing or rehabilitation care	Set amount determined by policy benefits

To be in compliance with the Act, insurance plans must consist of 10 essential health benefits (EHBs), including the following provisions:

- Ambulatory patient services
- Emergency services
- Hospitalization
- Maternity and newborn care
- Mental health and substance abuse disorder services, including behavior health services
- Prescription drugs
- Rehabilitative and habilitative services and devices
- Laboratory services
- Preventative services and wellness services, as well as chronic disease management
- Pediatric services, including oral and vision care

Disability (Loss of Income) Protection

Disability insurance is a form of insurance that insures the beneficiary's earned income against the risk that a disability will make working uncomfortable (as with psychological disorders), painful (as with back pain), or impossible (as with coma). It encompasses paid sick leave, short-term disability benefits, and long-term disability benefits.

Weekly or monthly cash benefits are provided to employed policyholders who become unable to work as a result of an accident or illness. Many disability policies do not start payment until after a specified number of days or until a certain number of sick leave days have been used. Payment is made directly to the individual and is intended to replace lost income resulting from an illness or other disability. It is not intended for payment of specific medical bills, and it should not be confused with a regular insurance plan, entitlement program, or workers' compensation, in which compensation is provided for an employee who is injured on the job or cannot work as a result of a job-related illness or other disability.

Dental Care

Dental benefits programs offer a variety of options in the form of either fee-for-service or managed care plans that reimburse a portion of a patient's dental expenses and may exclude certain treatments.

Dental coverage is included in many fringe benefit packages. Some policies are based on a co-payment and incentive program, in which preventive dental care (e.g., cleaning and x-ray films) is covered 100%, with most other coverage paid at 50%.

Vision Care

Vision care insurance may include reimbursement for all or a percentage of the cost for refraction, lenses, and frames. Some vision plans also pay for corrective procedures, such as laser eye surgery.

Medicare Supplement

Many Medicare beneficiaries purchase a supplemental health insurance policy to help defray medical costs not covered or only partially covered by Medicare. Federal regulations now require Medicare supplement contracts to be uniform in benefits to avoid confusion for the purchaser. Medicare supplements that cover Medicare recipients' out-of-pocket expenses, including the deductible and co-insurance payments, are called **Medigap** policies.

Special Risk Insurance

Special risk insurance protects a person in the event of a certain type of accident, such as an automobile or airplane crash, or for certain diseases, such as tuberculosis or cancer. There is usually a maximum benefit.

Liability Insurance

Liability insurance covers losses to a third party caused by the insured. There are many types of liability insurance, including automobile, business, and homeowners' policies. Liability policies often include benefits for medical expenses resulting from traumatic injuries, lost wages, and sometimes pain and suffering payable to individuals who are injured in the insured person's home or car, without regard to the insured person's actual legal liability for the accident.

Life Insurance

Life insurance provides payment of a specified amount on the insured's death, either to his or her estate or to a designated beneficiary or, in the case of an endowment policy, to the policyholder at a specified date. Life insurance policies sometimes provide monthly cash benefits if the policyholder becomes permanently and totally disabled. Sometimes the proceeds from life insurance are used to meet the expenses of the insured person's last illness.

Long-Term Care Insurance

Long-term care insurance is a relatively new type of insurance that covers a broad range of maintenance and health services for chronically ill, disabled, or mentally retarded individuals. Services may be provided on an inpatient basis (at a rehabilitation facility, nursing home, or mental hospital), on an outpatient basis, or at home. The **Health Insurance Portability and Accountability Act (HIPAA)** of 1996 improved access to long-term care services and coverage.

HOW BENEFITS ARE DETERMINED

Insurance benefits may be determined and paid in one of several ways:
- Indemnity schedules
- Service benefit plans
- Resource-based relative value scale (RBRVS)
- Determination of the usual, customary, and reasonable (UCR) fees

Indemnity Schedules

An indemnity health insurance plan, also known as *major medical,* is a more flexible yet more costly option. Many people refer to this as a traditional plan, because it preceded the advent of managed care (e.g., health maintenance organizations, preferred provider organizations, and point of service [POS] plans).

Indemnity plans, or schedules, are traditional health insurance plans that pay for all or a share of the cost of covered services, regardless of which physician, hospital, or other licensed healthcare provider is used. Because physicians and other providers are paid for each office visit, test, procedure, or other service they deliver, indemnity plans are often called fee for service plans.

Policyholders of indemnity plans and their dependents choose when and where to get healthcare services. In exchange for premiums that members pay, the indemnity plan reimburses members or the provider when claims are filed. When the policy is purchased, the subscriber is often given a schedule of indemnities (i.e., a fee schedule), which explains the benefit payment amounts. Indemnity benefits are usually paid to the person insured unless that person has authorized payment directly to the provider, which is a common practice.

Service Benefit Plans

In **service benefit plans**, the insuring company agrees to pay for certain surgical or medical services without additional cost to the person insured. There is no set fee schedule. In a service benefit plan, surgery with complications would warrant a higher fee than an uncomplicated procedure. Premiums are sometimes higher for this type of coverage, but often payments are larger. Frequently payment of benefits is sent directly to the physician and is considered full payment for services rendered. Consider this example: the service benefit plan states that it will pay $900 for a cholecystectomy. If Dr. Jones charges $1,500 for this procedure, he has the right either to accept the $900 as payment in full and write off the balance due, or to request payment of the remaining $600 balance from the patient or the **guarantor** (i.e., the individual or group responsible for payment).

Resource-Based Relative Value Scale

The CMS annually publishes physician fee schedule information on its Web site, in addition to the formula for calculating physician fee schedule payment amounts. Physician fee schedule amounts vary, depending on *facility* or *nonfacility*. Physicians who own their own facility (e.g., office) would not use the facility columns on the Medicare Fee Service Schedule. Entities such as hospitals, skilled nursing centers, nursing homes, and rehabilitation hospitals should all be classified as facilities. Facility rates are almost always lower than nonfacility rates, but when the physician treats the patient at a facility, he or she should receive facility rates. The amount of resources required to perform a service is determined through the use of *relative value units* (RVUs), which the CMS assigns to the *Current Procedural Terminology* (CPT) codes (see Chapter 19). This system was implemented to standardize payment while providing an adjustment for overhead costs in different geographic areas. The formula for calculating payment takes into consideration these elements: physician expense, malpractice, geographic practice cost index, and the conversion factor. Since Medicare introduced the **resource-based relative value scale (RBRVS)** in 1992, most third-party payers have adopted similar approaches in developing their fees.

Usual, Customary, and Reasonable Fee

Some insurance companies agree to pay on the basis of all or a percentage of a usual, customary, and reasonable (UCR) fee. Charges for a specific service are compared with a database showing (1) charges to other patients for the same service by the same type of physician and (2) charges to patients by other physicians performing the same or similar services in the same geographic area. The insurance company determines whether the provider's charge is UCR, and any amount over the allowed charge is not paid. Sometimes *UCR* is used synonymously with *fee allowance schedule* when that schedule is set relatively high.

HEALTH INSURANCE PROVIDERS

Health insurance providers include managed care plans, Blue Cross/Blue Shield (BC/BS), **commercial insurance** companies, and federal and state government programs, including Medicare, Medicaid, TRICARE, workers' compensation, and disability insurance.

Managed Care

Managed care is an umbrella term for all healthcare plans that provide healthcare in return for preset scheduled payments and coordinated care through a defined network of physicians and hospitals. **Managed care plans** are healthcare plans that provide healthcare in return for scheduled payments and that coordinate healthcare through a defined network of **primary care providers (PCPs)**, hospitals, and other providers. The passage of the Health Maintenance Organization Act in 1973 provided for federal aid to health insurance prepayment plans that met certain criteria. This brought about a rapid growth in **health maintenance organizations (HMOs)**; an HMO provides comprehensive healthcare to an enrolled group for a fixed periodic payment. Some of these plans pay by **capitation**, which means that the provider is paid a fixed amount for each individual enrolled in the plan during a specified period (usually 1 year), regardless of the expenses or number of services provided to the patient.

It is important for the medical assistant to be familiar with individual managed care contract benefits and with the procedures and processes for filing insurance claims. Reviewing a managed care plan's specific handbook, contracts, and required forms should always be part of a medical assistant's routine. This familiarizes the medical assistant with that plan's benefits and preauthorization and referral requirements, which enables him or her to discuss those requirements with the patient and to prepare the required forms and insurance claims properly. Procedure 20-1 describes the process for properly applying managed care policies and procedures.

PROCEDURE 20-1

Apply Managed Care Policies and Procedures

CAAHEP COMPETENCIES: II.C.II. 1., IV.C.IV.6., IV.P.IV.3., V. P.V.6., VII.P.VII.1., IX.A.IX.2.

ABHES COMPETENCIES: 3.t

GOAL: *To act within the guidelines of the managed care contracts that the physician and/or medical facility has partnered.*

EQUIPMENT and SUPPLIES

- Managed care contracts
- Managed care handbooks
- Forms from managed care organizations

PROCEDURAL STEPS

1. Determine which managed care organization the patient belongs to.
   <u>PURPOSE:</u> To make certain the right information is applied to the right patient.
2. Read and study the policies and procedures that are set forth by the managed care organization.
   <u>PURPOSE:</u> To understand and abide by the regulations that apply to a specific patient.
3. Make certain that a signature is on file for the patient.
   <u>PURPOSE:</u> The signature authorizes the provider to release medical information to the insurance carrier and authorizes the carrier to pay the provider directly.
4. Determine the procedures and services to be billed on the claim.
   <u>PURPOSE:</u> To ensure that all procedures and services are included in the review of the managed care plan.
5. Determine whether all procedures and services to be billed are covered by the managed care plan.
   <u>PURPOSE:</u> To understand which services are covered, which are noncovered, and which require special forms for billing. This also helps the medical assistant explain to patients the benefits covered and the steps that must be taken for procedures and services requiring preapproval.
6. Obtain any forms that are needed to process patient claims.
   <u>PURPOSE:</u> To submit the correct forms to the managed care organization.
7. Become familiar with the information in managed care policy manuals and handbooks.
   <u>PURPOSE:</u> By becoming familiar with handbooks and guidelines, the medical assistant will be able to assist patients in finding needed information.
8. Determine whom to contact in case of questions about the various managed care organizations.
   <u>PURPOSE:</u> To be able to refer patients to the best source of information when they have questions or concerns.
9. Attend seminars and workshops when offered by the managed care organizations.
   <u>PURPOSE:</u> To stay up-to-date on information and policies.
10. Use information gained on a daily basis when working with managed care organizations.

TABLE 20-2 Comparison of HMO Models

MODEL	STRUCTURE	BILLING MODEL
IPA	General or family practice physician or physician group that practices independently and may contract with several IPAs	Capitation or fee for service
Staff	One or more physicians hired by an HMO	Salaried
Group	Multispecialty group with or without a PCP (gatekeeper); may contract with several IPAs	Capitation or fee for service

HMO, Health maintenance organization; *IPA,* Independent practice association; *PCP,* primary care provider.

Managed Care Policies and Procedures

Managed care has been met with considerable controversy, and it has pros and cons that must be considered. It is important that medical assistants be well versed in the various types of managed care plans to fully understand their impact on healthcare costs.

Advantages of managed care include the following:

- Healthcare costs are usually contained.
- Established fee schedules are used.
- Authorized services are usually paid for.
- Most preventive medical treatment is covered.
- Patients' out-of-pocket expenses tend to be less than with traditional insurance.

Disadvantages of managed care include the following:

- Access to specialized care and referrals can be limited.
- Physicians' choices in the treatment of patients can be limited.
- More paperwork may be required.
- Treatment may be delayed because of preauthorization requirements.
- Reimbursement historically is less than with traditional insurance.

Models of Managed Care

The two basic models of managed care are the HMO and the preferred provider organization (PPO). The HMO can be structured as an independent practice association (IPA), a staff model, or a group model or as an exclusive provider organization (EPO) (Table 20-2).
Health Maintenance Organization. As mentioned, an HMO is a plan that contracts with a medical center or group of physicians to provide both preventive and acute care for the insured. HMOs are state-licensed health plans that are regulated by HMO laws, which require them to include preventive care, such as routine physical examinations and other services, as part of their benefits package. HMOs always require referrals to specialists, precertification, and preauthorization for hospital admissions, outpatient procedures, and treatments.

An HMO member is typically enrolled for a specified period (month, quarter, or year). If the HMO is a capitation plan, it receives a "per member per month" (pmpm) fee for each enrollee.

Providers receive payment according to various structures. The two most common structures are capitation and **fee for service.**

Capitation is payment in advance to the provider by the HMO for a contracted group of patients, regardless of how often the patients are seen and even if the patients are never seen by the provider. If the physician provides services that cost less than the capitation amount, the physician makes a profit. Conversely, if the physician's services cost more than the capitation amount, the physician takes a loss. Fees charged for services to group members may be billed directly to the IPA rather than to the patient. Fees for services to nonmember patients are handled in the same manner as any other fee for service. The payment structure is based on the type of HMO model and the contract negotiated between the HMO and the provider or providers. The most common HMO models are the IPA, staff model, group model, and EPO.

Independent Practice Association. An IPA is an independent group of physicians and other healthcare providers who are under contract to provide services to members of different HMOs, in addition to other insurance plans, usually at a fixed fee per patient. The physicians in the IPA, who have separately owned practices, formally organize a physician association and continue to practice in their own offices. A physician may be contracted with several IPAs. Payments to providers by an IPA can be structured either as a capitation or fee for service.

Staff Model. A staff model HMO hires physicians and pays them a salary. Rather than contracting with physicians to create a network, the HMO owns the network. Medical care is given or authorized by the patient's PCP. No capitation or fee for service payment structure is used with the staff model; however, the physicians may receive bonuses biannually or annually based on the number of patients treated and/or the cost savings.

Group Model. A group model HMO contracts with a multispecialty medical group to deliver care to its members. The HMO reimburses the physicians' group, which is responsible for reimbursing physician members and contracted healthcare facilities. This arrangement is similar to an IPA in that the multispecialty group may organize a physician association; however, the group members typically practice together in one facility. The payment structure to the providers can be either capitation or fee for service.

Exclusive Provider Organization. An EPO combines features of an HMO (e.g., an enrolled group or population, primary care providers, and an authorization system) and a PPO (e.g., flexible benefit design, and fee-for-service payments). The plan is referred to as "exclusive" because employers agree not to contract with any other plan. Members must choose medical care from network providers, with certain exceptions for emergency or out-of-area services. If a patient decides to seek care outside the network, he or she generally is not reimbursed for the cost of treatment. Technically, many HMOs can be considered EPOs; however, EPOs are regulated under insurance statutes rather than federal and state HMO regulations.
Preferred Provider Organizations. Sometimes called a *participating provider organization,* a PPO is a managed care network of physicians and hospitals that have joined to contract with insurance companies, employers, or other organizations to provide healthcare to subscribers for a discounted fee. The PPO model of managed healthcare preserves the fee-for-service concept that many physicians prefer. An insurer representing its clients contracts with a group of providers; the providers agree on a predetermined list of charges for all services, including those for both normal and complex

procedures. Unlike HMOs, PPOs have no capitation or prepaid care. Typically the patient pays deductibles or co-insurance payments of 20% to 25% of the predetermined charge, and the insurer pays the balance. A provider who joins a PPO does not need to alter the manner of providing care and continues to treat and bill the patients on a fee-for-service basis. When a patient covered under a PPO plan comes for treatment, the physician treats the patient and bills the PPO.

Technically PPOs are not HMOs, but they do have more patient care management than regular indemnity insurance plans. PPOs furnish their subscribers with a list of member-providers from which subscribers can receive healthcare at PPO rates. Rates are quite often lower than those charged to non-PPO patients. If a patient goes to a physician who is not in the PPO network, the out-of-pocket cost is higher.

CRITICAL THINKING APPLICATION   20-2

The physicians in the practice where Ann works are not members of a PPO that is often used in their geographic area. Many patients are confused when they have to pay a larger out-of-pocket fee for their medical services. How can Ann explain the reason for these higher fees to patients?

Blue Cross/Blue Shield

Blue Cross/Blue Shield is America's oldest and largest system of independent health insurers. It began in 1929 when an executive at Baylor University in Dallas came up with a plan for teachers to budget for their future hospital bills.

BC/BS offers incentive contracts to healthcare providers. If the provider chooses to sign a member contract, he or she becomes a **participating provider (PAR)**. Participating providers agree to write off the difference or balance between the amount charged by the provider and the approved fee established by the insurer. They also agree to bill the patient only for the deductible and co-pay/co-insurance amounts that are based on BC/BS-allowed fees and the full charge fee for any uncovered service. In turn, BC/BS agrees to reimburse providers directly and in a shorter time.

BC/BS identification (ID) cards (Figure 20-1) carry the subscriber's name and ID number with a three-character alphabetic prefix (or a single alphabetic prefix if it is a government policy). The letters are an important part of the number and must be included on the claim form.

Most BC/BS benefits are based on the fee-for-service or UCR schedules for payment, although certain types of managed care contracts also are available, primarily to group employers.

Medicaid

As mentioned, Title XIX of Public Law 89-97 under the Social Security Amendments of 1965 provided for agreements with states for assistance from the federal government in providing healthcare for the medically indigent. All states and the District of Columbia have Medicaid programs, but these programs vary widely. A person eligible for Medicaid in one state may not be eligible in another state, and the services may differ.

The federal government provides basic funding to the state, after which the states individually elect whether to provide funds for extension of benefits. The state determines the type and extent of medical care that will be covered within the minimum requirements established by the federal government. Some local areas and states are developing HMOs that serve only patients who qualify for Medicaid.

A physician may accept or decline to treat Medicaid patients. The physician who does accept Medicaid patients automatically agrees to accept Medicaid payment as payment in full for covered services. The patient cannot be billed for the difference between the Medicaid fee and the physician's normal fee. The patient can be billed for any services that are not covered by Medicaid. Eligibility for benefits is determined by the respective states.

Examples of those who qualify for benefits include the following:

- Individuals who are medically needy
- Recipients of Aid to Families with Dependent Children (AFDC)
- Individuals who receive Supplemental Security Income (SSI)
- Individuals who receive certain types of federal and state aid
- Individuals who are qualified Medicare beneficiaries (QMBs)—Medicaid pays for Medicare Part B premiums, deductibles, and co-insurance for qualified low-income elderly
- Individuals in institutions or receiving long-term care in nursing facilities and intermediate-care facilities

Depending on the state in which Medicaid is administered, Medicaid recipients are identified with a Benefits ID Card (BIC), a monthly sticker, a label, or a letter showing proof of eligibility. A BIC looks like a white credit card (Figure 20-2) and is verified by a

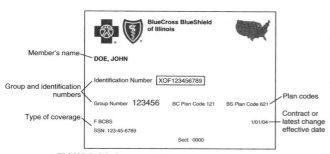

FIGURE 20-1 Blue Cross/Blue Shield identification card.

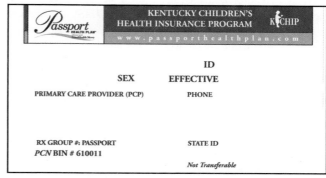

FIGURE 20-2 Medicaid Benefits ID Card.

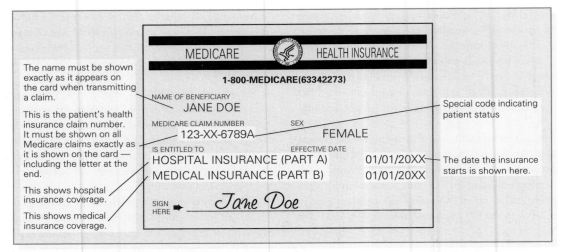

FIGURE 20-3 Medicare health identification card. (From Fordney MT: *Insurance handbook for the medical office*, ed 12, St Louis, 2012, WB Saunders.)

point of service (POS) device similar to a credit or debit card verification machine. The medical assistant must verify coverage each time the patient comes into the office, regardless of the type of ID the recipient is issued.

Medicare

Medicare is a federal health insurance program for the following:

- People age 65 years or older
- People who are permanently disabled or blind
- People receiving dialysis for permanent kidney failure or who have undergone kidney transplantation

Medicare was established July 1, 1966, under the Social Security Administration as a national health insurance program for those age 65 or older. Before Medicare was created, only 50% of the nation's elderly had any health insurance. Today Medicare is the world's largest insurance program. It serves more than 38 million older and disabled Americans. The scope of coverage increased in 1973 to include disabled persons younger than age 65 receiving Social Security benefits, railroad retirees, and civil service retirees. It also included disabled workers of any age, disabled widows, disabled dependent widowers, adults disabled before age 18 whose parents are eligible or are retired on Social Security benefits, children and adults with end-stage renal disease, and living kidney donors (including all expenses related to the kidney transplantation).

Medicare is administered by the CMS, which is a division of the Department of Health and Human Services (DHHS). The Medicare program is regulated by laws enacted by Congress. Medicare has two parts that cover healthcare services, Part A and Part B.

Medicare Part A

Part A is hospital insurance. Retired people 65 years of age or older and people who receive monthly Social Security or railroad retirement checks are automatically enrolled for hospital insurance benefits and pay no premiums for this insurance. Part A covers the following:

- Inpatient hospital care
- Skilled nursing facilities
- Home healthcare
- Hospice services

Part A is financed with special contributions deducted from employed individuals' salaries, with matching contributions from their employers. These sums are collected, along with regular Social Security contributions, from wages and self-employment income earned during a person's working years. A hospitalized patient on Medicare must pay a deductible toward hospital expenses. Typically the deductible amount changes annually by congressional enactment.

Medicare Part B

Part B is medical insurance. Those eligible for Part A are also eligible for Part B, but they must apply for this coverage and pay a monthly premium. Some federal employees and former federal employees who are not eligible for Social Security benefits and Part A may enroll in Part B. Certain disabled people younger than age 65 are also eligible. Part B covers the following:

- Outpatient hospital care
- Durable medical equipment
- Physicians' services
- Other medical services

A patient with Medicare Part B must meet an annual deductible before benefits become available, after which Medicare pays 80% of the covered, or allowed, benefits. Usually the physician accepts assignment of benefits for Medicare patients and is paid directly. In these cases the physician must accept the payment that Medicare allows and bills the patient only for 20% of the charge allowed by Medicare. If the physician does not accept assignment, the patient must pay the entire bill (which cannot be greater than the limit set by Medicare for nonparticipating physicians), and the patient receives a reimbursement check directly from Medicare.

Medicare health insurance cards (Figure 20-3) typically show nine numbers with a suffix of one or two alphabetic characters that denote the patient's status, such as wage earner (A), spouse of a wage earner (B), widow (D), or other designations. The health insurance claim number (HICN) or health identification card number (HIC#)

also identifies whether a person has Part A alone or both Part A and Part B insurance. If a patient's Medicare card has a claim number ending in the letter A, the HICN is the same as the person's Social Security number. If a patient's Medicare card has a claim number ending in B or D, the person's Social Security number is different from his or her issued HICN.

Many Medicare enrollees also carry private supplemental insurance that pays the deductible and the 20% co-payment not covered by Medicare. As mentioned, if the supplemental policy pays the deductible and the 20% co-payment, it is called a *Medigap policy.*

Medicare Advantage (formerly Medicare + Choice)

The Medicare Advantage program is commonly referred to as Part C, although Medicare does not label it as such. Medicare Advantage offers expanded benefits for a fee through private health insurance programs such as HMOs and PPOs that have contracts with Medicare. Patients must have a referral from their PCP before seeking treatment from another entity.

Medicare Part D

In 2006, drug and prescription benefits were added to Medicare, creating Part D. Medicare Part D gives Medicare recipients the option to choose, at a reduced cost, a prescription drug plan that pays for prescription drugs with just a small co-payment by the patient. Everyone with Medicare can get this coverage, which may help lower prescription drug costs and protect against higher costs in the future.

Private companies provide the Medicare prescription drug plans. Beneficiaries choose the drug plan and pay a monthly premium. As with other insurance, beneficiaries who decide not to enroll in a drug plan when they are first eligible may pay a penalty if they choose to join later.

TRICARE

TRICARE is the comprehensive healthcare program for family members of active duty personnel, military retirees and their eligible family members under the age of 65, and survivors of all uniformed services. (Before January, 1994, this program was known as CHAMPUS, created in 1966 under Public Law 89-614.)

The TRICARE program is managed by the military in partnership with civilian hospitals and clinics. It is designed to expand access to healthcare, ensure high-quality care, and promote medical readiness. All military hospitals and clinics are part of the TRICARE program and offer high-quality healthcare at low costs to plan users.

To be eligible for TRICARE, an individual must be a TRICARE or CHAMPVA recipient; must be entitled to retired, retainer, or equivalent pay; and must be listed in the Defense Department's Defense Enrollment Eligible Reporting System (DEERS), a computerized database that lists all active and retired service members. Coverage is also available for a TRICARE-eligible spouse under age 65 and dependent, unmarried children under age 21, or age 23 if in college full-time. Eligible spouses and children of active duty service members may enroll, as may TRICARE-eligible widows, widowers, and certain former spouses (those who have not remarried).

TRICARE offers three types of plans. More information about TRICARE eligibility requirements and the benefits of the three plans is available on the Evolve Web site *(evolve.elsevier.com/kinn).*

- TRICARE Prime: The Department of Defense's managed care plan, similar to a civilian HMO
- TRICARE Extra: A preferred provider network plan
- TRICARE Standard: A traditional fee-for-service plan (formerly CHAMPUS)

CHAMPVA

CHAMPVA, a health benefits program similar to TRICARE, was established in 1973 for the spouses and dependent children of veterans suffering total, permanent, service-connected disabilities and for surviving spouses and dependent children of veterans who had died as a result of service-related disabilities. The Department of Veterans Affairs (VA) shares with eligible beneficiaries the cost of certain healthcare services and supplies. After eligibility for CHAMPVA has been determined and ID cards issued, the insured may obtain covered services and supplies from any provider who is appropriately licensed or certified to perform the services offered. Exceptions include certain mental health categories and freestanding ambulatory surgical centers.

Workers' Compensation

Federal and all state legislatures require employers to maintain workers' compensation coverage to meet minimum standards, covering a majority of employees, for work-related illnesses and injuries, as long as the employee was not negligent in performing the assigned duties. The law also protects wage earners against the loss of wages and the cost of medical care resulting from occupational accident or disease. State laws differ as to the classes of employees included and the benefits provided.

No state's workers' compensation laws cover all employees. However, if a patient says that he or she was injured in the workplace or is suffering from a work-associated illness, the medical assistant should check with the patient's employer to verify the insurance coverage.

Compensation benefits include medical care benefits, weekly income replacement benefits for temporary disability, permanent disability settlements, and survivor benefits when applicable. The provider of service (e.g., doctor, hospital, therapist) accepts the workers' compensation payment as payment in full and does not bill the patient. Time limitations are set for the prompt reporting of workers' compensation cases. The employee is obligated to promptly notify the employer; the employer, in turn, must notify the insurance company and must refer the employee to a source of medical care.

The purpose of workers' compensation laws is to provide prompt medical care to an injured or ill worker so that the person may be restored to health and return to full earning capacity in as short a time as possible.

Disability Programs

Disability income insurance is a form of health insurance that provides periodic payments to an individual to replace income (actual or presumed) when a sickness, injury, or disability that is not a work-related condition results in the insured being unable to work.

PROCEDURE 20-2

Apply Third-Party Guidelines

CAAHEP COMPETENCIES: II.C.II. 1., IV.C.IV.6., IV.P.IV.3., V. P.V.6., VII.P.VII.2., IX.A.IX.2.

ABHES COMPETENCIES: 8.c

GOAL: *To ensure that claims are processed quickly and result in the highest allowable reimbursement.*

EQUIPMENT and SUPPLIES

- Insurance carrier contracts (sample provided in student workbook)
- Insurance carrier handbooks (sample provided in student workbook)
- Clerical supplies
- Forms from insurance carrier
- Insurance claim forms (CMS-1500)

PROCEDURAL STEPS

1. Determine the patient's health insurance plan.
   <u>PURPOSE:</u> To bill the correct health insurance plan for services rendered.
2. Review the rules and regulations that govern that particular organization.
   <u>PURPOSE:</u> To be sure that the claim is accurate according to the guidelines in place for the patient's policy.
3. Make certain that a signature is on file for the patient.
   <u>PURPOSE:</u> The signature authorizes the provider to release medical information to the insurance carrier and authorizes the carrier to pay the provider directly.
4. Determine the procedures and services that are to be billed on the claim.
   <u>PURPOSE:</u> To ensure that all procedures and services are included in the review of the managed care plan.

5. Determine whether all procedures and services to be billed are covered by the health insurance plan.
   <u>PURPOSE:</u> To understand which services are covered, which are not covered, and which require special forms for billing. This also assists the medical assistant in explaining to patients the benefits covered and the steps that must be taken for procedures and services requiring preapproval. Procedures and services that are not covered should not be billed on the health insurance claim form; the patient must pay for those services.
6. Make sure that the patient is aware of any procedures that will not be covered by the health insurance plan.
   <u>PURPOSE:</u> To ensure that the patient understands what is covered or not covered, what the patient's financial obligation is, and what special procedures (e.g., preauthorization) must be performed, when applicable.
7. Pay close attention to the blocks on the insurance claim form that are designated "for local use."
   <u>PURPOSE:</u> These blocks are designed to include information particular to certain policies. The carrier manual (for that insurance company) will provide instruction as to what information should be included in that block.
8. Submit the claim to the correct insurance company address or clearinghouse.

A disability insurance policy can be obtained through employer-sponsored and/or government-funded programs, or private policies can be purchased through a commercial insurance company.

COMMERCIAL INSURANCE

Many people are covered by health insurance issued by private (commercial) insurance companies (e.g., Aetna, Connecticut General, Metropolitan, and Prudential). Physicians and medical societies control neither the premiums paid nor the benefits received from such policies. For traditional types of policies, payment is normally made to the subscriber unless the subscriber or insured has authorized that payment be made directly to the physician.

UNDERSTANDING INSURANCE PLAN REQUIREMENTS

It is important for the medical assistant to be familiar with the particular procedures and processes for filing insurance claims set by individual insurance carriers, third-party payers, and government programs. The medical assistant also must be familiar with the handling of other tasks associated with an individual insurance plan or policy. Medical assistants should make it part of their routine to review the carrier's handbook, contracts, and required forms to familiarize themselves with the plan's benefits and preauthorization

and referral requirements. This equips the medical assistant to discuss those requirements with the patient and to prepare the required forms and insurance claims properly. Procedure 20-2 describes the process for properly applying third-party payer policies and procedures.

CRITICAL THINKING APPLICATION   20-3

Ann has been working with Mike Holland, who is having coronary bypass surgery in 1 week. Discuss the possible differences in Mike's coverage if he has Medicare, Medicaid, or commercial insurance. Should the medical assistant explain other bills, such as those to the hospital and anesthesiologist?

UTILIZATION MANAGEMENT/UTILIZATION REVIEW

Utilization management is a form of patient care review by health-care professionals who do not provide the care. It is a necessary component of managed care to control costs. A **utilization review** committee reviews individual cases to make certain that medical care services are medically necessary (the specificity of diagnosis coding is critical) and to study how providers use medical care resources. This committee also reviews all physician referrals and cases

Verification of Eligibility & Benefits Form

Today's Date: _____ Patient Name: _____

Date of Birth: _____ Social Security Number: _____

Primary Insurance: _____ Phone Number: _____

Plan Identification Number: _____ Group Number: _____

Insured's Name: _____ Insured's SS# _____

Is This Plan a: ☐ PPO In Network ☐ PPO Out of Network ☐ Commercial/Indemnity

If out of network:

What is the benefit for surgery? _____% of the doctor's fee or, $_____ for

procedure. Is the copay for office visits different? ☐ Yes ☐ No _____

Insurance Effective Date: _____ Deductible Amt: $_____

Has the deductible been met this year? ☐ Yes ☐ No If no, amount remaining: $_____

Is it a calendar year (if no, note renewal date) ☐ Yes ☐ No _____

Copay for Office Visits: $_____ Can we collect copay during post op period? ☐ Yes ☐ No

Do we bill separately for x-rays during the post op period (example: hands)? ☐ Yes ☐ No

Pre-Existing Conditions? _____

	Approved Facilities	Pre-Authorization Needed (Y/N)	Separate Deductible? Note $ and Max.	Dollar Out of Pocket Max Per Year?
Laboratory				
Diagnostic Tests				
Surgery				

Where Do We Send the Claim? _____

_____

I Spoke With: _____ Direct Line: _____

Employee Initials: _____

FIGURE 20-4 Sample Verification of Insurance Benefits form.

of emergency department visits and urgent care. For referrals, the committee reviews the referral and either approves or denies it, so it is important to submit exact documentation and precise statements. The medical assistant should contact the utilization review department directly; it should never be left to the patient or covered member to contact this department.

VERIFICATION OF INSURANCE BENEFITS

It is important to verify insurance benefits before providing services to patients. Verifying benefits is necessary to ensure that the patient

is covered by insurance and to determine what benefits will be paid for routine and special procedures and services. Verification protects the physician and the patient against unexpected medical care costs. An example of a Verification of Insurance Benefits form is shown in Figure 20-4. To verify benefits, the following steps should be taken (Procedure 20-3):

1. When a patient calls for an appointment, identify the type of insurance the patient has or the managed care organization to which the patient belongs.
2. When the patient arrives for the appointment, photocopy both sides of the patient's ID card. This is done to ensure the

PROCEDURE 20-3

Perform Verification of Eligibility and Benefits

CAAHEP COMPETENCIES: II.C.II. 1., IV.C.IV.6., IV.P.IV.3., V. P.V.6., VII.P.VII.6., IX.A.IX.2.

ABHES COMPETENCIES: 3.t

GOAL: *To confirm that the patient's insurance is in effect; to determine the benefits covered, exclusions, and noncovered procedures and services; and to determine whether precertifications are included or required.*

EQUIPMENT and SUPPLIES

- Patient record
- Verification of eligibility and benefits form
- Patient's insurance information
- Telephone and fax machine
- Pen

PROCEDURAL STEPS

1. When a patient calls for an appointment, identify the patient's insurance plan or managed care organization.
   <u>PURPOSE:</u> To prepare for and begin gathering required information to perform both insurance verification and insurance claim completion procedures.
2. At the time of the appointment, obtain and photocopy both sides of the patient's insurance ID card or cards.
   <u>PURPOSE:</u> To ensure that the correct ID, group, and policy numbers are obtained, in addition to the name, address, and phone number of the insurance carrier or carriers.
3. Complete the patient portion of the Verification of Eligibility and Benefits form, including demographic and insurance information for the patient and the contact information for the insurance plan. Complete one form for each of the patient's insurance plans.

<u>PURPOSE:</u> To document the information needed to perform the verification of eligibility and benefits. This form will later be filed in the patient's insurance record.

4. Contact the insurance carrier or carriers by phone to:
   - Verify that the patient is eligible for benefits and the insurance is in effect.
   - Determine the basic benefits, exclusions, and noncovered services of the insurance plan.
   - Determine whether there are deductibles, co-payments, or any other out-of-pocket expenses the patient is responsible for paying.
   - Determine whether preauthorization is required for referrals to specialists or for any procedures and/or services.
   <u>PURPOSE:</u> To confirm that the insurance is in effect and to determine benefits, preauthorizations, deductibles, and/or out-of-pocket expenses for which the patient is responsible.
5. Obtain the name, title, and phone number of the person to contact.
   <u>PURPOSE:</u> To identify and document the name of the individual providing the benefits and eligibility information and to serve as a reference if additional questions arise.
6. Document the information collected in the patient's medical record and on the Verification of Eligibility and Benefits form.

---

information obtained is correct, and because co-payments or amounts to be paid may appear on the back for hospital, office, and emergency department visits.

3. Contact the insurance carrier to verify that the patient is eligible for benefits and determine the basic benefits, exclusions or noncovered services; also find out whether preauthorization is required for referrals to specialists or for specific types of procedures and services.
4. Obtain the name, title, and phone number of the person contacted.
5. Document the information collected in the patient's medical record and on a verification of benefits form.
6. Give the patient a letter to read and sign that outlines his or her insurance plan's requirements and possible restrictions or noncovered items. This letter can also outline the patient's responsibility in helping with this process (Figure 20-5).
7. When referrals are required, explain the procedure to the patient; make sure he or she understands that without the referral, the patient is responsible for paying for the physician's services.
8. Collect any co-payments or deductibles.

▌ PRECERTIFICATION AND PREAUTHORIZATION

Many insurance companies require precertification or **preauthorization**, usually within 24 hours, if a patient is to be hospitalized or undergo certain procedures. In addition, most managed care systems require preauthorization for a patient to be referred to a specialist or even for certain laboratory tests or other procedures. Insurance claims for payment will be denied if proper authorization is not obtained.

When a new patient makes an appointment, it is standard procedure to ask what type of insurance the patient has and to collect the patient's and insured's personal, employment, and insurance information on a patient registration form. If the patient belongs to an HMO, the medical assistant should check that plan contract for precertification or preauthorization requirements. This information may be obtained verbally, but it should also be documented in writing or in the electronic medical record and should be obtained before any procedures or treatments are begun. The following information should be obtained and recorded on the preauthorization form (Figure 20-6) before the insurance carrier is contacted:

- Patient's name, address, phone number, and identification number or numbers

Doctor Sample, M.D.

1234 Any Street

Any Town, USA 12345

123-456-7890

Notice to Patients:

Due to multiple policy changes for the different insurance companies, this office is unable to keep up with the requirements for each patient's individual policy. There are multiple requirements stated in your policy; some of which are on the back of your insurance card and some of which are not.

Some of the most common requirements are:
- Referrals to or from Primary Care Physicians
- Prior Authorizations for some Procedures and Services
  - Hospital Admission
  - Pre-Admission Testing
  - Surgery
  - Outpatient Procedures: Laboratory, Radiology, etc.
- Co-pay amounts
  - Primary Care Physicians
  - Specialists
  - Testing: Laboratory, X-ray, etc.
- Pre-Admission Testing
- Second Opinions

Our office checks on these particular requirements for our patients. But if you do not ask the insurance company about a particular requirement, <u>point blank</u>, they will not volunteer any information.

IT IS YOUR RESPONSIBILITY TO BE AWARE OF AND FULFILL ALL THE REQUIREMENTS OF YOUR INSURANCE POLICY.

Our office will be happy to assist you in any matter in accomplishing this task — **but you are responsible for informing us of your insurance company requirements.**

I understand that should the insurance information I have provided be incorrect, and a claim is denied, I will be responsible for the bill.

Patient's Signature: _____ Date: _____

FIGURE 20-5 Sample Patient Responsibility Notification.

- Provider's name, address, phone number, and provider identification number (PIN)
- Insurance plan's name, address, and contact person
- Telephone number (or numbers) of the contact person and the fax number
- Preliminary diagnosis
- Planned surgery, diagnostic test, or reason for referring the patient to a specialist
- Name, address, and phone number of the facility or specialist

- Co-payment amount or deductible
- Hospital benefits for inpatient and outpatient surgery
- Participating hospitals, radiology service providers, laboratories, and physicians

Once the information has been collected, it should be faxed to the insurance company. In case of an emergency, the authorization may be obtained by phone; however, the form should be faxed as soon as possible afterward. The form is faxed back to the provider by the insurance carrier with the authorization number and other vital information.

Mary Jo Smith
College Clinic
4567 Broad Avenue, WH
Telephone No.: (555) 486-9002
Fax No.:(555) 487-8976

MANAGED CARE PLAN AUTHORIZATION REQUEST

**TO BE COMPLETED BY PRIMARY CARE PHYSICIAN
OR OUTSIDE PROVIDER**

☐ Health Net   ☐ Met Life
☐ Pacificare   ☐ Travelers
☐ Secure Horizons ☐ Pru Care
☐ Other

Member/Group No.: 54098XX

Patient Name: Louann Campbell   Date: 7-14-20XX

☐ Male   ☐ Female   Birthdate: 4-7-1952   Home Telephone Number: (555) 450-1666

Address: 2516 Encina Avenue, Woodland Hills, XY 12345-0439

Primary Care Physician: Gerald Practon, MD   Provider ID #: TC 14021

Referring Physician: Gerald Practon, MD   Provider ID #: TC 14021

Referred to: Raymond Skeleton, MD   Office Telephone Number: (555) 486-9002

Address: 4567 Broad Avenue, Woodland Hills, XY 12345

Diagnosis Code: 724.2   Diagnosis Low back pain

Diagnosis Code: 722.10   Diagnosis Sciatica

Treatment Plan: Orthopedic consultation and evaluation of lumbar spine; R/O herniated disc L4-5

Authorization requested for: ☐ Consult Only ☐ Treatment Only ☐ Consult/Treatment

☐ Consult/Procedure/Surgery   ☐ Diagnostic Tests

Procedure Code: 99244   Description: New patient consultation

Procedure Code: Description:

Place of service: ☒ Office ☐ Outpatient ☐ Inpatient ☐ Other   Number of Visits: 1

Facility: Length of Stay:

List of potential future consultants (i.e., anesthetists, surgical assistants or medical/surgical):

Physician's Signature: *Gerald Practon, MD*

TO BE COMPLETED BY PRIMARY CARE PHYSICIAN

PCP Recommendations: See above   PCP Initials: GP

Date eligibility checked: 7-14-20XX   Effective Date: 1-15-20XX

TO BE COMPLETED BY UTILIZATION MANAGEMENT

Authorized: Auth. No.   Not Authorized

Deferred: Modified:

Comments:

FIGURE 20-6 Sample preauthorization and/or referral form.

Obtaining preauthorization for referrals or certain procedures and services is required. Typically, the PCP, or "gatekeeper," is responsible for obtaining the authorization. A gatekeeper can be a PCP, a general or family practitioner, an internist, a pediatrician, and in some instances an obstetrician or a gynecologist.

Referral is a term used in managed care when a patient is referred from a PCP to a specialist. When completing a referral form, it is imperative that all necessary information be included (Procedure 20-4). Approval or denial of a referral can take anywhere from a few minutes to a few days. The three types of referral are as follows:

- A *regular referral* usually takes 3 to 10 working days for review and approval. This type of referral is used when the physician believes that the patient must see a specialist to continue treatment.

- An *urgent referral* usually takes about 24 hours for approval. This type of referral is used when an urgent situation occurs but is not life-threatening.

- A *STAT referral* can be approved by telephone immediately after it is faxed to the utilization review department. A STAT referral is used in an emergency situation as indicated by the physician.

A regular referral is the most common type and can be inconvenient for the patient. With most managed care plans, the member services department must be contacted to check the status of a referral. Remember this cardinal rule: never tell the patient the referral has been approved unless you have a hard copy of the authorization.

Authorization is a term used in managed care for an approved referral. A referral becomes an authorization after it is reviewed by

PROCEDURE 20-4

Perform Preauthorization (Precertification) and/or Referral Procedures

CAAHEP COMPETENCIES: II.C.II. 1., IV.C.IV.6., IV.P.IV.3., V. P.V.6., VII.P.VII.4., VII.P.VII.5., IX.A.IX.2.

ABHES COMPETENCIES: 3.u

GOAL: *Using the information in the case study (found in the Study Guide), to obtain precertification from a patient's HMO for requested services or procedures.*

EQUIPMENT and SUPPLIES

- Patient record
- Precertification/preauthorization form
- Referral form
- Patient's insurance information, including telephone and fax numbers of insurance carrier
- Telephone and fax machine
- Pen

PROCEDURAL STEPS

1. Assemble the necessary documents and equipment.
   <u>PURPOSE:</u> To avoid wasting time searching for information or equipment needed to perform the task.

2. Examine the patient's record and determine the service or procedure for which preauthorization is being requested, including, if applicable, the specialist's name and phone number and the reason for the request.
   <u>PURPOSE:</u> To correctly complete the required form for gaining authorization from the patient's insurance carrier for the specified treatment.

3. Complete the preauthorization and/or referral form, providing all pertinent information requested.
   <u>PURPOSE:</u> To document the required information for the insurance carrier, including:

- The patient's demographic and insurance information
- The physician's identification information, including the National Provider Identification (NPI) and/or group ID number or numbers
- The diagnosis and planned procedure or treatment, or the name and contact information of the physician to whom the patient is being referred.

4. Proofread the completed form.
   <u>PURPOSE:</u> To ensure the accuracy of the information.

5. Fax the completed form to the patient's insurance carrier.
   <u>PURPOSE:</u> To inform the insurance carrier of the patient's medical condition and to request the following:
- Preauthorization for the specified treatment
- A verification or authorization number
- Confirmation of the specific number of procedures, services, or treatment sessions allowed and/or authorization for referral of the patient to a specialist

6. Place a copy of the returned, completed approval form in the patient's medical record.
   <u>PURPOSE:</u> To ensure that the approved procedure and service (or procedures and services) and/or the referral is properly filed for future reference.

utilization management and/or the medical director and has been approved. If a referral is approved, the PCP's office receives a copy of the authorization by mail or fax. Always review the authorization thoroughly. The patient will receive a letter with an authorization number and the approved services. The patient must bring the authorization to the specialist's office on the day the services will be provided. An authorization provides the following information to both the referring PCP and the specialist:

- An authorization code, which may be alphabetic, numeric, or alphanumeric
- The date on which the referral request was received by the utilization review department
- The date on which the referral was approved and its expiration date
  - An authorization is typically good for 60 days.
  - If the authorization expires and services have not been provided, an extension may be requested. Utilization management will change the expiration date and fax a copy to the PCP and specialist or will generate a new authorization with a new number.

- If services are provided after the expiration date, the claim will be denied. If this happens, contact utilization management or member services, ask for an extension, and answer a few questions. Sometimes the patient, the specialist's office, or both must be involved in this process.
- A diagnosis code
- The name, address, and telephone number of the contracted specialist where services will be provided
  - Sometimes the PCP refers the patient to a specialist but does not receive approval for that specialist and must get approval for another.
  - Always be sure that any specialist to whom the physician refers a patient is contracted with the same managed care plan as the PCP.
- The Comments section: this is the most critical area of a referral, because this area designates the services that have been approved.
  - It includes the specified number of authorized visits to the specialist.

○ An authorization may be issued for (1) evaluation only, (2) evaluation and treatment plan, (3) evaluation and biopsy, (4) evaluation and one injection, and so on.

○ When authorization for only an evaluation and/or treatment plan is given, the medical assistant must inform the patient that no treatment will be given; only an evaluation and/or treatment plan will be provided.

The PCP's office is notified if a referral is denied because of insufficient information or lack of medical necessity. Some medical groups notify both the PCP and the patient. When the PCP's office provides the utilization management committee with the necessary information, the referral is reviewed again.

Managed care changes on a day-to-day basis. To compete in this market, some insurance companies have added a benefit that allows a member or patient to self-refer (meaning an authorization is not required to see a specialist). Many plans for senior citizens now have a **self-referral** and a co-payment, in addition to some other insurance coverage. The procedure for obtaining a self-referral is essentially the same as for a provider of service. An authorization form is completed by the patient or with the assistance of the referred provider and faxed to the insurance company for approval.

CRITICAL THINKING APPLICATION   20-4

Ann has obtained precertification and knows the benefits that will be paid toward Jeff England's bill. Discuss how Ann can best explain insurance benefits, exclusions, co-insurance, deductibles, and allowable amounts to Jeff. How can she explain the reasons for and the process of preauthorization to patients?

FEE SCHEDULES

A healthcare practitioner has three commodities to sell: time, judgment (expertise), and services. In every case the healthcare practitioner must place an estimate on the value of these services. Fees for medical procedures and services differ from office to office based on the type of practice and the needs of the facility. The physician or physicians establishing the practice normally set the fees for procedures and services. In the past, most physicians worked on a fee-for-service basis; that is, patients were charged for the provider's service based on each individual service performed.

In recent years, **third-party payers**, particularly government and managed healthcare organizations, have greatly influenced what healthcare providers can charge by establishing the allowable charge. The **allowable charge** (or **allowable amount**) is the maximum that third-party payers will pay for a particular procedure or service (see Procedure 20-4). When healthcare providers establish a fee schedule, other factors influence what the charge for a particular procedure or service can be; these factors include the RBRVS and the lesser used RVS.

As discussed earlier in this chapter, the CMS developed the first comprehensive RBRVS-based fee schedule, which was adopted by Medicare in 1992. The RBRVS-based fee schedule adjusts fees for differences in resources used to provide each service. The amount of resources required to perform a service is determined through the use of RVUs, which are assigned to the CPT codes developed by the

AMA with an adjustment for overhead costs in different geographic areas. Since Medicare's introduction of RBRVS, most third-party payers have adopted similar approaches in developing their fees.

Resource-Based Relative Value Scale

The RBRVS is one of the outcomes of the Medicare Physician Payment Reform that was enacted in the Omnibus Budget Reconciliation Act of 1989 (usually called *OBRA '89*). Originally, Medicare Part B had paid physicians using a fee-for-service system based on UCR charges. However, implementation of the RBRVS in 1992 changed this system to a fee scale consisting of three parts:

- Physician work
- Charge-based professional liability expenses
- Charge-based overhead

The physician work component includes the degree of effort invested by a physician in a particular service or procedure and the time it consumed. The professional liability and overhead components are computed by the CMS.

The RBRVS fee schedule is designed to provide national uniform payments, after adjustment to reflect the differences in practice costs across geographic areas. The fee schedule includes a conversion factor, which is a single national number applied to all services paid under the fee schedule. Conversion factors are changed by Congress, usually annually, at the request of the CMS.

Depending on the contract between the provider and the insurance carrier (especially Medicare, Medicaid, and other government programs), the provider either writes off the difference between the RBRVS schedule and his or her fee or passes on the nonallowed portion of the charge to the guarantor for payment.

Contracts between the provider of service and the insurance payer vary greatly, depending on the insurance or third-party payer. It is important for the medical assistant to know the contract terms for each different third-party payer and, upon receipt of payment, to examine the EOB from the insurance carrier closely to ensure that all benefits have been reimbursed appropriately and correctly.

DEDUCTIBLES AND CO-INSURANCE

Many types of health insurance plans (e.g., indemnity, managed care, and Medicare) require a deductible and co-insurance amount that the patient must pay out of pocket. These plans typically have an annual deductible amount the patient must pay before the plan pays anything. In addition, members usually must also pay a percentage of each charge (co-insurance payment). Most indemnity plans have an annual out-of-pocket limit on the amount members must pay for co-insurance payments. This type of plan takes the major expense out of medical bills and helps keep premium costs down.

Consider this example, Mrs. Jones' plan has a $500 deductible, after which the insurance company pays 95% of all charges; this leaves Mrs. Jones with a 5% co-insurance expense in addition to the deductible. She also is responsible for a $1,000 out-of-pocket expense maximum, which means that once Mrs. Jones has paid $1,000 total, the insurance company pays 100% of any balance remaining. Mrs. Jones has incurred a $10,000 charge for cardiac surgery performed by her physician.

- In Figure 20-7, Column A shows that Mrs. Jones' total out-of-pocket expense is $1,000. She paid the $500 deductible,

	Column A	Column B
Total charge	$10,000	$20,000
Deductible (paid by Mrs. Jones)	(500)	(500)
5% (Mrs. Jones' portion)	(500)	(500)
Total amount paid by Mrs. Jones	$1000	$1000
Total amount paid by insurance	$9000	$19,000

FIGURE 20-7 Calculation of deductible and co-insurance.

	Column A	Column B
Total charge	$10,000	$20,000
Deductible (paid by Mrs. Jones)	(500)	(500)
5% (Mrs. Jones' portion)	(500)	(500)
Allowable amount $8500	(1500)	
Allowable amount $8500 with write off		(1500)
Total amount paid by Mrs. Jones	$2500	$1000
Total amount paid by insurance	$7500	$17,500

FIGURE 20-8 Calculation of allowable amount.

and 5% of $10,000, or an additional $500. The insurance company then paid the remaining balance of $9,000.

- In Figure 20-8, Column B shows that the cardiac surgery in this instance cost $20,000. Mrs. Jones' total out-of-pocket expense remains $1,000; therefore, in this case the insurance company is responsible for payment of the balance of $19,000. Because her maximum out-of-pocket expense, according to the plan described, is $1,000, even though the charges were doubled, she still pays only the $1,000 total out-of-pocket expense.

With Medicare and some other plans, a limit is placed on the amount that will be reimbursed for any procedure or service. This limit is called an *allowable amount*. The allowable amount can be all or part of a charge for a service or procedure. For example, a provider typically charges $80 for a Level I office visit; however, the insurance company benefit's allowable amount is only $60. Depending on the contract between the provider and the insurance carrier, the provider will either write off the $20 difference or pass on the nonallowed portion of the charge to the guarantor for payment. Because contracts between carriers and providers vary greatly, it is important for the medical assistant to examine the EOB from the insurance carrier closely and to be knowledgeable about the contract provisions between the provider of service and all insurance carriers the provider uses.

Deductibles and co-insurance are generally deducted from the total charge for services rendered; however, depending on the policies and procedures of the provider, they can be calculated for each individual charge. Allowable amounts are almost always deducted from an individual charge.

The steps for calculating deductible, co-insurance, and allowable amounts are presented in Procedure 20-5. Calculating deductibles, co-insurance, and allowable amounts is relatively simple. The

deductible and co-insurance are subtracted from the total charge for the services and procedures. The sum becomes the patient's responsibility or, if the patient has a secondary insurance, it can be billed to the secondary insurance carrier. Deductibles and co-insurance are generally deducted from the total charge for services rendered; however, depending on the policies and procedures of the provider, they can be calculated for each individual charge. Allowable amounts are almost always deducted from an individual charge.

Using the example in Figure 20-7, if the allowable amount for Mrs. Jones' $10,000 cardiac surgery is $8,500, the $1,500 difference between the physician's charge and the allowed amount would be either written off or passed on to the patient as an out-of-pocket expense. In Figure 20-8, Column A, a line has been added to show the $8,500 allowable amount and that $1,500 has been billed to the patient. In Column B, the amount has been written off, or absorbed as a cost, by the provider. Notice, too, that the insurance carrier pays $1,500 less for the cardiac surgery charge in Figure 20-8 than in Figure 20-7.

CRITICAL THINKING APPLICATION   20-5

An elderly patient comes to the office complaining that Medicare did not pay her bill in full. "Medicare is supposed to pay 80% of all of my bills, and I have already paid my portion," she insists. What information does Ann need to get to the bottom of this problem? How can she explain situations like this to patients?

Patient Education

Understanding how insurance plans handle reimbursement of benefits is challenging both for patients and for medical assistants. However, it is important that patients understand how their insurance works. Many people, especially elderly individuals, believe that if they have health insurance, all charges for their healthcare will be covered. They do not always understand the intricacies of deductibles, co-payments, medical necessity, and allowable charges.

The responsibilities of a medical assistant include keeping the patient informed and answering questions as they arise. Often medical facilities provide their patients with informational brochures that explain how health insurance and reimbursement work and give definitions of some of the more common terms used in the insurance claims process. If patients are well advised and comfortable with insurance facts before treatment begins, the medical experience will go more smoothly, and collection of fees not covered by the carrier will be easier. The medical assistant must use good communication skills, patience, and tact when discussing third-party reimbursement issues with patients.

Legal and Ethical Issues

Throughout their careers, medical assistants must remember that an individual's medical record is personal and private. Conversations between patients and their healthcare providers (and staff) are considered privileged communication. Nearly every day a medical assistant is in a position to read and hear information of a private medical nature, and both the caregiver and the patient expect that this information will not leave the medical office.

PROCEDURE 20-5

Perform Deductible, Co-insurance, and Allowable Amount Calculations

CAAHEP COMPETENCIES: I.F.3., II.C.II. 1., IV.C.IV.6., IV.P.IV.3., V. P.V.6., VII.P.VII.1.2., IX.A.IX.2.

ABHES COMPETENCIES: 3.t

GOAL: *To calculate the patient's out-of-pocket expense or the amount to be billed to a secondary insurance carrier and to determine the amounts to be written off or passed on to the patient for payment.*

EQUIPMENT and SUPPLIES

- Explanation of benefits (EOB) form; *or* explanation of Medicare benefits [EOMB]) form, remittance advice (RA) form, or verification of eligibility and benefits form
- Patient accounts receivable ledger
- Calculator
- Pen
- Paper

PROCEDURAL STEPS

1. Assemble the required materials and equipment.
   <u>PURPOSE:</u> To save time looking for the information needed to properly perform the procedure.
2. Using the EOB, EOMB, and/or the RA form and/or the Verification of Eligibility and Benefits form, in addition to the patient accounts receivable ledger, perform the following:
   - Write down the total charge from the EOB and/or the patient accounts receivable ledger.
   - Subtract the deductible amount from the total charge. If the deductible exceeds the total amount, subtract only that amount of the deductible that equals the total charge, and stop—do not continue with the other steps. Proceed to the other steps only after all of the patient's deductible has been paid.
   <u>PURPOSE:</u> To calculate and record the appropriate amount of deductible that must be paid by the patient according to the terms of his or her insurance policy.
3. If it is determined that all of the patient's deductible has been met, identify the co-insurance amount that the patient must pay (e.g., 20%).
   - Multiply this amount (e.g., 20%) by the total charge.
   - Subtract the sum from the total charge balance.

<u>PURPOSE:</u> To calculate and record the appropriate amount of co-insurance that must be met (and paid) by the patient according to the terms of his or her insurance policy.

4. Record the deductible and, if applicable, co-insurance amount or amounts on separate lines in the patient balance due column of the patient's account receivable ledger.
   - The sum becomes the patient's responsibility.
   - If the patient has a secondary insurance carrier, the sum can be billed to the secondary insurance carrier.

<u>PURPOSE:</u> To maintain a current balance and audit trail on the patient accounts receivable ledger and, when appropriate, to submit a statement to the patient for payment and/or submit a claim to a secondary insurance company.

<u>NOTE:</u> If an allowable amount is shown on the EOB, EOMB, or RA and it is less than the amount of either the total charge or the individual charge for the date of service, proceed to steps 5 and 6. Otherwise, stop here.

5. Subtract the allowable amount of each individual charge from the actual (billed) charge.
6. Record the difference either in the adjustments or patient balance column.
   - If the provider of service writes off the difference as a courtesy, hardship adjustment, or as part of the contract the provider has with the insurance company, the amount is recorded in the adjustments column.
   - If the patient is responsible for paying the difference between the actual charge and the allowable amount, the amount is recorded in the patient balance column.

<u>PURPOSE:</u> To adjust and reconcile the patient accounts receivable ledger and deduct the appropriate allowable amounts from the patient ledger; or, to pass those amounts on to the patient for payment.

Unauthorized release of medical information carries over into the insurance claims processing area. Even though the patient expects the insurance form to be filled out and submitted for payment, this cannot be done without proper written release. This medical release form should be kept in the patient's chart, and it should be updated on a regular basis.

CLOSING COMMENTS

Managed care has often been criticized by the news media. Some types of managed care can create a physician-patient barrier that did not exist during the fee-for-service era. An extra effort in human relations by the medical assistant can help to overcome this barrier and put the patient at ease.

SUMMARY OF SCENARIO

There is still a lot of information on health insurance to digest, but Ann is now much more comfortable with its concepts and no longer feels that understanding the various topics is impossible. Ann understands that there are many different types of insurance carriers, including federal and state programs, commercial carriers, health maintenance organizations, and preferred provider organizations, and that each of these programs offers different benefits and has different requirements. She also understands that the best way to remember all the carriers and the benefits offered is to keep an up-to-date manual or computer record that keeps track of addresses, phone numbers, and benefits information for each carrier. In addition, she has learned that failure to verify benefits and

eligibility or authorization for referrals, treatments, or procedures can result in a denial of payment for services rendered.

Understanding how to calculate the deductibles, co-insurance, and allowed amounts for procedures and services benefits both the provider and patient. The provider's productivity, income, and losses can be easily tracked, and the patient can be educated as to the exact amounts he or she is responsible for paying.

Now that Ann understands the basics of health insurance, she can look forward to learning the procedure for completing insurance claim forms for various insurance carriers for reimbursement.

SUMMARY OF LEARNING OBJECTIVES

1. **Define, spell, and pronounce the terms listed in the vocabulary.**
   Spelling and pronouncing medical terms correctly bolster the medical assistant's credibility. Knowing the definition of these terms promotes confidence in communication with patients and co-workers.

2. **Discuss the purpose of health insurance.**
   Medical assistants should have an understanding of the purpose of health insurance. This will help in the workplace not only by facilitating their knowledge of the subject, but also in helping them educate patients. The trend for insurance policies to encourage preventive medicine can be appreciated.

3. **Differentiate among the various types of insurance policies.**
   Insurance policies fall into many different categories and are available in many different forms. The ability to differentiate among the various types of insurance policies gives medical assistants a solid background in what is available on the market, what is included in each policy category, and the function of each. It is also important for medical assistants to understand and appreciate that there are still many people in this country who cannot afford and do not receive high-quality healthcare.

4. **Explain the numerous classifications of insurance benefits available.**
   Insurance packages are often tailored to the needs of each individual or group, and the ways to combine benefits are limitless. Health insurance policies normally contain a combination of the different benefits, such as surgical, medical, hospitalization, and major medical.

5. **Explain how insurance benefits are determined.**
   Benefits are determined and paid in one of several ways: indemnity schedules, service benefit plans, UCR fees, and resource-based relative value scales. Medical assistants should become familiar with each of these methods and be able to differentiate the types of schedules, fees, and scales to determine which insurance payer uses them and how they affect reimbursement to the physician.

6. **Differentiate among the different types of managed care options.**
   "Managed care" is a broad term used to describe a variety of health plans developed to provide healthcare services at lower costs. When the

medical assistant is employed in a medical facility, he or she will undoubtedly be working with many types of managed care plans. Therefore, it is important to know the various types (e.g., HMO, IPA, and PPO) and understand how each one functions. The medical assistant should be well informed about the managed care policies most frequently seen in the practice.

7. **List and discuss other major third-party payers.**
   Other major third-party payers the medical assistant should become familiar with are BC/BS, Medicaid, Medicare, CHAMPVA, TRICARE, and workers' compensation. Medicare is the largest third-party insurer in the country, making high-quality healthcare affordable for the elderly and select other groups. Medicaid is another government-sponsored healthcare plan for individuals who qualify for these benefits. Workers' compensation covers employees who are injured or who become ill as a result of accidents or adverse conditions in the workplace. Disability programs reimburse individuals for monetary losses incurred as a result of an inability to work for reasons other than those covered under workers' compensation. The medical assistant should be familiar with the major plans that are presented in the practice.

8. **Explain the procedure for verifying insurance benefits.**
   Many problems for both the patient and the medical office can be prevented if the medical assistant develops and follows a procedure for verifying insurance benefits before services are rendered. This procedure includes gathering as much information as possible about the demographics of the patient and his or her insurance coverage. A pragmatic and tactful discussion with all new patients, to explain the medical office's established policy on insurance claims processing and the collection of fees not covered by the patient's policy, will pay off in the end.

9. **Discuss the different types of fee schedules.**
   It is important for both the medical assistant and patients to realize that fees for medical procedures and services differ from office to office based on the type of practice and the needs of the facility. Until the advent of managed care, most physicians operated on a fee-for-service basis in which the provider would render his or her services and charge accordingly. In recent years, government and managed care organizations have

greatly influenced what healthcare providers can charge. Many third-party payers base reimbursements on what is referred to as the allowable charge. Other fee schedule types include the RVS and the RBRVS.

10. **Explain how to make managed care referrals and obtain precertifications.**

Obtaining precertification, also known as *preauthorization,* and making referrals must be done according to the guidelines of the individual insurance companies. If the medical assistant is uncertain about the procedure, he or she should always refer to the company's insurance manual or check the process online, if possible.

11. **Perform eligibility and verification of benefits procedures.**

Verification of insurance benefits is done to make certain that physicians are reimbursed for the services they provide for patients and also so that patients know their financial responsibility in advance. The process for verifying insurance benefits is outlined in Procedure 20-3.

12. **Perform a preauthorization procedure.**

Preauthorization helps the medical assistant to ensure that the physician will be paid for the procedures and services provided to the patient. The process for obtaining preauthorization (precertification) is outlined in Procedure 20-4.

13. **Demonstrate how insurance benefits are determined by calculating deductible and co-insurance payments.**

Medical assistants should become proficient at calculating the amounts due to the physician, considering deductibles, co-payments, and co-insurance amounts. The process for calculating insurance payments is outlined in Procedure 20-5.

CONNECTIONS

Study Guide Connection: Go to Chapter 20 Study Guide. Read the Case Study and Workplace Applications and complete the assignments. Do online research for answers to the questions in the Internet Activities associated with third-party reimbursement.

Evolve Connection: For more information on third-party reimbursement, go to *evolve.elsevier.com/kinn* and visit related Web links for Chapter 20. Click on the Medical Assisting Exam Review and do the practice questions to sharpen your test-taking skills. To learn more about office software, do the exercises for the AltaPoint demonstration found on the CD.

THE HEALTH INSURANCE CLAIM FORM

Carline A. Dalgleish, Sharon Oliver, and Alexandra Patricia Adams

21

SCENARIO

The school where Machelle Van Cleve receives her medical assistant training offers an optional job-shadowing module. For her assignment she chose a nearby health center, where she observed the administrative responsibilities of the medical assistants employed in this multispecialty practice. Machelle found that some of the offices were organized and efficient, whereas others lacked a structured routine, especially in the insurance department. Machelle, a detail-oriented person who enjoyed her studies related to billing and coding, heard numerous comments from employees in the administrative area related to the volumes of work in the billing offices. Her office manager explained that the mountainous paperwork was created as a result of managed care requirements, rejected claims needing further research, and inconsistencies in the demands of the various insurance companies.

Machelle agreed that keeping up with the requirements and regulations of the many third-party payers and government entitlement programs must be an overwhelming task. She concluded that billing and reimbursement are at the heart of the medical facility, and the correct completion of insurance claim forms is central to the success of the practice. She realized that becoming familiar with the complexities of the insurance claims process would be challenging, but she was convinced that through education, organization, and dedication she could become a valuable employee and an advocate for the patients who needed her assistance in resolving issues related to their claims for reimbursement.

While studying this chapter, think about the following questions:

- What will Machelle find is one of the most important, and basic, tasks that must be done properly before even beginning the insurance claim preparation?
- Why is it important for Machelle to learn the specific insurance billing requirements of different insurance companies and third-party payers?
- What has Machelle learned about the importance of auditing claims before they are sent to the insurance carrier for reimbursement?
- What does Machelle know about reimbursement and insurance claims follow-up?

LEARNING OBJECTIVES

1. Define, spell, and pronounce the terms listed in the vocabulary.
2. Discuss the differences between paper claims and electronic claims.
3. Understand the guidelines for completing the CMS-1500 Health Insurance Claim Form.
4. Explain how to complete each of the blocks of the CMS-1500 claim form.
5. Gather information for use on insurance claim forms.
6. Complete a CMS-1500 claim form appropriately for various federal, state, and commercial third-party payers.
7. Differentiate between "clean" and "dirty" claims.
8. Discuss methods of preventing claims rejections.
9. Describe ways of checking the status of claims.

VOCABULARY

assignment of benefits The transfer of the patient's legal right to collect benefits for medical expenses to the provider of those services, authorizing the payment to be sent directly to the provider.

audit A process done prior to claims submission to examine claims for accuracy and completeness. An audit can be performed manually or, if computer billing software is used, electronically.

audit trail The path left by a transaction when it has been completed; often referred to when tracking medical services used by patients or researching claims.

clean claims Insurance claim forms that have been completed correctly (no errors or omissions) and can be processed and paid promptly if they meet the restrictions on covered services and blocks.

clearinghouse A centralized facility to which insurance claims are transmitted. Clearinghouses separate, check, and redistribute claims electronically to various insurance carriers and may offer additional services to the physician.

direct billing A method of electronic claims submission that uses computer software to allow a provider to submit an insurance claim directly to an insurance carrier for payment.

dirty claims Claims that contain errors or omissions; such claims must be corrected and resubmitted to an insurance carrier to obtain reimbursement.

electronic claims Claims that are submitted to insurance processing facilities using a computerized medium, such as direct data entry, direct wire, dial-in telephone digital fax, or personal computer download or upload.

electronic data interchange (EDI) The transfer of data back and forth between two or more entities using an electronic medium.

electronic (or digital) signature A scanned signature or other such mark that is accepted as proof of approval of and/or responsibility for the content of an electronic document.

Employer Identification Number (EIN) The number used by the Internal Revenue Service that identifies a business or individual functioning as a business entity for income tax reporting.

incomplete claim A claim that is missing information and is returned to the provider for correction and resubmission. Also called an *invalid claim*.

intelligent character recognition (ICR) The electronic scanning of printed blocks as images and the use of special software to recognize these images (or characters) as ASCII text for uploading into a computer database.

National Provider Identifier (NPI) A lifetime number consisting of 10 digits that Medicare used to replace the Provider Identification Number (PIN) and the Unique Provider Identification Number (UPIN). CMS met the compliance requirement of using the NPI on all claims in May 2008; most insurance carriers have followed the CMS and now also use the NPI.

paper (hard copy) claims Insurance claims that have been completed manually, on paper, and sent by surface mail.

provider Any company, individual, or group that provides medical, diagnostic, or treatment services to a patient.

provider identification number (PIN) Numbers assigned to providers by a carrier for use in the submission of claims.

rejected claims Claims returned unpaid to the provider for clarification of any question; these claims must be corrected before resubmission.

Unique Provider Identification Number (UPIN) A number assigned by fiscal intermediaries to identify providers on claims for services.

universal claim form The form developed by the Health Care Financing Administration (HCFA; now the Centers for Medicare and Medicaid Services [CMS]) and approved by the American Medical Association (AMA) for use in submitting all government-sponsored claims. Also known as the *CMS-1500 Health Insurance Claim Form*.

Medical insurance means many things to many people. To some, it is a mound of paperwork. To others, it is a mass of confusion and regulations that seem to constantly change. To a patient with an illness or injury, health insurance helps defray the high costs associated with healthcare.

The **universal claim form**, originally called the HCFA-1500, was first developed in 1988 by the Health Care Financing Administration (HCFA) and approved for use by physicians and providers of outpatient services when submitting Medicare Part B claims for reimbursement. In 2001 the HCFA was renamed the Centers for Medicare and Medicaid Services (CMS), and the claim form was renamed the CMS-1500 Health Insurance Claim Form, commonly known as the CMS-1500. The form was subsequently adopted by almost all health insurance companies and third-party payers for use in the submission of physicians' claims for reimbursement. The current version of the CMS-1500 was adopted in August, 2005. As of May, 2008, only the CMS-1500 (08-05) claim form may be used to submit insurance claims.

TYPES OF CLAIMS

A medical assistant may submit insurance claims to a third-party payer or an insurance carrier either on hard copy (paper) or electronically. Hard copy claims are insurance claims submitted manually, on paper, by surface mail (i.e., the U.S. Postal Service). Electronic claims are insurance claims that are submitted to an insurance carrier via electronic media, such as the Internet. Most of today's computer programs generate claims internally from the information entered into the database.

Hard Copy (Paper) Claims

Advantages and Disadvantages of Paper Claims

Paper (hard copy) claims have advantages and disadvantages. The advantages include minimal start-up costs (because the forms are readily available through many vendors) and the ability to attach documentation explaining unusual circumstances that might affect reimbursement. The cost in time, labor, and postage is higher with paper claim submission, and reimbursement is much slower. Paper claims also require a lot of storage space.

Intelligent Character Recognition

Insurance claims created on paper (hard copy) are processed at the insurance payer using **intelligent character recognition (ICR)**. ICR is a system that scans documents and captures claims information directly from the CMS-1500 form. Medicare, Medicaid, TRICARE (formerly CHAMPUS), and many other insurance carriers have adopted the ICR system. The ICR system has replaced the optical character recognition (OCR) process, which had been in use until the early twenty-first century.

At the insurance carrier, ICR scanners transfer the information on claim forms into computers. This transfer is done using a red bulb scanner, which causes the red preprinted portion of the CMS-1500 form to appear invisible to the computer. The scanner "captures" only characters printed in black ink on the form and transfers them to the computer's memory. The resulting image allows for "clean" recognition of the data entered on the CMS-1500 form; that is, the data characters are not obstructed by the lines and text of the form.

The benefits of ICR scanning include greater efficiency in processing claims, improved accuracy, more control over the data input, and reduced data entry cost for the insurance carrier.

The medical assistant should use the following rules to complete the paper CMS-1500 form correctly so that the insurance carrier can scan the claim:

- Entries should be clear and sharp; carbon copies are not acceptable.
- Use pica type (10 characters per inch). The equivalent computer font is Courier 10 or OCR 10.
- All uppercase letters should be used.
- All punctuation should be omitted.
- All birth dates should be in this format: MM DD YYYY (with a space between each set of digits).
- Each entry should be kept within its respective block; all characters (e.g., X, Y, N) must fall completely within the designated block.
- A blank space should be substituted for the following:
  - Dollar signs and decimal points in charges and in ICD-9-CM codes
  - Dashes preceding procedure code modifiers
  - Parentheses around telephone area codes
  - Hyphens in Social Security numbers
- Titles and other designations (e.g., Sr., Jr., II, or III) should be omitted unless they appear on the identification (ID) card.
- When the charge is expressed in whole dollars, two zeros should be used in the "cents" column.
- Do not enter the alpha character "O" for a zero (0).
- If a typewriter is used, do not use lift-off tape, correction tape, or correction fluid.
- Because photocopies of claims cannot be scanned, all resubmissions must be prepared using the original (red print) claim form.
- No handwritten data (other than signatures) may be included on the form.
- Nothing should be stapled to the form.

- The name and address of the insurance company should be inserted in the proper area in the top margin of the claim form.

Electronic Claims

As mentioned, **electronic claims** are insurance claims that are transmitted over the Internet from the provider to the health insurance company. Most claims-processing software is designed to permit electronic claims generation. A mandate included in the Health Insurance Portability and Accountability Act (HIPAA) required the development of "transaction and code sets" for all insurance-related information sent electronically, including claim form submissions, claim status requests, and remittance (payment) processing.

The transaction and code set for CMS-1500 electronic claims submission is the ASC X12N 837P (HIPAA 837 Health Care Claim: Professional [837P]). All insurance billing data entered into the computer software program (i.e., patient, provider, charge, diagnosis, and procedure) is reformatted by the software program to conform with the transaction and code sets format and guidelines. For more information on implementation guides for transaction and code sets, refer to the Evolve site at *evolve.elsevier.com/kinn*).

HIPAA 837 HEALTH CARE CLAIM: PROFESSIONAL (837P) OVERVIEW

As part of the Health Insurance Portability and Accountability Act of 1996, standards were developed to protect patients' health information when it was transmitted electronically. These standards, known also as *transaction and code sets*, mandate the format of insurance claims, remittance information, claims attachments, and claims status submitted electronically. The insurance claim form for physician and provider services is called the HIPAA 837 Health Care Claim: Professional, or 837P. This standard contains the format and establishes the data contents of the Health Care Claim Transaction Set (837) for use in the context of an **electronic data interchange (EDI)**; that is, data that are transmitted electronically via the Internet. This transaction set can be used to submit healthcare claim billing information, encounter information, or both from providers of healthcare services to payers, either directly or via intermediary billers and claims clearinghouses.

Since 2003, all insurance claims submitted electronically, regardless of whether the claim is submitted directly to the payer or to a clearinghouse, have had to be submitted using the 837P standard, to comply with the HIPAA mandates. Any provider, payer, employer, or other entity that does not use these standards can be removed from participation in federal programs such as Medicaid, Medicare, and TRICARE and also may face stiff civil and/or criminal fines and imprisonment. All vendors, providers, clearinghouses, employers, and health insurance carriers that transmit protected health information electronically must have updated software that conforms to the HIPAA standards, including but not limited to the 837P. These software upgrades will be transparent to the medical assistant entering data into the computer for insurance claims processing; in other words, the format, screens, steps, and processes for entering data into the computer for the purpose of generating insurance claim forms, whether on paper to be mailed or to be transmitted electronically, should look and feel the same as before the transaction and code sets were implemented.

The CMS Web site *(cms.gov)* provides more information about the Transaction and Code Sets for the HIPAA 837 Health Care Claim: Professional, and the standards for other electronically submitted data, such as the Claims Payment and Remittance Advice (835), Healthcare Claims Status (276/277), Coordination of Benefits (837), and Referral Certification and Authorization (278).

Electronic Claims Submission

Electronic claims can be submitted in several ways. Claims can be transmitted directly to the insurance carrier, also known as *direct billing,* or to a claims clearinghouse, which then submits the claims to the insurance carrier.

Direct Billing. **Direct billing** is the process by which an insurance carrier allows a **provider** to submit insurance claims directly to the carrier electronically. Most major insurance carriers, including Medicare and Medicaid, provide small computer programs to providers that are used to enter patient and insured information, charges, and provider detail directly into the program. These data are then transmitted electronically directly to the insurance carrier. Many carrier-direct systems are supplied free of charge to the provider, but the direct system can transmit only to specific carriers.

Clearinghouse Submission. A **clearinghouse** is a vendor that allows a provider to submit all the insurance claims generated by the provider to the clearinghouse using special software. The clearinghouse then **audits** and sorts the claims and sends them in batches electronically to each of the different insurance carriers. A clearinghouse charges the healthcare provider a small fee for the service of receiving claim transmissions, checking and preparing the claims for processing, consolidating claims so that one transmission can be sent to each carrier, and submitting claims in correct data format to the applicable insurance payer. Other services that clearinghouses typically provide include:

- Auditing claims to make sure all required fields are completed and the data are correct
- Reporting the number of claims submitted and the number of errors and their specifics
- Forwarding claims to insurance carriers that accept electronic claims (e.g., Medicare, Medicaid, Blue Cross/Blue Shield, and others) or to another clearinghouse that may hold the contracts with specific payers
- Keeping provider offices updated as new carriers are added to the database
- Generating informative statistical reports

Clearinghouses are also called *third-party administrators* (TPAs), and they are designed to receive electronic claims from any provider.

Advantages of Electronic Submission

Typically, with electronic claims processing, payments are received in less than half the time required for turnaround of paper claims. Very soon after claims have been transmitted, the clearinghouse sends the provider tracking reports that describe which claims were received, audited, and forwarded to the insurance carrier. These tracking reports also provide information regarding rejected claims and those needing additional information.

Electronic claims processing reduces payment turnaround time by shortening the payment cycle and can reduce average error rates to less than 1% or 2%. Some insurance companies even waive the attachment requirements for many procedures when claims are submitted electronically. For additional information on advantages and disadvantages, visit the Evolve site at *evolve.elsevier.com/kinn*).

CRITICAL THINKING APPLICATION   21-1

Machelle is interested in learning more about filing claims electronically. In the medical facility where she is doing her externship, she has asked to work with Frank Hern, who performs this procedure in the office. How can working closely with Mr. Hern benefit Machelle with regard to this subject?

DATA GATHERING GUIDELINES

When the first appointment is made for a patient, it is routine to ask the patient for all pertinent insurance information. Much of this information is on the Patient Registration form that is completed when the patient comes to the medical office for the initial visit; it is inserted into the medical chart and entered into the computer's patient database. This information should always be collected from every new patient seen by the provider. Returning or established patients should be asked during each visit whether their insurance information is complete and current. Many offices use a form that allows the patient to provide address and phone number updates, in addition to new insurance information.

The information needed to complete an insurance form (Table 21-1) is gathered from several sources: (1) the Patient Registration form, (2) the completed Verification of Eligibility and Benefits form, (3) referral and authorization information (when required by the insurance carrier), (4) the patient's medical record, (5) the encounter form or charge ticket, and (6) a photocopy of the patient's insurance card or cards, driver's license or state-issued ID card, and student ID (if applicable and available). The *Current Procedural Terminology* (CPT), *Health Care Common Procedural Coding System* (HCPCS), and *International Classification of Diseases, Ninth Revision, Clinical Modification* (ICD-9-CM) coding manuals and the individual insurance payer's claims processing manual or guidelines are also necessary resources for preparing insurance claims. Procedure 21-1 presents the steps for gathering patient and other information needed prior to completing the insurance claim form.

Verification of Eligibility and Benefits

Once the patient's and the insured's demographic and insurance information has been collected, the next step is to verify the patient's eligibility and benefits. This usually is done by phone, by calling the insurance carrier or carriers for the patient and confirming that the patient is covered by the insurance; this also provides an overview of the benefits available for the patient from the insurance policy. The information obtained over the phone should be verified by either fax or e-mail confirmation from the insurance carrier. For more information about verification of benefits and to see

TABLE 21-1 Information Required for Completion of CMS-1500 Form

BLOCK	INFORMATION NEEDED
	Completed Patient Registration form
	Photocopy of insurance card or cards—front and back
	Pertinent information from Verification of Eligibility and Benefits form
	Preauthorization and/or referral number (when applicable)
Section 1: Carrier Block	
Carrier Block	Insurance carrier's address
Section 2: Patient/Insured	
1	Type of insurance If patient's condition or illness is related to employment, auto accident, or some other type of accident, provide: • Date of onset of condition or accident • Responsible party's name, address, and phone number • Insurance carrier of responsible party, including address and phone number • Insurance ID number, policy, and/or group number
1a	Insured's identification (ID) number (primary insurance)
2	Patient's full name
3	Patient's date of birth and gender
4	Insured's name (primary insurance)
5	Patient's information • Permanent address (including apartment number if appropriate) • City, state, ZIP code • Telephone number
6	Patient's relationship to insured
7	Insured's information • Permanent address (including apartment number if appropriate) • City, state, ZIP code • Telephone number
8	Patient status • Employed? • Full- or part-time student?
9	Secondary (other) insured's name*
9a	Policy or group number of secondary insurance*
9b	Secondary insured's date of birth and gender*
9c	Secondary insured's employer or school name*
9d	Secondary insured's insurance plan or program name*
10a-c	If patient's condition or illness is related to employment, auto accident, or some other type of accident, make sure information is obtained as outlined in Block 1
11	Insurance policy, group, or FECA number of primary insurance
11a	Primary insured's date of birth and gender
11b	Primary insured's employer or school name
11c	Primary insured's insurance plan or program name

Continued

TABLE 21-1 Information Required for Completion of CMS-1500 Form—cont'd

BLOCK	INFORMATION NEEDED
11d	Determine whether the patient also is covered by a secondary health insurance plan
12	Confirm that the patient's release of information form has been signed and dated and is in the patient's record
13	Confirm that the insured's authorization of benefits form has been signed and dated and is in the patient's record
Section 3: Physician/Supplier	
14	Date illness, injury, or pregnancy began
15	Determine whether patient has had same or similar symptoms
16	From-To dates if patient was unable to work at current occupation
17	Name of ordering or referring provider
17a	Not required
17b	Ordering or referring provider's NPI number
18	From-To dates if patient encounter included an inpatient hospital stay
19	Determine whether insurance carrier in carrier block and Block 1 require any information entered in this field
20	Determine whether an outside lab was used; if so, enter charges billed to provider for outside lab services
21	ICD-9-CM code or codes for patient's condition, illness, or injury (maximum of four per claim)
22	Is Medicaid claim being resubmitted? If yes, provide reference number from original Medicaid claim submitted
23	If prior authorization and/or referral is required, provide authorization (approval) number from insurance payer
24A	From-To dates of service for current encounter
24B	POS code
24C	If an emergency, put a Y in this box
24D	CPT and/or HCPCS code CPT and/or HCPCS modifier(s) (maximum of four per charge line)
24E	Block 21 field or reference number (1, 2, 3 and/or 4)
24F	Total charge for CPT- or HCPCS-coded services listed in 24D. • If more than 1 day or unit is indicated in Block 24G, multiply the charge for the service(s) coded in Block 24D by the number of days/units in Block 24G; enter the result in Block 24F.
24G	Total number of days or units
24H	EPSDT or Family Plan code (Medicaid or AFDC)
24I	Qualifier ID code (if no NPI number is available)
24J	Rendering (treating) provider's NPI number—unshaded field PIN (if no NPI number is available)—shaded field
25	Rendering provider's federal tax ID number (EIN or SSN)
26	Patient's account number with rendering provider
27	Determine whether contract or agreement between provider and insurance carrier allows provider to accept assignment
28	Total charges from Block 24F, lines 1-6
29	Amount paid by patient, insured, or other insurance

TABLE 21-1 Information Required for Completion of CMS-1500 Form—cont'd

BLOCK	INFORMATION NEEDED
30	Balance due, if any amount paid is shown in Block 29
31	Signature of provider performing service or procedure
32	Address of facility where services were rendered
32a	NPI number of service facility in Block 32
32b	Qualifier ID number and PIN of facility in Block 32 (if no NPI is available)
33	Name, address, and phone number of performing (rendering) provider
33a	NPI number of provider in Block 33
33b	Qualifier ID number and PIN of provider in Block 33 (if no NPI is available)

*Only required if a secondary insurance exists and is to be submitted to the insurance carrier.
AFDC, Aid to Families with Dependent Children; *CPT, Current Procedural Terminology* coding method; *EIN,* Employer's Identification Number; *EPSDT,* Early and Periodic Screening, Diagnosis, and Treatment; *FECA,* Federal Employees Compensation Act; *HCPCS, Health Care Common Procedural Coding System* coding method ; *ICD-9-CM, International Classification of Diseases, Ninth Revision, Clinical Modification* coding method; *NPI,* National Provider Identifier; *PIN,* personal identification number; *POS,* place of service.

PROCEDURE 21-1

Gather Data to Complete CMS-1500 Form

CAAHEP COMPETENCIES: II.C.II.1., IV.C.IV.6., IV.P.IV.3., V. P.V.6., VII.P.VII.1., VII.P.VII. 2., VII.P.VII.3., IX.A.IX.2.

ABHES COMPETENCIES: 3.x

GOAL: *To gather all information and documentation required for completing an insurance claim.*

EQUIPMENT and SUPPLIES

- Patient Registration form
- Photocopy of patient's insurance card or cards, driver's license or state-issued identification card, and student ID (if applicable).
- Verification of Eligibility and Benefits form
- Preauthorization and/or Referral form
- Encounter form (charge ticket or superbill)
- ICD-9-CM coding manual
- CPT coding manual
- HCPCS coding manual

PROCEDURAL STEPS

1. Have the patient or patient's guardian complete the Patient Registration, Release of Information, and Authorization of Benefits form or forms in full and return them to the medical assistant.
   PURPOSE: To gather the required information to enter into the computer, so that the documents and files needed to ultimately receive the maximum reimbursement from the carrier. This process creates the record and allows the physician to begin documentation that will be used to complete the insurance claim form.
2. Ask for the patient's and the insured's driver's license and insurance card or cards. If the patient is a student, ask whether he or she has a student identification (ID) card; if so, request it from the patient. If a patient has more than one insurance policy, it is important to get the name, address, group, and policy number for each company.
   PURPOSE: To obtain state-issued identification of the patient so that the physician verifies that he or she is treating the right patient (who is eligible for benefits).

3. Photocopy the back and front of the patient's insurance card and place the photocopy in the medical record and/or the patient's insurance file. Most medical offices also photocopy the patient's and insured guarantor's driver's license or other state-issued ID card (and, when applicable, a student ID card) for verification of the patient's and insured's identity.
4. Confirm the patient's and insured's full name, address, phone number, date of birth, gender, and insurance information by comparing the Patient Registration form, insurance ID card, and state-issued ID card.
5. Determine whether someone other than the patient is the guarantor. The *guarantor* is the person or entity responsible for payment. The guarantor may be the patient, the insured, or a third party. If neither the patient nor the insured is the guarantor, obtain the guarantor's address, date of birth, and employer information, in addition to the guarantor's relationship to the patient (e.g., spouse, parent, self, or other).
6. Call the employer and confirm employment (optional). If the patient is insured under a group health plan, workers' compensation, TRICARE, or some other types of insurance, this information can be confirmed when verifying eligibility and benefits.
7. Confirm that the patient has signed and dated the Release of Information form.
   PURPOSE: To prove that the patient has agreed to allow the physician to release information to the insurance company or other third-party payor so that payment can be made on the claim.
8. Confirm that the insured has signed the Authorization of Benefits form. Signatures to authorize insurance billing, supplying of information to insurance companies, and acceptance of assignments of benefits

(if appropriate) should be obtained from all new patients and at the beginning of each new calendar year.

9. Contact the insurance carrier and perform a verification of benefits and insurance coverage.

10. Obtain any precertification or referral authorization or authorizations required by the insurance carrier or payer.

11. Code the diagnosis or diagnoses for the encounter using the ICD-9-CM coding manual.

12. Select any qualifying circumstance, physical or patient status, or other modifiers as appropriate.

13. Code the procedures and services rendered during the encounter using the CPT and/or HCPCS coding manual.

14. Select any CPT and/or HCPCS modifiers as appropriate.

15. Using Table 21-1 or a similar list of information to gather in preparation for insurance claim submission, confirm all information needed is available.

---

an example of a verification form, visit the Evolve site at *evolve. elsevier.com/kinn.*

Preauthorization and/or Referral

If any diagnostic or therapeutic services or procedures are to be rendered by the provider that require preauthorization approval, perform a preauthorization to obtain an authorization number. The authorization number, which confirms that precertification was performed, is placed in Block 23 on the CMS-1500 form. For more information about preauthorization and to see an example of the form, refer to the Evolve site at *evolve.elsevier.com/kinn.*

COMPLETING THE CMS-1500 FORM

The CMS-1500 Health Insurance Claim Form (Figure 21-1) is used by most health insurance payers for claims submitted by physicians and suppliers. The information needed to complete an insurance claim form includes the patient's and the guarantor's demographic and insurance information; the name, address, and phone number of the insurance company; the diagnostic, treatment, and procedures and services information; and the provider's billing information, including name, address, phone number, place of service, and the tax and provider identification numbers.

There are 33 blocks, or items, on the CMS-1500 form. These blocks are divided into three sections:

- **Section 1:** Carrier Block. The first section contains the address of the insurance carrier and is located at the top of the form (Figure 21-2).
- **Section 2:** Patient/Insured Section. The second section contains information about the patient and the insured; it includes Boxes 1 through 13.
- **Section 3:** Physician/Supplier Section. The third section contains information about the physician or supplier; it includes Boxes 14 through 33.

In the following guidelines, each of the 33 blocks contains the block title, description, and instructions for completing that block. Where applicable, special instructions are given for Medicare, Medicaid, TRICARE, group health plan, Federal Employees Compensation Act (FECA) and black lung (FECA/Black Lung) insurance, and other types of insurance. Procedure 21-2 provides detailed instructions on completing each section and block of the CMS-1500 claim form. (For hints on creating a work-friendly routine for completing insurance claims, refer to the Evolve site at *evolve.elsevier.com/kinn*).

Section 1: Carrier Block

The name and address of the payer is entered in this block. The payer is the carrier, health plan, third-party administrator, or other payer who will process the claim. Use the format shown in Figure 21-2.

Section 2: Patient/Insured Section—Blocks 1 to 8 (Figure 21-3)

Block 1: Type of Insurance. This block indicates the type of insurance the patient has. Indicate the type of health insurance coverage applicable to this claim by putting an X in the appropriate box (e.g., if a Medicare claim is being filed, mark the Medicare box). This information directs the claim to the correct payer and may establish primary liability. For example, if the claim is primary for Medicare, put an X in the Medicare box; if Medicare is secondary, put an X in the box for Other.

　　Block 1a: Insured's ID Number. The ID number of the person who holds the policy.

　　Block 2: Patient's Name. The name of the patient is the person who received treatment or supplies. The patient's last name should be entered first, then first name, and middle initial (e.g., Doe, John A.)

　　Block 3: Patient's Birth Date and Sex. The patient's birth date and sex help identify the patient and distinguishes patients with similar names.

　　Block 4: Insured's Name. The name of the person who holds the policy.

Primary and Secondary Insurance Determination. Generally, if the patient is insured, the patient's insurance is primary; any insurance carried by a spouse or other guarantor is considered secondary.

Determination of Primary and Secondary Insurance for a Child or Minor. In the case of a child whose mother and father both carry the child as a dependent on their insurance policies, primary and secondary insurance is determined by the birthday rule; that is, whichever parent's birth month and birth date falls first in a calendar year is considered primary. The year of the parent's birth is not used. Therefore, if the mother's birth month and day are February 20 and the father's are May 1, the mother's insurance is the primary insurance and the father's insurance is the secondary insurance.

　　Block 5: Patient's Address. The patient's permanent address and telephone number are entered here. Do not use a temporary or school address.

Text continued on p. 389

1500

HEALTH INSURANCE CLAIM FORM

APPROVED BY NATIONAL UNIFORM CLAIM COMMITTEE 08/05

PICA — PICA — CARRIER

1. MEDICARE (Medicare #) MEDICAID (Medicaid #) TRICARE CHAMPUS (Sponsor's SSN) CHAMPVA (Member ID#) GROUP HEALTH PLAN (SSN or ID) FECA BLK LUNG (SSN) OTHER (ID)

1a. INSURED'S I.D. NUMBER (For Program in Item 1)

2. PATIENT'S NAME (Last Name, First Name, Middle Initial)

3. PATIENT'S BIRTH DATE MM DD YY SEX M F

4. INSURED'S NAME (Last Name, First Name, Middle Initial)

5. PATIENT'S ADDRESS (No., Street)

6. PATIENT RELATIONSHIP TO INSURED Self Spouse Child Other

7. INSURED'S ADDRESS (No., Street)

CITY STATE

8. PATIENT STATUS Single Married Other

CITY STATE

ZIP CODE TELEPHONE (Include Area Code) ( )

Employed Full-Time Student Part-Time Student

ZIP CODE TELEPHONE (Include Area Code) ( )

9. OTHER INSURED'S NAME (Last Name, First Name, Middle Initial)

10. IS PATIENT'S CONDITION RELATED TO:

11. INSURED'S POLICY GROUP OR FECA NUMBER

a. OTHER INSURED'S POLICY OR GROUP NUMBER

a. EMPLOYMENT? (Current or Previous) YES NO

a. INSURED'S DATE OF BIRTH MM DD YY SEX M F

b. OTHER INSURED'S DATE OF BIRTH MM DD YY SEX M F

b. AUTO ACCIDENT? YES NO PLACE (State)

b. EMPLOYER'S NAME OR SCHOOL NAME

c. EMPLOYER'S NAME OR SCHOOL NAME

c. OTHER ACCIDENT? YES NO

c. INSURANCE PLAN NAME OR PROGRAM NAME

d. INSURANCE PLAN NAME OR PROGRAM NAME

10d. RESERVED FOR LOCAL USE

d. IS THERE ANOTHER HEALTH BENEFIT PLAN? YES NO ***If yes***, return to and complete item 9 a-d.

READ BACK OF FORM BEFORE COMPLETING & SIGNING THIS FORM.

12. PATIENT'S OR AUTHORIZED PERSON'S SIGNATURE I authorize the release of any medical or other information necessary to process this claim. I also request payment of government benefits either to myself or to the party who accepts assignment below.

SIGNED ____ DATE ____

13. INSURED'S OR AUTHORIZED PERSON'S SIGNATURE I authorize payment of medical benefits to the undersigned physician or supplier for services described below.

SIGNED ____

PATIENT AND INSURED INFORMATION

14. DATE OF CURRENT: MM DD YY ILLNESS (First symptom) OR INJURY (Accident) OR PREGNANCY(LMP)

15. IF PATIENT HAS HAD SAME OR SIMILAR ILLNESS. GIVE FIRST DATE MM DD YY

16. DATES PATIENT UNABLE TO WORK IN CURRENT OCCUPATION MM DD YY FROM TO MM DD YY

17. NAME OF REFERRING PROVIDER OR OTHER SOURCE

17a. 17b. NPI

18. HOSPITALIZATION DATES RELATED TO CURRENT SERVICES MM DD YY FROM TO MM DD YY

19. RESERVED FOR LOCAL USE

20. OUTSIDE LAB? YES NO $ CHARGES

21. DIAGNOSIS OR NATURE OF ILLNESS OR INJURY (Relate Items 1, 2, 3 or 4 to Item 24E by Line)

1. ___ . ___ 3. ___ . ___

2. ___ . ___ 4. ___ . ___

22. MEDICAID RESUBMISSION CODE ORIGINAL REF. NO.

23. PRIOR AUTHORIZATION NUMBER

24. A. DATE(S) OF SERVICE From MM DD YY	To MM DD YY	B. PLACE OF SERVICE	C. EMG	D. PROCEDURES, SERVICES, OR SUPPLIES (Explain Unusual Circumstances) CPT/HCPCS MODIFIER	E. DIAGNOSIS POINTER	F. $ CHARGES	G. DAYS OR UNITS	H. EPSDT Family Plan	I. ID. QUAL.	J. RENDERING PROVIDER ID. #
1									NPI	
2									NPI	
3									NPI	
4									NPI	
5									NPI	
6									NPI	

25. FEDERAL TAX I.D. NUMBER SSN EIN

26. PATIENT'S ACCOUNT NO.

27. ACCEPT ASSIGNMENT? (For govt. claims, see back) YES NO

28. TOTAL CHARGE $

29. AMOUNT PAID $

30. BALANCE DUE $

31. SIGNATURE OF PHYSICIAN OR SUPPLIER INCLUDING DEGREES OR CREDENTIALS (I certify that the statements on the reverse apply to this bill and are made a part thereof.)

SIGNED DATE

32. SERVICE FACILITY LOCATION INFORMATION

a. NPI b.

33. BILLING PROVIDER INFO & PH # ( )

a. NPI b.

PHYSICIAN OR SUPPLIER INFORMATION

NUCC Instruction Manual available at: www.nucc.org APPROVED OMB-0938-0999 FORM CMS-1500 (08/05)

FIGURE 21-1 CMS-1500 Health Insurance Claim Form.

1500

HEALTH INSURANCE CLAIM FORM

APPROVED BY NATIONAL UNIFORM CLAIM COMMITTEE 08/05

PICA

XYZ INSURANCE COMPANY
102 MAIN STREET
ANYTOWN, MO 63030

CARRIER

PICA

FIGURE 21-2 CMS-1500 claim form: Carrier Block.

PROCEDURE 21-2

Complete an Insurance Claim Form

CAAHEP COMPETENCIES: II.C.II. 1., IV.C.IV.6., IV.P.IV.3., V. P.V.6., VII.P.VII.1., VII.P.VII.2., VII.P.VII.3., IX.A.IX.2.

ABHES COMPETENCIES: 3.x

GOAL: *To accurately complete a CMS-1500 (formerly HCFA-1500) claim form.*

EQUIPMENT and SUPPLIES

- Patient Registration form
- Photocopy of patient's insurance ID card or cards
- Encounter form (charge ticket or superbill)
- Copy of the completed Verification of Eligibility and Benefits form
- Copy of the completed Preauthorization and/or Referral form (when applicable)
- Claims processing manual or guidelines for the insurance payer for which the insurance claim is being completed
- Patient's medical record
- Patient's ledger
- CMS-1500 Health Insurance Claim Form
- Typewriter or computer

PROCEDURAL STEPS

1. Determine the type of insurance (e.g., Medicare, Medicaid, TRICARE, CHAMPVA, group health plan, FECA/Black Lung, health maintenance organization [HMO], automobile or other liability policy, workers' compensation).
2. Review the Patient Registration form, medical record, financial ledger, Verification of Eligibility and Benefits form, and Preauthorization and/or Referral form to ensure that all the information needed to perform the procedure has been assembled. Table 21-1 lists the required information for completing the CMS-1500 form.
3. Refer to the claims processing manual or guidelines for the type of insurance to be submitted.
4. Complete each block (as appropriate) of the CMS-1500 form

SECTION 1: CARRIER BLOCK

- Enter the name and address of the payer to whom this claim is being sent in the following format:
  - First line: Name of carrier
  - Second line: First line of address
  - Third line: Second line of address, if needed
  - Fourth line: City, state, and ZIP code

SECTION 2: PATIENT/INSURED INFORMATION

- **Block 1** Put an X in the appropriate box to indicate the type of healthcare coverage that applies to this claim. Mark only one box.
  NOTE: One (1) character may be entered in any box in the field. Only one box can be marked.
  - Medicare—Put an X in this box when filing a Medicare claim.
  - Medicaid—Put an X in this box when filing a Medicaid claim.
  - TRICARE (CHAMPUS)—Put an X in this box when filing a TRICARE claim.

- CHAMPVA—Put an X in this box when filing a CHAMPVA claim.
- Group Health Plan—Put an X in this box when filing any type of group health insurance claim.
- FECA/Black Lung—Put an X in this box only when filing a claim for a patient who qualifies for these programs, which should be shown clearly on the insurance card.
- Other—Put an X in this box if the insurance type is:
  - HMO
  - Commercial insurance
  - Automobile accident
  - Liability
  - Workers' compensation

- **Block 1a** Enter the insured's ID number as shown on the health insurance ID card for the specific payer this claim addresses.
  NOTE: A total of twenty-nine (29) characters may be entered in this block.
  - Medicare—Use the Health Identification Card (HIC) number.
  - Medicaid—Use the Medicaid ID number.
  - TRICARE/CHAMPVA—Use the ID number on the card.
  - Group Health Plan—Use the ID number on the card.
  - FECA/Black Lung—Use the FECA/Black Lung ID number.
  - Other: Follow instructions in the carriers' instruction manual.

- **Block 2** Enter the patient's full last name, first name, and middle initial. Suffixes should be entered after the last name. Do not include titles or professional suffixes. Use commas to separate each name. Do not use periods. Use a hyphen for hyphenated names.
  NOTE: A total of twenty-eight (28) characters may be entered in this block.

- **Block 3** Enter the patient's birth date in eight (8)–digit format (MM/DD/YYYY). Enter an X in the correct box to indicate the gender of the patient. Only one box can be marked. Leave blank if the gender is for some reason unknown.
  NOTE: Two (2) characters may be entered for month and date, and four (4) characters may be entered for the year. One (1) character may be entered in the box denoting gender.

- **Block 4** Enter the insured's full last name, first name, and middle initial. Suffixes should be entered after the last name. Do not include titles or professional suffixes. Use commas to separate each name. Do not use periods. Use a hyphen for hyphenated names.
  NOTE: Twenty-nine (29) characters may be entered in this box.
  - Medicare—Enter the insured's name if the patient is not the insured individual. Leave blank if the patient is the insured.
  - Medicaid—Leave blank. The patient is considered the insured, because each patient is assigned his or her own Medicaid ID number.

○ TRICARE/CHAMPVA—Enter the insured's name if the patient is not the insured individual. Leave blank if the patient is the insured.

○ Group Health Plan—For employee-sponsored plans, the insured is the employee. Enter the insured's name if the patient is not the insured individual. Leave blank if the patient is the insured.

○ FECA/Black Lung—Leave blank. The patient is considered the insured, because each patient is assigned his or her own FECA/Black Lung ID number.

○ Other: Follow the carrier manual for the specific insurance being filed to accurately complete this section.

• **Block 5** Enter the patient's mailing address and phone number. The first line is for the address number and street; the second line is for the city and state; and the third line is for the ZIP code and phone number. Do not use punctuation in the address, other than a hyphen in a nine-digit ZIP code. Do not use hyphens in the phone number.
NOTE: Twenty-eight (28) characters are allowed for the street address; twenty-four (24) for the city; and three (3) for the state. Twelve (12) characters are allowed for the ZIP code; three (3) for the area code; and ten (10) for the phone number.

• **Block 6** Put an X in the box that indicates the relationship of the patient to the insured. Mark only one box.
NOTE: One (1) character may be entered in any box. Only one box should be marked.

• **Block 7** Enter the insured's address. The first line is for the address number and street; the second line is for the city and state; and the third line is for the ZIP code and phone number. Do not use punctuation in the address, other than a hyphen in a nine-digit ZIP code. Do not use hyphens in the phone number.
NOTE: Twenty-nine (29) characters are allowed for the street address; twenty-three (23) for the city; and four (4) for the state. Twelve (12) characters are allowed for the ZIP code; three (3) for the area code; and ten (10) for the phone number.

○ Medicare—Leave blank; the patient is the insured.

○ Medicaid—Leave blank; the patient is the insured.

○ Group Health Plan—Leave blank if the patient is the insured; otherwise, enter the insured's address and phone number.

○ FECA/Black Lung—Leave blank; the patient is the insured.

○ Other: Follow instructions in the carriers' instruction manual.

• **Block 8** Put an X in the appropriate box indicating marital status and employment status; also student status (if applicable). Mark only one box on each line.
NOTE: Only one (1) character may be marked in the boxes, and only one box per line should be marked.

• **Block 9** (Complete Blocks 9 and 9a-d only if YES is marked in Block 11d.) Use Blocks 9 and 9a-d when other group health coverage exists. Enter the last name, first name, and middle initial of the other insured if these are different from those shown in Block 2. Suffixes should be entered after the last name. Do not include titles or professional suffixes.

Use commas to separate each name. Do not use periods. Use a hyphen for hyphenated names.
NOTE: Twenty-eight (28) characters may be entered in this block.

• **Block 9a** Enter the group number or policy of the other insured.
NOTE: Twenty-eight (28) characters can be entered in this field.

• **Block 9b** Enter the other insured's birth date in an eight (8)—digit format (MM/DD/YYYY). Put an X in the correct box to indicate the gender of the other insured. Only one box can be marked. Leave blank if the gender is for some reason unknown.
NOTE: Two (2) characters may be entered for month and date, and four (4) characters may be entered for the year. One (1) character may be entered in the box denoting gender.

• **Block 9c** Enter the name of the other insured's employer or school.
NOTE: Twenty-eight (28) characters may be entered in this field.

• **Block 9d** Enter the name of the other insured's insurance plan or program.
NOTE: Twenty-eight (28) characters may be entered in this field.

• **Block 10a-c** Enter an X in the correct box to indicate whether one or more of the services described in Block 24 are for a condition or injury that occurred on the job or as a result of an automobile or other accident. Only one box on each line can be marked. Place the state postal code in the blank next to auto accident if the YES box is marked in that line.
NOTE: One (1) character may be entered per line in either box, and two (2) characters may be entered in the place/state field.

○ 10a: If the patient's condition is related to employment injury or illness, put an X in the YES box.

○ 10b: If the patient's condition is related to an automobile accident, put an X in the YES box and enter the two-letter state designation in the PLACE (State) field.

○ 10c: If the patient's condition is related to some other type of accident, put an X in the YES box.

• **Block 10d** Refer to the most recent instructions from the applicable public or private payer regarding the use of this field.
NOTE: Nineteen (19) characters may be entered in this field.

• **Block 11** Enter the insured's policy, group, or FECA number as it appears on the healthcare ID card. If Block 4 was completed, this block also must be completed.
NOTE: Twenty-nine (29) characters may be entered in this field.

○ Medicare—Use the HIC number.

○ Medicaid—Use the Medicaid ID number.

○ TRICARE/CHAMPVA—Use the ID number on the card.

○ Group Health Plan—Use the ID number on the card (usually the Social Security number).

○ FECA/Black Lung—Use the FECA/Black Lung ID number.

○ Other: Follow the carrier manual for the specific insurance being filed to accurately complete this section.

- **Block 11a** Enter the insured's birth date in an eight (8)-digit format (MM/DD/YYYY). Put an X in the box that indicates the gender of the insured.
  NOTE: Two (2) characters are allowed in the month and day spaces, and four (4) in the year space. One entry is allowed in the block to indicate gender.
- **Block 11b** Enter the name of the insured's employer or school.
  NOTE: Twenty-nine (29) characters are allowed in this block.
- **Block 11c** Enter the insurance plan or program name in this block. Some payers prefer an ID number of the primary insurer instead of a name in this block.
  NOTE: Twenty-nine (29) characters are allowed in this field.
- **Block 11d** Mark the appropriate box. If there is another health plan, Blocks 9 and 9a-d must be completed.
  NOTE: One (1) character may be entered in either box.
- **Block 12** Enter "Signature on File," "SOF," or the actual legal signature of the patient or an authorized person. When using a legal signature, enter the date signed in six (6)—digit (MMDDYY) or eight (8)—digit (MMDDYYYY) format.
  NOTE: Use the space available to enter the signature and date.
- **Block 13** Enter "Signature on File," "SOF," or the actual legal signature of the insured or an authorized person. When using a legal signature, enter the date signed in six (6)—digit (MMDDYY) or eight (8)—digit (MMDDYYYY) format.
  NOTE: Use the space available to enter the signature.

SECTION 3: PROVIDER/SUPPLIER INFORMATION

- **Block 14** Enter the date of the first time the present illness, injury, or pregnancy began in six (6)—digit (MMDDYY) or eight (8)—digit (MMDDYYYY) format. In the case of pregnancy, use the date of the last menstrual period (LMP).
  NOTE: Two (2) characters may be entered under MM and DD, and four (4) characters may be entered under the YYYY.
- **Block 15** Enter the first date the patient experienced the same or a similar illness in either six (6)—digit (MMDDYY) or eight (8)—digit (MMDDYYYY) format. Do not indicate previous pregnancies. Leave blank if unknown.
  NOTE: Two (2) characters may be entered under MM and DD, and four (4) characters may be entered under the YYYY.
- **Block 16** If the patient is employed and is unable to work in his or her current occupation, enter a six (6)—digit (MMDDYY) or eight (8)—digit (MMDDYYYY) date in the FROM and TO fields to explain the period in which the patient has been unable to work in his or her current occupation.
  NOTE: Two (2) characters may be entered under MM and DD, and four (4) characters may be entered under the YYYY.
- **Block 17** Enter the name (first name, middle initial, last name) and credentials of the professional who referred or ordered the service (or services) or supplies on the claim. Do not use a period or commas in the name. A hyphen can be used for hyphenated names.
  NOTE: Twenty-six (26) characters may be entered in this field.

For Medicare claims, the following services/situations require submission of the referring/ordering provider's information:
  ○ Medicare-covered services and items that are the result of a physician's order or referral
  ○ Parenteral and enteral nutrition
  ○ Immunosuppressive drug claims
  ○ Hepatitis B claims
  ○ Diagnostic laboratory services
  ○ Diagnostic radiology services
  ○ Portable x-ray services
  ○ Consultative services
  ○ Durable medical equipment
  ○ When the ordering physician is also the performing physician (as often is the case with in-office clinical laboratory tests)
- **Block 17a** If the referring provider, ordering provider, or other source does not have a National Provider Identifier (NPI) number, enter the qualifying ID number and the applicable personal identification number (PIN).
  NOTE: Two (2) characters may be entered in the qualifier field and seventeen (17) characters in the Other ID Number field.
- **Block 17b** Enter the NPI number of the referring provider, ordering provider, or other source, if available.
  NOTE: This field allows for entry of a ten (10)—digit NPI number.
- **Block 18** Enter the FROM and TO dates between which the patient was in the hospital, beginning with the admission date and ending with the discharge date; provide these dates in six (6)—digit (MMDDYY) or eight (8)—digit (MMDDYYYY) format. If the patient has not yet been discharged, leave the TO field blank. This block is used only when the hospitalization is related to the current illness or injury.
  NOTE: This field allows for entry of the following in each of the date fields: Two (2) characters may be entered under MM and DD, and four (4) characters under the YYYY.
- **Block 19** Refer to the most current instructions from the applicable public or private payer regarding the use of this field. Some payers ask for certain identifiers in this field. If identifiers are reported in this field, enter the appropriate qualifiers describing the identifier. Do not enter a space, hyphen, or other separator between the qualifier code and the number (see Table 21-3 for the list of qualifiers).
  NOTE: Eighty-three (83) characters are allowed in this field.
- **Block 20** Use this field when billing for purchased services. Put an X in the YES box if the reported services were performed by an entity other than the billing provider. Then enter the purchase price of those services. Marking the YES box indicates that an entity other than the one billing for the services performed the purchased services. Putting an X in the NO box indicates that no purchased services are included on the claim. When the YES box is marked, Block 32 must be completed. When billing for multiple purchased services, each service should be submitted on a separate claim form. Only one box can be marked. When entering the charge amount, enter the amount in the field to the left of the vertical line. Enter the number right justified to the left of the vertical line. Do not

use commas or a decimal point when reporting amounts. Negative dollar amounts are not allowed. Dollar signs should not be entered. Use "00" for the cents if the amount is a whole number. Leave the right-hand field blank.

NOTE: One (1) character may be entered in either box in the Outside Lab area, and eight (8) characters may be entered to the left of the vertical line and in the charges area.

- **Block 21** Enter the code(s) for the patient's diagnosis or condition. Up to four ICD-9-CM diagnosis codes can be listed. Relate lines 1, 2, 3, and/or 4 to the lines of service in Block 24E by line number. For the codes, use the highest level of specificity. Do not provide narrative descriptions in this field. When entering the code number, include a space (accommodated by the period) between the two sets of numbers. If entering a code with more than three beginning digits (e.g., E codes), enter the fourth digit on top of the period.

NOTE: This field allows for entry of three (3) characters before the period; one (1) character above or on the period; and four (4) characters after the period in each of the four line areas.

- **Block 22** List the original reference number for resubmitted Medicaid claims. Refer to the most current instructions from the applicable public or private payer regarding the use of this field.

NOTE: This field allows for entry of eleven (11) characters in the code area and eighteen (18) characters in the original reference number area.

- **Block 23** Enter any of the following: prior authorization number, referral number, mammography precertification number, or Clinical Laboratory Improvement Amendments (CLIA) number, as assigned by the payer for the current service. Do not enter hyphens or spaces in the number.

NOTE: Twenty-nine (29) characters are allowed in this field.

- **Block 24** The six service lines in Block 24 have been divided horizontally to accommodate submission of the NPI number and of supplemental information to support the billed service. The top area of the six service lines is shaded; this is the location for reporting supplemental information. It is NOT intended to allow billing for 12 blocks.

NOTE: The shaded area of lines 1 through 6 allows for entry of sixty-one (61) characters from the beginning of Block 24A to the end of Block 24G.

- **Block 24A** Enter the dates of service, both FROM and TO. If there is only one date of service, enter that date under FROM and leave TO blank, or re-enter the date placed in FROM.

NOTE: Two (2) characters are allowed for each section of month, day, and year.

- Enter the first date the service was provided, and the last date.
- If services were provided on the same day, enter the same date in the FROM and TO fields in Block 24A.
- Enter a date for each procedure, service, or supply in six (6)—digit (MMDDYY) or eight (8)—digit (MMDDYYYY) format.
- When FROM and TO dates are shown for a series of identical services, enter the number of days or units in column G.

- **Block 24B** Enter the appropriate two (2)—digit code from the Place of Service code list for each block used or service performed.

NOTE: Two (2) characters are allowed in the unshaded area.

- **Block 24C** Determine whether the services provided were an emergency. If required, enter Y for yes or N for no in the bottom, unshaded section of the field. An emergency is defined by federal or state regulations or programs, payer contracts, or as stated in the electronic 837P implementation guide.

NOTE: Two (2) characters may be entered in the unshaded area.

- **Block 24D** Enter the *Current Procedural Terminology* (CPT) or *Health Care Common Procedural Coding System* (HCPCS) code or codes and modifiers (if applicable) from the appropriate code set in effect on the date of service. This field accommodates entry of up to four (4) 2-digit modifiers. The procedure code must be shown without a narrative description.

NOTE: Six (6) characters may be entered in the unshaded area of the CPT/HCPCS field, and four sets of two (2) characters may be entered in the modifier area.

- The CPT or HCPCS code for the procedure or service is entered in the first section of Block 24D.
- The CPT or HCPCS modifier for the procedure or service (when applicable) is entered in the second section of Block 24D.
- Any additional CPT or HCPCS modifiers are entered in the remaining sections of Block 24D.

- **Block 24E** Enter the diagnosis code reference number (pointer), as shown in Block 21, to relate the date of service and the procedures performed to the primary diagnosis. When multiple services have been performed, the primary reference number for each service should be listed first and other applicable services should follow. The reference numbers should be 1, 2, 3, or 4, or multiple numbers as explained. ICD-9-CM diagnosis codes should be entered in Block 21 only. Do NOT enter them in Block 24E. Enter the numbers justified to the left. Do not use commas between the numbers.

NOTE: Four (4) characters may be entered in the unshaded area.

- **Block 24F** Enter the charge for the listed service or procedure. Enter the number right justified in the dollar area of the field. Do not use commas when reporting dollar amounts. Negative dollar amounts are not allowed. Dollar signs should not be entered. Enter "00" in the cents column area if the amount is a whole number.

NOTE: Six (6) characters may be entered to the left of the vertical line, and two (2) characters may be entered to the right of the vertical line in the unshaded area.

- **Block 24G** Enter the number of days or units. This is usually used for multiple visits, units of supplies, anesthesia units or minutes, or oxygen volume. If only one service is performed, enter 1. Enter numbers right justified in the field. No leading zeros are required. If reporting a fraction of a unit, use the decimal point (see Table 21-3 for a description of qualifiers).

NOTE: This field allows for entry of three (3) characters in the unshaded area.

- ○ Enter the number of days or units. If there is only 1 day or unit, the numeral 1 must be entered.
- ○ Some services require that the actual number or quantity billed be clearly indicated on the claim form (e.g., multiple ostomy or urinary supplies, medication dosages, or allergy testing procedures). When multiple services are provided, enter the actual number provided.
- ○ For anesthesia, show the elapsed time (minutes) in Block 24G.
- **Block 24H** If the claim is Early and Periodic Screening, Diagnosis, and Treatment (EPSDT) or Aid to Families with Dependent Children (AFDC) related, enter Y for yes or N for no in the unshaded area of the field. If the claim is family planning, enter Y, or leave blank if N is in the unshaded area of the field.
  NOTE: One (1) character is allowed in this field.
- **Block 24I** Leave blank if the rendering provider has an NPI number. If the provider of service does not have an NPI number, enter the qualifier number in the shaded area.
  NOTE: This field allows for entry of two (2) characters in the shaded area.
- **Block 24J** If the rendering provider has an NPI number, enter it in the unshaded area. If the provider of service does not have an NPI number, enter the provider's PIN number or other ID number in the shaded area.
  NOTE: Eleven (11) characters can be entered in the shaded area, and ten (10) characters for the NPI number are allowed in the unshaded area.
- **Block 25** Enter the provider's federal tax ID number or Social Security number. Put an X in the appropriate box (SSN or EIN) to show which was provided. Do not enter hyphens with numbers. Enter numbers left justified in the field.
  NOTE: Fifteen (15) characters may be entered for the federal tax ID number or Social Security number, and one (1) character may be entered for the description of which number is provided.
- **Block 26** Enter the patient account number, if desired.
  NOTE: This field allows for fourteen (14) characters.
- **Block 27** Put an X in the correct box (YES or NO) for accepting assignment. Only one box can be marked.
  NOTE: One (1) character is allowed per box.
- **Block 28** Enter the total charges for the services in Block 24F.
  NOTE: Seven (7) characters may be entered to the left of the vertical line, and two (2) characters may be entered to the right of the vertical line.
- **Block 29** Enter the total amount that was paid toward this claim by the patient or guarantor.
  NOTE: Six (6) characters may be entered to the left of the vertical line, and two (2) characters may be entered to the right of the vertical line.
- **Block 30** Enter the total amount due. (This information does not exist in the electronic 837P implementation guide.)
  NOTE: Six (6) characters may be entered to the left of the vertical line, and two (2) characters may be entered to the right of the vertical line.
- **Block 31** Enter "Signature on File," "SOF," or the actual legal signature of the practitioner or supplier. Enter the date the claim was signed in a six (6)–digit (MMDDYY) or an eight (8)–digit format.

- **Block 32** Enter the name, address, city, state, and ZIP code of the location where the services were rendered.
  NOTE: Seventy-eight (78) characters may be used in this block. Enter the name and address in the following format:
  - ○ First line: Name
  - ○ Second line: Address
  - ○ Third line: City, state, and ZIP code
- **Block 32a** Enter the NPI number of the service facility location.
  NOTE: Ten (10) characters may be entered in this space. If the service facility does not have an NPI number, leave Block 32a blank.
- **Block 32b** If the service facility does not have an NPI number, enter the two (2)–digit non-NPI number qualifier, followed by the PIN or other ID number. Do not enter a space, hyphen, or other separator between the qualifier and number.
  NOTE: Fourteen (14) characters may be entered in Block 32b.
- **Block 33** Identifies the provider requesting to be paid and should always be completed.
  NOTE: Three (3) characters are available for the area code; nine (9) characters for the phone number; and eighty-seven (87) characters for billing provider information. Enter the provider's or supplier's billing name and address using the following format:
  - ○ First line: Name
  - ○ Second line: Address
  - ○ Third line: City, state, and ZIP code
- **Block 33a** Enter the NPI number of the billing provider.
  NOTE: Ten (10) characters are allowed. If the billing provider does not have an NPI number, leave blank.
- **Block 33b** If the billing provider does not have an NPI number, enter the two (2)–digit non-NPI qualifier and PIN or other ID number.
  NOTE: Thirty-three (33) characters may be entered in this space. Do not put a space between the qualifier and ID number.

FINAL STEPS

1. Review the claim for accuracy and completeness.
   PURPOSE: To double-check that no blocks or fields are inaccurate or missing required information.
2. Run or prepare an insurance claims log for all claims completed. For paper claims, make a copy of the claim and place it in the tickler file.
   PURPOSE: To provide an audit trail of claims submitted.
3. For paper claims:
   a. Use a paper clip to add any attachments to be sent with the claim.
   b. Group all claims going to the same carrier and mail together in one large envelope.
   c. Address the envelope, weigh the contents, attach postage, and mail.
4. For claims to be submitted electronically, follow the computer software instructions for the software used.
   PURPOSE: To submit all claims electronically or by surface mail to the appropriate insurance carrier.

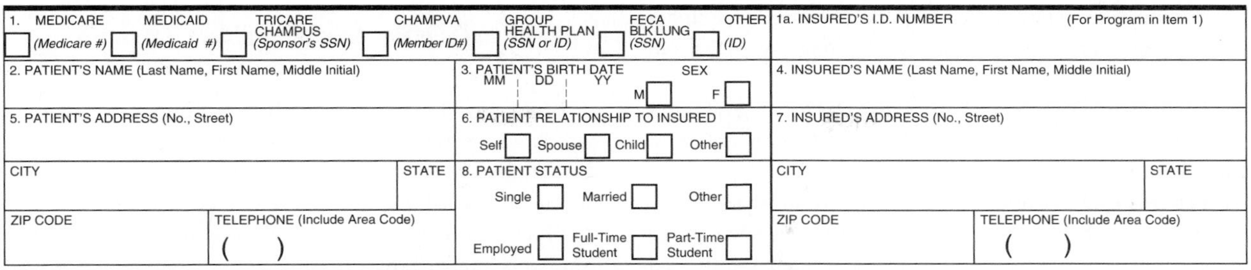
1. MEDICARE (Medicare #) | MEDICAID (Medicaid #) | TRICARE CHAMPUS (Sponsor's SSN) | CHAMPVA (Member ID#) | GROUP HEALTH PLAN (SSN or ID) | FECA BLK LUNG (SSN) | OTHER (ID)
1a. INSURED'S I.D. NUMBER (For Program in Item 1)
2. PATIENT'S NAME (Last Name, First Name, Middle Initial)
3. PATIENT'S BIRTH DATE MM DD YY SEX M F
4. INSURED'S NAME (Last Name, First Name, Middle Initial)
5. PATIENT'S ADDRESS (No., Street)
6. PATIENT RELATIONSHIP TO INSURED Self Spouse Child Other
7. INSURED'S ADDRESS (No., Street)
CITY STATE
8. PATIENT STATUS Single Married Other
CITY STATE
ZIP CODE TELEPHONE (Include Area Code) ( )
Employed Full-Time Student Part-Time Student
ZIP CODE TELEPHONE (Include Area Code) ( )

FIGURE 21-3 CMS-1500 claim form: patient and insured information, Blocks 1 to 8.

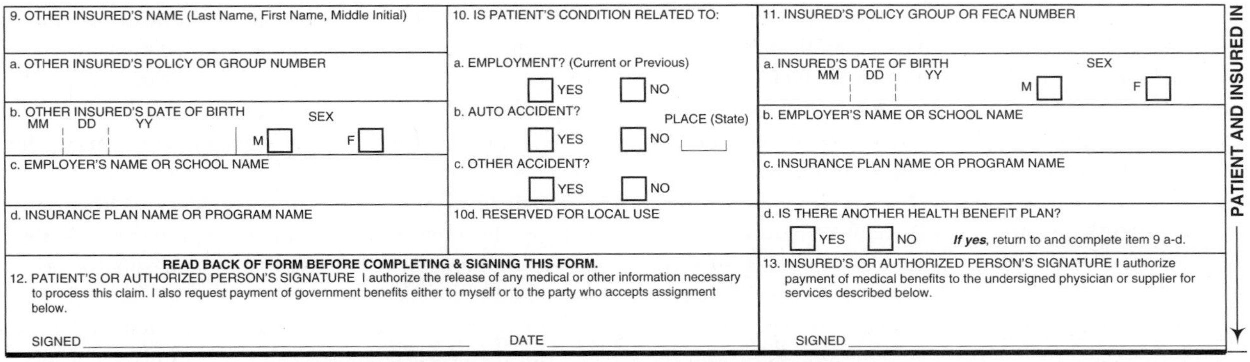
9. OTHER INSURED'S NAME (Last Name, First Name, Middle Initial)
10. IS PATIENT'S CONDITION RELATED TO:
11. INSURED'S POLICY GROUP OR FECA NUMBER
a. OTHER INSURED'S POLICY OR GROUP NUMBER
a. EMPLOYMENT? (Current or Previous) YES NO
a. INSURED'S DATE OF BIRTH MM DD YY SEX M F
b. OTHER INSURED'S DATE OF BIRTH MM DD YY SEX M F
b. AUTO ACCIDENT? YES NO PLACE (State)
b. EMPLOYER'S NAME OR SCHOOL NAME
c. EMPLOYER'S NAME OR SCHOOL NAME
c. OTHER ACCIDENT? YES NO
c. INSURANCE PLAN NAME OR PROGRAM NAME
d. INSURANCE PLAN NAME OR PROGRAM NAME
10d. RESERVED FOR LOCAL USE
d. IS THERE ANOTHER HEALTH BENEFIT PLAN? YES NO *If yes,* return to and complete item 9 a-d.
READ BACK OF FORM BEFORE COMPLETING & SIGNING THIS FORM.
12. PATIENT'S OR AUTHORIZED PERSON'S SIGNATURE I authorize the release of any medical or other information necessary to process this claim. I also request payment of government benefits either to myself or to the party who accepts assignment below.
SIGNED DATE
13. INSURED'S OR AUTHORIZED PERSON'S SIGNATURE I authorize payment of medical benefits to the undersigned physician or supplier for services described below.
SIGNED
PATIENT AND INSURED IN

FIGURE 21-4 CMS-1500 claim form: patient and insured information, Blocks 9 to 13.

Block 6: Patient Relationship to Insured.

- Self: Indicates that the patient is the insured.
- Spouse: Indicates that the patient is married to the insured.
- Child: Means that the patient is the insured's minor dependent.
- Other: May mean that the patient is an employee, that workers' compensation is the insurer, or that the patient is a ward or other dependent as defined by the insured's plan.

Block 7: Insured's Address. The insured's permanent address and telephone number are entered here. This address may be different from the patient's address in Block 5.

Block 8: Patient Status. These boxes are important for determining liability and for coordinating benefits.

- Single
- Married
- Other
- Employed: Put an X in this box if the patient is employed, whether full-time or part-time.
- Full-time student or part-time student: Put an X in the appropriate box, depending on the school's definition of full-time and part-time status. Generally, if the student is taking 6 or fewer credit hours, he or she is considered a part-time student.

Section 3: Patient/Insured Section—Blocks 9 to 13 (Figure 21-4)

NOTE: Blocks 11a-d are completed for the primary insurance. Blocks 9a-d are completed only if a secondary insurance claim is being submitted.

Block 9: Other Insured's Name. The name of the person who holds another policy on the patient. Block 9 is completed only if there is a secondary insurance policy and if that secondary policy is to be billed.

Block 9a: Other Insured's Policy or Group Number. The policy number of the insured in Block 9. See Block 1a for guidelines for Medicare, Medicaid, Group Health Plan, FECA/Black Lung, and Other ID numbers.

Block 9b: Other Insured's Date of Birth and Sex. The other insured's birth date and gender help identify the birth date and gender of the insured as indicated in Block 9. Block 9b is completed only if there is a secondary insurance policy and if that secondary policy is to be billed.

Block 9c: Employer's Name or School Name. This block identifies the other insured's employer or school name as indicated in Block 9. Block 9c is completed only if there is a secondary insurance policy and if that secondary policy is to be billed.

Block 9d: Insurance Plan Name or Program Name. The insurance plan name or program name identifies the name of the plan or program of the other insured as indicated in Block 9. Block 9d is completed only if there is a secondary insurance policy and if that secondary policy is to be billed.

Blocks 10a-c: Is Patient's Condition Related to: This block indicates whether the patient's condition is the result of an employment injury or illness, auto accident, or other accident.

Block 10d: Reserved for Local Use. Some third-party payers require that this box be used. Refer to the applicable third-party payer's instructions.

Block 11: Insured's Policy, Group, or FECA Number. Block 11 is completed for the primary insurance claim. The policy, group, or FECA number is the alphanumeric identifier for the insurance plan coverage. Workers' compensation claims use the carrier's alphanumeric identifier. The FECA number is the nine-digit alpha-numeric identifier assigned to the patient claiming a work-related condition under FECA.

Block 11a: Insured's Date of Birth and Sex. Block 11a is completed for the primary insurance claim. This information applies to the person identified in Block 1a.

Block 11b: Insured's Employer's Name or School Name. Block 11b is completed for the primary insurance claim. This refers to the name of the employer or school attended by the insured as indicated in Box 1a.

Block 11c: Insured's Insurance Plan Name or Program Name. Block 11c is completed for the primary insurance claim. The insurance plan name or program name refers to the name of the plan or program of the insured, as indicated in the Carrier Block (Section 1).

Block 11d: Is There Another Health Benefit Plan? This block indicates whether the patient has insurance coverage other than that indicated in Block 1. If there is a secondary coverage, put an X in the YES box; if not, or if no claim is being submitted using the secondary coverage, put an X in the NO box.

Block 12: Patient's or Authorized Person's Signature. The signature is an authorization for the release of any medical or other information necessary to process or adjudicate the claim. The signature of the patient or the patient's representative is required. In the case of computer-generated claims, an authorization form with the patient's signature must be kept in the patient's record authorizing the release of medical information. The phrase "Signature on File" may be entered in this field.

Block 13: Insured's or Authorized Person's Signature. The insured's or authorized person's signature indicates that there is a signature on file authorizing payment of medical benefits directly to the provider who appears in Blocks 31 and 32 of the claim. The signature of the patient or the patient's representative is required. In the case of computer-generated claims, an authorization form with the insured's signature must be kept in the patient's record authorizing the release of medical information. The phrase "Signature on File" may be entered in this field.

CRITICAL THINKING APPLICATION   21-2

It is office policy to request that patients assign benefits (payment) to the provider directly if the patient does not pay for services at the time of the encounter. One of the patients, Mr. Palmer, seems hesitant to sign Block 13 of the CMS-1500 form. How should Machelle explain the office policy to Mr. Palmer?

Physician/Supplier Section—Blocks 14 to 23
(Figure 21-5)

Block 14: Date of Current Illness, Injury, or Pregnancy. The date should be the date when the current illness or condition began, the date the injury happened or, in cases of pregnancy, the date of the last menstrual period (LMP).

Block 15: Same or Similar Illness. If the patient has had the same or a similar illness or condition, enter the onset date of the earlier condition. This block is used by the insurance carrier to determine whether any pre-existing condition existed, which might affect reimbursement.

Block 16: Dates Patient Unable to Work in Current Occupation. This section refers to the FROM and TO dates between which the patient was unable to work in his or her current occupation. If the patient has not returned to work, leave the TO field blank. This block is used to help determine an employee's long- or short-term disability payments.

Block 17: Name of Referring Provider or Other Source. The name of the referring provider, ordering provider, or other source that referred or ordered the service or procedure on the claim is entered in this block.

A *referring physician* is a physician who requests an item or service for the beneficiary for which payment may be made.

An *ordering physician* is a physician or, when appropriate, a non-physician practitioner who orders non-physician services for the patient.

Block 17a: Other ID. Block 17a currently is not reported (as of May 23, 2008); however, Block 17b must be reported when a service was ordered or referred by a physician.

Block 17b: NPI. The NPI refers to the individual national ID number (**National Provider Identifier**) that HIPAA assigns to each healthcare provider of services.

In the past, each insurance carrier, including government programs, assigned an identifier to each provider of service. Since 2007, as part of HIPAA, all allied healthcare providers of services have been assigned one individual NPI number that the provider can use regardless of which insurance carrier is billed for reimbursement. The NPI is a uniform, national ID number that has replaced Medicare's **Unique Provider Identification Number (UPIN)** and almost all other federal, state, and private insurance carriers' **provider identification numbers (PINs)**. However, the NPI does *not* replace the Social Security number (SSN), **Employer Identification Number (EIN)**, or federal Tax Identification Number (TIN) used by a

FIGURE 21-5 CMS-1500 claim form: physician or supplier information, Blocks 14 to 23.

provider of service. The SSN, EIN, and TIN are used for income and tax purposes and for reporting to the Internal Revenue Service.

Block 18: Hospitalization Dates Related to Current Services. These dates are the admission and discharge dates of the inpatient stay related to the services listed on the claim.

Block 19: Reserved for Local Use. Some payers ask for certain identifiers in this field. Refer to the applicable third-party payer's instructions. (To see a list of the identifiers that may still be used in some instances in this block, refer to the Evolve site at *evolve.elsevier.com/kinn*). Medicare has specific uses for this block if services were rendered by certain providers, or for certain services, drugs, or diagnostic tests. Refer to the *Medicare Claims Processing Manual* for instructions.

Block 20: Outside Lab?/Charges. This field refers to diagnostic laboratory services that have been rendered by an independent or separate provider as indicated in Block 32. Put an X in the YES box to indicate that an entity other than the provider billing for the service performed the diagnostic test and the provider in Block 33 paid the laboratory directly. Put an X in the NO box to indicate that no purchased tests are included on the claim. When the YES box is marked, the amount the provider was charged by the diagnostic laboratory is entered, and Block 32 should be completed with the name and address of the diagnostic laboratory or other entity.

Block 21: Diagnosis or Nature of Illness or Injury. This title refers to the signs, symptoms, complaint, or condition of the patient relating to the services on the claim. The diagnosis (ICD-9-CM) code or codes should be entered in this block. Enter one code for each of the four fields in the block. No more than four diagnosis codes should be used on one claim form.

Block 22: Medicaid Resubmission. The code and original reference number assigned by the insurance payer should be entered in this block if a Medicaid claim previously submitted has not been reimbursed; this also is done to resubmit the claim to Medicaid or its intermediary for payment.

Block 23: Prior Authorization Number. This is the payer-assigned number authorizing the service or services, procedure or procedures, and/or referral.

Physician/Supplier Section—Blocks 24 to 33
(Figure 21-6)

Block 24A: Date(s) of Service (lines 1-6). This date (or dates) is the actual month, day, and year that the service was provided.

Block 24B: Place of Service (lines 1-6). This block identifies where the services were provided. Enter the two-digit place of service (POS) code in Block 24B. Table 21-2 shows the two-digit place of service codes.

Block 24C: EMG (lines 1-6). This field is used to indicate whether the services provided involved an emergency. Enter a Y in this block if the services were provided in emergency circumstances. Medicare providers are not required to complete this item.

Block 24D: Procedures, Services, or Supplies (lines 1-6). In this field, identifying codes for reporting medical services and procedures are listed.

Block 24E: Diagnosis Pointer (lines 1-6). Enter the diagnosis code, or reference number, as shown in Block 21 to relate the date of service and the procedures performed to the primary diagnosis. Enter only one reference number per line item. When multiple services have been performed, enter the primary field number for each service (either a 1, a 2, a 3, or a 4). This is a required field. If two or more diagnoses are required for a procedure code (e.g., a Pap smear), the provider should reference only one of the diagnoses in Block 21.

Block 24F: $ Charges (lines 1-6). This is the total billed amount for each service line. If a series of services was performed on any one line, multiply the number of days or units (Block 24G) by the charge for one procedure or service and enter the total amount for all days or units.

Block 24G: Days or Units (lines 1-6). This title refers to the number of days that correspond to the dates entered in Block 24A, or to units, as defined in the CPT or HCPCS coding manual.

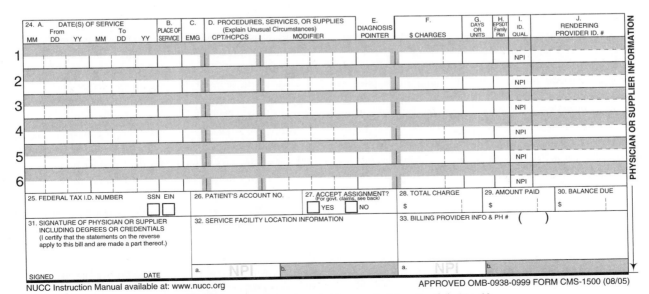

FIGURE 21-6 CMS-1500 claim form: physician or supplier information, Blocks 24 to 33.

TABLE 21-2 Place of Service Codes

CODE	DESCRIPTION	CODE	DESCRIPTION
11	Doctor's office	50	Federally qualified health center
12	Patient's home	51	Inpatient psychiatry facility
21	Inpatient hospital	52	Psychiatric facility — partial hospitalization
22	Outpatient hospital	53	Community mental health care (outpatient, 24-hour/day services, admission screening, consultation, and educational services)
23	Emergency department — hospital	54	Intermediate care facility/mentally retarded
24	Ambulatory surgical center	55	Residential substance abuse treatment facility
25	Birthing center	56	Psychiatric residential treatment center
26	Military treatment facility/uniformed service treatment facility	60	Mass immunization center
31	Skilled nursing facility (swing bed visits)	61	Comprehensive inpatient rehabilitation facility
32	Nursing facility (intermediate/long-term care facilities)	62	Comprehensive outpatient rehabilitation facility
33	Custodial care facility (domiciliary or rest home services)	65	End-stage renal disease treatment facility
34	Hospice (domiciliary or rest home services)	71	State or local public health clinic
35	Adult living care facilities (residential care facility)	72	Rural health clinic
41	Ambulance — land	81	Independent laboratory
42	Ambulance — air or water	99	Other unlisted facility

TABLE 21-3 Qualifiers Used to Report National Drug Code (NDC) Units

QUALIFIER	DESCRIPTION
F2	International unit
GR	gram
ML	milliliter
UN	unit

Table 21-3 shows the qualifiers to be used in this block. This field is most commonly used for multiple visits, units of supplies, or anesthesia minutes.

Block 24H: EPSDT/Family Plan (lines 1-6). This field identifies certain services covered under state plans. Refer to the appropriate insurance payer's guidelines (typically Medicaid or the Medicaid intermediary) for instructions on completing this block. Leave blank for Medicare, TRICARE, CHAMPVA, group health plans, FECA/Black Lung, and most other insurance types. (EPSDT stands for Early and Periodic Screening, Diagnosis, and Treatment, the child health program under Medicaid.)

Block 24I: Rendering Provider ID Qualifier (lines 1-6). The rendering provider is the person or company that rendered or supervised the care.

Block 24J: Rendering Provider ID Number (lines 1-6). Enter the NPI number of the individual performing/rendering the service

in the shaded portion of Block 24J. If there is no NPI number, enter the provider's PIN and the appropriate two-character qualifier.

Block 25: Federal Tax ID Number. This is the unique tax identifier assigned to the provider by the Internal Revenue Service. It may be either the provider's Social Security number or an EIN.

Block 26: Patient's Account Number. This is the account number assigned to the patient by the provider of service. The account number assists the provider in locating the patient's financial information and record.

Block 27: Accept Assignment? "Accepting assignment" means that the provider agrees to accept assignment under the terms of the Medicare program and some other insurance payers. Put an X in the YES box in this block if the provider will **accept assignment** of benefits; that is, that he or she is a participating physician and agrees to abide by the terms of the agreement to accept what the insurance company pays and write off the difference between the original charge and the allowable amount set by the insurance carrier.

Block 28: Total Charge. This is the amount billed on this claim form for all services rendered. Add the charges reported in Block 24F for all the lines of service on the claim form.

Block 29: Amount Paid. This is the amount received from the patient or other payers.

Block 30: Balance Due. This is the amount left after the patient has paid a co-pay or co-insurance.

Block 31: Signature of Physician or Supplier (include degrees or credentials). The signature is the verification from the provider that the claim is correct. The physician can place his **electronic (or digital) signature** on the claim by typing his or her name or initials (if allowed by the insurance carrier) in the block.

Block 32: Service Facility Location Information. Enter the name, address, city, state, and ZIP code for the site where services were rendered.

Block 32a [service facility NPI number]. Enter the NPI number of the service facility.

Block 32b [service facility's non-NPI identifier]. If the service facility does not have an NPI, enter the payer-assigned unique identifier of the facility and the qualifier number.

Block 33: Billing Provider Info & PH. Enter the address and phone number of the provider that wishes to be paid on this claim.

Block 33a [billing provider's NPI]. Enter the billing provider's NPI number.

Box 33b [billing provider's non-NPI identifier]. If the billing provider does not have an NPI number, enter the professional's payer-assigned unique identifier. The two-character qualifier for the non-NPI identifier is also entered here.

GUIDELINES FOR CLAIMS REVIEW BEFORE SUBMISSION

The following guidelines can help ensure that a clean claim is submitted.

- Proofread the form carefully for accuracy and completeness.
- Make certain any necessary attachments are included with the completed form.
- Follow office policies and guidelines for claim review and signatures.
- Forward the original claim to the proper insurance carrier either by mail or electronically.
- If creating a paper claim, make a copy of the completed and signed claim form for the office records.
- If a non-computer-generated insurance log is maintained, enter the appropriate information in the insurance log and record the insurance submission information on the patient's ledger.
- The patient's and/or insured's name, address, and ID, group, and/or policy number should be identical to the information printed on the insurance card.
- The patient's birth date and gender should correspond with the medical record.
- The word NONE should be entered in Block 11 if Medicare is the primary payer.
- The referring, consulting, or ordering provider's name and NPI number should be entered in Blocks 17 and 17a, if applicable.
- In Block 27 (Accept Assignment?), put an X in the YES box if the physician is a participating provider (PAR) or has an agreement with the insurance carrier or payer to accept assignment.
- Make sure the diagnosis is not missing or incomplete.
- The diagnosis must be coded accurately, according to the ICD-9-CM coding manual, and must correspond to the treatment.
- The patient must have authorized the release of information, and Block 12 should contain a handwritten signature, the words "Signature on File," or the acronym SOF.
- Section 2, the Patient/Insured Section (Blocks 1 through 13), should be completed accurately according to the guidelines of the insurance carrier.

- Fees for each charge must be listed individually, or they must be correctly computed if more than 1 day or unit is entered in Block 24G.
- All required fields of the diagnosis and procedure section of the claim form (Blocks 14 through 24J) should be accurate and completed according to the guidelines of the third-party payer or insurance company.
- The physician's signature must be on the form.
- The provider's federal TIN, EIN, or SSN should be double-checked to ensure accuracy.
- The physician's NPI number, corresponding to the insurance carrier being billed, should be entered in Block 24J and again in Block 33a. The provider's PIN, when applicable, should be entered in Block 33b, with the qualifying number, when applicable.

PREVENTING CLAIM REJECTION

It is important for the medical assistant to understand and comply with the guidelines specific to completion of a CMS-1500 form for each third-party payer and insurance company to prevent delays in reimbursement—or worse, denial of payment. The guidelines for Medicare, Medicaid, TRICARE, and workers' compensation can be found online at any of the fiscal intermediaries (e.g., Medicare billing guidelines are on the CMS Web site). Most computer software billing systems have built-in "claim scrubbers" that help in the process, and if claims are sent electronically through a clearinghouse, claims auditing is done before the clearinghouse submits the claim to the third-party payer. Claims without significant errors of any type are called *clean claims*. Claims with incorrect, missing, or insufficient data are called *dirty claims*.

Denied or Rejected Claims

The two main reasons for denial of payment are technical errors and insurance policy coverage issues. Technical errors include incorrect or incomplete information or typographic or mathematical errors. A common reason for insurance coverage rejection is that a procedure listed on the claim is not a covered service or is considered a pre-existing condition by the insurance payer.

Explanation of Benefits

The reason for a claim denial or reduction in reimbursement is listed on the explanation of benefits (EOB; Figure 21-7) of commercial carriers, the remittance advice (RA) for commercial carriers and on Medicaid claims, and the explanation of Medicare benefits (EOMB) on Medicare claims. The EOMB, EOB, and RA are hard copy or electronic forms that list the amount paid by the insurance company, in addition to information about any noncovered services, denied claims (and the reason), deductible and/or co-insurance amounts, and other information about the claim or claims submitted.

Some descriptive terms for claims include the following:

- **Clean claim**. A complete, accurate claim.
- Dingy or **dirty claim**. An inaccurate or **incomplete claim** returned for more information or correction.
- **Rejected claim**. A claim for which payment has been denied for any reason (e.g., non-covered service, pre-existing condition, or ineligibility).

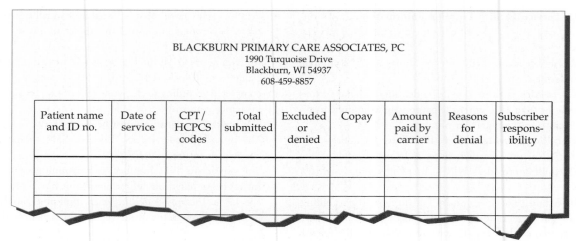

BLACKBURN PRIMARY CARE ASSOCIATES, PC
1990 Turquoise Drive
Blackburn, WI 54937
608-459-8857

Patient name and ID no.	Date of service	CPT/ HCPCS codes	Total submitted	Excluded or denied	Copay	Amount paid by carrier	Reasons for denial	Subscriber respons- ibility

FIGURE 21-7 Example of an explanation of benefits (EOB) form. (From Hunt SA: *Saunders fundamentals of medical assisting,* Philadelphia, 2002, WB Saunders.)

At times, a denied claim may involve policy issues beyond the control of the medical assistant. When this happens, he or she should contact the patient and discuss the problem. Normally, it is the patient's responsibility to resolve disputes regarding payment with the payer. The insurance policy is a contract between the company and the insured. However, the provider and those involved with the billing process in the medical facility should have a good understanding of the guidelines and requirements for the types of claims and various insurers handled most often in the facility and be willing to assist the patient wherever possible to ensure reimbursement.

CRITICAL THINKING APPLICATION   21-3
During her externship at the women's health center, Machelle sees a file containing a number of rejected claims. On closer examination, she notices that similar errors in certain blocks are repeatedly the cause for rejection. Discuss common errors on the CMS-1500 claim form and what can be done to prevent these mistakes and/or omissions.

CHECKING A CLAIM'S STATUS

It is often necessary to send a "tracer" to an insurance company to determine the status of a delinquent insurance claim. The accepted practice is to submit the tracer a day or two after the usual turnaround time of the payer, generally 30 to 60 days (10 to 14 days for an electronic submission). A tracer is typically a form letter asking the insurance company about the status of an unpaid insurance claim. An example of a tracer letter is shown in Figure 21-8. A claim's status can also be checked electronically using the ASC X12N transaction and code sets for the request and the response.
- ASC X12N 276 Health Care Claim Status Request
- ASC X12N 277 Health Care Claim Status Response

A duplicate copy of all submitted claims should be retained either in paper form or in the computer billing software. A structured routine for following up on claims unpaid within a specific time

frame should be created to prevent overlooking a claim that should be filed or that has not been paid. The Insurance Claim Register, tickler files, and reports from the insurance database all help to keep track of paid and pending claims. If software is used to file claims, an insurance pending report and an insurance aging report (among others) can be generated.

The insurance aging report (Figure 21-9) can be sorted by the age of the claim, typically 30, 60, 90, and 120 days (or more), and by the payer (e.g., Medicare, Medicaid, and so on). Any of these methods is useful for following up on claims that have yet to be paid.

If claims are submitted electronically, either directly or through a clearinghouse, the medical assistant might allow 10 business days for claim turnaround before expecting reimbursement. For paper claims, allow an additional week or two to account for the necessary manual processing and mailing time. The length of time between a claim's submission and its payment varies from payer to payer; an experienced medical assistant soon becomes familiar with the individual payment patterns of third-party payers and their claim turnaround times. Most states have laws that require payment within 45 days for clean claims.

Audit Trails

Electronic transactions leave behind a path or trail as they are processed, and this trail can be tracked or audited to provide a record. This record, called an **audit trail**, can be used to verify that the information was processed correctly or to locate the source of an error. If an office uses a computerized accounting program and submits claims electronically, the software is capable of printing out an insurance aging report by date, by patient name, or by carrier name. If paper claims are used, however, the medical assistant should establish a follow-up procedure for tracking insurance claims. This can be accomplished by using an insurance claims register or log (Figure 21-10). This document can be developed and updated with little effort using a spreadsheet computer program, such as Microsoft Excel, if the provider's office is computerized. If the provider uses physician financial management and billing

INSURANCE CLAIM TRACER

INSURANCE COMPANY NAME _____ DATE _____

ADDRESS: _____

PATIENT NAME _____ INSURED: _____

POLICY/CERTIFICATE NUMBER _____ GROUP NAME/NUMBER _____

EMPLOYER NAME AND ADDRESS: _____

DATE OF INITIAL CLAIM SUBMISSION _____ AMOUNT: _____

An inordinate amount of time has passed since submission of our original claim as described above. We have not received a request for additional information and still await payment of this assigned claim. Please review the attached duplicate and process for payment within seven (7) days.

If there is any difficulty with this claim, please check one of these below and return this letter to our office.

Claim pending because: _____
Payment of claim in process: _____
Payment made on claim: Date: _____ To whom: _____
Claim denied: (Reason) _____
Patient notified: Yes _____ No _____
Remarks: _____

Thank you for your assistance in this important matter. Please contact _____ in our office if you have any questions regarding this claim.

Office of: _____ M.D.

Address: _____

_____ TELEPHONE NUMBER: _____

FIGURE 21-8 Example of an insurance claim tracer. (From Fordney MT: *Insurance handbook for the medical office,* ed 12, St Louis, 2012, WB Saunders.)

Blackburn Primary Care Associates
Patient Aging

NAME	CURRENT 0 - 30	PAST 31 - 60	PAST 61 - 90	PAST 91 - 120	PAST over 120	Total Balance
Mary Smith Last Payment on 08/08/XX	$120.00					$120.00
John Payne Last Payment on 07/06/XX		$250.00				$250.00
Jack Desmonde Last Payment on 05/25/XX			$500.00			$500.00
Jill Jayne Last Payment on 04/02/XX		$80.00		$100.00		$180.00
Report Aging Totals Percent of Total Aging	$120.00 11.4%	$330.00 31.4%	$330.00 47.6%	$100.00 9.5%		$1,050.00 100.0%

FIGURE 21-9 Example of an accounts aging record. (From Hunt SA: *Saunders fundamentals of medical assisting,* Philadelphia, 2002, WB Saunders.)

INSURANCE CLAIMS REGISTER						Page No.		
Patient's Name Group/Policy No.	Name of Insurance Company	Claim Submitted		Follow-Up		Claim Paid		Difference
		Date	Amount	Date	Date	Date	Amt	
Jones, Bob	BC/BS	1-7-03	319.37			2/28/03	294.82	24.55
Carson, David	BC	1-8-03	268.08	2-10-03	3-10-03			
Linden, Jan	Medicaid	1-9-03	146.15	2-10-03				
Paul, Emma	Medicare	1-10-03	96.28	2-10-03				
Cortez, Jose	Unicare	1-10-03	647.09	2-10-03				
Dimico, Joe	Tricare	2-1-03	134.78	3-10-03				
Coldman, Billy	Aetna	2-4-03	607.67	3-10-03				
Fritz, Renee	Travelers	2-10-03	564.55	3-10-03				
Wong, Chang	Prudential	2-15-03	1515.79					
Billings, Harry	Allstate	2-21-03	121.21					
Green, James	BC	2-24-03	124.99					

FIGURE 21-10 Example of an insurance claims register.

software, an audit trail report can be generated automatically from the software program.

Another method of tracking claims is a tickler file (Figure 21-11), also called a *suspense* or *follow-up file*. With this method, a copy of each insurance claim is filed chronologically, and the file is checked periodically for unprocessed (delinquent) claims. When the claim is paid, the copy is removed and the information is posted on the patient's ledger card. Delinquent claims remaining in the file after the normal contract time limits are pulled and then traced. If the claim has been denied, a letter may be sent to the insurance carrier's appeals department, with a copy to the patient.

Patient Education

The medical assistant should be able to explain confusing technical issues to patients in simple, understandable terms. Patients, especially elderly ones, quickly become confused and frustrated by insurance issues, especially Medicare rules and regulations, which change nearly every year. The medical assistant should attempt to keep patients fully informed of changes in insurance guidelines and patiently explain why some procedures and services are paid for and others are not.

Legal and Ethical Issues

The practice of medicine and the responsibilities of the medical assistant are greatly affected by the legislative process. It is extremely important to stay current on the laws that affect medicine, federal and state insurance programs (e.g., Medicare, Medicaid, workers' compensation, and TRICARE) and the completion of the CMS-1500 claim form.

HIPAA is responsible for implementation of various laws that protect individuals' health insurance and privacy standards. Medical assistants should familiarize themselves with this important insurance law.

Because of the emphasis on compliance in medical practices today, every medical office must create and implement a plan to identify potential compliance problems and correct them before a liability risk is incurred. All providers are required to avoid fraud and abuse charges by following the regulations and guidelines provided by government entities and third-party payers.

CLOSING COMMENTS

Accurate completion of the CMS-1500 claim form begins with gathering the patient's and the insured's demographic and insurance information, the diagnoses and procedures and services performed, and the provider's identifying information. The Patient Registration form is used to collect the patient's and insured's information, and confirmation of all collected information is an important task that should not be neglected. Confirmation of the information can be obtained through photocopies of the patient's and insured's insurance cards, driver's licenses; verification of eligibility and benefits; and, where applicable, securing approval for procedures, services, and referrals from the insurance payer in advance. It is wise to have a checklist of all the information the medical assistant will need to complete an insurance claim correctly.

The CMS-1500 claim form (version 08-05) is generally accepted by all insurance payers. The requirements for completing each block of the CMS-1500 form vary slightly, depending on the type of insurance carrier (e.g., Medicare, Medicaid, group health plan). When completing an insurance claim for a specific insurance payer, it is important that the medical assistant use the claims processing manual or guidelines for *that* insurance carrier, to make certain the claim is completed according to the payer's specific requirements.

As mentioned, accurate and complete insurance claim forms submitted for payment are called *clean claims*. Clean claims result in reimbursement without delay, as long as no insurance policy limitations prevent or reduce payments. Insurance claims submitted with incorrect or missing information are called *dingy* or *dirty claims* and can be returned for additional information by the payer. This delays reimbursement for services rendered, and if the additional information is not forwarded quickly to the payer, can result in denial of payment. It is essential that procedures be in place to review all claims before submission to ensure that the claim is complete and the information is accurate. Unpaid claims result in a loss of revenue for the provider. Audit trails, insurance aging reports, tickler files, and/or insurance claims registers are valuable tools in insurance claims follow-up.

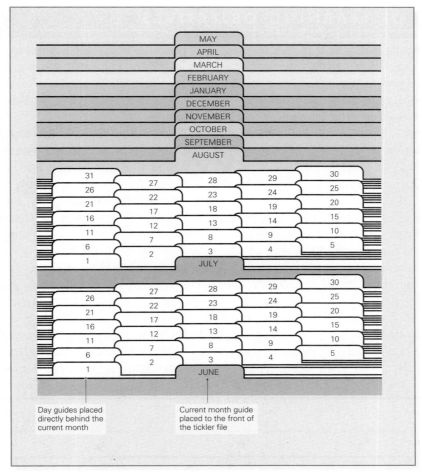

FIGURE 21-11 Example of an insurance claims tickler file. (From Fordney MT: *Insurance handbook for the medical office,* ed 12, St Louis, 2012, WB Saunders.)

SUMMARY OF SCENARIO

Machelle believes that she now has a better understanding of the insurance claims process. Before becoming a medical assisting student, she did not give much thought to what went on behind the scenes when she visited a medical office for her own personal healthcare. She now understands why all of the information is collected at the time of her visits to the doctor, including the patient registration form listing her demographic and insurance information.

Machelle has learned that the gathering of accurate data and verification of eligibility and benefits are some of the most important tasks performed, before she even begins to complete an insurance claim form. This information and the procedure to verify eligibility and benefits greatly reduce the chance of insurance claim denials or requests for additional information. No matter where

she works and regardless of whether the office is computerized, organization, communication, dedication, and attention to detail head the list of requirements for becoming successful.

Machelle has asked for her instructor's help in developing a reference manual for the various third-party payers common to her area; this will help her understand the requirements of the insurance carriers when submitting an insurance claim form. It also will greatly reduce the number of claims that are returned for more information, which delays reimbursement for services rendered.

Machelle is looking forward to more hands-on experience in the medical office where she is doing her externship so that she can gain as much knowledge as possible in every facet of medical assisting.

SUMMARY OF LEARNING OBJECTIVES

1. **Define, spell, and pronounce the terms listed in the vocabulary.**
   Spelling and pronouncing medical terms correctly bolster the medical assistant's credibility. Knowing the definition of these terms promotes confidence in communication with patients and co-workers.

2. **Discuss the differences between paper claims and electronic claims.**
   Insurance claims can be submitted in two forms: paper or electronic. Both have advantages and disadvantages; however, electronic claims normally have fewer errors and historically are paid faster.

3. **Understand the guidelines for completing the CMS-1500 Health Insurance Claim Form.**
   The insurance claim cycle begins when the patient first makes an appointment. The medical assistant should follow an established list of guidelines for completing the CMS-1500 claim form, including obtaining a signed authorization to release information and assign benefits, if applicable.

4. **Explain how to complete each of the blocks of the CMS-1500 claim form.**
   The CMS-1500 claim form had 33 blocks, and except for a few blocks that ask for standard information, completion requirements vary from payer to payer. To maximize reimbursement, the medical assistant should familiarize himself or herself with each major payer's unique requirements.

5. **Gather information for use on insurance claim forms.**
   The guidelines for gathering information needed to complete and submit an insurance claim are presented in Procedure 21-1. The medical assistant must have accurate, complete information to complete a claim form correctly.

6. **Complete a CMS-1500 claim form appropriately for various federal, state, and commercial third-party payers.**
   Accuracy in completing insurance claim forms is mandatory. The process for completing claim forms appropriately is outlined in Procedure 21-2.

7. **Differentiate between "clean" and "dirty" claims.**
   Clean claims are those that can be processed and paid quickly; dirty claims contain errors and/or omissions that often result in rejection, thus greatly slowing the reimbursement process.

8. **Discuss methods of preventing claims rejections.**
   Rejection and delay of claims cost the medical facility time and money. Proven methods of preventing claims rejections should be established and followed.

9. **Describe ways of checking the status of claims.**
   It is important to track claims once they have been submitted. An insurance claim register, or log, can be created and used as one method of tracking claims. A routine should be established for claims follow-up.

CONNECTIONS

Study Guide Connection: Go to the Chapter 21 Study Guide. Read the Case Study and Workplace Applications and complete the assignments. Do online research for answers to the questions in the Internet Activities associated with the health insurance claim form.

Evolve Connection: For more information related to the health insurance claim form, go to *evolve.elsevier.com/kinn* and visit related Web links for Chapter 21. Click on the Medical Assisting Exam Review and do the practice questions to sharpen your test-taking skills. To learn more about office software, do the exercises for the AltaPoint demonstration on the CD.

PROFESSIONAL FEES, BILLING, AND COLLECTING

22

SCENARIO

Jodie Bimmell, a registered medical assistant (RMA), has worked for Dr. Ted Crawford, an endocrinologist, for 3 years. She began as a receptionist, but she is proficient in mathematics and enjoys working with numbers. Because of Dr. Crawford's confidence in her abilities, he placed her in charge of the accounting functions for the practice 2 years ago. When patients are ready to leave, Jodie totals their bill and enters the charges and payments into the computerized billing system, which also allows her to schedule return appointments. Because Jodie also has learned quite a bit about medical insurance, she can answer most of the patients' questions about their coverage and the benefits or exclusions of their policies. She knows where to direct patients who have more complicated questions and how to follow up to ensure that they received an answer—one of the most important duties of a professional medical assistant. Jodie is able to decipher confusing explanations of benefits (EOBs) from insurance carriers and explain reimbursements to the patients. She has a great attitude about assisting patients with insurance questions and does not hesitate to call the insurance company or third-party payer on the patient's behalf. She provides patients with exceptional customer service.

Jodie knows to be careful when dealing with numeric transactions. Her handwriting is neat and legible, and she writes numbers the same way each time to prevent confusion and errors. She can work with a manual pegboard system in a pinch, but she uses the computerized billing system on a day-to-day basis. Jodie has some accounting background, which enables her to find errors easily and correct them. She is responsible for making sure the accounts balance on a daily, weekly, and monthly basis and considers errors a puzzle to solve and an opportunity to learn. She has never encountered an error she was unable to resolve by the end of the day.

Jodie provides a valuable service to Dr. Crawford's patients. She can be counted on to follow up on any detail that needs attention. When patients call her for assistance, she responds within 24 hours (often within 1 hour) with answers to their questions or a resource to help them. Jodie is willing to help any staff member with other duties when necessary and prides herself on being a patient advocate. She is an enthusiastic team player who puts the patients first.

While studying this chapter, think about the following questions:

- Why do the provider's usual fees influence the amount of reimbursement received from third-party payers?
- Why is professional courtesy used less frequently than in the past?
- How does the medical assistant effectively explain fees to patients?
- How can the medical assistant be a valuable patient advocate?

LEARNING OBJECTIVES

1. Define, spell, and pronounce the terms listed in the vocabulary.
2. List three values that are considered in determining professional fees.
3. Differentiate the terms *usual, customary,* and *reasonable.*
4. Discuss the value of fee estimates for patient treatment.
5. Explain basic bookkeeping computations.
6. Differentiate between bookkeeping and accounting.
7. Compare the manual and computerized bookkeeping systems used in ambulatory healthcare.
8. Identify procedures for preparing patient accounts.
9. Discuss the types of adjustments that may be made to a patient's account.
10. Explain both billing and payment options.
11. Describe the impact of both the Fair Debt Collection Practices Act and the Truth in Lending Act as they apply to collections.
12. Discuss procedures for collecting outstanding accounts.

VOCABULARY

account A statement of transactions during a fiscal period and the resulting balance.

account balance The amount owed on an account.

accounts receivable ledger A record of the charges and payments posted on an account.

credit An entry on an account constituting an addition to a revenue, net worth, or liability account; the balance in a person's favor.

credit cards Devices issued by a bank or other financial institution, retail stores, and other businesses that allow the card holder to make purchases prior to paying for them; the card holder is then billed, usually after interest has been added.

debit cards Cards that look like credit cards and by which money can be withdrawn, bills paid, or purchases made directly from the holder's bank account without the payment of interest.

debit An entry on an account representing an addition to an expense or asset account or a deduction from a revenue, a net worth, or a liability account.

decedent a person who is deceased.

disbursements Funds paid out.

fee profile A compilation or average of physician fees over a given period.

fee schedule A compilation of pre-established fee allowances for given services or procedures.

fiscal agent An organization under contract to the government (as well as some private plans) to act as financial representatives in handling insurance claims from providers of healthcare; also referred to as a fiscal intermediary.

instigate To goad or urge forward; to provoke.

intangible not made of physical substance; not able to be held or touched.

medically indigent Able to take care of ordinary living expenses but unable to afford medical care.

payables Balances due to a creditor on an account.

pegboard system An older method of tracking patient accounts that allows the figures to be proved accurate through mathematical formulas. It is still used in some small to medium practices; also called the write-it-once system.

posting Entering figures in an accounting system; transferring or carrying from a book of original entry to a ledger.

preponderance A superiority or excess in number or quantity; a majority.

professional courtesy Reduction or absence of fees to professional associates.

receipts Amounts paid on patient accounts.

receivables Total monies received on accounts.

secured A loan or line of credit that is backed by a pledge of payment and usually obtained using collateral.

transaction An exchange or transfer of goods, services, or funds.

trustee A person to whom property is legally committed to be administered for the benefit of a beneficiary or held by an administrator to be distributed to multiple individuals or businesses.

unsecured A debt that is not protected by collateral.

The practice of medicine is both a business and a profession, and the details of conducting the business aspects of the practice often are the responsibility of the medical assistant. Although service to the patient is the primary concern of the medical profession, a physician must charge and collect a fee for such services to continue providing medical care to patients. Many factors contribute to the determination of fees for the services and treatment rendered to the patient. The medical assistant is responsible for informing the patient about financial matters, for billing insurance companies or other third-party payers, and in some cases for making payment arrangements.

HOW FEES ARE DETERMINED

Setting fees is no simple matter. The physician has three commodities or values to sell: time, judgment, and services. Yet the value of these commodities is never exactly the same to any two individuals. Medical care has little value except to the patient receiving the care, and the value may not be consistent with the person's ability to pay. In every case, the physician must place an estimate on the value of the services. This estimated figure is known as the physician's *fee for service*. The value may then be modified by other considerations, such as an excessive length of time spent with the patient or an especially complicated group of illnesses suffered by one patient.

Impact of Managed Care

The **preponderance** of patients enrolled in health maintenance organizations (HMOs) and preferred provider organizations (PPOs) is an important consideration for the physician. Under managed care contracts, the physician agrees to accept predetermined fees for specific procedures and services instead of the fee-for-service method. The patient may have to make a co-payment, which is determined by the insurance contract and is collected at the time of service. A base capitation plan pays the provider a set amount for each patient enrolled in a group, and this amount is meant to cover all the patient's healthcare expenses in a given period. However, if one or two people in the group become very ill, the physician may actually lose money, because those patients may use all the groups' pooled money for that period.

Prevailing Rate in the Community

The economic level of the community plays a significant role in determining a physician's fees. Different communities have multiple cost-of-living scales, and this affects medical fees. The prevailing rate in the community must be taken into consideration by each physician. Interestingly, fees that are too low drive patients away just as quickly as fees that are too high, because the average person tends to judge the worth of a product by its cost, and low cost can be translated as low value.

Usual, Customary, and Reasonable Fees

Most insurance plans base their payments on a usual, customary, and reasonable (UCR) fee for a particular procedure.

- *Usual*—The physician's usual fee for a given service; the fee most frequently charged for the service.
- *Customary*—A range of the usual fees charged for the same service by physicians with similar training and experience who practice in the same geographic and socioeconomic area.
- *Reasonable*—The fee for an exceptionally difficult or complicated service or procedure that requires extraordinary time or effort by the physician.

For example, suppose Dr. Crawford's usual fee for new patients is $100. The customary charge for a first visit by other physicians in the same community with similar training and experience ranges from $75 to $125. Dr. Crawford's fee of $100 is within the customary range and would be paid by an insurance plan that pays on a usual and customary basis. However, if the range of usual fees in the community is $60 to $85, the insurance plan would allow only the maximum within the range, or $85. If Dr. Crawford spent 2 hours on a lengthy history and physical examination for a patient with a terminal illness, his charge of $175 might be considered reasonable, as long as he had documentation in the patient's chart to justify the charges. The Evaluation and Management (E/M) section of procedural coding manuals is carefully written to allow physicians to indicate the appropriate level, or extent, of the patient history, physical examination, and complexity of medical decision making.

CRITICAL THINKING APPLICATION 22-1

Jodie realizes that many of Dr. Crawford's patients are confused about insurance policies and managed care and that they are frustrated when payments are not as high as they expected. How can Jodie help patients better understand their policies? Is this duty truly a part of Jodie's job? Why or why not?

Fee Setting by Third-Party Payers

The physician does not act alone in determining fees. A third-party payer may provide a schedule of predetermined fees. Some require preapproval of the fee before service is rendered, and some require precertification before paying for certain services. Government programs, such as Medicare and Medicaid, have strict guidelines for reimbursement. The physician may have to adjust part of the fees to meet contractual obligations with the third-party payer.

Physician's Fee Profile

The **fiscal agent** (or *fiscal intermediary*) for government-sponsored insurance programs and some private plans keeps a continuous record of the usual charges submitted for specific services by each physician. When these fees have been compiled and averaged over a given period, usually a year, the physician's **fee profile** is established. The fee profile is used in determining the amount of third-party liability for services under the program. Physicians often object to the lag between a private fee increase and the point when it is reflected in payments by an insurance carrier. This interval can be as long as 2 to 3 years.

Insurance Allowance

In some individual cases, the physician may not want to charge the patient more than the person's insurance allows. This sometimes is a professional courtesy (which may be extended to healthcare professionals); in other cases, it is applied as the physician sees fit. Always charge the full fee first, with the understanding that after the insurance allowance has been received, the balance may be discounted or adjusted. If a smaller fee is quoted and charged at a discount, several things can happen:

- The lower fee can alter the physician's fee profile.
- Only the reduced fee can be recovered if it is necessary to bring litigation for payment.
- The insurance allowance may be reduced.
- The insurance company may take the position that the reduced fee is the physician's usual and customary fee and base its payment accordingly.
- Reducing fees and adjustments for professional courtesy may violate the physician's agreement with the third-party payer and could be considered fraudulent.

EXPLAINING FEES TO PATIENTS

Patients, especially new ones, naturally wonder how much their office visits and treatments will cost, but they often are reluctant to voice their concern. The first step in discussing financial issues is to make sure the conversation is held out of the hearing range of other patients. If the discussion is to be held during the checkout process, make sure this is done in a private area or that other patients are out of earshot. Patients are hesitant to discuss financial issues with strangers lingering.

Do not wait for the patient to ask about fees. The physician or the medical assistant should approach the subject if the patient does not do so. Be prepared to discuss costs with all patients and ask whether they have questions about the fees. The medical assistant might open the conversation by saying, "Mr. Conn, do you have any questions about the costs of your operation? If you do, I'll be glad to review them with you."

Never sidestep payment issues by saying, "Don't worry about the bill; let's just get you well first." The patient may later complain about the bill because he or she misunderstood the complexity of the service.

Even when the physician quotes a fee, the medical assistant often is responsible for explaining the physician's fees to the patient. Know how fees are determined and why charges vary. Develop a thorough knowledge of the physician's practice and policies so that handling perplexing situations involving fees becomes routine. Educate patients that the money spent for medical care is an excellent investment in the future. It is the rare patient who understands the intricate procedures involved in diagnosis and treatment, especially when third-party payers are involved, so be patient and understanding when questions arise about fees.

Explain that compliance with the physician's orders may actually save the patient money over time. Each patient should control and manage his or her current diseases and prevent symptoms from worsening or new disorders from developing; this ultimately reduces the patient's healthcare costs.

Discussion of Fees in Advance

Patients can better plan for medical expenses when fees are discussed before treatment. Most patients want to meet their financial obligations but rightfully insist on an accurate estimate of those costs before they commit to paying them. Misconceptions and complaints about overcharging and fee discrepancies often are eliminated when fees are explained to the patient before a procedure or surgery is scheduled, even to the point of describing how a fee is established. Some physicians offer a discount if a patient has no insurance and pays cash. Although some physicians will allow fee negotiation in special circumstances, most managed care contracts require the physician to charge the correct co-payment and do not allow further discounts.

Explanation of Additional Fees

When discussing patients' fees, remember to explain additional costs that extend beyond the physician's own charges. For example, if a patient is to undergo surgery, the person should know the costs of the operation, the anesthesiologist's and radiologist's charges, the laboratory fees, and the approximate hospital bill. If consultation becomes necessary, inform the patient that a separate bill will be sent by the consulting physician and that the consultation is for the benefit of the patient and the referring physician.

Fee Estimates

Most physicians give patients an estimate of medical expenses before hospitalization; these estimates often are developed in cooperation with local hospitals or surgery centers. Individual physicians occasionally work up their own estimate forms while in the treatment room with the patient. Patients must usually budget their money for medical procedures, and most physicians are willing to work with the patient to make payment arrangements, especially for expensive treatments or procedures, or when responding to emergency situations.

Estimates also are helpful when the patient is faced with long-term treatment. Always emphasize that the information is only an estimate and that the actual cost may vary somewhat. Estimate slips should be prepared in duplicate so that the patient has a copy. Retain the original in the patient's medical record. Using estimates (1) documents that a fee was quoted; (2) helps to eliminate the possibility of misquoting the fee later; and (3) simplifies collections by clarifying expected payments, which prevent misunderstanding and confusion over charges.

The Guarantor's Ultimate Responsibility

Patients must understand that the *guarantor* is the person ultimately responsible for the entire bill. The insurance policy is a contract between the policyholder or between a group of people (e.g., an employer) and an insurance company or managed care organization. The physician is not a party to this contract. Therefore, physicians and their staff are not responsible for pursuing insurance payment for the benefit of the patient. However, it is in the best interest of the staff to actively assist the patient if problems occur securing payment. This is true for two reasons.

First, the staff is almost always more knowledgeable about the insurance business than the patient. Many patients do not even read their insurance policies and have no idea what is and is not covered. Some patients expect insurance to pay all costs simply because they are paying a high premium or payment. The medical assistant may need to educate these patients about their policies and offer advice on how patients can effectively work with the insurance company to get answers to questions and make sure they are receiving all the benefits to which they are entitled.

Second, helping the patient secure payment means that the physician will be compensated for his or her services. If the medical assistant acts as a patient advocate with the insurance company, these efforts usually result in payment of the contracted amount of the bill. Make sure the proper co-payments are received and credited to patients' accounts.

Medical assistants gain knowledge about the insurance industry when they actively assist patients with their concerns. The more experience a medical assistant has in working with insurance and third-party payers, the more helpful he or she can be to patients. The medical assistant should keep a notebook with specific information about each type of policy the office handles; this will be a source of excellent guidance and suggestions when working with a particular payer.

Always be sure to secure guarantors in writing. Most patient information sheets have a section referring to the guarantor. A statement may be included that the guarantor signs, indicating an agreement to pay the costs of medical care. States have varying statutes that deal with guarantors, so be sure the office's policies reflect compliance with those laws. It is especially important to secure a written agreement to pay for services when the care will be long term or when a costly treatment or surgical procedure must be done.

Charging the Patient for Medical Services and Procedures

The slips attached to charts while the patient is in the office are called *encounter forms* (Figure 22-1; additional examples of encounter forms are available on the Evolve Web site). The encounter form provides information about the patient, such as the name, account

BRIAN R. BOYER, M.D.
Board Certified in Family Practice
9851 Regents Blvd.
Las Vegas, NV 89128
(702) 555-8978

LIC. # R66114
TAX I.D. # 60-2201741

PATIENT'S LAST NAME	FIRST	INITIAL	ACCOUNT NUMBER		DATE OF SERVICE
INSURANCE COMPANY			CO-PAY AMT.	VERIFY	

PAT. INFO.

✔ DESCRIPTION	NEW	ESTAB.	CODE/MD	FEE	✔ DESCRIPTION	CODE/MD	FEE	✔ DESCRIPTION		CODE/MD	FEE
1. OFFICE VISITS					**3. OFFICE PROCEDURES (CONTINUED)**			**4. INJECTIONS (CONTINUED)**			
Minimal	99201	99211			Addit. Shots	90472		Varivax	V05.4	90716	
Focused	99202	99212			Immun. Admin. (x1) Child	90465		Vitamin B12	J3420		
Expanded	99203	99213			Addit. Shots Child	90466		Influenza Child <3	V04.81	90655	
Detailed	99204	99214			Injection Admin	90772		Influenza, Adult		90658	
Comprehensive	99205	99215			IA-Finger, Toe	20600		Zostavax	053.71	90736	
Prev. Care Age und. 1	99381	99391			Wrist, Elbow, Ankle	20605		Menactra	V03.9	90734	
Age 1-4 yrs.	99382	99392			Shoulder, Hip, Knee	20610		Gardisil	V04.89	90649	
Age 5-11 yrs.	99383	99393			Venipuncture	G0001	36415				
Age 12-17 yrs.	99384	99394			**4. INJECTIONS**			**5. LABORATORY**			
Age 18-39 yrs.	99385	99395			Comvax - Hep B/HIB	90748		Stool Occult Blood		82270	
Age 40-64 yrs.	99386	99396			Depo-Medrol 40 mg	J1030		Urinalysis		81000	
Age 65 & up	99387	99397			Depo-Medrol 80 mg	J1040		Urinalysis w/Micro		81002	
Nursing Home -	99302	99312			DT - Child	V06.5	90702	Pregnancy Test		84703	
Home Visit - 45 Min.	99343	99349			DT - Adult	V06.5	90718	Blood Glucose Test		82948	
Home Visit - 60 Min.	99344	99350			DTaP	V06.1	90700	Hemocue-Hgb		83026	
2. OFFICE SURGERY					DTP	V06.1	90701	Wet Mount		87210	
Biopsy		11100			Hep A - .50 dose	V05.3	90633				
Excision Benign Lesion		114			Hep A - 1.0 dose	V05.3	90633				
Excision Malignant Lesion		116			Hep B - Child	V05.3	90744	**6. SUPPLIES/MISCELLANEOUS**			
Incision and Drainage		10			Hep B - Adult	V05.3	90746	Sm./Lg. Surgical Tray		A4550	
Laceration Repair		12			HIB	V03.81	90648	Wrist Brace	L3908	29125	
Location:					IPV	V04.0	90713	Rib Belt	L0210		
Length:					Kenalog - 10		J3301	Ankle Brace	L1906	29515	
3. OFFICE PROCEDURES					MMR	V06.4	90707	Arm Sling	A4565		
ECG-12 Lead		93000			Pneumovac	V03.82	90732	Finger Splint		29130	
-Rhythm Strip		93042			Pneumococcal	V03.82	90669	Elastic Band.	A4460		
Specimen Handling	P9600	99000			TB-Intradermal	V74.1	86580				
PAP Handling	Q0091	99000			Td	V06.5	90718				
Immun Admin (x1)	G0008	90471			TdAp (Adacel)	V06.1	90715				

DIAGNOSIS:	ICD-9 CM						
☐ Abdominal Pain	789.00	☐ Bronchitis, Chronic s/Exac	491.20	☐ Diarrhea	787.91	☐ Hyperthyroidisim	242.9	☐ Rhinitis, Allergic	477.0
☐ ADD a/Hyper	314.00	☐ Bronchitis, Chronic w/Exac	491.21	☐ Diverticulitis, Colon, w/o Hem	562.11	☐ Hypoglycemia, NOS	251.2	☐ Rhinitis, Chronic	472.0
☐ Abnormal Lab	796.4	☐ Bursitis, Olec	726.33	☐ Dysfunctional Bleeding	626.8	☐ Hypothyroidism	244.8	☐ Sciatica	724.3
☐ Abnormal PAP-Cervix	795.00	☐ Bursitis, Shoulder	726.19	☐ Dysmenorrhea	625.3	☐ Hordeolum (Stye)	373.11	☐ Sebaceous Cyst	706.2
☐ Abrasion, Unspec	919.0	☐ Carpal Tunnel Syndrome	354.0	☐ Edema	782.3	☐ Incont. Stress (female)	625.6	☐ Sinusitis, Acute	461.0
☐ Abscess	682.xx	☐ Cerumen Impacted	380.4	☐ Epicondylitis	726.31	☐ Influenza, NOS	487.1	☐ Sinusitis, Chronic	473.0
☐ Acne	706.1	☐ Cervicitis	616.0	☐ Erectile Dysfunction	302.72	☐ Ingrown Nail	703.0	☐ SOB/Dyspnea	786.05
☐ Actinic Keratosis	702.0	☐ Chest Pain, NOS	786.50	☐ Fever	780.6	☐ Insect Bite	919.4	☐ Sprain/Strain, Wrist	842.00
☐ Allergic Reaction, NOS	995.3	☐ Chondromalacia, Patella	733.92	☐ Funct. Dis.-Intestinal	564.89	☐ Insomnia, NOS	780.52	☐ , Ankle	845.00
☐ Allergy Drug Reaction, NOS	995.2	☐ Chronic Fatigue Synd	780.71	☐ Gastroenteritis	558.9	☐ Irritable Bowel Synd.	564.1	☐ , Cervical	847.0
☐ Amenorrhea	626.0	☐ Conjunctivitis, NOS	372.30	☐ GERD	530.11	☐ Malaise/Fatigue	780.79	☐ , Thoracic	847.1
☐ Anal Fissure	565.0	☐ Constipation, NOS	564.0	☐ Gout, Arthropathy	274.0	☐ Menopausal Sx	627.2	☐ , Lumbar	847.2
☐ Anemia, Iron Def.	280.0	☐ Contraception Surveill	V25.40	☐ Headache	784.0	☐ Mono	075	☐ , Knee/Leg	844.8
☐ Angina, Unstable or Initial	411.1	☐ Contusion	920-924.xx	☐ , Migraine Classic	346.00	☐ Nausea/Vomiting	787.01	☐ Syncope/Collapse	780.2
☐ Anxiety Reaction	300.00	☐ COPD	496	☐ , Tension	307.81	☐ Obesity, NOS	278.00	☐ Tendonitis, NOS	726.90
☐ Arteroscl. CVD (ASCVD)	429.2	☐ Corneal Abrasion	918.1	☐ HIV Disease	042	☐ Otitis Externa, NOS	380.10	☐ TIA, Hx	112.54
☐ Arthralgia, Unspec	719.40	☐ Cough	786.2	☐ Health Maint. Exam	V70.0	☐ Otitis Media, NOS	382.00	☐ Urethritis, NOS	597.80
☐ Arthritis, Osteo	715.00	☐ Counsel/Family Planning	V25.04	☐ Heart Failure, Diastolic	428.30	☐ Palpitations	785.1	☐ URI	465.0
☐ Arthritis, Rheum	714.0	☐ CVA	436	☐ Heart Failure, Systolic	428.20	☐ PAP smear	V76.2	☐ Urin. Tract Infect., Unspec	599.0
☐ Asthma, Unspec	493.90	☐ Cystitis, Acute	595.0	☐ Hematuria	599.7	☐ Peripheral Neuropathy	356.9	☐ Urticaria	708.0
☐ Atherosclerosis Extr., NOS	440.20	☐ D.D.D.	722.6	☐ Hemorrhoids	455.6	☐ Pernicious Anemia	281.0	☐ Vaginitis, NOS	616.10
☐ Atrial Fibrillation	427.31	☐ Dementia, Senile	290.0	☐ Hepatic Abn Enzymes	790.5	☐ Pharyngitis, Acute	462	☐ Vertigo, NOS	780.4
☐ Backache, NOS	724.5	☐ Depression, NOS	311	☐ Hepatitis B, Chronic	070.32	☐ Phlebitis	451.0	☐ Viral Warts	078.10
☐ Benign Essential Tumor	333.1	☐ Dermatitis, Atopic	691.8	☐ Hepatitis C, Chronic	070.54	☐ PMS	625.4	☐ Weight Loss, Abnormal	783.21
☐ BPH s/Obstr	600.00	☐ Dermatitis, Contact	692.xx	☐ Hepatitis Chronic, Unspec	571.40	☐ Pneumonia, Unspec	486	☐ Well Child	V20.2
☐ Breast, Fibrocystic	610.1	☐ DM, II, Cont.	250.00	☐ Hepatitis A, Exp	V01.7	☐ Pregnancy State, NOS	V22.2	☐ Wound, Simple, Unspec	879.8
☐ Breast, Lump	611.72	☐ DM, II, Uncont	250.02	☐ Herpes, Genital	054.10	☐ Prostatitis, Acute	601.0	☐ Well Woman Exam	V72.31
☐ Bronchitis, Acute	466.0	☐ DM, I, Cont.	250.01	☐ Hypercholesterolemia	272.0	☐ Prostatitis, Chronic	601.1		
		☐ DM, I, Uncont	250.03	☐ HTN, Benign	401.1	☐ Rectal Bleeding	569.3		

DIAGNOSIS: (IF NOT CHECKED ABOVE)

SERVICES PERFORMED AT:	DOCTOR'S SIGNATURE / DATE
☐ Office	
☐ Home	
☐ Hosp. (Name & Address)	ACCEPT ASSIGNMENT? ☐ YES ☐ NO

INSTRUCTIONS TO PATIENT FOR FILING INSURANCE CLAIMS:		TOTAL TODAY'S FEE	
1. Complete the patient portion of your insurance form.	5. Patients with health care insurance, please remember:	OLD BALANCE	
2. Sign and Date.	A. Professional services are charged to the patient, and not to the insurance company. We bill insurance as a professional courtesy.	TOTAL	
3. Attach this form to your insurance form.	B. Insured patients are expected to pay any amount not covered by insurance.	AMOUNT REC'D. TODAY	
4. Mail directly to your insurance company.	C. This office cannot accept responsibility for negotiating a settlement on a disputed claim.	BY: ☐ Cash ☐ Check	
		NEW BALANCE	

INSUR-A-BILL ® BIBBERO SYSTEMS, INC. • PETALUMA, CA • © 8/94 • (SB37705.01)   (REV. 03/08)

FIGURE 22-1 The encounter form is used by the physician and staff to document what was done to the patient during an office visit and to indicate when the physician wants the patient to return. The copies of the form may be used to bill third-party payers. (Courtesy Bibbero Systems, Petaluma, Calif.)

number, and previous balance. Current charges and payments for the visit are added after the physician sees the patient. The physician can indicate on the encounter form when the patient should return to the clinic. The medical assistant then schedules a return appointment and can even use the patient's copy of the encounter form to note the next appointment date and time.

The encounter form normally consists of three parts: a white top sheet, a yellow sheet, and a pink sheet. The colors can vary, but the white copy usually is kept as a permanent record by the office, and the yellow and pink copies are given to the patient. The patient uses the yellow copy for insurance billing (if it is not done by the office), and the pink copy is a receipt for the patient. Encounter forms sometimes are designed to work with a **pegboard system**, or they may be available in continuous forms that can be placed in the printer for computer use. Encounter forms have been known by many other names throughout the years, including *superbills, charge slips,* and *multipurpose billing forms.* Modern computer systems allow receipts to be printed directly from the computer.

COMPUTATIONS USED ON PATIENT ACCOUNTS

A business **transaction** is the occurrence of an event or of a condition that must be recorded. For example, when a service is performed for which a charge is made, when a debtor makes a payment on an account, when a piece of equipment is purchased, or when the monthly rent is paid, a business transaction has been completed. Each of these examples is a transaction that must be recorded in the accounting system. Medical assistants need to understand the difference between bookkeeping and accounting. Accounting is a four-stage process of recording, classifying, summarizing, and interpreting financial statements. The physician may have an accountant who provides periodic summaries and handles tax planning and payment for the physician. Bookkeeping is the recording stage of accounting. The medical assistant performs bookkeeping functions when posting a payment to a patient's account.

A patient's financial record is called an **account**. All of the patients' accounts together (in the entire practice) constitute the

accounts receivable ledger. Account (or ledger) cards vary in design (Figure 22-2), but all have at least three columns for entering figures:

- **Debit** column—located on the left; this column is used for entering charges and sometimes is called the *charge column*.
- **Credit** column—located to the right of the debit column; this column sometimes is headed *Paid* or *Payments* and is used for entering payments received on an account.
- Balance column—located on the far right; this column is used to record the difference between the debit and the credit columns.

An adjustment column is available in some systems and is used to enter professional discounts, write-offs, disallowances by insurance companies, and any other adjustments. In a computer system, when a patient is called up by name or identification number, the patient's balance appears. This is the individual patient's ledger.

Posting is the transfer of information from one record to another. Transactions are posted from the journal to the ledger; this is accomplished in one writing on the pegboard system. The **account balance** normally is a debit balance, which means that the charges exceed the payments on the account. A debit balance is entered simply by writing the correct figure in the balance column. A credit balance exists when payments exceed charges (e.g., when a patient pays in advance). This is common in obstetric practices. If a payment is made, that amount is entered and subtracted from the charge to arrive at the patient's account balance. If the patient or the patient's

insurance company pays more than the charge, the patient has a credit balance. Occasionally, an adjustment may be made to the patient's account; for instance, if the insurance company pays only $80 of a $100 charge, the physician may adjust $20 from the patient's account, especially if the physician is contracted to accept the allowed amount.

Discounts are also credit entries and are entered in the adjustment column; if there is no such column, the discount is entered in the debit column and enclosed in parentheses. When the entry is made this way, it is recognized as a subtraction from the charges. When columns are totaled, any figure in red or in parentheses is always subtracted. **Receipts** are cash and checks taken in payment for professional services. **Receivables** are charges for which payment has not been received; that is, amounts owed. **Disbursements** are cash amounts paid out. **Payables** are amounts owed to others but not yet paid.

All charges and payments for professional services are posted to the patient's account card or record daily. The record then becomes a reliable source of information for answering all inquiries from patients about their accounts. A separate account card or record is prepared for each patient at the time of the first visit or service. The record should include all information pertinent to collecting the account, such as:

- Name and address of the guarantor
- Insurance identification
- Social Security number
- Home and business telephone numbers
- Name of employer
- Any special instructions for billing

Billing statements to the patient and the patient's insurance carrier are prepared from the record. The patient's name, date, and diagnosis and the procedures performed are posted when the patient is leaving the office.

COMPARISON OF MANUAL AND COMPUTERIZED BOOKKEEPING SYSTEMS

Computerized Bookkeeping Systems

Computerized bookkeeping systems for medical offices vary in cost and capability. A computerized system reduces the time needed to balance the day sheet and the totals for monthly and year-to-date balances (Procedure 22-1). The software for these programs may need to be updated periodically. Several staff members can access the information in the computer at the same time, and output is legible over the long term compared to some handwritten information. Because computers are multiuse devices, several types of software programs can be housed on one computer. Manual systems are designed to do one thing and cannot provide information other than what has been posted on the system by hand.

Although most physicians have converted to an electronic billing system, some still use the pegboard for a number of reasons. Many rural physicians, those in practice for many years, and those that run small practices believe that conversion to an electronic system would not be worth the high cost involved in implementation. Although it is certainly the physician's choice as to the system the office uses, electronic medical records are more efficient. Nonetheless, the

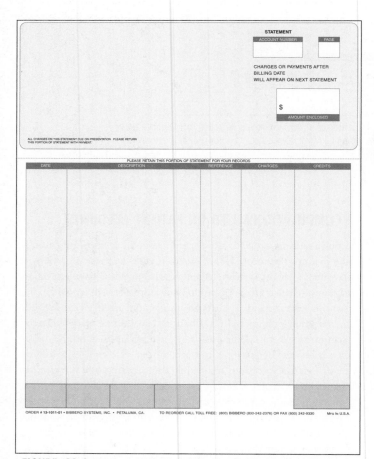

FIGURE 22-2 Patient account card used for computerized billing. (Courtesy Colwell Systems, Champaign, Ill.)

PROCEDURE 22-1

Use Computerized Office Billing Systems

GOAL: *To use the computer to perform office billing functions efficiently, accurately, and in a timely manner.*

EQUIPMENT and SUPPLIES

- Computer with billing software installed that contains a database of patients
- Physician's fee schedule
- Encounter forms
- Calculator

PROCEDURAL STEPS

1. Turn on the computer and open the applicable billing software program.
2. Generate a report that ages the accounts according to the last time a payment was made.
   PURPOSE: To determine the accounts that are 30, 60, 90, and 120 days old.
3. Review the accounts and determine whether any should be submitted to a collection agency.
   PURPOSE: To categorize accounts that are current and those that need outside collection action.
4. Run the software and print billing statements for all patients with a balance on their account.
   PURPOSE: To determine which patients need to be sent a statement. Some offices do not send bills to patients with less than $5 on their accounts to save postage and paperwork costs.
5. Review any notations in the computer billing system that relate to payment on the account.
   PURPOSE: To determine whether a patient has made payment arrangements on the account.
6. Determine whether any of the accounts need special handling.
   PURPOSE: To make sure that any follow-up activities have been done (e.g., calling the insurance company about denials, getting additional information from the physician).
7. Demonstrate sensitivity and professionalism in handling accounts receivable activities with patients.
   PURPOSE: To treat all patients fairly, to keep the billing information confidential, and to handle billing activities professionally.
8. Prepare the printed statements for mailing according to the billing cycle used by the clinic.
   PURPOSE: To mail a bill to a patient at the correct address in each month the person carries a balance.
9. Figure the best postage rate and use U.S. Postal Service (USPS) guidelines for mailing in bulk.
   PURPOSE: To save money on postage costs and send bulk mail in the most economical way.
10. Take the statements to the post office and mail.
    PURPOSE: To make sure the mail has been prepared according to USPS guidelines.

---

medical assistant benefits by learning how the manual pegboard system works. The bookkeeping concepts taught in using a manual system help the student understand the way a computerized system works. Whether manual or electronic, the physician's billing system must be accurate and cost effective and must allow quick retrieval of information.

Manual Bookkeeping Systems

Although we live in a technology-savvy world, there are many physicians who still use manual pegboard systems. Often, physicians who have been in practice for many years do not want to invest in a computerized billing system, because they may not plan to be in practice long enough to justify the cost. Usually, these doctors also still use a manual, written charting system. Additionally, some certifying exams still contain questions about manual systems. If the office experiences a power outage, the employees will have to use a manual system for the period in which patients are seen while the power is out. The medical assistant needs to be familiar with both manual and computerized bookkeeping systems. The pegboard is the most popular manual system for this purpose. The initial cost of materials for the pegboard system is slightly more than that for other manual accounting systems but is still less than the cost of most

billing management computer software systems. The pegboard is simple to operate, and once a medical assistant learns the pegboard system, computer systems are much easier to understand.

The system gets its name from the lightweight aluminum or Masonite board that is used. This board has a row of pegs along the side or top that holds the forms in place. The accounting forms are perforated for alignment on the pegs. All the forms used in any system must be compatible so that they can be aligned perfectly on the board. The pegboard system generates all the necessary financial records for each transaction in one writing, as follows:

- Encounter form
- Receipt
- Account (or ledger) card
- Accounting entry

The system also may include a statement and bank deposit slip. It provides current accounts receivable totals and a daily record of bank deposits and cash on hand, in addition to the record of income and expenses. The need for separate posting to patient accounts is eliminated, and the chance for error is reduced.

The pegboard system allows the medical assistant to keep control over cash, collections, and receivables and ensures that every cent is accounted for and properly entered. It provides a record of every patient, every charge, and every payment, plus a daily recap of earnings—a running record of receivables and an audited summary of cash—and requires little time.

Preparing Patient Accounts for Daily Transactions

If the medical facility uses a computerized billing system, turn on the computer and open the accounting software. Some advanced systems allow patients to check in at a computer in the reception area. When such a system is used, the patient must be taught how to enter his or her information. Once the patient has seen the physician and is ready to leave the office, he or she brings the encounter form to the checkout area. The medical assistant reviews the encounter form for the charges noted by the physician, and those charges are entered into the computer. Payments are noted after the charges have been entered.

Make sure the system has a reliable backup so that the patient account information is not lost. Back up the system daily to prevent the loss of all or part of patients' account information.

If a pegboard system is used, place a new day sheet on the board daily, even if there is still room left on the previous day sheet. This is helpful if a specific transaction needs to be looked up. The medical assistant can refer to a specific day sheet, rather than scan through several sheets, if he or she knows the date of the transaction. Most systems use no carbon required (NCR) paper on both encounter forms and account cards. If the encounter forms are shingled, lay the entire bank of receipts over the pegs, with the top one aligned with the first open writing line on the day sheet. The account card is placed underneath the encounter form but on top of the day sheet. Therefore, when the entry is recorded, the medical assistant writes on the encounter form, and the entry shows on the account card and the day sheet. Encounter forms should be used in numeric order. Save time by pulling account cards for all scheduled patients during morning preparation time.

Entering and Posting Transactions

When a computerized billing system is used, charges are entered into the computer at the end of the visit and payment is collected from the patient unless other arrangements have been made. The encounter form is referenced at the end of the visit. When a pegboard system is used, transactions are initiated before the patient goes to the exam room. The patient's ledger card is inserted under the first or next available receipt, with the first available writing line of the card aligned with the carbonized strip on the receipt. Enter the receipt number and date, the account balance in the space labeled *previous balance,* and the patient's name. The information recorded on the receipt is posted automatically to the ledger and the day sheet. The charge slip then is detached and clipped to the patient's chart to be routed to the physician.

After the service has been performed, the physician enters it on the encounter form and the patient or the nurse returns it to the medical assistant at the checkout desk. Charges are coded in the computerized billing system, and the computer also generates billing forms for insurance purposes. Whether a computerized or manual system is used, the charges posted to the patient's account should be taken from the physician's **fee schedule**. Computerized systems can automatically display the fees when a certain procedure code is entered.

When checking out a patient using a pegboard system, the medical assistant should insert the ledger card under the proper receipt and check the number previously entered to make sure the correct card is being used. Record the service by procedure code, post the charge from the fee schedule, enter any payment made, and write in the current balance (Procedure 22-2). If there is no balance, place a zero or a straight line in the balance column.

The transaction has now been posted to the journal and the account, and if payment was made by the patient, a receipt has been generated. The service receipt is given to the patient; no other receipt is necessary. The account card is ready for refiling.

File the encounter forms in numeric order for any internal audit. At the end of the month, the total of the encounter forms should equal the total of the charges recorded on the day sheets for the month (Figure 22-3).

Posting Other Payments and Charges

Payments may be received in the mail or may be brought in by patients some time after a service was performed. With a computer system, payments are simply entered into the computer and credited to the patient's account. With a manual system, payments are entered on the day sheet and the account card as described previously. Payments sent by mail do not require a receipt unless the patient specifically requests one.

The physician may have daily charges for visits to patients in a hospital or convalescent facility. Enter these charges on the day sheet and ledger card only. Surgery fees usually are recorded as one entry that includes the surgery and aftercare. All these charges are easily entered into a computer billing system.

CRITICAL THINKING APPLICATION   22-4

- Dr. Crawford sometimes forgets to write down information for billing when he goes to the hospital to check on his patients. Jodie has a difficult time entering the charges for hospital visits, because Dr. Crawford's records for these visits are not completely reliable. How might Jodie rectify this situation?
- How can Jodie help Dr. Crawford be more reliable in this area?

Summarizing Accounting Transactions

Computer systems figure the summary of accounting transactions automatically. Almost all systems have some type of error notification so that the medical assistant sees an error immediately and is prompted to correct it. With a manual system, all columns of the pegboard must be totaled and proved at the end of the day. Although all bookkeeping is done in ink, it is a good idea to write the totals in pencil until they have been proved. If an error is discovered, correct the entry in which it occurred. Do not attempt to erase or write over the incorrect entry. Simply draw one line through it and make a new entry on the first open writing line. Remember to reinsert the account card for these corrections. Also, if the entry included a receipt for the patient, make a new receipt and notify the patient of the correction.

PROCEDURE 22-2

Post Entries on a Day Sheet

GOAL: To post 1 day's charges and payments and compute the daily bookkeeping cycle using a pegboard.

EQUIPMENT and SUPPLIES

- Pegboard
- Calculator
- Pen
- Day sheet (a blank copy of an actual day sheet will work if no pegboard system is available)
- Receipts
- Ledger cards
- Balances from previous day
- Computer

PROCEDURAL STEPS

1. Prepare the board.
   - Place a new day sheet on the board.
   - Place a bank of receipts over the pegs, aligning the top receipt with the first open writing line on the day sheet.
2. Carry forward balances from the previous day.
   PURPOSE: To keep all totals current.
3. Pull ledger cards for the patients being seen that day.
4. Insert the ledger card under the first receipt, aligning the first available writing line of the card with the carbonized strip on the receipt.
   PURPOSE: To ensure that the staff member using the card correctly posts the entry to the receipt, ledger, and day sheet.
5. Enter the patient's name, the date, the receipt number, and any existing balance from the ledger card.
6. Detach the charge slip from the receipt and clip it to the patient's chart.
   PURPOSE: To allow the physician to indicate the service performed on the charge slip and return it to you.

7. Accept the returned charge slip at the end of the visit. If using a computerized system, pull up the patient's account on the screen.
8. Enter the appropriate fee from the fee schedule.
9. Locate the receipt on the board with a number matching the charge slip.
   PURPOSE: To make sure it is the correct receipt.
10. Reinsert the patient's ledger card under the receipt.
11. Write the service code number and fee on the receipt.
12. Accept the patient's payment and record the amount of payment and the new balance. Enter the payment amount into the computerized system, if applicable.
    PURPOSE: To bring the patient's account up-to-date and provide a current statement for the patient.
13. Give the completed receipt to the patient. Print the receipt using the computer, if applicable.
14. Follow your agency's procedure for refilling the ledger card.
15. Repeat steps 4 to 14 for each service of the day.
16. Total all columns of the day sheet at the end of the day. Computer systems provide this information electronically. Print daily reports if required at the end of the day.
    PURPOSE: To determine the total amount of the charges, receipts, and resulting balances for the day.
17. Write preliminary totals in pencil.
    PURPOSE: To facilitate any necessary changes.
18. Complete proof of totals and enter totals in ink.
19. Enter figures for accounts receivable control.
    PURPOSE: To complete the daily accounting cycle.

SPECIAL BOOKKEEPING ENTRIES

The following special entries sometimes are necessary. They may be performed either with a pegboard or a computer accounting system:

- Adjustments
- Credit balances
- Refunds
- Insufficient funds checks

Adjustments

At times a credit adjustment must be entered. This could be for professional discounts, insurance disallowances, account write-offs, or payments that come to the office after the account has been placed for collection (Procedure 22-3). If a patient or guarantor files for bankruptcy, the charge usually must be adjusted off the books.

If the system has an adjustment column or feature, enter adjustments there. Otherwise, because the adjustment is actually a subtraction from the charge, enter it in the charge column with the figure enclosed in parentheses or circled and with an explanation of the entry in the description column. When the column of figures is totaled, the circled figure is subtracted rather than added. The learner has a tendency to ignore the circled figures. This is incorrect; they must be subtracted.

Credit Balances

A credit balance occurs when a patient has paid in advance or an overpayment or duplicate payment is made (Procedure 22-4). For example, an overpayment occurs if the patient makes a partial payment and later the insurance allowance is more than the remaining balance. The difference between the total amount of money received and the amount owed must be entered in the balance column and enclosed within parentheses or circled. This indicates a credit balance. Some credit balances are created when an error is made in posting.

The credit balance is money owed to the patient. If the patient has paid in advance or wants to leave the overpayment in the account

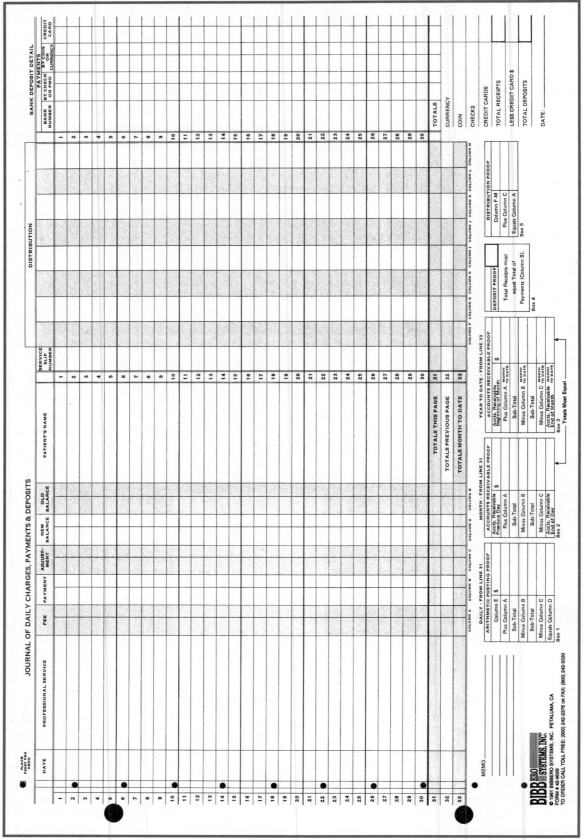

FIGURE 22-3 Sample day sheet used to log patient charges and receipts. (Courtesy Bibbero Systems, Petaluma, Calif.)

PROCEDURE 22-3

Post Adjustments

GOAL: *To process adjustments to patients' accounts accurately.*

EQUIPMENT and SUPPLIES

- Patient ledgers
- Office policy manual
- Explanation of benefits and remittance advice
- Bookkeeping system
- Clerical supplies
- Payments
- Calculator
- Computer

PROCEDURAL STEPS

1. Open checks that arrive in the mail as payment on patient accounts.
2. Paper-clip the check to the explanation of benefits (EOB) or remittance advice.
   PURPOSE: To keep the check with the EOB as payments are posted.

3. Post the payment to the patient's account using a computerized or manual system.
4. Determine whether an adjustment is necessary on the patient's account.
   PURPOSE: Adjustments may be necessary in cases of disallowed charges, noncovered services, and so on.
5. If necessary, review the office policy manual to ascertain the correct procedure for making adjustments to a patient's account.
   PURPOSE: To ensure that office policies are followed and are consistent with regard to patient accounts and adjustments.
6. If using a manual system, make sure the ledger card is aligned with the day sheet correctly.
7. Write the adjustment amount in the adjustment column of the ledger card.
8. Check the math to make sure the adjustment was posted correctly.

PROCEDURE 22-4

Process a Credit Balance

GOAL: *To return overpayments to patients in a timely manner.*

EQUIPMENT and SUPPLIES

- Patient ledgers
- Office policy manual
- Explanation of benefits and remittance advice
- Bookkeeping system
- Clerical supplies
- Payments
- Calculator
- Computer

PROCEDURAL STEPS

1. If necessary, review the office policy manual to determine the guidelines for credit balances.
   PURPOSE: To make sure office policy is followed.

2. Review the payment received and the explanation of benefits or remittance advice.
3. Post the payment to the patient's account using a computerized or manual system.
4. Determine whether an overpayment has been made.
5. Review the account to determine whether more insurance is expected on the account.
   PURPOSE: Some credit balances need not be made if more activity is expected on the account; only refund amounts that remain after the complete bill has been paid.
6. Adjust the credit balance off of the patient's account.
   PURPOSE: To refund the credit balance if it is due to the patient.

in anticipation of future charges, care must be taken in figuring the balance on future transactions. A charge increases the balance, but it reduces a credit balance.

Refunds

If a patient wants to have an overpayment refunded, write a check for the amount due and enter the transaction on the day sheet. In most cases, the refund results in a patient balance of zero (Procedure 22-5). Computer systems may automatically prompt a refund when the patient has a credit balance.

CRITICAL THINKING APPLICATION   22-5

Jodie receives a phone call from a patient who says that she is due a refund because her insurance company sent her an explanation of benefits for $654, and her balance was only $436. She demands an immediate refund, but Jodie has not yet received the check.

- What should Jodie do? Should she send the refund to the patient as requested?
- After investigating, Jodie suspects that the check sent to pay on the account was an error. What should she do in this situation?

PROCEDURE 22-5

Process Refunds

GOAL: *To process a patient's refund in a timely manner.*

EQUIPMENT and SUPPLIES

- Patient ledgers
- Office policy manual
- Explanation of benefits and remittance advice
- Bookkeeping system
- Clerical supplies
- Payments
- Calculator
- Computer

PROCEDURAL STEPS

1. Determine the amount of the refund to be processed.
   <u>PURPOSE:</u> To make sure the patient receives a refund in the correct amount.

2. Write a check for the amount of the refund using a computerized or manual system.
   <u>PURPOSE:</u> Always use a check to pay refunds so that the patient's name is on the back of the check as endorsement, proving the patient received the refund.

3. Give the check to the physician for a signature.
   <u>PURPOSE:</u> Most physicians prefer to sign their own checks.

4. Determine the correct mailing address for the patient.
   <u>PURPOSE:</u> To make sure the patient has not reported a change of address.

5. Make a copy of the check and put it in the patient's medical record.
   <u>PURPOSE:</u> To show that a check was mailed to the patient.

6. Mail the refund check to the patient.

PROCEDURE 22-6

Post Nonsufficient Funds Checks

GOAL: *To correctly note that a patient's check was returned because of insufficient funds.*

EQUIPMENT and SUPPLIES

- Patient ledgers
- Office policy manual
- Bookkeeping system
- Clerical supplies
- Calculator
- Computer

PROCEDURAL STEPS

1. Pull the ledger card for the patient who wrote the check or open the patient's account on the computer.
   <u>PURPOSE:</u> To post charges to the correct patient's account.

2. Determine the amount to be added back to the account as a result of the returned check.

   <u>PURPOSE:</u> The physician's bank usually charges a fee for all checks returned by the bank because of insufficient funds.

3. Post the total amount on the patient's ledger card or on the patient's computerized account.
   <u>PURPOSE:</u> To account for the original check amount plus the fee for the returned check.

4. Send a certified letter to the patient notifying him or her of the returned check and demand fast payment.
   <u>PURPOSE:</u> Many states require that certified mail be used when notifying patients about nonsufficient funds checks.

5. Note this collection activity in the patient's medical record and keep a copy, noting the numbers on the certified letter for reference.

Insufficient Funds Checks

A patient may send in a check without having sufficient funds to cover it in the bank; this check is later deposited to the physician's account. The bank will return the check to the medical facility marked NSF (nonsufficient funds). Two accounting functions must be performed. First, deduct the amount of the check from the practice's checking account balance. Then add that amount back into the patient's account balance, including an NSF fee (if applicable) in the paid column. Place that amount in parentheses and increase the balance by the same amount. Write "NSF check" in the description column (Procedure 22-6). Some offices do not charge an NSF fee if the physician's bank does not charge the physician a fee; however, charging a fee does serve as a deterrent to writing NSF checks in the future.

BALANCING THE ACCOUNTS RECEIVABLE AND ACCOUNTS RECEIVABLE CONTROL

The accounts receivable control is a daily summary of what remains unpaid on the accounts. Most offices also complete an end of day summary. These summaries help the medical assistant determine the outstanding accounts receivable; that is, the amount patients owe the clinic. In collections, this information is used to send letters asking patients to pay their accounts based on the age of the account. (Aging accounts receivables is discussed later in this chapter.)

PAYMENT OPTIONS

Physicians allow patients to pay for medical services in different ways, often determined by the amount of the total service. Sizeable fees might be divided into several payments, but patients should pay for regular office visits when the service is rendered.

Payment for medical services is accomplished in the following four ways:

- Payment at the time of service
- Billing after making payment arrangements
- Insurance or other third-party billing
- Billing and collection assistance

Payment at the Time of Service

Most patients pay their co-pay, co-insurance, or total bill at the time medical services are provided. A large percentage of patients have some type of health insurance for at least major expenses. Every practice should encourage time-of-service collection. Many offices now collect co-pays or co-insurance before the patient sees the physician. This may offend some patients, because they are being asked to pay before receiving services. The medical assistant should explain that this practice is followed merely to save the patient time after seeing the physician, because co-pays usually are a set amount for each visit. Patients without health insurance should pay after the charges for the day have been totaled. If patients get into the habit of paying their current charges before they leave the office, no further billing and bookkeeping expenses are incurred. Inform patients making an appointment that payment is expected at the time of service so that they are not surprised when asked for payment at the end of the visit. The medical assistant may say, "Your charge for today is $25. Will that be cash, check, credit, or debit card?"

Many offices accept **credit cards** for the convenience of their patients. **Debit cards** now are also widely accepted for payment. Computers have made the electronic transfer of funds easy and convenient. If a patient asks to be billed, the medical assistant may say, "Our normal procedure is to pay at the time of service unless other arrangements are made in advance."

Many patients are hesitant to ask about charges and are unsure whether to offer to pay or to wait until asked. Make it easier for patients by offering to accept their payments, because most people are prepared to pay small bills on a cash basis.

The medical assistant must believe that the physician and the facility have a right to charge for the services provided. Do not be embarrassed to ask for payment for the valuable services the physician provides. Remember that the practice is a business, and the physician must meet the obligations necessary to keep it fiscally healthy, including salary expenses. When tact and good judgment are used in billing and collecting, patients appreciate the service they receive and the help the medical assistant provides. Give each patient individual attention and personal consideration; also, be courteous and show a sincere desire to help the patient with financial problems.

CRITICAL THINKING APPLICATION   22-6

Mr. Page comes to Jodie's desk to pay his account. His credit card is declined. How does Jodie handle this situation?

- Mr. Page argues that he recently paid the balance of his account in full. What steps should Jodie take in this case?

Billing after Payment Arrangements

Most physicians prefer payment before or at the time of service. However, if fees for surgery or long-term care are involved, payment arrangements become necessary, and a regular system of billing must be established. The medical assistant therefore must explain to the patient the professional fees, the services the charges cover, and the office credit policies (Procedure 22-7). Most practices make payment arrangements with patients. The physician should decide what he or she expects of patients with regard to payments and how the patient will be informed. Although exceptions always occur to any rule, there must be a rule, which should be in writing and conveyed to the patient at the outset of the physician-patient relationship. Refer to the office policy and procedures manual for specific guidelines for payment arrangements in individual practices.

Using Credit for Medical Services

Because credit is so much a part of our economic system today, the physician's office usually accepts credit and debit cards for medical care. However, using a credit card can increase the total amount the patient will pay for the services. Suppose a patient uses a credit card to pay for minor surgery, and the physician's charge is $750. If the patient pays the balance in full during the next credit card billing cycle (which varies with every card), no charges above the $750 may be incurred. However, if the patient does not pay the entire bill, interest is charged on the account every month until the full bill is paid. In addition, late payment and over-the-limit fees can be astronomical, and the patient's credit card debt quickly can get out of control. Even small charges can multiply if the bill is not paid on time. In general, fees for routine office calls and small medical bills should be kept on a pay-as-you-go basis.

Some offices distribute information about credit cards or loans specifically for healthcare treatments. This is very popular for cosmetic surgeries, dental procedures, and laser eye surgeries. Offices that offer these types of procedures may want to investigate such alternative financing services. Although these options are valuable when used properly and repaid on time, they do create additional interest debt for the patient. Encourage patients to pay cash when obtaining medical services and to avoid using credit, because this saves them money in the long run. If the physician allows the patient to split large bills into two or three payments, the patient does not incur credit card interest charges.

PROCEDURE 22-7

Explain Professional Fees and Make Credit Arrangements with a Patient

GOAL: To assist the patient in paying for services by making mutually beneficial credit arrangements according to established office policy.

EQUIPMENT and SUPPLIES

- Patient's ledger
- Calendar
- Truth in Lending form
- Assignment of Benefits form
- Patient's insurance form
- Private area for interview

PROCEDURAL STEPS

1. Answer all questions about credit thoroughly and kindly.
2. Inform the patient of the office policy regarding credit.
   - Payment at the time of the first visit
   - Payment by bank card
   - Credit application

   PURPOSE: To ensure complete understanding of mutual responsibilities.
3. Have the patient complete the credit application.

   PURPOSE: To comply with office practices on the extension of credit.
4. Check the completed credit application.

   PURPOSE: To confirm that all the necessary information is included.

5. Discuss the possible arrangements with the patient and ask the person to decide which of them is most suitable.

   PURPOSE: To ensure better compliance. Patients usually keep a payment schedule if they have a voice in planning.
6. Prepare the Truth in Lending form and have the patient sign it if the agreement requires more than four installments.

   PURPOSE: To comply with legal requirements (Regulation Z of the Truth in Lending Act).
7. Be aware of the regulations of the Fair Debt Collection Act when working with patients on collections.

   PURPOSE: To abide by federal laws when collecting from patients.
8. Have the patient execute an assignment of insurance benefits.

   PURPOSE: To comply with credit policy.
9. Make a copy of the patient's insurance card and have the patient sign a consent for release of the information to the insurance company.

   PURPOSE: To ensure that a claim can be processed, because consent for the release of information is necessary on most insurance forms.
10. Keep credit information confidential.

    PURPOSE: To maintain patient confidentiality when performing billing and collection activities.

Truth in Lending Act

Regulation Z of the Truth in Lending Act (TILA), which is enforced by the Federal Trade Commission (FTC) and is part of the Consumer Credit Protection Act, requires that individuals be given certain information when credit is extended, such as the annual percentage rate (APR), the terms of the loan, and the total costs to the borrower. If an agreement exists between physician and patient that the physician will accept payment in more than four installments, the physician must provide a disclosure statement about finance charges (Figure 22-4), even if no finance charges are involved. The physician retains a copy of the form, and the original is given to the patient. Have the patient sign the agreement in your presence to document proof of signing. The disclosure statement must be kept on file for 2 years. Although the disclosure statement is designed as protection for the debtor, it can be a good collection tool for the creditor.

Although much less common than in the past, physicians occasionally permit their patients to pay in installments. As long as no specific agreement has been made for payment to the physician to be made in more than four installments and no finance charge is assessed, the account is not subject to TILA. In accepting such payments, the physician is not subject to the provisions of the regulation. However, the physician's office must make sure to send a statement for the full balance each billing cycle. If the statement is for only a partial payment, it becomes subject to TILA.

Helping patients budget their medical expenses is a fairly new aspect of the business side of medical practice. However, it is a real

service to patients and demonstrates that the physician and the office staff are sincerely interested in helping patients; it also may prevent many collection problems. The physician can write an office policy that allows interest charges if the patient does not comply with the original payment arrangements. This provision could help the medical assistant collect payment, because patients will not want interest charges added to the account.

Fair Debt Collection Practices Act

The Fair Debt Collection Practices Act requires that debt collectors act fairly in their collection efforts; it also restricts how and when a person can be contacted about an outstanding debt. Collectors are strictly limited as to whom they may contact about a debt. The medical assistant must work within the framework of this act when collecting for the physician.

Obtaining Credit Information

Credit information is confidential. It should be guarded as carefully as a confidential medical history and should never be disclosed to unauthorized persons. If a call is received about a patient's credit history, follow office policy and only release information according to that policy and legal guidelines in your state. When asking for credit information from patients in the office, do so in a private area where others cannot overhear the conversation. Provide a desk or table away from the reception area where a patient can sit in total privacy and complete a credit application. Credit information is

LEONARD S. TAYLOR, M.D.
2100 West Park Avenue
Champaign, Illinois 61820

Telephone 351-5400

FEDERAL TRUTH IN LENDING STATEMENT
For professional services rendered

Patient _____ Joseph Brookhurst
Address _____ 353 West Terry Lane
Birmingham, Alabama 35209
Parent _____

1. Cash Price (fee for service)	$	1200.00
2. Cash Down Payment	$	200.00
3. Unpaid Balance of Cash Price	$	1000.00
4. Amount Financed	$	1000.00
5. FINANCE CHARGE	$	–0–
6. Finance Charge Expressed As Annual Percentage Rate		–0–
7. Total of Payments (4 plus 5)	$	1000.00
8. Deferred Payment Price (1 plus 5)	$	1200.00

"Total payment due" (7 above) is payable to __Dr. Leonard S. Taylor__ at above office address in __five__ monthly installments of $ __200.00__ . The first installment is payable on __May 1__ 19 __xx__ , and each subsequent payment is due on the same day of each consecutive month until paid in full.

__4-15-2xxx__ _____
Date   Signature of Patient; Parent if Patient is a Minor

FORM 9402 COLWELL SYSTEMS, INC., CHAMPAIGN, ILLINOIS

FIGURE 22-4 Example of a disclosure statement used for compliance with the Truth in Lending Act. (Courtesy Colwell Systems, Champaign, Ill.)

personal, and great care must be taken to prevent misuse and identity theft. Never access a credit report on a patient unless it is necessary to process an application for credit privileges at the medical facility.

INSURANCE OR OTHER THIRD-PARTY PAYERS

Insurance billing in the medical office is a courtesy to patients. Often patients do not understand the policies and appreciate the assistance given by the medical office. Work diligently with patients to obtain the maximum reimbursement possible from insurance and third-party payers. Be a patient advocate by helping patients resolve issues with their policies so that patients obtain the benefits for which they pay.

Billing Procedures

Most physicians' offices and clinics send a billing statement to patients each month (Procedure 22-8). Billing can be accomplished using the following:

- Computer-generated statements
- Encounter forms
- Photocopied or scanned statements
- Online billing statements

The appearance of the statement makes a visual impact, just as a letter does; therefore, the statement heads should be printed or copied on clean, good-quality paper. Statements should be large enough to read easily and to allow itemization of charges. Envelopes should be imprinted with "Address Service Requested" in the appropriate place to maintain up-to-date mailing lists. A self-addressed return envelope included with the statement is convenient for the patient and encourages prompt payment.

PROCEDURE 22-8

Perform Billing Procedures

GOAL: To bill insurance companies for patient procedures and services and obtain the maximum legal reimbursement.

EQUIPMENT and SUPPLIES

- Patient ledgers
- Accounting system
- Calculator
- Claim forms
- Encounter forms
- Clerical supplies
- Computer

PROCEDURAL STEPS

1. Read the medical record or encounter form to determine the procedures and services to be billed.
   PURPOSE: To make sure all procedures and services performed by the provider are billed so that he or she can receive the correct reimbursement.

2. Determine the diagnosis code for each diagnosis noted by the provider.
   PURPOSE: To use the proper code to note each diagnosis.

3. Determine the procedure codes for all procedures noted by the provider.
   PURPOSE: To use the proper code to note each procedure.

4. Complete the claim form according to the directions for each block.

5. Determine the amount of money the provider is billing on the claim.
   PURPOSE: To bill for the correct amount in reimbursement.

6. Determine the address where the claim forms should be mailed.
   PURPOSE: To eliminate unnecessary delays in the carrier's receipt of the claim form.

7. Mail or electronically submit the claim form.

8. Note the date the claim should receive follow-up to make sure it is paid.

9. Bill the patient for the remaining balance, if any.
   PURPOSE: To clear the balance owed to the physician; to complete the claim form cycle accurately so that payment will not be delayed.

Computer-Generated Statements

Most statements now are computer generated. Patient accounts are established and stored in the computer so that a statement can be produced whenever needed. The statement provides information such as the service rendered on each date, the charge for each service, the date on which a claim was submitted to the insurance company, the date of payment, and the balance due from the patient. The computer may also be programmed to print messages on the statement, such as "Balance now 30 days past due."

Encounter Forms

Encounter forms usually are personalized for the practice. The form should have space for all the elements required to submit medical insurance claims, such as:

- Name and address of the patient
- Name of the insurance carrier
- Insurance identification number
- Procedure codes
- Fee for each service
- Diagnosis codes
- Place and date of service
- Physician's name and address
- Physician's signature

The encounter form often is used as a charge slip for office treatments. The physician checks or circles the services and procedures performed at the completion of the visit, and the form is taken to the checkout area. The medical assistant then totals the account and obtains payment from the patient.

Photocopied Statements

Some offices make a copy of the statements and mail them to patients each month as a bill. The copied statement should prominently display the balance due. Writing must be clear and legible. Usually, a window envelope is used for mailing, which means that the name and address on the ledger must be neat, correct, and positioned correctly for the envelope window. Office supply stores have stickers that can be attached to statements indicating that the bill is past due or close to collection action.

Online Billing Statements

If the medical facility uses a computer software system with e-billing capacity, patients can receive their statements by e-mail. Because of the security risk, the patient must agree to accept bills sent to them by e-mail. A computer hacker may be able to find information leading to identity theft when bills are sent and then paid using online systems. However, most facilities that accept online payments use a secure encrypted program to make the process safe for sensitive information. The patient could pay the bill using a credit card, debit card, or checking account. To use the checking account option, a patient usually is required to enter the bank's routing number and his or her checking account number. Some of these systems process the payment immediately; therefore, to avoid nonsufficient funds (NSF) charges, patients must take care that they have sufficient funds to cover the online payment before it is made.

Itemizing the First Statement

If the medical fee has been explained to the patient in advance, the monthly statement is merely a confirmation of what is owed, and there should be no misunderstanding. However, it is good business practice and a courtesy to the patient to itemize the charges on the first statement. This is essential if the statement is to be used for billing the patient's insurance. Patients are entitled to an understanding of the physician's statement for medical services.

Time and Frequency of Billing

Patients expect to receive statements from their creditors monthly, and they plan their budgets around first-of-the-month bills received. Punctuality in billing encourages prompt payment.

Statements should be sent at least once each month. Some offices send bills immediately after treatment; others bill all patients on the same day each month. Mailing statements twice a month (e.g., half of the accounts on the tenth and the remaining half on the twenty-fifth) is also a common practice.

Once-a-Month Billing

If a monthly pattern is followed, bills should leave the office in time to reach the patient no later than the last day of each month and preferably before the twenty-fifth to encourage payment around the first of the month. Planning ahead for the preparation of statements can lighten the burden of once-a-month billing.

Cycle Billing

Many physicians prefer to use the cycle billing system, in which certain portions of the accounts receivable are billed at given times during the month, instead of preparation of all statements at the end of the month. Large businesses, such as credit card issuers and banks, also use cycle billing. Sending statements in cycles has many advantages; for example, it prevents once a month peak workloads and stabilizes cash flow. In a small office where billing is done only once a month, the unexpected illness or absence of the medical assistant who prepares the statements can leave the physician in a financial bind because of a delay in billing. Most patients wait for their statement to send in a payment.

When statements are prepared, accounts are separated into fairly equal divisions, the number of divisions depending on how many times billing is done during a month. For example, if the office expects to bill twice a month, divide the accounts into two equal groups; for weekly billing, divide into four groups; and for daily billing, divide into 20 groups. Small alphabetic groups can be combined to keep the divisions nearly equal in the number of statements to prepare on each billing day. If the files are color coded, the medical assistant may want to use the same alphabetic breakdown in billing. Regardless of constant changes in the individual accounts, the mailing dates for accounts in each section remain the same. A schedule for processing and mailing is established, and the workload is apportioned throughout the entire month.

Cycle billing allows the medical assistant to continue all routine duties each day, handling the statements on a day-to-day or weekly schedule rather than in one intensive period at the end of the month. This means that whole days need not be sacrificed from other duties to get statements in the mail. When the billing is spaced throughout the month, more time and consideration can be given to each statement, itemization of bills is less burdensome, and the likelihood of error is reduced.

Patients generally accept the cycle billing system quickly and often with enthusiasm. However, if your office decides to change from a once-a-month billing system to a cycle billing system, patients should be notified in advance and the new plan should be explained to them. To explain the new system to established patients, enclose a notice in each statement for 2 months before the transfer, describing the plan and indicating the future dates on which each patient will receive the bill. Before a physician adopts the cycle billing system, particularly in a small community, several factors should be taken into consideration:

- What is the general income level of the community and how and when does the average patient get paid?
- Do local companies pay employees at various times during the month or are most paychecks handed out at the beginning of the month?
- Would cycle billing benefit patients in addition to the overall operation of the office?

PROFESSIONAL COURTESY

In the past, many physicians did not charge professional colleagues or their close family members for medical care; this concept is called **professional courtesy**. In some cases, giving professional courtesy represents the loss of a large amount of potential income. If a substantial outlay in the cost of materials is involved, the professional colleague probably will want to reimburse the physician for the materials used. Most physicians today subscribe to a health insurance plan. If the care they receive is covered by insurance, it is entirely ethical for the attending physician to accept the insurance benefits in payment for services.

Professional courtesy often is extended beyond fellow physicians and their dependents. Many physicians treat their own medical assistants and often their families without charge and grant discounts to nurses and medical assistants not in their direct employ. Student externs should never expect to be treated while serving in an externship capacity. Professional courtesy is sometimes extended to others in the healthcare field (e.g., pharmacists and dentists). Before offering professional courtesy to anyone, the physician must determine whether doing so violates any of his or her contracts or agreements with managed care providers or third-party payers. Some may have restrictions on eliminating or writing off co-pays or co-insurance amounts. Make sure the extension of professional courtesy never jeopardizes any contracts. The physician or office manager is responsible for adhering to all legal agreements, but the medical assistant must follow through. Never offer any type of discount that is outside of established office policy or that has not been authorized by the physician.

CRITICAL THINKING APPLICATION   22-7

Dr. Crawford has just finished seeing Dr. Franklin, who came to him as a patient. Dr. Franklin insists to Jodie that Dr. Crawford always extends him professional courtesy. This is not indicated on his account card, because several payments are shown on the record. Dr. Crawford has just left the office and is in an important meeting at the hospital.

- What should Jodie do?
- Does this event justify paging or calling the physician?

BILLING MINORS

Minors cannot be held responsible for payment of a bill unless they are emancipated. Bills for minors are usually addressed to a parent or legal guardian. If a bill is addressed to a minor, the parent or parents could take the attitude that they are not responsible because they never received the bill.

If the parents are separated or divorced, the parent who brings the child in for treatment is responsible for payment. Whatever financial agreement exists between the parents is strictly their personal business and should not concern the medical office. The responsible parent should be so informed from the beginning.

If a minor appears in the office and requests treatment and you can ascertain that the person is legally emancipated, the minor is responsible for the bill. It may be wise to make a determination either with the business manager or with the physician as to whether your office wishes to treat an emancipated minor. Minors can be treated for certain conditions, such as sexually transmitted diseases (STDs), pregnancy, and birth control without parental consent. In these cases, the medical assistant must determine where the bill should be sent, if the minor carries a balance on his or her ledger card. Be sure that office policy is followed and that the policies line up with local, state, and national laws.

COLLECTION PROCEDURES

Most patients truly want to pay the bills they owe. However, sometimes a patient may have difficulty meeting his or her obligations. The patient may have lost a job or insurance coverage. An emergency could arise that depletes finances. When patients must choose between paying their medical bills and having electricity, the physician often is forced to wait for reimbursement. Although a few patients absolutely refuse to pay for their medical care, most are honest and willing to pay but may need help with a payment plan. Terms can be arranged for collecting payment in full when the office and the patient cooperate with each other. The medical assistant should attempt to work out a plan that the patient can abide by, and the patient should be expected to make promised payments.

Collection problems can arise if the medical assistant fails to get the necessary insurance information. In some instances, if the insurance forms are not completed correctly, the claim may be denied. Minor errors, such as failing to name the responsible party or omitting accurate numeric information, delay payment to the physician.

MEDICAL CARE FOR THOSE WHO CANNOT PAY

The medical profession traditionally has accepted the responsibility of providing occasional medical care for individuals unable to pay for these services. Despite the increased scope of government-sponsored care for the **medically indigent**, physicians still spend thousands of dollars each year providing services before securing some type of payment.

In many instances medical care of the indigent is available through social service agencies. Medical assistants should learn about local organizations and agencies that can aid patients in obtaining the necessary assistance. The physician can provide only medical services. Other agencies provide hospitalization, for example, or arrange for paying the costs of special therapy, rehabilitation, or medications. Unfortunately, there is still another segment of the population that consists of uninsured employees who are not eligible for public assistance, are not covered under a group policy, and cannot afford the high premiums for private medical insurance. Give special attention to helping these people arrange payment of their medical bills. If a physician accepts a case in advance for which a fee will not be paid, complete records must still be kept on the patient. The only deviation in procedure is that the financial record indicates no charge (n/c) in the debit column.

FEES IN HARDSHIP CASES

Sometimes a physician is faced with the problem of deciding whether to reduce or cancel a fee in a hardship case. Before adjusting or canceling a fee, the physician or medical assistant should have a frank discussion with the patient about his or her financial situation. Find out whether the patient is entitled to any funds for medical care or an insurance settlement of some kind. For instance, if the patient's injuries are the result of a car accident, there may be insurance through the automobile policy. Circumstances may qualify the patient for local or state public assistance, such as crime victim assistance. Keep information about such agencies that are available in the area and direct the patient to the appropriate one.

Discuss the fee in advance and make payment arrangements if the circumstances of hardship are known before services are rendered. The physician may suggest that a medically indigent patient seek care at a county hospital with public assistance. A physician should be free to choose his or her form of charity and should not feel obligated to substantially reduce or cancel a fee when the circumstances are known in advance.

After the physician and patient have agreed on a fee, special circumstances may arise that create a hardship after the fact. If the physician then agrees to reduce the fee, the patient should be told that the reduction will be effective only after the adjusted amount is paid in full. For instance, if a fee of $500 is reduced to $350, the full amount of the $500 charge should appear on the ledger, and when $350 has been received, the remainder can be written off as an adjustment.

Pitfalls of Fee Adjustments

Problems can arise when a physician begins to reduce his or her fees. Patients may begin to expect fees to be reduced in all circumstances. Patients may even doubt the competency of a physician who habitually reduces fees. Make fee reductions the exception rather than the norm.

Take great care in reducing the fee for care of a patient who dies. The physician's sympathy is with the family in such instances, but the physician's generosity in reducing a fee could be misinterpreted and result in a suit for malpractice. The family may suspect that the fee was reduced because the physician knows he or she made an error.

If the physician agrees to settle for a reduced fee in a situation in which the patient is disputing the cost, take care to make sure the negotiations are without prejudice. By taking this precaution, the physician protects his or her right to collect the original sum should the patient refuse to pay the lowered fee. The offer of a discount,

therefore, should be made in writing, with insertion of the words "without prejudice," and a definite time limit for making payment should be stated. Prepare two copies of the agreement and have the signatures witnessed by a staff member. Keep the original for the physician and give a copy to the patient.

A fee should never be reduced on the basis of a poor result or as a means of obtaining payment to avoid the use of a collection agency. A reduction for these reasons degrades the physician and the practice of medicine.

MEDICARE AND ADVANCE BENEFICIARY NOTICES

Occasionally, Medicare requires that the physician give the patient an Advance Beneficiary Notice (ABN). This form is given when the physician, healthcare provider, or supplier thinks that Medicare probably or certainly will not pay for services or items. The patient decides whether he or she still wants to receive the services from the provider and completes the information on the form (Figure 22-5).

PREPARING ACCOUNTS FOR COLLECTION ACTIVITY

Sometimes it becomes necessary to aggressively attempt to collect the balances that patients owe the physician. Persuasive collection procedures include telephone calls, collection reminders and letters, and personal interviews (Procedure 22-9).

Before beginning collection action, determine which accounts have a balance due and how old the account is. Some accounts are grouped together, or "aged," according to the dates of the last payment activity, whereas others are grouped according to the original date of service. Others are grouped by month, beginning with the month the bill was first charged. Common account aging categories are:

0-30 days
30-60 days
60-90 days
90-120 days

Computer accounting systems can age the accounts and indicate the type of activity needed. A bill less than 30 days old might need a friendly call or reminder letter, whereas one that is over 120 days may need a final letter to encourage payment before the account is turned over to a collection agency. Always allow the physician a final review of the names of patients being sent to a collection agency. This practice prevents the embarrassing situation of sending a relative who may have an unfamiliar name to collections. Once the accounts are aged, choose the most appropriate type of collection activity according to office policy.

COLLECTION TECHNIQUES

The medical assistant can use a variety of techniques to collect patient accounts. Often more than one technique must be used to obtain payment. Always be courteous and kind when using collection techniques.

Telephone Collection Calls

A telephone call at the right time, in the right manner, is more successful than notes, a statement, or a collection letter. The personal

A. Notifier: John Doe, MD, College Clinic, 4567 Broad Avenue, Woodland Hills, XY 12345 555-486-9002

B. Patient Name: Mary Judd   **C. Identification Number:** 0920XX7291

Advance Beneficiary Notice of Noncoverage (ABN)

NOTE: If Medicare doesn't pay for D. __B12 injections__ below, you may have to pay.
Medicare does not pay for everything, even some care that you or your health care provider have good reason to think you need. We expect Medicare may not pay for the D. __B12 injections__ below.

D.	E. Reason Medicare May Not Pay:	F. Estimated Cost
B12 injections	Medicare does not usually pay for this injection or this many injections	$35.00

WHAT YOU NEED TO DO NOW:
- Read this notice, so you can make an informed decision about your care.
- Ask us any questions that you may have after you finish reading.
- Choose an option below about whether to receive the D. __B12 injections__ listed above.
  Note: If you choose Option 1 or 2, we may help you to use any other insurance that you might have, but Medicare cannot require us to do this.

G. OPTIONS: Check only one box. We cannot choose a box for you.

☒ **OPTION 1.** I want the D. __B12 injections__ listed above. You may ask to be paid now, but I also want Medicare billed for an official decision on payment, which is sent to me on a Medicare Summary Notice (MSN). I understand that if Medicare doesn't pay, I am responsible for payment, but **I can appeal to Medicare** by following the directions on the MSN. If Medicare does pay, you will refund any payments I made to you, less co-pays or deductibles.

☐ **OPTION 2.** I want the D. _____ listed above, but do not bill Medicare. You may ask to be paid now as I am responsible for payment. **I cannot appeal if Medicare is not billed.**

☐ **OPTION 3.** I don't want the D. _____ listed above. I understand with this choice I am **not** responsible for payment, and **I cannot appeal to see if Medicare would pay.**

H. Additional Information:

This notice gives our opinion, not an official Medicare decision. If you have other questions on this notice or Medicare billing, call **1-800-MEDICARE** (1-800-633-4227/**TTY:** 1-877-486-2048).
Signing below means that you have received and understand this notice. You also receive a copy.

I. Signature: *Mary Judd*	J. Date: *March 20, 20XX*

According to the Paperwork Reduction Act of 1995, no persons are required to respond to a collection of information unless it displays a valid OMB control number. The valid OMB control number for this information collection is 0938-0566. The time required to complete this information collection is estimated to average 7 minutes per response, including the time to review instructions, search existing data resources, gather the data needed, and complete and review the information collection. If you have comments concerning the accuracy of the time estimate or suggestions for improving this form, please write to: CMS, 7500 Security Boulevard, Attn: PRA Reports Clearance Officer, Baltimore, Maryland 21244-1850.

Form CMS-R-131 (03/11)   Form Approved OMB No. 0938-0566

FIGURE 22-5 The Advance Beneficiary Notice (ABN) form is used to notify patients that Medicare may not pay for certain items and services. (From Fordney M: *Insurance handbook for the medical office,* ed 12, St Louis, 2012, WB Saunders.)

---

contact of a telephone call often prompts patients to mail in their payment. In the absence of time to make calls, the collection letter is the next best approach, but if collections are a serious problem, it may be worth an extra salary to hire a person to do the telephoning.

Always treat patients with the utmost respect on the telephone. Keep their financial record close by in case they have questions about their bill; also have their insurance company's phone number handy. Remember that some patients may not understand anything about insurance or third-party payers, so guide them to that understanding and be their advocate in getting as much reimbursement as possible so that the patient's share is smaller. Never simply insist that insurance has paid and their balance is due. This puts the patient into a negative mindset. Try using phrases such as the following:

"Mrs. Diggs, it looks as if your insurance company paid late last month. I believe you have a co-pay for your surgery that amounts to $450. Is that what you were expecting? Would you

like to take care of the whole balance or split that into two payments?"

"Mr. Hildebrand, we're showing that you have a balance due from your surgery. Your insurance has paid, and it looks as if you owe $700. We would be happy to help you by splitting that into two or three payments. What would work for you?"

"Mrs. Crumley, it seems that you have a balance due of $450 from your surgery, and I called to see whether I could help you budget that. You could pay $50 this week and split the remaining $400 into two payments over the next 2 months? We would be happy to work with you on this balance."

Always abide by office policy when making payment arrangements in collection situations. Never be belligerent with a patient. If he or she becomes irate, simply state that the person can call back when ready to discuss a solution for paying the account, say goodbye, and gently hang up the phone. Never listen to explicatives or allow verbal abuse.

PROCEDURE 22-9

Perform Collection Procedures

GOAL: *To collect the maximum amount of funds on each account.*

EQUIPMENT and SUPPLIES

- Patient ledger
- Office policy manual
- Clerical supplies
- Scripts for telephone collections so that students can role play this activity
- Letters for collection efforts
- Telephone
- Letterhead and envelopes
- Copies of claim forms previously filed

PROCEDURAL STEPS

1. Become familiar with office policy regarding turning accounts over to collections.
   PURPOSE: To make sure the policy is followed when accounts are turned over to collection agencies.
2. Review the patient's ledger to determine whether it needs collection activity.
   PURPOSE: Some accounts may be past due, but patients may have made arrangements to pay them; in this case, collection activities should not commence.
3. Determine the type of collection activity the account needs.
   PURPOSE: An account that is only slightly past due does not need a harsh collection letter; determine the best approach for each particular account.
4. Begin collection efforts with telephone calls or postcards.
   PURPOSE: Many patients only need a small reminder that their account is past due.
5. Progress to more stringent collection efforts if the patient does not pay the account as promised.
6. Once all collection efforts have been exhausted, report the account to the physician for further disposition.
   PURPOSE: The physician should decide which accounts are given to collection agencies and which are simply written off as bad debts.
7. Document the final collection activity on the ledger and/or in the patient's medical record.

Written notification is a must before making a final demand for payment indicating that legal or collection proceedings will be started. Each case should be handled individually on the basis of the experience with the person involved.

GENERAL RULES FOR TELEPHONE COLLECTIONS

What to Do

- Call the patient when it can be done with privacy.
- Call between 8 AM and 9 PM.
- Determine the identity of the person with whom you are speaking. If you ask, "Is this Mrs. Noble?" and she answers, "Yes," it could be the patient's mother-in-law or daughter-in-law, who is also "Mrs. Noble." Use the person's full name. Include suffixes, such as "Thomas Melborn, III." This may sound too formal, but it helps to ensure that the correct person is on the phone.
- Be dignified and respectful. One can be friendly and formal at the same time.
- Ask the patient whether it is a convenient time to talk. Unless you have the attention of the called party, there is little to be gained by continuing. If told that it is an inopportune time, ask for a specific time to call back or get a promise that the patient will call the office at a specified time.
- After a brief greeting, state the purpose of the call. Make no apology for calling, but state the reason in a friendly, businesslike way. The physician expects payment, and the medical assistant is interested in helping the patient meet the financial obligation. Open the call with a phrase such as, "This is Alice, Dr. Crawford's financial secretary. I'm calling about your account." A well-placed pause at this point in the call sometimes gets an immediate response from the debtor with regard to the nonpayment.
- Assume a positive attitude. For example, convey the impression that the patient intended to pay and it is only a matter of working out some suitable arrangements.
- Keep the conversation brief and to the point; do not make threats of any kind.
- Try to get a definite commitment—payment of a certain amount by a certain date.
- Follow up on promises made by the patient. This is best accomplished by using a tickler file or a note on the calendar. If the payment does not arrive by the promised date, remind the patient with another call. If the medical assistant fails to do this, the whole effort has been wasted.

What Not to Do

- Do not call between 9 PM and 8 AM. To do so may be considered harassment.
- Do not make repeated telephone calls.
- Do not call the debtor's place of work if the employer prohibits personal calls.
- If a call is placed to the debtor at work and the person cannot take the call, leave a message asking the debtor to "call Mrs. Black at 727-9238" without revealing the nature of the call; that is, do not state that the call is from "Dr. Crawford's office" or "Dr. Crawford's medical assistant."
- Do not show hostility. An angry patient is a poorly paying patient. Insulted patients often do not pay at all.

Collection Letters or Reminders

Some consultants believe that a printed collection letter or reminder enclosed with a statement is more effective than a personal letter. Their attitude is that a patient may be embarrassed by a personal letter and feel that he or she has been singled out for attention. An impersonal printed message will probably encourage the debtor to send a payment. The printed form is a time saver and is recommended if a lack of time contributes to poor collection follow-up. Standard printed forms are readily available, or the medical assistant can design an original form.

Letters that are friendly requests for an explanation of why payment has not been made are effective in most cases. These letters should indicate that the physician is sincerely interested in the patient and wants to help resolve the financial obligations. Invite the patient to the office to explain the reasons for nonpayment so that payment arrangements can be made. To lessen the patient's embarrassment, these letters can suggest that previous statements may have been overlooked.

On receipt of such a letter, most patients make some effort to explain their failure to make payment. If a patient really is having financial difficulties, he or she may be able to get public assistance. If it is a temporary financial problem, the physician and the patient may together be able to work out a satisfactory installment plan for payment.

The medical assistant often is given a free hand in designing collection patterns and composing collection letters. Many medical assistants compose a series of collection letters, using model letters they have found effective. Such a series usually includes at least five letters in varying degrees of forcefulness.

Sometimes even a person with poor paying habits pays the bill if treated with respect and consideration. The medical assistant should never go beyond the authority granted by the physician in pursuing collections. If questions arise about special collection problems, always check with the physician before proceeding. This is particularly important with patients whom you do not know personally (e.g., patients whom the physician has seen in the hospital or at home and patients with no credit history). It is difficult to say whether the effects of pressing collections too hard (which can result in loss of patient good will) are more detrimental than the effects of not pursuing collections diligently enough (which can result in loss of revenue). The physician and the medical assistant should agree on general collection policies as outlined earlier in this chapter, and the policies then should be followed. In all cases in which an account is to be assigned to a collection agency, make sure the physician is aware of this and approves.

In most medical offices, the medical assistant signs collection letters using his or her title, such as "Medical Assistant" or "Financial Secretary" below the typewritten signature. Do not list "Collections" below the name, because the patient may assume that the account has been placed with a collection agency. Some physicians want to sign these communications personally, but generally the medical assistant who handles the accounts also signs the collection letters.

Personal Interviews

Personal interviews with patients sometimes can be more effective than a whole series of collection letters. By talking to a patient face to face, the medical assistant can come to an understanding of the problem more quickly, and an agreement about future payment plans can be reached.

Occasionally a patient may undergo a long course of treatment and yet make no attempt to pay anything on the account. Perhaps such a patient is only waiting for the physician or the medical assistant to suggest that a payment be made. When it is known in advance that the patient requires extensive treatment, the matter of payment should be discussed early in the course of treatment, the credit policy should be explained, and some agreement should be reached on a payment plan.

Because medical services are far more **intangible** than any commercial service, collection efforts must not be delayed too long. Any responsible, sincere patient will call or write the physician's office after receiving a second statement and explain the delay in payment or ask for a payment plan. This is best accomplished in a private, personal interview.

If the account ultimately must be referred to a collector, find a good agency with a high recovery rate. The value of medical accounts diminishes in direct proportion to the length of time that has elapsed since service was provided. Do not fight the law of diminishing returns. All collection activity is costly. Know when to stop and call on the services of a professional agency.

Special Collection Situations

Tracing "Skips"

When a statement is returned marked "Moved—no forwarding address," you may consider this account as a "skip." This generally is accepted as an indication that the patient is attempting to avoid liability for debts, although some skips are innocent errors. The person may have been careless in not leaving a forwarding address, or the mistake may have occurred in the physician's office; the wrong name or address may have been placed on the statement. However, immediate action should be taken with regard to returned statements. Do not wait until the next billing time to attempt to trace the debtor. The Internet can be a valuable tool in tracing skips. Using a search engine, such as Yahoo or Google, enter the patient's name. Patients might even be found on social networking sites, such as Facebook, and that information may provide clues about the person's whereabouts. Investigate the search results carefully so that collection efforts are directed at the right person.

Address Change Service. Two versions of address change service (ACS) are offered by the U.S. Post Office: one uses the traditional alpha participant code, and the other uses an intelligent mail barcode encoded with a business entity identifier (BEI) code. Both versions notify mailers electronically of a change of address (COA) or a reason for nondelivery. ACS is available for all classes of mail but must be used with either an ancillary service endorsement and a participant code or an intelligent mail barcode containing a BEI. If the mailer uses an ancillary service endorsement for manual notifications and does not participate in ACS, the USPS charges a higher fee per mail piece. For the fee structure, see the *Mailing Standards of the United States Postal Service Domestic Mail Manual*, available on the USPS Web site *(www.usps.com)*. Mailers who want to participate in ACS must acquire either an ACS participant code or a BEI code from the National Customer Support Center (NCSC) and apply it to their envelopes, address labels, or address blocks in the required format. The locations of the notation Address Service Requested are shown in Figure 22-6.

UNITED STATES POSTAL SERVICE
475 LENFANT PLZ SW
WASHINGTON DC 20250-5800

ADDRESS SERVICE REQUESTED[1]

ADDRESS SERVICE REQUESTED[3]

Presorted
First-Class Mail
U.S. POSTAGE PAID
Washington, DC 20250
Permit No.

ADDRESS SERVICE REQUESTED[4]

ADDRESS SERVICE REQUESTED[2]

NATIONAL CUSTOMER SUPPORT CENTER
UNITED STATES POSTAL SERVICE
6060 PRIMACY PKWY STE 201
MEMPHIS TN 38188-0001

FIGURE 22-6 Address Service Requested envelope from the U.S. Postal Service.

If all attempts fail, turn the account over to a collection agency without delay. Do not keep a skip account too long, because the trail may become so cold as time elapses that even collection experts will be unable to follow it.

SUGGESTIONS FOR TRACING SKIPS

- Examine the patient's original office registration card.
- Call the telephone number listed on the card. Occasionally a patient may move without leaving a forwarding address but will transfer the old telephone number. The new telephone number may be given when you call the old number.
- If you are unable to contact the individual by telephone, make a few discreet calls to the references listed on the registration card to get leads.
- Check the Internet to secure the names and telephone numbers of neighbors or the landlord and contact these people to secure information about the debtor's whereabouts.
- Do not inform a third party that the person owes you money. Simply state that you are trying to locate or verify the location of the individual.
- Check the debtor's place of employment for information. If the person is a specialist in his or her field of work, the local union or similar organizations may be contacted. Although they may not give you the person's current address, they will relay the message that you are seeking to contact him or her. Often people are stirred to pay a bill if they think their employer may learn of their payment failure.
- Do not communicate with a third party more than once. This is specifically forbidden by law (Public Law 95-109, Sec. 804) unless the third party requests the collector to do so.

Claims Against Estates

A bill owed by a deceased patient may be handled a little differently from regular bills. Courtesy dictates that a bill not be sent during the initial period of bereavement, but do not delay longer than 30 days. The person responsible for settling the affairs of the estate, called an executor, is assembling outstanding accounts and expects to receive the medical bills along with all others. Use the following format to address the statement:

Estate of (name of patient)
c/o (spouse or next of kin, if known)
Patient's last known address

Do not address the statement to a relative unless you have a signed agreement that that person will be responsible. If for some reason the statement cannot be addressed as just suggested (e.g., if the patient was in an assisted-living facility or a skilled nursing facility and no relative's name is available), seek information from the county seat in the county where the estate is being settled.

A will generally is filed within 30 days of a death. The name of the executor or administrator usually can be obtained by sending a request to the Probate Department of the Superior Court, County Recorder's Office, in the county where the **decedent** lived. The time limits for filing an estate claim are determined by the state where the decedent resided.

After the name of the administrator or executor of the estate has been obtained, send a duplicate itemized statement of the account to that person by certified mail, return receipt requested. If no response is received in 10 days, contact the executor or the county clerk where the estate is being settled and obtain forms for filing a claim against the estate. (Some states do not have special claim forms and accept simple itemized statements.) This claim against the estate must be made within a certain time, which varies from 2 to 36 months, depending on the state where it is filed.

The executor of the estate either accepts or rejects the claim, and if it is accepted, sends an acknowledgment of the debt. Payment often is delayed because of the legal complications involved in settling an estate, but if the claim has been accepted, the physician eventually receives the money. If the claim is rejected and there is full justification for claiming the bill, file a claim against the executor within a limited time, according to state laws. The time limit in such cases starts with the date on the letter of rejection sent in response to the original claim.

Because states have different time limits and statutes with regard to these issues, the medical assistant should contact the physician's attorney or the local court for the exact procedure to follow; or, the physician may prefer to turn such matters over to his or her legal counsel immediately.

Bankruptcy

Bankruptcy laws were passed to secure equal distribution of the assets of an individual among the individual's creditors. These are federal laws that apply in all the states. When notified that a patient has declared bankruptcy, do not send statements or make any attempt to collect on the account from the patient.

Chapter 7 bankruptcy usually is a "no asset" situation. Because the physician's fee is an **unsecured** debt, there is little purpose in pursuing collection. Chapter 13 is known as *wage-earner bankruptcy.* Under Chapter 13, the patient-debtor pays a fixed amount to a **trustee** that is agreed upon by the court. This is then passed on to the creditors. During this period, none of the creditors can attach the debtor's wages or otherwise attempt to collect the debt. It sometimes is beneficial to file a claim under Chapter 13, because small payments may be made by the debtor under the supervision of the court over a period of 3 years. However, the debts are paid in order, **secured** debts first; consequently, the physician may never receive payment from a debtor who has filed bankruptcy.

USING OUTSIDE COLLECTION SERVICES

When everything possible has been done internally to follow up on an outstanding account and the office has not received payment, the question arises as to what step to take next, as follows:

- Should the facility sue for the payment?
- Should the account be sent to a collection agency?
- Should the account be written off as a bad debt?

Before forcing an account, first consider the time element: Has the patient been given a fair chance to pay this bill? Have statements been sent regularly and has a systematic method of following the account been used? Ask whether there might be a misunderstanding about the fee charged. Was the first statement fully itemized? A large, unexplained bill may frighten a patient into making no payments at all because the whole balance looks too large.

If the correct registration forms to secure advance credit information were used, the medical assistant should know the patient's financial ability to pay. However, illness may have caused a loss of salary and resulted in temporary inability to pay. Try to analyze the situation thoroughly. Could the patient have been dissatisfied with the care received? For some unknown reason, a patient may feel that he or she was not treated correctly. Perhaps the patient expected a complete cure too soon. Only an explanation of the condition, prognosis, and care can enlighten such patients, and this is best handled by the physician. If payment of a bill is pressed too hard and the patient is dissatisfied for some reason, a malpractice suit may be filed by the patient to seek retribution against the physician. The court can approve a period longer than 3 years in special cases but cannot approve a period longer than 5 years for collecting patient accounts.

Using a Collection Agency

The medical assistant should try every means possible to collect accounts before they become delinquent. As soon as the account is determined uncollectible through the office (i.e., the patient has failed to respond to the final letter or has failed to fulfill a second promise on payment), send the account to the collector without delay. Skips should be assigned immediately.

Even though collection by an agency means sacrificing 40% to 60% of the amount owed, further delay only reduces the chances of recovery by the professional collector. If the agency finds that the case deserves special consideration, it will ask the physician's advice before proceeding further.

CRITICAL THINKING APPLICATION 22-8

- Jodie has had several complaints about the collection agency used by the office. Patients have called to report that the collectors are threatening and unprofessional. How should Jodie approach the collection agency about these complaints?
- The office manager refuses to take these patients seriously, saying that because they owe the money, the collection agency's job is to collect the account in whatever way necessary. Jodie does not agree with her philosophy. What should she do?

Working with the Collection Agency

The collection agency needs certain data to enable it to begin collection procedures on overdue accounts:

- Full name of the debtor
- Name of the spouse
- Last known address
- Full amount of the debt
- Date of the last entry on account (debit or credit)
- Occupation of the debtor
- Business address
- Any other pertinent data

After an account has been released to a collection agency, the office makes no further collection attempts. Once the agency has begun its work, a number of guidelines and procedures should be followed:

- Send no more statements.
- Mark the patient's ledger or stamp it so that everyone knows it is now in the hands of the collector.
- Refer the patient to the collection agency if he or she contacts the office about the account.
- Promptly report any payments made directly to your office (a percentage of this payment is due the agency).
- Call the agency if any information is obtained that will be of value in tracing or collecting the account.
- Do not push the agency with frequent calls. The representatives of the agency will report regularly and will keep the office posted on collection progress.

Posting Collection Agency Payments

Collection agencies charge different percentages to collect delinquent accounts, but the agency with the cheapest fee is rarely the most effective. Agencies pay the net back, which is the amount of money paid to the facility after the agency has been paid its fee. The net back is the figure that should be considered when using a collection agency, not simply the fee percentage. If a patient sends a payment after the account has been turned over to a collection agency, the payment must be recorded on the account card. Because the agency charges a fee for collection efforts, the amount credited to the patient's account might be less than the actual payment amount. For instance, if the agency charges 25%, a $100 payment results in a $75 credit to the patient's account and the agency keeps $25. When posting the payment, place the amount to be credited in the adjustment column on the day sheet (Procedure 22-10). Some offices prefer the payment to go directly to the collection agency;

PROCEDURE 22-10

Post Collection Agency Payments

GOAL: *To post payments received on an account after it has been turned over to a collection agency.*

EQUIPMENT and SUPPLIES

- Patient ledgers
- Office policy manual
- Bookkeeping system
- Clerical supplies
- Calculator

PROCEDURAL STEPS

1. Determine that a payment has been received on an account that is now being serviced by a collection agency.
2. Notify the collection agency that the payment has been made.

PURPOSE: The collection agency is entitled to a portion of the money collected when a payment is sent to the medical office.

3. Send a notice to the patient, if necessary, to explain that the payment has been forwarded to the collection agency for credit.
4. Instruct patients to forward additional payments straight to the collection agency.
5. If office policy dictates, deposit the payment to the physician's account and then forward the fee due to the collection agency to its address.
   <u>PURPOSE:</u> To honor the contractual obligations with the collection agency.

---

either way, the adjustment eventually must be credited to the patient's account.

Making the Decision to Sue

The physician must decide whether he or she will benefit or suffer loss of good will by suing for a bill rather than writing it off as a loss. Some physicians believe it is unwise to resort to the court to collect medical bills unless extraordinary circumstances apply.

An account must be considered a 100% loss to the physician before legal proceedings are started. Remember never to threaten to **instigate** legal proceedings unless the physician is prepared to carry out the threat and has decided to pursue legal action. If the physician decides in favor of a lawsuit, investigate thoroughly and obtain as much information as possible for the proceedings. Litigation to collect a bill generally is in order when the following are true:

- The patient can afford to pay without hardship.
- The physician can produce office records that support the bill.
- The physician can justify the amount of the bill by comparing it with fee practices in the community.
- The patient's general condition after treatment is satisfactory.
- The persuasive powers of an ethical collection agency have been exhausted, and the agency advises suing.
- The patient can be given ample warning of the physician's intention to sue.
- The defendant (whether a patient or a parent or legal guardian) is legally liable for the services rendered to the patient.
- The statute of limitations has ruled out any possible malpractice action.
- The physician is neither indignant nor in a negative frame of mind.

Small Claims Court

Many medical practices find the small claims court a satisfactory, inexpensive means of collecting delinquent accounts. The law places a limit on the amount of debt for which relief may be sought in small claims court. Because this varies from state to state (usually up to $10,000) and in some instances even within a state, this limit should be checked in local courts before recovery is sought in this manner.

Parties to small claims actions are not represented by an attorney at the hearing but may send another person to court on their behalf to produce records supporting the claim. Physicians often send their bookkeeper or medical assistant with records of unpaid accounts to show the judge.

If the court awards a judgment for the amount owed, the plaintiff in small claims court may also recover the costs of the suit. For a very small investment in time and money, the physician who uses this method saves the time of a regular court action and eliminates attorneys' fees.

After being awarded a judgment, the medical assistant still must collect the money. The only person in a small claims action who has the right of appeal is the defendant. An appeal by the defendant may have the judgment set aside. The plaintiff cannot file an appeal in a small claims action; the decision of the court is final.

The necessary papers for filing action and full instructions on the course to follow may be obtained from the clerk of the small claims court. A medical assistant who has never appeared in court probably would be wise to attend once as a spectator to preview the procedure; this should allow him or her to feel more at ease when appearing for the physician.

A collection agency to which an account may have been assigned may not file or handle a small claims action. It must either sue in the regular municipal or justice court or attempt to collect the debt in some other manner.

▌CLOSING COMMENTS

Billing and collecting are critical duties in the medical office, and a responsible medical assistant is a great asset in this important area.

Always maintain a positive attitude with patients and guarantors. Remember that those who are ill or facing challenges are not always at their best and may not respond in a positive way to calls about their accounts. Make every attempt to work with each patient to develop a workable plan to clear the account.

Patient Education

Most patients are unaware of the actual coverage they have through their insurance policies. The medical assistant should encourage patients to read the entire policy so that they become familiar with its limitations and exclusions. Tell patients that when calling the company with questions, they should always write down the date, time, and name of the person with whom they spoke. Using e-mail is helpful, because a record of the correspondence can easily be saved or printed. Making sure that patients have a general understanding of their health insurance coverage is well worth the effort.

Often patients do not dispute or question the company when a claim is rejected or not paid in the expected amount. Encourage them to call the company and question rejections if they do not understand why the claim was denied. Patients are paying for coverage, and they should receive all the benefits to which they are entitled.

Patients appreciate receiving an office policy brochure or booklet that informs them about payment and credit options. The patient can use the printed booklet as a reference whenever questions arise, and regular use of the booklet by most patients reduces the number of calls made to the office. Encourage patients to use the booklet. It should include helpful phone numbers or extensions and instructions on whom the patient should call at the medical facility for answers to questions.

Legal and Ethical Issues

A patient who has filed for bankruptcy cannot be contacted or billed further. A threat to take collection action must be fulfilled, or the creditor is in violation of the Fair Debt Collection Practices Act. Never say the physician intends to take action if he or she does not plan to follow through.

Because laws vary greatly from state to state, medical assistants should review the statutes pertaining to billing and collecting in the area where they live. Develop a good understanding of what is required of the small business, such as a physician's office, in collecting fees and billing for amounts due. Remember that laws change often, and constantly update policies to reflect current statutes.

SUMMARY OF SCENARIO

Jodie is a well-respected member of Dr. Crawford's office team. Her friendly attitude and flexibility attract patients, and she enjoys the interaction with them. She knows that there are only a few patients for whom she cannot work out some type of payment arrangement. She is professional in her dealings with those whom she contacts about outstanding accounts.

Dr. Crawford has noticed that more and more patients pay their accounts, and he attributes this to the care Jodie shows when working with them. She is never hesitant to ask for payment from patients, but at the same time, she is sensitive to their needs and struggles. She urges her patients to cooperate and to make a good attempt to pay their accounts; in return, Jodie arranges a payment schedule the patient can meet.

Although she initially was nervous about explaining fees to patients and asking for payment, Jodie has become more comfortable in doing this aspect of her job, since she understands the business aspect of the practice. The physician is operating the practice to make a profit and support his family, and the practice also is a source of support for the employees' families. Patients understand that physicians must charge for their services, and have become used to co-payments and co-insurance amounts. Many times, these fees are collected in advance, before the patient sees Dr. Crawford. This practice saves time on checkout, and most patients believe that the co-pay is a small cost compared to the entire fee that physicians charge to manage their care in one office visit.

Jodie has noticed that the usual, customary, and reasonable fees that Dr. Crawford charges his patients directly affect the reimbursements that are paid by various insurance and managed care companies. She has handled several claims in which the payer questioned the fee when it fell outside of the UCR ranges. Dr. Crawford commented that he uses professional courtesy much less frequently than in the past because of the many rules and regulations placed on providers by managed care companies. He still offers the occasional patient a professional discount when it does not violate the managed care contract that he holds with the insurer or managed care company.

Jodie's flexibility as an employee has paid off for Dr. Crawford several times. During a week-long period when the computer bookkeeping system was malfunctioning, Jodie was able to retrieve information from her backup disks and use a pegboard system until the system was repaired. Her preparation allowed the office to continue operations without skipping a beat. Most patients did not even notice that the computer was not in use for the week.

Many physicians still use the manual pegboard system out of habit and because it is a reliable method of keeping up with patient accounts. Some simply trust manual, written records more than computerized systems. This is a matter of personal choice; either system works in the physician's office.

Jodie has been able to fill in for other employees because of the versatility she gained from her medical assistant training. She has scheduled appointments and even assisted Dr. Crawford with minor office surgery. Jodie believes that performing other duties is a nice change periodically, and she keeps her skills sharp. She has proven herself to be a valuable and efficient employee.

SUMMARY OF LEARNING OBJECTIVES

1. **Define, spell, and pronounce the terms listed in the vocabulary.**
   Spelling and pronouncing medical terms correctly bolster the medical assistant's credibility. Knowing the definition of these terms promotes confidence in communication with patients and co-workers.

2. **List three values that are considered in determining professional fees.**
   Physicians offer the patient their time. They also make the most accurate judgments possible about the patient's medical condition. The services provided to the patient also figure into the fees set for various procedures.

3. **Differentiate the terms *usual, customary,* and *reasonable.***
   Many third-party payers use the UCR method of determining fees for procedures. The *usual* fee is what the physician normally charges for a given service. The *customary* fee is the range of fees charged by physicians with similar experience in the same geographic area. Services or procedures that are exceptionally complicated and that require extra time deserve a *reasonable* fee that may be higher than the usual fee.

4. **Discuss the value of fee estimates for patient treatment.**
   Providing estimates for medical care helps patients plan their finances when an illness or injury occurs. Providing estimates prevents misquoting of the fee later. The office staff should keep a copy of the estimate in the patient's chart to help prevent misunderstanding and confusion over the charges.

5. **Explain basic bookkeeping computations.**
   Basic bookkeeping allows the physician to keep track of the amounts patients owe to the practice and the amounts the practice owes to others. Accounting is the four-stage process of recording, classifying, summarizing, and interpreting financial statements. By recording the day's charges and payments made on account, the physician can take a daily, monthly, and annual snapshot of the financial health of the practice. Adjustments are sometimes necessary on patients' accounts. Practice expenses are tracked and used to prove income tax deductions and equipment depreciation. Meticulous financial records must be kept so that the physician can keep the facility in operation and make a healthy business profit.

6. **Differentiate between bookkeeping and accounting.**
   Bookkeeping is the recording stage of accounting. The medical assistant performs bookkeeping functions when posting a payment to a patient's account. Accounting is a four-stage process of recording, classifying, summarizing, and interpreting financial statements. The physician may have an accountant who provides periodic summaries and handles tax planning and payment for the physician.

7. **Compare the manual and computerized bookkeeping systems used in ambulatory healthcare.**
   Most medical facilities now use a computerized bookkeeping system, which allows for regular backup so that vital information is not lost. Computerized systems allow fast record retrieval, and a patient's account can be found and adjusted quickly when posting charges and payments. Manual systems, although more time-consuming, can provide the same information and are valuable when the computer system is down or malfunctioning.

8. **Identify procedures for preparing patient accounts.**
   Computer medical accounting systems allow report-writing; this function can be used to create an accounts receivables list of all patients who owe money and to generate a bill. When using a manual system, the medical assistant must check each ledger to determine whether a billing statement should be sent. Use the office policy and procedures manual to determine billing parameters.

9. **Discuss the types of adjustments that may be made to a patient's account.**
   Adjustments are common on patient accounts and may be made to write off a disallowed balance, post a nonsufficient funds check, and correct errors, among other transactions.

10. **Explain both billing and payment options.**
    Physicians usually bill for payment in cycles, which allows a consistent flow of income to the office. A section of patient accounts is billed either weekly or biweekly, and patients send in their payments by mail, bring them in personally, or use an online payment system. Payment is usually requested at the time of service, especially if the patient uses a managed care system that requires a co-pay.

11. **Describe the impact of both the Fair Debt Collection Practices Act and the Truth in Lending Act as they apply to collections.**
    These laws provide the framework of rules that must be followed when collecting debts or extending credit. They affect office practices because they designate specific actions that are allowed when contacting patients about their bills. The office policy and procedures manual should provide guidelines for collecting patient accounts.

12. **Discuss procedures for collecting outstanding accounts.**
    Most of today's medical offices use computerized letters to prompt patients to pay overdue bills. Often, a message can be added to monthly statements that is increasingly more urgent, depending on the age of the account. Outstanding balances are also collected using telephone calls, e-mails, and personal discussions with the patient or guarantor.

CONNECTIONS

📖 **Study Guide Connection:** Go to the Chapter 22 Study Guide. Read and complete the activities.

⊖ **Evolve Connection:** Go to the Chapter 22 link at *evolve.elsevier.com/kinn* to complete the Chapter Review and Chapter Quiz. Check out the other resources listed for this chapter to make the most of what you have learned from Professional Fees, Billing, and Collecting.

BANKING SERVICES AND PROCEDURES

23

Laura Anderson likes working with figures and has always been interested in bookkeeping. In high school she took all the bookkeeping and accounting courses offered, and during the summer months she helped out in the accounting department of the family business. She also worked part-time at City National Bank. Now, Laura wants to learn all she can about the financial transactions common to a medical practice. She is especially interested in electronic banking and all the possibilities it has to offer. Once her career in medical assisting is launched, Laura hopes to specialize in helping medical offices set up and run electronic medical record systems.

Although Laura has had considerable bookkeeping experience, she realizes that she still has a lot to learn about the daily financial duties in a medical office, including accounts payable, working with the business checkbook, making deposits, reconciling bank statements, and many other banking responsibilities.

Taking on the bookkeeping functions of a medical office involves not only responsibilities to the physician and employer, but also to patients and the vendors from whom the medical office purchases supplies. Laura realizes that to perform well in her upcoming career as a medical assistant, she must learn all she can about the topics pertinent to her special interest areas and stay current with the rapidly changing world of finance.

While studying this chapter, think about the following questions:

- How has banking changed over the years?
- How safe is Internet banking?

- How can an office manager know that an employee can be trusted with banking procedures?
- Why is making daily deposits a good idea?

LEARNING OBJECTIVES

1. Define, spell, and pronounce the terms listed in the vocabulary.
2. Describe banking procedures.
3. Explain how the Internet has changed traditional banking practices.
4. State the four requirements of a negotiable instrument.
5. Discuss the advantages of using debit cards.
6. Identify the three most common types of bank accounts.
7. Correctly write checks for bill payment.
8. Explain how to handle mistakes made in preparing a check.

9. Discuss precautions for accepting checks.
10. Discuss the actions necessary when a patient's check is returned.
11. Compare types of endorsements.
12. Prepare a bank deposit.
13. Accurately reconcile a bank statement for the office checking account.

VOCABULARY

disclaimer A denial of responsibility; a denial of a legal claim.

drawee A bank or facility on which a check is drawn or written.

drawer The person who writes a check.

e-banking Electronic banking via computer modem or over the Internet.

endorser The person who signs his or her name on the back of a check for the purpose of transferring title to another person.

holder The person who presents a check for payment.

maker Any individual, corporation, or legal party who signs a check or any type of negotiable instrument.

m-banking Banking through the use of mobile devices, such as cell phones and wireless Internet services.

negotiable Legally transferable to another party.

payee The person named on a draft or check as the recipient of the amount shown.

payer The person who writes a check in favor of the payee.

power of attorney A legal statement in which a person authorizes another person to act as his or her attorney or agent. The authority may be limited to the handling of specific procedures. The person authorized to act as the agent is known as the *attorney in fact*.

principal A capital sum of money due as a debt or used as a fund for which interest is either charged or paid.

reconciliation The process of proving that a bank statement and checkbook balance are in agreement.

Uniform Commercial Code (UCC) A unified set of rules covering many business transactions; it has been adopted in all 50 states, the District of Columbia, and most U.S. territories. It regulates the fields of sales of goods; commercial paper, such as checks; secured transactions in personal property; and particular aspects of banking, letters of credit, warehouse receipts, bills of lading, and investment securities.

Financial transactions in the professional office nearly always involve banking services and the use of checks. A medical assistant, therefore, must understand the responsibilities involved in accepting payments, endorsing and depositing checks, writing checks, and regularly reconciling bank statements. Payments received in the medical office should be deposited as soon as possible; ideally, on the same day. The medical assistant may very well be in charge of these financial responsibilities; therefore he or she must understand each transaction and its function.

BANKING IN TODAY'S BUSINESS WORLD

With the advent of the Internet, banking as we once knew it has changed. People once had to fight traffic and wait in line at crowded banks; today, they can sit in the comfort of their own homes and do their banking on the computer at any time of day. Banking transactions such as buying supplies, paying bills, and transferring funds between accounts can be done online. In addition, staff members have access to supply companies online and can review costs easily from the office instead of driving to numerous companies to compare prices.

Some banks have traded bricks and mortar to conduct all of their business online. The customers open their account online and deposits are made by using an application ("app") on a cell phone, tablet, or other electronic device. This type of banking service best fits the person who needs a simple account that can be accessed anytime and needs little maintenance.

In fact, people do not even have to sit in front of a computer terminal to conduct banking transactions. A physician may be sitting on a bus or a train or waiting for a flight and can carry out bank transactions. All this is possible just by turning on a laptop computer or using a mobile phone.

Online Banking

Online banking is a means of performing banking services electronically via the Internet. It also is called *personal computer (PC) banking, home banking, electronic banking,* **e-banking**, or *Internet banking.*

Many facilities have this capability, and most of them offer both basic and advanced services. With basic services, a customer usually can do the following:

- Check account balances
- Transfer funds between accounts
- Pay bills electronically
- Determine whether a check has cleared the bank
- Download account information
- View images of transactions (checks and deposits)

Online banking has advantages and disadvantages. One of the most obvious advantages is the ability to bank at one's own convenience in one's own home or office at any time. This can save considerable time and expense, especially if banking must be done daily. Many people find online banking a convenient and comprehensive method of money management. Other advantages include ease of use, portability, and availability.

Disadvantages of e-banking include learning to navigate the software. Service options are often more limited. In addition, some experts believe that there may be a slight increase in risk compared with conventional banking, although this has been debated by e-banking proponents. Despite the disadvantages, forecasts show that banking via the Internet is becoming more popular. The cost of online banking varies from bank to bank. Some charge a flat rate ($5 to $10 per month) with varying fees for additional transactions.

Online Convenience

Convenience probably is the number one reason people and businesses use the Internet for financial services. There is no frenzied drive to the bank during rush hour, waiting in line, or working around the confines of banking hours. Online banking is available 24 hours a day, 7 days a week. In addition to Internet banking services, clinic bills can be paid online, without the delay of mailing. Balance inquiries and various other transactions can be monitored easily. Costly fees for financial transactions left until the last minute can be avoided, because online transactions can be accomplished in a matter of seconds. Some banks now offer online transfers between banks, because many people have accounts at different banks.

Customer-Oriented Banking

Americans are becoming more and more mobile. They want to conduct business and take care of personal concerns on laptops or cell phones on their way to and from work. In addition, the rapid pace of life requires rapid or "instant" solutions; convenience has become a basic expectation of consumers where the banking industry is concerned.

Banks no longer consider customers as merely account numbers; to stay competitive, banks must look at the total customer picture. Many banks offer a type of interactive voice response system that operates through speech recognition, allowing customers to conduct business through a combination of talking into the telephone and using the telephone keypad. The call centers of some banks employ customer service personnel to answer questions and fulfill requests for all types of bank transactions.

Mobile banking, or **m-banking,** is a customer-oriented innovation that is emerging through the wireless technology market. Through the use of wireless devices, such as cell phones and wireless Internet services, customers can conduct a variety of financial transactions, set up alerts and notifications when bills are due, and make electronic transfers to pay these bills. Many banks offer applications (apps) that can be downloaded for free on smart phones and computers that will even let the user deposit checks from any location. Consider the services available through local banks when choosing the best banking facility for the physician's office.

ELECTRONIC FUNDS TRANSFERS

Electronic funds transfers (EFTs) are electronic payments of payroll, money owed to vendors or business establishments, and payments from government agencies. EFT payments are safe, secure, efficient, and less expensive than paper checks. The biggest advantage to using EFTs is the cost savings. The U.S. government pays $1.03 to issue each check payment, but only 10.5 ¢ to issue an EFT. Many EFTs are processed through an automated clearinghouse (ACH), which is an electronic network for financial transactions in the United States. An ACH processes large volumes of debit and credit transactions in batches. Rules and regulations that govern the ACH network have been established by the National Automated Clearing House Association (NACHA) and the Federal Reserve. The Federal Reserve banks, as a group, are the nation's largest clearinghouse operator. The Electronic Payments Network (EPN) is the only private-sector ACH in the country. Electronic processing becomes more prevalent each day, and business transactions are processed faster and more efficiently through electronic means. More information about clearinghouses can be found later in this chapter.

CRITICAL THINKING APPLICATION 23-1

Laura is excited about all the possibilities available with e-banking and m-banking. Where can Laura learn more about electronic banking and its advantages and disadvantages compared with conventional banking?

CHECKS

A check is a bank draft or order to pay a certain sum of money, payable on demand, to a specified person or entity. The concept of writing and depositing checks as a method of conducting financial transactions dates back as far as the Roman Empire. The word "check" was coined in England, where serial numbers were marked on these written orders of payment as a way to "check" on them. About 90% of all financial transactions in the United States are said to be accomplished by check.

A check is considered a **negotiable** instrument. For a check to be negotiable, it must:

- Be written and signed by a **maker**
- Contain a promise or order to pay a sum of money
- Be payable on demand or at a fixed future date
- Be payable to order or bearer

Debit Cards

The use of debit cards has vastly increased in the United States. Most debit cards are connected to a checking account. When the debit card is used, the amount of the transaction is immediately withdrawn from the available balance in the account. A pin number is assigned to the card for cash withdrawal and point of sale (POS) purchases. The cards usually have a MasterCard or Visa designation and can be used wherever those credit cards are accepted. The account can still be overdrawn, and in most situations, when there are not enough funds in the account to make a purchase, the card will be denied unless there is some type of overdraft protection on the account. Substantial fees may be charged if the bank elects to pay the debit when there are not enough available funds. Some banks now decline debit card charges at the point of sale when there are not sufficient funds in the account to pay the charge and do not charge any insufficient funds fees toward the attempted purchase. Stay abreast of recent banking legislation and always follow office policy when accepting debit cards as payment for medical services. The medical assistant may see various types of debit cards in the physician's office. Many states issue a debit card to individuals receiving child support payments or some types of state financial assistance.

ADVANTAGES OF USING DEBIT CARDS

Using debit cards to transfer funds has many advantages:
1. Debit cards are both safe and convenient, particularly for making payments online.
2. Transactions are completed quickly.
3. Expenditures are quickly calculated.
4. The cards can be used either as debit or credit cards. For debits, the user needs a personal identification number (PIN). For use as a credit card, the user often must provide identification.
5. Specific payments can be easily located online.
6. If stolen or lost, the debit card can be voided quickly with a minimum liability.
7. Receipts and statements provide a permanent, reliable record of disbursements for tax purposes.
8. The debit card statement provides a summary of receipts.
9. The cards usually can be used anywhere that accepts MasterCard or Visa.

Types of Checks

Medical assistants probably are familiar with the standard personal check, but many other types of checks also are used in business transactions.

Bank Draft

A bank draft is a check drawn by a bank against funds deposited to its account in another bank.

Cashier's Check

A cashier's check is a bank's own check drawn on itself and signed by the bank cashier or other authorized official. It is also known as an officer's or treasurer's check. A cashier's check is obtained by paying the bank cashier the amount of the check, in cash or by personal check. Many banks charge a fee for this service. Cashier's checks often are issued to accommodate a savings account customer who does not keep a checking account.

Limited Check

A check may be limited in the amount written on it and the time during which it may be presented for payment (e.g., 30, 60, or 90 days). A limited check often is used for payroll or insurance checks.

Money Order

Domestic money orders are sold by banks, some stores, and the U.S. Postal Service. Money orders often are used to pay bills by mail when a person does not have a checking account. The maximum face value varies, depending on the source. International money orders may be purchased for limited amounts, indicated in U.S. dollars, to send money abroad.

Traveler's Check

Traveler's checks, available at most banks, are designed for people who are traveling, because personal checks may not be accepted or carrying a large amount of cash might be inadvisable. Traveler's checks usually are printed in denominations of $10, $20, $50, and $100 and sometimes $500 and $1,000. They require two signatures from the purchaser, one at the time of purchase and the other at the time of use. The use of traveler's checks is becoming less common, because debit and credit cards are widely accepted throughout the world. However, the medical assistant may be presented with a traveler's check if a patient is on vacation or out of town and has a medical emergency. Follow office policy when determining whether this form of payment is acceptable.

Voucher Check

A voucher check has a detachable voucher form. The voucher portion is used to itemize or specify the purpose for which the check is drawn. It is used for the convenience of the **payer** and shows discounts and various other itemizations. This portion of the check, which is removed before the check is presented for payment, provides a record for the **payee** (Figure 23-1). Some government agencies use voucher checks to make various types of payments.

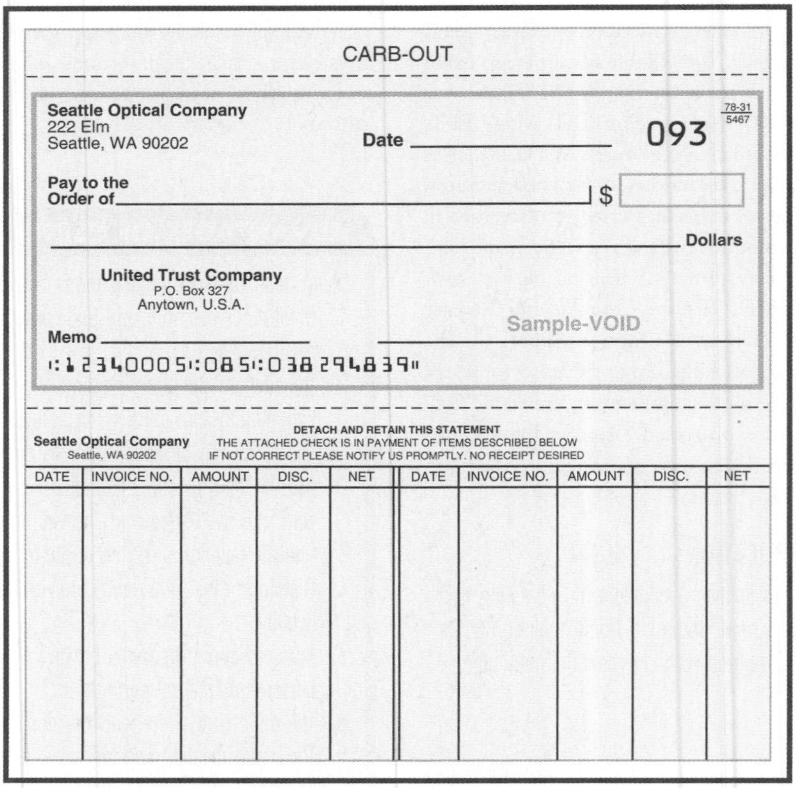

CARB-OUT

Seattle Optical Company
222 Elm
Seattle, WA 90202

78-31
5467

093

Date ____________

Pay to the Order of ____________ $

____________ Dollars

United Trust Company
P.O. Box 327
Anytown, U.S.A.

Memo ____________

Sample-VOID

:1234000 5:085:038 294839

DETACH AND RETAIN THIS STATEMENT

Seattle Optical Company
Seattle, WA 90202

THE ATTACHED CHECK IS IN PAYMENT OF ITEMS DESCRIBED BELOW
IF NOT CORRECT PLEASE NOTIFY US PROMPTLY. NO RECEIPT DESIRED

DATE	INVOICE NO.	AMOUNT	DISC.	NET	DATE	INVOICE NO.	AMOUNT	DISC.	NET

FIGURE 23-1 Page from a bank order book showing a sample voucher check.

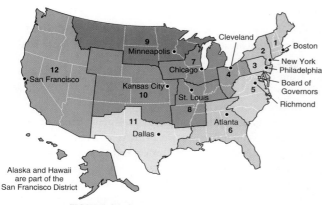

FIGURE 23-2 The 12 Federal Reserve districts.

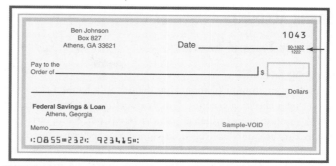

FIGURE 23-3 Sample check. The arrow indicates the American Bankers Association number. The numbers on the bottom left represent the bank's nine-digit routing number and the user's checking account number.

THE BANKING SYSTEM

The Federal Reserve

Wanting to provide the nation with a safer, more flexible, and stable monetary and financial system, Congress created the Federal Reserve in 1913 as the central bank of the United States. It consists of a seven-member Board of Governors with headquarters in Washington, D.C., and 12 Federal Reserve banks in major cities throughout the country (Figure 23-2). For additional information on the Federal Reserve System and its regional banks, visit its Web site at *www.federalreserve.gov.*

Routing and Account Numbers

A routing transit number (RTN) is a nine-digit code printed on the bottom left side of checks or other negotiable instruments. It identifies the bank upon which the check was drawn. Routing numbers also are used for direct deposits and bank wiring. The first two digits indicate the Federal Reserve district where the bank is located. The third digit indicates the particular district office, and the rest of the digits represent the individual bank identification number. Electronic payments can be made using the routing and account numbers and are processed at banks like regular checks.

American Bankers Association Number

The American Bankers Association (ABA) number appears in the upper right area of a printed check. The number is used as a simple means of identifying the area location of the bank on which the check is written and the particular bank in that area. The code number is expressed as a fraction (Figure 23-3):

$$\frac{90\text{-}1822}{1222}$$

In the top part of the fraction, before the hyphen, the numbers 1 to 49 designate cities in which Federal Reserve banks are located or other key cities; the numbers 50 to 99 refer to states or territories. The part of the number following the hyphen is a number issued to each bank for its own identification purposes. The bottom part of the fraction includes the number of the Federal Reserve district where the bank is located and other identifying information. The ABA number is used to prepare deposit slips and to identify each check.

How Checks Are Processed

When a check is presented for payment, the **drawee** (the bank or facility on which the check is drawn or written) pays the specified sum of money written on the face of the check to the **holder** (the person presenting the check for payment). Checks received by the bank are turned over daily to a regional clearinghouse, which cancels each one by stamping, mechanically punching, or embossing them. The identifying code numbers, printed on the face of the check with magnetic ink, enable this "clearing" process to be accomplished quickly and efficiently. Checks due from and to all banks outside a specific region are settled by means of computerized entries. The cancelled check is either kept by the financial institution or returned to the **drawer** (the person who wrote the check). Many banks no longer provide cancelled checks on a regular basis. If the drawer needs proof of payment, a copy of the check can be requested from the bank if the checks are not returned in the monthly bank statement.

Clearinghouses

As the use of checks increased, the system became confusing, because so many different banks were involved. At first, messengers were used for collection; however, this involved a lot of traveling and carrying a lot of cash. Then, in a London coffee shop, a solution came about when two bank messengers who were discussing the shortcomings of the system realized they had checks for each other. They decided to exchange them and save some time and effort. This practice evolved into a system of check clearinghouses, or networks of banks that exchange checks, which is still in use. Banks in the United States can present checks to the Federal Reserve System or private clearinghouses for regional and national check collection.

Magnetic Ink Character Recognition

As mentioned, characters and numbers printed in magnetic ink are found at the bottom of checks. They represent a common machine language, readable both by machines and humans. When a check is deposited, the amount of the check also can be printed in magnetic ink below the signature. Magnetic ink character recognition (MICR) identification facilitates processing through a high-speed machine that reads the characters, sorts the checks, and does the bookkeeping.

BANK ACCOUNTS

Common Types of Accounts

Checking Accounts

By placing an amount of money on deposit in a bank, a depositor can set up a checking account. Simply stated, a checking account is a bank account against which checks can be written. Many variations in checking accounts have been developed over the years. Instead of a straight, non-interest-bearing account, an individual might have an insured money market checking account, which bears interest at the daily money market rate if a certain minimum balance is maintained. However, most banks do not offer interest-bearing checking accounts for businesses.

A physician often requires three different checking accounts:
- An account for personal and family expenses
- A separate checking account for office expenses
- A high-yield, interest-bearing account for funds reserved for paying insurance premiums, property taxes, and other seasonal expenses

The medical assistant most likely will deal only with the office checking account.

Savings Accounts

Money that is not needed for current expenses can be deposited in a savings account. In most cases, savings accounts earn interest on the amounts deposited; that is, the bank pays the depositor a certain percentage monthly or quarterly to use the money in the savings account. An ordinary savings account draws interest at the lowest prevailing rate and has no minimum balance requirement and no check-writing privileges. A physician may deposit a certain percentage of income into a savings account each month.

Interest-Bearing Accounts

Interest is a charge (or payment) in exchange for the use of money. It usually is figured as a percentage of the **principal**. Simple interest is computed annually; compound interest is figured on the principal and on any previous interest that has been added to the original sum of money and can be computed using a variety of time increments (e.g., daily, monthly, quarterly, and so on). Interest-bearing checking accounts draw a small amount of interest, usually 1% or 2%, on the average daily balance. Savings accounts normally pay a higher rate of interest than checking accounts (e.g., 2% to 3%). However, these rates fluctuate with the financial market.

Money Market Savings Account

An insured money market savings account requires a minimum balance, anywhere from $500 to $5,000; it draws interest at money market rates (usually a higher percentage rate than for a regular savings account); and it allows a specified number of checks (frequently three) to be written per month. A minimum fee may be charged for each transaction. Such checks usually are written to transfer funds to a checking account. Some businesses transfer excess funds from the business checking account to a money market account over the weekend or over an extended holiday period to draw interest on the funds (Figure 23-4).

Individual Retirement Accounts

Individual retirement accounts (IRAs) are a type of individual savings plan that are allowed special tax treatment at the federal and sometimes the state level. This tax-favored status distinguishes an IRA from an ordinary savings account; specific rules must be followed to qualify for the tax savings. IRA rules are stricter than those for ordinary savings accounts.

Physicians and healthcare organizations may offer their employees an IRA. Several different types of IRAs are available (e.g., traditional, Roth, and education). For several reasons, IRAs often are used as a means of preparing for retirement:
- Savings grows tax-deferred.
- Tax deductions are realized for contributions (with traditional IRAs).
- Interest earned may not be taxed at withdrawal (with Roth IRAs).

IRAs come in all shapes and sizes. Individuals considering an IRA must make sure to study the rules of each one before deciding which is best for their needs.

CRITICAL THINKING APPLICATION   23-2

The physician knows that Laura worked part-time in a local bank before coming to the clinic. He tells her that he is considering changing banks and asks Laura to research the interest rates on money market accounts at local banks. How does Laura accomplish this task?

The Business Account

A business bank account is used for business or company operations and managing cash related to day-to-day business functions. Many different types of accounts are available for businesses today, including checking, savings, and money market accounts, in addition to other types of financial elements. Before a business account is set up, careful consideration should be given to each of these elements to determine which best meets the particular needs of the business.

What to Look for in a Business Account

Most businesses want "the most bang for their buck." They want the most services possible for the least amount of money, just as individuals do with personal accounts. Some of the services available for business accounts are:
- Business checking with interest, accruing interest with either checking or savings accounts
- Free checks and deposits with a maintained minimum balance (which varies from bank to bank)
- Overdraft protection by linking the account to a savings account or to a bank-issued credit or debit card
- Online banking

Perks for Businesses

Many financial institutions offer perquisites ("perks") for businesses that open accounts. These may include:
- Business Express: A computerized cash management system that allows access to account information by telephone.
- "Sweep" account: An account in which excess funds over a minimum balance are "swept" into a higher yielding

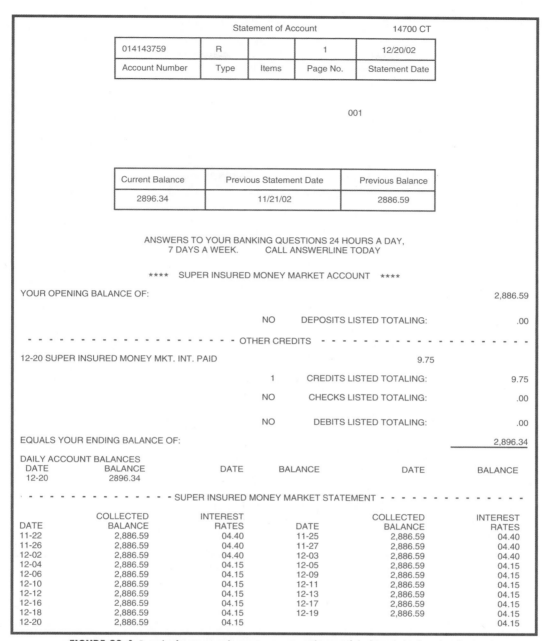

FIGURE 23-4 Example of a money market account statement. This type of check writing has limited privileges.

interest-bearing investment account. When the balance in the account drops below the minimum, funds are "swept" back into it automatically.

- Business checking with special features: A customized bank account designed for businesses with low to moderate transaction volumes and limited cash balances. This service helps business owners manage their day-to-day business and/or personal finances.
- Cash management account: Combines a checking account with a money market fund and a brokerage account. All cash activities are summarized on one monthly statement. This is ideal for business owners who do not have time to manage their money and/or investments.

- Other special features: Automatic bill paying, payroll preparation, smart phone applications, and timed business deposits.

Business Checks

The checkbook most widely used in the professional office is a ledger-type book with three checks per page and a perforated stub at the left side of the check (Figure 23-5). Checks may be bound in a soft cover or punched for a ring binder. The checks and matching stubs are numbered in sequence and preprinted with the depositor's name and account number, along with any additional information, such as address and telephone number. Numbered deposit slips in separately bound books are also supplied to the depositor.

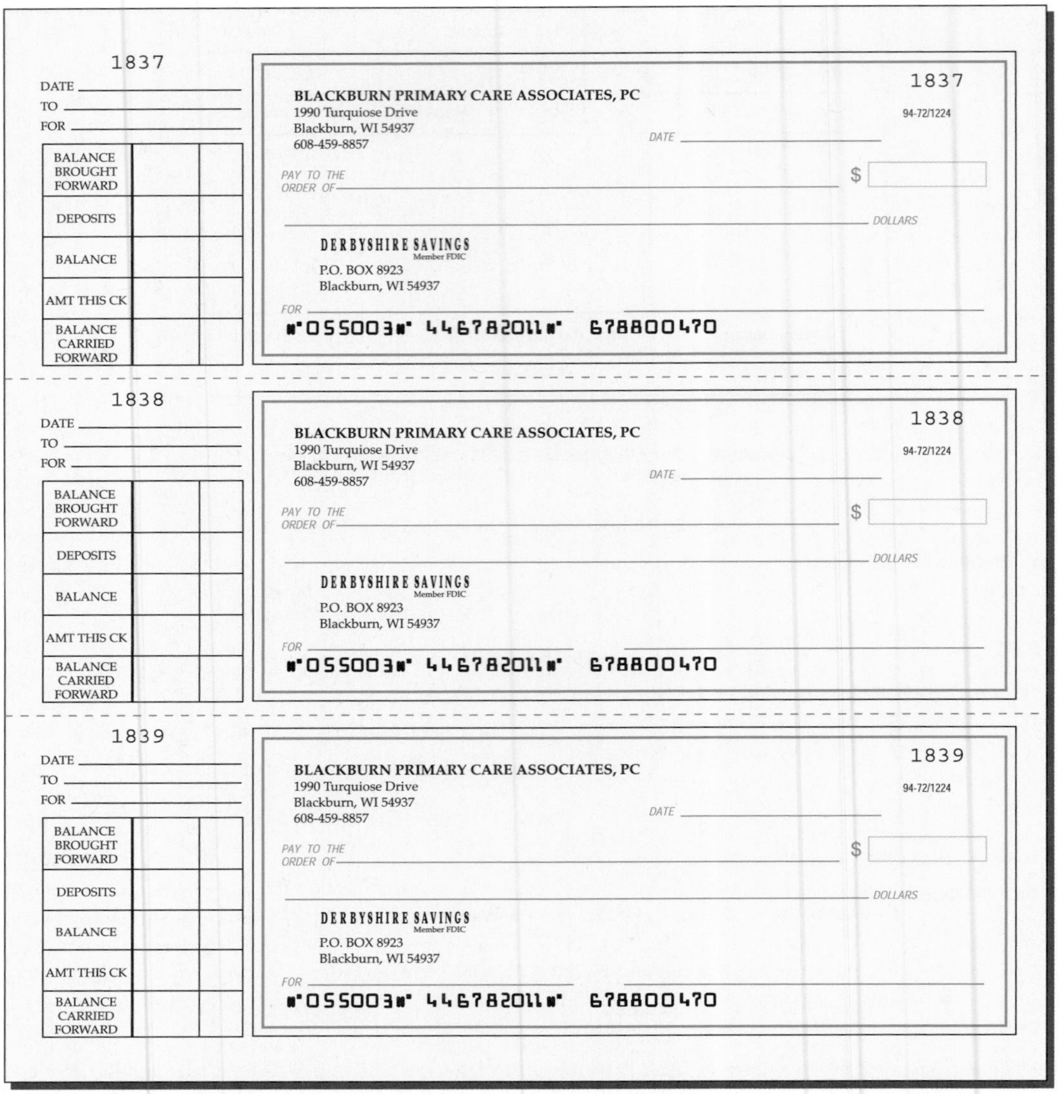
1837
DATE
TO
FOR
BALANCE BROUGHT FORWARD
DEPOSITS
BALANCE
AMT THIS CK
BALANCE CARRIED FORWARD

BLACKBURN PRIMARY CARE ASSOCIATES, PC
1990 Turquiose Drive
Blackburn, WI 54937
608-459-8857
1837
94-72/1224
DATE
PAY TO THE ORDER OF $
DOLLARS
DERBYSHIRE SAVINGS
Member FDIC
P.O. BOX 8923
Blackburn, WI 54937
FOR
⑈055003⑈ 446782011⑈ 678800470

1838
DATE
TO
FOR
BALANCE BROUGHT FORWARD
DEPOSITS
BALANCE
AMT THIS CK
BALANCE CARRIED FORWARD

BLACKBURN PRIMARY CARE ASSOCIATES, PC
1990 Turquiose Drive
Blackburn, WI 54937
608-459-8857
1838
94-72/1224
DATE
PAY TO THE ORDER OF $
DOLLARS
DERBYSHIRE SAVINGS
Member FDIC
P.O. BOX 8923
Blackburn, WI 54937
FOR
⑈055003⑈ 446782011⑈ 678800470

1839
DATE
TO
FOR
BALANCE BROUGHT FORWARD
DEPOSITS
BALANCE
AMT THIS CK
BALANCE CARRIED FORWARD

BLACKBURN PRIMARY CARE ASSOCIATES, PC
1990 Turquiose Drive
Blackburn, WI 54937
608-459-8857
1839
94-72/1224
DATE
PAY TO THE ORDER OF $
DOLLARS
DERBYSHIRE SAVINGS
Member FDIC
P.O. BOX 8923
Blackburn, WI 54937
FOR
⑈055003⑈ 446782011⑈ 678800470

FIGURE 23-5 Example of business checks with stubs. (From Hunt SA: *Fundamentals of medical assisting,* Philadelphia, 2002, WB Saunders.)

Computer-Generated Checks. Instead of ordering checks printed by the bank, the physician may use personalized checks that can be ordered from printing houses to fit the office computer's financial software program (e.g., Quicken). The checks may have one or more copies that serve as the record of checks written.

One-Write Check Writing. A one-write system of writing checks can save time and minimize errors in medical office disbursements. An office with a pegboard bookkeeping system may want to include one-write check writing. By using a combination check writing system, one check and one record of checks drawn handle both bill paying and payroll check writing.

When the check is written, a permanent record is created through the carbonized line of the check onto the record of checks drawn and the employee's payroll record, including a record of all deductions. Space is provided for the payee's address so that the check can be mailed in a window envelope. This not only saves time but also ensures that the check goes to the correct address. Suppliers of basic pegboard systems also can provide a check writing system such as the one described.

BILL PAYING AND CHECK WRITING

Establishing a Bill-Paying System

Establish a systematic plan for writing checks and paying bills. Some offices have incorporated an online bill paying system and pay bills as soon as they are received. For those using manual systems, check writing usually is done on a specific day or days of each month. An exception sometimes arises when a good discount can be had if a bill is paid within a specified time, such as 10 days. Such discounts usually are indicated at the bottom of invoices or billing statements.

Before writing a check, fill in the information on the check stub. Make this a habit so that no check is missing without the notation as to its payee and amount. When writing a check in payment of a

PROCEDURE 23-1

Write Checks in Payment of Bills

GOAL: *To correctly write checks for payment of bills.*

EQUIPMENT and SUPPLIES

- Checkbook
- Bills to be paid

PROCEDURAL STEPS

1. Locate the first bill to be paid. Before writing the check, fill out the stub or the place designated for recording expenditures. Include the date, name of payee, amount of the check, the new balance to be carried forward, and usually the purpose of the check.
   PURPOSE: To prevent the possibility of delivering or mailing a check without entering the information in the checkbook.

2. Complete both the check and the stub with pen, computer, or typewriter.
   PURPOSE: To eliminate the danger of alteration for any reason.

3. Date the check the day it is written (do not postdate).

4. Write the name of the payee after the printed words, "Pay to the Order of" with the necessary information following. Do not use abbreviations unless so instructed.

5. Leave no space before the name, and follow it with three dashes if space remains.

6. Omit personal titles from the names of payees.

7. If a payee is receiving a check as an officer of an organization, the name of the office should follow the name (e.g., John F. Jones, Treasurer).

8. Start writing at the extreme left of each space. Leave no blank spaces. Keep the cents notation close to the dollars figure to prevent alteration.

9. Verify that the amount of the check has been recorded correctly on the stub, in the box for the dollar ($) amount, and on the line where the amount is written in words.

10. If a check is written for an amount less than 1 dollar, the figures by the $ sign may be circled or enclosed in parentheses ($0.65) to emphasize the amount.

11. Obtain signatures on the checks from the physician or other authorized person.

---

statement or invoice, it is a good practice to write on the invoice the number of the check, the amount that was paid, and the date it was paid. If any question arises about whether or when the bill was paid, the check stub can be easily referenced. Handling and writing checks must be done with extreme care (Procedure 23-1). Extra checks and deposit slips should be kept in a safe place so that the routing and account numbers cannot be used by unauthorized individuals.

Designated Times

Rather than haphazardly paying bills as they are received in the office, the medical assistant should establish a routine for paying bills at designated times, such as on the fifteenth and thirtieth days of each month. Most vendors allow a 30-day cycle to elapse before adding interest or late fees.

One method of handling accounts payable is to create a chronologic tickler file with dividers for each pay cycle (e.g., the tenth of the month, the twentieth, and the thirtieth). Behind each of the dividers, the invoices can be arranged alphabetically if desired. When the date arrives, the medical assistant can pull all the bills from that section and prepare the checks.

Paying Bills to Maximize Money

In establishing the procedure for accounts payable, a medical assistant should keep in mind that most vendors allow 30 days to pay. When each invoice is received, check the "terms," which usually are located at the top of the document. A few vendors offer a discount (normally 1% to 2%) if bills are paid within a shorter time. If the terms say "Net 30," this means the total amount of the bill is due within 30 days. Remember to allow a certain number of days for

mailing (2 to 5, depending on where payment is sent). If the business checking account is an interest-bearing one, do not pay bills before their due date. In this way, the funds in the account continue to draw interest until it is time to write the check. Also, if the practice has a weekly service (e.g., a laundry or cleaning service) that bills several times a month, accumulate the invoices and issue only one check per month. Checks are costly, and some banks charge businesses a fee for each transaction.

Automatic Withdrawals and Deductions

Some routine bills that are due monthly or on a regular billing cycle, such as insurance premiums, rent payments, and utility bills, can be set up to be paid automatically through prior arrangements with the bank.

Online Bill Paying

An online bill paying account can be established with a bank or other business entity. The bank pays bills by automatically debiting the customer's account and crediting the merchant's account. More banks are offering this service; however, not all vendors accept electronic transfers in payment of bills. If a business decides to take advantage of online bill paying, the options should be researched carefully for their advantages and disadvantages.

Writing Checks

Instructions

Writing checks is a routine and basically simple function; however, certain guidelines should be followed to prevent potential problems.

Figure 23-6 shows the correct method for writing a check for an amount less than a dollar (top). The check on the bottom shows an incorrect method of check writing. Note the incomplete name and the space available for altering the check (e.g., $ 6.00 could easily be changed to $26.00 or more, and 00 could be made into 88). When writing in the numeric amount of a check, begin as far to the left in the block as possible. When inserting the written amount of the check, again start as far to the left as possible, allowing no space for added or altered words. Writing checks for less than a dollar is not recommended.

Checkbook Stubs

The check stub (the part that remains in the book after the check has been written and removed) is the depositor's own record of checks written: the date, amount, payee, and purpose (Figure 23-7). It is important to complete the stub before writing the check. This prevents the possibility of a check being written without the stub being filled out. If the stub is not completed and the check is sent out, no record exists of the payee and the amount taken from the account until the cancelled check is returned at a later date. Consequently, the account cannot balance, nor can the amount on hand be determined until the cleared check shows up online or on the monthly bank statement.

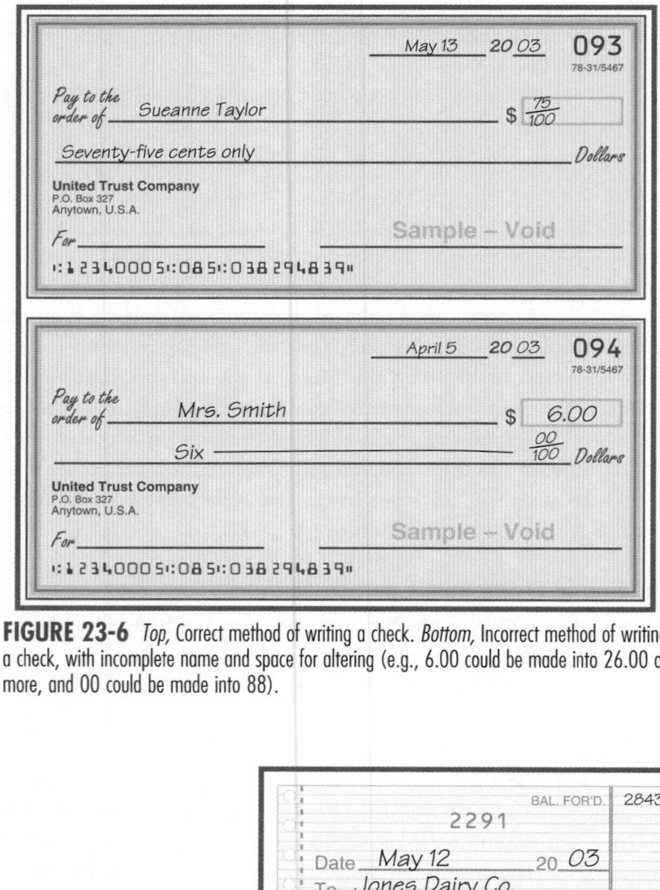

Signing Checks

After all checks have been written, place them on the physician's desk for signature, along with the invoices or other verifying information. In some practices the medical assistant in charge of financial matters is also allowed to sign the checks. To allow this, a **power of attorney** must be filed at the depositor's bank. The power of attorney may limit the check signing authorization to a certain amount or to a limited period. The medical assistant also is required to sign a signature card at the bank before writing any checks on the business account.

Handling Corrections

Do not cross out, erase, or change any part of a check. Checks are printed on sensitized paper so that erasures are easily noticeable, and the bank has the right to refuse to pay on any check that has been altered. (See Figures 23-6 and 23-7 for examples of correct and incorrect check writing.) If a mistake is made, write "VOID" on the stub and the check but do not throw out or destroy the check. It should be filed with the canceled checks so that it is available for auditing purposes.

Writing Cash Checks

A cash check is made payable to Cash or Bearer. Such checks are completely negotiable. Because these checks are easily cashed, it is poor policy to write cash checks until physically at the bank. These checks most often are used to replenish petty cash funds. Some bank personnel may require that the person receiving the cash endorse the check. Many experts in the banking business advise their customers not to endorse a check written for cash or petty cash; often, if a problem arises, the person who endorses the check is liable. A medical assistant should never endorse a check written for cash or petty cash, because he or she is not a party in the transaction.

FIGURE 23-6 *Top,* Correct method of writing a check. *Bottom,* Incorrect method of writing a check, with incomplete name and space for altering (e.g., 6.00 could be made into 26.00 or more, and 00 could be made into 88).

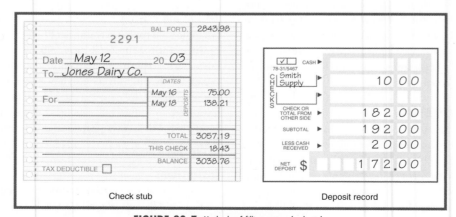

FIGURE 23-7 Methods of filling out a check stub.

Mailing Checks

When checks are sent through the mail, the check should not be visible through the envelope. Either place the check within a letter or fold it into a plain sheet of paper. Checks may be folded at the right end to conceal the amount of money written. Make sure the envelope is sealed before mailing. The medical assistant should personally mail all checks as soon as possible.

Special Problems with Checks

Special problems may arise when a check is written on nonexistent funds or when a payer, for a legitimate reason, wants to prevent the payee from cashing a check.

Overdraws or Overdrafts

When a depositor draws a check for more than the amount on deposit in the account, the account becomes overdrawn. In most states, issuing a check for more than the amount on deposit in the bank is illegal. Should this happen through error or oversight, the bank may refuse to honor the check and will return it to the bank that presented it for payment. Such a check is said to "bounce."

If a check is written by an established depositor, the bank may honor the check and notify the depositor that the account is overdrawn. If the bank thus pays or covers the check, it issues an overdraft on the depositor's account. Considerable fees ($10 to $35) normally are charged for an overdraft. The medical assistant should follow office policy regarding the charges for a returned check; some physicians may not charge the patient at all or will only charge the fee that the physician's bank charged to handle the patient's nonsufficient funds (NSF) check. Other physicians charge the highest fee allowed by law. States determine the maximum fee that can be charged for a returned check. Some accounts allow automatic withdrawals from savings accounts to cover overdrafts without additional charges.

If the check is returned to the physician's office unpaid, call the maker of the check immediately and ask him or her to forward the funds needed to cover the check and the fee. Most offices require that such payment be made in cash or through a money order. Legal remedies are available for the physician if the check remains unpaid.

Stop-Payments

A depositor or check writer who wants to rescind the check has the right to request that the bank stop payment on it. Stop-payment orders should be used only when absolutely necessary; as with overdrafts, most banks charge a fee for them. Reasons for stop-payment requests include:

- Loss of a check
- Disagreement about a purchase
- Disagreement about a payment

CRITICAL THINKING APPLICATION   **23-3**

When Laura arrives at the office on Monday morning, she discovers that a check is missing from the business checkbook and the stub is blank. What actions should Laura take to solve the problem?

▌PRECAUTIONS FOR ACCEPTING CHECKS

A medical assistant is presented with checks to pay for the physician's services every day. In most cases these are personal checks. Check fraud affects every financial institution and business throughout the United States. The best defense against check fraud is to train employees to detect some of the signs of a fraudulent check. The medical assistant can detect several signs of a phony check. If a check is not perforated on at least one side, it might be fraudulent. Also, the routing number and ABA number will be consistent with the physician's checking account numbers if the check is drawn on a local bank. Never accept a third-party check. For example, Mrs. Richards, a patient, receives a check written to her from her neighbor for $25. Mrs. Richards brings the check to her visit with the physician and presents it to the clinic to pay her co-pay. If the check is accepted and subsequently returned by the bank, obtaining reimbursement from the patient or the neighbor will be difficult.

Most patients who write checks to pay bills have no intention of committing fraud. However, checks should be examined while the patient is still in the office. Follow the guidelines in the office policy manual for accepting checks. The National Check Fraud Center suggests the following to minimize the chance of check fraud:

- Ask the bank to advise the office when new books of checks are ready, then either pick them up or use a parcel delivery service to have them delivered.
- Make sure cancelled checks and bank statements are in a secured area, such as a locking file cabinet. Do not throw them in the trash.
- Check bank statements immediately after receiving them. If check fraud is not reported within 30 days of receipt of a monthly statement, the bank does not have to reimburse the loss (**Uniform Commercial Code [UCC]** Code 4-406).
- Print a return address on an envelope or use printed stationery or return address stickers. If the return address is written in the maker's usual signature, it can be traced, duplicated, or forged.
- Do not discard credit card records or bills with trash. Instead, shred them.

For more information on how to prevent check fraud or what to do if fraud occurs, consult the National Check Fraud Center's Web site *(ckfraud.org)*.

▌Acknowledging Payment in Full

If a patient presents a check to the office and the notation of "payment in full" appears on any part of the check, front or back, it may be best to refuse to accept the check unless insurance has paid its portion and the patient owes no more on the bill. This notation is a type of restrictive endorsement, and it can prevent the physician from ever collecting any balance due. If the check is taken, however, the following **disclaimer** should be written on the back of the check above the normal endorsement: "This check is deposited under protest, without prejudice, and with preservation of all rights of the payee against the drawer of this check, according to UCC §1-207."

Research state law to determine whether any further regulations apply to acceptance of a check with a payment in full endorsement. A check is considered to have been accepted if it is deposited and cashed. The office may have little recourse against a patient who still owes money unless the previously mentioned disclaimer is used.

PRECAUTIONS FOR ACCEPTING CREDIT AND DEBIT CARDS

Just as the medical assistant must take precautions when accepting checks, care must also be taken when accepting a credit or debit card as payment for medical services. The first precaution should be to make certain that the person presenting the card is the person to whom it was issued. Always ask for a driver's license and compare the name on the card to the name on the driver's license. Follow office policy when those names do not match. Sometimes, a married couple may use each other's cards, but if the office is strict about the card acceptance policy, then the spouse may need to be present in the office for the medical assistant to accept the card. Some patients may also use blank cards that are purchased with cash to pay on their accounts. If allowed by office policy, these cards are acceptable and will pay just like a normal credit card. If a patient becomes belligerent about card denial, refer him or her to the office manager.

CRITICAL THINKING APPLICATION   23-4

A new patient wants to pay for his services at the end of the office visit. The charge is $75. The patient writes the check for $100 and asks Laura for $25 in currency in return. How should Laura handle the situation?

GUIDELINES FOR ACCEPTING CHECKS

- Scan the check carefully for the correct date, amount, and signature.
- Do not accept a check with corrections on it.
- If you do not know the person presenting a personal check, ask for identification and compare the signatures.
- Accept an out-of-town check, government check, or payroll check only if you are well acquainted with the person presenting it and it does not exceed the amount of the payment.
- Acceptance of a third-party check generally is unwise. A third-party check is one made out to your patient by a party unknown to you. A check from the patient's health insurance carrier is an exception.
- When accepting a postal money order for payment, make sure it has only one endorsement. Postal money orders with more than two endorsements will not be honored.
- Do not accept a check marked "Payment in Full" unless it does pay the account in full up to and including the date on which it is received. If a check so marked is less than the amount due, you will be unable to collect the balance on the account once you have accepted and deposited such a check. It is illegal for you to scratch out the words "Payment in Full."
- Accepting checks written for more than the amount due and returning cash for the difference between the amount of the check and the amount owed is poor policy. If the check is not honored by the bank, your office suffers the loss not only of the amount of the check but also of the amount returned in cash.

Returned Checks

Occasionally the bank may return a deposited check because of some irregularity, such as a missing signature or missing endorsement. More often, it is returned because the payer has insufficient funds on deposit to cover the check. If a check is stamped "NSF," contact the maker immediately. If the person cannot be reached, waste no time in tracking down all leads, such as referrals, numbers obtained from credit cards, driver's license, and so forth. Add the amount of the check plus the NSF fee back to the patient's account balance.

Charging Fees

To cover their overhead costs, most banks currently charge both the payer and payee a fee of $10 to $35 for a check that has been returned because of insufficient funds. The medical assistant customarily notifies the person who wrote the check that it has been returned. Often the individual has a plausible excuse and simply requests that the check be "run through again." If this is the case, it is a wise practice first to call the bank and ask whether sufficient funds are available; this prevents additional delays and fees. Some offices add these charges to the patient's account in an attempt to recoup the expense.

Legal Options

Many NSF problems can be cleared up quickly and easily with courtesy and tact, assuming the situation was simply a mistake or an oversight. Bad checks may be reported to several organizations, and once the writer is in their database, the person will have difficulty writing a check to any business. Credit associations often are a great help when such problems arise. Turn the account over to a qualified collection agency if unable to collect on the account within a short time.

Before taking legal action to collect a returned check, make sure documentation exists proving that attempts were made to collect the check. The best evidence of this is a certified letter sent to the patient with a return receipt requested. The office is notified when the maker of the check has signed for the documents. Keep all this information so that copies can be attached to the claim.

After all reasonable options for collecting NSF checks have been exhausted, a medical assistant may use a collection method that involves the court system. Bad checks also can be reported to the district attorney's office. As mentioned, writing a check without sufficient funds to cover it is illegal and can lead to charges of "theft by check."

The medical assistant also can file against the maker of the check in small claims court. This is a special court in which disputes are resolved inexpensively and quickly; it is a commonly used method that avoids costly attorney fees. Filing fees are about $20 to $35, and there usually is a charge for having the papers served. Some restrictions apply, however. The amount for which the plaintiff (individual or company initiating the suit) can sue in a small claims lawsuit varies from state to state. Contact the local Clerk of the District Court for the necessary forms and instructions for completing a small claims suit. For more information on filing small claims, refer to the government legal department's Web site.

CRITICAL THINKING APPLICATION 23-5

When opening the mail, Laura notices a form from the bank with a check attached. It is a check from Elliott Benson, a new patient seen in the office the previous week, which is being returned for insufficient funds. How should Laura handle this problem?

The medical assistant must be "proactive" rather than "reactive" when it comes to problem patients. He or she should discuss fees with the patient on the first visit and gather all the financial and insurance information necessary to make a judgment as to whether the patient is able and willing to pay. An experienced medical assistant can often sense a "red flag" during this initial information-gathering process. If this happens, requesting payment in advance might be wise. This practice should not be abused, however, and the medical assistant should follow the established office policy or discuss the matter with the office manager or physician when necessary.

ENDORSEMENTS

An endorsement is a signature plus any other writing on the back of a check by which the **endorser** transfers all rights in the check to another party. Endorsements are made in ink, with either pen or rubber stamp, on the back of the check across the left (or perforated) end.

Why an Endorsement Is Necessary

The Uniform Negotiable Instrument Act, which applies in all states, explains the need for an endorsement as follows:

"An instrument is negotiated when it is transferred from one person to another in such a manner as to pass title to another party. If payable to bearer, it is negotiated by delivery. If payable to order, it is negotiated by the endorsement of the holder completed by delivery."

The name of the last endorser of the check shows who last received the money. If a check is cashed for someone who did not endorse it and is returned for some reason, the bank charges the check to the last endorser, not to the last person receiving the money. For this reason, it is not wise to cash a check made payable to another party without having the endorsement of the person who delivered the check to you for cashing.

Types of Endorsements

Four principal kinds of endorsements can be used: blank, restrictive, special, and qualified. Blank and restrictive endorsements are most commonly used.

Blank Endorsement

In a blank endorsement, the payee signs only his or her name. This makes the check payable to the bearer. It is the simplest and most common type of endorsement on personal checks but should be used only when the check is to be cashed or deposited immediately.

Restrictive Endorsement

A restrictive endorsement specifies the purpose of the endorsement (Figure 23-8). It is used in preparing checks for deposit to the physician's checking account.

Pay to the Order of
Midwest National Bank
Main Branch
For Deposit Only
CARLOS MACAULEY
301-012697

FIGURE 23-8 Example of a restrictive endorsement.

Special Endorsement

A special endorsement includes words specifying the person to whom the endorser makes the check payable. For instance, a check naming Helen Barker as the payee may be endorsed to the physician by writing on the back of the check as follows:

Pay to the order of
Theodore F. Wilson, M.D.
Helen Barker

The check is still negotiable but requires Dr. Wilson's signature or endorsement.

Qualified Endorsement

With a qualified endorsement, the effect of the endorsement is qualified by disclaiming or destroying any future liability of the endorser. Usually the words "without recourse" are written above by an attorney who accepts a check on behalf of a client but who has no personal claim in the transaction.

Methods of Endorsement

Stamp

As checks from patients and other sources arrive, they should be recorded in the ledger and immediately stamped with the restrictive endorsement "For Deposit Only." This is a safeguard against lost or stolen checks.

Any endorsement should agree exactly with the name on the face of the check. If the name of the payee is misspelled, the payee usually must endorse the check the way the name is spelled on the face, followed by the correctly spelled signature. Section 3-203 of the UCC states: "Where an instrument is made payable to a person under a misspelled name or one other than his own, he may endorse in that name or his own or both; but signature in both names may be required by a person paying or giving value for the instrument." Most banks accept routine stamp endorsement that is restricted to deposit only if the customer is well known and maintains an established account.

Signature

Some insurance checks or drafts require a personal signature endorsement; a stamped endorsement is not acceptable. This is stated on the back of the check. In such cases ask the payee to endorse the check, then stamp immediately below the signature the restrictive endorsement "For Deposit Only."

Making Deposits

The medical assistant's financial duties include depositing checks and reconciling the bank statements with the checkbook. Checks should be deposited promptly for these reasons:

PROCEDURE 23-2

Prepare a Bank Deposit

GOAL: *To prepare a bank deposit for the day's receipts and complete appropriate office records related to the deposit.*

EQUIPMENT and SUPPLIES

- Currency
- Checks for deposit
- Deposit slip
- Endorsement stamp (optional)
- Computer or typewriter
- Envelope

PROCEDURAL STEPS

1. Organize currency.
   <u>PURPOSE:</u> To arrange currency in the best order for speedy and accurate presentation to the teller.
2. Total the currency and record the amount on the deposit slip.
3. Place restrictive endorsements on the checks using an endorsement stamp.

<u>PURPOSE:</u> To transfer the title and protect checks from loss or theft.
4. List each check separately on the deposit slip with the American Banking Association (ABA) number and the amount.
5. Total the amount of currency and checks and enter on the deposit slip.
6. Enter the amount of the deposit in the checkbook.
   <u>PURPOSE:</u> To record the current balance in the account.
7. Prepare a copy of the deposit slip for the office record, including the names of the payers.
   <u>PURPOSE:</u> For verification of checks deposited, if necessary.
8. Place the currency, checks, and deposit slip in an envelope for transporting to the bank.

- A stop-payment order may be placed.
- The check may be lost, misplaced, or stolen.
- Delay may cause the check to be returned because of insufficient funds.
- The check may have a restricted time for cashing.
- It is a courtesy to the payer.

Preparing the Deposit

Deposit slips are itemized memoranda of cash or other funds a depositor presents to the bank with the money to be credited to the account. All deposits must be accompanied by a deposit slip. A carbon or photocopy of the deposit slip should be kept on file (Procedure 23-2).

Several types of deposit slips (sometimes called *deposit tickets*) are available. The commercial slip is used for the office checking account. The deposit slips are printed with the number of the account in magnetic ink characters to correspond to the checks. Preprinted deposit slips are ordered along with the checks.

Some write-it-once accounting systems include a deposit slip that the bank accepts as the itemization if it is attached to the customer's numbered deposit slip. The deposit slip should be prepared before the medical assistant goes to the bank, and the money should be organized and ready to present to the bank teller.

Payments on patients' accounts generally are made by check, but some are made in currency (paper money). Each type of payment is recorded separately on the deposit slip. The currency usually is listed first. Organize the currency so that all the bills face in the same direction (e.g., with the black ink [portrait] side up). Place the largest denomination bills on top.

Some banks prefer that checks be recorded individually by the ABA number; others use just the maker's name. If the checks are arranged alphabetically by the names of the patient accounts, with

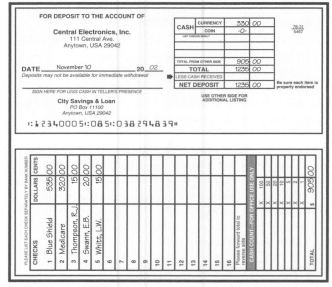

FIGURE 23-9 Front and back of a deposit slip.

these names included on your office copy of the deposit slip, you will have a ready reference of checks deposited should a question arise about a patient's payment. The following procedure should be used to prepare a deposit slip (Figure 23-9):

1. List all checks on the back of the deposit slip.
2. Transfer the total to the front of the slip.
3. Enter the amount of the total deposit on the deposit slip stub.

Money orders, whether postal, express, or others, are identified by "PO Money Order" or "Express MO." Remember that money orders cannot have more than two endorsements.

The deposit slip should be totaled carefully and the total entered in the checkbook. Any torn bills should be mended with transparent tape. Clip the currency together and clip the checks in a separate packet. Then place the entire amount in a heavy envelope for taking to the bank. A bank deposit should be made daily. Deposits can be made at any time during the business day. They can be made during the day or left in a drop box at night. Many banks require that deposits be made before 3 PM if the deposit is to be credited that business day.

Direct Deposits

Direct deposit is a plan in which payments are transferred, usually electronically, by a paying agency directly into the account of a recipient. Direct deposits are commonly used to pay salaries; paychecks are credited to employees' accounts (checking, savings, or any other type of account) at any financial institution.

Other Methods of Deposit

Advances in computer technology have allowed financial institutions to offer other methods of deposit to consumers and business customers. Some automated teller machines (ATMs) accept deposits, and checking accounts are available that allow the customer to conduct most banking services using the computer and ATMs. These types of accounts may limit the number of times the customer can use teller services without a fee.

Online banking allows customers to view their accounts, make transfers, order checks, pay bills, and perform numerous other transactions simply by logging onto the bank Web site and accessing the account with a password. Online banking also is an excellent way to research the checks that have cleared the bank and compute accurate bank balances.

BANK STATEMENTS AND RECONCILIATION

The bank periodically sends the customer a statement, which shows the status of the customer's account on a given date. This statement indicates the following:

- Beginning balance
- Deposits received
- Checks paid
- Bank charges
- Ending balance

Mailed Statements

Bank statements similar to the one in Figure 23-10 are prepared at regular intervals (usually once a month) and usually are mailed to the bank's customers. These statements may or may not include the accompanying cancelled checks, depending on the bank's policy and the type of account. The back of each page of the statement usually includes a reconciliation page so that the customer can determine what checks have still not cleared the bank, what deposits are not yet shown on the statement, and the accurate account balance.

Online Statements

Online statements, or e-statements, are an electronic version of a paper bank statement. Financial establishments that offer online banking services in an attempt to make banking easier for their customers claim that e-statements are a user-friendly way of viewing account balances and checking financial images online.

With e-statements, there is no need to continue receiving paper statements. The benefits include:

- The customer receives statements quickly and easily
- Statements can be saved in an electronic file for examination and printing at the customer's convenience.
- Fees are kept low, because paper and mailing costs are minimized.

Various banks offer different options, and fees vary. If the medical assistant has been authorized to set up an online banking account with the financial institution used by the medical facility, he or she should visit the bank to discuss the details of what is involved.

Reconciling the Bank Statement

The bank statement balance and the customer's checkbook balance usually differ, except in a relatively inactive account. The two balances must be reconciled. The **reconciliation** discloses any errors that may exist in the checkbook or, on rare occasions, in the bank statement (Figure 23-11).

The bank statement may include an entry for service charges that must be deducted from the checkbook balance. In all types of accounts, the bank may charge a fee for services. Usually in the case of an individual account, it is a flat fee; in a business account, the fee is based on services rendered. If the average or minimum balance is maintained at an established level, the bank may forego a service charge.

QUESTIONS TO ASK WHEN SEARCHING FOR A POSSIBLE ERROR
• Is your arithmetic correct?
• Did you forget to include one of the outstanding checks?
• Did you fail to record a deposit or did you record one twice?

Most banks ask to be notified within a reasonable time (e.g., 10 days) of any error found in the statement. The bank statement should be reconciled as soon as it is received. Most banks print a form for reconciliation on the back of the bank statement.

BANK STATEMENT RECONCILIATION FORMULA	
Bank statement balance	$ _____
Less outstanding checks	$ _____
Plus deposits not shown	$ _____
Corrected bank statement balance	$ _____
Checkbook balance	$ _____
Less any bank charges	$ _____
Corrected checkbook balance	$ _____

If the two corrected balances agree, stop there. If they do not agree, subtract the lesser figure from the greater figure; the difference usually provides a clue to the error (Procedure 23-3). For instance, if the shortage is $35, examine all the transactions for $35 on the

0821-402054

#821

||l|u|u|d|l|d|u|u|u|d|u|d|u|uuu|lll|u|d|u|u|u|d|u|u|u|d|l

N
2

CALL (888) 555-2932
24 HOURS/DAY, 7 DAYS/WEEK
FOR ASSISTANCE WITH
YOUR ACCOUNT.

PAGE 1 OF 2　　　THIS STATEMENT COVERS: 6/22/02 THROUGH 7/22/02

INTEREST CHECKING
0821-402054

SUMMARY

PREVIOUS BALANCE	252.10		MINIMUM BALANCE	142.55
DEPOSITS	68.74 +		AVERAGE BALANCE	220.00
INTEREST EARNED	.18 +		ANNUAL PERCENTAGE	
WITHDRAWALS	109.55 −		YIELD EARNED	.96 %
CUSTOMER SERVICE CALLS	.00 −			
INTERLINK/PURCHASE FEE	.00 −		INTEREST EARNED 1994	2.23
MONTHLY CHECKING FEE				
AND OTHER CHARGES	.00 −			

▶ **NEW BALANCE**　　　　211.47

USE YOUR EXPRESS CARD TO MAKE UNLIMITED PURCHASES AT RETAILERS DISPLAYING
THE INTERLINK SYMBOL. (A $1 MONTHLY FEE MAY APPLY.)

TRY IT TODAY AT ARCO . . . MOBIL . . . LUCKY . . . RALPHS . . . SAFEWAY & MORE!

CHECKS AND WITHDRAWALS	CHECK 202	DATE PAID 7/05	AMOUNT 15.05	CHECK 203	DATE PAID 7/15	AMOUNT 94.50

DEPOSITS				DATE POSTED	AMOUNT
	CUSTOMER DEPOSIT			7/22	68.74
	INTEREST PAYMENT THIS PERIOD			7/22	.18

BALANCE INFORMATION	DATE 6/22	BALANCE 252.10	DATE 7/05	BALANCE 237.05	DATE 7/15	BALANCE 142.55
					7/22	211.47

24 HOUR CUSTOMER SERVICE

EACH ACCOUNT COMES WITH 3 COMPLIMENTARY CALLS PER STATEMENT PERIOD.

CALLS TO 24 HOUR CUSTOMER SERVICE THIS STATEMENT PERIOD:　0

INTEREST INFORMATION

FROM	THROUGH	INTEREST RATE	ANNUAL PERCENTAGE YIELD (APY)
6/22	7/22	1.00%	1.01%

INTEREST RATE/APY AS OF 7/22/02 IF YOUR BALANCE IS

$ 0 - 4,999 . . . . .1.00%		1.01%
$ 5,000 - 9,999 . . . . .1.00%		1.01%
$ 10,000 AND OVER 1.00%		1.01%

CALL 1-800-555-2932 IN CALIFORNIA ANYTIME FOR CURRENT RATES.

MEMBER FDIC

STATEMENT

FIGURE 23-10 Example of a regular checking account statement.

statement and checkbook register and determine whether one of them has a posting error. Check the math and make sure all figures were added and subtracted correctly. Look at each figure and make sure none has been transposed. These tips usually catch the mistake.

SIGNATURE CARDS

When an account is first opened at a banking facility, the depositor is required to affix his or her handwritten signature to a card, which is kept on file at the bank. If a check comes through and some suspicion arises that the depositor's signature has been forged, the bank personnel compare the signature on the check with the original on the signature card.

In a business situation, as in a medical office, the physician often delegates the responsibility of paying bills to the medical assistant or other office staff members. In this case, any staff member who has been authorized to sign the medical facility's checks must go to the bank and add his or her handwritten signature to the signature card. Only those whose names appear on the signature card are authorized to sign checks, and the bank is responsible for verifying any questionable signatures.

BONDING

To protect their business establishments from embezzlement or other financial loss caused by employees who handle large sums of money,

THIS WORKSHEET IS PROVIDED TO HELP YOU BALANCE YOUR ACCOUNT

1. Go through your register and mark each check, withdrawal, Express ATM transaction, payment, deposit or other credit listed on this statement. Be sure that your register shows any interest paid into your account, and any service charges, automatic payments, or Express Transfers withdrawn from your account during this statement period.

2. Using the chart below, list any outstanding checks, Express ATM withdrawals, payments or any other withdrawals (including any from previous months) that are listed in your register but are not shown on this statement.

3. Balance your account by filling in the spaces below.

ITEMS OUTSTANDING	
NUMBER	AMOUNT
TOTAL	$

ENTER

The NEW BALANCE shown on this statement _ _ _ _ _ _ _ _ _ _ _ _ _ _ _ $_____

ADD

Any deposits listed in your register $_____
or transfers into your account $_____
which are not shown on this $_____
statement.   +$_____

TOTAL _ _ _ _ _ _ +$_____

CALCULATE THE SUBTOTAL _ _ _ _ _ _ _ $_____

SUBTRACT

The total outstanding checks and withdrawals from the chart at left _ _ _ _ _ _ _ _ −$_____

CALCULATE THE ENDING BALANCE

This amount should be the same as the current balance shown in your check register _ _ _ _ _ _ _ _ _ _ _ _ _ $_____

IF YOU SUSPECT ERRORS OR HAVE QUESTIONS ABOUT ELECTRONIC TRANSFERS

If you believe there is an error on your statement or Express ATM receipt, or if you need more information about a transaction listed on this statement or an Express ATM receipt, please contact us immediately. We are available 24 hours a day, seven days a week to assist you. Please call the telephone number printed on the front of this statement. Or, you may write to us at United Trust Company, P.O. Box 327, Anytown, USA.

1) Tell us your name and account number or Express card number.

2) As clearly as you can, describe the error or the transfer you are unsure about, and explain why you believe there is an error or why you need more information.

3) Tell us the dollar amount of the suspected error.

You must report the suspected error to us no later than 60 days after we sent you the first statement on which the problem appeared. We will investigate your question and will correct any error promptly. If our investigation takes longer than 10 business days (or 20 days in the case of electronic purchases), we will temporarily credit your account for the amount you believe is in error, so that you may have use of the money until the investigation is completed.

FIGURE 23-11 Reverse side of a bank statement, which is used for reconciling a checking account.

physicians often purchase fidelity bonds. Fidelity bonds reimburse the physician for any monetary loss caused by employees. Bonding normally requires a personal background investigation. The three types of bonding are:

- *Position-schedule bonding,* which covers a specific position rather than an individual, such as a bookkeeper or receptionist
- *Blanket-position bonding,* which covers all employees
- *Personal bonding,* which covers specific individuals

CLOSING COMMENTS

Patient Education

Medical assistants might want to encourage patients to pay for professional services with a personal check because of the numerous benefits checks offer. If a patient attempts to pay for services with a third-party check (other than an insurance reimbursement), the medical assistant should tactfully explain why this is not a wise

PROCEDURE 23-3

Reconcile a Bank Statement

GOAL: *To reconcile a bank statement for a checking account.*

EQUIPMENT and SUPPLIES

- Ending balance of previous statement
- Current bank statement
- Canceled checks for current month
- Checkbook stubs
- Calculator
- Pen

PROCEDURAL STEPS

1. Compare the opening balance of the new statement with the closing balance of the previous statement.
   <u>PURPOSE:</u> To determine that the balances are in agreement.
2. Compare the canceled checks with the items on the statement.
   <u>PURPOSE:</u> To verify that they are your checks and that they are listed in the correct amount.
3. Arrange the canceled checks in numeric order and compare with the checkbook stubs.
4. Place a checkmark on each stub for which a canceled check has been returned.
   <u>PURPOSE:</u> To locate any outstanding checks.

5. List and total the outstanding checks.
6. Verify that all previous outstanding checks have cleared.
7. Subtract the total of the outstanding checks from the bank statement balance.
   <u>NOTE:</u> Do not include any certified checks as outstanding, because their amount has already been deducted from the account.
8. Add to the total in step 7 any deposits made but not included in the bank statement.
   <u>PURPOSE:</u> To correct the credits in the bank statement balance.
9. Total any bank charges that appear on the bank statement and subtract them from the checkbook balance. Such charges may include service charges, automatic withdrawals or payments, and nonsufficient funds (NSF) checks.
   <u>PURPOSE:</u> To correct the checkbook balance.
10. If the checkbook balance and the statement balance do not agree, match the bank statement entries with the checkbook entries. Review deposit slips and transactions against the day sheet and read all columns. Correct any errors that are found.

---

practice. In addition, if a patient makes a mistake when writing a check, the medical assistant is responsible for pointing it out and requesting a new check, because corrections on the face of a check often render it useless.

If a patient's check is returned from the bank marked "nonsufficient funds," or "NSF," the medical assistant should immediately call the patient and explain the problem, requesting that he or she correct the matter as soon as possible. It is important to remember, however, that most overdrafts are simply the result of mathematic errors or a delay in deposited funds being available for withdrawal. Therefore, the medical assistant should be patient and courteous when discussing NSF issues with patients. However, patients need to know that overdrafts are costly not only to them but also to the medical facility.

Legal and Ethical Issues

If a mistake is made in preparing a check, do not destroy the check. Rather, write "VOID" across the face of the check, make a note on the check stub, and file the check with the canceled checks for auditing purposes.

A stop-payment order may be placed with the bank in an emergency, such as when a check is lost or a disagreement occurs with regard to a purchase or payment.

Do not accept a check made payable to another party without the endorsement of the person who gives the check to you. If the check is returned by the bank for any reason, the check will be charged to the last endorser, not the last person to receive the money.

SUMMARY OF SCENARIO

Laura has gained considerable knowledge through her experiences and work with the various aspects of the banking world. The goals she set for completing the assignments and competencies were accomplished in the time frame allowed by the instructor. She is comfortable now that she can readily apply this knowledge to whatever medical facility in which she finds work.

Laura spent extra time outside of class exploring online banking and bill paying on the Internet, and she found a wealth of information available. Laura

now plans to visit several banks in her area to see what kind of e-banking services they offer.

The versatility of the medical assistant's role and the variety of the opportunities available reinforce to Laura that she has made the right career choice. The more that she studies and learns, the more she can contribute to the physician's office, using her knowledge to help develop office policies, teach the other staff members how to use the more advanced aspects of the computer system, and make wise decisions about the banking services that will most benefit the clinic.

SUMMARY OF LEARNING OBJECTIVES

1. **Define, spell, and pronounce the terms listed in the vocabulary.**
   Spelling and pronouncing medical terms correctly bolster the medical assistant's credibility. Knowing the definition of these terms promotes confidence in communication with patients and co-workers.

2. **Describe banking procedures.**
   Banking procedures include withdrawals, deposits, writing checks, reconciling bank statements, paying bills, and other transactions.

3. **Explain how the Internet has changed traditional banking practices.**
   The Internet allows many banking transactions to be done at home through a personal computer or cell phone. It also allows access to bank account information 24 hours a day, 7 days a week.

4. **State the four requirements of a negotiable instrument.**
   To be negotiable, an instrument (e.g., a check) must (1) be written and signed by a maker, (2) contain a promise or order to pay a sum of money, (3) be payable on demand or at a fixed future date, and (4) be payable to order or bearer.

5. **Discuss the advantages of using debit cards.**
   Advantages of debit cards include safety and convenience, quick calculation of expenditures, and a permanent record for tax purposes. They are faster to use than writing a check and can be used when a person is out of town or on trips, whereas checks rarely are accepted outside the user's home town area.

6. **Identify the three most common types of bank accounts.**
   The three most common types of bank accounts are checking accounts, savings accounts, and money market savings accounts.

7. **Correctly write checks for bill payment.**
   The medical assistant may be required to write checks on the practice account to pay bills. The process for writing a check is outlined in Procedure 23-1.

8. **Explain how to handle mistakes made in preparing a check.**
   Normally, when a mistake is made on a check, the check should be marked "VOID" and a new check should be written. Some banks accept minor errors if the maker initials the error. Erasures are not allowed, nor is the use of correction fluid.

9. **Discuss precautions for accepting checks.**
   Scan the check carefully for the correct date, amount, and signature. Make sure the check is perforated on at least one side. Do not accept a check with corrections on it. If you do not know the person presenting a personal check, ask for identification and compare signatures.
   a. Acceptance of a third-party check generally is unwise. A third-party check is one made out to your patient by a party unknown to you. A check from the patient's health insurance carrier is an exception.
   b. Do not accept a check marked "Payment in Full" unless it does pay the account in full up to and including the date on which it is received.
   c. Do not accept checks written for more than the amount due and return cash for the difference between the amount of the check and the amount owed

10. **Discuss the actions necessary when a patient's check is returned.**
    When a deposited check is returned, the maker should be contacted immediately, informed of the situation, and asked to remedy the situation either by immediately depositing funds in his or her account to cover the check or by paying the bill by alternative means, such as cash or a money order.

11. **Compare types of endorsements.**
    Endorsements include (1) a blank endorsement, in which the payee simply signs his or her name on the back of the check; (2) a restrictive endorsement, which specifies in which bank and which specific account the funds are to be deposited; (3) a special endorsement, which names a specific person on the back of the check as payee; and (4) a qualified endorsement, which disclaims future liability. This type of endorsement is used when the person who accepts the check has no personal claim in the transaction.

12. **Prepare a bank deposit.**
    Bank deposits should be made on a daily basis. The process for preparing a bank deposit is outlined in Procedure 23-2.

13. **Accurately reconcile a bank statement for the office checking account.**
    Bank statements should be reconciled as soon as they arrive at the physician's office or should be printed from the bank's Web site for reconciliation. The process for reconciling a bank statement is outlined in Procedure 23-3.

CONNECTIONS

📖 **Study Guide Connection:** Go to the Chapter 23 Study Guide. Read and complete the activities.

ℰ **Evolve Connection:** Go to the Chapter 23 link at *evolve.elsevier.com/kinn* to complete the Chapter Review and Chapter Quiz.

24

FINANCIAL AND PRACTICE MANAGEMENT

SCENARIO

Brenda Newman is the office manager for Dr. Susan Wilkins, a neurologist who is beginning her second year of practice. Dr. Wilkins is financially savvy and takes care with the money she has invested in her business. She encourages her employees to plan for the future and offers them a retirement plan, in addition to opportunities for investing in mutual funds through payroll deduction. Her accountant, Grant Schmidt, assists Dr. Wilkins with the financial aspects of her practice and is always willing to counsel the employees of the clinic about finances.

Mr. Schmidt has taught Brenda several methods of keeping track of the practice's finances. Brenda is interested in learning more about general accounting rules and bookkeeping. She is able to perform computerized accounting duties and is also able to use a pegboard system. She works with patients when they need to make payment arrangements and has an excellent collection ratio.

Dr. Wilkins is cost conscious and does not order random supplies and equipment. Instead, she and Brenda plan the inventory for a 6-month period and order supplies every 6 months. By ordering in precise amounts, Dr. Wilkins saves money and uses the extra funds for staff development events and seminars. Each month, the budget is printed and reviewed during a staff meeting to ensure that the office is on track with expenses.

The team effort involving Dr. Wilkins, Brenda, and Mr. Schmidt results in a balanced budget for the clinic, and subsequently the staff is able to enjoy more benefits and perks.

While studying this chapter, think about the following questions:

- Why is a constant flow of income preferable to a once-a-month influx for a physician's office?
- Why should the person entering numbers on a manual system make all numerals exactly alike all the time?
- How have computers affected the management of finances in the physician's office?
- How do a practice's finances affect the income of the medical assistant?

LEARNING OBJECTIVES

1. Define, spell, and pronounce the terms listed in the vocabulary.
2. List the four items all financial records should show at any given time.
3. Describe how to establish and maintain a petty cash fund.
4. Differentiate between accounts payable and accounts receivable.
5. Explain the difference between a single-entry and a double-entry accounting system.
6. Explain the importance of a trial balance.
7. Describe common periodic financial reports.
8. Explain how to process an employee payroll accurately.
9. Explain the purpose of Form W-4.
10. State the types of employment records required by the Internal Revenue Service (IRS).
11. Discuss the basis for the withholding amounts taken from employees' earnings.
12. Explain the requirements of the Federal Insurance Contributions Act (FICA).
13. Discuss the importance of setting a budget each fiscal year.

VOCABULARY

accounts payable Debts incurred and not yet paid.

accounts receivable Amounts owed to the physician.

accounts receivable trial balance A method of determining that the journal and the ledger are in balance.

accrual basis of accounting Method of accounting in which income is recorded when earned and expenses are recorded when incurred.

admonition Counsel or warning against fault or oversight.

assets The entire property of a person, association, corporation, or estate applicable or subject to the payment of debts.

balance sheet A financial statement for a specific date that shows the total assets, liabilities, and capital of the business.

bookkeeping The recording of business and accounting transactions.

cash basis of accounting A method of accounting in which income is recorded when received and expenses are recorded when paid.

cash flow statement A financial summary for a specific period that shows the beginning balance on hand, the receipts and disbursements during the period, and the balance on hand at the end of the period.

controls A standard of comparison to make sure answers obtained are accurate.

disbursements journal A summary of accounts paid out.

entry A record or notation of an occurrence, transaction, or proceeding.

equities The monetary value of a property or of an interest in a property in excess of claims or liens against it.

in balance The state in which the total ending balances of patient ledgers equals the total of accounts receivable.

invoice A paper describing a purchase and the amount due.

liabilities Things that are owed; debts.

packing slip An itemized list of articles included in a shipping package, giving the quantity and description of the package contents.

petty cash fund A fund maintained to pay small, unpredictable cash expenditures.

statement A request for payment.

statement of income and expense A summary of all income and expenses for a given period.

subsidiary Supporting other documents or records.

trial balance A method of checking the accuracy of accounts.

A physician's business records are the key to good management practice. Physicians need and appreciate medical assistants who can keep accurate financial records and can conduct the administrative side of the practice in a businesslike fashion. Financial records that are complete, correct, and current are essential for:

- Prompt billing and collection procedures
- Accurate budgeting
- Professional financial planning
- Accurate reporting of income to federal and state agencies

More than half of today's physicians run independent practices. According to CNNmoney, shrinking insurance reimbursements, changing regulations, rising business and drug costs are among the factors preventing many from keeping their practices afloat. But some experts counter that doctors' lack of business acumen is also to blame. Unless the physician and staff stay abreast of regulations affecting finances, the physician may find his or her practice failing.

WHAT IS ACCOUNTING?

Accounting is a system of recording, classifying, and summarizing financial transactions. **Bookkeeping** is the recording part of the accounting process. Bookkeeping must be done daily. In a small practice, it is the responsibility of the administrative medical assistant; in a larger practice, it is done by the office manager or financial manager. Summaries are prepared and personal and business tax returns are filed with the Internal Revenue Service (IRS).

Accounting Bases

Two general bases, or methods, of accounting are used: the cash basis and the accrual basis. Most physicians use the **cash basis of accounting**, which means that charges for services are entered as income when payment is received, and expenses are recorded when they are paid. Merchants, on the other hand, generally use an **accrual basis of accounting**. Income is considered earned when services have been performed or goods have been sold, even though payment may not have been received. Expenses are recognized and recorded when incurred, even though they have not been paid.

Financial Summaries

The financial records of any business should show the following at all times:

- How much was earned in a given period
- How much was collected
- How much is owed
- The distribution of expenses incurred

The accountant can prepare monthly and annual summaries from the daily entries that provide a basis of comparison for any given period with another, similar period. Periodic analyses of financial records result in improved business practices, better time management, curtailment or elimination of unprofitable services, and better budgeting of expenses. With the appropriate software, these analyses can be done on the computer. The medical assistant may see notations such as AR/AP, which stand for **accounts receivable** (Procedure 24-1) and **accounts payable** (Procedure 24-2).

PROCEDURE 24-1

Perform Accounts Receivable Procedures

GOAL: *To collect amounts due to the physician or medical facility.*

EQUIPMENT and SUPPLIES

- Patient ledgers
- Office policy manual
- Telephone
- Letterhead and envelopes
- Clerical supplies

PROCEDURAL STEPS

1. Determine the billing cycle for the medical facility according to the office policy manual.
   PURPOSE: To determine which groups of accounts are billed at different times of the month, as specified by the billing cycle.
2. Prompt the computer to compile a report on the age of accounts receivable. Many programs have this as an easily accessed report option.
   PURPOSE: To determine which accounts have a balance due.
3. Divide the accounts into the following categories:
   0-30 days old
   30-60 days old

60-90 days old
90-120 days old
More than 120 days old

4. Determine the amounts due the physician and who owes these amounts.
   PURPOSE: To specify which accounts need to be billed.
5. Group accounts together when necessary.
   PURPOSE: Some physicians prefer to separate regular billings from past-due billings.
6. Print bills using the computer system or make copies of ledger cards.
7. Mail bills to patients.
8. Post payments to patients' accounts as they arrive at the office.
   PURPOSE: To credit payments to patients' accounts.
9. Demonstrate sensitivity and professionalism in handling accounts receivable activities.

CRITICAL THINKING APPLICATION   24-1

- Brenda has noticed several errors on encounter forms lately. These errors seem to be the result of a staff member not using a calculator to add up the charges when the patient is ready to check out. Brenda has approached the person who assists the patients in this area but has not seen any improvement. How might she convince the employee to follow precautions in adding charges? What are Brenda's options regarding the employee's job?
- How might Mr. Schmidt educate the staff about the importance of accurate financial records?

The Rules of Bookkeeping

Bookkeeping has many rules that the medical assistant must follow. First, use good penmanship so that the records are clearly legible, even years later. Use the same pen style and type of ink consistently. Keep columns of figures straight and write well-formed figures (a careless 9 may look like a 7; an open 0 may resemble a 6). Carry decimal points correctly. Ask the physician if any questions arise about bookkeeping issues (Figure 24-1).

Enter all charges and receipts immediately in the daily record or journal. Write a receipt in duplicate for any currency received. Writing receipts for checks is optional, but a consistent pattern should be followed. Post all charges and receipts to the patient ledger daily. Checks should be endorsed for deposit as soon as they are received. The **petty cash fund** should be used to pay for small, unpredictable expenses. Pay all other expenses by check. A cancelled check is the best proof of payment. Bills should be paid before their

FIGURE 24-1 When the medical assistant is unsure about financial information, he or she should ask the physician. When an unfamiliar statement arrives, check with the physician to make sure it should be paid.

due date after they have been checked for accuracy. Place the date of payment and the check number on paid bills.

Do not erase, write over, or blot out figures. If an error is made, a straight line should be drawn through the incorrect figure and the correct figure written above it. Bookkeeping procedures are not

PROCEDURE 24-2

Perform Accounts Payable Procedures

GOAL: *To determine the age of accounts and decide what collection activity is needed.*

EQUIPMENT and SUPPLIES

- Patient ledger cards with a balance due
- Pen
- Computer
- Calculator

PROCEDURAL STEPS

1. Prompt the computer to compile a report on the age of accounts receivable. Many programs will have this feature as an easily accessed report option. Divide the accounts into categories as listed below:
   0-30 days old
   30-60 days old
   60-90 days old
   90-120 days old
   PURPOSE: To determine how old the various accounts are and place the accounts into categories as to when the last payment was made.

2. If the computer program does not perform this function, manually pull all ledger cards that have a balance due and divide them into the categories listed under step 1.

3. Examine the accounts to see which are awaiting an insurance payment. Action need not be taken if an insurance payment is expected and is not long overdue. Return those ledgers to the ledger tray.
   PURPOSE: To avoid collection activity on accounts for which a payment is expected.

4. Follow the office procedure for collections on the accounts left. Collection reminder stickers may be placed on the statements sent to the patient, or a collection letter may be sent. Make sure the stickers are inside the envelope, not on the outside.
   PURPOSE: To prompt the patient to make a payment by pointing out the age of the account.

5. Call patients whose accounts are more than 90 days old. Attempt to make payment arrangements with the patient.
   PURPOSE: To attempt to collect from the patient or determine why the patient has not yet paid the account.

6. Send a collection letter to patients whose accounts are more than 120 days old, if indicated, to encourage the patient to pay the bill. If it is the office policy, mention that the account is in danger of being sent to a collection agency.
   PURPOSE: To reach patients who are not available by telephone.

7. Add the total accounts receivable for each category and arrive at a figure outstanding for each. The physician may want a report weekly or monthly on these figures.
   PURPOSE: To have a current accounting of the amounts owed to the physician and to double-check the amount outstanding according to the pegboard system or software system.

8. Note in the chart and/or on the ledger any arrangements made with patients regarding payment of the accounts. Send a follow-up letter to remind the patients of their payment agreements.
   PURPOSE: To document arrangements made and remind the patients of their obligation and promise to pay.

---

complicated, but they do require concentration to prevent errors. There is no such thing as almost correct financial records. Either the books balance, or they do not balance. The bookkeeping is either right or wrong.

Kinds of Financial Records

Daily Journal

The daily journal is the chronologic record of the practice (i.e., the financial diary). The day sheet is the daily journal for practices that use a manual pegboard system. Although more practices use computerized systems, some still use a manual pegboard; however, using a manual system helps the medical assistant to understand the theory of accounting in the medical office. All information about services rendered, charges, and receipts first is recorded in the daily journal. It is important to record every transaction.

The practice may earn income from sources other than the professional services rendered in and out of the office. Such sources include rentals, royalties, interest, and so forth. If the physician owns the entire building and rents a few offices to other professionals, he will have to claim rental income on his tax returns. Additionally, if he has published any textbooks or has other royalty income, that will also need to be listed on his annual returns. Usually a special place is provided in the journal for such income. Any income that is not practice related should be recorded separately from patient receipts.

Checkbook

Receipts usually are deposited in the checking account, and a record of the deposit is entered in the journal and on the check register. A copy of each deposit slip should be kept with the financial records. Bills usually are paid by check or through online bill paying services, and a record of the payment is entered on the check stub and in the disbursements section of the daily journal.

CRITICAL THINKING APPLICATION   24-2

- Brenda has noticed two checks missing from the business checkbook. Dr. Wilkins is out of town for a week and cannot be contacted. How might Brenda determine where the checks are or to whom they were written?
- What steps can be taken to resolve the problem of not knowing the amount of a missing check?

Disbursements Journal

In simplified accounting systems in which manual posting is used, the **disbursements journal** usually consists of a section at the bottom of each day sheet and a check register page at the end of each month, plus monthly and annual summaries. It must show the following:

- Every amount paid out
- Date and check number
- Purpose of the payment

When a computer system is used to post disbursements, the cash or check payments screen is used. Payment information is entered, and the computer prints the check, or the information is entered after the check has been manually prepared.

Petty Cash Records

A petty cash fund and voucher system should be established to take care of minor unpredictable expenditures, such as postage due, parking fees, small contributions, emergency supplies, and miscellaneous small items. In the average facility, $25 to $50 is sufficient for the petty cash fund. If a larger sum is available, the tendency is to pay too many bills out of petty cash instead of writing a check.

When the check for this fund is exchanged at the bank for small bills and coins, the money is placed in a cashbox or drawer that can be locked or kept in the safe at night. Only one person should be in charge of the petty cash fund. This person must be able to account for the full amount of the fund at any time.

CRITICAL THINKING APPLICATION   24-3

- Brenda has noticed that on several occasions, employees have borrowed money from the petty cash fund. Is this an acceptable practice? Why or why not?
- How might Brenda keep an accounting of money taken from the petty cash drawer if she is not the person actually in control of it?

ACCOUNTING SYSTEMS

The basic principles of accounting are the same, no matter which system is in place. Remember that accounting and bookkeeping are separate functions; accounting is a four-stage process of recording, classifying, summarizing, and interpreting financial statements. Bookkeeping is the recording stage of accounting. The medical assistant performs bookkeeping functions when posting a payment to a patient's account. Most accounting for physician offices or medical clinics is performed by using either a single-entry or double-entry system.

The single-entry system is very basic and usually is used in small businesses, such as a one-physician office or a partnership that sees a relatively small number of patients. Single-entry systems are inexpensive, easy to use, and require little training. The system requires three basic records: the general journal, the cash payment journal, and the accounts receivable ledger. The general journal is a record (e.g., a day sheet) where transactions are entered. The cash payment journal in its simplest form is a record (e.g., a checkbook) that is used to make payments. The accounts receivable ledger provides information about the amounts owed the physician.

Double-entry bookkeeping is also inexpensive but requires a trained, experienced bookkeeper or the regular services of an accountant. The transactions may be recorded manually or by computer. In addition to the basic journals used in a single-entry system, numerous **subsidiary** journals may be used. The system is based on the following accounting equation:

$$Assets = Liabilities + Proprietorship (Capital)$$

Every transaction requires an **entry** on each side of the accounting equation, and the two sides must always be in balance. For this reason the system is called *double-entry bookkeeping*, and it is the most complete accounting system. An understanding of the basics of double-entry bookkeeping can help clarify the principles of all systems.

Assets are the properties owned by a business, such as bank accounts, accounts receivable, buildings, equipment, and furniture. The rights to these assets are called **equities**. The equity of the owner is called *capital, proprietorship,* or *owner's equity.* The equities of the creditors to whom money is owed are called **liabilities**. The owner's equity, or capital, is what remains of the value of the assets after the creditor's equities or liabilities have been subtracted.

For example, if the physician purchased equipment for $1,000, paid $250 down, and signed a promissory note for $750, the accounting equation would be as follows:

Assets	$1,000	=	Liabilities	$750
			+	
			Capital	250
	$1,000			$1,000

The total value of the asset is $1,000. The owner's equity is $250, and the creditor's equity is $750. The accounting terms *capital, proprietorship, owner's equity,* and *net worth* are used interchangeably.

Few medical assistants are trained in accounting. If a double-entry system is used, a practice management consultant or the accountant who does most of the actual bookwork and reports usually sets it up. The medical assistant in this instance generally maintains only the daily journal, from which the accountant takes the figures once a month. The double-entry system provides a more comprehensive picture of the practice and its effect on the physician's net worth. Errors show up readily, and the system has many built-in accuracy **controls**; however, because of the time and skill required, it is not frequently used in a small practice.

END OF DAY SUMMARIZING

Most computer accounting systems perform end of the day summarizing automatically. If the office uses the pegboard system, the bottom of the day sheet has three sections to be completed that will show that the accounts have balanced for the day; similar functions are calculated in computerized systems. The medical assistant may be responsible for making sure the transactions made during the day are entered correctly and that the summary is in balance. Computerized systems may use different titles for the transactions, but they perform the same functions.

The first part of the end of day summary is the proof of posting section, which deals with the transactions that occurred that day on the day sheet. The second section is the month-to-date accounts receivable proof; adding the day's totals to the month-to-date totals should result in a sum that balances to the penny. The last section is the year-to-date accounts receivable proof, which adds the accounts, including the day's totals, to the year-to-date total.

The totals at the bottom of the second and third sections must be identical. If the end of the day summarizing does not balance, the medical assistant first should check the addition of each column, both horizontally and vertically; in most cases this reveals the error. Make sure the instructions are followed to the letter. To prevent frustrating mistakes, it is best to use a calculator, even when adding small numbers.

These calculations are helpful because they allow the physician to see the financial health of his or her practice. The physician can look at the end of day summaries and see exactly how much money has been paid in, in addition to how much money is outstanding and due from patients, to the day. The information helps the physician to know whether the practice finances are on track for the month and/or the year.

TRIAL BALANCE OF ACCOUNTS RECEIVABLE

A **trial balance** should be done once a month after all posting has been completed and before the monthly statements are prepared. The purpose of a trial balance is to disclose any discrepancies between the journal and the ledger. It does not prove the accuracy of the accounts. For example, if a charge or payment was posted to the wrong account or if the wrong amount was entered in the journal and then posted to the ledger, the totals would still "balance," but the accounts would not be accurate.

To begin, pull all the account cards with a balance, enter each balance on the calculator, and total the figures. This should equal the accounts receivable balance figure on the control. If there is no daily control, total all the charges, all the payments, and all the adjustments for the month, then do the following computation:

Accounts receivable at first of month	$ _____
Plus total charges for month	$ _____
Subtotal	$ _____
Less total payments for month	$ _____
Subtotal	$ _____
Less total adjustments for month	$ _____
Accounts receivable at end of month	$ _____

The end of the month accounts receivable figure must agree with the figure arrived at by adding all the account card balances. The accounts are then said to be **in balance**. If the two totals do not agree, the error must be located.

Locating and Preventing Errors

After checking the adding machine tape and verifying that no error in calculation has been made, the first step in locating an error in the trial balance is to find the difference between the two totals. Then search the daily journal pages and the account cards for an entry for the identical amount. Check each one found and verify that it was posted correctly. Of course, more than one error may add up to this amount.

If only one error was made and the amount of the error is divisible by 9, a figure may have been transposed. For example, if the difference is $81 (a number divisible by 9), the person who posted to the account may have written $209 instead of $290. If the amount of the error is divisible by 2, the amount may have been posted to the wrong column, reversing a debit and a credit.

A common error is entering the wrong amount in the previous balance column or in figuring the new balance. This kind of error shows up on the pegboard daily proof but could easily go undetected in the single-entry system. Carrying forward the wrong amount results in another common error total from one day to the next (e.g., carrying forward the beginning accounts receivable total rather than the ending accounts receivable total). There is always a chance of sliding a number, which means writing the first digit in the wrong column, such as writing 400 for 40 or 60 instead of 600.

Many bookkeepers prevent errors in the cents column by using a line (—) instead of writing two zeros when only even dollars are involved. For example, instead of writing $12.00, the bookkeeper writes $12.—. This eliminates the possibility of misreading zeros as other numbers. It also speeds the adding process when columns must be totaled. Make sure the same type of pen is used for all entries and that figures are written the same way. Scan for errors in every column. Try to spot figures in which the numbers have been transposed or that are unclear, thus increasing the chance that the numbers will be read incorrectly when adding.

If the medical assistant is unable to locate any numeric error, an account card may have been lost, overlooked, or transferred as paid in full. As a last resort, pull each account card and review it for errors. Compare the card to the day sheet and check to make sure that everything has been entered accurately. Computer programs often have checks and balance reports that can help the user find errors, but remember that the computer works with the data that were entered. If a $152 charge was entered instead of $125, the computer may not catch such a mistake.

CRITICAL THINKING APPLICATION 24-4

What should Brenda do if she has repeatedly reviewed records in search of an error and is still unable to find it? To whom should this be reported?

ACCOUNTS PAYABLE PROCEDURES

Invoices and Statements

If an item is not paid for at the time of purchase, the vendor usually includes a **packing slip** with delivery of the merchandise. A packing slip describes the items enclosed. The vendor may also enclose an **invoice**. An invoice describes the items and shows the amount due. Always check to verify that the items listed on the packing slip and invoice are included in the delivery.

Invoices should be placed in a designated folder until paid. The facility may be making more than one purchase from the same vendor during the month. Some vendors request that payment be made from the invoice; others expect to send a statement later. A **statement** is a request for payment.

Paying for Purchases

At the time of payment, compare the statement with the invoice to verify its accuracy, fasten the statement and invoice together, write the date, the amount paid, and the check number on the statement, and place it in the paid file.

CRITICAL THINKING APPLICATION   24-5

- Brenda does not recall ordering a certain item from the office supply company. However, it was included in her last shipment and listed on the packing list. How can she determine whether the item was ordered?
- How would Brenda correct this problem if the item had not been ordered?

Recording Disbursements

Disbursements are funds paid out. Disbursements are distributed to specific expense accounts, such as:

- Auto expenses
- Dues and meetings
- Equipment
- Insurance
- Medical supplies
- Office expenses
- Printing, postage, and stationery
- Rent and maintenance
- Salaries
- Taxes and licenses
- Travel and entertainment
- Utilities
- Miscellaneous
- Personal withdrawals

Each check used to pay an expense should be entered on the disbursement page showing the date, the name of the company to which the check was written, the number and amount of the check, and the payment allocated to one or more of the expense accounts. Always separate personal expenditures from business expenses. Business expenses are tax deductible and are considered in determining net income from the practice, but personal expenditures are not. Although personal expenses are not deductible in determining net income from the practice, some qualify as personal deductions in computing personal income tax, so a careful accounting should be kept. Deductible expenses would include property taxes, interest paid out, contributions, and so on.

Accounting for Petty Cash

The petty cash fund is a revolving fund (Procedure 24-3). Petty cash can be used for a variety of items, such as expendable supplies, business meals, local transportation, photocopy service, and other items.

To establish the petty cash fund, a check is written payable to Cash or Petty Cash and entered in the disbursements journal under Miscellaneous. This is the only time the petty cash check is charged to Miscellaneous. Each time the fund is replenished, the amount of the check is spread among the various accounts for which the money was used. This is determined from a record of expenditures. The headings of the columns should correspond to headings in the disbursements journal to which they will be posted.

A pad of petty cash vouchers is kept in or near the cash box. For every disbursement from the fund, the person who handles the fund

---

PROCEDURE 24-3

Account for Petty Cash

GOAL: *To establish a petty cash fund, maintain an accurate record of expenditures for 1 month, and replenish the fund as necessary.*

EQUIPMENT and SUPPLIES

- Form for petty cash fund
- Pad of vouchers
- Disbursement journal
- Two checks
- List of petty cash expenditures

PROCEDURAL STEPS

1. Determine the amount needed in the petty cash fund.
2. Write a check in the determined amount.
   <u>PURPOSE:</u> To establish a fund.
3. Record the beginning balance in the petty cash fund.
4. Post the amount to Miscellaneous on the disbursement record.
   <u>PURPOSE:</u> To account for the original amount in the fund.

5. Prepare a petty cash voucher for each amount withdrawn from the fund.
   <u>PURPOSE:</u> The vouchers will be used for internal audit.
6. Record each voucher in the petty cash record and enter the new balance.
   <u>PURPOSE:</u> To record the current balance and determine the need to replenish the fund.
7. Write a check to replenish the fund as necessary.
   <u>NOTE:</u> The total of the vouchers plus the fund balance must equal the beginning amount.
8. Total the expense columns and post to the appropriate accounts in the disbursement record.
   <u>PURPOSE:</u> To record expenditures in the correct expense category.
9. Record the amount added to the fund.
10. Record the new balance in the petty cash fund.

should either have a receipt or prepare a voucher. The total of the petty cash vouchers and receipts plus the amount of cash in the box must always equal the original amount of the fund.

At the end of the month or sooner if the fund is depleted, a check is written to Cash to replenish the fund. However, instead of being charged to Miscellaneous, as was done when the fund was established, the amount of the check is divided among the various accounts affected.

Avoid the habit of borrowing from the petty cash fund. This **admonition** applies both to the physician and to the medical assistant. If the physician requests cash from the fund, request a personal check or an office check in exchange for cash from the fund when it is time to replenish the money. Although many offices use petty cash to make change, it is best to have a separate change fund to prevent errors. If the incorrect change is made and the petty cash drawer is shorted, the person responsible for petty cash will not be able to balance the fund.

COMMON PERIODIC FINANCIAL REPORTS

Financial summaries are compiled monthly and annually. They may be prepared either by the medical assistant manually or on the computer or by the accountant. Common summary reports include the following:

- Statement of income and expense
- Cash flow statement
- Trial balance
- Accounts receivable trial balance and aging analysis
- Balance sheet

The **statement of income and expense**, also known as the *profit and loss statement,* covers a specific period. It lists all the income received and all expenses paid during the period. The total income is called *gross income* or *earnings.* The income after deduction of all expenses is the *net income.*

A **cash flow statement** starts with the amount of cash on hand at the beginning of the month (or for any specified period). It then lists the cash income and the cash disbursement made throughout the period and concludes with a statement of the amount of cash remaining on hand at the end of the period.

A trial balance is necessary to determine that the books are in balance. All the columns in the disbursements journal must be totaled at the end of the month. The combined totals of all the expense columns must equal the total of the checks written. If the figures do not balance, recheck every entry until the error is found.

The **accounts receivable trial balance** is done before the monthly statements are sent out. First, record the total of the accounts receivable ledger at the end of the previous month; then add the charges for the current month and subtract the adjustments and the payments received. The remainder should equal the total of the accounts receivable ledger at the end of the current month.

The **balance sheet**, also known as a *statement of financial condition,* shows the financial picture of the practice on a specific date. Often it is done only once a year. The balance sheet is set up using the following accounting equation:

$$\text{Assets} = \text{Liabilities} + \text{Proprietorship}$$

The title of the statement had its origin in the equality of the elements: the balance between the sum of the assets and the sum of the liabilities and proprietorship. An aging analysis shows the amount of outstanding receipts in aging groups, such as current, 30 days, 60 days, 90 days, and 120 days.

At the end of the accounting year, it is very simple to combine the monthly reports to compile the annual summaries. The annual summaries simplify the reporting of income for tax returns.

RECENT LEGISLATION FOR SMALL BUSINESSES AND THEIR EXPENSES

Several new laws have been passed that relate to the small business and its financial accounting. First, as of January 1, 2013, the amount allowed for mileage is 56.5¢ for business miles driven. This rate fluctuates, depending on the cost of fuel, and has been changed midyear on some occasions. Employees are allowed 24¢ for driving when the purpose is medically related. Charitable organizations can claim 14 cents per mile when driving for business reasons.

PAYROLL RECORDS

Handling payroll records, whether for one employee or dozens of employees, involves frequent reporting activities (Procedure 24-4). Government regulations require the withholding of taxes from employees and payment of certain taxes by both employees and employers. To comply with government regulations, complete records must be kept for every employee. All records of employment taxes must be kept for at least 4 years. These should be available for review by the IRS. These records include:

- Social Security number of the employee
- Number of withholding allowances claimed
- Amount of gross salary
- All deductions for Social Security and Medicare taxes; federal, state, and city or other subdivision withholding taxes; state disability insurance; and state unemployment tax, where applicable

CRITICAL THINKING APPLICATION 24-6

On Friday Brenda hired a new employee, who reported to work on Monday. The new employee states that she cannot produce her Social Security card. Can Brenda allow the individual to work? How can Brenda verify a Social Security number?

Payroll Reporting Forms

Each employee and each employer must have a tax identification number. The Social Security number is the employee's tax identification number. Any person who does not have a Social Security number should apply for one, using Form SS-5, available online or from any Social Security Administration office.

The employer applies for a number for federal tax accounting purposes using Form SS-4, available at Social Security Administration offices. In states that require employer reports, a state employer number must also be obtained. This number is called the *employer identification number (*EIN) (formerly called the tax identification number).

PROCEDURE 24-4

Process an Employee Payroll

GOAL: To process payroll to compensate employees and make accurate deductions.

EQUIPMENT and SUPPLIES

- Checkbook
- Computer and payroll software, if applicable
- Pen
- Tax withholding tables
- Federal Employers Tax Guide

PROCEDURAL STEPS

1. Make sure all information and paperwork have been collected from the employees, including a copy of the Social Security card, a W-4 form, and an I-9 form.
   PURPOSE: To make sure the employee is eligible to work in the United States and to determine the withholding amounts to deduct from paychecks.
2. Review the time cards for all employees. Determine whether any employees need counseling because of late arrivals or habitual absences.
   PURPOSE: To address problems immediately and help correct habits that can lead to employee termination.

3. Figure the salary or hourly wages due the employee for the period worked.
   PURPOSE: To ascertain the amount owed to the employee.
4. Figure the deductions that must be taken from the paycheck. These usually include but are not limited to:
   - Federal, state, and local taxes
   - Social Security withholdings
   - Medicare withholdings
   - Other deductions (e.g., insurance, savings, and so on)
   - Donations to organizations, such as the United Way
   PURPOSE: To comply with federal, state, and local laws and deduct amounts for insurance, savings plans, and so on.
5. Write the check for the balance due the employee. Most software can print the checks and explanations of deductions.
6. Have employees sign for their paychecks if that is the office policy.
   NOTE: Make certain that the person is not an independent contractor, in which case a 1099 Form (IRS) should be issued.

Before the end of the first pay period, the employee should complete an Employee's Withholding Allowance Certificate (Form W-4) showing the number of withholding allowances claimed. Otherwise, the employer must indicate withholding on the basis of a single person with no exemptions.

The employee should complete a new form when changes occur in marital status or in the number of allowances claimed. Each employee is entitled to one personal allowance and one for each qualified dependent. Because employees can claim allowances based on their job situation, being the head of the household, and having dependent care expenses totaling more than $1,500, they may find that their allowances equal more than just a personal exemption and an exemption for their dependents. However, employees should be warned to take care in listing too many allowances, because this affects the amount of tax taken from their paycheck. If too little tax is taken out during the year, the employee may owe a significant amount of money to the IRS the following year.

The employee may elect to take fewer or no allowances, in which case the tax withheld will be greater and a refund may be due when the employee's annual tax report is filed. If an employee claims more than 10 withholding allowances or an exemption from withholding and his or her wages would normally be more than $200 per week, the employer is required to send copies of these W-4 forms to the IRS.

A supply of all the necessary forms for filing federal returns, preprinted with the employer's name, will be furnished to an employer who has applied for an employer identification number. Extra forms may be obtained from the IRS office.

CRITICAL THINKING APPLICATION 24-7

- Mr. Schmidt has explained to Brenda that the more withholding deductions an employee claims, the less tax is taken from the paycheck. If Brenda's new employee wants to claim seven deductions and she has only three children and is single, can she do so legally? Why or why not?
- Why might it be risky to claim all the deductions to which a person is legally entitled?

Income Tax Withholding

Employers are required by law to withhold certain amounts from employees' earnings. These amounts must be reported and forwarded to the IRS to be applied toward payment of income tax. The amount to be withheld is based on:

- Total earnings of the employee
- Number of withholding allowances claimed
- Marital status of the employee
- Length of the pay period involved

The Federal Employer's Tax Guide includes tables to be used in determining the amount to be withheld. One table is for single people and unmarried heads of households and one is for married individuals. The tables cover monthly, semimonthly, biweekly, weekly, and daily or miscellaneous periods.

Employers Income Tax

A physician practicing as an individual is not subject to withholding tax but is expected to make an estimated tax payment four times a year. The accountant prepares four copies of Form 1040-S, Declaration of Estimated Tax for Individuals, for the ensuing year when the annual income tax return is prepared. The first form and the quarterly estimated tax for the next year are filed at the same time as the tax return. The remaining three forms, with the estimated tax due, must be filed on June 15, September 15, and January 15. It may be the business manager's responsibility to see that these returns are filed when due. The employer also contributes to Social Security and Medicare in the form of a self-employment tax.

Social Security, Medicare, and Income Tax Withholding

The Federal Insurance Contributions Act (FICA) provides for a federal system of old age, survivors, disability, and hospital insurance. The tax rate is reviewed frequently and is subject to change by Congress. As of 2009, the wage base for Social Security tax was $113,700 and the tax rate was 6.2% each for employers and employees. All wages are subject to the Medicare tax at a rate of 1.45% each for both employees and employers.

Quarterly Returns

Each quarter of the year, all employers subject to income tax withholding (including withholding on sick pay and supplemental unemployment benefits) of Social Security and Medicare taxes must file an Employer's Quarterly Federal Tax Return (Form 941) on or before the last day of the first month after the end of the quarter. Due dates for this return and full payment of the tax are April 30, July 31, October 31, and January 31. If deposits equaling full payment of taxes due have been made, the due date for the return is extended 10 days.

Annual Returns

The employer is required to furnish two copies of Form W-2, the Wage and Tax Statement, to each employee from whom income tax or Social Security tax has been withheld or from whom income tax would have been withheld if the employee had claimed no more than one withholding allowance. The forms should be given to employees by January 31. If employment ends before December 31, the employer may give the W-2 form to the terminated employee any time after employment ends. If the employee asks for Form W-2, the employer should give the employee the completed copies within 30 days of the request or the final wage payment, whichever is later.

Employers must file Form W-3, the Transmittal of Income and Tax Statement, annually to transmit wage and income tax withheld statements (Form W-2) to the Social Security Administration. These forms are processed by the Social Security Administration, which furnishes the IRS with the income tax data that it needs from those forms. Form W-3 and its attachments must be filed separately from Form 941 on or before the last day of February after the calendar year for which the W-2 forms are prepared.

Federal Unemployment Tax

Employers also contribute under the Federal Unemployment Tax Act (FUTA). Generally, credit can be taken against the FUTA tax for amounts paid into a state unemployment fund up to a certain percentage. Employers are responsible for paying the FUTA tax; it must not be deducted from employees' wages. For 2012 the FUTA tax was 6.2% of the first $7,000 in wages paid to each employee during the calendar year.

For deposit purposes, the FUTA tax is figured quarterly, and any amount due must be paid by the last day of the first month after the quarter ends. The formula for determining the amount due is set forth in the Federal Employer's Tax Guide.

An annual FUTA return must be filed on Form 940, Employer's Annual Federal Unemployment Tax Act (FUTA) Tax Return, on or before January 31 following the close of the calendar year for which the tax is due. Any tax still due is payable with the return. Form 940 may be filed on or before February 10 after the close of the year if all required deposits were made on time and if full payment of the tax due is deposited on or before January 31.

State Unemployment Taxes

All the states and the District of Columbia have unemployment compensation laws. In most states, the tax is imposed only on the employer, but a few states require employers to withhold a percentage of wages for unemployment compensation benefits. An employer may be subject to federal unemployment tax and not subject to state unemployment tax. In some states, for instance, an employer with fewer than four employees is not subject to the state unemployment tax. The regulations for a specific state should be checked.

State Disability Insurance

Some states require employees to be covered by disability or sick pay insurance. The employer may be required to withhold a certain amount from the employee's salary to pay for this insurance.

Budgets

Growing businesses must develop budgets that aid the planning of finances over a certain period. Medical offices should establish a new budget before the beginning of each fiscal year. The best way to begin a budget is to look at the expenses from the previous year (Figure 24-2). These expenses should be divided into categories, then a total should be derived for each category. Each month should represent

FIGURE 24-2 Inventory supplies and equipment before developing the annual budget. Once a good inventory has been completed, more accurate projections can be made for the expenses for the coming year.

approximately $\frac{1}{12}$ of the total budget, not including large capital expenses.

In the individual categories, examine expenses for those that could be eliminated or those that were under budget. For example, if $3,345 was spent on office supplies and the budget was $3,000, either more money needs to be allotted for this category or cuts in spending are necessary. If $3,345 was spent and the budget was $4,000, the excess may be placed in another category for the next year. Even quarterly and semiannual expenses should be annualized and then divided by 12 to obtain a monthly expense amount.

CRITICAL THINKING APPLICATION   24-8

■ Brenda has developed a preliminary budget for next year. She realizes that several pieces of equipment need to be replaced. However, Dr. Wilkins has said she does not want to make any capital purchases over the next 2 years. How might Brenda approach Dr. Wilkins about the needed equipment?

■ How might leasing equipment benefit the office? How can Brenda determine whether this would be more or less expensive than purchasing the equipment?

By monitoring expenses on a monthly basis, the physician can see whether the facility is over budget, under budget, or right on target. Categories in which overspending has occurred can be reconciled by taking funds from another category (e.g., category B) and adding them to the overspent category (category A). However, the amount taken must be subtracted from category B and added to category A. Those subtracted funds are no longer available in category B. Specific notes should be kept when categories are overspent so that an adjustment can be made for the next fiscal year.

The following categories should be considered for the physician's operating budget:

- Insurance
- Rent
- Depreciation
- Loan payments
- Advertising and promotions
- Legal and accounting
- Miscellaneous expenses
- Supplies
- Salaries and wages
- Utilities
- Dues, subscriptions, and fees
- Taxes
- Repairs and maintenance
- Medical equipment
- Administrative equipment
- Medication and pharmacy expenses

The physician should investigate whether leasing equipment might be a better option for the facility. Some leasing programs are very progressive and provide service contracts at no additional cost. Because depreciation costs are high, leasing might be the best answer to a new equipment need.

Insurance

Insurance coverage is one of the physician's major expenses. Almost every physician carries some type of malpractice insurance for protection against the cost of legal liabilities. Property and fire insurance are mandatory, and most physicians carry workers' compensation insurance to cover employee injuries and accidents. The medical assistant may be asked to shop for the best insurance rates at the time of renewals.

CLOSING COMMENTS

The physician comes to rely heavily on the person who manages the office's finances. It is important that this individual keep information confidential. The entire staff must be conscious of the costs involved in operating a medical office and should adhere to their respective budgets as closely as possible. The physician then may be willing to spend more money on pay increases and benefits to reward employees.

All office employees must attempt to save money and resources wherever possible. Medicare plays a pivotal role in a physician's income. For example, Medicare has recently cut costs for certain cardiovascular services, such as stress tests and echocardiograms, up to 35% to 40%. Private insurers usually follow Medicare's lead when determining their own costs, Medicare reimbursements are calculated according to a formula based on the current status of the economy; therefore, when the economy is poor, reimbursements to physicians go down, but medical equipment and supply costs continue to rise. Because reimbursements are critical to the physician's income, some doctors are forced out of medicine, leaving a gap in the availability of medical services to the community.

Patient Education

In some cases patients may not fully understand the costs involved in providing high-quality medical care. The medical assistant may need to educate the patient about the basic costs involved with the procedures performed in the office. Patients do not need a lengthy explanation but may be set more at ease by knowing that the physician does not set fees arbitrarily. The physician's office is a small business, like thousands of other small businesses, and should be able to pay its overhead and expenses.

Legal and Ethical Issues

A person who keeps financial records holds a position of great trust and responsibility. Some physicians require the person placed in charge of the office finances to be *bonded*. This means that the facility has done a security check on the individual and the person was found worthy to be placed in a position of responsibility. A bond is issued by an entity on behalf of a second party, guaranteeing that the second party will fulfill an obligation or series of obligations to a third party. In the event that the obligations are not met, the third party recovers its losses via the bond.

Records must be accurate and completed on a daily basis. Daily journals should be kept indefinitely to support tax returns.

SUMMARY OF SCENARIO

Brenda has learned much about the financial management of a physician's office. She is never hesitant to call the practice accountant, Mr. Schmidt, whenever a question arises. As she gains more experience, she comes to understand the budgeting process, cost management, and the various methods of accounting practice.

Many factors can affect the finances of a medical practice. However, a physician who is fairly conservative about spending and careful with investments likely will do well as a member of the community's healthcare professionals. Dr. Wilkins lives by this philosophy and also encourages her employees to manage money wisely. This attitude among the staff members promotes a sense of teamwork and cooperation for the benefit of all.

SUMMARY OF LEARNING OBJECTIVES

1. **Define, spell, and pronounce the terms listed in the vocabulary.**
   Spelling and pronouncing medical terms correctly bolster the medical assistant's credibility. Knowing the definition of these terms promotes confidence in communication with patients and co-workers.

2. **List the four items all financial records should show at any given time.**
   (1) How much was earned in a given period, (2) how much was collected, (3) how much is owed, and (4) the distribution of expenses incurred.

3. **Describe how to establish and maintain a petty cash fund.**
   Most offices pay for small, incidental expenses with petty cash. The process for maintaining a petty cash fund is outlined in Procedure 24-3.

4. **Differentiate between accounts payable and accounts receivable.**
   Accounts payable refers to the amounts of money owed by a business and not yet paid; *accounts receivable* refers to amounts owed to the business that are not yet paid.

5. **Explain the difference between a single-entry and a double-entry accounting system.**
   The single-entry accounting system uses three basic records: the general journal, the cash payment journal, and the accounts receivable ledger. The general journal is a record (e.g., a day sheet) in which transactions are recorded. The cash payment journal in its simplest form is a record (e.g., a checkbook) that is used to make payments. The accounts receivable ledger provides information about the amounts owed to the physician. The double-entry system, which is more difficult to use than the single-entry system, requires an entry on each side of the accounting equation, and each side must always balance.

6. **Explain the importance of a trial balance.**
   A trial balance reflects discrepancies between the journal and the ledger. It does not reveal errors in the individual accounts but shows errors in the overall balances of accounts.

7. **Describe common periodic financial reports.**
   Five common reports are used for accounting in the small business office: (1) the statement of income and expense (lists all the income received and all expenses paid during a set period), (2) the cash flow statement (lists cash income and cash disbursement made during a period, noting the beginning and ending balances on hand), (3) the trial balance (determines whether all of the books are in balance), (4) the accounts receivable trial balance (an equation that double checks the total of all

   A/R prior to sending monthly statements), and (5) the balance sheet (depicts the financial picture of the practice on a specific date).

8. **Explain how to process an employee payroll accurately.**
   Employee payroll is an essential function related to practice finances. The process for employee payrolls is outlined in Procedure 24-4.

9. **Explain the purpose of Form W-4.**
   The Employee's Withholding Allowance Certificate, or Form W-4, specifies the number of withholding allowances the employee is claiming. The more allowances claimed, the less money is taken from the employee's paycheck.

10. **State the types of employment records required by the Internal Revenue Service (IRS).**
    The IRS requires that several employment records be kept for at least 4 years: the employee's Social Security number; the number of withholding allowances claimed; the amount of gross salary; all deductions for Social Security and Medicare taxes; federal, state, and city or other subdivision withholding taxes; state disability insurance; and state unemployment tax.

11. **Discuss the basis for the withholding amounts taken from employees' earnings.**
    Several deductions are taken from the employee's wages as required by law. They are based on the employee's total earnings, the number of withholding allowances claimed, the employee's marital status, and the length of the pay period involved. The wage base for Social Security tax currently is $106,800.

12. **Explain the requirements of the Federal Insurance Contributions Act (FICA).**
    FICA requires that a certain amount be deducted from an employee's wages and designated for Medicare and Social Security programs. The current percentages are 1.45% for the Medicare contribution and 6.2% for Social Security. Both the employer and the employee contribute these amounts.

13. **Discuss the importance of setting a budget each fiscal year.**
    The physician's office must set a budget each fiscal year to prepare for all the expenses involved in running the office. Without a well-planned budget, the physician cannot control expenses. The expenditures from the past year should be evaluated when planning the new budget, paying particular attention to the expense categories that exceeded expected amounts.

CONNECTIONS

Study Guide Connection: Go to the Chapter 24 Study Guide. Read and complete the activities.

Evolve Connection: Go to the Chapter 24 link at *evolve.elsevier.com/kinn* to complete the Chapter Review and Chapter Quiz. Check out the other resources listed for this chapter to make the most of what you have learned from Financial and Practice Management.

MEDICAL PRACTICE MANAGEMENT AND HUMAN RESOURCES

25

SCENARIO

Katherine Martinson is the office manager for Dr. Michael Collins, a family practitioner in a group practice in a metropolitan area. The office usually carries a full schedule of patients each day. Katherine has been instrumental in the seamless operation of the facility. Before joining Dr. Collins, Katherine worked for a physician in the same group of doctors, Dr. Grant Bradley, who retired last year. She worked as an administrative medical assistant for 6 years before that. Her strength and ability to motivate employees led Dr. Collins to approach her about becoming his office manager once Dr. Bradley retired.

Katherine is a consummate professional, but she knows the importance of treating each employee as an individual. At weekly staff meetings, the employees offer input on the various procedures followed in the office. Katherine regularly consults with the staff members and always asks for input as to how the office can function more effectively. She implements many of the staff members' suggestions in the day-to-day activities of the office. She knows that employees need to feel a part of the team, and by trying the procedures others suggest, she validates them as an asset to the facility.

When a position is open, Katherine is careful about whom she hires, always checking at least three references per applicant and verifying each previous place of employment. She trains each employee in every aspect of the job and keeps checklists that reflect that the employee has been given instruction in certain skills.

Katherine makes sure each person has the tools needed to do his or her job. She also explains overhead costs to employees and helps them understand what is involved in the daily operation of the practice. With this information, the employees are more conservative about using supplies and more careful with equipment. Major changes are presented to the entire staff, and although Dr. Collins makes the final decision, he and Katherine seek the input of the employees. The cooperative attitude between management and the employees of the office provides a good atmosphere for teamwork, and Katherine and the physician are pleased with the results.

While studying this chapter, think about the following questions:

- How friendly should office managers become with the staff members?
- Why is checking references important when hiring a new staff member?
- How should negative employee evaluations be handled?
- How can the office manager promote an atmosphere of teamwork?

LEARNING OBJECTIVES

1. Define, spell, and pronounce the terms listed in the vocabulary.
2. Explain the importance of management in the medical office.
3. Discuss the desirable qualities of a medical office manager.
4. List and discuss the three types of leaders.
5. Discuss several types of power and whether power is a positive or negative entity.
6. Identify several ways in which employees are motivated.
7. Explain the difference between intrinsic and extrinsic motivation.
8. List several ways to prevent burnout.
9. Discuss what to look for when reviewing resumés and applications.
10. Explain why the telephone voice of an applicant is important.
11. List and discuss legal and illegal interview questions.
12. Identify the follow-up activities the office manager should perform after an interview.
13. Explain the importance of mentors for new employees in the medical office.
14. Describe how to conduct a performance review for an employee.
15. List the various types of staff meetings.
16. Explain how to arrange a group meeting.

VOCABULARY

advocate A person who defends or pleads the cause of another; one that supports or promotes the interests of another.

affable Pleasant and at ease in talking to others; characterized by ease and friendliness.

agenda (ah-jen′-duh) A list or outline of things to be considered or done.

ancillary (an′-suh-ler-e) Subordinate; auxiliary.

appraisal An expert judgment of the value or merit of; judgment as to quality.

blatant Completely obvious, conspicuous, or obtrusive, especially in a crass or offensive manner; brazen.

burnout Exhaustion of physical or emotional strength or motivation, usually as a result of prolonged stress or frustration.

chain of command A series of executive positions in order of authority.

cohesive Sticking together tightly; exhibiting or producing cohesion.

disparaging (dis-pahr′-uh-jing) Slighting; having a negative or degrading tone.

embezzlement Stealing from an employer; to appropriate goods, services, or funds for personal use without permission.

extrinsic (eks-trin′-zik) External to a thing, its essential nature, or its original character.

impenetrable Incapable of being penetrated or pierced; not capable of being damaged or harmed.

incentives Things that incite or spur to action; rewards or reasons for performing a task.

liaison A close bond or connection; a person with a connection, contract, link, or conspiracy with another person or group.

mentors Trusted counselors or guides.

meticulous (meh-tiku′-luhs) Marked by extreme or excessive care in the consideration or treatment of details.

micromanage To manage with great or excessive control or attention to details.

motivation The process of inciting a person to some action or behavior.

quackery practicing or pretending to have the ability to cure or treat a patient without qualifications to do so.

reprimands Criticisms for a fault; severe or formal reproofs.

retention The act of keeping in possession or use; keeping in one's pay or service.

subordinate Submissive to or controlled by authority; placed in or occupying a lower class, rank, or position.

targeted Directed or used toward a target; directed toward a specific desire or position.

The management of a professional medical office can greatly influence the success of the operation. Good management allows the physician to see and treat patients in a functional environment with the confidence that the business side of the facility is operating as it should be. A well-managed office is not something that just happens. Great effort and teamwork are necessary to ensure that the day-to-day activities are carried out efficiently and that the many details needing attention are handled expeditiously.

Although most medical assistants do not enter office management right after graduation, they certainly want to succeed and to advance their career. The information in this chapter can help the medical assistant understand what makes a good manager. Those traits can be developed as a new employee after graduation. Additionally, the medical assistant will learn the employment process from the office manager's point of view. This information also is valuable to a new medical assistant who is applying for a position. By studying office management, the medical assistant prepares for future management positions, but also learns to see both sides of the coin and understand why managers make certain decisions and enact policies.

TODAY'S OFFICE MANAGERS

The office manager in today's medical facilities must be versatile and able to perform several tasks at one time. The office manager is responsible for many more duties if the office is small and has a smaller patient load. These professionals must know how to complete almost all the tasks in the office and have good people management skills. In larger offices, human resources duties may be performed by a separate office, or an accountant may take care of all financial management issues. However, the more duties the office manager can perform, the more valuable he or she is to the clinic. Always be open to learning management duties, because taking on management positions usually results in an increase in salary and benefits. A sharp medical assistant who is ready to learn will advance quickly and find a variety of opportunities in the healthcare industry.

WHO'S IN CHARGE?

If the office has only one medical assistant, that person must be able to assume many management responsibilities with cooperation from the physician. When the office has two medical assistants, one administrative and one clinical, the administrative medical assistant often is expected to assume management duties. In an office with a larger staff, a **chain of command** must be established.

A facility with three or more employees should designate one person as supervisor or office manager. This individual needs management skills and the ability to deal with personnel matters. Other employees answer to the office manager, and the office manager answers to the physician or physicians. A chain of command allows the office staff to consult with the physician regarding administrative or clinical problems, complaints, or grievances; however, it prompts employees to allow individuals whom the physician has placed in charge to have the first opportunity to solve problems. It also allows the physician to check on the operation of the office, disseminate information on policy changes, and correct errors or grievances by dealing with one person instead of all employees.

QUALITIES OF AN EFFECTIVE MANAGER

- Uses good judgment
- Has good health
- Has the ability to organize
- Is willing to learn
- Possesses original ideas
- Has leadership ability
- Is fair with all employees
- Is flexible
- Has a sense of fairness
- Cares about employees
- Remains calm during crises
- Is open to constructive criticism
- Has good communication skills
- Uses good listening skills
- Is approachable

A medical assisting career is challenging and offers great opportunities for advancement. A recently graduated medical assistant, whose first position may have been as a receptionist, can be given more responsibilities based on good work and eventually may become the office manager of a large staff.

Management problems often can be prevented by defining carefully the areas of authority and the responsibilities of each employee. Many physicians say that friction among workers is their most common personnel problem. The importance of the chain of command cannot be overemphasized, and the physician must not undermine the office manager's authority by circumvention. When employees know what is expected of them, they can plan both their daily and long-term work more effectively.

Duties of the Medical Office Manager

The duties performed by medical office managers vary from place to place and practice to practice. Some physicians take a much more active role in office management than others. The best management plan for the physician is to hire a trustworthy, reliable office manager and then allow the person to run the business aspects of the office. This frees the physician to concentrate on taking care of patients.

Some of the tasks performed by the medical office manager include:

- Preparing and updating the policies and procedures manuals
- Making sure employees follow the policies and procedures manuals
- Developing job descriptions
- Recruiting new employees
- Performing orientation and training
- Conducting performance and salary reviews
- Dismissing employees
- Planning staff meetings
- Maintaining staff harmony
- Establishing work flow guidelines

- Ensuring compliance with all federal and state regulations
- Improving office efficiency
- Supervising the purchase and care of equipment
- Educating patients
- Eliminating time-wasting tasks for the physician
- Marketing the practice
- Performing customer service

Office management can best be accomplished by developing a thorough office policy and procedures manual and then enforcing its contents except in extraordinary circumstances. This is discussed later in the chapter.

The Power of Influence

Managers have a great deal of influence over the people they supervise. A successful manager must be interested in people and enjoy working with them on a daily basis. It is said that if one helps others get what they want in life, the individual usually also gets what he or she wants. An effective manager discovers the **motivation** behind employees' drives to be a part of the profession in which they are employed and then helps them achieve their individual goals. In turn, most employees are enthusiastic about working toward the facility's goals as a productive team member.

Successful managers know that their employees should be encouraged to perform at optimum levels, and they are confident enough in their own skills to give credit to employees who develop ideas and concepts for the team. These managers know how to let their employees help them "look good." A manager with a group of outstanding employees usually is looked on as an effective leader.

CRITICAL THINKING APPLICATION 25-1
When Katherine began as Dr. Collins' office manager, she found several supportive employees, but a few were concerned about their new boss. How can a new manager help employees be at ease during the first few weeks?

The Manager as a Leader

Leaders nurture other people. They take the time to discover what makes people tick and then give them opportunities that will help them rise to new levels of responsibility. Leaders have a strong belief in people, and they express confidence in their abilities, seeing them as successes rather than failures. Often this belief exists before people prove themselves, and that provides motivation for them to reach their potential.

Perhaps most important, leaders listen to their people. Few things are more frustrating than an employee attempting to talk to a manager who is working on some project or typing on the computer. Listening involves eye contact and questions to ensure that the employee is understood. Being willing to take the time to listen is a step toward success as a manager.

Instead of sitting across from employees at a desk, try sitting beside them in the chairs that are usually placed in front of a desk. When discussing issues with employees, this simple change in position places the office manager on an equal plane with the employee and implies more of a team effort. At times this positioning might be inappropriate, such as during discussions about disciplinary matters. Still, when attempting to get an employee to cooperate or come over to the office manager's way of thinking, position can play a large role in getting people "on the same page."

Types of Leaders

The three basic types of leaders are the charismatic leader, the transactional leader, and the transformational leader. Each has positive qualities, and all can be successful in business.

Charismatic leaders have a special way of inspiring an unswerving allegiance and devotion from their followers. They encourage people to overcome great obstacles and buy into their vision for the organization or business. They also tend to trust people in **subordinate** positions and earn trust in return.

Transactional leaders are structured and organized. They make sure their subordinates understand their duties and roles. These leaders are fair and provide rewards when they have been earned. The transactional leader is hardworking, a planner, and strict about budgets and time frames.

Transformational leaders are innovative and able to bring about change in an organization. These leaders are relationship builders. They stress shared values and strive to create a common ground among team members. Transformational leaders are the most effective when an organization is experiencing change and reorganization.

Styles of Management

Some managers are democratic and willing to listen to employees. These managers are fair-minded and ask the opinions of the staff when making decisions. In contrast, the autocratic manager is more of a dictator, making demands and insisting that tasks be done in a certain way—his or her way. The laissez-faire manager is easygoing and does not make a lot of demands on employees. This is a "go with the flow" manager who lets employees work on their own and does not **micromanage**.

Theories X, Y, and Z

Douglas McGregor, an American social psychologist, developed Theory X and Theory Y to distinguish two types of management. His book, *The Human Side of Enterprise,* published in 1960, explains these management types. In 1981, William Ouchi offered his own management theory, calling it Theory Z.

All these theories include several assumptions. Theory X, for example, suggests that humans dislike working and avoid it whenever possible. Because it is unpleasant, management must push, coerce, or threaten workers to do their jobs. Workers, according to Theory X, do not like responsibility and prefer to be directed than to lead. McGregor says that Theory X is applied best to large-scale employers, such as those involved in factories or manufacturing. Theory X is considered "hard" management.

Theory Y is virtually the opposite of Theory X. Theory Y holds that people enjoy work and that it is a normal component of life, as are rest and play. McGregor says that these humans, when motivated, work toward the goals of the organization. People seek and accept responsibility, enjoy job satisfaction, and are imaginative and creative. Theory Y applies to workers such as managers and other professionals. Theory Y is considered "soft" management.

Ouchi's Theory Z is a combination of American and Japanese management theories. Theory Z considers characteristics such as long-term employment, collective decision making, individual responsibility, and a holistic view of the employee and his or her family.

Maslow's Hierarchy of Needs

Maslow's hierarchy of needs, first discussed in the chapter on communications, also can be applied to management. The triangle of needs begins with physiologic needs (air, food, water, sleep) and safety needs. Moving upward, social needs and then esteem needs are addressed. The last need is self-actualization.

In the workplace, physiologic needs are met with lunch breaks, rest times, and days off. The worker's salary helps the person meet other physiologic needs, such as shelter. Safety needs are addressed in this theory as having a safe place to work and a sense of security through savings, health insurance, and retirement programs. Social needs are met through interaction with co-workers, working as a team, and enjoying the work family at events away from the office. Needs related to esteem include feeling appreciated, valued, and being recognized for good work. Continuing to set higher goals and working to reach them are steps toward self-actualization.

Frederick Herzberg believed that job enrichment had to exist for a worker to be motivated. He theorized that several factors affect job satisfaction, some negative and some positive. The six factors that can lead to job dissatisfaction include:
- Company policy
- Supervision
- Relationship with supervisors
- Work conditions
- Salary
- Relationship with co-workers

The six factors that lead to job satisfaction include:
- Achievement
- Recognition
- The work product
- Responsibility
- Advancement
- Growth

In his book, *The Motivation to Work,* Herzberg states three points:
1. Jobs must be satisfying and must motivate employees to grow and reach their full capabilities.
2. Employees who show greater ability should be given more responsibility.
3. If the job does not allow the employee to use his or her full ability, a different employee who can grow and find motivation in the work should be placed in that position.

These are only a few of the many theories about employment and management. The theory of management by objectives suggests that goal setting serves as a basis for greater job efficiency and better employee motivation and commitment and that it leads to planning for results instead of just planning to work. Some managers believe in the theory of management by walking around, which suggests that the more visible and engaged the manager is with his or her employees, the more productive they will be. Supervisors develop and modify their management style as they gain more experience. The medical assistant who understands the type of manager he or she has may find it easier to understand the manager's actions and preferences. This realization can lead to better job performance and promotions for the medical assistant.

Leading During Transitions and Change

Change is a part of the life of every person and every business. Most people initially are hesitant to face change, and many people try to avoid it completely. However, a business cannot experience growth without change. The manager who can lead subordinates through periods of change is a valuable asset to the organization. Employees need guidance on maintaining focus on the tasks at hand. The manager should remain visible to employees during times of change and communicate frequently through status reports and updates on policies and procedures.

The book *Who Moved My Cheese?* by Spencer Johnson, MD, is an innovative story that all managers should read. Any manager or employee experiencing a time of change should study this simple, short book. The opening quotes renowned author A.J. Cronin:

"Life is no straight and easy corridor along which we travel free and unhampered, but a maze of passages, through which we must seek our way, lost and confused, now and again checked in a blind alley. But always, if we have faith, a door will open for us, not perhaps one that we ourselves would ever have thought of, but one that will ultimately prove good for us."

Who Moved My Cheese? stresses several points about change that the good manager should remember:

- Change happens.
- Anticipate change.
- Monitor change.
- Adapt to change quickly.
- Move with the change.
- Enjoy change.
- Be ready to change again quickly and enjoy it again.

The simplicity of this advice does not diminish its truth. Change happens in everyone's job and personal life. Those who learn to adapt quickly and move forward do not become casualties of change.

The Role of Power

Power is the ability to influence employees so that they carry out their directives. Leaders use many types of power.

- *Coercive power* is manipulative, and the leader often makes threats or uses fear to accomplish goals. The fear of losing a job is a manipulation of power.
- *Granting rewards* is a more positive use of power. When the leader is able to give employees some type of reward for a job well done, most employees strive to reach their goals.
- *Expert power* is a factor when the leader is knowledgeable about a subject. Employees respect leaders who know their job and how things should be done. Most people look up to a person who has a high degree of knowledge about a given subject. Employees frequently are frustrated when they must work for someone who knows nothing about procedures or the service offered.
- *Legitimate power* is that of position or status. It does not really matter who the president of the United States is; the office itself carries the weight of power. Therefore, the individual who serves as president holds legitimate power.

- *Referent power* is granted from subordinates to those who lead by example. It is a power based on the admiration of the leader. Mentors, parents, and teachers often are the objects of referent power.

CRITICAL THINKING APPLICATION   **25-2**

- Katherine is a respected office manager in the office where she works, but several other managers in the office building are not as well liked. What makes a strong, effective office manager?
- Everyone has worked for at least one supervisor whom they did not like. What traits make a poor office manager?

Abuse of Power and Authority

Unfortunately, many managers may abuse the power they have. A manager who puts up barriers and erects emotional walls with employees has difficulty forming a **cohesive** team. Some managers use other people as tools to get what they want, and other managers stick to their own level or stature, relating only to the inner circle of decision makers in the facility.

When an organization has no checks and balances, power is easily abused. Working with a manager who cannot look inside himself or herself and see mistakes is difficult. Some managers stress rules and conformity, leaving no gray areas where subordinates are concerned. Some show a false humility and pretend to care, but most employees can see right through this half-effort at a relationship. Others only hire "yes" people, who agree with everything the manager says. All these are abuses of power and indications of a poor manager.

The Power of Motivation

A number of factors can motivate a person to reach a goal, including:

- A challenge
- Money
- Praise
- Satisfaction
- Freedom
- Fear
- Family
- Insecurity
- Competition
- Fulfillment
- Integrity
- Honor
- Reputation
- Responsibility
- Prestige
- Needs
- Love

Any of these motivators can prompt an employee to action. There are two general types of motivation. *Intrinsic motivation* is internal, or originates within a person. Intrinsic motivation is long term and can be focused toward a lifelong goal. **Extrinsic** *motivation* is external and more material in nature. Generally, extrinsic motivation is more short lived and less satisfying than intrinsic motivation.

CRITICAL THINKING APPLICATION   25-3

- Katherine knows that employees have different reasons and motivations for working. Some must work to help support their families, and others work simply because of a love for their field. How can Katherine discover her employees' motivations for working?
- How does this knowledge benefit the office manager?
- Can this knowledge help Katherine achieve her goals?

THE NEW OFFICE MANAGER

The medical assistant will encounter various reactions when entering a facility as the new office manager. Often, he or she will face negative reactions from employees. They may have felt an intense loyalty to the previous manager and may resent that the person was terminated, or they may have settled into a routine with an office manager they had had for many years. As mentioned earlier, most individuals resist change, and getting accustomed to a new supervisor can be extremely stressful. A new office manager wants to create a positive work environment; therefore, he or she must find ways to win the support of current employees.

The first thing a new office manager can do to begin garnering support is nothing. Never storm into an office and begin making radical changes in the first few days. Always observe for at least a few weeks and make notes about problem areas. Then, meet with the physician and share the information observed and present a plan for changes. Ask for the physician's input, because he or she may know the history of difficult situations and can provide guidance in moving forward with plans for change.

After discussing these plans with the physician, use strategy when attempting to move employees toward achieving office goals. Schedule individual meetings with employees and allow them to tell you three things they like about their jobs, three things they dislike, and three things they need to do their jobs more effectively. Surprisingly, the employee may need only a truly insignificant item, such as his or her own box of file folders or a stapler that works with larger stacks of paper.

Once all the meetings have been held, review the information the employees provided and create a plan of action. The information provides a preliminary road map for management, because the employees' responses give the new manager an excellent idea about what is important to them and where the problem areas are in the office. Also, choose one item from each employee's list of what they need to do their job more effectively and obtain it within 1 week of the interviews. Employees will be impressed that the new manager is interested in their opinions and wants to meet their needs for the good of the office.

Hold a staff meeting a week later, and wherever possible, move toward eliminating the issues the employees do not like about their jobs. Ask for input, and perhaps even more important, ask for their assistance in improving the work environment. If the new manager follows this process, the employees will realize that he or she can get things done, is interested in their input, and often acts based on their input. Do not change a slew of policies or procedures too quickly; remember that change is difficult for most people. However, indicate to the employees that their issues are important and will be addressed.

Distribute memos frequently that communicate with employees in a way that makes them feel like part of a team. Be willing to ask for input and try suggestions for dealing with problems in the flow of the workday.

Realize that some employees still will resist, which may make the new office manager feel frustrated. At some point staffing changes may be necessary, and this might include terminating employees who do not get onboard with the office moving in a positive direction. Although any terminations are stressful for the entire office, realize that this is a common situation when new managers begin their positions. This process is the first step in building a functional team.

CREATING A TEAM ATMOSPHERE

Teamwork is critical in the medical profession. In the physician's office, the manager must promote an atmosphere in which the employees are willing to work together toward common goals. Morale in the office may be low because of recent changes in policies or procedures, changes in staff or management, recent terminations of employees, lack of business, or any number of other reasons. The wise manager takes steps to improve employee morale constantly, including scheduling frequent meetings and keeping the employees abreast of changes and developments that affect them (Figure 25-1). Employees like to be kept "in the loop." Some managers try to shield employees from negative information, but this practice can cause rumors to circulate and worsen morale.

Managers can improve morale by scheduling activities that involve the families of employees and by making an obvious effort to include them in various events. One of the most effective ways to improve employee morale is to communicate. Regular staff meetings, e-mails, and memos are critical for good communication and smooth operation of the medical facility.

FIVE ESSENTIAL ELEMENTS OF TEAMWORK

1. *Mutual accountability:* Each person on the team holds the others accountable for the success of the organization.
2. *Common purpose and performance goals:* Short-term and intermediate goals must relate to the long-term goals of the group.
3. *Small size:* Most successful teams have a small number of members; fewer than 10 is optimum.
4. *Common approach:* All team members must learn to work together toward the goal.
5. *Complementary skills:* A variety of talents, skills, and abilities is needed for a successful team.

From Katzenbach JR, Smith DK: *Wisdom of teams: creating the high-performance organization,* Boston, 1992, Harvard Business School Publishing.

Use of Incentives and Employee Recognition

The staff of the physician's office should feel satisfaction with the working conditions and atmosphere in the facility. The office manager plays a part in ensuring that this happens.

Incentives give employees reason to perform over and above the level expected of them. If the staff meets or exceeds a goal that has

FIGURE 25-1 Communication is vital when building a team. Employees appreciate good communication with management. Sharing good and bad news openly with employees leads to fewer rumors and eases workers' concerns.

been set, the physician may elect to provide tickets to a sports or entertainment event for the entire staff. A paid day off is always a great incentive for accomplishing a goal. Some physicians have an incentive program that is related to collections for a given period. These ideas provide a goal for the employees to work toward and an opportunity to expand their efforts as a team.

Recognition is a strong method of improving employee morale and encouraging outstanding performance. Certificates for peak performance are a great way to motivate employees. For instance, the office manager may decide to award a certificate each month to the employee who provides the best customer service. Patients could even be involved by allowing them to nominate employees for this honor. When an award is at stake, most employees enjoy participating and striving to accomplish the goals that have been set.

CRITICAL THINKING APPLICATION　　25-4

One of Katherine's employees, Jewel, is very sensitive about performing perfectly on the job. She is an excellent employee, but she has a few weaknesses. However, she has received a lot of recognition for the good things she has done at work. Katherine still feels that she needs to discuss with Jewel the areas where her performance is weak, but she knows it will upset her. How might Katherine deal with this sticky situation? How can Katherine reassure Jewel that she is pleased with her overall performance?

Problem Employees

Occasionally, problem employees disrupt the efficiency of the physician's office. Counseling these employees to find the source of their difficulties is the first step toward resolution. Many employees can be redirected to become productive staff members with a little patience and understanding on the manager's part. However, some employees have negative attitudes that seem **impenetrable**.

The manager must never hesitate to counsel the employee who is not performing at the expected level, and this includes employees with attitude problems. Establish a set regimen of counseling. Many offices allow one verbal warning before written reprimands go into

the employee's file. If the manager does not make a habit of writing formal **reprimands**, there may be insufficient documentation of problems with the employee once the manager is ready to terminate him or her. Even small offenses, such as being tardy, should at least be noted in the employee's file. The manager should never be in a position in which the termination of an employee cannot be justified by written documents.

Problem Patients

Patients can be quite challenging to the physician's staff and office manager. Most patients are genuinely concerned about their health and are cooperative with the physician's instructions. However, a few patients require extra understanding, which may lead to intervention by the office manager. Types of problem patients may include those who are:

- Complainers
- Angry
- Needy
- Demanding
- Violent
- Nonpaying
- Noncompliant
- Drug seeking
- Reschedulers

The office manager may act as a **liaison** between the patient and the physicians when issues arise that are somewhat complicated. Some patients may feel ignored or mistreated. Others may have a general lack of trust that makes complying with the physician's orders difficult for them. Cultural differences, social issues, and financial problems all can affect patient compliance and attitude. The rare patient may have a personality disorder or psychological problems that are frustrating as they receive medical treatment.

The time may come that the physician decides to discontinue care for a difficult patient. If that happens, the physician must notify the patient in writing and send the letter by certified mail, return receipt requested. Because some patients refuse to sign for mail, a copy of the same letter can be sent by regular mail. The physician must tell the patient that care is to be discontinued, inform the patient what day will be the final one the physician will provide care, and urge the patient to seek medical care from a new physician. The letter does not have to detail the reasons for the physician's decision, but those reasons should be explained in the patient's medical record. Always follow office policy in terminating patient care.

Preventing Burnout

Burnout is defined as exhaustion of physical or emotional strength or motivation, usually as a result of prolonged stress or frustration. Medical professionals are particularly susceptible to burnout because of the intensity of their jobs. Even small decisions could affect a patient's life. Therefore the office manager should take measures to help employees avoid burnout.

Some of the causes of burnout include a stressful, disorganized home or work environment; poor human relations skills; a feeling of being out of control of one's life; excessive expectations from supervisors or family members; long work hours or time away from family and friends; and not being able to relax either at home or in the work environment.

TIPS FOR PREVENTING BURNOUT

- Ask for help.
- Devote specific times to introspection or meditation.
- Understand what can be changed and what cannot be changed.
- Get some exercise.
- Organize and prioritize tasks.
- List tasks that are displeasing and delegate them to others, if possible.
- Understand personal limitations.
- Take short vacations at least twice a year.
- Identify goals and try to perform only tasks that lead to reaching them.
- Consider options, including changing jobs.
- Personalize work space with pictures and comforting items.
- Get a good understanding of a position and the stress involved before accepting it.

Keeping the Management Relationship Professional

When people work together for an extended period, they often become **affable**, and sometimes relationships develop into close friendships. This is a normal occurrence, but the office manager must be careful about becoming too close to his or her employees. When the relationship is friendly, reprimanding an employee when needed sometimes is difficult. Some employees take advantage of a good relationship with the office manager and may begin to arrive late or call in sick more than usual. A healthy respect for each other must be maintained. The manager can have a good rapport with employees without becoming overly friendly, and this is the best policy. Some facilities have strict rules about fraternization with subordinates outside the work facility. It is advisable to keep the relationship on a professional level at all times.

CRITICAL THINKING APPLICATION 25-5

- The clinical medical assistants usually celebrate payday by going out to eat after work every other Friday. After about 6 months on the job, they invite Katherine to join them. Should she go with the employees? Why or why not?
- Most offices plan parties for Christmas or at other times during the year. Are these good for employee morale, or should they be avoided?

The professional office manager serves as a liaison between the employees and the physician, but can also serve in the same capacity for the patients. Some patients have issues that, for whatever reason, they cannot seem to talk about with the physician; however, they may reveal this information to the medical assistant or the office manager. Employees may have similar situations.

Both the medical assistant and the office manager should serve as a patient **advocate**, but they can never hold back information the physician needs to know. For instance, if a patient tells the medical assistant or office manager that he has really been smoking, although he told the physician he had quit, the information must be given to the physician. Never suggest to or tell a patient that information can be withheld from the physician. If the patient asks the medical assistant to keep information from the physician, the medical assistant must refuse.

In the same manner, a medical assistant may have made a medication error and is afraid to tell the physician. The office manager must relay the information to the physician, who can determine whether the error could be harmful to the patient. Fortunately, most situations between the medical assistants and the physician are not life-threatening. The office manager who is fair and who also serves as an advocate for the medical assistant tries to rectify situations in a positive manner.

LAWS AFFECTING EMPLOYMENT

Numerous laws affect the way that employees are treated from the interview through the end of employment. The office manager should be familiar with these laws and how they affect the practice.

- Fair Labor Standards Act
  - Prescribes standards for wages and overtime pay
  - Requires that employees must be paid minimum wage and time and a half for overtime hours, as they apply
  - Prohibits those under age 18 from performing certain kinds of work and restricts the hours of workers under age 16
- Occupational Safety and Health Act
  - Regulates conditions affecting employees' safety and health in the workplace
- Workers' Compensation
  - Regulates the benefits of employees who have been injured on the job
  - Determines pay for employees who are not working because of an on-the-job injury
- Family and Medical Leave Act
  - Requires employers of 50 or more employees to offer up to 12 weeks of unpaid, job-protected leave to eligible employees for the birth of a child, an adoption, or a personal or family illness
- Pregnancy Discrimination Act
  - Forbids employers to refuse to hire a woman based upon pregnancy, childbirth, or related medical conditions
  - Requires employers to hold open a job for a pregnancy-related absence the same length of time that a job would be held open for employees on sick or disability leave
- Americans with Disabilities Act
  - Prohibits discrimination against individuals with disabilities (see Chapter 7)
- Age Discrimination Act
  - Prevents discrimination in hiring on the basis of age
  - Prevents discrimination in promoting, discharging, and compensating employees

Many more federal and state laws affect employers and employees. When a position is available at the medical office, the person conducting the interviews and making hiring decisions must be familiar with the laws that govern the practice.

SELECTING THE RIGHT STAFF MEMBERS

The most important asset to any medical facility is the staff that cares for the patients. From the physician to the receptionist, all play a vital role in the well-being of those who visit the office. Selecting staff members who can be molded into a cohesive team is not an easy task. Care should be taken to choose employees who have the necessary skills and the right personality for the office. Never try to select employees who are all alike. A variety of personality types works better than several similar personalities.

Understanding the Needs of the Office

The office manager should discuss with the physician the type of employee needed when an opening arises. Ask what qualities the physician desires in the person who occupies that particular position and the tasks for which the person will be responsible. Once the need has been established and the duties confirmed, the office manager can begin the recruiting process.

One of the most effective methods of finding new employees is through word of mouth. Ask other office managers, physicians, or medical professionals if they are aware of a person looking for employment who has the skills needed in the office. Keep a file of resumes that can be accessed when an opening occurs in the office. Often the physician or office manager may know of a person working in another area of the clinic or perhaps in a nearby hospital who may be interested in a job change. Be careful in approaching a person who is already employed. There is no harm in asking if a person is interested, but if the reply is negative, do not pursue the issue further.

Employment agencies can be used to find staff members, but they may charge a fee for their services. The office manager may want to contact a local medical assisting school to secure an extern. If the extern proves to be an asset to the office, he or she may be offered the permanent position. Online job postings and newspaper ads are another option for finding employees, but many resumes may be submitted from people who are not qualified, especially when the economy is not at its best. When creating an ad for the newspaper, list the basic requirements for the position. Briefly describe the office and location and the personality type sought. Some offices also list a few of the benefits offered to attract applicants and also may disclose a salary range.

Reviewing Resumés and Applications

Once several resumés or applications have been submitted, the office manager should set aside a quiet time to review the documents. Divide them into three stacks: stack one should contain resumés of individuals who will be called for an interview; stack two should consist of possible candidates but not the strongest; and stack three should contain applicants who will not be called.

During this preliminary review process, look for several items. First, make sure the documents are neatly prepared, free of error, and completely legible (Figure 25-2). The person hired probably will write in patients' charts, so this is a good opportunity to make sure the handwriting can be read easily. Second, look for gaps between positions. Make sure any lengthy time of unemployment is explained. The application should be filled out completely, and no notations of "see resume" should be included. The application provides important information, and an applicant who does not fill it out completely might be classified as lazy and prone to taking shortcuts. Watch for inconsistencies or oversights, including information that seems incomplete. Also look for resumés **targeted** toward the job opening available in the clinic. Targeted resumés are written specifically for a

certain position. With today's computer capabilities, job seekers can target their resumés for each job for which they apply, and this strategy tells the manager that the applicant has enough interest in the job to demonstrate that he or she meets their specific requirements.

Once the entire original stack of resumés has been reviewed and separated, return to the stack of potential interviews. Careful judgment and objectivity must be used in the search for an employee suitable for the practice. Before interviewing any applicant, the manager needs to know several details:

- What personal qualities and abilities must the applicant have?
- What responsibilities are involved with the position?
- What salary range is the physician willing to offer?
- How soon will the position be open?

Once these facts are clear, the manager should review the final resumés and applications with the following questions in mind:

- Do the applicant's handwriting and/or grammar meet the office's standards?
- Has the applicant been employed previously? What duties were performed?
- If previously employed, how long was the applicant in the last position? Why did the applicant leave?
- What are the applicant's skills? Do these meet the requirements for the position as set forth in the office procedures manual?
- Does the applicant seem to accept and enjoy responsibility?
- What is the applicant's formal education? Is he or she registered or certified? If not, is the applicant interested in taking the examination?
- Is the applicant a member of a professional organization? Does he or she attend meetings?

Arranging the Personal Interview

If the applicant sent a letter asking for an interview, note whether the letter was correctly typed and included essential contact information and whether the person also provided an attractive resumé. Amazingly, some resumés do not include a contact telephone number! Managers can schedule interviews by e-mail, but speaking to applicants directly has its advantages. By conducting a prescreening interview with the applicant on the phone, the manager has an opportunity to judge the person's telephone voice, attitude, and communications skills. In addition, the manager may want to ask several questions about the person's education and experience. Because the employee probably will speak with patients on the telephone, clarity of speech is important. Those who perform well during the prescreening should be scheduled for an interview.

CRITICAL THINKING APPLICATION   25-6

- Katherine was impressed with Carol Limpken's resumé and application, but when scheduling an interview on the telephone, she noticed that Carol's grammar was not as professional as Katherine would like. Should this influence Katherine's decision to hire Carol?
- Why is speech such an important issue in the medical office?

APPLICATION FOR POSITION / Medical or Dental Office
AN EQUAL OPPORTUNITY EMPLOYER

(In answering questions, use extra blank sheet if necessary)

No employee, applicant, or candidate for promotion, training or other advantage shall be discriminated against (or given preference) because of race, color, religion, sex, age, physical handicap, veteran status, or national origin.

Date of Application

PLEASE READ CAREFULLY AND WRITE OR PRINT ANSWERS TO ALL QUESTIONS. DO NOT TYPE.

A. PERSONAL INFORMATION

Name - Last   First   Middle   Social Security No.   Area Code/Phone No. ( )

Present Address: - Street   (Apt #)   City   State   Zip   How Long At This Address?:

Previous Address: - Street   City   State   Zip   Person to notify in case of Emergency or Accident - Name:

From: To: Address: Telephone:

B. EMPLOYMENT INFORMATION

For What Position Are You Applying?:   □ Full-Time □ Part-Time □ Either   Date Available For Employment?:   Wage/Salary Expectations:

List Hrs./Days You Prefer To Work   List Any Hrs./Days You Are Not Available: (Except for times required for religious practices or observances)   Can You Work Overtime, If Necessary? □ Yes □ No

Are You Employed Now?: □ Yes □ No   If So, May We Inquire Of Your Present Employer?: □ No □ Yes, If Yes:
Name Of Employer: Phone Number: ( )

Have You Ever Been Bonded? □ Yes □ No   If Required For Position, Are You Bondable? □ Yes □ No □ Uncertain   Have You Applied For A Position With This Office Before? □ No □ Yes   If Yes, When?:

Referred By / Or Where Did You Learn Of This Job?:

Can You, Upon Employment, Submit Verification Of Your Legal Right To Work In The United States?: □ Yes □ No
Submit Proof That You Meet Legal Age Requirement For Employment? □ Yes □ No

Language(s) Applicant Speaks or Writes (If Use Of A Language Other Than English is Relevant To The Job For Which The Applicant Is Applying:

C. EDUCATIONAL HISTORY

Name & Address Of Schools Attended (Include Current)	Dates From	Thru	Highest Grade/Level Completed	Diploma/Degree(s) Obtained/Areas of Study
High School				
College				Degree/Major
Post Graduate				Degree/Major
Other				Course/Diploma/License/ Certificate

Specific Training, Education, Or Experiences Which Will Assist You In The Job For Which You Have Applied.

Future Educational Plans

D. SPECIAL SKILLS

CHECK BELOW THE KINDS OF WORK YOU HAVE DONE:

□ BLOOD COUNTS	□ DENTAL ASSISTANT	□ MEDICAL INSURANCE FORMS	□ RECEPTIONIST
□ BOOKKEEPING	□ DENTAL HYGIENIST	□ MEDICAL TERMINOLOGY	□ TELEPHONES
□ COLLECTIONS	□ FILING	□ MEDICAL TRANSCRIPTION	□ TYPING
□ COMPOSING LETTERS	□ INJECTIONS	□ NURSING	□ STENOGRAPHY
□ COMPUTER INPUT	□ INSTRUMENT STERILIZATION	□ PHLEBOTOMY (Draw Blood)	□ URINALYSIS
OFFICE EQUIPMENT USED: □ COMPUTER	□ DICTATING EQUIPMENT	□ POSTING	□ X-RAY
		□ WORD PROCESSOR	□ OTHER:

Other Kinds Of Tasks Performed Or Skills That May Be Applicable To Position: Typing Speed   Shorthand Speed

(PLEASE COMPLETE OTHER SIDE)

FIGURE 25-2 Application for employment. Candidates for jobs in the medical office should complete applications accurately, leaving no blanks or unanswered questions. (Courtesy Bibbero Systems, Petaluma, Calif., *www.bibbero.com*.)

E. EMPLOYMENT RECORD

LIST MOST RECENT EMPLOYMENT FIRST

May We Contact Your Previous Employer(s) For A Reference? ☐ Yes ☐ No

1) Employer

Work Performed. Be Specific:

Address   Street   City   State   Zip Code

Phone Number   (   )

Type of Business   Dates   Mo. | Yr.   Mo. | Yr.
From   To

Your Position   Hourly Rate/Salary
Starting   Final

Supervisor's Name

Reason For Leaving

2) Employer

Worked Performed. Be Specific:

Address   Street   City   State   Zip Code

Phone Number   (   )

Type of Business   Dates   Mo. | Yr.   Mo. | Yr.
From   To

Your Position   Hourly Rate/Salary
Starting   Final

Supervisor's Name

Reason For Leaving

3) Employer

Worked Performed. Be Specific:

Address   Street   City   State   Zip Code

Phone Number   (   )

Type of Business   Dates   Mo. | Yr.   Mo. | Yr.
From   To

Your Position   Hourly Rate/Salary
Starting   Final

Supervisor's Name

Reason For Leaving

F. REFERENCES — FRIENDS / ACQUAINTANCES NON-RELATED

(1)
Name   Address   Telephone Number   (☐ Work ☐ Home)   Occupation   Years Acquainted

(1)
Name   Address   Telephone Number   (☐ Work ☐ Home)   Occupation   Years Acquainted

Please Feel Free To Add Any Information Which You Feel Will Help Us Consider You For Employment

READ THE FOLLOWING CAREFULLY, THEN SIGN AND DATE THE APPLICATION

"I certify that all answers given by me on this application are true, correct and complete to the best of my knowledge. I acknowledge notice that the information contained in this application is subject to check. I agree that, if hired, my continued employment may be contingent upon the accuracy of that information. If employed, I further agree to comply with Company/Office rules and regulations."

Signature: _____   Date: _____

FIGURE 25-2, cont'd

Set a time for the personal interview when the applicant can be given undivided attention. An applicant who is being considered for employment should have an opportunity to see the office during a period of a fairly normal amount of activity. The prospective employee who is interviewed in a peaceful, quiet office on the physician's day out may not be prepared for the activity on a normal working day.

Before interviewing any applicant, become thoroughly familiar with the federal, state, and local fair employment practice laws affecting hiring practices. Both men and women receive protection from on-the-job discrimination, sexual harassment, mandatory lie detector tests, and unfair discharge. Title VII of the Civil Rights Act of 1964, as amended by the Equal Employment Opportunity Act of 1972, prohibits inquiries into an applicant's race, color, gender, religion, and national origin. Inquiries about medical history, arrest records, or previous drug use also are illegal. Most states have laws designed to protect the rights of job applicants, and these laws may impose additional restrictions. Office managers must research the laws that pertain to employment in their own states.

If an actual application has not been submitted, have the applicant complete it at the time of the interview. The application form can serve as a check of the applicant's penmanship and thoroughness and becomes a permanent record if the individual is hired. Tell the candidate whether the form should be completed in the applicant's own handwriting and be sure to state this on the instructions. Check to see whether the applicant was **meticulous** about following instructions and filling in all the blanks. This serves as an indication of the individual's capacity for following directions.

The Interview

The manager's first priority is to make sure the applicant feels at ease (Figure 25-3). Shake his or her hand and ask a few social questions before starting the interview (Procedure 25-1). In general, use good manners and see that the person to be interviewed is comfortable. Most people feel some butterflies in the stomach when interviewing, but the manager will get a better idea of the person's capabilities if he or she is relaxed and able to discuss strengths and background openly.

Stress interviews usually are a waste of time. In a stress interview, the potential employee is placed in a difficult situation; for instance,

FIGURE 25-3 Put the job applicant at ease. Candidates perform at their peak when they are relaxed and calm.

the interviewer may call and invite the potential employee to the office for a "casual second interview." Upon arrival, he or she enters a room where several individuals are sitting at a table, prepared to grill the prospective employee. Although those who will be placed in higher management positions may be expected to survive such a situation and perform under that type of stress, the regular employee placed in such situations might assume that the employer will be highly demanding throughout the course of employment, and this might lead a great prospect to refuse opportunities at that particular office. The potential employee may not express his or her strengths and abilities as well when intentionally placed into a stress interview situation. Some interviewers make up nerve-wracking scenarios that might happen in the office and then ask the prospect, "How would you handle that?" Although the medical profession is certainly demanding, the interview should be a time for honest exchange of information and accurate evaluation of the potential employee.

Begin with a few open-ended questions that cannot be answered with a simple "yes" or "no," such as, "What were your duties during your last position?" When interviewing a recent graduate who does not have experience, ask questions such as, "What subject did you perform well in at school?" When speaking with the candidate, make a mental note of whether he or she displays essential personal qualities, such as the ability to converse easily, the capacity to listen, and a bright smile. The applicant should be interested enough in the position to ask intelligent questions and appear interested in the office and the physician's specialty.

Avoid inquiries that involve the applicant's privacy. The questions should be related to the available position and the applicant's ability to do the job. At all stages of the interview, the interviewer should avoid questions about age, race, marital status, and other discriminatory areas.

An interview is a two-way exchange of information between the applicant and the interviewer. If the applicant appears to be one who will receive serious consideration, explain what will be expected as an employee. Office policies regarding appearance, working hours, overtime, time off, and vacations may be discussed at this stage. Salary and other fringe benefits should be discussed once the manager is ready to offer the job. If the manager fails to mention these items, the applicant may be hesitant to inquire.

Some employers request a credit check before offering employment, especially if the individual will be handling practice finances. It can safely be assumed that one who is unable to handle personal financial affairs will be a poor risk in handling office finances. The medical assistant may also be required to submit to criminal background checks, drug screens, and even personality tests before or just after being offered a position. The medical assistant must be prepared to deal with the information obtained by such inquiries. If a long time has passed since the incident happened, be honest and explain that it was a mistake, it happened several years ago, and retribution has been made. Be prepared to answer questions about such events during the job interview.

Review the job description for the position being filled. The person being interviewed must understand the required duties and responsibilities of the job. Ask whether the applicant has any questions, and close the interview on a positive note. Let the candidate know when a decision will be made and what further contact the office will initiate.

PROCEDURE 25-1

Interview Job Candidates Effectively

GOAL: *To evaluate job candidates fairly and choose the best person to fill an available position in the medical facility.*

EQUIPMENT and SUPPLIES

- Candidate's completed job application
- Candidate's resumé
- Private area in the medical office
- Clerical supplies

PROCEDURAL STEPS

1. Review the job requirements the candidate will need to perform.
   <u>PURPOSE:</u> To evaluate candidates properly, the employer must determine the tasks the new employee will be expected to perform.
2. Match each job application with the corresponding resumé.
3. Separate strong candidates from moderate candidates and poor candidates.
   <u>PURPOSE:</u> To screen the best candidates and invite them to interview for the position.
4. Review each resumé and job application again and determine which candidates should be brought to the office for an interview.
5. Call each candidate and schedule an appointment for an interview.
6. Evaluate the applicant's speaking voice while making the appointment or the interview.
   <u>PURPOSE:</u> To determine the candidate's professionalism and ability to speak clearly and with clarity on the telephone.
7. Select several interview questions in advance to ask all of the applicants.
   <u>PURPOSE:</u> To avoid having to think of questions during the interview.
8. Note whether the applicant arrives on time for the interview.
   <u>PURPOSE:</u> If the candidate does not arrive on time for the interview, he or she may be a habitually late employee.
9. Introduce yourself to the applicant and proceed to a private area to conduct the interview.

10. Make the applicant feel as much at ease as possible.
    <u>PURPOSE:</u> Most individuals are a little nervous during job interviews, and if helped to relax, they are able to present their qualifications and skills confidently.
11. Ask the applicant the chosen questions.
12. Evaluate the answers and make notations about the candidate that are not demeaning or unprofessional.
    <u>PURPOSE:</u> Demeaning comments in an employee's file eventually may be seen if there is a subsequent lawsuit, and this can reflect poorly on the person who made the comments.
13. Ask the candidate whether he or she has any questions.
    <u>PURPOSE:</u> Evaluate the types of questions the employee asks; determine whether they are intelligent questions and whether they indicate a true interest in the position.
14. Offer strong candidates a brief tour of the facility.
15. State a date by which a hiring decision will be made and suggest that the candidate call the facility that day, if desired.
16. Evaluate all applicants fairly according to their experience and training.
17. Select the best three candidates and call them for a second interview, if desired.
18. Discuss the final hiring decisions with the physician or others with influence.
    <u>PURPOSE:</u> Some physicians want to make the final hiring decisions.
19. Make the final hiring decision.
20. Call the candidate to come to the office to discuss the position.
21. Negotiate salary and benefits.
22. Offer the position.
23. If the offer is declined, call the next candidate to the office to discuss the position until a satisfactory candidate accepts and agrees to a start date.

During the hiring process, the manager may want to invite serious prospects to lunch with the staff or for coffee in the more relaxed atmosphere of the employee lounge. This presents an opportunity to discover whether the applicant's personality will mesh with the atmosphere of the office. Employees appreciate being asked their opinion on those who are potential team members. An extensive list of interview questions can be found in Chapter 58.

Follow-Up Activities

When the interview is over, immediately take a few moments to rate the applicant while the interview is fresh in the memory. Jot down some notes so that the applicant will be remembered easily when the final decisions are being made as to who will be hired. Do not trust the impressions to memory, especially if several applicants have been

interviewed. Never write harmful personal statements; instead, be objective and fair. Should the potential employee ever have cause to bring the physician to court for discrimination in hiring practices, there should be no **disparaging** information written down that would reflect negatively on the physician or office manager.

Always carefully check all references and follow through on any leads for information. Use the telephone in checking references, because people sometimes are less than candid in a letter; furthermore, letter writing is time-consuming, and a reply may never be sent. If the e-mail address for a reference is provided, this is an excellent way to check a reference, and the printed version may be added to the applicant's file.

Prepare a checklist before placing the call. When speaking with the person called, be sure to "listen between the lines." Note the tone of the replies to the questions. Do not ask questions that might incriminate the person answering them. The following questions are effective as an introduction:

- When did (the applicant) work for you?
- For how long?
- What were the duties and responsibilities?
- Did the employee assume responsibility well?

Some employers provide information only on the date of hire, job title, and date of termination of the employment. However, if the employer states, "She worked in our office from May, 2011, to July, 2012, and is NOT eligible for rehire," the reasonable assumption is that the employee did not perform well. The tone of voice and emphasis on the word "not" should be clues that this person is probably not right for the job. Still, if all other references are glowing, call and ask the applicant about the facility that gave the negative response. There could be a reasonable explanation for what might have been a bad experience. Respect the company's policy and do not press for further information.

Any person who is granted an interview should send a thank you letter to the person who interviewed him or her. Watch the mail to see whether any of the applicants perform this important follow-up task.

A second interview may be granted when the field is narrowed to two or three candidates. The physician may want to participate in these interviews. Some offices conduct a group interview with several staff members present. Remember that these interviews become more and more stressful for the candidate, and the manager should expect some nervousness. Do not "count off" in the interview for mild nervousness.

Making the Selection

Once the final interviews have been conducted, the best candidate must be chosen. Never rely strictly on a "gut instinct" about a potential employee. Base hiring decisions on logical conclusions drawn from all contacts with the applicant, including:

- Grammar and enunciation
- Appropriate manners
- Professional appearance
- Work history
- Match to required job skills
- Friendly, personable attitude

Some offices create a score sheet for interviews that lists the needs of the office and allows the office manager to assign points according to how the applicant fits.

When a decision has been reached to hire someone, it is best to bring the successful candidate back into the office to offer the position and negotiate the final details. The office manager may want to wait until the first-choice candidate has actually accepted the offer before notifying anyone else that the job has been filled. Do not expect the potential employee to answer the offer on the spot. Twenty-four hours is a reasonable time to consider the offer.

Remember to notify all final candidates for the position that it has been filled so that they can continue their job search. They may have hesitated to accept other interviews, and it is unfair to keep individuals who are seeking employment hoping for a telephone call from the physician's office. Good etiquette requires dropping them a note or calling to say that the position is filled. Although this is a

rare practice in today's busy clinics, all of the applicants who interviewed were surely the manager's best candidates and professional individuals. Therefore, they deserve a brief call and a wish for success in their job search. Thank the individual for applying, and offer to keep his or her application on file, if the candidate was especially impressive.

PAPERWORK FOR NEW EMPLOYEES

The office manager should develop a checklist of the paperwork needed for newly hired staff and all of the information that should be covered with the new employee at the onset of the job. Basic new employee paperwork often includes:

- Job application
- Form I-9 (Employment Eligibility Verification)
- W-4 Form (Employee's Withholding Allowance Certificate)
- Notice of Workers' Compensation coverage
- Consent for background check, drug testing, and search (if applicable)
- Acknowledgement of receipt of company handbook or policy manual
- Agreements regarding pay, wage deductions, benefits, schedule, work location, and so on
- Notices of at-will employment status
- Acknowledgement of ethics statement
- Occupational Safety and Health Administration (OSHA) compliance acknowledgement or checklist

All of these forms, once signed, should be kept in the employee's personnel file. Other forms and paperwork may be necessary that vary from state to state and company to company. Make certain that Form I-9, Employment Eligibility Verification, is completed. Form I-9 is required by the federal government and used by the employer to make certain that the newly hired individual is eligible to work legally in the United States. A person who cannot provide the required documentation should not be allowed to remain as an employee. Employees should also understand the at-will employment status. Under the *at-will employment* principle, the employee or the employer can terminate employment for good cause, bad cause, or no cause, unless an express contract is signed for a specific term or the employee is a member of a collective bargaining group, such as a union.

ORIENTATION AND TRAINING: CRITICAL FACTORS FOR SUCCESSFUL EMPLOYEES

The hiring process does not end with hiring a new employee. Orientation and training help new employees to understand what is expected and to develop to their full potential (Figure 25-4). One of the most critical errors made when bringing new staff members aboard is not providing them with a fair orientation and training period.

Some managers assign a mentor to assist the new employee during the initial probationary period. A **mentor** is a guide whom the new staff member can approach with questions and concerns. Using this type of "buddy" system is a good practice, because the new person does not feel isolated and alone during the first few weeks on the job.

FIGURE 25-4 Training an employee well contributes greatly to the person's success.

Acquaint the new employee with the following:
- Staff members and their names
- Physical environment and layout of the office
- Nature of the practice and specialty
- Types of patients seen in the office
- Office policies
- Short- and long-range expectations

All new employees should be required to read the office policy and procedures manual. It is advisable for the manager to require the employee to sign a statement verifying that the manual (or manuals) have been read.

Make sure all federal and state regulations that apply to new employees are met. OSHA training must be provided to employees at risk for exposures *before they begin any duties.* Training required by the Health Insurance Portability and Accountability Act (HIPAA) also must be completed. Make certain that the employee's file is complete before allowing the employee to work even 1 hour. The manager must meet this federal requirement to prove that the employee is eligible to work in the United States (Figure 25-5).

CRITICAL THINKING APPLICATION 25-7

Katherine is bringing in a new employee who must begin work on the following Monday, because the staff has been short one person for approximately 2 weeks. However, Katherine will be going on vacation the same day. How can she ensure that the new employee is trained properly?

Job Description

The job description is a tool designed to inform employees about the duties they are expected to perform. Well-written job descriptions list the essential functions of the job and reveal the chain of command the employee should follow when questions or concerns arise. These documents provide a good guideline for employees so that they will understand exactly what is expected of them and their responsibilities at work.

The job description should include a statement that says the employee must perform any additional duties as assigned by the supervisor. With this statement in place, the employee cannot say, "That is not my job." All employees should be willing to pull together and assist with any tasks, but this statement gives added weight to assignments that are not specified in the written job description.

An effective manager understands the phrase "inspect what you expect." When duties are assigned, the manager should ensure that the tasks were completed correctly and in a timely manner. New employees should be monitored to make sure their delegated tasks are being done and done right. Without inspection, the manager cannot know whether the new employee is meeting expectations. Once employees have earned a degree of trust, inspecting their work is not as necessary as in the beginning. As mentioned earlier, many managers practice a skill called "management by walking around." By strolling through the areas where subordinates work, managers can observe and hear about issues that might be brewing, while at the same time improve morale by offering encouragement and praise.

Staff Development Training

Continuous training and staff development are vital aspects of any medical office. Constant advancements and technologic changes occur, and employees must be kept up-to-date on those changes. Meetings should be held at least quarterly to ensure that the staff is using the latest techniques and current regulations when dealing with issues that confront the medical facility. Watch the mail for seminar opportunities that will allow employees to earn continuing education units (CEUs) or learn new skills that will benefit the office. Get input from employees about what they would like to learn and look for those opportunities. Professional organizations, such as the American Association of Medical Assistants (AAMA) and the American Medical Technologists (AMT), offer CEUs on a regular basis; therefore, encourage all staff members to be certified and to join professional organizations. Most hospitals have numerous continuing education classes that they allow physician's office employees to attend.

Delegation of Duties

Delegating duties to subordinates allows managers to concentrate on the most critical aspects of their own jobs. Delegation also provides an opportunity for the employees to grow and learn new skills. Some managers are hesitant to assign duties to employees because they believe the tasks are too important not to be completed by the manager. This hesitation suggests either a refusal to release control or mistrust of the employees. However, this type of manager soon is overrun with tasks and unable to complete them. Managers should place trust in employees who have earned it and allow them to prove their abilities. Mistrust is a symptom of a poor hire. Discover the strengths of individual employees and then assign them tasks that will allow them to use those strengths. If a medical assistant was hired to do administrative duties but is good with phlebotomy, encourage and allow the employee to assist with venipunctures whenever needed.

OMB No. 1615-0047; Expires 08/31/12

Department of Homeland Security
U.S. Citizenship and Immigration Services

Form I-9, Employment
Eligibility Verification

Read instructions carefully before completing this form. The instructions must be available during completion of this form.

ANTI-DISCRIMINATION NOTICE: It is illegal to discriminate against work-authorized individuals. Employers CANNOT specify which document(s) they will accept from an employee. The refusal to hire an individual because the documents have a future expiration date may also constitute illegal discrimination.

Section 1. Employee Information and Verification *(To be completed and signed by employee at the time employment begins.)*

Print Name: Last	First	Middle Initial	Maiden Name

Address *(Street Name and Number)*	Apt. #	Date of Birth *(month/day/year)*

City	State	Zip Code	Social Security #

I am aware that federal law provides for imprisonment and/or fines for false statements or use of false documents in connection with the completion of this form.

I attest, under penalty of perjury, that I am (check one of the following):

☐ A citizen of the United States

☐ A noncitizen national of the United States (see instructions)

☐ A lawful permanent resident (Alien #) _____

☐ An alien authorized to work (Alien # or Admission #) _____
until (expiration date, if applicable - *month/day/year*) _____

Employee's Signature	Date *(month/day/year)*

Preparer and/or Translator Certification *(To be completed and signed if Section 1 is prepared by a person other than the employee.)* I attest, under penalty of perjury, that I have assisted in the completion of this form and that to the best of my knowledge the information is true and correct.

Preparer's/Translator's Signature	Print Name

Address *(Street Name and Number, City, State, Zip Code)*	Date *(month/day/year)*

Section 2. Employer Review and Verification *(To be completed and signed by employer. Examine one document from List A OR examine one document from List B and one from List C, as listed on the reverse of this form, and record the title, number, and expiration date, if any, of the document(s).)*

List A	**OR**	List B	**AND**	List C
Document title:				
Issuing authority:				
Document #:				
Expiration Date *(if any)*:				
Document #:				
Expiration Date *(if any)*:				

CERTIFICATION: I attest, under penalty of perjury, that I have examined the document(s) presented by the above-named employee, that the above-listed document(s) appear to be genuine and to relate to the employee named, that the employee began employment on *(month/day/year)* _____ **and that to the best of my knowledge the employee is authorized to work in the United States. (State employment agencies may omit the date the employee began employment.)**

Signature of Employer or Authorized Representative	Print Name	Title

Business or Organization Name and Address *(Street Name and Number, City, State, Zip Code)*	Date *(month/day/year)*

Section 3. Updating and Reverification *(To be completed and signed by employer.)*

A. New Name *(if applicable)*	B. Date of Rehire *(month/day/year)* *(if applicable)*

C. If employee's previous grant of work authorization has expired, provide the information below for the document that establishes current employment authorization.

Document Title:	Document #:	Expiration Date *(if any)*:

I attest, under penalty of perjury, that to the best of my knowledge, this employee is authorized to work in the United States, and if the employee presented document(s), the document(s) I have examined appear to be genuine and to relate to the individual.

Signature of Employer or Authorized Representative	Date *(month/day/year)*

Form I-9 (Rev. 08/07/09) Y Page 4

FIGURE 25-5 The I-9 Employment Eligibility Verification form is designed to help the employer gather the documents necessary to prove that an employee is eligible to work in the United States.

LISTS OF ACCEPTABLE DOCUMENTS
All documents must be unexpired

LIST A	LIST B	LIST C
Documents that Establish Both Identity and Employment Authorization	**Documents that Establish Identity**	**Documents that Establish Employment Authorization**

OR ... AND

LIST A	LIST B	LIST C
1. U.S. Passport or U.S. Passport Card	1. Driver's license or ID card issued by a State or outlying possession of the United States provided it contains a photograph or information such as name, date of birth, gender, height, eye color, and address	1. Social Security Account Number card other than one that specifies on the face that the issuance of the card does not authorize employment in the United States
2. Permanent Resident Card or Alien Registration Receipt Card (Form I-551)		
3. Foreign passport that contains a temporary I-551 stamp or temporary I-551 printed notation on a machine-readable immigrant visa	2. ID card issued by federal, state or local government agencies or entities, provided it contains a photograph or information such as name, date of birth, gender, height, eye color, and address	2. Certification of Birth Abroad issued by the Department of State (Form FS-545)
		3. Certification of Report of Birth issued by the Department of State (Form DS-1350)
4. Employment Authorization Document that contains a photograph (Form I-766)	3. School ID card with a photograph	
	4. Voter's registration card	4. Original or certified copy of birth certificate issued by a State, county, municipal authority, or territory of the United States bearing an official seal
5. In the case of a nonimmigrant alien authorized to work for a specific employer incident to status, a foreign passport with Form I-94 or Form I-94A bearing the same name as the passport and containing an endorsement of the alien's nonimmigrant status, as long as the period of endorsement has not yet expired and the proposed employment is not in conflict with any restrictions or limitations identified on the form	5. U.S. Military card or draft record	
	6. Military dependent's ID card	
	7. U.S. Coast Guard Merchant Mariner Card	5. Native American tribal document
	8. Native American tribal document	
	9. Driver's license issued by a Canadian government authority	6. U.S. Citizen ID Card (Form I-197)
	For persons under age 18 who are unable to present a document listed above:	7. Identification Card for Use of Resident Citizen in the United States (Form I-179)
6. Passport from the Federated States of Micronesia (FSM) or the Republic of the Marshall Islands (RMI) with Form I-94 or Form I-94A indicating nonimmigrant admission under the Compact of Free Association Between the United States and the FSM or RMI	10. School record or report card	8. Employment authorization document issued by the Department of Homeland Security
	11. Clinic, doctor, or hospital record	
	12. Day-care or nursery school record	

Illustrations of many of these documents appear in Part 8 of the Handbook for Employers (M-274)

Form I-9 (Rev. 08/07/09) Y Page 5

FIGURE 25-5, cont'd

USING PERFORMANCE REVIEWS EFFECTIVELY

A new employee should be granted a probationary period. A period of 60 to 90 days has been traditional, but many employers believe that 2 weeks is sufficient to determine whether the employee will be able to learn and adapt to the position. Set a definite date for a performance review covering the probationary period at the time of initial employment. This review should not be squeezed in between patient visits or be given a token few minutes at the end of a day. Schedule a time that provides the opportunity to relax and talk. Tell the new employee how well expectations have been met and whether there are any deficiencies. Then give the employee an opportunity to ask questions. Sometimes an employee fails to perform because he or she was never told what was expected. Although the probationary period does not always allow time to train an individual fully for a specific position, it is fair to assume that the potential for being a satisfactory employee can be judged at this time. Now is the time to talk out any problems and make suggestions for improvement. Sometimes the employee is released after an unsuccessful probationary period.

The performance **appraisal** includes a judgment of both the quality and quantity of work, personal appearance, attitudes and team spirit, dependability, self-discipline, motivation, attendance, punctuality, and any other qualities essential to satisfactory performance of the job in question (Figure 25-6). The supervisor is responsible for ongoing performance appraisals of all employees, complimenting whenever possible and appropriate and offering helpful criticism when necessary. A formal performance appraisal at the end of the probationary period and at regular 6-month intervals thereafter, with a report to the physician-employer, is helpful for the employee's salary review (Procedure 25-2).

When negative information is to be relayed to the employee during a performance appraisal, sandwich the negative comment between two positive ones whenever possible. For instance, tell the employee, "Jewel, you are a pro at greeting patients and making them feel at home. I would like to see you improve your time management skills, however, because I feel you are spending too much time with each individual patient. I must confess that they feel a part of the clinic family. Just watch the time and keep making them feel so welcome!"

Managers also may use the "feel, felt, found" approach when talking with employees about their performance. For example, "Jewel, I feel the same way you do about the patients taking up a lot of our time. I know there are some that want to talk with us for hours, and I have felt the pressure of wanting to make them feel comfortable but having so much to do, too. I have found that if I

PROCEDURE 25-2

Conduct a Performance Review

GOAL: *To evaluate job performance fairly and determine the strengths and weaknesses of employees using accurate documentation.*

EQUIPMENT and SUPPLIES

- Employee's file
- Past evaluations of employee
- Notes and/or reports regarding employee behavior
- Private area in the medical office
- Clerical supplies

PROCEDURAL STEPS

1. Set an appointment with the employee to conduct the review.
2. Allow the employee to complete a self-evaluation of his or her own work.
   PURPOSE: To gain insight into how the employee sees his or her own work performance and to allow input as to how the employee feels that he or she has performed during the evaluation period.
3. Review the self-evaluation, then document additional information about the employee and his or her performance.
4. Share the information with any other supervisor or the physician, if dictated by office policy or if additional input is necessary.
   PURPOSE: To accommodate any additional input (e.g., by the physician) that needs to be documented and discussed during the review.

5. Complete the final written review and proofread it for accuracy and completeness.
6. Discuss the review with the employee during the evaluation appointment.
   PURPOSE: To promote an understanding of what is expected by the employer.
7. Progress through the interview and explain the results of the evaluation to the employee.
8. Allow the employee to respond to any of the points raised during the evaluation but do not allow an argumentative attitude.
   PURPOSE: To gain insight into the employee's reasons for any poor performance without allowing belligerence.
9. Allow the employee to respond in writing to the evaluation for a limited time (e.g., 5 days).
   PURPOSE: To give the employee a chance to insert his or her input into the performance report.
10. Ask the employee to sign the evaluation to document that it was reviewed with him or her. (The employee does not have to agree with the evaluation to sign it.)
11. Give a copy of the evaluation to the employee.
12. File the evaluation in the employee's file.

PERFORMANCE EVALUATION AND DEVELOPMENT PLAN (OFFICE AND CLERICAL)

NAME: ______________________ DATE OF EVALUATION: ______________________

DATE OF HIRE: ______________________ DEPARTMENT: ______________________

JOB TITLE: ______________________ SUPERVISOR: ______________________

DATE APPOINTED THIS JOB: ______________________ MANAGER: ______________________

LAST REVIEW DATE: ______________________ LAST REVIEW RATING: ______________________

NEXT REVIEW DATE: ______________________ CURRENT REVIEW RATING: ______________________

PURPOSE

The purpose of this evaluation is to:

1. SET GOALS WITHIN SCOPE OF PRESENT JOB.
2. COMMUNICATE OPENLY ABOUT PERFORMANCE.
3. EVALUATE PAST PERFORMANCE.
4. DISCUSS FUTURE DEVELOPMENT PLANS FOR GROWTH.

INSTRUCTIONS

1. Supervisor to review form prior to completion. If specific items are not applicable they should be left blank.
2. Supervisor and employee to review job description prior to review.
3. In "COMMENTS" section supervisor may indicate which factors should be more heavily weighted in this particular evaluation.
4. Comments should be specific and job-related. All appropriate evaluation factors should be commented on to some degree.

I. POSITION OBJECTIVES AND MAJOR RESPONSIBILITIES. Summarize specific responsibilities of the job.

____

____

____

II. ACCOMPLISHMENTS AND/OR IMPROVEMENTS. What specific accomplishments and/or improvements has employee made since last review with respect to set goals?

____

____

____

PLEASE CONSIDER THE EMPLOYEE'S DEMONSTRATED PERFORMANCE AND MARK THE CIRCLE WHICH MOST CLOSELY DESCRIBES THAT PERFORMANCE.

4 - Performance consistently far exceeds expectations and requirements.
3 - Performance consistently exceeds normal expectations and job requirements.
2 - Performance consistently meets expectations and job requirements
1 - Performance usually meets expectations and minimum job requirements.
0 - Performance does not meet job requirements.

– CONTINUED, NEXT PAGE –

FORM # 72-119 © 1987 BIBBERO SYSTEMS, INC. PETALUMA, CA

TO REORDER CALL TOLL FREE: 800-BIBBERO /(800 242-2376) OR FAX: (800) 242-9330 MFG IN U.S.A.

FIGURE 25-6 Performance evaluation and development plan. Performance evaluations should be considered tools that help employees reach their personal goals and the goals of the organization. (Courtesy Bibbero Systems, Petaluma, Calif.)

Continued

7. <u>DEPENDABILITY:</u> CONSIDER ATTENDANCE, PUNCTUALITY, IDLE TIME AND RELIANCE WHICH CAN BE PLACED ON EMPLOYEE TO PERSEVERE AND CARRY THROUGH TO COMPLETION ALL ASSIGNED TASKS

○ 0   ○ 1   ○ 2   ○ 3   ○ 4

8. COMPLIANCE WITH COMPANY POLICIES: DOES THE EMPLOYEE COMPLY WITH RULES AND REGULATIONS WHICH APPLY TO SAFETY, FAIR EMPLOYMENT PRACTICES AND GENERAL ADMINISTRATIVE PROCEDURE.

○ 0   ○ 1   ○ 2   ○ 3   ○ 4

9. SPECIFIC PERFORMANCE	1	2	3	4	COMMENTS
A. Ability to handle scheduling:					
B. Willingness to work OT when necessary:					
C. Handling of calls and follow-up:					
D. Maintenance of equipment:					
E. Ability to handle patient complaints:					
F. Tact in dealing with patients:					
G. Speed (in specific technical procedures):					
H. Secretarial accuracy:					
I. Professional terminology:					
J. Assisting procedures:					
K. Laboratory techniques:					
L. X-ray techniques:					
M. Physical therapy:					
N. Collections:					
O. Medical Insurance:					
P. Bookkeeping:					

10. PERSONAL	1	2	3	4	COMMENTS
A. Grooming:					
B. Professional conduct:					
C. Energy, enthusiasm:					
D. Ability to handle stress:					

ADDITIONAL COMMENTS: _____

FIGURE 25-6, cont'd

explain that I have a meeting or another patient to assist, they are very understanding and not offended. Perhaps you can try that approach, too."

Peer Evaluations

Some innovative companies use peer evaluations of employees to get a different view of the work performed by a worker. Asking co-workers to assist in the evaluation process can promote teamwork and cooperation. The rare employee offers a poor evaluation because of a personal problem with another staff member, but for the most part, employees provide fair, unbiased evaluations, knowing that they also will be evaluated when it is their turn.

A process known as a *360-degree evaluation* is an excellent tool for evaluating any employee, including managers. Such evaluations usually consist of a questionnaire that is given to those who work closely with the employee, and they provide input about the employee's performance.

Poor Evaluations Made Easier

No supervisor enjoys giving an evaluation that is not a positive one. It is difficult to know where to begin when the employee has not performed as expected or hoped. Perhaps the best way to open the conversation is to say, "Rebecca, your review today is not going to be a positive one. It seems that we do not have a meeting of the minds about your duties and our expectations of you. Let's talk about your performance and discuss whether this position is a good match for you."

The manager should have good documentation of the problems that led to the poor evaluation. If so, these can be reviewed with the employee with specific times, dates, and descriptions of incidents. If the manager does not document these issues, the conversation can become an argument and grow quite heated. Firm dates and times leave little room for argument and place the manager on the offensive. The employee may be apprehensive or even defensive at this point, but the phrasing will certainly get his or her attention, and the discussion should produce either the motivation to improve or the clarity that termination is in order.

CRITICAL THINKING APPLICATION 25-8

While Katherine is explaining to a particularly poor employee why Katherine plans to terminate her, the employee begins screaming and accusing Katherine of discrimination and harassment. How should Katherine handle this situation? What are Katherine's options if the employee does not stop the inappropriate behavior?

Terminating Employees

Dismissing an employee is unpleasant at best, but if the ground rules are decided in advance, written into the policy manual, and explained to all employees, the problem is partially solved. The policies must be applied equally and impartially to all. The final decision for dismissal probably will be made by the physician, but it may be based on the recommendation of the office manager or supervisor. Unless there are mitigating factors that suggest otherwise, the person who does the hiring should do the firing.

A probationary employee who does not prove satisfactory should be dismissed at the end of the probationary period, with tact and a full explanation of the reasons for dismissal. In all fairness, an individual should be told why the employment is being ended and not be given weak excuses or untruths that do not help correct deficiencies. If the manager is not straightforward in giving the reason for dismissal, the employee will not have the opportunity to grow and improve his or her performance.

An employee who has been in service for some time and is offering unsatisfactory performance should be warned and given an explanation of the specific improvements expected (Figure 25-7). If a second chance does not produce improvement in performance or attitude, dismissal must follow. It should be done privately, with tact and consideration.

Most practice consultants believe that firing should come close to the end of the day, after all other employees have left, and that the break should be clean and immediate. If the office policy provides for 2 weeks' notice when an employee resigns, the physician may want to offer 2 weeks' pay unless the circumstances that led to the dismissal were extremely **blatant**. A dismissed employee should never be allowed to train or influence a replacement.

The exit meeting should be planned just as carefully as the employment interview. Be honest with the employee. Discuss both the employee's assets and liabilities and give the reasons for the termination. There is no need to dwell on the employee's deficiencies. These should have been thoroughly discussed at the warning interview, and the employee need only be told that the necessary improvements have not been made. Do listen to the employee's feedback, unless it becomes lengthy or abusive. This may reveal some important administrative problems that need correction.

After dismissing an employee, do not leave that person in the office unattended. Request and get the office keys and any other equipment in the employee's possession immediately before the dismissed employee leaves the building. Most states have strict payday laws that do not allow holding the final paycheck for any reason. Do not offer to give the employee a good reference unless it can be done sincerely. If there is any indication that an employee may become abusive or violent once told about the termination, the supervisor should bring a representative from the Human Resources Department or Security to the final interview. It is possible that an employee can "snap" and suddenly become violent; however, more often it is the warning flags raised by an employee's behavior before termination that justify care in the termination interview. This is why supervisors must always document any strange or suspicious behavior and any breach of policy or procedures in the employee's personnel file. Documenting everything creates a clear picture of the employee's actions throughout the time of employment. The supervisor must be willing to confront an employee about his or her actions at the workplace. Document employee behavior as instructed in the office policy manual.

Certain breaches of conduct, such as **embezzlement**, insubordination, and violation of patient confidentiality, are grounds for immediate dismissal without warning.

Occasionally an employee voluntarily terminates a job without giving a valid reason. The physician or office manager may want to follow up with a letter to the former employee to determine whether a problem prompted the resignation. The employee may reveal

TERMINATION / REHIRE EVALUATION FORM

Employee Name_____ Social Security No._____

Department _____ Title _____

Termination Date _____

Reason for Termination: _____Resigned _____Laid Off_____Retired

Evaluation of Job Performance	Excellent	Very Good	Average	Poor	Unacceptable
Quality (accuracy, etc.)	☐	☐	☐	☐	☐
Quantity (productivity, consistency, etc.)	☐	☐	☐	☐	☐
Knowledge of Duties	☐	☐	☐	☐	☐
Reliability (absenteeism)	☐	☐	☐	☐	☐
Punctuality	☐	☐	☐	☐	☐
Ability to Cooperate with Co-workers	☐	☐	☐	☐	☐
Relationship with Patients	☐	☐	☐	☐	☐
Overall Attitude (willingness and commitment)	☐	☐	☐	☐	☐
Initiative	☐	☐	☐	☐	☐
Judgment	☐	☐	☐	☐	☐

Recommendation for Rehiring: _____

_____

_____

Comments:_____

_____

_____

_____

_____

_____

_____

_____

_____ Date _____

Supervisor's Signature

FORM # 72-123   PERSONNEL RECORDS ORGANIZING SYSTEMS • © 1987 BIBBERO SYSTEMS, INC. • PETALUMA, CA.
TO REORDER CALL TOLL FREE: (800) BIBBERO (800-242-2376) OR FAX (800) 242-9330   MFG IN U.S.A.

FIGURE 25-7 Termination form. Document the reasons for terminating an employee and make sure supporting documentation shows warnings and previous counseling efforts. (Courtesy Bibbero Systems, Petaluma, Calif.)

serious issues with other personnel or with the office that need to be addressed and corrected.

Fair Salaries and Raises

Medical office managers should recruit employees who will remain with the office for a long time. There are always situations when a part-time worker returns to college, or someone working during the summer months goes back to school. However, good employee **retention** is the goal.

To keep good employees, the practice must pay them a fair salary with regular raises if they perform as expected. The office manager can find information about salary comparisons on the Internet. Check the job duties and descriptions found on the Web and see whether the salary the medical facility offers is comparable to that for similar jobs in the area.

Merit raises are increases based on an employee's commendable performance. Cost of living increases are given when earned, usually after specific periods or annually, and are based on national statistics and trends. An employee who is promoted should also be awarded a salary increase. When the office pays a fair salary for work done, the physician retains happy employees.

STAFF MEETINGS

Some formal mechanism must be used to keep the office manager and other key employees current on the daily business affairs of the practice. One of the most common complaints from office personnel is that they are unable to discuss problems with the physician. The solution to this problem may be to hold regular staff meetings, which may be scheduled as frequently as weekly but should be held no less often than quarterly (Figure 25-8). Some of the best ideas on improvement come from the office staff; the expression and exchange of good ideas should be encouraged.

Set aside a specific time for regular meetings at an hour when the most people can attend with the least disruption (Procedure 25-3). The meetings need not be long or overly formal, but to be effective, they must be planned and organized. There must be a leader, and someone should be appointed to take notes. The effectiveness of the leader, a person who can balance firmness with fairness, is an important aspect of the meeting. This usually is either the physician or the office manager or supervisor. All members of the staff should be encouraged to submit ideas for discussion.

Draw up a simple **agenda** listing the issues to be discussed and prepare any supporting data needed for the meeting. There are many kinds of staff meetings. They may be purely informational,

FIGURE 25-8 Periodic staff meetings are important tools for improving communication and resolving problems.

problem-solving, or brainstorming meetings. They may be work sessions for updating manuals, training seminars, or whatever is necessary to the individual practice. Meetings also may be scheduled to discuss new ideas and any changes in office procedures. Some meetings are held simply to resolve specific problems. The staff meeting must not be allowed to deteriorate into a gripe session. Individual complaints should be handled privately.

The meeting agenda might be similar to that of any business meeting:

1. Reading of the last meeting's minutes
2. Discussion of any unfinished business
3. Discussion of any problems in the clinical area
4. Discussion of any problems in the administrative area
5. Discussion of any problems in common areas
6. Adjournment

Some physicians like to combine the staff meeting with a breakfast or lunch. The time or place is not important as long as it is neutral and meets the needs of the practice. Meetings should be conducted regularly, democratically, and without interruption. Always follow up on the items discussed; otherwise, the only result will be frustration and a reluctance to discuss problems at future meetings.

SEEING THE WHOLE PICTURE

The office manager must keep a bird's-eye view on the office operations. He or she must look at the whole picture when difficulties arise. Remember, there are always two sides to every story, and there is usually truth intermingled with falsity. Do not form the habit of taking every word that an employee says as 100% accurate. This is not meant to suggest that all employees are not truthful, but rather to encourage the office manager to look at all sides before making critical decisions.

See issues from the employees' point of view. Try to understand their perspective when dealing with everyday situations in the medical facility. Do not become closed minded as a manager, unable to grasp what the employees see as important.

PROCEDURE 25-3

Arrange a Group Meeting

GOAL: *To plan and execute a productive meeting that will result in achieved goals and applied concepts for office procedures.*

EQUIPMENT and SUPPLIES

- Meeting room
- Agenda
- Visual aids and equipment
- Handouts
- Stopwatch or clock
- Computer or word processor
- Paper
- List of items for the agenda

PROCEDURAL STEPS

1. Determine the purpose of the meeting and draft a list of the items to be discussed. Include the desired results of the meeting.
   PURPOSE: To keep the focus on the issues at hand and make the meeting a productive one.
2. Determine where the meeting will be held, the time and date of the meeting, and the individuals who should attend.
   PURPOSE: To have the demographic information about the meeting on hand before posting a notice. Only necessary staff members should attend so that those not directly involved in the issues to be discussed can continue their regular duties.
3. Send a memo, e-mail, or letter at least 10 days in advance, if possible, to the individuals who should attend the meeting. Send a copy to any supervisors who should be kept informed about the issues to be raised in the meeting.
   PURPOSE: To allow for rescheduling if the key personnel cannot attend on the originally planned time and date; also to keep managers informed of important details in areas for which they are ultimately responsible.
4. Be sure that the notice includes the following information:
   - Date
   - Time
   - Place
   - Directions (if not held in a common meeting room or if held away from the office)
   - Speakers and/or meeting topics
   - Cost and registration information, if applicable
   - List of items individuals should bring to the meeting
   PURPOSE: To fully inform those who should attend the meeting of the demographic information and their responsibilities.
5. Finalize the list of items to discuss and place them in priority order.
   PURPOSE: To keep the focus of the meeting on the issues at hand and to avoid discussion of nonrelated items; also to make sure the time spent in the meeting is productive for all involved.
6. Delegate any tasks that others can accomplish and follow up to be sure they fulfill their duties before the meeting.
   PURPOSE: To ensure that all needed information and items are available for the meeting.
7. Assign a staff member to take notes and keep time during the meeting.
   PURPOSE: To have notes so that a permanent record of what was discussed and the decisions made can be written after the meeting.
8. Make a list of all items that need to be taken to the meeting, including equipment such as microphones, projectors, screens, computers, disks containing presentations, and so on.
   PURPOSE: To be fully prepared and to have all needed items in place during the meeting.
9. Compile the final agenda for the meeting.
10. On the meeting day, transport all necessary items to the meeting room. Begin and end the meeting on time. Stay on track and follow the agenda.
    PURPOSE: Following the plan and showing consideration for the time staff members devote to meetings can promote a positive attitude for meetings and encourage group participation.
11. Follow up whenever necessary on items discussed in the meetings. Distribute a synopsis of the meeting to all the individuals who attended and keep a copy in a binder or folder.
    PURPOSE: To keep a permanent record of the meeting and the items discussed and decided.

OFFICE MANAGEMENT TOOLS

Patient Information Booklet

Only a very small percentage of practices have a booklet that explains the information basic to the operational and service aspects of the practice. Yet, the physician and staff can easily compile a patient information booklet cooperatively during a staff meeting. Experience has shown that if such a booklet is given to every new patient, the number of incoming telephone calls can be reduced by an average of 20% to 30%. It also can reduce misunderstandings and forgotten instructions. The booklet must be tailored to the specific practice.

The patient information booklet should be an introduction to the practice. If possible, it should be mailed to a new patient before the first visit. A supply also may be left with referring physicians' offices to be given to patients coming to your office. It should be designed to fit easily into a No. 10 business envelope. The cover should show the name of the practice, its location, and the practice logo, if there is one. Consider using a photograph of the medical building for easy identification by the new patient and a map to the office. Many offices save the booklet as a .pdf file so that it can be emailed to the patient.

A statement of philosophy frequently is included in the introduction, followed by a description of the practice. For example:

The doctors and staff would like to welcome you to our office. We work as a team with the goal of providing prompt and thorough care for your problems. We are always working to improve our care and service in any way possible. Our practice is limited exclusively to the musculoskeletal system and its disorders. Therefore, it is important for each patient to have a primary care physician, such as a pediatrician, a family physician, or an internist, to oversee the patient's primary medical care. Our role is most effective as a consultant to your primary care physician.

Describe the office policy regarding appointments and cancellations, telephone calls, and the function of the answering service. If a separate business telephone line is available, make sure to include this information. For example:

This office has two receptionists available to answer telephone calls during regular office hours. The office is very busy, and occasionally you will be asked to hold for a brief period. Please be patient with this. If you want to speak to a doctor, your call usually will be returned during the next available break period or at the end of the office day. We receive many calls during the day, and it is unfair to the patients who have scheduled appointments to interrupt the doctor continually for telephone calls. Therefore, the receptionist usually will take a message, and your call will be returned as soon as possible. Please inform the receptionist if your problem is urgent, and she will let the doctor know this.

Describe any **ancillary** or laboratory services provided, how test results are reported, and your policy on prescription renewals. Patients need to know the provisions for emergency procedures: What hospitals does the practice use regularly? What is the night and weekend coverage? Hospitalization procedures and postoperative care and follow-up may also be included:

One of the doctors in the group is always on call for emergencies. You may reach him or her by calling our office telephone number (714) 555-2323; the answering service will put you in touch with the doctor on call at that time. Our doctors are on staff at St. Joseph Hospital (714) 555-3333, and for children, Children's Hospital of Orange County (714) 555-4444. In case of emergency, call 911.

List all physicians in the practice; state their educational backgrounds, training, and board certifications; and define their specialties. List the names of key clinical and administrative staff members, such as registered nurses and nurse practitioners, medical assistants, the office manager, and the business manager. Provide the practice address, a map of how to get there, and information about the parking facilities.

Do not just stack these folders in the reception room for patients to pick up. Have the receptionist write the patient's name on the folder, hand it to the patient when he or she registers for the first appointment, and suggest that the patient keep it for future reference.

Financial Policy Folder

A separate, small folder covering the financial policies of the office can eliminate many questions and possible misunderstandings. Tailor the financial policy folder to the specific practice. Keep it small enough to fit into the billing envelope and send it out with the first monthly statement. If the practice sends out a welcome package before the patient's first visit, include the financial policy folder. Otherwise, present one at the first visit.

Spell out policies regarding billing and collection procedures and make it clear that patients are responsible for the uninsured portion of the fees. If payment is expected at the time of service, put this in the folder. Keep the language simple and straightforward so that the message is clear:

We ask that our services be paid for at the time they are rendered. You will be provided with an encounter form so that you may bill your insurance company and be reimbursed for services paid at the time of your visit. Simply attach the encounter form to your insurance form and mail it to the insurance company. The appropriate diagnoses and charges will be on the encounter form. There is usually a greater charge for the initial visit, because this involves more time than follow-up visits. If you are sent to an outside office for laboratory testing or special x-ray procedures, you will be billed separately by that office. We will be available to help if special circumstances arise involving difficulty with forms or receiving reimbursement. We will bill your insurance if you have a special situation such as surgery, prepaid health plans, Medicaid, or Senior Savers. We will complete disability papers as promptly as possible. However, you must obtain the necessary forms from your employer or the disability office.

The financial policy folder should also clearly state that the ultimate responsibility for payment lies with the patient.

Patient Instruction Sheets

In most medical offices, some patient procedures are performed over and over again. Instead of attempting to instruct a patient orally each time, why not develop clearly stated instruction sheets that can be reviewed with the patient and then give the patient the written instructions to take home? The following are some suggestions for patient instruction sheets:

- Preparation for an x-ray procedure or laboratory tests
- Preoperative and postoperative instructions
- Diet sheets
- Performing an enema
- Dressing a wound
- Taking medications
- Using a cane, crutches, walker, or wheelchair
- Care of casts
- Exercise therapy

MEDICAL PRACTICE ACTS

Medical practice acts existed as early as colonial days. However, these acts were later repealed, and in the mid-nineteenth century, practically none of the states had laws governing the practice of medicine. As one might expect, a rapid decline in professional standards followed. The general welfare of the people was endangered by medical **quackery** and inadequate care. By the beginning of the twentieth century, medical practice acts were established by statute and were again in effect in every state. The purpose of the medical practice acts is to:

- Define what is included in the practice of medicine in that state

- Govern the methods and requirements of licensure
- Establish the grounds for suspension or revocation of license

All physicians' offices must follow the laws and regulations set forth by the city and state where the practice is located (see Procedure 7-5). Medical assistants are required to report situations in which the law is being broken or that may lead to harm to another person, including the patient (see Procedure 7-6). However, before taking action that could do irreparable harm to another person's character, verify the facts and follow the facility's chain of command.

PHYSICIAN LICENSURE AND REGISTRATION

A graduate of a medical school must be licensed before beginning the practice of medicine. Licensure is regulated by state statutes through the Medical Practice Acts. It is important for a medical assistant to understand licensing and other laws and regulations intended to protect patients, physicians, medical assistants, and other healthcare workers.

Licensure

A Doctor of Medicine (MD), Doctor of Osteopathy (DO), or Doctor of Chiropractic (DC) degree is conferred upon graduation from a medical or chiropractic school. The license to practice medicine or chiropractic is granted by a state board, frequently known as the State Board of Medical Examiners or Board of Registration. Licensure may be accomplished by examination, reciprocity, or endorsement.

Examination

Every state requires medical doctors to pass a written examination. The Federation of State Medical Boards and the National Board of Medical Examiners agreed in 1990 to establish a single licensing examination, the Federation Licensing Examination (FLEX), for graduates of accredited medical schools. Medical graduates in the United States must pass the FLEX examination, the U.S. Medical Licensing Examination (USMLE), or the National Board of Medical Examiners' Examination (NBME). Osteopathic physicians pass the National Board of Osteopathic Medical Examiners' Comprehensive Osteopathic Medical Licensing Examination (COMLEX).

Reciprocity

Some states grant the license to practice medicine by *reciprocity*; that is, they automatically recognize that the requirements of the state in which the license was granted meet their standards.

Endorsement

Most graduates of medical schools in the United States have been licensed by endorsement of the National Board certificate. In simpler terms, a state offers a license to a physician based on the examinations taken to grant the license, not by virtue of the license granted from another state. Licensure by endorsement is granted on a case-by-case basis. Graduates who have not been licensed by endorsement are required to pass a state board examination.

In all states, graduates of foreign medical schools who are seeking licensure by endorsement must meet the same requirements as graduates of medical schools in the United States, in addition to various other qualifying factors.

Exemptions

Some graduates may not want to engage in the practice of medicine; their interests may lie in research, administration, or even in the practice of law with a special interest in medical liability. In such instances, licensure is not required. Licensed physicians in the Armed Forces, Public Health Service, and Veterans Affairs facilities need not be licensed in the state in which they are employed. However, the Department of Defense is encouraging states to require full licensure of military personnel.

Registration and Reregistration

After a license has been granted, reregistration is required annually or biennially. A physician can be *concurrently* registered in more than one state. The issuing body notifies the physician when reregistration is due. A medical assistant can aid the physician by being aware of when the registration fees are due, preventing a possible lapsing of the registration.

Many states require proof of continuing education in addition to payment of a registration fee. CEUs are granted to physicians for attending approved seminars, lectures, scientific meetings, and formal courses in accredited colleges and universities. A total of 50 hours per year is the average requirement for a license renewal. A medical assistant may be expected to help the physician arrange to complete the required units for license renewal.

Revocation or Suspension

Under certain conditions, the license to practice medicine may be revoked or suspended. Grounds for revocation or suspension of the license to practice medicine fall within one of three categories:

- *Conviction of a crime:* This may include felonies (e.g., murder, rape, larceny) and narcotics violations.
- *Unprofessional conduct:* Failure to uphold the ethical standards of the medical profession may be indicated by betrayal of patient confidence, giving or receiving rebates, and excessive use of narcotics or alcohol.
- *Personal or professional incapacity:* Such incapacity is difficult to label or prove. For example, advanced age or an injury may reduce the apparent capacity of some physicians. Certain illnesses can affect the memory or judgment necessary to practice medicine.

A physician studies many years to learn the profession before becoming licensed by the state to practice medicine. A medical assistant is not licensed to practice medicine and must never prescribe or attempt to diagnose a patient's ailment; this is the illegal practice of medicine. For this reason, a medical assistant must use great care in discussing patients' complaints and treatment with them, because patients identify the medical assistant's remarks as being the opinion of the physician.

CLOSING COMMENTS

Successful office managers care about their employees and the vision for the office. They must be strong promoters of the office mission statement. The areas of authority and responsibility must be clearly defined to prevent management problems. A solid office policy and procedures manual helps the office manager to run an efficient office.

Leadership is an important quality for any manager, and the medical office manager is no exception. The manager should develop good leadership skills, be fair and open minded, and treat employees and patients as he or she would want to be treated. These actions help ensure a pleasant, productive working environment.

Patient Education

Educate patients in the policies and procedures of the office by providing patient information folders or brochures. When these documents are prepared and given to patients formally, the patient is better informed and fewer calls come to the office.

Legal and Ethical Issues

Office managers must stay abreast of current employment laws and regulations for all the different agencies that govern the medical office. Joining an office manager's association helps the manager keep the office up-to-date and in compliance. Periodic checks on the Web sites of various organizations, such as OSHA, also help the manager stay aware of the most recent changes in policies and rules.

Documentation is a critical aspect of the office manager's duties. The manager should keep detailed notes on the performance of employees and always discuss poor performance with employees. Never allow bad habits to go unmentioned. To the extent that it is possible, treat employees in a similar fashion and extend fairness to all.

SUMMARY OF SCENARIO

Katherine has had an effect on all the staff members at Dr. Collins's office. She treats her employees well and is fair about office policies and procedures. Her subordinates appreciate her flexibility and professionalism as she deals with the many issues surrounding the operation of a medical office. Katherine treats the employees as team members, never speaking to them as if she were superior to them. She shares vital information with the staff so that they feel a part of the whole team, and she believes that even some negative information should be related to the staff so that everyone is aware of the challenges the office faces. She makes good hiring decisions and firmly believes in a good orientation and training program. Dr. Collins has placed a great deal of trust in Katherine, and she has performed well, proving to be reliable in her position as office manager.

Katherine knows that she should display a friendly attitude toward her staff members when appropriate to do so. She is kind and considerate and treats the staff as individuals. She does not fraternize with them but is open to having lunch with the staff at various times and participates in all casual office activities. She maintains a healthy distance so that she can be an effective manager, but she listens to those who are experiencing difficulty and is compassionate about helping whenever possible.

Katherine knows that she must be diligent in checking references so that she brings reliable, qualified individuals on board as staff members. Unless she receives acceptable references, she will not hire a medical assistant to become a part of her team. Once she hires someone, she conducts a thorough training program and takes special care to share the experience and skills of the new staff member with the rest of the team.

When Katherine must give a negative employee evaluation, she states that fact at the beginning of their meeting. Although she is compassionate, she is able to point out a staff member's shortcomings in a detailed, fair way. She usually is willing to give an employee time to improve, but if he or she fails to perform, Katherine does not hesitate to end the employment.

Katherine uses patient information folders as management tools. She has instructed her staff to explain the folders to patients fully and to tell them about the information in them. Because the staff takes the time to review the folders with patients, calls to the office have been reduced and the staff believes that patients are much more informed. They understand office policies much better, and the staff finds that they repeat basic information much less frequently. Katherine heads a cooperative team that functions well together every day, making the office efficient and the work environment a pleasant one of which to be a part.

SUMMARY OF LEARNING OBJECTIVES

1. **Define, spell, and pronounce the terms listed in the vocabulary.**
   Spelling and pronouncing medical terms correctly bolster the medical assistant's credibility. Knowing the definition of these terms promotes confidence in communication with patients and co-workers.

2. **Explain the importance of management in the medical office.**
   The physician counts on the office manager to run the business aspects of the office so that he or she can focus efforts on good patient care. A high degree of trust is placed in the office manager.

3. **Discuss the desirable qualities of a medical office manager.**
   A good office manager is fair and flexible. Good communications skills are necessary, as is attention to details. The manager should care about the employees and have a sense of fairness. The ability to remain calm in a crisis is important, as are the use of good judgment and the ability to multitask.

4. **List and discuss the three types of leaders.**
   Charismatic leaders inspire allegiance and dedication and encourage individuals to overcome great obstacles. *Transactional leaders* are structured, organized, hardworking, and planners. *Transformational leaders* are excellent during times of transition and effective at building relationships.

5. **Discuss several types of power and whether power is a positive or negative entity.**

Power can be both a positive and a negative entity. Power should not be used in a manipulative or coercive manner. *Expert power* is based on a high degree of knowledge about a certain subject. The use of rewards is a way of invoking power, and *legitimate power* is that of position or status. *Referent power* is granted from subordinates to those who lead by example.

6. **Identify several ways in which employees are motivated.**

   Employees are motivated by various factors, including money, praise, insecurity, honor, prestige, needs, love, fear, satisfaction, and many others. An effective manager attempts to discover what motivates employees to do a good job.

7. **Explain the difference between intrinsic and extrinsic motivation.**

   Intrinsic motivation comes from within the employee. Extrinsic motivation has an outside source.

8. **List several ways to prevent burnout.**

   Asking for help, first and foremost, can prevent burnout. Managers often take on too many duties and do not delegate as much as they should. Exercise and rest help prevent burnout, as does understanding one's personal limitations. Focused goals are important and help keep the manager working toward the most critical tasks.

9. **Discuss what to look for when reviewing resumés and applications.**

   Resumés and applications should be reviewed for accuracy and completeness. Gaps in employment dates should be explained fully, and the office manager should verify any references given. Documents should be legible, and the information should be consistent and without oversights.

10. **Explain why the telephone voice of an applicant is important.**

    The telephone voice of an applicant is important because most employees have occasion to answer the telephone while at work. The employee's voice should be clear and easily understandable. Good grammar skills must be used to reflect a professional image.

11. **List and discuss legal and illegal interview questions.**

    Title VII of the Civil Rights Act of 1964, as amended by the Equal Employment Opportunity Act of 1972, prohibits inquiries into an applicant's race, color, gender, religion, and national origin. Inquiries regarding medical history, arrest records, or previous drug use also are illegal. Most states have laws designed to protect the rights of job applicants, and these laws may impose additional restrictions. Office managers must research the laws that pertain to employment in their own states.

12. **Identify the follow-up activities the office manager should perform after an interview.**

    After interviewing a prospective candidate, the office manager should verify the facts on the resumé and application and check several references. A comparison should be made between the candidates and the top two or three chosen for a possible second interview. It is wise to involve other staff members when choosing new employees for the office.

13. **Explain the importance of mentors for new employees in the medical office.**

    Mentors help new employees by offering information about policies and procedures. The mentor can be an advocate that the new employee can approach when questions arise about any aspect of the medical office.

14. **Describe how to conduct a performance review for an employee.**

    Performance reviews can be productive, positive experiences, or they can lead to termination of employment. The process for conducting a performance review is outlined in Procedure 25-2.

15. **List the various types of staff meetings.**

    Staff meetings may be held to relay information, solve a problem, or brainstorm ideas. Some meetings are designed as work sessions, whereas others may be scheduled to discuss new policies or changes in procedures.

16. **Explain how to arrange a group meeting.**

    Meetings will be held on at least a monthly basis in most physicians' offices. The process for arranging a group meeting is outlined in Procedure 25-3.

CONNECTIONS

📖 **Study Guide Connection:** Go to the Chapter 25 Study Guide. Read and complete the activities.

⊖ **Evolve Connection:** Go to the Chapter 25 link at *evolve.elsevier.com/kinn* to complete the Chapter Review and Chapter Quiz. Check out the other resources listed for this chapter to make the most of what you have learned from Medical Practice Management and Human Resources.

MEDICAL PRACTICE MARKETING AND CUSTOMER SERVICE

26

SCENARIO

Monica Ray is a medical assistant who is also pursuing a bachelor's degree in marketing. She has worked for Dr. Julie Todd and Dr. Robert Todd for 2 years. Based on her career interests, the physicians have agreed to allow her to develop some new marketing strategies for their obstetrics and gynecology office. Because medical facilities are now so competitive, Monica knows that any physician who wants growth in the practice must market his or her services to the public. Also, physicians cannot depend only on insurance reimbursements to provide them a strong income through the life of the practice. Today, physicians must market themselves and their services to the public to ensure practice growth.

Monica is highly computer literate and can design Web pages. She plans to incorporate several ideas she found on other physicians' Web sites, including a method of online scheduling. She is also aware of the importance of social networking and wants to create a brand for the clinic using resources such as Facebook, Twitter, and YouTube. She is quite creative and is excited about the challenge of providing such a service to the patients of the clinic and about growing the patient base using social networking. Monica knows that planning is involved in any project, including creating the facility's Internet presence. She plans to speak to every employee of the office to get input regarding the design and content of the site. Patients will be able to provide her with additional suggestions on features they would like to see.

This new development for the office is just one way Monica hopes to incorporate more formal customer service techniques. She plans to share the information she is learning in the classroom with the physicians and staff at the clinic. Monica and the physicians are fortunate that the staff is enthusiastic and eager to try new methods of customer service; often employees are highly resistant to new techniques. The physicians will set specific goals with the help of the employees and devise a reward system for reaching them. An exciting few months are ahead for this innovative group of medical professionals!

While studying this chapter, think about the following questions:

- How important is an Internet presence to today's medical office?
- Why has "customer service" become a buzzword in the medical industry?
- How can social networking grow the practice patient base?
- Which is more important: the internal customer or the external customer?

LEARNING OBJECTIVES

1. Define, spell, and pronounce the terms listed in the vocabulary.
2. List the four steps to follow when preparing to implement a medical marketing strategy.
3. Explain the term *target market*.
4. Discuss how suggestion boxes might help the medical facility make improvements.
5. List and discuss the four Ps of marketing.
6. Explain the five steps for developing a plan in marketing.
7. Discuss how community involvement can make a difference in marketing efforts.
8. State the difference between advertising and public relations.
9. Determine ways to promote a new practice.
10. Prepare a presentation using PowerPoint.
11. Discuss applications of electronic technology in effective communication.
12. Organize technical information and summaries.
13. Discuss responses that help the medical assistant identify with the patient.
14. Explain the concept of the internal customer.
15. Design a presentation for a marketing event.
16. Locate resources and information for patients and employers.
17. Advocate on behalf of the patient and family and be able to deal and communicate with family members.

VOCABULARY

branding The process involved in creating a unique name and image in the customer's mind, mainly through advertising campaigns with a consistent theme.

marketing The process or technique of promoting, selling, and distributing a product or service.

objective Something toward which effort is directed; aim, goal, or purpose of action.

outreach The process of using marketing and education strategies to reach and involve diverse audiences through the use of key messages and effective programs.

prosthetic (prohs-thet′-ik) The surgical or dental specialty concerned with the design, construction, and fitting of prostheses, which are artificial devices that replace missing parts of the body.

tangible (tan′-juh-buhl) Capable of being appraised at an actual or approximate value; capable of being precisely identified or realized by the mind.

target market A specific group of individuals toward whom the marketing plan is focused.

Each medical office needs a mission statement that defines the reason for its existence. The physician's philosophy of medicine and reasons for pursing medicine as a career greatly influence the mission statement. With this statement in place, the staff can develop goals that will assist them in meeting the mission. The goals can be met through a **marketing** and **outreach** plan for the practice and by providing excellent customer service to patients and visitors to the facility.

DEVELOPING MARKETING STRATEGIES

If a business is to grow, marketing strategies are critical. A marketing strategy is designed to promote the services offered by the organization and encourage new business. Four steps are generally followed when preparing to implement or change medical marketing strategies:

1. Assess what has been done in the past.
2. Evaluate what is being done now to increase patient flow.
3. Decide what objectives are important and how meeting these objectives will be measured.
4. Develop a plan with various means of marketing the practice and a specific methodology for implementing each phase.

CRITICAL THINKING APPLICATION   26-1

Monica knows that the office has never attempted any formal marketing in the past. Because no one at her office is familiar with this task, who might she contact for advice and assistance?

■ Even though her fellow staff members are not familiar with marketing, could they provide workable ideas?

■ What are some ideas for marketing a medical practice?

Branding

The concept of **branding** is fairly new to the medical profession. Branding, applied to the physician's office, is the process involved in creating a unique concept or image that customers think of in association with the practice. Branding aims to establish a significant and differentiated presence in the market that attracts and retains loyal customers. This can be accomplished using a name, logo, tagline, catch-phrase, symbol, or design that makes your organization distinct and unique among others. A brand is a valuable element in a marketing campaign. The art of creating and maintaining a brand in the marketplace is called *brand management*. Global brands include Facebook, Apple, FedEx, and MasterCard; people all over the world recognize those brands. A local brand is one that is marketed in a small geographic area; for example, the Baylor Health Care System in Texas uses a distinct blue color on its Web sites, and its logo includes a flame symbol, easily identifying any Baylor facility throughout the area.

Branding helps the medical practice to stand out, ideally as a trusted authority in healthcare. Additionally, the physician can attract the types of cases that he or she is most interested in through branding; if the physician is interested in fibromyalgia, diabetes, or any other specific disease or condition, it may be incorporated into the practice through branding. The practice might use a tag line after the clinic name, such as:

Woodridge Clinic: The Diabetes Center
San Jose Family Practice: Caring for Each Family Member

The market climate has shifted to a highly competitive environment, and many physicians are forced to market their practice to gain any part of the local market share. Without a reasonably full schedule of patients, the physician cannot cover the costs of running the practice, and the business may not survive. The medical assistant can play a role in practice branding by following office procedures, treating patients with excellent customer service skills, and keeping a positive, enthusiastic attitude during every workday and with every patient.

SEVEN REASONS TO BRAND A MEDICAL PRACTICE

1. People prefer to buy brands, because they reduce perceived risk.
2. People buy brands for status.
3. People refer more often and more passionately to a brand that they like and trust.
4. You can build and accelerate your reputation through branding.
5. You can attract more of the cases you like through branding.
6. Branding will give you a competitive advantage.
7. A branded practice will be worth more than a nonbranded practice.

Knowing the Target Market

During the strategic phase of developing a marketing plan, the physician and office manager must identify the **target market** for the services provided by the clinic. The target market is the group or groups of individuals the office wants to reach. Reaching the target market means that the specific groups are made aware of the clinic and what it has to offer. With managed care restrictions and regulations, competition for patients has become keen among physicians, and a facility that does not pursue growth runs a great risk of not surviving.

Answer the following questions when considering the target market:

- What specific outcomes do we hope to accomplish?
- What are the needs and desires of our target market?
- What are the characteristics of a typical member of the target market?
- How can the target market be reached in the most cost-effective ways?

Staff meetings are excellent times to brainstorm about reaching target markets. The staff can explain the needs of the patients who are active at the medical office. If patients have made suggestions, they should be discussed and weighed with regard to which would benefit the patient population of the facility (Figure 26-1).

> ### CRITICAL THINKING APPLICATION 26-2
> What community resources could Monica seek as she is determining the target market of the practice? What information does she need to begin her search?

Suggestion boxes are a great way to solicit patient input. Ask patients for ideas about how the clinic could operate more smoothly and what additional services they would like to see introduced. Check the suggestion box frequently. If the patient leaves his or her name on the suggestion form, a good customer service tactic is to reward the patient for the suggestion. Mail the individual a coupon for a free lunch at a local restaurant or a free car wash at a local

detailing shop. Involving other businesses in marketing efforts helps both attract new customers. Businesses in a central location, such as a strip mall, can work together to refer customers to each other.

Ethics, Marketing, and Public Relations

Not many years ago, advertising about the physician and his services was considered completely unethical. However, today's healthcare industry is highly competitive, and advertising is no longer considered unethical. Because competition for patients is so great, medical assistants who work in physicians' offices must use some marketing techniques to get new patients and keep the ones already coming to the clinic. This practice may not seem "right" to some employees, but the healthcare industry has changed over the past few decades, and physicians must invite change to be competitive. After all, the medical office is still a business. The goal of any business is to make money so that the owners can pay business costs and make a reasonable profit and employees can earn a healthy wage with which to support their own families.

The Four Ps

The four Ps of marketing are product, placement, price, and promotion. A physician's office offers medical services as a product. Some offices have **tangible** retail products that they also offer, such as vitamins, skin-sensitive cosmetics, or **prosthetic** devices. Placement involves the actual location of the medical office. The office may be located in an urban area close to large neighborhoods of young professionals or in a rural area with a few people living several miles apart. Placement can greatly influence the traffic to the facility. Placement also can refer to the setup of the office, the specific suite in a shopping strip where the office is located, or even the placement of retail objects on a shelf. Price is simply the amount of money charged for goods and services provided. Promotion refers to the methods used to get the product or services to the consumers (or, in the case of the medical office, to patients).

> ### CRITICAL THINKING APPLICATION 26-3
> - How can Monica investigate the charges for similar procedures at other clinics in her area?
> - Why is this information important to Monica?

Deciding What Services to Offer

Once the physician and office manager have identified the target market, decisions can be made about the services that should be offered to patients. For instance, suppose the office is situated in a neighborhood of young families. Both parents are very likely to work outside the home, so evening hours would be beneficial to these patients. The physician may decide to extend office hours to 8 PM twice a week and to open from 9 AM to noon on Saturdays. If several schools are in the area, particularly junior high and high schools, the physician may want to offer a special price on sports physicals during the fall. Because these physicals are required, if the physician offers them at a reasonable price, the entire family may decide to seek medical care from the physician.

FIGURE 26-1 Friendly staff members are the best marketing tools. A smile is an excellent way to make patients feel welcome in the medical facility.

FIGURE 26-2 Offer services that are important in the geographic area of the office. College students may need to see a physician for minor illnesses, and they appreciate offices that provide short office visits for a reasonable fee.

If the office is located in a college town, the physician may want to offer a special student rate for short office visits (Figure 26-2). If a number of older adults live in the area, a senior citizen discount might be appropriate. Input from patients and staff members is valuable in determining what services to offer in the medical facility.

Developing a Plan for Marketing

The facility may use several specific planning steps for events, marketing strategies, and any number of other ideas the physician would like to implement. These steps are:

- Assessment
- Research
- Planning
- Execution
- Evaluation

Assessment is the phase of planning in which the problem or goals are reviewed. This is another excellent time for brainstorming. Research allows the physician or office manager to investigate the needs of the target market and then decide what the medical office can do to meet those needs. Planning of the concept follows, and once a firm plan is in place, it is executed, or carried out. Afterward, the participants evaluate what went well and what problems occurred so that future efforts will be even more successful.

Try this simple assessment tool, which will help clarify the patient population: Keep a log of all patients for a specific period; include the reason for the visit; the patient's age, ZIP code, gender, and marital status; and the number and ages of children. These simple demographics can provide a great base picture of the types of individuals using the physician's services.

PROMOTING THE PRACTICE

The physician and office manager should constantly watch for ways to promote the medical practice and keep its name in the public eye. Some of these methods are free, whereas others require detailed budgeting and planning.

The physician can allot a large portion of the practice budget to advertising and promotional costs. Some clinics publish a health-related magazine and mail it or send it electronically to their patient base. Magazine and newspaper ads can be effective tools, but finding free sources to promote the practice eases the budget and will allow expansion in other areas.

Tapping into Free Community Resources

By becoming a member of various civic organizations, such as the Chamber of Commerce, the practice will receive notice of upcoming events and should plan to participate in them regularly. The more the public sees the physician in the community, the more likely this will affect the growth of the practice. Many good promotional activities are relatively free to the physician. Some newspapers offer an advice column in which different types of professionals give general medical advice to those who write in with questions. Physicians volunteer to answer these questions in print, and in return the office address, the office telephone number, and often the physicians' pictures are featured. This is an excellent way to generate patient calls and inform the public about the specialties and types of cases the physician handles.

CRITICAL THINKING APPLICATION   26-4

- Monica knows there are many opportunities and free resources in her area. Where should she begin to look?
- How might Monica's clinic partner with other businesses and services to provide excellent care to patients and to help one another at the same time?

Getting involved in the local community is another way to promote a medical practice. Some physicians sponsor Little League football teams, baseball teams, or bowling leagues. Sometimes entire staffs participate in charity events and marathons, wearing T-shirts with the clinic name printed on the back.

The physician or staff may have specific charities they support annually, or they may participate in United Way activities, which distribute funds to many different types of worthy organizations through payroll deductions. Some medical facilities have volunteer programs in which employees receive recognition for participation in various activities. A good example is blood donations. Many blood centers offer pins and recognition certificates for the number of pints of blood volunteers donate. The office staff may set a goal to reach a certain number of donated pints in a year, and as recognition certificates are collected, the staff may want to display them in a prominent place in the office. This is an indication to patients that the staff is concerned about the community and is volunteer minded. From a public relations standpoint, this is valuable to the medical office, because patients tend to expect medical professionals to be volunteer oriented.

Health fairs are a great way to promote the services offered by the clinic, resulting in name recognition and increasing public visibility. Some health fairs are huge, highly publicized events, whereas others are small, often held at a local shopping mall or grocery store. All these events could be worthy projects for the physician and the medical office.

CRITICAL THINKING APPLICATION   26-5

- What community organizations might help Monica in her efforts to make the office an integral part of the community?
- What resources and community organizations are available in your area that would be good avenues for practice marketing and community service?

Advertising Plans and Agencies

Most physicians' offices do not use advertising agencies to promote their practices, but occasionally an agency might be useful. If the practice schedules or sponsors a very special event that needs extensive planning, a public relations firm or advertising agency might be consulted. Unfortunately, the cost of these groups usually is high and beyond the reach of sole practitioners or small group practices. However, the money may be well spent if the event is critical and attendance is important to its success.

There is a difference between advertising and public relations. Advertising involves creating or changing attitudes, beliefs, and perceptions by influencing people with purchased broadcast time, print space, or other forms of written and visual media. Broadcast time could take the form of television commercials, radio broadcasts, or audiovisual aids. Print could be in a newspaper, magazine, or trade journal, and written and visual media may be a flier, brochure, or billboard. Public relations is a similar field but relies more on news broadcasts or reports, magazine or newspaper articles, and radio reports to reach the audience. Most public relations efforts are free, but often it is difficult to get others interested enough in the activities the medical office is planning to warrant coverage.

Communication as a Marketing Tool

Many medical offices use communications tools to market the practice and improve customer service. Sending out a monthly newsletter by mail or electronically provides health information and news about upcoming events. The newsletter can be personalized for the office and might even include news about patients and the medical staff, as long as permission is obtained.

Sending birthday cards is an excellent public relations tool. Some offices sign the greetings at staff meetings, and they are placed in a tickler file for the proper mailing date. Consider sending holiday greetings to wish patients well.

Automated call distribution is becoming a popular means of communicating with large numbers of people. A computer dials multiple numbers at the same time and plays a recorded message, which can be the actual physician with news about a new procedure or new associate joining the practice. Although many people block such calls to their homes and an equal number hang up, the success rate for automatic call distribution is actually quite good. Many individuals listen and respond to the calls, especially if they come from someone they know and the information is important. For instance, if a medical clinic were planning to move to another part of the city, a program could be initiated to notify all patients with telephone numbers that the office will be moving after a certain date. The message could include the address of the new location and even prompt patients to "press 1" if they need to schedule an appointment. The same principle could be applied to news about an upcoming health fair, a special seminar about a certain illness, or even an article that will be in the Sunday paper about the clinic.

Promoting a New Practice

Most physicians who open a new practice place an ad in local newspapers to announce the event. Usually a picture of the physician is included, and a map to the exact location may be available on the ad. Some physicians purchase clinics from others who are moving or retiring, but many open a freestanding clinic in a new building, and the word about the new facility must be spread for the business to be a success.

Providing business cards for all employees is a good way to increase public knowledge about the facility. Some offices offer incentives for patient referrals from the staff or other patients, but the physician must ensure that no state statutes or ethical standards prohibit this practice. The incentive could be a simple coffee cup with the clinic's logo on it or a book about a healthcare issue. Recognition is the important factor where referrals are concerned. A thank you card is the minimal acceptable "thanks" for patient referrals.

Some physicians hold an open house when the new facility opens. Often, those individuals who assisted with the business from its inception attend the open house to lend support to the owners. Bankers, attorneys, accountants, and other physicians often show their support by attending the open house. Place pictures from this event on the facility's Web site, in the local newspaper, or in the monthly newsletter. Choose an employee who is a proficient writer and assign him or her the task of writing and sending press releases to media outlets when the physician or practice is involved with a newsworthy event.

Developing and Giving Presentations

Today's medical assistant should be comfortable when speaking in front of individuals and groups. By developing additional skills, the medical assistant increases his or her value to the physician. Developing and giving presentations is not difficult, although one of the most prevalent fears in the United States is the fear of speaking in public (Procedures 26-1 and 26-2).

There are many different types of speeches, but remember that all public speaking is persuasive. The speaker is attempting to get the audience to do something, whether to buy a new medical product or convince people to participate in a clinical trial. The speaker always has a purpose and must be credible to persuade listeners to act. Credibility underlies all persuasion. When the speaker is proficient at this art, the audience's questions are answered, their concerns addressed, and their needs fulfilled, while at the same time the speaker's goals are met. If the speaker does a good job, the audience feels satisfied after hearing a persuasive speech. Persuasion should be nonadversarial and gentle so that the audience feels comfortable in making a decision.

In his book, *Presenting to Win: The Art of Telling Your Story*, Jerry Weissman calls persuasion "audience advocacy," by which he means the ability to view the self, a company, a story, or a presentation through the eyes of the audience. Answer the question, "What's in it for me?" which the audience is constantly thinking. To motivate the audience, the speaker must do the following:

PROCEDURE 26-1

Design a Presentation

GOAL: *To gain skill in designing presentations that can be used for a variety of projects in the medical facility.*

EQUIPMENT and SUPPLIES

- Information about the presentation's subject
- Software (e.g., PowerPoint), if needed
- Computer access
- Peripheral computer equipment, if needed

PROCEDURAL STEPS

1. Determine the goals of the presentation.
   <u>PURPOSE:</u> The goals and purpose of the presentation must be determined before beginning so that the presenter is sure to reach those goals.
2. Write an outline of the entire presentation.
   <u>PURPOSE:</u> The outline helps the presenter prepare so that no important points are left out of the presentation.
3. Build the presentation using software (e.g., PowerPoint), highlighting the major points of the presentation.
4. Evaluate the audience and adjust the presentation to appeal to that audience.
   <u>PURPOSE:</u> The presenter must know the audience to ensure a successful presentation.

5. Rehearse the presentation several times in front of a mirror.
   <u>PURPOSE:</u> Rehearsing in front of a mirror builds confidence.
6. Make a list of all equipment and materials to take to the presentation.
   <u>PURPOSE:</u> A list helps the presenter remember all items that need to be taken to the presentation.
7. Arrive for the presentation 15 to 30 minutes early, depending on the preparation and setup required.
   <u>PURPOSE:</u> Arriving early gives the presenter the opportunity to set up the presentation before the audience arrives.
8. Deliver the presentation within the prescribed period.
9. Ask the audience whether anyone has any questions about the information in the presentation.
   <u>PURPOSE:</u> A question and answer period allows the presenter to interact with the audience.
10. Thank the audience and remove all equipment and supplies when appropriate.
11. Send a thank you note to the organization for allowing the presentation, if appropriate.

- Know the audience
- Research the audience to know their needs, what they care about, and what they want to know
- Link all presentation information to the audience's needs
- Know the purpose of the presentation
- Rehearse the presentation repeatedly

When designing the content of the presentation, keep the audience in mind and nail down the most important points that must be conveyed to them.

Overcoming Anxiety

Because the fear of public speaking is so common, the speaker must develop ways to overcome it and make a successful presentation. Find the actions that promote relaxation and practice them before giving a speech. Look for a sympathetic face in the audience, and speak directly to that person. Never begin a presentation with an apology of any type, such as, "I didn't have much time to prepare," or "I'm not very good at presentations." This undermines the authority of the speaker. Greeting as many of the guests as possible before the presentation helps to develop a rapport and may reduce anxiety. In addition, the guests feel welcome and special because the speaker took the time to make introductions.

During the Presentation

Make sure the audience can hear everything that is said. The presentation cannot be effective if it cannot be heard. Make all movements purposeful; if a hand gesture is used, make it and then relax the arms. Do not wander around the room. If moving from place to place, go to a spot and then stop. Constant movement distracts from the message of the presentation.

Most individuals speak faster when making a presentation, so slow the pace just a little. Speak so that all the people in the back of the room can hear, but not so loudly that the people in the front rows have to cover their ears. Possibly most important, remember to relax. The physical reactions felt before speaking, such as an increase in pulse rate and a rush of adrenaline, are natural. Do not allow negative thoughts to enter your mind. Instead, deal with fear by knowing the topic and being confident about the message.

PREPARING A PRESENTATION

Answer these important questions when preparing a presentation:
- Who is the audience?
- What are the key points?
- When is the presentation?
- How long is the presentation?
- What will the physical surroundings be?
- Why should the audience listen?
- How will the presentation be done?

PROCEDURE 26-2

Prepare a Presentation Using PowerPoint

GOAL: *To enhance presentations using PowerPoint as a visual aid.*

EQUIPMENT and SUPPLIES

- Information about the presentation's subject
- Software (e.g., PowerPoint), if needed
- Computer access
- Peripheral computer equipment, if needed

PROCEDURAL STEPS

1. Open the PowerPoint program.
2. Have the outline of the presentation available.
3. Click on the "new slide" icon in the program.
4. Create the title slide using the slide layout section on the right side of the screen.
5. Create additional slides using the slide layout section or design the slides manually.
6. Limit the number of words on the slides so that a concise message results.
   <u>PURPOSE:</u> Too many words on one slide make the message difficult to understand.
7. Make sure the font is as large as possible on the slide, beginning with a size 18 font and increasing from there.
   <u>PURPOSE:</u> The font on a presentation must be easy to read from the back of the room.
8. Do not use more than three font types per slide.
   <u>PURPOSE:</u> More than three font types makes the presentation difficult to read.
9. Avoid using more than three text-only slides in a row.
   <u>PURPOSE:</u> Use clip art, photographs, graphs, and other items to enhance the presentation.
10. Insert photos or clip art into the presentation by clicking on "Insert," then clicking on "Picture," then choosing "Clip art" or "From file."
11. Format the background of each slide, or of all slides, by clicking on "Format," then "Background," and then choose a color or fill effects.

<u>PURPOSE:</u> A consistent background makes the presentation look more professional.

12. Click on "Slide show" and adjust the slide transitions so that the slides appear and disappear as desired and are timed correctly.
13. Click on "Custom animation" to change the entrance and exit of the slides to the effect that is desired.
14. Save the presentation frequently while working on it.
    <u>PURPOSE:</u> Saving the presentation frequently ensures that the work will not be lost.
15. Click on "View" on the task bar, then on "Slide sorter," which allows the slides to be moved around in the presentation.
16. To run the show continuously, click on "Slide show," then on "Set up show," then click the box labeled "Loop continuously until escape" in the "Show options" box.
    <u>PURPOSE:</u> Running the show continuously is helpful for situations in which the presentation can be watched while people are passing through an exhibit hall, and so on.
17. Make sure the presentation has been saved.
18. Practice giving the presentation several times to smooth all transitions and to become familiar with the content.
    <u>PURPOSE:</u> The more the presentation is practiced, the more comfortable the presenter will be.
19. Anticipate questions the audience may ask and have answers prepared.
    <u>PURPOSE:</u> Anticipating questions helps the presenter better prepare for the presentation and ensures that the presenter knows the material.
20. Offer other visual aids, such as handouts, if appropriate, when giving the presentation.
    <u>PURPOSE:</u> Visual aids help the audience remember the presentation and may prompt them to take any action the presenter wants them to take.

DESIGNING PRESENTATION CONTENT

Remember these points when designing a presentation:

- Use bulleted points consistently.
- Use white space between bullets.
- Align text systematically in one area of a slide and place graphics on the other side.
- Make sure visuals deal with the subject of the presentation and are necessary.
- Time the transition between slides.
- Make bulleted points appear in a systematic way so that readers see text as the speaker is talking and not before or after the points are mentioned.
- If a physical process is demonstrated, use visuals to enhance the demonstration.
- Choose the most readable font.
- Use hyperlinks effectively.
- Use midrange colors for backgrounds.
- Rehearse the narration.
- Use titles for charts and illustrations.
- Organize content well.

Building a Practice Web Site

One of the most popular and beneficial marketing tools for the physician is a professional Web site. If the physician or an office staff member has sufficient knowledge to construct a Web site, there is little or no cost to the doctor if free Web site services are used. Businesses that host Web sites on the Internet offer very reasonable costs, starting at around $25 a month.

Four basic steps are involved in building a Web site for a medical practice:

1. Define the objectives of the Web site.
2. Design the pages.
3. Locate a Web server to which the pages can be uploaded.
4. Upload the pages to the server.

Defining Objectives

When defining the **objectives** of the practice, consider the physician's goals. The physician and staff should discuss who the audience will be and what will be included on the site. Most Web Sites designed for physicians' offices and clinics are informational, developed for both patient and public use. Once the objectives have been clearly defined, specific content can be written to place on the Web Site. The practice website is a perfect example of the need to organize technical information and summarize activities in which patients might be interested. The objectives developed by the physician and staff need to be transformed into activities that will attract and interest the patients as well as the local community.

Designing Pages

When the objectives have been clarified, begin developing ideas about what the site will look like on the computer screen. Color choices, animation, and fonts enhance the look that is being created and make a strong statement about the medical facility. The menus should be designed so that viewers can navigate easily through the site. Most users appreciate a means to go back to the page previously viewed and grow frustrated with sites that have an excessive number of pop-up boxes. Consistency is important, so it is a good idea to keep the same design theme on each page of the Web site.

The most important part of the Web site is the text. It has been said that every word in a book must add to the story, and this is a good way to look at the text in a Web site. Avoid too much repetition and remain clear about what is being communicated on the site. Headings and titles help clarify the theme of each page. Use a spell-checker before uploading the message and making it available for public viewing.

Photographs, graphics, music, and video can add fun to the Web site, but be careful not to overdo them. Graphics often are large files that take time to download. Most people will not wait longer than about 10 seconds for a Web page to load before clicking elsewhere. When designing Web page graphics, remember that smaller is better. Graphics can be found by searching for "index of GIF files" or "GIF library." Once an appropriate file has been found, it should be copied onto the hard drive by right-clicking the graphic and selecting "Save picture as." Music can be found by searching for "mid" or "midi." The search can even specify a certain singer, song, or composer. Always respect any copyrights that are designated on any file used. Many Web sites offer these files for free.

For a more professional-looking Web site, consider purchasing Web development software, such as Macromedia's Dreamweaver or Microsoft's FrontPage. These feature-rich products are fairly inexpensive and can help the medical assistant create very attractive, easy to maintain Web sites. Most products integrate tutorial and "help" features that explain how to use them.

Hyperlinks are words or graphics on a Web page that take the viewer to another page or another Web site when clicked. To add a hyperlink, simply highlight the text field or graphic, select the hyperlink icon, and specify the destination address (uniform resource locator [URL]). Always specify the full URL to ensure that the link directs the user to the desired page.

The main page should always be assigned the file name "index.htm" or "default.htm." Other pages on the Web site can be assigned any name; however, keep the names short and do not use special characters.

Locating a Web Server

At this point, the design of the Web site is complete, but the files reside on the computer hard drive, not on the Internet. Now the pages are ready to be uploaded, or published, to a Web server that will allow them to be viewed on the Internet. The Internet service provider (ISP) that the office uses for e-mail and online services may offer free Web space to its customers. If not, a number of companies provide Web space at no charge, but the user usually is required to use banners on the site that advertise the ISP or other services. If no banner ads are desired, the medical facility may want to use a paid provider. Some Web hosting companies provide other services free of charge, such as simple Web page editors and e-mail addresses.

Uploading Pages

When a free Web server is used, instructions and passwords are sent to the users that describe how to upload files to the server. The password is necessary so that other people cannot alter the files. Copying the files from the local hard disk to the Web server is a simple process. The hosting site prompts the user for the name of the directory on the hard drive where the files are stored and for the names of the specific files to be uploaded. To avoid confusion, make sure the files saved on the server have the same file names used on the hard drive.

Once all the files have been uploaded, test the page on the Web server and make sure it functions properly and that all files have been uploaded correctly. It also is a good idea to test the page using a different computer to ensure that graphic files are being read from the server and not from the local hard drive.

Evaluating the Web Site

Include an e-mail address where viewers of the Web site can interact with the creator with comments. When viewers have this option, problems with the site can be readily identified and corrected. It also is advisable to check the site every few days to make sure it is functioning properly.

CRITICAL THINKING APPLICATION   26-6

Monica is considering a frequently asked questions (FAQ) section for the Web site. How might this help patients?
- What kinds of questions might be asked in this section?
- How might the inclusion of this section benefit employees?

Counters often can be added to the Web site that will indicate how many people viewed it. This helpful tool allows the medical facility to track how many people are viewing which pages.

Social Media and Networking

Social media can be considered a two-way street that allows a communication response to regular media, which is a one-way street, such as a newspaper article or a television report. Regular media allows only limited ability to give a response; one can write a letter to the editor of a newspaper, but the letter is not an immediate two-way response. Social media is sometimes called *consumer-generated media* (CGM) and is considered a blending of technology and social interaction that creates a thing of value. This technology has become important to businesses of all types and continues to evolve. Creative, tech-savvy people are producing innovative ideas for medical facilities to attract new patients.

Developing along with social media is another important concept, Web 2.0. This is the term used to describe the cumulative changes in the ways that end-users and software developers use the Web, resulting in application features that facilitate information sharing, interoperability, user-centered design, and collaboration. Instead of just reading content on the Web, users interact in a virtual community or social network. Many Web sites now contain icons representing Facebook, Twitter, YouTube, Pinterest, and other types of social media to promote interaction, with the hope of creating a loyal customer or user who will return to the site or business repeatedly.

Earlier in the chapter, we considered Baylor Health Care System in Texas with regard to its branding messages. The organization has incorporated social media to interact with those in need of the services that the hospital system offers, but also uses games, craft ideas, health tips, and other interesting applications that a user may enjoy just for fun. Baylor uses Facebook as a resource, a platform to share medical news and health information, and to connect with its "fans." The system uses Twitter to announce classes on healthcare issues, present surveys, share news related to healthcare, and allow patients to comment on care received at Baylor facilities. For example, a tweet mentions an article about Baylor's Animal Therapy Program and points the user to Baylor's Pinterest board, where photos of the animals, procedures for obtaining therapy animals, and videos of patients using the therapy animals can be found. The Baylor YouTube Channel offers videos with instructions about making an emergency kit for a family, Ask the Expert videos cover subjects such as stress, cervical cancer, and anterior cruciate ligament (ACL) injuries and also presents healthy cooking demonstrations for cancer patients. Baylor uses all of these aspects of social media to their best advantage in an effort to meet its organizational goals, recruit new users to its services, and retain current users.

From just this one example, it is easy to understand how an aggressive, well-planned social media approach can positively affect the financial health of a facility. These processes put individuals "into" the Web, making the experience more interactive and responsive. The medical assistant who can use social media in a professional way will be a valuable asset to the medical practice.

SOCIAL NETWORKING SITES OF INTEREST TO MEDICAL ASSISTANTS

- Healthranker
- Organized Wisdom
- Peoples MD
- Trusera
- FitLink
- Limeade
- American Well
- Daily Strength
- Group Loop
- Health 2.0
- Mamaherb
- MDJunction
- Patients Like Me
- Real Mental Health
- Real Self
- Right Health
- Twit2Fit
- Vitals

HIGH-QUALITY CUSTOMER SERVICE IN THE MEDICAL PRACTICE

Treating the Patient as a Customer

The best way to increase the number of patients in a medical office is through word of mouth. When patients are satisfied with the treatment they receive, they refer other patients to the physician. However, if they are dissatisfied, they will tell everyone they know!

Because patients often have a choice about who provides their healthcare services, it is important that the physician's office become the patient's first choice. Some patients are so loyal to a certain physician that even if their healthcare coverage no longer pays for visits, they continue to see that doctor. This happens because of the attitude of the physician and his or her office staff.

Medical assistants, whether just out of school or already established in their careers, must provide patients with good customer service. Patients do not hesitate to tell the physician if the medical assistant is not cordial and helpful. Providing excellent customer service is mandatory for every employee of the practice.

Helpful Attitude

The physician and staff should project a helpful attitude in every contact with the patient. They should sincerely ask, "How may I help you?" and then take steps to assist the patient in whatever way possible. Instead of pointing in the general direction of the radiology department, a staff member should take the patient there and introduce him or her to the receptionist. Instead of telling a patient on the telephone, "Ann handles the insurance billing. I'll transfer you to her," say, "One moment, Mrs. Brown, let me see if Ann is at her desk." Place Mrs. Brown on hold, call Ann, and let her know that she has a call. Then return to Mrs. Brown, tell her that Ann is at her desk, and transfer the call at that time. Be courteous and kind to every patient and visitor to the office. Good customer relations must be one of the primary goals of the medical facility. Patients count on the staff members to be reliable and available to help them to the best of their abilities.

Phrases That Undermine Successful Customer Service

The following are some phrases that should never be used when relating to patients and visitors.
- "I don't know."
  Say instead: "Although I don't know the answer, I will find out for you." The medical assistant will not know the answer to every question but must be willing to find out the information.
- "I don't care."
  Say instead: "We do care about your concerns and want to help." If the medical assistant cannot honestly make this statement, he or she should consider another profession.
- "I can't be bothered."
  Say instead: "I truly want to give this matter my full attention. Where can I contact you once I have looked into the matter?" Some people may expect immediate attention and service, but they may have to be patient and wait their turn to receive assistance.
- "Ask someone else."
  Say instead: "I will be happy to find out who handles that for you." The medical assistant should never project the attitude that the patient's concerns are unimportant.
- "It's not my job."
  Say instead: "I am not one of the employees who files insurance, but I will be happy to ask Amanda, our insurance supervisor, to contact you and answer your questions." Do not ever tell the patient or a supervisor that a certain duty is not a responsibility. Find the right person to help the patient.
- "It's not my fault."
  Say instead: "I was not involved with that decision, but I know that our office manager would be happy to speak with you about it." Although blame should never be placed on another employee, any touchy issue should be referred to the office manager, especially if the medical assistant is not the final decision-making authority.
- "I didn't do it."
  Say instead: "I will see if I can get to the root of this issue." Be willing to assist the patient even if you are not involved in the situation at hand.
- "I know that."
  Say instead: "Yes, I understand. Let me try to help you." Do not use sarcasm and never make snippy remarks to patients.
- "I'm right, you're wrong."
  Say instead: "Our policy is clear about this matter, but let's see if we can come up with a compromise." Accusatory remarks should never be made to a patient.

All these alternate phrases give the patient or visitor a more positive view of both the office and those who work in the facility.

Identifying with Patients

Patients appreciate staff members who can identify with the problems they are facing. This is especially effective when a patient is upset or angry. For example, if a patient comes to the office complaining that charges were placed on his account for procedures that were not performed, the medical assistant may respond with a phrase such as, "Mr. Roberts, I understand that you're upset about these additional charges. I know I would be upset if I were billed for something I didn't receive. Let me help you by doing this ..."

Identifying with the patient shows understanding on the part of the staff member, no matter how upset the patient may be. Always acknowledge and restate the patient's concern. It proves that the medical assistant was listening and is interested in resolving the problem.

Remember, it costs much more to find new customers than to keep existing customers happy. Providing helpful, personal service impresses even the most difficult patient. To patients and visitors to the clinic, the employees to whom they speak represent the whole company. Perceptions and opinions likely will be formed based on experiences with only one person. Each individual employee must be aware that to the patient, each employee is the healthcare facility.

What Do Patients Expect?

First, patients expect to be treated according to the Golden Rule. They expect their concerns to be met with responsiveness, which means that the medical assistant should have a caring attitude. They also expect the professionals in the medical office to be knowledgeable about their field or specialty. An insurance biller should know more than just the basics of insurance filing. The office manager should have a certain degree of authority to handle problems and complaints. Patients also expect confidentiality and trust from the staff of the medical office. They expect an organized office that runs on schedule. They also expect that if a staff member promises to do something, it is as good as done. Patients' expectations can be better assessed by using customer service evaluation forms. For an example of a customer service evaluation form, visit the Evolve site at *evolve.elsevier.com/kinn.*

Remembering the Internal Customer

Most of us do not have problems figuring out who the external customers are in a medical practice. Patients, their families and friends, and visitors to the office are external customers. But who is the internal customer?

Internal customers are employees and staff members of the facility. Although they work for the business, they also are served by the business. If they are not pleased with the atmosphere of the medical facility, they are sure to look elsewhere for employment. Keeping the internal customer is just as important as keeping the external customer.

CLOSING COMMENTS

Providing good customer service is a commitment that must be made by every employee of the medical facility, every single day. There will be times when the customer is not right, but he or she should be treated with dignity and respect at all times. In addition, an expert customer service provider has a knack for making the customer think he or she was right all along! The medical office is no exception to the requirements for providing good service to its patients, and doing so results in an excellent reputation for the clinic, built by those who matter most—the patients.

Patient Education

A practice's marketing and public relations efforts provide endless opportunities for patient education. Most physicians agree that part of the obligation of the medical profession is to educate patients about healthcare issues. The practice's public relations and marketing staffs can work together to provide information to patients of the facility and to the general public. Many physicians attend health fairs, where brochures and pamphlets can be distributed about

conditions such as diabetes, heart disease, hypertension, and other disorders. Screenings for cholesterol and blood pressure checks are good ways to market a practice and gain new patients.

The medical assistant who knows how to build and maintain a simple Web site can be of great value to the physician. The practice's Web site could provide opportunities for educating patients, in addition to special sections for upcoming events, an online newsletter, and appointment setting. The Web site address should be included on stationery, business cards, and other documents used to promote the facility. Using Facebook, Twitter, YouTube, and other types of social media will place the healthcare facility in strategic positions to thrive amid the fierce competition of today's healthcare industry.

Legal and Ethical Issues

The physician must take care that patients do not use the information in brochures or on the practice Web site as medical advice or as a substitute for the physician's counsel. When attaching links to other Web sites, be sure they are reputable. The patient may consider information on the practice's Web site to be an extension of the physician's advice, so make sure everything on the Web site is accurate.

The physician should carefully review all printed information used to promote the medical facility. Make sure no misleading statements are included. A disclaimer should be used to remind patients that the information given in brochures and on Web sites is only general information. Patients should discuss specific medical issues with the physician.

SUMMARY OF SCENARIO

Monica knows that without growth, many businesses eventually fail. She is confident that with a simple marketing plan, the clinic will experience steady, continuous expansion. She has spoken to all the office staff members and gained input from both employees and patients of the clinic. Many offered excellent suggestions that Monica can incorporate into her marketing plan.

One of her first activities was to develop an annual calendar of special events and outreach efforts. A monthly newsletter and the practice Web site will be the main thrusts of her marketing plan. The newsletter will be available both in print and online. The patients in the office database who have e-mail addresses will receive automatically a computer-generated e-mail message containing a link that will take them directly to the online newsletter. Inside, patients will find health information and details about upcoming events.

Monica also planned one special activity for each month of the year. She scheduled a blood drive, a Christmas toy drive, and mini–health fair. Because both Dr. Julie and Dr. Robert Todd are dedicated to students who want to pursue medicine, Monica even planned a career day for high school students interested in becoming physicians, inviting representatives from the medical school that the Todds attended. Because this is considered a public service, Monica was able to get press coverage on the local radio station and in the newspaper at no cost.

Monica visited a new restaurant close to the office that serves heart-healthy dishes, met with the manager, and discussed ways the two businesses could help each other. They decided to provide a "buy one entrée, get one free" coupon to patients who referred other patients to the clinic. In turn, Dr. Robert Todd agreed to hold his free nutrition seminars at the restaurant. This arrangement has proved to work well for both businesses. Monica obtained this new agreement by making an effective presentation to the restaurant manager. Her skills in putting an interesting, informative presentation together helped her secure the agreement.

An Internet presence is important to businesses that want to grow in today's society. Consumers often look on the Internet first when planning purchases, shopping, or looking for community resources. Monica plans to track responses to each event promoted on the practice Web site to determine what efforts were the most effective in promoting the clinic. The Web site will allow her to count the number of times it is accessed and which pages were the most popular. She will keep the physicians informed and be open to their suggestions throughout the year. Monica is anxious to see the results of her marketing efforts and feels confident of success. Social media enhances the Web site, offering patients several options to increase their knowledge about health-related subjects and find opportunities to participate in events that will promote good health.

SUMMARY OF SCENARIO—cont'd

The staff members understand that no matter what efforts are used to promote the facility and obtain new patients, it is their responsibility to provide exceptional customer service so that the patients will be happy with their experience. In the medical industry today, customer service has become as important as in the retail world. Patients have choices as to who provides their healthcare, so they must be treated cordially and fairly by medical professionals who truly want to serve their needs. The success and growth of the facility depends on customer service. Monica knows that the medical office has more than one type of customer, and that the internal customers (employees) are critical to the clinic's success. She includes other employees in marketing decisions and often asks for their input. The more involved employees feel in company decisions, the more they feel as if they are a part of the community that is created in the individual facility. Monica has helped to create a fun, exciting workplace, and she looks forward to going to work every single day.

SUMMARY OF LEARNING OBJECTIVES

1. **Define, spell, and pronounce the terms listed in the vocabulary.**
   Spelling and pronouncing medical terms correctly bolster the medical assistant's credibility. Knowing the definition of these terms promotes confidence in communication with patients and co-workers.

2. **List the four steps to follow when preparing to implement a medical marketing strategy.**
   When preparing to implement marketing strategies, first evaluate what currently is being done toward the marketing effort. Then decide on the objectives of the marketing plan and how they will be measured. Finally, develop a specific plan and timeline for implementing each phase.

3. **Explain the term *target market*.**
   A target market is a very specific group of people or individuals whom the medical facility wants to serve. Geography, lifestyle, and personality all are ways to classify individuals into specific target markets. When identifying a target market ask, "Who is our patient?" "What does our patient want?" and "Why is it wanted?" These questions can help the medical facility design a marketing plan to meet the needs of these individuals.

4. **Discuss how suggestion boxes might help the medical facility make improvements.**
   Suggestions from patients and employees should always be welcomed in the medical office. Often these people see the facility from a different point of view, and their suggestions can enhance the atmosphere and the services offered.

5. **List and discuss the four Ps of marketing.**
   The four Ps of marketing are product, placement, price, and promotion. The *product* in a medical office includes the services and any actual retail items that might be sold. *Placement* relates to the location of the office and its convenience for the patients and to the placement of retail items in the facility. *Price* represents the charges for goods and services, and *promotion* entails the ways in which the services are promoted to the general public and the target market.

6. **Explain the four steps for developing a plan in marketing.**
   The facility first should assess the efforts that have been made in the past, then research the results of those efforts. Next the plan is developed, which should include very specific steps for each aspect of the endeavor. After the plan has been executed, the staff must evaluate its effectiveness and determine whether the goals were met. The evaluation is important in planning future marketing strategies.

7. **Discuss how community involvement can make a difference in marketing efforts.**
   Involvement in the community is an excellent way to promote the medical profession and remain in the public eye. These efforts can result in new patients for the facility. The public sees medical professionals as caring and compassionate; volunteer activities reinforce this attitude and help meet patients' expectations.

8. **State the difference between advertising and public relations.**
   Advertising is a medium that attempts to create or change attitudes, beliefs, and perceptions through purchased broadcast time, printed material, or other forms of communication. Public relations is a similar field but relies more on news broadcasts or reports, magazine or newspaper articles, and radio reports to reach the audience.

9. **Determine ways to promote a new practice.**
   A new medical practice can be promoted by placing an announcement in the newspaper about its opening. Some physicians hold an open house, inviting the public to visit the office. A Web site is an excellent promotional tool and should be listed on business cards and stationery. Community service and volunteer activities that mention the practice also help spread the word about the services available.

10. **Prepare a presentation using PowerPoint.**
    PowerPoint is a user-friendly program that can produce effective presentations. The process for preparing a presentation using PowerPoint is outlined in Procedure 26-2.

11. **Discuss applications of electronic technology in effective communication.**
    The Internet is a form of communication, and the physician can make use of it by developing a Web site for the practice. The Web site might highlight a featured procedure, explaining it in detail. Space can be devoted to providing the background information on the physicians and medical assistants at the clinic. Directions with maps are popular additions to physician Web sites. In addition, many doctors place their new patient forms on their Web site so that the forms can be filled out before a patient's first visit. The physician's Web site is a valuable communications tool that can help employees provide patients with even better customer service.

12. **Organize technical information and summaries.**
    The clinic Web site is the perfect place to provide patients with technical information about the physician's specialty and the procedures and

treatments available at the clinic. The Web site might have a procedure tab along the top of the home page that leads to all the procedures done in the office, with a brief description of each. Graphics or photos make the pages more interesting. Summaries of estimated costs might be appropriate. The patient must be able to navigate the Web site easily and find information quickly.

13. **Discuss responses that help the medical assistant identify with the patient.**

    Identifying with the patient is an effective customer service tool. The medical assistant should express his or her understanding of the patient's concerns and then tell the patient that the situation can be resolved and how it will be resolved. Four magic words in customer service are, "Let me help you."

14. **Explain the concept of the internal customer.**

    External customers are those who visit the facility, such as patients. However, staff members and employees are *internal customers,* who want to derive a sense of satisfaction from working for the medical office. Internal customers are just as important as the external customers.

15. **Design a presentation for a marketing event.**

    A sharp, effective presentation helps the medical assistant secure permission to hold or promote a marketing event. The process for designing a presentation is outlined in Procedure 26-1.

16. **Locate resources and information for patients and employers.**

    Many physicians include a "links" page on their Web site that displays several other businesses and organizations that might be of interest to the patient. Examples of such organizations include the local blood bank; hospitals where the physician has staff privileges; local branches of national organizations, such as the American Heart Association or American Association of Retired Persons; various insurance Web sites; the Web site for the Centers for Medicare and Medicaid Services (CMS); and numerous others. Patients appreciate access to information on businesses and organizations.

17. **Advocate on behalf of the patient and family and be able to deal and communicate with family members.**

    The professional medical assistant must be a patient advocate and must be willing to assist patients with their healthcare needs. Communicate with the patient and family members just as if they were your own family. Always follow up when referring patients to community resources. Medical assistants must want to help patients with reasonable tasks, and their attitude must reflect that helping is a pleasure, not an obligation.

CONNECTIONS

Study Guide Connection: Go to the Chapter 26 Study Guide. Read and complete the activities.

Evolve Connection: Go to the Chapter 26 link at *evolve.elsevier.com/ kinn* to complete the Chapter Review and Chapter Quiz. Check out the other resources listed for this chapter to make the most of what you have learned from Medical Practice Marketing and Customer Service.

27

EMERGENCY PREPAREDNESS AND ASSISTING WITH MEDICAL EMERGENCIES

Cheryl Skurka, CMA (AAMA), has been working for Dr. Peter Bendt for approximately 6 months. During that time, a number of patient emergencies have occurred in the office, and even more potentially serious problems have been managed by the telephone screening staff. Cheryl is concerned that she is not prepared to assist with emergencies in the ambulatory care setting. She decides to ask Dr. Bendt for assistance, and

he suggests that she work with the experienced screening staff to learn how to manage phone calls from patients calling for assistance.

Dr. Bendt is participating in a community-wide preparedness effort focused on both natural and human-made disasters, and he expects his practice and employees to be ready to respond if needed. This includes both creating plans to maintain the safety of patients and employees in the facility and providing assistance as needed in a community emergency.

While studying this chapter, think about the following questions:

- What should Cheryl learn about the medical assistant's responsibilities in an emergency situation?
- What are some of the general rules for managing a medical emergency in an ambulatory care setting?
- What types of questions does the telephone screening staff ask if a patient calls with a medical emergency?
- What information from these phone calls should be documented?
- Is it important for Cheryl to be able to recognize life-threatening emergencies and to be prepared to respond to them?
- What are some of the typical patient emergencies that occur in a healthcare facility?

- How should Cheryl instruct a patient to control bleeding from a hemorrhaging wound?
- What safety practices should be followed in the healthcare facility to protect patients and employees from potential harm?
- What is the medical office's responsibility in preparing for community emergencies?
- Are there common health emergency topics for patient education that Cheryl should be prepared to present?
- What legal factors should Cheryl keep in mind when handling ambulatory care emergencies?

LEARNING OBJECTIVES

1. Define, spell, and pronounce the terms listed in the vocabulary.
2. Apply critical thinking skills in performing the patient assessment and patient care.
3. Describe patient safety factors in the medical office environment.
4. Evaluate the work environment to identify safe and unsafe working conditions.
5. Identify environmental safety issues in the healthcare setting.
6. Develop environmental, patient, and employee safety plans.
7. Discuss fire safety issues in a healthcare environment.
8. Demonstrate the proper use of a fire extinguisher.
9. Describe the fundamental principles for evacuation of a healthcare facility.
10. Role-play a mock environmental exposure event and evacuation of a physician's office.
11. Discuss the requirements for proper disposal of hazardous materials.
12. Define the important features of emergency preparedness in the ambulatory care setting.
13. Maintain an up-to-date list of community resources for emergency preparedness.

14. Describe the medical assistant's role in emergency response.
15. Summarize the typical emergency supplies and equipment.
16. Demonstrate the use of an automated external defibrillator.
17. Summarize the general rules for managing emergencies.
18. Demonstrate telephone screening techniques and documentation guidelines for ambulatory care emergencies.
19. Recognize and respond to life-threatening emergencies in the ambulatory care setting.
20. Perform professional-level cardiopulmonary resuscitation (CPR).
21. Administer oxygen through a nasal cannula to a patient in respiratory distress.
22. Identify and assist a patient with an obstructed airway.
23. Determine the appropriate action and documentation procedures for common ambulatory care emergencies.
24. Assist and monitor a patient who has fainted.
25. Control a hemorrhagic wound.
26. Apply patient education concepts to medical emergencies.
27. Discuss the legal and ethical concerns arising from medical emergencies.

VOCABULARY

arrhythmia (uh-rith'-mee-uh) An abnormality or irregularity in the heart rhythm.

asystole (ay-sis'-toh-le) The absence of a heartbeat.

cyanosis (si-an-oh'-sis) A blue coloration of the mucous membranes and body extremities caused by lack of oxygen.

diaphoresis (di-uh-fuh-re'-sis) The profuse excretion of sweat.

ecchymosis (e-ki-moh'-sis) A hemorrhagic skin discoloration commonly called *bruising.*

emetic (eh-met'-ik) A substance that causes vomiting.

fibrillation Rapid, random, ineffective contractions of the heart.

hematuria (hi-ma-tuhr'-e-uh) Blood in the urine.

idiopathic Pertaining to a condition or a disease that has no known cause.

mediastinum (meh-de-ast'-uhn-um) The space in the center of the chest under the sternum.

myocardium (my-oh-kar'-de-um) The muscular lining of the heart.

necrosis (neh-kroh'-sis) The death of cells or tissues.

photophobia An abnormal sensitivity to light.

polydipsia Excessive thirst.

thrombolytics Agents that dissolve blood clots.

transient ischemic attack (TIA) Temporary neurological symptoms caused by gradual or partial occlusion of a cerebral blood vessel.

The medical assistant typically is responsible for making the healthcare facility as accident-proof as possible. This requires attention to a number of factors. For example, cupboard doors and drawers must be kept closed; spills must be wiped up immediately; and dropped objects must be picked up. The medical assistant also should make sure that all medications are kept out of sight and away from busy patient areas. If children are in the office, all sharp objects and potentially toxic substances must be kept out of reach. In addition, the medical assistant should never leave a seriously ill patient or a restless, depressed, or unconscious patient unattended.

SAFETY IN THE HEALTHCARE FACILITY

Patient Safety

Patient safety is a critical component of the quality of care provided in a healthcare facility. The U.S. Department of Health and Human Services (DHHS) has conducted extensive research on the features of safe patient environments in physicians' offices. The DHHS has found the following factors to be crucial to patient safety:

- Open lines of communication must be established among all employees about possible safety issues, and employees must work together to solve these problems before a patient is injured.
- If an injury occurs (e.g., a medication is administered to the wrong patient), policies and procedures must be in place so that all employees recognize the potential for an error and protocols are established for preventing a similar problem in the future.
- Procedures must be standardized in the facility's policy and procedures manual so that all employees can refer to specific guidelines on how procedures should be performed. For example, in the case of a blood spill, the policy and procedures manual must outline a specific, step-by-step procedure for cleaning up the spill that safeguards both patients and staff members.
- The facility must provide ongoing staff training in patient safety factors.
- Staff members must work as a team to maintain a safe environment for patients. For example, all staff members must follow Standard Precautions to prevent the spread of disease in the facility.

Throughout this text, you have learned about situations that could result in serious harm to your patients. You must constantly be on guard to protect patients from possible injury. For example, studies have shown that healthcare workers frequently confuse drug names, which results in administration of the wrong medication; they also fail to identify a patient correctly before performing a procedure and neglect to perform hand sanitization consistently, thus promoting the spread of infectious diseases. The medical assistant is an important link in the delivery of quality and *safe* care. Can you think of anything you have learned thus far in your studies that could help keep patients safe in the physician's office? Procedure 27-1 presents a scenario about patient safety. Follow the step-by-step procedure to learn what you can do to protect your patients from possible harm.

Employee Safety

The healthcare facility should safeguard patients as well as staff members from the possibility of accidental injury. Data compiled by the Occupational Safety and Health Administration (OSHA) reveal that the leading causes of accidents in an office setting are slips, trips, and falls. You must think and work safely to prevent accidents. Following are some suggestions from OSHA for vigilant accident prevention methods (Procedure 27-2):

1. Use proper body mechanics in all situations (see Chapter 32). For example, bend your knees and bring a heavy item close to you before lifting rather than bending from your back; push heavy items rather than pulling them; and ask for assistance when transferring patients.
2. Constantly check the floors and hallways for obstructions and possible tripping hazards, such as telephone and computer cables or boxes.
3. Store supplies inside cabinets rather than on top, where they can fall off and injure someone; store heavier items on lower shelves so they do not have to be lifted any higher than necessary.
4. Clean up spills immediately; slippery floors are a danger to everyone.

PROCEDURE 27-1

Develop a Patient Safety Plan: Order the Correct Medication From the Pharmacy

GOAL: *To telephone the correct medication prescription into the pharmacy.*

SCENARIO: *The physician writes an order to be phoned into the pharmacy for a new patient diagnosed with depression. You think the order reads, Avinza, 30 mg po bid. The pharmacist asks you for the physician's DEA number, because Avinza is a narcotic analgesic. You ask the physician for clarification and are told the order was for Avanza, an antidepressant. Look up both medications in a drug reference. What could have happened if a powerful narcotic had been ordered for the patient instead of the antidepressant the physician intended?*

EQUIPMENT and SUPPLIES

- Notepad and pen
- Patient's record
- PDR or other drug reference

PROCEDURAL STEPS

1. Review the physician's written order for a prescription or repeat the order back to the physician if it is a verbal order. If it is a verbal order, write the order down and have the physician review it to make sure you have the correct medication before calling the pharmacy.
   <u>PURPOSE:</u> To make sure you can clearly read the order and/or have adequately verified a verbal order.

2. If you are unfamiliar with the medication, look it up in a drug reference.
   <u>PURPOSE:</u> To prevent possible errors, you should be familiar with all medications ordered.

3. After you have become familiar with the medication, if the order does not match the patient's diagnosis, ask the physician for clarification.
   <u>PURPOSE:</u> If you are not absolutely sure what the physician's handwriting means, do not hesitate to ask for clarification.

4. Refer to the office's policies and procedures manual to review the procedure for calling in a prescription order to the pharmacy.

5. Clarify any questions with the office manager to prevent any future errors.

PROCEDURE 27-2

Evaluate the Work Environment to Identify Safe and Unsafe Working Conditions: Develop an Environmental Safety Plan

GOAL: *To assess the healthcare facility for possible safety issues and develop a safety plan.*

SCENARIO: *Work with a partner to evaluate environmental safety in the laboratory at your school. Record your results and discuss them with the class. After all members of the class have shared their observations, develop a safety plan for your laboratory.*

EQUIPMENT and SUPPLIES

- Pen and paper
- Policies and procedures for environmental safety issues in the facility

PROCEDURAL STEPS

1. Check the floors and hallways for obstructions and possible tripping hazards, including torn carpets, possible spills, protruding electrical cords, and so on.
   <u>PURPOSE:</u> To prevent accidental falls.

2. Check storage areas to make sure the tops of cabinets are clear, and that heavier items have been stored closer to the floor.
   <u>PURPOSE:</u> To prevent injuries from items falling off shelves and to limit the lifting of heavy items.

3. Assess the location and security of handrails placed around the facility. They should be placed at all stairs, in restrooms, and in any other areas where staff members or patients may need assistance.
   <u>PURPOSE:</u> Handrails help safeguard staff members and patients and provide assistance where needed.

4. Examine all electrical plugs and outlets to prevent electrical overload.
   <u>PURPOSE:</u> Overloading electrical outlets could cause a fire.

5. Check all equipment to make sure it is in safe working condition.

6. Make sure all lights are working (both inside and outside the facility), that lighting is adequate, and that light fixtures are in good condition.
   <u>PURPOSE:</u> Adequate lighting both inside and outside the facility helps prevent accidents, and faulty fixtures can be a fire hazard.

7. Check the working condition of smoke alarms and examine all fire extinguishers.
   <u>PURPOSE:</u> To monitor the function of smoke detectors and make sure fire extinguishers are charged.

8. Make sure evacuation routes are posted throughout the facility, along with floor plans with clearly marked exit routes.
   <u>PURPOSE:</u> Every room in the facility must have a map with exit routes marked on it to make sure even those who are unfamiliar with the facility's floor plan can safely reach an exit in case of an emergency.

9. Record your observations and share them with the class.
   <u>PURPOSE:</u> To compile a comprehensive list of problem areas.

10. Based on group discussion, develop a plan of action for improving the safety of the laboratory.
    <u>PURPOSE:</u> The student-generated safety plan can be incorporated into the laboratory's policies and procedures manual.

5. Use a step stool to reach for things, not a chair or a box that could collapse or move.

6. Have handrails available as needed in the facility; use them and encourage patients to use them.

7. Do not overload electrical outlets.

8. Perform a safety check of the facility routinely; look for unsafe or defective equipment, torn carpeting that could catch heels, adequate lighting both inside and outside the facility, and so on.

A primary concern for personnel and patient safety is infection control. Chapter 27 discussed Standard Precautions in detail and the responsibility of employers to provide appropriate and adequate personal protective equipment (PPE). The goal is to protect staff members from occupational exposure to blood-borne pathogens while at the same time safeguarding patients in the facility. OSHA's guidelines include managing sharps and providing current safety-engineered sharps devices; providing hepatitis B immunization free of charge to all employees at risk of exposure to blood and body fluids; using latex-free supplies as much as possible to prevent allergic reactions in both staff members and patients; identifying all chemicals in the facility with Material Safety Data Sheets (MSDS; see Chapter 51) and adequately storing potentially dangerous substances; and performing proper hand hygiene consistently throughout the workday.

Another serious concern that faces all of us today is the prevention of workplace violence. Unfortunately, rarely does a week go by without reports of violence in a public place. Employees in a healthcare facility are no exception. We started the text with information about and exercises in communication techniques in the workplace—problem solving, therapeutic communication, and assertive behavior. All of these are helpful in dealing with a difficult patient. Employers should provide training on how to identify potentially violent patients and should discuss safe methods for managing difficult patients. Many employers offer training on how to manage assaultive behaviors.

In addition to these concerns, staff members should constantly be on the alert for possible safety hazards in and around the building, such as improper lighting, unlimited access to the facility, and inadequate use of security systems. Procedure 27-3 presents a scenario that deals with employee safety. Follow the steps of this procedure to learn how to handle such a situation.

Environmental Safety

Personal safety guidelines were discussed in Chapter 12. These include numerous work safety practices, such as office security, management of smoke detectors and fire extinguishers, posting of designated fire exit routes, and securing certain items (e.g., narcotics, dangerous chemicals) in locked storage areas in the facility.

The medical assistant must be prepared to use a fire extinguisher to prevent injury to patients and to protect the medical facility (Procedure 27-4). An ABC fire extinguisher is effective against the most common causes of fire, including cloth, paper, plastics, rubber, flammable liquids, and electrical fires. Most small extinguishers empty within 15 seconds, so it is important to call 911 immediately if the facility fire is not small and confined. If the fire is small, no heavy smoke is present, and you have easy access to an exit route, use the closest fire extinguisher. However, do not hesitate to evacuate the facility if you believe any danger exists to yourself or to others.

METHODS OF FIRE PREVENTION AND RESPONSE

- Properly store potentially flammable chemicals and supplies according to manufacturers' guidelines.
- Properly maintain electrical equipment, cords, and outlets throughout the facility.
- If a fire is suspected, immediately disconnect oxygen supplies or turn off oxygen tanks to prevent an explosion.
- Smoke alarms should be located throughout the facility, checked periodically, and replaced as needed.
- Make sure that fire safety equipment is available and current; fire extinguishers should be inspected at least annually; if an extinguisher is discharged, it must be replaced immediately.
- Fire extinguishers should be located in multiple sites throughout the facility and mounted on the wall for easy access.
- If you smell smoke or suspect a fire, immediately notify the fire department (or call 911) and evacuate the facility. Do not use elevators if a fire is suspected.

CRITICAL THINKING APPLICATION 27-1

Cheryl is in the middle of a busy day; patients are in all of the examination rooms, and the waiting room is full. She walks past the patient bathroom and smells smoke. She opens the door and sees smoke and flames coming from the waste basket. What should she do? Write down your response to this scenario and share it with your classmates.

Each facility should have a policy and procedure in place for evacuating the building. According to OSHA, the facility's plan first should identify the situations that might require evacuation, such as a natural disaster or a fire. The following provisions should be included in the facility's evacuation plan:

- An emergency action coordinator must be designated, and all employees must know who this individual is. This person is in charge if an emergency occurs.
- The coordinator is responsible for managing the emergency at the facility and for notifying and working with community emergency services.
- Evacuation routes with clearly marked exits must be posted in multiple locations throughout the facility. Maps of floor diagrams with arrows pointing to the closest exits are an easy means of finding the closest door out, even for individuals unfamiliar with the facility.
- Exit doors must be clearly marked, well lit, and wide enough for everyone to evacuate.
- Identify hazardous areas in the facility that should be avoided during an emergency evacuation.
- Designate a meeting place outside the facility for all those evacuating to make sure everyone got out of the facility safely.
- Employees should be trained to assist any co-worker or patient with special needs.
- A designated individual must check the entire facility, including restrooms, before exiting. He or she must make sure to close all

PROCEDURE 27-3

Develop an Employee Safety Plan: Manage a Difficult Patient

GOAL: *To communicate with an angry patient in a safe, therapeutic manner. The following procedure is part of an overall employee safety plan.*

SCENARIO: *You are working at the admissions desk when an extremely angry patient comes storming into the office, screaming about a mistake on his bill. Although the facility uses an outside billing center, you recognize that you should attempt to help the patient and try to diffuse the situation. Remember: Call 911 immediately and alert any available security if you or one of your co-workers is being threatened with violence.*

EQUIPMENT and SUPPLIES

- Telephone
- Patient record
- Policies and procedures manual

PROCEDURAL STEPS

1. Although it is important to safeguard patient privacy, do not ask an angry patient into an isolated room; do not close the door.
   UNDERLINE: PURPOSE: To protect yourself, remain in an open area. If you are in a room with an angry patient, keep the door open and stand close to the door so that you can leave the room quickly if necessary.
2. Alert other staff members to the situation, if possible.
   PURPOSE: To have assistance nearby; call 911 immediately if you feel physically threatened.
3. If you do not feel physically threatened, allow the patient to blow off steam.
   PURPOSE: Attempting to interrupt the patient to give a logical reason for the problem will only make him angrier. Allowing him to continue to yell helps him release the anger so that you can work on a reasonable solution to the problem. Call 911 if at any time you feel threatened.
4. When the patient begins to slow down, offer supportive statements, such as, "I understand it is frustrating to receive a bill you think is unfair." Continue to make supportive statements until the patient is calmer (think of it as the patient screaming his way up a mountain; sooner or later, he is going to run out of steam; when he begins to slow down, you can then start offering supportive statements).

PURPOSE: Providing verbal support helps diffuse the situation and gives the patient the opportunity to become calmer and reach a rational level where you can discuss the problem.

5. Once you can discuss the situation, ask the patient for the details of the problem. Gather as much information as possible so you can work together on a possible solution.
6. After determining the problem, suggest a possible solution to the patient. For example, tell him that you will contact the billing office with the information and will make sure they get back to the patient as soon as possible.
   PURPOSE: Use therapeutic techniques, including restatement, reflection, and clarification, to gather details and work on a possible solution with the patient. Make sure you follow up with the action to prevent future outbursts.
7. Report the incident to your supervisor and document the patient's problem and the agreed-upon action in the patient's medical record, taking care not to use judgmental statements.
   PURPOSE: Documenting the patient's problem and the agreed-upon solution allows for continuity of care if follow-up is needed. The patient's medical record is a legal document, and all judgmental statements must be avoided.
8. Discuss your approach to managing the difficult patient at the next staff meeting. With your supervisor's permission, summarize your approach and include it as part of the facility's Employee Safety Plan.
   PURPOSE: The safety plan should be reviewed frequently, and revisions should be made as needed.

PROCEDURE 27-4

Demonstrate the Proper Use of a Fire Extinguisher

GOAL: *To role-play the safe and proper use of a fire extinguisher.*

EQUIPMENT and SUPPLIES

- Portable, office-size ABC fire extinguisher that has been discharged

PROCEDURAL STEPS

Role-play the following with a discharged ABC fire extinguisher.

1. Pull the pin from the handle of the extinguisher.

2. Aim the discharge from the extinguisher toward the bottom of the flames.
   PURPOSE: Aiming the fire extinguisher directly onto the fire may spread the flames.
3. Squeeze the handle of the extinguisher so that it begins to discharge.
4. Sweep the extinguisher from side to side toward the base of the fire until it is out or until fire officials arrive.
5. Check on the safety of all patients and other personnel.

PROCEDURE 27-5

Participate in a Mock Environmental Exposure Event: Evacuate a Physician's Office

GOAL: To role-play an environmental disaster and implement an evacuation plan.

SCENARIO: Role-play the following scenario with your lab group: The building next door to the physician's office where you work is on fire. One member of the group is the designated emergency action coordinator, two individuals are responsible for helping patients with special needs out of the facility, and one person is designated to be the last to leave after the building is clear. In a community emergency situation, certain staff members may be designated to provide immediate assistance to survivors. Two medical assistants are sent to help with fire victims. How could medical assistants help in this situation? After the evacuation is complete, meet in a designated spot to discuss the process and see whether any aspects of the evacuation plan could be improved. Document the steps taken throughout the mock environmental event.

EQUIPMENT and SUPPLIES

- Pen and paper
- Policies and procedures for evacuation of the facility and response to an environmental disaster

PROCEDURAL STEPS

1. In an actual emergency, an emergency action coordinator is in charge.
   <u>PURPOSE:</u> All employees must know who this individual is (usually it is the office manager) and must follow his or her lead in safely responding to the emergency situation.

2. The coordinator is responsible for managing the emergency at the facility and for notifying and working with community emergency services.
   <u>PURPOSE:</u> The coordinator or someone designated by the coordinator must notify community emergency services of the fire; the coordinator works with emergency services to provide care at the scene.

3. Fire victims are being cared for across the street, where a triage and treatment center has been set up by the police, fire, and emergency responder units in the city. Two medical assistant staff members are sent to assist with the victims, as follows:
   - Use therapeutic communication techniques to calm and care for victims
   - Implement appropriate Standard Precautions
   - Monitor and record vital signs
   - Gather pertinent health histories
   - Observe victims for possible complications, such as breathing problems, shock, angina, and so on.
   - Immediately report to emergency responders any life-threatening changes in a patient's status
   - Use first aid skills as needed

4. The coordinator designates an employee to shut down any combustibles (e.g., oxygen tanks) immediately.
   <u>PURPOSE:</u> To prevent an explosion if the fire spreads.

5. Using the posted evacuation routes, staff members follow floor plan diagrams to the closest safe exit. Any hazardous areas in the facility that should be avoided during the emergency evacuation are identified.
   <u>PURPOSE:</u> Evacuation routes must be posted throughout the facility, and exit doors must be clearly marked, well lit, and wide enough for everyone to evacuate. The doors facing the building on fire should not be used, because this could be a hazard.

6. Assistance is provided for employees and patients with special needs who may require extra help during the evacuation.

7. One staff member is delegated to check that everyone has left the facility and that fire doors have been closed before he or she leaves the building.
   <u>PURPOSE:</u> To make sure the building is clear and that any fire is contained. This person should leave immediately if there is danger.

8. All evacuated personnel and patients should meet in a designated area to count heads and make sure everyone exited the facility safely.
   <u>PURPOSE:</u> To make sure everyone safely evacuated the facility.

9. After everyone has been accounted for and the office patients are secure, staff members who are not needed should report to the triage area to provide assistance to rescue workers and victims.

10. Discuss with the class the evacuation exercise and response to a community disaster.

11. Document your role in the exercise. What were the strengths and weaknesses of the group's response to an environmental emergency?
    <u>PURPOSE:</u> To reflect on the learning activity.

---

doors when leaving to try to contain the fire or other disaster (Procedure 27-5).

DISPOSAL OF HAZARDOUS WASTE

Chapter 27 explained the management of biohazardous waste; the use of PPE when the potential exists for exposure to blood and body fluids; the importance of flushing the eyes with an eye wash unit if they are exposed to potentially infectious material; and the consistent

use of sharps containers. Regardless of individual responsibilities in the facility, all employees must be aware of potentially dangerous situations and must comply with all safety measures to protect themselves and their patients.

OSHA defines regulated waste as any contaminated item that might release blood or other potentially infectious material; contaminated supplies that are caked with dried blood or other potentially infectious material; contaminated sharps; and waste products that contain blood or other potentially infectious material.

Healthcare facilities must make special arrangements for the disposal of regulated waste, which often costs as much as 10 times more than regular garbage disposal. It therefore is important to put only supplies contaminated with blood or body fluids into red bag collection systems and sharps containers. Steps for the proper disposal of hazardous materials in the physician's office include the following:

- Place signs on or near the biohazard container to identify its purpose and the materials that should be deposited there. All biohazardous waste containers should display a biohazard label.
- Make sure all biohazardous waste containers are covered and have a foot pedal for opening and closing the container. This prevents the spread of infectious material and reduces the likelihood that noninfectious material will be tossed inside. Biohazard containers should be kept only in treatment areas where contaminated materials are likely to be produced.
- Place a regular garbage container next to a biohazard container to encourage staff to use the biohazard bags only as needed.
- Place only sharps in sharps containers; gauze, bandages, and so on belong in a contaminated waste container. Noninfectious packaging material and other items belong in the regular trash.

EMERGENCY PREPAREDNESS

Ambulatory care centers and hospitals may be the first to recognize and initiate a response to a community emergency. If an infectious outbreak is suspected, Standard Precautions should be implemented immediately to control the spread of infection. If the problem has the potential to affect a large number of individuals in the community (e.g., suspected food contamination), a communication network should be established to notify local and state health departments and perhaps federal officials. Your employer may participate in an annual community disaster preparedness drill designed to help facilities improve their response to natural disasters and other emergencies.

Local governments are responsible for creating a Local Emergency Management Authority (LEMA) that coordinates police, fire, emergency medical services, public health, and area healthcare response to community-wide emergencies. These agencies are responsible for developing an all-hazards response plan that would be appropriate for any community emergency. Local officials turn to state, regional, or federal officials for assistance as needed.

Every healthcare facility should have a policy that includes specific procedures for the management of emergencies on site. When a new employee starts on the job, part of the orientation process is to review the site's policies and procedures manual. As a new employee, be sure to get answers to any questions you have about emergency management in that particular facility.

Staff members should discuss emergencies that may occur and should have an emergency action plan for rapid, systematic intervention. For instance, local industries may present unique problems that call for very specialized care. Plan for these, and ask the physician's advice on the procedures to follow and the supplies to have on hand. If the facility has several employees, each should be assigned specific duties in the event of an emergency. Organization and planning make the difference between systematic care for patients and complete chaos.

EMERGENCY PLAN FOR A NATURAL DISASTER OR OTHER EMERGENCY IN AN AMBULATORY CARE FACILITY

- Evacuate the facility as needed.
- Include procedures for the protection of patients' medical records. If the facility uses electronic health records (EHRs), make sure this information is backed up on other systems or on flash drives.
- In the case of a community emergency, provide care to the extent possible within the facility.
- Coordinate services between the ambulatory facility and other local healthcare systems, including hospitals and public health departments.
- Provide staff and supplies as needed to help in a community emergency.
- Maintain up-to-date phone trees to notify staff members of an emergency.
- Educate patients on emergency preparedness.

CRITICAL THINKING APPLICATION   27-2

A chemical plant is located about 3 blocks from Dr. Bendt's office. The office staff is brainstorming ideas about what should be done if an accident occurs at the plant. Based on what you have learned so far about emergency preparedness, what do you think should be included in the office's emergency plan?

Community Resources for Emergency Preparedness

Most communities have an emergency medical services (EMS) system. This system includes an efficient communications network (e.g., the emergency telephone number 911), well-trained rescue personnel, properly equipped ambulances, an emergency facility that is open 24 hours a day to provide advanced life support, and a hospital intensive care unit for victims.

More than 100 poison control centers in the United States are ready to provide emergency information for the treatment of victims of poisoning. Every healthcare facility is required to post a list of local emergency numbers. This list should be kept in plain sight and should be known to all office personnel. A good place to post this vital information is next to all the phones in the facility. Include on the list the numbers for the local EMS system, poison control center, ambulance and rescue squad, fire department, and police department (Procedure 27-6).

TELEPHONE NOTIFICATION NUMBERS FOR EMERGENCY PREPAREDNESS

- Local hospital numbers, including emergency department, infection control officer, administration contacts, and public affairs office
- Local and state Health Department numbers
- Centers for Disease Control and Prevention (CDC) Emergency Response Office: 770-448-7100

PROCEDURE 27-6

Maintain an Up-to-Date List of Community Resources for Emergency Preparedness

GOAL: To develop and maintain a list of community agencies that would respond to a natural disaster or other emergency.

SCENARIO: Your employer asks you to develop a list of groups in your community that are part of the community-wide emergency preparedness plan that has been mandated by the state and federal governments. Using multiple resources, develop a comprehensive list of emergency services for your area.

EQUIPMENT and SUPPLIES

- Telephone
- Internet access
- Pen and paper
- Electronic record

PROCEDURAL STEPS

1. Start with an online search for the area Local Emergency Management Authority (LEMA) office, sponsored by the Department of Homeland Security. If available, investigate the Web site for information about the emergency preparedness plan in your community. You can begin the search at www.ready.gov/america

   PURPOSE: To develop emergency preparedness plans by starting with the federal and state governments.

2. Gather contact information for local police, fire, and emergency medical services (EMS); post this information next to all telephones in the facility.

   PURPOSE: To ensure that emergency services contact information is immediately available in case of an emergency in the facility.

3. Investigate services provided by your local Public Health office and the American Red Cross.

   PURPOSE: To coordinate services available to potential victims in the community.

4. Organize the information gathered about community resources for emergency preparedness. With your supervisor's approval, post a copy of this information in all appropriate locations in the facility. Prepare a database in the computer that can be updated as the information changes.

The Centers for Disease Control and Prevention (CDC) recommends that all healthcare facilities be aware of possible agents of bioterrorism, including anthrax, botulism, plague, and smallpox. The physician is responsible for diagnosing and reporting any suspected cases, but the medical assistant may be involved in patient care and certainly will participate in preventing the spread of infection in the facility. As with any suspected infectious disease, Standard Precautions (see Chapter 27) should be used to control disease transmission. These precautions should be implemented with all patients, regardless of their diagnosis or possible infection status.

Infection control procedures for bioterrorism threats include the following:

- Sanitize hands routinely.
- Wear disposable gloves when the potential exists for contamination with blood and body fluids.
- Use masks/eye protection or face shields if the potential exists for being splashed by secretions or blood and body fluids.
- Wear gowns to protect skin and clothes as needed; remove them promptly and wash the hands to prevent transmission of infectious material.
- Sanitize, disinfect, and sterilize equipment, supplies, and environmental surfaces.
- Dispose of contaminated waste in appropriate biohazard containers.

Community emergency preparedness plans are required by the federal government so that a coordinated response is in place if a natural disaster occurs, such as Hurricane Katrina, which devastated New Orleans. The federal government requires all healthcare facilities, including private physicians' offices, to be prepared to provide medical services and to contribute medical supplies if a natural disaster or other emergency occurs in the area.

Emergency preparedness plans are designed to coordinate the care provided by all healthcare facilities and agencies in the community, including local emergency management agencies, EMS, fire departments, law enforcement agencies, the American Red Cross, and the National Guard. Each of these groups can provide crucial services during any community emergency.

Medical assistants also can contribute to rescue and emergency efforts. Services that might be performed by trained medical assistants include providing emergency first aid at the site of a disaster; conducting patient interviews in an empathetic manner while using therapeutic communication to help calm victims and gather important health-related information; helping with mass vaccination efforts or antibiotic distribution; performing documentation and electronic health record management; ensuring compliance with the procedures required by Standard Precautions; assisting with patient education efforts; and performing phlebotomy and laboratory procedures according to their skill level.

PSYCHOLOGICAL ASPECTS OF AN EMERGENCY SITUATION

Everyone involved in an emergency situation experiences a certain amount of anxiety and stress. The Centers for Disease Control and Prevention (CDC) recommends that a facility's emergency preparedness plan consider the following steps to minimize these negative psychological effects on both healthcare workers and patients:

- Provide fact sheets for employees and patients to help them understand the dangers of certain emergencies, and encourage employee participation in disaster drills.

- Plan in advance for effective communication and action in response to an emergency; the plan should include methods for coordinating a response with local and state agencies and media sources.
- Put into place a method for clearly explaining emergency situations to patients and healthcare workers; offer immediate evaluation and treatment of an infectious outbreak.
- Treat acute anxiety with reassurance and explanation; provide follow-up counseling for employees as needed.

Further information on emergency preparedness can be found at the following CDC sites:

- Emergency preparedness planning: www.bt.cdc.gov/planning
- Coordinating Office for Terrorism Preparedness and Emergency Response (COTPER): www.bt.cdc.gov

ASSISTING WITH MEDICAL EMERGENCIES

First aid is defined as the immediate care given to a person who has been injured or has suddenly taken ill. Knowledge of first aid and related skills often can mean the difference between life and death, temporary and permanent disability, or rapid recovery and long-term hospitalization. The medical assistant may be responsible for initiating first aid in the office and continuing to administer first aid until the physician or the trained medical team arrives. Every medical assistant should successfully complete a course for the professional in cardiopulmonary resuscitation (CPR) and should continue to hold a current CPR card as long as he or she is employed.

Basic knowledge of CPR and life support skills needs to be updated regularly, because procedures change as new techniques are developed. For example, both the American Red Cross and the American Heart Association (AHA) now recommend the inclusion of training on automated external defibrillators for all healthcare workers.

Medical assistants need up-to-date training in current emergency practices. They should encourage their local professional chapters to offer workshops on management of emergencies in the ambulatory care setting, as well as community-wide emergency preparedness. Being prepared for both types of emergencies is important. The facility's employees must be ready to respond both to emergencies on site and to natural disasters or other emergencies that affect the community.

Medical assistants are not responsible for diagnosing emergencies, especially over the telephone, but they are expected to make decisions about emergency situations on the basis of their medical knowledge and training. If any doubt exists about how to manage a particular situation or emergency phone call, the medical assistant should not hesitate to consult the physician, the office manager, or some other more experienced member of the healthcare team.

THE MEDICAL ASSISTANT'S ROLE IN PERFORMING EMERGENCY PROCEDURES

- Perform only the emergency procedures for which you have been trained.
- If an emergency occurs in the facility, notify the physician.
- If a physician cannot be located, immediately contact the local emergency medical services (EMS) team.

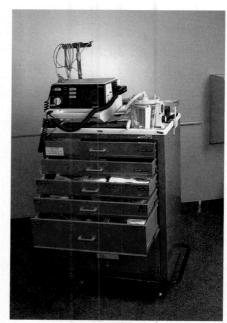

FIGURE 27-1 Office emergency cart with defibrillator. Drawers are marked for easy retrieval of emergency supplies.

Emergency Supplies

Emergency supplies consist of a properly equipped "crash cart" or box of items needed for a variety of emergencies (Figure 27-1). The contents vary to some degree, depending on the types of emergencies the particular office might expect to encounter. Emergency supplies should be kept in an easily accessible place that is known to all personnel in the office, and the supplies should be inventoried regularly. Expiration dates of medications and sterile supplies must be checked weekly or monthly, along with the status of available oxygen tanks and related supplies, and the cart should be replenished with fresh supplies after every use.

Emergency pharmaceutical supplies should include certain basic drugs, such as epinephrine, which has multiple uses in emergency situations. As a vasoconstrictor, it controls hemorrhage, relaxes the bronchioles to relieve acute asthma attacks, is administered for an acute anaphylactic reaction, and is an emergency heart stimulant used to treat shock. Epinephrine should be available in a ready-to-use cartridge syringe and needle unit. These units are supplied in 1-mL cartridges.

Other drugs used include atropine, digoxin (Lanoxin), nitroglycerin (Nitrostat), and lidocaine (Xylocaine). Atropine reduces secretions, increases respiratory rate and heart rate, and is a smooth muscle relaxant. It is administered in a cardiac emergency for **asystole**, or it can be used to treat bradycardia. Digoxin is a cardiac drug used to treat **arrhythmia** and congestive heart failure (CHF); it is good for emergency use because it has a relatively rapid action. Nitroglycerin is a vasodilator that is given to relieve angina; it acts by dilating the coronary arteries so that an increased volume of oxygenated blood can reach the **myocardium**. Lidocaine is used intravenously to treat a cardiac arrhythmia and locally as an anesthetic, and sodium bicarbonate corrects metabolic acidosis, which typically occurs after cardiac arrest.

Emergency medical supplies also should include an **emetic**, such as syrup of ipecac, which causes vomiting soon after the syrup is swallowed, and activated charcoal, an antidote that is swallowed to absorb ingested poisons. Narcan, an antidote administered intravenously for narcotic drug overdoses, acts to raise blood pressure and increase respiratory rate. Antihistamines for the treatment of allergic reactions and for anaphylaxis need to be available to treat any allergic responses to medications administered in the facility. Such antihistamines include Benadryl for minor reactions and Solu-Medrol, a corticosteroid, for severe anaphylactic reactions.

Other medications also may be found on a crash cart. These include isoproterenol (e.g., Isuprel, Medihaler-Iso, Norisodrine), an antispasmodic used to treat bronchospasms (such as those experienced during an asthma attack) that also is effective as a cardiac stimulant; metaraminol (Aramine) (50%, in a prefilled syringe) for severe shock; phenobarbital, amobarbital sodium (Amytal), and diazepam (Valium) for convulsions and/or sedative effects; furosemide (Lasix) for CHF; and glucagon, which is used primarily to counteract severe hypoglycemic reactions (low blood glucose) in diabetic patients taking insulin.

BASIC EMERGENCY SUPPLIES

Equipment
- Adhesive tape in 1- and 2-inch widths
- Airways—variety of types and sizes
- Alcohol wipes
- Ambu bag with assorted sizes of facial masks
- Antimicrobial skin ointment
- Bandage scissors
- Cotton balls and cotton swabs
- Cardiopulmonary resuscitation (CPR) masks—both adult and pediatric
- Defibrillator
- Elastic bandages in 2- and 3-inch widths
- Filter needles
- Flashlight with batteries
- Gauze pads, 2 × 2- and 4 × 4-inch widths, and roller bandage—both sterile and nonsterile
- Gloves, sterile and nonsterile, in multiple sizes
- Hot and cold packs (instant type)
- Intravenous catheters, tubing, solutions (variety of types, including D_5W and Ringer's lactate), and tourniquet
- Laryngoscope with blades
- Lubricant
- Personal protective equipment (PPE), including impervious gowns, splash guards or goggles, and booties
- Portable oxygen tank with regulator, mask, and nasal cannula
- Roller gauze (Ace bandages and gauze dressing) in various sizes
- Sharps container
- Sphygmomanometer—both pediatric and adult regular and large sizes
- Splints—various sizes
- Sterile dressings—miscellaneous sizes, including two abdominal pads
- Steri-Strips or suturing material
- Suction machine and catheters
- Syringes and needles in assorted sizes and gauges
- Tongue blades
- Tubex cartridge system
- Venipuncture supplies and butterfly units

Medications
- Activated charcoal, bottle of 30 to 50 g
- Amobarbital (Amytal)
- Antihistamine, injectable and oral
- Atropine
- Dextrose
- Diazepam (Valium)
- Digoxin (Lanoxin), injectable
- Diphenhydramine (Benadryl)
- Epinephrine (Adrenalin), injectable
- Furosemide (Lasix)
- Glucagon and/or glucose tablets
- Ipecac syrup
- Isoproterenol (Isuprel), aerosol inhaler and injectable
- Lidocaine (Xylocaine), injectable and spray
- Metaraminol (Aramine)
- Narcan
- Nitroglycerin tablets
- Phenobarbital, injectable
- Sodium bicarbonate, injectable
- Solu-Medrol
- Sterile water and saline for injection

Defibrillators

The medical assistant may be required to assist the healthcare team with defibrillation of emergency patients. Defibrillation is indicated when a patient is in ventricular **fibrillation** (VF). VF is a severe cardiac arrhythmia that is caused by uncoordinated, rapid firing of the electrical system of the heart, which makes it impossible for the ventricles to empty. In the absence of ventricular emptying, the patient has no pulse, blood pressure drops to zero, and the patient could die within 4 minutes unless help is given immediately.

Defibrillators are devices that send an electrical current through the myocardium by means of handheld paddles (in a healthcare facility) or self-adhesive pads applied to the chest. This electrical shock causes momentary asystole, giving the heart's natural pacemaker an opportunity to resume the heart rate at a normal rhythm.

An automated external defibrillator (AED) has a computerized system that analyzes a cardiac rhythm and delivers voice-prompt instructions on how to operate the device (Figure 27-2 and Procedure 27-7). AEDs uses self-adhesive pads that record and monitor the cardiac rhythm, and the device instructs the rescuer when to deliver the electrical charge. The apex-anterior position is the most commonly used paddle position, with the anterior (sternum) pad placed to the right of the upper sternum, and the apex pad placed under the patient's left nipple at the left middle axillary line (Figure 27-3). To defibrillate a female patient, the apex pad is placed next to or underneath the left breast.

Precautions for Automated External Defibrillators

- Neither the patient nor the caregiver should be in contact with any metal during defibrillation. Do not place the AED pad over jewelry, and remove the patient's glasses to prevent injuries.
- When available, a pediatric-dose AED system should be used for children 1 to 8 years of age (it should not be used on infants younger than 1 year old). These systems deliver a reduced shock dose for victims up to about 8 years old or weighing 55 pounds.

- All clothing (including bras) must be removed; pads must be applied directly to the skin. If the individual has a great deal of hair on the chest, try to push the hair aside before applying the pads; or, apply the pads and quickly remove them to remove hair form the area, then reapply new pads. The machine will prompt you by stating "Check electrode" if the connection is poor.
- To prevent burns, make sure the patient is lying on a dry surface and the chest is dry before applying the pads.
- If the patient has an implanted defibrillator or pacemaker, it will be obvious from the bulged area under the surface of the skin on

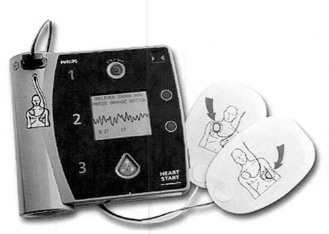

FIGURE 27-2 Fully automated external defibrillator. (From Aehlert B: *Mosby's comprehensive pediatric emergency care*, St Louis, 2005, Mosby.)

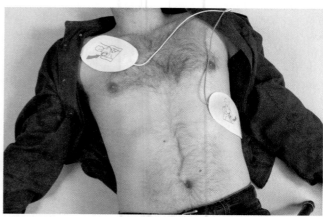

FIGURE 27-3 Connect the adhesive pads to the automated external defibrillator (AED) cables; apply the pads to the patient's chest at the upper right sternal border and at the lower left ribs over the cardiac apex. (From Chapleau W: *Emergency medical technician: making the difference*, St Louis, 2007, Mosby.)

PROCEDURE 27-7

Maintain Provider/Professional-Level CPR Certification: Use an Automated External Defibrillator

GOAL: *To defibrillate adult victims with cardiac arrest. Most adult victims in sudden cardiac arrest are in ventricular fibrillation. The survival rate for victims with ventricular fibrillation is as high as 90% when defibrillation occurs within the first minute of collapse; however, the survival rate declines 7% to 10% with every minute defibrillation does not occur.*

EQUIPMENT and SUPPLIES

- Practice automated external defibrillator (AED)
- Approved mannequin

PROCEDURAL STEPS

These steps are to be performed only on an approved mannequin.

If the healthcare worker witnesses a cardiac arrest, an AED should be used as soon as possible. If cardiopulmonary resuscitation (CPR) has already been started, continue performing CPR until the AED machine is turned on, pads are applied, and the machine is ready.

1. Place the AED near the victim's left ear. Turn on the AED.
2. Attach electrode pads to the victim's bare dry chest as pictured on the AED. Place the electrodes at the sternum and apex of the heart. Make sure the pads are in complete contact with the victim's chest and that they do not overlap (see Figure 27-3).

3. All rescuers must clear away from the victim. Press the ANALYZE button. The AED analyzes the victim's coronary status, announces whether the victim is going to be shocked, and automatically charges the electrodes (Figure 1).

(From Chapleau W: *Emergency medical technician: making the difference*, St Louis, 2007, Mosby.)

4. All rescuers must clear away from the victim. Press the SHOCK button if the machine is not automated. You may repeat 3 analyze-shock cycles.

5. Deliver 1 shock, leaving the AED attached, and immediately perform CPR, starting with chest compressions.

6. After 5 cycles (about 2 minutes) of CPR, repeat the AED analysis and deliver another shock, if indicated. If a nonshockable rhythm is detected, the AED should instruct the rescuer to resume CPR immediately, beginning with chest compressions.

7. If the machine gives the "No Shock Indicated" signal, assess the victim. Check the carotid pulse and breathing status and keep the AED attached until EMS arrives.
   <u>PURPOSE:</u> Continue to monitor breathing and circulation, because these can stop at any time. Keep the AED pads in place to diagnose ventricular fibrillation quickly if it occurs.

---

the chest. Apply the AED pads at least 1 inch away from implants to prevent interference.

GENERAL RULES FOR EMERGENCIES

A medical assistant will face two types of emergencies in the ambulatory care setting: office emergencies and home emergencies. Common office emergencies and their management are discussed later in this chapter. Besides dealing with actual emergency situations on site, a medical assistant frequently is the first person to interact with patients facing potential emergencies at home. It is estimated that one-third of the telephone calls received in a physician's office involve some type of problem that requires attention. An immediate decision must be made on how to manage that problem: by giving home care advice, scheduling an appointment, or, in life-threatening cases, notifying EMS. Many facilities, under the direction and approval of the physician, create a reference list of appropriate questions for specific patient complaints.

Regardless of how emergency phone calls are managed in the facility where you work, consider the following general rules when faced with an emergency:

- It is most important to stay calm. Reassure the patient and make him or her as comfortable as possible.
- Assess the situation to determine the nature of the emergency. Decide whether the need is immediate. This decision requires calm judgment and medical knowledge.
- Obtain as much information as possible to determine the appropriate action.
- Immediately refer any concerns to the office supervisor or physician.

Telephone Screening

Each time the phone rings in a healthcare facility, a person with a possible life-or-death situation may be on the other end of the line. One of the most important tasks performed by medical assistants every day is answering the phones and managing patients' needs efficiently and appropriately. Emergency action principles serve as a guide for managing emergency phone calls in an ambulatory care setting:

- If the patient's situation is life-threatening, activate EMS/911.
  - *Never put a caller with a life-threatening emergency on hold, and always be the last to hang up.*

- Remain on the line until help arrives and you have talked to EMS personnel.
- Immediately record the names of the caller and the patient, the location, and the phone number in case the connection is lost.
- If you are unsure how to manage the emergency situation, contact the physician.
- If the patient is referred to an emergency department (ED), call the ED to notify the staff of the patient's arrival, and make a follow-up call to determine the patient's condition.
- Gather as much information as possible about what is wrong with the patient and when the problem started. Obtain details about the patient's condition, including:
  - What is the patient's level of consciousness? Alert, responsive, lethargic, or confused? Did the patient lose consciousness at any time? If so, for how long?
  - What is the character of the patient's respirations (and pulse if the caller is able to determine this): normal, rapid, shallow, or difficult?
  - Is there bleeding? If so, how much and from where?
  - Is there a suspected head or neck injury? If so, has the patient been moved? Is there a suspected fracture? Where?
  - Does the patient have a history of this problem?
  - Any there other symptoms, such as fever, vomiting, diarrhea, or pain?
- Details about what has been done for the patient:
  - Medication: What, when? Dose, effectiveness? Current allergies?
- Thoroughly document the information gathered and any actions taken, including notification of EMS, whether the patient was sent to the ED or an appointment was scheduled, all home care recommendations, and whether the physician was notified and when.

Based on the outcome of the telephone interaction, a decision is made about when the practitioner will see the patient (Procedure 27-8). Emergency calls require activation of EMS or immediate attention as soon as the patient arrives. Urgent calls require a same-day appointment if the patient has an acute condition or is in severe discomfort. This would include a young child with a high fever or a patient who complains of moderate to severe abdominal pain. The new patient will have to be worked into the day's schedule, which may cause a delay in currently scheduled appointments. Patients

PROCEDURE 27-8

Perform Patient Screening Using Established Protocols: Telephone Screening and Appropriate Documentation

GOAL: To assess the direction of emergency care and to document information appropriately in the patient's record.

SCENARIO: Cheryl is working with the telephone screening staff when they receive a call from the mother of a 5-year-old patient. The mother reports that her son fell and cut his arm. What type of information should Cheryl gather about the injury? What action should be taken? How should the incident be documented?

EQUIPMENT and SUPPLIES

- Notepad and pen or pencil
- Patient's medical record
- Facility's emergency procedures manual
- Appointment book or computer program
- Area emergency numbers

PROCEDURAL STEPS

1. Stay calm and reassure the caller.
   PURPOSE: To enable you to gather accurate details about the patient's condition.
2. Verify the identity of the caller and the injured patient.
3. Immediately record the name of the caller and the patient, the location, and the phone number.
   PURPOSE: To be able to contact the caller if the connection is lost.
4. Determine whether the patient's condition is life threatening. Quantify the amount of blood loss, whether the patient is alert and responsive, and whether breathing is normal. Notify emergency medical services (EMS) if necessary.
   PURPOSE: Notify emergency services immediately if the patient is in danger.
5. If EMS is notified, stay on the line with the caller until EMS personnel arrive at the scene.
   PURPOSE: Never break a phone connection in the case of a life-threatening emergency.
6. If emergency services are not needed, gather details about the injury to determine whether the patient can be seen in the office or should be referred to an emergency department (ED). Consider the following questions:

- Is there a suspected head or neck injury? Has the patient been moved?
- Is there a possible fracture? If so, where?
- Are there any other symptoms?
- Is there anything pertinent in the patient's health history that would complicate the situation?
- Has the caller administered any first aid? If so, what was done?

7. Based on the information gathered, determine when the patient should be seen in the office if he or she has not been referred to an ED.
   PURPOSE: Most emergencies are scheduled for an immediate office visit. This may require altering the current appointment schedule.
8. At any point in this process, do not hesitate to consult the physician or experienced staff or refer to the facility's emergency procedures manual to determine how to manage the patient's problem.
9. Always allow the caller to hang up first, just in case more information or assistance is needed.
10. Document the information gathered, the actions taken or recommended, any home care recommendations, and whether the physician was notified.
    PURPOSE: To have a legal record of the management of the emergency and a comprehensive description of the patient's condition and recommended management.

7/13/XX 1:25 PM Patient's mother reports child fell against a window and lacerated his arm. Bleeding is moderate but controlled. No reported signs of dyspnea or altered consciousness. Mother will bring child to office immediately for physician assessment. Cheryl Skurka, CMA (AAMA)

---

with other, less urgent problems can be scheduled for appointments within the next 3 to 4 days.

Management of On-Site Emergencies

An emergency can occur at any time to anyone. Always follow Standard Precautions when at risk for coming into contact with blood or body fluids. When an emergency occurs, it is impossible to determine the level of infection. All body fluids must be considered infectious, and appropriate precautions must be taken to prevent cross-contamination. If the situation is life-threatening, notify EMS and stay with the patient until you are relieved by the EMS provider or the physician. It is important to document all details of the incident in the patient's medical record.

DOCUMENTATION OF AN ON-SITE EMERGENCY

1. Patient's name, address, age, and health insurance information
2. Allergies, current medications, and pertinent health history
3. Name and relationship of any person with the patient
4. Vital signs and chief complaint
5. Sequence of events, beginning with how the problem occurred, any changes in the patient's overall condition, and any observations made regarding the patient's condition
6. Details regarding procedures or treatments performed on the patient

CRITICAL THINKING APPLICATION 27-3
Cheryl is working the front desk when a patient comes into the office limping. She tells Cheryl that she fell in the parking lot and hurt her ankle. Cheryl helps the patient into an exam room and begins to interview her. Role-play the situation with a classmate and make a list of at least 10 questions Cheryl should ask the patient.

Life-Threatening Emergencies

If a patient in the facility shows any signs of unresponsiveness, the clinician must be brought to the patient immediately. If no clinician is available in the facility, EMS must be activated. Even when a physician is present, the physician may order you to call 911 for immediate emergency care. Put on gloves before you begin to assess the patient, because any emergency situation may involve exposure to blood or body fluids.

Unresponsive Patient

If a patient is able to talk to you, he or she has an open airway. If the patient does not respond to a simple question (e.g., "Are you OK?"), gently shake the person's shoulder to check responsiveness. If the patient does not respond, you must assume that the patient is unconscious. Immediately call for help and activate EMS if that is office policy.

To care for an unresponsive patient, first assess the patient's respirations to determine whether the person is breathing. When the patient collapsed, the tongue may have gone limp and occluded the trachea. Just by changing the individual's position and opening the airway, you may provide all the assistance the patient needs to breathe independently.

If the patient is face down, roll the victim onto his or her back while supporting the head, neck, and back. Apply the head tilt–chin lift movement to open the airway. The tongue is attached to the lower jaw, so moving the jaw forward automatically opens the patient's airway. If a head or neck injury is suspected, the neck should be manipulated as little as possible; therefore, the airway should be open with the jaw-thrust maneuver. Both of these actions relieve possible obstruction of the trachea by the tongue.

Check for breathing no longer than 10 seconds by looking for a rise in the chest and by listening or feeling for air exchange (Figure 27-4). Breathing may stop suddenly for a variety of reasons, including shock, disease, and trauma. If no breaths are detected, artificial ventilation must be started immediately, because death can occur within 4 to 6 minutes. Barrier devices should be kept on hand for artificial respiration (Figure 27-5), and these should be used if rescue breaths are required (Procedure 27-9).

After giving the patient 2 slow breaths, check for signs of normal breathing or movement. If no signs of responsiveness are evident, check for cardiac circulation at the carotid pulse (in an adult or a child) or at the brachial pulse (in an infant) (Figure 27-6). Gently feel for the pulse while continuing to assess the patient for possible signs of recovery for 5 to 10 seconds. If a pulse is present, continue ventilating the lungs with slow breaths every 4 to 5 seconds (adult) or every 3 seconds (child or infant). If the pulse is absent, begin cycles of 30 chest compressions at a rate of about 100 per minute followed by 2 slow breaths.

FIGURE 27-4 Checking for breathing in an unconscious patient.

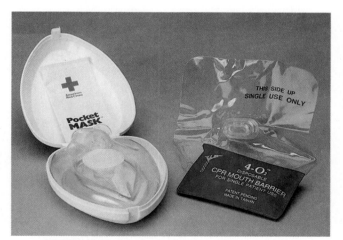

FIGURE 27-5 Cardiopulmonary resuscitation (CPR) mouth barriers.

When both breathing and pulse stop, the victim has suffered sudden death. Sudden death has many causes, including heart disease, choking, drowning, poisoning, suffocation, electrocution, and smoke inhalation. CPR must be started immediately to attempt to revive the patient and to prevent permanent damage to body organs, especially the brain. Continue CPR until the victim begins to move, an AED is available and ready to use, professional help arrives, or you are too exhausted to continue. If the patient has a pulse but is not breathing, continue rescue breathing and occasionally monitor the pulse until help arrives.

Refer to the *Standard First Aid Manual* of the American Red Cross or the *American Heart Association CPR Manual*, or the organizations' Web sites, for specific procedures and precautions in the management of respiratory and cardiac emergencies. As stated earlier, all healthcare workers should have a current Certification for the Professional in CPR.

Maintain Provider/Professional-Level CPR Certification: Perform Adult Rescue Breathing and One-Rescuer CPR; Perform Pediatric and Infant CPR

GOAL: *To restore breathing and blood circulation when respiration or pulse (or both) has stopped.*

EQUIPMENT and SUPPLIES

- Disposable gloves
- Cardiopulmonary resuscitation (CPR) ventilator masks for adults, children, and infants
- Approved mannequins

PROCEDURAL STEPS

These steps are to be performed only on approved mannequins.

TO PERFORM CPR ON AN ADULT VICTIM

1. Establish unresponsiveness. Tap the victim and ask, "Are you OK?" Wait for the victim to respond.
   <u>PURPOSE:</u> To determine whether the victim is conscious.
2. Activate the emergency response system. Put on gloves and get a ventilator mask.
   <u>PURPOSE:</u> As soon as it is determined that an adult victim requires emergency care, activate emergency medical services (EMS). Most adults with sudden, nontraumatic cardiac arrest are in ventricular fibrillation. The time from collapse to defibrillation is the single most important predictor of survival.
3. Tilt the victim's head by placing one hand on the forehead and applying enough pressure to push the head back; with the fingers of the other hand under the chin, lift up and pull the jaw forward. Look, listen, and feel for signs of breathing. Place your ear over the mouth and listen for breathing. Watch the rising and falling of the chest for evidence of breathing (Figure 1). If breathing is absent or inadequate, open the airway and place the ventilator mask over the victim's mouth and nose.
   <u>PURPOSE:</u> To open the airway and determine whether the victim is breathing.

4. Give 2 slow breaths (1½ to 2 seconds per breath for an adult; 1 to 2 seconds per breath for an infant or child), holding the ventilator mask tightly against the face while tilting the victim's chin up to keep the airway open (Figure 2). Remove your mouth from the mouthpiece between breaths to allow time for the patient to exhale between breaths.

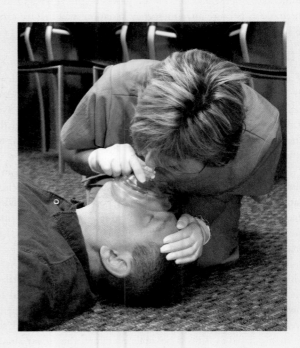

5. Check the patient's pulse (at the carotid artery for an adult or older child; at the brachial artery for an infant). If a pulse is present, continue rescue breathing (1 breath every 4 to 5 seconds—about 10 to 12 breaths per minute for an adult; 1 breath every 3 seconds—about 12 to 20 breaths per minute for an infant or child). If no signs of circulation are present, begin cycles of 30 chest compressions (at a rate of about 100 compressions per minute for an adult) followed by 2 slow breaths.
6. To deliver chest compressions, kneel at the victim's side a couple of inches away from the chest. Hand placement is over the sternum, between the nipples but above the xiphoid process.
7. Place the heel of your hand on the chest over the lower part of the sternum.
8. Place your other hand on top of the first and interlace or lift your fingers upward off the chest (Figure 3).
   <u>PURPOSE:</u> This position gives you the most control, allowing you to avoid injuring the victim's ribs as you compress the chest.

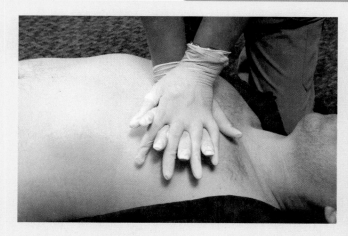

9. Bring your shoulders directly over the victim's sternum as you compress downward, keeping your elbows locked (Figure 4).

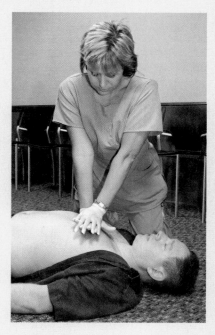

10. Depress the sternum at least 2 inches in an adult victim. Relax the pressure on the sternum after each compression but do not remove your hands from the sternum.
    PURPOSE: The depth of compression is needed to circulate blood through the heart. Movement of the hands may cause injury to the victim.

11. After performing 30 compressions (at a rate of about 100 compressions per minute), perform the head tilt–chin lift maneuver to open the airway, and give 2 slow rescue breaths.

12. After 5 cycles of compressions and breaths (30:2 ratio, about 2 minutes) recheck the breathing and carotid pulse (Figure 5). If a pulse is present but breathing is not, continue rescue breathing (1 breath every 5 seconds, about 10 to 12 breaths per minute) and re-evaluate the victim's breathing and pulse every few minutes. If no signs of circulation are present, continue 30:2 cycles of compressions and ventilations, starting with chest compressions. Continue giving CPR

until an automated external defibrillator (AED) is available or EMS relieves you.

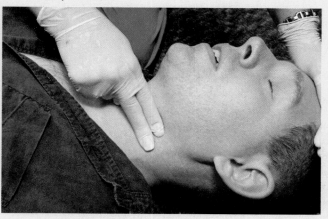

TO PERFORM CPR ON A CHILD

The procedure for giving CPR to a child ages 1 through 8 is essentially the same as that for an adult. The differences are as follows:

- Perform 5 cycles of compressions and breaths on the child (30:2 ratio, about 2 minutes) before calling 911 or the local emergency number or using an AED. If another person is available, have that person activate EMS while you care for the child.
  PURPOSE: It is important to provide immediate circulation of oxygenated blood to a child to prevent brain damage. Most pediatric cardiac arrests occur because of a secondary problem, such as airway occlusion, rather than a cardiac problem. If you know there is an airway obstruction, clear the obstruction and then proceed with CPR.

- Use only one hand to perform chest compressions (Figure 6).
  PURPOSE: The pediatric sternum requires less force to achieve the needed depression.

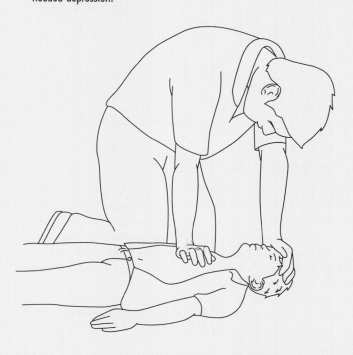

PROCEDURE 27-9—cont'd

- Breathe more gently.
- Use the same compression-to-breath ratio as used for adults, 30 compressions followed by 2 breaths per cycle; after 2 breaths, immediately begin the next cycle of compressions and breaths.
- After 5 cycles (about 2 minutes) of CPR without response, use a pediatric AED if available.
- Continue until the child responds or help arrives.

INFANT CPR

Infant cardiac arrest typically is caused by lack of oxygen from drowning or choking. If you know the infant has an airway obstruction, clear the obstruction; if you do not know why the infant is unresponsive, perform CPR for 2 minutes (about 5 cycles) before calling 911 or the local emergency number. If another person is available, have that person call for help immediately while you attend to the baby.

RESCUE BREATHING FOR AN INFANT

Use an infant ventilator mask or cover the baby's mouth and nose with your mouth.
- Give 2 rescue breaths by gently puffing out the cheeks and slowly breathing into the infant's mouth, taking about 1 second for each breath (Figure 7).

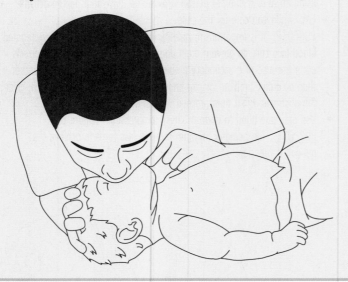

TO PERFORM CPR ON AN INFANT

- Draw an imaginary line between the infant's nipples. Place two fingers on the sternum just below this intermammary line.
- Gently compress the chest.
- Compression rate should be 100 to 120 per minute.
- Administer 2 breaths after every 30 compressions.
- After about five 30:2 cycles, activate EMS.
- Continue CPR until the child responds or help arrives.

13. Remove your gloves and the ventilator mask valve, and discard them in the biohazard container. Disinfect the ventilator mask per the manufacturer's recommendations. Sanitize your hands.
14. Document the procedure and the patient's condition.

▌Cardiac Emergencies

Chest pain or angina can be associated with heart and lung disease, as well as a few other conditions. It can be quite serious; a patient with chest pain is treated as a cardiac emergency until a physician has ruled this out. A heart attack, or *myocardial infarction*, usually is caused by blockage of the coronary arteries, which reduces the amount of blood delivered to the myocardium. The most common signal of a heart attack is an uncomfortable pressure, squeezing, fullness, or pain in the center of the chest. This may spread to the shoulder, neck, jaw, or arms. The pain may not be severe. The lips and fingernails may be blue, which is a sign of **cyanosis** (Figure 27-7), or the patient may have a gray, ashen appearance. Frequently, the patient clutches the chest in pain. This pain may radiate from the **mediastinum** down the left arm and up the left side of the neck. The pulse may be rapid and weak, and the patient often complains of nausea. Other symptoms include sweating *(diaphoresis)*; indigestion; shortness of breath (SOB); cold, clammy skin; and a feeling of weakness *(general malaise)*. Unfortunately, most people deny that the problem is serious until they require immediate medical attention.

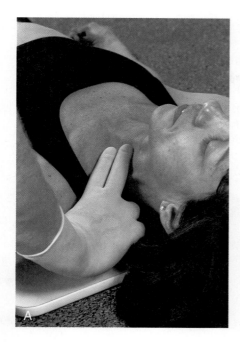

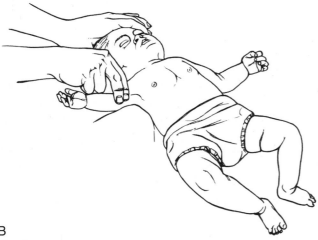

FIGURE 27-6 A, In an adult, check for a carotid pulse. **B,** In an infant, check for a brachial pulse.

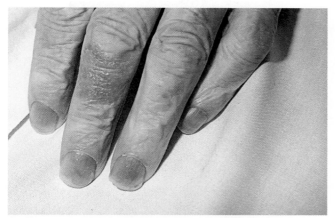

FIGURE 27-7 Cyanosis of the nail beds. (From Henry MC, Stapleton ER: *EMT prehospital care,* ed 3, Philadelphia, 2004, Saunders.)

SIGNS AND SYMPTOMS OF MYOCARDIAL INFARCTION IN WOMEN

Women may experience symptoms that are different from those traditionally associated with a heart attack. These include a combination of the following:

- Back pain or aching and throbbing in the biceps or forearms
- Shortness of breath (SOB)
- Clammy perspiration
- Dizziness (vertigo)—unexplained light-headedness or syncopal episodes
- Edema, especially of the ankles and/or lower legs
- Fluttering heartbeat or tachycardia
- Gastric upset
- Feeling of heaviness or fullness in the mediastinum

Immediately report any of these signs or symptoms to the physician. If the physician is not available, activate EMS. Use a wheelchair to move the patient to an examination room. Breathing will be easier if the patient's head is slightly elevated, or if the patient is in Fowler's position. Keep the patient quiet and warm. Loosen all tight clothing. Take vital signs, including both apical and radial pulses. The physician may order oxygen started on the patient to relieve dyspnea (Procedure 27-10). Bring the emergency cart into the room and open the medication drawer so that the physician can quickly prepare the medications needed. These may include epinephrine (adrenaline), atropine, digitalis, calcium chloride, or morphine.

If the patient is conscious, ask about any medication that he or she has recently taken or is carrying. If the patient has an established heart disorder, the person may be carrying nitroglycerin tablets; these tablets are administered sublingually and may be given with the patient's consent (Figure 27-8). If the physician is in the office or is on the way, connect the patient to the electrocardiograph machine and record a few tracings. If the patient becomes unresponsive before the physician or EMS arrives, it may be necessary to start rescue breathing if there is no evidence of respirations. If chest pain progresses to cardiac arrest and loss of circulation, CPR must be performed until help arrives.

Choking

Choking is usually caused by a foreign object, often a bolus of food, lodged in the upper airway. The victim may clutch the neck between the thumb and the index finger (Figure 27-9); this universal distress signal should be viewed as a sign the victim needs help. If the victim has good air exchange or only partial airway obstruction and can speak, cough, or breathe, do not interfere, but encourage the patient to continue coughing until the object is expelled. Monitor the patient for signs of respiratory distress, such as pallor and cyanosis. If the patient has a pronounced wheeze or a very weak cough, he or she has a partial airway obstruction with poor air exchange and may need help. If the patient is unable to speak, breathe, or cough, a complete airway obstruction exists, and quick action must be taken to clear the airway. With complete obstruction, the patient eventually loses consciousness from lack of oxygen to the brain. This condition may lead to respiratory and cardiac arrest. If the object is not

PROCEDURE 27-10

Perform First Aid Procedures: Administer Oxygen

GOAL: *To provide oxygen for a patient in respiratory distress.*

EQUIPMENT and SUPPLIES

- Portable oxygen tank
- Pressure regulator
- Flow meter
- Nasal cannula with connecting tubing
- Physician's order
- Patient's medical record

PROCEDURAL STEPS

1. Gather equipment and sanitize your hands.
2. Greet and identify the patient, introduce yourself, and explain the procedure.
   <u>PURPOSE:</u> A nasal cannula is applied with a nasal prong in each nostril and the tab resting above the upper lip. Patients who will be using oxygen at home need to be taught how to open an oxygen tank or to use an oxygen compressor. It is vital that patients and their families understand the dangers of oxygen use in the home. They must avoid open flames and not smoke when oxygen is in use, because it is combustible. The physician typically writes an order for the number of liters of oxygen to be delivered and for home healthcare services to set up the equipment in the patient's home.
3. Check the pressure gauge on the tank to determine the amount of oxygen in the tank.
4. If necessary, open the cylinder on the tank one full counterclockwise turn, then attach the cannula tubing to the flow meter.
5. Adjust the administration of the oxygen according to the physician's order. Usually the flow meter is set at 12 to 15 liters per minute (LPM). Check to make sure oxygen is flowing through the cannula.

6. Insert the tips of the cannula into the nostrils and adjust the tubing around the back of the patient's ears (Figure 1).

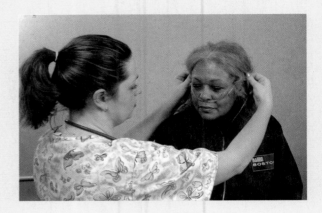

7. Make sure the patient is comfortable, and answer any questions he or she may have.
8. Sanitize your hands.
9. Document the procedure, including the number of liters of oxygen being administered and the patient's condition. Continue to monitor the patient throughout the procedure and document any changes in condition.

7/24/XX 3:05 PM R – 28 and labored. Oxygen initiated at 4 L/min via nasal cannula per physician order. Pt observed for signs of dyspnea and tachypnea. Cheryl Skurka, CMA (AAMA)

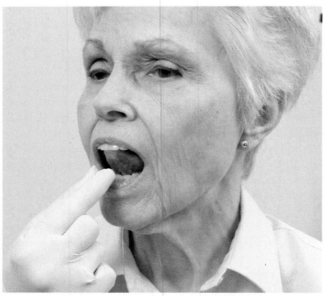

FIGURE 27-8 Nitroglycerin is administered beneath the patient's tongue.

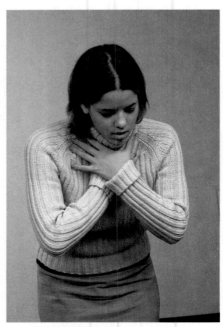

FIGURE 27-9 Universal sign of choking.

removed, the victim may die within 4 to 6 minutes. Procedure 27-11 presents the steps involved in clearing an obstructed airway in an adult. The procedure for removal of a foreign airway obstruction is exactly the same for a child older than 1 year of age.

To dislodge a foreign object from the airway of an infant up to 1 year of age, place the baby face down over your forearm and across your thigh. The head should be lower than the trunk, and you should support the baby's head and neck with one hand. Using the heel of your other hand, deliver 5 blows to the back, between the infant's shoulder blades (Figure 27-10, *A*). Holding the baby between your arms, turn the infant face up, keeping the head lower than the trunk. Using two fingers, deliver 5 thrusts to the midsternal area at the infant's nipple line (Figure 27-10, *B*). Examine the infant's mouth, and if the object is visible, pluck it out with your fingertips. *Never perform a finger sweep on an infant.* A baby's oral cavity is too small for a finger sweep, and such an action may only push the obstruction farther into the airway. If the obstruction is not visible, administer 2 rescue breaths by covering the baby's nose and mouth with your

mouth, or use a pediatric ventilator mask if available. Repeat the sequence until the foreign body is expelled or help arrives.

If a choking victim is in the late stages of pregnancy, chest compressions should be delivered to prevent possible trauma to the infant. If the patient is obese and you are unable to wrap your arms around the abdomen, perform chest compressions as you would for a pregnant woman.

The abdominal thrust maneuver also can be performed on yourself if you are choking and no one is nearby to help you. Press your fist into your upper abdomen with quick, upward thrusts, or lean forward and press the abdomen quickly against a firm object, such as the back of a chair.

Cerebrovascular Accident (Stroke)

A cerebrovascular accident (CVA), or stroke, is a disorder of the cerebral blood vessels that results in impairment of the blood supply to part of the brain. This interruption in normal circulation of blood through the brain leads to some degree of neurological damage,

---

PROCEDURE 27-11

Perform First Aid Procedures: Respond to an Airway Obstruction in an Adult

GOAL: *To remove an airway obstruction and restore ventilation.*

EQUIPMENT and SUPPLIES

- Disposable gloves
- Ventilation mask (for unconscious victim)
- Approved mannequin to practice unconscious foreign body airway obstruction (FBAO) removal

PROCEDURAL STEPS

The technique for an unresponsive victim is to be performed only on an approved mannequin.

1. Ask, "Are you choking?" If the victim indicates yes, ask, "Can you speak?" If the victim is unable to speak, tell the victim you are going to help.
   PURPOSE: If the victim is unable to speak, is coughing weakly, and/or is wheezing, he or she has an obstructed airway with poor air exchange, and the obstruction must be removed before respiratory arrest occurs.
2. Stand behind the victim with your feet slightly apart.
   PURPOSE: With an obstructed airway, the victim may lose consciousness at any time. The rescuer must be prepared to lower the unconscious victim to the floor safely.
3. Reach around the victim's abdomen and place an index finger into the victim's navel or at the level of the belt buckle. Make a fist of the opposite hand (do not tuck the thumb into the fist) and place the thumb side of the fist against the victim's abdomen above the navel. If the victim is pregnant, place the fist above the enlarged uterus. If the victim is obese, it may be necessary to place the fist higher in the abdomen. It may be necessary to perform chest thrusts on a victim who is pregnant or obese.
   PURPOSE: The fist should be placed in the soft tissue of the abdomen to avoid injury to the sternum or rib cage.

4. Place the opposite hand over the fist and give abdominal thrusts in a quick inward and upward movement (Figure 1).
   PURPOSE: Abdominal contents pushing against the diaphragm force trapped air out of the lungs, and with it the obstruction.

(From Chapleau W: *Emergency medical technician: making the difference,* St Louis, 2007, Mosby.)

5. Repeat the abdominal thrusts until the object is expelled or the victim becomes unresponsive.

Unresponsive Adult Victim

1. Carefully lower the patient to the ground, activate the emergency response system, and put on disposable gloves.
2. Immediately begin cardiopulmonary resuscitation (CPR) with 30 compressions and 2 breath cycles using the ventilator mask.
   PURPOSE: Higher airway pressures are maintained with chest compressions than with abdominal thrusts.

PROCEDURE 27-11—cont'd

3. Each time the airway is opened to deliver a rescue breath during CPR, look for an object in the victim's mouth and remove it if visible. If no object is found, immediately return to the cycle of 30 chest compressions.
4. A finger sweep should be used only if the rescuer can see the obstruction.
5. Continue cycles of 30 compressions to 2 rescue breaths until the obstruction is removed or emergency medical services (EMS) arrives.
6. If the obstruction is removed, assess the victim for breathing and circulation. If a pulse is present but the patient is not breathing, begin rescue breathing.
7. Once the patient has been stabilized or EMS has taken over care, remove your gloves and the ventilator mask valve and discard them in the

biohazard container. Disinfect the ventilator mask per the manufacturer's recommendations. Sanitize your hands.
8. Document the procedure and the patient's condition.

7/22/XX 8:35 AM Pt in waiting room clutching throat and coughing weakly. After confirming pt choking, abdominal thrusts performed until foreign body expelled. Pt breathing without difficulty; R – 18 and regular. Incident reported to physician. Cheryl Skurka, CMA (AAMA) _____

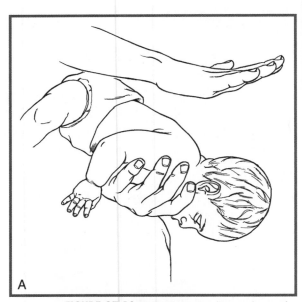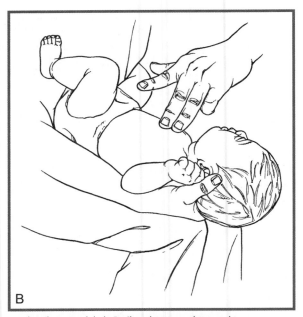

FIGURE 27-10 A, Back blows are administered to an infant supported on the arm and thigh. **B,** Chest thrusts are administered in the same position as for cardiac compressions. (From Henry MC, Stapleton ER: *EMT prehospital care,* ed 3, Philadelphia, 2004, Saunders.)

temporary or permanent, depending on the severity of oxygen deprivation to the brain cells.

A minor stroke, or **transient ischemic attack (TIA)**, usually does not cause unconsciousness, and symptoms depend on the location of the circulatory problem in the brain, as well as the amount of brain damage. TIA symptoms are temporary and may include headache, confusion, vertigo, ringing in the ears *(tinnitus)*, temporary paralysis or weakness of one side of the body, transient limb weakness, slurred speech, and vision problems. TIA episodes indicate that the patient is at risk for a major stroke.

Symptoms of a major stroke include unconsciousness, paralysis on one side of the body, difficulty breathing and swallowing, loss of bladder and bowel control, unequal pupil size, and slurring of speech.

Home recommendations for a patient who has suffered a major stroke should begin with notifying the physician and/or activating EMS. Keep the patient lying down and lightly covered. Maintain an open airway. To prevent choking, position the head so that any secretions drain from the side of the mouth. If the patient is lying on the floor, did not fall, and shows no indications of a head or neck injury, he or she can be placed in the recovery position as follows (Figure 27-11):

1. Place the patient's arm that is farthest from you alongside and above the head; place the other arm across the chest.
2. Bend the leg that is closest to you, and after placing one arm under the patient's head and shoulder and the other hand on the flexed knee, roll the patient away from you while you stabilize

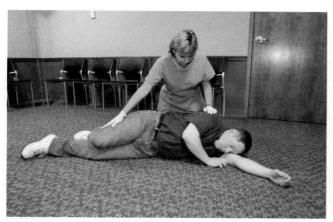

FIGURE 27-11 Recovery position.

the head and neck. The patient's head should be resting on the extended arm.

The recovery position uses gravity to drain fluids from the mouth and keep the trachea clear. Keep the patient in this position until the person is alert or help arrives. Do not give the patient anything to eat or drink. Vital signs should be measured at regular intervals and recorded for the physician.

Advances in early treatment of strokes show great promise in preventing long-term neurological deficits. However, to prevent permanent brain damage, **thrombolytics** must be administered intravenously within 3 hours of the onset of symptoms. If a patient does not know when the symptoms began (e.g., the person woke up with the symptoms) or cannot accurately tell the physician when the symptoms started, the time allotted for administration begins from the point at which the patient last was known to be asymptomatic. Intracranial hemorrhage must be ruled out before treatment begins. The earlier the treatment starts, the better are the neurological outcomes. The best possible outcomes are seen in patients who received thrombolytic therapy within 90 minutes of the onset of symptoms.

CRITICAL THINKING APPLICATION   **27-4**

Thomas Antonio, a 67-year-old patient, calls to report that when he woke up this morning, the left side of his face was drooping and he had difficulty seeing out of his left eye. The symptoms went away in about 2 hours, and he is feeling fine now. The schedule does not show any openings for 2 days. When should Cheryl make an appointment for Mr. Antonio? What questions should Cheryl ask him?

Shock

Shock is a state of collapse caused by failure of the circulatory system to deliver enough oxygenated blood to the body's vital organs. Injury, hemorrhage, infection, anesthesia, drug overdose, burns, pain, fear, or emotional stress can cause this physiologic reaction. Shock can be immediate or delayed, and it is potentially fatal. Many different types of shock can occur, but the signs and symptoms are universal. The most common indicators are a pale, gray, or cyanotic appearance; moist but cool skin; dilated pupils; a weak, rapid pulse; marked hypotension; shallow, rapid respirations; lethargy or restlessness; nausea and vomiting; and extreme thirst.

If a patient shows signs of shock, maintain an open airway and check for breathing and circulation. Place the patient supine with the legs elevated approximately 1 foot to return the blood from the legs to vital organs. Loosen all tight clothing and cover the patient with a blanket for warmth. Do not move the patient unnecessarily. Fluids may be given by mouth if the patient is alert. Because shock can evolve into a life-threatening situation, only basic first aid should be administered, and the patient should be transported to the hospital as soon as possible.

TYPES AND CAUSES OF SHOCK

- Anaphylactic—a severe allergic reaction
- Insulin—severe hypoglycemia caused by an overdose of insulin
- Psychogenic or mental—excessive fear, joy, anger, or emotional stress
- Hypovolemic or hemorrhagic—excessive loss of blood
- Cardiogenic—myocardial infarction, pulmonary embolism, or severe congestive heart failure
- Neurogenic—dilation of blood vessels as a result of brain or spinal cord injury
- Septic—systemic infection

COMMON OFFICE EMERGENCIES

The remainder of this chapter highlights typical emergencies seen in the ambulatory care setting or in telephone triage situations. Table 27-1 summarizes common emergencies, the questions that should be asked, and possible actions for home care.

Fainting (Syncope)

Fainting, or *syncope*, is a common emergency. It usually is caused by a transient loss of blood flow to the brain (e.g., a sudden drop in blood pressure), which results in a temporary loss of consciousness. It can occur without warning, or the patient may appear pale; may feel cold, weak, dizzy, or nauseated; and may have numbness of the extremities before the incident. The greatest danger to the patient is an injury from falling during the attack. Therefore, if a patient has syncopal symptoms, immediately place the individual in a supine position. Loosen all tight clothing and maintain an open airway. Apply a cold washcloth to the forehead. Measure and record the patient's pulse, respiratory rate, and blood pressure, and report the findings to the physician. Keep the patient in a supine position for at least 10 minutes after the person regains consciousness. A complete patient history can help determine the possible causes of the attack (e.g., a history of heart disease or diabetes). Document the details of the episode and how long it took the patient to recover completely (Procedure 27-12).

If the patient does not recover quickly, the physician may activate EMS for transport to the hospital. Syncope might be a brief episode in the development of a serious underlying illness, such as an abnormal heart rhythm, that could lead to sudden cardiac death.

Poisoning

Poisonings are considered medical emergencies and are the sixth leading cause of accidental pediatric death in the United States. Poisoning can occur by oral intake, absorption, inhalation, or

TABLE 27-1   Telephone Screening of Possible Emergency Situations

EMERGENCY SITUATION	SCREENING QUESTIONS	HOME CARE ADVICE
Syncope	• Was the patient injured? • Does the patient have a history of heart disease, seizures, or diabetes?	• Does not necessarily indicate a serious disease. If injured by a fall, the patient may need to be evaluated and treated. • The patient should get up very slowly to prevent a recurrence, take it easy, and drink plenty of fluids. • If the patient is to be seen, someone should accompany him or her to the physician's office.
Animal bites	• What kind of animal (pet or wild)? • How severe is the injury? • Where are the bites? • When did the bites occur?	• The health department or police should be notified. Every effort must be made to locate the animal and monitor its health. • If the skin is not broken, wash well and observe for signs of infection.
Insect bites and stings	• Does the patient have a history of anaphylactic reaction to insect stings? • Does the patient have difficulty breathing, have a widespread rash, or have trouble swallowing?	• If the patient has a history of anaphylaxis and an EpiPen, the EpiPen should be used immediately and emergency medical services (EMS) notified. • Activate EMS if the patient is having systemic symptoms. • An antihistamine (Benadryl) relieves local pruritus.
Asthma	• Does the patient show signs of cyanosis? • Has the patient used prescribed inhalers?	• If a patient with asthma is unable to speak in sentences, has poor color, and is struggling to breathe even after using an inhaler, he or she should be seen immediately, or EMS should be activated.
Burns	• Where are the burns located, and what caused them? • Are signs of shock present: moist, clammy skin, altered consciousness, rapid breathing and pulse? • Are signs of infection present (foul odor, cloudy drainage) in a burn more than 2 days old?	• Activate EMS for burns on the face, hands, feet, or perineum; those caused by electricity or a chemical; and burns associated with inhalation. Activate EMS if signs of shock are present. • The patient must receive a tetanus shot if he or she has not had one in more than 10 years. • Schedule an urgent appointment if signs of infection are reported.
Wounds	• Is the bleeding steady or pulsating? • How and when did the injury occur? • Does the patient have any bleeding disorders or is the patient taking anticoagulant drugs? • Is the wound open and deep?	• Pulsating bleeding usually indicates arterial damage; activate EMS. • If the injury was caused by a powerful force, other injuries also may have resulted. • For patients taking anticoagulants or with diabetes or anemia, schedule an urgent appointment. • A gaping, deep wound requires sutures.
Head injury	• Did the patient pass out or have a seizure? Is the patient confused or vomiting? Is a clear fluid draining from the nose or ears?	• If the answer is "yes" to any of these questions, EMS should be activated.

injection. Over-the-counter (OTC) medications (e.g., acetaminophen); detergents and bleach; plants; cough and cold medicines; and vitamins cause most cases of poisoning seen in young children. Other typical household poisons include drain cleaner, turpentine, kerosene, furniture polish, and paint (Figure 27-12). Signs and symptoms of poisoning, which vary greatly, include burns on the hands and mouth, stains on the victim's clothing, open bottles of medicines or chemicals, changes in skin color, nausea or stomach cramps, shallow breathing, convulsions, heavy perspiration, dizziness or drowsiness, and unconsciousness.

If you receive a phone call about a suspected poisoning, tell the caller not to hang up and not to leave the victim unattended. Call the local poison control center and forward all directions to the caller. Syrup of ipecac, which causes vomiting within 15 to 20 minutes, should be used only if ordered by the physician or the poison control center, because some chemicals can cause serious

PROCEDURE 27-12

Perform First Aid Procedures: Care for a Patient Who Has Fainted

GOAL: *To provide emergency care for and assessment of a patient who has fainted.*

EQUIPMENT and SUPPLIES

- Patient's record
- Sphygmomanometer
- Stethoscope
- Watch with second hand
- Blanket
- Footstool or box
- Pillows
- Oxygen equipment, if ordered by physician:
    - Portable oxygen tank
    - Pressure regulator
    - Flow meter
    - Nasal cannula with connecting tubing

PROCEDURAL STEPS

1. If warning is given that the patient feels faint, have the patient lower the head to the knees to increase the blood supply to the brain (Figure 1). If this does not stop the episode, have the patient lie down on the examination table or lower the patient to the floor. If the patient collapses to the floor when fainting, treat with caution because of possible head or neck injuries.

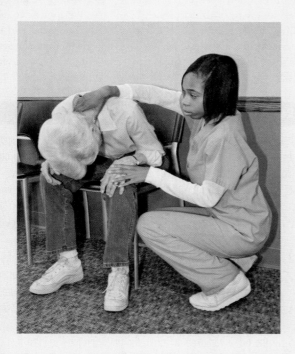

2. Immediately notify the physician of the patient's condition and assess the patient for life-threatening emergencies, such as respiratory or cardiac arrest. If the patient is breathing and has a pulse, monitor the patient's vital signs.

3. Loosen any tight clothing and keep the patient warm, applying a blanket if needed.

4. If a head or neck injury is not a factor, elevate the patient's legs above the level of the heart using the footstool with pillow support if available (Figure 2).
   <u>PURPOSE:</u> Elevating the legs assists with venous blood return to the heart. This may relieve symptoms of fainting by elevating the blood pressure and increasing blood flow to vital organs.

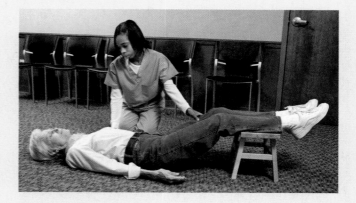

5. Continue to monitor vital signs and apply oxygen by nasal cannula if ordered by the physician.

6. If vital signs are unstable or the patient does not respond quickly, activate emergency medical services (EMS).
   <u>PURPOSE:</u> Fainting may be a sign of a life-threatening problem.

7. If the patient vomits, roll the patient onto his or her side to prevent aspiration of vomitus into the lungs.

8. Once the patient has completely recovered, assist the patient into a sitting position. Do not leave the patient unattended on the examination table.

9. Document the incident, including a description of the episode, the patient's symptoms and vital signs, the duration of the episode, and any complaints. If oxygen was administered, document the number of liters and how long oxygen was administered.

7/29/XX 4:18 PM Pt in waiting room states she feels faint. Pt lowered to floor, clothing loosened, legs elevated. Physician notified. P 88 and regular, R 22, BP 112/60. Syncopal episode persisted for 90 sec, feeling of vertigo lasted 10 min post syncope. Pt transferred to exam room via wheelchair after recovery. Cheryl Skurka, CMA (AAMA) _____

FIGURE 27-12 Hazardous household materials. (From Henry MC, Stapleton ER: *EMT prehospital care*, ed 3, Philadelphia, 2004, Saunders.)

irritation to the tissues if vomited. Do not induce vomiting if the victim is semiconscious or is experiencing convulsions, because of the risk of aspiration of stomach contents into the lungs. If syrup of ipecac is recommended, give 2 teaspoons to infants 9 to 12 months old after the child drinks about 4 ounces of warm water. For a child 1 to 4 years old, administer 1 tablespoon after the child drinks 4 to 8 ounces of warm water. If the patient is to be seen by the physician or sent to the hospital, tell the caller to bring the container of poison or a sample of the vomitus with him, so that the chemical contents of the substance can be verified.

WHAT TO ASK WHEN A POISONING IS REPORTED

- Victim's name, weight, and age
- Name of the poison taken and any information on the label
- How much was taken
- How long ago the poison was ingested
- Whether vomiting has occurred
- Any pertinent symptoms, such as difficulty breathing or an altered state of consciousness
- Any first aid that has been given

CRITICAL THINKING APPLICATION   27-5

A young mother calls in a panic to report that her 18-month-old daughter swallowed at least half a bottle of cough syrup. The child is fussy and very sleepy, and the mother wants to give her ipecac immediately. What should Cheryl do?

Animal Bites

Potential complications from animal bites include rabies, tetanus, and local skin infection. Any animal bite that is extensive or deep should be seen by a physician. Human infection with rabies is rare; however, if the bite is made by a domestic animal, the animal should be kept quarantined and under observation for 10 days for monitoring for signs of the disease. The animal should not be killed, because a positive finding of rabies is almost impossible to make if the animal has been dead for an extended time. If the bite is that of a bat,

raccoon, or any other wild animal, the animal is assumed to be rabid, and the patient must undergo a series of rabies vaccine injections. Local skin infection can be prevented by immediately cleansing the area with antimicrobial soap and water. If the bite breaks the skin (including human bites), the patient's tetanus immunization status must be checked and, if needed, a booster or the entire four-dose tetanus series must be administered as indicated.

Insect Bites and Stings

The bite or sting of an insect can be irritating and painful because of the chemical toxin injected by the insect, but it usually is not serious. Typical symptoms—inflammation, itching *(pruritus)*, and edema—are local and are confined to the area of the bite. In rare cases, a severe allergic reaction may occur; this is a potentially dangerous situation that can lead to anaphylaxis. Signs and symptoms of a systemic allergic reaction include a dry cough, a feeling of tightening in the throat or chest, swelling or itching around the eyes, widespread hives *(urticaria)*, wheezing, dyspnea, and hypotension. Difficulty talking is a sign of urticaria or edema in the throat and may indicate the onset of complete airway obstruction. This is a sign of a true emergency. Epinephrine and oxygen should be ready for immediate administration on the physician's orders. Antihistamines and corticosteroids may be used, but these agents act considerably slower than epinephrine. If acute anaphylactic shock develops, death may occur within 1 hour without medical intervention.

If the stinger is still lodged in the skin, scrape it off with a dull knife, a credit card, or a fingernail. Be careful not to squeeze the stinger, because this injects more venom into the skin. Apply an ice bag to the site to relieve pain and slow absorption of venom. Calamine lotion or hydrocortisone cream may be applied to relieve itching. If the patient has a history of allergies, especially to insect venom, he or she should have access to an EpiPen injection system; this should be used immediately after the sting. The patient should be transported to the nearest hospital for immediate care.

REMOVAL OF A TICK

Ticks can cause a number of diseases, including Rocky Mountain spotted fever and Lyme disease. The tick embeds its head into the skin to obtain blood, and it should be removed intact by the following method:
1. Do not handle ticks with uncovered fingers; use tweezers to prevent personal contamination.
2. Place the tips of the tweezers as close as possible to the area where the tick has entered the skin.
3. With a slow, steady motion, pull the tick away from the skin. Try not to squeeze or crush the tick. If the tick's entire body is not removed, make an appointment with a physician to have the site evaluated.
4. After removal, place the tick directly into a sealable container. Disinfect the area around the bite site using standard procedures.
5. If the tick is removed at home, the physician may suggest that it be brought to the office to be tested for disease.

Asthma Attacks

Asthma is characterized by expiratory wheezing, coughing, a feeling of tightness in the chest, and shortness of breath (SOB). During an asthma attack, two different physiologic responses occur. The lining of the respiratory tract becomes inflamed and edematous and produces mucus, which results in narrowing of the air passages. At the same time, bronchospasms occur, which also constrict the airways. The quality and severity of attacks vary greatly among patients, and treatment must be individualized to minimize or eliminate chronic symptoms (see Chapter 46). If the patient is prescribed a bronchodilator inhaler, it should be used at the first indication of symptoms. Depending on the severity of the attack, give the patient an appointment for the same day as the call, or consult the physician. The physician may recommend that the patient go directly to the ED for emergency respiratory care.

Seizures

Seizures may be **idiopathic**, or they may result from trauma, injury, or metabolic alterations, such as hypoglycemia or hypocalcemia. A *febrile* seizure is transient and occurs with a rapid rise in body temperature over 101.8° F (38.8° C). Febrile seizures typically occur in children between 6 months and 5 years of age. Many different types of seizures occur, but all are caused by a disruption in the electrical activity of the brain. (The different types of seizures are discussed in Chapter 44.)

If a patient suffers a grand mal seizure, which involves uncontrolled muscular contractions, the most important point is to protect the patient from possible injury. Clear everything away from the patient that could cause accidental injury, and observe him or her until the seizure ends. Do not place anything into the person's mouth, because it may damage the teeth or tongue and force the tongue back over the trachea. Do not hold the patient down, because this may result in muscle injuries or fractures. If unconsciousness persists after the seizure has subsided, place the patient in the recovery position to maintain an open airway and allow drainage of excess saliva. After the seizure is over, let the patient rest or sleep, but never leave the person alone. If the physician is not in the office, check the office policies and procedures manual to determine how to manage the situation.

Call 911 for emergency assistance in any of the following situations:

- The patient does not regain consciousness within 10 to 15 minutes.
- The seizure does not stop within a few minutes.
- The patient begins a second seizure immediately after the first one.
- The patient is pregnant.
- Signs of head trauma are present.
- The patient is known to have diabetes.
- The seizure was triggered by a high fever in a child.

Abdominal Pain

Abdominal pain is a symptom caused by many different problems, which can range from acute discomfort to life-threatening complications. The clinician should see every patient who reports abdominal pain; the question is how soon the patient should be seen. A patient with acute onset of severe, persistent abdominal pain, especially when this is accompanied by fever, should receive medical attention as soon as possible. Abdominal pain has a variety of causes, including intestinal infection, appendicitis, ectopic pregnancy, inflammation, hemorrhage, obstruction, and tumor.

Treatment in the ambulatory care setting depends on the cause of the pain; however, the medical assistant should observe the following general guidelines:

- Keep the patient warm and quiet.
- Have an emesis basin available.
- Administer nothing by mouth (NPO).
- Do not apply heat to the abdomen unless so instructed by the physician.
- Administer analgesics as ordered.
- Check and record the patient's vital signs and follow the physician's orders.

SCREENING GUIDELINES FOR ASSESSING ABDOMINAL PAIN

- Assess for shock-related signs and symptoms: **diaphoresis**; cold, clammy skin; cyanosis or gray pallor; rapid respirations; altered state of consciousness
- Is the pain severe and constant or does it come in waves?
- Has the patient had any bloody or tarry stools?
- Is the patient's temperature higher than 101° F?
- Could the patient be pregnant or has she missed a menstrual period?
- Has the patient experienced continuous vomiting or severe constipation?
- Are any urinary symptoms present, such as frequency, hematuria, or flank pain?
- Does the patient have chest pain, shortness of breath, or a continuous cough?
- Does the patient have a history of serious illness, such as diabetes, heart disease, or cancer?

Sprains and Strains

Sprains are tears of the ligaments that support a joint; *strains* are injuries to a muscle and its tendons. Both types of injury may damage surrounding soft tissues and blood vessels, as well as nearby nerves. With a sprain, the victim develops edema and **ecchymosis** around the injury, and any movement of the joint, especially a twisting one, produces pain. Usually no swelling or discoloration is seen with a strain, and only mild tenderness is noted unless the injured muscle or tendon is used.

Tendon strains and ligament sprains take several weeks to heal, whereas muscle tears usually heal in 1 to 2 weeks, because muscle has such a rich blood supply. (The details of orthopedic injuries are discussed in Chapter 43.) These injuries are treated by elevating the affected area and applying mild compression and ice. Swelling is reduced if ice is applied within 20 to 30 minutes of the injury. After 24 to 36 hours, alternating applications of mild heat and ice usually are indicated. The patient may be advised to immobilize the part.

Fractures

A fracture is a break or crack in a bone, which can result from trauma or disease. Fractures are very painful and affect the patient's ability to freely move the injured part. When a patient with a fracture is brought into the office, the medical assistant should make the patient as comfortable as possible. Place the patient in a position that supports the affected area at the joints above and below the suspected fracture and does not place strain on the injury. Notify the physician immediately and proceed according to the orders given. Emergency treatment for fractures includes preventing movement of the injured part through splinting, elevation of the affected extremity, application of ice, and control of any bleeding. If a patient with an open fracture is seen in an ambulatory care setting, he or she should be transported to the ED. (Fractures are discussed in greater detail in Chapter 43.)

Burns

Burns are among the most common causes of injury in the United States. Burn injuries can result from flame, heat, scalds, electricity, chemicals, or radiation. The skin surface may be reddened, blistered, or charred. The depth and extent of a burn are the major determinants in classifying its severity. The extent of the pain is directly proportional to the extent of the surface area burned, as well as the depth and nature of the burn.

To screen a burn injury, the medical assistant must know what caused the burn, its location and approximate size, the depth of the burn, and whether any additional injuries occurred. If the patient reports a chemical burn, it is important to have the person immediately remove all clothing that may have come into contact with the chemical and flood the affected area with running water to flush the irritant off the skin. If the chemical is not quickly flushed away or remains in the patient's clothing, the agent will continue to burn the skin and may do very serious damage.

The percentage of the body surface area burned can be estimated using the Rule of Nines (Figure 27-13). This is an assessment tool that helps caregivers quickly calculate the amount of burned tissue. With the Rule of Nines, the body is divided into areas approximately equal to 9% of the total body surface area. When a burn

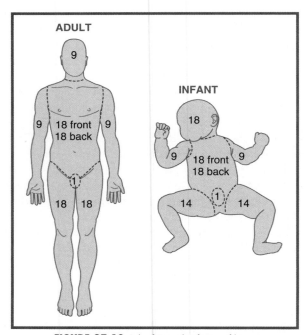

FIGURE 27-13 Rule of Nines classification of burns.

victim is assessed, the affected regions are combined to yield an estimate of the total percentage of burned tissue. Partial-thickness burns over 15% of the total body surface and full-thickness burns of less than 2% can be treated in the ambulatory care setting if the patient can be seen immediately. Patients with larger body surface area involvement or other complications should be transported immediately to a hospital, preferably one with a burn unit. (A complete description of burns and their management is given in Chapter 38.)

Tissue Injuries

Patients may report any of several different types of wounds. A *contusion* is a closed wound with no evidence of injury to the skin; it typically is caused by blunt trauma, appears swollen and discolored, and is painful. A contusion results in a painful bruise, but the skin remains intact. A scrape on the surface of the skin (e.g., a skinned knee, rug burn) is called an *abrasion*. A deeper, more jagged wound is called a *laceration*. Additional tissue damage may occur around a laceration, and, depending on its depth, the wound may need to be repaired surgically. A *puncture* wound occurs when an object is forced into the body (e.g., stepping on a nail). If an object is lodged in body tissues, the best course is to leave it there, stabilize it as much as possible with rolled-up material, and transport the individual to a clinic or ED. The puncture may have severed blood vessels, and if the object is removed, considerable bleeding may occur. An injury in which tissue is torn away (e.g., complete or partial removal of a finger) is known as an *avulsion*.

Lacerations are common presentations in a primary care physician's office. A lacerated wound shows jagged or irregular tearing of the tissues. The severity depends on the cause of the laceration, the site and extent of the injury, and whether the area is contaminated. The injury that caused the laceration also may have damaged blood vessels, nerves, bones, joints, and organs in the body cavities.

When the patient arrives at the facility, put on gloves and notify the physician immediately. Have the patient lie down, and cover the injured area with a sterile dressing; use a dressing that is thick enough to absorb the bleeding (Procedure 27-13). Reassure the patient and explain your actions as much as possible. Ask the patient when he or she last received a tetanus inoculation, and record the date in the patient's record. If it has been longer than 10 years, the physician probably will want a booster injection given.

Wounds that are not bleeding severely and that do not involve deep tissue damage should be cleaned with antimicrobial soap and water to remove bacteria and other foreign matter. If the laceration is extremely dirty, the physician may want the area irrigated with sterile normal saline solution.

A butterfly closure strip may be used over small lacerations to hold the edges together. If the wound is superficial and has straight edges, it may be closed with a microporous tape (e.g., Steri-Strips) (Figure 27-14), which eliminates the discomfort of suturing and suture removal. Another wound closure option is a tissue adhesive product such as Dermabond fluid or Liquiband, which forms a strong, flexible closure similar in strength to nylon suture material. Tissue adhesive products are very useful for closing simple lacerations in children while providing an antimicrobial and waterproof coating to the wound site that lasts several days, even with repeated washing.

PROCEDURE 27-13

Perform First Aid Procedures: Control Bleeding

GOAL: *To stop the hemorrhaging from an open wound.*

EQUIPMENT and SUPPLIES

- Gloves, sterile if available
- Appropriate personal protective equipment (PPE) according to Occupational Safety and Health Administration (OSHA) guidelines, including:
  - Impermeable gown
  - Goggles or face shield
  - Impermeable mask
  - Impermeable foot covers if indicated
- Sterile dressings
- Bandaging material
- Biohazard waste container
- Patient record

PROCEDURAL STEPS

1. Sanitize your hands and put on appropriate PPE.
   PURPOSE: To follow Standard Precautions.
2. Assemble equipment and supplies.
3. Apply several layers of sterile dressing material directly to the wound and exert pressure.
   PURPOSE: Direct pressure to a wound slows or stops the bleeding. Sterile supplies are needed to prevent wound infection.
4. Wrap the wound with bandage material. Add more dressing and bandaging material if the bleeding continues.
5. If bleeding persists and the wound is on an extremity, elevate the extremity above the level of the heart. Notify the physician immediately if the bleeding cannot be controlled.
6. If the bleeding still continues, maintain direct pressure and elevation; also apply pressure to the appropriate artery. If the bleeding is in the arm, apply pressure to the brachial artery by squeezing the inner aspect of the middle upper arm. If the bleeding is in the leg, apply pressure to the femoral artery on the affected side by pushing with the heel of the hand into the femoral crease at the groin. If the bleeding cannot be controlled, emergency medical services (EMS) may need to be activated.
7. Once the bleeding has been brought under control and the patient has been stabilized, discard contaminated materials in an appropriate biohazard waste container.
8. Disinfect the area, then remove your gloves and discard them in a biohazard waste container.
9. Sanitize your hands.
10. Document the incident, including details of the wound, when and how it occurred, the patient's symptoms and vital signs, treatment provided by the physician, and the patient's current condition.

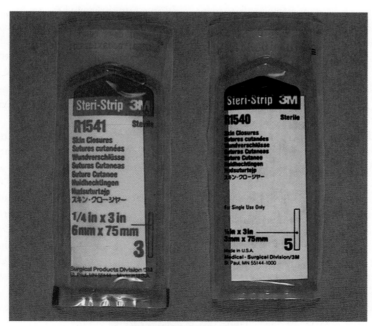

FIGURE 27-14 Steri-Strips.

After the clinician closes the wound, the medical assistant typically applies a sterile dressing to the site. The size and thickness of the dressing depend on the type of wound. (Various wound dressings and techniques for their application are discussed in Chapter 57.)

Nosebleeds (Epistaxis)

A nosebleed, or *epistaxis*, is a hemorrhage that usually results from the rupture of small vessels in the nose. Nosebleeds can be caused by injury, disease, hypertension, strenuous activity, high altitudes, exposure to cold, overuse of anticoagulant medications (e.g., aspirin), and nasal recreational drug use. Bleeding from the anterior nostril area usually is venous, whereas bleeding from the posterior region usually is arterial and is more difficult to stop. Treatment of epistaxis varies according to the amount of bleeding and the presence of other conditions, as well as the use of anticoagulant medications.

If the bleeding is mild to moderate and from one side of the nose, the patient should sit up, lean slightly forward, and apply direct pressure to the affected nostril by pinching the nose. Continue constant pressure for 10 to 15 minutes to allow clotting to take place. Repeat if the bleeding cannot be controlled, insert a clean gauze pad into the nostril, and notify the physician. If the physician is not available, proceed with standard EMS protocols. Bleeding should be considered a medical emergency if it is bilateral and continuous, or if it occurs in a patient who has a bleeding disorder or is undergoing anticoagulant therapy.

Head Injuries

The severity of head injuries can vary greatly. The history of the injury (i.e., details about what it is and how it happened) is crucial for determining appropriate management. With a head injury, the patient may appear normal; may experience dizziness, severe headache, mental confusion, or memory loss; or may even be unconscious. Loss of consciousness may be brief or prolonged; it may appear immediately or may be delayed. The victim may experience vomiting; loss of bladder and bowel control; and bleeding from the nose, mouth, or ears. The pupils of the eyes may be unequal and nonreactive to light.

All head injuries must be considered serious. Notify the physician or contact EMS immediately. If evidence of a neck injury is seen, stabilize the neck and do not attempt to move the victim. Do not administer anything by mouth. Keep the patient warm and quiet. Watch the pupils of the eyes and record any changes. Measure vital signs and record the extent and duration of any unconsciousness. If the patient is at home or is sent home after the physician's assessment, he or she should be watched closely for 24 hours after the injury for any change in mental status.

Foreign Bodies in the Eye

The eye is a delicate organ with a unique structure that demands special handling. This kind of emergency is most uncomfortable, and it often is extremely difficult to keep the patient from rubbing the eye. Tell the patient not to touch the eye in any way. The physician may order ophthalmic topical anesthetic drops to relieve pain. The patient should be placed in a darkened room to wait for the physician because **photophobia** is common with eye irritations. If a contusion and swelling are present, cold, wet compresses can help.

Ask the patient to close both eyes and cover them with eye pads until the physician arrives. The physician may order an eye irrigation to remove the object. Unless the foreign object is clearly visible, do not attempt to search for it or to remove it. (Eye care is presented in greater detail in Chapter 37.)

Heat and Cold Injuries

Exposure to extremes in temperature can cause minor to severe injuries. Heat injuries occur most often on hot, humid days and result in cramps, heat exhaustion, or heatstroke. Heat-related muscle cramps may be the first sign of *heat exhaustion*, which is a serious heat-related condition. Patients with heat exhaustion appear flushed and report headaches, nausea, vertigo, and weakness. *Heatstroke,* the most dangerous form of heat-related injury, results in a shutdown of body systems. Patients with heatstroke have red, hot, dry skin; altered levels of consciousness; tachycardia; and rapid, shallow breathing. This is a true medical emergency. If heat-related problems are recognized in the early stages and are adequately treated, the patient does not usually develop heatstroke. Management of heat-related conditions includes getting the person out of the heat; loosening clothing or removing perspiration-soaked clothing; and giving the person cool drinks if he or she is alert. An effective way to lower the victim's temperature is to apply cool, wet cloths and then fan the moist skin, so that heat is released from the body by evaporation.

The two types of cold-related injuries are frostbite and hypothermia. *Frostbite*, which is the actual freezing of tissue, occurs when skin temperature falls to a range of 14° F to 25° F (−10° C to −3.9° C). Prolonged exposure of the skin to cold causes damage similar to a burn. The tissue may appear gray or white, may be swollen, and may have clear blisters, or, in full-thickness frostbite, may show signs of tissue **necrosis**, including blackened areas and severe deformity. The more advanced the frostbite, the more serious is the tissue damage and the more likely the body part will be lost. Frozen tissue has no feeling, but as thawing occurs, the patient reports itching, tingling, and burning pain. Mild frostbite can be managed by applying constant warmth to the affected areas by immersing the area in warm water (no warmer than 105° F [40.6° C]) or by wrapping it in warm, dry clothing. Friction should never be used, because this would increase tissue damage. If blisters have formed, or if evidence of full-thickness frostbite is seen, the patient should be transported to the nearest ED.

Hypothermia is a medical emergency that may result in death unless the patient receives immediate assistance. Systemic hypothermia occurs when the core body temperature drops below 95° F (35° C). Signs and symptoms of hypothermia include shivering, numbness, apathy, and loss of consciousness. If hypothermia is suspected, activate EMS and care for any life-threatening conditions until help arrives. Remove the victim's wet clothing and wrap the victim in blankets while moving him or her to a warm place. If the victim is alert, give warm liquids and apply heating pads (using a barrier to prevent burns) to help slowly raise the core body temperature.

Dehydration

A person dehydrates when more water is excreted than is taken in. Dehydration can be a very serious health emergency, leading to convulsions, coma, and even death. Infants, young children, and older adult patients are at greatest risk of developing serious complications from dehydration. Severe dehydration may be caused by excessive heat loss, vomiting, diarrhea, or lack of fluid intake. Symptoms include vertigo; dark yellow urine or no urine output for 8 to 10 hours; extreme thirst; lethargy or confusion; and abdominal or muscle cramps. If the patient shows any of these symptoms and is unable to retain fluids, schedule an urgent appointment or recommend that the patient be taken to the ED. Replacement of lost fluids is vital, so the patient should be encouraged to drink water, tea, sports drinks, fruit juice, or Pedialyte.

Diabetic Emergencies

Diabetes mellitus is caused by a malfunction in the production of insulin in the pancreas or by an inability of the cells to use insulin. Insulin is required on the cellular level so that glucose can be used for energy. Two different diabetic emergencies are caused by *hyperglycemia* (high blood glucose levels) or by *hypoglycemia* (low blood glucose levels).

Insulin shock is caused by severe hypoglycemia, because the patient with diabetes has taken too much insulin, has not eaten enough food, or has exercised an unusual amount. Signs and symptoms, which have a rapid onset, include tachycardia, profuse sweating (diaphoresis), headache, irritability, vertigo, fatigue, hunger, seizures, and coma. It is important to provide glucose immediately, preferably in the form of glucose tablets, because they have a known concentrated quantity of glucose.

Diabetic coma results from severe hyperglycemia, which develops because the body is not producing enough insulin; the patient ate too much food or is very stressed; or the patient has an infection. Symptoms of impending diabetic coma develop more slowly than those of insulin shock; these include general malaise, dry mouth, polyuria, **polydipsia**, nausea, vomiting, SOB, and breath with an acetone (or "fruity") smell. If the patient or caregiver calling for an appointment reports these symptoms, notify the physician immediately, because the patient typically would be admitted to the hospital.

In an emergency situation, if a patient diagnosed with diabetes mellitus shows signs and symptoms of a diabetic emergency, the patient should be given glucose. If the problem is caused by insulin shock (hypoglycemia), the patient will improve quickly after receiving glucose; if it is caused by diabetic coma (hyperglycemia), a small amount of added glucose will not affect the patient's condition, and he or she must be transported to the hospital regardless. (Diabetes mellitus is covered in detail in Chapter 45.)

CLOSING COMMENTS

Patient Education

Emergencies can occur anywhere. Patients need to learn how to handle emergency situations both by the example of healthcare workers and through instruction. The medical assistant must remain calm, screen the situation, call for help, and be prepared to administer appropriate first aid. Brochures on home safety can be used to help teach patients methods for preventing accidents in the home.

All patients, even children, should understand how to contact EMS. This is especially important for families with members who have chronic diseases that are potentially life threatening, such as heart conditions, severe allergic reactions, diabetes, and asthma. Patients should be encouraged to post next to the telephone emergency numbers such as those for the local EMS and poison control center, and for the primary care physician. Families with young children need to "child-proof" their homes, being especially careful to keep potentially poisonous substances stored where children cannot get into them. Placing "Mr. Yuk" stickers on containers of poisonous substances can be an excellent educational tool for young children.

Medical assistants must remember to keep their American Red Cross or American Heart Association certifications current, and they should take advantage of community workshops to maintain and extend their skills. Post a list of community safety workshops in an area where it can be seen by patients, and encourage them to attend. Your participation in emergency care workshops, as well as encouraging others to participate, may help to save lives.

Legal and Ethical Issues

The medical assistant works in the healthcare environment as the physician's agent. Although you are responsible for your own actions, the physician is legally responsible for the care you administer to patients while working in the healthcare facility. You are responsible for knowing the limitations placed on medical assistants in your state and for adhering strictly to your employer's emergency care policies and procedures. Medical assistants are not qualified to diagnose a patient problem but are responsible for acting appropriately in a medical emergency. In addition to legal responsibilities, you have an ethical responsibility to your patients to provide the highest standard of care. Always act in the best interest of the patient, and never hesitate to ask the physician and/or the office manager for immediate assistance when faced with a medical emergency.

Most states have enacted Good Samaritan laws to encourage healthcare professionals to provide medical assistance at the scene of an accident without fear of being sued for negligence. These statutes vary greatly, but all have the intent of protecting the caregiver. A physician or other healthcare professional is not legally obligated to provide emergency care at the site of an accident, regardless of the ethical and moral considerations. Legal liability is limited to gross neglect of the victim or willfully causing further injury to the victim. As a caregiver, you are required to act as a reasonable person and cannot be held liable for personal injury resulting from an act of omission. Good Samaritan statutes provide for evaluation of the caregiver's judgment but are in effect only at the site of an emergency, not at your place of employment.

If you have not been trained in CPR, you cannot be expected to perform the procedure at the emergency site. However, in many states, a healthcare provider with CPR training and skills who is present at the scene can be declared negligent if cardiac arrest occurs and he or she does not administer CPR to the victim.

If the victim is conscious, or if a member of his or her immediate family is present, obtain verbal consent to perform emergency care. Consent is implied if the patient is unconscious and no family member is present.

Many types of emergencies can be handled in the physician's office. In an emergency situation, decisions that must be made quickly can determine whether the patient lives. A medical assistant must be prepared to act calmly and efficiently in all emergency situations.

Medical assistants also can play a key role in community response to natural or human-made disasters. The medical assistant is cross-trained to perform multiple administrative and clinical duties that would prove very useful in an emergency. These include management of medical records, interacting professionally with

patients, performing diagnostic tests, performing phlebotomy and administering medications, assisting with procedures, and administering first aid and CPR as needed. Because of this wide range of skills, medical assistants serve as useful volunteers on local emergency response teams. Investigate agencies and organizations that are committed to emergency preparedness in your community, and see how a medical assistant could help these organizations if an emergency arises.

SUMMARY OF SCENARIO

Cheryl has learned through her work with the telephone screening team and involvement with emergencies in the office how important it is to gather complete information about emergency situations and to act calmly and knowledgeably when managing patient problems. She knows she needs to maintain her certification in CPR for the Professional and to continue to participate in workshops on emergency care to be prepared for the wide variety of patient problems seen in the ambulatory care setting. Working with the screening staff has reinforced the importance of documenting all interactions on the telephone and information gathered during patient visits.

Cheryl recognizes that medical assistants in the office must follow the facility's policies and procedures manual for handling emergencies. They must plan ahead and complete their designated duties if an emergency occurs; use

community emergency services as needed; and keep emergency supplies and equipment well stocked and ready for any potential emergency situation. She recognizes that understanding first aid practices for common patient emergencies allows her to assist patients by providing instruction on the phone or by performing specific skills when emergencies occur in the facility.

Cheryl has investigated her legal standing as a medical assistant in her home state and recognizes her responsibilities when a patient calls or shows up at the office with a medical emergency. She will continue to refer to the more experienced screening staff or to Dr. Bendt when she has questions, but she now feels more confident in managing emergency situations at work. She also recognizes her role as part of the healthcare team if an emergency situation arises in her community.

SUMMARY OF LEARNING OBJECTIVES

1. **Define, spell, and pronounce the terms listed in the vocabulary.**
   Spelling and pronouncing medical terms correctly bolsters the medical assistant's credibility. Knowing the definitions of these terms promotes confidence in communication with patients and co-workers.

2. **Apply critical thinking skills in performing the patient assessment and patient care.**
   Completing the Critical Thinking Application exercises throughout the chapter can help the student medical assistant become more adept at critical analysis of real-life situations.

3. **Describe patient safety factors in the medical office environment.**
   The medical assistant must be constantly on guard to protect patients from possible injury. Methods for achieving this goal include communicating openly about patient safety issues; following standard procedures when delivering patient care; and working as part of a team to secure patients' safety (see Procedure 27-1).

4. **Evaluate the work environment to identify safe and unsafe working conditions.**
   See Procedure 27-2.

5. **Identify environmental safety issues in the healthcare setting.**
   Medical assistants must be constantly on the alert for potentially unsafe conditions; must consistently follow the guidelines established by OSHA for infection control; and must follow safety procedures to prevent workplace violence.

6. **Develop environmental, patient, and employee safety plans.**
   See Procedures 27-1 to 27-3.

7. **Discuss fire safety issues in a healthcare environment.**
   Combustibles should be stored properly; electrical equipment must be monitored for safety; smoke detectors and fire extinguishers should be checked routinely; and the facility should be evacuated if a fire breaks out.

8. **Demonstrate the proper use of a fire extinguisher.**
   See Procedure 27-4.

9. **Describe the fundamental principles for evacuation of a healthcare facility.**
   An emergency action coordinator should be designated. This person is in charge of delegating duties to staff members. Exit maps should be posted in multiple areas around the facility. Patients and staff members should be evacuated safely and should meet in a designated spot to make sure all staff members and patients have escaped.

10. **Role-play a mock environmental exposure event and evacuation of a physician's office.**
    See Procedure 27-5.

11. **Discuss the requirements for proper disposal of hazardous materials.**
    OSHA has established specific rules about biohazard waste disposal including the use of sharps containers and red bag collection systems. These must be used properly to avoid disease transmission.

12. **Define the important features of emergency preparedness in the ambulatory care setting.**

    Ambulatory care centers may be the first to recognize and initiate a response to a community emergency. Standard Precautions should be implemented immediately to control the spread of an infection. A communication network should be established to notify local and state health departments and perhaps federal officials. Every healthcare facility should have a standard policy with specific procedures for the management of emergencies on site. The CDC recommends that a facility's safety plan consider multiple steps to minimize the negative psychological effects of an emergency situation.

13. **Maintain an up-to-date list of community resources for emergency preparedness.**

    See Procedure 27-6.

14. **Describe the medical assistant's role in emergency response.**

    Medical assistants can be of considerable help in a community emergency. They can provide therapeutic communication to gather patient data; monitor injured victims; perform first aid and monitor vital signs; and help with any medically related service.

15. **Summarize the typical emergency supplies and equipment.**

    A physician's office must have a centrally located crash cart or emergency bag stocked with all emergency supplies, equipment, and medication. This material must be inventoried consistently and maintained. This chapter provides a detailed list of materials that should be readily available for an on-site emergency, including a defibrillator if indicated by the physician's practice.

16. **Demonstrate the use of an automated external defibrillator.**

    See Procedure 27-7.

17. **Summarize the general rules for managing emergencies.**

    Management of emergencies requires a calm, efficient approach. The medical assistant should assess the nature of the emergency and determine whether EMS should be activated, or whether the patient requires an immediate or urgent appointment. As many details about the situation as possible should be gathered, and the physician should be consulted when the medical assistant is in doubt.

18. **Demonstrate telephone screening techniques and documentation guidelines for ambulatory care emergencies.**

    Telephone screening is one of the medical assistant's most important tasks. Emergency action principles should be used to determine the level of a patient's emergency. These include determining whether the situation is life threatening and obtaining the patient's contact information, as well as all pertinent information about the injury and the patient's signs and symptoms. This information must be shared with the physician, and all details must be documented in the patient's chart (see Procedure 27-8).

19. **Recognize and respond to life-threatening emergencies in the ambulatory care setting.**

    Life-threatening emergencies require immediate assessment, referral to the physician, and, if the physician is not present, activation of EMS.

While waiting for assistance, the medical assistant should check for breathing and circulation. Rescue breaths or CPR is administered if indicated. Depending on the patient's signs and symptoms, the patient should be monitored for signs of a heart attack; the Heimlich maneuver is performed for an airway obstruction; the patient is evaluated for signs of a CVA and is assessed for shock. The medical assistant should ask for help when indicated and should perform appropriate procedures based on the patient's presenting condition.

20. **Perform professional-level CPR.**

    See Procedure 27-9 for instruction on performing adult, pediatric, and infant rescue breathing and CPR.

21. **Administer oxygen through a nasal cannula to a patient in respiratory distress.**

    See Procedure 27-10.

22. **Identify and assist a patient with an obstructed airway.**

    Procedure 27-11 presents instructions for assisting an adult with an obstructed airway. Infants with an obstructed airway should receive alternating back blows and chest thrusts with attempted rescue breaths until the item is dislodged or help arrives.

23. **Determine the appropriate action and documentation procedures for common ambulatory care emergencies.**

    The medical assistant should always follow Standard Precautions when caring for a patient with a medical emergency. Documentation of emergency treatment should include information about the patient; vital signs; allergies, current medications, and pertinent health history; the patient's chief complaint; the sequence of events, including any changes in the patient's condition since the incident; and any physician's orders and procedures performed.

24. **Assist and monitor a patient who has fainted.**

    See Procedure 27-12.

25. **Control a hemorrhagic wound.**

    See Procedure 27-13.

26. **Apply patient education concepts to medical emergencies.**

    Patients should know how to contact emergency personnel, and families with young children should have telephone numbers for poison control posted. Educating patients about how to care for minor emergencies at home is an important part of telephone triage in the ambulatory care setting. Encouraging patients to participate in community safety workshops and to become certified in CPR may help prevent emergencies and save lives.

27. **Discuss the legal and ethical concerns arising from medical emergencies.**

    Good Samaritan laws, which vary from state to state, are designed to protect any individual from liability, whether a healthcare professional or a layperson, if he or she provides assistance at the site of an emergency. The law does not require a medically trained person to act, but if emergency care is given in a reasonable and responsible manner, the healthcare worker is protected from being sued for negligence. This protection, however, does not extend to the workplace.

CONNECTIONS

Study Guide Connection: Go to the Chapter 27 Study Guide. Read and complete the activities.

Evolve Connection: Go to the Chapter 27 link at *evolve.elsevier.com/kinn* to complete the Chapter Review and Chapter Quiz. Peruse other resources listed for this chapter to increase your knowledge of Emergency Preparedness and Assisting With Medical Emergencies.

CAREER DEVELOPMENT AND LIFE SKILLS

28

SCENARIO

Lisa Walker is 1 month away from graduating from her medical assisting program. She has been an excellent student and is looking forward to beginning her career in the medical field. Lisa wants to begin her job search now so that she will be employed soon after her externship ends.

Lisa participated in several volunteer activities while she attended school. She plans to list these experiences on her resumé. She met many office managers and physicians while doing volunteer work, and she will be contacting those people in hopes of obtaining more job leads.

Lisa began saving for interview clothing when she first began school. She is on a strict budget, but she found several outfits appropriate for interviews at secondhand clothing shops and discount stores. Her best-looking suit cost only $25!

Not a person afraid to interview, Lisa looks forward to sharing her skills and experience with potential employers. She looks on each interview as a practice session for the next one, and this helps her relax more and present a true picture of herself to the office manager. She has a great smile and projects a natural friendliness and positive attitude.

Lisa has given much thought to what she wants from her first job as a medical assistant. She knows that she may not start at a high salary, but she also realizes that there are benefits and perquisites ("perks") to working in a physician's office. She plans to commit to working for 2 years on her first job, gaining experience before looking for her next job at a higher salary and with additional benefits.

Lisa is excited about her future as a medical assistant. She is ready to put the training she received to work with patients. She is determined to perform exceptionally well at her externship site and to go above and beyond her assigned duties to impress the staff in that facility, who will become references for her first paid position. Lisa is dedicated to being the best medical assistant possible and to becoming indispensable to her employer.

While studying this chapter, think about the following questions:

- How can the medical assistant prepare for his or her first job throughout the duration of training?
- What is meant by "writing your resumé every day"?
- How can the medical assistant organize the job search?
- How can the new medical assistant employee make a positive, lasting impression on co-workers and supervisors?

LEARNING OBJECTIVES

1. Define, spell, and pronounce the terms listed in the vocabulary.
2. Discuss the reasons job search training is important to a medical assistant.
3. List three expectations employers have of employees.
4. Understand the three types of employee skill strengths.
5. Explain the two best job search methods.
6. Describe some of the errors that should be avoided on a resumé.
7. List the four phases of the interview process.
8. Explain the importance of having demographic information about former jobs before appearing for an interview.
9. List and discuss legal and illegal interview questions.
10. Discuss the importance of the probationary period for a new employee.
11. List some common early mistakes of which a new employee should be aware.
12. Understand the importance of maintaining liability coverage once employed in the industry.
13. Explain why a performance appraisal rating is usually not perfect.
14. Organize a job search.
15. Prepare a resumé.
16. Complete a job application.
17. Interview for a job.
18. Negotiate a salary.

VOCABULARY

counteroffer Return offer made by one who has rejected an offer or a job.

default To fail to pay a financial debt, such as a student loan.

deferment Postponement, especially of a student loan.

genuineness Expressing sincerity and honest feeling.

intolerable Not tolerable or bearable.

mock Simulated; intended for imitation or practice.

networking Exchange of information or services among individuals, groups, or institutions; also, meeting and getting to know individuals in the same or similar career fields and sharing information about available opportunities.

pertinent (pur′-tuh-nent) Having a clear, decisive relevance to the matter at hand.

proofread To read and mark corrections.

rectify (rek′-tuh-fy) To correct by removing errors.

subtle Ingenious; artful; delicate.

succinct (suhk-sinkt′) Marked by compact, precise expression without wasted words.

synopsis Condensed statement or outline.

vocation The work in which a person is regularly employed.

Each day a person exists is a small portion of a whole—a part of a person's entire lifetime. The events that happen during a day, no matter how small, shape the future. In the same way, the events that happen in the life of a medical assistant play a role in shaping his or her career. Every day, the medical assistant "writes a resumé"—through actions that reveal strengths, highlight skills, and summarize accomplishments—that builds on his or her **vocation**. Each duty performed becomes a part of the medical assistant's sum of experience and is important in the overall growth of the individual. Each action taken can have an impact on the future for the medical assistant. If the actions are professional, accurate, and performed to the individual's utmost ability, the resumé the medical assistant is writing will be one that leads to greater opportunities. If the medical assistant performs poorly, the resumé will be one that does not reflect trustworthiness and dependability. The small decisions made each day greatly affect the overall impression the medical assistant makes in the workplace.

Most people seeking employment have never had any type of formal training in the job search process. A newly graduated medical assistant should take advantage of job search training for three reasons:

- It will reduce the amount of time spent searching for a job.
- It will increase the chances of receiving better wages through negotiation.
- It will help eliminate the fears of looking for work and interviewing.

WHAT DOES THE EMPLOYER WANT?

Employers have three basic desires when they interview individuals for a job:

- They want a person who has a neat appearance and looks as if he or she fits the job (Figure 28-1).
- They want an individual who is dependable and can prove that he or she has been a reliable team member in other job positions.
- They want a person with the skills to do the job.

From the beginning of the job search process, a medical assistant's attitude is the most critical part of his or her potential success in getting a job (Figure 28-2). A good attitude is not a trait that can

be developed overnight. For this reason, a medical assistant must have a positive outlook in all situations so that the **genuineness** of his or her demeanor is clear during job interviews. The attitude displayed during training and externships is likely to be the same attitude that will be evident on the job. Make it a positive, enthusiastic one.

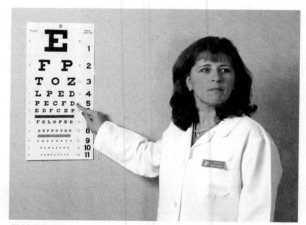

FIGURE 28-1 A professional appearance is mandatory in the medical office.

FIGURE 28-2 A great attitude is the best personal asset. Employers in the medical profession want medical assistants who have a positive attitude with patients.

ASSESSING STRENGTHS

Before promoting himself or herself as a potential employee, a medical assistant must first determine the strengths that make him or her a valuable team member. The three types of skill strengths are job skills, self-management skills, and transferable skills.

Job skills are the abilities the medical assistant needs to perform the job. These include such skills as performing venipuncture, billing insurance, answering the telephone, scheduling appointments, giving injections, and handling other tasks.

Self-management skills relate to the medical assistant's personality and character traits. They include such attributes as honesty, integrity, and enthusiasm.

Transferable skills can be taken from one job to another. For instance, if the medical assistant has the ability to communicate effectively, this skill can be used on every job. Leadership is a transferable skill, as are the ability to follow directions and the ability to manage people.

DEVELOPING CAREER OBJECTIVES

Each medical assistant has a reason for entering the healthcare field. This basic desire should influence decisions concerning his or her career choices. Because medical assisting is such a versatile profession, a medical assistant has numerous options after graduation.

Medical assistants should take some time to think about what they want from their career. While attending school and subsequently completing an externship, ideas may surface about the area of healthcare in which the medical assistant most wants to work.

When developing career objectives, the medical assistant should start by asking several questions:

- Where am I today?
- Where do I want to be in 5 years?
- Where do I want to be in 10 years?
- What additional skills do I need to get where I want to go?

Write down the questions and answers and go into specific detail. Set realistic goals and develop a plan as to how and when they will be reached. It is helpful to put a list of goals in a prominent place at home, where you can see them each day. Some people use a spiral notebook, the front of the refrigerator, or Post-it notes attached to a mirror in the area where they get dressed. Keep goals in a visible place to keep them in mind even on the more difficult days, when they seem far from sight.

KNOWING PERSONAL NEEDS

When searching for a job, the medical assistant must evaluate all of his or her needs. Most people have a minimum salary they require, in addition to certain benefits. For example, if the medical assistant is a single mother, she may require a moderate salary and insist on health insurance benefits. We also have intrinsic needs, which are internal desires important to us personally.

A helpful activity is to write a **synopsis** of a typical day on an ideal medical assisting job. Imagine the type of office, the job title, the daily duties, and the salary and benefits that would be a part of the ideal job (Figure 28-3). This can help you develop a focus and a goal to work toward as your career develops.

FINDING A JOB

Many people have misconceptions about the job market that exists today. Fortunately, the medical field is not an industry that sees high levels of unemployment. Usually, healthcare percentages remain high even in a poor economy. Graduation from a medical assisting program does not guarantee that the student will obtain employment. Completion of the program gives the medical assistant the job skills needed to work, but a good attitude and positive outlook are essential for success in the job search. In addition, the medical assistant should always be open to new and better opportunities.

Some job seekers assume that potential employers will not interact with students until they graduate. However, prospecting before graduation is a smart idea, and there are **subtle** ways of introducing

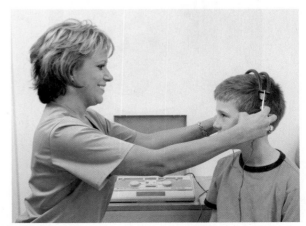

FIGURE 28-3 Enjoyment of the job is paramount. Medical assistants should enjoy their work and give compassionate, friendly care to all patients.

oneself to a facility without bluntly asking for employment. Many also think they must have work experience to be hired, but employers are more interested in attitude and "teachability" than a long resumé full of experience. In fact, many physicians like hiring students fresh from school so that they can teach them specifically how they want procedures done before the new graduate gets used to doing them another way.

Two Best Job Search Methods

Although there are many ways to find employment, two methods have proved to be the best and most effective: networking and direct contact with employers.

Networking is the exchange of information or services among individuals, groups, or institutions. When related to a job search, networking involves meeting and getting to know individuals in the same or similar career fields and sharing information about available opportunities. A medical assistant should begin to form a network of friends, business associates, co-workers, and acquaintances early in training, and he or she should stay in contact with these people throughout the job search effort and beyond (Figure 28-4). E-mail, Facebook, MySpace, and other electronic advances make staying in touch with former classmates and instructors very easy.

How does one network? One way is by joining professional medical assisting organizations. The members who attend regular meetings often know about job leads in the area. The medical assistant should also tell his or her personal physician or physicians about being in school and the approximate time of graduation. Friends and family members can be on the lookout for potential opportunities and may help by asking their personal physicians if they are aware of positions that will open for applications soon. Always keep a few resumés on hand; the opportunity to network could come at any time.

Networking is not limited to job searching, and many organizations are formed to develop networks of individuals or groups that assist one another and refer clients to one another. However, these groups are useful to the person who is looking for employment, and by attending meetings and get-togethers held for networking purposes, medical assistants may happen onto the ideal job for which they have been looking.

> **CRITICAL THINKING** APPLICATION   28-4
>
> Lisa knows that networking is a great way to find employment. She is making a list of people with whom she can share her resumé or inform that she is now ready to seek employment as a medical assistant.
> - How many relatives can you think of who are good prospects for networking?
> - How many professional people can you think of who are good prospects for networking?

Direct contact with employers is also an effective method of job searching. Medical assistants often know of specific clinics or facilities they would like to investigate as job possibilities. Compile a list of these places and learn as much about them as possible. If the facility has a Web site, read it thoroughly. Ask for brochures or patient information packets offered by the employer. Some have an annual report that lists details about the organization. All this information helps the medical assistant get a good basic idea of why the facility exists and what it does for the community.

Contact with employers does not necessarily begin only after the student has graduated. Students can begin networking and contacting employers from the very start of their enrollment at school. The student can keep a file of potential employers. Take a drive around the area where your home is located and make note of the medical facilities close by. Then, determine the facilities that are good prospects for employment and begin researching them. Call to find out who supervises medical assistants in the facility. In a physician's office, this usually is the office manager. Then call the office manager and ask to make an appointment to learn about the facility. Even the busiest people usually are willing to help a student investigate healthcare facilities in the area.

Do not tell the office manager that the objective of the appointment is a job offer. The goal at this point is to learn about the facility, what it offers the community, and what roles the medical assistants in the facility perform. Suggest that the appointment be set at the office manager's convenience. Then treat the appointment like an actual job interview, dressing appropriately and arriving on time. Do not be late or cancel without calling first. Have a list of questions about the facility prepared in advance and do not take too much of the office manager's time. Take notes about what the office manager says about the facility so that you can refer to them after graduation, during the actual job search.

After the appointment with the office manager, ask for a business card and always send a thank you note or letter. Remember this critical point! This helps the office manager remember the name of the medical assistant, and it is a pleasant addition to the daily mail. Everyone enjoys being recognized for his or her efforts, and the office manager will appreciate the thank you note.

Toward time for graduation, determine the possibility of performing an externship at one of the facilities you visited early in training. Check with school regulations to determine whether this

FIGURE 28-4 Stay in touch with classmates. They are excellent networking contacts and may be able to provide job leads.

is possible. Then the office manager can be approached about allowing the student to extern in the office. Be sure to follow school guidelines when investigating these possibilities. Some schools allow students to secure their own externship sites, but this must be discussed with the externship supervisor at school. Performing an externship at a medical facility usually is the first practical experience the student has in the medical field and can be used as a reference in building a resumé.

After the externship is complete, the medical assistant may want to send a resumé to all the office managers he or she met through the direct contact efforts made earlier in training. A professional resumé with a cover letter that refers to the earlier meeting will prompt the office manager to remember the student. Ask in the cover letter whether any opportunities are available in the facility. Mention that the facility and staff were impressive on the first meeting and that the facility would be an exciting place to begin a career. In the letter request that, if the office manager does not have any positions available at that time, he or she keep the resumé on file or pass it along to an acquaintance who is looking for an additional staff member.

Internet and the Job Search

The Internet opens a whole new world of opportunity when it comes to job searches. The medical assistant can find a gargantuan amount of information about writing resumés, interviewing, and follow-up methods, but perhaps most important, the Internet can provide information about who is hiring right now.

Many databases provide information about job openings. Monster, Yahoo! Jobs, and the Online Career Center are a few examples. The search can be targeted to specific geographic areas, certain career fields, or even specific job titles. Conduct a search in a selected state (or metropolitan area), then look for jobs in the medical profession, then narrow the field even more by asking for information on jobs specifically for medical assistants.

The medical assistant also can express interest in a job by perusing the company Web site and then contacting the employer directly on the "contact us" page. Anyone looking at the Web site should be able to find an e-mail address to use for gathering additional information. Mention that the school encourages quality businesses as potential employers and ask for information that could be presented to a class. Most employers are happy to get the word out about their company and may give all kinds of pamphlets and "freebies" to share with a class. By sending a thank you note and staying in touch with the company, the medical assistant creates a new lead for the job search.

Just remember, the information available to one medical assistant on the Internet is also available to every other medical assistant. The Internet is great for researching positions and companies, but networking and direct contact are still the most successful ways to obtain a job. All the elements of the medical assistant's "whole package"—the resumé, application, interview, follow-up, attitude, appearance, and job skills—combine to make an impression on the employer. Will that impression be favorable enough to result in a job offer?

Traditional Job Search Methods

The more traditional job search methods may be effective but usually are not as successful as networking and contacting employers directly.

School Career Placement Offices

Students usually have lifetime access to their school placement offices. Take advantage of the job search classes held at the school and seek advice regularly from the placement officers. They can suggest facilities that have job openings and will often make appointments for interviews. The placement office should be the first resource for the student's job search.

Newspaper Ads

Newspaper ads normally produce a huge number of applicants and resumés for the employer. A resumé or application must stand out in the crowd to be noticed when it arrives at the facility. Some applicants use clear envelopes, which draw attention to the resumé quickly in a stack of mail.

Employment Agencies

Employment agencies usually charge a fee for their services. Even when the employer pays the fee, the medical assistant may be offered a lower wage to compensate for the fee. These agencies can be useful, however, especially in salary negotiations. The agency knows the salary range the employer is willing to pay. This means that medical assistants can command a salary within that range and are not short-changed by asking for a salary that is much lower than the employer is willing to pay.

> **CRITICAL THINKING** APPLICATION   28-5
>
> Lisa keeps an eye on the local newspapers for ads that mention a need for medical assistants.
> - What current ads in local papers are interesting and would prompt sending a resumé?
> - What factors might the medical assistant consider in choosing ads to which he or she will respond?
> - How can the medical assistant determine which are good potential employers?

Professional Organizations

Joining local chapters of medical assistant organizations, such as the American Association of Medical Assistants (AAMA) or the American Medical Technologists (AMT), can help the student in many ways. Not only is valuable information exchanged at the meetings, but the medical assistant also may hear of positions becoming available in various medical facilities. Participating in professional organizations is a form of networking with the added benefit of continuing educational opportunities.

Volunteering

By volunteering in medical offices or facilities, the medical assistant meets other professionals who may be able to provide job leads. Volunteer activities should be added to the resumé, because these valuable experiences often can be used in the physician's office as well. It does not matter that the position was not a paid job; experience counts, whether paid or not.

Mailing Resumés

Mailing a large number of resumés is not a very effective method of searching for a job. Out of 100 resumés sent, one or two potential employers may respond with a request for an interview. It is much more effective to network first, then follow up with a good cover letter and resumé. Resumés can be used when contacting employers directly, and this approach allows the medical assistant to meet at least one employee of the facility when the document is delivered. Be sure to ask for a business card and write down the name of the person to whom the resumé was delivered. For impressive facilities, send a note of thanks to the person who accepted the resumé, asking to be considered for future positions.

Cold Calling

Cold calling is contacting employers by phone and prospecting for available positions. If the medical assistant asks, "Are you hiring?" at the beginning of the conversation, he or she should expect a negative answer and has just wasted the call. This is all but useless in the job search effort. However, an assistant who calls for information about the clinic and schedules an appointment with the office manager may have more success. Most office managers are open to talking with a medical assistant about the profession and will gladly make an appointment if it can be at their convenience. Some would not even consider interrupting their day just to talk with a student medical assistant, but most are happy to help new graduates obtain answers to questions and get started in their medical career. However, do not waste the time the person has offered. Prepare a list of questions in advance and be sure to ask about the interviewer's career in the healthcare industry. People enjoy talking about themselves and their accomplishments, and valuable information may be gleaned from hearing how the office manager started in healthcare. Never attempt to get a job over the phone. Even when interested employers call and ask questions, attempt to set up an interview to discuss your qualifications in person.

Performing Well on Externships

Performing well on externships may be one of the best ways to secure a job. If an opening exists, the medical assistant extern is already oriented to the practice and may be the perfect fit for the job. Perform duties assigned on the externship as if they were final examinations at school. Even if the office does not have a position available at that time, there may be one soon, or the office manager or physician may know of an office that has an opening. Do the best job possible, and an employment offer may be waiting at the conclusion of the externship. Be ready to learn from the moment the externship begins until the moment it ends.

Organizing the Job Search

Seeking a job is a full-time job. The new medical assistant must put forth effort, have stamina, and be persistent. Do not expect to get a job with the first practice that offers an interview. By keeping track of opportunities found, the medical assistant is more likely to obtain employment soon after graduation (Procedure 28-1).

A job lead is any information that could lead to a position, either now or in the future. Some of the most promising job leads for the newly graduated medical assistant come from the externship experience. Be friendly and meet as many people as possible while completing this part of training. Ask for business cards and stay in contact with the medical professionals you meet at the externship site and nearby hospitals. Be willing to shake hands and make introductions

at all times so that the circle of promising contacts for job leads continues to expand.

The medical assistant would be wise to keep a record of all job leads (Figure 28-5). The name and address of the facility, a contact name, and phone numbers all are important pieces of information. Keep track of where the lead was obtained; if it was provided by an individual, thank that person properly, especially if the lead results in a job offer. These records are an excellent starting place when making calls to set up job interviews. Remember, the placement office at school is a resource for job leads but should not be the only source used for obtaining leads. Each medical assistant graduate must take personal responsibility for finding and following up on job opportunities.

The job lead is not the only information that should be recorded during job search efforts. Keep a record of arrangements when an interview is secured, including information such as the following:

- Day, date, and time of the interview
- Directions to the interview site
- Name of the interviewer
- Items to bring to the interview
- Information about the company or facility

As soon as the interview is over, make a few notes about what happened during the interview. After several interviews, remembering which facility offered what salary, which had medical benefits, and which was closest to home may be difficult. By keeping accurate records, the medical assistant can follow up in the appropriate manner and send a note or letter of appreciation to the person who conducted the interview (Figure 28-6).

DEVELOPING A RESUMÉ

A resumé is a fact sheet that summarizes an applicant's qualifications, education, and experience. Medical assistants must determine what to include in the resumé, remembering that they are "selling" themselves to an employer (Procedure 28-2). The resumé should be developed before cover letters are written or job applications are completed so that strengths can be identified and highlighted on all job search documents.

Many types of resumés can be used. Three of the most common are the chronologic resumé, the functional resumé, and the targeted resumé. A chronologic resumé highlights the medical assistant's abilities in a logical order, such as most recent jobs back to the beginning of the individual's career (Figure 28-7). A functional resumé highlights specific skill sets, emphasizing the most important abilities or the most valuable experiences the medical assistant has had (Figure 28-8). A targeted resumé is perhaps the most effective; it emphasizes the skills that relate specifically to the job for which the medical assistant is applying (Figure 28-9).

The medical assistant should target the resumé to the specific job for which he or she is applying. This means that the job requirements should be compared with the skills on the resumé, and those skills should be highlighted in the document using action words (Figure 28-10). Of course, to do this effectively, the medical assistant must actually know the job requirements. Clinical and administrative duties are likely to be similar from place to place, but the ad for the position may provide further information about the scope of duties. The medical assistant should read this information carefully and

PROCEDURE 28-1

Organize a Job Search

GOAL: To devote adequate time to and organize the job search in an efficient way so that proper follow up can be conducted.

EQUIPMENT and SUPPLIES

- Record of a job lead form
- Record of an interview form
- Copies of your resumé
- List of interview questions
- Contact information for former employers and references
- Map of geographic area or printout from Internet mapping program
- Internet access
- Computer
- Job search Web links
- Local newspapers
- Contact information for friends and family

PROCEDURAL STEPS

1. Format the resumé as an accurate, up-to-date document.
   <u>PURPOSE:</u> If the resumé is kept on a computer, it can be easily updated and targeted for various job opportunities.
2. Make copies of the record of job lead and record of interview forms.
3. Research job search Web sites and newspapers for job leads.
4. Network and contact employers directly to obtain job leads.
   <u>PURPOSE:</u> Networking and direct employer contact are the best two methods of searching for a job.
5. Gather information on job leads and complete a record of job lead form for each one.

<u>PURPOSE:</u> Employers are impressed when the person being interviewed is familiar with the company; much information can be found on the company's Web site.

6. Prepare a targeted copy of the resumé for each job lead.
   <u>PURPOSE:</u> Targeted resumés are designed to highlight the candidate's skills for a particular job, and the resumé can easily be tailored for each specific company on a computer.
7. Take the resumé to the facility and ask to complete an application or (see step 8).
8. E-mail the resumé to the facility according to directions listed in the job advertisement.
9. Document all activity on each job lead.
   <u>PURPOSE:</u> The job search should be an organized process.
10. Schedule interviews for as many facilities as possible.
    <u>PURPOSE:</u> The more interviews, the better prepared the candidate will be.
11. Keep a record of job details on the record of the interview form for later reference.
    <u>PURPOSE:</u> Keeping a record of the details about each job possibility helps keep them organized and is useful for comparing job offers.
12. After an interview, send a thank you note to the interviewer.
    <u>PURPOSE:</u> Never fail to send a thank you note, because this gesture may be the deciding factor in securing the job.
13. Compare opportunities when making a choice between offered positions.

should emphasize on the resumé that those responsibilities are part of his or her skill set.

Compose the resumé and save it on the computer, a CD, or other storage device. Keep a copy on a flash drive so that the information is readily available if needed when away from the primary computer. Remember to keep the flash drive in the car or in a purse or backpack. Then, as each job opportunity presents itself, the resumé can be modified to fit the job. For instance, if the resumé lists back-office skills first and the job is for an administrative position, the administrative skills should be moved to the top to draw more attention to them. This is easy to accomplish when the resumé is on a computer, because the medical assistant can cut and paste where necessary to make changes and save several versions of the resumé. Then an original can be printed on high-quality paper for every job for which he or she applies.

A resumé is an important job search tool, but it should never be expected to get the medical assistant a job on its own merit. Resumés are one of many tools that should be used when looking for employment. Developing a professional resumé takes some effort but proves

to be a good time investment. Give the document some thought and follow generally accepted guidelines for constructing it.

CRITICAL THINKING APPLICATION 28-6

Lisa has drafted her resumé and given a copy to three of her instructors. One recommended that Lisa remove the mention of her volunteer experience, because it was not in the medical field.

- Should Lisa do this? Why or why not?
- How can experience outside the medical field be beneficial to a new graduate?

Critical Resumé Errors

The first error that should be prevented on a resumé is just that—any error. The resumé should have no errors at all; many employers automatically disqualify a job candidate if one is found.

One medical assistant who was having trouble finding a job consulted her placement director at school. The director suggested

Record of a Job Lead

Job Title _____ Medical Office/Facility Name _____

Phone Number_____ Fax Number _____

Contact Name _____ Contact Title _____

Contact Phone Number/Extension _____

Physician(s) _____ Office Manager _____

Office/Facility Address _____

City _____ State _____ Zip _____

Referred By _____ Phone Number _____

Date First Contacted _____ Person Spoken To _____

Information Submitted:

☐ Cover Letter   ☐   Résumé   ☐   References

Date Sent _____   Date Sent _____   Date Sent _____

First Interview Scheduled: Day/Date _____   Time _____

Interviewer Name _____   Phone _____

Second Interview Scheduled: Day/Date _____   Time _____

Interviewer Name _____   Phone _____

Travel Directions _____

_____

_____

Office/Facility Information _____

_____

Basic Job Duties _____

_____

Miscellaneous Information _____

_____

_____

_____

(staple a business card to this form from the office/facility – use back for additional information)

FIGURE 28-5 Record of a job lead.

Record of an Interview

Job Title _____ Medical Office/Facility Name _____

Phone Number_____ Fax Number _____

Contact Name _____ Contact Title _____

Contact Phone Number/Extension _____

Physician(s) _____Office Manager _____

Office/Facility Address _____

City _____ State _____ Zip _____

Interviewer Name _____ Phone _____

Travel Directions _____

_____

_____

Office/Facility Information _____

_____

Basic Job Duties _____

_____

Benefits/Salary Discussed _____

_____

Hours/Days to Work _____

General Impression of Office and Personnel _____

Questions as a result of interview _____

_____

Self-Evaluation of Interview Performance _____

_____

Thank-you sent ❑ yes ❑ no Date _____ Job Offer ❑ yes ❑ no (use back for notes)

Other Follow-up _____

_____

(staple a business card to this form from the office/facility – use back for additional information)

FIGURE 28-6 Record of an interview.

PROCEDURE 28-2

Prepare a Resumé

GOAL: *To write an effective resumé for use as a tool in obtaining employment.*

EQUIPMENT and SUPPLIES

- Scratch paper
- Pen or pencil
- Former job descriptions, if available
- List of addresses of former employers and schools and names of supervisors
- Computer or word processor
- Quality stationery and envelopes

PROCEDURAL STEPS

1. Perform a self-evaluation by making notes about your strengths as a medical assistant. Consider job skills, self-management skills, and transferable skills.
   <u>PURPOSE:</u> To determine the strongest aspects of your abilities so that they can be highlighted on the resumé.

2. Explore formatting and decide on a professional resumé appearance that best highlights your skills and experience. Use the templates available in word processing software or design your own.
   <u>PURPOSE:</u> To construct an attractive document.

3. Place your name, address, and two telephone numbers where you can be contacted at the top of the resumé.
   <u>PURPOSE:</u> To make sure potential employers have a means of contacting you.

4. Write a job objective that specifies your employment goals.
   <u>PURPOSE:</u> To give the prospective employer an idea of what you are looking for in a medical assisting position.

5. Provide details about your educational experience. List degrees and/or certifications you have obtained.

6. Provide details about your work experience. Include all contact information and names of supervisors. Do not include salary expectations or reasons for leaving former jobs. Use former job descriptions to detail work experience from previous employment.
   <u>PURPOSE:</u> No negative information should be put on the resumé. Salaries should not be discussed; if a certain salary is listed on the resumé, it may limit the amount the facility offers the medical assistant.

7. Include information on the resumé that exhibits dependability, punctuality, positive work ethics, initiative, the ability to adapt to change, and a responsible attitude.

8. Prepare a cover letter and a list of references. Send the references with the resumé only when requested.

9. Type the resumé carefully and make sure the document has no errors.
   <u>PURPOSE:</u> Resumés submitted with errors often are discarded without consideration.

10. Proofread the resumé. Allow another person to read it as well and look for missed errors.
    <u>PURPOSE:</u> To make sure the resumé is error free.

11. Print the resumé on high-quality paper. Review the resumé again for errors and to make sure it looks attractive on the printed page.

12. Target each resumé to a specific person or position. Do not send generic resumés to each prospective employer.
    <u>PURPOSE:</u> Targeted resumés get better results during the job search.

13. For all resumés that are distributed, follow up with a phone call to arrange an interview.
    <u>PURPOSE:</u> A resumé sent without follow-up usually is ineffective.

---

that she come in for a **mock** interview. About halfway through the interview, the placement director realized the problem. The medical assistant had worked for 2 years at a local grocery store and had misspelled the name of the store on the resumé. From an employer's point of view, a person who cannot spell the name of a facility where she worked for a length of time, even though she cashed a paycheck with the company name on it, might well make critical errors in charting or in other aspects of her duties. Within a week after this error was corrected, the medical assistant found a job.

Never list salary expectations on the resumé. If the medical assistant lists a salary of $26,620 for the last job held, the future employer might not offer more than $27,000 to $28,000, realizing that this is a step up from the last salary. If the employer had been willing to pay $32,000, the medical assistant lost an opportunity for much higher wages.

Avoid using "I" or other personal pronouns on the resumé. If abbreviations are used on the resumé, be sure to spell them out for clarity the first time they are used if they are not well-known

abbreviations. Never include personal information, such as height, weight, age, marital status, number of children, or any other information that is not **pertinent** to the job requirements.

Do not list dates along the left-hand side of the paper. This is distracting and draws attention away from the points that should be emphasized. A resumé must be visually appealing and easy to read. The medical assistant should make good use of spacing, margins, indention, capitalization, and underlining to ensure an attractive document. Proofread the document several times to be sure it has no errors. Having someone else **proofread** it can be helpful, because often the writer of a document misses errors when proofreading.

Never include a photograph with the resumé. Photographs can be a discriminatory factor in the hiring process, and the medical assistant should be wary of any employer who requests a photograph with the resumé.

One of the most senseless errors common to resumés is not including the appropriate contact information, such as an address, telephone number, and e-mail address. Two phone numbers are

Ruby Dunham
9362 Caesar Creek Road
Mytown, OH 45458
(937) 555-1899
rdunham@comcast.net

Education

• 1998: A.S. in Medical Assisting, Community College, Mytown, OH

Experience:

1995–present: Medical Transcriptionist, Community Hospital, Mytown, OH

• Transcribe 55 wpm
• Specialist in medical terminology
• Excellent attendance record
• Detail oriented
• Increased personal productivity each quarter

1990–1995: Secretary, State University School of Medicine, Mytown, OH

• Coordinated schedules of four full-time professors
• Maintained office supply and assistant budget
• Created final examination scheduling guidelines for department
• Developed excellent written communication skills
• Familiar with a variety of office machines

1986–1990: Shift Manager, Burger World, Mytown, OH

• Managed 10 employees, including hiring, training, evaluating, and firing
• Developed excellent oral communication skills and team player concept
• Improved inventory supply techniques, reducing losses by 10%
• Maintained cleanliness standards highest in chain
• Developed customer-focused service goals for store

FIGURE 28-7 Chronologic resumé.

Max Bryan
1234 Rolling View Court
Mytown, OH 45431
(937) 555-3137
maxbryan@yahoo.com

OBJECTIVE

• An entry level position in medical assisting, with the opportunity to utilize and refine skills and training

EDUCATION

• 1998: A.S. in Medical Assisting, Community College, Mytown, OH
  Dean's list senior year, cumulative GPA 3.5

STRENGTHS

• Possess excellent interpersonal and communication skills
• Demonstrate consistent positive attitude and high energy
• Caring and compassionate
• Responsible, self-motivated, precise in work
• Experienced in customer-focused service

ACCOMPLISHMENTS

• Tutored students in medical assisting and 12-lead EKG courses
  Received excellent evaluations and positive results
• Certified Medical Assistant, active member of local AAMA
• Experienced in MS Office programs
• Consistent "excellent" ratings in clinical externships

COMMUNITY ACTIVITIES

• 1995–present: Organized, recruited, and trained 20 others for church hand bell choir, direct weekly practices and monthly performances
• 1996–present: Teach community CPR twice yearly to high school students
• Vice-President Student Government, Community College, Mytown, OH. Recruited members, organized fund-raisers, campaigned successfully for policy changes

EMPLOYMENT

• 1996–present: Tutor, Community College, Mytown, OH
• Waiter, Scott's Place, Mytown, OH

FIGURE 28-8 Functional resumé.

suggested, such as a cell phone number and a home phone number, so that an office manager has a better chance of reaching the candidate to schedule an interview. Place an e-mail address on the front page so that potential employers can make contact quickly. Make sure the e-mail address is professional; do not use something like "babydoll@yahoo.com." If an interview time becomes available late in the day, having access to job candidates by e-mail may make a difference in who is scheduled and who ultimately gets the job.

Argument about Length

Professionals disagree about the acceptable length of a resumé. One page may be considered the ideal length, but a person who has worked for 10 years will never get all his or her skills and experience on a single page. A medical assistant without previous work experience may easily fit the resumé on one page.

Recent trends indicate that a good rule of thumb is to allow one page for every 6 years of experience. If a person has a 20-year career, the resumé would be approximately three pages long. This is a general guideline; the document should be as **succinct** as possible while clearly communicating the applicant's strengths and background. Make sure your contact information, such as name, phone number, and an e-mail address, are also provided on each subsequent page of the resumé. If the front page or cover letter is somehow

misplaced, the employer will be able to use the information at the top of the page to contact the applicant. Number the pages if the resumé is longer than one page.

Purpose of a Resumé

The purpose of a resumé is not to get the medical assistant a job, although this is a commonly held belief. The purpose of the cover letter is to get the employer to look at the resumé. The purpose of the resumé is to get the applicant an interview. The purpose of the interview, of course, is to get the job. Remember this and use the resumé as a tool, along with other strategies for job searching.

The medical assistant should be the one who writes the resumé, or at the very least should have a hand in its composition. Professional resumé services may be helpful, but the person who knows the most about the experience and education gained is the medical assistant.

Roscoe Patterson
3472 Vienna Woods Lane
Mytown, OH 45449
(937) 555-8874
rpatt@aol.com

Job Target:

• A long-term medical assistant position in a busy and varied medical office

Education:

• 1992: BA in Art History, State University, Mytown, OH
• 1998: AS in Medical Assisting, Community College, Mytown, OH

Capabilities:

• Excellent interpersonal skills and caring attitude
• Detail oriented, with strong analytical and problem-solving abilities
• Utilize solid organizational and time-management abilities in coordinating multiple projects
• Self-starter, take initiative to ensure jobs get done properly and efficiently
• Upbeat, personable, and highly energetic
• Ability to communicate in Spanish and American Sign Language

Accomplishments/Achievements:

• Campaigned for and raised consistent 15% annual increase in contributions and grants, allowing expansion of exhibits and needed renovations to art museum
• Maintained museum budget with 100% accountability
• Organized annual "Art Ball" for 100 contributors under budget
• Museum employee of the year 1995
• Certificates in CPR and EKG; Certified Nursing Assistant; will sit for CMA exam this November

Work History:

• 1998–present: Certified Nursing Assistant, Friendly Nursing Home, Mytown, OH
• 1992–1998: Assistant to the Curator, Mytown Museum of Art, Mytown, OH

FIGURE 28-9 Targeted resumé.

USEFUL ACTION WORDS

Accelerated	Manage
Actively	Motivated
Adapted	Organized
Administered	Originate
Analyze	Participated
Approve	Perform
Completed	Pinpointed
Conceived conduct	Plan
Control	Proficient
Coordinate	Program
Created	Proposed
Delegate	Proved
Demonstrate	Provide
Develop	Recommended
Direct	Reduced
Effect	Reinforced
Eliminated	Reorganized
Established	Responsibilities
Evaluate	Revamped
Expanded	Review
Expedite	Revise
Founded	Schedule
Generated	Significantly
Implemented	Simplify
Improved	Solve
Increased	Strategy
Influence	Streamline
Interpret	Structure
Launched	Successfully
Lead	Supervise
Lecture	Support
Maintain	Teach

FIGURE 28-10 Use action words when describing your skills on the resumé.

CRITICAL THINKING APPLICATION 28-7

Lisa has been asked by a potential employer to e-mail her resume. She has used an unusual font on her cover letter and on the top of the resume.

■ What concerns should Lisa have about e-mailing the document?

■ How can Lisa make sure her document arrives in a readable format?

■ How can she ensure that it will look exactly as she designed it when it is opened?

COVER LETTER

When sending a resumé, always include a cover letter (Figure 28-11). This is the introduction to the resumé and the person sending the document. A cover letter should always be sent to an individual, not to the facility or "to whom it may concern." The name of the person to whom the resumé should be sent usually can be obtained with a simple phone call. Ask for the name of the office manager, or, if this information is not obtained, address the cover letter specifically to the physician.

The purpose of the cover letter is to gain attention. Many potential employers schedule an interview with an individual based strictly on the content of the cover letter. Some are general letters that provide basic information without targeting the requirements of a specific job. An executive briefing, as described by Martin Yate in his book *Cover Letters That Knock 'Em Dead*, is a variation on the traditional cover letter. It provides a comprehensive picture of a thorough professional, plus a personalized, fast, and easy to read synopsis that details exactly how the applicant meets the major job requirements. This type of cover letter is extremely effective, but the applicant must have some idea of the job requirements in advance. To produce a dynamic executive briefing, the medical assistant should choose the most important qualifications listed in the ad for the job and then explain how he or she fits those qualifications (Figure 28-12).

Remember, direct supervisors are not always the first recipient of the resumé, so the impression made by the cover letter may make the difference in getting to the next step in the hiring process. Make it easy for screeners to find the strengths that match the job description. The cover letter should be brief but interesting. Use the same paper stock weight and color as the resumé. Be sure to include

Brutis Walter
2345 Morrow Court
Mytown, OH 45310
(937) 555-7426

May 23, 1998

Andrea Foreman, CMA
Office Manager
Family Health, Inc.
123 Timberleaf Drive
Mytown, OH 45432

Ms. Foreman:

I will be graduating from Community College with an A.S. in Medical Assisting on June 9 and am interested in an entry-level medical assistant position in your office. I will consider part-time or temporary work to gain experience in a diverse office such as yours.

My training includes hands-on experience in pediatrics, cardiology, internal medicine, obstetrics, and geriatrics. My administrative training would allow me to fill in wherever needed in the office. I am highly motivated and have supported myself and paid my own way through college. I understand responsibility and am a true team player. Belinda Mallet, RN, a fellow church member, told me the office will be short-staffed this summer owing to vacations and a maternity leave. I believe I could help your office run smoothly this summer, and beyond.

I look forward to hearing from you. I am available Tuesday and Thursday afternoons and Friday mornings until graduation. I will call you next Tuesday to set up an appointment for an interview. Thank you for your consideration.

Very truly yours,

Brutis Walter

FIGURE 28-11 Basic cover letter.

EXECUTIVE BRIEFING

Allison Aubrey, R.M.A.
3040 Wood Branch Drive
Austin, Texas 78716
512-434-9902

James Richardson, M.D.
Family Practice Clinic
5508 Lamar Blvd.
Austin, Texas 78752

Dear Dr. Richardson:

Although my attached resume will provide you with a general outline of my work history, my problem-solving abilities, and some of my achievements, it may take longer than a few moments to peruse. For your convenience, I have listed your specified requirements for the medical assistant position at the Lakewood office below, and the skills I have developed that match those specifications. I hope this briefing will allow you to quickly determine my eligibility for the position and will prompt you to contact me for an interview.

Your Requirements:	My Skills:
1. Two years' experience as a medical assistant.	1. Three years' experience as a registered medical assistant.
2. Ability to work with a larger supervisory team in planning, budgeting, and policy formulating.	2. Experience as employee council president, intricately involved in planning and budgeting.
3. Familiarity with HIPAA regulations.	3. Trained in HIPAA compliance and received three certificates for continuing education related to HIPAA compliance.
4. Ability to work with others as a team.	4. Awarded "Employee of the Quarter" honors twice during past year, and nominated for "Employee of the Year" by my coworkers.

I know that my experience and abilities will be of benefit to your organization. I look forward to discussing my qualifications and your requirements in person. I am confident that we can develop an exceptional working relationship and that I am the right individual for your organization. I will telephone you on Monday to arrange an interview to take place at your convenience.

Sincerely yours,

Allison Aubrey, R.M.A.

FIGURE 28-12 Executive briefing.

contact information, such as an address and at least two phone numbers, even if these are on the attached resume. The supervisor may separate the two documents, so each one must include a method of contact. Never start a cover letter with the sentence, "I saw your ad in the newspaper" or a similar phrase. Be creative with the opening line and try to capture the reader's attention.

A cover letter should be one to three paragraphs long. The final section should include a call to action that prompts an interview. If the document concludes with a request for a meeting, the medical assistant should state when he or she will call for a time and date.

▌JOB APPLICATIONS

Many facilities require a job application along with a resumé (Figure 28-13). Arrive 15 minutes before the scheduled interview to allow time to fill out an application.

A job application can be considered a legal document if the person is hired; therefore, it should be filled out neatly, correctly, and completely (Procedure 28-3). Always read the application before filling it out, so that directions make sense and information is not placed in the wrong area of the form. Carry a planner or address book to the interview so that former employers' and supervisors' names, addresses, and phone numbers are handy. The medical

assistant should not have to ask for a phone book to get an address. Have all of this information ready when it is needed.

Applications often ask for a date when the medical assistant would be available for work. Be careful with this question. If the applicant currently has a job, yet writes that he or she is "immediately available," it may indicate that the applicant intends to quit without notice. On the other hand, the current employer may be aware that the person is seeking other employment and may have granted him or her permission to quit immediately once a new job is found.

Be careful on the sections that ask the reason for leaving former positions. Think about the answers to be listed in those spaces and try to put the information in as positive a light as possible. Ask the

APPLICATION FOR POSITION / Medical or Dental Office
AN EQUAL OPPORTUNITY EMPLOYER

(In answering questions, use extra blank sheet if necessary)

No employee, applicant, or candidate for promotion, training or other advantage shall be discriminated against (or given preference) because of race, color, religion, sex, age, physical handicap, veteran status, or national origin.

PLEASE READ CAREFULLY AND WRITE OR PRINT ANSWERS TO ALL QUESTIONS. DO NOT TYPE.

Date of Application

A. PERSONAL INFORMATION

Name - Last First Middle		Social Security No.	Area Code/Phone No. ( )	
Present Address: - Street (Apt #) City	State	Zip		How Long At This Address?:
Previous Address: - Street City State Zip From: To:		Person to notify in case of Emergency or Accident - Name: Address: Telephone:		

B. EMPLOYMENT INFORMATION

For What Position Are You Applying?:	☐ Full-Time ☐ Part-Time ☐ Either	Date Available For Employment?:	Wage/Salary Expectations:
List Hrs./Days You Prefer To Work	List Any Hrs./Days You Are Not Available: (Except for times required for religious practices or observances)		Can You Work Overtime, If Necessary? ☐ Yes ☐ No
Are You Employed Now?: ☐ Yes ☐ No	If So, May We Inquire Of Your Present Employer?: ☐ No ☐ Yes, If Yes: Name Of Employer: Phone Number: ( )		
Have You Ever Been Bonded? ☐ Yes ☐ No	If Required For Position, Are You Bondable? ☐ Yes ☐ No ☐ Uncertain	Have You Applied For A Position With This Office Before? ☐ No ☐ Yes If Yes, When?:	
Referred By / Or Where Did You Learn Of This Job?:			
Can You, Upon Employment, Submit Verification Of Your Legal Right To Work In The United States?: ☐ Yes ☐ No Submit Proof That You Meet Legal Age Requirement For Employment? ☐ Yes ☐ No		Language(s) Applicant Speaks or Writes (If Use Of A Language Other Than English Is Relevant To The Job For Which The Applicant Is Applying:	

C. EDUCATIONAL HISTORY

Name & Address Of Schools Attended (Include Current)	Dates From	Dates Thru	Highest Grade/Level Completed	Diploma/Degree(s) Obtained/Areas of Study
High School				
College				Degree/Major
Post Graduate				Degree/Major
Other				Course/Diploma/License/Certificate

Specific Training, Education, Or Experiences Which Will Assist You In The Job For Which You Have Applied.

Future Educational Plans

D. SPECIAL SKILLS

CHECK BELOW THE KINDS OF WORK YOU HAVE DONE:		☐ MEDICAL INSURANCE FORMS	☐ RECEPTIONIST
☐ BLOOD COUNTS	☐ DENTAL ASSISTANT	☐ MEDICAL TERMINOLOGY	☐ TELEPHONES
☐ BOOKKEEPING	☐ DENTAL HYGIENIST	☐ MEDICAL TRANSCRIPTION	☐ TYPING
☐ COLLECTIONS	☐ FILING	☐ NURSING	☐ STENOGRAPHY
☐ COMPOSING LETTERS	☐ INJECTIONS	☐ PHLEBOTOMY (Draw Blood)	☐ URINALYSIS
☐ COMPUTER INPUT	☐ INSTRUMENT STERILIZATION	☐ POSTING	☐ X-RAY
OFFICE EQUIPMENT USED: ☐ COMPUTER	☐ DICTATING EQUIPMENT	☐ WORD PROCESSOR	☐ OTHER:
Other Kinds Of Tasks Performed Or Skills That May Be Applicable To Position:		Typing Speed	Shorthand Speed

ORDER # 72-110 • © 1976 BIBBERO SYSTEMS, INC. • PETALUMA, CA. • (REV. 1/95)
TO REORDER CALL TOLL FREE: (800) BIBBERO (800-242-2376) OR FAX (800) 242-9330 MFG IN U.S.A.

(PLEASE COMPLETE OTHER SIDE)

FIGURE 28-13 Application for employment. (Courtesy Bibbero Systems, Petaluma, Calif.)

E. EMPLOYMENT RECORD

LIST MOST RECENT EMPLOYMENT FIRST   May We Contact Your Previous Employer(s) For A Reference? ☐ Yes ☐ No

1) Employer	Work Performed. Be Specific:
Address Street City State Zip Code	
Phone Number ( )	
Type of Business Dates Mo. Yr. Mo. Yr. From To	
Your Position Hourly Rate/Salary Starting Final	
Supervisor's Name	
Reason For Leaving	

2) Employer	Worked Performed. Be Specific:
Address Street City State Zip Code	
Phone Number ( )	
Type of Business Dates Mo. Yr. Mo. Yr. From To	
Your Position Hourly Rate/Salary Starting Final	
Supervisor's Name	
Reason For Leaving	

3) Employer	Worked Performed. Be Specific:
Address Street City State Zip Code	
Phone Number ( )	
Type of Business Dates Mo. Yr. Mo. Yr. From To	
Your Position Hourly Rate/Salary Starting Final	
Supervisor's Name	
Reason For Leaving	

F. REFERENCES — FRIENDS / ACQUAINTANCES NON-RELATED

(1) ___ Name   Address   Telephone Number   (☐ Work ☐ Home)   Occupation   Years Acquainted

(1) ___ Name   Address   Telephone Number   (☐ Work ☐ Home)   Occupation   Years Acquainted

Please Feel Free To Add Any Information Which You Feel Will Help Us Consider You For Employment

READ THE FOLLOWING CAREFULLY, THEN SIGN AND DATE THE APPLICATION

"I certify that all answers given by me on this application are true, correct and complete to the best of my knowledge. I acknowledge notice that the information contained in this application is subject to check. I agree that, if hired, my continued employment may be contingent upon the accuracy of that information. If employed, I further agree to comply with Company/Office rules and regulations."

Signature: _____   Date: _____

FIGURE 28-13, cont'd

PROCEDURE 28-3

Complete a Job Application

GOAL: *To complete an accurate, detailed job application legibly so as to secure a job offer.*

EQUIPMENT and SUPPLIES

- Record of a job lead form
- Record of an interview form
- Copies of your resumé
- Contact information for former employers and references
- Contact information for friends and family

PROCEDURAL STEPS

1. Read the entire job application before completing any part of the document.
   PURPOSE: Reading through the entire application helps prevent errors while filling out the document.
2. Gather any information that may be necessary to answer all questions on the application.
   PURPOSE: The candidate should have all information available for completing a job application.
3. Begin to complete the application legibly.
   PURPOSE: The interviewer evaluates the candidate's handwriting to make sure it would be legible on medical records.
4. Answer each question on the document or write "not applicable."
5. Do not leave any space blank.
   PURPOSE: Leaving a space blank on the application may suggest that the candidate did not want to answer a certain question or accidentally overlooked it. By writing "not applicable" on such questions, the candidate demonstrates competence and attention to detail.
6. Do not write "see resumé" anywhere on the document.
   PURPOSE: Many supervisors view this practice as laziness. Always fill out the job application completely and do not leave blank spaces.
7. Be completely honest about every fact written on the document.
8. Include information on the resumé that exhibits dependability, punctuality, positive work ethics, initiative, the ability to adapt to change, and a responsible attitude.
9. Sign the document and date it.
10. Proofread the document and make sure none of the information conflicts with the resumé.
    PURPOSE: Proofreading helps the candidate to catch any errors before submitting the application.
11. Submit the application.

---

advice of your placement counselor if you are unsure what to say in these sections.

If there are sections available for listing special skills and qualifications, fill them out fully. Describe cardiopulmonary resuscitation (CPR) and first aid certifications and any professional organizations of which you are a member. If references are requested, list the name, title, employer, and a means of contact. Be sure to get permission before using someone as a reference.

One of the most common mistakes on job applications is writing "see resumé." This is an indication of laziness and must be avoided. Even if the same information is found on the resumé, the application must be completed in its entirety. If the exact information is not included on the job application, that legal document is incomplete. In addition, most job applications include a disclaimer that if a false or incomplete statement is made on the application, the individual can be dismissed from any position for which he or she was hired. So make sure all the information given is accurate.

JOB INTERVIEW

A medical assistant may interview with the office manager, the physician, or both, and other staff members may be brought in for part of the interview. This is especially true in offices with a cohesive team of employees.

The interview usually is the most stressful of the job search steps. Some individuals dread job interviews and become extremely nervous at the prospect of interviewing. Others are very comfortable and consider the interview as much for their own purposes as for the employer's. Either way, the more interviews the medical assistant has, the more comfortable he or she will be with each subsequent interview.

An interview has four phases: preparation for the interview, the interview itself, the follow-up, and the negotiation.

Preparation for the Interview

When preparing for an interview, the medical assistant should learn everything possible about the employer. Look on the Internet for information about the facility. Practice answering possible interview questions. Prepare an outfit to wear to interviews. It is wise to drive to the interview site on a day preceding the interview date if the location is unfamiliar to avoid getting lost on the day of the important event. The better prepared the medical assistant is, the more comfortable he or she will be while interviewing.

The critical part of the interview is the medical assistant's ability to present himself or herself as the best candidate for the job. By preparing to answer interview questions before the interview, the medical assistant will be much more prepared. Although no one can guess exactly what questions will be asked, some standard interview questions are very common (Figure 28-14). Review these questions thoroughly, answer them in writing, then study them before the interview. Then when the medical assistant is asked, "What are your three greatest strengths?" he or she can confidently answer, "I am professional, reliable, and honest."

When preparing on the day of the interview, be conservative with wardrobe choices. For women a skirt and blouse or business suit is appropriate. For men a business suit is the best choice. Depending

TOP 100 INTERVIEW QUESTIONS

1. Tell me about yourself.
2. Why do you want to work for this company?
3. Why should I hire you?
4. How do you work under pressure?
5. What type of job or salary do you expect to make in 5 years?
6. How do you handle criticism?
7. What do you think your co-workers think about you?
8. What is your opinion of the company you last worked for?
9. Describe your last supervisor.
10. What is your view of management?
11. What would you like to change about yourself and how would you do it?
12. What is your best asset?
13. What adjectives would you use to describe yourself?
14. What aspects of your life are you most happy with?
15. How would you describe the perfect job?
16. Why did you leave your last job?
17. Why did you choose this type of profession?
18. What salary do you expect?
19. What are your strongest and weakest personal qualities?
20. What motivates you?
21. What have you learned from some of your previous jobs?
22. What personal characteristics are necessary for success in your chosen field?
23. What do you know about this facility and our competitors?
24. What were your major courses of study in school?
25. Do you plan to continue your education?
26. Did school meet your expectations or were you disappointed?
27. How did you pay for your education?
28. Sell this pen to me.
29. To what extent do your grades reflect how much you have learned?
30. Do you feel your education was worthwhile?
31. What were the major responsibilities of your last job?
32. What has been your most rewarding experience at work?
33. What was your single most important accomplishment for the company on your last job?
34. What was the toughest problem you have ever solved and how did you do it?
35. How do you see yourself fitting in with our company?
36. What skills did you learn on your last job that can be used here?
37. What would you do if you were fired in two years?
38. What kinds of additional education do you think you need to meet your career goals?
39. How long do you plan to stay with our company?
40. What immediate contribution could you make if you came to work for us today?
41. Do you feel that you have received good general training?
42. If you were starting school all over again, what courses would you take?
43. How much money do you hope to earn in 5 years? 10 years?
44. Do you think that your extracurricular activities were worth the time spent?
45. Are you interested in making money or do you have other reasons for entering this career field?
46. Do you prefer working with others or by yourself?
47. Can you take instructions or criticism without being upset?
48. Tell me a story.
49. What do you know about the opportunities in the field in which you are trained?
50. How long do you expect to work?
51. Have you ever had any difficulty in getting along with a co-worker, classmate, or instructor?
52. Which of your school years was most difficult?
53. Do you like routine work?
54. Define cooperation.
55. Will you fight to get ahead?
56. Do you have an analytical mind?
57. Are you willing to go where the company sends you?
58. What job in this company would you choose if you could?
59. Do you think that employers should consider grades?
60. What have you done that shows initiative and willingness to work?
61. What benefits did you receive from your last employer?
62. What has been your most important accomplishment during your school years?
63. Have you ever helped to reduce operating costs, and how?
64. Have you ever developed or helped develop any programs, and how did you do this?
65. What do you think determines a person's progress in a company?
66. What would you do if a personal problem interfered with your work?
67. What would you do if you became bored with your job?
68. What would you do if you had a personality clash with a supervisor?
69. How will you be getting to work each day?
70. Do you have reliable transportation?
71. How do you feel about working with someone who is HIV positive?
72. What person has most influenced your life?
73. What is the last book you read?
74. Who do you most admire?
75. Who is your favorite relative?
76. What will previous supervisors say about you?
77. What makes a good supervisor?
78. Why would you be successful in this job?
79. Why have you held so many jobs?
80. Can you explain this gap in your employment history?
81. Have you ever been fired from a position?
82. Do you have adequate child care arrangements that will allow you to be at work when scheduled?
83. What is your philosophy of life?
84. How many other positions are you considering?
85. Why were your grades in school so low?
86. Are you a member of any professional organizations?
87. How old were you when you began to support yourself?
88. Do you participate in continuing education activities or seminars?
89. Have you had the hepatitis B injection series?
90. Where did you perform your externship?
91. How many days of school did you miss?
92. Why did you decide to attend the college/school you attended?
93. What kind of boss do you prefer?
94. How do you usually spend your weekends?
95. Why types of people seem to rub you the wrong way?
96. What planning procedures do you use?
97. What frustrates you about your current job?
98. What is unique about you?
99. What have you done that indicates you are qualified for this job?
100. Do you have any questions?

FIGURE 28-14 Top 100 interview questions.

on the office situation, one may be given very specific instructions on wardrobe. Some office managers or physicians even tell the potential employee to arrive in jeans. Is this a test? The physician may be curious as to whether the medical assistant can follow directions and actually wear jeans. Obtain a hint about clothing by visiting the office before the interview, even if it is just to ask for directions. That way, the potential employee can see what the office staff members are wearing. A similar wardrobe should be sufficient for an interview. If the staff wears scrubs, then wear neatly pressed scrubs with clean shoes; do not wear the slouchy scrubs one might find in a hospital surgical suite. Conservative business suits should always be acceptable in an interview.

Be sure clothing is fresh, wrinkle free, and well fitting and that shoes are clean and shined. It is a good idea to carry a planner or other method of taking notes during the interview; this makes a good impression and indicates interest in the job. Always arrive 15 minutes early for the interview. Do not wear heavy perfumes or colognes, do not chew gum, and do not wear excessive jewelry. Never take anyone along on a job interview, especially children, even if they are older.

Pay particular attention to other aspects of appearance (Figure 28-15). Make sure your hair is clean and styled attractively, your teeth are clean, and your breath is fresh. Nails are also important and should be clean and well groomed, because the medical assistant should give the interviewer a firm handshake. However, nails should not be excessively long or painted in highly visible colors. Remember the appearance guidelines that applied to the externship; some employers will react negatively to tattoos, extravagant hairstyles, or other excessive wardrobe choices. Always dress appropriately and conservatively for an interview. Once hired, the new employee may be allowed to wear more diverse styles but must comply with the employee handbook or procedure manual. Expect to be a little nervous. Any interview can be a stressful situation. The better prepared the medical assistant is, the more of a success the interview will be.

Take a professional binder to the interview with extra copies of your resume and reference list. Include a list of both former employees and references, as well as the dates of employment, supervisors'

FIGURE 28-15 Present a professional appearance during the job interview and be sure to smile often. (From Yoder-Wise P: *Leading and managing in nursing*, ed 4, 2006, St Louis, Mosby.)

names and their spelling, and any other demographic information that might be needed to accurately complete paperwork (this could also be saved into documents or applications in a smart phone). This will help to avoid the embarrassment of asking to look up an address in a phone book or calling to obtain the information.

Interview

The interviewer should not ask any illegal questions, including those that are related to age, sex, nationality, religion, marital/family status, affiliations/organizations, and disabilities. For instance, the interviewer may ask "Are you legally eligible to work in this country?" However, the interview cannot legally ask "What nationality are you?" If the job involves some travel, the interviewer cannot legally ask "What are your child care arrangements?" However, the interviewer can ask "Can you travel and work overtime if necessary?"

Employers may ask illegal questions, whether intentionally or accidentally, and the way that the medical assistant answers the questions can influence the employer's hiring decision. If the medical assistant is openly offended, then the sometimes abrasive comments that patients make may be offensive as well. If the illegal question is answered, the interviewer may use the information in the answer to weed out the medical assistant as a candidate. The best approach is to politely address the question, either by answering it directly or by redirecting the interviewer back to the job requirements. For example, if the interviewer asks if the candidate plans to put children in day care (which might be a way of determining the age of the dependent children and thus the likelihood of absenteeism due to the children's illnesses), the medical assistant could answer, "I will be able to meet the work schedule and the responsibilities that this job requires." Some questions that might normally be considered illegal, such as "What organizations are you a member of?" might be job related. The employer may be interested in knowing that the medical assistant is a member of various professional organizations, such as the American Association of Medical Assistants or the American Medical Technologists.

During the actual interview, maintain good eye contact. Many supervisors refuse to hire people who seem uncomfortable looking them directly in the eyes. Never take control of the interview. Allow the supervisor to ask questions at his or her own pace. Do not fidget in the chair and observe the interviewer's body language for clues as to how interested he or she might be. Do not volunteer any negative information; be honest and do not exaggerate experience or lengths of employment. Never speak negatively about former employers.

Be careful when answering questions such as, "Tell me about yourself." Most female medical assistants might begin to answer this question with a phrase like, "I'm a recent graduate, and I am married and have two children." The answer to this question should not reflect information about personal issues. Focus all answers on professionalism and the strengths that will be an asset to the medical office.

Remember that the interview is centered on the medical assistant, so freely discuss the skills and attributes that you would bring to the job. The better prepared the medical assistant is, the smoother the interview will go. Be able to prove the skills you claim and explain how they meet the needs of the company or facility. Avoid a "know it all" attitude, which indicates overconfidence and reluctance to take direction. Always express an interest in the employer and his or her

PROCEDURE 28-4

Interview for a Job

GOAL: *To project a professional appearance during a job interview and to be able to express the reasons the medical assistant is the best candidate for the position.*

EQUIPMENT and SUPPLIES

- Record of a job lead form
- Record of an interview form
- Job application
- Copies of your resumé
- Contact information for former employers and references
- Contact information for friends and family
- Sample interview questions

PROCEDURAL STEPS

1. Prepare for the interview by studying sample interview questions and researching basic information about the facility.
   PURPOSE: Employers are impressed by candidates who have researched the company and know some details about its operation.
2. Know all the information on the resumé so that it can be discussed confidently during the interview.
3. Prepare clothing that reflects a professional image for the facility in which the medical assistant is hoping to gain employment.
   PURPOSE: Most medical facilities prefer conservative dress.
4. Gather all materials that might be needed during the interview, such as copies of your resumé, contact information, and copies of earned certificates.
   PURPOSE: All information must be handy and prepared before the interview.
5. Arrive for the interview at least 15 minutes early.
   PURPOSE: Arrive early in case forms must be completed before the interview.

6. Stand and shake hands with the interviewer when he or she appears.
   PURPOSE: A confident, firm handshake is a positive gesture.
7. Listen intently to the interviewer as the position is described and be ready to explain how you fit the requirements for the position.
   PURPOSE: The interviewer evaluates how well the candidate listens and answers questions.
8. Answer all interview questions confidently, smiling when appropriate and displaying a positive, responsible attitude.
9. While answering interview questions, stress dependability, punctuality, positive work ethics, initiative, and the ability to adapt to change.
10. Ask intelligent questions after the interviewer finishes.
    PURPOSE: The questions asked at the end of an interview should indicate an interest in the position and should not focus on how the candidate would benefit from the job, but rather on what the candidate can do for the company.
11. Determine a day and time when the next contact will be made.
12. Express interest in the position.
    PURPOSE: Employers expect some type of confirmation that the candidate is interested in the job.
13. Send a thank you note or letter to the interviewer within 24 hours of the interview.
    PURPOSE: A thank you note is impressive and reinforces the candidate's interest in the position.
14. Follow up as appropriate on the interview.

---

projects, rather than in what the employer can do for the employee. Ask intelligent questions at the end of the interview if given the opportunity. Never let your first question be, "How much will I be paid?" Money, although important, cannot appear to be your primary concern.

Before the interview ends, the medical assistant should ask when a decision will be made and if it would be acceptable to call to follow up (Procedure 28-4).

CRITICAL THINKING APPLICATION   28-8

Lisa is enjoying a good interview when the interviewer, a male supervisor, asks her if she is married. When Lisa replies that she is not, he asks if she has a steady boyfriend.

- What might the supervisor's motive be with this line of questioning?
- How should Lisa respond?
- Are these questions inappropriate or do they serve a purpose?

Follow-Up after the Interview

Follow-up is critical after an interview. Always send a written thank you note or letter to the person who conducted the interview. Many employers wait to see who sends a thank you letter before making the final hiring decision. Limit follow-up calls to one or two a week. Most employers give an indication of when the hiring decision will be made. The company should notify all those who interviewed once a decision has been made, unless specific protocols were set during the interview about follow-up. For instance, if the office manager says a decision will be made on Friday and the final three candidates will be called for a second interview, the medical assistant knows if a call is not received to continue the job search. Although not all companies provide this type of notification, it is considered professional etiquette to tell the candidates who interviewed for the job if they are no longer under consideration. Never place all your hope in one job; continue to prospect and interview until an offer is made and accepted. In addition, always be on the watch for the next job opportunity.

REASONS PEOPLE DO NOT GET HIRED

The following is a ranked list of reasons interviewers do not hire job candidates. The list was compiled from the results of a nationwide survey of 153 companies performed by Northcentral Technical College, Wausau, Wisconsin.

1. Poor personal appearance
2. Lack of interest or enthusiasm
3. Overemphasis on money
4. Poor voice, diction, grammar
5. Lack of planning
6. No purpose or goals
7. Condemnation of past employers
8. Poor eye contact
9. "Limp fish" handshake
10. Late to interview
11. Lack of tact
12. Lack of maturity
13. Lack of courtesy
14. Asking no questions
15. Overbearing, "know-it-all" attitude
16. Lack of confidence and poise
17. Failure to participate in activities
18. Making excuses, evading unfavorable factors on record
19. Indecisiveness
20. Just shopping around
21. No interest in company
22. Sloppy application form
23. Wanting a job for a short time
24. Unwillingness to relocate
25. Cynical attitude
26. Low moral standards
27. Laziness
28. Intolerance or strong prejudices
29. No sense of humor
30. Narrow interests
31. Inability to take criticism
32. No appreciation of the value of experience
33. Radical ideas
34. Too aggressive during interview

Negotiation

The negotiation stage of job acceptance can be as stressful as the actual interviews. A medical assistant should know the lowest salary he or she can afford and should ask for a little more than that figure. Bracket salary requests: instead of asking for $13 per hour, ask for a salary in the "mid to high twenties." Let the employer mention a figure first or a range of salary. Usually the person who mentions a salary range first has the disadvantage. If the medical assistant requests $13 per hour and the facility was willing to pay $16 per hour, the medical assistant probably will get $13.

Never say "no" to a job offer on the spot. Request at least 24 hours to consider the offer (Procedure 28-5). A medical assistant should not let the salary amount be the main factor in the decision whether to accept a position. Before accepting or rejecting a job offer, consider whether the position carries any authority, the benefits, the hours, the distance from home, and the potential for advancement. People accept jobs for reasons other than the salary; remember the value of experience.

YOU GOT THE JOB!

Once the job offer has been made and accepted, a start date will be determined. Before the first day, use the computer to map several ways to get to work. If you are unsure of the traffic flow, leave home extra early the first day so that you are guaranteed to arrive on time.

Most employees are placed on a 30- to 90-day probationary period, during which employment may be terminated for unsatisfactory performance. The probationary period also provides the employer and employee an opportunity to learn about each other. The medical assistant will interact with other co-workers, patients, and providers. A new medical assistant should volunteer to help others and efficiently complete the duties assigned. Use the probationary period as a testing ground, carefully observing ways in which the office might run in a smoother manner. However, do not make numerous suggestions for change during this period. Discover why certain methods are used and make an effort to fit in with the rest of the team before suggesting that the office routine be changed. Remember, the people at the office may have been employed for a substantially longer time and may resent suggestions from a new staff member. Learn the office rhythms, procedures, and culture first and demonstrate a team-oriented attitude. After new employees prove their responsibility and good attitude, other staff members will be open to suggestions about improvements for the office.

Common Early Mistakes

Some medical assistants make mistakes early on a new job. Never be disruptive to the office by gossiping or complaining. A medical assistant must realize that procedures may be performed in many different ways and that the way he or she was taught in school probably is not the only correct way. Be open to learning new ideas, concepts, and procedures. Although some mistakes are to be expected, make sure that once a mistake has been pointed out, it is corrected. Do not make the same mistakes over and over.

Supervisors may work closely with the medical assistants. Some expect medical assistants to carry out orders on their own. Do not make too much supervision necessary or force the office manager to constantly check the work you have done. Finish all assigned duties in a timely manner and avoid procrastination. When significant problems arise, discuss them openly with the supervisor and attempt to find a quick resolution. Limit absences and tardy days to a minimum and miss work only when absolutely necessary, especially during the probationary period.

Being a Good Employee

A medical assistant can be a better employee in several ways. First and foremost, arrive 15 minutes before the scheduled shift and do not leave early. Even the best medical assistant cannot benefit an

PROCEDURE 28-5

Negotiate a Salary

GOAL: *To develop negotiation skills that will help the medical assistant obtain the salary and benefits he or she requires.*

EQUIPMENT and SUPPLIES

- Record of a job lead form
- Record of an interview form
- Information about job offers received
- Contact name at medical facility

PROCEDURAL STEPS

1. Study the job offer at hand.
2. Determine whether the offer is sufficient as it stands.
3. Make a list of what additional salary requirements and/or benefits are needed at a minimum.
   <u>PURPOSE:</u> Know the minimum salary and benefits you can accept when evaluating a job offer.
4. Arrive at the second or subsequent interview appointment to discuss the job with the hiring supervisor.
5. Thank the supervisor for the offer that has been presented and express interest in the position.
6. Express the additional salary and/or benefits desired.
   <u>PURPOSE:</u> The candidate should be able to express what he or she needs with regard to salary and benefits.
7. Discuss whether the facility would be willing to increase the offer to match your desires.
8. Express valid reasons that explain why the additional benefits should be offered, based on past performance, experience, or other valid factors.
9. Discuss reasonable compromises regarding the additional salary and/or benefits.
   <u>PURPOSE:</u> The ability to compromise is a valuable employee trait.
10. Ask what level of performance is expected for salary and/or benefits to be increased.
11. Be courteous and diplomatic during all negotiations.
12. Express interest in and promise serious consideration of the position.
13. Determine the next contact time with the supervisor.
14. Weigh the offer and compromises to make a good decision about the job offer.

---

office if he or she does not come to work. Be honest and demonstrate trustworthiness and professionalism. Get along with co-workers in the facility. A medical assistant should be able to resolve simple problems with others easily without involving the supervisor. Reflect a friendly attitude toward others, even if they are difficult to get along with. Arrive every single day ready to learn. The medical assistant's education does not end on graduation from school. The medical field is one of constant change, and those who work in it must learn and change along with it.

A medical assistant should constantly be performing assigned duties and should not expect frequent breaks in the medical office. Most offices are fast paced, and the supervisor expects the medical assistant to keep up with the activity. Even during slow periods, there is always a counter to clean or filing to do. Be supportive of the leadership in the facility and ask for more responsibility if necessary. Take the initiative to perform duties that are cumbersome or repetitive and get them done quickly.

Always treat patients with compassion. Remember that they are not always at their best when ill, so be kind and courteous to them and their families. The patients are the reason the facility exists. Treat them with great respect and care.

Remember that medical assistants can be held individually responsible for their actions even though they work as an agent of the physician-employer. Although the physician is usually the person against whom professional liability lawsuits are brought, the medical assistant can still be named in a lawsuit. For this reason, it is wise to carry individual professional liability coverage once employed in the medical industry. The coverage should be maintained throughout the medical assistant's career.

CRITICAL THINKING APPLICATION 28-9

On Lisa's second day at the externship site, she clearly sees a co-worker taking and using a controlled drug from the storage area.
- What should Lisa do?
- What potential problems arise with this situation?
- To whom should Lisa report this incident, if anyone?

Dealing with Supervisors

Supervisors appreciate employees who come to them when they have questions, but who are able to handle minor decisions on their own. Never hesitate to approach supervisors when an issue at hand needs their attention. Do not allow a situation to go unaddressed and then say, "I didn't want to bother you with that." The office manager is responsible for dealing with difficult issues, and these should be handled immediately when they arise.

A medical assistant should never attempt to cover up a mistake; admitting the error is a much better approach to solving the problem. When talking with the supervisor, do not hesitate to speak and do not avoid the subject. State the problem clearly and explain what routes are available to **rectify** the situation. Work with the supervisor to resolve issues and accept the advice given with a positive attitude.

Performance Appraisals

Performance appraisals usually are done after the initial probationary period and annually thereafter. The performance appraisal is designed to inform the employee of his or her strengths and weaknesses on the job, according to the supervisor's point of view. Most of these appraisals offer a scale to rate the employee's performance, such as 1 to 5. Do not expect to receive a perfect appraisal, because employees are seldom perfect in all aspects of their jobs. If the supervisor gives perfect scores to an employee, there is no room for growth or improvement. It is the rare employee who completes all duties and meets every expectation without any errors.

When asked to sit down with your supervisor for a performance appraisal, expect to address areas that need improvement. Ask questions and work with the supervisor to improve in the areas that may need more effort or a different approach.

If the employee strongly disagrees with any area of the performance appraisal, he or she should discuss this with the supervisor. There may have been a misunderstanding as to the duties involved. Clarify this calmly and patiently and strive to do better next time.

Asking for a Raise

Most facilities have some type of schedule for pay increases. Some offer a cost of living increase on an annual basis; others use a merit system, offering raises only when earned and deserved based on performance.

There may come a time when the medical assistant feels the need to ask for a raise. Before doing so, a little self-reflection is important to determine whether a raise is in order. Has attendance been exemplary? How many times was the medical assistant tardy? Does he or she work well with little supervision? Has he or she performed all the expected duties well and in a timely manner?

Approach the supervisor at a relatively calm part of the day and ask how a salary raise might be earned in the near future. Do not expect a raise of more than 3% to 5% at any given time, unless the employee is promoted to another position or given additional duties. If the supervisor is unable to grant a raise, determine whether the reasons are valid. If they are not, the medical assistant may want to pursue other employment options. The medical assistant will find that finding a job is always easier if one already has a job, so do not quit outright unless the work environment is **intolerable**. Begin networking again and discover the options available.

Leaving a Job

Always offer at least 2 weeks' notice when resigning from a job. Prepare a written notice of resignation and take it to the supervisor in person. Do not just leave it on a desk or place it in the interoffice mail.

Resigning from a job just as an attempt to get a salary increase is a dangerous practice. Once the employer doubts the employee's loyalty, the future usually is not bright for the employee at that facility. Resign only after a final decision has been made. If the medical assistant is resigning to take another position, the current employer may be expected to make a **counteroffer**. However, be wary about accepting counteroffers. What led you to look for a new job in the first place? Has the situation been resolved? Ask yourself these questions before agreeing to stay with the current employer. Often employees who accept a counteroffer and stay at their original job find that few changes are made, and the employee ends up leaving the position in the long run.

LIFE SKILLS

To be successful in the job search, the medical assistant must have the basic entry-level skills needed to perform in the workplace. Even more important, he or she must develop certain life skills that are essential to excel in any profession. If these skills are not developed and refined, the medical assistant may find fewer opportunities and advancements available, as well as less impressive salaries and benefits. Perhaps even more important, the medical assistant who does not have his or her personal life in order will not be able to offer their employer their best performance every day. He or she will be expected to give a full day's work for a full day's pay on every single shift. Although personal issues do affect work performance, the medical assistant must make a good effort to put personal problems aside when working.

The most important life skill one can have is the willingness to change. Many employees insist on doing things the same way they have always been done, and they resist any changes in policy or procedure. However, a medical assistant who does not welcome and work hard to adjust to change is a failure waiting to happen.

Personal Growth

Personal growth is a comprehensive term that applies to many aspects of a person's mental, physical, and spiritual health. This growth is a result of goals that are set for self-improvement. Without clear goals, people rarely experience personal growth that is initiated from within. Growth may happen as a result of some outside influence, but a conscious effort toward personal growth is an innate decision.

No matter how great the training or how many opportunities are placed in front of a person, fear and doubt can sabotage efforts to improve the self-image, confidence, and future potential of an individual. Personal growth involves such traits as self-control, self-esteem, problem-solving skills, decision-making skills, and stress management.

Self-Control

Self-control is a vital trait in the medical office. Some patients are not at their best because of their illness, and this may make them less than cordial toward the staff. Remember that this is usually a temporary situation. A medical assistant must exercise self-control and must not respond in kind to patients who are disagreeable.

Self-control is important in other areas of the medical office. Never remove drugs from the storage areas without permission and be careful when dealing with petty cash. A medical assistant must get enough rest during the work week that he or she can care for the patients in an enthusiastic manner.

Self-Esteem

Everyone has certain strengths and weaknesses. Good self-esteem is the result of knowing what those strengths are and overcoming the weaknesses. It is having a positive outlook about oneself and others. A person with good self-esteem is motivated, able to express love, and capable of handling criticism. A person's self-esteem improves if he or she has developed adaptive skills. Especially in the medical profession, one thing that is guaranteed in the workplace is change.

Change can be positive or negative; this depends mostly on the way it is viewed by the individual.

A person is not doomed to live with poor self-esteem forever. With a degree of effort and open mindedness, an individual can work toward better self-esteem, which can make a tremendous difference in the individual's future potential.

Problem-Solving Skills

For individuals to work together, they must have a degree of trust and be willing to make suggestions for the good of the group. The phrase "two heads are better than one" is still true when it comes to problem solving. Employees usually want to play a part in solving the problems in the workplace, and they appreciate knowing that their opinions make a difference. A medical assistant who can listen to the concerns of others and is willing to give and take will be an excellent problem solver.

Decision-Making Skills

People who know how to make good decisions usually are successful. Thinking through a decision requires logic, and it is best to take some time to think carefully of all the pros and cons. Unfortunately, a medical assistant may not always have time to consider decisions in a leisurely fashion, especially when dealing with emergencies. A good decision maker is honest in identifying the real problems and attempts to keep personal feelings isolated from the process.

There are several steps in making a sound decision. The problem must be specifically defined and evaluated so that the individual understands clearly what needs to happen to resolve the situation. Gather as much information as possible and consider all alternatives. It sometimes is helpful to choose an alternative and consider all the ramifications of making a decision using that alternative. Then, when the best alternative has been determined, the decision should be made and put into action. Care should be taken to avoid making a decision simply because it is easy and comfortable, because more problems could arise later as a result of not addressing the true problem in the beginning.

CRITICAL THINKING APPLICATION   **28-10**

Lisa has been on several interviews and likes the prospect of working for three different physicians. If an offer is made at each office, how can Lisa decide which to accept? What will help Lisa make this decision?

Stress Management

The demands of the medical profession make it a stressful environment at times. Stress is not always bad. In fact, some stress is a positive motivator toward a goal. A *stressor* is a stimulus that prompts a reaction from the body. Positive stress, or *eustress,* includes exhilarating activities or success, which often leads to higher expectations from the person experiencing the eustress. The opposite is distress, which includes disappointment, failure, or embarrassment. Stress management is a conscious effort to control the stressors and resulting reactions so that the body and mind operate evenly, even when stress is present in an individual's life.

By learning to recognize the signs of stressful overload, a medical assistant can possibly ward off the negative reactions that are so physically and mentally draining to the body. Many people notice a headache or fatigue when overly stressed. Breathing correctly is one way to reduce stress. Often an accelerated breathing pattern that is quick and shallow is a stress indicator. Breathing from the abdomen at a slower pace, inhaling through the nose, and exhaling through the mouth, may help reduce tension. Taking time for relaxing activities and getting plenty of exercise are other methods of stress reduction.

Planning a Budget

A newly graduated medical assistant should formulate a simple budget and live within that budget. Track spending with checkbook ledgers, bill stubs, receipts, and daily records for 3 months before developing a firm budget, so that you have a realistic accounting of where money goes when it leaves the checkbook. Use that information to design a reasonable spending plan for monthly income that accounts for monthly, quarterly, and annual expenses, as well as special expenses.

Even if you make only a small salary, building savings is important. A medical assistant should set aside 5% to 10% of the net income in a savings account. The money in savings should not be touched except in emergencies. Establish a separate emergency fund, which ideally should hold 3 to 6 months' salary. This way, enough cash is available to pay bills for 3 months in case of a sudden job loss or emergency. No one can do this immediately when beginning a new job, but it can be done over a period of time if one is committed to the effort.

Avoid going into debt whenever possible. If credit cards are used at all, they should be used conservatively and not for impulse purchases. Instead of using credit, set spending goals and save for a purchase or use layaway programs. Always make more than the minimum payment on credit cards to prevent excessive interest from accruing on the account. Even better, pay off the entire balance when the statement is received each month, avoiding charges higher than what can be paid with the monthly salary in addition to other bills. Everyone should work toward being debt free as soon as possible.

In his book *The Total Money Makeover,* author Dave Ramsey recommends avoiding credit card use altogether and paying off all debts in order from smallest to largest to become debt free. Avoiding debt helps keep finances manageable whether the economy is up or down.

Student Loans

Student loans are designed to provide the opportunity to obtain an education. They must be paid back. If an individual **defaults** on a student loan, he or she becomes ineligible for future student loans until the original loan is paid back, and amounts owed may be deducted from tax refunds involuntarily. Remember that interest is accrued on loans, so the student will owe more than was actually borrowed. Although small loans may run around $50 per month once they are due, larger loans can result in payments in excess of $1,000 per month. Never incur more student loan debt than absolutely necessary and make every effort to pay off the loan as early as possible, even if that means making extra payments or a larger lump-sum payment in addition to the required monthly amounts. If the student can avoid loans by saving for school expenses and paying for each semester in cash, the education will cost less, because no interest charges will be added to the tuition costs.

There is never a reason to default on a student loan. The medical assistant should contact the company that services the student loan and explain any problems that are preventing repayment of the debt. These companies want to work with students to clear their accounts. Often a **deferment** is available, which allows the student to postpone the payments for a period of time. Deferments may be available if the student is unemployed, attending school to continue his or her education, suffering economic hardship, completing a graduate fellowship, completing rehabilitation training, or in other situations. The medical assistant should contact the lender to find out whether he or she is eligible for a deferment. (For tips on how to avoid defaulting on a loan, along with an in-school deferment form, visit the Evolve site at *evolve.elsevier.com/kinn*.)

Guideline Budget

Dealing with personal finances can be a stressor. Developing a realistic budget helps a medical assistant plan his or her spending. When careful planning is implemented, more can be accomplished with less money if a commitment has been made to staying on budget and resisting the temptation to spend.

Start by evaluating your monthly expenses. The easiest way to do this is to save every single receipt and a copy of each bank transaction for 3 months. Then, divide the receipts into the appropriate month and determine where your money is going. Put the receipt amounts in specific categories, such as:

- Rent/mortgage
- Child care
- Utilities
- Food
- Car payments
- Car expenses
- Credit/debts
- Professional dues
- Household expenses
- Medical/dental care
- Child support
- School expenses
- Student loans

Budgets should be designed and planned to be as personal as possible. Using the information from the receipts, you can easily determine which categories fit your individual budget. Budget forms are readily accessible on the Internet or can be designed using computer programs, such as Microsoft Word or Excel. A sample budget outline is shown in Figure 28-16. Take an honest look at each item listed and determine the amount you spend monthly in each category. Compare these amounts with your monthly income and see whether your current budget is positive or negative. Remember that the gross salary is the amount earned before taxes and other deductions. The net salary is the take-home pay. Adjustments may be needed to bring the budget into balance.

Getting a Paycheck

Nothing is more exciting than receiving the first paycheck from a new job. Still, the recipient must handle finances responsibly so that financial obligations can be met. Employees who handle their personal finances well can better focus on work responsibilities and those in their personal life.

MONTHLY INCOME	AMOUNT
Net Income	
Spouse Net Income	
Child Support	
Other Income	

MONTHLY EXPENSES	AMOUNT
Rent	
Gas	
Electric	
Home/Renters Insurance	
Water/Sewage	
Trash	
Home Telephone	
Cell Telephone	
Pager	
Cable TV/Satellite	
Internet/DSL	
Child Care	
Lawn Care	
Clothing	
Food - Home	
Food - Work or School	
Food - Eating Out	
Laundry/Dry Cleaning	
Medical Expenses	
Dental Expenses	
Life Insurance	
Medical Insurance	
Dental Insurance	
Eyeglasses	
Prescriptions	
Automobile Payment	
Automobile Insurance	
Repairs	
Gas/Oil	
Furniture	
Beauty/Barber Shop	
Pet Expenses	
Student Loan	
Other Loans	
Credit Cards	
Church/Charities	
Birthdays	
Anniversaries	
Christmas	
Vacation Planning	
Entertainment	

FIGURE 28-16 The guideline budget.

Several deductions will be taken from the employee's paycheck, such as Federal Insurance Contributions Act (FICA) and Medicare contributions, in addition to optional deductions, such as those for medical and dental insurance, disability insurance, vision care, retirement funds, and others, depending upon what is offered by the employer. If the employee knows the amount of all the deductions on the paycheck, he or she can figure the FICA and Medicare contributions to estimate the net amount of the check each pay period and know the amount of money that will be available toward the budget. The current FICA deduction is 12.4% of the income earned for the period, and the Medicare deduction is 3.8%. By calculating these deductions from the gross salary for the period minus optional deductions, the net salary can be determined. Always bring questions to the attention of the payroll manager immediately so that payroll issues can be rectified quickly.

Dangerous Habits

Some individuals practice dangerous habits with regard to finances. For instance, if this month's bills are arriving and last month's have not been paid, frustration and depression may result. Some people may even avoid opening letters or bills just so they do not have to deal with seeing the balance due. Writing checks on funds that are not in the checking account is not only unwise, it is also illegal. All states have laws against writing insufficient funds checks, and most legislation considers this a form of theft. A person can be arrested for writing "hot" checks. People headed for financial disaster also purchase daily items, such as bread and milk, with a credit card. All these behaviors are signs of financial trouble.

CLOSING COMMENTS

The period surrounding graduation is a celebration, but also a busy time that requires much planning. Cooperate with the school in securing externship sites and make an effort to obtain a site that will be the most beneficial to the career you want. Do not take an externship just because it is close to home. Think about the skills that will be offered and learn as much as possible. Then perform well, so that the staff and physicians are happy to offer a good reference to potential employers. Strive to attain goals, and once they are reached, set additional goals to continue moving forward in life.

Even though the medical assistant educational experience ends, remember that there is constantly something new to learn in the medical profession. Join professional societies and participate in as many educational seminars and continuing education classes as possible. Remain in a continual state of learning and be determined to be the best medical assistant you can be.

Patient Education

Some patients assume that the people who assist the physician in the office are all nurses. The medical assistant should always specify that he or she is a medical assistant, especially when making initial introductions. There should never be any representation that the medical assistant is the "office nurse." If a patient uses that term, correct him or her in a friendly manner.

A medical assistant may find it necessary to educate the patient about the definition of a medical assistant. An occasional rare patient

may not have heard of the profession. Explain the type of training that was completed, emphasizing that medical assistants are trained specifically for work in a physician's office. If patients have any questions about the medical assistant's qualifications, refer them to the office manager or physician.

STEPS FOR ACHIEVING GOALS

- Decide what you want.
- Write down the goal.
- Set the date for accomplishment.
- Read the goal three times a day.
- Think of the goal often.
- See yourself accomplishing the goal.
- Develop a plan of action for reaching the goal.
- Do not discuss the plan with others who might be discouraging.
- Be confident.
- Act successful, and you will be!

Legal and Ethical Issues

Always be completely honest when completing a job application and offering information on a resumé. Most facilities stipulate that if an individual is not truthful on these documents, his or her employment can be terminated when the deception is discovered. Employers are more interested in honesty and a forthright explanation than in minor problems that affect the job performance.

If a medical assistant has had some brush with the law that requires disclosure on the job application, the best policy is to be honest and to deal with the ramifications of telling the truth. Most businesses can verify whether a potential employee has any type of criminal record. A solid explanation of the facts, admission of a past mistake, and excellent, current references often prompt an employer to have faith and make a positive decision about offering employment.

SUMMARY OF SCENARIO

The end of medical assistant training is a time of great excitement and perhaps a small bit of apprehension. Lisa is prepared to accept the challenges ahead as she readies herself for her future in her new career. She has begun her externship and has been expanding her network of acquaintances in the medical profession for several months. Lisa has met many office managers and a few physicians and has learned a great deal about several area medical facilities. Through her research, she has decided that she would like to work with one of three local physicians who need a medical assistant. One is a pediatrician, another is a well-known neurologist, and the third is a family practitioner just out of medical school. Lisa has gathered information about all of these professionals, and each has invited her for a job interview.

Lisa knows that she will need to be at her best, so she takes care of herself and gets plenty of rest. She has a long list of interview questions and has taken

the time to write out answers to the questions in preparation for her interviews. She is careful about her grooming every day that she reports to the externship, because she knows that the physician at her site is her first reference in the medical field. In addition, she knows that she may be called for an interview any day that might be scheduled just after her workday ends. Looking professional prepares her for this each day.

Lisa is comfortable during her interviews because she is well prepared. She has identified her strengths and can share them with a potential employer. She is focused on her objectives and knows her minimum requirements to accept a position. She has a healthy self-esteem, and her good decision-making skills will help her to determine which position is right for her. Her enthusiasm and excitement show in her eyes, and she is dedicated to making a difference in the lives of her patients and co-workers.

SUMMARY OF LEARNING OBJECTIVES

1. **Define, spell, and pronounce the terms listed in the vocabulary.**
   Spelling and pronouncing medical terms correctly bolster the medical assistant's credibility. Knowing the definitions of these terms promotes confidence in communication with patients and co-workers.

2. **Discuss the reasons job search training is important to a medical assistant.**
   Because approximately 85% of individuals do not have any formal training in job search skills, taking the time to learn the best methods puts the medical assistant at an advantage. Training reduces the time spent looking for work and increases the benefits and salary offered when good negotiating skills are used. The medical assistant also is more comfortable during interviews and throughout the job search process.

3. **List three expectations employers have of employees.**
   Employers have three basic expectations of their medical assistant employees. They want an employee with a good appearance, who looks as if he or she fits in the medical profession. A medical assistant should also be dependable and have the skills to do the job for which he or she was hired.

4. **Understand the three types of employee skill strengths.**
   Three types of skill strengths may be used by employees. Job skills are those used to actually perform a job, such as venipunctures or scheduling appointments. Self-management skills usually are part of the medical assistant's personality; these include honesty and dependability. Transferable skills are those that can be taken from one job to another or used on any job. Examples include the ability to communicate effectively and to lead and manage individuals.

5. **Explain the two best job search methods.**
   Networking and contacting employers directly are the two best methods of searching for a job. Networking involves developing a network of individuals who can assist the medical assistant in finding employment. This group may include co-workers, other students, relatives, or friends who provide leads to potential employers. Contacting employers directly includes taking resumés to specific offices or making appointments to gain knowledge about the facility and then later using that knowledge during the job search. These two methods are more effective than most traditional means of finding a job.

6. **Describe some of the errors that should be avoided on a resumé.**
   Any error should be avoided on a resumé. Medical assistants must make sure everything is spelled correctly, but they cannot rely on the computer's spell-check feature alone. They must proofread the document and have someone else proofread it to catch errors that may have been overlooked. Salary expectations should never be stated on the resumé, and a photograph should not be included. Personal information, such as height and weight, also are not included.

7. **List the four phases of the interview process.**
   The four phases of the interview process include the preparation, the actual interview, the follow-up, and the negotiation. The preparation includes all efforts made before the actual interview in obtaining information about the company, deciding on the wardrobe, and making sure

nails are groomed and shoes are shined. The interview itself is designed to help the employer and potential employee get to know each other and discover whether they are compatible. The follow-up is perhaps the most critical stage, wherein the medical assistant should send a thank you letter and continue to stay in touch with the facility until the job is filled. The negotiation includes discussion of the salary and benefits that will be offered to the new employee.

8. **Explain the importance of having demographic information about former jobs before appearing for an interview.**
   Demographic information on other employers should be taken to interviews and kept handy when filling out job applications. A medical assistant should never have to ask for a phone book to look up the address of a former employer. This demonstrates a lack of preparation and planning on the part of the potential employee.

9. **List and discuss legal and illegal interview questions.**
   Employers may intentionally or accidentally ask illegal interview questions, and the medical assistant has three choices in this situation: (1) refusing to answer the question, which may indicate that he or she will not tolerate difficult patients; (2) answering the question directly, which may cost the medical assistant the position; or (3) relating the question back to the position, which indicates maturity and the ability to be tactful and polite.

10. **Discuss the importance of the probationary period for a new employee.**
    The probationary period is a time for the new medical assistant to become oriented to the facility. It also allows the employer to assess whether the medical assistant fits with the team and performs the duties of the job in a satisfactory way. During this time, the medical assistant should demonstrate that he or she is a productive team member with an excellent attitude. There should never be idle time; rather, when all duties are completed, the medical assistant should look for ways to assist others.

11. **List some common early mistakes of which a new employee should be aware.**
    A new employee in the medical office should avoid arriving late or being absent, especially during the probationary period. He or she should never participate in office gossip and should make a good attempt to get along with every employee. A medical assistant should not make excessive supervision necessary and should be open to learning new ways of performing procedures. A new employee who fits in with the team finds the job more rewarding.

12. **Understand the importance of maintaining liability coverage once employed in the industry.**
    Because patients can bring professional liability suits against any personnel involved in their care, the medical assistant should maintain professional liability coverage throughout their career in the healthcare industry.

13. **Explain why a performance appraisal rating is usually not perfect.**
    No employee is perfect, so performance appraisals rarely have perfect ratings. Even an employee who is doing an excellent job has room for

improvement in some area. Without comments that suggest improvement, the employee may not feel that the position offers growth potential. Constructive comments help a medical assistant perform better and take on more responsibility.

14. **Organize a job search.**
Time management and organizational skills help the medical assistant launch an effective job search (see Procedure 28-2).

15. **Prepare a resumé.**
The resumé must be accurate and error free (see Procedure 28-1).

16. **Complete a job application.**
Job applications must be filled out accurately and completely (see Procedure 28-3).

17. **Interview for a job.**
The interview is the job search step that most influences hiring decisions (see Procedure 28-4).

18. **Negotiate a salary.**
The medical assistant should develop skills in negotiating salary after he or she has determined the minimum amount in both benefits and pay that can be accepted (see Procedure 28-5).

CONNECTIONS

Study Guide Connection: Go to the Chapter 28 Study Guide. Read and complete the activities.

Evolve Connection: Go to the Chapter 28 link at *evolve.elsevier.com/kinn* to complete the Chapter Review and Chapter Quiz. Check out the other resources listed for this chapter to make the most of what you have learned from Career Development and Life Skills.

GLOSSARY

abandonment To withdraw protection or support; in medicine, to discontinue medical care without proper notice after accepting a patient.

abstract An outline or summary of the diagnostic statement and/or procedures and services performed. In procedural coding, the outline or summary assists in ensuring that all procedures and services are included in an insurance claim submission and that nothing is omitted or added to the encounter form or charge ticket; as a verb form, *abstract* also means to compile this outline or summary for use in procedural coding.

academic degree A title conferred by a college, university, or professional school upon completion of a program of study.

account A statement of transactions during a fiscal period and the resulting balance.

account balance The amount owed on an account.

accounts payable Debts incurred and not yet paid.

accounts receivable Amounts owed to the physician.

accounts receivable ledger A record of the charges and payments posted on an account.

accounts receivable trial balance A method of determining that the journal and the ledger are in balance.

accreditation (u-kre-duh-ta'-shun) The process through which an organization is recognized for adherence to a group of standards that meet or exceed the expectations of the accrediting agency.

accrual basis of accounting A method of accounting in which income is recorded when earned and expenses are recorded when incurred.

acronyms Abbreviations, such as ECG for electrocardiography.

act The formal action of a legislative body; a decision or determination of a sovereign state, a legislative council, or a court of justice.

adage (a'-dij) A saying, often in metaphoric form, that embodies a common observation.

add-on codes Codes that indicate additional or supplemental procedures carried out along with the primary procedure.

admonition Counsel or warning against fault or oversight.

advance An amount of money or credit furnished in anticipation of repayment.

advent Coming into being or use.

adverse event An injury caused by medical management rather than the underlying condition of the patient.

advocate (ad'-vuh-kat) One who pleads the cause of another; one who defends or maintains a cause or proposal.

affable Pleasant and at ease in talking to others; characterized by ease and friendliness.

agenda (ah-jen'-duh) A list or outline of things to be considered or done.

aggressive Forceful or intended to dominate; hostile, injurious, or destructive, especially when referring to a behavior caused by frustration.

allegation (a-li-ga'-shun) A statement by a party to a legal action of what the party undertakes to prove; an assertion made without proof.

alleviate To partly remove or correct; to relieve or lessen.

allied health fields Occupational disciplines in which professionals involved with the delivery of healthcare or related services assist physicians with the diagnosis, treatment, and care of patients in many different specialty areas.

allocating (a'-luh-ka-ting) Apportioning for a specific purpose or to particular persons or things.

allopathic (al-o-path'-ik) A term used to contrast homeopathic medicine with mainstream medicine; allopathic medicine is characterized by an effort to counteract the symptoms of a disease by administration of treatments that produce effects opposite to the symptoms.

allowed charge (allowable amount) The maximum amount of money that many third-party payers allow for a specific procedure or service.

alphabetic filing Any system that arranges names or topics according to the sequence of the letters in the alphabet.

Alphabetic Index Volume 2 of the ICD-9-CM coding manual; it lists conditions, injuries, illnesses, and diseases in alphabetical order by main terms, modifying terms, and subterms. It also contains the Classification of Factors Influencing Health Status and Contact with Health Service (V Codes) and the index for Supplemental Classification of External Causes of Injury and Poisoning (E Codes).

alphanumeric Of or relating to systems made up of combinations of letters and numbers.

ambiguous (am-bi'-gu-wus) Capable of being understood in two or more possible senses or ways; unclear.

ambulatory (am'-bu-la-tor-ee) Able to walk about and not be bedridden.

amenities Things that contribute to comfort, enjoyment, or convenience.

amenity (uh-me'-nuh-te) Something conducive to comfort, convenience, or enjoyment.

amiable (a'-me-uh-buhl) Having qualities that make one liked and easy to deal with.

ancillary (an'-suh-ler-e) Subordinate; auxiliary.

ancillary diagnostic services Services that support patient diagnoses (e.g., laboratory or radiologic services).

and In the context of the ICD-9-CM, *and* should be interpreted as *and/or.*

animate To fill with life; to give spirit and support to expressions.

annotating Furnishing with notes that are usually critical or explanatory.

annotations (a-nuh-ta′-shun) Notes added by way of comment or explanation.

appeal A legal proceeding by which a case is brought before a higher court for review of the decision of a lower court.

appellate (uh-pe′-lut) Having the power to review the judgment of another tribunal or body of jurisdiction, such as an appellate court.

application software Computer programs designed to perform specific tasks.

appraisal An expert judgment of the value or merit of something; judgment as to quality.

arbitration (ar-buh-tra′-shun) The hearing and determination of a cause in controversy by a person or persons either chosen by the parties involved or appointed under statutory authority.

arbitrator (ar-buh-tra′-ter) A neutral person chosen to settle differences between two parties in a controversy.

archived To have filed or collected records or documents.

arrhythmia (uh-rith′-mee-uh) An abnormality or irregularity in the heart rhythm.

artificial intelligence The aspect of computer science that deals with computers taking on the attributes of humans, such as mimicking human thought. For example, expert systems can make decisions, such as software designed to help a physician diagnose a patient, given a set of symptoms.

assault An intentional, unlawful attempt of bodily injury to another by force.

assent To agree to something, especially after thoughtful consideration.

assessment The physician's determination of what is or may be wrong with the patient based on the findings from the history and physical examination (H&P). The assessment includes a preliminary, interim, or final diagnosis.

assets The entire property of a person, association, corporation, or estate applicable or subject to the payment of debts.

assignment of benefits The transfer of the patient's legal right to collect benefits for medical expenses to the provider of those services, authorizing the payment to be sent directly to the provider.

asystole (ay-sis′-toh-le) The absence of a heartbeat.

audit A formal examination of an organization's or individual's accounts or financial situation; a methodic examination and review.

audit trail The path left by a transaction when it has been completed; often referred to when tracking medical services used by patients or researching claims.

augment To make greater, more numerous, larger, or more intense.

authenticated Proved; with regard to medical records, it applies to a signature, initials, or computer keystroke by the maker of the record to verify that the record is correct.

authorization An alphanumeric designation or a number given by the insurance company authorizing approval of a procedure or service. This does not guarantee payment.

automatic call routing A software system that answers phones automatically and routes calls to staff after the caller responds to prompts; also used to call a large number of patients to remind them of appointments or make announcements.

avert To see coming and ward off or avoid.

backorder An ordered item that is not delivered when promised or demanded but will be filled at a later date.

backup Any type of storage that prevents the loss of files with hard disk failure.

bailiff An officer of some U.S. courts who usually serves as a messenger or usher and who keeps order at the request of the judge.

balance sheet A financial statement for a specific date that shows the total assets, liabilities, and capital of the business.

battery A willful and unlawful use of force or violence on the person of another. *Also,* offensive touching or the use of force on a person without his or her consent.

benchmarks Items or factors that serve as standards against which other items or factors can be measured or judged.

beneficence (buh-ne′-fuh-sens) The act of doing or producing good, especially performing acts of charity or kindness.

beneficiary The individual entitled to receive benefits from an insurance policy or program or a governmental entitlement program offering healthcare benefits. Also called a *participant, subscriber, dependent, enrollee,* or *member.*

benefits Services or payments provided under a health plan, employee plan, or some other agreement, including programs such as health insurance, pensions, retirement planning, and many other options that may be offered to employees of a company or an organization.

birthday rule An insurance rule that applies as follows: when an individual is covered under two insurance policies, the insurance plan of the policyholder whose birthday comes first in the calendar year (month and day, not year) becomes the primary insurance.

bits The smallest units of information inside the computer, each represented either by the digit "0" or "1"; 8 bits equal 1 byte.

blatant Completely obvious, conspicuous, or obtrusive, especially in a crass or offensive manner; brazen.

bleak Not hopeful or encouraging.

bond A durable, formal paper used for documents.

bookkeeping The recording of business and accounting transactions.

bookmark A command in a browser that marks the Internet protocol (IP) address of a Web site so that it can be saved and recalled quickly without typing the entire Web address.

branding The process involved in creating a unique name and image in the customer's mind, mainly through advertising campaigns with a consistent theme.

browsers Software programs that allow users to view Web pages on the Internet (e.g., Internet Explorer, Firefox).

budget A plan for the coordination of resources and expenditures; the amount of money available or required for a particular purpose.

bundled codes CPT codes designating procedures or services that are grouped together and paid for as one procedure or service, according to the National Correct Coding Initiative (NCCI) edits, established by the Centers for Medicare and Medicaid Services (CMS).

burnout Exhaustion of physical or emotional strength or motivation, usually as a result of prolonged stress or frustration.

business associates Individuals or organizations that perform or assist a covered entity in the performance of a function or activity involving the use or disclosure of individually identifiable health information.

byte A unit of data that contains 8 binary digits, or bits.

cache (kash) Special, high-speed storage that either can be part of the computer's main memory or a separate storage device. One function of a cache is to store Web sites visited in the computer memory for faster recall the next time the Web site is requested.

capitation   A payment method used by many managed care organizations in which a fixed amount of money is reimbursed to the provider for patients enrolled during a specific period of time, no matter what services were received or how many visits were made.

caption   A heading, title, or subtitle under which records are filed.

carriers   In insurance terms, companies that assume the risk of an insurance policy.

case management   The process of assessing and planning patient care, including referral and follow-up, to ensure continuity of care and quality management.

cash basis of accounting   A method of accounting in which income is recorded when received and expenses are recorded when paid.

cash flow statement   A financial summary for a specific period that shows the beginning balance on hand, the receipts and disbursements during the period, and the balance on hand at the end of the period.

categorically   Placed in a specific division of a system of classification.

category   In the CPT manual, the element indented one level below a subsection; it usually refers to a specific anatomic site or to procedures and/or services.

Category I codes   Five-digit primary procedure or service codes, found in the Tabular Index, that are selected when performing insurance billing or statistical research.

Category II codes   Special codes that can help providers track revenue and reimbursement; these codes are alphanumeric and end in the letter F.

Category III codes   Codes for a new or experimental procedure or service, otherwise referred to as "Emerging Technology"; these codes are alphanumeric and end in the letter T.

caustic (kos'-tik)   Capable of burning, corroding, or damaging tissue by chemical action. *Also,* marked by sarcasm.

CD burner   A device that can "write" data on a blank compact disk (CD) or copy data from one CD to a blank CD.

certification (ser-tuh-fuh-ka'-shun)   The attesting of something as being true as represented or as meeting a standard; the result of having been tested, usually by a third party, and awarded a certificate based on proven knowledge.

chain of command   A series of executive positions in order of authority.

channels   Means of communication or expression; courses or directions of thought.

characteristics   Distinguishing traits, qualities, or properties.

chief complaint (CC)   The reason the patient has sought medical care, usually taken down in the patient's own words. It is recorded in the history documentation in the medical record, preceded by the abbreviation CC.

chiropractic (ki'-ruh-prak-tik)   A medical discipline that focuses on the nervous system and involves manual adjustment of the vertebral column to affect the nervous system, thereby treating various disorders, and also to promote patient wellness.

chronologic order   Of, relating to, or arranged in or according to the order of time.

circumvent (suhr-kuhm-vent')   To manage to get around, especially by ingenuity or strategy.

cited   Quoted by way of example, authority, or proof or mentioned formally in commendation or praise.

Civilian Health and Medical Program of the Department of Veterans Affairs (CHAMPVA)   A health benefits program run by the Department of Veterans Affairs (VA) that helps eligible beneficiaries pay the cost of specific healthcare services and supplies.

Civilian Health and Medical Program of the Uniformed Services (CHAMPUS)   See TRICARE.

clarity   The quality or state of being clear.

clauses   Groups of words containing a subject and predicate and functioning as a member of a complex or compound sentence.

clean claims   Insurance claim forms that have been completed correctly (no errors or omissions) and can be processed and paid promptly if they meet the restrictions on covered services and blocks.

clearinghouse   A centralized facility to which insurance claims are transmitted. Clearinghouses separate, check, and redistribute claims electronically to various insurance carriers and may offer additional services to the physician.

clinical trials   Research studies that test how well new medical treatments or other interventions work in the subjects, usually human beings.

code first   When more than one code is necessary to identify a given condition, *code first* or *use additional code* is used. A *code first* note is found at a manifestation code. A *use additional code* note is found at the etiology code when the underlying condition is sequenced first followed by the manifestation.

Code of Federal Regulations (CFR)   A coded delineation of the rules and regulations published in the *Federal Register* by the various departments and agencies of the federal government. The CFR is divided into 50 titles that represent broad subject areas and chapters that provide specific detail.

coding   Converting verbal or written descriptions into numeric and alphanumeric designations.

cohesive   Sticking together tightly; exhibiting or producing cohesion.

co-insurance   A policy provision frequently found in medical insurance whereby the policyholder and the insurance company share the cost of covered losses in a specified ratio (e.g., 80/20 means that 80% is covered by the insurer and 20% by the insured).

collect on delivery (COD)   A method of payment used when an article or item is delivered, and payment is expected before the item is released.

comfort zone   A place in the mind where an individual feels safe and confident.

commensurate (ku-men'-su-rut)   Corresponding in size, amount, extent, or degree; equal in measure, proportionate.

commercial insurance plans   Plans that reimburse the insured for expenses resulting from illness or injury according to a specific fee schedule as outlined in the insurance policy and on a fee-for-service basis. Sometimes called *private insurance.*

competent   Having adequate abilities or qualities; having the capacity to function or perform in a certain way.

complainant (kuhm-pla'-nuhnt)   The person making a complaint against another person and/or organization.

complementary and alternative medicine (CAM)   A group of diverse medical and healthcare systems, practices, and products that are not generally considered part of conventional medicine. Complementary medicine is used in combination with conventional medicine (allopathic or osteopathic); alternative medicine is used instead of conventional medicine.

computerized physician/provider order entry (CPOE)   A process of electronic data entry of medical practitioner or provider instructions for the treatment of patients.

concise (kun-sice′)   Expressing much in brief form.

concurrently   Occurring at the same time.

condescending   Assuming an air of superiority.

congruent (kun-gru′-unt)   Being in agreement, harmony, or correspondence; conforming to the circumstances or requirements of a situation.

connotation (kah-nuh-ta′-shun)   An implication; something suggested by a word or thing.

contamination (kun-ta-mu-na′-shun)   The process by which something is made impure, unclean, or unfit for use by the introduction of unwholesome or undesirable elements.

continuation pages   The second and following pages of a letter.

continuing education units (CEUs)   Credits for courses, classes, or seminars related to an individual's profession that are designed to promote education and to keep the professional up-to-date on current procedures and trends in the field; CEUs often are required for licensing.

continuity of care   Continuation of care smoothly from one provider to another, so that the patient receives the most benefit and no interruption in care.

contraindications (kahn-truh-in-duh-ka′-shuns)   Factors, such as symptoms or conditions, that make a particular treatment or procedure inadvisable.

contributory negligence   Statutes in some states that may prevent a party from recovering some damages if he or she contributed in any way to the injury or condition.

controls   A standard of comparison to make sure answers obtained are accurate.

conventional medicine   Medicine as practiced by holders of the Doctor of Medicine (MD) and Doctor of Osteopathy (OD) degrees and by their allied health professionals, such as physical therapists, psychologists, and registered nurses.

conventions   Abbreviations, punctuation, symbols, instructional notations, and related entities that help guide the medical assistant or coder in the selection of an accurate, specific code.

cookies   Messages sent to a Web browser from a Web server that identify users and can prepare custom Web pages for them, possibly displaying their name on return to the site.

co-payment   A sum of money that is paid at the time of medical service; a form of co-insurance.

counteroffer   Return offer made by one who has rejected an offer or a job.

courier   A messenger, especially one on official or diplomatic business; a service that provides delivery and transportation services for documents and/or packages.

covered entities   As defined by HIPAA, organizations that transmit information in an electronic form during a transaction.

credentialing (kri-den′-shuh-ling)   The process of extending professional or medical privileges to an individual; the process of verifying and evaluating that person's credentials.

credibility   The quality or power of inspiring belief.

credit   An entry on an account constituting an addition to a revenue, net worth, or liability account; the balance in a person's favor.

credit cards   Devices issued by a bank or other financial institution, retail stores, and other businesses that allow the card holder to make purchases prior to paying for them; the card holder is then billed, usually after interest has been added.

critical thinking   The constant practice of considering all aspects of a situation when deciding what to believe or what to do.

cross-training   Training in more than one area so that a multitude of duties may be performed by one person or so that substitutions of personnel may be made in an emergency or at other necessary times.

culpability   Meriting condemnation, responsibility, or blame, especially as wrong or harmful.

cultivate   To foster the growth of something; to improve by labor, care, or study.

cursor   A symbol on the monitor screen that shows the location of the next character to be typed.

curt   Marked by rude or peremptory shortness.

cyanosis (si-an-oh′-sis)   A blue coloration of the mucous membranes and body extremities caused by lack of oxygen.

cyberspace   The nonphysical space of the online world of computer networks in which communication takes place.

damages   Loss or harm resulting from injury to person, property, or reputation; compensation in money imposed by law for losses or injuries.

database   A collection of related files that serves as a foundation for retrieving information.

debit   An entry on an account representing an addition to an expense or asset account or a deduction from a revenue, a net worth, or a liability account.

debit cards   Cards that look like credit cards and with which money can be withdrawn, bills paid, or purchases made directly from the holder's bank account without the payment of interest.

decedent (di-se′-dent)   A legal term for a deceased person.

decodes   Converts, as in a message, into intelligible form; recognizes and interprets.

deductibles   Specific amounts of money a patient must pay out of pocket before the insurance carrier begins paying. Usually this amount ranges from $100 to $500. This deductible amount is met on a yearly or per-incident basis.

default   To fail to pay a financial debt, such as a student loan.

defendant   A person required to answer in a legal action or suit; in criminal cases, the person accused of a crime.

defense mechanisms   Psychological methods of dealing with stressful situations that are encountered in day-to-day living.

deferment   Postponement, especially of a student loan.

demeanor (di-me′-nur)   Behavior toward others; outward manner.

demographic (de-muh-gra′-fik)   The statistical characteristics of human populations (as in age or income) used especially to identify markets.

dependents   The spouse, children, and sometimes domestic partner or other individuals designated by the insured who are covered under a healthcare plan.

depleted   Lessened markedly in quantity, content, power, or value.

detrimental (de-truh-men´-til)   Obviously harmful or damaging.

device driver   The program or commands given to a device connected to a computer that enable the device to function. For instance, a printer may come equipped with software that must be loaded onto the computer first so that the printer will work.

diagnosis   The concise, technical description of the cause, nature, or manifestations of a condition or problem. *Initial diagnosis:* The physician's temporary impression, sometimes called a *working diagnosis. Differentiated diagnosis:* A comparison of two or more diseases with similar signs and symptoms. *Clinical diagnosis:* The conclusion the physician reaches after evaluating all findings, including laboratory and other test results.

diagnostic statement   Information about a patient's diagnosis or diagnoses that has been extracted from the medical documentation.

diaphoresis (di-uh-fuh-re´-sis)   The profuse excretion of sweat.

dictation (dik-tay´-shun)   The act or manner of uttering words to be transcribed.

diction   The choice of words, especially with regard to clearness, correctness, or effectiveness.

digital subscriber line (DSL)   A high-speed, sophisticated modulation scheme that operates over existing copper telephone wiring systems; often referred to as "last-mile technologies," because DSL is used for connections from a telephone switching station to a home or office and not between switching stations.

digital video disk (DVD)   An optical disk that holds approximately 28 times more information than a CD; a DVD is most commonly used to hold full-length movies. Compared with a CD, which holds approximately 600 megabytes, a DVD can hold approximately 4.7 gigabytes. Also called a *digital versatile disk.*

direct billing   A method of electronic claims submission that uses computer software to allow a provider to submit an insurance claim directly to an insurance carrier for payment.

direct filing system   A filing system in which materials can be located without consulting an intermediary source of reference.

dirty claims   Claims that contain errors or omissions; such claims must be corrected and resubmitted to an insurance carrier to obtain reimbursement.

disability income insurance   Insurance that provides periodic payments to replace income when an insured person is unable to work as a result of illness, injury, or disease.

disbursements   Funds paid out.

disbursements journal   A summary of accounts paid out.

disclaimer   A denial of responsibility; a denial of a legal claim.

discrepancies   Differences between conflicting facts, claims, or opinions.

discretion (dis-kre´-shun)   The quality of being discreet; having or showing good judgment or conduct, especially in speech.

disk drives   Devices that load a program or data stored on a disk into the computer.

disparaging (dis-pahr´-uh-jing)   Slighting; having a negative or degrading tone.

disparities (di-spar´-uh-tes)   Fundamentally different and often incongruous elements; elements that are markedly distinct in quality or character.

disposition (dis-puh-zi´-shun)   The tendency of something or someone to act in a certain manner under given circumstances.

disruption   An unexpected event that throws a plan into disorder; an interruption that prevents a system or process from continuing as usual or as expected.

dissection (di-sek´-shun)   The separation into pieces and exposure of parts for scientific examination.

disseminate (di-se´-muh-nat)   To disperse throughout.

divulge (duh-vuhlj´)   To make known, as a confidence or secret.

docket   A formal record of judicial proceedings; a list of legal cases to be tried.

domain name   The initial part of a URL listing; the domain and name of the host or server, indicating the publisher of a Web page or site.

domestic mail   Mail sent within the boundaries of the United States and its territories.

downcoding   A change in a code or codes for entries submitted for reimbursement. This change usually is made by the insurance company, generally because the code submitted in some way does not match the company's specifications.

drawee   A bank or facility on which a check is drawn or written.

drawer   The person who writes a check.

drug of choice   The drug an abuser uses most frequently to satisfy the craving for a certain feeling; the user's preferred drug.

due diligence   The effort made by an ordinarily prudent or reasonable party to prevent harm to another party or oneself; doing everything possible to prevent something negative from happening; also called *due care.*

due process   A fundamental constitutional guarantee that all legal proceedings will be fair; that one will be given notice of the proceedings and an opportunity to be heard before the government acts to take away life, liberty, or property; a constitutional guarantee that a law will not be unreasonable or arbitrary.

duty   Obligatory tasks, conduct, service, or functions that arise from one's position, as in life or in a group.

e-banking   Electronic banking via computer modem or over the Internet.

ecchymosis (e-ki-moh´-sis)   A hemorrhagic skin discoloration commonly called *bruising.*

e-commerce   Short for *electronic commerce;* used to describe the sale and purchase of goods and services over the Internet; doing business over the Internet.

editing   To prepare for publication or public presentation; to alter, adapt, or refine, especially to bring about conformity to a standard or to suit a particular purpose.

effective date   The date on which an insurance policy or plan takes effect so that benefits are payable.

electronic (or digital) signature   A scanned signature or other such mark that is accepted as proof of approval of and/or responsibility for the content of an electronic document.

electronic claims   Claims that are submitted to insurance processing facilities using a computerized medium, such as direct data entry, direct wire, dial-in telephone digital fax, or personal computer download or upload.

electronic data interchange (EDI)   The transfer of data back and forth between two or more entities using an electronic medium.

electronic fund transfer (EFT)   The movement of funds between different accounts in the same or different banks using wire transfer, automated teller machines (ATMs), or computers, without the use of paper documents.

electronic health record (EHR)   An electronic record of health-related information about a patient that conforms to nationally recognized interoperability standards and that can be created, managed, and consulted by authorized clinicians and staff from *more than one health-care organization.*

electronic media   The means of electronic transmission, including the Internet, private networks, dial-up phone lines, and fax modems; includes information moved from one place to another while stored on an electronic device.

electronic medical record (EMR)   An electronic record of health-related information about an individual that can be created, gathered, managed, and consulted by authorized clinicians and staff *within a single healthcare organization.*

electronic remittance advice (ERA)   An explanation that accompanies checks and relays details of the payment sent to the provider from the insurance company or other third-party provider.

eligibility   A term that describes whether a patient's insurance coverage is in effect and eligible for payment of insurance benefits.

e-mail   Short for *electronic mail;* communications transmitted via computer or computer network.

emancipated minor   A person under legal age who is self-supporting and living apart from parents or a guardian; a mature minor considered by the courts to possess a sufficient understanding of self-care and responsibility.

embezzlement   Stealing from an employer; to appropriate goods, services, or funds for personal use without permission.

emetic (eh-met′-ik)   A substance that causes vomiting.

empathy (em′-puh-the)   Sensitivity to the individual needs and reactions of patients.

Employer Identification Number (EIN)   The number used by the Internal Revenue Service that identifies a business or individual functioning as a business entity for income tax reporting.

encodes   Converts from one system of communication to another; converts a message into code.

encounter   Any contact between a healthcare provider and a patient that results in treatment or evaluation of the patient's condition; it is not limited to in-person contact.

encroachments   Actions that advance beyond the usual or proper limits.

encrypted (in-kript′-ed)   Encoded; converted from one system of communication to another.

endorser   The person who signs his or her name on the back of a check for the purpose of transferring title to another person.

entry   A record or notation of an occurrence, transaction, or proceeding.

enunciate (e-nun′-se-at)   To utter articulate sounds; the act of being very distinct in speech.

enunciation (e-nun-se-a′-shun)   The utterance of articulate, clear sounds.

environment   The state of a computer, usually determined by the programs running and hardware and software characteristics.

eponym   A name or term for something that is based on the name of a person (or occasionally a place or thing). Traditionally in medicine, discoveries often are named after the person or people who made the discovery.

e-prescribing   The use of electronic devices to communicate with pharmacies and send prescribing information, taking the place of writing a prescription by hand and physically giving it to a patient; new or refill prescriptions can be submitted electronically, cutting down on fraud and errors.

equities   The monetary value of a property or of an interest in a property in excess of claims or liens against it.

erroneous (eh-ro′-ne-uhs)   Containing or characterized by error or assumption.

established patient (EP)   A patient who has received professional services (face to face) from the physician, or from another physician of the *exact* same specialty *and subspecialty* who belongs to the same group practice, within the past 3 years.

etiology   The science and study of the causes of disease. The cause of a disorder; a claim may be classified according to the etiology.

euthanasia (yu-thuh-na′-zhe-uh)   The act or practice of killing or permitting the death of hopelessly sick or injured individuals in a relatively painless way for reasons of mercy.

excludes   Exclusion terms are always written in italics, and the word *excludes* often is enclosed in a box to draw particular attention to these instructions. Exclusion terms may apply to a chapter, a section, a category, or a subcategory. The applicable code number usually follows the exclusion term. An *excludes* note under a code indicates that the terms excluded from the code are to be coded elsewhere. The term *Excludes* means "DO NOT CODE HERE."

exclusions   Limitations on an insurance contract for which benefits are not payable.

expediency (ik-spe′-de-un-se)   A means of achieving a particular end, as in a situation requiring haste or caution.

expert witnesses   People who provide testimony to a court as experts in certain fields or subjects to verify facts presented by one or both sides in a lawsuit, often compensated and used to refute or disprove the claims of one party.

explanation of benefits (EOB)   A letter or statement from the insurance carrier describing what was paid, denied, or reduced in payment. It also contains information about amounts applied to the deductible, the patient's co-insurance, and the allowed amounts.

explanation of Medicare Benefits (EOMB)   An explanation of benefits from Medicare (see *explanation of benefits [EOB]*).

external noise   Sounds or factors outside the brain that interfere with the communication process.

externalization   The attribution of an event or occurrence to causes outside the self.

externship (or internship)   A training program that is part of the medical assisting course of study in an educational institution. This part of training is taken in the actual business setting of that field of study; the terms are interchanged in some areas of the country.

extrinsic (eks-trin′-zik)   External to a thing, its essential nature, or its original character.

fee for service   An established schedule of fees set for services performed by providers and paid by the patient.

fee profile   A compilation or an average of physicians' fees over a given period.

fee schedule   A compilation of pre-established fee allowances for given services or procedures.

feedback   The transmission of evaluative or corrective information to the original or controlling source about an action, event, or process.

felony A major crime, such as murder, rape, or burglary; punishable by a more stringent sentence than that given for a misdemeanor.

fermentation (fur-men-ta′-shun) An enzymatically controlled transformation of an organic compound.

fervent Exhibiting or marked by great intensity of feeling.

fibrillation Rapid, random, ineffective contractions of the heart.

fidelity (fuh-de′-luh-te) Faithfulness to something to which one is bound by pledge or duty.

fine A sum imposed as punishment for an offense; a forfeiture or penalty paid to an injured party or the government in a civil or criminal action.

fiscal agent An organization under contract to the government (and some private plans) to act as financial representatives in handling insurance claims from providers of healthcare; also referred to as a *fiscal intermediary.*

fiscal intermediary An organization that contracts with the government to handle and mediate insurance claims from medical facilities, home health agencies, or providers of medical services or supplies.

fiscal year An accounting period of 12 months during which a company determines earnings and profit; the fiscal year does not necessarily begin in January; the business determines the beginning of its fiscal year.

flash drive A small, portable device that can carry 2 to 8 gigabytes or more of information and that plugs into a USB port; also called a *thumb drive, jump drive,* or *portable drive.*

flush Directly abutting or immediately adjacent, as set even with an edge of a type page or column; having no indention.

gametes (ga′-meets) Mature male or female germ cells, usually possessing a haploid chromosome set and capable of initiating formation of a new diploid individual; a sex cell, whether sperm or ovum.

genome (jeh′-nom) The genetic material of an organism.

genuineness Expressing sincerity and honest feeling.

gigabyte (GB) Approximately 1 billion bytes.

girth A measure around a body or an item.

gleaned Gathered bit by bit (e.g., information or material); picked over in search of relevant material.

government plans Entitlement programs or healthcare plans that are sponsored and/or subsidized by the state or federal government, such as Medicaid and Medicare.

gradients A change in parameters or the value of a quantity, such as temperature or pressure; a change in response with distance from the stimulus; a graded difference in physiological activity along an axis, as of the body or embryonic fluid.

grammar The study of the classes of words, their inflections, and their functions and relations in the sentence; a study of what is preferred and what should be avoided in inflection and syntax.

grief Reaction to an unfortunate outcome; a deep distress caused by bereavement, a loss, or a perceived loss.

group policy Insurance written under a policy that covers a number of people under a single master contract issued to their employer or to an association with which they are affiliated.

guarantor The person responsible for paying a medical bill.

guardian ad litem Legal representative for a minor.

guidelines Found at the beginning of each section of the coding manual, guidelines are the specific definitions of items that must be read to appropriately interpret and report the procedures and services contained in that section.

hard copy The readable paper copy or printout of information.

hardware The physical components of the computer system, such as the central processing unit (CPU), monitor, and printer.

harmonious Marked by accord in sentiment or action; having the parts agreeably related.

HCPCS *Health Care Common Procedural Coding System;* also called *Level II codes.* HCPCS codes were created by the CMS to report supplies, materials, injections, and certain procedures and services not defined in the CPT manual.

health insurance Insurance protection, provided in return for periodic premium payments, that provides reimbursement of expenses resulting from illness or injury. It includes accident, disability income, medical expense, and accidental death and dismemberment insurance. Also known as *accident and health insurance* or *disability income insurance.*

Health Insurance Portability and Accountability Act (HIPAA) A law enacted in 1996 to improve the portability and continuity of health insurance coverage; to combat waste, fraud, and abuse in health insurance and healthcare delivery; to promote the use of medical savings accounts; to improve access to long-term care services and coverage; to simplify the administration of health insurance; and to serve other purposes. As a result, standards have been created for electronic health information transactions and for the privacy of health information. Also known as the Kassebaum-Kennedy Act.

health maintenance organization (HMO) An organization that provides a wide range of comprehensive healthcare services for a specified group at a fixed periodic payment. HMOs can be sponsored by the government, medical schools, hospitals, employers, labor unions, consumer groups, insurance companies, and hospital-medical plans.

healthcare providers Providers of medical or health services, individually or as organizations, that furnish, bill for, or are paid for services or products.

hematuria (hi-ma-tuhr′-e-uh) Blood in the urine.

history and physical examination (H&P, HPE) At the patient's first visit with a new physician or an established provider or upon admission to a hospital, the history and physical examination (H&P) are documented. The H&P normally includes the chief complaint, a review of systems (ROS), the patient's personal and family medical history, a physical examination, an assessment of the findings from the history and physical exam, and a treatment plan for the patient, also referred to as Medical Decision Making (MDM).

holder The person who presents a check for payment.

holistic (ho-lis′-tik) A health viewpoint that considers all the systems of the body and their interdependence, rather than breaking down the body into discrete parts.

homeopathy (ho-me-uh′-puh-the) A type of alternative medicine that attempts to stimulate the body to recover by itself; a system of therapy based on the concept that disease can be treated with minute doses of drugs thought capable of producing the same symptoms in healthy people as the disease itself.

honorarium A payment in recognition of acts or professional services, usually on a special occasion.

hospice (hos′-pus) A concept of care that involves health professionals and volunteers who provide medical, psychological, and spiritual support to terminally ill patients and their loved ones.

HTML The acronym for *hypertext markup language,* the language used to create documents for the Internet.

HTTP   The acronym for *hypertext transfer protocol,* which defines how messages are formatted and transmitted over the Internet. When a URL is entered into the computer, an HTTP command tells the Web server to retrieve the requested Web page.

hub   A common connection point for devices in a network with multiple ports, often used to connect segments of a local area network (LAN).

icons   Pictures, often on the monitor screen "desktop," that represent programs or objects. Clicking on an icon directs the user to the program.

idealism   The practice of forming ideas or living under the influence of ideas.

idiopathic   Pertaining to a condition or a disease that has no known cause.

impaired   Being in a less than perfect or less than whole condition; it includes having handicaps or functional defects and being under the influence of drugs, alcohol, and/or controlled substances.

impenetrable   Incapable of being penetrated or pierced; not capable of being damaged or harmed.

implied consent   Presumed consent, such as when a patient offers an arm for a phlebotomy procedure.

implied contract   A legally enforceable agreement that arises from conduct, from assumed intentions, from some relationship among the immediate parties, or from the application of the legal principle of equity.

in balance   The state in which the total ending balances of patient ledgers equals the total of accounts receivable.

incentives   Things that incite or spur to action; rewards or reasons for performing a task.

incidental disclosure   A secondary use of health information that cannot reasonably be prevented, is limited in nature, and occurs as a result of another use or disclosure that is permitted.

includes   When this term appears under a subdivision, such as a category (three-digit code) or two-digit procedure code title, it indicates that the code and title include these terms. Other terms also classified to that particular code and title are listed in the Alphabetic Index.

incomplete claim   A claim that is missing information and is returned to the provider for correction and resubmission. Also called an *invalid claim.*

incurred   To become liable or subject to; to bring down upon oneself.

indemnity plans   Traditional health insurance plans that pay for all or a share of the cost of covered services, regardless of which physician, hospital, or other licensed healthcare provider is used. Policyholders of indemnity plans and their dependents choose when and where to get healthcare services.

indicators   An important point or group of statistical values that, when evaluated, indicates the quality of care provided in a healthcare facility.

indicted (in-di′-ted)   Charged with a crime by the finding of a jury according to due process of law.

indigent (in′-di-junt)   A needy or poor person who is unable to provide the basic necessities of life; totally lacking in something of need.

indirect filing system   A filing system in which an intermediary source of reference (e.g., a card file) must be consulted to locate specific files.

individual policy   An insurance policy designed specifically for the use of one person and his or her dependents. An individual policy generally does not offer some of the amenities of a group policy (e.g., lower premiums). Often called *personal insurance.*

individually identifiable health information   Any part of a patient's health record that is created or received by a covered entity.

inferred   Derived as a conclusion from facts and premises.

infertile   Not fertile or productive; not capable of reproducing.

inflection (in-flek′-shun)   A change in the pitch or loudness of the voice.

informed consent   A consent, usually written, that states understanding of what treatment is to be undertaken and of the risks involved, why it should be done, and alternative methods of treatment available (including no treatment) and their attendant risks.

infractions (in-frak′-shuns)   Breaking the law; minor offenses against the rules, usually punishable by fines.

initiative   Energy or aptitude to cause or facilitate the start of something or to cause something to happen.

innate   Existing in, belonging to, or determined by factors present in an individual since birth.

innocuous (i′-nuh-kyu-wus)   Having no effect, adverse or otherwise; harmless.

input   Information entered into and used by the computer.

instigate   To goad or urge forward; to provoke.

insubordination (in-suh′-bor-din-a-shun)   Disobedience to authority.

insured   An individual or organization covered by an insurance policy according to the policy terms; usually, the individual or group that pays the premiums. Blue Cross/Blue Shield refers to this person or group as the *subscriber.*

intangibles (in-tan′-juh-buls)   Qualities that cannot be perceived, especially by touch, or cannot be precisely identified or realized by the mind.

integral (in′-ti-grul)   Essential; being an indispensable part of a whole.

integrated delivery system (IDS)   A network of healthcare providers and organizations that provides or arranges to provide a coordinated continuum of services to a defined population and is willing to be held clinically and fiscally accountable for the clinical outcomes and health status of the population served.

integrated   Formed, coordinated, or blended into a functioning or unified whole; to incorporate into a larger unit.

intelligent character recognition (ICR)   The electronic scanning of printed blocks as images and the use of special software to recognize these images (or characters) as ASCII text for uploading into a computer database.

interaction   A two-way communication; mutual or reciprocal action or influence.

intercom   A two-way communication system with a microphone and loudspeaker at each station for localized use.

intermittent   Coming and going at intervals; not continuous.

internal noise   Factors inside the brain that interfere with the communication process.

***International Classification of Diseases, Ninth Revision, Clinical Modification* (ICD-9-CM)**   The manual that establishes the system for classifying disease to facilitate collection of uniform and comparable health information for statistical purposes, for indexing medical records for data storage and retrieval, and to facilitate payment.

international mail   Mail that is sent outside the boundaries of the United States and its territories.

***International Statistical Classifications of Diseases and Related Health Problems, Tenth Revision, Clinical Modification* (ICD-10-CM)** The current ICM rules manual, which contains the greatest number of changes in the ICD-CM system in ICD history. To allow more specific reporting of diseases and newly recognized conditions, the ICD-10-CM contains approximately 55,000 more codes than the ICD-9-CM.

interoperable The capability of a system to work with or use the parts or equipment of another system.

interval Space of time between events.

intolerable Not tolerable or bearable.

intrinsic (in-trin′-zik) Belonging to the essential nature or constitution of a thing; indwelling, inward.

introspection (in-truh-spek′-shun) An inward, reflective examination of one's own thoughts and feelings.

invariably (in-var′-e-uh-buh-le) Consistently; not changing or capable of change.

invasive Involving entry into the living body, as by incision or insertion of an instrument.

invoice A paper describing a purchase and the amount due.

jargon The technical terminology or characteristic idiom of a particular group or special activity, as opposed to lay terms.

judicial (ju-di′-shuhl) Of or relating to a judgment, the function of judging, the administration of justice, or the judiciary.

jurisdiction (jur-uhs-dik′-shun) A power constitutionally conferred on a judge or magistrate to decide cases according to law and to carry sentence into execution; jurisdiction is original when it is conferred on the court in the first instance, called original jurisdiction; or it is appellate when an appeal is given from the judgment of another court.

jurisprudence (jur-uhs-proo′-dens) The science or philosophy of law; a system or body of law or the course of court decisions.

justice With regard to medical ethics, the fair distribution of benefits and burdens among individuals or groups in society with legitimate claims on those benefits.

kilobyte (KB) Approximately 1,024 bytes.

language barrier Any type of interference that inhibits the communication process and is related to languages spoken by the people attempting to communicate.

law A binding custom or practice of a community; a rule of conduct or action prescribed or formally recognized as binding or enforceable by a controlling authority.

learning style The way an individual perceives and processes information to learn new material.

liabilities Things that are owed; debts.

liable (li′-uh-buhl) Obligated according to law or equity; responsible for an act or circumstance.

liaison A close bond or connection; a person with a connection, contract, link, or conspiracy with another person or group.

libel A written defamatory statement or representation that conveys an unjustly unfavorable impression.

litigious (luh-ti′-juhs) Prone to engage in lawsuits.

main term The primary or key word or words abstracted from a medical record that are used to begin the code search in the Alphabetic Index. A main term can identify a procedure or service performed; an organ or anatomic site; a condition, illness, or injury; or an eponym, abbreviation, or acronym.

Main Text See Tabular Index.

maker Any individual, corporation, or legal party who signs a check or any type of negotiable instrument.

malediction (ma-luh-dik′-shun) Speaking evil or the calling of a curse.

managed care plans An umbrella term for all healthcare plans that provide healthcare in return for preset monthly payments and coordinated care through a defined network of primary care physicians and hospitals.

manifestation (ma-nuh-fuh-sta′-shun) Something that is easily understood or recognized by the mind. *Also,* an indication of the existence, reality, or presence of something, especially an illness.

marketing The process or technique of promoting, selling, and distributing a product or service.

matrix Something in which a thing originates, develops, takes shape, or is contained; a base on which to build.

m-banking Banking through the use of mobile devices, such as cell phones and wireless Internet services.

media A term applied to agencies of mass communication, such as newspapers, magazines, and telecommunications.

mediastinum (meh-de-ast′-uhn-um) The space in the center of the chest under the sternum.

Medicaid A federal- and state-sponsored health insurance program for the medically indigent.

medical savings accounts (MSAs) Tax-deferred bank or savings accounts that are combined with a low-premium, high-deductible insurance policy; they are designed for individuals or families who choose to fund their own healthcare expenses and medical insurance.

medically indigent Able to take care of ordinary living expenses but unable to afford medical care.

Medicare A federally sponsored health insurance program for those over age 65 and for individuals under age 65 who are disabled.

Medigap A term sometimes applied to private insurance products that supplement Medicare insurance benefits.

megabyte (MB) Approximately 1 million bytes.

megahertz (MHz) The measuring device for microprocessors. A megahertz is 1 million cycles of electromagnetic currency alternation per second and is used as a unit of measure for the clock speed of computer microprocessors.

mentors Trusted counselors or guides.

meticulous (meh-tiku′-luhs) Marked by extreme or excessive care in the consideration or treatment of details.

microfilm A film with a photographic record of printed or other graphic matter on a reduced scale.

micromanage To manage with great or excessive control or attention to details.

misdemeanor (mis-duh-me′-nuhr) A minor crime, as opposed to a felony, punishable by fine or imprisonment in a city or county jail rather than in a penitentiary.

mitigating To cause to become less harsh or hostile; to make less severe or painful.

mock Simulated; intended for imitation or practice.

modem Short for *modulator-demodulator;* a device that allows information to be transmitted over telephone lines at speeds measured in bits per second (bps). The modem speed generally is listed somewhere on the unit.

modifiers Terms that serve as the means to report or indicate that a service or procedure performed has been altered by some specific circumstance but not changed in its definition or code.

modifying terms Key words selected after the main term has been chosen to help further define or describe the procedure or service performed.

monotone A succession of syllables, words, or sentences in an unvaried key or pitch.

morale (mo-ral′) The mental and emotional condition, enthusiasm, loyalty, or confidence of an individual or group with regard to the function or tasks at hand.

motivation The process of inciting a person to some action or behavior.

multimedia The presentation of graphics, animation, video, sound, and text on a computer in an integrated way or all at once. CD-ROMs are efficient multimedia devices.

multitasking Performing multiple tasks at the same time.

municipal (myu-ni′-suh-puhl) courts Courts that sit in some cities and larger towns and that usually have civil and criminal jurisdiction over cases arising within the municipality.

myocardium (my-oh-kar′-de-um) The muscular lining of the heart.

mysticism The experience of seeming to have direct communication with God or ultimate reality.

National Provider Identifier (NPI) A lifetime number consisting of 10 digits that Medicare uses to replace the Provider Identification Number (PIN) and the Unique Physician Identification Number (UPIN).

naturopathy (na-chu-ra′-puh-the) An alternative to conventional medicine in which holistic methods are used, in addition to herbs and natural supplements, with the belief that the body will heal itself. Naturopathic physicians currently can be licensed in 15 states, Puerto Rico, and the Virgin Islands.

near miss A situation in which an error is caught or corrected before it affects the patient.

necrosis (neh-kroh′-sis) The death of cells or tissues.

negligence (ne′-gli-jents) Failure to exercise the care a prudent person usually exercises; implies inattention to one's duty or business; implies want of due or necessary diligence or care.

negotiable Legally transferable to another party.

networking Exchange of information or services among individuals, groups, or institutions. *Also,* meeting and getting to know individuals in the same or similar career fields and sharing information about available opportunities.

new patient (NP) A patient who has *not* received any professional services (face to face) from the physician or another physician of the *exact* same specialty *and subspecialty* who belongs to the same group practice, within the past 3 years.

nonmaleficence (non-mal-fe′-zens) Refraining from the act of harming or committing evil.

no-show A person who fails to keep an appointment without giving advance notice.

nosocomial (no-suh-ko′-me-uhl) Originating or taking place in a hospital.

notations Found in both the Alphabetic Index and the Tabular Index, notations are instructions or guides in classification assignments, defining category content or the use of subdivision codes; also called *instructional notations.*

notebook Although often used interchangeably with "laptop," this term was created to identify a smaller, thinner, and lighter device, partially designed to fit on tray tables on airplanes.

numeric filing The filing of records, correspondence, or cards by number.

objective information Information gathered by watching or observing a patient.

objective Something toward which effort is directed; aim, goal, or purpose of action.

obliteration (uh-bli-tuh-ra′-shun) The act of making undecipherable or imperceptible by obscuring or wearing away.

Office for Civil Rights (OCR) The division of the federal government that enforces privacy standards.

Office of the Inspector General (OIG) An office of the U.S. Department of Health and Human Services that conducts audits, investigations, and inspections involving laws pertaining to health and human services.

opinions Formal expressions of judgment or advice by an expert; formal expressions of the legal reasons and principles on which a legal decision is based.

optimistic Inclined to put the most favorable construction on actions and events or to anticipate the best possible outcome.

ordinance (or′-di-nens) Authoritative decree or direction; law set forth by a governmental authority, specifically, municipal regulation.

osteopathic (us-te-uh-path′-ik) A term describing the type of medicine that is based on the theory that disturbances in the musculoskeletal system affect other bodily parts, causing many disorders that can be corrected by various manipulative techniques in conjunction with conventional medical, surgical, pharmacologic, and other therapeutic procedures.

other potentially infectious materials (OPIM) Substances or materials other than blood that have the potential to carry infectious pathogens, such as body fluid, urine, semen, and others.

OUTfolder A folder used to provide space for the temporary filing of materials.

OUTguide A heavy guide used to replace a folder temporarily removed from the filing space.

output Information processed by the computer and transmitted to a monitor, printer, or other device.

outreach The process of using marketing and education strategies to reach and involve diverse audiences through the use of key messages and effective programs.

outsourcing The practice of subcontracting work to an outside company.

overhead The ongoing administrative expenses of a business that cannot be attributed to any specific business activity but are still necessary for the business to function (e.g., rent, utilities, insurance).

packing slip A list of items included in a shipment.

pandemic (pan-de′-mik) A condition in which most people in a country, a number of countries, or a geographic area are affected.

paper (hard copy) claims Insurance claims that have been completed manually, on paper, and sent by surface mail.

parameters Any set of physical properties, the values of which determine characteristics or behavior.

paraphrasing To express an idea in different wording in an effort to enhance communication and clarify meaning.

participating provider (PAR)   A physician or other healthcare provider who enters into a contract with a specific insurance company or program and by doing so agrees to abide by certain rules and regulations set forth by that particular third-party payer.

patient status (PS)   The state of a patient as either new or established; appears in the Evaluation and Management section of the CPT.

payables   Balances due to a creditor on an account.

payee   The person named on a draft or check as the recipient of the amount shown.

payer   The person who writes a check in favor of the payee.

peer review organizations (PROs)   Groups of medical reviewers contracted by the Centers for Medicare and Medicaid Services (CMS) to ensure quality control and the medical necessity of services provided by a facility.

pegboard system   An older method of tracking patient accounts that allows the figures to be proved accurate through mathematic formulas. It is still used in some small to medium practices; also called the *write-it-once system.*

per diem   By the day; per day. An allowance for daily expenses.

perceiving (pur-sev'-ing)   How an individual looks at information and sees it as real.

perception   A quick, acute, and intuitive cognition; a capacity for comprehension.

perjured testimony   The voluntary violation of an oath or vow either by swearing to what is untrue or by omission to do what has been promised under oath; false testimony.

perks   Extra advantages or benefits of working in a specific job that may or may not be commonplace in that particular profession; a shortened form of perquisites.

persona (pur-so'-nuh)   An individual's social facade or front that reflects the role in life the individual is playing; the personality a person projects in public.

personal digital assistant (PDA)   A handheld computer capable of functions such as mobile telephony, Web browsing, and media playing. PDAs typically include an appointment calendar, to-do list, address book, note programs, and e-mail and/ or Web capabilities.

personal health information (PHI)   The patient's own information that pertains to his or her health.

personal health record (PHR)   An electronic record of health-related information about an individual that conforms to nationally recognized interoperability standards and that *can be drawn from multiple sources but that is managed, shared, and controlled by the individual.*

pertinent (pur'-tuh-nent)   Having a clear, decisive relevance to the matter at hand.

petty cash fund   A fund maintained to pay small, unpredictable cash expenditures.

philanthropist (fu-lan'-thruh-pist)   An individual who makes an active effort to promote human welfare.

philosopher   A person who seeks wisdom or enlightenment; an expounder of a theory in a certain area of experience.

phlebotomy (fli-bah'-tuh-me)   An invasive procedure used to obtain a blood specimen for testing, experimentation, or diagnosis of disease.

phonetic (fuh-ne'-tik)   Constituting an alteration of ordinary spelling that better represents the spoken language, that uses only characters of the regular alphabet, and that is used in a context of conventional spelling.

photophobia   An abnormal sensitivity to light.

phrases   Groups of words with a specific grammatical function, such as a noun phrase or an adjective phrase.

physical status   The physical condition of the patient.

physician office laboratories (POLs)   Laboratories owned by a private physician or corporation, such as the laboratory inside a physician's office or a freestanding laboratory.

physiologic noise   Internal interferences comprised of biologic factors within a speaker or listener that hinder effective and accurate communication.

pitch   Highness or lowness of a sound; the relative level, intensity, or extent of some quality or state.

place of service (POS) codes   Codes used on professional claims to specify the facility or location where the service or services were rendered.

plaintiff   The person or group bringing a case or legal action to court.

policyholder   A person who pays a premium to an insurance company and in whose name the policy is written in exchange for the insurance protection provided by a policy of insurance.

polydipsia   Excessive thirst.

portfolio   A set of pictures, drawings, documents, or photographs either bound in book form or loose in a folder.

posting   Entering figures in an accounting system; transferring or carrying from a book of original entry to a ledger.

postmortem   Done, collected, or occurring after death.

potentially compensable event (PCE)   An adverse occurrence, usually involving a patient, that could result in a financial obligation for a business or organization.

power of attorney   A legal instrument authorizing a person to act as the attorney or agent of the grantor.

practicum   Another word for the externship; a training program that is a part of the medical assisting course of study in the actual business setting of a medical office or facility. (This term is used by the Commission on Accreditation of Allied Health Education Programs [CAAHEP] to designate the externship.)

preauthorization   A process required by some insurance carriers in which the provider obtains permission to perform certain procedures or services or refers a patient to a specialist.

precedence (pre-sed'-ens)   To surpass in rank, dignity, or importance; to be, go, or come ahead or in front of.

precedents (pre'-suh-dens)   A person or thing that serves as a model; something done or said that may serve as an example or rule to authorize or justify a subsequent act of the same kind.

precertification   A process required by some insurance carriers in which the provider must prove medical necessity before performing a procedure.

preclude   To rule out in advance.

premium   The periodic (monthly, quarterly, or annual) payment of a specific sum of money to an insurance company, for which the insurer in return agrees to provide certain benefits.

preponderance   A superiority or excess in number or quantity; a majority.

preponderance of the evidence   Evidence of greater weight or more convincing than the evidence offered in opposition to it; evidence that as a whole shows that the fact sought to be proven is more probable than not.

prerequisite (pre-re'-kwe-zut)   Something that is necessary to an end or to carry out a function.

pressboard A strong, highly glazed composition board resembling vulcanized fiber; heavy card stock.

prevalent Generally or widely accepted, favored, or practiced.

primary care provider (PCP) A general practice or nonspecialist provider or physician responsible for the care of a patient for some health maintenance organizations. Also called a *gatekeeper*.

principal A capital sum of money due as a debt or used as a fund for which interest is either charged or paid.

principal diagnosis The initial identification of the condition or complaint the patient expresses in the outpatient medical setting based on the physician's assessment as documented in the medical record.

privacy officer A person designated to ensure compliance with privacy standards for a covered entity.

proactive Acting in anticipation of future problems, needs, or changes.

processing (pro′-ses-ing) How an individual internalizes new information and makes it his or her own.

procrastination (pruh-kras-tuh-na′-shun) Intentional postponement of doing something that should be done.

procurement (pro-kuhr′-ment) To get possession of, to obtain by particular care and effort.

professional behaviors Actions that identify the medical assistant as a member of a healthcare profession, including being dependable, providing respectful patient care, exercising initiative, demonstrating a positive attitude, and working as an effective team member.

professional courtesy Reduction or absence of fees to professional associates.

professionalism The conduct or qualities characterized by or conforming to the technical or ethical standards of a profession; exhibiting a courteous, conscientious, and generally businesslike manner in the workplace.

proficiency (pruh-fi′-shun-se) Competency as a result of training or practice.

profit sharing Offer of a part of a company's profits to employees or other designated individuals or groups.

progress notes Notes used in the medical record to track the patient's progress and condition.

proofread To read and mark corrections.

prosthesis (prohs-thet′-ik) An artificial device that replaces missing parts of the body.

protected health information (PHI) Any individually identifiable health information that may be transmitted and/or maintained in electronic form.

provider An individual or individuals qualified by education, training, licensure or regulation, and facility privileging who perform a professional service within their scope of practice and independently report that professional service. *Also,* a company that provides medical care and services to a patient or the public.

provider identification number (PIN) A number assigned to providers by a carrier for use in the submission of claims.

provisional diagnosis A temporary diagnosis made before all test results have been received.

proxemics (prok-se′-miks) The study of the nature, degree, and effect of the spatial separation individuals naturally maintain.

prudent Marked by wisdom or judiciousness; shrewd in the management of practical affairs.

public domain The realm embracing property rights that belong to the community at large, are unprotected by copyright or patent, and are subject to use or appropriation by anyone.

purging The process of moving active files to inactive status.

putrefaction (pyu-truh-fak′-shun) Decomposition of animal matter, which results in a foul smell.

quackery The pretense of curing disease.

quality assurance (QA) Activities designed to increase the quality of a product or service through process or system changes that increase efficiency or effectiveness.

quality control An aggregate of activities designed to ensure adequate quality, especially in manufactured products or in the service industries.

queries Requests for information from a database.

ramifications (ra-muh-fuh-ka′-shuns) Consequences produced by a cause or following from a set of conditions.

ream A quantity of paper weighing 20 lb or consisting of, variously, 480, 500, or 516 sheets.

reasonable cause Circumstances that would make it unreasonable for the covered entity, despite the exercise of ordinary business care and prudence, to comply with the administrative simplification provision that was violated.

reasonable diligence The business care and prudence expected from a person seeking to satisfy a legal requirement under similar circumstances.

reasonable doubt Doubt based on reason and arising from evidence or lack of evidence; it is not doubt that is imagined or conjured up, but doubt that would cause reasonable persons to hesitate before acting.

receipts Amounts paid on patient accounts.

receivables Total payments received on accounts.

recipient The receiver of some thing or item.

reciprocity The mutual exchange of privileges; a recognition of one state or institution of the licenses or privileges granted by the other.

reconciliation The process of proving that a bank statement and checkbook balance are in agreement.

recourse A turning to something or someone for help or protection.

rectify (rek′-tuh-fy) To correct by removing errors.

referral An insurance term used when a primary care provider wants to send a patient to a specialist. Typically, the provider must obtain authorization from the insurance carrier in advance to refer a patient.

reflection (re-flek′-shun) The process of considering new information and internalizing it to create new ways of examining information.

reimbursement Payment of benefits to the physician for services rendered according to the guidelines of the third-party payer.

rejected claims Claims returned unpaid to the provider for clarification of any question; these claims must be corrected before resubmission.

relevant Having significant and demonstrable bearing on the matter at hand.

remittance advice (RA) An explanation of benefits from Medicaid (see *explanation of benefits [EOB]*).

reparations (re-puh-ra′-shuns) Amends, acts of atonement, or satisfaction given as a result of a wrong or injury.

reprimands Criticisms for a fault; severe or formal reproofs.

reproach An expression of rebuke or disapproval; a cause or occasion of blame, discredit, or disgrace.

requisites (re'-kwuh-zuhts) Entities considered essential or necessary.

resource-based relative value scale (RBRVS) A fee schedule designed to provide national uniform payment of Medicare benefits after adjustment to reflect the differences in practice costs across geographic areas.

respondent (ri-spahn'-dunt) The person required to make answer in a civil legal action or suit; similar to a defendant in a criminal trial.

retention schedule A method or plan for retaining or keeping medical records and for their movement from active, to inactive, to closed filing.

retention The act of keeping in possession or use; keeping in one's pay or service.

reverse chronologic order Arranged in order so that the most recent item is on top and older items are filed further back.

rider A special provision or group of provisions that may be added to a policy to expand or limit the benefits otherwise payable. It may increase or decrease benefits, waive a condition or coverage, or in any other way amend the original contract.

robotics Technology dealing with the design, construction, and operation of robots in automation.

router (rau'-ter) A device used to connect any number of LANs, which communicate with other routers and determine the best route between any two hosts.

salutation (sal-yu-ta'-shun) An expression of greeting, goodwill, or courtesy by words or gestures.

sarcasm A sharp and often satirical response or ironic utterance designed to cut or inflict pain.

scanner A device that reads text or illustrations on a printed page and can translate the information on that page into a form the computer can understand.

screen Something that shields, protects, or hides; to select or eliminate through a screening process.

screening A system for examining and separating into different groups; in the medical office, determining the severity of illness that patients experience and prioritizing appointments based on that severity.

search engines Programs that search documents for keywords and return a list of documents containing those words.

section One of the six primary divisions of the main body of the CPT.

secured A loan or line of credit that is backed by a pledge of payment and usually obtained using collateral.

see A direction to the coder to look in another place; this instruction must always be followed. It is found in the Alphabetic Index, volumes 2 and 3.

see also A direction to the coder to look elsewhere if the main term or subterm (or subterms) for that entry are not sufficient for coding the information. If a code number follows, *see also* is enclosed in parentheses. If there is no code number, *see also* is preceded by a dash.

see category A direction to the coder to see a specific category (three-digit code); this instruction must always be followed.

self-insured (or self-funded) plan An insurance plan funded by an organization having a large enough employee base that it can afford to fund its own insurance program.

self-referral Occurs when a patient or an insured individual refers himself or herself to a specialist without requesting the referral from the primary provider (e.g., a woman seeking an annual gynecologic examination). Managed care guidelines may require the patient to report the self-referral.

sentinel events Unexpected occurrences involving death or serious physical or psychological injury, or the risk thereof.

sequentially (si-kwen'-shuh-le) Of, relating to, or arranged in a sequence.

server A computer or device on a network that manages shared network resources.

service benefit plans Plans that provide benefits in the form of certain surgical and medical services rendered rather than cash. A service benefit plan is not restricted to a fee schedule.

shingling A method of filing in which a report is laid on top of the older report, resembling the shingles of a roof.

slander Oral defamation; a harmful, false statement made about another person.

SOAP notes A system of charting comprising the *s*ubjective findings, *o*bjective findings, *a*ssessment, and *p*lan for treatment.

socioeconomic Relating to a combination of social and economic factors.

sociologic Oriented or directed toward social needs and problems.

staff privileges The permission granted by a facility to a healthcare professional to practice in that facility.

standards Items or indicators used as a measure of quality or compliance with a statutory or accrediting body's policies and regulations. *Also,* models or examples established by authority, custom, or general consent; something set up and established by authority as a rule for the measure of quantity, weight, extent, value, or quality.

STAT Medical abbreviation for immediately; at this moment.

statement A request for payment.

statement of income and expense A summary of all income and expenses for a given period.

stationers (sta'-shuh-nerz) Sellers of stationery.

statutes (sta-choots) Laws enacted by the legislative branch of a government.

stereotype Something conforming to a fixed or general pattern; a standardized mental picture that is held in common by many and represents an oversimplified opinion, prejudiced attitude, or uncritical judgment.

stipulate To specify as a condition or requirement of an agreement or offer; to make an agreement or covenant to do or forbear from doing something.

stock options Offers of stocks for purchase to a certain group of individuals or certain groups, such as employees of a for-profit hospital.

stressors Stimuli that cause stress.

subcategory In the CPT manual, the element indented one level below a category, usually a procedure or service unique to a specific category.

subjective information Information gained by questioning the patient or taking it from a form.

subluxations (suh-blek-sa'-shuns) Slight misalignments of the vertebrae or a partial dislocation.

subordinate Submissive to or controlled by authority; placed in or occupying a lower class, rank, or position.

subpoena (suh-pe'-nuh) A writ or document commanding a person to appear in court under a penalty for failure to appear.

subpoena duces tecum A legally binding request to appear in court and provide records or documents that pertain to a particular case.

subsection In the CPT manual, the element indented one level below a section; it usually describes an anatomic site or organ system (e.g., Integumentary, Cardiology).

subsidiary Supporting other documents or records.

substance number A number based on the weight of a ream of paper containing 500 sheets.

subtle Difficult to understand or perceive; having or marked by keen insight and ability to penetrate deeply and thoroughly. *Also,* ingenious, artful, delicate.

succinct (suhk-sinkt') Marked by compact, precise expression without wasted words.

superfluous (suh-puhr'-flu-uhs) Exceeding what is sufficient or necessary.

superuser A special account on a computer system that is used for system administration; also, a person in a facility who is able to make system-wide changes to a computer system.

surrogate (suhr'-uh-gat) A substitute; to put in place of another.

switch In networks, a device that filters information between LAN segments and reduces overall network traffic and increases speed and bandwidth use efficiency.

synopsis Condensed statement or outline.

system software The operating system and all utility programs that allow the computer to function and perform operations.

tablet A wireless, portable personal computer with a touch screen interface, usually smaller than a notebook but larger than a smart phone (e.g., Apple iPad, Samsung Galaxy, Dell Streak).

Tabular Index Volume 1 (Main Text) of the ICD-9-CM coding manual. It contains all the diagnostic codes in alphanumeric order, which are grouped into 17 chapters of diseases and injuries.

tactful Having a keen sense of what to do or say to maintain good relations with others or to prevent offense.

tangible (tan'-juh-buhl) Capable of being appraised at an actual or approximate value; capable of being precisely identified or realized by the mind.

target market A specific group of individuals toward whom the marketing plan is focused.

targeted Directed or used toward a target; directed toward a specific desire or position.

TCP/IP The acronym for *transmission control protocol/Internet protocol;* a suite of communications protocols used to connect users or hosts to the Internet.

tedious (te'-de-yus) Tiresome because of length or dullness.

telecommunications The science and technology of communication by transmission of information from one location to another via telephone, television, telegraph, or satellite.

telemedicine The use of telecommunications in the practice of medicine to compensate for the great distances that can separate healthcare professionals, colleagues, patients, and students.

teleradiology The use of telecommunication devices to enhance and improve the results of radiologic procedures.

template A predeveloped page layout used to make new pages with a similar design, pattern, or style; a standardized file type used in computer software as a preformatted example on which to base other files.

terabyte (TB) Approximately 1 trillion bytes.

testimony A solemn declaration usually made orally by a witness under oath in response to interrogation by a lawyer or authorized public official.

thanatology (tha-nuh-tah'-luh-je) The study of the phenomena of death and of psychological methods of coping with death.

third-party administrator (TPA) An organization that processes claims and performs other business-related functions for a health plan.

third-party payers Entities that make payment on an obligation or debt but are not parties to the contract that created the debt.

thrombolytics Agents that dissolve blood clots.

tickler file A chronologic file used as a reminder that something must be dealt with on a certain date.

tolerance The need to use more and more of a substance to get the same feeling as the body learns to tolerate the drug.

transaction An exchange or transfer of goods, services, or funds.

transactions As defined by HIPAA, transmissions of information between two parties to carry out financial or administrative activities related to healthcare.

transcription A written copy of something made either in longhand or by machine.

transient ischemic attack (TIA) Temporary neurologic symptoms caused by gradual or partial occlusion of a cerebral blood vessel.

transposed Altered in sequence; interchanged.

treatises (tree'-te-ses) Systematic expositions or arguments in writing, including a methodic discussion of the facts and principles involved and the conclusions reached.

triage (tree'-azh) Identification of the severity of patients' conditions and the allocation of treatment according to a system of priorities, which is designed to maximize the number of survivors and provide treatment for the sickest patients first.

trial balance A method of checking the accuracy of accounts.

TRICARE A government-sponsored program under which authorized dependents of military personnel receive medical care. Originally called *CHAMPUS.*

trustee A person to whom property is legally committed to be administered for the benefit of a beneficiary or held by an administrator to be distributed to multiple individuals or businesses.

unbundled codes Codes in which the components of a major procedure are separated and reported separately.

Uniform Commercial Code (UCC) A unified set of rules covering many business transactions; it has been adopted in all 50 states, the District of Columbia, and most U.S. territories. It regulates the fields of sales of goods; commercial paper, such as checks; secured transactions in personal property; and particular aspects of banking, letters of credit, warehouse receipts, bills of lading, and investment securities.

unique identifiers Codes used instead of names to protect the confidentiality of the patient in a method of anonymous HIV testing.

Unique Provider Identification Number (UPIN) A number assigned by fiscal intermediaries to identify providers on claims for services.

universal claim form The form developed by the Health Care Financing Administration (HCFA; now the Centers for Medicare and Medicaid Services [CMS]) and approved by the American Medical Association (AMA) for use in submitting all government-sponsored claims. Also known as the *CMS- 1500 Health Insurance Claim Form.*

unsecured A debt that is not protected by collateral.

upcoding   A deliberate increase in a CPT code, despite the lack of documentation, to the next highest reimbursable code so as to obtain higher reimbursements.

URL   The acronym for *uniform resource locator;* specifies the global address of documents or information on the Internet. The URL provides the IP address and the domain name for the Web page, such as microsoft.com.

use additional code   A *use additional code* note is found at the etiology code when the underlying condition is sequenced first, followed by the manifestation. A term that appears only in the Tabular Index (Volume 1) in subdivisions in which the user should add further information, by means of an additional code, to give a more complete picture of the diagnosis. In some cases, *if desired* follows the term. For the purpose of coding, the *if desired* phrase will not be used. When the term *use additional code if desired* appears, disregard "if desired" and assign the appropriate additional code.

utilization review   A review of individual cases by a committee to make sure that services are medically necessary and to study how providers use medical care resources.

vehemently (ve′-uh-ment-le)   In a manner marked by forceful energy; intensely, emotionally.

veracity (vuh-ra′-suh-te)   A devotion to or conformity with the truth.

verbiage   A manner of expressing oneself in words.

verdict   The finding or decision of a jury on a matter submitted to it in trial.

versatile (vur′-suh-til)   Embracing a variety of subjects, fields, or skills; having a wide range of abilities.

vested   Granted or endowed with a particular authority, right, or property; to have a special interest in.

virtual reality   An artificial environment presented to a computer user that feels as if it were a real environment, often involving use of special gloves, earphones, and goggles to enhance the experience.

vocation   The work in which a person is regularly employed.

volatile (vah′-luh-til)   Easily aroused; tending to erupt in violence. *Also,* capable of vaporizing at a low temperature, such as an explosive substance.

watermark   A marking in paper resulting from differences in thickness usually produced by the pressure of a projecting design in the mold or on a processing roll; it is visible when the paper is held up to the light.

willful neglect   Conscious, intentional failure or reckless indifference to the obligation to comply with the administrative simplification provision violated.

with   In the context of the ICD-9-CM, the terms *with, with mention of,* and *associated with* in a title dictate that both parts of the title must be present in the diagnostic statement to allow assignment of the particular code.

work ethics   A set of values based on the moral virtues of hard work and diligence.

workers' compensation   Insurance against liability imposed employers cover medical expenses and lost wages to employees who are injured on the job and to pay benefits to dependents of employees killed in the course of or arising out of their employment.

INDEX

Page numbers followed by "f" indicate figures, "t" indicate tables, and "b" indicate boxes.